# Intellectual Property

*Text and Essential Cases*

# Intellectual Property

## Text and Essential Cases

### Fourth edition

**Rocque Reynolds**

BA, LLM, PhD (Syd)
Professor, School of Law & Justice, Southern Cross University
Solicitor of the Supreme Courts of New South Wales and Australian Capital Territory

**Natalie P Stoianoff**

BSc, LLB, MAppSc (UNSW)
Professor, Faculty of Law, University of Technology, Sydney
Fellow of the Taxation Institute of Australia
Solicitor of the Supreme Court of New South Wales

**Angela Adrian**

BBA, MIM, JD, LLM, PhD (London)
Senior Lecturer in Law, School of Law & Justice, Southern Cross University
Attorney-at-Law (Louisiana) and Solicitor (England & Wales)

**Alpana Roy**

BA, LLB (Hons), PhD (Sydney)
Lecturer, Faculty of Law, University of Technology, Sydney

FEDERATION PRESS
2012

Published in Sydney by
   The Federation Press Pty Ltd
   PO Box 45, Annandale, NSW, 2038.
   71 John St, Leichhardt, NSW, 2040.
   Ph (02) 9552 2200. Fax (02) 9552 1681.
   E-mail: info@federationpress.com.au
   Website: http://www.federationpress.com.au

First edition      2003
Second edition     2005
Third edition      2008
Fourth edition     2012

National Library of Australia
Cataloguing-in-Publication entry

   Intellectual property : text and essential cases / Rocque Reynolds ... [et al].

   4th ed.
   Includes index.

   978 186287 870 9 (pbk)

   Intellectual property – Australia.

346.94048

Typeset by The Federation Press, Leichhardt, NSW.
   Printed by Ligare Pty Ltd, Riverwood, NSW.

# Foreword to the First Edition

## *The Hon Justice WMC Gummow, AC*

### *High Court of Australia*

That students enjoy their courses in intellectual property is a truth universally acknowledged by them, wherever in the common law world the tuition takes place. This book will add to that enjoyment by Australian students.

The authors are well aware of the speed with which the subject now moves. This is apparent from the discussion of Moral Rights (Ch 7), Plant Breeder's Rights (Ch 15) and Circuit Layouts (Ch 16). One result of this legislative activity, to which must be added the many other changes over the last 15 years or so to the *Copyright Act 1968* (Cth) and the patents legislation, is that the statute law in this country diverges to a significant extent from that of the United Kingdom. That country in turn now is heavily influenced, indeed directed, by the dictates of the European Union.

These developments emphasise the need for texts with a specifically Australian orientation, as has this book. Of some 46 cases which the authors extract (some cases being extracted for more than one passage), 35 are decisions of Australian courts and several are of Privy Council decisions on Australian appeals. Of that 35, the great bulk are judgments of the Federal Court of Australia. This is indicative of the pre-eminent position which that Court has achieved in its quarter century of life. In this significant measure, the Court has achieved the aspirations of its chief architects, Mr RJ Ellicott QC and Sir Nigel Bowen, both experts in intellectual property law.

The authors are to be congratulated on the scope of their efforts, the perceptive text in which various points of view are put and weighed, and upon their choice of cases. By their efforts the teaching and understanding of intellectual property in Australia is further advanced.

High Court of Australia
Canberra
28 January 2003

# List of Chapters

## Part I Introduction

## Part II Copyright and Neighbouring Rights

## Part III Patents

## Part IV Passing Off, Trade Marks and Related Actions

## Part V Designs, Plant Breeder's Rights, Circuit Layouts and Confidential Information

For detailed Table of Contents *see over*

# Contents

**PART III**
**PATENTS**

## PART IV
## PASSING OFF, TRADE MARKS AND RELATED ACTIONS

# PART V
## DESIGNS, PLANT BREEDER'S RIGHTS, CIRCUIT LAYOUTS AND CONFIDENTIAL INFORMATION

# Preface

Since 2008 the field of intellectual property has undergone much development and change in Australia, both judicially and legislatively. The influence of technology, and society's reaction to that technology, comprise a significant part of these developments. The two major industries that have given rise to much of these developments are the life sciences, particularly genetic engineering, and the information and communications technology (ICT) industries.

Copyright has experienced a series of High Court decisions that have dealt with the concept of idea and expression, originality and authorship, and the parameters of authorisation such as in *Roadshow Films Pty Ltd v iiNet Ltd*. In each case some facet of the information and communications technology industry has been explored. Meanwhile, the Full Federal Court in *National Rugby League Investments Pty Ltd v Singtel Optus* has taken a narrow view of the private and domestic use exceptions to infringement which may have wider implications for mobile technology and cloud computing providers. The Australian Law Reform Commission is currently undertaking a review of the *Copyright Act 1968* to determine whether the exceptions are sufficient and appropriate given the ever evolving digital environment.

Meanwhile, the role and effectiveness of our patent regime has been called into question on numerous occasions. There have been several reviews on the issue of patenting genes and other biological materials, and more generally on what is patentable subject matter. At the time of writing, the Federal Court is contemplating whether genes are patentable subject matter under current legislation. Trade marks law has also undergone judicial development particularly on the front of what is capable of protection and what constitutes infringement. On the issue of confidentiality and privacy the issue of a tort of invasion of privacy has been raised in the courts time and again, and which has also attracted several reviews at federal and State level resulting in expected federal legislation on an action of serious invasion of privacy.

The status of Australia's intellectual property regime in relation to its major developed trading partners has been called into question by the executive arm of government, namely IP Australia. This has led to new legislation aimed at raising the quality of patents granted through improvements to the robustness of our patent examination criteria and procedures, opposition procedures, enhancing competition and introducing the experimental use exception to infringement while expanding the free access to patented inventions for regulatory approvals. This same legislation, *Intellectual Property Laws Amendment (Raising the Bar) Act 2012* which received Royal Assent on 15 April 2012, will also bring about procedural improvements to the trade marks regime to reduce delays in the resolution of applications and has provided improvements to the enforcement regime for both trade marks and copyright in line with the requirements under the Agreement on Trade Related Aspects of Intellectual Property (TRIPS). Meanwhile the federal government's *Tobacco Plain Packaging Act 2011* and corresponding amendment of the *Trade Marks Act 1995*, the subject of a High Court challenge, seek to restrict the rights granted to a trade mark owner where the product in question is tobacco.

What each of the developments of the past four years has in common is the need to deal with the tension between the rights of the intellectual property owner and the rights of society to access the protected subject matter. Entwined with that are the basic human rights to better health, to privacy and enhanced living standards. Perhaps we are seeing the objectives stated in Article 7 of the *TRIPS Agreement* finally at play:

> The protection and enforcement of intellectual property rights should contribute to the promotion of technological innovation and to the transfer and dissemination of technology, to the mutual advantage of producers and users of technological knowledge and in a manner conducive to social and economic welfare, and to a balance of rights and obligations.

But certainly, what is in question now relates to Australia's compliance with Article 8.1 of TRIPS and, in particular, the proviso:

> Members may, in formulating or amending their laws and regulations, adopt measures necessary to protect public health and nutrition, and to promote the public interest in sectors of vital importance to their socio-economic and technological development, provided that such measures are consistent with the provisions of this Agreement.

The foreshadowed adoption of the *TRIPS Protocol* announced in early 2011 has yet to be presented as a Bill. This proposed introduction of compulsory licensing provisions for the production of generic pharmaceuticals bound for export to least developed nations experiencing health crises would certainly emphasise a growing trend in favour of the rights of society. Only time will tell.

This edition of our book explores these changes and is based on the law available to us as at 1 May 2012.

# Acknowledgments

Thank you first to our research assistant, Albert Surjadiredja, for his excellent work.

The authors gratefully acknowledge the *Max Planck Institute for Intellectual Property, Competition and Tax Law*, Munich, Germany, for supporting Natalie Stoianoff during the initial research and drafting of this book.

The authors wish to thank the following for permission to reproduce materials:

LexisNexis for *All England Law Reports*, *Australian Law Reports* and *Intellectual Property Reports*

Council of Law Reporting for NSW for *New South Wales Law Reports*. © Council of Law Reporting for New South Wales 2003.

Incorporated Council for Law Reporting for England and Wales for cases reported in the official law reports.

Thomson Reuters for *Commonwealth Law Reports*, *Federal Court Reports* and *Federal Law Reports*. Reproduced with the express permission of Thomson Reuters © Thomson Reuters

# Table of Cases

(References in **Bold** are to extracts or summaries of cases)

# Table of Statutes

# Part I

# Introduction

Chapter 1

# Opening Your Eyes to IP

As we say elsewhere in this book – learning about intellectual property law is a bit like stepping into a new dimension. One suddenly becomes aware that there is a whole economy or market in ideas, creative works, inventions and trade marks which remains largely invisible to the general public. A person who rides on a roller coaster, for example, probably does not give a thought to whether the owner of the funfair has paid a licence fee for using the invention. The home gardener probably doesn't know whether his or her nursery has the right to cultivate seedlings. Many people will not have wondered how songwriters collect their licence fees each time a song is played on the radio, in a club, at a school camp or in a church, temple or synagogue. On the other hand, there are some aspects of intellectual property law which we probably notice everyday. There are detailed copyright notices on videos, DVDs and university photocopying machines, for example, as well as on films, books and CDs. Newspapers report on the cost of patented drugs, the battles over genetically modified foods and bio-prospecting. Trade marks form part of the visual landscape of our lives. In this text we want to open your eyes to the way intellectual property is developed, marketed, managed and protected and the legal framework which supports this economy. In order to do this it is important, first, to identify the types of subject-matter that are protected as intellectual property.

## What is Intellectual Property?

The type of subject-matter protected as intellectual property is gradually expanding. The core intellectual property rights are copyright, patents and trade marks which are covered by the *Copyright Act 1968* (Cth), the *Patents Act 1990* (Cth) and the *Trade Marks Act 1995* (Cth). Copyright gives the copyright owner of a literary, dramatic, musical or artistic work, or of a film, sound recording, broadcast or printed edition of a work, the exclusive right to copy, publish, perform, communicate or adapt the subject-matter and, in some instances, to commercially lease that subject-matter. Under the *Copyright Act 1968* it is not necessary to register or complete any formalities in order to acquire these rights. Under the *Patents Act*

*1990*, an inventor who registers a patentable invention has the exclusive right to "exploit" the invention – that means the right to make, hire, sell, use or import the invention. The registered owner of a trade mark has the exclusive right to use the mark "as a trade mark". Each of these forms of intellectual property rights is a property right and may be assigned, licensed and otherwise commercially dealt with. They will be considered in Parts II (Copyright and Neighbouring Rights), III (Patents) and IV (Passing Off, Trade Marks and Related Actions) of this text.

From these core intellectual property rights, new intellectual property rights have developed in three different ways. First, new forms of subject-matter have been given protection similar to copyright or patents law through the passing of specialised legislation. Thus, under the *Designs Act 2003* (Cth) the registered owner of a design has an exclusive right to make and deal with products embodying the design. Under the *Plant Breeder's Rights Act 1994* (Cth) the registered owner of a plant variety has the exclusive right to produce, reproduce, sell, import and export propagating material for that plant variety. The *Circuit Layouts Act 1989* (Cth) gives the maker of an eligible layout the exclusive right to copy, make and exploit it. Like copyright and patents, these rights are proprietary rights which may be dealt with as a form of personal property.

The second way in which the range of subject-matter protected as intellectual property has expanded is through the common law evolution of the actions of confidentiality and passing off. Confidentiality agreements are a common part of commercial life today and one of the ways in which a person might protect information that is not protected by the statutory intellectual property regimes. For example, a contract of employment may require an employee to keep information regarding customer lists confidential even though that information might not be protected under copyright law. A manufacturer may impose a duty of confidentiality on a prospective joint venturer in respect of a planned new product even though that product may not be eligible for registration and protection under the *Patents Act*. These intellectual property rights are considered in Part V (Designs, Plant Breeder's Rights, Circuit Layouts and Confidential Information).

Passing off occurs when a trader misrepresents his or her goods or services as having a quality associated with another trader's goods or services or as having some other connection with that trader's goods or services. Thus, a passing off may occur if a trader puts another's name on his or her goods or if the trader misrepresents that the goods are endorsed by another. This action has proved to be very flexible and responsive to new forms of trading and is a powerful weapon in the hands of a trader to protect his or her reputation or name. It is often used in conjunction with an action for trade mark infringement and we will therefore consider it in Part IV (Passing Off, Trade Marks and Related Actions).

The third and more controversial way in which the range of protected subject-matter has expanded is by extending the nature of interests characterised as intellectual property. Moral rights, performers' protection and resale royalty rights for visual artists are examples of this form of development. Moral rights give the author of a literary, dramatic, musical or artistic work, the maker of a film, performers in live performances, and performers in recordings of live performances, rights in relation to attribution and the right not to have the work, film or performance subject to derogatory treatment. Performers' protection gives a performer, including a performer of expressions of folklore, the right to take action against a person who makes an unauthorised recording of a live performance or broadcasts that performance. Resale royalty rights give a visual artist a right to receive a royalty each time a visual artwork worth more than $1000 is commercially resold by an art professional. None of these rights are property rights and they cannot be assigned. Authors and performers, however, may waive their rights and the resale royalty right of visual artists may pass by succession. Moral rights and artists' resale royalty rights subsist for the copyright period which is generally 70 years after the death of the author. Performers' protection lasts for 20 to 50 years after the performance. Moral rights and performers' protection are covered by the *Copyright Act 1968*; resale royalty rights are granted under the *Resale Royalty Right for Visual Artists Act 2009* (Cth). Each of these rights will be considered in Part II (Copyright and Neighbouring Rights).

The extension of the concept of intellectual property to cover such personal interests means that there is no real limit to what might be characterised as intellectual property in the future. It is sometimes suggested, for example, that indigenous culture and knowledge should be protected as intellectual property even though an indigenous community's interest in such culture or knowledge would not normally be characterised as a property right. The development of moral rights, performers' protection and resale royalty rights provide examples of this process in action.

To sum up, the term intellectual property today embraces those interests which are protected by the *Copyright Act 1968*, which includes moral rights and performers' protection; the *Resale Royalty Right for Visual Artists Act 2009*; the *Patents Act 1990*; the *Trade Marks Act 1995*; the *Designs Act 2003*; the *Plant Breeder's Rights Act 1994* and the *Circuit Layouts Act 1989*. Intellectual property also covers the two common law actions of passing off and breach of confidentiality.[1]

## Intellectual Property Themes

In this text we focus on a number of themes which we believe are important to a full understanding of intellectual property law. First, in so far as intellectual property is a form of personal property, the law protects it in a way which some people will find unacceptable. The intellectual property owner, for example, may be able to protect that property at the expense of other interests such as freedom of speech, public health and knowledge sharing. The owner may be granted a remedy to protect that property even if the owner suffers no actual damage. The ongoing debate as to whether intellectual property is a "good thing" and whether it can survive the digital, biotech age can best be understood as an honest disagreement as to the proper limits of this right of property. At the end of this text we hope that you will be able to make an intelligent contribution to this debate.

---

1    We might compare this list to the definition of intellectual property in the World Intellectual Property Organization's (WIPO's) *Agreement on Trade Related Aspects of Intellectual Property* (TRIPS). Article 1.2 of TRIPS provides that "for the purposes of this Agreement, the term 'intellectual property' refers to all categories of intellectual property that are the subject of sections 1 through 7 of Part II". Sections 1 through 7 of Part II of the TRIPS Agreement cover copyright and "related rights", that is, moral rights and performers' rights; trade marks; geographical indications; industrial designs; patents, which includes plant breeder's rights; layout (topographies) of integrated circuits and protection of undisclosed information.

Secondly, intellectual property law is conducted in an international context and this is reflected in Australia's domestic law. This means that international and bilateral treaties commonly impose minimum standards for intellectual property protection and may require Australia to extend protection for intellectual property to citizens and nationals of other party states. Under more recent international agreements, Australia may be subject to trade sanctions if it fails to comply with these minimum standards or offer such protection.

The impetus for this global regulation of intellectual property has traditionally come from IP producers who seek to protect their worldwide manufacturing and distribution networks. At the same time, however, IP importing countries who want access to these international products may introduce IP laws so as to encourage IP producers to export to their countries. The desire for access to overseas-produced seed, for example, was one of the principal drivers for the introduction of plant breeder's rights in Australia in the 1980s.

We can understand this international movement if we realise that intellectual property law does not protect or commodify ideas, plants or life as such, but rather it facilitates their marketing and distribution by commodifying the right to deal with them. For example, the introduction of copyright laws in the early 18th century did not lead to the commodification of literary expression – this was already a commodity. Rather it led to the emergence of the modern publishing industry and the birth of the distribution networks that we still see today. International agreements allowed these same publishers to extend their networks worldwide. Similarly, the introduction of plant breeder's rights in Australia 20 years ago did not suddenly turn seeds into a commodity – they were already a commodity. Rather, the introduction of plant breeder's rights led to the separation of growing and marketing in many agricultural sectors and the emergence of specialist marketing companies which relied on modern production and distribution networks built on intellectual property licensing agreements and access to internationally produced seed.[2] This distinction is well recognised in patent law. As any patent attorney will attest, the grant of a patent does not turn an invention into a successful commodity, rather it allows the inventor to deal with marketers and manufacturers who will work to turn that invention into a successful commodity in a global market.

This distinction is also useful when thinking about intellectual property law reform. Much of the international debate regarding the extension of intellectual property rights to indigenous cultural property and traditional knowledge, for example, has turned on the question of whether it would be harmful to indigenous communities to commodify culture and knowledge. We would suggest that there is already a market for the products of indigenous culture and traditional knowledge and to this extent they might already be said to have been commodified. The extension of intellectual property rights to indigenous culture and traditional knowledge would have other effects. It could facilitate the development of modern worldwide distribution networks for these "products". Alternatively, exclusive dealing rights might, in certain limited circumstances, allow communities to actually prevent dealing with the "products". Or again, rights in the nature of

---

2   See Rocque Reynolds, *Plant Breeder's Rights and Contract Growing in the Pasture Seeds Industry. A Market in Transition*, RIRDC, Canberra, 2007.

moral rights would give communities some recognition and control over the use of their cultural products once they had been dealt with.

Finally, the relationship between technology and intellectual property law is a constantly changing and fascinating one. Not only does changing technology pose challenges for law reformers and drafters but it also opens up new possibilities and challenges for intellectual property owners. Sometimes the path taken by the intellectual property owner is obvious, profitable and successful – such as the online distribution of legal research databases. Sometimes the process is slow and difficult – such as the recording industry's attempt to develop a profitable online music distribution model. In patent law and plant breeder's rights the relationship between technology and intellectual property law is particularly complex. Biotechnology is breaking down the distinctions between life and technology, discovery and invention, which have previously framed our common sense view of what is a patentable invention. At the same time, gene regulation technology (so called "terminator genes") could render plant breeder's rights redundant.

## The Law, the Textbook and Online Updates

This text contains a detailed analysis of the law of intellectual property as at 1 May 2012, including the *Intellectual Property Laws Amendment (Raising the Bar) Act 2012* (Cth). This Act has been described as a "major reform" of the intellectual property system and the culmination of two years of extensive consultation with interested parties.[3] It draws on a number of past inquiries including the Advisory Council on Intellectual Property's *Patents and Experimental Use* 2005, *Review of Trade Mark Enforcement* 2004 and *Should the jurisdiction of the Federal Magistrate's Service be extended to include patent, trade mark and designs matters?* 2003; the Senate Standing Committee on Community Affairs' *Inquiry into Gene Patents* 2009; the Australian Law Reform Commission Report 99, *Genes and Ingenuity: Gene Patenting and Human Health* 2004; IP Australia's *Review of Penalties and Damages* 2008; and the Australian Institute of Criminology's *Intellectual Property Crime Enforcement in Australia* 2008.

The Act amends the *Copyright Act 1968,* the *Trade Marks Act 1995*, the *Patents Act 1990*, the *Designs Act 2003* and the *Plant Breeder's Rights Act 1994*. It seeks to raise the quality of granted patents; provide free access to patents for research and regulatory purposes (the experimental and regulatory use exception); streamline and simplify patent, trade mark, design and plant breeder's rights procedures; and to bring provisions relating to patent and trade mark attorneys into line with other professionals. The Act also strengthens trade mark and copyright enforcement by increasing trade mark penalties, allowing exemplary damages in trade mark cases and facilitating confiscation of counterfeit goods.

One of the features of this textbook is that it contains extracts of essential cases at the end of each chapter. In most cases, the extracts have been chosen because they are the leading or authoritative statement of the legal point in issue. However, in some cases, an extract might have been selected because it provides an excellent statement of the legal principles in issue or because it provides

---

3    Commonwealth, *Parliamentary Debates*, Senate, 22 June 2011, p 3485 (Kim Carr).

an historical background for the legal issue or an overview of the authoritative case law. We hope that, as critical readers of this text, you will take account of these matters and use the cases as springboards to consider additional case law whenever the opportunity for further research or inquiry arises.

References to legislation in the text are to Commonwealth statutes unless otherwise specified.

# Part II

# Copyright and Neighbouring Rights

---

## Chapter 2

# Copyright – Its Birth and Nature

### The Great Question of Literary Property and the Birth of Copyright

The *Copyright Act 1968* (Cth) s 8 provides that, subject to the Crown prerogative, copyright does not subsist "otherwise than by virtue of this Act". That is, copyright is a statutory right and common law copyright, if any, is abolished. This little section rounds off one of the great debates of the 17th and 18th centuries which was known at the time as "The Great Question of Literary Property". The "great question" was whether authors had, or should have, a property right in their published literary works which was separate from the chattel right in the paper and ink which comprised the book itself. It was generally accepted that authors had an equitable right to prevent publication of unpublished works[1] but once the work was published debate raged as to the nature, if any, of the authors' right in the work.

Two powerful arguments framed the debate as it was conducted inside and outside the courts. On the one hand, it was argued that, according to principles of natural law, an author should own the "fruits of his labour". On the other, it was argued that, also according to principles of natural law, property was only property in so far as it could be occupied, that is only in so far as the owner was able to protect it and exclude others from it. Once words and ideas were published in the public arena, it was said, an author could no more own them than a person might own the sunshine or the air. The first of these arguments was a popularised version of John Locke's argument in *Two Treatises of Government*, published in 1690, regarding the creation of private property from the commons.[2] The second argument is familiar to all law students today as a traditional, but criticised, legal definition of property. In the 17th century, however, the test might have been more popularly associated with Thomas Hobbes who wrote in *Leviathan*, published in 1651:

> To this war of every man, against every man, this also is consequent; that nothing can be unjust ... It is consequent also to the same condition, that there can be no propriety,

---

1    *Macklin v Richardson* (1770) 27 ER 451.
2    John Locke, *Two Treatises of Government*, Dent, London, 1924 (first published 1690).

no dominion, no *mine* and *thine* distinct; but only that to be every man's, that he can get; and for so long, as he can keep it.[3]

Why this question should reach its peak in England only at this time is a matter of great debate itself. Books had been written for some 5000 years, the printing presses had been running for more than 200 years and a substantial book trade had existed at least since the second century BC. Cicero's friend, Pomponius Atticus (109-32 BC), for example, kept writer slaves who copied books for the trade, and historians calculate that in a large scriptorium up to 400 books a day may have been produced by the simple expedient of having one slave read aloud to the rest.[4] For lawyers, however, it is possible to identify two distinct events which brought the great question of literary property into sharp relief. These were the dismantling, in 1641, of the licensing system for printing and publishing literary works and the subsequent enactment of the first copyright Act, the *Statute of Anne* (8 Anne c 19) in 1709.

In Benjamin Kaplan's influential series of lectures, *An Unhurried View of Copyright*,[5] the author begins his history of copyright law with a consideration of the system of press licensing established by the Tudor monarchs (1485-1603) following the introduction of Caxton's printing press into England in 1476. The system, which continued until the abolition of the Star Chamber in 1641, was based on the Crown prerogative to grant licences and patents to individuals authorising them to print or import books. It was policed by the Stationers Company which was given a charter to act as a "literary constable" to license printing presses, censor books and to search out, seize and destroy illicit presses and seditious, heretical literature. In exchange, the Stationers Company obtained a substantial monopoly in the printing and selling of books. The Star Chamber partially enforced the system through its criminal jurisdiction over treason, sedition and heresy. Kaplan concludes his survey of the period with the rhetorical flourish, "How does this relate to copyright? To mangle Sir Henry Maine's aphorism, copyright has the look of being gradually secreted in the interstices of the censorship".[6] This idea of copyright as an objectionable form of publisher's privilege still enjoys currency today although Kaplan himself is careful to distinguish the censorship/ licensing system from copyright law itself:

> The patents for the books, in that they conferred exclusive rights, bear some family resemblances to the later institution of copyright. They did not however, stand on any notion of original composition, for they might be granted for ancient as well as new works.[7]

The first copyright Act, the *Statute of Anne*, was passed in 1709. Under that Act the right to print or reprint a book was vested, for the first time, in the hands of the author rather than in the hands of the person registered with the Stationers Company. The right could be sold or licensed to publishers and others. Some commentators, loosely relying on Kaplan, have suggested that the *Statute of Anne*

---

3    Thomas Hobbes, *Leviathan: Or the matter, forme and power of a Commonwealth ecclesiasticall and civil*, edited with foreword by Michael Oakeshott, Blackwell, Oxford, 1955, p 83.
4    See S Dahl, *History of the Book*, 2nd ed, Scarecrow Press, Metuchen, 1968.
5    Benjamin Kaplan, *An Unhurried View of Copyright*, Columbia University Press, 1967.
6    Benjamin Kaplan, *An Unhurried View of Copyright*, Columbia University Press, 1967, p 4.
7    Benjamin Kaplan, *An Unhurried View of Copyright*, Columbia University Press, 1967, p 4.

was primarily an economic right designed to protect the interests of publishers following the collapse of the Stationers' monopoly.[8] More literary scholars have suggested that the Act represented a new and romantic image of the author as the creator of the work and the emergence of the professional writer-scholar who was no longer supported by a patronage system.[9] Historians might see both of these suggestions as examples of the relentless move from Crown privilege to private industry. Kaplan's own conclusion is more measured. "I doubt", he writes, "that the statute was any more grounded on a thoughtful review of policy than the defeat of official licensing had been. ... It is hard to know how far the interests of authors were considered in distinction from those of publishers".[10] The preamble of the Act partially reflects all of these interests.

> An act for the encouragement of learning, by vesting the copies of printed books in the authors or purchasers of such copies, during the times therein mentioned. Whereas printers, booksellers, and other persons have of late frequently taken the liberty of printing, reprinting, and publishing, or causing to be printed, reprinted, and published, books and other writings, without the consent of the authors or proprietors of such books and writings, to their very great detriment, and too often to the ruin of them and their families: for preventing therefore such practices for the future, and for the encouragement of learned men to compose and write useful books; may it please your Majesty, that it may be enacted, and be it enacted by the Queen's most excellent majesty, by and with the advice and consent of the lords spiritual and temporal, and commons, in this present parliament assembled, and by the authority of the same; That from and after the tenth day of April, one thousand seven hundred and ten, the author of any book or books already printed, who hath not transferred to any other the copy or copies of such book or books, share or shares thereof, or the bookseller or booksellers, printer or printers, or other person or persons, who hath or have purchased or acquired the copy or copies of any book or books, in order to print or reprint the same, shall have the sole right and liberty of printing such book and books for the term of one and twenty years, to commence from the said tenth day of April, and no longer; and that the author of any book or books already composed, and not printed and published, or that shall hereafter be composed, and his assignee or assigns, shall have the sole liberty of printing and reprinting such book and books for the term of fourteen years, to commence from the day of the first publishing the same, and no longer.

The *Statute of Anne* presented a puzzle for lawyers. Did it create a new, hitherto unknown, copyright vested in authors or did it declare an existing common law copyright? If the latter, did the common law right survive the statute and exist in perpetuity or were all rights in the nature of copyright henceforth limited to statute? The question was eventually answered in the great cases of

---

8   S Ricketson's opening chapter in *The Berne Convention and the Protection of Literary and Artistic Works: 1886-1986*, Kluwer, London, 1987, pp 3-4, partially adopts this argument. See also Jane C Ginsberg, "The Tale of Two Copyrights: Literary Property in Revolutionary France and America" in B Sherman and A Strowel (eds), *Of Authors and Origins: Essays on Copyright Law*, Clarendon Press, Oxford, 1994, pp 131-158.

9   Mark Rose, "The Author as Proprietor: *Donaldson v Beckett* and the Genealogy of Modern Authorship" in B Sherman and A Strowel (eds), *Of Authors and Origins: Essays on Copyright Law*, Clarendon Press, Oxford, 1994, pp 23-55; Paul Edward Geller, "Must Copyright Be Forever Caught between Marketplace and Authorship Norms?" in B Sherman and A Strowel (eds), *Of Authors and Origins: Essays on Copyright Law*, Clarendon Press, Oxford, 1994, pp 159-201.

10   Benjamin Kaplan, *An Unhurried View of Copyright*, Columbia University Press, 1967, pp 6-7.

*Millar v Taylor*[11] in 1769 and *Donaldson v Becket*[12] in 1774 in favour of those who propounded a common law copyright based on the natural right of the author as the creator of a work. In *Donaldson v Becket* and *Jefferys v Boosey*[13] in 1854 it was further decided that the common law right had been abolished by the passing of the *Statute of Anne* and that henceforth copyright was purely a creature of statute.

*Millar v Taylor* concerned the copyright in James Thomson's book of poetry, *The Seasons*, which was owned by Millar. Following the elapse of the statutory period under the *Statute of Anne*, Taylor printed 1000 copies of the book and these copies were offered for sale. Millar sued for loss of profit and benefit. The Court of Kings Bench, in its first split decision under Lord Mansfield, found that there was a common law copyright and that it was not taken away by the *Statute of Anne* (Willes and Ashton JJ and Mansfield LJ; Yates J dissenting).

Willes J avoided the "too metaphysical" Lockean arguments advanced by counsel. "Metaphysical reasoning", he said, "is too subtle; arguments from the supposed modes of acquiring the property of acorns, or a vacant piece of land in an imaginary state of nature are too remote".[14] Instead, Willes J appealed to what he called "natural justice", a concept which still owed a lot to Locke. He referred to the importance of encouraging literary works, the desire that strangers should not reap where they have not sown, the author's entitlement to the "fruits of his own labour", the public advantage of authors being able to feed themselves and their families, and the small impact such a right would have on the price of books.[15] In addition, Willes J argued, the Courts of Equity had historically granted injunctions for breach of copyright even though the formalities required under the *Statute of Anne* had not been complied with. In other words, Willes J found proof of the existence of a common law right in an examination of the practices of the equity justices.

Ashton J also found the philosophical arguments regarding property inadequate as legal tools. Such arguments were suitable for things in a primitive and imaginary state, he said, but they were too crude to deal with the subtleties and developments of the common law. They "lose sight of the present state of the world; and end their enquiries where they should begin".[16] Property, he said, no longer depended on the crudeness of occupancy or on the myth of a commons. The types of property had been expanded to include objects hitherto unknown to the law and property no longer depended on its utility. All that was required, Ashton J held, was that the thing have a "distinguishable existence" and an "actual value" to the true owner.[17] Copyright in a literary work in general, and *The Seasons* in particular, met these criteria:

> The present claim is founded upon the original right to the work, as being the mental labour of the author; and that the effect and produce of the labour is his. It is a personal,

---

11    (1769) 98 ER 201.

12    (1774) 1 ER 837.

13    (1854) 4 HLC 815.

14    (1769) 98 ER 201 at 218 referring to Chapter 5 para 31 of John Locke's *An Essay Concerning the True Original, Extent and End of Civil Government* first published in 1690. See EA Burtt (ed), *The English Philosophers from Bacon to Mill*, Modern Library, New York, 1939, p 415.

15    (1769) 98 ER 201 at 218.

16    (1769) 98 ER 201 at 220-221.

17    (1769) 98 ER 201 at 221.

incorporeal property, saleable and profitable; it has indicia certa: for though the sentiments and doctrine may be called ideal, yet when the same are communicated to the sight and understanding of every man, by the medium of printing, the work becomes a distinguishable subject of property, and not totally destitute of corporeal qualities.[18]

Ashton J concluded: "The best rule, both of reason and justice seems to be, 'to assign to everything capable of ownership, a legal and determinate owner'".[19]

Lord Mansfield, like Willes J, found proof of the existence of a common law copyright in the practices of the Equity justices.[20] Like the other judges he found the arguments of the philosophers inadequate but based his arguments not on any principle of labour but on the moral rights of the author as expounded by John Milton (1608-1674).[21]

> The author may not only be deprived of any profit, but lose the expense he has been at. He is no more master of the use of his own name. He has no control over the correctness of his own work. He cannot prevent additions. He cannot retract errors. He cannot amend; or cancel a faulty edition. Anyone may print, pirate, and perpetrate the imperfections, to the disgrace and against the will of the author; may propagate sentiments under his name, which he disapproves, repents and is ashamed of.[22]

Yates J's three hour dissent provides a comprehensive statement against a common law copyright and is based on general principles of property law and on legal history. He accepts the maxim that "nothing can be an object of property which is not capable of sole and exclusive enjoyment"[23] and concludes that the words and ideas in a literary work are no more capable of being owned than the sunshine or light. He accepts that a person may be entitled to the "fruits of his labour" but he adds, we "must not expect these fruits to be eternal". The author in this regard is like the inventor and both the author and the inventor owe the extent of their property to the legislature rather than to the common law.[24] As a matter of precedent Yates J rejects the injunctions of the courts of equity, the decrees of the Star Chamber and the practices of the Stationers Company as evidence of the common law. The equity courts could not determine the content of the common law;[25] the criminal jurisdiction of the Star Chamber could not determine the content of the civil law;[26] and the charter powers of the Stationers Company were no proof of a common law of property.[27]

---

18 (1769) 98 ER 201 at 221-222.
19 (1769) 98 ER 201 at 221.
20 (1769) 98 ER 201 at 252.
21 "The single opinion of such a man as Milton", stated Mansfield LJ, "speaking, after much consideration, upon the very point is stronger than any inferences from gathering acorns and seizing vacant pieces of ground; when the writers, so far from thinking of the very point, speak of an imaginary state of nature before the invention of letters": *Millar v Taylor* (1769) 98 ER 201 at 253. See John Milton, "Areopagitica or A Speech for the Liberty of Unlicensed Printing to the Parliament of England 1644" in *Areopagitica and Other Prose Works*, Dent, London, 1927, pp 1-41.
22 Lord Mansfield in *Millar v Taylor* (1769) 98 ER 201 at 252.
23 (1769) 98 ER 201 at 233.
24 (1769) 98 ER 201 at 231-232.
25 (1769) 98 ER 201 at 241.
26 (1769) 98 ER 201 at 239.
27 (1769) 98 ER 201 at 240.

*Donaldson v Becket*[28] came before the House of Lords as an appeal against a decree of the Court of Chancery regarding *The Seasons* and other works by Thomson. Copyright in these works, under the *Statute of Anne*, had expired in 1757. In 1768 Donaldson printed and published copies of the works and in 1769 an alleged right to print the works was sold to Becket by the executors of Millar's will. Based on the decision in *Millar v Taylor*, Becket successfully sought an injunction against Donaldson who appealed to the House of Lords on the ground that he was authorised to print, publish and sell the works unless Becket could prove a "title paramount to the statute".[29] The House of Lords referred the matter to the 12 common law judges for opinion. The judges were split in their advice. By a majority of eight to three they advised that there was a common law copyright in published works but by a majority of six to five they advised that it had been taken away by statute. Lord Mansfield did not speak and the House of Lords reversed the decree.

*Jefferys v Boosey*[30] concerned Vincenzo Bellini's unpublished opera, *La Sonnambula*. Bellini assigned his rights in the opera to Giovanni Ricordi according to the laws of Milan. On a visit to London, Ricordi assigned the rights to the plaintiff, Jefferys, who published the work. In an action against Boosey for breach of copyright, Boosey argued that no copyright subsisted in the work, at least in England. The judges were still divided on the question of whether there had indeed been a common law copyright but agreed that copyright was now a "creature of statute". On this basis the court held that Boosey had not infringed copyright in the opera because the *Statute of Anne* did not vest copyright in a foreign national who composed a work in another country nor did the statute vest copyright in the first publisher of the work in England.

Despite the fact that by a substantial majority the 18th century judges[31] held that there was a common law copyright which vested in authors, such a view now appears to be unpopular, at least amongst text book writers. The rather flighty language of the judges in favour of a common law right, together with their appeals to natural law and to moral rights, hold little attraction as a form of legal discourse today.[32] Whether there was in fact a form of copyright at common law is still, therefore, a moot point and, while studying copyright law, it is worth remembering that at the time of its birth this was indeed a "great question".[33]

Whatever its origins, the idea of an author's property right in his or her work which was separate from the chattel right took hold and has since been enshrined in statutory form throughout the world. Over the 18th and 19th centuries the types of works to which it applied, the duration of the right and the rights granted

---

28    (1774) 1 ER 837.

29    (1774) 1 ER 837 at 839.

30    (1854) 4 HLC 815.

31    See a head count of judicial opinion in Sir William Holdsworth, *A History of the English Law*, Methuen, London, 1936-1966, Vol 6, p 379n.

32    The views of Yates J and the occupancy theories of property are not popular either. In *Pacific Film Laboratories Pty Ltd v Commissioner of Taxation (Cth)* (1970) 121 CLR 154 at 168, Windeyer J commented that "[t]he views of Yates J as to the nature of copyright as property can be disregarded now".

33    See, for example, Ronan Deazley, *On the Origin of the Right to Copy*, Hart Publishing, Oxford and Portland Oregon, 2004; and Ronan Deazley, "The Myth of Copyright at Common Law" (2003) 62 *Cambridge LJ* 106.

gradually expanded. In the United Kingdom the *Engraving Copyright Act* was introduced in 1734 (8 Geo II c 13); the *Print Copyright Act* in 1777 (17 Geo III c 57) and the *Sculpture Copyright Act* in 1798 (38 Geo III c 71). A performance right was introduced in 1833 under the *Dramatic Copyright Act* (3 and 4 Will IV c 15) and later extended to musical works by amendment to the 1842 *Copyright Act* (5 and 6 Vict c 45). A *Lectures Copyright Act* (5 and 6 Will IV c 65) was introduced in 1835 and in 1862 a *Fine Arts Copyright Act* (25 and 26 Vict c 68) which covered paintings, drawings and photographs was enacted.

In the United Kingdom this ad hoc, piecemeal approach to the protection of authors' rights was subject to sustained criticism.[34] There was also concern that the legislation did not meet the United Kingdom's obligations under the first international convention on copyright, the *International Convention for the Protection of Literary and Artistic Works* which had been concluded at Berne on 9 September 1886 (the Berne Convention).[35] In 1911 the United Kingdom Parliament passed the *Copyright Act 1911* (1 and 2 Geo V c 46) which repealed 20 separate statutes relating to copyright and replaced them with one consolidated statute which covered literary, dramatic, musical and artistic works (s 1). Sound recordings were protected as musical works (s 19) and some cinematographic films were protected as dramatic works (s 35(1)). In order to meet the requirements of the Berne Convention the Act also extended copyright to architectural works (as artistic works) and choreographic works (as dramatic works) and all registration and other formality requirements for obtaining copyright protection were abolished. The Act vested in the author the right to publish, reproduce and perform a work, deliver a lecture, dramatise a novel or make a non-dramatic version of a dramatic or artistic work and, in the case of literary, dramatic and musical works, to make a record, piano roll, cinematographic film or other "mechanical reproduction" (such as a music box) of the work (s 1).

## The International Context

In the age of empire into which copyright was born, the international aspects of copyright protection were always important. In 1886 the first international convention on copyright, the *Berne Convention for the Protection of Literary and Artistic Works*, was finalised and signed by 10 nations – Belgium, France, Germany, Haiti, Italy, Liberia, Spain, Switzerland, Tunisia and the United Kingdom.[36] In reaching agreement on the terms of the convention the primary concern for copyright-producing nations was to protect the work of their authors in other countries. For copyright consuming nations, such as Sweden (which did not sign until 1904), as for developing countries today, a primary concern was to ensure access to and translation rights for copyright works. Before the Berne

---

34    See *The Royal Commission into Copyright*, Command 2086, HMSO, London, 1878; and Board of Trade, *Report of the Committee on the Law of Copyright*, Command 4976, HMSO, London, 1909.

35    This was three years after the *Paris Convention on the Protection of Industrial Property* 1883 which was the first international intellectual property convention and covered patents, trade marks and designs.

36    For a detailed account of the development and first 100 years of the Berne Agreement, see S Ricketson, *The Berne Convention for the Protection of Literary and Artistic Works 1886-1986*, Kluwer, London, 1987.

Convention the usual method of achieving these aims had been through bi-lateral agreements and, in the case of colonial powers such as Spain, France, Portugal and the United Kingdom, by passing imperial legislation. Today, more than 160 states are members of the Berne Union.

The central plank of the Berne Convention was the adoption of the principle of national treatment or reciprocity. Under this principle an author whose work was made in one Union country and infringed in another was entitled to the same protection and remedies in the country of infringement as a national of that country (Art 5). By itself, the principle of national treatment had certain shortcomings. A domestic law, for example, might require registration of a work or other formalities in order to obtain protection and in many cases foreign authors would not have complied with these requirements. Article 5(2) therefore provided that the exercise of Berne Convention rights would not be subject to any formalities, although a member country could still impose formalities on its domestic authors. To give an example, in the United States a domestic author may be required to register a work in order to receive damages in infringement proceedings but, since signing the Berne Convention in 1989, the United States has finally agreed that a foreign author need not adopt these formalities in order to receive similar protection in the United States.[37] Another shortcoming of the principle of national treatment is that the level of copyright protection, the duration of copyright, the works covered and the remedies available might differ significantly between member countries. Country A might therefore be required to offer substantial protection to authors from Country B even though neither that author nor an author from Country A would receive comparable protection in Country B. Recognition of these shortcomings led to the second aspect of the Berne Convention which was the establishment of minimum standards for the protection of copyright.

The original Berne Convention covered "literary and artistic works" which included books, musical works, dramatic works, maps and paintings, engravings and designs (Art 4). Since 1886 the convention has been subject to five major revisions. These were at Berlin in 1908, Rome in 1928, Brussels in 1948, Stockholm in 1967 and Paris in 1971. In 1908 the convention was extended to include architectural works, pantomimes and choreographic works and, in 1948, cinematographic films and photographs were included. Authors were given exclusive broadcast rights in 1928 and in the same year moral rights were introduced (Art 6bis). Although moral rights are not strictly a form of copyright they are often dealt with under copyright legislation and are referred to as a "neighbouring right".

The Berne Convention is not the only international copyright agreement and not all copyright material is covered by it. The *Rome Convention for the Protection of Performers, Producers of Phonograms and Broadcasting Organisations 1961*, the *Geneva Convention for the Protection of Producers of Phonograms Against*

---

37   The *Universal Copyright Convention* (UCC) was drafted under the auspices of the United Nations Educational, Scientific and Cultural Organisation (UNESCO) in 1952 and is more generous than Berne in allowing developing countries to use copyright material. The UCC provides that the application of the copyright symbol © shall be sufficient to achieve copyright protection for a foreign author in a contracting state whose domestic laws require formalities (Art III). If a country is a party to both the UCC and Berne, however, Berne shall prevail and no formalities may be required. The only countries which are signatories to the UCC and not Berne are Cambodia and Laos.

*Unauthorised Duplication of their Phonograms 1971*, the *Vienna Agreement for the Protection of Typefaces and other International Deposit 1973* and the *Brussels Convention Relating to Distribution of Programme-Carrying Signals Transmitted by Satellite 1974* extended the reach of copyright law to include sound recordings and television and radio broadcasts as well as introducing another neighbouring right known as performers' protection.

An important development during the 1970s and 1980s on the international scene was the growing voice of developing countries. These countries sought to limit the extent of copyright protection, facilitate the use of works for scholarly and educational purposes and to protect folklore. A protocol to the 1967 Stockholm revision of the Berne Convention partially addressed these concerns (but was not binding) as had the introduction of the *Universal Copyright Convention* (UCC) under the auspices of the United Nations Educational, Scientific and Cultural Organisation (UNESCO) in 1952. However, the strength of this voice waned in the late 1980s and since 1990 international copyright agreements have tended to reflect a commitment to free trade principles rather than to development issues.

This new direction in copyright law has not been led by the World Intellectual Property Organization (WIPO), the international body established to administer the Berne Convention but by the *General Agreement on Trade and Tariffs* (GATT) and the World Trade Organization (WTO). GATT, an international agreement committed to freeing up world trade, was first signed in 1947, and is regularly renegotiated. As part of the negotiations known as the Uruguay Round (1986-1994) intellectual property was added to the range of trade matters subject to the GATT and is now governed by the *Agreement on Trade Related Aspects of Intellectual Property 1995* (TRIPS). TRIPS covers trade marks, designs, patents, confidential information, geographical indicators and circuit layouts as well as copyright. In relation to copyright TRIPS requires members to abide by the Berne Convention, protect computer programs and databases as literary works, grant commercial leasing rights to owners of copyright in computer programs and cinematographic works and extend performers' protection. These provisions have since been adopted and developed by WIPO which in 1996 completed the *WIPO Copyright Treaty* (on computer programs and digital rights) and the *WIPO Performances and Phonograms Treaty*.

The significance of TRIPS does not lie in its comparatively minor substantive provisions but in its treatment of intellectual property as a trade commodity. Members are required to abolish impediments to free trade in intellectual property and to institute effective enforcement and customs procedures to prevent piracy and other infringements of intellectual property rights. Failure to meet the requirements of the agreement may lead to disputes procedures in the WTO and eventual trade sanctions. This has been particularly important in the field of patents (especially for pharmaceutical products) but has also been applied in copyright cases. In January 1999, for example, the European Community notified a dispute against the United States in relation to an amendment to s 110(5) of the United States *Copyright Act Title 17*.[38] The amendment allowed small businesses, within certain limits, to play music on radios and televisions to their customers without breaching the public performance right of the copyright owner. The WTO

---

38    Australia, Brazil, Japan, Switzerland and Canada reserved their right to intervene.

Disputes Settlement Body held that this was an unauthorised detraction from the rights of the copyright owner as provided for under the Berne Convention and ordered the United States to repeal the provision.[39] It might be noted that the interests of developing nations were not completely ignored under TRIPS – developing countries were allowed an extended period of time to meet their obligations under the agreement.

In addition to its obligations under TRIPS, Australia has now signed a free trade agreement with the United States which requires Australia to further extend the level and range of its intellectual property protection. The *US Free Trade Agreement Implementation Act 2004* (Cth) commenced on 16 August 2004 and most Parts of the Act came into effect on 1 January 2005. The Act brought in a number of significant changes including the extension of the copyright term and improved copyright and moral rights protection for performers, including performers of expressions of folklore.

All of these changes are dealt with in detail in the text.

## Copyright in Australia

On 25 July 1828, by virtue of the *Australian Courts Act 1828* (9 Geo IV c 83), United Kingdom statutes then in force were received as part of the law of what are now the Australian States of New South Wales, Victoria and Queensland. Similar legislation was eventually passed in the other States and Territories. The reception date in Western Australia was 1 June 1829, in South Australia 28 December 1836 and in the Australian Capital Territory and the Northern Territory the reception date was 1 January 1911. Statutes passed in the United Kingdom after the reception date did not apply unless expressed to do so. The effect of these different reception dates, together with the already ad hoc nature of United Kingdom copyright law, was that the protection offered to both British and colonial authors was highly inconsistent. In light of this generally unsatisfactory situation and possibly spurred on by the passing of the *Colonial Laws Validity Act* in 1865 (28 and 29 Vict c 63), a number of colonies were moved to pass their own copyright laws. Thus Victoria (in 1869), South Australia (in 1878), New South Wales (in 1879) and Western Australia (in 1895) passed relatively consolidated copyright laws which remained in force until after federation.[40]

Given the international context of intellectual property law it is not surprising that the Australian Constitution gave the Australian Parliament power under s 51(xviii) to make laws with respect to "copyrights, patents of inventions and designs and trade marks". The new Federal Parliament passed the *Copyright Act 1905* (Cth) but this Act was repealed in 1912 when the *Copyright Act 1912* (Cth) declared the *Copyright Act 1911* (UK) to be in force in Australia subject to

---

39 The Panel Report in *United States – Section 110(5) of the US Copyright Act* WT/DS160/R was adopted by the Disputes Settlement Body (DSB) on 27 July 2000. In the same decision the DSB upheld the "homestyle exemption" which allowed the public playing of a single radio or television commonly used in private homes so long as there was no charge for this and the transmission is not retransmitted.

40 For a discussion of the inadequacies of this colonial system of copyright protection, see Senator Keating's Second Reading Speech to the Senate on the Bill for the first Commonwealth Federal *Copyright Act 1905* in *Hansard*, Senate, 24 August 1905, pp 1425-1432.

any modifications made by the Australian Act itself (s 8). The 1911 Act applied in Australia as a piece of imperial legislation rather than as an ordinary Act of the Australian Parliament and therefore was not restricted to Australian territorial jurisdiction.[41] In 1931 the *Statute of Westminster* (22 Geo V c 4) was passed which provided that no Act of the United Kingdom Parliament would apply to any part of the Dominions unless there was an express request and consent to such application. In the absence of such a request from Australia the *Copyright Act 1958* (UK) which repealed the 1911 Act in the United Kingdom did not apply in Australia.[42] The 1911 Act therefore remained in force in Australia until it was repealed by the *Copyright Act 1968* (Cth) which came into effect on 1 May 1969.

One of the most important innovations of the 1968 Act was the introduction of a new category of protected subject-matter known by the unfortunate title of "Part IV Subject-matter other than Works". Under Part IV, copyright subsisted in television and radio broadcasts, and in cinematographic films and sound recordings as independent forms of copyright subject-matter. A new form of copyright in the printed edition of a work was also introduced. The *Copyright Act 1968* has been extensively amended in the ensuing decades to take account of changing forms of distribution and production and in order to meet Australia's international obligations. Some of the most important of these amendments have been the inclusion of computer programs as literary works in 1984;[43] the introduction of performers' protection in 1993;[44] the regulation of parallel importation of books (1991),[45] sound recordings (1998),[46] computer programs, electronic literary and music items (2003);[47] the introduction of a new digital communication right;[48] the extension of moral rights;[49] the introduction of some protection for expressions of folklore under the *US Free Trade Agreement Implementation Act 2004*; and the introduction of a new set of defences in 2006, including fair dealing for the purposes of parody or satire.[50]

Australian colonies became members of the Berne Union in 1887 by virtue of being part of the British Empire and, even after federation, Britain continued to act for Australia in many international matters. In 1912, for example, Britain acceded to the Rome revision of the Berne Convention on Australia's behalf and Australia did not become a member of the Berne Union in its own right until 1928. Since then Australia has signed and ratified most of the major international copyright agreements including the *Universal Copyright Convention* in 1969, the *Geneva Convention for the Protection of Producers of Phonograms Against Unauthorised Duplication of their Phonograms* in 1974, the *Brussels Convention Relating to Distribution of Programme-Carrying Signals Transmitted by Satellite*

---

41  *Gramophone Company Ltd v Leo Feist Inc* (1928) 41 CLR 1.
42  See *Copyright Owners Reproduction Society Ltd v EMI (Australia) Pty Ltd* (1958) 100 CLR 597.
43  *Copyright Amendment Act 1984.*
44  *Copyright Amendment Act 1989* and *Copyright Amendment (Re-enactment) Act 1993.*
45  *Copyright Amendment Act 1991.*
46  *Copyright Amendment Act (No 2) 1998.*
47  *Copyright Amendment (Parallel Importation) Act 2003.*
48  *Copyright Amendment (Digital Agenda) Act 2000.*
49  *Copyright Amendment (Moral Rights) Act 2000*; *US Free Trade Agreement Implementation Act 2004.*
50  *Copyright Amendment Act 2006* (Cth).

in 1990, the *Rome Convention* in 1992, the TRIPS Agreement in 1995, the *WIPO Copyright Treaty* and the *WIPO Performances and Phonograms Treaty*.

## Copyright and the Crown Prerogative

The *Copyright Act 1968* s 8A preserves "any prerogative right or privilege of the Crown". The Crown prerogative to publish certain books, as it was understood in England in 1769, was described by Yates J in *Millar v Taylor*[51] in the following terms:

> The books are Bibles, Common-Prayer Books, and all extracts from them (such as primers, Psalters, Psalms) and almanacs. Those have relation to the national religion, or Government, or the political constitution. Other compositions to which the King's right of publication extends, are the statutes, Acts of Parliament, and State-papers. The King's right to all these is, as head of the Church, and of the political constitution.

It is unlikely that the Crown prerogative would be understood in these broad terms in Australia today but the precise extent and nature of the Crown prerogative today in Australia is contested in both the academic literature and the case law. It has been argued that the Crown has a prerogative in the printing and publishing of legislation[52] but the question of copyright in a judge's reasons for decisions has been subject to disagreement.[53] The significance of the Crown prerogative in relation to copyright is diminished in so far as any defence available to infringement of copyright under the *Copyright Act* is also available for infringement of the prerogative or privilege in the nature of copyright (s 8A(2)).

## General Principles Regarding the Nature of Copyright

Despite the misgivings of Yates J in *Millar v Taylor*,[54] the *Copyright Act 1968* describes copyright as a personal right which is transmissible by assignment, by will and by devolution (s 196). Copyright has a number of distinctive features. As the name suggests, copyright originally granted the copyright owner exclusive rights in the copying of the subject-matter – through publication, reproduction or performance. If there was no copying then there was no infringement. Thus, if Painter B independently and fortuitously creates a painting which is identical to Painter A's painting there is no infringement of copyright. If a hundred monkeys over a hundred days with a hundred computers fortuitously rewrite even a well known novel there is no infringement of copyright. This is the primary difference between copyright and patents. A patent gives a monopoly right over the invention regardless of copy. If Inventor B independently makes a drip-less teabag

---

51    (1769) 98 ER 201 at 243.

52    *Attorney-General (NSW) v Butterworth and Co (Australia) Ltd* (1938) 38 NSW (SR) 195.

53    See CJ Bannon, "Copyright in Reasons for Judgment and Law Reporting" (1982) 56 *ALJ* 59, for example, and M Taggart's response in "Copyright in Written Reasons for Judgment" (1984) 10 *Syd L Rev* 319. Taggart argues that the Crown does not own the copyright in a judgment either under the *Copyright Act* or under the prerogative in judgments. If copyright subsists in judgments it is owned by the judges. See also Mark Perry, "Judges' reasons for judgments – to whom do they belong?" (1998) 18(2) *NZULR* 257.

54    (1769) 98 ER 201.

which is the same as the drip-less teabag for which Inventor A owns the patent then Inventor B has infringed Inventor A's patent despite the fact that Inventor B had no knowledge of the patent or Inventor A's teabag.

Copyright is different from and separate to the chattel right in the subject-matter. Furthermore, the copyright and the chattel right may be owned by different people. If I buy a book, for example, I have bought the chattel but I have not thereby acquired the copyright in the book as a literary work. I might sell the book, lease it, lend it or give it away but I may not exercise the rights of the copyright owner. I may not photocopy the book, make it available online, perform a dramatic version of it in public or make a translation of it. Up until 2006 I could not even make a Braille copy of it for my visually impaired friend. As one can imagine, many disputes have arisen because parties have failed to deal with the copyright separately from the chattel.

In *Pacific Film Laboratories Pty Ltd v Commissioner of Taxation (Cth)*,[55] the Commissioner of Taxation applied sales tax to the photographic prints developed by Pacific Film Laboratories and paid for by its customers. Pacific Film objected to the assessment on the ground that the customer owned the copyright in the film negatives, that Pacific Film was authorised by the customer to reproduce prints from these negatives, that Pacific Film had no property right in these prints and therefore was not selling anything to the customer which might be taxed. The High Court rejected this argument as based on a confusion between the chattel right in the print and the copyright in the negative. The customer had authorised Pacific Film to reproduce the negatives but the chattel produced in the process of this reproduction was owned by Pacific Film.

This general provision is partly modified by s 198 which provides that if an unpublished manuscript in a literary, dramatic, musical or artistic work forms part of a bequest then, unless the contrary intention appears in the will, the bequest will be read as including any copyright in the unpublished work owned by the testator at the time of his or her death. This section reverses the decision of the Court of Appeal in *Re Dickens*[56] regarding copyright in an unpublished manuscript by Charles Dickens known as "The Life of Christ". In his will Dickens left his papers, including the unpublished manuscript, to his sister-in-law. His residual estate was left to a beneficial trust. The sister-in-law purported to sell the copyright in "The Life of Christ" to Associated Press and the residual beneficiaries sued. The court held that the copyright in the literary work and manuscript as a chattel were separate and, although the sister-in-law owned the manuscript itself, the copyright in that manuscript had passed with the residual estate. Section 198 does not apply to published works and in that case the general rule applies.[57]

## Authorship and the idea-expression dichotomy

The fundamental principle of copyright law is that copyright does not protect ideas but only protects the form of expression. This principle arises directly from the original concept of copyright as an author's right. The author's craft is the

---

55   (1970) 121 CLR 154.

56   [1935] 1 Ch 267.

57   For transitional provisions regarding bequests, see *Copyright Act 1968* s 240.

craft of expression and copyright protects the author's craft. The idea-expression dichotomy is explicitly maintained in the TRIPS Agreement which provides that "[c]opyright protection shall extend to expressions and not to ideas, procedures, methods of operation or mathematical concepts as such" (Art 2).

Two examples of the principle are traditionally given. A book which explains a system of accounting, it is said, would be protected as a literary work but the ideas in the book would not be protected. Therefore, it would be an infringement of copyright to reproduce the text of the book but it would not be an infringement of copyright in the book to use or put into practice the system of accounting outlined in the book.[58] Similarly, the text of a recipe for a rabbit pie may be protected as a literary work but the recipe itself would not be protected. It would therefore be an infringement to reproduce the text of the recipe but it would not be an infringement to make the rabbit pie.[59] Both the accounting system and the recipe are classified as mere ideas and therefore not protected by copyright.

In copyright law the principle is applied in two different ways. Positively, the principle is applied to afford copyright protection to an author's expression regardless of the fact that the ideas expressed by the author existed in the public domain, were common or lacked novelty. Thus, in *Walter v Lane*,[60] the respondents argued that copyright did not subsist in a journalist's verbatim report of a public speech by Lord Rosebery because the report consisted only of matters which were "publici juris". The House of Lords rejected this argument, Lord Davey stating:

> [The respondents] say that Lord Rosebery was the author of his speech and gave it to the world ... The reporter they say (with a pardonable jingle), is the reproducer and not the producer of the speech ... In my opinion the reporter is the author of his own report. He it was who brought into existence in the form of a writing the piece of letterpress which the respondent has copied.[61]

Applying similar reasoning, it has been held that the author of a translation owned the copyright in a translation despite the fact that the ideas in the translation were not new and that they had been expressed in other terms before.[62] Similarly, copyright subsists in a photograph of a particular scene despite the fact that the scene itself is public.[63]

Negatively, the idea-expression dichotomy is applied to exclude mere information or ideas from copyright protection apart from their form of expression. Thus, in *Chilton v Progress Printing and Publishing Company*,[64] the English Court of Appeal found that copyright did not subsist in a racing tip although

---

58   This example is loosely taken from the famous United States case of *Baker v Selden* 101 US 99 (1879).

59   This example appears to have first been used by counsel for the defendant in *Cuisenaire v Reed* [1963] VR 719.

60   [1900] AC 539.

61   [1900] AC 539 at 551.

62   *MacMillan v Khan Bahadur Shamsul Ulama Zaka* [1895] ILR 19 Bom 557 (India). The *Copyright Act 1911* added the right to translate a work to the rights of the copyright owner. This does not prevent an infringing translator from claiming copyright in a translation: *Byrne v Statist Co* [1914] I KB 622.

63   For an obiter discussion of this point, see *Bauman v Fussell* [1978] RPC 485.

64   [1895] 2 Ch 29. See also *Walter v Steinkopff* [1892] 3 Ch 489 and *Springfield v Thame* (1903) 89 LT 242. Copyright does not subsist in news but in the form in which that news is expressed.

copyright would have subsisted in the written expression of that racing tip had it been claimed.

In *Donoghue v Allied Newspapers Ltd*,[65] a popular jockey, Donoghue, was interviewed over a period of time by a journalist. News of the World published a number of articles written by the journalist based on these interviews. The articles had titles such as "Steve Donoghue's Racing Secrets", "Enthralling Stories of the King of Sports" and "My Greatest Derby". Some of the articles were in the form of dialogues with Donoghue. Donoghue had been paid for these interviews but subsequently the information in the articles was updated and a further article appeared in another newspaper under the title "My Racing Secrets. By Steve Donoghue". Donoghue sought to prevent further circulation of the articles. Farwell J "reluctantly" found that Donoghue was neither the author nor a joint author of the articles because he had supplied only the ideas for the article and there was no copyright in an idea.

The application of the idea-expression dichotomy is thought to be fundamental to balancing the interests between copyright owners and the social interest in "free and open communication".[66] In *IceTV Pty Ltd v Nine Network Australia Pty Ltd*[67] the High Court expounded on the balancing act required:

> The information/expression dichotomy, in copyright law, is rooted in considerations of social utility. Copyright, being an exception to the law's general abhorrence of monopolies, does not confer a monopoly on facts or information because to do so would impede the reading public's access to and use of facts and information. Copyright is not given to reward work distinct from the production of a particular form of expression.[68]

## Functionality and the idea-expression dichotomy

Special problems arise in applying the idea-expression dichotomy to functional works such as computer programs or instruments. In Australia a computer program has been narrowly defined to mean the expression of the set of instructions which cause the computer to perform that particular function.[69] It would not, therefore, be an infringement of the copyright in a computer program to produce another program which performs the same function unless one also reproduced the expression of the set of instructions used in that computer program.

In *Autodesk Inc v Dyason (No 1)*,[70] the appellants owned the copyright in a computer program known as AutoCAD which was designed to aid architectural drawing and design. In order to discourage piracy the appellants developed a hardware device called an "AutoCAD lock" without which the computer program could not run. Thus, even if the program were copied it could not be used without the AutoCAD lock, only one of which was supplied with each program purchased. The respondent developed a circumvention device called an Auto Key

---

65   [1938] Ch 106.
66   *Telstra Corp Ltd v Phone Directories Co Pty Ltd* [2010] FCAFC 149 citing *IceTV Pty Ltd v Nine Network Australia Pty Ltd* (2009) 239 CLR 458
67   (2009) 239 CLR 458.
68   (2009) 239 CLR 458 at [28].
69   *Data Access Corporation v Powerflex Services Pty Ltd* (1999) 202 CLR 1 and see the definition of computer program in *Copyright Act 1968* s 10(1).
70   (1992) 173 CLR 330.

lock which performed the same function as the AutoCAD lock but was designed quite differently. The respondents sold their lock for less than the cost of buying another AutoCAD program. At first instance Northrop J, applying a very broad interpretation of computer program, found that both locks were computer programs, that they performed the same function and that the difference in the form of expression used in the two locks to achieve this particular function was irrelevant. Northrop J held that the respondents had infringed the appellant's copyright because the function of the AutoCAD lock had been reproduced in material form by the Auto Key lock.[71] In the High Court Northrop J's judgment was criticised both for the broad definition of computer program and also for the emphasis placed on the function of the locks rather than on the form of expression by which the function was achieved. The judgment was said to have ignored the traditional distinction between an idea and its expression. Dawson J, who delivered the leading judgment said:

> Indeed, the significance placed by Northrop J upon the function of the two locks would appear to disregard the traditional dichotomy in the law of copyright between an idea and the expression of an idea … There is a particular difficulty in distinguishing an idea from its expression in the case of a utilitarian work, such as a computer program, which, in contrast to literary works of an artistic kind, is intended to be useful rather than to please. But it has been held that the idea of a utilitarian work is its purpose or function and that the method of arriving at that purpose or function is the expression of the idea: see *Whelan Associates v Jaslow Dental Laboratory* (1986) 797 F 2d 1222, at p 1236 citing *Baker v Selden* (1879) 101 US 99.[72]

Dawson J's reference to American case law is unfortunate in this context because the application of the idea-expression dichotomy to functional works has developed quite differently in the United States. Under the United States *Copyright Act Code 17* s 102, copyright subsists in an "original work of authorship" but is limited in s 102(b) in terms which are arguably wider than the terms of the TRIPS Agreement:

> In no case does copyright protection for an original work of authorship extend to any idea, procedure, process, system, method of operation, concept, principle, or discovery, *regardless of the form in which it is described, explained, illustrated, or embodied in such work*. (emphasis added)

Although influential American commentators, such as Nimmer,[73] have argued that s 102(b) should be read as a statement of the general principle that copyright subsists in the expression of an idea but not in the idea itself, this interpretation has not been adopted by United States courts. Instead the exemption has given rise to two important limitations to copyright in United States law which do not apply in Australia.

First, it has been held that where there is a merger between an idea (or function) and its expression then copyright does not subsist in that expression. Thus, in *Baker v Selden*,[74] copyright did not subsist in accounting forms designed

---

71    *Autodesk Inc v Dyason* (1989) 15 IPR 1 at 25.
72    (1992) 173 CLR 330 at 344.
73    Melville B Nimmer and David Nimmer, *Nimmer on Copyright,* M Bender, New York, 1999 §2[18][C][2].
74    101 US 99 (1879).

especially to enable a new method of accounting to be performed. The United States Supreme Court held that to grant copyright in the accounting forms would indirectly give a monopoly over the method of accounting itself because there was a merger between the method of accounting (the idea) and the forms themselves (the expression). To allow such a monopoly over an idea would be against the purposes of copyright protection as provided under the United States Constitution:

> The Congress shall have power … to promote the progress of the sciences and useful arts, by securing for limited times to authors and inventors the exclusive right to their respective writings and discoveries.[75]

Nearly one hundred years later, in *Whelan Associates v Jaslow Dental Laboratory*,[76] it was argued that copyright could not subsist in a computer program designed to keep records in a dental clinic because there was a merger between the idea of the program (or its function) and its expression. The argument was rejected on the basis that there were a number of different ways that such a program could be expressed and therefore there was no merger in that case.

Although there have been many obiter statements in Australian and English cases[77] supporting the existence of a merger doctrine in Australian copyright law, the leading computer software case in the High Court impliedly rejects its application. In *Data Access Corporation v Powerflex Services Pty Ltd*,[78] the High Court found that copyright subsisted in a computer compression table. Whilst acknowledging that such a finding would effectively prevent competitors developing compatible computer software because the function of the compression table could not be achieved without reproducing the compression table itself, the High Court left it to the legislature to fix the problem.[79] Interestingly, the necessary legislation came into effect on the same day that the High Court handed down its decision.[80] These amendments allowed reproductions of computer programs to be made for the purposes of making interoperable programs as well as for the ordinary running of the computer, making back-up copies, security testing and for correcting programming errors.[81]

A controversial extension of the United States functionality exemption was made in *Lotus Development Corporation v Borland International Inc*,[82] a case which Nimmer has referred to as the computer software case of the century.[83] In *Lotus v Borland* the First Circuit Court of Appeals held that copyright could not subsist in a computer menu command structure because it was a "method of operating" a computer (just as a gear shift mechanism might be a method of operating a car or a button might be the method of operating a video or food processor). The menu command structure was therefore excluded from protection

---

75    United States Constitution Art 1 s 8.
76    *Whelan Associates v Jaslow Dental Laboratory* 797 F 2d 1222 (1986).
77    See Davey LJ in *Hollinrake v Truswell* [1894] 3 Ch 420 at 428 and Dawson J in *Autodesk Inc v Dyason (No 1)* (1992) 173 CLR 330 at 344 for two examples.
78    (1999) 202 CLR 1.
79    (1999) 202 CLR 1 at 42.
80    *Copyright Amendment (Computer Programs) Act 1999* Sch 1.
81    See *Copyright Act 1968* ss 47C-47F.
82    49 F 3d 807 (1995); 33 IPR 233.
83    Melville B Nimmer and David Nimmer, *Nimmer on Copyright,* M Bender, New York, 1999, §13.3[F][3][e] n 17.

under s 102(b). The exemption applied despite the fact that the court found that there were other ways of expressing the menu command structure, that is, the exemption applied even though there was no merger between the idea or function of the menu command structure and its expression.[84] Again, the United States court came to this conclusion by interpreting s 102(b) in the light of the broader public purposes of copyright protection as provided for under the United States Constitution. In *Data Access*, by comparison, the Australian High Court refused to adopt these public policy issues as part of its reasoning despite being urged to do so by the respondents.

Despite the fact that the distinction between an idea and its expression has been criticised and despite the fact that there is no express reference to it in the *Copyright Act 1968*, it remains a fundamental feature of Australian copyright law. As Dawson J commented in *Autodesk Inc v Dyason (No 1)*, "it is true that it is often difficult to separate an idea from its expression, but it is nevertheless fundamental that copyright protection is given only to the form in which ideas are expressed, not to the ideas themselves".[85]

## Copyright and this Textbook

In this chapter the birth and nature of copyright law have been sketched in their international context. In Chapter 3 the categories and types of subject-matter in which copyright is said to subsist will be considered in more detail. In Chapter 4 the exclusive rights of the copyright owner will be examined by reference to actions for infringement of those rights. In addition, in Chapter 4 we will consider other actions available to the copyright holder besides infringement to protect the interests of the copyright owner and offences provided for under the Act. One of the distinctive features of the *Copyright Act 1968* is its lack of broad principles. Unlike the United States copyright regime, there are no broad constitutional principles to uphold, there is no general fair use exemption to copyright infringement and there are no free speech principles which might function to ensure that important works remain "in the public domain". Australian courts have sometimes been reluctant to take an active role in balancing the rights of the copyright owner against the public interest in ensuring access to copyright material.

One of the results of this is that the *Copyright Act* contains numerous detailed limitations on the rights of the copyright owner. Such limitations typically take the form of a defence in infringement proceedings. These defences will be considered separately in Chapter 5, "Balancing the Interests", but the table of defences which is provided in that chapter could prove useful when considering the rights of the copyright owner.

The other way that the *Copyright Act* balances the interests of the public and the copyright owner is by granting compulsory licences. A compulsory licence authorises a member of the public to exercise one or more of the rights of the copyright owner without the owner's consent but still requires the member to pay for that use. Compulsory licences are particularly important in the educational field

---

84    *Lotus Development Corporation v Borland International Inc* 49 F 3d 807 (1995); 33 IPR 233 at 243.

85    (1992) 173 CLR 330 at 344.

and in the music industry. Anyone is free to play or broadcast any published CD in public, for example, but records must be kept of such use and an agreed licence fee eventually paid (ss 108 and 109). Educational institutions may reproduce one article from a printed periodical journal for educational purposes so long as they have an agreement to pay for this use with the appropriate collecting agency (s 135ZJ). Compulsory licences are also considered in Chapter 5.

Copyright is a form of personal property which may be licensed and sold. In Chapter 6, "Dealing with Copyright", the rules relating to ownership and licensing of copyright will be considered together with the remedies for infringement of copyright which occurs when a person exercises the rights of the copyright owner without permission. We shall also examine the role of collecting agencies and the regulatory structure necessary to enable copyright dealings to be carried on effectively at a commercial level.

In Chapter 7, we will examine copyright's neighbouring rights, that is, moral rights, performers' protection and resale royalty rights for visual artists. We will also consider the inadequacies of copyright law and moral rights with respect to indigenous cultural property and proposals to protect it.

The legislative history of copyright law has necessitated the drafting of detailed transitional provisions. The general rule is that the *Copyright Act* extends to subject-matter made before the commencement of the Act but, if the Act grants copyright in a new form of subject-matter, the Act will only apply to infringing actions after the commencement of the Act. Part IX of the Act contains provisions relating to transitional arrangements and these will be referenced in the footnotes.

This general rule is not always followed. In the case of copyright for performers in sound recordings and live performances, which were introduced under the *US Free Trade Agreement Implementation Act 2004*, the rights were made retrospective. That means that a performer on an old Beatles' album, and the band itself, suddenly became owners of the copyright in the sound recording and shared this ownership with the recording studio. This extraordinary provision will be considered in more detail in Chapter 6.

# CASES

## *Pacific Film Laboratories Pty Ltd v Commissioner of Taxation (Cth)*

High Court of Australia: Barwick CJ, McTiernan, Windeyer,
Owen and Walsh JJ
(1970) 121 CLR 154

The Commissioner of Taxation applied sales tax to the photographic prints developed by Pacific Film Laboratories and paid for by its customers. Pacific Film objected to the assessment on the ground that the customer owned the copyright in the film negatives, that Pacific Film was authorised by the customer to reproduce prints from these negatives, that Pacific Film had no property right in these prints and therefore was not selling anything to the customer which might be taxed. The High Court rejected this argument as based on a confusion between the chattel right in the print and the copyright in the negative.

**Barwick CJ:** [162] But it is objected that there could not in any case be a sale of a print or duplicate either to the photographer or to any other person because of the provisions of the *Copyright Act 1912*. It has been assumed in argument that the person ordering the print was the owner of the copyright in the negative or transparency. This may or may not be so, but I am prepared to assume it as fact. Because the negative or transparency was the subject of copyright it is said that the appellant as the producer of the print [162] or duplicate as a reproduction of the negative or transparency could not have any general property in the print which he could transfer by sale to any person including the owner of the copyright. It is submitted that it would have no more than a lien for the amount agreed to be paid for the production of the print or duplicate. The fact that he owned the sensitized paper or the film on which the print or duplicate was made to appear and such of the chemicals as remained on the paper or film at the end of the process of making the print or duplicate did not give him any general property in the print or duplicate as reproductions of the copyright work, the negative or transparency as the case may be.

The *Copyright Act 1912* (Cth) which was in force during the period relevant to the assessment in this case carried the *Copyright Act 1911* of the United Kingdom into operation in Australia. Section 1 sub-s 2 (a) of the Act of 1911 gives to the author of a photograph the sole right to reproduce the photograph and to authorize its reproduction. By s 2 sub-s 1, copyright shall be deemed to be infringed by any person who without the consent of the owner of the copyright does anything, the sole right to do which is by the Act conferred on the owner of the copyright. By s 7, all infringing copies of any work in which copyright exists shall be deemed to be the property of the owner of the copyright who accordingly may take proceedings for the recovery of possession thereof or in respect of the conversion thereof. But s 8 provides that where proceedings are taken in respect of the infringement of the copyright in any work and the defendant establishes that he was not aware nor had reasonable ground for suspecting that copyright existed in the work the plaintiff shall not be entitled to any remedy other than an injunction.

There are, in my opinion, several clear answers to this submission. In the first place, there is authority for the proposition that the property in a chattel may be in one person and the copyright in another: *In re Dickens; Dickens v Hawksley* [1935] 1 Ch 267. In the second place, an authority to reproduce a copyright work given by the owner of the copyright allows the authorized person to produce the copy as his own property and indeed unless the authority to reproduce it provides otherwise, he is free to dispose of the reproduction, cf Copinger and Skone James' *Law of Copyright*, 10th ed (1965), p 378, s 1027. In the third place, whilst of course the *Copyright Act* enables the copyright owner to recover possession of infringing copies of the copyright work or damages **[164]** for the conversion of such infringing copies there were in this case no infringing copies, the owner of the copyright on the supposition made, authorized the making of the copy and its delivery to himself. It seems to me that even if the agreement between the owner of the copyright and the appellant had been no more than an agreement for the rendering of services the print produced by the appellant could not have been claimed by the owner of the copyright as his own nor could he have recovered it in detinue before it had been delivered to him but if as I think the agreement was an agreement for the sale of the print or duplicate by the appellant to the owner of the copyright it seems to me necessarily to follow that not only was there no property in the owner of the copyright in the print viewed as a chattel at any time before the delivery of the print to the owner of the copyright but that it was intended that property in the print or duplicate should pass on delivery of the print or duplicate.

In my opinion, the appellant had general property in the print or duplicate when produced with the authority of the copyright owner: it was not an infringing copy of the negative or transparency as the case may be though possibly it might have become so if sold to some person other than the owner of the copyright: this was so because of the limited nature of the authority to reproduce given by the owner of the copyright. But the rights given by s 7 to recover infringing copies, though subject to s 8, only arise when the copy is the infringing copy: that is to say, it is the sale which attracts the operation of the section in the case supposed. But that conclusion denies that the authorized reproducer had no general property in the print or duplicate. As I have said, the appellant, in my opinion, had the general property in the print or duplicate which it manufactured out of its own materials and none the less so because the copyright in the negative or transparency was in some other person, or as has been supposed in the member of the public ordering the print or duplicate.

In my opinion, the delivery of the prints or duplicates by the appellant for an agreed sum was a sale of those prints or transparencies within the meaning of s 17 of the Act. Accordingly, in my opinion, the sale value of those sales was rightly included in an assessment by the respondent Commissioner of the appellant. The question whether the sale value assigned by the Commissioner in the assessment was the correct sale value is not a question which is before this Court on the case stated.

## *Walter v Lane*
House of Lords: Earl of Halsbury LC, Lord Davey, Lord James of Hereford,
Lord Brampton and Lord Robertson
[1900] AC 539

The Earl of Rosebery delivered five speeches at public lectures in 1896 and 1898. Journalists, employed by the appellant, attended the meetings, took down the speeches verbatim in short hand and the speeches were published in *The Times*. In 1899 the respondents published a book of the speeches which they admitted they had copied from *The Times*. The respondents unsuccessfully argued that copyright did not subsist in *The Times* reports of the speeches.

**Lord Davey:** [550] My Lords, the question in this appeal is whether the proprietors of *The Times* by assignment from their reporter are entitled to copyright in the reports published in their newspaper of certain speeches delivered by Lord Rosebery on public occasions. Copyright is the right of multiplying copies of a published writing. There is no copyright in a speech although delivered on a public occasion … It is not disputed in the present case that the thoughts and words of Lord Rosebery's speeches were communicated by him to the public, and no question is raised as to the existence of any right in the orator. This case raises only a question of statutory copyright in *The Times* report, and must be decided on the provisions of the Copyright Act (5 & 6 Vict c 45).

Now, what has the respondent done? He has admittedly copied and republished for his own profit certain sheets of letterpress forming parts of *The Times* newspaper. A sheet of letterpress is a book within the meaning of the Act, and, not-**[551]**withstanding the decision of Malins V-C in *Cox v Land and Water Journal Co* (1869) LR 9 Eq 324, I have no doubt that a newspaper is within the Act. In *Walter v Howe* (1881) 17 Ch D 708 Sir George Jessel differed from the Vice-Chancellor, and his decision has since been followed. Prima facie, therefore, the respondent has fringed the appellants' copyright in their newspaper. His defence is that the appellants have no copyright in this portion of their published work because it was compiled from, or consisted only of, matters which were publici juris. They say that Lord Rosebery was the author of his speech and gave it to the world for any to reproduce who would, and that nobody, therefore, can claim to be the "author" within the meaning of the Act of a report of his speech. The reporter, they say (with a pardonable jingle), is the reproducer and not the producer of the speech. That is true in a sense, and if *The Times* were claiming a property in the speech itself and seeking prevent anybody else from publishing any other report of it, the argument would be cogent. But the appellant's claim is of a more modest description. They seek only to prevent the respondent multiplying copies of their own report of the speech and availing himself for his own profit the skill, labour, and expense by means of which that report was produced and published. But for the fact that the Court of Appeal thought differently, and one of your Lordships agrees with the learned judges, I should say that there is no answer to this claim.

In my opinion the reporter is the author of his own report. He it was who brought into existence in the form of a writing the piece of letterpress which the respondent has copied. I think that he and he alone composed the report. The materials for his composition were his notes, which were his own property, aided to some extent by his memory and trained judgment. Owing to the perfection which the art of shorthand writing has attained in recent yews, memory and judgment bear a less important part in the composition of a report a speech than was formerly the case. But the question whether the composer has copyright in his report does not **[552]** seem to me to vary inversely with or to depend on his skill in stenography. Nor, as it appears to me, does the fact that the subject-matter of the report had been made public property, or that no originality or literary skill was demanded for the composition of the report have anything to do with the matter. Again, it is said that the lucidity of diction and perfection of expression which characterise the eminent person named render an exact reproduction of his words a comparatively easy and almost mechanical task. But is it argued that the reporter of the hesitating or half-completed utterances of an inferior speaker might have copyright, though the reporter of Lord Rosebery may not? or does the question of copyright in the report depend on the clearness of thought and speech of the orator? In my opinion the question must be decided on general considerations, and not on any grounds which are personal either to the orator or to the reporter. Copyright has nothing to do with the originality or literary-merits of the author or composer. It may exist in the information given by a street directory: *Kelly v Morris* LR 1 Eq 697; or by a list of deeds of arrangement: *Cate v Devon and Exeter Constitutional Newspaper Co* (1889) 40 Ch D 500; or in a list of advertisements: *Lamb v Evans* [1893] 1 Ch 218. I think those cases right, and the principle on which they proceed directly applicable to the present case. It was of course open to any other reporter to compose his own report of Lord Rosebery's speech, and to any other newspaper or book to publish that report; but it is a sound principle that a man shall not avail himself of another's skill, labour and expense by copying the written product thereof. To quote the language of North J in another case: "For the purposes of their own profit they desire to reap where they have not sown, and to take advantage of the labour and expenditure of the plaintiffs in procuring news for the purpose of saving labour and expense to themselves."

For these reasons I agree with my noble and learned friend in thinking that the judgment of the Court of Appeal should be reversed, and that of North J restored.

**Lord James of Hereford: [553]** The question, therefore, to be decided is whether there is any copyright in the reports of speeches made in public with the object that they should be published. The determination of this question depends upon the construction to be placed the provisions of the *Copyright Act* of 1842. It may be that the matter published in the columns of a newspaper is a "book" within s 2 of that Act; but the plaintiffs in the suit have to establish that the proprietors of *The Times* are the "authors" of such book within the meaning of s 3 ... The plaintiffs do not claim copyright in the speech itself, but, as stated by Lord Lindley in the Court of Appeal, the report of the speech is something different from and beyond the speech, and the question to be solved is whether this difference represents a "something" of which any one can regarded as the "author" within the meaning of the *Copyright Act*.

Whilst the Act supplies no definition of the word "author," and whilst it may be difficult for any judicial authority to give **[554]** a positive definition of that word certain considerations controlling the meaning of it seem to be established. A mere copyist of written matter is not an "author" within the Act, but a translator from one language to another would be so. A person to whom words are dictated for the purpose of being written down is not an "author." He is the mere agent or clerk of the person dictating, and requires to possess no art beyond that of knowing how to write. The person dictating takes a share in seeing that the person writing follows the dictation, and makes it his care to give time for the writing to be made. But an "author" may come into existence without producing any original matter of his own. Many instances of the claim to authorship without the production of original matter have been given at the bar. The compilation of a street directory, the reports of proceedings in courts of law, and the tables of the times of running of certain railway trains have been held to bring the producers within the word "author"; and yet in one sense no original matter can be found in such publications. Still there was a something apart from originality on the one hand and mere mechanical transcribing on the other which entitled those who gave these works to the world to be regarded as their authors.

## *Donoghue v Allied Newspapers Ltd*
High Court of Justice, Chancery Division: Farwell J
[1937] 3 All ER 503

Donoghue was interviewed over a period of time by a journalist and a number of articles were subsequently published by *News of the World*. Donoghue sought an injunction, as a joint author and owner of the copyright in the articles, to prevent further publication. The court held that Donoghue was neither the author nor a joint author of the articles because he had supplied only the ideas for the article and there was no copyright in an idea.

**Farwell J: [506]** The first question that I have to determine is whether the plaintiff is or is not either the sole or the joint owner of the copyright in these articles, that is to say, in the original articles which appeared in the *News of the World*. If Mr Donoghue has no copyright, either as sole owner or as **[507]** joint owner, in these articles, then of course this action necessarily fails, and it is unnecessary then for me to consider the further question which I shall have to consider if that is not the position, namely, as to the effect of the agreement of 4 April 1931, and whether that agreement amounts to an equitable assignment of Mr Donoghue's copyright to the *News of the World*. It is necessary, in considering whether Mr Donoghue is the owner or part owner of the copyright in this book, to see what it is in which a copyright exists under the *Copyright Act 1911*. This, at any rate, is clear, and one can start with this beyond all question, that there is no copyright in an idea, or in ideas. A person may have a brilliant idea for a story, or for a picture, or for a play, and one which, so far as he is concerned, appears to be original, but, if he communicates that idea to an author or a playwright or an artist, the production which is the result of the communication of the idea to the author or the artist or the playwright is the copyright of the person who has clothed the idea in a form, whether by means of a picture, a play, or a book, and the owner of the idea has no rights in that product. On the other hand, this, I think, is equally plain, that, if an author employs a shorthand writer to take down a story which the author is composing, word for word, in shorthand, and the shorthandwriter then transcribes it, and the author then has it published, the author and not the shorthandwriter is the owner of the copyright. A mere amanuensis does not, by taking down word for word the language of the author, become in any sense the owner of the copyright. That is the property of the author. I think the explanation of that is this, that that in which the copyright exists is the particular form of language by which is conveyed the information which is to be conveyed. If the idea, however brilliant and however clever it may be, is nothing more than an idea, and is not put into any form of words, or any form of expression such as a picture or a play, then there is no such thing as copyright at all. It is not until it is (if I may put it in that way) reduced into writing, or into some tangible form, that you get any right to copyright at all, and the copyright exists in the particular form of language in which, or, in the case of a picture, in the particular form of the picture by which, the information or the idea is conveyed to those who are intended to read it or to look at it.

In the present case, apart altogether from what one may call merely the embellishments, which were undoubtedly supplied wholly by Mr Felstead, the ideas of all these stories, and, in fact, the stories themselves, were supplied by the plaintiff; but, in my judgment, upon the evidence, it is plain that the particular form of language by which those stories were conveyed was the language of Mr Felstead and not that of the plaintiff. Although many of the stories were told in the form of dialogue, and to some extent Mr Felstead no doubt tried to reproduce the story as it was told to him by the plaintiff. Nevertheless the particular form of language in which those adventures or stories were conveyed to the public was the language of Mr Felstead, and not the language of Mr **[508]** Donoghue. *Evans v Hulton (E) & Co Ltd*, is, I think, very near to the present case, and I feel that, if I were to decide in favour of the plaintiff on this first point, I really should be disregarding the decision of Tomlin J, in that case. No doubt it is quite true, as Mr Clark very ably pointed out, that the facts are not on all fours, but, if one looks closely into the circumstances of the case before Tomlin J, I think one is driven to the conclusion that the principles upon which that judgment turns are really the principles which I have to apply in this case. No doubt in that case the person who supplied the information was a foreigner, and no doubt he did not convey the information in a form which would have been at all adaptable to an article in a newspaper, and to that extent it may be that the person who wrote it down and supplied the article had more to do, possibly, than in this present case. But, as it seems to me, the principle upon which Tomlin J, proceeded in that case is the one which I am bound to apply here. What Tomlin J, said at p 56 was this:

> One thing is reasonably plain, I think, that probably Mr Zeitun would not himself claim that he was capable of producing in the English tongue a literary work which would find a market. He certainly agrees that he has never attempted to do so, And

I should doubt his capacity to do so. The fact that he is the subject-matter of the production in the sense that it is an incident from his life, for which he provided the material, does not seem to me to make him in any sense the joint author with Mr Evans of the manuscript which was in fact written, and, upon the facts which I have stated, I find that he did not take any part in producing the express matter which is the original literary work, the subject-matter of copyright.

What I understand the judge to mean by "the express matter" is that which I have endeavoured to define as the particular form of language in which the information is conveyed, and, although it may be that, in the present case, the plaintiff could give more help to Mr Felstead than Mr Zeitun could give, in *Evans v Hulton (E) & Co Ltd*, to the author of the manuscript, nevertheless, although Mr Donoghue supplied all the substance of the articles, the articles themselves, and the information which was in them, were conveyed in language which was the language of Mr Felstead, and for which Mr Donoghue himself was not responsible.

I come to the conclusion, with some regret, that the plaintiff has failed to show that he is the owner or part owner of the copyright in these articles. The articles in this paper *Guide and Ideas* were published as being the adventures of Steve Donoghue, entitled "My Racing Secrets. By Steve Donoghue," and no doubt that was because, both in that case and in the earlier case, the persons who are responsible for the papers desired to lead the public to believe that what they were reading was something of which Steve Donoghue himself was the author, and I think it is probable that so describing the articles does have the effect, under the *Copyright Act 1911*, s 6, of throwing the onus, in a case of this kind, on the defendant company. But, notwithstanding that, it appears to me that I am forced to come to the conclusion—although, as I say, rather unwillingly—that Mr Donoghue was not the author, or even the joint **[509]** author, of the articles in the *News of the World*. It must necessarily follow that he cannot sustain this action, and that the action fails, accordingly, and must be dismissed with costs.

# Chapter 3

# Subsistence of Copyright*

On 13 December 1999 the Nine Network sought an interlocutory injunction to prevent the Australian Broadcasting Corporation from making an Australian broadcast of the New Year's Eve fireworks display which was to take place on Sydney Harbour as part of the Year 2000 celebrations.[1] Nine claimed to have paid Sydney City Council $450,000 for the Australian broadcast rights in the fireworks display. But what exactly had it purchased?

Nine could not claim to have purchased any rights to the fireworks display as a spectacle for, as we know from *Victoria Park Racing and Recreation Grounds Co Ltd v Taylor*,[2] there is no property in a spectacle. Rather, Nine based its argument on copyright. Sydney City Council, it argued, owned the copyright in at least certain parts of the fireworks display and Nine had purchased from the copyright owner the right to broadcast those parts of the display.

The *Copyright Act 1968* is surprisingly straightforward in setting out the subject-matter in which copyright subsists. Section 32 provides that copyright subsists in four types of "works". These are:

(1) original literary works, which are defined to include tables, compilations and computer programs;[3]

(2) original dramatic works;

(3) original musical works; and

(4) original artistic works (which includes paintings, sculptures, engravings, drawings, photographs, buildings, models of buildings and works of artistic craftsmanship).[4]

Part IV of the Act provides that copyright subsists in four types of "subject-matter other than works". These are:

(1) sound recordings (s 85);

---

\* For presumptions relating to subsistence of copyright in civil proceedings, see *Copyright Act 1968* ss 126(a) and 126A.

1 *Nine Network Australia Pty Ltd v Australian Broadcasting Corporation* (1999) 48 IPR 333.

2 (1937) 58 CLR 479.

3 Section 10(1).

4 Section 10(1).

(2)  cinematographic films (s 86);

(3)  television broadcasts and sound broadcasts (s 87); and

(4)  published editions of works (s 88).

Copyright will be presumed to subsist in the work or other subject-matter if the defendant does not put the issue in question[5] but the plaintiff still needs to identify the subject-matter in which copyright is said to subsist. In this case Nine identified a number of such items. It argued that copyright subsisted in drawings which had been made as part of the planning for the fireworks display. These were a drawing of a face superimposed on the Harbour Bridge, a drawing of the word "Eternity" in copperplate writing also superimposed on the Harbour Bridge and a set of drawings of stylised sea creatures. In addition, Nine claimed that copyright subsisted in "sculptures" which were built in accordance with these drawings – the construction of the face on the Harbour Bridge, the construction of the word "Eternity" on the Harbour Bridge and the constructed sea creatures. Finally, Nine claimed that copyright subsisted in the script or schedule of the fireworks display itself which Nine characterised as a dramatic work.

The application for an injunction was refused on the ground of delay and so there is no reasoned decision regarding the subsistence of copyright. However, we begin this chapter with this tale for two reasons. First, it illustrates the importance of identifying the actual subject-matter in which copyright is said to subsist. Although it is often said, quoting Petersen J in *University of London Press Ltd v University Tutorial Press Ltd*,[6] that "what is worth copying is worth protecting",[7] this does not mean that copyright law provides a general prohibition against unfair copying. Some valuable products have failed to gain protection either because they have fallen between the cracks of the definitions of different subject-matters[8] or because the *Copyright Act 1968* has lagged behind technological advances.[9] Second, Nine's application illustrates the possibly wide-ranging effects which copyright law can have. In this case, for example, copyright law may have succeeded in indirectly giving Channel Nine control over a spectacle which the common law would not have envisaged. As we shall see, such issues arise often in copyright cases.

## Connecting Factors and Material Form

In order for copyright to subsist in subject-matter that subject-matter must have a connecting factor with Australia. The connecting factor may arise either because of the author's or the subject-matter's connection with Australia or because of Australia's international obligations.

---

5    Section 126(a).

6    [1916] 2 Ch 601.

7    [1916] 2 Ch 601 at 610.

8    M Cuisenaire's rods, for example, were neither sculptures nor works of artistic craftsmanship: *Cuisenaire v Reed* [1963] VR 719.

9    The initial difficulty faced by Beaumont J in trying to fit computer programs within the definition of "literary work" before the 1984 amendments is demonstrated in *Apple Computer Inc v Computer Edge Pty Ltd* (1983) 50 ALR 581.

## Connecting factors

The connecting factors for works are set out in s 32.[10] The Act distinguishes between unpublished and published works. Copyright subsists in an unpublished literary, dramatic, musical or artistic work if the author was a qualified person at the time the work was made or for a substantial part of this time. Copyright subsists in a published work which is first published in Australia or if the author was a qualified person. If the artistic work is a building or is attached to or forms part of a building, copyright subsists in the work if the building is situated in Australia.

The connecting factors for Part IV "subject-matter other than works" are set out in Division 3 of Part IV. Copyright subsists in sound recordings and films made in Australia, first published in Australia or where the maker was a qualified person. Copyright subsists in printed editions of works first published in Australia or whose publisher was a qualified person.[11] Copyright subsists in a broadcast made from a place in Australia by the Australian Broadcasting Corporation, the Special Broadcasting Corporation or a licensee under the *Broadcasting Services Act 1992*.

A number of these terms are defined. A "qualified person" is defined as an Australian citizen or resident and, in the case of Part IV subject-matter, a body corporate incorporated under the laws of the Commonwealth or a State.[12]

"Made" is defined in s 22(1) in relation to literary, dramatic, musical or artistic works as the time when the work was "first reduced to writing or some other material form". Writing is defined as "a mode of representing or reproducing words, figures or symbols in a visible form".[13] Material form "in relation to a work or an adaptation of a work, includes any form (whether visible or not) of storage of the work or adaptation, or a substantial part of the work or adaptation, (whether or not the work or adaptation, or a substantial part of the work of adaptation, can be reproduced)".[14] Under this definition, a literary work might be made either when it is reduced to writing or when it is put in the form of electrical impulses in a computer program object code. In *Roland Corporation v Lorenzo and Sons Pty Ltd*,[15] Pincus J held that a literary work was made at the moment that it was typed into a computer.[16] In *Green v Broadcasting Corporation of New Zealand*,[17] the Privy Council impliedly accepted that a dramatic work might be reduced to material form when a performance is recorded on video tape for broadcast.

A sound recording is deemed to have been made when the first record embodying the recording is produced; and a film is made when the first copy of the film is

---

10    For transitional provision regarding subsistence of copyright in works, see *Copyright Act 1968* s 211.

11    Copyright does not subsist in a printed edition which simply reproduces a previous edition of the same work (s 92(2)).

12    For transitional provisions regarding qualified persons, see s 211 (works) and s 220 (sound recordings).

13    Section 10(1).

14    Before the *US Free Trade Agreement Implementation Act 2004*, it was necessary that the work or adaptation could itself be reproduced from the form of storage.

15    (1991) 105 ALR 623.

16    (1991) 105 ALR 623 at 631.

17    [1989] 2 All ER 1056.

produced. That is, in each case copyright subsists once the object itself is made. There is no requirement that a copy of a broadcast be "made" and therefore it need not be reduced to material form and copyright will subsist in a broadcast even though there may be no copy of it at all.

"Publication" is narrowly defined. It refers to making copies of the work or subject-matter available, usually for sale or hire. Thus, s 29(1) defines publication as the supply of reproductions of a work, sound recording or an edition of a work to the public and a film is said to have been published if copies of the film have been sold, let or offered for sale or hire to the public. The publication must be authorised (s 29(1)) and s 29(4) provides that a publication which is not intended to satisfy the reasonable requirements of the public is "merely colourable" and is to be disregarded.[18]

This narrow definition of publication means that merely making the subject-matter public does not constitute a publication. Thus, a cinema showing of a film is not a publication of the film (although supplying copies to the cinema owner may be). A performance of a literary, dramatic or musical work or the exhibition of an artistic work is not a publication of the work. A building is not published by constructing it nor can one say that a building or sculpture is published if photographs or engravings of the building or sculpture are made available to the public (s 29(3)). Section 29(2) provides that the supply of a record of a literary, dramatic or musical work to the public is not a publication of the work although it may be a publication of the sound recording. Thus, copyright does not subsist in an unrecorded unwritten speech or in an unrecorded improvised musical work or in an unrecorded, unwritten dramatic work. In such cases the works have neither been made nor published. This is one of the reasons that Channel Nine, in the case discussed above, had to claim copyright in the script for the fireworks display as a dramatic work rather than in the display itself.

In recognition of the international nature of copyright law, s 29(5) provides that, if a work or other subject-matter is published in one country within 30 days[19] of its first publication in another Berne country, the latter publication is still treated as a first publication.

In *Francis Day and Hunter v Feldman*,[20] the Canadian copyright owners wanted to publish the song "You Made Me Love You – I Didn't Want to Do It" in England within the time frame (then 14 days) necessary to achieve copyright protection under the *Copyright Act 1911* (UK). They sent 12 copies of the work to an English music publisher with instructions to "copyright" the work in England on 5 May 1913.[21] In accordance with those instructions the publishers sent a copy of the work to the Copyright Receipt Office at the British Museum, filed one copy in their own office and exposed six copies of the work for sale in their retail shop. The next day they sent the remaining four copies to a person responsible for receiving works for university libraries. The song was not advertised and did not sell immediately. Two months later, however, following public performances of

---

18    For transitional provisions regarding publications, see ss 209 and 211(2).

19    This is 14 days for works published before the *Copyright Act 1968*. For transitional provisions regarding international publication, see s 209.

20    [1914] 2 Ch 728.

21    As we have seen, there were no formalities or registration requirements under the *Copyright Act 1911*. Had there been then the English publisher's job may have been a little easier.

the song, further copies were sent to the English retailers and an English edition was printed. The publishers eventually sold a quarter of a million copies of the work. In subsequent infringement proceedings the question arose as to whether the initial actions constituted a first publication in the United Kingdom for the purposes of copyright subsistence under the *Copyright Act 1911*. The trial judge held that there had been a publication at that time. Although the initial supply of works was insignificant and the anticipated demand was insignificant, there was "an intention from the first to satisfy the public demand" in England.[22] This decision was upheld on appeal.

In *Bodley Head Ltd v Flegon*,[23] the question arose as to whether a clandestine circulation, in the former Soviet Union, of Alexander Solzhenitsyn's novel *August 14* was a publication. Brightman J found that there was no evidence that such a clandestine circulation had taken place but commented obiter that it would be difficult to say that such a small, illegal and possibly dangerous operation could truly be said to satisfy the reasonable requirements of the public.[24]

## Material form

Some text writers and many judges have said that, in order for copyright to subsist, the subject-matter must be reduced to a material form, that is, the subject-matter must be written down or recorded in some way. This is neither historically nor actually correct. The *Lectures Copyright Act 1835* (5 and 6 Will IV c 65) extended copyright to unfixed oral lectures,[25] the *Berne Convention* Art 2(2) provides that the requirement for material form is optional and, under the *Copyright Act 1968*, there is no requirement that broadcasts be fixed in a material form. Any requirement for material form in relation to other subject-matter under the *Copyright Act* arises indirectly through the requirement that the subject-matter be "made" or "published". It is also possible that some commentators have confused the principle that copyright protects the form of expression, rather than the idea, with a requirement that copyright will only protect something in a material form.

In his looseleaf service Ricketson has suggested that the requirement for material form might appropriately be dropped as a requirement in Australian copyright law. Ricketson suggests that there is no good reason why the "utter-ances of celebrated conversationalists" such as Dr Samuel Johnson, the Reverend Sydney Smith and Oscar Wilde should not be protected. If you are worried that this might mean that copyright protection will be afforded to the bon mots, impromptu ditties and party tricks of your dinner guests, Ricketson takes this suggestion even further. "Could it not be argued", he asks, rhetorically, "that a work is equally fixed in a material form at the time when it is originally conceived by the author and held in that person's brain prior to disclosure to the world?"

Although this tabula rasa view of the human mind is a little wayward, Ricketson's more important point is that the value of the requirement for material

---

22   [1914] 2 Ch 728 at 735.
23   [1972] 1 WLR 680.
24   [1972] 1 WLR 680 at 687.
25   Although it was necessary for the lecture to be registered prior to its being given.

form today is primarily evidentiary. One's concern with the dinner party guest's contribution and the random thoughts of one's friends probably has less to do with the fact that the work is not fixed in a material form than with the difficulty of proving that there is in fact a work, or an author, at all. Not only would it be difficult to prove the form of expression of the work but it might also be difficult to prove that the work originated with your friend.

The question of material form also arises in relation to infringement because a reproduction of a work only constitutes an infringement of copyright if it is a reproduction in material form. This aspect of material form is considered in the next chapter.

## General Principles Regarding Subsistence of Copyright

### Originality

The first and most important requirement for subsistence of copyright in literary, artistic, dramatic and musical works is that they be "original". There is no similar requirement applying to Part IV films, sound recordings, broadcasts and printed editions of works.

Originality was introduced as a general requirement of copyright works only in the *Copyright Act 1911*. Before this the term had been used in the *Sculpture Copyright Act 1814* (54 Geo III c 56) and the *Fine Arts Copyright Act 1862* (25 and 26 Vict c 68) but not in the *Copyright Act 1842* (5 and 6 Vict c 45), the *Dramatic Copyright Act 1833* (3 and 4 Will IV c 15) or the *Lectures Copyright Act 1835* (5 and 6 Will IV c 65). In 1917 in *Sands and McDougall Pty Ltd v Robinson*,[26] the Australian High Court rejected an argument that the term imported a requirement of novelty or inventiveness into copyright law. The High Court held that "originality" was not an additional requirement imposed in relation to copyright subject-matter but was equivalent to the old requirement of "authorship" under the *Copyright Act 1842* (5 and 6 Vict c 45).

The High Court expressly endorsed the test for authorship in *Walter v Lane*[27] as the test for originality. The requirement for originality has two aspects. Originality requires that the form of expression "originate" with the author and is not copied or produced by a "mere conduit" or amanuensis. Thus, in *Walter v Lane*,[28] the journalist was the author or originator of the work, not a mere conduit of Lord Rosebery's words. In *Cummins v Bond*,[29] a spiritualist medium, who at a series of séances produced by automatic writing a large volume of material entitled "The Chronicle of Cleophas", was held to have originated the work even though the parties themselves believed that the "true originator ... is some being no longer inhabiting this world, and has been out of it for a length of time sufficient to justify the hope that he has no reasons for wishing to return to it".[30] Cleophas was one of the two on the road to Emmaus to whom Christ appeared

---

26    (1917) 23 CLR 49.
27    [1900] AC 539.
28    [1900] AC 539.
29    [1927] 1 Ch 169.
30    [1927] 1 Ch 169 at 172.

after the resurrection (Luke 24). The fact that the Chronicles were written in 16th and 17th century English, a language which Cleophas could not have known, rather than in ancient Aramaic, a language which the medium could not have understood, led Eve J to hold that the medium was much more than a mere conduit of an author from the "other side".

This finding illuminates the second aspect of originality. The work is said to have originated with the author if it is the product of the author's skill, labour and expertise or experience. In the words of Kearney J in *Ogden Industries Pty Ltd v Kis (Australia) Pty Ltd*:[31]

> The *locus classicus* on the meaning of original is the following statement by Petersen J in *University of London Press Ltd v University Tutorial Press Ltd* applied in *Ladbroke (Football) Ltd v William Hill (Football) Ltd*:[32]
>
>> The word "original" does not in this connection mean that the work must be the expression of original or inventive thought. Copyright Acts are not concerned with the originality of ideas but with the expression of thoughts and in the case of "literary work" with the expression of thought in print or writing. The originality which is required relates to the expression of the thought. But the Act does not require that the expression must be an original or novel form, but that the work must not be copied from another work – that it should originate with the author. Hence, if the work originates from the author in the sense that it is the result of his skill, labour or experience, and it is not copied from another, then it will be an original work for the copyright purposes.[33]

Lord Atkinson in *MacMillan and Co Ltd v K and J Cooper*[34] laid down the general principle for calculating the amount of labour, skill and expertise required to establish originality in the following terms:

> What is the precise amount of knowledge, labour, judgement or literary skill or taste which the author of any book or other compilation must bestow upon its composition ... cannot be defined in precise terms. In every case it must depend largely on the special facts of that case, and must in each case be very much a question of degree.[35]

Lord Atkinson's statement has been constantly affirmed and attempts to definitively quantify the amount of skill, labour or expertise required to constitute originality have proved futile. In *Ladbroke (Football) Ltd v William Hill (Football) Ltd*,[36] for example, three of the judges expressed the requirement in three different formulations when deciding whether a betting coupon was an original literary work. Lord Hodson held that a work arranged without the exercise of "more than negligible work, labour or skill" will not be entitled to copyright.[37] Lord Evershed found that the particular work in question displayed "considerable skill, labour and judgment"[38] and so attracted copyright. Lord Devlin held that

---

31    (1982) 45 ALR 129.
32    [1964] 1 All ER 465 at 479.
33    (1982) 45 ALR 129 at 133, quoting Petersen J in *University of London Press Ltd v University Tutorial Press Ltd* [1916] 2 Ch 601 at 608-609.
34    (1924) 93 LJ PC 113.
35    (1924) 93 LJ PC 113 at 121.
36    [1964] 1 All ER 465.
37    [1964] 1 All ER 465 at 475.
38    [1964] 1 All ER 465 at 472.

a work must be the result of "substantial skill, industry or experience"[39] in order to attract copyright.

Despite these different formulations there are some guidelines which may be drawn from the cases. In line with the idea-expression dichotomy, it does not matter that the work is drawn from a common stock of knowledge, the amount of labour refers to the labour expended in the expression of the work (*University of London Press Ltd v University Tutorial Press Ltd;*[40] *Erica Vale v Thompson and Morgan*[41]). The quantum is not referable to the amount of time taken to complete the work. As Peterson J said in *University of London Press Ltd v University Tutorial Press Ltd:*[42]

> If time expended is to be the test, the rapidity of an author like Lord Byron in producing a short poem might be an impediment in the way of acquiring copyright, and, the completer his mastery of his subject, the smaller would be the prospect of the author's success in maintaining his copyright[43]

The labour, skill and expertise does not necessarily require the exercise of literary or artistic merit or skill although it is interesting to note that the inclusion of "literary skill and taste" in Lord Atkinson's general statement suggests that this is one type of skill or expertise which might be taken into account. Labour, skill and expertise has been found to have been exercised in the selection and arrangement of information (*Ladbroke (Football) Ltd v William Hill (Football) Ltd;*[44] *University of London Press Ltd v University Tutorial Press Ltd;*[45] *Collis v Cater, Stoffell and Fortt Ltd*[46]) as well as in the updating of information in a computer program (*A-One Accessory Imports Pty Ltd v Off Road Imports Pty Ltd*).[47]

Preparatory work will be included in the consideration of the labour, skill and expertise if the preparatory work has as one of its objects the preparation of the alleged copyright work. Thus, in *Olympic Amusements Pty Ltd v Milwell Pty Ltd,*[48] the calculation of betting odds for a gaming machine was taken into account in determining the amount of labour, skill and expertise involved. In *Ladbroke (Football) Ltd v William Hill (Football) Ltd,*[49] Lord Devlin held that it was not necessary that the preparatory work "should have as its sole, or even as its main, object the preparation of a document ... It is sufficient that the preparation of the document is an object of the work done".[50]

---

39   [1964] 1 All ER 465 at 478.

40   [1916] 2 Ch 601.

41   (1994) 29 IPR 589.

42   [1916] 2 Ch 601.

43   [1916] 2 Ch 601 at 609. Compare Whitford J at first instance in *Gleeson v H Denne Ltd* [1975] RPC 471 at 483 regarding a sketch of a clerical collar, "I should myself have thought that the production of a drawing with speed might, on the face of it, indicate a high degree of skill".

44   [1964] 1 All ER 465.

45   [1916] 2 Ch 601.

46   (1898) 78 LT 613.

47   (1996) 143 ALR 543.

48   (1999) 162 ALR 199, upheld on appeal in *Milwell Pty Ltd v Olympic Amusements Pty Ltd* (1999) 161 ALR 302. (Note, the appeal was reported before the trial judgment.)

49   [1964] 1 All ER 465.

50   [1964] 1 All ER 465 at 479.

Finally, copying does not always destroy originality. Although Petersen J said in *University of London Press Ltd v University Tutorial Press Ltd*[51] that "the Act does not require that the expression must be an original or novel form, but that the work must not be copied from another work – that it should originate with the author",[52] this does not mean that no copying at all is allowed. The significant word in this statement is that the "work" should not have been copied and the "work" refers to the work as a whole. Copyright can therefore subsist in a work which includes copied material (such as compilations or adaptations of musical works)[53] so long as the work as a whole is the product of the requisite level of labour, skill and expertise to constitute originality. This applies even if the copied part of the new work constitutes an infringement of an earlier work. Thus, in *A-One Accessory Imports Pty Ltd v Off Road Imports Pty Ltd*,[54] the fact that the applicant's database constituted an infringement of another company's copyright did not prevent copyright subsisting in the applicant's work so long as it was the product of the requisite level of labour, skill and expertise. Such reasoning may not meet the moral expectations of some but it does reflect the principles of authorship and originality. It also means that both the original author and the "copying" author may have actions against a person who infringes the second work.

Most of these examples relate to original literary works but the same principles of originality apply to artistic, dramatic and musical works. For example, in *Interlego AG v Croner Trading Pty Ltd*,[55] the Privy Council held that a drawing which had been partly copied from an earlier drawing was not an original artistic work because there was little visually significant difference between the earlier and the later drawings.[56] In the related Australian Federal Court case Gummow J expressly rejected this test on the basis that it introduced a requirement of novelty into the principle of originality.[57] He held that the later drawings were original on account of the skill, labour and expertise exercised in their execution.

The test for originality is often criticised for being too low although there have been some cases where the requisite level of skill, labour and expertise was found not to exist. In *GA Cramp and Sons Ltd v Frank Smythson Ltd*,[58] copyright was said not to subsist in a selection of tables to be included in the back of a diary because the selection was of "an obvious and commonplace character" and that no "meritorious distinctiveness" could be detected in it.[59] Unfortunately, the original compiler of the tables was deceased and there was no evidence before the court of the actual amount of labour, skill or expertise which may have gone into this selection so the usefulness of the case is questionable.[60] In *Leslie v Young and Sons*,[61] the

---

51   [1916] 2 Ch 601.
52   [1916] 2 Ch 601 at 608-609.
53   *Wood v Boosey* (1868) 3 LR QB 223.
54   (1996) 143 ALR 543.
55   [1989] 1 AC 217.
56   [1989] 1 AC 217 at 258.
57   *Interlego AG v Croner Trading Pty Ltd* (1992) 111 ALR 577 at 609.
58   [1944] All ER 92.
59   [1944] All ER 92 at 96.
60   Today, the work will be presumed to be original unless the contrary is established: s 129.
61   [1894] AC 335.

House of Lords held that copyright did not subsist in a local railway timetable where the only labour expended was to change the already published British Rail timetables by showing the starting point of the trip as Penrith and by excluding some small stations in between.

The test for originality has become a hot topic in recent years, especially in relation to automated databases and compilations where the question arises as to whether there is any author at all. This question was nascent in early telephone directories cases but not discussed. In the United States case of *Feist Publications Inc v Rural Telephone Service*,[62] the United States Supreme Court held that copyright did not subsist in a white pages telephone directory as a literary work because it lacked the requisite originality. The court held that originality was not determined by the fact that a compilation was made by the "sweat of the brow" or "industrious collection". Rather, something in the nature of "intellectual production" was required and, in the case of directories, this might be demonstrated by the selection, coordination and arrangement of factual material. In this case Rural Telephones could not be said to have selected the material because it had a statutory requirement to list everyone who subscribed to its service. The court also held that it could not be said to have arranged or coordinated the material. An alphabetical listing in this case was not only unoriginal, it was "practically inevitable".

By comparison in 2001, Finkelstein J in the Australian case of *Telstra Corporation Ltd v Desktop Marketing Systems Pty Ltd*,[63] determined that a telephone directory was an original work despite the fact that it displayed no "intellectual production". The judge directly compared the two different interpretations of originality and held that in Australia "industrious collection" was still sufficient to establish originality.[64] This decision was upheld on appeal where Black CJ noted that Telstra users were required to supply the relevant data and Telstra was required to publish it. However, the judge held that "industrious collection" could also include "industrious receipt".[65] The Australian decision has now been called into question.

In *IceTV Pty Ltd v Nine Network Australia Pty Ltd*[66] the High Court discussed the relationship between authorship and originality although it had not been addressed directly by the applicants in that case. The court stated that the ideas of authorship and originality are "coextensive", that the policy of the *Copyright Act 1968* was to protect "authors" and therefore, that the question of authorship should not be ignored. The High Court also suggested that the test of originality in *Telstra Corporation Ltd v Desktop Marketing Systems Pty Ltd*[67] needed to be reconsidered in the light of this requirement.

The opportunity for such reconsideration arose in *Telstra Corporation v Phone Directories Company Pty Ltd*[68] where Gordon J held that copyright did not subsist in either the White Pages or the Yellow Pages telephone directories because they

---

62    499 US 340 (1991); 20 IPR 129 (1991).
63    (2001) 51 IPR 251.
64    *Telstra Corporation Ltd v Desktop Marketing Systems Pty Ltd* (2001) 51 IPR 251.
65    *Desktop Marketing Systems Pty Ltd v Telstra Corporation Ltd* [2002] FCAFC 112.
66    (2009) 239 CLR 458.
67    (2001) 51 IPR 251.
68    [2010] FCA 44.

did not have an "author". Although the High Court's comments may have been considered obiter, Gordon J denied this on the basis that they were statements of the "central concepts" of copyright law.[69] She also denied that she was bound by the decision in *Telstra Corporation Ltd v Desktop Marketing Systems Pty Ltd*[70] on the basis that it "did not deal directly with the issue of authorship"[71] and because the High Court had expressed doubt about it.

In coming to her decision that copyright did not subsist in the directories because they did not have an author, Gordon J noted that the directories were made by many people (often not identified), using automated computer software whose architecture controlled the appearance and form of the entry, together with rules and procedures which were either programmed into the software or, on rare occasions, applied by individuals. Citing *IceTV Pty Ltd v Nine Network Australia Pty Ltd*[72] Gordon J held that the "theoretical underpinnings" of the *Copyright Act 1968* strike a balance between rewarding authors of original works against the "public interest in maintaining a robust public domain in which further works are produced".[73]

The author is the person or persons who bring the work into existence in material form.[74] To be considered an author of a literary work the person must exercise "independent intellectual effort" and/or "sufficient effort of a literary nature". This may include a consideration of "creative spark" and "exercise of skill and judgement". However, and very importantly, "substantial labour" or "substantial expense" is insufficient.[75] Because authorship and originality are coextensive the test for originality is the same.

In the case of compilations the author or authors will be those who gather or organise the collection of material and who select, order or arrange its fixation in material form. Gordon J noted that copyright protects a particular form of expression, not work per se therefore it is not helpful to refer to the "commercial value" of a work because that directs attention to the information rather than the form of expression.[76] The judge concluded:

> The various computer systems … were the result of the work of various entities over a number of years. Although the Applicants, as the ultimate purchaser of such systems, were often responsible for prescribing and overseeing the implementation of the requirements, only in a few cases was the software designed and created by the Applicant's employees. Although the computer systems were not relied upon as an independent copyright work in this proceeding, the Applicants did rely upon the intellectual effort of Sensis employees in customising the programs. On the evidence before the Court, it is not possible to determine who created and had the benefit of the whole or any part of the various computer systems … at any time.[77]

---

69    [2010] FCA 44 at [46].
70    (2001) 51 IPR 251.
71    [2010] FCA 44 at [46].
72    (2009) 239 CLR 458.
73    [2010] FCA 44 at [20].
74    [2010] FCA 44 at [20].
75    [2010] FCA 44 at [20].
76    [2010] FCA 44 at [20].
77    [2010] FCA 44 at [87].

This is an important decision which, following *IceTV Pty Ltd v Nine Network Australia Pty Ltd*, positions authors, rather than copyright owners and those who benefit from the commercial exploitation of a work, at the centre of copyright law. The decision is particularly important in relation to databases where there may be no identifiable author or authors. This is a problem which has been long recognised internationally, including in the European Union where the 1996 Directive of the European Parliament and of the Council on the Protection of Databases has been adopted. The directive recognises that a database may not have an author in the copyright sense and therefore seeks to protect the "maker" of the database where there has been "substantial investment" in obtaining, verifying or presenting material in the database. The directive also protects databases which do have an author in the usual sense. Both the High Court and Gordon J noted that Australia does not have similar legislation and that, if it is desirable to protect makers of databases such as Telstra, then this is a matter for Parliament.[78]

## Work

There seems to be no reason why copyright should not subsist in Mohammed Ali's famous impromptu poem "I, We" (at least once it is reduced to material form) or in Colin McCahon's painting comprising the words "I am". On the other hand, there seems to be every reason why copyright should not subsist in my doodles on the note pad beside the telephone, even if I do doodle "I, We" or "I am". There are three ways in which we might approach this problem. First, one might argue that I have not expended the necessary labour, skill or expertise to reach the original-ity threshold for my doodle, whilst Ali and McCahon have. The originality test is notoriously low, however, and it might not be an adequate discriminator. The second way we might discriminate between Ali's poem and McCahon's painting on the one hand and my doodle on the other is to apply the principle of de minimus non curat lex to the interpretation of the word "work" under the Act. Finally, one might discriminate between the poem and the painting on the one hand and my doodle on the other on the basis that the first two are "works" and my doodle isn't. Courts and commentators have sometimes conflated these last two arguments.

De minimus non curat lex translates as "the law is not concerned with trifling matters". Although the principle is most often invoked in criminal law it has also been held to be a principle of statutory interpretation.[79] *Halsbury's Laws of England* explains the application of the principle to statutory interpretation in the following way:

> Unless the contrary intention appears, an enactment by implication imports the principle of legal policy expressed in the maxim *de minimus non curat lex* ...; so if an enactment is expressed to apply to matters of a certain description it will not apply where the description is satisfied only to a very small extent.[80]

---

78   See *IceTV Pty Ltd v Nine Network Australia Pty Ltd* (2009) 239 CLR 458 at [135-138] and *Telstra Corporation v Phone Directories Company Pty Ltd* [2010] FCA 44 at [29-30].

79   *Farnell Electronic Components Pty Ltd v Collector of Customs* (1996) 142 ALR 322.

80   *Halsbury's Laws of England*, 4th ed, Vol 44(1), para 1441.

In *Farnell Electronic Components Pty Ltd v Collector of Customs*,[81] it was held that the "applicability or otherwise of the maxim depends upon the context in which it falls to be considered".[82] In the case of copyright one of the factors which might be considered would be the nature of the work in question. In the case of works of fine art, for example, the amount of time expended in the creation of the work may be of less importance than the way the work is received or used. Thus, Ali's poem may qualify as a literary work even though it was quickly and seemingly effortlessly created because it was presented as a literary work (in this case a poem) and received as such. My mere scribble, however, may fall below the limit despite the fact that strictly speaking it may be literary, it may be a work and possibly, may even be said to be original.

Furthermore, the application of the maxim does not depend simply on the size of the work. Copyright has been found to subsist in a single stylised letter applied to Boss sound equipment (*Roland Corporation v Lorenzo and Sons Pty Ltd*[83]), in the title of a song (*Francis Day and Hunter Ltd v Twentieth Century Fox Corp Ltd*[84]) and in headings, at least where the headings were in different languages (*Lamb v Evans*[85]).

In *Exxon Corporation v Exxon Insurance Consultants International Ltd*,[86] the English Court of Appeal, unanimously upholding the trial judge's decision, held that copyright did not subsist in the single invented word "Exxon" as an original literary work.[87] Some commentators and judges have suggested that this is an example of the application of the de minimus principle to copyright law.[88] We would disagree with such an interpretation. On the one hand, it is hard to argue that the name of a multinational oil company is a "trifling matter" with which the courts should not be concerned. On the other, it is significant that neither the trial judge nor the Court of Appeal referred to the de minimus principle in coming to their decisions. Instead, the judges sought to give a positive definition of the term "work".

Although the court found that the word "Exxon" was original (being the product of substantial labour, skill and expertise) and "literary" (in so far as it was to do with the alphabet and writing), the court held that it was not an "original literary work" when the term was considered as a whole. In coming to this decision the court rejected the applicant's submission that the word was a "work" in the sense that a work was anything that was "produced or accomplished by effort, exertion, or exercise of skill ... something produced by the exercise of

---

81   (1996) 142 ALR 322.
82   (1996) 142 ALR 322 at 327. Under a customs by-law "paper catalogues and paper price lists relating exclusively to products ... of a country other than Australia" were duty free. The Federal Court applied the de minimus principle in the interpretation of the term "exclusively" and found that customs duty was not due on the catalogue in question when only 81 out of the 40,000 items listed in the catalogue were in fact available in Australia.
83   (1991) 105 ALR 623.
84   [1940] AC 112.
85   [1893] 1 Ch 218.
86   [1982] Ch 119.
87   The company had won on a passing-off and trade marks case in the lower court and appealed only on the copyright issue.
88   See, for example, Thomas J in *Kalamazoo (Australia) Pty Ltd v Compact Business Systems Pty Ltd* [1990] 1 Qd R 231 in the Queensland Supreme Court quoting S Ricketson, *The Law of Intellectual Property*, LBC, Sydney, 1984, paras 5.61 to 5.63.

creative talent or expenditure of creative effort".[89] Instead, the court endorsed the comments of the trial judge, Graham J, who compared the invented word "Exxon" to Lewis Carroll's "jabberwocky". Although the word jabberwocky might be protected as part of the poem "Jabberwocky", Graham J said, "the word itself and by itself cannot be considered as a 'literary *work*', the subject of copyright under the Act".[90] The court held that the invented word, Exxon, lacked the necessary coherency of a work in so far as it had no meaning apart from its use as a trade mark applied to the applicant's products.[91]

The Australian *Concise Oxford Dictionary* defines a work as a "literary or musical composition". In *Exxon* the court seems to be using the term "work" in this sense where a "composition" implies some coherency in the work considered as a whole. In *Exxon* the court cited two early cases, *Davis v Comitti*[92] and *Hollinrake v Truswell*,[93] in support of its approach.[94] In *Davis v Comitti* copyright was held not to subsist in a card which comprised the face of a barometer. Chitty J held that the card was meaningless in so far as it was a "mere adjunct" to the barometer, "[b]y reading the printed matter on the card alone no intelligible proposition is arrived at".[95] In *Hollinrake v Truswell* it was held that copyright did not subsist in a cardboard cut-out in the shape of a woman's arm together with the words upon it. The Lord Chancellor, Lord Herschell said:

> The words and figures found on the "chart" do not in combination convey any intelligible idea, nor could they be of the slightest use to anyone, apart from the cardboard upon which they are printed.[96]

These cases, which delineate the limits of copyright protection, should be distinguished from the United States functionality cases. In *Baker v Selden*,[97] for example, the accounting forms were literary works but were excluded from protection because they were functional. In the cases from the English courts there was no literary or dramatic work because the words and phrases in question lacked the coherency required of a "work".

An analogous construction of "original dramatic work" was given in *Green v Broadcasting Corporation of New Zealand*,[98] where the Privy Council held that a collection of catchphrases used by a host on an unscripted television talent show was not a dramatic work because "a dramatic work must have sufficient unity capable of performance".[99] The Australian courts have not considered this question directly.

---

89  [1982] Ch 119 at 139, rejecting the Webster's Dictionary definition of "work". One might note that this is the same as the test for originality and would therefore, if accepted, have rendered the word "work" otiose.

90  *Exxon Corporation v Exxon Insurance Consultants International Ltd* [1982] Ch 119, Graham J at 132, endorsed by Stephenson LJ at 138.

91  *Exxon Corp v Exxon Insurance Consultants International Ltd* [1982] Ch 119 at 144.

92  (1885) 52 TL(NS) 539.

93  [1894] 3 Ch 420.

94  *Exxon Corporation v Exxon Insurance Consultants International Ltd* [1982] Ch 119 at 142-143.

95  (1885) 52 TL(NS) 539 at 426.

96  [1894] 3 Ch 420 at 424-425.

97  101 US 99 (1879).

98  [1989] 2 All ER 1056.

99  [1989] 2 All ER 1056 at 1058.

# Categories of Works in which Copyright Subsists

Defining the proper limits of the subsistence of copyright is important for two reasons. It can determine whether an identified subject-matter is entitled to copyright protection as a whole and it can determine in particular cases whether copyright has been infringed. Although these two aspects of subsistence are usually indistinguishable this is not always the case. It may be clear, for example, that "The Phantom of the Opera" is a dramatic work but it may not be clear that a chandelier swinging out over an audience will be protected as part of that dramatic work. It may be clear that "The Man from Snowy River" is a literary work but it may not be clear that the rhyming structure and rhythm of the poem will be protected as part of that literary work. In considering the question of subsistence it is useful to remember that the work may be considered at these different levels of generality

## Literary works other than computer programs

Literary work is defined in the *Copyright Act 1968* s 10(1) to include tables and compilations and, since 1984, to include computer programs or compilations of computer programs. Computer programs will be considered below on the basis that the definition and case law regarding computer programs has, since 1984, developed quite distinctly from the definition of literary works generally.

A literary work need not display literary merit. Thus, in *Maple and Co v Junior Army and Navy Stores*[100] in 1882, the English Court of Appeal held that copyright subsisted in a catalogue of furniture as a "book" which was defined in the 1842 *Copyright Act* (5 and 6 Vict c 45) to include "every volume, part or division of a volume, pamphlet, sheet of letterpress, sheet of music, map, chart or plan, separately published". In *Trade Auxiliary Co v Middlesborough and District Tradesmen's Protection Association*,[101] the same court held that copyright subsisted in a list of bills of sale.[102] Even before the express inclusion of compilations and tables within the definition of literary work, copyright was found to subsist in a chemist's catalogue (*Collis v Cater, Stoffell, and Fortt Ltd*[103]) and in a list of solicitors and their addresses (*Waterlow Directories Ltd v Reed*[104]) in so far as they displayed the requisite originality. More recently, copyright has been found to subsist in a football betting coupon (*Ladbroke (Football) Ltd v William Hill (Football) Ltd*[105]); in a computer compression table (*Data Access Corporation v Powerflex Services Pty Ltd*[106]); in a weight watcher's program comprising recipes, intake charts and some menus (*Skybase Nominees Pty Ltd*

---

100  (1882) 21 Ch D 369.

101  (1888) 40 Ch D 425.

102  This was so even though the Act at the time recited in its preamble that the purpose of the Act was "to afford greater encouragement to the production of literary works of lasting benefit to the world" (*Copyright Act 1842* (5 and 6 Vict c 45) s 2). Although the court did not address the question directly it seems that the "lasting benefit" to the world need not be of a literary nature.

103  (1898) 78 LT 613.

104  (1990) 20 IPR 69.

105  [1964] 1 All ER 465.

106  (1999) 202 CLR 1.

*v Fortuity Pty Ltd*[107]) and in a television program guide (*Nine Network Australia Pty Ltd v IceTV Pty Ltd*[108]). As Petersen J said in *University of London Press Ltd v University Tutorial Press Ltd*:[109]

> In my view the words "literary work" cover work which is expressed in print or writing irrespective of the question of whether the quality or style is high. The word "literary" seems to be used in a sense somewhat similar to the word "literature" in political or electioneering literature and refers to written or printed matter.[110]

As we have seen, a literary work need no longer be in writing but it seems it need not be related to the letters of the alphabet either. The *Copyright Act 1968* s 10 provides that compilations and tables are included as literary works if they are "expressed in words, figures or symbols". A literary work has therefore been found to include a compilation of blank billing forms (*Kalamazoo (Australia) Pty Ltd v Compact Business Systems Pty Ltd*[111]) and a list of newspaper bingo numbers (*Express Newspapers plc v Liverpool Daily Post and Echo plc*[112]).

If a literary work need not display literary merit, need not be written and need not be related to the letters of the alphabet what is it that positively constitutes subject-matter as a literary work? The classic test was formulated by Davey LJ in *Hollinrake v Truswell*[113] where the alleged literary work was the cardboard cut-out in the shape of a woman's arm together with the words and figures on it:

> Now, a literary work is intended to afford either information and instruction, or pleasure, in the form of literary enjoyment. The sleeve chart before us gives no information or instruction. It does not add to the stock of human knowledge or give … any instruction by way of description or otherwise; it is certainly not calculated to afford literary enjoyment or pleasure. It is a representation of the shape of a lady's arm, or more probably of a sleeve designed for a lady's arm, with certain scales for measurement upon it. It is intended, not for the purposes of giving information or pleasure, but for the practical use in the art of dress making.[114]

The requirement that a literary work afford information, instruction or literary pleasure in the form of literary enjoyment has been broadly interpreted and has been held to include codes comprising either foreign or invented words (*DP Anderson and Co Ltd v Lieber Code Co*[115]) and in the *Apple Computer* cases the term was held to include computer source codes.[116]

---

107 (1996) 36 IPR 529.
108 [2007] FCA 1172.
109 [1916] 2 Ch 601.
110 [1916] 2 Ch 601 at 608.
111 [1990] 1 Qd R 231.
112 [1985] 3 All ER 680.
113 [1894] 3 Ch 420.
114 [1894] 3 Ch 420 at 428.
115 [1917] 2 KB 469.
116 In the Apple cases the trial judge, all members of the Full Federal Court and all members of the High Court agreed that a source code was a literary work. The difficulty in the case related to the object code. The trial judge's decision is reported in *Apple Computer Inc v Computer Edge Pty Ltd* (1983) 50 ALR 581, the Full Federal Court decision in *Apple Computer Inc v Computer Edge Pty Ltd* (1984) 53 ALR 225 and the High Court decision in *Computer Edge Pty Ltd v Apple Computer Inc* (1986) 161 CLR 171.

In *Exxon Corporation v Exxon Insurance Consultants International Ltd*,[117] Stephenson J accepted that a literary work should afford "information and instruction, or pleasure in the form of literary enjoyment" but commented, "whatever those last six words may add to the word 'pleasure'".[118] We would suggest that these words are potentially important in so far as they may help distinguish between literary and musical works on the one hand and between literary and artistic works on the other. In *Joy Music Ltd v Sunday Pictorial Newspapers (1920) Ltd*,[119] for example, a popular song was allegedly reproduced by a written "take-off" of the words of the song printed in a newspaper. The court accepted that copyright subsisted in the words of the song as a literary work but declined to compare the metre and rhythm of the two works on the basis that copyright did not subsist in these aspects of a literary work. The plaintiff may have been more successful had they claimed protection as a musical work. Similarly, if the arrangement and look of an EE Cummings poem were reproduced but the words were not reproduced it is likely that this would not be held to be an infringement of the literary aspects of the work although there may be an argument that the work is protected as an artistic work.[120] Although both the metre and the arrangement of a literary work may add to its pleasure, they do so by offering pleasure to the ear and the eye rather than to the capacity to comprehend meaning from the arrangement of words, figures and symbols that might be said to be the specifically literary pleasure protected under copyright law.

The requirement that a literary work afford information, instruction or pleasure in the form of literary enjoyment has imposed some important limitations on the range of literary works and its status today has been reinforced. In *Hollinrake v Truswell*,[121] *Davis v Comitti*[122] and *Exxon*,[123] as we have seen, copyright was held not to subsist in the alleged literary works because they lacked the necessary coherency to afford information, instruction or literary pleasure when considered as a work. In *Statuscard Australia Pty Ltd v Rotondo*[124] the visual display of a computer screen, comprising a grid of lines devoid of all information, was held not to be a literary work because it afforded no information, and was held not to be an artistic work because it was not original. Most notoriously, the requirement that a literary work afford information, instruction or literary pleasure was applied by Beaumont J at first instance in *Apple Computer Inc v Computer Edge Pty Ltd*[125] to hold that a computer program in object code was not a literary work. In the Full Federal Court on appeal, this question was not addressed and, in the High Court, four judges considered it but split two each side. Mason and Wilson JJ, who held that a computer program in object code was a literary work endorsed the Full Federal Court's statement that Davey

---

117 [1982] Ch 119.
118 [1982] Ch 119 at 143.
119 [1960] 2 QB 60.
120 This relationship will be explored further in the discussion of artistic works.
121 [1894] 3 Ch 420.
122 (1885) 52 TL(NS) 539.
123 *Exxon Corporation v Exxon Insurance Consultants International Ltd* [1982] Ch 119.
124 [2008] QSC 181.
125 (1983) 50 ALR 581.

LJ's definition of a literary work was not intended to be "comprehensive or exhaustive".[126] They concluded that:

> It is not correct to describe an object program as *merely* a sequence of electrical impulses within the computer. Electrical impulses there are, but these impulses serve to identify a set of instructions in machine readable language designed to guide the machine in its basic operations.[127]

Gibbs CJ, who held that an object code was not a literary work, said that the question was whether the object code was a "work" which had been reduced to the material form of a ROM:

> It seems to me a complete distortion of meaning to describe electrical impulses which cannot be perceived by the senses and are not intended to convey any message to a human being and which do not represent words, letters, figures, letters, figures or symbols, as a literary work; still less can a pattern of circuits be so described.[128]

Object codes are today expressly included within the definition of computer program and the question of whether they fit within the traditional definition of literary work no longer arises. The case is interesting, however, for its demonstration of the possible width of the term "literary work".

As we shall see, "computer program" is defined very narrowly in the Act and only includes the computer language itself, not the databases, software application, or visual interface as such. The question of whether a particular database or software application is a traditional literary work must still be determined according to general principles. The digital spare parts catalogues in *A-One Accessory Imports Pty Ltd v Off Road Imports Pty Ltd*[129] and *TR Flanagan Smash Repairs Pty Ltd v Jones*[130] were held to be literary works applying these principles. On the other hand, the collection of words such as "save", "type" and "delete" which were the subject of dispute in *Data Access v Powerflex Services Pty Ltd*[131] would probably not be a literary work. Although the point was not argued, such a collection of words would probably fail to qualify as a literary work because they lack the necessary coherency to constitute a "work," fall foul of the de minimus principle, or because they lack the necessary skill, labour or expertise required to constitute originality.[132] This case is discussed below.

## Computer programs

Computer program is defined in s 10 as "a set of statements or instructions to be used directly or indirectly in a computer in order to bring about a certain result". This rather succinct definition came into effect on 4 March 2001 as part of the *Copyright Amendment (Digital Agenda) Act 2000*. It replaces the 1984 definition of computer program (which had been rushed into effect following the outcry

---

126 *Computer Edge Pty Ltd v Apple Computer Inc* (1986) 161 CLR 171 at 192.
127 (1986) 161 CLR 171 at 194.
128 (1986) 161 CLR 171 at 184.
129 (1996) 143 ALR 543.
130 (2000) 172 ALR 467.
131 (1999) 202 CLR 1.
132 See the High Court's comments on this point in *Data Access v Powerflex Services Pty Ltd* (1999) 202 CLR 1 at 34-35.

against Beaumont J's decision in *Apple Computer Inc v Computer Edge Pty Ltd*[133] and reflects the 1999 decision of the High Court in the leading computer program case, *Data Access v Powerflex Services Pty Ltd.*[134]

The most important thing to note about the definition is its narrowness. It does not protect the application of that computer program but only the actual computer language used in the writing of the computer program, whether that language is in object code or source code. Nor does it cover the data which the program navigates. For example, the actual computer language used in writing MYOB would be protected as a computer program but MYOB itself, that is the words and layout used in the software as it appears on the screen, for example, is not protected as a computer program. Nor is any data, such as a dictionary, included within the definition. If the appearance or dictionary, for example, are to receive copyright protection, they must fit within one of the other categories of subject-matter such as a literary work, artistic work or film.

In *Data Access v Powerflex Services Pty Ltd*,[135] the High Court provided the following negative definition of a computer program:

> [S]omething is not a "computer program" within the meaning of the definition in s 10(1) unless it is intended to express, either directly or indirectly, an algorithmic or logical relationship between the function desired to be performed and the physical capabilities of the "device having digital processing capabilities". Thus, in the sense employed by the definition, a program in object code causes a device to perform a particular function "directly" when executed. A program in source code does so "after ... conversion to another language, code or notation".[136]

In *Data Access* the appellant owned the copyright in a computer program known as the Dataflex program. The respondent had developed a computer program known as Powerflex or PFXplus. In order to enhance compatibility between the two programs the respondent had reproduced approximately 300 of Data Access's "reserved words" into its software package so that, to users of the two systems, the two packages would appear to operate in a similar way. The "reserved words" were words such as save, drive, direct and edit which appeared on the screen during the operation of the program and, one might also assume, may have appeared as part of the source code for the Dataflex program. Data Access did not argue that the words were traditional literary works; rather, Data Access claimed that copyright subsisted in the words either individually as "computer programs" or together as a compilation of computer programs.

This argument was accepted by the Federal Court at first instance where Jenkinson J found that each of the reserved words was a computer program within the 1984 definition because it was a translation of the set of instructions in source code and object code which were intended to cause the computer to function.[137] On appeal to the Full Federal Court this decision was overturned. The Full Court held that the words were not themselves an expression of the set of instructions which caused the computer to function. Rather, the words were

---

133  (1983) 50 ALR 581.
134  (1999) 202 CLR 1.
135  (1999) 202 CLR 1.
136  (1999) 202 CLR 1 at 26.
137  *Data Access Corporation v Powerflex Services Pty Ltd* (1996) 33 IPR 194 at 197-198.

a mere "trigger" to activate that underlying set of instructions (just as the word "wash" on a washing machine button might be the mere trigger for causing a washing machine to function).[138] This decision appears to have conflated the two concepts of functionality and lack of coherency and the court did not itself explain why a "mere trigger" was excluded from copyright protection.

In the High Court a different approach was taken. The High Court held that the reserved words which appeared on the screen of the computer during the operation of the Data Access program (and possibly appeared in the computer program itself) neither expressed an algorithmic or logical relationship intended to cause a computer to function nor were they a "conversion" or translation of such a relationship.[139] The words might be included within the set of instructions so defined but they did not express this functional relationship.

Under the 1984 definition of computer program "related information" was expressly included as part of the computer program. Related information might include such things as databases or the cinematograph film to be shown on a DVD. In *Data Access* the question arose as to whether the reserved words could be protected as "related information". The High Court was divided on the meaning of "related information" in the 1984 definition and it is significant that the new definition does not use the term. The majority (Gleeson CJ, McHugh, Gummow and Hayne JJ) asserted (obiter) that related information was any data included in a computer program which did not express the requisite algorithmic or logical relationship. It included data or information which formed part of the computer program but was "irrelevant to its structure, choice of commands and combination and sequencing of commands".[140] An example of such data or information would be the information in an electronic encyclopaedia, for example, as opposed to the set of instructions which causes the computer to sift the information in the encyclopaedia. In the opinion of the majority, reproducing such related data would infringe the copyright in the computer program if the related data was a substantial part of the computer program. Gaudron J expressly disagreed with this definition and held that data or information was only "related information" if it was related to the structure of the computer program in some way. She gave as an example the look up table in *Autodesk Inc v Dyason (No 1)*.[141] Both approaches were unsatisfactory in the light of the High Court's restricted definition of a computer program and would have led to years of litigation as to the substantiality, relatedness or otherwise of any data in a computer program.

Under the new definition, the reference to related data has been excluded, and in *Australian Video Retailers Association Ltd v Warner Home Video Pty Ltd*[142] Emmett J held that this exclusion meant that copyright protection of computer programs did not extend to original content which a computer program was designed to reproduce or copy. Thus, in the case in point, the commercial rental right in a computer program only extended to the language of the computer

---

138  *Powerflex Services Pty Ltd v Data Access Corporation* (1997) 37 IPR 436 at 451.

139  In copyright law "version" has the limited of meaning of "translation". "Conversion" was assumed by the High Court to be similarly limited. The right to translate a work is one of the rights included in the adaptation right which is considered in Chapter 4.

140  *Data Access v Powerflex Services Pty Ltd* (1999) 202 CLR 1 at 33.

141  (1992) 173 CLR 330.

142  *Australian Video Retailers Association Ltd v Warner Home Video Pty Ltd* (2001) 53 IPR 242.

program which caused a DVD to function, it did not extend to the film which was shown when the DVD was played. Despite Emmett J's comments to the contrary, this represents yet a further limitation on the level of protection for computer programs and may have significant implications in relation to rights which may attach to computer programs (such as the commercial rental right) but which do not extend to other subject-matter such as films.

The fact that the "content" of computer programs is not protected as a computer program but must fit within other categories of computer subject-matter reflects a familiar distinction in copyright law. Early films, for example, were only protected under the *Copyright Act 1911* in so far as they were dramatic works. It was only in the *Copyright Act 1968* that a film, as such, was protected as a separate form of expression. The rights, however, which subsist in a film are still much narrower than the rights subsisting in a dramatic work. As you learn about the difference between works and subject-matter other than works, you may like to consider whether a computer program would be better classified as a form of Part IV subject-matter.

## Dramatic works

The definition of a dramatic work appears to have gradually widened since the first *Dramatic Copyright Act 1833* (3 and 4 Will IV c 15). In 1906 in *Tate v Fullbrook*,[143] the defendants had used the plaintiff's comic devices of a car, six characters, certain scenes such as an explosion, and the plaintiff's acting style in an allegedly infringing performance. The plaintiff's dialogue had not been reproduced. The English Court of Appeal held that there was no infringement because copyright could not subsist in such scenic effects, situations or what was then known as "gag" (that is, improvisations, interjections or interpolations into a written script). The court held that copyright subsisted only in the written form of a dramatic work which was meant to be published or printed. Non-copyright effects might be referred to only for the purpose of determining whether there had been a substantial taking of the copyright material.[144] This decision was founded on the argument that copyright in dramatic works had evolved from copyright in "books" and that each type of dramatic work referred to in the definition clause (tragedy, comedy, play, opera, farce) was similarly literary in character. Kennedy LJ said he was "not prepared to accept that a 'dramatic piece' can exist without words".[145]

It is arguable that the *Copyright Act 1911* impliedly rejected this narrow definition by defining a dramatic work to include "any piece for recitation, choreographic work, or entertainment in dumb show,[146] the scenic arrangement or acting form of which is fixed in writing or otherwise". In similar language the *Copyright Act 1968* provides that a dramatic work includes a choreographic or "other dumb show" and a scenario or script for a film (s 10). Like the 1911 Act, the 1968 definition extends the definition of dramatic work beyond traditional dialogue-based

---

143  [1908] 1 KB 821.
144  [1908] 1 KB 821 at 832.
145  [1908] 1 KB 821 at 834.
146  One might think of mimes, clowns or some forms of performance art.

productions and it is apparent that non-verbal, non-literary and purely corporal elements of a production may be protected, subject to the requirement for the work to have been made or published.

In *Hexagon v Australian Broadcasting Commission*,[147] the original producers of the Alvin Purple movies sought relief against the ABC for passing off and copyright infringement when the ABC made a television series based on Alvin Purple, using the same actor and the same writer. Needham J in the Supreme Court of New South Wales found that copyright in the script for the film had been infringed. However, the producers also argued that copyright subsisted in "the kind of situations and style shown in the film".[148] This argument potentially raised important questions regarding which elements might be considered as part of the "expression" of a dramatic work today. Needham J thought the point was "an interesting one" but did not find it necessary to decide it.[149] Similarly, in *Telstra Corp Ltd v Royal and Sun Alliance Insurance Australia Ltd*,[150] Merkel J considered, but did not determine, two related questions. These were whether Telstra's brief synopsis for a television advertisement featuring the famous Goggomobil was a dramatic work for the purposes of the *Copyright Act* and, secondly, whether the film of the advertisement was a dramatic work.

The Privy Council did consider this issue in *Green v Broadcasting Corporation of New Zealand*.[151] Green was a well known presenter of a talent show on English television. The New Zealand Broadcasting Corporation broadcast a similar television show with the same title. Green sued for passing off and breach of copyright. He succeeded in the passing-off action in the New Zealand Court of Appeal but failed on the copyright action which he appealed to the Privy Council. Copyright was said to subsist in two different dramatic works. The first was a script. In the absence of any evidence as to the contents of the script the Privy Council was unable to find an infringement. The second dramatic work was said to be the "dramatic format" of the show which included the title, the use of a device called a "clapometer", and the use of sponsors to introduce competitors and the repetition of certain catch phrases such as "for (name of contestant) opportunity knocks", "this is your show folks, and I do mean you" and "make up your mind time". The Privy Council impliedly accepted that all of these literary and non-literary elements (including props such as the clapometer) might be taken into account in determining whether there was a dramatic work in which copyright subsisted. However, as we have seen, the Privy Council held that, even taken together, these elements did not constitute a dramatic work because "a dramatic work must have sufficient unity capable of performance".[152]

In Australia a similar test was adopted by Tamberlin J in *Aristocrat Leisure Industries Pty Ltd v Pacific Gaming Pty Ltd*[153] where the alleged dramatic work was the written specifications for a digital poker machine. The specifications described the odds to be paid by the machine, the combination of "cards" which

---

147  (1975) 7 ALR 233.
148  (1975) 7 ALR 233 at 252.
149  (1975) 7 ALR 233 at 252.
150  (2003) 57 IPR 453.
151  [1989] 2 All ER 1056.
152  [1989] 2 All ER 1056 at 1058.
153  (2000) 50 IPR 29.

would "pay" and the situations when the screen would become a video style racing match which would allow the player to win bonus points. Tamberlin J declined to find that the specifications were a dramatic work. The games, said Tamberlin J:

> lack the element of *performance* by characters, and are insufficiently predetermined … There is no apparent "plot", nor is there any choreography, script, characterisation or interaction between characters and there is a strong element of unpredictability and randomness. None of these elements are essential or individually determine the question, but, weighing them cumulative, I am led to the conclusion that the specifications do not give rise to any dramatic work.[154]

The judge expressly acknowledged that a "performance" need not be by human beings and that a script for "The Simpsons" or "South Park" may well be a dramatic work in so far as it calls for a performance by characters.[155] It is interesting to consider in this context whether either the fireworks or the fireworks technicians could be said to be characters for the purposes of determining whether the script for the New Year's Eve fireworks display was a dramatic work in the *Channel Nine* case.

In *Australian Olympic Committee Inc v Big Fights Inc*,[156] Lindgren J considered a number of films made of the 1956 Olympic Games and whether they were cinematographic productions and therefore dramatic works within the terms of the 1911 definition. The decision in so far as it relates to the definition of a cinematographic production is not of importance here but in the course of his decision he held that "[t]he expression 'dramatic work' itself also suggests that the action must be staged, contrived or directed and not simply recorded".[157] In this case films of sporting events were held not to be dramatic works. A similar result would arise under the *Copyright Act 1968* today if one applied the Privy Council decision in *Green v Broadcasting Corporation of New Zealand* or Tamberlin J's definition in *Aristocrat Leisure Industries Pty Ltd v Pacific Gaming Pty Ltd*.

## Musical works

There are musical works which have rhythm but no melody, sound without rhythm, compositions of found sounds, compositions made through sampling, and adaptations and arrangements of other musical works. Musical works might be composed for orchestras, hand clapping, or the human voice[158] alone, for example, and are not restricted to works for traditional musical instruments.[159]

---

154  (2000) 50 IPR 29 at 44.

155  (2000) 50 IPR 29 at 43.

156  (1999) 46 IPR 53.

157  (1999) 46 IPR 53 at 67.

158  The musical line for voices in a musical work is part of the musical work: *Robertson v Lewis* [1976] RPC 169 and *CBS Records Australia Ltd v Guy Gross* (1989)15 IPR 385. Words will still be protected separately as a literary work.

159  There is no reason why a musical work for wind chimes would not be protected as a musical work, but see *Komesaroff v Mickle* (1986) 77 ALR 502 at 509 where King J held that a moving sand painting was not a work of artistic craftsmanship because it was "produced by the operation of forces acting in the confines of the product". The cases can be distinguished in so far as a musical work can be defined by reference to its effects rather than by reference to how it is produced.

Adaptations, arrangements[160] and sampled works may qualify as original musical works in their own right provided they display the requisite degree of labour, skill and expertise. In *CBS Records Australia Ltd v Guy Gross*,[161] the singer, Collette, had collaborated with Gross to produce a cover version of Anita Ward's song, "Ring My Bell". A demo tape of this arrangement was made and sent to CBS Records who subsequently asked Collette to record another cover version of the song with them. Collette did this and the new recording was released by CBS Records. Gross sued CBS Records for infringement of his copyright in the demo tape arrangement of "Ring My Bell". The court found the demo tape arrangement was an original musical work and in the judgment drew a distinction between differences arising from "mere interpretation" and actual original arrangement:

> As to whether any copyright subsists in the (demo tape) version is a point of difficulty. For copyright in an arrangement to subsist, the difference from the work arranged must be such that a new original work can be identified. Differences resulting from mere interpretation, particularly differences brought about by an arrangement of a work to suit the qualities of a particular singer's voice, do not result in the creation of an original work. Particularly is this so in the area of popular music where the latitude given to the performer may be greater than that in the classical works ... creational composition is required to bring into being an original work.[162]

It should be noted that, to the extent that the reference to "creational composition" seems to import a requirement of novelty into the originality requirement, the decision is inconsistent with Gummow J's decision in *Interlego AG v Croner Trading Pty Ltd*[163] and the criticism of the Privy Council decision in that case.[164]

It has sometimes been suggested that traditional music will not be protected because it lacks originality, material form or both. Before 2005 it was also thought that a traditional musician whose performance was recorded would be disadvantaged because it was the maker of the film, rather than the performer, who owned the copyright.[165] These concerns were sometimes overstated and some of them have now been addressed. For example, live performers are now joint owners of the copyright in a sound recording of the performance and have moral rights in relation to both the performance itself and recordings of the performance; the performer also has performers' protection to prevent unauthorised dealings with recordings of the performance. In addition, general copyright principles can be used to ensure that, whilst traditional music in the abstract might lack originality, an adaptation or arrangement of the music may be original enough to attract copyright protection. The biggest problem with protecting traditional music today might not be in proving subsistence but in proving infringement. This is because it may be difficult for the musician to prove that the alleged infringer copied the musician's version of the work rather than some other version. This was

---

160  *Wood v Boosey* (1868) 3 LR QB 223.
161  (1989) 15 IPR 385.
162  (1989)15 IPR 385 at 392.
163  (1992) 111 ALR 577.
164  *Interlego AG v Tyco Industries Inc* [1989] 1 AC 217.
165  See J McKeough and A Stewart, "Intellectual Property and the Dreaming" in E Johnson, M Hinton and D Rigney (eds), *Indigenous Australians and the Law*, Cavendish, Sydney, 1997, pp 53-79.

the problem confronting the plaintiff in *Robertson v Lewis*[166] who was unable to prove that Vera Lynn's recording was an infringement of the plaintiff's particular arrangement of an old Scottish air.

## Artistic works in general

Artistic work is defined in s 10(1) to mean:

(a)   a painting, sculpture, drawing, engraving or photograph, whether the work is of artistic quality or not;

(b)   a building or a model of a building, whether the building or model is of artistic quality or not; or

(c)   a work of artistic craftsmanship whether or not mentioned in paragraphs (a) or (b);

but does not include a circuit layout within the meaning of the *Circuit Layouts Act 1989*.

Some of these terms are further defined in s 10. A drawing includes a "diagram, map, chart or plan"; an engraving includes an "etching, lithograph, product of photogravure, wood-cut, print or similar work, not being a photograph"; photograph means "a product of photography or a process similar to photography, other than an article or thing in which visual images forming part of a cinematographic film have been embodied, and includes a product of xerography" and sculpture includes a "cast or model made for the purposes of sculpture". A building is defined to include "a structure of any kind".

There are two general points to note about the definition of artistic work. First, the definition is partly exclusive. Courts do not have to determine whether the particular subject-matter is an "artistic work" but rather whether it can be classified as a "painting", a "sculpture" or a "building", for example. These categories of artistic work are close and if a work does not fit one category it may well fall into another or may be characterised in more than one way. A crayon work might be classified as a drawing if it is determined that crayon is not a paint; a textured painting might be classified as a sculpture if it is thought that a painting suggests flatness; a charcoal monochrome might be accepted as a painting if it is thought that a drawing must have lines; a painted table might be protected as a work of artistic craftsmanship or a sculpture if it is thought that it is not a painting. Although it may sometimes be unimportant whether a work is protected as a sculpture or a painting or as a work of artistic craftsmanship, this is not always so. Section 68 of the Act, for example, would allow a person to publish a book of photographs of public sculptures without infringing the copyright in the sculptures but would not extend to allow publication of photos of paintings, even if the paintings had been in a public space. A work of artistic craftsmanship, but not a sculpture, may retain its copyright protection even after a corresponding design of it has been industrially applied (see ss 74-77A).

The second point to note is that, except for works of artistic craftsmanship, the above works need not be of "artistic quality".[167] To say that something is artistic

---

166   [1976] RPC 169. This case contains an interesting obiter consideration of the application of *Walter v Lane* [1900] AC 539 to musical works.

167   The provision that artistic works need not have artistic quality was not expressly included in the *Copyright Act* 1911 although it had developed under case law. The modern authoritative

may mean two things. It may mean that the work in question displays more than mere commonplace or "workaday" standards of execution or that it is part of the artistic scene, a branch of the fine arts, for example. The *Macquarie Dictionary* refers to both of these senses:

> artistic 1. conformable to the standards of art; aesthetically excellent or admirable. 2. of, like, or befitting an artist.

Copyright in artistic works, therefore, has been held to extend to drawings of machine parts, building plans,[168] a design for a sliding drawer[169] and for a solar water panel as well as to structures such as a swimming pool[170] and a half-size tennis court.[171] It has been held to cover very simple drawings subject to their meeting the requirement of originality. In *Kenrick and Co v Lawrence and Co*,[172] copyright was found to subsist in a simple drawing, to be used on a voting form, of a hand ticking a box. The court noted that in the case of simple drawings it might be difficult to prove that the alleged infringer has in fact copied the work. The fact that artistic works need not be of artistic quality has raised few problems in relation to two dimensional subject-matter such as drawings and paintings but causes some difficult problems in relation to three dimensional subject-matter such as industrial moulds, casts and functional objects which might arguably be classified as sculptures or engravings.

## Paintings, drawings and photographs

Butterworths *Australian Legal Dictionary* defines a painting as "in ordinary language, a surface which has been covered in whole or part with a film of coloured matter, which is applied wet and subsequently dries". That is, the Dictionary defines a painting by reference to its medium rather than by reference to its ordinary meaning as a "thing" entitled to copyright protection.

There are considerable problems with this media-based definition of a painting. As Cleasby B commented in *Woodward v London and North Western Railway Co*,[173] such a definition would cover "everything which has painting done upon it by a workman".[174] The media definition of painting would encompass other artistic works including sculptures, works of artistic craftsmanship and buildings as well as ordinary utilitarian articles in which copyright might not normally subsist. It would exclude all digital works including those which emulated painting techniques. A particular work in oil pastels, a medium which is somewhere between a paint and a crayon, may fail to gain protection as a painting and also

---

statement of the principle is found in the House of Lord's decision in *LB (Plastics) Ltd v Swish Products Ltd* [1979] RPC 551 and the High Court's decision in *SW Hart and Co Pty Ltd v Edwards Hot Water Systems* (1985) 159 CLR 466.

168  *Ancher, Mortlock, Murray and Woolley Pty Ltd v Hooker Homes Pty Ltd* [1971] 2 NSWLR 278

169  *LB (Plastics) Ltd v Swish Products Ltd* [1979] RPC 551.

170  *Darwin Fibreglass Pty Ltd v Kruhse Enterprises Pty Ltd (t/as Viking Swimming Pools and Spas)* (1998) 8 NTLR 46.

171  *Half Court Tennis Pty Ltd v Seymour* (1980) 53 FLR 240.

172  (1890) 25 QBD 99.

173  (1878) 3 Ex D 121.

174  (1878) 3 Ex D 121 at 123. In that case, the judge declined to find that a painted rug was a painting within the terms of the *Carriers Act 1830* (UK).

fall outside the definition of a drawing in so far as the particular work was not concerned with aspects of line. The fact that the definition might fail to encompass even a simple mixed media work such as one made in oil pastels plus charcoal plus a photograph indicates the inadequacy of the media-based approach.

Rather than focus on the medium in which the work is made the English Court of Appeal, in *Merchandising Corporation of America v Harpbond*,[175] defined a painting by reference to its ordinary meaning as a thing in which copyright subsists. In that case the defendants commissioned an artist to paint a portrait of Adam Ant sporting his then new Prince Charming make-up which comprised two parallel red lines on the cheek, shaved and eye-shadowed eyebrow, a pigtail, a beauty spot and a red heart above the left eyebrow. In addition, the defendants altered old photographs of Adam Ant and superimposed the new make-up. The plaintiffs alleged breach of copyright in a drawing made by Adam Ant of the new look, in a photograph of Adam Ant sporting his new look and in the make-up itself as a painting. The Court of Appeal held that there was no substantial reproduction of the sketch or the photograph. The court also held that copyright did not subsist in facial make-up as a painting within the ordinary meaning of the word. This was for two reasons. In the ordinary meaning of the word a face, even made up, is not a painting and if one considered the make-up without the face then it was a mere idea. It is probably impossible to give a comprehensive definition of the ordinary meaning of the word painting as a thing entitled to copyright protection and Lawton J said "it is a question of fact in any particular case whether that which is under discussion is or is not a painting".[176] The court expressly rejected an argument that a painting must be a two-dimensional work of art.

In the fine arts a drawing has traditionally been defined by reference to its content – it is a work of art which emphasises the line, regardless of its medium.[177] In copyright law a slightly wider definition has evolved and the cases include within the definition of a drawing a wide range of two dimensional visual works which are not paintings, photographs or films, including abstract works. As the court said in *Elwood Clothing v Cotton On Clothing*:[178]

> There can be a drawing in the form of a pattern, using shapes, colours and other elements in order to give pleasure, or … simply as here to attract attention and to convey a visual impression – a certain 'look and feel'. It is not inconsistent … to suggest that the object represented by the pictorial line may be a shape, form, or pattern that is not a recognisable image, and may be in an abstract style.[179]

As we have seen, some particular problems may arise in the characterisation of writing as an artistic work. Under s 10 of the *Copyright Act 1968* writing is defined as a form of visible representation of words, figures and symbols. Because

---

175 [1983] FSR 32.

176 [1983] FSR 32 at 46.

177 Although the distinction between a drawing and a painting may be practically unimportant under the *Copyright Act* it has arisen in other circumstances. In 2004, Craig Ruddy's Archibald Prize winning portrait "David Gupilil – two worlds" was challenged on the basis that it was not "painted" as required under the Archibald trust. The work was basically a crayon line-based drawing on flocked wall paper.

178 [2008] FCAFC 197.

179 [2008] FCAFC 197 at [49].

it is a visual representation there may be occasions when an author wants to protect the words as an artistic work rather than as a literary work. This issue was addressed in a comprehensive manner by the Full Federal Court in *Elwood Clothing Pty Ltd v Cotton On Clothing Pty Ltd*.[180] The matter related to the design of T shirts and swing tags which comprised an arrangement of words, numbers and graphics. The distinctive features of the design included the placement of the numbers on the shoulders and the v-shape of the design, both of which accentuated the male form.

The respondent admitted to copying the "look and feel" of the design but noted that they had used different words and numbers on their T shirts and swing tag. Both parties agreed that, if the design was classified as a literary work rather than an artistic work, there was no infringement. The primary question therefore was whether the design was an artistic or literary work. Both the trial judge and the Full Court held that each of the designs was a drawing and therefore an artistic work. Furthermore, although a design might be both a literary work and an artistic work, in this case, because of the semiotic insignificance of the words, the designs were not literary works.

> To the extent that the words and numbers convey some semiotic meaning it is trifling when compared with ... "the selection and arrangement of the various elements (text, colour, font, shape, and so on)". The drawing, so constituted, makes a visual impression notwithstanding the presence of words and numbers ...
>
> The artistic quality of the work consists of the layout, balancing, form, font, positioning, shaping and interrelationship of the various elements. Any meaning conveyed by the numerals and text is so obscure, subjective to the reader and subservient to the artistic aspect that the numerals and text do not amount to a literary work.[181]

It is the application of specifically visual labour, skill and expertise which constitutes a design as an artistic rather than a literary work. It is therefore important to note that the Full Court is not adding an extra requirement to this by suggesting that the meaning of the words must always be insignificant to constitute an artistic work. Rather, in this case, the semiotic insignificance of the words meant the design was not also a literary work.

A compilation of artistic works and literary works was held to be a literary work in *Kalamazoo (Australia) Pty Ltd v Compact Business Systems Pty Ltd*[182] although, more commonly, words and figures have been held to be part of a drawing. In *Lincoln Industries v Wham-O Manufacturing Co* Davison CJ in the New Zealand Court of Appeal explained why:

> The statutory definition of "drawings" ... "includes any diagram, map, chart or plan" and each of these in ordinary experience conveys the concept of drawn lines in combination with words and figures. Words and figures are an integral part of drawings of the kind referred to.[183]

---

180 [2008] FCAFC 197 at [49]. See also *Millar and Lange Ltd v Polak* [1908] 1 Ch 433; *Roland Corporation v Lorenzo and Sons* (1991) 105 ALR 623; *Lott v JBW and Friends Pty Ltd and Endeavour Corporation Design* (2000) 76 SASR 105; and *Cortis Exhaust Systems Pty Ltd v Kitten Software Pty Ltd* [2001] FCA 1189.
181 [2008] FCAFC 197 at [60] and [62].
182 [1990] 1 Qd R 231.
183 (1984) 3 IPR 115 at 122.

Unlike paintings and drawings, a photograph is defined in the *Copyright Act 1968* by reference to its method of production. Under s 10 a photograph is a product of photography or a process similar to photography. It includes a xerox but does not include images from a cinematographic film (s 10). A photograph within a cinematographic film is part of that film (s 25).[184] We have considered the question of originality above and noted that some people suggest that originality is difficult to prove in relation to a photograph. Anyone who has ever taken a photo, however, knows the difference that angle, light, time and composition can make and the usual tests relating to originality are readily applicable to the first photograph. In relation to xeroxes and reprints the questions of originality may be different. A simple xerox of a work will usually fail to satisfy the tests for originality as a photograph but an overhead of the same work, modified, enhanced, cropped or otherwise dealt with may satisfy the test.

## Digital works and moving pictures

In Harry Potter's world paintings not only walk and talk but also wander off and, at the end of the day, snooze. Portrait subjects wander off to visit others and, at the end of the day, they snooze. Our artistic works may not yet be quite so mobile but moving images are an ordinary part of our visual landscape. From simulated three dimensional architectural designs to complex media works in an art gallery it is commonplace to think of moving artistic works. However, it is not clear how these works are protected under the *Copyright Act 1968* either because they change form or because they fall between the gaps of the different classifications of artistic works.

In *Komesaroff v Mickle*,[185] for example, King J held that a picture made by sand moving between sheets of glass could not be a work of artistic craftsmanship because "it must be possible to define the work ... and this can only be done by reference to a static aspect of what has been referred to by counsel as a 'work of kinetic art'".[186] There is little to commend this judgment and it is out of step with cases such as *Galaxy Electronics Pty Ltd v Sega Enterprises*[187] which found that a computer video game was a film even though the order of play could change with each game. It is also out of step with *TR Flanagan Smash Repairs Pty Ltd v Jones*[188] where the possibility of a catalogue being changed was not seen as an insurmountable obstacle to copyright subsistence.

A more serious problem in relation to moving images is that they may not fit within any of the traditional definitions of a painting, drawing or photograph. It will need a brave and wizardly judge to make the leap to rethink these traditional

---

184   The definition of engraving specifically excludes those forms of engraving which are photographs. Thus, an engraving made by the process of photo-lithography will be classified as a photograph rather than as an engraving. This distinction is of importance for determining the duration of copyright (ss 33, 35, 212) and in the past was important for determining authorship of the photo. Before 1968 the author of a photo was the person who owned the equipment by which the photograph was made. Today, the author of a photograph is the person who took the photograph (s 10) subject to the s 127 presumptions. See s 208 for transitional positions.

185   [1987] VR 703.

186   [1987] VR 703 at 710.

187   (1997) 145 ALR 21.

188   (2000) 172 ALR 467.

definitions in the light of what, one must admit, is relatively old technology. The fact that this has not yet been done is perhaps a little peculiar but not inexplicable. Until recently, it was generally assumed that moving pictures would be protected either as computer programs or as cinematographic films. The narrow definition of computer program in *Data Access Corporation v Powerflex Services Pty Ltd*[189] closed the first avenue and it seems that the second may also be under challenge despite the fact that a cinematographic film is defined specifically by reference to its ability to be shown as a "moving picture" (s 10).

In *Aristocrat Leisure Industries Pty Ltd v Pacific Gaming Pty Ltd*,[190] the moving art work in question was of spinning symbols which looked like an old fashioned poker machine reel. Had these images been static works on paper there is little doubt that they would have been characterised as paintings or drawings. At trial the defendant conceded, however, that the moving images were a cinematographic film and therefore the question of whether they would constitute a drawing was not considered. It is interesting to note that the trial judge, Tamberlin J, expressed reservations about this concession and expressed the opinion that, had he had to decide the issue he would have held that the moving images were not a cinematographic film. He drew an unlikely distinction between images which only "appear to move" and those with a real "element of progression or movement":

> It is literally true that the specific symbols appear to rotate on the reels but there is no element of progression or movement in the symbols themselves as there is in a traditional movie film, which is comprised of marginally different pictures, which when repeated quickly, give the impression of motion. I appreciate that the language is not to be restricted by any static view anchored in previous technology but there is a real difficulty in accepting that the aggregate of the symbol images in the present case constitutes a "moving picture".[191]

On appeal[192] this question was not raised but Tamberlin J's decision acts as a warning that protecting a moving artistic work by classifying it as a cinematographic film might not be an option. In addition, it must be remembered that the exclusive rights attaching to cinematographic films are not as broad as those for works, the moral rights afforded are different, the duration of copyright is shorter and ownership is determined differently.

## Sculptures and engravings

Is a frisbee or a drive shaft a sculpture? Is a mould for a frisbee an engraving? Such questions pose considerable difficulties for courts. If the frisbee or its mould were displayed in an art gallery by an artist and was intended to function as a specifically artistic work, most Australian judges would have little difficulty in classifying such a work as a sculpture even though there may be some question as to who "made" the work and whether it has an author at all. We could

---

189  (1999) 202 CLR 1.
190  (2000) 50 IPR 29.
191  (2000) 50 IPR 29 at 45.
192  *Pacific Gaming Pty Ltd v Aristocrat Leisure Industries Pty Ltd* (2001) 116 FCR 448.

confidently say that, in most cases, an Australian judge would not bat an eye at Du Champ's "Fountain".

But, if the frisbee is just a frisbee and the drive shaft is just a drive shaft how is the judge to act? As we have seen, the *Copyright Act 1968* does not exclude functional objects from protection on the basis of their functionality nor can the judge simply rely on the workaday standard of production of the object to exclude it from protection. The question is further complicated because the dictionary definitions of sculpture and engraving refer to both the process of producing something ("engraving" something or the "art of sculpture") and the "thing" itself (an engraving or sculpture). Courts have diverged on the important question of how to interpret these terms. The New Zealand Court of Appeal has focused on the method of producing an object in order to determine whether it is an engraving or sculpture. The Australian Federal Court is divided. Pincus J has been making a valiant effort to prevent the ever increasing reach of the *Copyright Act 1968* by defining sculptures and engravings by reference to their ordinary meaning as works of art traditionally protected under the *Copyright Act*. This effectively excludes industrial objects such as mouldings from protection under the Act. Carr J, on the other hand, has followed the more expansive New Zealand approach and defined sculptures by reference to the method of producing them. Carr J's approach was accepted "in principle" (but not decided) on appeal to the Full Federal Court in *Burge v Swarbrick*[193] and the matter was not considered in the final appeal to the High Court.[194]

In *Lincoln Industries Ltd v Wham-O Manufacturing Co*,[195] the New Zealand Court of Appeal considered claims of copyright infringement in relation to the manufacture of a plastic frisbee by a plastics injection-moulding process. In this case, a rough sketch was made of the proposed finished frisbee, a wooden model of the frisbee was made, a detailed diagram was made from the wooden model for the making of a mould and the mould was made partly in accordance with the diagram and partly through trial and error on a lathe. Finally, melted plastic was injected into the mould. Once the plastic set the mould was opened to reveal the finished frisbee. The question arose as to whether copyright subsisted in any of these "things".

The New Zealand Court of Appeal made three findings. First, they held that the "engraved" plate from which an engraving is made is also an engraving.[196] Secondly, they found that the mould was a plate because it was made by a process of "engraving" the metal on the lathe. Thirdly, the plastic frisbee, which was made by pressure from the "plate" (the mould) was a print or an engraving within the terms of the New Zealand Act because it had been made by the process of pressure from an engraved plate. What the court had done was to define the terms in the Act not as "things" with a common meaning but by reference to the manner in which they were made. Applying such reasoning, all products of injection moulding from sheds to straws would be engravings entitled to copyright protection.

---

193  *Burge v Swarbrick* [2005] FCAFC 257 at [60].

194  *Burge v Swarbrick* (2007) 234 ALR 204.

195  (1984) 3 IPR 115.

196  This was in accordance with English authority in *James Arnold and Co Ltd v Maifern Ltd* [1980] RPC 397.

On the question of whether the wooden model or the frisbee were sculptures, the New Zealand court held that a frisbee was not a sculpture but that the wooden model was a sculpture. After quoting extensively from dictionaries the Court of Appeal commented that "it seems to us inappropriate to regard utilitarian objects such as flying plastic disks, manufactured as toys, by an injection moulding process, as items of sculpture".[197] The rejection, however, was not based on the utilitarian nature of the frisbee but on the process by which it was made. Davison CJ held that forcing melted plastic into a mould was neither original nor expressive of the artist's idea. The wooden model, on the other hand, was an original creation which expressed the artist's idea of a frisbee and could therefore be classified as a sculpture in so far as it was the "creation of expressive form in three dimensions".[198]

In *Greenfield Products Pty Ltd v Rover-Scott Bonnar Ltd*[199] the applicants, relying on the *Wham-O* case, argued that moulds used to produce pulleys and clutch plates for a ride on mower were engravings and that parts of the drive mechanism were sculptures. Pincus J, in the Australian Federal Court, rejected these arguments.

In relation to the definition of sculpture the judge said that the word sculpture must be given its "ordinary meaning, in accordance with orthodox principles of interpretation".[200] Although the judge expressly agreed with the conclusion of the New Zealand court that a frisbee was not a sculpture he did not consider the reasoning of the New Zealand court nor explain how the drive mechanism differed from the wooden model of the frisbee which that court had found was a sculpture.

In relation to engravings Pincus J pointed out that not all cutting could be called engraving, despite the dictionary definition.[201] In particular, he rejected the New Zealand finding that cutting metal from a block on a lathe could be considered engraving. "In current usage", Pincus J stated, "the physical meaning is confined to cutting, marking or otherwise working a surface".[202] Having noted that the term engraving referred to both the process and the product he concluded:

> No consideration of policy, or other orthodox approach, could justify straining the English language so far as to call the moulds engravings ... In particular, I cannot, with respect, agree with the view that a frisbee is an image or that it is a print.[203]

Having rejected the approach of the New Zealand court regarding the definition of engraving as a process it is suggested that Pincus J was here relying on the ordinary meaning of the word engraving considered as a "thing" which is protected.

It is interesting to note that, in *Talk of the Town v Hagstrom*,[204] Pincus J had an opportunity to reconsider his decision in *Greenfield Products Pty v Rover-Scott Bonnar Ltd* regarding the definition of "engraving". In *Talk of the*

---

197  (1984) 3 IPR 115 at 131.
198  (1984) 3 IPR 115 at 131.
199  (1990) 95 ALR 275.
200  (1990) 95 ALR 275 at 284.
201  (1990) 95 ALR 275 at 285.
202  (1990) 95 ALR 275 at 285.
203  (1990) 95 ALR 275 at 285.
204  (1990) 99 ALR 130.

*Town* the applicants argued that the moulds used to make extruded PVC sections for use in the building trade were engravings under the *Copyright Act 1968* as determined by the New Zealand Court of Appeal and that there was an important question to try regarding the difference between Pincus J's decision in *Greenfield* and the New Zealand court's decision in *Wham O*. Pincus J declined to find that there was an important question to try and said that he adhered to what he had said in the earlier case "with the exception that the suggestion that engraving is typically on a flat surface is overstated".[205] Pincus J continued:

> I remain unconvinced that a reader of the definition of "engraving" set out above, would think it to be intended to cover a mould or a die of the ordinary kind. I can see that arguments might arise at the margin, such as with respect to a mould for making artistic works in low relief. But the idea that a mould or a die used for making a frisbee is an "engraving" within the definition, as is the frisbee itself, appears to me (with the greatest respect) to be difficult to reconcile with the ordinary meaning of the language actually used in the definition.[206]

Strengthening his opposition to the New Zealand decision he concluded: "I note further that the word 'plate' is defined in the Act as including a mould, but neither 'engraving' nor 'artistic work' includes 'plate' as defined".[207]

Despite this strong stance, Pincus J's approach has not been endorsed by other judgments in the Federal Court and, at the time of writing, there appears to be a swing back to the New Zealand position represented by Carr J's decision in *Swarbrick v Burge*.[208] It may be that, commendable as Pincus J's approach is, it is out of step with the rest of the *Copyright Act 1968* which, on the whole, does not distinguish between industrial and aesthetic works. A strict application of Pincus J's approach might mean that the question of whether an industrial product is protected or not may depend on the chance occurrence of whether or not copyright drawings were made of the product at an early part of the design product.

## Works of artistic craftsmanship

In *George Hensher Ltd v Restawile Upholstery (Lancs) Ltd*,[209] Lord Simon of Glaisdale provides an engaging, erudite history of the growth of the Arts and Crafts movement in England in the 1860s. The movement, which took its name from the Arts and Crafts Exhibition Society formed in 1888 and is associated with the names of William Morris, John Ruskin and Augustus Welby Pugin, promoted the value of the well crafted object over the products of mass production and industrialisation. As Lord Simon argues, however, the movement also saw itself as separate from the realm of the fine arts which, at the time, was almost exclusively concerned with the art of easel painting and sculpture. The products of the movement ranged from wallpaper to cutlery and included the work of bookbinders, glaziers, printers, woodworkers and even printers. The fact that

---

205  (1990) 99 ALR 130 at 136.
206  (1990) 99 ALR 130 at 136.
207  (1990) 99 ALR 130 at 136. The status of *James Arnold and Co Ltd v Maifern Ltd* [1980] RPC 397 in Australian copyright law is therefore still undecided.
208  [2004] FCA 813.
209  [1976] AC 64 at 89-92.

the *Copyright Act 1911* (UK) included works of artistic craftsmanship for the first time can be attributed directly to the influence of the movement.

Despite its birth in an anti-industrial sentiment it was quickly accepted that works of artistic craftsmanship need not be handmade or unique. In addition, a model or prototype of an object which is later mass produced may qualify as a work of artistic craftsmanship if it displays the requisite degree of artistic craftsmanship. Thus, in *George Hensher Ltd v Restawile Upholstery (Lancs) Ltd*,[210] it was accepted that a prototype for an industrial product (in that case, a three-piece lounge set) could in principle qualify as a work of artistic craftsmanship. In *Coogi Australia Pty Ltd v Hysport International Pty Ltd*,[211] Drummond J held that the first roll of fabric in a commercial run was a work of artistic craftsmanship. Whether later individual products of a mass production process could qualify as works of artistic craftsmanship will depend on the process itself. In most cases later articles will lack sufficient originality to be works in their own right.[212]

Unlike other categories of artistic works, such as drawings and possibly sculptures and engravings, works of artistic craftsmanship require some form of artistic quality. However, it is the craftsmanship, not the work itself, which must be artistic: see Lord Simon's comments in *George Hensher Ltd v Restawile Upholstery (Lancs) Ltd*.[213]

In *Burge v Swarbrick*,[214] a case relating to the plug and mouldings for a racing yacht,[215] the JS 9000, the High Court had an opportunity to consider the meaning of the phrase "work of artistic craftsmanship" for the first time. The High Court noted that the phrase had two distinct roles within the *Copyright Act*. First, it characterised those works which had been afforded copyright protection as a result of the Arts and Crafts Movement as discussed above. Secondly, since 1989, works of artistic craftsmanship were in a special category of three dimensional artistic works in so far as they maintained their full copyright protection even after a design for the work had been industrially applied.[216] Other three dimensional artistic works, such as sculptures, do not have this protection and instead are forced to rely on the lesser protection of the *Designs Act 2003* (Cth).[217]

The High Court asked why works of artistic craftsmanship should be afforded such protection and concluded that it was to encourage "real artistic effort".[218]

---

210 [1976] AC 64.

211 (1998) 157 ALR 247.

212 In *Coogi Australia Pty Ltd v Hysport International Pty Ltd* (1998) 157 ALR 247, Drummond J held that copyright did not subsist in the later works because s 32 only applied to works when they were "first made". This argument is not terribly convincing and the originality argument mentioned above is probably a more useful way of thinking about the problem.

213 [1976] AC 64 at 91-92. The High Court effectively rejected the approach taken by Finkelstein J in *Muscat v Le* (2003) 204 ALR 335.

214 [2007] HCA 17.

215 The plug is a handcrafted full scale model of the yacht, the mouldings are parts of the boat itself which are taken from inverted moulds, which in turn have been taken from the plug.

216 See reg 17 of the *Copyright Regulations 1969* (Cth) which provides that a design has been industrially applied if it has been applied to more than 50 articles.

217 See the designs/copyright overlap defences in ss 74-77A of the *Copyright Act* discussed in Chapter 5, "Using artistic works as designs and applying artistic works industrially".

218 In the absence of any reasons being given in the Explanatory Memorandum to the Copyright Amendment Bill 1988 (Cth) which introduced this change, the High Court relied on the reasoning of Drummond J in *Coogi Australia Pty Ltd v Hysport International Pty Ltd* (1998) 157 ALR 247.

On this basis the court held that the question of whether a work was a work of artistic craftsmanship is not determined by assessing the beauty or aesthetic appeal of a work nor by assessing any harmony between its visual appeal and its utility. Rather, the question is to be determined by assessing "the extent to which the particular work's artistic expression, in its form, is unconstrained by functional considerations".[219] The court explained the rationale for its new test in the following way:

> The more substantial the requirements in a design brief to satisfy utilitarian considerations of the kind indicated with the design of the JS 9000, the less the scope for that encouragement of real or substantial artistic effort. It is that encouragement which underpins the favourable treatment by the 1989 Act of certain artistic works which are applied as industrial designs but without design registration. Questions of fact and degree inevitably arise.[220]

Although the evidence of the person who made the work may be taken into account in assessing this matter, the issue is to be determined objectively by the courts.[221]

Applying this test in this case the court held that the plug was not a work of artistic craftsmanship because the objective evidence of the design brief showed that the intention and purpose of the design was to produce a fast, two-handed racing yacht. Further, in so far as the mouldings could be understood to be reproductions in a material form of the plug, their separate status as works of artistic craftsmanship did not need to be considered.

The decision in *Burge v Swarbrick* does not mean that yachts or other utilitarian works can never be works of artistic craftsmanship (works of artistic craftsmanship traditionally have a utilitarian purpose). Rather, the High Court's decision means that only those artistic works whose process of production allows a certain amount of artistic freedom will be afforded the broader protection offered by the *Copyright Act* once they have been industrially applied.[222]

In so far as the High Court's test requires the decision maker to look to the process by which the work came into existence, rather than to the object itself, the test has much to commend it.

First, by focusing on the process rather than the product the High Court has provided a way forward for thinking about prototypes, moulds and other intermediate works produced in the design process. Although a prototype or mould will probably be destroyed in the process of creating the final product, and although the prototype or mould may not be of the highest standard of craftsmanship (for example, the outside of a mould may be rough and unsightly) it is the production of the mould, from which a final product will be taken, which may involve the most artistic effort. Once the prototype or mould is protected then the ensuing products will also be protected indirectly.

Secondly, the High Court's test may also be useful in drawing fine line distinctions between industrial designs which are protected under the *Designs Act* and

---

219  [2007] HCA 17 at [83].
220  [2007] HCA 17 at [84].
221  [2007] HCA 17 at [63]. This accords with the decision of the English Court of Appeal in *Merlet v Mothercare Pty Ltd* (1984) 2 IPR 465, a case relating to a well-made baby's rain cape.
222  Compare the approach of the Full Federal Court in *Sheldon v Metrokane* (2004) 135 FCR 34.

works of artistic craftsmanship which are afforded the greater protection of the *Copyright Act*. A set of crockery, for example, may fall into either category and it is not possible to determine what category this may be by looking at the thing itself. Industrial designs may be beautiful and well crafted, they may even be made and marketed in such a way as to simulate works of artistic craftsmanship, but it is in the process of design that one may be able to determine into which category they fall.[223]

There are some dangers, however, in looking behind the thing itself. If courts are to rely on design briefs, promotional literature and other objective manifestations of the process of design it is important to realise that sometimes the aesthetic content or purpose of the design might "go without saying". For example, if a practising artist were to design a bicycle rack[224] or belt buckle[225] it might "go without saying" that the aesthetic concerns of the artist will be paramount in its design. The design brief, however, might focus on the utilitarian aspects of the design so as to provide practical guidance to the artist/designer. Similarly, documents developed for potential investors in a new yacht may seek to emphasise the practical attractions of yacht design and its commercial potential rather than the aesthetic vision of the designer. Courts must take care not to be blinded by the language of the documents in question.

## Buildings and models of buildings

Before 1968 copyright in buildings and other structures subsisted only in "architectural works of art" which were defined as buildings or structures having artistic character or design. Copyright protection only extended to protect these artistic features.[226] In *Vincent v Universal Housing Company Ltd*,[227] the question arose as to whether a lily pond surrounded by stone work in a sunken garden, flights

---

223  The examples used by the High Court are traditional and unhelpful. References to wallpaper, tapestry, stained glass windows, pieces of jewellery and Tiffany artefacts at [75] take us no further than Lord Simon's examples in *George Hensher Ltd v Restawile Upholstery (Lancs) Ltd* [1976] AC 64 at 91-92. The works of a cobbler, dental mechanic, or wheelwright are not works of artistic craftsmanship. They lie at one extreme, the hand-painted tiles lay at the other:

> In between lie a host of crafts some of whose practitioners can claim artistic craftsmanship, some not – or whose practitioners sometimes exercise artistic craftsmanship, sometimes not. In the former class, for example, are glaziers. The ordinary glazier is a craftsman, but he could not properly claim that his craftsmanship is artistic in the common acceptation. But the maker of stained glass windows could properly make such a claim; and, indeed, the revival of stained glass work was one of the high achievements of the Arts and Crafts movement. In the latter class is the blacksmith – a craftsman in all his business, and exercising artistic craftsmanship perhaps in making wrought-iron gates, but certainly not in shoeing a horse or repairing a ploughshare. In these intermediate – or rather, straddling – classes come, too, the woodworkers, ranging from carpenters to cabinet-makers: some of their work would be generally accepted as artistic craftsmanship, most not. Similarly, printers, bookbinders, cutlers, needleworkers, weavers – and many others. In this straddling class also fall, in my judgment, the makers of furniture. Some of their products would be, I think, almost universally accepted as 'works of artistic craftsmanship'; but it would be a misuse of language to describe the bulk of their products as such. (quoted by the High Court in *Burge v Swarbrick* [2007] HCA 17 at [81])

224  Cf *Brandir Int'l v Cascade Pac Lumber Co* 834 F 2d 1142 (2d Cir 1987).

225  Cf *Kieselstein-Cord v Accessories by Pearl Inc* 632 F 2d 989 (2nd Cir 1980).

226  *Copyright Act 1911* (UK) s 35(1).

227  [1928-1935] MacG Cop Cas 275.

of steps and low stone walls was a structure within the terms of the 1911 Act. Romer LJ held that either together or separately these features did comprise a structure although the report suggests that the lawn, paths and flower beds in the landscaped garden were not considered part of the structure. The report does not explain what level of coherency is necessary between the disparate components of the structure and the usefulness of this judgment is therefore limited.

In accordance with the Berne Convention, the requirement to display such architectural merit was deleted with the passing of the *Copyright Act 1968*. Today copyright subsists in buildings and models of a building and a building is defined to include "a structure of any kind" (s 10).

In ordinary usage we might expect an architectural structure to include bridges, dams and other similar constructions but a "structure of any kind" may widen this definition substantially. Under the current definition, copyright has been held to subsist in a concrete slab and inserted posts which formed a half-size tennis court (*Half Court Tennis Pty Ltd v Seymour*[228]). In *Darwin Fibreglass Pty Ltd v Kruhse Enterprises Pty Ltd (t/as Viking Swimming Pools and Spas)*,[229] Mildren J found that copyright subsisted in a fibreglass swimming pool as a building and in a mould for the swimming pool as a model of a building. Mildren J held that a model of a building includes not only a representational model of the building but also a "three dimensional image which is a copy of an object or which is to be copied to make the actual object itself".[230] Mildren J's definition of a "structure" under the Act was wide but not unhelpful. He states that a structure need not have steps, doors, a roof or windows; it need not be inhabited by humans or animals and continues:

> I think that the word "structure" implies something which is of some substance, and is usually erected upon or constructed upon or in the ground with an element of permanence, although it need not be a fixture, so that prima facie a prefabricated building ... may still remain a structure even though it is in the process of being moved or is left temporarily unattached to the soil. I do not see why buildings ... need be built from concrete or stone ... It flows from this that it is not necessary that the building or structure be built from the ground in situ.[231]

A significant level of copyright litigation relates to buildings, especially in the highly competitive project home market and one might expect the incidence of such cases to increase in the future as architects become more involved in the future treatment of their buildings under moral rights provisions. There seems to be a problem in relation to renovating buildings if one tries to abide by all the requirements of the *Copyright Act*. On the one hand, the addition of a building extension which sympathetically reflected the principal architectural features of the original facade has been held to be an infringement of the copyright in the original building (*Meikle v Maufe*[232]). On the other hand, one can imagine that an unsympathetic extension which did not repeat significant architectural features might, today, be held to be an infringement of the moral rights of the author of the original building.

---

228  (1980) 53 FLR 240.
229  (1998) 41 IPR 649.
230  (1998) 41 IPR 649 at 656.
231  (1998) 41 IPR 649 at 656.
232  [1941] 3 All ER 144.

Despite the fact that significant commercial buildings such as the National Gallery of Australia, Centre Point Tower and Stadium Australia will require refurbishment and updating at least every 20 years, the only provision for this under the *Copyright Act 1968* is that it is not an infringement of copyright in a building to "reconstruct" a building (s 73). Whether a reconstruction covers a repair, renovation or refurbishment is moot.

## Categories of Subject-Matter other than Works in which Copyright Subsists

Copyright in cinematographic films, sound recordings, broadcasts and published editions of works subsists independently of the works which are embodied in them (s 113). Thus, copyright in a sound recording is independent of the copyright in the musical work recorded. In the case of a film, copyright may subsist in the cinematograph film itself, but it may also subsist in the screen play for the film (dramatic work), the music (musical works), and lyrics (literary work). This independence of subsistence is subject to the s 110(2) defence which provides that, where a film is caused to be seen or heard in public after the expiration of copyright in the film, then there is no infringement of the copyright in the works included within the film.

Copyright in Part IV subject-matter also subsists independently (s 113(2)). Thus, copyright will subsist in a television broadcast independently of the copyright in the film which is broadcast: see *Phonographic Performance Company of Australia Ltd v Federation of Australian Commercial Television Stations.*[233]

The independence of different copyright subject-matters is important to keep in mind because the rights attaching to the different subject-matters are quite different, the copyright may be owned by different people, the duration of the copyright may vary and there may be different defences available depending on the classification of the subject-matter. To give the most striking example, a work is infringed by "reproducing" that work but a cinematographic film, sound recording, broadcast or printed edition of a work is infringed by "copying". A musical work might, therefore, be infringed by the making of a sound alike version of the work but a sound recording will only be infringed if the actual sounds recorded are copied (for example, by ripping the CD).[234]

### Sound recordings[235]

A sound recording is defined in s 10 as the aggregate of sounds embodied in a record and a record is defined as a disc, tape, paper, electronic file or other device in which the sounds are embodied. Taken literally, this means that the soundtrack to a film could constitute both a sound recording and a substantial part of a film. In order to avoid this possibility s 23(1) provides that sounds embodied in a

---

233  (1998) 195 CLR 158.

234  *CBS Records Australia Ltd v Telmak Teleproducts (Aust) Pty Ltd* (1987) 79 ALR 604.

235  The label or P symbol on a record will be prima facie evidence of the maker, year and country of first publication: *Copyright Act 1968* s 138.

sound-track associated with visual images forming part of a film shall be deemed not to be a sound recording.

The relationship between sound recordings and films is quite complex. In *Phonographic Performance Company of Australia Ltd v Federation of Australian Commercial Television Stations*,[236] it was accepted by all parties and the High Court that s 23(1) prevents the maker of a film from acquiring a separate copyright, as a sound recording, in the sound-track of the film.[237] However, the majority held that the section did not operate to destroy the copyright in a sound recording even if it were embodied in the sound-track of a film. Thus the owner of the copyright in the sound recording of Boom Crash Opera's *Dancing in the Storm* did not lose its copyright in the sound recording even when that recording was used on the sound-track of the Australian film, *The Big Steal*. The High Court held that, despite s 23(1), the broadcast of the film also constituted a broadcast of the sound recording. The majority emphasised that the copyright in the sound recording subsisted in the sounds recorded, not in the medium, that is, not in the record or sound-track on which the sounds were recorded.

The case also considered s 110(3) which provides that, where sounds are included in a sound-track but are also included in a sound recording which was not made directly or indirectly from the film, then there is no infringement of copyright in the film by virtue of any use made of the sound track. Thus, the playing of the original sound recording of *Dancing in the Storm* would not constitute an infringement of the film, *The Big Steal*, but playing the sound-track of the film, including *Dancing in the Storm,* would be an infringement of both the film and the sound recording.

## Cinematographic films[238]

A cinematographic film is defined in s 10(1) as:

> the aggregate of the visual images embodied in an article or thing so as to be capable by the use of that article or thing:
> (a)  of being shown as a moving picture; or
> (b)  of being embodied in another article or thing by the use of which it can be shown;
> and includes the aggregate of the sound embodied in a sound-track[239] associated with such visual images.

Section 24 provides that a visual image is embodied in an article or thing if the images can be reproduced from that article or thing. Applying this definition, a video tape has been held to be a cinematographic film[240] and in *Galaxy Electronics Pty Ltd v Sega Enterprises* Wilcox J held that a computer-generated video game was a cinematographic film:

---

236  (1998) 195 CLR 158.
237  (1998) 195 CLR 158 at 167.
238  For transitional provisions regarding cinematographic films, see ss 221 and 222.
239  Sound-track is defined in s 10.
240  *Netage Pty Ltd v Cantley* (1985) 6 IPR 200 at 208-209.

It does not matter that they were embodied in a different form, ie three-dimension vertices of the polygram model, rather than a two dimensional image. The statutory definition says nothing about the form of embodiment.[241]

We have discussed some of the problems relating to moving visual images above. Section 10 provides that a photograph in a cinematographic film is not a photograph and s 25 provides that photographs within cinematographic films are protected as cinematographic films. In *Aristocrat Leisure Industries Pty Ltd v Pacific Gaming Pty Ltd*,[242] however, Tamberlin J expressed the obiter opinion that the visual images of a cinematographic film must themselves display some "element of progression or movement".[243] Under this definition a slide show would not be a cinematographic film nor would a series of individual, relatively unrelated photographs, even if they were embodied in a video tape or film.

In *Galaxy Electronics Pty Ltd v Sega Enterprises*,[244] the alleged cinematographic film was the computer-generated images in a video game known as Virtua Cop. The Full Federal Court held that even though the exact sequence of visual images changed each time somebody played the game the game was a cinematographic film. The court based its decision on the finding that the full range of images had been embodied in the program prior to the playing of the game. The court's decision in this case is more generous than King J's decision in *Komesaroff v Mickle*[245] regarding variable subject-matter but it still assumes some prior limitations on the form of the copyright subject-matter. As interactive works become more sophisticated and responsive the question of how to characterise them will become a question of some difficulty.

## Published editions of works[246]

Copyright subsists in a published edition of a literary, dramatic, musical or artistic work or a collection of these works. The copyright includes the published edition of a newspaper or magazine as well as a book.[247] Like other Part IV subject-matter there is no requirement that the published edition be original although s 92(2) provides that copyright will not subsist in an edition which reproduces a previous edition of the same work or works. Copyright can therefore subsist in a published edition even though it is substantially similar to the published edition of another work or works. This allows publishers to publish series in similar styles without losing their copyright protection.

The published edition right was introduced in the *Copyright Act 1956* (UK) following the report of the Gregory Committee in 1952 which noted the ease with which editions of literary and musical works could be copied using photo-lithography and other means.[248] The Committee also noted that once a work

---

241  (1997) 145 ALR 21 at 29.
242  (2000) 50 IPR 29.
243  (2000) 50 IPR 29 at 45.
244  (1997) 145 ALR 21.
245  (1986) 77 ALR 502.
246  For transitional provisions regarding published editions of works, see s 224.
247  *Nationwide News Ltd v Copyright Agency Ltd* (1996) 136 ALR 273.
248  *UK Parliament: Report of the Copyright Committee*, Cmd 8662, London, HMSO 1952.

was out of copyright there was nothing to prevent a competitor from copying a publisher's edition of the work. The United Kingdom Act was amended to provide limited protection for publishers against the reproduction by photographic or similar processes of the typographical arrangement of a published edition of a literary, dramatic or musical work. Thus, it is not an infringement of the copyright in a published edition to reproduce similar layout in another edition of the work – the right is restricted to copying the published edition by photographic means. In Australia, the published edition right was introduced in the 1968 Act following the recommendations of the Spicer Committee.[249]

"Published edition" is not defined in the Australian Act and, unlike the United Kingdom legislation, is not restricted to typographical arrangements. In *Nationwide News Ltd v Copyright Agency Ltd*,[250] the right was interpreted broadly: "Published edition copyright", held Sackville J, "protects the presentation embodied in the edition":[251]

> The general principle of copyright law is that copyright does not extend to ideas, but only to the expression of those ideas. But in the case of a published edition copyright, what is protected is not a particular collocation of words or musical notes, or a photographic representation. Published edition copyright protects the presentation embodied in the edition. This form of copyright, as the legislative history shows, protects such matters as typographical layout. However, it also protects other aspects of presentation, such as juxtaposition of text and photographs and use of headlines. In the present case, a considerable volume of evidence was adduced on the importance of layout and presentation to magazines and newspapers. In modern times, the work of typesetters is shared among sub-editors, layout artists or designers and production editors. It is clear that layout is often extremely important in attracting readers to read a particular story or magazine. It is also clear that the choice of layout, type-size, headings and colour is a skilled operation.[252]

In this case the court held that the published edition referred to the edition as a whole so that one article copied from a newspaper did not represent a substantial part of the protected subject-matter.[253]

## Broadcasts

Provisions relating to copyright in broadcasts[254] have been simplified by the *Copyright Amendment (Digital Agenda) Act 2000* which abolished the distinctions between free to air and cable services and between subscription and non-subscription services. The new provisions are consistent with the more media-neutral approach of the *Broadcasting Services Act 1992*.

The *Copyright Act 1968* s 91 provides that copyright subsists in a television broadcast or sound broadcast made from a place in Australia, by the Australian Broadcasting Corporation, by the Special Broadcasting Corporation or under a licence or a class of licence granted under the *Broadcasting Services Act 1992*.

---

249 *Report of the Committee to Consider Alterations in the Copyright Law of the Commonwealth*, AGPS, Canberra, 1963.
250 (1996) 136 ALR 273.
251 (1996) 136 ALR 273 at 291
252 (1996) 136 ALR 273 at 290-291.
253 (1996) 136 ALR 273 at 291-292.
254 For transitional provisions regarding broadcasts, see s 223.

Under the *Broadcasting Services Act* licences are granted to individuals for national, commercial or community broadcasting services, for subscription broadcasting services (for example, Pay TV) and narrow casting services (for example, Sky Channel), open narrow casting services and international broadcast service. Alternatively, the Australian Communications and Media Authority may provide a general authorisation, known as a class licence, which allows any person to provide a specified type of service without the need for an individual licence.

In ordinary language "broadcast" has two meanings – it is a generic term for a communication made by a television or other communications service or it can refer to a communication made to the general public as opposed to narrow casting which is a communication made to a selected part of the public. It is the first meaning which is reflected in s 10 of the *Copyright Act* and copyright therefore subsists in narrow casts as well as broadcasts.[255]

Section 10 defines a broadcast as a "communication to the public" delivered by "a broadcasting service" under the *Broadcasting Services Act*. A broadcasting service is defined under this Act as a service that delivers "television programs" or "radio programs" to people having appropriate receiving equipment regardless of the means of delivery, that is, by use of the radio frequency spectrum, cable, optical fibre, satellite or any other means (s 6). Dial up services and teletext services are specifically excluded from the *Broadcasting Services Act* definition.[256]

In *Network Ten Pty Ltd v TCN Channel Nine Pty Ltd*,[257] which dealt with the broadcast of segments of Channel Nine television programs on Ten's infotainment program "The Panel", the majority in the High Court (McHugh ACJ, Gummow and Hayne JJ; Kirby and Callinan JJ dissenting) overturned a Full Federal Court decision that any single image broadcast was a television broadcast for the purposes of copyright protection. The High Court commented that "there can be no absolute precision as to what in any of an infinite possibility of circumstances will constitute a 'television broadcast' "[258] but, as a general rule, the term referred to a "program" and television commercials were discrete television broadcasts in their own right.[259] As Finkelstein J commented when the matter was referred back to the Federal Court, the High Court thereby implicitly rejected the idea that the medium was the message as espoused by Marshall McLuhan in his seminal work *Understanding Media*.[260]

---

255 This interpretation is consistent with usage in the *Broadcasting Services Act 1992* where "broadcast" is often used as a general term for a communication to the public whilst a "narrowcast" is a type of broadcast. See the definition of narrow casting in *Broadcasting Services Act* s 18.

256 *Broadcasting Services Act 1992* s 6 provides that broadcast services do not include "(a) a service (including a teletext service) that provides no more than data, or no more than text (with or without associated still images); or (b) a service that makes programs available on demand on a point-to-point basis, including a dial-up service; or (c) a service, or a class of services, that the Minister determines, by notice in the *Gazette*, not to fall within this definition".

257 (2004) 205 ALR 1.

258 (2004) 205 ALR 1 at 21.

259 (2004) 205 ALR 1 at 19-21.

260 First edition, McGraw Hill, New York, 1984. Finkelstein J in *TCN Channel Nine Pty Ltd v Network Ten Pty Ltd (No 2)* [2005] FCAFC 53 at [3]. The Federal Court had already rejected an alternative argument that a broadcast was the totality of images transmitted from the time a service started transmitting: *TCN Channel Nine Pty Ltd v Network Ten Pty Ltd* (2002) 190 ALR 468.

"Program" is not defined under the *Copyright Act* but is defined under the *Broadcasting Act* as "matter the primary purpose of which is to entertain, to educate, or to inform an audience" and includes "advertising or sponsorship matter". This definition would therefore cover sporting events and news as well as films, serials, game shows, reality TV and music shows.

## Duration of Copyright[261]

As a general rule copyright continues to subsist in works, films and sound recordings under the *Copyright Act 1968* until 70 years after the end of the calendar year in which the author of the work died or in which the film or sound recording was published. Copyright in television and sound broadcasts continues until the end of 50 years from the end of the calendar year in which the broadcast was made and copyright in printed editions of works continues until 25 years after the end of the calendar year in which the edition was published. The duration of copyright in works, films and sound recordings was increased from 50 to 70 years under the *US Free Trade Agreement Implementation Act 2004* but does not extend to works, films or sound recordings subject to Crown copyright.

The duration of copyright protection has relentlessly increased and one must question the policy reasons supporting such an increase. Under the *Statute of Anne* copyright subsisted in a book for 14 to 21 years. Today, Art 7 of the Berne Convention provides that the term of protection for copyright in works shall be the life of the author plus 50 years from the first of January of the year following the author's death. For cinematographic films the Convention provides that copyright shall subsist for 50 years from the date in which the film was published or made. The period of protection for photographs may be reduced to 25 years from the making of the photograph and there are special provisions relating to pseudonymous and anonymous works and films.[262] The Rome Convention, which covers sound recordings and broadcasts, provides for a minimum period of 20 years from the making of the broadcast or recording (Art 14). There are no international standards for printed editions of works. Australia's copyright legislation meets these international requirements and partly extends them (s 33 as to works, ss 93-96 as to other subject-matter, ss 180 and 181 for Crown copyright).

In 1995 the European Union extended the duration of copyright in works to 70 years after the death of the author.[263] In 1998 the United States[264] adopted this period for works and extended the period for "works made for hire" to up to 120 years from the year in which it was made.

---

261  For transitional provisions regarding duration, see *Copyright Act 1968* s 210 (works), s 212 (photographs) and ss 233-237 (Crown copyright and copyright subject-matter made or published by international organisations). For application of the US-Australia Free Trade Agreement extension, see *US Free Trade Agreement Implementation Act 2004* Sch 9, Part 6, cl 131, which applies the extended term retrospectively.

262  The *Universal Copyright Convention* provides for shorter periods but, in the case of a country which is a signatory to both conventions, the Berne Convention prevails. Article 12 of the TRIPS Agreement substantially adopts the Berne provisions. Australia is bound by the higher requirements of the US-Australia Free Trade Agreement.

263  European Council Directive 93/98/EEC of 29 October 1993.

264  The *Copyright Act Title 17* (US) was amended by the *Sonny Bono Copyright Term Extension Act* (US) passed in 1998.

It is difficult to support these long protection periods from a policy point of view. They cannot be justified, as they were in the great copyright cases of the 18th century, by reference to the need to support the writer or artist; nor can they be justified on the basis that the copyright owner, as a question of moral rights, should be able to control the use of their works well after their deaths. From an economic point of view it is difficult to argue that such protection is needed as a form of incentive and, in the case of some works, such as computer programs they may even act as a disincentive to effort. One can only imagine that it is large corporations and publishing houses, who do not want Winnie the Pooh or Mickey Mouse to become part of the public domain, that are driving this rather irrational growth.

| Duration of Copyright | | |
|---|---|---|
| **Subject-Matter** | **Duration*** | **Section** |
| Published literary, dramatic and musical works, and published or unpublished artistic works other than an unpublished engraving | From time made to 70 years after year of author's death | s 33(2) |
| Literary, dramatic and musical works which had not been published, performed, broadcast or of which records of the work had not been sold at time of author's death (excluding computer programs) | From time made to 70 years after year first published, performed etc | s 33(3) |
| Engravings unpublished at time of author's death | From time made to 70 years after year of publication | s 33(5) |
| Genuinely anonymous or pseudonymous published works | 70 years after year of publication | s 34(1) |
| Sound recordings | 70 years after publication | s 93 |
| Cinematographic films made in Australia or by qualified person | From time made to 70 years after publication | s 94(1) |
| Cinematographic films not made in Australia, not made by qualified person but first published in Australia | 70 years from publication only | s 94(2) |
| Television and sound broadcasts | 50 years after calendar year broadcast first made | s 95 |
| Printed editions of works | From time made to 25 years after year published | s 96 |
| Literary, musical and musical works subject to Crown copyright | From time made to 50 years after year published | s 180(1) |
| Artistic works, other than engravings and photographs, subject to Crown copyright | 50 years from year made | s 180(2) |
| Engravings and photographs subject to Crown copyright | From time made to 50 years after year published | s 180(3) |
| Sound recordings and films subject to Crown copyright | 50 years from year first published | s 181 |
| Works made by or under the direction of international organisation | From time made to 70 years from year of first publication | s 187 |
| Sound recordings and films made by or under direction of international organisation | From time made to 70 years after first publication | s 188(1) |
| Printed editions of works made by or under control of international organisation | From time made to 25 years after first publication | s 188(2) |

\* The time is generally taken from the end of the calendar year in which the relevant event took place.

## Crown Copyright and International Organisations

Division 1 of Part VII of the *Copyright Act 1968* sets out special rules regarding Crown copyright. If a literary, dramatic, musical or artistic work, a sound recording or film is "made by, or under the direction and control of the Commonwealth or a State", copyright will subsist in it even if it would otherwise not be entitled to protection.[265] This is especially important in regard to material made outside Australia by an unqualified person. The duration of copyright in such material will be determined from the time it is made or published rather than from the death of the author.[266]

Similarly, copyright will subsist in works, recordings, films and printed editions of works made or first published by or under the direction or control of an organisation declared by regulation to be an international organisation.[267] The *Copyright Regulations 1969* Sch 12 sets out the organisations to which these provisions apply. These include a number of United Nations bodies, the Asian Development Bank, the International Coffee, Tin and Wheat Councils, the South East Asia Treaty Organisation and the International Criminal Police Organisation.

## International Provisions Relating to Subsistence

In accordance with Australia's international obligations, s 184 provides that Regulations may be made extending the provisions of the *Copyright Act 1968* to subject-matter made or published in another country, buildings situated in another country, subject-matter made by a citizen, national or resident of another country or bodies incorporated in another country and broadcasts made from another country.

The *Copyright (International Protection) Regulations 1969* extend copyright protection under the *Copyright Act* to works, published editions of works, films and sound recordings having the necessary connecting factor to countries who are parties to the Berne Convention, the Universal Copyright Convention, the Rome Convention, the *WIPO Copyright Treaty*, the *WIPO Performers and Phonograms Treaty*, and countries who are members of the World Trade Organization. Protection is also extended to television and encoded broadcasts from the United States and certain performances from Rome Convention, WPPT and WTO countries.

Under s 185 the Governor-General may make Regulations denying copyright protection to copyright subject-matter if the author or maker is a citizen or national (not resident in Australia) of a country or a corporation incorporated in a country, which in the opinion of the Governor-General, does not provide adequate protection to Australian works. No Regulations have been made under this section.

---

265  Section 176(1) (works), s 178(1) (films and sound recordings).
266  Sections 180 and 181.
267  Section 187 (works) and s 188 (films, sound recordings and published editions).

# CASES

## *Sands and McDougall Pty Ltd v Robinson*
High Court of Australia: Isaacs, Gavan Daffy and Rich JJ
(1917) 23 CLR 49

The respondents produced a map of Europe which the appellants reproduced. The appellants argued that copyright did not subsist in the respondent's map because the *Copyright Act 1911* had introduced a new requirement of originality or novelty into Australian copyright law which was different from the requirements of authorship under *Walter v Lane* [1900] AC 539.

**Isaacs J**: **[55]** The Act certainly makes some radical changes in the law of literary property. It entirely abolishes, by sec 31, the common law right of an author analogous to copyright in unpublished works – though preserving the personal right where a trust or confidence exists; and of course leaving untouched questions of fraud and passing off. It substitutes for the common law right referred to, the statutory right mentioned in sec 1. But if the argument advanced be correct, the statutory right – that is, the only such right – in respect of unpublished works would not arise unless the work were "original" in the inventive sense.

But, in addition, that argument overlooks the obvious fact that in copyright law the two expressions "author" and "original work" have always been correlative; the one connotes the other, and there is no indication in the Act that the Legislature intended to depart from the accepted signification of the words as applied to the subject-matter. Indeed, the circumstance of reciprocal connotation is the key to the meaning of the enactment. We find in the *Oxford Dictionary,* vol I, p 571, col 1, "author" defined as "the person who originates or gives existence to anything." ...

**[56]** Turning now to the Convention, which was the public bargain Parliament was carrying into effect, we find in various articles (*eg*, 2, 8, 11, 12 and 14) the expression "original work." I apprehend that the signatories in employing that term were not attempting to affect *Walter v Lane*,[268] but, except where the context contrasts "original" with translations or reproductions, were using a time honoured and universal phrase then current and well understood in relation to copyright.

By art 1 the contracting States are constituted into a Union for the protection of the rights of authors over their literary and artistic works. Art 2 is specially important. It first defines "literary and artistic works," then it says that translations, etc, shall be protected as "original works without prejudice to the rights of the author of the original work." Here we have two senses of the word "original," the first in the sense relevant to this case; but neither assists the appellants. Then the article declares: "The contracting countries shall be bound to make provision for the protection of the above-mentioned works." This fact, by affording a distinct reason for the use of the expression, greatly adds to the **[57]** improbability of the Imperial Parliament intending by a subtle implication to attach a new meaning to the word "original," a meaning which would undoubtedly cut down the rights of foreign authors in whose countries *Walter v Lane* was not an authority.

---

[268] [1900] AC, 549.

## *Ladbroke (Football) Ltd v William Hill (Football) Ltd*

House of Lords: Lord Reid, Lord Evershed, Lord Hodson, Lord Devlin and
Lord Pearce (note that Lord Devlin retired on 10 January 1964)
[1964] 1 All ER 465

The respondents were bookmakers who each week produced a betting coupon. The
appellants produced a similar coupon which they admitted was largely copied.
The appellants used different headings and gave different odds but had the same
arrangement of 16 different lists of bets.

**Lord Devlin:** [478] My Lords, I think that this appeal can be determined on quite a short
point. It is an important point and one that has led to a difference of judicial opinion. The
respondents are bookmakers who devoted a great deal of time, skill and experience to
the preparation of a fixed odds betting coupon for football matches. There is an infinity
of ways of betting on the results of the fifty-four League matches that are played every
Saturday during the season. The simplest and obvious way is for the bookmaker to offer
odds against the punter picking winners out of the whole list; the more winners that he
wagers that he will pick the greater the odds. Then you can have "restricted" lists of
selected matches in which there can be all sorts of variations; the punter can be invited
to pick home wins, away wins and draws in various combinations. Then you can invite
him to forecast scores full-time and half-time. The respondents' coupon contains sixteen
different lists of matches, each list permitting of a number of different wagers which
the punter can make against odds fixed according to tables given in the coupon. It is
common ground that the preparation of a coupon with bets of this sort requires a great
deal of industry and skill. Among other things, skill is required in the selection of types
of wagers that will appeal to punters while offering a good profit to the bookmaker, in
arranging them on the coupon and giving them attractive headings.

That a document prepared in this way can be the subject of copyright is not disputed.
Nor is it disputed that the appellants copied it. They were newcomers in a field in which
the respondents had been successful pioneers. They thought rightly that the types of
wagers selected by the respondents would be those shown by experience to be both attractive and profitable, and that they would do better to rely on the respondents' selection than
to make their own. They also adopted to a large extent the arrangement and the headings.
If the argument did not go beyond this point, it would, I think, be plain that there was a
breach of copyright. There is copyright in every original literary work, which by definition
includes compilation, so that there can be copyright in such productions as timetables and
directories, provided always they are "original". The requirement of originality means that
the product must originate from the author in the sense that it is the result of a substantial
degree of skill, industry or experience employed by him. The appellants argue that the
skill, industry and experience admittedly employed by the respondents was not employed
in the production of the coupon. It was employed, they say, in the selection of types of
wager. These wagers were, so to speak, the articles which the respondents offered for
sale to the public. Like other salesmen, the respondents had as a matter of business to
decide what sort of wares they were going to offer. The making of that choice is a matter
of business which, it is argued, is irrelevant for the purposes of copyright. So the skill
and labour devoted to the work of selection must be exorcised. What is left, that is, the
skill and labour required to express in writing a business decision, is negligible; and so
there is no originality. This is the short point taken by the appellants which found favour
with Lloyd-Jacob J at the trial and with Diplock LJ dissenting in the Court of Appeal.

My lords, both on principle and on authority, it appears to me to be an unsound
point. Any selection, for an example an anthology, requires a process of decision between
alternatives, and I cannot see that it matters whether the decision is made on literary or

on business grounds. An anthology of saleable poems is as much entitled to protection as an anthology of beautiful poems. It is pointed out, quite rightly, that an anthology is different from a list that is descriptive of articles for sale, since the anthology is itself the thing that is to be offered for sale. But if this distinction was a good one, there could never be a copyright in a catalogue **[479]** of goods. Such a proposition would be contrary to *Collis v Cater, Stoffell and Fortt, Ltd.*[269] This case was applied by the Court of Appeal in *Purefoy Engineering Co Ltd v Sykes Boxall & Co Ltd,*[270] where it was described as a decision that had never been doubted. I do not think that your lordships should now overrule it, or that it can be distinguished on the grounds adopted by Diplock LJ in the Court of Appeal. *Masson Seeley & Co Ltd v Embosotype Manufacturing Co*[271] is another case in which Tomlin J held that there was copyright in a trade catalogue.

I do not think that it is necessary in this type of case that the work done should have as its sole, or even as its main, object the preparation of a document such as a list or catalogue or race card. It is sufficient that the preparation of the document is an object of the work done. If that be so, the work cannot be split up and parts allotted to the several objects. The value of the work as a whole must be assessed when the claim to originality is being considered. If, when the work of selection is being done, there is no intention of listing results, the matter might well be different. A line could then be drawn between the work of selecting and the work of recording a selection independently made. No such line can be drawn in the present case which is, to my mind, much stronger than the ordinary case in which goods are being catalogued. The whole object of the work done was the production of the coupon.... .

I would therefore dismiss the appeal.

## *Telstra Corporation v Phone Directories Company Pty Ltd*
Federal Court of Australia: Gordon J
[2010] FCA 44

Does copyright subsist in the White and Yellow Pages? Instead of relying on arguments relating to the amount of work, the type of work or the commercial value of the work, the court, relying on *IceTV Pty Ltd v Nine Network Australia Pty Ltd,*[272] answers this question by reference to the "theoretical underpinnings" of the *Copyright Act 1968* and holds that copyright does not subsist in a work unless that work has an "author". This decision throws the protection of automated databases into question.

**Gordon J:** 20. The centrality of authorship is self evident.
1. The "theoretical underpinnings" of the *Copyright Act* strike a balance between rewarding authors of original literary works against policy considerations concerning "the public interest in maintaining a robust public domain in which further works are produced": *IceTV* [2009] HCA 14; 254 ALR 386 at [24] and [71]. The genesis of copyright legislation in England was to protect the rights of authors of work from the reproduction of their work without their consent: see *IceTV* [2009] HCA 14; 254 ALR 386 at [25].
2. The *Copyright Act* fixes on the author: ss 32, 33, 35 and 127 of the *Copyright Act*; IceTV [2009] HCA 14; 254 ALR 386 at [22]-[25] and [96]-[97] and *Vawdrey*

[269] (1898) 78 LT 613.
[270] (1955) 72 RPC at p 95.
[271] (1924) 41 RPC 160.
272 (2009) 239 CLR 458.

*Australia Pty Ltd v Krueger Transport Equipment Pty Ltd* (2009) 83 IPR 1 at [147] per Lindgren J.

3.  The author is the person or persons who bring the work into existence in its material form: s 10(1), 31 and 32 of the *Copyright Act* and *IceTV* [2009] HCA 14; 254 ALR 386 at [26], [33] and [98]-[99]. To be considered as an author of a literary work the person or persons must have exercised "independent intellectual Effort" (*IceTV* [2009] HCA 14; 254 ALR 386 at [33] and [48]) and/or "sufficient effort of a literary nature" (*IceTV* [2009] HCA 14; 254 ALR 386 at [99]).

4.  The *Copyright Act* provides for the possibility of joint authors: s 10(1) of the *Copyright Act* and *IceTV* [2009] HCA 14; 254 ALR 386 at [23] and [100] …

5.  The *Copyright Act* also provides for compilations – the bringing into existence of a literary work which gathers and organises material from various sources: *IceTV* [2009] HCA 14; 254 ALR 386 at [72], quoting *William Hill (Football) Ltd v Ladbroke (Football) Ltd* [1980] RPC 539 at 550 per Diplock LJ. The fact a work is a compilation will itself inform the issues of authorship to be considered: *IceTV* [2009] HCA 14; 254 ALR 386 at [99]. The author or authors will be those who gather or organise the collection of material and who select, order and arrange its fixation in material form: ss 10(1), 31 and 32 of the *Copyright Act* and of *IceTV* [2009] HCA 14; 254 ALR 386 at [73]-[74] and [99]. However, it is a question of fact and degree which one or more of them will have expended "sufficient effort of a literary nature" to be considered an author under the *Copyright Act*: *IceTV* [2009] HCA 14; 254 ALR 386 at [99].

6.  Original works emanate from authors: ss 32, 33 and 35 of the *Copyright Act* and *IceTV* [2009] HCA 14; 254 ALR 386 at [22], [24], [33], [48] and [96]. Authorship and originality are correlatives: *IceTV* [2009] HCA 14; 254 ALR 386 at [33], [34], [47]-[49], [52] and [54]. In that context, as mentioned in [20(3)] above, "originality" under the *Copyright Act* means that "the creation (ie the production) of the work required some independent intellectual effort" and/or the exercise of "sufficient effort of a literary nature": *IceTV* [2009] HCA 14; 254 ALR 386 at [33], [47]-[48] and [99]; see also at [187]-[188] and discussion of the need for some "creative spark" and exercise of "skill and judgment". The phrases adopted are different. However, each phrase confirms that for a work to be sufficiently original for the subsistence of copyright, "substantial labour" and/or "substantial expense" is not alone sufficient. More is required. What that more is will, of course, vary from case to case but must involve "originality" by an identified author in an identified work. Where the expression of the work is dictated by the nature of the information the subject of expression without such effort, it will go against a finding of originality: *IceTV* [2009] HCA 14; 254 ALR 386 at [42] and [170].

7.  The *Copyright Act* does not protect facts, ideas or information contained in a work, to ensure a balance is struck between the interests of authors and those in society: *IceTV* [2009] HCA 14; 254 ALR 386 at [28] and the cases cited therein. The *Copyright Act* does not provide protection for skill and labour alone: *IceTV* [2009] HCA 14; 254 ALR 386 at [49], [52], [54] and [131].

8.  The *Copyright Act* protects the particular form of expression of the information: *IceTV* [2009] HCA 14; 254 ALR 386 at [26], [28], [40], [70], [102] and [160]; *Hollinrake v Truswell* [1894] 3 Ch 420 at 424 per Lord Herschell LC; *Victoria v Pacific Technologies (Australia) Pty Ltd* (No 2) (2009) 177 FCR 61 at [17] per Emmett J; see also *Larrikin Music Publishing Pty Ltd v EMI Songs Australia Pty Limited* [2010] FCA 29 at [40], [41] and [212]. Copyright is not given to reward work distinct from the production of a particular form of expression: *IceTV*

[2009] HCA 14; 254 ALR 386 at [28] and [31]. Accordingly, it is "unhelpful to refer to the 'commercial value' of the information, because that directs attention to the information itself rather than to the particular form of expression": *IceTV* [2009] HCA 14; 254 ALR 386 at [31] and [166].

9.  As compilations often contain facts and information, it is necessary to focus on the nature of the skill and labour required to create the work and ask whether it is directed to the originality of the particular form of expression: *IceTV* [2009] HCA 14; 254 ALR 386 at [31], [33], [47]-[48], [52] and [54].

10. "Fixation" or identification of the original work is essential: ss 8 and 31-35 of the *Copyright Act* and *IceTV* [2009] HCA 14; 254 ALR 386 at [15], [24]-[28] and [102]-[105]. Copyright does not subsist in a work unless and until the work takes a material form: *IceTV* [2009] HCA 14; 254 ALR 386 at [26] and [103] …

21. As explained above (see [20(6)]), originality is closely tied to authorship. It requires that works originate with an author and that "the creation (that is the production) of the work [involve] some independent intellectual effort, but neither literary merit nor novelty or inventiveness as required in patent law": *IceTV* [2009] HCA 14; 254 ALR 386 at [33] and [48]. This view is consistent with a long line of authority: see *University of London Press Ltd v University Tutorial Press Ltd* [1916] 2 Ch 601 at 608-609 per Peterson J; *Robinson v Sands and McDougall Pty Ltd* [1916] HCA 51; (1916) 22 CLR 124 at 132-133 per Barton J; *Sands and McDougall Pty Ltd v Robinson* [1917] HCA 14; (1917) 23 CLR 49 at 52 per Isaacs J; *Victoria Park Racing and Recreation Grounds Co Ltd v Taylor* [1937] HCA 45; (1937) 58 CLR 479 at 511 per Dixon J; *Football League Ltd v Littlewoods Pools Ltd* [1959] Ch 637 at 651 per Upjohn J; *Autodesk Inc v Dyason* [1992] HCA 2; (1992) 173 CLR 330 at 347 per Dawson J; *Interlego AG v Croner Trading Pty Ltd* [1992] FCA 624; (1992) 39 FCR 348 at 379 per Gummow J; *Data Access Corporation v Powerflex Services Pty Ltd* (1999) 202 CLR 1 at [22], [95] and [122] per Gleeson CJ, McHugh, Gummow and Hayne JJ; *Sawkins v Hyperion Records Ltd* (2005) 64 IPR 627 at [31] per Mummery LJ; *Victoria v Pacific Technologies (Australia) Pty Ltd* (No 2) (2009) 177 FCR 61 at [18] per Emmett J.

22. Moreover, at [47] and [48] of *IceTV* [2009] HCA 14; 254 ALR 386, French CJ, Crennan and Kiefel JJ stated:

[47] Much has been written about differing standards of originality in the context of the degree or kind of "skill and labour" said to be required before a work can be considered an "original" work in which copyright will subsist. "Industrious collection" or "sweat of the brow", on the one hand, and "creativity", on the other, have been treated as antinomies in some sort of mutually exclusive relationship in the mental processes of an author or joint authors. They are, however, kindred aspects of a mental process which produces an object, a literary work, a particular form of expression which copyright protects. A complex compilation or a narrative history will almost certainly require considerable skill and labour, which involve both "industrious collection" and "creativity", in the sense of requiring original productive thought to produce the expression, including selection and arrangement, of the material.

[48] It may be that too much has been made, in the context of subsistence, of the kind of skill and labour which must be expended by an author for a work to be an "original" work. *The requirement of the Act is only that the work originates with an author or joint authors from some independent intellectual effort.* … (Emphasis added, citations omitted).

23. Similar warnings were contained in the joint judgment of Gummow, Hayne and Heydon JJ at [187] and [188]:

[187] … This concerns the submission by the Digital Alliance that this Court consider the Full Court's decision in *Desktop Marketing* and, to the contrary of *Desktop*

*Marketing*, affirm that there must be some "creative spark" or exercise of "skill and judgment" before a work is sufficiently "original" for the subsistence of copyright.

[188] It is by no means apparent that the law even before the 1911 Act was to any different effect to that for which the Digital Alliance contends. It may be that the reasoning in *Desktop Marketing* with respect to compilations is out of line with the understanding of copyright law over many years. These reasons explain the need to treat with some caution the emphasis in *Desktop Marketing* upon "labour and expense" per se and upon misappropriation. However, in the light of the admission of *Ice* that the Weekly Schedule was an original literary work, this is not an appropriate occasion to take any further the subject of originality in copyright works. (Citations omitted).

24. As these passages make clear, care must be taken not to extend the notion of originality beyond that which the *Copyright Act* was and is intended to protect.

## *Interlego AG v Croner Trading Pty Ltd*
Federal Court of Australia: Black CJ, Lockhart and Gummow JJ
(1992) 111 ALR 577

Tyco and Lego are competitors in the plastic toy brick market. The Lego Corporations alleged copyright infringement against Croner Trading Pty Ltd on the basis that the importation of Tyco bricks by Croner constituted an infringement of Lego's copyright in their drawings of the bricks (ss 37 and 38 *Copyright Act 1968*). Croner argued that copyright did not subsist in a set of drawings made after 1969 because they lacked originality in so far as they had been copied from earlier drawings.

### Gummow J: Post-1969 drawings

[607] Whereas the respondent admits that the appellants owned any copyright which subsisted in the pre-1969 drawings, but submits that copyright does not subsist by reason of s 218, the respondent contests existence of copyright in the post-1969 drawings on the ground of lack of originality. Ownership is admitted. The primary judge accepted that the post-1969 drawings did not amount to original artistic works. As will become apparent, I have reached the contrary conclusion …

[608] The relevant facts were not in dispute. Mr Pucek had drawing No 5 in front of him when he drew drawing No 8. However, he did not trace drawing No 5. Some of the scales were different, and there were five main differences between the two drawings:

(a) The flow rib which ran longitudinally along the inside of the brick in drawing No 5 was removed. This required changes to three of the perspectives in drawing No 8.

(b) In drawing No 5, the edges of the tube endings were rounded on both the inside and the outside. In drawing No 8, the edges of the tube endings are rounded only on the inside.

(c) The thickness of the upper wall is visibly less in drawing No 8 than as shown in drawing No 5.

(d) The corners of the brick are radiused in drawing No 8.

(e) The knob radius in drawing No 8 is increased.

It took Mr Pucek half a day to complete the drawing.

The appellants relied on a number of cases which considered copyright in artistic works. Most of these principles were not disputed by the respondent. Though recognising that a slavish copy of an earlier work will not enjoy copyright (*Ladbroke (Football) Ltd v*

*William Hill (Football) Ltd* [1964] 1 All ER 465 at 469) and that originality must pertain not to ideas but to their expression (*University of London Press Ltd v University Tutorial Press Ltd* [1916] 2 Ch 601 at 608), the appellants contended that drawings which derive from earlier drawings can still be seen as distinct original artistic works, each attracting its own copyright. This proposition was supported by reference to *LB (Plastics) Ltd v Swish Products Ltd* [1979] RPC 551 where Whitford J said at 569:

> The draughtsmen called on both sides made it quite plain that even where there has been a previous drawing or some sketches have been made which are in part redrawn, the making of any drawing of the kind I have to consider is a skilled business involving hours of labour, although the end result may seem relatively simple… .

**[609]** In contrast, the respondent sought to rely on a number of cases concerning copyright in literary works, which apply a *de minimis* principle in relation to the subsistence of copyright: *Noah v Shuba* [1991] FSR 14 at 33; *Exxon Corp v Exxon Insurance Consultants International Ltd* [1982] Ch 119. In developing its submission the respondent referred to the reasons of the Judicial Committee in the Hong Kong case. Their Lordships rejected the Hong Kong Court of Appeal's finding of copyright in the later (post-1972) drawings on two grounds. The first was the fear of a "perpetual monopoly" being established if "minor changes" to a work could result in a fresh copyright (at 255-6). The respondent did not pursue such an argument. In speaking of "minor changes" the argument does not use the language of copyright law. Further, the "monopoly" conferred in respect of works is essentially protection against copying. The second ground for their Lordships' decision was that the changes incorporated in the later drawing were not "visually significant" (at 266). These words were taken, with acknowledgment, by their Lordships from remarks of Whitford J in *Rose Plastics GmbH v William Beckett & Co (Plastics) Ltd* [1989] FSR 113 at 123. But a perusal of that judgment shows that plainly Whitford J was speaking of infringement, not of the subsistence of artistic copyright.

There is no doubt that the test of whether one drawing based on another attracts a separate copyright is a visual one. The question for the court is whether the later drawing is merely a copy of the earlier, or is a new artistic work. The difficulty with the approach of the Privy Council lies in the adoption of a notion of "significance".

The appellants submit that this would introduce into copyright law an element of "novelty" that has no place there. It is well established that in copyright law originality is a concept distinct from novelty in design law and patent law and from obviousness in patent law. Whilst the author of what is claimed to be an original artistic work must have expended a significant amount of his skill and labour, "originality" does not mean novelty or uniqueness and does not require inventiveness in the sense of patent law. In this field as in that of literary copyright the courts have been impressed by the precept that "prima facie what is worth copying is worth protecting": *University of London Press Ltd v University Tutorial Press Ltd* [1916] 2 Ch 601 at 610. The degree of skill and labour required of the artist will vary with the nature of the work. Authorities for these propositions may be found in Laddie et al, supra, §3.25 and see also *Sands & McDougall Pty Ltd v Robinson*, supra. There is no rule that an artistic work based on another cannot for that reason alone attract a distinct copyright.

In this case, there was no question about the labour involved …

**[610]** The learned primary judge erred in so far as he held that the differences between drawing No 5 and drawing No 8 were not sufficiently significant to give rise to fresh copyright. Since there was copyright in drawing No 8, then (as explained above) it should be held that copyright subsisted in all the post-1969 drawings.

### *Exxon Corp v Exxon Insurance Consultants International Ltd*
Court of Appeal: Stephenson and Oliver LJJ, Sir David Cairns
[1981] 3 All ER 241

Exxon was the new corporate name devised by the appellant, a multinational oil company, after extensive research and consultation. The respondents, a company with no connection with the appellant, used the name. The appellant sought an injunction for breach of copyright and passing off. Graham J, at trial, found in favour of the appellants on the passing-off issue but found against them on the copyright issue on the ground that the corporate name "Exxon" was not an original literary work. The trial judge's decision, *Exxon Corporation v Exxon Insurance Consultants International Ltd*,[273] is worth reading and was cited extensively on appeal where his decision was upheld.

> **Stephenson LJ: [243]** Graham J in his judgment posed the basic question, and in my judgment posed it rightly, as being the question—
>> 'whether it is proper to construe "original literary work" in s 2 of the Copyright Act 1956 as covering a single invented word even if considerable time and work **[244]** were expended on it and, if so, whether the word Exxon here is such a work. There are, I think no decided cases which deal specifically with the precise point that I have to decide. The answer, therefore, must in the end depend on the proper construction of the words in the 1956 Act according to general principles and the facts of the case.' (See [1981] 2 All ER 495 at 502, [1981] 1 WLR 624 at 632.)
>
> He answered the question in this way ([1981] 2 All ER 495 at 503, [1981] 1 WLR 624 at 634-635):
>> 'As I have already stated, the question that I have to decide is, shortly stated, whether Exxon is an "original literary work" within s 2 of the 1956 Act? I do not think it is. What is it then, one may ask. It is a word which, though invented and therefore original, has no meaning and suggests nothing in itself. To give it substance and meaning, it must be accompanied by other words or used in a particular context or juxtaposition. When used as part of any of the plaintiffs' corporate names, it clearly has a denominative characteristic as denoting the company in question. When used, as I assume it is, with the plaintiffs' goods, it would clearly have the effect of denoting origin or quality. It is in fact an invented word with no meaning, which is a typical subject for trade mark registration, and which no doubt, with adequate user, is capable also of becoming, if it has not already become, distinctive of the plaintiffs and their goods at common law. It is not in itself a title or distinguishing name and, as I have said, only takes on meaning or significance when actually used with other words, for example indicating that it is the name of a company, or in a particular juxtaposition as, for example, on goods. Nothing I have said above is intended to suggest that I consider that a word which is used as a title can, as a matter of law, never in any circumstances be the subject of copyright, and I would disagree with dicta in previous cases to the contrary effect. Such a word would, however, I think have to have qualities or characteristics in itself, if such a thing is possible, which would justify its recognition as an original literary work rather than merely as an invented word … the mere fact that a single word is invented and that research or labour was involved in its invention does not in itself in my judgment necessarily enable it to qualify as an original literary work within s 2 of the 1956 Act.'
>
> The learned judge then went on to consider an analogy with Lewis Carroll's Nonsense poem 'Jabberwocky', and came to the conclusion that the words 'Jabberwock' or

---

273 [1981] 2 All ER 495.

'Jabberwocky', if used alone without any poem, could not form the subject of copyright, the legal reason being—

'that the word alone and by itself cannot properly be considered as a "literary work", the subject of copyright under the Act. It becomes part of a "literary work" within the Act when it is embodied in the poem, but it is the poem as a composition which is a work within the Act and not the word itself.'

(See [1981] 2 All ER 495 at 594, [1981] 1 WLR 624 at 635; Graham J's emphasis.)

I have quoted extensively from Graham J's judgment in order to adopt it gratefully. It seems to me that the learned judge asked the right question and gave it the right answer ...

## Data Access Corporation v Powerflex Services Pty Ltd
High Court of Australia: Gleeson CJ, Gaudron, McHugh,
Gummow and Hayne JJ
(1999) 202 CLR 1

Data Access Corporation developed a computer software program which allowed a programmer to develop customised database applications or databases. The program included "reserved words" such as "print" and "type". Powerflex made a compatible software program which included the reserved words so that to the user of the program there was little difference between the Data Access and Powerflex programs. On appeal to the High Court the question was whether the reserved words individually or together were a computer program and whether Powerflex had copied a computer program.

### Gleeson CJ, McHugh, Gummow and Hayne JJ:

**[14]** 1. *Is each of the Reserved Words a "computer program" within the meaning of s 10(1) of the Act?*

18. The appellant contends that each of the Reserved Words is itself a "computer program" within the meaning of the definition in s 10(1) **[15]** of the Act. In order to determine the validity of the appellant's submissions, it is convenient to divide the definition of "computer program" into its component parts.

19. The definition of "computer program" requires that each Reserved Word be: (i) "an expression," (ii) "in any language, code or notation," (iii) "of a set of instructions (whether with or without related information)" (iv) "intended, either directly or after either or both of the following: (a) conversion to another language, code or notation; (b) reproduction in a different material form; to cause" (v) "a device having digital information processing capabilities to perform a particular function."

20. Each of the first four of these elements qualifies what follows and the scope of the definition is marked out by the requirement of an intention that the device be caused "to perform a particular function". In form, the definition of a computer program seems to have more in common with the subject matter of a patent than a copyright. Inventions when formulated as a manner of new manufacture traditionally fell within the province of patent law, with the scope of the monopoly protection being fixed by the terms of a public document, the patent specification. In Australia claims to computer programs which are novel, not obvious and otherwise satisfy the *Patents Act 1990* (Cth) and which have the effect of controlling computers to operate in a particular way, have been held to be proper subject matter for letters patent, as "achieving an end result which is an artificially created state of affairs of utility in the field of economic endeavour",[274]

---

[274] *CCOM Pty Ltd v Jiejing Pty Ltd* (1994) 51 FCR 260 at 295.

within the meaning of *National Research Development Corporation v Commissioner of Patents*[275] ...

**[24]** 52. In our opinion, the second view is the preferable one. The definition of "computer program" begins with the words "an expression, in any language, code or notation". The phrase relates to a singular expression (the word "an" is used) and the words "any language" envisage that the expression will be in a particular language, whatever that language might be. However, the "expression" must be of a "set of instructions" which has a particular intention.

53. The meaning of the phrase "expression ... of a set of instructions" was referred to in the Explanatory Memorandum to the Copyright Amendment Bill 1984:[276]

"The phrase 'expression ... of a set of instructions' is intended to make clear that it is not an abstract idea, algorithm or mathematical principle which is protected but rather a particular expression of that abstraction. The word 'set' indicates that the instructions are related to one another rather than being a mere collection."

54. It is the particular selection, ordering, combination and arrangement of instructions within a computer program which provide its expression. A computer program in a particular language may be relatively inefficient because it uses many instructions to achieve the function that a single instruction could achieve. A computer program in a particular language may also operate relatively inefficiently because of the way it is structured, in terms of the ordering of the instructions and the sequence in which they are executed. Considerations of efficiency are largely a function of the particular language which is used. It is the skill of the programmer in a particular language which determines the expression of the program in that language.

55. The Explanatory Memorandum states that it is a "*particular* expression" of an abstract idea which is protected.[277] As a particular expression is a function of the language of the expression, whether a word or words is or are a relevant expression of a set of instructions needs to be asked separately for each language in which there is purportedly a set of instructions.

56. For an item to be a computer program, it must not only be an "expression ... of a set of instructions", but the expression of that set of instructions must also be designed to achieve a particular purpose. That is to say, it must be "intended ... to cause a device having digital information processing capabilities to perform a particular function". The emphasis on a singular function in the phrase "a *particular* function" indicates that it is necessary to identify precisely the relevant function.

**[25]** 57. As we have already indicated, the only operations which a computer is physically capable of performing are those logic operations which are hard wired into its circuits. This physical limitation manifests itself at every level of computer programming, at different levels of abstraction. At the lowest level, when programming in object code, the limitation is perhaps most evident. That is because the computer program is written in terms which are closely related to physical events within the processor and memory of the computer. In higher level languages, the physical limitations of the computer manifest themselves to a programmer in a more subtle way. In the particular language in which a programmer is working, there is a limited set of commands which can be used. Each of these commands has its own syntactical and grammatical rules which must be followed in order for the command to be successfully recognised by the compiler program which converts the commands into object code. This is because each command in the high level language is nothing more than a "pre-packaged set" of sequences of the logic

---

[275] (1959) 102 CLR 252 at 275-277.
[276] At par 16.
[277] Explanatory Memorandum, Copyright Amendment Bill 1984, par 16 (emphasis added).

operations which the computer is capable of performing. The compiler program, upon reading a command, merely opens the pre-packaged set and launches the corresponding logic operations which the computer is capable of performing. If a set of instructions in a high level language is intended to cause a computer to perform a particular function, it is an expression which intends to express an algorithmic or logical relationship between the desired function and the physical capabilities of the computer, albeit indirectly. Owing to programming errors, or what are commonly called "bugs", it may not actually do so. The presence of "bugs" in a computer program, however, does not disentitle it to copyright protection, because as the Explanatory Memorandum stated:[278]

"The phrase 'intended ... to cause' is used in preference to words such as 'capable ... of causing' to cover the situation where the program, as written, may not operate for technical reasons such as the presence of a programming error."

58. It is the ability to express in a computer language an algorithmic or logical relationship between an identifiable function which is desired to be performed and the physical capabilities of the computer, which is the true skill of the programmer. This remains true even if the programmer is working via the medium of a high level language and is unaware of the physical capabilities of the computer. It is the expression of this skill which is intended to be protected by the Act.

59. In our opinion, the foregoing conclusion also explains the reference in the definition of "computer program" to "a set of instructions **[26]** (whether with or without any related information)". The Explanatory Memorandum stated:[279]

"The phrase 'whether with or without related information' is intended to make clear that the protected program may include material other than instructions for the computer (such as information for programmers or users of the program, or data to be used in connection with the execution of the program)."

60. The distinction between "data" or "related information" on the one hand and "instructions for the computer" on the other indicates that Parliament has conceived of a "set of instructions" that are truly "instructions for the computer" in the sense that they are referable to the computer's physical capabilities. The inclusion in the definition of "computer program" of the words "(whether with or without related information)", in parenthesis, effected the legislative intent that the inclusion of "related information" within the "expression ... of a set of instructions" would not take that expression outside the definition. "Data" or "related information" is that part of the computer program which is not in any sense referable to the computer's physical capabilities. The examples given in the Explanatory Memorandum indicate that it may be a wide category. It is unnecessary to consider what may constitute "information" which is not "related information", a matter removed from the task of construing the phrase "set of instructions".

61. In our opinion, whether what is claimed to be a "computer program" is an "expression ... of a set of instructions ... intended ... to cause a device having digital information processing capabilities to perform a particular function" must be answered separately for each language in which the item in question is said to be a computer program.

62. Moreover, something is not a "computer program" within the meaning of the definition in s 10(1) unless it intends to express, either directly or indirectly, an algorithmic or logical relationship between the function desired to be performed and the physical capabilities of the "device having digital information processing capabilities". Thus, in the sense employed by the definition, a program in object code causes a device to perform a particular function "directly" when executed. A program in source code does so "after ... conversion to another language, code or notation".

[278] Explanatory Memorandum, Copyright Amendment Bill 1984, par 19.
[279] Explanatory Memorandum, Copyright Amendment Bill 1984, par 18.

## *Green v Broadcasting Corporation of New Zealand*
High Court of New Zealand: Ongley J
(1983) 2 IPR 191

This is a decision of the High Court of New Zealand where the question arose whether the "dramatic format" of a television game show was a dramatic work.

**Ongley J: [199]** It is the copyright of the title scripts and dramatic format which the plaintiff claims to own. In order to establish a claim for breach of copyright he must show that copyright subsists in these things as original literary, dramatic or musical works.

It is a difficult though not impossible task to establish copyright in a title. In *Francis Day & Hunter Ltd v 20th Century Fox Corp Ltd* [1940] AC 112 at 123 (the case involving the song title of "The Man who Broke the Bank of Monte Carlo") Lord Wright said:–

"As a rule a title does not involve literary composition and is not sufficiently substantial to justify claims of protection. That statement does not mean that in particular cases a title may not be on so extensive a scale and of so important a character as to be a proper subject of protection against being copied ...

"There might be copyright in a title 'as for instance in a whole part of title for something of that kind requiring invention' but this could not **[200]** be said of the facts in the present case. There may have been a certain amount, but not a high degree, of originality in thinking of the theme of the song and even achieving a title, though it is of the most obvious. To 'break the bank' is a hackneyed expression, and Monte Carlo is, or was, the most obvious place at which that achievement or accident might take place."

I find myself quite unable to elevate the title "Opportunity Knocks" to the status of a literary work. Even if it were possible to do so it could not be said to be an original work. It is a hackneyed expression which is used in all sorts of different contexts and while it may have been apt for the plaintiff's popular television production there was no literary skill involved in compiling it.

As to copyright in scripts, I find that the *Concise Oxford Dictionary* gives a secondary meaning of the word "script" as "text of broadcaster's announcement or talk; typescript of film-play". It is a necessary condition for the existence of copyright that something should exist in writing or other notation: *Copinger and Skone James on Copyright*, para 165. Copyright can undoubtedly exist in the script of an original television production; but here there were no scripts that could be or were in fact reproduced or adapted by the defendant.

The main spoken features of the entertainment were the individual performances, the interviews with sponsors and the *ad libitum* commentary of Mr Green himself. Interspersed amongst these features were the spoken catchphrases which occurred in each show but apart from those few spoken words the content of the show by its very nature differed with every production. There was really no evidence that any part of the show was reduced to a written text which could properly be called a script. The plaintiff said on this topic in his evidence in chief as recorded in the notes of evidence at p 3, line 4: "In the year 1956, I wrote the scripts of Opportunity Knocks Shows, such as they were, because we would have what we would call the introductions, our stock phrases like 'For So-and-So, Opportunity Knocks', phrases such as 'This is your show, folks, and I do mean you'. The other part of the writing dealt with interviews with the people and one could not really call it writing because you were really only finding out what the artists wanted to talk about."

There is nothing to indicate that during any period later than 1976 the writing associated with the production amounted to any more than was there described by the plaintiff. The catchphrases from the plaintiff's show were, in my view, copied by Television Two. It stretches coincidence beyond reasonable limits of probability to suggest that they found their way into the New Zealand production by chance. I take the same view of the introduction of the clapometer and the idea of using sponsors but the fact that those features were copied does not determine the case. For copyright to subsist it must be shown that there was a script of which they formed part. One would not think that writing was needed for the catchphrases and as I understand the passage from the plaintiff's evidence quoted above he expressly excluded the catchphrases **[201]** from such writing as there may have been. The same can be said in respect of the sponsors. The idea of using a sponsor cannot be the subject of copyright. The spoken exchanges between the plaintiff and the sponsor could be if they were reduced to writing but, of course, they were not and even had they been taken from a script there is no evidence of their having been copied. The clapometer does not lend itself to incorporation in a script. No writing has been produced in evidence in this action in which, in my view, copyright could subsist.

One comes then to the format of the production. It is described as a dramatic format and as I have already said I have some difficulty with this concept. Using the meaning attributed to it in relation to the claim for passing off, I take it to be the form in which the entertainment is presented to the public, including any special characteristics. The question is whether that can be described as a dramatic work. "Dramatic work" is defined in the Copyright Act 1962 as follows:–

"'Dramatic work' includes a choreographic work or entertainment in dumb show if reduced to writing in the form in which the work or entertainment is to be presented, but does not include a cinematograph film as distinct from a scenario or a script for a cinematograph film."

In *Copinger and Skone James* it is said, at para 164, in relation to a dramatic work: –

"It was thought that under the Act of 1911, a sketch or dramatic performance might acquire copyright protection if filmed or recorded at the moment of performance, but it would seem clear that this is not so under the Act of 1956. There must be some existing writing or notation before a copyright work comes into existence ...

"In the circumstances, there seems, therefore, under the present law, to be little difference between a literary and a dramatic work, so far as concerns the kind of material in which copyright subsists. In either case it would appear to be a necessary condition for the existence of copyright that something should exist in writing or other notation."

My attention has not been drawn to any case in which the format of television entertainment has been made the subject of protection under the Copyright Act. I think it is too vague a concept for that to be done. If it were capable of exact formulation copyright in it could not subsist unless it were reduced to writing. No writing has been produced in this case which is said to comprise the format of "Opportunity Knocks".

For the reasons given, I find that it has not been established that the plaintiff has copyright of the title, scripts or dramatic format of his production of "Opportunity Knocks".

## *Greenfield Products Pty Ltd v Rover-Scott Bonnar Ltd*
### Federal Court of Australia: Pincus J
### (1990) 17 IPR 417

The applicants in this case alleged breach of copyright in parts of a ride-on mower. Relying on New Zealand authority the applicants argued that moulds used to produce pulleys and clutch plates for the mower were engravings and that parts of the drive mechanism were sculptures. Pincus J rejected these arguments. Note, however, that Pincus J's narrow interpretation of the terms "sculpture" and "engraving" have not been generally adopted.

**Pincus J: [426] Copyright in Three-Dimensional Objects**
There are no two-dimensional objects; the above heading is intended as a shorthand way of referring to the applicant's claim to copyright in certain moulds and in a drive mechanism, as opposed to its claim to copyright in drawings. The relevant parts of the statement of claim are paras 11(iii) (on p 4) and 13 (on pp 10 and 11). These allege, in effect, that there is copyright in "moulds used in connection with the casting of" certain pulleys and clutch plates and in a certain drive mechanism.

It was argued on behalf of the applicant that the Copyright Act, as presently construed, is wide enough to encompass such objects. Under Part III of the Act, copyright may subsist in, inter alia, an artistic work and the applicant contends that the moulds and the drive mechanism [427] are artistic works. The expression "artistic work" is defined in s 10 to mean, inter alia: "A painting, sculpture, drawing, engraving or photograph, whether the work is of artistic quality or not".

Each of the words "sculpture" and "engraving" is separately defined:
"'Sculpture' includes a cast or model made for purposes of sculpture".
"'Engraving' includes an etching, lithograph, product of photogravure, wood cut, print or similar work, not being a photograph".
It was argued on behalf of the applicant that copyright can subsist in the moulds and machine parts because they are "engravings" and that the drive mechanism is an "artistic work", being made up of its components which are themselves sculptures and therefore artistic works.

It is convenient to take the latter point first. Although the definition of "sculpture" is not exhaustive, insofar as the word remains undefined it must be given its ordinary meaning, in accordance with orthodox principles of construction. It is for that reason that I rejected evidence proffered on behalf of the respondent to prove what "sculpture" means in certain circles. The word "sculpture" is, at least in this context, not a technical term so as to make evidence admissible on the issue of statutory construction.

It appears to me clear that neither the moulds nor the drive mechanism, nor the parts of the latter, are sculptures in the ordinary sense. It is true, as was pointed out in the course of argument, that some modern sculptures consist of or include parts of machines, but that does not warrant the conclusion that all machines and parts thereof are properly called sculptures, and similar reasoning applies to moulds. I respectfully agree with the conclusion arrived at in the New Zealand Court of Appeal, in *Lincoln Industries Ltd v Wham-O Manufacturing Co* (1984) 3 IPR 115 at 131 that frisbees are not sculptures under the Copyright Act 1962 (NZ); that conclusion is consistent with mine.

I therefore reject the submission that there can be copyright in the drive mechanism. I do so with more confidence having regard to the concept of infringement by copying objects made from a copyright drawing; the development of that doctrine would have been unnecessary if machinery were itself the subject of copyright.

A submission which is not quite so easily disposed of is that the moulds are "engravings" under the Act; this has some support from the *Lincoln Industries* case just referred to and from the reasons of the Court of Appeal of Hong Kong in *Interlego AG v Tyco Industries Inc* [1987] FSR 409 at 421 and 453. In the former case, there was evidence that the frisbee moulds were made by use of a tool, cutting metal blanks on a lathe. The Court remarked: "We see no reason why the process involved in the production of the die or mould, particularly the creation of the cuts to produce the ribs or rings should not be regarded as the act of engraving within the provisions of s 2(1)(a) of the Act, and the mould or die so created an 'engraving' just as a 'print' is an engraving in terms of the extended definition in s 2 the Act." (at 127)

The definition of "engraving" in issue there differed slightly from that with which I am concerned, but the difference is not of present significance.

I do not well understand why the Court thought that working at a lathe cutting into a rotating piece of metal with a tool is the work of engraving. One can use a tool fixed in a lathe to inscribe a pattern onto the surface of metal or other materials, but even that would not, perhaps, ordinarily be **[428]** called engraving. It is true that dictionary definitions of engraving refer to cutting, but it is not all cutting which is engraving; for example, to cut a piece of steel rod into lengths is not to engrave it. Nor, in my opinion, is the process of cutting metal from a block spinning on a lathe a process of engraving the block, in the ordinary sense of the word. The term does not cover shaping a piece of metal or wood on a lathe, but has to do with marking, cutting or working the surface – typically, a flat surface – of an object. The Second Edition of the *Oxford English Dictionary* cites usages of the word "engrave" which appear to support the New Zealand decision. For example, a translation of the *Metamorphoses* has: "The fatall steele … he waues Deepe in his guts, and wounds on wounds ingraues." But that was published in 1626 and no modern similar example is given. More generally, the text under "engrave" supports the view that in current usage the physical meaning is confined to cutting, marking or otherwise working a surface. The same may be said of the dictionary's treatment of "engraving", except that "engraving" can mean the product as well as the process.

I note that the Court of Appeal went on to say (129) that each frisbee made from a mould is an "image produced from an engraved plate" and therefore a "print". I was urged by Mr Hanger QC to adopt what he described as the "flexible approach" evinced in this decision, particularly as it has at least the tentative approval of the Hong Kong Court of Appeal in the *Interlego* case.

No consideration of policy, or other orthodox approach, could justify straining the English language so far as to call the moulds engravings. Despite the respect which one must have for any decision of the New Zealand Court of Appeal, I find myself unable to follow the approach in the *Lincoln Industries* case. In particular, I cannot, with respect, agree with the view that a frisbee is an image or that it is a print. Similarly, in my opinion, the moulds from which these machine parts are made are not engravings. It is unnecessary to consider the question whether "engraving" in the Act includes such objects as were dealt with in *James Arnold and Co Limited v Maifern Limited* [1980] RPC 397.

I should add that I am by no means convinced that the New Zealand decision, even if correct, produces success for the applicant on this point; as was pointed out on behalf of the respondent, the basis of that decision appears to have been that operations which involve cutting to create a shape are properly called engraving. But here there was no evidence that the moulds were produced by any sort of cutting.

The applicant also contended that the machine parts are themselves "engravings". Counsel did not shrink from the proposition that a machined steel shaft, however enormous, is an "engraving". That seems to me preposterous.

I therefore arrive at the conclusion that the applicant's claim to copyright in the moulds and machine parts is ill-founded and cannot succeed, because they cannot be the subject of copyright.

## *Burge v Swarbrick*
High Court of Australia: Gleeson CJ, Gummow, Kirby,
Heydon and Crennan JJ
[2007] HCA 17; 234 ALR 204; 81 ALJR 950

This case was the first time the High Court had an opportunity to consider the meaning of the phrase "work of artistic craftsmanship". The High Court held that in determining whether something was a work of artistic craftsmanship (rather than an industrial design) one must look objectively at the evidence to determine to what extent "the particular work's artistic expression, in its form, is unconstrained by functional considerations".

**Gleeson CJ, Gummow, Kirby, Heydon, and Crennan JJ:**

*The significance of the 1989 Act*

50. In its form after the changes made by the 1989 Act, the Copyright Act employed the expression "a work of artistic craftsmanship", both as a criterion to mark out the nature, duration and ownership of copyright in artistic works (Pt III, Div 1, ss 31-35) and to differentiate the protection given where artistic works were applied as industrial designs without a design registration (Pt III, Div 8, ss 74-77A). The statute in this amended form is to be considered with respect to subsequent events as a coherent whole. The phrase "a work of artistic craftsmanship" should be read consistently. There has been debate as to the extent to which a statute in its unamended form may be construed with respect to past events by reference to amendments [*Commissioner of State Revenue (Vic) v Pioneer Concrete (Vic) Pty Ltd* [2002] HCA 43; 209 CLR 651 at 669 [51]-[52], 670 [54]]. But however that may be, the phrase "a work of artistic craftsmanship" was introduced by the 1989 Act into the "overlap" provisions of Pt III, Div 8 of the Copyright Act upon a particular legislative view of the purpose it would serve. That view, as Drummond J indicated in *Coogi* (1998) 86 FCR 154 at 168, was the encouragement of "real artistic effort" in industrial design.

51. Several consequences for this appeal follow from this state of affairs. First, as the facts of this case demonstrate, encouragement of "real artistic effort" to industrial design may be constrained by the nature of the functional purposes to be served by the object to which industrial design is applied and by the marketing imperatives for mass production. The evidence of the marketing of the JS 9000 class of racing yacht, described in the first part of these reasons, is illustrative of these constraints. It is these constraints which make it difficult to support the Plug as "a work of artistic craftsmanship".

52. Secondly, the need after the 1989 Act to read consistently throughout the Copyright Act the phrase "a work of artistic craftsmanship" [*Commissioner of Stamps (SA) v Telegraph Investment Co Pty Ltd* [1995] HCA 44; 184 CLR 453 at 463, 479] entails caution, lest too little weight be given to the need for a real or substantial artistic element in what is posited for any purpose of the Copyright Act as "a work of artistic craftsmanship".

53. Thirdly, the 1989 Act places some check upon entire acceptance of what had been said earlier with respect to the 1956 UK Act in the most significant judicial treatment of the scope and purpose of the special treatment given the phrase "a work of artistic craftsmanship". This was the speech of Lord Simon of Glaisdale in *George Hensher Ltd v Restawile Upholstery (Lancs) Ltd* [1976] AC 64; [1975] RPC 31. …

59. There are further points respecting statutory construction to be made here. First, the statutory expression is "artistic craftsmanship", not "artistic handicraft", notwithstanding that the aesthetic of the Arts and Crafts movement may have been that of the living artisan in his workshop. Lord Simon noted that some leaders of the Arts and Crafts movement recognised that they would have to come to terms with the machine, and referred to a lecture by Frank Lloyd Wright, "The Art and Craft of the Machine". Lord Simon concluded [1976] AC 64 at 91:

"The Central School of Arts and Crafts, though foremost a school of handicrafts, had as a declared aim to encourage 'the industrial application of decorative design.' So, although 'works of artistic craftsmanship' cannot be adequately construed without bearing in mind the aims and achievements of the Arts and Crafts movement, 'craftsmanship' in the statutory phrase cannot be limited to handicraft; nor is the word 'artistic' incompatible with machine production: see *Britain v Hanks Brothers and Co* (1902) 86 LT 765. [Wright J restrained the pirating of metal models of toy soldiers and horses, as being protected by the 1814 Act.]"

60. Secondly, coming to terms with machine production involves acceptance that a prototype such as the Plug may qualify as "a work of artistic craftsmanship" even though it was to serve the purpose of reproduction and then be discarded. Doubts upon the matter expressed by several of the Law Lords in *Hensher* [1976] AC 64 [at 77 per Lord Reid, 84 per Viscount Dilhorne] were somewhat misplaced. These doubts influenced the reasoning of the Full Court in the present case, a matter as to which it will be convenient to say more later in these reasons.

61. Thirdly, whilst not denying an enduring distinction between fine arts and useful or applied arts, in dealing with artistic craftsmanship there is no antithesis between utility and beauty, between function and art. In that regard, Lord Simon said in *Hensher* [1976] AC 64 at 91:

"A work of craftsmanship, even though it cannot be confined to handicraft, at least presupposes special training, skill and knowledge for its production … 'Craftsmanship', particularly when considered in its historical context, implies a manifestation of pride in sound workmanship – a rejection of the shoddy, the meretricious, the facile."

Lord Simon further said [1976] AC 64 at 91:

"Even more important, the whole antithesis between utility and beauty, between function and art, is a false one – especially in the context of the Arts and Crafts movement. 'I never begin to be satisfied,' said Philip Webb, one of the founders, 'until my work looks commonplace.' Lethaby's object, declared towards the end, was 'to create an efficiency style.' Artistic form should, they all held, be an emanation of regard for materials on the one hand and for function on the other." …

*Was the Plug "a work of artistic craftsmanship"? – the evidence*

63. The answer to the question whether the Plug is a "work of artistic craftsmanship" cannot be controlled by evidence from Mr Swarbrick of his aspirations or intentions when designing and constructing the Plug. His evidence was admissible. But the operation of the statute does not turn upon the presence or absence of evidence of that nature from the author of the work in question. The matter, like many other issues calling for care and discrimination, is one for objective determination by the court, assisted by admissible evidence and not unduly weighed down by the supposed terrors for judicial assessment of matters involving aesthetics [cf *Attorney-General v Trustees of National Art Gallery of NSW* (1944) 62 WN (NSW) 212; *In re Pinion dec'd* [1965] Ch 85; Picarda, *The Law and Practice Relating to Charities*, 3rd ed (1999) at 61-62; Cowen, "An Artist in the Courts of Law", (1945) 19 *Australian Law Journal* 112].

64. The statute does not give to the opinion of the person who claims to be the author of "a work of artistic craftsmanship" the determination of whether that result was obtained; still less, whether it was obtained because he or she intended that result. Given the long period of copyright protection, the author, at the stage when there is litigation, may be unavailable. Indeed, as Pape J noted in *Cuisenaire* [1963] VR 719 at 730, the author may be dead. Again, intentions may fail to be realised. Further, just as few alleged inventors are heard to deny the presence of an inventive step on their part, so, it may be expected, will few alleged authors of works of artistic craftsmanship be heard readily to admit the absence of any necessary aesthetic element in their endeavours [cf *Wellcome Foundation Ltd v VR Laboratories (Aust) Pty Ltd* [1981] HCA 12; 148 CLR 262 at 286-287].

65. This is not to deny the admissibility of such evidence, nor to disparage the good character of such witnesses, and certainly not that of Mr Swarbrick; it is to reaffirm the

well-recognised dangers of hindsight which are present in various fields of intellectual property law, as in many other disputes that come to litigation.

66. The various aspects of the definition of "a work of artistic craftsmanship" which are discussed above with reference to *Hensher* have particular significance here. The primary judge considered "craftsmanship" and "aesthetic appeal" as distinct and consecutive questions, before going on and "considering both aspects together" [[2004] FCA 813; 138 FCR 353 at 367]. This was an error in the construction and application of the Copyright Act and requires re-examination of what transpired at the trial.

67. Upon that footing, the primary judge started his analysis of the evidence from the proposition that the evidence of intention of the author of the alleged work was important, albeit not essential [[2004] FCA 813; 138 FCR 353 at 363-364]. Whilst allowing that Mr Swarbrick was "scarcely a disinterested person", the primary judge gave very great weight to his evidence as to that intention. His Honour accepted that Mr Swarbrick had intended to design and build a yacht of "great aesthetic appeal", that the JS 9000 had "a high level of aesthetic appeal" and that this was the outcome intended by Mr Swarbrick [[2004] FCA 813; 138 FCR 353 at 366].

68. The primary judge added that Mr Swarbrick had not been cross-examined on these views. The appellants properly dispute this. They point, among other things, to the passage in his lengthy cross-examination:

"Your main concerns with design, I suggest to you, were to provide yachts for that market performing in accordance with the design brief you had set for yourself? – Yes. I wanted a well mannered, easily balanced boat that was fast by contemporary standards."

69. The "design brief" referred to was that set out in an affidavit by Mr Swarbrick. This stated that the market at which the JS 9000 was aimed comprised persons who, in no particular order, were reasonably experienced amateur sailors, aged 45 or more, who wanted a yacht of good performance, capable of racing, but for typical use in day sailing, relatively simple to sail with a minimum crew size, and visually attractive.

70. The promotional material and business plan described earlier in these reasons are relatively contemporaneous evidence. They are confirmatory of that design brief but, it should be noted, do not give prominence to matters of visual and aesthetic appeal. However, the primary judge gave this material little apparent weight, beyond saying that the documentary evidence did not lead him to doubt Mr Swarbrick's evidence at the trial. ...

73. Taken as a whole and considered objectively, the evidence, at best, shows that matters of visual and aesthetic appeal were but one of a range of considerations in the design of the Plug. Matters of visual and aesthetic appeal necessarily were subordinated to achievement of the purely functional aspects required for a successfully marketed "sports boat" and thus for the commercial objective in view.

*Conclusions respecting the Plug*

74. This state of the evidence must strongly influence the answer to the question whether the Plug was "a work of artistic craftsmanship", within the meaning of the Copyright Act and allowing for the "overlap" provision made by the 1989 Act.

75. With wallpaper, a tapestry, stained glass window, piece of jewellery or Tiffany artefact, there is considerable freedom of design choice relatively unconstrained by the function or utility of the article so produced. But, as the evidence disclosed, that was not the case with the design constraints upon a class of yacht such as the JS 9000. ...

83. It may be impossible, and certainly would be unwise, to attempt any exhaustive and fully predictive identification of what can and cannot amount to "a work of artistic craftsmanship" within the meaning of the Copyright Act as it stood after the 1989 Act. However, determining whether a work is "a work of artistic craftsmanship" does not

turn on assessing the beauty or aesthetic appeal of work or on assessing any harmony between its visual appeal and its utility. The determination turns on assessing the extent to which the particular work's artistic expression, in its form, is unconstrained by functional considerations. To decide the appeal it is sufficient to indicate the following.

84. The more substantial the requirements in a design brief to satisfy utilitarian considerations of the kind indicated with the design of the JS 9000, the less the scope for that encouragement of real or substantial artistic effort. It is that encouragement which underpins the favourable treatment by the 1989 Act of certain artistic works which are applied as industrial designs but without design registration. Questions of fact and degree inevitably arise.

85. In the present case, notwithstanding what Mr Swarbrick later said on the matter after litigation was on foot, the earlier statements in the promotional material and in the business plan, with the evidence of Mr Hood, should have led the primary judge to conclude that the Plug was not "a work of artistic craftsmanship" because the work of Mr Swarbrick in designing it was not that of an artist-craftsman.

## *Galaxy Electronics Pty Ltd v Sega Enterprises*
Federal Court of Australia: Lockhart, Wilcox and Lindgren JJ
(1997) 145 ALR 21

Wilcox J in this case determines that a video game is a cinematographic film under the *Copyright Act 1968* even though there is no image "embodied" in the video tape which precedes the image shown on the screen and despite the fact that the format of the video game might vary each time someone played it.

**Wilcox J: [23] The games**
The respondents, Sega Enterprises Pty Ltd (Sega) and Avel Pty Ltd (Avel), are respectively the manufacturer and exclusive Australian licensee of two video games, "Virtua Cop" and "Daytona USA Twin". The appellant, Galaxy Electronic Pty Ltd (Galaxy), imported into Australia machines containing copies of the computer program that generated the visual images and sounds constituting the game "Virtua Cop" and displayed them for sale or hire at its premises. The appellant, Gottlieb Electronics Pty Ltd (Gottlieb), did the same things in relation to "Daytona USA Twin". Both appellants concede that, if the video games are a "cinematograph film", their actions constitute an infringement of the respondents' rights; but they say the games are not cinematograph films.

It is not necessary to describe both games in detail. They are similar in nature. The description given by the learned trial judge, Burchett J in *Sega Enterprises Ltd v Galaxy Electronics Pty Ltd* (1996) 35 IPR 161 at 162-3, was not challenged. I gratefully adopt it.

"There are two video games with which the cases are concerned, one entitled "Virtua Cop" and the other "Daytona USA". Each presents on the video screen a series of images resembling, more or less, a traditional movie film. In the case of Virtua Cop, an extremely simple but violent tale is told of assaults by police upon a criminal organisation. In the case of Daytona USA, what is involved is car racing. The parties were agreed that it is sufficient to concentrate upon Virtua Cop, since the two video games are constructed upon the same principle. In Virtua Cop, the protagonists are two police officers (with whom the players of the game identify) whose investigations are resisted, first, at a cargo wharf, next, at a construction site, and finally at their antagonists' evil headquarters. To begin with, there is a brief introduction, followed by the main part of the game in which the player must keep shooting quickly and accurately, with a make-believe weapon or "input" device, at the correct villainous targets, so that the various assaults will progress according to the script.

At the end, there is a triumphant finale, when the police congratulate each other and the dastards are led away in handcuffed defeat. Only the successful player will reach this denouement, and only the very skilled can possibly do so without numerous setbacks along the way, caused by misdirected responses, or failures to respond, to the actions depicted on the screen. For example, if the player's shot misses a criminal, the player may himself be shot by the criminal; and if this happens a predetermined number of times, the assault fails, and the game ends. Also, each time a criminal is merely winged, he may react differently, depending on where he has been hit. Thus, except for the opening and closing sequences, the events represented on the screen will show differences from screening to screening, except where the player's responses are all correct.

What this means, it will be appreciated, is that the apparatus is designed to screen the simple story only when the correct responses to a series of cues are fed into it by the player; and when incorrect responses are given, a number of variations will result."

[24] Burchett J detailed the way "Virtua Cop" was created. He said (at IPR 163-4): "Graphic designers developed the scenes, and representations of the characters. In doing so, they made drawings and models, and decided, for instance, how a particular character would walk. Sets were made up. A "test version" was prepared on a computer and copied onto a video tape. Further detailed sketches of scenes to be depicted on the screen were prepared by hand. These sketches were used as the basis for the preparation of the computer program, according to which particular scenes were ultimately enabled to be depicted on the screen. The program itself was extremely sophisticated. It calculated the three-dimensional position of each part of each object and character at each stage of all movements. An example of the sophistication involved is the windscreen of a car, which is shown three-dimensionally, with a superimposed two-dimensional image of a reflection of the sky appearing on it.

Sound effects, music, and very simple dialogue were also required. Over 80 sound effects were selected from a sound library or created, and then manipulated, for inclusion in the program. Dialogue was recorded, and that recording was also manipulated and included in the program. Music was added after composition on a synthesiser.

When all the work had been completed and was brought together, it was represented by a highly specialised piece of computer equipment, suitable, and suitable only, for bringing Virtua Cop to the screen. Although, as I have said, sketches, models and video tape were used in the course of the creation of the program, in the finished product, the screen images were not represented by anything comparable to the tiny translucent images which characterise the original technology of cinematograph film. A closer analogy could be drawn to video tape, containing magnetic fields that may be transformed into visual images upon a screen. But the respondents argue that even this analogy misses the mark. According to their contention, Virtua Cop is not represented in any form until it is born on the screen out of the union between the player's input and the computer program that calculates the three-dimensional reference points, not images, by reference to which the images themselves are made to appear on the screen. The respondents say that the visual images were not stored in any manner; mathematical co-ordinates of models of objects, together with animation and texture mapping data, were stored in digital form, and are used by the controlling program to create images on the screen. In doing so, the respondents say, the "micro-computer controls the sequence of visual displays and aural effects in response to a player's actions and this generates a different game play for each player within the overall limitations of objects and scenes available to be generated by the controlling program". Thus, they contend, "the visual imagery ... is an artefact of real-time computer graphics in that the images on the screen are synthesised on the fly by the controlling program". On this basis, their argument asserts it is "not correct to say that the two-dimensional screen images themselves are stored in the computer like some form of "digital movie" and simply played back during the game."

The parties called "the respondents" by his Honour are, of course, the present appellants.

Burchett J noted (at 164) that the expert called to give evidence on behalf of Sega and Avel, while disputing the ultimate conclusion, conceded the technical accuracy of the proposition put by Galaxy and Gottlieb... .

[29] Against this background, I have come to share the opinion of Burchett J that the critical question in these cases is the application to them of the word "embodied". The definition of "cinematograph film" refers to "the aggregate of the visual images *embodied* in an article or thing ...". Section 24 sets out circumstances under which "visual images shall be taken to have been *embodied* in an article or thing". I also agree that the word "embodied" refers to the giving of a material or discernible form to an abstract principle or concept. The Lord Chancellor's *Iolanthe* song neatly illustrates this meaning. According to his Lordship, the abstract concept of excellence achieves material manifestation in the law; and the law, in turn, is manifested in his noble person.

It seems inherent in both the dictionary definition and the Iolanthe illustration that the abstraction must pre-exist the material manifestation. Counsel for the appellants argue that the images visible to players of the games do not exist before the moment of visibility; accordingly, it cannot be said that they represent an embodiment of pre-existing images. Counsel make the point that computer-generated images are fundamentally different to film or video images; in the latter case the images are fixed on celluloid or videotape before the moment of projection and viewing.

This analysis is superficially attractive; but, I think, unsound. The visual images depicted in these video games did exist before the game was played. They existed in the minds of their creators and the drawings and models they made. The images were embodied in the computer program built into the video game machine so as to be capable, by the use of that program, of being shown as a moving picture. It does not matter that they were embodied in a different form, ie three-dimension vertices of the polygon model, rather than a two-dimensional image. The statutory definition says nothing about the form of embodiment. Nor does it matter that the images seen by players are created by computer calculations only immediately before their appearance on the screen of the video game machine. Although that means, in a sense, that they are new, they are exact recreations of images previously devised by the graphic designers. Similarly, of course, it is unimportant that the images could not be seen on the screen as a moving picture until generated by the computer, any more than it matters that a length of video tape is incapable of being seen as a moving picture until passed through a video player.

Counsel for the appellants emphasise the circumstance that the sequence of images seen in any particular game reflects player input. It may be true that no two sequences will be identical. But that does not mean the sequence is incapable of coming within the definition of "cinematograph film". As is demonstrated by analogous American cases, a question of degree is involved. The question in those cases was whether the subject video game was an "audiovisual work". The legislation defined "audiovisual works" as "works that consist of a series of related images which are intrinsically intended to be shown by the use of machines, or devices such as projectors, viewers, or electronic equipment, together with accompanying sounds, if any, regardless of the nature of the material objects, such as films or tapes, in which the works are embodied". In *Stern Electronics Inc v Kaufman* 669 F 2d 852 (1982) it was contended that there was no copyright in the subject game because it was neither fixed in a tangible medium of expression nor original. Both contentions arose from the fact that the sequence of some of the images appearing on the screen during each play of the game varied according to player actions. Speaking for the United States Court of Appeals, Second Circuit, Newman J said at 855–6:

[30] "If the content of the audiovisual display were not affected by the participation of the player, there would be no doubt that the display itself, and not merely the written computer program, would be eligible for copyright. The display satisfies the statutory definition of an original "audiovisual work", and the memory devices of the game satisfy the statutory requirement of a "copy" in which the work is "fixed"… .

We agree with the District Court that the player's participation does not withdraw the audiovisual work from copyright eligibility. No doubt the entire sequence of all the sights and sounds of the game are different each time the game is played … Nevertheless, many aspects of the sights and the sequence of their appearance remain constant during each play of the game. These include the appearance … of the player's spaceship, the enemy craft, the ground missile bases and fuel depots, and the terrain over which (and beneath which) the player's ship flies, as well as the sequence in which the missile bases, fuel depots, and terrain appears. Also constant are the sounds heard whenever the player successfully destroys an enemy craft or installation or fails to avoid an enemy missile or laser. It is true, as appellants contend, that some of these sights and sounds will not be seen and heard during each play of the game in the event that the player's spaceship is destroyed before the entire course is traversed. But the images remain fixed, capable of being seen and heard each time a player succeeds in keeping his spaceship aloft long enough to permit the appearances of all the images and sounds of a complete play of the game … The repetitive sequence of a substantial portion of the sights and sounds of the game qualifies for copyright protection as an audiovisual work."

At 857 he said:

"We need not decide at what point the repeating sequence of images would form too insubstantial a portion of an entire display to warrant a copyright, nor the somewhat related issue of whether a sequence of images … might contain so little in the way of particularised form of expression as to be only an abstract idea portrayed in non-copyrightable form … Assessing the entire effect of the game as it appears and sounds, we conclude that its repetitive sequence of images is copyrightable as an audiovisual display."

The following year a similar question came before the Seventh Circuit of the United States Court of Appeals, with a similar result. The case was *Midway Manufacturing Co v Artic International Inc* 704 F 2d 1009 (1983). Speaking for the court, Cummings CJ observed that it was not immediately obvious that video games fell within the definition of "audiovisual works", the reason being that, each time a video game is played, a different sequence of images appears on the screen. But he held that the phrase "series of related images" might be construed to refer, not only to a set of images displayed in a fixed sequence, but also "to any set of images displayed as some kind of unit". At 1011-12 he said:

"The person playing the game can vary the order in which the stored images appear on the screen by moving the machine's control lever. That makes playing a video game a little like arranging words in a dictionary into sentences or paints on a palette into a painting. The question is whether the creative effort in playing a video game is enough like writing or painting to make each performance of a video game the work of the player and not the game's inventor.

We think it is not. Television viewers may vary the order of images transmitted on the same signal but broadcast on different channels by pressing a button that changes the channel on their television … Playing a video game is more like changing channels on a television than it is like writing a novel or painting a picture. The player of a video game does not have control over the sequence of images that appears on the video game screen. He cannot create any sequence he wants out of the images stored on the game's circuit boards. The most he can do is choose one of the limited number of sequences the **[31]** game allows him to choose. He is unlike a writer or a painter because the video game in effect writes the sentences and paints the painting for him; he merely chooses one of the sentences stored in its memory, one of the paintings stored in its collection."

Upon analysis, the present case seems to fall directly within the terms of the s 10 definition of "cinematograph film", without the necessity of resorting to s 24. However, that section puts the matter beyond doubt. The visual images that constitute the moving picture are taken to have been "embodied" in the computer program because the computer program was so treated in relation to those images as to be capable of reproducing them.

Counsel for the appellants argue it is not enough that a particular article was capable of producing particular sounds or visual images. If capability is the test, they say, every piano would have to be held a "sound recording" of Beethoven's "Moonlight Sonata". Every piano is capable of producing the notes that constitute that work. Counsel have in mind that the term "sound recording" is defined by s 10 as meaning "the aggregate of the sounds embodied in a record" and a "record" includes any "device in which sounds are embodied".

I accept capability is not enough. It is important to note the requirement of s 24 that the article or thing "has been so treated in relation to those sounds or visual images" that they are capable of being reproduced from the article or thing. There must have been a treatment of the article or thing that is related to specific sounds or visual images. This can be said of a computer program, not of a piano. It is necessary to include a keyboard in a piano, if it is to be capable of reproducing the notes that constitute the "Moonlight Sonata". But the inclusion of a keyboard is not something done "in relation to" those particular sounds; it is done in relation to piano music generally.

I think Burchett J was correct in holding that the aggregate of the visual images generated by the playing of each of the two subject video games constituted a "cinematograph film" within the meaning of s 10 of the Copyright Act.

# Chapter 4

# Exclusive Rights of the Copyright Owner, Actions and Offences

In Chapter 2 we saw that the rights of the copyright holder have expanded as a result of international arrangements and legislative amendment. Legislative amendment, however, has not been the most significant form of expansion. A much more significant influence has been the ability of the existing definitions of the copyright owner's rights to incorporate new forms of reproduction and distribution technologies. This has been fuelled by the willingness of copyright owners to exploit new forms of technology and has been facilitated by the broad and largely ahistorical definitions of the rights adopted by courts. The expansion has largely been accomplished without any new "great debate" on the proper nature and extent of the rights of the copyright owner.

A striking example of this is the *Napster* case in the United States.[1] Under the *Copyright Act Title 17* (US) s 106, the copyright owner has the right "to distribute copies or phonorecords of the copyrighted work to the public for sale or other transfer of ownership, or by rental, lease or lending". Napster was a small internet start-up company which developed a Musicshare software program. The program facilitated peer-to-peer sharing of sound recordings online by providing MP3 technology to compress digital music. It also provided a centralised search engine for identifying music available from the computers of other logged-on Napster users. In addition, the software enabled users to transfer music directly from one user's computer to another via the internet, that is, the transfer did not go through the Napster site. Members of the recording industry sought an injunction against Napster on the basis that it was authorising unlawful reproduction and distribution of musical works and sound recordings by its users.

Napster raised a number of defences against the granting of an interlocutory injunction including arguments based on authorisation and fair dealings. However, the question of whether peer-to-peer sharing was or should be caught within the distribution right was barely touched upon. Although this was only an interlocutory proceeding the omission is still striking.

It is important when studying infringement of copyright to understand that the copyright owner is not necessarily trying to prevent the conduct but may be trying to benefit economically from it. When photocopiers became a common part

---

1    *A and M Records Inc v Napster* (2000) 50 IPR 232.

of library facilities, for example, the copyright owners did not seek to ban them. Rather, they tried to identify a way of exploiting and benefiting from the new technology. To this end, the literary copyright owners' organisation at the time, the Australian Copyright Council, supported proceedings against a university for authorising infringement of copyright. Success in this action led to the introduction of a licence scheme for photocopying for educational usage. Today, individual authors may receive more from this licence than they do from publishing agreements. In this context you may like to think about what the recording industry was trying to achieve in the Napster case.

This chapter outlines the exclusive rights of the copyright owner and examines cases on the direct and indirect infringement of these rights. As well as actions for infringement under s 115, the *Copyright Act 1968* provides other avenues for protection of copyright including actions for conversion and detinue (s 116), actions in relation to circumvention devices and electronic rights management information (ss 116A, 116B and 116C) and actions in relation to broadcast decoding devices (s 135AN and s 135ANA). In addition, the Act provides for a number of offences in relation to copyright. These actions and offences are also considered in this chapter. There are many detailed defences to copyright infringement and it is probably fair to say that without these defences the enforcement and management of copyright would be unwieldy and maybe even impossible. The defences will be dealt with separately in the next chapter but you may find it useful to refer to the table of defences provided there while reading this chapter.

## Exclusive Rights of the Copyright Owner

The *Copyright Act 1968* s 31(1) provides that, in relation to literary, dramatic and musical works, copyright is the exclusive right:

- to reproduce the work (or an adaptation of the work) in material form;
- to publish the work (or an adaptation of the work);
- to perform the work (or an adaptation of the work) in public;
- to communicate the work (or an adaptation of the work) to the public;
- to make an adaptation of the work;
- to enter into a commercial rental arrangement for sound recordings of dramatic, musical or literary works (other than computer programs);
- to enter into a commercial rental arrangement for a computer program; and
- to authorise the doing of one of these acts (s 13(2)).

In relation to an artistic work, copyright is the exclusive right:

- to reproduce the work in material form;
- to publish the work;
- to communicate the work to the public; and
- to authorise the doing of one of these acts (s 13(2)).

Copyright in subject-matter other than works is dealt with in Part IV ss 85-88. Section 85(1) provides that copyright in sound recordings is the exclusive right:

- to make a copy of the sound recording;
- to cause the recording to be heard in public;

- to communicate the sound recording to the public;
- to enter a commercial rental arrangement in respect to the sound recording; and
- to authorise the doing of one of these acts (s 13(2)).

The copyright in cinematographic films is the exclusive right:

- to make a copy of the film;
- to cause the film to be seen and/or heard in public;
- to communicate the film to the public (s 86); and
- to authorise the doing of one of these acts (s 13(2)).

The copyright in television and sound broadcasts is the exclusive right:

- to make a film or sound recording of the broadcast or a copy of that film or sound recording;
- to re-broadcast or communicate the broadcast to the public (s 87); and
- to authorise the doing of one of these acts (s 13(2)).

In the case of a printed edition of a work or works, copyright is the exclusive right

- to make a facsimile copy of the edition (s 88); and
- to authorise the doing of this act (s 13(2)).

## General Principles of Infringement

The *Copyright Act 1968* provides that copyright is infringed if a person who is not the owner of the copyright "does ... any act comprised in the copyright" in Australia without the licence of the copyright owner[2] or authorises a person to do any of those acts.[3] Section 14 of the Act provides that a reference to the infringement of copyright material includes a reference to an infringement of a "substantial part" of the material. This is often referred to as "direct infringement" of copyright although the term is not used in the Act.

In establishing infringement it is irrelevant that the infringer creates a new and original work or that the taking was necessary in order to make the work function. Such issues may, however, be important for establishing a defence. Thus, it has been held that reproducing a substantial part of a spare parts catalogue is an infringement even though the part taken was used in a new and original work.[4] In *Data Access Corporation v Powerflex Services Pty Ltd*,[5] we saw that reproducing a compression table in a computer program was a breach of the reproduction right even though the reproduction was necessary in order to make a compatible computer program. Today such a use may be subject to the defence under s 49D.

---

2    Section 36 as to works; s 101 as to Part IV subject-matter. "Any act comprised in the copyright" is defined as one of the exclusive rights of the copyright holder: s 13(1).

3    Section 36 as to works and s 101 as to Part IV subject-matter. See also s 13(2) which includes authorisation within the exclusive rights of the copyright holder.

4    *TR Flanagan Smash Repairs Pty Ltd v Jones* (2000) 172 ALR 467.

5    (1999) 202 CLR 1.

As well as direct infringements, the *Copyright Act* provides that it is an infringement of copyright if a person, without the licence of the copyright owner, imports, sells or otherwise deals with infringing works and other subject-matter.[6] Similarly, it is an infringement of copyright to permit a place of public entertainment to be used for an infringing performance of a work.[7] These forms of infringement are usually referred to as "indirect infringements". An indirect infringement of a substantial part of the material also constitutes an infringement under s 14 of the Act.

Knowledge on the part of the alleged infringer is not required for establishing direct infringement, except in the case of authorisation where it may be one of the factors taken into account. Knowledge is expressly required for the establishment of indirect infringement and, in every case, is relevant to the question of remedies.

Before turning to infringement in detail we will consider the application of the idea-expression dichotomy to infringement proceedings, the meaning of substantiality under s 14 and the law on authorisation of an infringement. The question of whether the alleged infringer is the owner of the copyright or has a licence from the copyright holder is often contested in copyright litigation and will be considered in Chapter 6 "Dealing With Copyright".

## The idea-expression dichotomy in infringement proceedings

Copyright subsists in the original form of expression of a work and not in its ideas (where "original" is used in its copyright sense of being the product of labour, skill and expertise rather than in its popular sense of being novel). It follows from this that there can be no infringement of copyright if the alleged infringer has not taken the author's form of expression but has taken only the author's idea.[8]

It is easy to misstate this principle and say that there is no infringement if a person takes the author's idea. This is a logical fallacy which can be illustrated by the following case. In *Cuisenaire v Reed*,[9] M Cuisenaire developed a mathematical learning program based on wooden rods of different colours and lengths. Each rod represented a different number so that, under the system, two little white rods with a value of one would equal one little red rod with a value of two and so on. M Cuisenaire wrote up a chart which set out in words and numbers the colour and the value for each rod. Copyright subsisted in the chart as a literary work. The defendant produced a set of rods made in accordance with the information in the chart. One of the questions for the court was whether the defendant's little wooden rods were a reproduction of the plaintiff's literary work. Pape J compared the written chart to the rods and found that the rods did not reproduce the form of expression of the literary work.

It would be incorrect to say that in this case there was no infringement because the author's idea was taken. If M Cuisenaire had made drawings of the rods, for example, and the alleged infringer produced a set of rods by reproducing

---

6    Sections 37 and 38 as to works; ss 102 and 103 as to Part IV subject-matter.

7    Section 39 as to works.

8    Whether a case is argued on the basis of lack of subsistence or lack of infringement is a matter of pleading.

9    [1963] VR 719.

those drawings, there would have been an infringement. In both cases it could be said that the alleged infringer had taken the author's idea. The difference between the two cases lies in the fact that in the first case the alleged infringer has not reproduced the expression of information, instruction and pleasure which is protected as a literary work. In the second case, the visual aspects of the expression in the artistic work have been reproduced.

It may be difficult to establish that a person has taken the author's form of expression when the author and the alleged infringer have drawn on common sources, themes or ideas. Conversely, it may be difficult to establish that a person has not taken the author's form of expression when the person has relied on the author's work as a source. In each case, however, the question is the same. One should not ask whether the alleged infringer has taken the author's idea but whether the alleged infringer has taken the author's form of expression.[10]

Thus, in *Pike v Nicholas*[11] the plaintiff and the defendant had both entered a contest which required them to write an essay on the same topic. The court held that the plaintiff could not show that the defendant had reproduced his form of expression although there were some similarities in the work, many similar sources and even similar use of those sources. In *Harman Pictures NV v Osborne*,[12] on the other hand, the writer John Osborne had admittedly referred to the plaintiff's book (among others) on the charge of the light brigade in order to write his screen play on the same subject. On an interlocutory motion the court made a careful comparison of the two works and made a prima facie finding that Osborne had reproduced the author's form of expression, not just his ideas.[13]

## Substantiality

The *Copyright Act 1968* s 14 provides that a reference to the doing of an act in relation to copyright subject-matter includes doing the act in relation to a substantial part of the subject-matter and that the reproduction, adaptation or copying of subject-matter includes the reproduction, adaptation and copying of a substantial part of the copyright subject-matter. Thus, even though a plaintiff may establish copying, reproduction or other similar conduct regarding the work there will be no infringement unless this has been in respect of a substantial part of the work.

A substantial part of the work need not be a discrete part of the work. For example, an allegedly infringing work might take the subject-matter and composition of an artistic work but not its painting technique or its colour scheme. Whether the parts taken constitute a substantial part of the original work is a question to be determined according to principles established by case law.

---

10   As an exercise, imagine that you are a journalist or an academic who wants to report and comment upon Lord Rosebery's speech in *Walter v Lane* [1900] AC 539 but you missed his presentation. In deciding how you might use the published speech without infringing copyright you will gain little assistance in contemplating the public nature of Lord Rosebery's speech or the fact that you want to refer to his ideas. Rather your attention will be directed towards ensuring that you do not take the author's form of expression.

11   (1869) 5 LR Ch App 251.

12   [1967] 1 WLR 731.

13   A person in the position of John Osborne is advised to keep records of his or her research as evidence that any similarities are a result of the common sources and materials (and maybe coincidence) rather than a reproduction of the copyright owner's form of expression.

The classic statement of the test for substantiality of a work was given by Lord Reid in *Ladbroke (Football) Ltd v William Hill (Football) Ltd*:[14]

The question of whether (an author) has copied a substantial part depends much more on the quality than on the quantity of what he has taken. One test may be whether the part which he has taken is novel or striking, or merely a commonplace arrangement of ordinary words or well-known data.[15]

Thus, in *Hawkes and Son (London) Ltd v Paramount Film Service Ltd*[16] a newsreel of the Prince of Wales opening a hospital in Suffolk included a part of the Colonel Bogey March played by a boys' band on the day. Despite the fact that only 20 seconds of a four-minute musical work was played, Lord Hanworth MR held that it was a substantial part of the work because "it would be recognised by any person".[17] Slessor LJ held that it was a substantial part "looked at from any point of view, whether it be quantity, quality or occasion", "anyone would know it" and it was "a vital, and an essential part".[18] Romer LJ held that there was a substantial taking because the 28 bars taken contained "the principal air ... the air which everyone who heard the march played through would recognise as being the essential air".[19]

Substantiality has, over the years, often been decided by reference to the originality or otherwise of the part taken. Thus in *Ladbroke (Football) Ltd v William Hill (Football) Ltd*,[20] the order, layout and presentation of the coupon in question was held to be an original and protected part of the compilation literary work and was therefore considered to be a substantial part of the work. In *Bauman v Fussell*,[21] on the other hand, the alleged infringer had made a painting based on a photograph of a cock fight. The positioning of the cocks was the same but the colours used in the painting were "heightened" giving the painting a more dramatic style. The majority held that the positioning of the cocks was not a sufficiently original part of the work and therefore did not represent a substantial part of the work.[22]

This approach has been particularly important in relation to compilations, the classic statement of which is that of Lord Pearce in *Ladbroke (Football) Ltd v William Hill (Football) Ltd*:[23]

The reproduction of a part which by itself has no originality will not normally be a substantial part of the copyright and therefore will not be protected. For that which would not attract copyright except by reason of its collocation will, when robbed of that

---

14 [1964] 1 All ER 465.

15 [1964] 1 All ER 465 at 469.

16 Slessor LJ at [1934] 1 Ch 593 at 607.

17 [1934] 1 Ch 593 at 604.

18 [1934] 1 Ch 593 at 604.

19 [1934] 1 Ch 593 at 605.

20 [1964] 1 All ER 465.

21 [1978] RPC 485.

22 In the unfortunate early computer program case, *Autodesk Inc v Dyason (No 1)* (1992) 173 CLR 330 the High Court held that a look-up table was a substantial part of the computer program because "but for" the inclusion of the look-up table the computer program would not function. This approach was criticised in *Data Access Corporation v Powerflex Services Pty Ltd* (1999) 202 CLR 1.

23 [1964] 1 All ER 465.

collocation, not be a substantial part of the copyright and therefore the courts will not hold its reproduction to be an infringement.[24]

The High Court has split on the correctness of this approach. In *IceTV Pty Ltd v Nine Network Australia Pty Ltd*,[25] French CJ, Crennan and Kiefel JJ endorsed the originality test for substantiality as expressed by Lord Pearce. The co-majority, comprising Gummow, Hayne and Heydon JJ, however, rejected the approach on the basis that it ignored the fact that at least some original work may be taken under the *Copyright Act*.

The case involved the production of an electronic television guide by IceTV which had initially been compiled by watching and recording details of what was on television. The IceGuide was updated by referring to Weekly Schedules produced by the Nine Network. The Weekly Schedules included time and title information as well as synopses, viewer and classification details. They were distributed to aggregators such as newspapers and TV magazines. Channel Nine did not object to the production of the initial IceTV Guide but rather to the reproduction by IceTV of the time and title information from Nine's Weekly Schedule in the IceGuide updates.

Although Gummow, Haynes and Heydon JJ agreed that there was "extremely modest skill and labour"[26] involved in producing the work in question, they held that it was the factual nature of the part taken which rendered it not substantial:

> In assessing the quality of the time and title information, as components of the Weekly Schedule, baldly stated matters of fact or intention [such as time and title information: author] are inseparable from and co-extensive with their expression. ... if the facts are divorced from the other elements constituting the compilation in suit, as is the case here, then it is difficult to treat the IceGuide as the reproduction of a substantial part of the Weekly Schedule in the qualitative sense required by the case law.[27]

Non-copyright aspects may be taken into account in determining substantiality. In *Tate v Fullbrook*[28] in 1906, for example, the English Court of Appeal held that non-copyright gag and scenic effects might be taken into account as evidence of the substantiality of the part taken.

Because Part IV subject-matter does not require originality it has sometimes been suggested that it is the quantity, rather than the quality, which should be considered in determining the substantiality of the part taken. However, this position has not been accepted in Australia. In the Panel cases, *TCN Channel Nine Pty Ltd v Network Ten Pty Ltd (No 2)*[29] and *Network Ten Pty Ltd v TCN Nine Pty Ltd*,[30] the Full Federal Court and the High Court insisted that the question of quality should be considered in relation to Part IV subject-matter and, in addition, that this question is not confined to elements which are intrinsic to the work itself. As Finkelstein J said in the Federal Court:

---

24    [1964] 1 All ER 465 at 481.
25    (2009) 239 CLR 458.
26    (2009) 239 CLR 458 at [168].
27    (2009) 239 CLR 458 at [170].
28    [1908] 1 KB 821 at 872.
29    [2005] FCAFC 53.
30    *Network Ten Pty Ltd v TCN Nine Pty Ltd* (2004) 218 CLR 273. See *Nationwide News Pty Ltd v Copyright Agency Ltd* (1996) 65 FCR 399 for an application of this principle to a published edition of a work.

The effect of the authorities seems to be this. The test of substantiality – that is the notion of quality – is not confined to an examination of the intrinsic elements of the plaintiff's work. The test of substantiality may involve a broader enquiry, an enquiry which encompasses the context of the taking.[31]

Thus the aesthetic significance of the part taken,[32] the economic significance of the part taken[33] and the use to which the part taken would be put[34] were all considered in that case. In considering use it is important not to confuse the issue of substantiality with the issue of fair dealing. In relation to substantiality the question of use arises in so far as a competitive use, for example, will be evidence of the importance or significance of the part taken to the work as a whole. In relation to the fair dealing defences the issue of use goes to the question of whether the use fits within one of the defences – ie research or study; criticism or review; reporting the news; or parody or satire. Before the parody and satire fair dealing defence was introduced in Australia, as part of the 2006 copyright amendments, Conti J, at first instance in *TCN Channel Nine Pty Ltd v Network Ten Pty Ltd*,[35] suggested that the fact that the part taken was to be used for the non-competing use of satire or parody meant that the part taken was not substantial. This was rejected on appeal.

The application of the substantiality test to the excerpts taken in the Panel case proved to be difficult when the case was referred back to the Federal Court. The majority held that six of the 11 contested segments were substantial whilst the minority held that only three of these were substantial. The difference between the two decisions is interesting. The majority considered the fact that the parts taken were funny or memorable to be proof of their substantiality, regardless of their significance to the original story. Hely J's minority decision, on the other hand, looked at the significance of the part taken to the issue being discussed in the broadcast. Thus, for the majority a nine-second segment of a child interviewee yawning was substantial because it was "memorable".[36] The minority judgment found it not substantial because it was "fleeting in nature and on the periphery of the original broadcast, making little, if any, contribution to the subject-matter of the broadcast". Hely J concluded: "The footage taken is only incidental to the source broadcast, and is trivial, inconsequential or insignificant in terms of the broadcast".[37]

## Substantiality and parody

It has sometimes been suggested that the fact that non-copyright factors may be taken into account means that if the purpose of the taking is for parody or satire this will be proof of insubstantiality. No matter how much one might like

---

31   [2005] FCAFC 53 at [16].
32   [2005] FCAFC 53 at [11].
33   [2005] FCAFC 53 at [12].
34   [2005] FCAFC 53 at [14].
35   (2001) 184 ALR 1. See also *Joy Music Ltd v Sunday Pictorial Newspapers (1920) Ltd* [1960] 2 QB 60 for a similar early misapplication of the substantiality test to parodic takings.
36   [2005] FCAFC 53 at [38].
37   [2005] FCAFC 53 at [66].

to support such an idea as part of a principle of free speech it must be said that it does not form part of Australian law today.

An attempt by Conti J in *TCN Channel Nine Pty Ltd v Network Ten Pty Ltd*[38] to allow an otherwise infringing taking on the basis that it was for an alternative purpose and in particular, for a satirical purpose, failed to find any support on appeal.[39] Similarly, the reasoning in *Joy Music Ltd v Sunday Pictorial Newspapers (1920) Ltd*[40] has been subject to much criticism. In that case McNair J suggested that if the part taken was taken for the purposes of parody and the resulting parody displayed enough labour, skill and expertise to qualify as an original work in its own right, then the part taken was not substantial. Such reasoning is not in accordance with case law, principle or statutory interpretation and in *Schweppes Ltd v Wellingtons Ltd*[41] Falconer J, commenting on McNair J's suggestion, said that, put in this way, it was "not a correct statement of the law".[42]

Before 2007 parody and satire could be protected if they fitted within the fair use provisions for the purposes of news or criticism but this was a question which arose only after the question of substantiality had been decided. As McHugh ACJ, Gummow and Hayne JJ said in *Network Ten Pty Ltd v TCN Channel Nine Pty Ltd*: "It would be quite wrong to approach an infringement claim on the footing that the question of the taking of a substantial part may be by-passed by going directly to the fair dealing defences".[43] Much of this discussion is now moot as the 2006 copyright amendments introduced a new parody and satire defence which is discussed in the next chapter.

## Authorisation

The statutory concept of authorisation was first introduced in the *Copyright Act 1905*.[44] This is an important addition to the copyright owner's armoury and allows the copyright owner to take action either against the person actually copying, performing or otherwise dealing with the copyright material or against the person who authorised the infringing act.

Section 36(1A) as to works and s 101(1A) as to Part IV subject-matter provide that, in determining whether a person has authorised an infringing act, the matters which the court must take into account include (a) the extent (if any) of the person's power to prevent the doing of the act; (b) the nature of the relationship between the alleged authoriser and the person doing the act; and

---

38  (2001) 184 ALR 1.

39  *TCN Channel Nine Pty Ltd v Network Ten Pty Ltd* (2002) 190 ALR 468 and *Network Ten Pty Ltd v TCN Channel Nine Pty Ltd* (2004) 218 CLR 273 at [113].

40  [1960] 2 QB 60.

41  [1984] FSR 210.

42  [1984] FSR 210 at 212. Falconer J agreed that McNair J's decision was correct in so far as McNair J found that only two words of the chorus had been taken and this did not amount to a substantial part of the work (at 213).

43  *Network Ten Pty Ltd v TCN Channel Nine Pty Ltd* (2004) 218 CLR 273 at [21]. At the time of writing the High Court had referred the question of substantiality back to the Full Federal Court.

44  Authorisation can be distinguished from the concept of liability as joint tortfeasors in so far as it does not require a common design. It can be distinguished from vicarious liability on the basis that it does not arise out of the status of the legal relationship as such.

(c) whether the person took "*any other* reasonable steps" to prevent or avoid the doing of the act, including whether the person complied with relevant industry codes. These provisions were introduced into the *Copyright Act 1968* in 2001 and partly codify the case law on authorisation[45] and questions of authorisation must now be determined "primarily by reference to" these provisions.[46]

Section 39B as to works and s 112E as to audio-visual items[47] provide a "safe harbour" for any person (including a carrier or carriage service provider) who provides facilities for making or facilitating the making of a communication. Under these provisions such a person is not taken to have authorised an infringement "merely because" another person uses the facilities so provided to do something included in the copyright. As the High Court stated in *Roadshow Films Pty Ltd v iiNet* these sections seem to have been enacted "from an abundance of caution".[48] As we shall see from the case law on authorisation, it is difficult to see how such activity could amount to authorisation in any case.

The leading common law case on the meaning of authorisation is *University of New South Wales v Moorhouse*,[49] where the High Court held that a person authorised an infringing act if the person "sanctioned, approved or countenanced" the infringing act.[50] Although express acts of approval are not necessary to constitute authorisation under this test, mere inactivity is insufficient. In seeking to establish the requisite mental element the High Court approved the statement in *Corporation of the City of Adelaide v Australasian Performing Right Association Ltd*[51] that "Inactivity or indifference, exhibited by acts of commission or omission may reach such a degree from which an authorisation or permission may be inferred".[52]

In the *Moorhouse* case, the High Court held that the university had authorised infringing reproduction of literary works in so far as it had provided photocopiers and books and had "reasonable grounds to suspect"[53] possible infringements. The university was found to be in a position to prevent infringing copying. In so far as the university had taken steps to prevent infringing copying these steps were not "reasonable or effective".[54] The court found that certain conduct of the university suggested that it assumed and accepted that infringing copying would take place.

As a result of this decision a compulsory licensing scheme was introduced whereby educational institutions are entitled to reproduce copyright works upon payment of a fee by the institution.[55] In addition, s 104B of the Act now provides that, if a person makes an infringing copy of a work or audio-visual item on a machine, including a computer, in a library or archive, the library or archive will

---

45   [2011] FCAFC 23 at [22].

46   [2011] FCAFC 23 at [21].

47   An audio-visual item is a sound recording, film, television or radio broadcast (s 100A).

48   [2012] HCA 16 at [113] (Gummow and Haynes JJ). See also at [26] (French CJ, Crennan and Kiefel JJ).

49   (1975) 133 CLR 1.

50   (1975) 133 CLR 1 at 12, approving *Corporation of the City of Adelaide v Australasian Performing Right Association Ltd* (1928) 40 CLR 481 at 489 and 497.

51   (1928) 40 CLR 481 at 489 and 497.

52   *University of New South Wales v Moorhouse* (1975) 133 CLR 1 at 12, approving *Corporation of the City of Adelaide v Australasian Performing Right Association* (1928) 40 CLR 481 at 504.

53   (1975) 133 CLR 1 at 14.

54   (1975) 133 CLR 1 at 17.

55   *Copyright Act 1968* Part VB.

not be taken to have authorised the infringement if a prescribed notice is given on or near the machine.

Both directors and employees of companies have been found to be liable for authorisation of infringement if they have "authorised, procured or directed" the infringing conduct. See *Microsoft Corporation v Auschina Polaris Pty Ltd*[56] regarding the liability of directors and *Microsoft Corporation v Goodview Electronics Pty Ltd*[57] for a discussion of the liability of employees. In *Sony Music Entertainment (Australia) Ltd v CEL Music Pty Ltd*,[58] the non-executive Label Manager of a recording company was held liable for authorisation of infringement.

Authorisation is not established without proof of an infringing act. Thus, in *WEA v Hanimex Corporation Ltd*,[59] WEA asserted that Hanimex's radio advertisements authorised infringement of its copyright in Madonna's "Like A Virgin" album. The text of one of the advertisements was as follows.

> *First voice (miserable)*: Madonna's bent. And Bowie's completely deformed. Springsteen's a crumpled heap … Boy George is covered in horrible blisters … (disappears under).
>
> *Second voice*: If you don't want your favourite recordings ruined, use Fuji GTI car tapes. The only tape that won't melt, warp, twist or bend even on the hottest dashboard.
>
> *First voice (breaks down completely)*: … and what's this horrible gooey blob? Oh no, it's Paul McCartney.
>
> *Second voice*: Fuji. The world's most developed audio tape.

Gummow J held on two grounds that Hanimex had not authorised an infringement. First, authorisation is not complete until the unlawful act has occurred. In this case there was no proof of any actual infringing act. Secondly, Gummow J found as a matter of impression that the substance of the advertisements was not the invitation, incitement or approval of an infringing act but the promotion of the physical properties of the product.

Finally, although courts do not look favourably on copyright owners who rely on third parties to enforce their rights, those third parties cannot simply contract out of their liability for authorisation. See *Australasian Performing Right Association Ltd v Metro on George*[60] and the discussion regarding permitting a place of public entertainment to be used for the performance of a work (s 39, below).

Applying the authorisation principles to technology manufacturers, sellers and providers has proved to be contentious. In *Sony Corporation v Universal City Studios Inc*,[61] the United States Supreme Court declined to find the manufacturers of home video recorders liable for authorisation on the basis, inter alia, that the manufacturer and the consumer lacked the necessary connection and relationship of control to ground authorisation. In particular, the manufacturers were not in a position to prevent infringing use. Similarly, in *CBS Songs Ltd v*

---

56    (1996) 142 ALR 111.
57    (2000) 49 IPR 578.
58    (2002) 54 IPR 289.
59    (1987) 77 ALR 456.
60    (2004) 210 ALR 244.
61    464 US 417 (1984).

*Amstrad Consumer Electronics plc*,[62] the House of Lords held that, though the manufacturers of twin-deck tape recorders facilitated the copying of sound recordings, they did not authorise the infringement because the manufacturer was not in a position to prevent infringing copying.[63] These cases were approved by the High Court in *Australian Tape Manufacturers Association Ltd v Commonwealth*.[64]

In *Cooper v Universal Music Australia Pty Ltd*[65] Cooper was the owner and operator of the MP3s4FREE website which included hyperlinks to music stored on remote websites. The Federal Court held that he had authorised internet users to copy, and remote websites to communicate, sound recordings in breach of the owners' copyright. In coming to this conclusion Branson J, in the Full Federal Court, considered the factors set out in s 101(1A). He held that the "power to prevent" the doing of acts comprised in the copyright is not limited to having the power to prevent each act of infringement at the time it was done but includes the "power to not facilitate the doing of that act by, for example, making available to the public a technical capacity calculated to lead to the doing of that act".[66] In this case Cooper had done more than merely provide facilities for copying and communicating sound recordings; he had created and maintained the website whose principal content was links to often infringing copies. It was irrelevant that he had deliberately designed the site to operate automatically.[67]

In considering the nature of the relationship between Cooper and the person doing the infringing act, Branson J found that Cooper had a commercial interest in attracting users to his website for the purpose of copying music files.[68] Such a relationship contributed to the judge's final decision that Cooper had authorised the infringement. Finally, the disclaimers on the website (which misstated Australian copyright law) did not constitute a reasonable step to avoid infringement.

In *Universal Music Australia Pty Ltd v Sharman License Holdings Ltd*[69] (the *Kazaa* case) Sharman Networks Ltd (Sharman) and LEF Interactive Pty Ltd (LEF) controlled the file sharing system, Kazaa, which networks computers on which it is installed to allow registered users to find and download digital music and other files. Ms Hemming was the sole director and shareholder of LEF and CEO of Sharman. Sharman Holdings was a holding company which was not shown to have done any particular act in relation to the case. Sharman sought to rely on the s 112E safe harbour provision but the Federal Court held that, although Sharman was a person who provided facilities facilitating the making of a communication, the section does not give a general immunity against a finding of authorisation and does not preclude the possibility that a person who falls

---

62   [1988] AC 1013.
63   Lord Templeman noted that, although the manufacturers "conferred on the purchaser the power to copy [they] did not grant or purport to grant the right to copy": [1988] AC 1013 at 1054. This distinction between conferring a power to copy as opposed to authorising infringing copying is a useful distinction which has been somewhat obscured in Australia by the wording of s 101(1A).
64   (1993) 176 CLR 480 at 498. In this case a levy on blank tapes to be paid by the vendor was held to be a tax and unconstitutional in so far as it did not comply with the requirements of a tax Bill under s 55 of the Constitution
65   [2006] FCAFC 187.
66   [2006] FCAFC 187 at [41].
67   [2006] FCAFC 187 at [43].
68   [2006] FCAFC 187 at [48].
69   (2005) 220 ALR 1.

within its ambit may, for other reasons, be an authoriser. In this case the court held that Sharman had authorised the infringement, taking into consideration the factors set out in s 101(1A).

The High Court has had an opportunity to address this issue in *Roadshow Films Pty Ltd v iiNet Ltd*,[70] a case relating to the liability of an internet service provider (ISP) for authorisation of infringement. In this case major film companies unsuccessfully sued iiNet, the third biggest ISP in Australia, for authorisation of copyright infringement in films which were downloaded and made available online by iiNet customers using BitTorrent protocol. iiNet had refused to comply with infringement notices from the appellants which "required" iiNet to disconnect services to IP addresses where the infringing conduct was allegedly taking place. iiNet refused to comply with these notices partly on the basis that the IP addresses referred to particular modems rather than to individual users, and partly because it was not prepared to rely on the evidence of infringement provided by the film companies. The film companies argued that iiNet had authorised the making available of the films by "standing by and allowing this to happen without doing anything about it"[71] and further argued that iiNet "could not avoid secondary infringement unless it implemented a system designed to achieve the removal of infringing material by iiNet customers from the BitTorrent clients on those customers' computers".[72]

In rejecting the film companies' argument French CJ, Crennan and Kiefel JJ emphasised the importance of looking to the question of legal authorisation of infringement by reference to the wording of s 101(1A) rather than relying on synonyms such as "sanction, approve or countenance":

> In both the United Kingdom and Canada, it has been observed that some of the meanings of "countenance" are not co-extensive with "authorise". Such meanings are remote from the reality of authorisation which the statute contemplates.[73]

In particular, in applying s 101(1A) they held that mere inactivity, although arguably within the definition of "countenance", did not necessarily amount to authorisation unless the alleged authoriser had the power to prevent the primary infringement. This was so even if such inactivity may have provided encouragement and support to infringing users.[74] In this case they found that iiNet had no involvement with any part of the BitTorrent system and therefore no power to control or alter it; that under its contract iiNet did not grant the customer any right to use the internet for infringing purposes; and that, even if iiNet did discontinue its service to a particular customer that customer could simply go elsewhere to continue infringing activity. In relation to the infringement notices the court held that it was reasonable for iiNet to ignore the notices because of the risk of relying on untested allegations made by the companies. This was not mere indifference.[75]

Gummow and Hayne JJ, in a separate judgement, focused on the tortious nature of the action for copyright infringement and affirmed the "general rule of

---

70    [2012] HCA 16.
71    [2012] HCA 16 at [111].
72    [2012] HCA 16 at [59].
73    [2012] HCA 16 at [68] (referenes omitted).
74    [2012] HCA 16 at [68]-[69].
75    [2012] HCA 16 at [65]-[76].

the common law that in the absence of a special relationship one person has no duty to control another person to prevent the doing of damage to a third".[76] They warned against relying on US cases such as *A and M Records Inc v Napster* and *Metro-Goldwyn-Mayer v Grokster* which were decided on the basis of contributory infringement and vicarious liability rather than authorisation.[77] Gummow and Hayne JJ also sought to delineate the proper limits of authorisation and rejected the argument that "mere indifference" was sufficient to establish authorisation. They distinguished *Moorhouse* on the basis of the high level of control which the University had in relation to the particular infringing action in question.[78]

## Direct Infringement of Exclusive Rights

### The right to reproduce a work in a material form (s 31)

It is an infringement of the rights of the copyright owner to "reproduce" a work without the owner's consent. It is an infringement of the copyright owner's right in sound recordings or films to "copy" that recording or film. There is an important difference between these two rights. This difference might be understood by drawing a rough analogy with biological processes. Copying is like cloning something. In cloning, either the whole or part of the thing itself is replicated. Thus, a sound recording might be copied if the whole of the recording, one track of the recording or one instrumental track from the master tape is replicated on a CD or a DVD, for example. Reproduction is broader than this. It may include copying but it also includes the creation of a new thing by taking certain features of the original and mixing them with other, separate features. Thus, a musical work might be reproduced by making a sound alike version of it. A painting might be reproduced by photocopying (which is like a "copy") but it might also be reproduced by taking features of the painting such as its subject-matter, design and colour scheme and including them in another work. A dramatic work might be reproduced by copying the script verbatim or by taking the plot, the characters, the dramatic structure and the story line and writing a new play.[79] This section considers reproduction of works. In the following section we consider copying of recordings and films.

Reproduction has been defined broadly both in the case law and under the *Copyright Act 1968*. Section 21 contains a number of deeming provisions relating to the definition of reproduction under the Act. These cover the making of sound recordings or films of works; the digitalisation of works; the reproduction

---

76    [2012] HCA 16 at [108], citing *Brodie v Singleton Shire Council* (2001) 206 CLR 512 at 551.

77    In *A and M Records Inc v Napster* (2000) 50 IPR 232 the US Supreme Court held the supplier of peer-to-peer software, for sharing music and other files online, liable for both vicarious and contributory infringement. In this case Napster had a centralised indexing system and had the ability to exclude people from that system. In *Metro-Goldwyn-Mayer v Grokster* 243 F Supp 2d 1073 (2003), on the other hand, the supplier of the peer-to-peer software did not provide a centralised indexing system and had no practical ability to exclude users from using the software. In this case the US Ninth Circuit Court of Appeal declined to find the supplier liable for either vicarious or contributory infringement.

78    [2012] HCA 16 at [130].

79    Traditionally, "copying" has been used as a generic term for all forms of direct copyright infringement. We have tried to use the term "taking" but as you read cases you must make a decision as to how the term is being used in the particular case.

of computer programs and the three-dimensional reproduction of two-dimensional artistic works (and vice versa). Thus s 21 provides that:

- a literary, dramatic or musical work will be deemed to have been reproduced in a material form if a sound recording or film is made of the work (s 21(1));
- a work is taken to have been reproduced if it is converted into or out of a digital or other electronic machine-readable form (s 21(1A));
- a computer program is taken to have been reproduced if an object code is produced from a source code "by any process, including compilation" (s 21(5)(a));
- a computer program is taken to have been reproduced if a source code is derived from an object code "by any process, including decompilation" (s 21(5)(b));[80]
- an artistic work will be deemed to have been reproduced if a two-dimensional work is produced in three-dimensional form or if a three-dimensional work is produced in two-dimensional form (s 21(3)).

Reproduction need not be exact or perfect. This arises from both general principles of statutory interpretation and the ordinary meaning of the word. As Megarry J said in *British Northrop Ltd v Texteam Blackburn Ltd*[81] regarding the reproduction right under the United Kingdom Act:

> [S]ection 48(1) [of the *Copyright Act 1956* (UK)] necessarily indicates that "reproduction" is not confined to a copy of complete precision, from its use of the words "version", "converting" and "form" ... . Furthermore, I do not think that the work "reproduction", in its normal use, carries any implication of exactitude of likeness between that which is produced and the reproduction itself. Not every reproduction is a perfect reproduction ...[82]

Reproduction in copyright law involves three elements – a causal connection between the two works, objective similarity with the part taken and the production of something in material form. The causal connection requires that the alleged infringer either directly or indirectly takes from the original work. This is sometimes referred to as "subjective copying". The requirement for similarity means that even if a causal connection has been established there will be no infringement unless there is a sufficient degree of similarity between the part taken and the alleged infringing work.[83] If we want to maintain the biological analogy, the plaintiff must establish both paternity and family resemblance. The requirement that the reproduction be in material form effectively separates the reproduction and performance rights. Without this requirement it would be difficult to say that a recitation of a literary work was not a reproduction of that work.

---

80   This leaves the question of what constitutes an adaptation of a computer program. Although this is discussed below we note here that an adaptation in relation to a computer program is now defined as a version of the program which is not a reproduction: s 10.
81   [1974] RPC 57.
82   [1974] RPC 57 at 72.
83   Note, there need not be similarity between the protected work and the infringing work *as a whole*. The protected work, for example, may form only a small part of the infringing work.

## Causal connection

In *SW Hart and Co Pty Ltd v Edwards Hot Water Systems*,[84] Wilson J warned against artificially separating the two questions of causal connection and objective similarity. He stressed that the two elements may be interdependent:

> If a case is to succeed where there is no evidence of access to the copyright drawings, the similarity of the impugned product to the drawings will be required to be so strong as to itself sustain, without more, an inference of copying. On the other hand, in a case where there is strong evidence in support of an inference of copying such evidence as there is of similarity may take on added significance. It must, of course, still amount to a sufficient similarity of a substantial part of the copyright work. But such dissimilarities as are apparent may be seen as no more than a deliberate attempt to obscure what has actually taken place.[85]

In *Clarendon Homes (Aust) Pty Ltd v Henkley Arch Pty Ltd*,[86] the Full Federal Court considered when such an inference may be drawn. The plaintiff must show "in the absence of evidence of access, that the similarities are so striking as to preclude the possibility of the defendant having arrived at the result independently".[87]

Many cases, however, have still been lost because the plaintiffs have failed to prove the necessary causal connection. In *Robertson v Lewis*,[88] the applicants failed to prove a causal connection between Vera Lynne's recording of a traditional Scottish tune and a copyright arrangement of the tune. The court accepted evidence that pipers were likely to have known the air from different sources.[89]

In establishing a causal connection courts have accepted that reproduction may be unconscious but it is a question of fact in each case whether the necessary causal connection exists. In *Francis Day & Hunter v Bron*,[90] the plaintiff failed to prove infringement of the musical work "In a Little Spanish Town" by the defendant's "Why". Although there was similarity between the two works and the court expressly accepted that as a question of law unconscious reproduction was possible, the plaintiffs failed to prove that the defendant had any familiarity with the work at all.[91]

---

84   (1985) 159 CLR 466.
85   (1985) 159 CLR 466 at 484. Wilson J continued: "In *Ancher, Mortlock, Murray and Woolley Pty Ltd v Hooker Homes Pty Ltd* [1971] 2 NSWLR 278 Street J ... noted the fine line that may exist between the conduct of an architect who, having inspected an original plan or house, then proceeds to embody the architectural concepts in an original plan prepared by him and that of an architect who merely proceeds by way of copying what he has seen. His Honour observed (p 284) that it may be that only after making a finding of copying, that is to say, of unfair or unconscientious use of the author's plan or building, that significance will attach to the degree of similarity. In finding an infringement in the case before him, His Honour acknowledged that his assessment had been coloured by the unmeritorious use made by the defendant of the plaintiff's plans and houses".
86   (1999) 46 IPR 309.
87   (1999) 46 IPR 309 at 314.
88   [1976] RPC 169.
89   This was so even though the recording used the name of the arrangement as its title rather than the traditional name of the tune.
90   [1963] Ch 587.
91   See *Andritz Sprout-Bauer Australia Pty Ltd v Rowland Engineering Sales Pty Ltd* (1993) 28 IPR 29 for an example of an unconscious reproduction of an artistic work.

The causal connection between the protected work and the alleged infringing work may be direct, as when an artist produces a drawing of a painting which the artist has seen. The causal connection may be indirect, as when an artist produces a drawing of a painting, which the artist has never seen, by looking at a photograph of the painting. In this case, when the protected work, the causal path and the product are all similar in kind, the concept of indirect reproduction is generally accepted as uncontentious.

Indirect reproduction becomes more contentious when the causal path is through a different type of copyright work (a drawing made from a written description of a painting which the artist has not seen) or through an unprotected medium (as when an artist reproduces a drawing of a chair by looking at a chair made in accordance with the original drawing of a chair). The concept becomes particularly troublesome when the product of this process is itself an unprotected thing. For example, a carpenter infringes a drawing of a chair by looking at a chair made in accordance with that drawing and then making another chair.

In these latter examples copyright law appears to be extending into areas of industry and commerce which were never contemplated by the 18th century judges who championed the rights of the author in *Millar v Taylor*[92] and *Donaldson v Becket*.[93] As Deane J said in *SW Hart and Co Pty Ltd v Edwards Hot Water Systems*:[94]

> The convoluted path by which a three-dimensional object has been held to be an infringement of the copyright in a technical drawing which has neither been factually copied nor even seen illustrates the incursions which copyright – with its extended life but more limited protection, its lack of any requirement of novelty or true inventiveness and its minimal standards of originality – is capable of making into what would ordinarily be seen as the proper domains of the law of patents and the law of industrial designs.[95]

In *Frank M Winstone (Merchants) Ltd v Plix Products Ltd*,[96] the respondent's kiwi fruit tray had been adopted by the kiwi fruit marketing authority as a standard. The appellant engaged a designer who produced a similar tray by referring to the authority's written specifications and verbal instructions from the appellants. The resulting tray was held to be a reproduction of the respondent's copyright in drawings of the tray and "and other artistic works"[97] despite its causal link through a generically different medium.

In *King Features Syndicate Inc v Kleeman Ltd*,[98] the defendants were held to have reproduced the plaintiff's drawings of Popeye by producing brooches based on other brooches made in alleged infringement of the drawings. In *LB (Plastics) Ltd v Swish Products Ltd*,[99] the defendants were held to have reproduced the

---

92    (1769) 98 ER 201.

93    (1774) 1 ER 837.

94    (1985) 159 CLR 466.

95    (1985) 159 CLR 466 at 495.

96    (1985) 5 IPR 156.

97    This is a New Zealand case and therefore the moulds and plastic kiwi fruit containers were characterised as sculptures or engravings.

98    [1941] AC 417.

99    (1979) 1A IPR 359.

plans for the plaintiff's commercial drawers by producing drawers using reverse engineering techniques (for example, they examined the plaintiff's drawer slides in order to develop their own drawer design). It is interesting to note that in each of these cases there was some evidence of access to the original drawings although the court did not emphasise this point in its reasoning.

This is unfortunate because, without some reference to such access, the principle of indirect reproduction gives an advantage to the plaintiff which is based purely on the fortuitous existence of drawings. There are, however, some limitations to the application of the principle and recent cases do indicate some willingness on the part of judges to restrict it. In *Purefoy Engineering Co Ltd v Sykes, Boxall & Co Ltd*,[100] the plaintiffs argued that the defendant's catalogue of machine tooling parts was an indirect reproduction of their catalogue because it had been made by copying actual machine tooling parts. Evershed MR rejected the argument on the basis that in establishing indirect infringement "the intermediate stage or subject ... must in some real and intelligible sense ... be a 'copy' or representation of the original work".[101]

A similar principle has been applied in Australia but without detailed discussion. In *Talk of the Town v Hagstrom*,[102] the applicant produced plastic extrusions for use in the building trade. The respondent had copied the applicant's moulds (or dies) to produce their own plastic extrusions but, as we have seen, Pincus J held that there was no copyright in the moulds as artistic works. The applicant therefore argued that the respondents had indirectly copied the applicant's drawings of the moulds. Pincus J rejected this argument because the moulds "were not made by direct use of the drawings". He continued:

> There is an affidavit ... which explains that a sketch of the extruded product desired to be made is prepared and, from that, a working drawing for a die is made. The die prepared from that working drawing, however, is not the final version. It is tried and recut until the desired result is achieved. In these circumstances, there is plainly no breach of copyright based on drawings ...[103]

In *Gleeson v H Denne Ltd*,[104] the requisite causal connection between a sketch of a clerical shirt and the alleged infringing shirt was not established when, on the evidence, a priest had pointed to the shirt and said to a salesman, "I don't suppose your firm could make this sort of thing?"[105] The salesman subsequently asked the firm's tailor to make a shirt with a tunnel collar. In this case there was some connection between the shirt indicated and the sketch protected but the English Court of Appeal held that there was no causal link because it was only the "idea" which was passed on, not the form of visual expression which was protected in the sketch.[106]

---

100   (1955) 72 RPC 89.
101   (1955) 72 RPC 89 at 99.
102   (1990) 99 ALR 130.
103   (1990) 99 ALR 130 at 136.
104   [1975] RPC 471.
105   [1975] RPC 471 at 489.
106   [1975] RPC 471 at 490.

*Objective similarity*

Even if the requisite causal connection has been found it is still necessary to establish that there has been a reproduction in the sense that there is some objective similarity between the protected work and the allegedly infringing subject-matter. As a matter of principle it is not necessary to establish that there is overall similarity between the copyright work as a whole and the alleged infringing work as a whole. Similarly, it is not necessary that there be similarity between a discrete part of the original work and the allegedly infringing material. As Lord Millet commented in slightly different circumstances regarding reproduction of an artistic work:

> It must be borne in mind that this is an action for infringement of copyright. It is not an action for passing-off. The gist of an action for passing off is deceptive resemblance … An action for infringement of copyright, however, is very different. It is not concerned with the appearance of the defendant's work but with its derivation. The copyright owner does not complain that the defendant's work resembles his. His complaint is that the defendant has copied all or a substantial part of the copyright work.[107]

This is not to say that there can never be overall similarity or similarity between discrete parts of the material in question but rather, that it is not necessary. In establishing similarity courts are in the position of a visitor looking at a new baby trying to find a family resemblance. First, the court might ask itself whether features of the original have been taken and appear in the new subject-matter ("Oh look, he's got your nose!"). Alternatively, the court might ask whether there is a resemblance between the two works overall ("Ah, she looks just like you"). Finally, the court might ask itself whether the new subject-matter calls the original to mind ("Every time I look at her I am reminded of you"). The three approaches are related to each other but only the first is necessary. In so far as the new subject-matter displays enough protected features then it will probably resemble the original and if there is a strong enough resemblance then it will probably remind an observer of the original.[108]

In determining similarity, unlike substantiality, only those features in which copyright subsists are considered. It follows from this that what one compares varies according to the type of work in question. In the case of musical works one compares the essentially musical aspects of the works. Thus, in *Francis Day & Hunter v Bron*,[109] Lord Wilberforce compared the musical structure of the two works, the treatment of the primary musical theme, the use of musical repetition, the melody, the harmonic structure, the metre and rhythm and the beat.[110] None of these was decisive by itself and Wilberforce LJ concluded:

> [O]ne must resist the temptation … to atomise what is a living phrase. One must not lose sight of the musical character and the aural appeal of the sentence as a whole.[111]

---

107  *Designer Guild Ltd v Russell Williams (Textiles) Ltd* [2001] 1 All ER 700 at 708, using "copying" here in the broader sense of reproduction.

108  Courts have rarely distinguished these three approaches and one case, or even one judgment, may apply to one or more of them. Compare, for example, the approaches of the judges in *Hanfstaengl v Baines* [1985] AC 20.

109  [1963] Ch 587.

110  [1963] Ch 587 at 594-596.

111  [1963] Ch 587 at 596.

Swinfen Eady LJ took a similar approach in *Rees v Melville*[112] in relation to the reproduction of a dramatic work where he is reported to have said:

> In order to constitute an infringement it is not necessary that the words of the dialogue should be the same, the situations and incidents, the mode in which the ideas are worked out and presented might constitute a material part of the whole play, and the court must have regard to the dramatic value and importance of what, if anything, was taken, even although the portion might in fact be small and the actual language not copied. On the other hand, the fundamental idea of the play might be the same, but if worked out separately and on independent lines they might be so different as to bear no real resemblance to each other.[113]

Artistic works are compared visually by reference to what is protected as a visual work rather than by reference to the content of the visual work. Courts have been quite sophisticated in identifying these specifically visual features. Thus, in *McCrum v Eisner*,[114] the plaintiff owned the copyright in a series of postcards called the "Recruit Series". One of the postcards depicted a very hot, weary and disconsolate recruit looking with dismay at a notice which read "Recruits. Orders of the day: Eight Hours drill. Eight hours route march. Eight hours trench work. By Order. God Save the King". Under the drawing was the legend, "And then we have all the rest of the day to ourselves". The defendant, who appeared to lack the applicant's mordant humour, produced a postcard which also showed a recruit looking at a notice which gave a fairly dull and detailed timetable for the day beginning with 6am reveille and 7am breakfast and ending with 10pm lights out. Under the drawing was the same legend, "And then we have the rest of the day to ourselves". The copyright owner sued for infringement of the drawing. Petersen J acknowledged that a reproduction need not be exact but emphasised the importance of distinguishing between an idea and its expression in determining whether there had been an infringement. In this case, although the second postcard called the first to mind there was not enough visual similarity between the two to constitute infringement.

The need to distinguish between the specifically visual aspects of the artistic work which are protected and the idea in the work is particularly important when the comparison is being made between a two-dimensional artistic work, such as a diagram and a three-dimensional object made in accordance with that diagram. Thus, in *Burke and Margot Burke Ltd v Spicers Dress Designs*,[115] Clauson J, to the continuing scorn of many feminist commentators, found that copyright in a drawing of a slim model wearing a dress had not been infringed by making the dress. This was because there was no objective similarity between the two things – the pile of fabric which comprised the dress and the stylised drawing of the model wearing a dress. Had the real dress been put on a model and posed in a similar fashion, the judge commented, he may have been able to find the necessary visual similarity:

---

112  (1914) MacG Cop Cas 168.
113  (1914) MacG Cop Cas 168 at 174.
114  (1918) 87 LJ Ch 99.
115  [1936] Ch 400.

But when I look upon the frock, it seems quite impossible to say that the frock, and nothing more – is a reproduction of the sketch. It is not like it at all.[116]

This does not mean that clothing designers are not protected. These days, to ensure protection, clothes designers claim copyright in the drawings, patterns and prototype of garments. See *Muscat v Le*[117] for a discussion of clothes and copyright.

In the case of literary works it is not just the exact order of the words but also the ordering of ideas and the layout of the literary work which are protected and which must be compared in order to establish objective similarity. This may be illustrated by Jenkinson J's approach in *Zeccola v Universal City Studios Inc*[118] where a literary work was allegedly infringed by a film. In that case the Full Federal Court compared the "occurrences narrated or otherwise given verbal representation in the works" with their portrayal "by the visual images and sound of the cinematograph film". Jenkinson J concluded, "in my opinion the greater the number of those occurrences so portrayed the more completely is such a work reproduced".[119] This is similar to the approach taken in the case of musical and dramatic works, that is, identification of the specifically literary aspects in which copyright subsists and determining whether these aspects have been repeated in the allegedly infringing work.

This is particularly clear in the case of literary compilations where the questions of subsistence and infringement have been closely intertwined. Thus, in *Ladbroke (Football) Ltd v William Hill (Football) Ltd,*[120] it was the "ordering" of the lists and the "selection" of the bets in which copyright subsisted as an original work and it was the taking of these parts which constituted infringement. As in the case of dramatic works such an approach requires careful consideration of the limits of the form of expression in which copyright subsists. In *Joy Music Ltd v Sunday Pictorial Newspapers (1920) Ltd,*[121] for example, the court declined to compare the metre and rhythm of the two works on the basis that copyright did not subsist in these aspects of a literary work.

A problem arises when comparing literary works due to the fact that literary works are generally in writing and writing has, historically, been a visual form of representation. Judges have, therefore, sometimes judged the similarity between the original literary work and its infringement by comparing them visually rather than by reference to the specifically literary aspects of the work which are protected. Thus, in *Cuisenaire v Reed,*[122] for example, Pape J concluded that there was "no ... visual resemblance"[123] between the rods and the written chart in question. Applying similar logic, translations were found, in the past, not to be a reproduction of a literary work; dramatisations were not a reproduction of a non-dramatic literary work; and a picture version of a book could not be

---

116 [1936] Ch 400 at 406.
117 (2003) 204 ALR 335.
118 (1982) 46 ALR 189.
119 (1982) 46 ALR 189 at 196.
120 [1964] 1 All ER 465.
121 [1960] 2 QB 60 at 69-70.
122 [1963] VR 719.
123 [1963] VR 719 at 734.

considered to be a reproduction of a literary work. It is for this reason that they are today characterised as adaptations under the *Copyright Act 1968* s 10. Until the advent of digital technology courts continued to use this approach without much discussion.

Digital technology effectively separated the form of literary expression that is protected as a literary work from its form of representation. Two literary works which are exactly the same in format, content and language, for example, may have no visual similarity if one is in digital form and the other is in a hard copy form or if they are in different digital forms. Courts had to deal with this change directly in relation to computer programs.

If you wanted to "duplicate" (to use a neutral term) a computer program to use in a new software package in another code, you might use decompiler software which will dump the program in object code and write it up in a code similar to a source code. From this point you could change the source code into any other code you liked. Alternatively, if you had access to a source code for a computer program you might write it up in any object code suitable to your hardware and software requirements or use a compiler to do it for you. In neither of these cases would there be any visual similarity between the original and the "duplicate" but the arrangement and expression of the set of instructions would still be the same. In *Data Access Corporation v Powerflex Services Pty Ltd*,[124] it was held that this process was similar to translation and, consistently with the older approach, this was held to be an adaptation. Reproduction, in this case, seemed to be limited to copying. This part of the decision has since been overturned by the *Copyright Amendment (Digital Agenda) Act 2000* which amends s 21 of the *Copyright Act 1968*. Section 21 provides that a work is taken to have been reproduced if it is converted into or out of a digital or other electronic machine-readable form (s 21(1A)); a computer program is taken to have been reproduced if an object code is produced from a source code "by any process, including compilation" (s 21(5)(a)) and a computer program is taken to have been reproduced if a source code is derived from an object code "by any process, including decompilation" (s 21(5)(b)).

Confronted by the separation of the form of expression and its form of repre-sentation, it follows that the use of visual comparison for establishing similarity of literary works is no longer either philosophically or practically appropriate. The legislative amendments also ensure that such an approach is blocked, at least so far as digital works are concerned. We would suggest that it should be avoided in the case of all literary works.

### Material form

Material form as we have seen, is defined under s 10 as any form (whether visible or not) of storage of a work or adaptation, or a substantial part of the work or adaptation (whether or not the work or adaptation, or a substantial part of the work or adaptation can be reproduced from it). A live performance or live broad-cast of a work therefore is not a reproduction of the work because it is not a form of storage. Although a *tableau vivant* was held to be a reproduction of an artistic

---

124 (1999) 202 CLR 1.

work in *Bradbury, Agnew and Co v Day*[125] under the *Copyright Act 1911*, this is no longer good law. The *Copyright Act 1911* did not contain the limited definition of material form and s 1 of that Act provided that it was an infringement of copyright to reproduce the work "in any material form whatsoever".

The reproduction need not be another work or other copyright material. Thus, the reproduction may be another work or other subject-matter or even an unprotected object. In *Zeccola v Universal City Studios Inc*,[126] both the script for the film "Jaws" and the novel on which it was based were found, prima facie, to have been reproduced in a material form by a film, "Great White". In *SW Hart Pty Ltd v Edwards Hot Water Systems*,[127] a technical drawing of a solar panel was found to have been reproduced by the production of a solar panel.

### Applying these principles to electronic devices

The current definition of material form is different in two ways from the definition of material form applying before the commencement of the *US Free Trade Agreement Implementation Act 2004*. Under the old definition, material form was a form of storage, whether visible or not, *from which a work could be reproduced*. In addition, there was no reference to substantiality under the old definition. These changes are significant because the old definition of material form had been interpreted narrowly so as to limit the reproduction right in relation to computer programs in particular and the operation of electronic devices generally.

In 2001 in *Pacific Gaming Pty Ltd v Aristocrat Leisure Industries Pty Ltd*,[128] for example, the Full Federal Court held that the data stored on an EPROM for a computerised poker machine game was not a reproduction in material form of the table of specifications for the game which the plaintiffs had lodged with the poker machine regulatory agency. The court held that, whilst the EPROM may have been made in accordance with the instructions contained in the table of specifications, it could not be said that the table of specifications could be reproduced from the EPROM. The EPROM was therefore not a reproduction in material form of that table under the definition of material form then applying.

More significantly, the limitation was applied where the ordinary operation of an electronic device entailed some level of ephemeral reproduction or copying of minute quantities of copyright subject-matter into RAM. If such ephemeral reproduction or copying were to be considered as reproduction or copying under the *Copyright Act 1968* then the mere reading of material on screen, the playing of a computer program, the operation of a washing machine or the running of a DVD would constitute an infringement of the copyright in a computer program and any of the added content, such as a film or literary work. Australian courts have avoided this broad interpretation of the reproduction right by relying on a narrow definition of material form, but the reasoning applied in the cases has been different.

---

125  [1916] WN 114.
126  (1982) 46 ALR 189.
127  (1985) 159 CLR 466.
128  (2001) 116 FCR 448.

In *Dyason v Autodesk Inc*,[129] Sheppard J doubted whether the ephemeral and volatile transient holding of data in RAM could be said to be a form of storage within the then definition of material form under s 10. He acknowledged that, at a policy level the running of a program could be compared to reading a book but was reluctant to take this argument too far.[130] In *Australian Video Retailers Association Ltd v Warner Home Video Pty Ltd*,[131] Emmett J held that the transient storage of parts of the computer program in question was not storage in a material form because a computer program could not be reproduced from RAM without the use of specialised equipment.[132] In *Kabushiki Kaisha Sony Computer Entertainment v Stevens* Sackville J,[133] and on appeal Lindgren J (with whom French J agreed),[134] also followed this reasoning in relation to the DVD in question but acknowledged that, in other circumstances and with different technology, it might be possible to reproduce the work from RAM and thereby bring the usage within the statutory definition of reproduction in material form then applying.

In coming to this conclusion the Full Court expressly rejected the opposite conclusion of Tamberlin J in *Microsoft Corporation v Business Boost Pty Ltd*[135] who held that the requirement for storage in material form was met by storage in RAM because a computer might be left on for a long period of time and the requirement for storage did not refer to a specific duration. Tamberlin J did not address the requirement that a storage in material form meant storage in a form from which the work might itself be reproduced. The Full Court also rejected the heavily criticised United States decision of *MIA Systems Corporation v Peak Computer Inc*[136] which held that storage in RAM amounted to an infringing reproduction. The Full Court distinguished the decision on the basis of the wording of the United States Code.

Each of these decisions is unsatisfactory in so far as they rely on fine distinctions relating to the current status of technology rather than the proper extent of the copyright owner's exclusive rights. There is little consideration of the general policy issue of whether a user of an authorised computer program or other work should be able to use it in a fashion comparable to a reader's right to read a copyright book.

At the time there was only one defence which could have been applied to avoid a finding of reproduction. Section 47B provided a defence where the reproduction of an authorised computer program is made as part of the normal running of that computer program. However, the s 47B defence only applied to the reproduction of computer programs and did not cover other works or subject-matter other than works.

---

129  *Dyason v Autodesk Inc* (1990) 96 ALR 57.
130  *Dyason v Autodesk Inc* (1990) 96 ALR 57 at 87-88.
131  *Australian Video Retailers Association Ltd v Warner Home Video Pty Ltd* (2001) 53 IPR 242.
132  *Australian Video Retailers Association Ltd v Warner Home Video Pty Ltd* (2001) 53 IPR 242 at 255.
133  *Kabushiki Kaisha Sony Computer Entertainment v Stevens* (2002) 200 ALR 55; affirmed on appeal to the High Court: *Stevens v Kabushiki Kaisha Sony Computer Entertainment* (2005) 224 CLR 193.
134  *Kabushiki Kaisha Sony Computer Entertainment v Stevens* (2003) 200 ALR 96.
135  *Microsoft Corporation v Business Boost Pty Ltd* (2000) 49 IPR 573.
136  *MIA Systems Corporation v Peak Computer Inc* 991 F 2d 511 (9th Circuit 1993).

The new definition of material form would make each of the above fact situations infringing – subject only to the requirement of substantiality. However, the new definition has been accompanied by a new defence. Sections 43B and 111B provide that copyright in subject-matter is not infringed if the reproduction is incidentally made as part of the technical process of using a copy of the subject-matter. The defence does not apply if the reproduction is made from an infringing copy of the subject-matter. It is expected that this defence will cover each of the fact situations referred to above.

## The right to make a copy of a sound recording or film (ss 85 and 86)

Under ss 85 and 86 the copyright owner has the exclusive right to make a copy of a sound recording or film. Copy is defined in s 10(1) in relation to a film as "any article or thing in which the visual images or sounds comprising the film are embodied". There is no equivalent definition of a copy in relation to a sound recording. Section 21 provides that a sound recording or film is taken to have been copied if it is converted into or from a digital or other machine readable form and any article embodying the recording or film is taken to be a copy of that recording or film. Section 24 provides that sound or visual images will be taken to be embodied in an article or thing if that thing has been treated so that the sounds and visual images are capable, with or without the aid of another device, of being reproduced from the article or thing. This section appears to be in conflict with s 10(5) and (6) introduced by the *US Free Trade Agreement Implementation Act 2004* which provide that, for the purposes of the definition of copy under s 10(1) (that is, in relation to a film), such a copy includes any form (whether visible or not) of storage of a film or sound recording, or a substantial part of a film or sound recording whether or not the copy can be reproduced. The object of the amendments appears to be to bring the copying provisions into line with the reproduction provisions, especially in relation to the application of the copying right to the use of electronic devices.

The right to make a copy of a sound recording or film is significantly narrower than the right to reproduce or adapt a work. The right to reproduce may be infringed by making a "sound alike" musical work or a "look alike" film. The right to adapt a musical work or a screenplay might be infringed by making a version of the work in a different medium. The right to make a copy of a sound recording or film, by comparison, is infringed only by the making of another sound recording or film which must be "an actual embodiment of the very sounds or images" in the copyright sound recording or film (*CBS Records Australia Ltd v Telmak Teleproducts (Aust) Pty Ltd*).[137]

In *CBS Records Australia Ltd v Telmak Teleproducts (Aust) Pty Ltd*,[138] a sound alike compilation by Telmak called "Chart Sounds 16 Hit Songs" was found not to be an infringement of CBS recordings of the songs. Similarly, whilst the defendant's film "Great White" may have infringed the copyright in the screen-

---

137  (1987) 79 ALR 604.
138  (1987) 79 ALR 604.

play for "Jaws" it could not infringe the copyright in the film "Jaws" because the defendant's film did not embody the very images or sounds of the original film.[139] This does not mean that the copy must be identical to the original film or sound recording. An infringing copy may be made by copying the sounds from a master tape of a recording, for example, and remixing them, adding to them, subtracting from them or by sampling. *Polygram Records Inc v Raben Footwear Pty Ltd*[140] is an interesting example of the difficulty faced by plaintiffs in establishing that the "very sounds" of the alleged copyright sound recording have been copied.

### The right to publish a work (s 31)

In *Avel Pty Ltd v Multicoin Amusements Pty Ltd*,[141] the High Court defined the right to publish a work under s 31 as the right to "make public that which had not previously been made public in the copyright territory".[142] That is, the exclusive right to publish is exhausted upon first publication.

*Avel* provides a cautionary tale for all those who would negotiate a copyright agreement – make sure that you are buying or selling something which exists. In this case, Avel had an exclusive agreement with an American manufacturer of amusement machines to "sell and distribute" the machines in Australia. A second importer, Multicoin Amusements Pty Ltd, bought machines from the United States manufacturer and imported them for sale in Australia. Avel was unable to prove that the machines had been imported for sale without the licence of the copyright owner and therefore could not establish indirect infringement under s 37 or s 38. Avel therefore alleged that its right to "sell and distribute" the machine amounted to an exclusive licence to publish the artwork and computer program in Australia and that, by offering the machines for sale, Multicoin had directly infringed this right.

Avel based its argument on the definition of publish under s 29 – that is, a work is deemed to have been published if reproductions of the work or an edition of a work have been made available to the public. There is no requirement under s 29 that this be for a first time. The High Court held that there was a difference between publication for the purposes of establishing subsistence and publication for the purposes of infringement. The court acknowledged that there was "an element of artificiality" in confining the definition of s 29 but held that the confinement was dictated by "general concepts of copyright law", by considerations of policy and by the fact that ss 37 and 38 (which require knowledge on the part of the alleged infringer who imports or sells an infringing article) would be rendered otiose if the sale of copyright matter could constitute a direct infringement (which does not require knowledge on the art of the alleged infringer).[143] The court also noted that the confinement of the right to publish to first publication was in accordance with the House of Lords decision in *Infabrics Ltd v Jaytex Ltd*.[144]

---

139 *Zeccola v Universal City Studios Inc* (1982) 46 ALR 189.
140 (1996) 35 IPR 426.
141 (1990) 171 CLR 88.
142 (1990) 171 CLR 88 at 88.
143 (1990) 171 CLR 88 at 88.
144 [1982] AC 1 regarding "publication" of a printed shirt.

To what extent the right to publish can be divorced from the s 29 definition is unclear. For example, does the first broadcast of a work or the first online publication of a work infringe the right to publish? Whilst s 29 requires that a work be published in a material form there is no such requirement in Mason J's definition. The question was not raised in *Avel* and is perhaps simply moot today because both the broadcast and the online publication would constitute an infringement of the right to communicate the work to the public.

## The right to perform a work in public (s 31) and the right to cause a film or sound recording to be heard or seen in public (ss 85, 86)[145]

These rights are closely related. The copyright owner of a work has the exclusive right to perform the work in public whilst the owner of the copyright in a film or sound recording has the exclusive right to cause it to be seen or heard in public. There are two questions to be answered in determining the extent of these rights. Has there been a performance or has the Part IV subject-matter been caused to be heard or seen? Has it been in public?

Performance covers not just live performances but "any mode of visual or aural presentation" including presentations on television, radio, film, computer monitor and other forms of reception equipment. It includes the delivery of a lecture, speech, address or sermon (s 27(1)). Before the introduction of the broadcast right (which is now included in the communication right), the performance right was found to cover the act of broadcasting a work on radio.

Thus, in *Chappell and Co v Associated Radio of Australia Ltd*,[146] a radio broadcaster was found to have infringed the performance right in a musical work by broadcasting that work. Today, s 27 provides that a communication or the operation of equipment to make a communication does not constitute either a performance under s 31 or causing a film or sound recording to be heard or seen in public under ss 85 and 86.

If the reception equipment (as opposed to the communication equipment) is used to perform or cause a film or sound recording to be heard or seen in public, the relevant act shall be deemed to be effected by the operation of the reception equipment. Thus, subject to s 199, the operation of a radio or television may constitute a performance of the copyright material included in the broadcast. Where the relevant act is effected through the operation of reception equipment the occupier of the premises is deemed to have infringed the s 31 performance right or the ss 85 and 86 rights if the equipment was provided by or with the consent of the occupier whether or not the occupier operates the equipment (s 27(4)).

Section 199 provides that copyright in an authorised reading or recitation included in a television or radio broadcast and copyright in a sound recording or a film included in a television or radio broadcast is not infringed by a person who, by the reception of the broadcast causes the work, recording or film to be performed or seen or heard in public.[147] Section 199 does not apply to works,

---

145   For transitional provisions relating to performance of works, see s 246.
146   [1925] VLR 350.
147   This limitation only applies to authorised broadcasts in the case of films although, even in the case of unauthorised broadcasts, no action may be brought against the person receiving the film.

however, and therefore, a person who plays a recording in a shop may have breached the copyright in the musical work but not in the sound recording itself.

*Australasian Performing Right Association Ltd v Telstra Corporation Ltd*[148] concerned the playing of music on hold over the telephone. On trial in the Federal Court before Gummow J, APRA argued that the reception equipment, in this case the telephone, was partly activated by the current passing in the telephone wires. APRA argued on this basis that, although Telstra could not be liable for breach of the performance right in so far as it operated communication equipment, Telstra could be held liable for breach of the performance right in so far as it could be said to operate the reception equipment. Gummow J rejected the argument because it would "deny the natural effect of the subsection" and noted that even old fashioned radios were "to some extent activated by the signal".[149] Gummow J's finding on this point was not appealed and today s 27(3) expressly overturns this decision.

The exclusive rights in this case are limited to performances in public and causing a film or sound recording to be seen or heard in public and most of the relevant case law has been concerned with the question of what constitutes "in public". There have been two main tests for the determination of this question and both are derived from *Jennings v Stephens*.[150] In that case a performance of a play before a ladies club in a small country town was held to be a performance in public even though the audience was restricted to members and their guests, the performers were not paid and there was no entrance fee. Wright MR and Romer LJ held that the performance was in public because the meeting "formed part not of the domestic, that is the private life of a member, but of her out-side, that is to say, of her public life". The size of the audience and the presence or absence of visitors were irrelevant for determining whether the performance was public or private.[151] The case distinguished *Duck v Bates*[152] which had found that a performance for patients, nurses and visitors at Guys Hospital was of a quasi-domestic character and was not a performance in a "place of entertainment". *Duck v Bates* has consistently been recognised as a borderline case.

Greene LJ in *Jennings v Stephens*,[153] on the other hand, held that the question of whether a performance was "in public" should not be determined by looking at the relationship between the audience and the performers but by looking at the relationship between the audience and the copyright owner. The question was whether the audience was part of the copyright owner's public "because the wrong of infringement is defined by reference to the statutory rights of the owner".[154]

---

In such a case the reception of the unauthorised broadcast may be taken into account when assessing damages in actions for breach of the communication right.

148  (1995) 131 ALR 141 (FC); (1993) 118 ALR 684 (Gummow J).
149  (1993) 118 ALR 684 at 691.
150  [1936] 1 All ER 409.
151  [1936] 1 All ER 409 at 418.
152  (1884) 13 QBD 843.
153  [1936] 1 All ER 409.
154  [1936] 1 All ER 409 at 420.

The relationship between the two tests was explained by Lord Wheatley in *Performing Right Society Ltd v Rangers Football Club*:[155]

> What is the underlying reasoning behind the exclusion of domestic or quasi-domestic performances? It is to be found in the relationship between the audience and the owner of the copyright. In a situation where a person organises a private party in his own home, then it seems reasonable to assume that the unauthorised publication or use of the copyright work is not redounding to the financial disadvantage of the owner of copyright, since the selected audience is not enjoying the work under conditions in which they would normally pay for the privilege in one form or another.[156]

Both of the tests have been criticised. The first because it is said to be based on the logical fallacy that anything that is not domestic is therefore public. The second because of its circularity – whether the performance impacts on the proprietary right of the copyright owner depends on whether the performance is one to which the copyright owner has an exclusive right. At trial in *Australasian Performing Right Association Ltd v Commonwealth Bank of Australia*,[157] Gummow J considered these criticisms and sought to endorse the domestic-public test at the expense of the test of the copyright owner's public. That there is a difference between the two tests was demonstrated by that judge's approach to the broadcast right in *Australasian Performing Right Association Ltd v Telstra Corporation Ltd*[158] where he found that the private and confidential nature of a telephone conversation precluded the playing of music on hold from being a broadcast "to the public".[159] This finding was overturned on appeal to the High Court.

In the High Court, Dawson and Gaudron JJ, with whom Toohey and McHugh JJ agreed, noted the difference in wording between the right to perform a work "in public" and the right to broadcast "to the public". The right to broadcast to the public may be wider than the right to perform in public in so far as it "makes clear that the place where the relevant communication occurs is irrelevant".[160] In this case, however, nothing turned on the distinction. Rather, the High Court decision is important because it endorses the test of what constitutes the copyright owner's public. Although there remains an element of circularity in the test it at least has the advantage (over the domestic-public test) of being able to deal with changing technologies which have, over the years, tended to privatise and segment the public.

Thus, the radio cases found that the public need not be in the one place but may be constituted by having different people in different places, even when they may be individual different people in different places by themselves.[161] Despite the fact that a broadcast no longer constitutes a performance, this approach

---

155 [1975] RPC 626.
156 [1975] RPC 626 at 634.
157 (1992) 111 ALR 671 at 685.
158 (1993) 118 ALR 684.
159 (1993) 118 ALR 684 at 697.
160 *Telstra Corporation Ltd v Australasian Performing Right Association Ltd* (1997) 191 CLR 140.
161 *Chappell and Co v Associated Radio of Australia Ltd* [1925] VLR 350. This decision is to be preferred to the rather unfortunate Privy Council decision in *Mellor v Australian Broadcasting Commission* [1940] 2 All ER 20 which found that a radio broadcast constituted a performance in public by assuming that it would in some circumstances at least be heard by two or more people listening together.

was confirmed in *Rank Film Production Ltd v Dodds*,[162] which held that the transmission of videos into motel rooms constituted a performance in public, partly because of the public nature of the audience (any member of the public could stay at the motel) and partly because of the fact that the paying guests were part of the copyright owner's public (there was evidence that motels paid licence fees for the playing of videos). *Australasian Performing Right Association Ltd v Telstra Corporation Ltd*[163] extended this further by finding that playing music on hold to people in different places, in the privacy of their own homes and through the relatively confidential medium of the phone constituted a broadcast "to the public". We can expect changing technology to extend this definition even further to include more interactive situations where the work is chosen by the audience, for example, or encrypted for a limited portion of the public.

## The right to communicate to the public (ss 31, 85, 86, 87)

The right to communicate a work or other subject-matter to the public was introduced by the *Copyright Amendment (Digital Agenda) Act 2000*. Fortunately, the communication right is not quite as broad as it might seem. "Communicate" is defined in s 10 of the *Copyright Act 1968* as "make available online or electronically transmit (whether over a path, or a combination of paths, provided by a material substance or otherwise)".[164] It thus covers two distinct acts which can be distinguished on technical grounds. A transmission transfers data from one location to another. The making available right does not require that data be moved (although there is no reason why it should not move). If data is simply linked to the internet without being transferred from one location to another then it may, subject to the public requirements, be said to infringe the right to make the subject-matter available online but it would not constitute a transmission in electronic form. On the other hand, an email sent to a public mailing list would constitute a transmission but it should also constitute an infringement of the making available right.[165]

---

162  [1983] 2 NSWLR 553.

163  (1993) 118 ALR 684.

164  The communication right replaces and enlarges the previous exclusive rights to broadcast to the public and to transmit to subscribers of a diffusion service. The earlier rights had been criticised on a number of grounds. The broadcast and diffusion rights were technology specific. The broadcast right covered only wireless broadcasts made to the public (over the air television and radio broadcasts and broadcasts of on-hold music over mobile phones, for example, but not cable television). The diffusion right covered cable services but only if they were part of a subscriber service (cable television transmissions to subscribers and transmission of on-hold music over conventional phones, for example). There was no diffusion right attaching to sound recordings and broadcasts. Finally, the rights did not cover on-demand interactive services such as the internet.

165  The Explanatory Memorandum to the Copyright (Digital Agenda) Bill 2000 item 35 seems to assume that the transmission right covers non-interactive broadcast-like functions and that the making available right would cover on-demand interactive services. Such an assumption accords with previous discussion papers but the wording of the amendments does not appear to support such a limited interpretation. The *Copyright Reform and the Digital Agenda Discussion Paper*, July 1996, for example, gave linking a server containing copyright material to the World Wide Web and uploading copyright material to a www site as examples which might breach the making available right but the same discussion paper classified emailing an article as part of a commercial service as a breach of the transmission right but not of the making available right. (See Table 1 "Examples of How the Proposed New Rights would be Exercised in Practice" in the Discussion Paper.)

The communication must be "to the public". The discussion papers preceding the introduction of the new right recommended against codifying the test of "to the public" and both the discussion paper and the Explanatory Memorandum endorsed the copyright owner's public test from *Australasian Performing Right Association Ltd v Telstra Corporation Ltd*.[166] The amendments did make one important definitional change regarding the public, however. "To the public" is now defined in s 10 to mean to the public "within or outside Australia". Thus, even though it is only an infringement of copyright to do *in Australia*, or authorise the doing *in Australia*, of one of the exclusive rights of the copyright owner, this definition of "to the public" means that making a work available online to the public outside Australia would still constitute an infringement.

Section 22(6) provides that a communication other than a broadcast is taken to have been made by the person responsible for the content of the communication.[167] This is meant to exempt carriers and carriage service providers[168] from liability for infringement of the communication right.[169] As we have seen, carriers and carriage service providers are also protected from liability for authorising infringement under s 39B as to works and s 112E as to subject-matter other than works.

It is important to distinguish the right to communicate from the right to perform a work or other subject-matter. Neither the communication of copyright material nor the operation of reception equipment infringes the right to perform a work under s 31 (s 27(2)(3)) or the right to cause a film or sound recording to be seen or heard in public under ss 85 and 86. Once the subject-matter has been communicated, however, the performance rights under ss 31, 85 and 86 are infringed if the subject-matter is displayed or exhibited to the public (s 27(3)). Thus, it would be an infringement of the communication right to upload a sound recording online or to broadcast the sound recording from a radio station. It would not be an infringement of the performance right, however, to operate your computer or radio to hear the sound recording although it would be an infringement of the performance right to amplify it to be heard by the public. If you download the sound recording from the computer or tape it from the radio then, subject to any exemptions, you may have infringed the exclusive right to copy.

One question which has not been determined is when the communication right is exhausted. It could be argued that the making available right should be treated as analogous to the publication right and that the transmission right should be treated as analogous to the broadcasting and diffusion rights. In this case the making available right would be exhausted after a first making available whilst the transmission right would not be. There are strong arguments against such an interpretation. First, it is not very elegant to have the one communication right being exhausted at different times. Secondly, there is nothing in the legislative

166  (1993) 118 ALR 684.

167  Section 22(6A) provides that, to avoid doubt, a person is not responsible for determining the context of a communication merely because the person gains access to an online communication or receives the electronic transmission which constitutes the communication.

168  Under the *Copyright Act 1968* s 10 "carrier" and "carrier service provider" have the same meaning as they do under the *Telecommunications Act 1997*. Under the *Telecommunications Act* a carriage service is a service for carrying communications by means of guided and/or unguided electromagnetic energy (s 7) and a carrier service provider is defined, inter alia, as the supplier of a listed carrier service using a network owned by one or more owners of a carrier's licence (s 87).

169  Explanatory Memorandum to the Copyright (Digital Agenda) Bill 2000 item 26.

history to suggest that the making available right was meant to be limited in this way. Finally, the very size and pervasiveness of the internet presents policy reasons both for and against the exhaustion of the making available right. On the one hand, one might say that the internet is so large and covers so many potential publics that one act of making available should not exhaust the copyright owner's rights. The copyright owner should continue to have the right to determine when and how the work should be made available to all these different members of the public. On the other hand, one might say that the internet is so large, so open, so accessible, that once copyright subject-matter has been made available online then the copyright owner can no longer expect to control further acts of making available and the copyright owner's right to make it available should be taken to be exhausted.[170] As we have seen, in the *Napster* case for example, the courts have tended to treat the internet as simply one form of distribution and not as a fundamental challenge to the assumptions about the rights of the copyright owner. In this case, it is possible that the courts will not limit the make available right in this way.

## The right to make an adaptation of the work (s 31)

The adaptation right is the right to translate a literary, musical or dramatic work or a computer program.[171] The right does not apply to artistic works or to Part IV subject-matter. The right to adapt is not defined in the Act although s 10(1) defines an adaptation as:

- a translation of a literary work;
- a dramatic version of a non-dramatic literary work;
- a non-dramatic version of a dramatic literary work;
- a picture version of a literary work;
- in relation to computer programs, a version of the work (whether or not in the language, code or notation in which the work was originally expressed) not being a reproduction of the work;
- in relation to a musical work, an arrangement or transcription.

Although the word "version" is used in relation to dramatisations and computer programs, the Full Federal Court, in *Powerflex Services Pty Ltd v Data Access Corporation*,[172] held that within the context of the *Copyright Act 1968* "version" was intended to have only its narrow meaning of "translation". In *Coogi Australia Pty Ltd v Hysport International Pty Ltd*,[173] Drummond J explained the effect of this restricted interpretation:

> In ordinary usage, the term "version" is applicable to a wider range of renderings of the original literary work than is the term "translation": a version can apply to as literal as possible a rendering of the original into another language, as well as to a work in the same or another language that is only recognisable as related to the original because that

---

170  In many cases making subject-matter available also constitutes an infringement of the reproduction right and this difference may be moot. However, in some cases, such as linking a server to an internet site, there may be no reproduction.
171  *Powerflex Services Pty Ltd v Data Access Corporation* (1997) 37 IPR 436 at 457.
172  (1997) 37 IPR 436.
173  (1998) 157 ALR 247.

is the identifiable source of the theme of the version. The term "translation" has a much narrower reach. In ordinary speech, Piave's libretto in Italian for Verdi's opera "Macbeth" could fairly be called a version of Shakespeare's play; it could not, however, be properly described as a translation of the English original.[174]

In the *Data Access* case the respondent had carefully studied the Data Access program in order to ensure that the Powerflex program commands would perform the same function as Data Access's macro commands. The respondent, however, had written his own program to achieve this outcome. Even though there was some objective similarity between the Data Access and the Powerflex macros in source code the Full Court held that there had been no adaptation or translation of the Data Access program:

> In our view, the process of devising a source code to perform the same function as is performed in some other source code expressed in original language does not involve creating a version of the original source code.[175]

In relation to computer programs the Full Court held, and the High Court upheld,[176] that a version of a computer program could be produced either by the translation of a computer program from one language to another or by the compilation and decompilation of a computer program.

In *Coogi Australia Pty Ltd v Hysport International Pty Ltd*,[177] the respondent examined the applicant's knitted fabrics and produced a computer program to make a similar type of fabric. Although there was some incidental similarity between the original and the resulting computer programs, Drummond J declined to find that there had been an adaptation because the process of making the new program lacked the close connection with the original text required of a translation:

> Translation, as that term is ordinarily used, connotes more than conveying in different language the same idea expressed in another language. It describes a closer connection between the original and the translated text than that. I do not think an activity could be described in ordinary speech as a translation unless it involves the expenditure of effort on the original words or text to render them into words or text in a different language that conveys with precision the same meaning as that conveyed by the original.[178]

## The right to make a facsimile copy of a published edition of a work (s 88)

The published edition right was introduced in the *Copyright Act 1956* (UK) following the report of the Gregory Committee in 1952[179] which noted the ease with which editions of literary and musical works could be copied using photolithography and other means. The Committee also noted that once a work was out of copyright there was nothing to prevent a competitor copying a publisher's edition of the work. The United Kingdom Act was amended to provide limited protection for publishers against the reproduction by photographic or similar

174  (1998) 157 ALR 247 at 275-276.
175  (1997) 37 IPR 436 at 455.
176  *Powerflex Services Pty Ltd v Data Access Corporation* (1997) 37 IPR 436 at 454-455 (FC) and *Data Access Corporation v Powerflex Services Pty Ltd* (1999) 202 CLR 1 at 39 (HC).
177  (1998) 157 ALR 247.
178  (1998) 157 ALR 247 at 278.
179  United Kingdom Parliament, *Report of the Copyright Committee,* Cmd 8662, HMSO, London, 1952.

processes of the typographical arrangement of a published edition of a literary, dramatic or musical work. Thus, it is not an infringement of the copyright in a published edition to reproduce similar layout in another edition of the work – the right is restricted to copying the published edition by photographic means.

In Australia, the published edition right was introduced in the 1968 Act. Unlike the United Kingdom Act the protection is not restricted to the typographical arrangement. Like the United Kingdom Act, however, it provides only for a limited form of protection against the copying by photographic, or similar means, of a published edition.

In *Nationwide News Ltd v Copyright Agency Ltd*,[180] News Limited argued that the collecting agency CAL had authorised the infringement of published editions of News Limited's newspapers by entering into licence agreements with educational institutions for the photocopying of literary works including newspaper articles. The court accepted that copyright could subsist in the published edition of a newspaper or a magazine. It also found, in relation to the two articles under consideration, that they had been photocopied by the educational institution. However, the court found that the published edition copyright had not been infringed because the layout of the articles copied constituted an insubstantial part of the published edition as a whole.

The *Copyright Amendment (Digital Agenda) Act 2000* amended s 88 by substituting the right to make a "facsimile copy" of a published work for the previous right to make a "reproduction" of the work by means that include a photographic process. The amendment achieves its end of being more clearly technology neutral whilst still limiting the right to the right to copy rather than the broader right of reproduction.

## Commercial rental arrangements for sound recordings and computer programs (ss 31 and 85)

The TRIPS Agreement provided that authors of computer programs and films (Art 11) and producers of sound recordings and others having rights in a sound recording (Art 14) should be granted the right to authorise or prohibit the commercial rental of their copyright subject-matter. This was subject to a possible exemption. Member countries were not required to extend the protection to films unless the commercial rental of films was leading to widespread copying of films and the impairment of the rights of the copyright owner.

In Australia, under the *Copyright (World Trade Organization Amendments) Act 1994*, the commercial rental right was granted to the authors of computer programs (s 31), to producers of sound recordings (s 85) and to the authors of literary (other than computer programs), musical and dramatic works included in a sound recording (s 31). Australia did not extend the right to cover films and the rights do not cover sound recordings purchased before the amending Act came into force (s 85).

A commercial rental agreement is defined in s 30A and covers rentals made in the course of conducting a business for payment in money, kind or service. Lending arrangements by municipal libraries and friends, for example, are not covered.

---

180 (1996) 136 ALR 273.

Section 31(5) provides that the right does not extend to entry into a commercial rental arrangement if the computer program is not the "essential object of the rental". In *Australian Video Retailers Association Ltd v Warner Home Video Pty Ltd*,[181] the question arose as to whether the commercial rental of DVDs containing films could be said to be a commercial rental arrangement for a computer program. Relying on the narrow definition of computer program in *Data Access v Powerflex Services Pty Ltd*[182] as that language which causes a device to operate, Emmett J held that the computer program was not the essential object of the rental. He held that the computer program did not include the film itself but only those parts of the DVD which allowed the viewer to navigate the film and that, even though this power to navigate was an attractive feature for viewers, this was not the essential object of the rental – rather the film was the essential object of the rental. Emmett J, in other words, held that the phrase "essential object of the rental" referred to the subjective purpose of the rental, not to the objective subject matter being rented.[183]

## Indirect Infringement of the Copyright Owner's Rights

The *Copyright Act 1968* provides that it is an infringement of copyright if a person, without the licence of the copyright owner, imports for commercial dealing or commercially deals with articles which, if they were made in Australia, would constitute an infringement of copyright. It is also an infringement to allow a public place of entertainment to be used for an infringing performance of a work in public.

### Importing and dealing with infringing articles (ss 37 and 38 (works) and ss 102 and 103 (subject-matter other than works))[184]

Sections 37 (works) and 102 (other subject-matter) provide that it is an infringement of copyright for a person to import an article for the purpose of:

- selling, letting for hire, or offering by way of trade or exposing for sale or hire;
- distributing the article for purposes of trade or for any other purpose which will prejudicially affect the copyright owner; or
- exhibiting the article in public by way of trade,

without the licence of the copyright owner, if the importer knew or ought reasonably to have known that the making of the article would, if it had been made in Australia by the importer, have constituted an infringement of copyright.

Sections 38 (works) and 103 (other subject-matter) provide that it is an indirect infringement of copyright for a person to:

---

181  *Australian Video Retailers Association Ltd v Warner Home Video Pty Ltd* (2001) 53 IPR 242.
182  *Data Access v Powerflex Services Pty Ltd* (1999) 202 CLR 1.
183  *Australian Video Retailers Association Ltd v Warner Home Video Pty Ltd* (2001) 53 IPR 242 at 259-261.
184  Section 130A provides that in actions for infringement under ss 37, 38, 102 or 103 if the act involves an article which is a copy of a sound recording it is presumed that the sound recording is an infringing copy unless the defendant proves otherwise.

- sell, let for hire, by way of trade offer or expose for sale or hire an article; or
- by way of trade exhibit an article in public,

without the licence of the copyright owner if the person knew or ought reasonably have known that the making of an article constituted an infringement of copyright or, in the case of an imported article, would have constituted an infringement of copyright if the article had been made in Australia by the importer.

Although the provisions were introduced primarily to combat international trading in pirated copyright material they also cover unlicensed importation and dealing with lawfully made copyright material. Thus, if X on a shopping spree in Bali, were to buy cheap CDs from a local shop and import them into Australia for one of the prescribed purposes this would, prima facie, be an infringement even if the CDs were not pirate copies but lawfully made. There would be no infringement if X could establish that she had a licence from the copyright owner either express or implied but this licence must be positively given.

The requirement that the licence be positively given arises because there is no term implied by law in the sale of copyright material which allows the purchaser to import the article for commercial dealing. This may be contrasted with the purchase of a patented article where such a term will be implied as a matter of law and must be expressly limited by the owner of the patent.

The High Court explained the difference between copyright and patented material regarding this matter in *Interstate Parcel Express Co Pty Ltd v Time-Life International (Nederlands) BV*.[185] In that case Time Incorporated, an American company, owned the copyright in a number of cookery books and had granted an exclusive licence to Time-Life (a Netherlands company) to publish the books throughout the world, other than in North America. Interstate Parcels carried on business in Australia as Angus and Robertson Bookshops and wanted to sell the books. At the time, the Australian dollar was worth more than the American dollar and Interstate Parcels bought more than 16,000 of the books from an American book wholesaler rather than from the Australian wholesaler who carried them under agreement with Time-Life. The American book wholesaler had lawfully acquired legal copies of the book in the ordinary course of trade from the company which had an agreement with Time Incorporated to distribute the books to the United States book trade. There were no restrictions placed on either the distributor or wholesaler as to how and where the books might be sold and any such restriction may have been unlawful under United States law. Interstate Parcels imported the books for sale in Australia and sold them retail for less than they would have been able to buy them wholesale in Australia.

Interstate Parcels, relying on case law relating to patents,[186] argued that in so far as the books were lawful copies sold in the ordinary course of trade, without any restrictions imposed on their use, there was a licence implied by law given by Time Incorporated to buyers and anyone claiming title through such buyers, to use the books however and wherever they pleased and that this included importing

---

185  (1977) 138 CLR 534.
186  *Betts v Willmott* (1871) LR 6 Ch App 239; *Societe Anonyme des Manufactures de Glaces v Tilghman's Patent Sand Blast Co* (1883) 25 Ch D 1; *National Phonograph Co of Australia Ltd v Menck* (1911) 12 CLR 15; *Anilin und Soda Fabrik v Isler* [1906] 1 Ch 605.

the books and selling them in Australia. The High Court rejected the argument and distinguished the case of copyright from that of patented inventions.

In the case of patents the rights of the patentee include the monopoly rights to "make, use, exercise and vend" the patented invention. Unless a licence to use or sell the invention were implied, the sale of a patented invention would be "quite futile"[187] because the buyer would be unable to exercise any of the rights normally associated with a chattel owner. As both a matter of business efficacy and a matter of law, it was therefore necessary to imply a licence to use and sell the invention, although this implied licence could be displaced. The High Court noted that the exclusive rights of the copyright owner did not extend so far and, therefore, there was no requirement of law to imply a licence for sale or importation of the copyright subject-matter.

In the absence of a licence implied by law it may be possible to argue that a licence may be implied in the contract in order to give the agreement business efficacy. This argument had been relied on by Interstate Parcels in the first instance. On appeal, the High Court noted that the existence of the exclusive agreement between Time-Life and Time Incorporated told against such an implication.

In implying a licence to import or deal with the copyright material the cases have highlighted a number of factors. Unlike patents, the *mere absence of a restriction* on the dealing with copyright material does not imply a licence to import and deal with copyright subject-matter. The existence of exclusive distribution agreements with another party (*Interstate Parcel Express Co Pty Ltd v Time-Life International (Nederlands) BV*)[188] or with the defendant (*Lorenzo and Sons Pty Ltd v Roland Corporation*)[189] may prevent the implication of a licence. Evidence that different spelling or formats have been published for different markets may indicate the lack of a licence (*Interstate Parcel Express Co Pty Ltd v Time-Life International (Nederlands) BV*)[190] just as the fact that sound equipment bought in Hong Kong was not wired for Australia was evidence of a lack of a licence to import the accompanying manuals into Australia (*Lorenzo and Sons v Roland Corporation*). The licence required by ss 37 and 102 is a licence to import and deal with the article for one of the specified purposes (*Computermate Products (Aust) Pty Ltd v Ozi-Soft Pty Ltd*).[191] The licence may be given for specified transactions by particular parties or to the world "at large" (*Computermate Products (Aust) Pty Ltd v Ozi-Soft Pty Ltd*).[192]

Liability under the importing and dealing sections is limited by the requirement that the importer must know or ought reasonably to have known that the making of the article would, if it had been made in Australia by the importer, have constituted an infringement of copyright. Courts have commented that this is an unusual provision in so far as it determines liability for importation by reference to something that the importer had no intention of doing and in fact, never did – that is, making the article in Australia. In *Raben Footwear Pty*

---

187  *Interstate Parcel Express Co Pty Ltd v Time-Life International (Nederlands) BV* (1977) 138 CLR 534, Gibbs J at 542.
188  (1977) 138 CLR 534.
189  (1992) 23 IPR 376.
190  (1977) 138 CLR 534.
191  (1988) 83 ALR 492 at 495.
192  (1988) 83 ALR 492 at 495.

*Ltd v Polygram Records Inc*,[193] the appellant importers argued that the defence could be made out if they could show that they had no knowledge of an exclusive licence to manufacture the relevant CDs in Australia which they would have infringed had they themselves made the CDs in Australia. The respondents supported a strict liability interpretation whereby the importer's knowledge that the licence to import did not grant a right to make the articles in Australia was sufficient to establish the necessary knowledge. The court took a middle road and held that the importer's knowledge regarding the licence to import was not conclusive of the question but might be taken into account in assessing it.

The licence must be given by the "copyright owner" but there is no owner of the copyright in the right to import copyright subject-matter and the question of who is the copyright owner for the purpose of this indirect infringement has not been authoritatively determined by the courts. Where there is only one copyright owner there is no problem. In *Time-Life*, for example, the court was not concerned with the agreement between the wholesaler and Interstate Parcels but with the non-existent agreement between Time Incorporated and Interstate Parcels. In the New Zealand case of *J Albert and Sons Pty Ltd v Fletcher Construction Co Ltd*,[194] on the other hand, the plaintiffs owned the right to reproduce certain musical works in New Zealand but the Australasian Performing Right Association (APRA) was the owner of the right to transmit the record to a subscriber service. The plaintiff imported a Musak tape to transmit lawfully to a subscriber service and the plaintiffs sued for indirect breach under the equivalent New Zealand legislation. APRA was not joined as a party to the proceedings. The parties agreed that the plaintiff was the owner from whom the licence to import was required and the court heard no argument on the matter.

The decision in *Time-Life* effectively foreclosed the practice of parallel importing – that is the importation of lawful copyright material for sale in Australia – without the licence of the copyright owner and thereby indirectly maintained the territorial distribution and publishing agreements common in the publishing industry. Such agreements have been subject to intense criticism by consumer groups and amendments have since been made to the *Copyright Act 1968* to limit the effect of the decision by allowing importation of books, sound recordings and computer programs in certain limited circumstances. These provisions are considered in Chapter 5, "Balancing the Interests".

## Permitting a place of public entertainment to be used for the performance of a work (s 39)

The copyright in a literary, dramatic or musical work is infringed by a person who permits a place of public entertainment to be used for the performance in public of a work where the performance would constitute an infringing act. The section does not apply if the person establishes that he or she was not aware, and had no reasonable grounds for suspecting that the performance would be an infringement of copyright or if permission to use the place was given gratuitously or for

---

193  (1997) 145 ALR 1.
194  [1974] 2 NZLR 107.

a nominal or cost only fee (s 39). The permission must be for the performance of the actual infringing work rather than for the performance of works generally.[195]

Although the High Court in *University of New South Wales v Moorhouse*[196] held that "authorise" has the same meaning as "permit", early cases drew a distinction between "permitting" a place to be used for an infringing performance and "authorising" an infringing performance. Thus, in *Australasian Performing Right Association and J Leist v J Turner and Sons*[197] the owner of a hall was held not to have authorised an infringing performance because he had not "given formal approval to" or "sanctioned, approved or countenanced" the performance.[198] On the other hand, he was held to have given permission for the use of the hall for the infringing performance on the basis that he had been notified that the performance would be an infringing performance but had nevertheless gone ahead with the letting, arguing that he was "entitled to disregard anything told to him" by APRA. He had done nothing to prevent or hinder the performance of the works.[199] In this case the New South Wales Supreme Court held that he should have broken the contract in order to avoid liability.

Subsequent cases have taken a less severe line regarding the breaking of a contract for the letting of a place of public entertainment and the courts seem to look poorly on copyright owners relying on lessors to enforce their rights. In *Corporation of the City of Adelaide v Australasian Performing Right Association Ltd*,[200] a majority in the High Court held that the Adelaide Corporation, which had entered into a contract for letting a public space for the "performance of a vocal concert", did not have to break the contract upon being advised that the concert would involve an infringing performance. This was so even though the agreement gave the Town Clerk power to cancel as he saw fit. Higgins J endorsed the statement of the lower court which said that "mere indifference or omission cannot be treated as 'permission' unless the Corporation had the power to permit the performance, and unless there was some duty to interfere".[201] The duty to interfere must be reasonable and Higgins J held that it was not reasonable to expect the Corporation to "smash the lease".[202] Gavan Duffy and Starke JJ noted that the clause in question did not give the Corporation any control over JC Williamson Ltd, the performer or the songs sung and concluded:

> The power to prevent that which a man can legally prevent may be evidence of his consent to its coming into, or continuing in, existence; but no inference of consent should be drawn against one who having no legal right remains quiescent and declines to alter his legal relations in order to acquire such a right.[203]

---

195  *Performing Right Society v Ciryl Theatrical Syndicate* [1924] 1 KB 1 at 15.
196  (1975) 133 CLR 1 at 12.
197  (1927) 27 SR (NSW) 344.
198  (1927) 27 SR (NSW) 344 at 348.
199  (1927) 27 SR (NSW) 344 at 349.
200  (1928) 40 CLR 481.
201  (1928) 40 CLR 481 at 498.
202  (1928) 40 CLR 481 at 499. Compare the modern case *Australasian Performing Right Association v Metro on George Pty Ltd* (2004) 210 ALR 244 regarding contracting and authorisation.
203  (1928) 40 CLR 481 at 505.

To this extent the s 39 cases on permission may be distinguished from the covenant cases such as *Atkin v Rose*[204] where a failure to take legal action to prevent a breach of covenant was held to constitute a permission to breach.

## Other Civil Actions

The *Copyright Act 1968* provides four main actions in relation to unlawful copyright dealings.[205] These are actions for infringement (s 115), actions in conversion or detinue (s 116), actions in relation to circumvention devices and electronic rights management (Part V, Div 2A, Subdivs A and B) and actions in relation to broadcast decoding devices (Part VAA, Div 2, Subdivs A, B and C).

Whilst most copyright dealings are conducted amicably outside of the court room, the threat of legal proceedings can act as a powerful tool to force others to enter into negotiation or to refrain from their planned course of action. If wrongly used such threats can turn copyright dealings into mere bluff and bullying. For this reason s 202 of the Act provides that a person may take an action against any other person who by way of "circulars, advertisements or otherwise" threatens to take action against the first person for infringement of copyright, for detinue or conversion. In similar patent legislation the term, "circulars, advertisements or otherwise", has been held to include a letter to a prospective customer of the alleged infringer even though that letter was written in response to a direct inquiry by the potential customer.[206]

The court is empowered to grant a declaration that the threats were unjustifiable, an injunction against their continuance and damages unless the court is satisfied that the action in relation to which the threat was issued would constitute an infringement. Mere notification that copyright exists does not constitute a threat and an act done by a solicitor or barrister in his or her professional capacity does not render them liable under s 202.[207] It is common in s 202 for the defendant to make a counterclaim in respect of the alleged infringement or other action.

Section 202A provides a similar ground for threats of legal proceedings in relation to technological protection measures.

## Actions in conversion and detinue

Under the common law, conversion is an intentional unlawful dealing with chattels in a manner inconsistent with the owner's actual or constructive right of possession. Detinue is the wrongful detention of goods after a lawful request for their return. In actions for conversion or detinue the owner may request the delivery up of the goods or their value. Under s 116 the owner of the copyright in a work or other subject-matter may bring an action for conversion or detention in

---

204 [1923] 1 Ch 522.

205 The statutory limitation period is six years with respect to infringements under the 1968 Act (s 134). For transitional provisions regarding the limitation period, see s 230.

206 *Skinner v Perry* [1893] 10 RPC 1; *C and P Development Co (London) Ltd v Sisabro Novelty Co Ltd* (1953) 70 RPC 277.

207 See the trial judge's decision in *SW Hart and Co Pty Ltd v Edwards Hot Water Systems* (1980) 30 ALR 657.

relation to an "infringing copy" or a device used or intended to be used for making infringing copies. The action is based on the legal fiction that the copyright owner is the owner of the infringing copy from the time it is made or of the device from the time it was used or intended to be used to make an infringing device.

An infringing copy is defined in s 10 as, inter alia, a reproduction or copy of the copyright material. The conversion therefore does not relate to the copyright as a chose in action but to the chattel, at least in so far as the chattel is a reproduction or copy of the copyright material. If the copyright material forms only part of the chattel and can be severed from it, an order for delivery up of that part only may be made or damages may be calculated as a percentage of the value of the chattel.[208]

The action has formed part of copyright law at least since 1842 and has been constantly criticised as potentially oppressive in so far as the infringing copies may have a much greater value than the copyright itself, considered as a chose in action.[209] As Lord Scarman remarked obiter in *Infabrics Ltd v Jaytex Ltd*:

> And what if the infringing copy is engraved on a silver chalice or a gold medallion? The language of the subsection is, I think, clear: it bestows on the owner of the copyright the rights and remedies to which at common law an owner of goods is entitled for conversion. It treats the owner of the copyright as if he were the owner of the infringing copies. Since at common law the damages of conversion are ordinarily measured by reference to the value of the goods converted, I would not think it legitimate to construe the section otherwise, though the result will be injustice in some cases.[210]

Because the action under the *Copyright Act 1968* relates to the infringing copy rather than the copyright material it follows that manufacture does not constitute a conversion because the object of the conversion did not exist before its manufacture.[211] Under the common law mere damage to the goods does not constitute a dealing inconsistent with the owner's right of possession.[212] Failure to return the goods after a lawful request is, however, a conversion. In the case of manufacture or mere possession of infringing articles the copyright owner is therefore advised to first bring an action for detinue and then seek conversion damages.

## Actions in relation to technological protection measures, electronic rights management and broadcast decoding devices

The *Copyright Act 1968* Part V (Actions in Relation to Circumvention Devices and Electronic Rights Management Information) and Part VAA (Broadcast Decoding Devices) were first introduced as part of the digital agenda reform in 2001 in order to meet Australia's obligations under the WIPO *Copyright Treaty* and the WIPO *Performances and Phonograms Treaty*. They were extensively amended by the *Copyright Amendment Act 2006* to meet Australia's obligations under Art 17.4.7(a)(i) of the US-Australia Free Trade Agreement, to clarify the limits of the actions and put in place certain exemptions.

---

208  *Blackie and Sons Ltd v Lothian Book Publishing Company Pty Ltd* (1921) 29 CLR 396.
209  See *Autodesk Inc v Yee* (1996) 139 ALR 735 for a discussion of these criticisms.
210  *Infabrics Ltd v Jaytex Ltd* [1982] AC 1 at 26. The action has been abolished in the United Kingdom.
211  *Caxton Publishing Co Ltd v Sutherland Publishing Co Ltd* [1939] AC 178.
212  *Penfolds Wines Pty Ltd v Elliot* (1946) 74 CLR 204.

They provide private civil actions and criminal offences in relation to the circumvention of technological protection measures, electronic rights management information and unauthorised access to encoded broadcasts.

### Technological protection measures

There are three civil actions in relation to technological protection measures (TPMs). The owner or exclusive licensee may take an action against any person who circumvents an access control technological protection measure (s 116AN); or who manufactures a circumvention device for a technological protection measure (s 116AO); or who provides a circumvention service for a technological protection measure (s 116AP). In addition, anyone who does any of these acts may be liable for an offence (Part V, Div 5, Subdiv E, ss 132APA-132APE).

These have proved to be contentious provisions and the disagreements regarding technological protection measures go to the heart of copyright law and copyright wars. Besides the battle between those who design technical barriers and those who seek to circumvent them, there are broader policy debates regarding the responsibility of copyright owners to protect their material rather than simply relying on infringement proceedings and criminal actions; the extent to which the use of TPMs may lead to geographic market segmentation and anti-competitive conduct; and the extent to which TPMs interfere with the statutory balance of interests between copyright owners and users by preventing otherwise lawful access to copyright material.

A technological protection measure is defined in s 10(1) as a device, product, technology or component (including a computer program), which in the normal course of its operation prevents, inhibits or restricts the doing of an act comprised in the copyright, or is an access TPM. An access control TPM is defined as a device, product, technology or component that in the normal course of its operation controls access to the work or other subject-matter. A device, product, technology or component is said to control access if it requires the application of information or a process to gain access to the subject-matter.[213] TPMs do not include devices or other measures which prevent non-infringing copies of computer programs or games or films being played on machines acquired in different parts of the world or which limit the use of other goods and services in a machine which incorporates a computer program.

A circumvention service or device is defined as a service or device which is promoted, advertised or marketed as having the purpose or ability to circumvent a TPM; has no other or only limited other commercially significant purpose; or is primarily or solely designed to produce or facilitate the circumvention of the TPM (s 10(1)). Neither s 116AO nor s 116AP applies if the device is only a circumvention device because it was promoted, advertised and marketed as having the necessary purpose where this advertising etc was not done by the person who is being sued or under the direction or at the request of that person.[214]

---

213 See definitions of "access control technological protection measure" and "technological protection measure" and "controls access" in s 10(1). An access control TPM is defined as a device, product, technology or component that in the normal course of its operation controls access to the work or other subject-matter. A device, product, technology or component is said to control access if it requires the application of information or a process to gain access to the subject-matter.

214 These are defences to the actions and the onus is on the defendant to establish the defence.

These provisions seek to achieve a balance in relation to the policy issues referred to above in three ways. First, the definition of TPM only applies to protection measures which "prevent, inhibit or restrict" an infringing act. Therefore, an access code in a Sony computer game which could not be read by CD burners and therefore did not appear in an infringing copy (which therefore could not be played on a Sony PlayStation) was held not to be a TPM in *Stevens v Kabushiki Kaisha Sony Computers Entertainment*.[215] As the High Court noted, this protection measure only prevented access after the infringing act had taken place.

Second, the definition as amended in 2006, explicitly excludes geographical access codes and measures designed to limit the use of machines to particular products. Thus, it would not be an offence to circumvent an access code which prevented a person from playing a computer game on an Australian machine if that game had been lawfully obtained in the United States. Similarly, it would not be an offence to circumvent a protection measure which sought to prevent the playing of an Apple product on a PC. (This, of course, is subject to the general law of copyright infringement and does not allow reproduction of the computer program unless it fits into one of the defences considered in the next chapter.)

The third balancing provision is that the three actions (and their mirror offences) are subject to a number of important exceptions. In a civil action therefore, a person is not liable if the action was done to facilitate interoperability (ss 116AN(3), 116AO(3), 116AP(3)); to enable encryption research (ss 116AN(4), 116AO(4), 116AP(4)); to allow computer security testing (ss 116AN(5), 116AO(5), 116AP(5)); or if it is for the purposes of law enforcement and national security (ss 116AN(7), 116AO(6), 116AP(6)). In addition, s 116AN (relating to use of a circumvention device for an access TPM) is further limited by exemptions which allow a person to identify and disable "an undisclosed capability to collect or disseminate personally identifying information about the online activities of a natural person" (s 116AN(6)); non-profit libraries and archives to make acquisition decisions (s 116AN(8)); and a person to do a prescribed act (s 116AN(9)). The prescribed acts are set out in Sch 10A to the *Copyright Regulations 1969* and include the reproduction of computer programs to make interoperable products; the reproduction and communication of copyright material by educational and other institutions assisting people with disabilities; the reproduction and communication of copyright material by libraries, archives and cultural institutions for certain purposes; the inclusion of sound recordings in broadcasts and the reproduction of sound recordings for broadcasting purposes; and access in the case of a malfunctioning TPM.[216] The onus is on the defendant to establish the defence (ss 116AN(10), 116AO(7) and 116AP(7)).

In actions relating to TPMs the court may grant an injunction and either an account of profits or damages, and an order that the circumvention device be destroyed or otherwise dealt with. In assessing damages the court may award additional damages having regard to the flagrancy of the breach, the need to deter similar acts, the conduct of the defendant, the benefit accruing to the defendant, and any other relevant matters (s 116AQ).

---

215 (2005) 224 CLR 193.
216 Section 249(2) places certain limitations on the Governor-General's ability to make regulations in respect of TPMs in accordance with Australia's obligations under the US-Australia Free Trade Agreement and a review must be held in respect of prescribed acts at least once every four years.

## Electronic rights management information

Under s 116B the copyright owner may take action against a person who removes or alters electronic rights management information (RMI) from copy material without the permission of the copyright owner or exclusive licensee and the person knew or ought reasonably to have known that the removal or alteration would induce, enable, facilitate or conceal an infringement of copyright in the material. An action also lies against any person who imports, communicates or distributes copyright material to the public where the RMI has been removed or altered if the person knew that the RMI had been removed or altered without the permission of the copyright owner or exclusive licensee and the person knew or ought reasonably to have known that the importation, communication or distribution would induce, enable, facilitate or conceal an infringement of copyright (ss 116C and 116CA).

In actions relating to RMI the court may grant an injunction and either an account of profits or damages. In assessing damages the court may award additional damages having regard to the flagrancy of the breach, the benefit accruing to the defendant, and any other relevant matters (s 116D).

## Unauthorised access to encoded broadcasts

Part VAA contains four civil actions relating to unauthorised access to encoded broadcasts and a number of mirror offences. The actions relate to making or dealing with an unauthorised decoder (s 135AOA); making a decoder available online (s 135AOB); causing unauthorised access to an encoded broadcast (s 135AOC); and unauthorised commercial use of a subscription broadcast (s 135AOD).

An encoded broadcast is defined as a subscription broadcast or an encrypted broadcast (other than a subscription or radio broadcast) delivered by a commercial broadcasting service or national broadcasting service within the meaning of the *Broadcasting Services Act 1992* (Cth).

Under s 135AOA a channel provider or any person with an interest in the copyright in an encoded broadcast or its content may bring an action against a person who makes an unauthorised decoder or sells, hires, trades with the intention of making a commercial advantage; exhibits in public by way of trade or with the intention of making a commercial advantage; exposes for sale; distributes; imports (for the purposes of selling, trading, distributing); or who makes an unauthorised decoder available online. This only applies if the extent of the above dealing will prejudicially affect a channel provider or anyone with an interest in the copyright in the broadcast or its content. The person must know or ought reasonably to know that the unauthorised decoder will be used to gain access to an encoded broadcast without the permission of the broadcaster but this will be presumed unless the defendant proves otherwise.

Section 135AOB provides an action against a person who makes an authorised decoding device for a subscription broadcast available online to an extent that will prejudicially affect certain parties. Again, there is a presumption that the person had the relevant knowledge in the action. Section 135AOC provides an action against a person who allows unauthorised access to an encoded broadcast and s 135AOD provides an action against a person who uses a subscription broadcast (or the sounds or images from the broadcast) by way of trade or with the intention of obtaining a commercial advantage or profit. In each of these cases an "affected party" may take action and the affected party is defined as a person with an interest in the copyright in the relevant broadcast; or the content of the broadcast; or a relevant channel provider.

In actions under this Division the court may grant an injunction and either an account of profits or damages, and an order that the circumvention device be destroyed or otherwise dealt with. In assessing damages the court may award additional damages having regard to the flagrancy of the breach, the need to deter similar acts, the benefit accruing to the defendant, and any other relevant matters (s 135AOE). The court may also order that the decoder to be destroyed or otherwise dealt with (s 135AOF).

## Offences

One of the important amendments introduced by the *Copyright Amendment (Digital Agenda) Act 2000* and the *Copyright Amendment Act 2006* was the introduction of new offences relating to circumvention devices, broadcast decoding devices and electronic rights management information (RMI) in s 132(5B)-(5F)). The amendments were made in order to meet the requirement under the WIPO *Copyright Treaty* and the WIPO *Performance and Phonograms Treaty* to provide adequate legal protection and effective legal remedies and to meet Australia's obligation under the US-Australia Free Trade Agreement.

The offences relate to the provision of, commercial dealing in, and importation of, circumvention devices and broadcast decoding devices but there is no offence relating to using such devices. The offences prohibit the alteration and removal of RMI and dealing with articles where the RMI has been altered or removed. RMI is the information one usually sees on videos and computer programs regarding ownership of copyright and conditions for the use of the copyright material. The offences and civil actions only relate to RMI which is electronically attached to the copyright material.

Many of the offences in the table below are drafted to include an indictable, a summary and a strict liability version of the offence with different penalties associated with each. Under s 132AK an indictable offence is classified as an "aggravated offence" if it involves converting copyright subject-matter from analogue to digital or other electronic machine-readable form.

| | |
|---|---|
| s 132AC | Commercial scale infringement prejudicing copyright owner. |
| s 132AD | Making infringing copy commercially. |
| s 132AE | Selling or hiring out infringing copy. |
| s 132AF | Offering infringing copy for sale or hire. |
| s 132AG | Exhibiting infringing copy in public commercially. |
| s 132AH | Importing infringing copy commercially. |
| s 132AI | Distributing infringing copy. |
| s 132AJ | Possessing infringing copy for commerce. |
| s 132AL | Making or possessing device for making infringing copy. |
| s 132AM | Advertising supply of infringing copy. |
| s 132AN | Causing work to be performed publicly. |
| s 132AO | Causing recording or film to be heard or seen in public. |

| | |
|---|---|
| s 132APC | Circumventing an access control technological protection measure. |
| s 132APD | Manufacturing etc a circumvention device for a technological protection measure. |
| s 132APE | Providing etc a circumvention service for a technological protection measure. |
| s 132AQ | Removing or altering electronic rights management information. |
| s 132AR | Distributing, importing or communicating copies after removal or alteration of electronic rights management information. |
| s 132AS | Distributing or importing electronic rights management information. |
| s 135ASA | Making unauthorised decoder. |
| s 135ASB | Selling or hiring unauthorised decoder. |
| s 135ASC | Offering unauthorised decoder for sale or hire. |
| s 135ASD | Commercially exhibiting unauthorised decoder in public. |
| s 135ASE | Importing unauthorised decoder commercially. |
| s 135ASF | Distributing unauthorised decoder. |
| s 135ASG | Making unauthorised decoder available online. |
| s 135ASH | Making decoder available online for subscription broadcast. |
| s 135ASI | Unauthorised access to subscription broadcast etc. |
| s 135ASJ | Causing unauthorised access to encoded broadcast etc. |
| ss 135L; 135ZY; 135ZZP | Offences relating to inspection of records. |
| s 135ZZQ | Offence relating to identity cards of a collecting society. |
| s 172 | Offences by witnesses before Tribunal. |
| s 173 | Offences relating to Tribunal. |
| ss 203A; 203D; 203E; 203F; 203G | Offences relating to activities by libraries and archives. |
| s 47A | Offence relating to retention of records by print disability radio licensees. |
| s 126B | Offence relating to chain of ownership documents. |

## Private International Law

Copyright, as we have seen, is territorial. Only acts committed in Australia constitute an infringement of copyright under the *Copyright Act 1968*. The principle of territoriality is not affected by the principle of national treatment which, through legislative provision, protects foreign authors and works made in foreign jurisdictions in so far as they are breached by an act done in Australia. In each of these cases Australian courts assume jurisdiction in the matter.

If the act which constitutes an infringement of copyright subject-matter is committed outside Australia, for example, by the unauthorised screening of an Australian film in a number of different countries, different rules apply. Under private international law, copyright and patents are classified as "immovable" property and Australian courts have determined that they have no jurisdiction to hear and determine such matters.[217] The Australian copyright owner, therefore, cannot bring proceedings in Australia in respect of these infringements and must bring individual actions in each of the different jurisdictions. In each jurisdiction, the protection afforded to the copyright owner is determined in accordance with the principles of national treatment and the law of that jurisdiction.[218]

---

217 *Potter v BHP* (1906) 3 CLR 479 and *Norbert Steinhardt and Son Ltd v Meth* (1961) 105 CLR 440 regarding patents. For copyright cases, see United Kingdom decision *Tyburn Productions Ltd v Conan Doyle* (1990) 19 IPR 455 and the New Zealand High Court decision of *Atkinson Footwear Ltd v Hodgskin International Services Ltd* (1994) 31 IPR 186.

218 See WIPO Background Paper, *WIPO Forum on Private International Law and Intellectual Property*, WIPO/PIL/ 01/9, Geneva, January 2001.

# CASES

## *Blackie and Sons v Lothian Book Publishing Company Pty Ltd*
High Court of Australia: Starke J
(1921) 29 CLR 396

This case illustrates the way in which courts approach the question of substantiality and reproduction where the authors use common sources.

**Starke J: [397]** The plaintiff, Blackie & Sons Ltd, is a well-known English publishing company, and the defendant, the Lothian Book Publishing Co Proprietary Ltd, is an Australian publishing company. The plaintiff published a number of Shakespeare's dramatic works under the name of "The Warwick Shakespeare." One of the works so published was the historical play called "The Life of King Henry the Fifth." It was prepared for the plaintiff by Dr GC Moore Smith, Professor of English Language and Literature in the University of Sheffield, and was first published in the United Kingdom on 26th December 1895. The defendant also published a number of Shakespeare's works, under the name of "The Australasian Shakespeare." One of the works so published by the defendant was also the historical play "The Life of King Henry the Fifth." It was prepared for the defendant by Mr J Le Gay Brereton, BA, who, at the time of its preparation, was the librarian of the Fisher Library in the University of Sydney, and afterwards became Professor of English Literature in that University. This work was first published in Australia in the year 1918. ...

[399] The question whether the defendant has infringed that copyright is more difficult in the circumstances of this case.

During the trial particulars were delivered of the passages in the defendant's book which the plaintiff asserted were copied from the plaintiff's book. These particulars are to be found partly in a copy of the defendant's book underlined in red ink, and partly in a copy of the plaintiff's book marked with a pencil circle in the margin. It is, of course, clear that the plaintiff has not acquired the right to the materials which were common sources of information or the work of other authors. The defendant was free to use common materials as well as Professor Moore Smith and the work of authors other than Professor Moore Smith without infringing the plaintiff's copyright. The question is whether the defendant's book or any substantial part thereof was copied from the plaintiff's book, or whether it was the result of independent labour and research and a resort to sources of information that were open to all or from works other than the plaintiff's book? "It is not sufficient," as Mr Justice *Story* said in *Emerson v Davies*,[219] "to show, that it" (the defendant's book) "may have been suggested by" the plaintiff's book, "or that some parts and pages of it have resemblances" to the plaintiff's book. "It must be further shown, that the resemblances in those parts and pages are so close, so full, so uniform, so striking, as fairly to lead to the conclusion" that the one was copied from the other in whole or in a substantial part. In the editor's note to the defendant's edition of Henry the Fifth Professor Brereton says that in its preparation he has made full use [400] of the labours of his predecessors, and was indebted particularly to the edition of Henry the Fifth by Porter and Clarke (1st fol ed), Moore Smith (Warwick edition) and Verity (Pitt Press), and had constantly referred to standard works of reference. The plaintiff relied upon this statement and the resemblances to its book which are to be found in the defendant's book, but it adduced no further evidence. Unfortunately Professor Brereton has long since destroyed his manuscript notes, which might perhaps have afforded some help in

---

[219] 3 Story, at p 787.

solving the question of fact here involved, and unfortunately also his memory as to the precise sources of his notes and comments is far from clear. But Professor Brereton is a scholar of repute and well acquainted with Shakespearian literature. And I have no doubt, and find as a fact, that the defendant's book was the result of some independent knowledge and considerable labour, research and skill on the part of Professor Brereton. Apart from his oath on the subject, which I accept, there is internal evidence in Professor Brereton's book that in its preparation he resorted to the sources of information open to all and to the works of other authors just in the same manner as did Professor Moore Smith. [His Honour referred to a few instances of this internal evidence.] Nevertheless, without attributing the *animus furandi* to Professor Brereton, it is still possible, owing to ignorance of the copyright law or carelessness, that he has made more use of the plaintiff's book than can be justified. This has led me to a detailed examination of the two books and a consideration of the various works which Professor Brereton in his evidence stated that he had consulted. And for the purpose of this examination I took it to be clear that, as to literary works, the object of the Copyright Act is not to accord protection to ideas but to the particular form of expression in which an author conveys his ideas or information to the world. (See *Hollinrake v Truswell*;[220] *University of London Press Ltd v University Tutorial Press Ltd*;[221] *Copinger on Copyright*, 5th ed, p 2.) It may be that Professor Brereton derived some of his ideas from Professor Moore Smith, but, as Mr *Dixon* very properly said, it was legitimate for Professor Brereton in preparing his edition to acquaint himself with the views of scholars, including Professor **[401]** Moore Smith, and to allow those views to influence him in annotating his edition of Henry the Fifth. It would be unreasonable in this judgment to deal specifically with every passage in the defendant's book which has been challenged, though I have considered each of them. And I can do justice to the parties by indicating in general terms my findings in point of fact. The plan and arrangement of the defendant's book was not copied from the plaintiff's book. It is a common form (see Deighton's and Verity's editions of Henry the Fifth), but it was really adopted from the plan pursued by Professor Wallace, the general editor of "The Australasian Shakespeare," in his annotated edition of Twelfth Night, which was the first of the series of Shakespeare's plays published by the defendant. The text of the play was not copied from the plaintiff's book. It is founded on the first folio edition, and was an independent selection by Professor Brereton. Parts of the general introduction to the defendant's book are taken from the plaintiff's book under a colourable disguise, but the rest of the introduction was gathered from various sources. The part that was taken commences with the words "The source from which Shakespeare drew the historical material for his play" on page VIII of the defendant's book and ends with the words "They have sealed their own doom" on page XII. I do not say that Professor Brereton was not to some extent assisted by his own knowledge and by other sources of information in this part of the introduction, but the internal evidence satisfies me that the defendant's illustrations of Shakespeare's divergence or deviation from history were taken from the plaintiff's book. Mr Boswell Stone, in his edition of Henry the Fifth, had no doubt collected all the illustrations mentioned by Professor Brereton, and Mr Verity has noted some with acknowledgment to Mr Stone, but the plaintiff's book and not these authors was the source from which Professor Brereton took his illustrations and developed this part of his introduction. [His Honour in an appendix set forth the resemblances which led him to the conclusion already stated.] The introductory comments to Act I, Scene I, beginning with the words "This scene" and ending with the words "charm of his eloquence" are also taken under colourable disguise from the plaintiff's book. The arrangement of the note, the use of the words **[402]** "main theme" for "main action," "many sided genius" for

---

[220] [1894] 3 Ch 420, at p 424.
[221] [1916] 2 Ch, 601, at p 608.

"genius," "charm of his eloquence" for "his charm of speech," and the identical words "moral reformation" are coincidences which the fact that both authors were giving a short summary of the same scene does not explain. The appendices A, B and C and the glossary in the defendant's book were not copied from the plaintiff's book. I am satisfied that Professor Brereton resorted in the main for his glossary to Schmidt's Lexicon, to the Shakespearian glossary by Mr Onians and to the new English Dictionary edited by Sir James Murray. I ought, perhaps, to note the word "gross" in the defendant's glossary. There is an erroneous reference to line 106 which also appears in the plaintiff's book. The reference was probably taken from the plaintiff's book, and much stress was placed upon the fact. It is an isolated instance, and trivial in itself. The notes upon the text remain for consideration. Here the resemblances between the plaintiff's and the defendant's books are certainly remarkable. Some of these resemblances arise from the nature of the case, namely, the fact that two-scholarly men were expounding the meaning of some word or passage in simple language for the use of students. I am convinced, however, that the great bulk of these resemblances arise from the fact that Professors Moore Smith and Brereton resorted to many of the same authorities, though it must be mentioned, in passing, that Professor Brereton had also the advantage of Mr Verity's annotated edition of Henry the Fifth, which was not published when Professor Moore Smith prepared his book. Still, Professor Brereton did take either verbatim or under colourable disguise some notes from the plaintiff's book. The internal evidence of some of the notes satisfies me of this fact. [In an appendix his Honour set out these cases side by side.] As to the rest of the notes I find that they were not taken from the plaintiff's book.

Ought I on these facts to hold that the defendant has infringed the plaintiff's right? Has the defendant, to use the words of the statute, reproduced a substantial part of the plaintiff's book (see *Chatterton v Cave*;[222] *Leslie v Young & Sons*);[223] or, as *Page Wood* V-C said in *Jarrold v Houlston*,[224] has an unfair or undue use been made **[403]** of the work protected by copyright? The question is, in truth, one of fact and not of law: "it is a question of degree, which must depend upon the circumstances of each particular case" (*Sweet v Benning*,[225] per *Jervis* CJ; *Chatterton v Cave*[226]). *Moffatt & Paige Ltd v Gill*[227] was much relied upon for the plaintiff, but the decision affords but little assistance in the present case. The facts in the two cases are quite dissimilar. It is undoubted that the books in question here are in direct competition for use in schools and for students in the Universities of Australia, and were intended so to be. The choice of Professors in Australian Universities as editors of the defendant's series of Shakespeare's plays was well calculated to assist the defendant in that competition. Even the remuneration of Professor Brereton depends upon the successful sale of the book prepared by him. In these circumstances it was the special duty of the defendant and its editor to avoid the appropriation of the labour and research of its rivals. The defendant did, in my opinion, appropriate a substantial and valuable portion of the plaintiff's general introduction to its book. It is true, but nothing to the point, to say that the information could have been derived from other sources. A considerable amount of labour and independent research was thus saved, and a useful and interesting addition was made to the general introduction of the defendant's book. The notes cannot be considered apart from the introductory comments for the purposes of infringement. The quantity of notes taken is not very considerable, and, taken by themselves, these notes are not, in my opinion, of any outstanding value.

---

[222] 3 App Cas, 483.
[223] [1894] AC, at p 341.
[224] 3 K & J, 708 at p 714.
[225] 16 CB, 459, at p 481.
[226] 3 App Cas, 483.
[227] 86 LT, 465.

From about 110 pages of notes the defendant has taken about 50 separate notes. The notes in the defendant's book cover about 89 pages. The material and sometimes the very note taken from the plaintiff is intermixed with material the result of Professor Brereton's own knowledge or of independent labour and research on his part. In some cases in the notes acknowledgment is made to Professor Moore Smith, but this is the exception and not the rule. The defendant's book is by no means a "servile imitation" of the plaintiff's work, and is largely a "compilation from other common or independent sources" ...

[404] Giving, however, the fullest consideration to all these facts, the appropriation by the defendant of the plaintiff's labour and research is, I find, on the whole, substantial and material, and beyond what was a fair and legitimate use of the plaintiff's book in all the circumstances of the case. The extracts were made, I do not doubt, for the purpose of enhancing the value of the defendant's book, and I see no reason for saying that the defendant did not achieve its purpose. Further, these extracts saved the defendant and its editor some labour and research.

It is not for the Court to make the way of the taker of copyright matter easy. It is a sound principle of copyright law that the Court should not allow one man to take away the result "of another man's labour, or, in other words, his property," unless it is satisfied that the part taken is "so slight, and the effect upon the total composition was so small," "as to render the taking perfectly immaterial," or, what is much the same thing, that the part taken is an unsubstantial part (*Hogg v Scott*;[228] *Chatterton v Cave*[229]).

## *TCN Channel Nine Pty Limited v Network Ten Pty Limited (No 2)*
### Federal Court of Australia: Sundberg, Finkelstein and Hely JJ
### [2005] FCAFC 53

Channel Ten broadcast segments of Channel Nine programs on Ten's info-tainment program "The Panel". After an appeal to the High Court regarding the interpretation of the term "broadcast" the matter was referred back to the Full Federal Court to determine whether the segments taken were substantial. The case is important for its consideration of substantiality in relation to Part IV subject-matter.

> **Finkelstein J (with whom Sundberg J agreed):** 28. It is now clear that the starting point for any enquiry into substantiality (of a broadcast copyright) is not, as the judge would have it, "primarily quantitative". Nor is the principal enquiry whether harm has been caused to the plaintiff's commercial interests. The first thing that must be done is to look at the part taken, compare it with the copyright work and ask whether it is possible to conclude from that comparison whether that part is a "substantial part" of the plaintiff's programme. The question will often boil down to one of the following (dependent on the type of programme): Does what has been taken amount to "essentially the heart" of the copyrighted work?: *New Era Publications International, ApS Carol Publishing Group* 904 F 2d 152, 158 (2nd Circ, 1987). Is what has been taken "the essential part of the copyright work?": *Cable / Home Communications Corporation v Network Productions, Inc* (902) F 2d 829, 844 (11th Circ, 1990). Is what has been taken "at least an important ingredient" of the copyright work?: *Salinger v Random House* 881 F 2d 90, 99 (2nd Circ, 1987). Have the best scenes been taken from the programme?: *Hi-Tech Video Productions Inc v Capitol Cities / ABC* 804 F Supp 950, 956 (WD Mich, 1992). Are the excerpts "highlights" from the programme?: *New Boston Television Inc v Entertainment*

---

[228] LR 18 Eq, 444, at p 458.
[229] 3 App Cas, at pp 490, 495.

*Sports Programming Network Inc* 215 US PQ 755, 757 (D Mass, 1981). Are the excerpts central to the programme in which it appeared?: *Roy Expert Company Establishment of Vaduz Liechtenstein, Black Inc v Columbia Broadcasting System Inc* 503 F Supp 1137, 1145 (2nd Circ, 1980). Does the portion used "constitute the 'heart' – the most valuable and pertinent portion – of the copyright material?": *Los Angeles News Service v CBS Broadcasting, Inc* 305 F 3d 924, 940 (9th Circ, 2002).

29. If what has been taken does not meet any of those descriptions that will often be the end of the enquiry. There will, however, be borderline cases where an enquiry based on a visual comparison will not yield a result. Take as an example a programme that has no "core" or "heart". Here I have in mind two cinematograph films by the 1960s icon Andy Warhol. The films are "Sleep" and "Empire", films that few people have seen. "Sleep" has been described as "one of the most famous of unseen films": F Camper, "The Lover's Gaze", *Chicago Reader Movie Review*, section 1, 28 April, 2000. It is a six-hour (some say longer) film taken by a stationary 16 mm camera of a man sleeping. The reviewer Jonas Mekas writing in the *Village Voice* (September, 1963) queried whether the film was: "An exercise in hypnosis? Test of patience? A Zen joke?" *Empire* is a single shot from late dusk to early morning of the Empire State Building taken from the 44th floor of the Time-Life Building. Mr Koch described *Empire* as "the most profoundly mute motion picture ever filmed": S Koch, *Stargazer: Andy Warhol's World and His Films* (2nd ed, M Boyars, New York, 1985) at 60. The film has no plot and only two things happen. The sun moves through the sky and, at dusk, floodlights are turned on to illuminate the upper floors of the Empire State Building. If part of "Sleep" or "Empire" is taken, no amount of visual comparison would enable a tribunal to determine whether that part is a substantial part of the film. It would be necessary to consider factors such as the plaintiff's financial interest as well as the defendant's purpose to resolve the issue.

30. There is one other aspect of the judge's test for substantiality which, with respect, I think is wrong. It is the judge's acceptance of Ten's submission that "matters of technical significance ... to the broadcast may also be relevant". According to the judge (at 273) those matters encompass the "technical considerations associated with the infrastructure of production". If by accepting Ten's submission the judge meant that it is either necessary or permissible to enquire into the means by which a programme is created and broadcast then in my view he is in error. It cannot make any difference to the test of substantiality if, say, there is a live broadcast of a sporting event using several television cameras and microphones near the scene that send their signals to a control room where they are combined and then transmitted to television sets or whether the broadcast is of a video recording of the event. At any rate "matters of technical significance" is not the interest protected by the copyright.

31. The final thing that remains to be done is to apply the correct test to the extracts taken from Nine's programmes. Here I will not repeat the description of the programmes; the programmes have been sufficiently described in previous judgments. I will provide enough of a description so that the reasons for reaching my conclusions will be understood. For that purpose I will in large measure paraphrase Nine's description of the programmes for it appears to be accepted by Ten that those descriptions are reasonably accurate.

32. Ten infringed Nine's copyright in the television broadcast when it broadcast the following extracts.

33. The Inaugural Allan Border Medal Dinner: Ten copied 10 seconds of the programme. The programme centred upon the dinner and presentation of the inaugural Allan Border Medal for the Australian cricket player of the year. The extract was of Glen McGrath's reaction to the announcement that he was the winner of the award, his displayed emotion and the congratulations from his surrounding team mates. The cameras were trained on the winner to capture that moment. The cameras then followed Mr McGrath as he moved towards the stage. The excerpt was plainly a material and

important part of the programme. The evidence of Mr Burns was that the announcement of Glen McGrath as the Australian cricketer of the year was "the highlight of the dinner".

34. Midday (Prime Minister singing Happy Birthday): Ten copied 17 seconds of the programme. The presence of the Prime Minister on the Midday show was a key part of that day's programme. The footage of the Prime Minister singing Happy Birthday to Australian cricketing legend, Sir Donald Bradman, was a key and memorable feature. One of the panellists, Mr Gleisner, said the footage should be included in the Midday's shows "best of" special.

35. Wide World of Sports (Grand Final Celebration/Glen Lazarus cartwheel): Ten copied eight seconds of the programme. The footage of the Glen Lazarus cartwheel was, on any view, a "highlight". Mr Lazarus was a prop (affectionately known as "the brick with eyes"). He was playing his very last game of rugby league and was able to celebrate it with a win in the 1999 grand final.

36. Australia's Most Wanted (re-enactment of stabbing by party gatecrashers): Ten copied 26 seconds of the programme. "Australia's Most Wanted" is a programme directed at unsolved crimes and seeking public assistance in relation to particular crimes that are the subject of re-enactments on the programme. The re-enactment was of a gang of youths who gatecrashed a party. The gatecrashers intimidate the innocent partygoers. The gatecrashers then force entry into the house and one of them stabs a young man. The intimidation and break-in sequence coupled with the climactic stabbing scene is very dramatic and clearly central to the programme in which it appeared.

37. Pick Your Face (Keri-Anne Kennerley): Ten copied 20 seconds of the programme. This programme is a game show for children. The identification by contestants of the faces they have assembled is an important part of the show. One of the Panel members, Mr Gleisner described the excerpt of the child who wrongly identified Keri-Anne Kennerley (from faces shown on a board) as a "little highlight".

38. The Today Show (child yawning): Ten copied nine seconds of the programme. The footage rebroadcast involved part of an interview by Richard Wilkins with Alex Breden, and his mother. Alex was a child celebrity who featured on the HBA health insurance advertisements. The extract showed Alex yawning while being interviewed. It is a memorable part of the interview.

39. There has been no infringement by taking extracts from the following programmes: A Current Affair (brothel masquerading as introduction agency); The Today Show (Boris Yeltsin); The Crocodile Hunter (scuba diving); The Today Show (Prasad interview); and Nightline (Kevin Gosper interview). In each case the extracts were very short, but as I have previously said quantity does not dictate the answer. I have found that these extracts have not infringed Nine's copyright because the extracts were insignificant (de minimis is another description) in the context of Nine's programme (or, if it be relevant, the segment of the programme from which they were taken). Moreover, as the judge pointed out, the taking of these extracts caused absolutely no injury to Nine's interests.

**Hely J: Substantiality**

47. The term 'substantial' is imprecise and ambiguous. It takes its meaning from the context. Ten submits that in the present context, 'substantial' is a reference to taking 'the substance of' the source television broadcast. That submission pays insufficient regard to the statutory language, which is expressed in terms of '**a** substantial **part**' of a television broadcast, which is a different thing. There may be many parts of a television broadcast which qualify as a substantial part of that broadcast.

48. Both parties accepted that in determining whether a substantial part of a copyright work or other subject matter is taken, the relevant comparison is between the part taken and the copyright work or subject matter: see *Auto Desk Inc v Dyson (No 2)* (1993) 176 CLR 300 ('*Auto Desk (No 2)*') at 305. The issue is not the importance of the part taken

to the defendant's product: *Designer Guild Ltd v Russell Williams (Textiles) Ltd* [2001] 1 All ER 700 at 709 ...

### Individual Consideration of the Panel segments

62. It remains for me to consider whether individual Panel Segments represent a substantial part of the source programmes. Subject to the foregoing discussion, this is largely a matter of impression as the text of 'substantial part' under the Act imparts criteria of 'fact and degree': 78 ALJR 585 at [100] (Kirby J). As is apparent from the table set out above, quantitatively each of the Panel Segments is but a small proportion of the source programme.

63. Nonetheless, in my opinion, three of the Panel Segments are a substantial part of the television broadcast from which they have been taken. The first is 'Midday' (Prime Minister singing). Programmes such as 'Midday' which extend over a significant period of time are often punctuated by highlights. The footage of the Prime Minister singing Happy Birthday to Australia's cricketing legend, Sir Donald Bradman, is one such highlight. The re-broadcast of this potent footage provided entertainment in its own right, apart altogether from any additional contribution made by members of the panel.

64. The second is 'Australia's Most Wanted' (Aria Award). The footage taken is part of a re-enactment of an unsolved stabbing that had taken place at a residential home. The crux of the re-enactment is the intimidation of the innocent partygoers and the forcible entry into the home culminating in the stabbing, all of which are shown on the footage taken. The footage shown is highly dramatic, and reproduces the essence of the original story, rather than something which is merely incidental to the originating broadcast. The fact that the Panel used the footage as the foundation for a humorous assertion that the boys dancing in another piece of footage shown were the same gang that stabbed the partygoer does not negate substantiality.

65. The third is 'Pick Your Face' (Kerri-Anne Kennerley). Pick Your Face is a game show for children, in which child contestants are asked to identify a celebrity from a partial picture. The particular portion shown in the Panel Segment is a child mistakenly identifying a partial picture as depicting Ms Kerri-Anne Kennerley. In my opinion, the Panel Segment provided a substantial part of the entertainment value of the programme from which it is taken, and the footage re-broadcast is funny in its own right. The member of the Panel who introduced the footage, Mr Gleisner, described the excerpt as a 'little highlight' from the programme.

66. In my opinion, the following Panel Segments are not a substantial part of the source programme:

- 'A Current Affair' (Masquerade of Introduction Agency): the original programme is an exposé of questionable business practices conducted by an introduction agency. The Panel Segment relates to disguises worn by alleged victims of the introduction agency who were interviewed during the programme. The Panel Segment strings together disconnected parts of the source broadcast, without conveying anything of significance in relation to the original story. The extracts are trivial, inconsequential or insignificant in the context of the source broadcast.

- 'The Inaugural Allan Border Medal Dinner' (Prime Minister embarrassed): this Panel Segment takes a portion of a live Nine broadcast during which a number of awards are presented. The particular segment re-broadcast shows the passage of the winner of the inaugural Allan Border medal, Mr Glen McGrath, from his seat to the stage. The Panel re-broadcast 10 seconds of a source work that was 2 hours 11 minutes 44 seconds in length. The portion taken does not include any critical moments or highlights of the original broadcast such as Mr McGrath receiving the award or giving his acceptance speech. The material used by the

Panel is only incidental to the source broadcast, and the part taken is trivial, inconsequential or insignificant in terms of the source broadcast.

- 'The Today Show' (Boris Yeltsin): this Panel Segment takes a portion of the Today Show, a Nine program that presents a series of magazine-style segments. The particular portion taken is footage of successive Russian Prime Ministers who had been dismissed by President Boris Yeltsin. The footage taken is incidental to the source broadcast and is trivial, inconsequential or insignificant in terms of that broadcast.

- 'Wide World of Sports' (Grand Final celebrations): this Panel Segment takes a portion of Nine's live broadcast of the National Rugby League grand final. The particular portion taken features one of the players, Mr Glen Lazarus, performing a cartwheel as part of the post-match celebrations. He was not the only player to do so, and the footage taken does not show that there were other players following suit doing cartwheels of their own. The part taken is fleeting in character, and is not in any sense a highlight of the broadcast. Even if it be accepted that the original broadcast had as its subject matter both the grand final itself as well as the post-match presentations, the footage taken was only incidental to the source broadcast, and was trivial, inconsequential or insignificant in terms of that broadcast.

- 'The Today Show' (Child yawning): this Panel Segment takes another portion of the Today Show. The particular part taken is nine seconds in length during which a child is shown yawning in an interview with the presenter, Mr Richard Wilkins. The part taken is fleeting in nature and on the periphery of the original broadcast, making little, if any, contribution to the subject matter of that broadcast. The footage taken is only incidental to the source broadcast, and is trivial, inconsequential or insignificant in terms of that broadcast.

- 'Crocodile Hunter' (Scuba diving): this Panel Segment takes a portion of a show featuring Mr Steve Irwin, who is promoted by Nine as the 'Crocodile Hunter'. During the programme Mr Irwin is filmed in various marine environments, and the show climaxes with him swimming in the open ocean with sharks. The particular portion shown in the Panel Segment depicts Mr Irwin in a large tank in which various marine creatures are swimming. The dialogue during the footage is Mr Irwin's description of a wobbegong shark that is also in the picture. The Panel Segment is humorous, but there was nothing funny about the original broadcast. The footage taken is used in an entirely different context from the original broadcast, and in that broadcast it is trivial, inconsequential or insignificant.

- 'The Today Show' (Prasad interview): the part taken is from an interview with the manager of a hostel for homeless people, in which a number of homeless people can be seen gesticulating in the background. The source broadcast is a human interest story. The Panel's focus is on matters which are no more than background in the source broadcast, and barely noticeable. Again, the footage taken is trivial, inconsequential or insignificant in terms of the source broadcast.

- 'Nightline' (Kevin Gosper interview): Nightline is a late night news and current affairs programme broadcast by Nine. The particular part taken shows Mr Kevin Gosper, an Australian Vice President of the International Olympic Committee, expressing relief at being cleared of all corruption allegations. The part taken is fleeting in nature, and so taken out of context that it does not give the impression of a reproduction of a material part of the original story. Again, the footage taken is trivial, inconsequential or insignificant in terms of the source broadcast.

## *Cooper v Universal Music Australia Pty Ltd*
### Full Federal Court of Australia: French, Branson and Kenny JJ
### [2006] FCAFC 187

In this extract the Federal Court takes into account the factors set out in ss 36(1A) and 101(1A) to determine that Cooper, the owner and operator of the MP3s4FREE website (which included hyperlinks to music stored on remote websites), had authorised copyright infringement. The extract also considers the application of the ss 39B and 112E "safe harbour" provisions for any person (including a carrier or carriage service provider) who provides facilities for making or facilitating the making of a communication.

### Branson J: Did Mr Cooper Authorize?

28. The issue of whether Mr Cooper authorized internet users in Australia to copy, and operators of remote websites to communicate to the public, music files constituting sound recordings in which the Record Companies hold copyright must be determined primarily by reference to s 101(1A) of the Act (see [15] above). The appropriate starting point is to have regard to the matters identified in pars (a)-(c) of s 101(1A).

### Power to Prevent (s 101(1A)(a))

29. Mr Cooper submitted that he did not have any power to prevent the doing of the acts comprised in the copyright of the sound recordings in issue because he did not have power to prevent:

    (a)  a person from making an MP3 file from a sound recording in another format (eg from a compact disc);

    (b)  a person from making an MP3 file generally accessible over the internet; and

    (c)  a person from accessing an MP3 file that another person had made generally accessible over the internet.

30. The above submission appears to overlook that the copyright in a sound recording is infringed each time that it is copied without proper authority. The making of a particular unauthorized copy is no less an infringement of the owner's copyright because other unauthorized copies are also made or are likely to be made.

31. Additionally, Mr Cooper submitted that to facilitate copying or communication is not to authorize it. He placed reliance on observations made by Lord Templeman in *CBS Songs Ltd v Amstrad Consumer Electronics plc* [1988] AC 1013 and by Sackville J, with whom Jenkinson and Burchett JJ agreed, in *Nationwide News Pty Ltd v Copyright Agency Limited* (1996) 65 FCR 399 at 422. His Honour there observed that:

> 'a person does not authorise an infringement merely because he or she knows that another person might infringe the copyright and takes no step to prevent the infringement.'

For the reasons given below (see in particular [37] and [43]) I conclude that Mr Cooper did not merely facilitate the infringements of copyright upon which the case of the Record Companies relied. He engaged in additional relevant conduct so as to take himself outside the purview of his Honour's observation.

32. Before considering the extent (if any) of Mr Cooper's power to prevent the copying or communication to the public of sound recordings in which the Record Companies hold copyright, it is necessary to determine what is meant by *'power to prevent'* in s 101(1A)(a). The appellants contended, in effect, that unless Mr Cooper had power, at the time of the making of an infringing copy of a sound recording, to prevent that copy being made, he had no power to prevent within the meaning of s 101(1A)(a). Unless s 112E of the Act, which is set out in paragraph [16] above, were enacted simply out of an abundance of caution, it presupposes that a person who merely provides facilities

for making a communication might, absent the section, be taken to have authorized an infringement of copyright in an audio visual item effected by use of the facility. This presupposition is inconsistent with the submission of the appellants. However, in my view, it is consistent with the ordinary understanding of authorization. The following hypothetical situation may be considered. One person has a vial which contains active and highly infectious micro-organisms which are ordinarily passed from human to human by the coughing of an infected person. He or she authorizes another person to break the vial in a crowded room knowing that this will result in some people in the room becoming infected with the micro-organisms. Most people would, I think, regard the first person as having authorized the infection not only of those in the room, but also the wider group thereafter directly infected by them, notwithstanding that he or she had no power to prevent those who were in the room from coughing.

33. In determining what is meant by '*power to prevent*' in s 101(1A)(a) it is appropriate then to turn to relevant authorities concerning authorization in the context of copyright law, and in particular, to the Australian authorities as it is these to which the legislature may be presumed to have given particular attention when enacting s 101(1A)(a).

34. In *University of New South Wales v Moorhouse* (1975) 133 CLR 1 the High Court unanimously held that the University had infringed Mr Moorhouse's copyright in a book of short stories by authorizing the making of an infringing copy of one of the stories. The relevant circumstances were that a copy of Mr Moorhouse's book was held on open shelves in the University's library and the University placed a coin-operated photocopier in that library. Jacobs J, with whom McTiernan ACJ agreed, identified at 21 the real question to be determined as whether there was in the circumstances an invitation to be implied that the person who made the infringing copy might, in common with other users of the library, make such use of the photocopying facilities as he thought fit. His Honour found that such an invitation was to be implied. He concluded that it was immaterial that the library was not open to all comers, that use of the photocopier was not intended to generate a profit to the University and that the University did not know that users of the photocopier were doing acts comprised in authors' copyrights – and may even have been entitled to assume that users would obey the law of copyright.

35. In a separate judgment Gibbs J, after noting at 12 that a person cannot be said to authorize an infringement of copyright unless he or she has some power to prevent it, said at 13 that:

'a person who has under his control the means by which an infringement of copyright may be committed – such as a photocopying machine – and who makes it available to other persons, knowing, or having reason to suspect, that it is likely to be used for the purpose of committing an infringement, and omitting to take reasonable steps to limit its use to legitimate purposes, would authorize any infringement that resulted from its use.'

36. It seems to me that both Jacobs and Gibbs JJ concentrated on the behaviour of the University in making the photocopier available for use in the library rather than on the issue of the University's capacity to control the use of the photocopier once it had been made available to library users. The observation of Gibbs J that a person cannot be said to authorize an infringement unless he or she has some power to prevent it must be understood in this context. That is, the relevant power which the University had to prevent the copyright infringement must be understood to have been, or at least to have included, the power not to allow a coin-operated photocopier in the library.

37. Some support for this understanding of *Moorhouse* can be found in *Australian Tape Manufacturers Association Ltd v Commonwealth* (1993) 176 CLR 480. In that case at 498 Mason CJ and Brennan, Deane and Gaudron JJ identified a distinction between the mere sale of an article, such as a blank tape or a video recorder, where there is a likelihood that the article will be used for an infringing purpose and the circumstances

of *Moorhouse*. Their Honours noted that in *Moorhouse* the University not only failed to take steps to prevent infringement; it provided potential infringers with both the copyright material and the means by which it could be copied.

38. Some, albeit limited, support for understanding the reference in s 101(1A)(a) to *'the person's power to prevent the doing of the act concerned'* to include the person's power to avoid the means of infringement becoming available for use can, in my view, be found in *Australasian Performing Right Association Limited v Jain*. In that case the Full Court, which concluded that Mr Jain had authorized the infringement of copyright in question, said at 61:

'The judgment of the members of the High Court in the Moorhouse case establishes that one of the meanings of the word "authorize" in the context in which it is here used is "countenance". It may be that not every act which amounts to the countenancing of something is an authorisation. Every case will depend upon its own facts. Matters of degree are involved. But the evidence in the present case reveals … a studied and deliberate course of action in which Mr Jain decided to ignore the appellant's rights and to allow a situation to develop and to continue in which he must have known that it was likely that the appellant's music would be played without any licence from it.'

39. Additionally, as mentioned in [32] above, the introduction of s 112E into the Act suggests that, absent that section, a mere provider of facilities for making communications could have been held to have authorized copyright infringements effected by the use of those facilities. I do not accept, as Mr Cooper contended, that s 112E was introduced into the Act simply out of an abundance of caution. The supplementary explanatory memorandum for the Copyright Amendment (Digital Agenda) Bill indicates otherwise by stating that the new s 112E:

'has the effect of expressly limiting the authorisation liability of persons who provide facilities for the making of, or facilitating the making of, communications.'

40. Mr Cooper placed considerable weight on a suggested analogy between his website and Google. Two things may be said in this regard. First, Mr Cooper's assumption that Google's activities in Australia do not result in infringements of the Act is untested. *Perfect 10 Inc v Google Inc* 416 F Supp 2d 828 (CD Cal 2006) upon which Mr Cooper placed reliance is a decision under the law of the United States of America which includes the doctrine of 'fair use'. Secondly, Google is a general purpose search engine rather than a website designed to facilitate the downloading of music files. The suggested analogy is unhelpful in the context of Mr Cooper's appeal.

41. I therefore reject the contention that unless Mr Cooper had power, at the time of the doing of each relevant act comprised in a copyright subsisting by virtue of the Act, to prevent its being done, he had no relevant power within the meaning of s 101(1A)(a). I conclude that, within the meaning of the paragraph, a person's power to prevent the doing of an act comprised in a copyright includes the person's power not to facilitate the doing of that act by, for example, making available to the public a technical capacity calculated to lead to the doing of that act. The evidence leads to the inexorable inference that it was the deliberate choice of Mr Cooper to establish and maintain his website in a form which did not give him the power immediately to prevent, or immediately to restrict, internet users from using links on his website to access remote websites for the purpose of copying sound recordings in which copyright subsisted.

42. I conclude that, within the meaning of s 101(1A)(a), Mr Cooper had power to prevent the copying in Australia of copyright sound recordings via his website. He had that power because he was responsible for creating and maintaining his MP3s4FREE website. As stated above, the principal content of the website comprised links to other websites and files contained on other servers. Senior counsel for Mr Cooper conceded that, in effect, the overwhelming majority of the files listed on the website were the subject

of copyright. The website was structured so that when a user clicked on a link to a specific music file a copy of that file was transmitted directly to the user's computer.

43. It is immaterial, in my view, that Mr Cooper's website operated automatically in the sense that, although he could edit links on the site, he did not control the usual way in which links were added to the site. The evidence also leads to the inexorable inference that it was the deliberate choice of Mr Cooper to establish his website in a way which allowed the automatic addition of hyperlinks.

44. I also conclude that, within the meaning of s 101(1A)(a), Mr Cooper had power to prevent the communication of copyright sound recordings to the public in Australia via his website. Again he had that power because he was responsible for creating and maintaining his MP3s4FREE website with the characteristics referred to above.

45. For the above reasons, I find that, within the meaning of s 101(1A)(a), the extent of Mr Cooper's power to prevent copyright infringements via his website was considerable.

### Nature of Relationship (s 101(1A)(b))

46. Mr Cooper submitted that he did not have any relationship with people who made MP3 files generally accessible over the internet or with people who downloaded such files from remote websites via hyperlinks on his website. The findings of the primary judge do not suggest any relationship between Mr Cooper and those who made MP3 files generally accessible over the internet. However, the same cannot be said of his Honour's findings concerning those who downloaded music files via Mr Cooper's website.

47. An aspect of the nature of the relationship existing between Mr Cooper and those users of the internet who obtained copyright sound recordings from the internet via his website is that the users were attracted to Mr Cooper's website and obtained the sound recordings by clicking on hyperlinks on that website. The primary judge found that Mr Cooper's website was user friendly and allowed internet users readily to select from a variety of catalogues of popular sound recordings.

48. His Honour also found that Mr Cooper benefited financially from sponsorship and advertisements on the website; that is, that the relationship between Mr Cooper and the users of his website had a commercial aspect. Mr Cooper's benefits from advertising and sponsorship may be assumed to have been related to the actual or expected exposure of the website to internet users. As a consequence Mr Cooper had a commercial interest in attracting users to his website for the purpose of copying digital music files.

### Other Reasonable Steps Including Compliance with Industry Codes of Practice (s 101(1a)(c))

49. Mr Cooper did not suggest, other than by reference to disclaimers on his website, that he took any reasonable steps to avoid the infringements of copyright. As those disclaimers misstated Australian copyright law in a material way, the inclusion of them on the website did not constitute a reasonable step to prevent or avoid the infringement of copyright. In any event, I would have attributed little, if any, weight to them as, on his Honour's findings, their intended purpose was merely cosmetic.

50. The reasons for judgment of the primary judge make no reference to any relevant industry codes. It appears that the parties agreed at trial that there were no relevant industry codes to which his Honour could have regard.

51. I conclude that Mr Cooper did not establish that he took any reasonable steps to prevent or avoid the use of his website for copying copyright sound recordings or for communicating such recordings to the public.

### Mr Cooper Authorized

52. Having taken into account the matters identified above, and the name of his website, I conclude that Mr Cooper infringed the Record Companies' respective copyrights in sound recordings by in Australia authorizing internet users to do acts comprised in those copyrights, namely make copies of the sound recordings. I also conclude that Mr Cooper

infringed the Record Companies' respective copyright in sound recordings by authorizing operators of remote websites to communicate those sound recordings to the public in Australia.

## *Frank M Winstone (Merchants) Ltd v Plix Products Ltd*
### Court of Appeal of New Zealand: Cooke, Richardson and Somers JJ
### (1985) 5 IPR 156

The respondent's kiwi fruit tray was adopted by the kiwi fruit marketing authority as a standard. The appellant engaged a designer to produce a tray by referring to the authority's written specifications and verbal instructions from the appellants. The resulting tray was held to be a reproduction of the respondent's copyright in drawings of the tray even though the copying had been indirect and through a different medium.

### Cooke J: [160] Indirect copying

Describing this as the threshold question, Mr Smellie contended that the Judge was wrong in holding that indirect copying can be perpetrated through the medium of a verbal description of the copyright work. In developing his argument in this Court counsel modified the argument that he had presented in the High Court on this topic by adopting a suggestion in a recently published (1984) work on *Intellectual Property* by Staniforth Ricketson, paras 9.30 and 9.31. The suggestion is made in the interests of manufacturers or traders who, the author says, often unknowingly use intermediate versions of copyright works. It is suggested that there should be no infringement if the medium worked from was generically different from the copyright work. As we understand Mr Smellie, he invites us to see the verbal Specifications and Instructions in this case as generically different from the drawings, patterns, moulds and packs in which he acknowledges copyright to subsist.

Mr Smellie argues that copyright has already been taken beyond the intention of the framers of the original legislation and that to treat indirect copying as an infringement in a case like the present would be a further extension and of a kind which should only be made by Parliament. Mr Crew retorts that the suggested limitation is inconsistent with basic principle and would amount to an infringer's charter.

Two decisions of the English Court of Appeal were the subject of particular discussion in argument. In *Solar Thomson Engineering Co Ltd v Barton* [1977] RPC 537 it was held – we do not think that the passage was obiter, but that does not matter for our purposes – that instructions given by the defendant to his designer afforded a sufficient causal link to give the designer's version of a rubber ring the quality of an indirect reproduction of a sectional drawing of the plaintiff's ring. Buckley LJ's judgment that this was a breach of the plaintiff's copyright was applied here by Prichard J and Mr Smellie accepts that it did afford the Judge considerable support. He argued, however, as Mr Ricketson does in his book that *Solar Thomson* is inconsistent with the earlier decision in *Purefoy Engineering Co Ltd v Sykes Boxall & Co Ltd* (1955) 72 RPC 89.

In *Purefoy* the plaintiff and the defendant made similar standard parts to be used by customers in the manufacture of jigs. In making and offering for sale such parts the defendant did not infringe the plaintiff's copyright. Each party issued a catalogue illustrating its range of products. The question, so far as the case is relevant to the present argument, was whether the defendant's catalogue could be treated as an indirect copy of the plaintiff's catalogue and hence as infringing the copyright in that **[161]** catalogue. It was held not. That decision seems readily understandable. The defendant's catalogue was in no sense derived from that of the plaintiff, for the latter merely followed the making of and described the plaintiff's range of parts. The parts were not made from the catalogue.

The case is distinguishable from the present on that point; what is more important is that as a general proposition the concept of indirect copying is accepted in the judgment of Sir Raymond Evershed MR.

There can be no doubt that in principle a reproduction may be the result of indirect copying. We see no sound reason for introducing a generic limitation; and in this and other cases it could be most difficult to apply. The question must always be whether the work alleged to be an infringement can fairly be said to be a reproduction of the copyright work or of a substantial part of that work. If words alone enable a drawing to be reproduced, it seems to us that copyright in the drawing is infringed. It would be dangerous to hold otherwise. And if words alone were capable of enabling a copyright painting to be reproduced, we see insufficient reason for a different conclusion, although that precise point need not now be decided. The textbook already mentioned refers to the possibility of a painting, based on a copyright literary work, enabling a person seeing only the painting to reproduce the literary work. Such a case can safely be left until it ever arises, but again we would be disposed to answer it by the same principle.

In the present case the written words were sufficient to enable the defendants to copy at least a substantial part of each of the plaintiff's copyright designs. Accordingly we hold that infringement is established.

## *Zeccola v Universal City Studios Inc*
Federal Court of Australia: Lockhart, Fitzgerald and Jenkinson JJ
(1982) 46 ALR 189

This case provides an interesting example of the treatment of originality and how to establish similarity in relation to a literary work.

**Lockhart and Fitzgerald JJ: [192]** Counsel for the appellants submitted that both films, "Jaws" and "Great White" are genre films based upon the idea of a savage monster menacing a community. Each is a film about a killer shark terrorizing human beings and it was said that neither film was entitled to protection as there is no copyright in that general idea.

The difficulties involved in severing films into parts which are capable of characterization as original works and other parts that are not is obvious. Indeed, it is the subject of only limited exploration by the laws of this country and the United Kingdom. We were referred to certain decisions of United States courts where this question has been considered from time-to-time and we have found those cases helpful in resolving the questions before us. In general, there is no copyright in the central idea or theme of a story or play, however original it may be; copyright subsists in the combination of situations, events and scenes which constitute the particular working out or expression of the idea or theme. If these are totally different the taking of the idea or theme does not constitute an infringement of copyright.

Of necessity certain events, incidents or characters are found in many books and plays. Originality, when dealing with incidents and characters familiar in life or fiction, lies in the association, grouping and arrangement of those incidents and characters in such a manner that presents a new concept or a novel arrangement of those events and characters. We accept that where a story is written based on various incidents which, in themselves, are commonplace, a claim for copyright must be confined closely to the story which has been composed by the author.

Another author who materially varies the incidents and characters and materially changes the story is not an infringer of the copyright. If a literary or dramatic work is not wholly original there is no copyright in the unoriginal part so as to prevent its use. Additional factors may fall for consideration where the alleged infringement is by cinematograph film.

**[193]** The primary judge closely analysed the two films "Jaws" and "Great White". Notwithstanding that the subject-matter of the film "Jaws" was not particularly striking his Honour held the view, in essence, that the combination of the principal situations, singular events and basic characters was sufficient to constitute an original work that was susceptible of protection under the law of copyright in this country. In our opinion his Honour's finding has not been shown to be in error. It must be remembered that all his Honour did was make his findings on the basis that a prima facie case was established. He did not make any final or definitive finding on this, or indeed any other question … The primary judge correctly realized that two questions were involved in the resolution of what is the major issue: namely, the degree of objective similarity between the appellants' film and the respondent's novel and screenplay and, given sufficient objective similarity, whether copying was established. In relation to the question of copying, the appellants sought to show that the inspiration for the film "Great White" came partly from the imagination of its producer, Dr Tucci, and partly from a book by one Ramon Bravo called "Carnada" which is published only in Spanish.

His Honour was provided with a copy of the novel and screenplay "Jaws", but did not have time to read them in the circumstances **[194]** attending the claim for inter-locutory relief. However, the proceedings before him were conducted on the basis that the screenplay closely followed the novel and that the film "Jaws" closely followed the screenplay. Thus the exercise of comparison between the novel and the screenplay "Jaws" on the one hand, and the film "Great White" on the other hand, was regarded as appropriately undertaken by a comparison of the two films. Further, all his Honour had of the book "Carnada" was a translation in condensed form. His Honour, with some degree of fortitude, viewed both films, one after the other.

The comparative exercise which his Honour undertook was central to his decision. He considered that there was such a marked degree of similarity between the two films that there was an inescapable inference of copying and that the respondent had an excellent chance of success at the trial. The strength of his views in relation to the similarity between the two films influenced the attitude which he took to much of the evidence, including expert evidence, and to the appellant's denial of copying, most of which was held to be inadmissible.

**Jenkinson J: [196]** It was submitted for the appellants that those of the similarities which were found in occurrences patterned according to the commonplace in animal or human behaviour or character, or in drama or cinematographic art, or in a particular genre of either of those two fields of activity, should be disregarded in determining whether copyright had been infringed. It is unnecessary to express an opinion upon the correctness of the submission in its application to copyright in a film conceived as analogous to copyright in a novel or a dramatic work, but I have assumed, for the purpose of disposing of this appeal, that the appellants' construction of s 86(a) is correct, because I incline to the opinion that it is correct and because the appellants by their counsel maintain it. Accordingly it is the copyright in the novel and the scenario and script deriving from s 31(1)(a)(i) and 21(1) which is here in question: see s 113. Cinematographic reproduction of such works is, in my opinion, necessarily more completely reproduction within s 21(1) the more faithfully the occurrences narrated, or otherwise given verbal representation in the works, are portrayed by the visual images and sound of the cinematograph film, which s 10(1) defines; and in my opinion the greater the number of those occurrences so portrayed the more completely is such a work reproduced. If it should happen that some or all of those occurrences are commonplace within one or more **[197]** of the conceptual frames of reference specified in the appellants' submission, that circumstances cannot, in my opinion, diminish the significance for the purposes of s 31(1)(a)(i) of a similarity discerned between an occurrence communicated in the literary or the dramatic work and an occurrence communicated in the film.

# Chapter 5

# Balancing the Interests

There is a tension at the heart of copyright law. Copyright law recognises a public interest in granting private ownership rights to the author or maker of copyright material but it also recognises a public interest in ensuring access to this material in certain circumstances. For example, public policy may favour the right of a person to reproduce a work for the purposes of criticism, review or news or for use by the Crown. Competition policy may favour the parallel importation of copyright works or the development of interoperable computer software. As a matter of fairness (and a desire not to clog up the courts with minor matters) it could be argued that unavoidable ephemeral reproductions made for the purpose of communicating a work should not open the user to additional licence fees. As a matter of public policy it may be desirable to ensure that educational institutions or organisations assisting people with a disability have the right to reproduce works for educational and related purposes. One of the distinctive features of Australian copyright law is that there is no general fair use exemption to infringement of copyright which would allow the court to take on the role of balancing these interests. This role has been left to the legislature. This has two main effects. First, the provisions designed to achieve this balance are numerous and very detailed. Secondly, the *Copyright Act 1968* requires constant amendment so as to take account of changing methods of using copyright material.

Balancing these interests under the *Copyright Act* is achieved in three different ways. The first is by providing that certain uses of copyright material do not constitute an infringement of one or more of the designated rights of the copyright holder. Such uses constitute a defence to an infringement proceeding. In these cases the user is not liable for any licence fees and the permitted uses are therefore sometimes referred to as free use provisions.

The second way is to limit the rights of the copyright holder by imposing compulsory licence schemes. In this case the user has the right to exercise certain of the exclusive rights of the copyright holder without permission but the user is still required to pay a licence fee for this use. The compulsory licence fee is generally set by negotiation between representatives of the copyright owner and user bodies (such as the Australasian Performing Right Association (APRA) and the Hotels Association regarding licence fees for performance of sound recordings in hotels). Disputes between the parties are taken to the Copyright Tribunal of Australia.

The third way in which some balance is reached is by limiting the remedies available in respect to certain breaches. Generally damages are not available for innocent infringement. In addition, the *US Free Trade Agreement Implementation Act 2004* limited the remedies available against internet carriage service providers. Under these provisions, internet carriage service providers, if they meet certain conditions relating to industry codes of practice, are not liable for damages, account of profits or other monetary relief. Instead, the court may order them to remove infringing material, discontinue an account, disable access to certain locations or some other less burdensome remedy (ss 116AA-116AJ). These provisions will be dealt with in the next chapter.

Electronic distribution of copyright material has had a significant effect on the balance of interests. In the past, an informal fair use exemption was maintained simply because it was too difficult or expensive for copyright owners to identify casual, private infringers. This was particularly so in the case of private photocopying or home copying of sound recordings and films. So entrenched were these private usages that in 1988 Lord Templeman was able to say in *CBS Songs Ltd v Amstrad Consumer Electronics plc*[1] in relation to home copying of sound recordings:

> From the point of view of society the present situation is lamentable. Millions of breaches of the law must be committed by home copiers every year. Some home copiers may break the law in ignorance, despite extensive publicity and warning notices on records, tapes and films. Some home copiers may break the law because they estimate that the chances of detection are non-existent. Some home copiers may consider that the entertainment and recording industry already exhibit all the characteristics of undesirable monopoly – lavish expenses, extravagant earnings and exorbitant profits – and that the blank tape is the only restraint on further increase in the price of records. Whatever the reasons for home copying, the beat of Sergeant Pepper and the soaring sounds of the Miserere from unlawful copies are more powerful than law abiding instincts or twinges of conscience. A law which is treated with such contempt should be amended or repealed.[2]

At that time, the Australian Federal Government attempted to deal with the issue of home copying by amending the *Copyright Act 1968*. The amendment was two pronged. It allowed home taping of sound recordings and at the same time introduced a levy on blank audio tapes. The levy was to be paid by the blank tape vendors and distributed to copyright holders by approved collecting agencies. The amendments were challenged on constitutional grounds. In *Australian Tape Manufacturers Association Ltd v Commonwealth*,[3] the High Court unanimously accepted that the amendments were a law in respect to copyright under s 51(xviii) of the Constitution but in a 4:3 decision held that the levy was a tax and therefore the amendments were invalid in so far as they included non-tax provisions within a tax Bill in breach of the requirements of s 55 of the Constitution.

In 2006 the Commonwealth finally addressed this problem in a more successful and comprehensive manner by introducing a number of new exemptions

---

1    [1988] AC 1013.
2    [1988] AC 1013 at 1060.
3    (1993) 176 CLR 480.

relating to private and domestic use. The new exemptions allow time shifting of broadcasts (s 11); format shifting of works in books, newspapers and periodicals (s 43C); format shifting of photographs (s 47J); copying sound recordings (s 109A); and format shifting of films (s 110AA).[4]

Besides the private and domestic use exemptions, the most important 2006 amendments were the addition of a fair use exemption for parody and satire (ss 41A and 103A); an exemption allowing use of copyright materials for "certain purposes" amounting to a "special case" (s 200AB); and provisions to allow educational institutions to take advantage of new technologies to cache materials for educational purposes (s 200AAA).

The 2006 amendments mark the most significant change to the balance of interests between copyright owner and users in Australia for more than a decade but it is important to note that they are still drafted to comply with the requirements of Art 13 of the TRIPS Agreement (see below). The effectiveness of these types of exemptions, however, is constantly under challenge through the use of contract law in relation to copyright dealings, especially in the electronic environment. Using contract law, copyright owners are able to restrict access to and use of copyright material even when such access or use is subject to free use provisions under the Act. A university law library, for example, which acquires an electronic reference work is not liable for infringement of copyright if the library makes the work available online within the library premises (s 49). Under a licensing agreement with the publisher of the electronic work, however, the publisher may limit such access to university students and staff so that neither local practitioners nor casual library users can access the work. This effectively prevents the university library from performing one of its traditional roles of being an information resource for its local community. Except for s 47H in relation to reproduction of computer programs, the *Copyright Act 1968* makes no reference to the validity and enforceability of such contracts.

At the same time, contracts have also been used by copyright owners to try to improve access to copyright material. This is particularly important in the free software and open source movements which make computer source codes available, either free or for a charge, on condition that the user of the source code makes the source code available together with any modifications made to it.[5]

In June 2001 the Copyright Law Review Committee released an issues paper in response to a reference from the Attorney-General to consider the relationship between copyright and contract law. Under the terms of reference the government noted the importance of maintaining an "appropriate balance" between the rights of copyright owners and the rights of copyright users; the rapid growth of electronic commerce which had facilitated the use of contract law to set terms and conditions on access to and use of copyright material; and that, with the exception of s 47H, the *Copyright Act 1968* being silent as to whether private agreements can displace the reasonable access provisions under the Act. The Committee was required to inquire into and report on the extent to which trade in copyright material is subject to agreements which exclude or modify the exemptions to the exclusive rights of the copyright holder both online and

---

4    *Copyright Amendment Act 2006* (Cth) Sch 6 which came into effect on the first of January 2007.

5    See Donald Rosenberg, *Open Source: The Unauthorized White Papers*, M&T Books, NY, 2000.

offline; the ability of copyright owners and users to enforce these agreements and whether, as a matter of policy, such agreements should be enforceable under the Act.[6]

In October 2002 the Copyright Law Review Committee released its final report, *Copyright and Contract*.[7] In that report the Committee recommended that any provision which seeks to exclude the operation of defences provided under ss 40, 41, 42, 103A, 103B, 103C (fair dealing), ss 43 and 104 (professional advice and judicial proceedings), ss 43A and 111A (temporary reproductions or copies in the course of communications) or ss 48A, 49, 50, 51AA, 51A, 52, 110A and 110B (library usages) of the *Copyright Act 1968*, should have no effect. In relation to the remaining exemptions the Committee recommended that codes of conduct and model licences should be developed where relevant. At the time of writing these recommendations had still not been adopted.

## Defences and Compulsory Licences[8]

### Defences

| Copyright | Use | Section |
|---|---|---|
| *Fair Dealing and General Defences* | | |
| Works and audio-visual items (avi) | Fair dealing for research or study. NB see special defence for external students, s 40(1A). | s 40 (works); s 103C (avi) |
| Works and avi | Fair dealing for criticism or review. | s 41 (works); s 103A (avi) |
| Works and avi | Fair dealing for reporting news. | s 42(works); s 103B (avi) |
| Works and avi | Fair dealing for purpose of parody or satire. | s 41A (works) s 103AA (avi) |
| Various | Private and domestic use. | s 111 (broadcasts); s 43C (books etc); s 47J (photographs); s 109A (sound recordings); s 110AA (analogue videos). |
| All | Use by libraries, archives, educational institutions and people with a disability: certain purposes amounting to a special case. | s 200AB |
| *Educational Uses* | | |
| Published works | Short extracts in collection of works for educational use. NB. There are significant limitations on this use. | s 44 |
| Works | Non-multiple reproductions by student or teacher in class (eg by overhead projector) or in exam question or answer. | s 200(1) |

---

6    See Copyright Law Review Committee, Terms of Reference and Discussion Paper <http://www.law.gov.au/clrc>.

7    Copyright Law Review Committee, *Copyright and Contract*, AGPS, Canberra, 2002.

8    For background reading, see Copyright Law Review Committee, *Simplification of the Copyright Act 1968 Part 1 Exceptions to the Exclusive Rights of Copyright Owners*, AGPS, Canberra, 1998.

| | | |
|---|---|---|
| Sound recording, work or broadcast | Making sound recording of sound broadcast by educational institution for educational purposes. | s 200(2), (2A) |
| Literary, dramatic or musical work | Performance by teacher or student in class for the purposes of educational instruction. | s 28 |
| All | Proxy caching | s 200AAA |
| Published literary or dramatic work | Multiple copies of insubstantial part for a course of study. | s 135ZMB |
| **_Artistic Works_** | | |
| Sculpture or work of artistic craftsman-ship permanently situated in public space | Painting, drawing, engraving or photographing the work or including it in film or TV broadcast. | s 65 |
| Building or model of building | Painting, drawing, engraving or photographing the work or including it in film or TV broadcast. | s 66 |
| Artistic work | Incidental inclusion in film or television broadcast. | s 67 |
| Artistic work | Publication of the painting, drawing, engraving, photograph, film or TV broadcast made under ss 65-67 not an infringement. | s 68 |
| Artistic work | Author may use an artistic work in later work so long as later does not repeat or imitate the main design of the earlier work. | s 72 |
| Building and building plans | May reconstruct building. | s 73 |
| Artistic work where correspond-ing design applied industrially | No infringement to reproduce the artistic work by applying the work or corresponding design to an article. | ss 74-77 |
| **_Films_** | | |
| Film depicting news | Causing newsreel to be seen or heard in public after expiration of 50 years after calendar year in which the events depicted occurred. | s 110(1) |
| Work incorporated into a film | Causing film to be seen or heard in public after expiration of copyright in film. | s 110(2) |
| Film soundtracks | Where sounds embodied in a sound-track are also embodied in a non derived sound recording then use of the sound recording is not an infringement of copyright in the film. | s 110(3) |
| **_Performances_** | | |
| Extract of reason-able length from published literary or dramatic work | Reading or recitation in public or inclusion of read-ing or recitation in sound or television broadcast, with acknowledgment. | s 45 |
| Literary, dramatic or musical work | No infringement when operate reception equipment (eg TV or radio) or play record (eg CD) at premises where people reside or sleep as part of amenities provided exclusively to residents, inmates and their guests. | s 46 |
| Sound recording | No infringement when cause to be heard in public at premises where people reside or sleep as part of amenities provided exclusively to residents, inmates and their guests or as part of charitable activities of a club or society. | s 106 |

| *Communication, Broadcasting and Technical Processes* | | |
|---|---|---|
| Sound recording not made by qualified person or not made in Australia | If copyright only subsists in a sound recording by virtue of s 89(3) (ie first published in Australia), it may be broadcast or caused to be heard in public. | s 105 |
| Works and avi | Making temporary copy of work or avi as part of technical process for sending or receiving authorised communications. | s 43A (works); s 111A (avi) |
| Work, sound recording | Making a film or sound recording for the purposes of making broadcast where maker of both is the same. | s 47(1) (literary, dramatic or musical work); s 70(1) (artistic work); s 107 (sound recording)* |
| Literary, dramatic or literary work, sound recording or film | Making film or sound recording of broadcast for purposes of simulcast. | s 47AA (literary, dramatic or musical work); s 110C (sound recording or film) |
| All | Reproductions incidentally made as part of technical process of using the work or subject-matter. | s 43B (works); s 111B (Part IV) |
| All | Safe harbour provisions. | s 39B (works); s 112E (avi) |
| *Computer Programs* | | |
| Authorised computer program | Reproduction made as part of the normal running for purposes for which program made or for purpose of studying ideas behind the program. | s 47B(1) and (3) |
| Authorised computer program | Reproduction for purposes of making back-up or spare copy. | s 47C |
| Authorised computer program | Reproduction or adaptation for purposes of making interoperable program or article. | s 47D |
| Authorised computer program | Reproduction to correct errors. | s 47E |
| Authorised computer program | Reproduction for security testing of program, system or network. NB an agreement which excludes or limits operation of ss 47B(3), 47C, 47D, 47E or 47F has no effect. | s 47F |
| *Importing* | | |
| Certain books and published editions | Parallel importing allowed in certain circumstances. NB Doesn't include books of musical works, computer manuals or periodical publications. | s 44A (works); s 112A (published editions) |
| Recorded works and sound recordings | Parallel importing allowed in certain circumstances. | s 44D (works); s 112D (sound recording) |
| Literary, dramatic or musical work embodied in non-infringing accessory or sound recording | Not infringed by importing the accessory with the article or sound recording. | s 44C (articles); s 44D(4) (sound recordings) |
| Non-infringing copies of computer programs | Parallel importation allowed. | s 44E |

| Electronic literary and musical items and published editions of them. | Parallel importation allowed. | s 44F (electronic literary and musical works); s 112DA (published editions of these electronic works) |
|---|---|---|
| | *Libraries, Archives and Key Cultural Institutions* | |
| All | Librarian in Parliamentary Library dealing with material for sole use of Member of Parliament. | s 48A (works); s 10A (Part IV) |
| Article or published work in library collection | Librarian may reproduce and supply to person for research or study and make electronic works available online within library premises. NB also applies to accompanying illustrations, s 53. | s 49 |
| Article or published work in library collection | Librarian may reproduce for and communicate to another library for inclusion in the second library or for purposes referred to above (s 48A, s 49). NB also applies to accompanying illustrations, s 53. | s 50 |
| Unpublished works, sound recordings and films in library collection | Librarian may reproduce and communicate an unpublished work, sound recording or film for research or study, use by member of parliament or with view to publication. NB see s 52 re subsequent publication. NB also applies to accompanying illustrations, s 53. | s 51(works); s 110A (sound recording or film) |
| Work in Australian Archives | Archives may reproduce and communicate a reference, working or replacement copy. NB also applies to accompanying illustrations, s 53. | s 51AA (works) |
| Work, sound recording or film in library collection or key cultural institution | Librarian may reproduce or communicate a work for the purpose of preservation, replacement, administration, making available online within the library. NB also applies to accompanying illustrations, s 53. | ss 51A and 51B (works); ss 110B and 110BA (sound recordings and films); s 112AA (published editions of works) |
| Unpublished literary, dramatic and musical works in library collection | First publication (and certain subsequent publications) will not be an infringement of publication right if identity of copyright owner unknown and notification of publication given. May also broadcast, electronically transmit, perform in public or make a record of the publication without infringing copyright in unpublished work. | s 52 |
| | *Judicial Proceedings and Statutes* | |
| All | Judicial proceedings, reports of judicial proceedings and in relation to professional advice by legal practitioner, patent attorney or trade marks attorney. | s 43 (works); s 104 re Part IV subject-matter (Part IV) |
| All | Making one copy by reprographic means of a statute, judgment order, reasons for decisions etc. | s 182A |
| | *Miscellaneous* | |
| Writing on approved Agvet chemical label | Reproduction of writing not an infringement. | s 44B |

\*     Note the limit set on live performers' consent under s 100AH (as inserted by the *US Free Trade Agreement Implementation Act 2004*).

## Compulsory licences

There are four areas of copyright usage which, for reasons of public policy, history or convenience are subject to compulsory licence schemes. These are use by educational institutions or institutions assisting people with disabilities; certain uses in the music industry; use of copyright material by the Crown; and certain technical uses for the purposes of making a broadcast.

### Compulsory Licences

| 1. | Sound recording or film of a work or sound recording for the purposes of making a broadcast where the maker of the broadcast and recording are different. | ss 47(3), 70(3), 107(3) |
|---|---|---|
| 2. | Making of records of musical works previously recorded. | ss 54-64 |
| 3. | Performing published sound recordings in public. | s 108 |
| 4. | Broadcasting published sound recordings. | s 109 |
| 5. | Making a sound broadcast of a literary or dramatic work or its adaptation by the holder of a print handicapped radio licence. | s 47A |
| 6. | Copying and communicating broadcasts by educational and other institutions. | Part VA ss 135A-135ZA |
| 7. | Reproducing and communicating works etc by educational and other institutions. | Part VB ss 135KB-135ZZH |
| 8. | Retransmission of free-to-air broadcasts. | Part VC ss 135ZZI-135ZZZE |
| 9. | Crown copyright. | Part VII Division 2 ss 182B-183E |

## Fair dealing

The four fair dealing provisions in Australia are limited and do not amount to a general fair use defence. These fair dealing defences apply to works and audio-visual items.[9] It is a defence to an action for infringement of copyright that the dealing was for the purpose of criticism and review (s 40 as to works; s 103A as to audio-visual items[10]) or for the purpose of research and study (s 40 as to works; s 103C as to audio-visual items) or for the purpose of reporting the news (s 42 as to works; s 103B as to audio-visual items) or for the purpose of parody or satire (s 41A as to works; s 103AA as to audio-visual items). The onus is on the defendant to establish that the dealing was for one of the specified purposes and that the dealing was fair in all the circumstances.[11] If the purpose is criticism and review or reporting news in the press (as opposed to news on television, radio, film or other forms of electronic communication), the defendant must also prove that there has been "sufficient acknowledgment" of the work or audio-visual item.

---

9    An audio-visual item is a sound recording, cinematographic film, television or radio broadcast (s 100A). The fair dealing defences therefore do not extend to dealings with published editions of works.

10   An "audio-visual item" is a sound recording, cinematographic film, sound broadcast or television broadcast (s 100A).

11   *De Garis v Neville Jeffress Pidler Pty Ltd* (1990) 95 ALR 625 at 629 citing *Sillitoe v McGraw-Hill Book Co (UK) Ltd* [1983] FSR 545 at 558.

The courts have often referred to public interest as a separate ground either for a defence to infringement or as a matter to be taken into account in determining whether to grant a remedy under the *Copyright Act 1968*. Although no cases have been determined on this basis we consider these comments below.

### Fair dealing for purposes of criticism and review (ss 40 and 103A)

In *De Garis v Neville Jeffress Pidler Pty Ltd*,[12] Beaumont J, relying on the *Macquarie Dictionary*, defined criticism as:

> the act or art of analysing and judging the quality of a literary or artistic work, etc: literary criticism. The act of passing judgement as to the merits of something ... A critical comment, article or essay; a critique.[13]

He similarly relied on the Macquarie's definition of a review as a "critical article or report, as in a periodical, on some literary work, commonly some work of recent appearance; a critique".[14]

It has been said that in determining whether the dealing is for the relevant purpose the court will look at the purposes of the taker rather than the ultimate user. Thus, in *De Garis v Neville Jeffress Pidler Pty Ltd*,[15] a press clipping service was found to have reproduced press clippings for the purpose of commercial dealings rather than for the purposes of criticism, review or for reporting the news. This was so even though some of its customers may in fact have used the press clippings for such purposes. Strictly applied, this interpretation might prevent a research assistant for a freelance reviewer, for example, from relying on the defence.

In *Time Warner v Channel 4 Corp*,[16] Henry LJ explained that the defence was necessary so as "to prevent copyright owners of works which they have put into the public domain from picking and choosing as to who may review their works, when they may do so, and what clips they may use".[17] It follows that, although the dealing must be fair, the criticism or review itself need not be. Nor is it necessary that the extracts used in the review or criticism be representative of the subject-matter. In *Pro Sieben Media AG v Carlton UK Television Ltd*,[18] Robert Walker LJ in the English Court of Appeal commented:

> If the fair dealing is for the purpose of criticism that criticism may be strongly expressed and unbalanced without forfeiting the fair dealing defence; an author's remedy for malicious and unjustified criticism lies ... in the law of defamation, not copyright.[19]

The criticism or review may be of the copyright subject-matter itself or of another work or audio-visual item. The criticism or review might also be of the

---

12    (1990) 95 ALR 625.
13    (1990) 95 ALR 625 at 631.
14    (1990) 95 ALR 625 at 631.
15    (1990) 95 ALR 625 at 629, citing *Sillitoe v McGraw-Hill Book Co (UK) Ltd* [1983] FSR 545 at 558, which in turn cited *University of London Press Ltd v University Tutorial Press Ltd* [1916] 2 Ch 601 at 613.
16    (1993) 28 IPR 459.
17    (1993) 28 IPR 459 at 468.
18    [1999] 1 WLR 605.
19    [1999] 1 WLR 605 at 613.

ideas underlying the protected material. Thus, a program which criticised Stanley Kubrick's decision not to allow "A Clockwork Orange"[20] to be exhibited in the United Kingdom and a criticism of the philosophy and practices of the Church of Scientology[21] have both been accepted as criticism and review for the purposes of the fair dealing defence.

It has sometimes been said that the fair dealing defences cannot be used to justify a hidden purpose.[22] That is, simply calling something a criticism or review will not suffice to establish the defence. In *Pro Sieben Media AG v Carlton UK Television Ltd*,[23] the defendant television station, Carlton, had copied part of Pro Sieben's television interview with a man whose partner was pregnant with eight live embryos.[24] Whilst Pro Sieben's broadcast was an uncritical, rather sentimental look at the couple,[25] the Carlton program was an attack on cheque book journalism and its effect on truth in reporting. Carlton used the Pro Sieben program, together with others, to illustrate the problem. At trial, evidence was given for Carlton by a person the Court of Appeal described as a "nightmare witness". This witness made a vitriolic attack on cheque book journalism generally and Pro Sieben in particular. The Court of Appeal commented that the trial judge had probably been influenced by this witness when he found that the purpose of the dealing had not been for criticism and review. The Court of Appeal, however, held that the relevant purpose must be determined objectively by reference to the use of the material rather than subjectively by reference to the intent of the taker. In this case, viewed objectively, the alleged infringing program itself provided a balanced and "muted" criticism of the effects of cheque book journalism and therefore was within the purposes allowed by the defence.

The taking need not be solely for the relevant purpose but may be "associated with" that purpose. In *TCN Channel Nine Pty Ltd v Network Ten Pty Ltd*,[26] Channel Ten broadcast segments of Channel Nine television programs on its infotainment program "The Panel". The Full Federal Court considered whether the fair dealing provisions were available to Channel Ten. (This issue was not reconsidered on appeal to the High Court in *Network Ten Pty Ltd v TCN Nine Pty Ltd*.)[27]

The Full Federal Court upheld the trial judge's finding that a segment taken from "Days of Our Lives", which showed Marlena levitating after being possessed by the devil, was used for the purposes of criticism and review in the sense that it passed judgment on the television show, its script writers and plot. This was

---

20   *Time Warner v Channel 4 Corp* (1993) 28 IPR 459.

21   *Hubbard v Vosper* [1972] 2 QB 84.

22   Before the introduction of the fair dealing defence in the 1911 Act the "fair user" defence had concentrated on the intent of the taker. In *Johnstone v Bernard Jones Publications Ltd and Beauchamp* [1938] 1 Ch 599, Morton J considered whether the motive of the taker was relevant under the new fair dealing provisions. The judge found that he did not have to make a determination whether this was so in the circumstances of the case but since then judges and commentators have incorrectly referred to the case as authority for the proposition that the defence cannot be held to justify a hidden motive.

23   [1999] 1 WLR 605 at 617.

24   Carlton had also taped the whole of the broadcast in order to select the extract used.

25   Part of the interview showed the couple buying eight teddy bears in a toy shop, for example, even though medical opinion held that the chance of bringing eight live embryos to term was slight and the attempt to do so, dangerous.

26   (2002) 190 ALR 468.

27   (2004) 218 CLR 273.

so even though the use of the extract also involved a "measure of satire and humorous entertainment".[28] Similarly, the Full Federal Court upheld a finding of the trial judge, Conti J, that a segment showing Isaac Hayes disappearing in a "pea souper" of an artificial fog on stage at the 72nd Academy Awards was criticism and review of the making and staging of the Academy Awards. This was so despite the "humorous, if not hilarious" treatment of the footage by The Panel. On the other hand, the fact that The Panel members thought that the interviewer from Nine's program "Crocodile Hunter" looked just like "Uncle Arthur" from "The Comedy Company" was found by the trial judge not to be criticism and review in so far as it did not have the necessary element of "passing judgment".[29] Again this finding was upheld on appeal.

The question of whether the dealing has been fair is determined by the courts "after a detailed consideration of all the circumstances of the case".[30] In a passage approved by Beaumont J in *De Garis v Neville Jeffress Pidler Pty Ltd*,[31] Lord Denning in *Hubbard v Vosper*[32] considered some of the factors which might be taken into account in determining such "fairness":

> It is impossible to define what is a "fair dealing". It must be a question of degree. You must consider first the number and extent of the quotations and extracts. Are they altogether too many and too long to be fair? Then you must consider the use made of them. If they are used as a basis for comment, criticism or review, that may be fair dealing. If they are used to convey the same information as the author, for a rival purpose, that may be unfair. Next, you must consider the proportions. To take long extracts and attach short comments may be unfair. But, short extracts and long comments may be fair. Other considerations may come to mind also. But, after all is said and done, it must be a matter of impression. As with fair comment in the law of libel, so with fair comment in the law of copyright. The tribunal of fact must decide.[33]

It has been argued that it cannot be fair to criticise or review an unpublished work but, in *Hubbard v Vosper*,[34] Lord Denning held that the fact that the copyright material had only been distributed to members of the Church of Scientology did not prevent the defence being raised. In *Commonwealth v John Fairfax & Sons Ltd*,[35] Mason J, when considering whether the defence was available in relation to dealings with unpublished, leaked government documents, said that "the absence of consent, express or implied, or such circulation by the author of an unpublished literary work as to justify criticism or review is ordinarily at least an important factor in deciding whether there has been 'a fair dealing' under s 41".[36]

Sections 41 and 103A provide that the defence will not be made out even if the purpose is for criticism and review, unless there has been "sufficient

---

28    To use the words of Conti J as trial judge in *TCN Channel Nine Pty Ltd v Network Ten Pty Ltd* (2001) 184 ALR 1 at 57.

29    Conti J as trial judge in *TCN Channel Nine Pty Ltd v Network Ten Pty Ltd* (2001) 184 ALR 1 at 60.

30    *University of New South Wales v Moorhouse* (1975) 133 CLR 1, Gibbs J at 12 regarding s 49.

31    (1990) 95 ALR 625 at 633.

32    [1972] 2 QB 84.

33    [1972] 2 QB 84 at 94.

34    [1972] 2 QB 84.

35    (1980) 147 CLR 39.

36    (1980) 147 CLR 39 at 55.

acknowledgment" of the work or audio-visual item. Sufficient acknowledgment in relation to a work is defined in s 10(1) as an identification of the work by title or other description plus the name of the author (unless the work is anonymous, pseudonymous or the author directs otherwise). In relation to audio-visual items the question of what constitutes sufficient acknowledgment is "at large" in the words of Conti J in *TCN Channel Nine Pty Ltd v Network Ten Pty Ltd*.[37] Conti J suggested that the display of the Channel Nine logo would be sufficient to establish this element of the defence, especially as this was the usual means of identifying the company and the use of the correct name of the company was likely to be meaningless to the ordinary viewer. This part of the decision was not appealed.

### Fair dealing for purposes of study and research (ss 40 and 103C)

Research and study are different from mere gathering of information by a government task force, for example, even when that information gathering is organised toward an identified end or is complex.[38] In *De Garis v Neville Jeffress Pidler Pty Ltd*,[39] Beaumont J again referred to the *Macquarie Dictionary* definition. Research is "1. diligent and systematic enquiry or investigation into a subject in order to discover facts or principles: *research in nuclear physics*".[40] Study is "1. application of the mind to the acquisition of knowledge, as by reading, investigation or reflection; 2. the cultivation of a particular branch of knowledge: *The study of law*. 3. a particular course of effort to acquire knowledge: *to pursue special medical studies* ... 5. a thorough examination and analysis of a particular subject".[41]

As with fair dealing for the purposes of criticism and review, it is the use of the reproducer or copier for example, not the use of the ultimate user, which determines the relevant purpose. For this reason the *Copyright Act 1968* sets out detailed provisions which allow librarians to deal with copyright material on behalf of another person if the material is for that person's research and study (ss 49-51, 110A).

The *Copyright Act* sets out the factors to be taken into account in determining whether the use has been a fair dealing for the purposes of research or study. These factors are the purpose and character of the dealing, the nature of the work or audio-visual item, the availability of the work or audio-visual item, the market effect of the dealing and the amount and substantiality of the part copied (ss 40(2) and 103C(2)).

If the dealing is by way of reproducing a literary, dramatic or musical work, s 40(3) deems the reproduction of all or part of an article in a periodical journal to be a fair dealing. This provision does not apply if another article in that publication is also reproduced for the purpose of different research or a different course of study (s 43(4)). This provision causes many problems for large educational institutions such as universities that may want to reproduce different articles from the same journal but for different faculties. The institution will not only

---

37    (2001) 184 ALR 1 at 42.
38    See *Re Attorney-General of British Colombia and Messier* (1984) 8 DLR (4th) 306.
39    (1990) 95 ALR 625.
40    (1990) 95 ALR 625 at 629.
41    (1990) 95 ALR 625 at 630.

have to keep records of what it has reproduced but will also have to decide which faculty gets preference.

Under the research and study provisions the dealing is deemed to be fair if only a reasonable proportion of other published literary, dramatic or musical works is reproduced (s 40(5)). (This deeming provision does not apply to unpublished works, other subject-matter or to works in a periodical.) A reasonable proportion is defined for the purposes of this section only as 10 per cent of the number of pages in the published edition or a single chapter or, in the case of electronic publications, 10 per cent of the words or a single chapter. Users cannot aggregate these provisions over time or by taking parts of both electronic and hard copy publications (s 40(6) and (7)).[42]

It is interesting to note that there is a special wide defence available to external students for dealings with literary works other than lecture notes. In this case the fair dealing is not restricted to purposes of research and study but encompasses any fair dealing "for the purpose of, or associated with, an approved course of study or research by an external student of an educational institution" (s 40(1A)).

### Fair dealing for the purpose of reporting the news (ss 42 and 103B)

Although the point has not been taken, the courts have applied the same principles regarding fair dealing under the news reporting defences as under the criticism and review defences. The fair dealing principles are general enough to take into account any differences which may arise from the different uses of the copyright material. The main question which remains under this defence is whether the use is for the proper purpose – that is "for the purpose of, or associated with, the reporting of news by means of newspaper, magazine or similar periodical" (ss 42(1)(a) and 103B(1)(a)) or "by means of a communication or in a cinematographic film" (ss 42(1)(b) and 103B(1)(b)). In the case of newspaper, magazine or similar periodical news reports, sufficient acknowledgment is required and this will be determined in accordance with the definition in s 10(1).[43]

In *De Garis v Neville Jeffress Pidler Pty Ltd*, Beaumont J relied on the *Macquarie Dictionary* definition of "news" as including "1. a report of any recent event, situation etc; 2. a report of events published in a newspaper, journal, radio, television, or any other medium; 3. information, events etc considered as suitable for reporting: *it's very interesting, but it's not news*; 4. information not previously known: *that's news to me*".[44]

---

42    Note that there is another definition of reasonable portion in s 10(2), (2A), (2B) and (2C) which is not affected by the research and study provisions (s 40(8)).

43    When *Hawkes and Son (London) Pty Ltd v Paramount Film Service Ltd* [1934] 1 Ch 593 was decided the fair dealing defence under the *Copyright Act 1911* (UK) extended to "private study, research, criticism, review or newspaper summary" (s 2(1)). The court held that a cinematographic film newsreel was not a newspaper summary and therefore the defence did not apply. In his judgment Romer LJ considered whether the defence would apply if the newsreel were taken to be a newspaper summary. Romer LJ held that if it would not be a fair dealing to print the words and music of a song in a newspaper report of the Prince of Wales' visit then it could not be a fair dealing to play that music in a newsreel of the same visit. In other words, the judge did not take the difference in technology into account.

44    (1990) 95 ALR 625 at 633.

Mason J, on an application for an interlocutory injunction in *Commonwealth v John Fairfax & Sons Ltd*,[45] was "inclined to allow that 'news' ... is not restricted to 'current events'".[46] Thus, in the 1980 High Court case he was prepared to accept that leaked government documents regarding Australia's involvement in East Timor in 1975-1976 might be classified as news.

The *Copyright Act 1968* provides that the use of the copyright material may be "associated with the reporting of news" and it is perhaps on this basis that Conti J as trial judge in *TCN Channel Nine Pty Ltd v Network Ten Pty Ltd* was prepared to hold that "the relevant news need not totally inhere in the work or audio-visual item"[47] in question. This question was not discussed on appeal. Thus, commentary on the material may be taken into account in determining whether the copyright material is being used for the appropriate purpose. In addition, the copyright material may be used in association with news for which it was not originally made. In *TCN Channel Nine Pty Ltd v Network Ten Pty Ltd*,[48] the Full Court and the trial judge were prepared to accept that footage of a drunk President Boris Yeltsin of Russia might be used "in association with" a report on the then pending Australian referendum on the Republic. On balance, however, both at trial and on appeal to the Full Federal Court it was held that the footage in that case, together with The Panel's discussion, tipped in favour of humour and entertainment rather than news.[49]

This does not mean that news may not be humorous or entertaining. As Hill J said in *Nine Network Australia Pty Ltd v Australian Broadcasting Corporation*[50] when considering the 2000 fireworks display on Sydney Harbour:

> For my part I find the distinction between news and entertainment a very difficult one. It is not one I think which can be resolved by looking at the dictionary definition of the word. In some ways it may well be as difficult as the issue that has dominated the news press over the last few months of some suggestion of difference between commentary and info-tainment or entertainment.
>
> In my view the fact that humour is used does not necessarily negate the fact that what is being broadcast may be news. Hopefully the fact that news coverage is interesting or even to some entertaining likewise does not negate the fact that it could be news. As I have already said, the celebrations of the City of Sydney this New Year's Eve are of both national and international significance. The reporting and showing of a part of them on TV by Channel Two as national broadcaster could well fall within s 42.[51]

In *Hawkes and Son (London) Ltd v Paramount Film Service Ltd*,[52] the defendants were held to have infringed the copyright in the musical work, the "Colonel Bogey March". A substantial part of the work had been reproduced in a cinematographic newsreel of the Prince of Wales visiting the new quarters of the Naval School at Holbrook in 1934. Part of the newsreel showed the boys doing

---

45    (1980) 147 CLR 39.
46    (1980) 147 CLR 39 at 56.
47    (2001) 184 ALR 1 at 53.
48    (2002) 190 ALR 468.
49    (2002) 190 ALR 468 at 491 and (2001) 184 ALR 1, Conti J at 53. Not discussed in High Court decision: *Network Ten Pty Ltd v TCN Nine Pty Ltd* (2004) 218 CLR 273.
50    (1999) 48 IPR 333.
51    (1999) 48 IPR 333 at 340.
52    [1934] 1 Ch 593.

a march past with a band playing the musical work in question. At the time the fair dealing defence for news under the *Copyright Act 1911* (UK) only applied to a "newspaper summary" (s 2(3)) and the English Court of Appeal held that the defence did not extend to cover news reports in a cinematographic film.

Today, the defence extends to cinematographic films and communications. Communications include making the material available online and electronic transmissions including email and broadcasts. Applying general principles, the playing of a musical work or a sound recording in the course of reporting the news would be expected to constitute a fair dealing if the playing formed part of the news being reported or was "associated with" the reporting of news. However, s 42(2) limits this general principle by providing that playing a musical work in the course of reporting the news is not a fair dealing "if the playing of the work does not form part of the news being reported". There is no similar provision in s 103B in relation to sound recordings so a wider usage may be allowed for such subject-matter.

Section 110 provides a special defence in relation to newsreels. If a film comprises images which were "a means of communicating news" at the time they were made then the film may be shown in public 50 years after the principal events in the film took place without infringing the copyright in the film, sound recording or underlying works. Newsreels would be covered by this defence as, arguably, would a film of still news photographs. Whether a film of a newsworthy event made by a freelance film maker or a lucky bystander would be covered by the exemption will be determined according to the particular facts of the case. You may like to consider the possible fate of the images of the planes flying into the World Trade Towers in New York on September 11 2001.

### Fair dealing for the purpose of parody or satire (ss 41A and 103AA)

This defence was introduced by the 2006 amendments and at the time of writing there has been no Australian case law addressing the extent of the exemption. However, the concepts have been discussed in Australian case law, especially by the trial judge in *TCN Channel Nine Pty Ltd v Network Ten Pty Ltd*,[53] a case decided before the defence was introduced in Australia. In that case Conti J considered the extent to which the purpose of the taking could be taken into account in determining whether what had been taken was substantial. Conti J drew a distinction between parody and burlesque on the one hand and satire on the other whereby the essence of parody and burlesque is imitation, whilst satire is a form of criticism which does not necessarily involve imitation or take-off. Conti J:

> It is appropriate that I should interpolate at this point to say something about the words 'parody' and 'burlesque', and what I consider to be their distinctiveness of meaning from the word 'satire', and I do so in the particular context of my discussion of authorities in [16] above. The Macquarie Dictionary definitions of the three notions indicate that the essence of parody is imitation, consistently with the observation made in AGL as above extracted, and that burlesque is in the nature of vulgarising parody by way, for instance, of a vulgarising or debasing caricature, whereas satire is described as being a form of ironic, sarcastic, scornful, derisive or ridiculing criticism of vice, folly or abuses, but

53   (2001) 184 ALR 1.

not by way of an imitation or take-off. Nevertheless that dictionary's attribution of '…satirical imitation' has caused me to research further into the true or essential meaning of satire. In the work of a highly respected Australian academic, Professor Margaret Rose, published by the Cambridge University Press in 1993 and titled Parody: Ancient, Modern, and Post Modern, the author distinguishes between both the Aristotle-originated word 'parody', and the conceptually similar Italian-originated word 'burlesque', on the one hand, and the Latin-originated word 'satire' on the other hand. Such distinction referable essentially to imitation, though sometimes blurred at the edges by everyday usage, assists an understanding as to why parody (and burlesque) will not avoid copyright infringement, [remember this was before the parody and satire defence was introduced: authors] since imitation is in the nature of copying, in contrast to satire which involves the drawing of a distinction between the satirist and the author, composer etc.[54]

Two problems arise in relation to this definition. First, based on these definitions it is difficult to distinguish between the parody and satire defence on the one hand and the criticism and review or news defences on the other. Secondly, and related to this difficulty, it may be thought there is no need for a specific defence in relation to satire because it does not involve imitation.

Conti J's association of parody and satire with criticism is not surprising in the context of "The Panel" litigation which held that parody and satire might be considered forms of criticism and review, or news, and therefore covered by the existing fair dealing defences. The introduction of a specific parody and satire defence ensures that the parody and satire need not be for the purposes of criticism and review or news but might simply be humour for its own sake.

On the second point, the reason there needs to be a separate satire defence even though there is not necessarily any imitation in satire is because satire may include criticism, comment or humour relating to a work other than the work or other subject-matter which has been taken. Thus, if a part of a film is used to make a satiric film on an unrelated topic this may be covered by the parody and satire defence even though the satire does not relate to the film taken.

What amounts to a fair dealing in the case of parody or satire has yet to be determined. In particular, the question arises as to whether the policy imperatives which have given such a broad reach to the fair dealing provisions in relation to criticism, review and news are applicable to this new defence.

## Private and domestic use (ss 43C, 47J, 109A, 110AA, 111)

The *Copyright Amendment Act 2006* introduced five new defences which allow very limited time and format shifting of certain copyright subject-matter for private and domestic use whether or not this use occurs on or off domestic premises (s 10(1)). The defences allow time shifting of broadcasts (s 111); format shifting of works in books, newspapers and periodicals (s 43C); format shifting of photographs (s 47J); format shifting of sound recordings, other than sound recordings downloaded from the Internet (s 109A); and format shifting of analogue videos to electronic form (s 110AA). In each case the subject-matter being copied or reproduced must be a non-infringing copy owned by the person relying on the defence. In addition, the defence is taken not to have ever applied if the copy or reproduction is sold or otherwise dealt with. In *National Rugby League Investments Pty Ltd v Singtel*

---

54    (2001) 184 ALR 1 at 14.

*Optus*,[55] the Full Federal Court held that Optus could not rely on the s 111 defence to support its TV Now subscription service which allowed subscribers to have free-to-air television programs recorded and then played back at a time of the subscriber's choosing on the subscriber's compatible mobile device or personal computer. The decision turned on whether Optus and/or the subscriber could be said to be the "maker" of the allegedly infringing copy. The court rejected the argument that the maker was simply the subscriber who initiated the recording. Instead, the court held that the "maker" was the one who captured the broadcast and then embodied its images and sounds (in this case, Optus),[56] either alone or jointly and severally with the subscriber who instigated the copying.[57] Whilst the defence was not available to Optus, it was available to individual subscribers, none of whom was a party to the proceedings.

## Certain purposes amounting to a special case (s 200AB)

The *Copyright Amendment Act 2006* introduced a new "certain purposes" defence (s 200AB) which allows a body administering a library or archive to use copyright subject-matter for the purpose of maintaining or operating the library or archive; or a body administering an educational institution to use copyright subject-matter for the purpose of giving educational instruction; or a person with a print, visual or hearing disability or another person to use copyright subject-matter in order to obtain a copy or reproduction of the subject-matter in another form in order to reduce the difficulty caused by the disability.

This defence is subject to certain limitations. The use must amount to a "special case"; the use must not conflict with a normal exploitation of the subject-matter; and the use must not unreasonably prejudice the legitimate interests of the copyright owner. Furthermore the use must not be made partly for the purpose of obtaining a commercial advantage or profit (although cost recovery is permitted).

The Act provides that the first three limitations have the same meaning they have under Art 13 of the TRIPS Agreement which allows members to limit the exclusive rights of the copyright owner in "certain special cases" which "do not conflict with the normal exploitation of the work" and "do not unreasonably prejudice the legitimate interests of the right holder".

The application of this "three step test" under TRIPS was considered by the Disputes Settlement Body (DSB) of the World Trade Organization in the dispute between the United States and the European Communities regarding the business and home style exemptions under s 110(5) of the *Copyright Act Title 17* (US) (previously mentioned in Chapter 2 of this text).[58] The home style exemption allowed the public playing of a single radio or television commonly used in private homes so long as there was no charge for this and the transmission is not retransmitted. The business exemption allowed the public performance of non dramatic musical works on radios and televisions in some small businesses in limited circumstances.

---

55   [2012] FCAFC 59.
56   [2012] FCAFC 59 at [67].
57   [2012] FCAFC 59 at [76].
58   The Panel Report in *United States – Section 110(5) of the US Copyright Act WT/DS160/R 15* was adopted by the Disputes Settlement Body on 27 July 2000.

The DSB took a narrow approach to each element of the test. In relation to the first step the DSB held that "certain" meant that the exception or limitation must be "clearly defined" (para 6.108). It further held that a case is "special" when it is not normal – that is, it must be "limited in its field of application or exceptional in its scope". In other words, the DSB commented, the exception or limitation must be "narrow in a quantitative as well as a qualitative sense" (para 6.109). It is not enough that the exception or limitation is drafted to meet a special policy purpose (para 6.111). Applying this test the DSB held that the home style exemption was well defined and limited in its scope and reach and therefore came within the definition of a "certain special case" but that the business exemption did not.

In relation to the second step of the test – that the exception or limitation "not conflict with a normal exploitation of the work" – the DSB noted that if "normal" meant the full use of all exclusive rights then the Art 13 exception clause would be devoid of meaning (para 6.167). The DSB held that the term "normal" had both empirical and normative connotations and therefore covered actual and potent-ial exploitation (para 6.178) which "generate significant or tangible revenue" (para 6.180). The use conflicts with normal exploitation if it "enters into economic competit-ion with the ways that rights holders normally extract economic value from that right … and thereby deprive them of significant or tangible commercial gains" (para 6.183). Applying this test the DSB held that the home style exemption did not conflict with the normal exploitation of the work but that the business exemption did.

Finally, in relation to the third test – that exceptions or limitations "do not unreasonably prejudice the legitimate interests of the right holder" – the DSB held that "interests" are not limited to a legal right or title, or to economic advantage or detriment, but may include "something that is of importance to a natural or legal person" (para 6.223). Similarly, "legitimate" interests are not limited to lawful interests but include "interests that are justifiable in the light of the objectives that underlie the protection of exclusive rights" (para 6.224). "Prejudice" connotes "damage, harm or injury" and "not unreasonable" is said by the DSB to connote a "slightly stricter threshold than 'reasonable' ", a term which the DSB interprets in the more European sense of "proportionate" (para 6.225). In this case the DSB treated the legitimate interests of the rights owners as the economic value of the exclusive rights. Although this facilitated the measurement of the level of prejudice, the DSB emphasised that this was an "incomplete and thus conservative" way of looking at legitimate interests (para 6.227). The DSB concluded that "prejudice to the legitimate interests of right holders reaches an unreasonable level if an exception or limitation causes or has the potential to cause an unreasonable loss of income to the copyright owner" (para 6.229). In this case the DSB held that the home style exemption did not breach the requirement but that the business exemption did.

## Public interest

It has sometimes been suggested that there is no infringement of copyright if it is against the public interest to enforce copyright. The strongest obiter state-ment of this principle was the rather cranky remarks of the court in the English Spycatcher case, *Attorney-General v Guardian Newspapers Ltd (No 2)*,[59] but in

---

59    [1988] 3 All ER 545.

that case the court believed that the author, Peter Wright, did not own copyright in the work at all.[60]

In Australia the extent of this alleged exemption is very narrow and is based on the court's inherent jurisdiction to decline a discretionary remedy and its duty to prevent the legal system being misused. However, this inherent power must be offset against the importance of protecting property rights, including copyright. In *A-One Accessory Imports Pty Ltd v Off Road Imports Pty Ltd (No 2)*,[61] for example, Drummond J rejected the defendant's argument that a remedy should not be granted for infringement of copyright on the basis that the work infringed was itself an infringing work. He summed up the Australian position in the following terms:

> Where it is against public policy to enforce copyright because, eg, the copyright work is libellous, obscene or otherwise involves a publication contrary to the public interest, the courts will not give any remedy. See *Glyn v Western Feature Film Company* [1916] 1 Ch 261; *Attorney-General v Guardian Newspapers Ltd. (No 2)* [1988] 3 All ER 545 at 654. Even if copyright can exist in a compilation consisting entirely of parts pirated from other works, Copinger and Skone James, supra, at para 3-48, suggests that public policy might well justify the court, in such a case, refusing all relief for infringement of that copyright.
>
> However, where, as here, the work in question consists of a compilation of pirated and original work, there is no reason, on grounds of public policy, that I can see to deny all relief to the owner of copyright in the compilation: it is the entire compilation which has copyright and there is nothing in the *Copyright Act 1968* (Cth) which operates to make that entity an illegal work. The cases I referred to in my reasons of 27 March 1996, particularly *Redwood Music Ltd v Chappell & Co Ltd* [1982] RPC 109, show that there is good reason for holding that the owner of copyright in such a mixed work is entitled to a remedy for an infringement of that copyright. Counsel for the respondents yesterday drew my attention to the recently reported decision in *ZYX Music GmbH v King* (1995) 31 IPR 207. The passage in Lightman J's reasons at 214-15 supports my conclusion in this regard.
>
> Copyright is essentially a private proprietary right. Because there is no significant element of public interest involved in that statutory right or in its enforcement, it is appropriate, in my opinion, to have close regard to equitable rules governing the grant of injunctions and accounts of profit in deciding whether or not a particular copyright owner is entitled to any of those statutory forms of relief provided for by s 115. There is a suggestion in *Hayward Brothers v Lely & Co* (1887) 56 LT 418 at 421 that relief in respect of infringement of copyright in a compilation consisting of original material, including some original material tainted with a misrepresentation, might be limited to an injunction as to the parts not so tainted, as a consequence of the application of the equitable maxim requiring clean hands. In my opinion, since the A-One catalogue contains so much material pirated from the 1984 Phoenix catalogue and the 1991 Link catalogue, it would be inequitable to treat the applicants as standing in the position of an author of an entirely original work. Adopting the approach in *Moody v Cox and Hatt* [1917] 2 Ch 71 at 87-8, I think that the dirt on the applicants' hands, constituted by their extensive copying of the works of others, is so closely related to the equity claimed in the form of an injunction to restrain Off Road's use of its own infringing catalogue as to justify denying the applicants relief under s 115(2) of the *Copyright Act 1968* (Cth) analogous to discretionary equitable relief, by way of an injunction (and an account of the profits so earned by Off Road).[62]

---

60    See also Mason J in *Commonwealth v John Fairfax & Sons Ltd* (1980) 147 CLR 39 at 57 and Ungoed-Thomas J in *Beloff v Pressdram Ltd* [1973] 1 All ER 241 at 259 who suggested obiter that public interest may be a defence to copyright infringement.

61    (1996) 144 ALR 559.

62    (1996) 144 ALR 559 at 561-562.

## Educational use and assistance for people with a disability and certain purposes

The educational market is an attractive and potentially lucrative one for copyright owners. To have a book set as required reading in an educational institution brings not only prestige but also cash to the publisher and the author. From the point of view of students and educational institutions, on the other hand, accessing copyright educational material is necessary but potentially very expensive. In balancing the interests of copyright owners and users of educational material the *Copyright Act 1968* takes a softly softly approach. The Act provides for very limited free usage and three compulsory licence schemes. Part VA of the Act institutes a compulsory licence scheme for educational institutions and institutions assisting people with an intellectual disability to allow the institution to copy and communicate radio and television broadcasts. Part VB institutes a compulsory licence scheme which allows educational institutions and institutions assisting people with a print disability or an intellectual disability to reproduce and communicate works. Section 47 establishes a compulsory licence scheme for the broadcast of works by the holder of a print disability licence.

There are a number of defences allowing incidental usage of copyright material in the classroom. A teacher or a student, in the course of educational instruction, may perform or communicate a work or film or play a sound recording or broadcast without infringing the relevant performance or communication rights. The defence is very limited and does not cover the annual school play, for example (s 28). A teacher or student may reproduce a work by writing it on the board, showing it on an overhead projector or reproducing it in a question or answer in an examination (s 200(1)). In addition, the *Copyright Amendment Act 2006* allows for the proxy caching of material on a computer system operated by the institution for later access by staff and students for educational purposes (s 200AAA).

In addition, there are a number of defences allowing certain limited reproductions of works. Multiple reproductions of two pages or 1 per cent (whichever is the greater)[63] of a literary or dramatic work may be made (s 135ZG). Such insubstantial parts may also be made available online or transmitted electronically. A short extract of a work may be included in a collection of works (the collection may be in the form of a book, film or sound recording) subject to a number of restrictions. The collection must be for educational use, the work must not have been published for educational use, the collection must be principally composed of non-copyright material, there must be sufficient acknowledgment and no more than two works by the same author must be represented in the collection (s 44). Multiple copies of an insubstantial part of a published literary or dramatic work may be reproduced or communicated if the reproduction or communication is carried out on the premises of an educational institution for the purpose of a course of study provided by that institution (s 135ZMB). This is subject to many restrictions. The part must be less than 1 per cent of the number of words in the work; or less than 2 per cent if it is a reproduction or communication of an electronic format that is likely to change. Further insubstantial reproductions or

---

63    The whole of a work cannot be reproduced or communicated under this section. A potential copyright infringer cannot get around the limitations in this clause by reproducing only two pages at a time unless that person is prepared to wait 14 days between reproductions.

communications of the work cannot be made within 14 days and no more than one part of the work may be online at the same time.

Under the Part VB compulsory licence scheme, an educational institution may reproduce or communicate an article in a periodical, a work in an anthology or, if it is otherwise not available for a reasonable price, a whole work in hard copy or electronic form. An institution assisting people with a print disability may make a sound recording, a Braille version, large print, photographic or electronic version of a work if these are not already reasonable available. An institution assisting a person with an intellectual disability may reproduce, copy, make available online or transmit electronically any work, film, sound recording or film or a work included in a broadcast where this is done for the purposes of assisting the person. In all of these cases, however, it is important to remember that the use must still be paid for and the institution must serve a remuneration notice on the appropriate collecting agency.

Historically, radio has played an important part in providing educational services in Australia. The *Copyright Act 1968* provides that in the case of sound broadcasts which were made in order to be used for educational instruction ("School of the Air" was a popular example for many decades) there is no infringement of either the copyright in the broadcast or the underlying works if a copy is made by an educational institution for educational instruction at that institution (s 200(2), (2A)). This use is extended by the Part VA compulsory licence scheme which allows the relevant institution to copy or communicate a broadcast for educational purposes upon service of an appropriate remuneration notice.

A remuneration notice advises the appropriate collecting agency that the institution undertakes to pay equitable remuneration for the usage under the compulsory licence. The institution will indicate whether it will pay according to a records system (in which case they will pay per usage) or by way of a sampling system (in which case they will pay an annual rate calculated subject to an agreed sampling procedure of the actual usage). The amount of equitable remuneration in either case may be agreed between the parties or determined by the Copyright Tribunal.

These licences are not cheap. Under the 2008 Part VB agreement between Universities Australia and the Copyright Agency Limited (CAL), Australian universities pay $23.55 million per annum for the right to reproduce works for educational purposes. In 2010 educational institutions paid an additional $32.98 million to Screenrights for usage under the Part VA compulsory licence.

Note that the certain purposes defence may be used by a body administering an educational institution or to assist a person with a disability (s 200AB) and that the strict limitations of s 200AB do not operate to limit other defences under the Act (s 200AB(6)).

## Artistic works

Most of the defences relating to artistic works are quite minor and are designed to deal with works in public spaces or allow certain limited traditional usages of works. Thus, it is not an infringement of the copyright in a building or model of a building (s 66) or in a sculpture or work of artistic craftsmanship displayed in a public space (s 65) to paint, draw, engrave, photograph or film the work or to include it in a television broadcast. Amateur *plein air* painters and those taking holiday snaps therefore have a good defence should the copyright owner seek to prevent their undertakings or have their treasured works seized. The incidental inclusion of any artistic work in a film or television broadcast is also protected (s 67). This would extend to paintings on the wall behind the interviewee in a television broadcast or even the poster on the toilet door on a film set but would not extend to films specifically about the painting, for example. It is worth noting that if an artistic work is the subject of a direct television broadcast it might not constitute an infringement if the broadcast is not reduced to a material form. This is because the rights of the copyright owner in a work includes the right to reproduce in a material form but does not include the right to broadcast the work (s 31(10)(b)). A work, film or broadcast made under ss 65, 66 and 67 may be published without constituting an infringement (s 68).

Two traditional usages of artistic works are also allowed under the Act. First, even if the copyright in an artistic work has been assigned the artist may reproduce the artistic work in a later work so long as the later work does not repeat or imitate the main design of the original work (s 72). Secondly, there is no infringement in a building, model of a building, architectural drawing or plans if the building is reconstructed (s 73) but, as previously mentioned, the relationship between reconstruction, repair, renovation and refurbishment has not been considered by the courts.

## Using artistic works as designs and applying artistic works industrially[64]

The broad definition of artistic work to include industrial plans and diagrams means that a diagram, for example, may be both an artistic work under the *Copyright Act 1968* and a representation of a design entitled to protection under the *Designs Act 1906* or the *Designs Act 2003*. If someone were to reproduce the diagram by making a three-dimensional article such an action might constitute a reproduction of the artistic work under the *Copyright Act* and the application of a design to an article in contravention of the *Designs Act*. In other words, without some specific provision there may be dual coverage of the one subject-matter.

This is significant for two reasons. On the one hand, the *Designs Act* (which we consider later in the text) has a shorter protection period than the *Copyright Act* (being up to 10 years rather than the life of the author plus 70 years). If a designer could protect a design by relying on the *Copyright Act* rather than the *Designs Act*, the *Designs Act* would be rendered largely useless. This is so even though the *Designs Act* grants a monopoly to the registered owner of the design which does not rely on proof of subjective copying. In practice it seems that most designs infringements result from subjective copying rather than from independent development. Secondly, the shorter period of the designs monopoly would also be rendered useless if, upon expiration of the monopoly period, the designer could resort to the *Copyright Act* for protection of the design.

Given this situation one might wonder why special legislation to protect designs was passed at all. The reason is largely historical. At the time of the first designs statute in 1787, copyright law had proved inadequate to protect

---

64    For transitional provisions relating to the industrial application of artistic works, see *Copyright Act 1968* s 218.

industrial applications and there was no copyright infringement by the making of a three-dimensional representation of a two-dimensional work. The first designs statute applied only to the design of muslins and other named fabrics and it was only gradually that the designs regime extended to protect the wide variety of designs for industrial products which it does today.

In the light of this possible dual protection the legislature today is faced with a number of possibilities. The legislature could provide that copyright does not subsist in a design which could be registered under the *Designs Act*. The legislature might provide that a designer has to elect at a certain point in time which protection is being sought. The legislature might provide that copyright in a registrable design expires at the same time as the design monopoly. Over the years, various approaches have been taken to this problem and provisions dealing with the designs–copyright overlap have been subject to significant amendment.[65]

Under ss 74-77A of the *Copyright Act* the latest approach is to provide that it is not an infringement of copyright to reproduce an artistic work by embodying a "corresponding design" in a product. A "corresponding design" is defined in s 74 as:

> in relation to an artistic work, means visual features of shape or configuration which, when embodied in a product, result in a reproduction of that work, whether or not the visual features constitute a design that is capable of registration under the *Designs Act 2003*.

For the purposes of this definition, embodied in, in relation to a product, includes woven into, impressed on or worked into the product (s 74(2)). Note that the definition effectively limits the concept of a corresponding design to three-dimensional aspects of a product – that is, it covers the shape and configuration of a product but not its pattern or ornamentation. In particular it would not cover merely two-dimensional aspects of an artistic work as applied to the surface of an object.

Broadly speaking, this means that, subject to limitations mentioned below, if a person reproduced a drawing of a chair by making the chair there would be no infringement of copyright. If a person reproduced a drawing of a chair by applying the drawing of the chair to a T shirt the defence would not apply and there would be an infringement of copyright. The defence applies whether or not the "corresponding design" has been registered under the *Designs Act*.

In the case of an artistic work where the "corresponding design" is or has been registered under the *Designs Act*, s 75 of the *Copyright Act* simply provides that it is not an infringement of copyright in the artistic work to reproduce the work by embodying that design or any other corresponding design in a product.

In the case of a "corresponding design" which has not been registered the provisions are a little more complex. Section 77 of the *Copyright Act 1968* applies to an artistic work, other than a building, model of a building or work of artistic craftsmanship, where a "corresponding design" has not been registered under the *Designs Act 1906* or *2003* or is not registrable but the corresponding design has been applied industrially and products embodying the design have been sold, hired or offered or exposed for sale or hire (that is, dealt with) in Australia or elsewhere. (Note that buildings, models of buildings and artistic works have traditionally not been registrable under the *Designs Act* in any case. A building or

---

65    For a detailed consideration of the history of legislative responses to the designs–copyright overlap, see Gummow J's judgment in *Interlego AG v Croner Trading Pty Ltd* (1992) 111 ALR 577.

model of a building is defined in s 77(5) in accordance with this traditional practice.) Section 77 also applies where the design has been disclosed in a complete patent specification or in a representation accompanying a designs application. In each of these cases there is no infringement of copyright to reproduce the artistic work by embodying it in a product at any time after the corresponding work has been so dealt with or disclosed.

Under reg 17 of the *Copyright Regulations 1969* a design is taken to be applied industrially for the purposes of s 77 if it is applied to more than 50 articles or to one or more articles (other than hand-made articles) manufactured in lengths or pieces. This definition is not exhaustive and in *Press-Form Pty Ltd v Henderson's Ltd*[66] Gummow J held that a public display of a prototype for the purposes of attracting or sealing a sale was an industrial application for the purposes of s 77.[67] Where there are two or more articles of the same general character which are intended to be used together then they will be counted as a single article. A design is taken to be applied to an article, for the purposes of this regulation, if the design is applied to the article by a process (whether a process of printing, embossing or otherwise) or if the design is reproduced on or in the article in the course of the production of the article.

Section 76 provides special rules for cases where a corresponding design has been falsely registered under the *Designs Act*. The general rule is that the corresponding design will be deemed never to have been registered and so s 77 applies. This is subject to the provision that if the alleged copyright infringer was acting bona fide with the consent of the person falsely registered under the *Designs Act* then the design will be deemed to have been registered for the purpose of relying on the s 75 defence.

A lot of case law arises under these provisions because infringements tend to occur in commercial circumstances where the parties can afford to or are inclined to take action. As a matter of practice the most contentious issue has been whether the "corresponding design" is a "design" under the *Designs Act*. This question of what is a design will be dealt with in detail when we consider the *Designs Act* but it is worth noting that a "design" must be embodied in a product and a mere drawing on paper, for example, has been held not to be a design to which the *Designs Act* applies.[68] Furthermore, s 77 of the *Copyright Act* provides that the defence does not apply in relation to "designs" which are excluded by regulation from registration under the *Designs Act*. Under reg 4.06 medals; certain usages of the word ANZAC; certain representations of Australian currency; scandalous designs; and Arms, seals, flags and emblems of the Commonwealth, a State or Territory, a city, town or public authority or of another country are prescribed designs.

It is notable that the ss 74-77 defences, as written, only apply when the reproduction constitutes a finished product. Section 77A was added in 2004 to ensure that reproductions and communications of a three-dimensional product in the process of making such a finished product, or the making of a cast or mould for the purposes of making such a finished product, are not infringements where the making, selling or otherwise dealing with the finished product would not be an infringement under the previous provisions.

---

66  (1993) 26 IPR 113.
67  See also *Safe Sport Australia Pty Ltd v Puma Australia Pty Ltd* (1985) 4 IPR 120.
68  *Re Littlewood's Pools Ltd* (1949) 66 RPC 309.

## Performances

The performance right in works, as we saw, is restricted to performances in public as is the right to cause a sound recording or film to be seen or heard. Sections 46 and 106 partially codify the case law relating to what constitutes "in public" by providing that it is not an infringement of copyright in a literary, dramatic or musical work to operate "reception equipment" (a radio or television for example) or to play a sound recording in premises where people reside or sleep so long as this performance is provided only for residents, inmates and their guests. Sound recordings may also be played as part of the activities of a non-profit charity, society or similar organisation. Note that these defences do not apply to films and therefore were not available to the motel owners in *Rank Film Production Ltd v Dodds*.[69]

The Act also provides for what might be characterised as a traditional use by allowing a public reading or recitation from a published literary or dramatic work so long as there is sufficient acknowledgment and the extract is of a reasonable length. The recitation or reading may be included in a sound or television broadcast (s 45).

We have already noted s 110 which provides that film news footage may be shown in public 50 years after the events portrayed rather than the usual 50 years after the film was published. Note, however, that the defence only applies to copyright in the film and does not extend to works which may be incorporated in the film.

## Communications and broadcasting

Beside the private and domestic use defences considered above there are a number of very technical defences relating to broadcasting and communications. If a person has a licence to broadcast a work or sound recording the Act provides that the person may film or record the work or recording for the purposes of making that broadcast. If, however, a different person makes the film or recording then equitable remuneration is due to the owner of the copyright in the original work or sound recording (ss 47, 110, 70). Similarly, if a person has a licence to transmit a free-to-air broadcast the person has the right under a compulsory licence to also transmit a work, film or sound recording included in that broadcast if the person agrees to pay equitable remuneration. On the other hand, there is no infringement or payment necessary if the re-transmission is necessary only in order to deal with different time zones (Part VC). The *Broadcasting Services Act 1992* requires broadcasters in certain circumstances to make simultaneous digital and analogue broadcasts. If a recording of a literary, dramatic or musical work or of a film or sound recording is made for this purpose there is no copyright infringement (ss 47AA and 110C).

Sections 43A and 111A provide that a temporary copy of a work or audio-visual item may be made in the process of making or receiving an authorised communication. The exemptions do not cover temporary storage of material in the operation of a digital appliance and so would not cover modern photocopiers and portable CD players, for example, which temporarily store material before

---

69    (1983) 2 IPR 113.

it is printed or received by the listener. It is restricted to caching made in the process of communicating a work and is meant to limit the liability of Internet Service Providers (ISPs) for reproductions and copies made in the process of communicating copyright material. It also allows browsing of copyright material without risk of infringement.[70]

These narrow defences have been substantially broadened by the *US Free Trade Agreement Implementation Act 2004* which introduced s 43B and s 111B into the *Copyright Act 1968* and limited the liability of ISPs for infringement. Under s 43A and s 111B there is no infringement of copyright if a reproduction is made incidentally as part of the technical process of using a copy of the work. This would cover the cases of reading online, playing a DVD and operating an electronic device such as a DVD player. The defence effectively addresses the problems considered in *Stevens v Kabushiki Kaisha Sony Computer Entertainment*[71] as to whether a transient reproduction amounts to a reproduction or copy for the purposes of infringement. The limitation on the remedies available against ISPs will be considered in the next chapter.

## Computer programs

A reproduction of a computer program may be made as part of the normal running of the program or for making a back-up or spare copy of the program (ss 47B and 47C). Reproductions of the computer program may be made for the purposes of studying the program (s 47B), correcting errors (s 47E), testing for security (s 47F) and in order to make interoperable programs (s 47D). These defences only apply to authorised computer programs and only to the extent necessary to achieve the stated purpose. These rights in relation to computer programs cannot be excluded by contract (s 47H).

## Parallel importation of books, sound recordings, computer programs, electronic literary or musical items and non-infringing accessories

As we have seen, importing copyright articles for the purposes of commercial dealing or commercially dealing with copyright articles without the licence of the copyright owner is an indirect infringement of copyright under ss 37 and 38 (works) and ss 102 and 103 (Part IV subject-matter). These provisions are powerful commercial weapons in the hands of copyright holders and have been subject to criticism both by consumer groups and potential competitors, especially in the book publishing and sound-recording industries. It has been argued that the provisions maintain high prices by limiting competition and, over time, the Act has been amended to allow parallel importation, first, of books, then sound recordings, computer programs and, finally, electronic literary and musical items (meaning a book or periodical in electronic form or sheet music in electronic form) regardless of whether there is a printed form of the work (s 10(1)) plus published

---

70   For a discussion of caching generally, see Intellectual Property and Competition Review Committee, *Review of Intellectual Property Legislation Under the Competition Principles Agreement, Final Report*, 2000, pp 108-113.

71   (2005) 224 CLR 193.

editions of these works. Each new importable item has been subject to fewer and fewer restrictions and we shall deal with each of them in turn.

Following a report by the Copyright Law Review Committee in 1988[72] and the Prices Surveillance Authority in 1989[73] regarding parallel importation of books, the *Copyright Amendment Act 1991* inserted provisions in the *Copyright Act 1968* allowing parallel importation of copyright books in limited circumstances (s 44A as to works in books; s 112A as to published editions of works). In 1998 the *Copyright Amendment Act (No 2) 1998* was passed allowing parallel importation of certain sound recordings (s 44D as to sound recording of works; s 112 as to sound recordings). This amendment followed the Prices Surveillance Authority report in 1990[74] and a number of legislative attempts to implement the recommendations over the next seven years. Most recently, the question of parallel imports has been addressed by the Intellectual Property and Competition Review Committee in 2000.[75] The Committee recommended the wholesale repeal of limitations on parallel importing under the *Copyright Act 1968* with a 12-month transitional period for the book industry.

In the case of books a person may import one "non-infringing" copy of a published book (defined in s 10 as a book whose making did not constitute an infringement of copyright) for a customer who undertakes not to deal with the book in a manner specified in s 37. A person may also import two or more non-infringing copies of any published book for a non-profit library. Books which have been published overseas since the commencing date of the provisions may be imported into Australia without infringement of copyright if the books have not also been published in Australia. In the case of books published in Australia or published overseas before the commencement of the parallel importing provisions a person may only import non-infringing copies if the publisher is first given an opportunity to supply the book within 90 days. These provisions therefore serve the dual purposes of ensuring that Australian readers have access to works published anywhere in the world and allowing publishers to maintain their effective monopoly so long as they meet the demands of Australian readers.

In the case of sound recordings a person may import any non-infringing copy of a sound recording which has been published in Australia or overseas with the consent of the copyright owner. This prevents the parallel importation of pirated recordings. If the sound recording was made or published in a country which does not provide copyright protection for sound recordings the provisions identify an imputed owner for the purposes of determining whether such consent has been granted. The burden is on the defendant to prove that the imported copy is not an infringing copy (s 130A). The difficulty this imposes on the defendant has been commented upon by Hill J in *Australian Competition and Consumer Commission v Universal Music Australia Pty Ltd*.[76] In that case Warner Brothers

---

72    Copyright Law Review Committee, *The Importation Provisions of the Copyright Act, 1968*, AGPS, Canberra, 1988.

73    Prices Surveillance Authority, *Inquiry into Book Prices, Interim Report, Report No 24*, AGPS, Canberra, 1989.

74    Prices Surveillance Authority, *Inquiry into the Prices of Sound Recordings, Report No 35*, AGPS, 1990.

75    Intellectual Property and Competition Review Committee, *Report on Parallel Importation under the Copyright Act*, 2000, and *Review of Intellectual Property Legislation Under the Competition Principles Agreement, Final Report*, 2000.

76    (2001) 115 FCR 442 at 449.

and Universal Music Australia were found liable for breach of restrictive trade practices under the *Trade Practices Act 1974* (now the *Competition and Consumer Act 2010*) ss 45 and 47 for conduct engaged in against record stores which sold cheap parallel import CDs.[77]

In 2003 the Act was further amended to allow parallel importation and dealing with non-infringing copies of a computer program (s 44E) or electronic literary or musical item (s 44F) or a published edition of electronic literary or music items (s 112DA). The materials are non-infringing if they were made in a "qualifying country" and did not constitute an infringement under the laws of that country (s 10AB and s 10AC). A qualifying country is defined as a country that is a party to the Berne Convention or a member of the WTO and has laws protecting subsistence and ownership of copyright in accordance with the TRIPS Agreement (s 10). In an action for infringement it is presumed that the copy is not a non-infringing copy unless the defendant proves otherwise (ss 130B and 130C).

These defences would be useless if the copyright owner could get around them by claiming that the importation of a sound recording, for example, constituted an indirect infringement of the copyright in the label or packaging associated with the sound recording. For this reason s 44C provides that the importation of an article does not constitute an infringement of copyright in a "non-infringing accessory". Section 10 defines an accessory "in relation to an article" as "a label affixed to, displayed on, incorporated into the surface of, or accompanying, the article; the packaging or container in which the article is packaged or contained; a label affixed to, displayed on, incorporated into the surface of, or accompanying, the packaging or container in which the article is packaged or contained; a written instruction, warranty or other information provided with the article; a record embodying an instructional sound recording, or a copy of an instructional cinematograph film, provided with the article". Section 10AD provides that an accessory also includes a copy of any work or other subject-matter, other than a feature film, that is embodied in or included with an article which contains a copy of a computer program or electronic literary or music work. Feature film is defined narrowly and thus the section would not normally capture short video clips in electronic games, for example, but does prevent the importation of pirated DVDs on the basis that they are an accessory to some other non-infringing computer program or electronic work.

In *The Polo/Lauren Company v Ziliani Holdings,*[78] Polo/Lauren unsuccessfully argued that the well-known Polo logo embroidered on its shirt was not a label because the use of the words "in relation to" in s 10 meant that the label had to be conceptually distinct from the article; that the logo was not a label because it was primarily decorative rather than informative; and that the trial judge had conflated the notion of trade mark and label. The Full Court accepted that a label had to be conceptually distinct from the article but held that in this case it was.[79] The Full Court rejected the argument that the logo was purely decorative because, considered objectively, the logo also had a functional purpose of identifying the clothes as Polo/Lauren.[80] Finally, the Full Court recognised

---

77    For the relationship between the *Copyright Act 1968* and the *Trade Practices Act 1974*, now the *Competition and Consumer Act 2010* see Chapter 6, "Dealing With Copyright".

78    [2008] FCA 49.

79    [2008] FCA 49 at [22].

80    [2008] FCA 49 at [29].

that a label is a physical object whilst a trade mark is an intangible property and that therefore, in a legislative sense, a label is not a trade mark. "Nonetheless, where a trademark is physically manifested and incorporated into an article … the trademark is being used to identify the article with its sources. Its purpose is to label the goods: it is a label".[81]

In 2003 the Act was also amended to deal with the significant problem of trade marks on imported copyright material. As we shall see, in broad terms a trade mark is not infringed by the importation of goods to which a trade mark has been lawfully applied overseas with the consent of the registered owner of the trade mark.

The 2002 amendments to the *Copyright Act* attempt to ensure that the *Trade Marks Act 1995* is not used to indirectly prohibit otherwise lawful parallel importations of copyright material. Section 198A provides that there is no trade mark infringement if the trade mark is applied to goods that have been imported under the parallel importation provisions of the *Copyright Act* if the trade mark was applied before importation by the registered owner of the trade mark or by a person who at the time of application was the "owner" of a trade mark and had been a registered owner of the trade mark in the past. This section arguably widens the trade marks defence but it is doubtful whether it clarifies the question of who is a registered owner or owner of a trade mark for the purposes of determining whether the trade mark is or is not infringing.

## Libraries, archives and key cultural institutions

There is a need to balance the interests of libraries and library users against the interests of copyright owners and authors. The balance is partly achieved under the *Copyright Act 1968* which provides a number of exemptions to copyright infringement for libraries carrying out their functions. In addition, under the *Public Lending Right Act 1985* the Federal Government provides some compensation to "creators" whose books are included in library collections "in recognition of their loss of income from their books being available for loan from, or for use in, public lending libraries in Australia; and to support the enrichment of Australian culture by encouraging Australian persons to create books and by encouraging publishers to publish books in Australia".[82]

Libraries have an important role in collecting, maintaining and disseminating information and in the past a national, State or university library might realistically aim to maintain a comprehensive collection, at least in nominated areas, in order to carry out this role. Such an aim is unrealistic and arguably unnecessary given the ease with which electronic information can be stored and shared. In the words of the Intellectual Property and Competition Review Committee:

> The Committee believes that libraries are more, not less, important in the information age. We are also convinced of the fundamental importance of allowing Australia's libraries to act as a system built on a base of resource sharing and cooperation, if the goal of widespread access to information is to be achieved. It has long been the case that no library could aspire to an all-embracing collection and acquire all relevant material for users.

---

81   [2008] FCA 49 at [31].
82   *Public Lending Right Act 1985* s 3.

If anything, new technologies, and the continued rapid growth in the knowledge base make it even more unlikely that such an aspiration could be fulfilled ... However, whilst undermining the classical notion of libraries as a comprehensive store of knowledge, the development of a "digital library" creates new scope for libraries to provide effective access to widely dispersed information.[83]

Ideally, from a user's point of view, a "digital library" would allow the user to access the library's resources without having to physically attend the library; allow libraries to co-operate nationally and internationally to provide an internationally comprehensive collection; and enable libraries to address chronic funding shortages by instituting such co-operative arrangements. From the copyright owner's point of view such a scenario is somewhat of a nightmare and copyright owners have expressed the opinion that the defences applying to library usage pose a threat to the rights of the copyright owner.[84] At the extreme, copyright owners may believe that the birth of the "digital library" will reduce their potential sale of electronic resources to one. On the whole, the copyright owners' view has prevailed and legislative responses have sought to maintain the status quo by equating digital works with hard copy works and limiting access to most electronic works to in-library viewing. The potential of the "digital library" may never be realised and, under the *Copyright Act* ss 48-53, only the following limited acts do not constitute an infringement of copyright.

*Making electronic works available online.* If an article in a periodical journal or a work has been acquired by a library or archive in electronic form the library or archive may make the work or article available online within the premises of the library in such a manner that users cannot make an electronic reproduction of it or communicate it (s 49). Under s 50 the article or work may be reproduced and supplied to another library for this purpose. Section 49 does not authorise the digitalisation of a work or article acquired in non-electronic form and therefore does not allow libraries to provide electronic, online reserve services, for example.

*Research and study.* An authorised archivist or librarian of a non-profit library may reproduce and supply one article in a periodical journal, part of one article, two or more articles in a periodical journal if they are for the same research or course of study, or a reasonable part of a published work for a person who has requested a reproduction for the purposes of research and study and has made a declaration to that effect. Section 49(5AA) provides that "reasonable portion" is defined for the purposes of this section in accordance with s 10(2) and (2A): that is, 10 per cent of the published work in electronic or hard copy form (where the work is more than 10 pages long) with special provisions for work published in chapters.

"Supply" includes making the article available to the person online or electronically transmitting it to that person. If a work or article is communicated to a person under this section then the person must be notified that the communication

---

83    Intellectual Property and Competition Review Committee, *Review of Intellectual Property Legislation Under the Competition Principles Agreement, Final Report*, 2000, p 90.

84    See submissions to the Copyright Law Review Committee *Copyright and Contract* review. For a summary of issues arising from these submissions, see Copyright Law Review Committee, *Paper for Meeting With the Copyright Law Review Committee on 4 October 2001* <http://www.law.gov.au/clrc>.

is made under this section, that it may be subject to copyright and the library or archive must destroy any reproduction made for the purposes of the communication as soon as possible (s 49). Under s 50 the article or work may be reproduced and supplied to another library for this purpose.

An authorised librarian of a non-profit library or archivist may reproduce and supply the whole of a published work or more than a reasonable part of a published work for such a person if the work is part of the library or archive collection and the librarian or archivist has first ascertained that a new copy of the work cannot be obtained within a reasonable time and at a reasonable price (s 49). Under s 50 the article or work may be reproduced and supplied to another library for this purpose. The s 49 and s 50 defences do not apply if the library or archives imposes a charge which exceeds the cost of reproducing and supplying the reproduction.

An authorised librarian may reproduce and communicate a thesis or other similar literary work or an unpublished work which forms part of a university library or archival collection if the reproduction or communication is for a person who satisfies the librarian that the person requires it for the purposes of study or research (s 51).

*Adding to collection of another library.* An authorised librarian may reproduce and supply one article, part of one article, two or more articles from a periodical journal on the same subject, a work or part of a work to another library for inclusion in its collection. If the librarian reproduces and supplies the whole of a work or more than a reasonable part of a work the librarian must be satisfied that a new copy of the work cannot be obtained within a reasonable time, at an ordinary commercial price. In the case of electronic articles, even if less than a reasonable part is reproduced and supplied, the librarian must be satisfied that the part cannot be obtained by itself or together with a reasonable portion of the article within a reasonable time at an ordinary commercial price (s 50). The Copyright Law Review Committee reports that at least some universities have given evidence that this is one of the free uses which is often restricted under licensing agreements with publishers.[85]

*Publications of unpublished works.* Copyright is not infringed in a manuscript or reproduction of a literary, dramatic, musical work, or artistic work which has not been published 50 years after the death of the author and which forms part of the collection of a library or archive, if the manuscript is reproduced or communicated by an authorised librarian or other person with a view to publication of the work (s 51).

*Preservation and other purposes.* The Australian Archives may make or communicate a work held in its collection for use as a reference or working copy at its central office or in a regional office (s 51AA). A library or archives may make and communicate a work, sound recording or film held in its collection for preservation purposes, administrative purposes or to replace a damaged or stolen copy if a copy of the work, recording or film cannot be obtained within a reasonable time and at an ordinary commercial cost. Replacement and preservation copies

---

85    See Copyright Law Review Committee, *Law and Contract – Issues Paper* and *Paper for Meeting With the Copyright Law Review Committee on 4 October 2001* <http://www.law.gov.au/clrc>.

may be made available online for administrative purposes (in the case of works) or for viewing by library users within the premises of the library or archives in such a manner that they cannot be communicated or reproduced by the viewer (s 51A as to works, s 110B as to sound recordings and films). The *Copyright Amendment Act 2006* made special provisions applying to libraries, archives and declared key cultural institutions for the preservation of works, sound recordings, films and published editions of works of historical and cultural significance to Australia (s 51B as to works, s 110BA as to sound recordings and films and s 112AA as to published editions of works).

*Certain purposes.* Note that the certain purposes defence may be used by a body administering a library or archive (s 200AB) and that the strict limitations of s 200AB do not operate to limit other defences under the Act (s 200AB(6)).

*Members of parliament.* An authorised librarian of a parliamentary library may reproduce or otherwise deal with a copyright work for the purpose of assisting a member of a parliament to perform his or her duties (s 48A as to published works, s 51 as to unpublished works). Under s 50 a published work may be reproduced and supplied to another library for this purpose.

## Crown copyright and legal proceedings

A compulsory licence scheme authorises the Crown in right of the Commonwealth or a State or a person authorised in writing[86] by the Crown to exercise any of the rights of the copyright holder in copyright subject-matter if such exercise is "for the services of the Commonwealth or State" (ss 182B-183A). Meeting the defence needs of another country is deemed to be "for the services of the Commonwealth" (s 183(2)). On the other hand educational purposes are deemed not to be "for the services of the Crown" presumably because educational usages are otherwise dealt with (s 183(11)). The Crown is required to notify the copyright owner of the use unless this would be contrary to the public interest. Alternatively, the Crown may notify a relevant collecting society. In either case the terms of the licence may be agreed between the parties or determined by the Copyright Tribunal. In *Re Australasian Performing Right Association Ltd's Reference; Re Australian Broadcasting Commission,*[87] the Full Federal Court rejected an argument by the ABC that it was the Crown for the purposes of s 183.

Any of the rights of the copyright owner may be exercised with impunity if they were exercised for the purposes of judicial proceedings, reporting judicial proceedings or in the course of giving or seeking legal professional advice from a legal practitioner, patent attorney or trade marks attorney (ss 43 and 104). In addition, a single photocopy of certain "prescribed works" may be made without infringing the copyright or any prerogative right or privilege which the Crown may have in the work. These works are State, Commonwealth and Territory statutes and instruments plus judgments, orders, awards and reasons for decisions of courts and statutory tribunals (s 182A). The Copyright Law Review

---

86   The authorisation may be given after the act has taken place: *Copyright Act 1968* s 183(3).
87   (1982) 45 ALR 153.

Committee is currently considering whether the provision should be extended to cover multiple copies.[88]

The breadth of the statutory licence for Crown use was considered by the High Court in *Copyright Agency Ltd v New South Wales*.[89] The matter related to the use of survey plans which had been lodged with the State Government under various statutes. The Copyright Agency Limited (CAL), representing the surveyors, had demanded payment under the statutory licence scheme for Crown use. The Crown argued that it had an implied licence, apart from the s 183 statutory licence, to use the plans. The Crown did not argue any statutory defences to copyright infringement.

Certain of the Crown uses were not challenged in the case – eg making a working copy of the survey in order to effect registration and the issuing of title. However, post-registration uses, including the copying of the plans for public purposes and the communication of the plans to the public, were considered.

The High Court noted that the *Copyright Act* did not distinguish between commercial and public usages for the purpose of the statutory licence scheme even though, as a matter of legislative history, some limitations had been considered by the drafters. The High Court also noted that other countries including the United Kingdom and New Zealand did provide some limitations. Therefore, although these uses were required or authorised by legislation, the High Court held that the Crown was still required to pay remuneration for these uses under the statutory licence scheme for Crown use.

The High Court further held that there was no implied licence apart from s 183 for the Crown to use the surveys in the contested manner. The contested usages did not relate to the private interests of the applicant; the nature of the relationship between the surveyor, the Crown and the client meant that the issue of remuneration had not been factored in; the legislative history of the statutory licence scheme did not distinguish between public and commercial usages; and there was no necessity to imply a licence to allow the Crown to make the contested usages.

## Compulsory licences in the music industry

Before learning about intellectual property you may not have wondered whether a particular radio station had the right to play a piece of music, whether a café had the right to play the radio or have a juke box on or whether a night club or pub had to control what the band might play. You probably did not think about whether the congregation of a local church was allowed to sing hymns. If, in a relaxed moment, you wondered why singers made cover versions of songs and why there were hundreds of recorded versions of "Stairway to Heaven" you probably did not think it was a legal issue.

Sound-recording companies have never succeeded in establishing the effective control over their industry that book publishers have enjoyed. The *Copyright Act*

---

88   The power of live performers to negotiate compulsory licences in relation to Crown copyright is limited by the *US Free Trade Agreement Implementation Act 2004*, inserting s 100AH in the *Copyright Act*.

89   (2008) 233 CLR 279.

*1968* ensures that smaller players in the music industry have a slice of the market and that the public is able to hear and perform music. Section 105 provides that, if a sound recording was not made in Australia or was not made by a qualified person and therefore only receives copyright protection because it was first published (usually under the international provisions) in Australia, it may be played in public or broadcast without any infringement of copyright. Other published sound recordings may be played in public (s 108) or broadcast (s 109) if the person who plays or broadcasts the sound recording pays or agrees to pay equitable remuneration to the copyright owner. If the sound recording has not been published in Australia it may not be performed or broadcast under these licences until seven weeks after its first publication. The amount of equitable remuneration may be agreed between the parties or determined by the Copyright Tribunal.

The most significant compulsory licence allows any manufacturer to make a sound recording for retail sale of any musical work which has previously been recorded so long as the recording was made in or imported into Australia for retail sale or made in or imported into a country named in Sch 8 to the *Copyright Regulations 1969* for retail sale (ss 54-64). In the usual case the original manu-facturer has a one month grace period before the second manufacturer is allowed to sell the new recording. In the case of cinema sound tracks and sound tracks for musicals and other dramatic works, however, the second manufacturer may not sell the new recording without the permission of the person who owns the copyright in the musical work. This means that a sound alike version of "Cats" cannot be sold without the licence of Andrew Lloyd Webber or his assignee.

Before the introduction of the *Copyright Amendment (Moral Rights) Act 2000* the compulsory licence scheme was subject to the general proviso that a new recording of an adaptation of a musical work must not "debase" the musical work. In *Schott Musik International GMBH and Co v Colossal Records of Australia Pty Ltd*,[90] the court held that a techno dance version of the "O Fortuna" chorus from "Carmina Burana" did not debase the original. The majority held that the question must be determined musicologically by reference to the work. Hill J, in the minority, held that the question should be determined by reference to the fame of the author and the manner in which the sound recording was used. Today the original work would be protected from debasement, if it is protected at all, through the assertion of the author's moral rights and it is arguable that Hill J's approach reflects the new statutory approach. Moral rights are considered in more detail in Chapter 7.[91]

90   (1997) 145 ALR 483.
91   Note that live performers have limited rights in relation to the negotiation of compulsory licences: see *US Free Trade Agreement Implementation Act 2004*, inserting s 100AH in the *Copyright Act*.

# CASES

## *De Garis v Neville Jeffress Pidler Pty Ltd*
Federal Court of Australia: Beaumont J
(1990) 95 ALR 625

The respondents provided a press clipping service and were sued by two journalists, one employed by a newspaper, the other an independent contractor, for breach of copyright in their published articles on the basis that the articles had been reproduced by the press clipping service for distribution to its paying subscribers. The respondents raised the three primary fair dealing defences.

**Beaumont J: [628]** *Section 40 – fair dealing for the purpose of research or study*
The material provisions of s 40 are as follows. A fair dealing with a literary work for the purpose of research or study does not constitute an **[629]** infringement of the copyright of the work: s 40(1). In determining whether a dealing by way of copying the whole or part of the work constitutes a fair dealing, regard shall be had to: (a) the purpose and character of the dealing; (b) the nature of the work; (c) the possibility of obtaining the work within a reasonable time at an ordinary commercial price; (d) the effect of the dealing upon the potential market for, or value of, the work; and (e) in the case where part only of the work is copied – the amount and substantiality of the part copied taken in relation to the whole work: s 40(2). Notwithstanding s 40(2), a dealing with a literary work by way of copying, for the purposes of research or study, of not more than a "reasonable portion" of the work (as defined in s 10(2)) shall be taken to be a fair dealing: s 40(3).

Can it be said that the Jeffress' dealing with the work (assuming, for the moment, without deciding, that the dealing is "fair") is done by Jeffress "for the purpose of research" within the meaning of s 40(1)?

It will be recalled that Jeffress did not call any evidence. There is no direct evidence of the actual method of operation of the "press-clipping and media research bureau" (as it is stated in the order form), but it is, I think, reasonable to infer that Jeffress has established an effective method of retrieval of material published in newspapers by reference to subject matter. Is this "research" within the meaning of s 40?

According to the *Macquarie Dictionary*, "research" may be defined as: "1. diligent and systematic enquiry or investigation into a subject in order to discover facts or principles: *research in nuclear physics* ..."

In my view, "research" in s 40 is intended to have this dictionary meaning.

In my opinion, Jeffress' dealing with the work is not something done for the purpose of research. Although the retrieval of the material may be a complicated exercise, it does not follow that the purpose of Jeffress is research. Its purpose, which is purely commercial, is to supply a photocopy of material already published in return for a fee. This is an activity engaged in by Jeffress in the ordinary course of trade, which, in my view, is in the nature of an information audit and should be distinguished from research activity of the kind contemplated by s 40: see *Re Attorney-General (British Columbia) and Messier* (1984) 8 DLR (4th) 306.

There is another reason why s 40 cannot apply here. The relevant purpose required by s 40(1) is that of Jeffress, not that of its customer. That is to say, even if a customer were engaged in research, this would not assist Jeffress. In *Sillitoe v McGraw-Hill Book Co (UK) Ltd* [1983] FSR 545, Judge Mervyn Davies said at 558: "The onus of showing that an exception applies is on the defendants. Mr Jeffs contended that s 6(1) is widely drawn and not limited to the actual student, so that if a dealing is fair and for the purposes of private study the sub-section applies whether the private study in mind is one's own or that of somebody else. Here, he said, the dealing was for the purpose of private study by the examinees who would acquire the notes. I do not accept that argument. To my mind s 6(1) authorises what would otherwise be an infringement if one is engaged in private study or research. The authors of the Notes, when writing the Notes and thus 'dealing' with the original work, were not engaged in private study or research. To my mind *University of London Press Ltd v University Tutorial Press Ltd* [1916] 2 Ch 601 at 613, affords some support for this view."

[630] In the *University of London case,* above, Peterson J said at 613: "The defendants on these facts contend that their publication of the three papers set by Professor Lodge and Mr Jackson is a fair dealing with them for the purposes of private study within s 2, sub-s (1), of the Act of 1911, and is therefore not an infringement of copyright. It could not be contended that the mere republication of a copyright work was a 'fair dealing' because it was intended for purposes of private study; nor, if an author produced a book of questions for the use of students, could another person with impunity republish the book with the answers to the questions. Neither case would, in my judgment, come within the description of 'fair dealing'. In the present case the paper on more advanced mathematics has been taken without any attempt at providing solutions for the questions, and the only way in which the defendants have dealt with this paper is by appropriating it, except that there are 11 lines of criticism of it, dividing the questions into easy, troublesome, and difficult questions."

It follows, in my view, that the activities of Jeffress cannot be characterised as "research" for the purposes of s 40.

Is the dealing done for the purpose of "study".

The *Macquarie Dictionary* definitions of the noun "study" include the following: "1. application of the mind to the acquisition of knowledge, as by reading, investigation or reflection. 2. the cultivation of a particular branch of learning, science, or art: *The study of law*. 3. a particular course of effort to acquire knowledge: *to pursue special medical studies* … 5. a thorough examination and analysis of a particular subject …"

In my view, "study", where used in s 40 is intended to have this dictionary meaning. In *Messier's case,* above, the question for determination before the court was whether a "nursing audit committee" was relevantly a "research group" for the purposes of the Evidence Act, RSBC 1979. If it was, then a report of the committee would attract an evidentiary privilege under the legislation. After citing the dictionary definition of "research", "study", "inquiry" and "investigation", MacKinnon J pointed out the dichotomy between the process of gathering facts, on the one hand, and conducting a course of study or research, on the other.

Again, even if "study" were the purpose for which a subscriber retained the services of Jeffress, it cannot be said that "study" was the purpose of Jeffress.

It follows, in my view, that s 40 has no application in the present case.

*Section 41 – fair dealing for the purpose of criticism or review*
A fair dealing with a literary work does not constitute an infringement of the copyright in the work if it is for the purpose of criticism or review, whether of that work or another work, and a "sufficient acknowledgment" of the work is made: s 41. A "sufficient acknowledgment" means an acknowledgment identifying the work by its title or other description and also identifying the author: s 10(1).

The origins of this defence were explained by Lord Hatherley in *Chatterton v Cave* (1878) 3 App Cas 483 at 492: "Books are published with an expectation, if not a desire, that they will be criticised in reviews, and if deemed valuable that parts of them will be used as affording illustrations by way of quotation, or the like – and if the quantity taken be neither [631] substantial nor material, if, as it has been expressed by some judges, 'a fair use' only be made on the publication, no wrong is done and no action can be brought."

On the other hand, a work cannot be published under the pretence of quotation: see *Mawman v Tegg* (1826) 2 Russ 385; *Commonwealth v John Fairfax & Sons Ltd* (1980)

147 CLR 39 at 54-7, 32 ALR 485, *Commonwealth v Walsh* (1980) 147 CLR 61 at 63; 32 ALR 500, Lahore, *Copyright Law*, p 7562.

The *Macquarie Dictionary* definition of "criticism" includes the following: "1. the act or art of analysing and judging the quality of a literary or artistic work, etc: *literary criticism*. 2. the act of passing judgment as to the merits of something ... 4. a critical comment, article or essay; a critique."

In my opinion, "criticism" in the context of s 41 is used in these senses. It has been held that criticism of any kind, and not only literary criticism, is within the provision: see *Sillitoe's case,* above, at 559.

The *Macquarie* definition of "review" includes the following: "1. a critical article or report, as in a periodical, on some literary work, commonly some work of recent appearance; a critique ..."

In my opinion, "review" is used in s 41 in this sense.

It would seem that the word "review" in the sense in which it is to be understood in s 41 is cognate with the word "criticism". It may be said that one is the process and the other is the result of the critical application of mental faculties. The extent of Jeffress' input, there being no material or evidence (apart from the order form) to support a contrary inference, appears to be limited only. The process involves scanning media for particular subjects according to the requests of subscribers. It does not appear to extend to the passing of a judgment as to the merit of the articles identified. Once an article is located which falls within the description of the nominated subject matter, the quality of that article is immaterial for the purposes of the exercise. The task undertaken is one of *location* rather than evaluation. This is the concern of the subscriber and will depend upon his or her particular purpose for subscribing.

In my view, the activities of, and service provided, by Jeffress cannot be characterised as either "criticism" or "review" for the purposes of s 41.

*Fair dealing for the purpose of reporting news – s 42*
By s 42(1), a fair dealing with a literary work does not constitute an infringement of copyright if it is for the purpose of, or associated with, the reporting of news in a newspaper, magazine or similar periodical and a sufficient acknowledgment of the work is made.

It may be accepted that the "reporting of news" in this context can go beyond a report of events which are current. In *John Fairfax,* above, Mason J said of s 42(1) (CLR at 56; ALR at 496): "I am inclined to allow that 'news', despite its context of 'the reporting of news' 'in a newspaper, magazine or similar periodical' is not restricted to 'current events'."

In *Hawkes & Son (London) Ltd v Paramount Film Service Ltd* [1934] Ch 593, the owners of the copyright in the musical march "Colonel Bogey" sued for infringement. The defendants exhibited a "news reel" film recording a motion picture of the scene at the public opening of a new school, together with the accompanying sounds, including the playing by a band of part of "Colonel Bogey". It was held that there had been an actionable **[632]** infringement; and that the playing of "Colonel Bogey" was not a "newspaper summary" within the meaning of the English legislation, as it then stood: see *Copinger and Skone James*, p 207, para 515. Romer LJ said at 609:

"Then it is said by the defendants that they are protected by the first proviso to s 2, sub-s (1), of the Act, which enacts that amongst the acts which shall not constitute an infringement of copyright are: 'Any fair dealing with any work for the purposes of private study, research, criticism, review, or newspaper summary.' Mr Macgillivray has asked us to hold that a cinematograph screen when displaying items of news is a newspaper within the meaning of that proviso. I see obvious difficulties in so holding. But let me assume it is a newspaper. Even then, what the defendants have done cannot be described as a fair dealing with any work for the purposes either of criticism, review, or newspaper summary. Test it in this way. The item of news with which we are dealing is the item of news that on a certain day the Prince of Wales reviewed the boys of the Naval School in question, and that they marched past him to the tune of 'Colonel Bogey'. Of course, any newspaper is entitled to say that, and that would be a summary of an item of news. The paper would also, of course, be entitled to publish a photograph of the boys marching past the Prince of Wales. But what they would not be entitled to do would be to say: 'For the benefit of those who were not able to be present, we publish the principal 28 bars of the "Colonel Bogey" march.' That is just what the defendants have done. They have, for the benefit of those who were not present, photographed the boys marching past the Prince of Wales; and have also provided, for the people who would see that, a representation of the 'Colonel Bogey' march."

In *Pacific & Southern Co Inc v Duncan* (1984) 744 F 2d 1490; *cert denied*, (1985) 471 US 1004, the United States Court of Appeals for the Eleventh Circuit held that a television news clipping service's unauthorised videotaping of a television station's copyrighted news feature story did not constitute fair use.

Johnson J said at 1496:

"The purpose and character of TV News Clips' use of WXIA's work heavily influences our decision in this case. TV News Clips copies and distributes the broadcast for unabashedly commercial reasons despite the fact that its customers buy the tapes for personal use. The district court characterised TV News Clips as a 'full-fledged commercial operation' ... TV News Clips denies that its activities have a commercial purpose; instead, it says that its purpose is 'private news reporting', meant to provide the public with a record of news reports. Of course, every commercial exchange of goods and services involves both the giving of the good or service and the taking of the purchase price. The fact that TV News Clips focuses on the giving rather than the taking cannot hide the fact that profit is its primary motive for making the exchange.

This commercial nature of the use militates quite strongly against a finding of fair use, for the Supreme Court emphasised in *Sony*, ... that a commercial purpose makes copying onto a videotape cassette 'presumptively unfair'."

Johnson J added at 1496: "We also note that TV News Clips' use is neither productive nor creative in any way. It does not analyse the broadcast or improve it at all. Indeed, WXIA expressed concern over the technical **[633]** inferiority of the tapes. TV News Clips only copies and sells. As the uses listed in the preamble to s 107 indicate, fair uses are those that contribute in some way to the public welfare. Until recently a few courts had automatically considered unproductive or uncreative uses to be unfair ... Although the Supreme Court has rejected 'productive use' as an absolute prerequisite to a defence of fair use, it has recognised that the distinction between productive and unproductive uses could be 'helpful in calibrating the balance' ... The unproductive nature of TV News Clips' use affects the balance in this case": see also *Georgia Television Co v TV News Clips of Atlanta Inc* (1989) Copyright Law Decisions 22,583 and 23,002; and see William F Patry, *The Fair Use Privilege in Copyright Law*, 1985, pp 143–6.

As has been said, in order to justify its conduct under s 42(1), Jeffress must first establish that its activity was carried out for the purpose of, or is associated with, "the reporting of news".

The *Macquarie* definition of "news" includes: "1. a report of any recent event, situation etc. 2. the report of events published in a newspaper, journal, radio, television, or any other medium. 3. information, events, etc, considered as suitable for reporting: *it's very interesting, but it's not news. 4. information not previously known: that's news to me ...*"

In my opinion, the reference to the "reporting of news" in s 42(1) is intended to comprehend these matters, subject to the possible extension mentioned by Mason J in *John Fairfax,* supra. It follows, in my view, that the reproduction by Jeffress of the review written by Mr de Garis was not done for the purpose of the reporting of news. Nor, in my opinion, was the conduct of Jeffress "associated" with such a purpose. The work of which Mr de Garis was the author was itself a literary review. Its reproduction by Jeffress had nothing to do with the reporting of news within the meaning of s 42(1).

Further, the defence provided by s 42(1) is only available where the reporting is in a newspaper, magazine or similar periodical. In considering Mr Moore's claim, I deal later with the meaning of the term "newspaper" where used in s 35(4). In my view, that reasoning is applicable here also, with the consequence that, in my opinion, the reproduction by Jeffress cannot be said to be reporting in a newspaper, magazine or similar periodical.

In any event, Jeffress has not, in my view, established that its dealing was "fair" for the purposes of s 42(1). The notion of "fairness" in this context has been considered in a number of cases.

In *Hubbard v Vosper* [1972] 2 QB 84, Lord Denning MR said at 94: "It is impossible to define what is 'fair dealing'. It must be a question of degree. You must consider first the number and extent of the quotations and extracts. Are they altogether too many and too long to be fair? Then you must consider the use made of them. If they are used as a basis for comment, criticism or review, that may be fair dealing. If they are used to convey the same information as the author, for a rival purpose, that may be unfair. Next, you must consider the proportions. To take long extracts and attach short comments may be unfair. But, short extracts and long comments may be fair. Other considerations may come to mind also. But, after all is said and done, it must be a matter of impression. As with fair comment in the law of libel, so with fair dealing in the law of copyright. The tribunal of fact must decide."

**[634]** In the *University of New South Wales v Moorhouse* (1975) 133 CLR 1; 6 ALR 193 Gibbs CJ said (CLR at 12; ALR at 200): "The principles laid down by the Act are broadly stated, by reference to such abstract concepts as 'fair dealing' (s 40) and 'reasonable portion' (s 49) and it is left to the courts to apply those principles after a detailed consideration of all the circumstances of a particular case."

In the present case, Jeffress took the whole of Mr de Garis' work and supplied it to its customers for its own reward in the course of a trading activity. Jeffress did not comment on the material or attempt any analysis of its content: see *Duncan's case, supra*. In the circumstances, the dealing cannot be said to be "fair".

## TCN Channel Nine Pty Ltd v Network Ten Pty Ltd
Federal Court of Australia: Sundberg, Finkelstein and Hely JJ
(2002) 190 ALR 468

Channel Ten broadcast segments of Channel Nine's programs on Ten's infotainment program, "The Panel". The Full Federal Court addressed the question of whether the fair use defences applied to the parts taken. This question was not considered on appeal to the High Court or in the case remitted back to the Full Federal Court.

### Hely J: Fair dealing
**[487]** 96. At first instance both parties professed reliance on the decision of the United Kingdom Court of Appeal in *Pro Sieben Media AG v Carlton UK Television Ltd* [1999] 1 WLR 605. The court there held that the test of whether an extract from a copyright work had been used for one of the purposes laid down in the corresponding provisions of the Copyright, Designs and Patents Act 1988 (UK) is an objective one (at 614):

The words "in the context of" or "as part of an exercise in" could be substituted for "for the purpose of" without any significant alteration of meaning.

97. That decision was followed by the UK Court of Appeal in the subsequent case of *Hyde Park Residence Ltd v Yelland* [2001] Ch 143. In that case, whether a work was

used "for the purpose of reporting current events" was a matter to be ascertained by a reading of the relevant parts of the work in question. However, both cases make it clear that the intentions and motives of the user of the copyright material are highly relevant in relation to the issue of fair dealing.

98. After reviewing the authorities, and the submissions of the parties, the primary judge summarised the principles emerging from the authorities involving fair dealing defences as follows:

(i)   Fair dealing involves questions of degree and impression; it is to be judged by the criterion of a fair minded and honest person, and is an abstract concept;

(ii)   Fairness is to be judged objectively in relation to the relevant purpose, that is to say, the purpose of criticism or review or the purpose of reporting news; in short, it must be fair and genuine for the relevant purpose, because fair dealing truth of purpose [sic];

(iii)   Criticism and review are words of wide and indefinite scope which should be interpreted liberally; nevertheless criticism and review involve the passing of judgment. Criticism and review may be strongly expressed;

(iv)   Criticism and review must be genuine and not a pretence for some other form of purpose, but if genuine, need not necessarily be balanced;

(v)   An oblique or hidden motive may disqualify reliance upon criticism and review, particularly where the copyright infringer is a trade rival who uses the copyright subject matter for its own benefit, particularly in a dissembling way; "the path of criticism is a public way";

(vi)   Criticism and review extends to thoughts underlying the expression of the copyright works or subject matter;

(vii)   "News" is not restricted to current events; and

(viii)   "News" may involve the use of humour though the distinction between news and entertainment may be difficult to determine in particular situations.

[**488**] 99. Nine submitted on the hearing of the appeal that the criticism or review must be of the work itself, but this may include the doctrine or philosophy underlying the work. However, s 103A expressly provides that the criticism or review may relate to "the first-mentioned audio-visual item, another audio-visual item or a work".

100. Nine's written submissions on the appeal also challenged principle (ii) in the summary of the trial judge quoted above. It was submitted that the requisite purpose must be that of the respondent rather than some third party, and there was no evidence before the trial judge that Ten itself (as distinct from Working Dog Pty Ltd and its Executive Producer, Mr Hirsh) had a relevant purpose of criticism or review or of news reporting. Contrary to the position which it had adopted at first instance, Nine's submission then proceed upon the basis that it was incumbent upon Ten to call evidence as to the actual purposes, intentions and motives of those who produced the programs.

101. Ten engaged Working Dog Pty Ltd (Working Dog), referred to by the primary judge as "its contracted production team", to produce for it a television program which would, amongst other things, involve criticism and review and the reporting of news events. The purpose of Working Dog in the production of these programs was the purpose of Ten. Consistently with the decisions of the UK Court of Appeal earlier referred to, the "purpose" referred to in ss 103A and 103B is to be ascertained objectively, and it was neither necessary nor appropriate for officers of Ten or of Working Dog to give evidence that they had a sincere belief that he or she was criticising a work or an audio-visual item or reporting news.

102. Nine also submits that to the extent that it is discernible, Ten's purpose in re-broadcasting the Nine material was to entertain, provide program content and achieve ratings. This purpose is the same purpose that Nine, its trade rival, had in broadcasting the material originally. It does not ground a fair dealing defence.

103. Ten accepted the proposition that if it had used the Panel Segments as a "potted" substitute for entertainment, so that a television viewer could obtain ready and easy access to the same in a shorter time, such kind of activity on its part would constitute an unfair dealing. Ten denied that it had used any of the Panel Segments in that way, and the primary judge found that its denial was justified.

104. Ten's purpose in broadcasting its program The Panel may have been, as Nine asserts, to entertain and to achieve ratings. If it does so by means of a program involving or including criticism, review or reporting of news in which there is fair dealing with material in which copyright would otherwise subsist, then Ten is not disentitled from relying on the ss 103A and 103B defences by reason only of the commercial nature of its activities. Criticism may involve an element of humour, or "poking fun at" the object of the criticism. The fact that news coverage is interesting or even to some people entertaining, does not negate the fact that it could be news: *Nine Network Australia Pty Ltd v Australian Broadcasting Corporation* (1999) 48 IPR 333 at 340 [34]–[37]. News may be reported with humour and still fall within the ambit of s 103B. ...

**[491]** 109. I turn, then, to the particular Panel Segments that were the subject of submissions on the appeal whether on the part of Nine as the appellant, or on the part of Ten pursuant to its notice of contention.

### 1. The Today Show (Boris Yeltsin)

110. At [72](i), the primary judge said:

> ... news may involve the use of humour, but ... there can nevertheless be considerable difficulty in distinguishing news from entertainment (see [58] above). As a matter of judgment and impression, I prefer the conclusion that the purpose of this re-broadcast, evident from The Panel discussion, was that of entertainment rather than the reporting of news ...

Ten submits that the primary judge reached this conclusion upon the erroneous basis that there could be no overlap between news and entertainment. His Honour specifically acknowledged that there could be such an overlap, but came to the conclusion, as a matter of judgment and impression, that this Panel Segment fell upon one side of the line rather than upon the other. This is a matter on which different persons might legitimately hold different conclusions. I am not persuaded that his Honour erred in coming to the conclusion which he did.

### 2. Midday

111. At [72](ii), the primary judge found that:

> ... the purpose of Nine's dealing with the subject footage of "Midday" was to satirise aspects of Ms Kennerley's performance as presenter of "Midday", and certain supposed personality traits and political allegiances. I do not think that on balance, and as an issue of fact and degree, it can rightly be postulated that The Panel here engaged in criticism or review of "Midday", and that such was its purpose.

112. In context, the issue is whether the purpose for which the Panel Segment was shown was criticism or review of the broadcast of which the Panel Segment formed part, or criticism or review of some other broadcast of the Midday program. An appraisal of Ms Kennerley's role as the presenter of the Midday show could amount to criticism or review of the television broadcast constituted by the "Midday" program, but there was no real connection between the Panel Segment and such discussion as there was of Ms Kennerley's role. The Panel Segment was shown for its own sake, either as something worth seeing again, or for the benefit of those who had missed it when it was originally broadcast by Nine. I agree with the primary judge's conclusions.

**[492]** 113. The primary judge also rejected Ten's claimed entitlement to a defence under s 103B(1)(b) on the purported basis that the Prime Minister's singing of "Happy Birthday" to Sir Donald Bradman was "newsworthy". It may be accepted that unusual or incongruous moments in the life of a world leader may be "news", and elsewhere in his reasons, the primary judge accepted that "news" for the purposes of s 103B(1) was not restricted to current events. But a contention that The Panel was reporting an item of news, namely that the Prime Minister had sung Happy Birthday to Sir Donald Bradman on the Midday show some 14 days earlier, and that the Panel Segment was shown for the purpose of or in association with the reporting of that news is, to my mind, an exaggeration or distortion of the facts. The Panel Segment was simply shown for its entertainment value. No error has been shown in the primary judge's conclusion in this respect.

### 3. A Current Affair

114. The primary judge found that there was a fair dealing for the purpose of criticism or review of the program from which the Panel Segment was taken, on the basis that Ten was criticising Nine's broadcast for inadequately protecting by means of ineffective disguises the anonymity of interviewees who wished to keep their identity secret. That was sufficient to "marginally weigh" the balance in favour of Ten's establishment of the s 103A defence.

115. In assessing whether a defence of fair dealing exists, it is necessary to have regard to the true purpose of the critical work. As Henry LJ said in *Time Warner Entertainment Co Ltd v Channel 4 Television Corporation plc* (1993) 28 IPR 459 at 468, the question to be answered is as follows:

> … is the program incorporating the infringing material a genuine piece of criticism or review, or is it something else, such as an attempt to dress up the infringement of another's copyright in the guise of criticism, and so profit unfairly from another's work? As Lord Denning said in *Hubbard v Vosper* [1972] 2 QB 84 at 93, "it is not fair dealing for a rival in the trade to take copyright material and use it for its own benefit".

What is required in order to enliven the defence is that the copying take place as part of and for the purpose of criticising or reviewing the broadcast in question: *Ashdown v Telegraph Group Ltd* [2001] EWCA Civ 1142; [2001] 4 All ER 666 at [61].

116. The Panel discussion did not involve a criticism of Nine's selection of disguises for the interviewees; the discussion proceeded upon the basis that the interviewees chose their own disguises. Thereafter The Panel attempted to poke fun at the disguises which the interviewees wore. I agree with the submission of Mr Bannon SC that The Panel were not criticising Channel Nine's failure to protect people who wished to remain anonymous, which might have amounted to a criticism of the television broadcast. Rather, The Panel were simply poking fun at the disguises which the people had chosen, and using the Panel Segment for the purposes of entertainment.

117. For these reasons, in my opinion, Nine has established that the primary judge fell into error in upholding the fair dealing defence in relation to this Panel Segment.

### 4. & 5. Days of Our Lives

118. The primary judge found that these Panel Segments would have attracted the defence of fair dealing for the purposes of criticism or review on the footing of an innuendo of loss of originality and novelty of theme. I agree with that **[493]** conclusion. The fact that humour was also involved is beside the point. I do not agree with Nine's submission that Ten re-broadcast melodramatic aspects in order to entertain persons who did not see the material as originally broadcast.

### 6. Simply the Best

119. The primary judge held that the s 103A defence of criticism or review was not made out. He did so on the basis of a "paucity of evidence" which left no "viable basis for comprehending, much less resolving, what was the true nature of the alleged criticism, and what was the purported basis therefore".

120. Ten contends that the comments by The Panel members clearly reveal the purpose of criticism or review in relation to the set (and underlying artistic work) used in

Nine's programs; and that once this is accepted, there is no need to enquire further as to the nature or basis for the criticisms made.

121. Criticism or review may be unbalanced or strongly expressed and nevertheless fall within s 103A. Nonetheless, it has to be recognisable as criticism or review. As I read his Honour's decision the defence failed because the so-called criticism or review in relation to the set was not recognisable as such. I agree with his Honour's conclusions in this regard.

### 7. The Inaugural Allan Border Medal Dinner

122. The primary judge would have upheld a fair dealing defence of reporting of news in respect of this re-broadcast. However, was it news that Glenn McGrath did not notice the Prime Minister's attempt to congratulate him at the dinner? There is no suggestion that Mr McGrath deliberately ignored the Prime Minister, or that on the actual night anyone thought that the Prime Minister had been publicly embarrassed. The only public embarrassment was created by The Panel's publicising of a background and unnoticed incident. It was done by showing the footage in slow motion (unlike the original). Section 103B proceeds upon the basis that the news exists independently of the Panel Segment, and the defence is attracted if the Panel Segment is broadcast for the purpose of or in association with the reporting of that news. Yet here, if there is any news, it arises by reason of the slowing down of the footage so as to display a hitherto unnoticed incident which, had it been noticed, might have been a source of embarrassment for the Prime Minister. I agree with Nine's submission that it is not a fair dealing for the purpose of reporting news to use footage in a particular way so as to create the appearance of a public embarrassment and then to assert that the re-broadcast of the footage was merely the report of a public embarrassment.

123 Nine's appeal in relation to this Panel Segment should be upheld.

### 8. The Sunday Program

124. The primary judge held that this was "perhaps the clearest exemplification" of the s 103B(1)(b) defence. The theme of The Panel commentary on this re-broadcast was that the allegations of drug-taking made on the Nine footage by a so-called Sports Performance Consultant constituted gross exaggeration, yet had been inappositely made in the context of the pending Olympic Games in Sydney.

125. Nine submits that it was not necessary for Ten to re-broadcast Nine's copyright in the expansive manner in which it did for the purpose of reporting the news that 70–80% of elite athletes take drugs. Whether excessive use was made of the material in which copyright subsists so as to negative the fair dealing defence is very much a matter of impression. I agree with the impression formed **[494]** by the primary judge. Nine has not established that the conclusion reached by the primary judge in this respect was erroneous.

### 9. The Today Show (Prasad interview)

126. The primary judge held that this Ten re-broadcast encaptures the perils of live interviews on television, and on balance, found that the purpose of using the Panel Segment was to lightly and humorously criticise the Nine broadcast.

127. Ten's rebroadcast involved the "splicing" or "merging", in a compressed fashion, of elements of the original broadcast that were temporally separated. Nine submits that the splicing distorted the impact of the background interference in the interview in order to achieve a humorous result. Ten contends that the editing did not affect the fairness of the dealing, but rather more plainly conveyed the criticism being made, although the nature and content of the so-called criticism was never clearly identified.

128. The primary judge's conclusion was one which he reached "not without some difficulty". With respect, I do not agree with that conclusion. The broadcast of the Panel Segment was made for its own sake, or, as Nine put it, "watch this for fun" rather than as something shown as part of an exercise of criticism or review. The Panel members

giggled about homeless men coming into the background of the interview. Any humour that existed in that respect was accentuated by the splicing. In my view, the fair dealing defence was not made out.

**10. Newsbreak**

129. The primary judge would have upheld a defence of fair dealing for the purpose of criticism or review. There was a technical glitch in the source program which involved the appearance of the presenter of "Newsbreak" being accidentally shrunk or abbreviated to a very small size. The Panel commentator showed the Panel Segment in association with the commentary that live television is fraught with peril.

130. Nine submits that the "content of the re-broadcast (a technical glitch suffered in the Newsbreak programme) may be humorous. But while criticism or review may be humorous, humour without criticism or review does not ground a fair dealing defence".

131. Whilst there is force in Nine's submissions, what Ten has done is to draw attention, in a humorous way, to a fault appearing in the original television broadcast by Nine. The primary judge characterised that as an exercise in criticism or review. I agree with that characterisation. It has not been shown that his Honour was in error in coming to the conclusion which he did.

## *Interlego AG v Croner Trading Pty Ltd*
### Federal Court of Australia: Black CJ, Lockhart and Gummow JJ
### (1992) 111 ALR 577

The respondent Croner had imported toy blocks into Australia and sold them. Lego sued for indirect infringement of copyright under ss 37 and 38 of the *Copyright Act 1968* on the basis that the blocks were a reproduction of copyright drawings of the Lego blocks. As we saw in Chapter 3, the drawings were found to be original works under the Act and it was also held that the maker of the blocks imported by Croner had reproduced them. The question was whether this reproduction constituted an infringement under the *Copyright Act* or whether the alleged infringer could rely on the s 77 defences. In this judgment Gummow J provides a detailed history of the law relating to the designs-copyright overlap but here we have extracted only his consideration of the law as it stands today.

**Gummow J: [614]** The only remaining question on this part of the appeal is whether the respondent can mount a similar defence under s 77 as it presently stands in response to an application for an injunction to prevent continued infringement of copyright in the post-1969 drawings.

The relevant new provisions inserted by the 1989 Act read as follows:

"74. In this Division:
'corresponding design', in relation to an artistic work, means a design that, when applied to an article, results in a reproduction of that work, but does not include a design consisting solely of features of two-dimensional pattern or ornament applicable to a surface of an article.

77. (1) This section applies where:
   (a) copyright subsists in an artistic work (other than a building or a model of a building, or a work of artistic craftsmanship) whether made before the commencement of this section or otherwise;
   (b) a corresponding design is applied industrially, whether in Australia or elsewhere, by or with the licence of the owner of the copyright in the work in the place where the industrial application happens;

(c)   at any time on or after the commencement of this section, articles to which the corresponding design has been so applied (in this section called 'articles made to the corresponding design') are sold, let for hire or offered or exposed for sale or hire, whether in Australia or elsewhere; and

(d)   at that time, the corresponding design is not registrable under the Designs Act 1906 or has not been registered under that Act.

(2) It is not an infringement of the copyright in the artistic work to reproduce the work, on or after the day on which articles made to the corresponding design are first so sold, let for hire or offered or exposed for sale or hire, by applying that, or any other, corresponding design to an article."

Again, the appellants contend that the post-1969 drawings are not designs within the meaning of the 1906 Designs Act, and again they must fail. The appellants' other two arguments in relation to the previous **[615]** wording of s 77 are now expressly excluded: para (b) applies whether industrial application occurs in Australia or elsewhere; and para (d) applies not only if the design has not been registered, but also if it "is not registrable" under the 1906 Act.

Pressed into this corner, the appellants submit that there are outstanding factual issues which the respondent has to establish if it is to bring its case within the defence given it by s 77 of the 1989 Act, and that it has failed to do so. Paragraph (a) clearly applies: copyright subsists in the post-1969 drawings. It might be argued that para (b) has not been satisfied because the respondent has not adduced proof of industrial application since 1 October 1990. However, the terms of para (c), which refer to sale on or after the commencement of the section of articles to which the design has been applied, make it clear that the relevant application might occur prior to 1 October 1990. This leaves para (c). It is conceded that the respondent has not adduced evidence of any sales in Australia by any member of the Lego group of articles made according to corresponding designs in the post-1969 drawings. In view of the course of the trial, no criticism should attach to the respondent in this connection.

Counsel for the respondent suggested alternative courses to meet that situation. One would involve waiving the requirement to adduce evidence on the ground that the appellants' objection is not bona fide. Order 33 Rule 3 of the Federal Court Rules provides:

"The Court may at any stage of the proceedings –

(a)   dispense with compliance with the rules of evidence for proving any matter which is not bona fide in dispute ..."

This rule should not be applied lightly: *Arnotts Limited v Trade Practices Commission* (1990) 24 FCR 313 at 360, 369. It clearly refers to the waiving of the rules of evidence, rather than of the need to adduce any evidence at all. Secondly, the respondent suggests that this Court order the administration of interrogatories. But at this stage in the proceedings it would not be desirable for us to interrupt the disposition of the appeal in this way ...

The preferable course is for this Court to grant an injunction to restrain sale of the bricks produced in infringement of the appellants' drawings, but to suspend the operation of the injunction, and to grant the respondent leave to re-open its case before the primary Judge to tender evidence to show sales by the Lego group in Australia since 1 October 1990 and to establish before his Honour the alleged defence under s 77. The primary Judge may entertain an application to achieve this end by the administration of interrogatories. The matter will be entirely in his Honour's hands.

This disposes of the copyright and design issues.

# Chapter 6

# Dealing with Copyright

In Chapter 3 we saw that copyright is infringed by a person who, not being the owner of the copyright and without the licence of the copyright owner, does any of the acts comprised in the copyright. The question of who is the owner of the copyright or whether a licence has been granted is therefore of fundamental importance in copyright law. Traditionally, the first owner of the copyright is the author of the work or the maker, or publisher of the film, sound recording, broadcast or published edition. This is subject to special provisions relating to works made under a contract of employment, journalistic works, commissioned portraits, photographs and engravings[1] and copyright subject-matter made by or under the direction of the Crown.[2]

This traditional position was significantly altered, however, by the *US Free Trade Agreement Implementation Act 2004* which made the live performer on a sound recording a joint owner of copyright together with the maker of the sound recording. Surprisingly, this conferral of copyright on performers was made retrospective so Jimmy Barnes, for example, will now be one of the owners in his old recordings as well as in his future recordings. The rather complex limitations and dealings relating to the conferral of these retrospective rights are discussed below.

It is sometimes relatively clear that a person is entitled to do one of the acts comprised in the copyright but it may not be easy to determine whether the person's entitlement arises because the person is the owner of the copyright or a licensee. If the person is a licensee it may be difficult to determine whether the person is an exclusive licensee or not. In copyright law such distinctions are important for two main reasons. First, different formalities are required for transmission of ownership and the granting of licences. Secondly, the owner and an exclusive licensee have the right to take action for infringement of copyright. This right is not available to a non-exclusive licensee. In this chapter we consider the law relating to first ownership of copyright, the manner in which copyright might be transmitted or licensed and the formalities required for copyright dealings as well as the remedies available for breach of copyright. We conclude our examination of the law of copyright by considering non-judicial mechanisms for

---

1    *Copyright Act 1968* s 35 as to works and ss 97-100 as to other subject-matter.
2    Sections 176(2) and 177 as to works, s 178 (2) as to films and sound recordings.

the enforcement and protection of copyright with particular reference to the role of collective agencies and the Copyright Tribunal of Australia.

Because the copyright owner or licensee may not be the author or performer of the copyright subject-matter the licensing and assignment of copyright must take account of the separate moral rights of authors as well as the rights of performers. These will be considered in the next chapter, "Neighbouring Rights".

## First Ownership

Since the *Statute of Anne* the general rule has been that copyright is first owned by the author of the work (*Copyright Act 1968* s 35(1)).[3] Authorship is determined according to the general principles established in *Walter v Lane*[4] and *Donoghue v Allied Newspapers Ltd*.[5] If two or more authors produce "a work of joint authorship", copyright vests in them as tenants in common.[6]

A work of joint authorship is defined in s 10(1) as a work that is produced by the collaboration of two or more authors and in which the contribution of one author is not separate from the contribution of the other authors.[7] The definition requires that each person be an "author". Donoghue, therefore, was not a joint author of the newspaper articles about him in *Donoghue v Allied Newspapers Ltd*[8] and the man who asked the medium to contact Cleophas in *Cummins v Bond*[9] was not a joint author of the resulting chronicles even though he attended the séance. More importantly, in *Bulun Bulun v R and T Textiles Pty Ltd*,[10] von Doussa J found that the Aboriginal customary owners of the right to reproduce an image were not joint authors for the purposes of maintaining a copyright infringement case nor did they have an equitable interest which would ground a copyright action. von Doussa J, however, did hold that the artist was in a fiduciary relationship with the traditional owners in relation to the artistic work question. The inadequacies of current copyright law in dealing with indigenous communal cultural property will be considered in the next chapter.

This general rule of first ownership is subject to special provisions relating to works created under a contract of service (s 35(6)); newspaper journalists (s 35(4)); certain commissioned photographs, paintings, engravings and portraits (s 35(5));[11] and in works made or published by or under the direction or control of the Crown (Part VII, Division 1) or an international organisation (s 187).

---

3    For transitional provisions regarding authorship of photographs, see s 208. For presumptions regarding ownership, authorship and publisher, see ss 126B and 129 as to ownership, s 127 as to authorship, s 128 as to publisher, s 130 as to sound recordings and s 131 as to cinematographic films.

4    [1900] AC 539.

5    [1938] Ch 106.

6    *Lauri v Renard* [1892] 3 Ch 402; *Acorn Computers Ltd v MCS Microcomputer Systems Pty Ltd* (1984) 57 ALR 389.

7    Under this definition an encyclopaedia or dictionary might not be classified as a work of joint authorship if different authors make distinct and separate contributions.

8    [1938] Ch 106.

9    [1927] 1 Ch 169.

10   (1998) 157 ALR 193.

11   For transitional provisions regarding works made under a contract of service, works made by newspaper journalists and commissioned photographs, portraits and engravings, see s 213.

Copyright in Part IV films, sound recordings, broadcasts and published editions of works is first owned by the "maker" of the film (s 98), sound recording (s 97), broadcast (s 99) or the publisher of a published edition of a work (s 100). The maker of a film is the person (including a corporation) who undertakes the arrangements for the production of the film, that is, the producer owns the copyright in the film (s 22(4)). If the film is not a commissioned film the maker also includes the director of the film (s 98(4)). In *Seven Network (Operations) Ltd v TCN Channel Nine Pty Ltd*,[12] the Federal Court gave a broad definition of the maker of a film to include a joint venturer who had the idea to make a film about a group of troubled boys walking the Kokoda trail, and who arranged for the selection of the boys, parental consents, travel arrangements, funding, insurance and gear for the trip. The Full Court said "the idea for the trek *and for the filming of it*" was his and therefore the person was a maker of the film and a joint owner. The maker of a broadcast is the person who provided the broadcasting service (s 22(6)). The maker of a sound recording other than a sound recording of a live performance is the person who owned the first record of the sound recording (s 22(3)). The makers of a sound recording of a live performance, by virtue of the *US Free Trade Agreement Implementation Act 2004*, are the person or persons who own the record on which the first recording is made and the performer or performers who performed the performance unless that is also the person who owns the first record. That is, the performer in that case would not have two shares in the copyright (s 22(3A)). If a sound recording or film is made in pursuance of an agreement for valuable consideration with another person that person shall own the copyright (ss 97(3) and 98(3)). Films or sound recordings made or published by or under the direction or control of the Crown (Part VII, Division 1) or an international organisation (s 188) are owned by the Crown or the organisation.

## Works made under a contract of service

Where an original work is made by the author in pursuance of the terms of the author's employment under a contract of service, the copyright is owned by the employer rather than by the author (s 35(6)). Similarly, where the performer in a live performance was employed under a contract of employment or apprenticeship to perform in that performance then that performer's employer is taken to be a maker of the sound recording of the performance (s 22(3B)). There are two different questions to address in relation to these provisions. Was there a contract of service? Was the work made in pursuance of the terms of employment?

Whether a person is employed under a contract of service or under a contract for services is determined according to general principles of employment law. The traditional test for determining this distinction is the "control" test which asks whether the master controls not only what is to be done but also how it is to be done.[13] In the case of more skilled or professional positions (plumber, builder, computer programmer, doctor, journalist, academic, lawyer, for example)

---

12    (2005) 222 ALR 569.
13    *Collins v Hertfordshire County Council* [1947] KB 598.

including many positions which require the creation of intellectual property, such a test may not be useful or easily applied. In these cases the importance of the control test "lies not so much in its actual exercise ... as in the right of the employer to exercise it".[14] Other indicia may also be considered including "the mode of remuneration, the provision and maintenance of equipment, the obligation to work, the hours of work and provision for holidays, the deduction of income tax and the delegation of work by the putative employee".[15]

In the United Kingdom the "organisation" or "integration" test was proposed by Lord Wright in *Montreal v Montreal Locomotive Works*[16] and developed by Lord Denning in the copyright case of *Stevenson Jordan and Harrison v MacDonald and Evans*:[17]

> One feature which seems to run through the instances is that, under a contract of service, a man is employed as part of the business, and his work is done as an integral part of the business; whereas, under a contract of services, his work, although done for the business, is not integrated into it but is only an accessory to it.[18]

Applying this test in *Beloff v Pressdram*,[19] the Chancery Division in the English High Court determined that the well-known political correspondent for the *Observer*, Nora Beloff, was employed under a contract of service. In Australia the High Court has rejected the organisation test as a separate or alternative test to the control test but accepted that it may be taken into account as one of the indicia in determining the nature of the relationship.[20]

A more difficult question in relation to copyright is whether the work was made "in pursuance of the terms of employment". In *Stevenson Jordan and Harrison v MacDonald and Evans*,[21] a case concerning a book of lectures written by a middle level manager, Evershed MR emphasised the fact of control. Even though the lectures were important and advantageous for the company Evershed MR found that they were not made in pursuance of the terms of employment because the company could not direct the manager to give such lectures.[22]

This general test has been refined in two cases relating to patents and designs. In *Spencer Industries Pty Ltd v Collins*[23] and *Courier Pete Pty Ltd v Metroll Queensland Pty Ltd*[24] the Federal Court distinguished between "ordinary duties" and a "residual area of duties" in which it was open to the employer to expressly or implicitly direct the employee to use technical skills for additional duties, including creating new products.[25] In both cases the court found that neither of the sales people involved had "an ongoing expectation of creativity" nor had they

---

14    *Stevens v Brodribb Sawmilling Co Pty Ltd* (1986) 160 CLR 16, Mason J at 27.
15    *Stevens v Brodribb Sawmilling Co Pty Ltd* (1986) 160 CLR 16, Mason J at 27.
16    [1947] 1 DLR 161.
17    [1952] 1 TLR 101.
18    [1952] 1 TLR 101 at 111.
19    [1973] 1 All ER 241.
20    *Stevens v Brodribb Sawmilling Co Pty Ltd* (1986) 160 CLR 16, Mason J at 27, Wilson and Dawson JJ at 36-37.
21    [1951] 1 TLR 101.
22    [1952] 1 TLR 101 at 111.
23    (2003) 58 IPR 425.
24    [2010] FCA 735.
25    [2010] FCA 735 at [24].

been specifically directed to produce the products in issue.[26] They were therefore found to be the owners of the intellectual property in dispute.

In *Redrock Holdings Pty Ltd v Hinkley*,[27] on the other hand, Harper J emphasised integration of the work rather than control of the employee. In this case Hinkley, the 17-year-old author, had started his computer library before he was employed by Redrock to develop a Macintosh version of MobileNet Mail to be used by Telstra, British Telecom and Optus. During his employment with Redrock, Hinkley used the library of applications in the development of Redrock products and also added to the library. In some ways the library was simply a tool and Redrock did not seek to control his work on the library. In fact, it was irrelevant to Redrock whether or not Hinkley used a library to develop its products. What was important, however, was that because of the way in which Hinkley had written the Redrock programs the library was fully integrated into them. The programs developed by Hinkley could not run without accessing the library. Furthermore, future modifications of programs developed by Hinkley or Redrock would require modification of the library and therefore access to the source code of the library.[28] The court found that the copyright in the library was owned by Redrock.

The result of *Redrock* is that Hinkley lost one of his most valuable programming tools and Redrock was under no obligation to grant a licence to him for use of the library. Unfair as this may seem the obiter comments of Harper J on this point should be noted:

> If Mr Hinkley proposed to fulfil his obligations to his employer by drawing upon the library by means which might in the absence of prior agreement blur the question of ownership of the copyright in the library, it fell to Mr Hinkley, as the only repository of the relevant information, to place his employer in a position from which the employer and employee, both being fully informed of the relevant facts, could either negotiate a mutually satisfactory resolution to the copyright problem or go their separate ways.[29]

## Print media exemption

Journalists, photojournalists and other employees of newspapers, magazines and similar periodicals have traditionally had greater ownership rights than other employees. Until 1998, print media employees, unlike other employees, owned the copyright in their artistic, literary and dramatic works even though those works were made in the course of employment or under an apprenticeship. These rights were subject to the provision that the newspaper proprietor owned the copyright in such works for limited purposes. Those limited purposes were publication of the work in any newspaper, magazine or similar periodical or for broadcasting the work. The exemption was not extended to radio or television journalists and it was never decided whether the owner's publication right was exhausted after first publication.[30]

---

26   [2010] FCA 735 at [41].

27   (2001) 50 IPR 565.

28   Hinkley had left Redrock an object code version of the library but Redrock argued that this was unsatisfactory: (2001) 50 IPR 565 at 579. This emphasises the importance of owning the copyright – if Redrock owned the copyright in the library they could keep developing it.

29   (2001) 50 IPR 565 at 574.

30   See *Avel Pty Ltd v Multicoin Amusements Pty Ltd* (1990) 171 CLR 88.

As forms of distribution and publication changed there were disputes between journalists and newspaper proprietors regarding the extent of the newspapers' rights, especially regarding syndication of news articles and the provision of press clipping services. The introduction of the internet raised new but similar issues. It was not clear, for example, whether the newspapers' rights extended to online media reports, e-zines, online archives or other electronic databases. Journalists were concerned that their works were being exploited without consent or compensation. Newspapers expressed concern that they would be unable to exploit new forms of communication and delivery. Following an inquiry by the Copyright Law Review Committee in 1992 the Committee, in a split decision, recommended that any special position for journalists be abolished. This was not a politically sustainable position and in 1997 the Federal Parliament introduced a modified form of journalists' copyright in the *Copyright Amendment Act (No 1) 1998*.

The new s 35(4) provided that a newspaper proprietor owns the copyright in literary, artistic and dramatic works made under a contract of service subject to two very narrow exemptions. The author of the work owns the right to reproduce the work for the purpose of including it in a "book". The author also owns the right to make a facsimile copy of the work included in a paper edition of the newspaper. The drafting of this section is unfortunate and raises as many problems as it solves. A book is not defined but the history of copyright law indicates that it has been very broadly interpreted in the past. There seems little reason, for example, to restrict a book to hard copy non-electronic forms of literary work. In addition, the right to make a facsimile copy is not supported by any other rights such as publication rights. Its practical use is therefore limited to allowing the journalist to make a copy for the purposes of including it in his or her portfolio.

*De Garis v Neville Jeffress Pidler Pty Ltd*[31] was a decision made under the old provisions. In that case the question arose as to who owned the right to publish a journalist's work in a press clipping service. The court held that a press clipping service was not a "newspaper, magazine or similar periodical" and therefore the newspaper proprietor did not have the right to allow publication of the work in such a service. Under the new provisions different questions arise but the result is less certain. If the press clipping service can be characterised as a "book" then the journalist may own the right to reproduce the work in such a service. In addition, the journalist owns the right to photocopy the works from a newspaper and may sell this right to the press clipping service. The journalist, however, does not own the right to publish these copies and therefore the press clipping service could do little with these copies except read them.

## Domestic photographs, portraits and engravings

A person who commissions a photograph for a private or domestic purpose,[32] or a portrait or an engraving, owns the copyright in that photograph, portrait or engraving (s 35(5)). This is subject to the proviso that, if the person tells the artist that the work is for a particular purpose, the artist may restrain the person from

---

31  (1990) 95 ALR 625.

32  Before 1998 the section covered all commissioned photographs, not just domestic or private photographs.

exercising any other copyright. The proviso protects the professional reputation of the artist who may, for example, take a different approach to a portrait destined for the family living room as opposed to a portrait destined for publication in an art journal.

Applying the exemption in a commercial environment has raised a number of problems, especially regarding originality. In *Con Planck Ltd v Kolynos Inc*,[33] an artist who owned the copyright in an artistic work showed the work to a potential client for an advertising campaign. The client liked the work but requested that it be done in new colours to suit the client's product. The English High Court held that the work in its new colour scheme comprised a new, original engraving which had been made for the client for valuable consideration. Therefore, even though the artist had owned the copyright in the first artistic work the client was the first owner of the copyright in the final engraving.

In yet another poker machine case, *Cope Allan (Marrickville) Ltd v Farrow*,[34] the plaintiff manufacturers, who traded under the wonderful name of Nutt and Muddle and Sons, claimed ownership in the engravings which constituted the panels of their poker machines on the basis that they were engravings made on commission. The Supreme Court of Victoria, on a motion for an interlocutory injunction, held that the plaintiffs had failed to establish a prima facie case because the author of the engravings had originally made drawings for the plaintiff based on written specifications and only subsequently produced engravings from these drawings. The judge held that the copyright in the original drawings "extends to the finished product".[35] Given the interlocutory nature of this decision we would suggest that it should not be relied on to support this rather significant claim.

A portrait was defined by the Vice Chancellor in *Duke of Leeds v Earl of Amherst*[36] as a representation or a "correspondence" of a person taken "after life" rather than "from life".[37] On appeal the Lord Chancellor remarked obiter that a portrait might include a representation of someone who has already died unless the representation was completely "ideal" or imagined.[38] This has been interpreted broadly and, in *Leah v Two Worlds Publishing Co Ltd*,[39] Vaisey J held that a painting of a dead boy by a spiritualist medium who had never seen him (or any other material image), but who had come to a likeness of the boy through speaking to the father over the phone, was a portrait within the terms of the Act. A portrait may include props such as armour and horses, other people and even historical scenes and, in *Duke of Leeds v Earl of Amherst*, a painting of the Duke of Schomberg on horseback in full armour against a background of a battle was held to be a portrait. A painting might be a portrait even though the picture is "bad" and the likeness is poor.[40]

These decisions are consistent with the considered obiter statements of Roper J in the famous Australian case of *Attorney-General v Trustees of National Art*

---

33    [1925] 2 KB 804.
34    (1984) 3 IPR 567.
35    (1984) 3 IPR 567 at 571.
36    (1845) 14 LJ Ch 73.
37    (1845) 14 LJ Ch 73 at 74 in trial judgment.
38    (1845) 14 LJ Ch 73 at 81-82 on appeal.
39    [1951] Ch 393.
40    *Duke of Leeds v Earl of Amherst* (1845) 14 LJ Ch 73 at 81 on appeal.

*Gallery of New South Wales*,[41] who held that the question of whether Dobell's painting of Joshua Smith was a portrait within the terms of the Archibald bequest was a discretionary matter for the trustees.[42] In dicta, however, the judge canvassed the arguments put by counsel regarding the meaning of the term and concluded that the fields of caricature, fantasy and portrait were not mutually exclusive.[43]

This question does keep the trustees busy. One of the contestants in the 2003 Archibald Prize competition argued that neither Richard Bell's painting "I am not sorry" nor Paul Worstead's painting "Me" were portraits within the terms of the bequest. Richard Bell's portrait portrays, against a red background, a head in the shape of the iconic Ned Kelly helmet above a black t-shirt with the words "White Girls" printed on it. Paul Worstead's self-portrait portrays a rather sad looking rabbit, standing with folded arms, with the words "Autism as metaphor" written above it. Being within the discretion of the trustees, it is unlikely that these matters will come to court – but they are interesting examples of the possible limits of the genre.

## Copyright material made or published by or under the direction or control of the Crown or an international organisation

The Commonwealth or the State is the owner of any work, sound recording or film made or published by or under the direction and control of the Crown.[44] These provisions are subject to any agreement made with the author or maker of the copyright material.[45] An international organisation is the owner of a work, sound recording, film or printed edition made or published by or made under its control or direction.[46]

In *British Broadcasting Co v Wireless League Gazette Publishing Co*,[47] it was held that the radio guide published by the British Broadcasting Company was not published by or on behalf of the Crown even though such a program was required to be published under the terms of the BBC's broadcast licence. This was explained in *Copyright Agency Ltd v New South Wales*[48] where the Full Federal Court considered the meaning of the expression "under the direction or control" of the Crown and held that the question to be answered is whether the Crown is "in a position to determine whether or not a work will be made, rather than simply determining that, *if it is to be made at all,* it will be made in a particular way or in accordance with particular specifications".[49]

---

41    (1945) 62 WN(NSW) 212.
42    (1945) 62 WN(NSW) 212 at 214.
43    (1945) 62 WN(NSW) 212 at 215.
44    Sections 176(2) and 177 as to works, s 178(2) as to films and sound recordings.
45    Section 179.
46    Section 187 as to works, s 188 as to sound recordings, films and printed editions.
47    [1926] Ch 433. See *Commonwealth v Oceantalk Australia Pty Ltd* (1998) 151 ALR 567 for a recent discussion of ss 176 and 177.
48    [2007] FCAFC 80.
49    [2007] FCAFC 81 at [126].

## The live performers' copyright

The new live performers' copyright in the sound recording of a live performance, together with the retrospective nature of this right, has significantly extended the reach of copyright ownership. Not only will it give Jimmy Barnes copyright in a sound recording of his live performance (past and present) but it will also give copyright to an unknown triangle player who appeared 10 years ago in the finale of a show.

The rights go beyond just musical recordings, however, because live performance is defined broadly to mean a performance of a dramatic work (including an improvisation) including a puppet work; a performance (including an improvisation) of a musical work; the reading, recitation or delivery of a literary work or improvised literary work; performance of a dance, circus act or variety act and the performance of an "expression of folklore" (s 22(7)). Performer is defined as a person (including the conductor) who contributes to the sounds of the performance (s 84). The inclusion of an expression of folklore in this definition is significant in so far as it extends protection to certain indigenous performers whose work has not otherwise been reduced to material form or which includes stories taken from ancient times, which might be thought to be outside the protection of copyright. We will consider the meaning of the term "expression of folklore" in Chapter 7 when we consider performers' moral rights and the possible extension of moral rights to indigenous communities.

The definition of performance provides that the performance must be live but need not be in the presence of an audience (s 22(7)). This is an unusual definition from the music industry's point of view at least. The music industry, for example, traditionally distinguishes between live performances and studio performances on the basis of whether there is an audience or not. It may be that other factors must be taken into account including where the recording was made; how and when it was edited; whether tracks were laid separately or at different times and the intention of the performers. None of these factors alone would be sufficient, however, to distinguish a live performance from a studio performance. A recording made by a musician in an ABC radio studio, rather than in an ABC recording studio, would normally be characterised as a live performance rather than a studio performance. Modern recording equipment allows significant editing at the time of making the recording, including the laying down of tracks separately. Perhaps one of the most distinctive factors would be that, in general, a live performance is considered as a singular event and will be recorded in a single take rather than in multiple takes over time (although there may be engineers and producers who, as a matter of aesthetics, prefer a single take even in the studio). In addition, a live performance has an element of simultaneousness between the performance and the reception which is not present in non-live performances. These examples come from the music industry but more difficult questions may arise in relation to sound recordings of dramatic works, folklore and circus acts, for example, where there is a less developed industry usage regarding live performances. We would suggest that any definition of live performance should take into account its specific industry usage rather than simply borrow blindly from the music industry.

Despite the wide definitions of performance and performer it is likely that it still will not cover fly-on-the-wall documentaries except to the extent that they can be characterised as a dramatic or musical work or circus act or expression of folklore, for example. The real life teacher in the French documentary of a small one teacher school in rural France, for example, lost his attempt to be recognized as a copyright owner in the commercially successful 2002 film, *Être et Avoir*. We would suggest that, depending on the way the documentary was made, a similar result would eventuate in Australia in relation to a sound recording made at the school. A different result might arise in the case of expressions of folklore or circus acts, for example, if a sound recording were made in a fly-on-the-wall style. Similarly, a sound recording made of street kids rapping would seem to be caught by the new provisions despite the strong belief of documentary makers (whether in sound or visual media) that participants in documentaries should not, as a matter of principle, be paid. It may be that courts will try to import into the definition of "performer" a requirement for some notion of professionalism or calling which would recognise the rights of professionals and indigenous people whilst still respecting the documentary tradition.

One of the more surprising aspects of these new copyright provisions is that they are retrospective. The *US Free Trade Agreement Implementation Act 2004* contains special provisions for dealing with what are called pre-commencement sound recordings of live performances – that is, a relevant sound recording in which copyright subsisted at the date of commencement of the section (that is January 2005) and where at least one person has become a maker by virtue of the *US Free Trade Agreement Implementation Act 2004*. Under s 100AE the "former owners" and the "new owners" of the copyright each own half of the copyright as tenants in common. Where there is more than one former owner they will own their half in the same proportions as they previously owned the whole of the copyright. The new owners own their share as tenants in common. If the new owner has died at the time of commencement then the copyright will devolve as though the new owner owned the copyright immediately before his or her death. If the copyright devolves to more than one person then that person is considered to be one person for the determination of the shares in the copyright referred to above.

The new owner does not necessarily acquire this copyright for nothing. Section 116AAA requires that if the performer's acquisition of property under the new provisions results in an acquisition of property other than on just terms then the parties are to negotiate compensation, for the acquisition of those rights, either between themselves or have the amount determined by a court of competent jurisdiction. The section does not actually require a party to pay "just terms" for the property, rather, the failure to achieve just terms brings the compensation provisions into play. This is in accordance with modern constitutional law principles which have held that, although the requirement of just terms in general requires the payment of market value, the requirement to pay just terms is largely limited to procurement by the government and does not extend to third party acquisitions or legislation which relates to the adjustment and regulation of competing claims, rights and liabilities between the parties: see the High Court's discussion of a similar point in relation to the *Circuit Layouts Act 1989* in *Nintendo Co Ltd v Centronics Systems Pty Ltd*.[50] The Act does not give

---

50   *Nintendo Co Ltd v Centronics Systems Pty Ltd* (1994) 181 CLR 134 and also *Mutual Pools and Staff Pty Ltd v Commonwealth* (1997) 190 CLR 513. Compare *PJ Magennis Pty Ltd v Commonwealth* (1949) 80 CLR 382 and *Trade Practices Commission v Tooth* (1979) 142 CLR 397.

any guidance on what constitutes appropriate compensation under the Act except that compensation and damages paid in other actions must be taken into account. In so far as the claim of the new owner may vary from that of the triangle player on the superstar's album to the superstar whose fame has made a producer rich, the terms will be determined on a case-by-case basis although it can be expected that it will be determined by reference to some idea of market value.

Although the performer on a sound recording of a live performance has the same exclusive rights as the other owners of a sound recording there are limitations with respect to pre-commencement recordings. In particular the former owner (and successors in title) or a person authorised by the former owner may do any act comprised in the copyright or any other act in relation to copyright as if each new owner had granted a licence or permission to the former owner to do the act (s 100AF, although this may be varied by agreement). In addition, the new owner's remedies are limited in the case of infringement and other civil actions (s 100AG). Finally, the new owner has little or no role to play in relation to compulsory licences (s 100AH).

## Transmission of Ownership and Licensing Agreements

### Transmission of ownership[51]

Ownership of copyright may pass by assignment, by will or by devolution by operation by law (*Copyright Act 1968* s 196). Under s 197 copyright not yet in existence is also assignable and vests in the purported assignee or successor at the time that the copyright comes into existence. This is subject to the usual rules regarding priority of interests and if there is a person with a prior claim then copyright will not vest in the future assignee at all by virtue of this provision.

As we saw in Chapter 2, in accordance with the distinction between the chattel right and the copyright, a bequest of Charles Dickens' unpublished manuscript failed to pass the copyright in the work at common law.[52] This position is today partly overturned by s 198 which provides that, where a manuscript of an unpublished literary, dramatic or musical work or an unpublished artistic work is bequeathed, the bequest shall be read as including the copyright in the work. The application of s 198 is expressly subject to the appearance of a contrary testamentary intent and does not apply to published works or other subject-matter whether published or not. Any copyright may therefore be subject to a bequest.

Property is said to devolve by operation of law when, without any voluntary act on the part of any party, it passes from one person to another.[53] The question of whether the copyright has been devolved by law rather than by assignment may be particularly important in cases where the formalities required for an assignment have not been met. Succession of estates on death, proceedings in bankruptcy or insolvency and changes of an official incumbent have been held to be examples of devolution by operation of law[54] but the transmission of copyright

---

51    For transitional provisions relating to assignment, see ss 239 and 248.
52    *Re Dickens* [1935] 1 Ch 267.
53    *O'Brien v Komesaroff* (1982) 150 CLR 310, Mason J at 319-320.
54    *O'Brien v Komesaroff* (1982) 150 CLR 310, Mason J at 320, approving *Francisco v Aguirre* (1892) 29 P 495 at 497.

under a deed of partnership is not.[55] In *Murray v King*,[56] Sheppard J held that a sale by a court appointed receiver constituted a devolution by law.[57]

The most common form of transmission of ownership of copyright is by assignment. Only the exclusive rights of the copyright owner may be assigned (including the right to authorise).[58] In *Kervan Trading Pty Ltd v Aktas*,[59] Bryson J held that the indirect infringement actions under ss 102 and 103 of the *Copyright Act* are not exclusive rights of the copyright holder but provide a practical way for copyright owners to establish an infringement. The copyright owner therefore cannot assign the right to import and deal with the copyright material.[60] At most, all the copyright owner could do would be to grant a non-exclusive licence to the would-be importer/dealer and, as we shall see, a non-exclusive licence does not give the licensee standing to sue.

The exclusive rights of the copyright owner are "divisible". That is, they may be partially assigned and may be divided in a number of different ways (s 196). The assignment may only apply to one or more classes of the exclusive rights; the rights may be assigned to apply for a set period of time or for a specified geographical area in Australia and a part of a class of rights may be assigned even though it is not separately specified as a right under the *Copyright Act*. This provision allows the copyright owner to exploit the copyright in a wide-ranging manner. A copyright holder may therefore assign just the paperback publication rights, for example, for a particular area and/or for a specified time.

Once the copyright has been assigned the *Copyright Act* and the courts, in the past, have done little to protect any moral interest which the copyright owner may have in the material. This is partly ameliorated by the introduction of moral rights. These rights, which give authors, performers, directors, screenwriters and producers of works and films the right to have their authorship attributed to the material, the right not to have another person falsely attributed as the author and the right not to have the material treated in a derogatory manner, are considered in the next chapter.

## Licensing of copyright[61]

A licence provides permission or consent to do something.[62] It does not create any estate or interest in a property but only makes an act lawful which would otherwise be unlawful. In infringement proceedings the onus of proving an absence of licence, permission or consent to do the infringing act lies on the party alleging infringement because it constitutes one of the elements of the breach not an excuse, defence or justification.[63]

---

55    *O'Brien v Komesaroff* (1982) 150 CLR 310.

56    (1984) 55 ALR 559.

57    The remaining judges in that case found that the question did not need to be addressed.

58    *Devefi Pty Ltd v Mateffy Pearl Nagy Pty Ltd* (1993) 113 ALR 225.

59    (1987) 8 IPR 583.

60    *Kervan Trading Pty Ltd v Aktas* (1987) 8 IPR 583 at 587.

61    For transitional provisions relating to licensing, see ss 228, 239 and 248.

62    See *Banks v Transport Regulation Board (Vic)* (1968) 119 CLR 222 at 230 for Windeyer J's comments.

63    *Avel Pty Ltd v Multicoin Amusements Pty Ltd* (1990) 171 CLR 88, Mason CJ, Deane and Gaudron JJ at 94-95, Dawson J at 119.

A licence may be given to the world at large (for example, a notice on sheet music that anyone may perform the musical works)[64] or to one or more people (known as a sole licence where it is only given to one person) and, in the ordinary case, the licensor retains the right to do the licensed action. Under the *Copyright Act 1968* there is provision for the granting of an "exclusive licence" which is defined in s 10 as:

> a licence in writing, signed by or on behalf of the owner or prospective owner of copyright, authorising the licensee, to the exclusion of all other persons, to do an act, which by virtue of this Act, the owner of the copyright would, but for the licence, have the exclusive right to do ...

The phrase, "all other persons", has been interpreted to include the owner of the copyright and, therefore, upon the grant of an exclusive licence even the copyright owner is excluded from doing the licensed act.[65] Like assignment, the exclusive licence is limited to the exclusive rights of the copyright owner and therefore the indirect infringement provisions cannot be subject to an exclusive licence.

A licence may be "bare" (that is, without consideration) or contractual (supported by consideration). A bare licence may be revoked at will, or at least with reasonable notice. Thus, in *Trumpet Software Pty Ltd v Ozemail Pty Ltd*,[66] Ozemail could not rely on the bare licence printed on the free computer shareware, Trumpet Winsock, as permission to do the infringing act in the face of Trumpet's express refusal to grant permission to do that act. It has been suggested that if the bare licence has been acted upon by the licensee to the detriment of the licensee, then the copyright owner may be estopped from revoking the licence, either completely or without the granting of notice.[67]

In copyright cases, the question of whether a contractual licence may be assigned to someone else has been determined by reference to the terms of the licence. In *Beck v Montana Constructions Pty Ltd*,[68] Jacobs J held that there was an implied term in an architectural contract that the owner of the land for which the plans were made might assign the right to the purchaser of the land for the same use. In *Devefi Pty Ltd v Mateffy Pearl Nagy Pty Ltd*,[69] on the other hand, the court found that a licence to reproduce engineering diagrams by erecting the building could not be assigned because the licence was inextricably bound up in a contract for the ongoing provision of personal supervisory services by the engineer.

Although the *Copyright Act 1968* does not expressly provide for divisibility of copyright for the purposes of licensing, it has been held as a matter of statutory construction that the exclusive rights of the copyright owner may be partially

---

64    *Mellor v Australian Broadcasting Commission* [1940] AC 491.

65    See Denning MR in *Murray (Inspector of Taxation) v Imperial Chemical Industries Ltd* [1967] Ch 1038 at 1051 regarding exclusive licences. See *Computermate Products (Aust) Pty Ltd v Ozi-Soft Pty Ltd* (1988) 83 ALR 492 for a useful discussion of licences under the *Copyright Act 1968*.

66    (1996) 34 IPR 481.

67    The Full Federal Court in *Computermate Products (Aust) Pty Ltd v Ozi-Soft Pty Ltd* (1988) 83 ALR 492 at 495, citing *Waltons Stores (Interstate) Ltd v Maher* (1988) 76 ALR 513.

68    (1963) 5 FLR 298.

69    (1993) 113 ALR 225.

licensed.[70] As Bryson J remarked in *Kervan Trading Pty Ltd v Aktas,* copyright is "almost infinitely subdivisible" for these purposes.[71]

There are special provisions relating to the licensing of copyright in the recording of a live performance. In particular, all members of a group of performers will be taken to have granted a licence or permission if the group's agent, acting within the authority of the agency, grants the appropriate consent (s 113A). A performer is said to have granted consent to use the recording of a live performance if the consent was for a specific purpose and the recording was used for those purposes (s 113B). Finally, s 113C deals with the situation where one owner of the copyright in a published sound recording of a live performance enters into an agreement with a third person to do an act comprised in the copyright but the owner cannot locate or identify other owners or representatives of other owners of the copyright. In this case the first owner is held to have the permission or licence of the other owners to do the act (including, by necessity, authorising the act (s 13(c)). If the owner receives any amount on account of the agreement then the owner must hold the other owner's share on trust for four years. If, at the end of this period, the other owner has not been located or identified then the first owner may retain the amount. Note that the first owner is only required to make reasonable initial inquiries, the first owner is not required to keep seeking the other owner during this four-year period. Even if the other owner is located or identified he or she cannot prevent the first owner doing an act comprised within the copyright during the term of the agreement.

## Implied terms

In the case of an assignment or a licence (whether in writing or not) terms may be implied according to general principles of construction. Thus, the term must be reasonable and equitable; it must be necessary to give business efficacy to the agreement so that no term will be implied if the agreement is effective without it; it must be so obvious that "it goes without saying"; it must be capable of clear expression; and it must not contradict any express terms of the agreement.[72]

The general principle of copyright law is that the acquisition of a chattel does not give the person who acquires the chattel a right to exercise the copyright in relation to the chattel, either by licence or assignment. Thus, a person who borrows a book does not acquire the right to reproduce the book and the purchaser of an art work does not acquire the right to publish the work. The supremacy of this principle was highlighted in *Interstate Parcel Express Co Pty Ltd v Time-Life International (Nederlands) BV*[73] where, as we saw in Chapter 4, the High Court held that the lawful purchase of a book did not imply a licence to import and

---

70    *PM Sulcs and Associates Pty Ltd v Detroit Diesel-Allison Australia Pty Ltd* (1997) 39 IPR 328 at 334 and *Sega Enterprises Ltd v Galaxy Electronics Pty Ltd* (1998) 39 IPR 577 at 580.

71    (1987) 8 IPR 583 at 587.

72    See *Codelfa Construction Pty Ltd v State Rail Authority of New South Wales* (1982) 149 CLR 337, Mason J at 347, citing the Privy Council in *BP Refinery (Westernport) Pty Ltd v Hastings Shire Council* (1977) 180 CLR 266 at 283 and applied in a copyright case in *Moorhead v Brennan* (1991) 20 IPR 161 at 165.

73    (1977) 138 CLR 534.

sell the book in breach of the indirect infringement provisions of the *Copyright Act 1968*.

This principle is subject to the proviso that if the chattel or copyright material is acquired for a particular purpose there will be an implied licence to use the material to carry out that purpose. Thus, in *Beck v Montana Constructions Pty Ltd*,[74] an architect was held to have given a licence to the property owner to use architectural plans for the purpose of constructing the building. This included a licence for the property owner's surveyors and builders to copy the plans for the purpose of obtaining building approval.[75] In *Kervan Trading Pty Ltd v Aktas*,[76] the court held that a person who had a licence to import and deal with certain films had an implied licence to reproduce those films in Australia. This implication was necessary as a matter of business efficacy because under the contract the importer/dealer was only given one copy of the film and the consideration paid suggested that the contract was not meant to be restricted to just one sale of one film in Australia.[77]

In Australia the courts have been cautious about implying a licence to deal with copyright in chattels acquired by a person. In defence of this caution the courts have emphasised both the personal nature of copyright as separate either from the chattel right or other intellectual property rights as well as the role of the detailed defence provisions in balancing the interests of the copyright owner and user. The courts have been adept in finding ways in which the agreement could be effective without the benefit of the implied term. Thus, in *R and A Bailey and Co v Boccaccio Pty Ltd*,[78] the Supreme Court of New South Wales declined to hold that there was an implied right to import and deal with an artistic work which comprised a trade mark even though the importation and trading did not constitute an infringement in the trade mark itself. The court held that it was not necessary, either as a matter of law or business efficacy, to imply such a term because the importer could have removed and replaced the labels before dealing with them commercially.[79] In that case the court also noted that, in the light of the High Court's decision in *Interstate Parcel Express Co Pty Ltd v Time-Life International (Nederlands) BV*,[80] Australian courts were unlikely to follow the United Kingdom decisions which readily implied a licence to exercise the copyright for the purposes of repairing a chattel or making spare parts.[81]

---

74   (1963) 5 FLR 298.
75   The High Court considered implied terms in relation to architectural plans in *Concrete Pty Ltd v Parramatta Designs and Developments Pty Ltd* (2006) 231 ALR 663 and found that an implied licence to use the plans ran with the land in light of the statutory provisions relating to development applications, the original relationship between the parties, and the circumstances in which the plans were brought into existence.
76   (1987) 8 IPR 583.
77   (1987) 8 IPR 583 at 588-589.
78   (1986) 77 ALR 177.
79   As we saw in Chapter 5, the severity of this approach has been overcome by s 44C which allows the importation of "non-infringing accessories" which includes labels on non-infringing material (s 10).
80   (1977) 138 CLR 534.
81   *R and A Bailey and Co v Boccaccio Pty Ltd* (1986) 77 ALR 177 at 187-188 referring to *Solar Thomson Engineering Co Ltd v Barton* [1977] RPC 537 regarding repairs and *British Leyland Corporation Ltd v Armstrong Patents Co Ltd* [1986] AC 577 regarding spare parts.

The courts have been more inclined to imply a term into an agreement where the term protects the economic interests of the copyright owner. Thus, in *Moorhead v Brennan*,[82] the Supreme Court of New South Wales construed a publishing agreement between a publisher and a novelist to include an implied term that the publisher would not impede or obstruct opportunities to receive royalties and fees from persons who proposed to publish the work under licence. In that case the publisher was found to have breached the implied term by refusing to grant a licensing agreement to a British publishing house because he disagreed with their feminist principles and felt he was being made a victim of their "lesbian feminist politics and philosophy". In an entertaining judgment Bryson J concluded that it was unreasonable for the publisher to refuse to enter a publishing agreement with Women's Press on the basis that they would not publish his "publisher's note" to the novel and "still more unreasonable to tell a British publisher who wanted the book that the note stood the sole surviving witness to a remembered past and hoped-for future of gender detente and peaceable sexual co-existence".[83]

## Invalid agreements and the Competition and Consumer Act

In the 1970s and 1980s the courts were active in developing the modern principles of contractual fairness which have since been adopted by legislatures in consumer protection and trade practices legislation. In copyright law this judicial activity was brought into play in three cases where young or relatively inexperienced performers had assigned their (in two cases, world wide) copyright, including future copyright, under contracts which imposed no obligation on the purchasers to publish or exploit the copyright. The contracts had been entered into generally without independent legal advice. In each of the cases the courts held the contracts to be invalid but on different grounds in each case.

In the first, *A Schroeder Music Publishing Co Ltd v Macauley*,[84] the House of Lords upheld the decision of the trial judge and the Court of Appeal to declare the contract void on the basis that it was a restraint of trade. Lord Reid held that a contract in restraint of trade was void because the public interest required that a person should be as "free as far as practicable to earn a livelihood and to give to the public the fruits of his particular abilities".[85] Lord Diplock rejected Lord Reid's explanation of restraint of trade as based on 19th century laissez-faire economic theories and held that restraint of trade was one species of the general category of unconscionable contract and offered "protection of those whose bargaining power is weak against being forced by those whose bargaining power is stronger to enter into bargains which are unconscionable".[86]

A few days after this judgment Lord Denning, in *Clifford Davis Management Ltd v WEA Records Ltd*,[87] dealt with a similar contract relating to the assignment of copyright in Fleetwood Mac songs. He said that such a contract could not be

---

82    (1991) 20 IPR 161.
83    (1991) 20 IPR 161 at 172.
84    [1974] 3 All ER 616.
85    [1974] 3 All ER 616 at 621.
86    [1974] 3 All ER 616 at 623.
87    [1975] 1 All ER 237.

said to be a "restraint of trade" but was "restrictive of trade".[88] In granting an interim injunction he concluded that it could be said that "there was such an inequality of bargaining power that the agreement should not be enforced and that the assignment of copyright was invalid".[89]

In *O'Sullivan v Management Agency and Music Ltd*,[90] the performer Gilbert O'Sullivan was successful in having his contract set aside, his copyright re-assigned, a delivery up of the master tapes and an account of profits on the basis that the contract was the result of undue influence on the part of the manager and his company who were in a fiduciary relationship with the performer. The decision of the lower court that the contract was also in restraint of trade was not subject to appeal.

Under the *Competition and Consumer Act 2010* Part IV (previously the *Trade Practices Act 1974* Part IV) certain restrictive trade practices are proscribed. Under s 45, provisions in contracts, arrangements and understandings which restrict the supply or acquisition of goods or services to a person or class of people or which lessen competition are unenforceable. Similarly, covenants which lessen competition are unenforceable (s 45C). Secondary boycotts (s 45D), misuse of market power (ss 46 and 46A), exclusive dealing (s 47), resale price maintenance (s 48) and acquisition of assets and shares which lessen competition (ss 50 and 50A) are subject to substantial penalties under Sch 2, Part 2-2. Section 51(1) provides that if the action complained of was authorised by legislation other than Acts relating to patents, trade marks, designs or copyrights, then there will be no contravention of Part IV. The application of restrictive trade practices to intellectual property rights is dealt with separately and more narrowly under s 51(3).

Section 51(3) provides that if the act complained of was committed in order to give effect to a condition of a licence or assignment of a patent, a registered design, an eligible layout under the *Circuit Layouts Act 1989* or copyright there will be no contravention of Part IV. The exclusion does not cover ss 46 and 46A or s 48; therefore, neither misuse of market power nor resale price maintenance can be justified by reference to an intellectual property agreement.

The exclusion is said to apply only to the extent that the condition in question "relates to" the patented invention, products made by using the invention, the article to which a design is applied, the copyright subject-matter or an eligible layout. There has been some debate as to when a condition might be said to "relate to" one of these objects. On the one hand, it has been suggested that the object must be considered only as a physical thing apart from the intellectual property which subsists in it. Under this interpretation a condition "relates to" the object only if it is concerned with physical attributes of the object such as packaging and quality. The s 51(3) exclusion therefore would not apply to any conditions relating to licensing and assignment of the intellectual property subsisting in the object.[91] This interpretation is not convincing, however, in so far as it renders the exemption unnecessary (because such conditions would not normally constitute a

---

88    [1975] 1 All ER 237 at 239.
89    [1975] 1 All ER 237 at 241.
90    [1985] QB 428.
91    Ricketson takes this further and argues that "subject-matter in which copyright subsists" is restricted to the original literary work itself and therefore the exemption would not extend to physical aspects of books which are reproductions of the original literary work: S Ricketson, *The*

restrictive trade practice). The better interpretation is a purposive one, whereby the purpose of the section is to allow the intellectual property owner to license and assign the IP rights which subsist in the named objects without risk of contravening Part IV of the *Competition and Consumer Act 2010*. At the same time, the section tries to prevent the IP agreement from being used as a cover for imposing restrictive trade practices outside the legitimate exercise of the intellectual property owner's rights subsisting in the objects. In this case the "object" is the object including the intellectual property which subsists in it. Thus, a geographical limitation for the publication of a literary work would be a condition "relating to" the object in which intellectual property subsists. A condition which required the licensee to use a particular printing press for publishing the book would not be a condition relating to the book unless it was also concerned with quality of reproduction, for example. It is interesting to note that none of the defendants in *Australian Competition and Consumer Commission v Universal Music Australia Pty Ltd*[92] appears to have raised the s 51(3) exclusion in relation to the threats to review the terms of their agreements with record stores who were selling parallel import CDs.

## Formalities

There are two formal requirements for the effective assignment of copyright or the granting of an exclusive licence. The assignment or agreement must be in writing and must be signed by or on behalf of the copyright owner.[93] Non-exclusive licences need not be in writing.

The writing need not expressly mention copyright and a term may be implied into a written contract or the contract may be construed to include the copyright. Thus, in *Greenfield Products Pty Ltd v Rover-Scott Bonnar Ltd*,[94] a term was implied into a written agreement to sell the company including its goodwill in order to give the contract business efficacy. In *Murray v King*,[95] a written agreement which referred to the "assets" of the company was held to include the copyright owned by the company. The court held that the question of whether the words in a written agreement cover copyright is a matter of interpretation and parol evidence may be admitted for the purposes of determining the subject-matter intended to be assigned.[96]

In *Murray v King*, the agreement was between the bankruptcy receiver and the purchaser of the bankrupt estate. The receiver in bankruptcy was neither the owner of the copyright nor the agent of the copyright owner and the question arose as to whether the agreement could be said to have been signed by the copyright owner or on behalf of the copyright owner as required under s 196. Morling and Spender JJ held that the receiver did sign "on behalf of" the copyright owner. Morling J held that "on behalf of" meant "for the benefit of" the copyright owner

---

   *Law of Intellectual Property: Copyright, Designs and Confidential Information*, Looseleaf service, LBC, Sydney, para 15.190.
92   (2001) 115 FCR 442.
93   Section 196 as to assignments and see definition of "exclusive licence" in s 10.
94   (1990) 95 ALR 275.
95   (1984) 55 ALR 559.
96   (1984) 55 ALR 559, Spender J at 576, citing *EW Savory Ltd v World of Golf Ltd* [1914] 2 Ch 566.

who in this case was the bankrupt partnership.[97] In *Beloff v Pressdram*,[98] on the other hand, an agreement signed by the editor of a newspaper purporting to assign the copyright in an unpublished memorandum was held not to have been signed by or on behalf of the copyright owner who, in this case, was the company which owned the newspaper.

Before 1968, agreements for the assignment of copyright not yet in existence were not effective but created an equitable interest. Under s 197 such agreements may be made and copyright passes at the time the work comes into existence but not before.[99] Assignments of both future copyright (s 197) and equitable interests in copyright[100] must be in writing and signed by the person who would be the owner of the copyright once it came into existence, apart from the agreement in question.

In the case of equitable interests it is important to distinguish between the assignment of an equitable interest and the creation of an equitable interest. Where the purported assignor is both the legal and equitable owner of the copyright and grants an equitable interest the better view is that in this case the owner is creating an equitable interest rather than assigning it and thus the requirement for writing does not apply. Where the purported assignor is the equitable owner but not the legal owner of the copyright and grants a right to another person then this is an assignment which requires writing.

Thus, in *Acorn Computers Ltd v MCS Microcomputer Systems Pty Ltd*[101] an unwritten agreement was made between Acorn and another company. Under the agreement all the assets in the company, including existing and future copyright, was to pass to Acorn. The respondents argued that the lack of writing rendered the purported assignment ineffective. The court rejected the argument on the basis that the contract "created" an equitable interest in Acorn in the copyright material rather than assigned an equitable interest in the copyright material:

> It is normally the consequence of such a transaction that, value having been given, an equitable interest in the subject thereof arises in the party giving it ... In such a case the equitable interest arises not by way of transfer but by activation in Equity of the conscience of the receiver of the valuable consideration. A trust is created; there is no transfer or assignment; there is no transmission of an equitable interest.[102]

This principle may be of practicable importance in cases where there have been verbal agreements, for example, between an employer and an employee or a director and company regarding the ownership of future copyright.

---

97   (1984) 55 ALR 559, Morling J at 571, citing Lord Hatherly in *Gillespie v City of Glasgow Bank* (1879) 4 App Cas 632 at 642.

98   [1973] 1 All ER 241.

99   *Chaplin v Leslie Frewin (Publishers) Ltd* [1966] Ch 71, construing s 36 of the *Copyright Act 1956* (UK).

100  *Conveyancing Act 1919* (NSW) s 23C; *Property Law Act 1974* (Qld) s 11; *Law of Property Act 1936* (SA) s 29; *Conveyancing and Law of Property Act 1884* (Tas) s 60(2); *Property Law Act 1958* (Vic) s 53; *Property Law Act 1969* (WA) s 34; *Imperial Acts (Substituted Provisions) Act 1986* (ACT) Sch 2 Part 11 cl 1(c); *Law of Property Act No 1 2000* (NT) s 10.

101  (1984) 57 ALR 389.

102  (1984) 57 ALR 389, Smithers J at 393.

## Remedies and Standing for Civil Actions

The court's power to grant relief under the *Copyright Act 1968* is discretionary and the court may withhold relief on the basis of acquiescence and laches.[103] Acquiescence occurs when the plaintiff abstains from interfering whilst his or her rights are being violated.[104] Laches refers to undue delay in bringing proceedings in relation to the breach[105] which evidences acquiescence or causes the defendant to alter his or her position. Although the principles of acquiescence and laches are equitable in origin, Thomas J in *Kalamazoo (Aust) Pty Ltd v Compact Business Systems Pty Ltd*[106] held that they should not be so restricted. It is not clear whether he meant that they should be available in the case of damages as well as injunction and account or whether he thought it was necessary to make this point because of the statutory nature of injunction and account under the *Copyright Act*. Drummond J in *A-One Accessory Imports Pty Ltd v Off Road Imports Pty Ltd (No 2)*,[107] on the other hand, noted that, although the award of damages under s 115(2) is created by a form of words which suggests that it too is discretionary, the proprietary nature of copyright and the award of damages for infringement should not be forgotten and concluded, "I do not think that there is a discretion to deny a copyright owner who has established an infringement of his copyright the remedy by way of damages also provided for by the section".[108]

The remedies are similar for each of the civil actions but subject to some differences. In the case of an action for infringement under s 115 the court may grant an injunction and either damages or an account of profits. Damages may not be awarded if the infringement is "innocent", that is, if it is established that the defendant was not aware or had no reasonable grounds to suspect that the act was an infringement. In such a case an account of profits may still be awarded. Additional damages in the nature of exemplary or punitive damages may be awarded if the court is satisfied that it is proper to do so having regard to the flagrancy of the breach, any benefit accruing to the defendant and any other relevant matter. Under the 2001 digital amendments the fact that the infringement involved the conversion of a hardcopy or analogue form of the copyright subject-matter into a digital or other electronic machine-readable form may also be taken into account in determining additional damages (s 115(4)). In addition, where there has been an infringement relating to communication and because of this communication it is likely that other infringements have occurred and, together, these are on a commercial scale, the court may take this into account when determining relief (s 115(5)).

In an action for conversion under s 116 the court may grant any remedy available for such an action. This would normally include an order to deliver up the goods or damages and, at one time, was thought not to include an injunction.[109]

---

103 See *Kalamazoo (Aust) Pty Ltd v Compact Business Systems Pty Ltd* (1985) 5 IPR 213 for an example of the application of these principles to copyright cases.
104 *Ramsden v Dyson* (1888) LR 1 HL 129.
105 *Orr v Ford* (1988) 167 CLR 316.
106 (1985) 5 IPR 213.
107 (1996) 144 ALR 559.
108 (1996) 144 ALR 559 at 562.
109 *Re Wait* [1927] 1 Ch 606.

Under the *Copyright Act* no damages or pecuniary relief other than costs may be awarded if the infringement is "innocent". Although the relief available under s 116 is additional to the relief available under s 115 the court is not to grant any relief for conversion or detinue if the court is satisfied that the relief granted under s 115 is sufficient. There is no provision for additional damages in relation to s 116 actions.

In actions relating to circumvention devices, electronic rights management information and broadcast decoding devices (ss 116, 116B, 116C and Part VAA) the court may grant an injunction and either damages or an account of profits. Additional damages may be awarded having regard to the flagrancy of the breach, the benefit accruing to the defendant and other relevant matters. In the case of broadcast decoding devices the court may direct that the device be destroyed or otherwise dealt with (ss 135AN(6), 135ANA(6)).

In addition to these substantive remedies the *Copyright Act* provides three significant pre-trial procedures which facilitate the effective prosecution of copyright actions. Under Part V, Division 7 the copyright owner or exclusive licensee may give notice to the Chief Executive Officer of Customs objecting to the importation of goods which, if made in Australia, would constitute an infringement of copyright. The notice stays in effect for two years during which time the CEO may seize such goods if they are imported into Australia for the purposes of selling or otherwise dealing with the goods. The goods will be released to the importer if the copyright owner or exclusive licensee fails to institute proceedings within the prescribed time of 10 days[110] and that person is also responsible for any reasonable costs associated with the storage of the goods.[111] In addition to the customs seizure provisions the courts may also exercise their inherent jurisdiction to grant ex parte interlocutory relief in the form of an Anton Piller order or Mareva injunction. An Anton Piller order compels the defendant to allow the plaintiff to enter and remove any material relevant to the case.[112] A Mareva injunction is an order preventing the defendant from removing or otherwise dealing with assets in a way which would render a subsequent judgment ineffective.[113]

Note that a "new owner", that is a performer in a live performance who has been granted copyright under the *US Free Trade Agreement Implementation Act 2004* in relation to a sound recording made before January 2005, has limited remedies in relation to these pre-commencement sound recordings. In particular, in an action for infringement (s 115), conversion (s 116) and in actions relating to circumvention devices, electronic rights management and broadcast decoding services (s 116A, s 116B and s 116C), a new owner is not entitled to damages (other than additional damages) or an account of profits. In addition, in an action for conversion the new owner is not entitled to any other pecuniary remedy (other than costs) or delivery up of an infringing copy (s 100AG).

---

110  *Copyright Regulations 1969* reg 22.
111  The *Intellectual Property Laws Amendment (Raising the Bar) Act 2011* streamlines these procedures.
112  *Anton Piller KG v Manufacturing Processes Ltd* [1976] 1 Ch 55 and *EMI (Australia) Ltd v Bay Imports Pty Ltd* [1980] FSR 328.
113  *Mareva Compania Naviera SA v International Bulkcarriers SA (The Mareva)* [1980] 1 All ER 213.

## Injunction

An injunction orders someone to do something or, more commonly, refrain from doing something. In copyright law an injunction is commonly requested to prevent an apprehended infringement of copyright or to prevent the continuation of infringing behaviour. The injunction might be interlocutory, in which case it is given before the court makes its final decision and the order does not determine the substantive rights of the parties. Alternatively, the injunction might be final which means that it is granted as the remedy or part of the remedy based on a final determination of the substantive issues between the parties. In *Nine Network Australia Pty Ltd v Australian Broadcasting Corporation*,[114] for example, Channel Nine requested an interlocutory injunction to prevent the ABC from filming the New Year's Eve fireworks display. In *A and M Records Inc v Napster*,[115] the recording companies sought an interlocutory injunction against Napster requiring it to cease operating the music-sharing service in infringing ways pending the outcome of the trial. In *Australasian Performing Right Association Ltd v Tolbrush Pty Ltd*,[116] on the other hand, the court granted a permanent injunction against the defendant shop keepers in the face of their persistent refusal to acknowledge that playing musical works on the radio and tapes in their shops was an infringing act. The principles under which an interlocutory or final injunction are ordered are different although in practice many parties do not proceed beyond the interlocutory stage.

In the case of an interlocutory injunction the court may make an order if it is satisfied that the claim is not frivolous or vexatious, that is, that there is a "serious question to be tried" and if the "balance of convenience" favours the granting of the injunction. This test, which was laid down by Lord Diplock in *American Cyanamid Co v Ethicon Ltd*,[117] a patent case approved by Gibbs CJ in *Australian Coarse Grain Pool Pty Ltd v Barley Marketing Board of Queensland (No 1)*,[118] is important in so far as it rejects the suggestion that an interlocutory injunction will not be granted unless the court is satisfied that the applicant has established a prima facie case of infringement.[119]

The court will not normally grant an interlocutory injunction unless the plaintiff gives undertakings as to damages for loss to the defendant in the event that the defendant were to win at trial. Nor will the court normally grant an interlocutory injunction, no matter how strong the plaintiff's case, if damages for the continued infringing use before the final determination of the matter would be an adequate remedy in the event that the plaintiff won. Conversely, if damages would not be an adequate remedy for continued use the court, before granting an injunction, must consider the effect on the defendant on the contrary hypothesis that the defendant were to succeed at trial. If the undertaking represents an adequate remedy for the defendant's loss and the plaintiff would be able to pay then there would be no ground to refuse the interlocutory injunction.[120] Where there is doubt

---

114  (1999) 48 IPR 333.
115  (2000) 50 IPR 232.
116  (1985) 62 ALR 521.
117  [1975] AC 396.
118  (1982) 46 ALR 398.
119  *Beecham Group Ltd v Bristol Laboratories Pty Ltd* (1968) 118 CLR 618.
120  *American Cyanamid Co v Ethicon Ltd* [1975] AC 396 at 408.

as to the adequacy of damages then other questions must be addressed in order to determine the balance of convenience. Lord Diplock warned that it would be "unwise to attempt even to list all the various matters which need to be taken into consideration in deciding where the balance lies, let alone to suggest the relative weight to be attached to them". He concluded that, where other factors appear to be balanced it is a counsel of prudence to preserve the status quo.[121]

Despite this warning, some factors which may be important in determining whether to grant an interlocutory injunction in infringement or other civil proceeding under the *Copyright Act 1968* may be whether the defendant has commenced the wrongful act, the nature of the market for the copyright material, the relative size and competitiveness of the plaintiff and the defendant (a large, well known defendant might effectively destroy the plaintiff's chances of success if the defendant gets an opportunity to start dealing with infringing products at that time), whether the copyright work was produced for one specific purpose which would be lost if the injunction did not issue and whether there is a going rate for the licensing of the use.

Although it was once thought that, as a general principle of law and equity, a final injunction would not be granted where damages were an adequate remedy, this is not reflected in the *Copyright Act* which appears to favour the granting of an injunction over damages in the case of innocent infringement or dealings. An injunction is not usually granted for a conversion but, as there can be no conversion under the *Copyright Act* without an infringement, the point is of little real importance. The court will normally exercise its discretion to grant a final injunction for infringement when it is established that the infringement is likely to re-occur[122] and, in accordance with its characterisation of copyright as a proprietary interest, will grant an injunction even when there has been no damage to the plaintiff or even, one can imagine, where the infringement has brought a benefit to the plaintiff.[123]

## Damages

Damages may be awarded for each of the civil actions under the *Copyright Act 1968*. This is subject to the proviso that damages cannot be awarded in addition to an account of profits and further provided that damages may not be awarded under ss 115 and 116 if the infringement or conversion is innocent (ss 115(3) and 116(3)). The measure of damages is different according to the action and additional damages may be awarded except for s 116 actions.

### Innocence

Section 115(3) provides:

> Where, in an action for infringement of copyright, it is established that an infringement was committed but it is also established that, at the time of the infringement, the defendant was not aware, and had no reasonable grounds for suspecting, that the act constituting

121 [1975] AC 396 at 408.
122 *Australasian Performing Right Association Ltd v Tolbrush Pty Ltd* (1985) 62 ALR 521.
123 See the comments of Romer LJ in *Hawkes and Son (London) v Paramount Film Services* [1934] 1 Ch 593 at 608.

the infringement was an infringement of the copyright, the plaintiff is not entitled under this section to any damages ... but is entitled to an account of profits.

Under s 116(3) the court may not award damages if it is established that the defendant was not aware or had no grounds for suspecting that copyright subsisted in the subject-matter, that the articles converted or detained were infringing copies or that the article converted or detained was a device for making infringing copies.

These sections have been narrowly construed. In *Olympic Amusements Pty Ltd v Milwell Pty Ltd*,[124] a case involving copyright in the prize scale for a poker machine, the trial judge found that the defendant was entitled to the protection offered by the first limb of s 115(3) because, on the trial judge's assessment, the defendant was a " 'rough and ready' type of businessman, not well informed about the law relevant to his business and not curious about it".[125] This decision was overturned on appeal and the Full Federal Court held that the onus is on the defendant in relation to the first limb to establish positively that he was not aware that the action was infringing. Mere denial of infringement or ignorance is not enough. In order to obtain the protection of the section the court held that the defendant must establish:

(i) an active, subjective, lack of awareness that the act constituting the infringement was an infringement of the copyright, and (ii) that, objectively considered, [the defendant] had no reasonable grounds for suspecting that the act constituted an infringement.[126]

The most common fact situations in which the innocence limitation has been raised have been for mistake of law and mistaken identity. Neither is sufficient by itself to establish innocence. In *Milwell Pty Ltd v Olympic Amusements Pty Ltd*,[127] the Full Court rejected the trial judge's finding that the defendant had no reasonable grounds for suspecting that his actions were infringing because an ordinary person would not think that copyright would subsist in a prize scale for a poker machine (as opposed to a book, for example).[128] The Full Court endorsed the statement of Mann J in *Pollock v JC Williamson Ltd*[129] that ignorance of the obscurities of copyright law is no defence. In that case, the question turned on the performance rights of the translator of a dramatic work:

I do not think I could admit a mere belief that the law was otherwise ... as a "reasonable ground" within [s 8 of the *Copyright Act 1911*], even if such belief has been proved. It is a branch of the law directly affecting the defendant's business, and where there is shown to be no reasonable ground of ignorance of the relevant facts, I do not think that the section can be applied by reference to the varying degrees of legal obscurity which may be thought to surround particular questions.[130]

In *Kalamazoo (Aust) Pty Ltd v Compact Business Systems Pty Ltd*,[131] on the other hand, the fact that the market for printing substitute business forms

---

124  (1999) 162 ALR 199.
125  (1999) 162 ALR 199 at 212.
126  *Milwell Pty Ltd v Olympic Amusements Pty Ltd* (1999) 161 ALR 302 at 314.
127  (1999) 161 ALR 302.
128  (1999) 161 ALR 302 at 314.
129  [1923] VLR 225.
130  [1923] VLR 225 at 235.
131  (1985) 5 IPR 213.

had continued for more than 20 years, that neither the plaintiff nor defendant had believed that copyright subsisted in the forms and that the plaintiff had partly facilitated the defendant's actions over that period of time led Thomas J to conclude that, up until notification of the action, the defendants had no reasonable ground for suspecting that their actions were infringing.

Merely mistaking the identity of the copyright owner is no defence but if a defendant has acted reasonably in trying to identify the copyright owner and yet makes an error, the limitation under s 115(3) may be available. In *Golden Editions Pty Ltd v Polygram Pty Ltd*,[132] the defendants obtained non-exclusive licences from New Breed to manufacture and reproduce certain sound recordings by Cat Stevens and The Carpenters. New Breed claimed to be the "owner of the master tapes" but made no representations regarding its entitlement to grant copyright licences. The copyright owners, Polygram, sued for damages and Golden Editions relied on ss 115(3) and 116(3). The trial judge, in a decision upheld on appeal, held that, despite these facts and given the defendant's experience in the recording industry, the defendant had no reasonable grounds for suspecting that his actions were not infringing. Beazley J:

> This is so, notwithstanding that Mr Hughes believed he was dealing with a reputable broker and that he had a non-exclusive license. The particular matters which put him on inquiry were his awareness that he was licensing (or even possibly licensing) the original sound recordings; his knowledge that Cat Stevens and The Carpenters had recorded for Island and A and M; his knowledge that Island and A and M owned the copyright in the original sound recordings; the possibility that they were still selling the original sound recordings in Australia in 1991; the clause in the lease agreements to which I have referred and Mr Hughes' understanding of the meaning of that clause. Mr Hughes did not make any enquiries, and in this case, I consider that he did so at his peril.[133]

### Measure of damages for infringement and conversion

The purpose of compensatory damages is to "compensate the defendant for the loss suffered as a result of the defendant's breach".[134] In quantifying the amount of damages for infringement of copyright Lord Wright MR in *Sutherland Publishing Co Ltd v Caxton Press*[135] said that the measure of compensatory damages was "the depreciation caused by the infringement to the value of the copyright as a chose in action". The value of the copyright might be seriously depreciated, for example, "by the issue of a cheap and inferior infringement which vulgarises the work". Thus, in *Prior v Lansdowne Press Pty Ltd*, the court did not determine the amount of damages solely by reference to the licence fee the plaintiff may have received for the particular use which the defendant made (reproducing part of a literary work in a newspaper) but by reference to the general market and the effect of publication on the ability of the plaintiff to exploit this market. In *Milpurrurru v Indofurn Pty Ltd*, von Doussa J found that the possibility that the indigenous artists would have licensed the use of the art works in question for use as a carpet design was "extremely remote", but that, nevertheless, the use did

---

132  (1996) 135 ALR 638.
133  *Polygram Pty Ltd v Golden Editions Pty Ltd* (1994) 30 IPR 183 at 193-194.
134  *Autodesk Australia Pty Ltd v Cheung* (1990) 94 ALR 472 at 475.
135  [1936] 1 Ch 323.

depreciate the "freshness" of the works and the possibility of their being used for educational or other similar purposes. In this case, that fact that the artists had taken action quickly meant that the effect was likely to be small and the amount of compensatory damages was accordingly modest.[136]

In *Autodesk Australia Pty Ltd v Cheung*,[137] Wilcox J warned against applying the *Sutherland Publishing Co Ltd v Caxton Press*[138] formula too literally and noted that an infringement may actually increase the residual capital value of the copyright. An unauthorised broadcast of a song, for example, might cause an increase in demand for a recording of the song.[139] In this situation it may be more appropriate to calculate the damage by reference to the licence fee which the defendant would have paid[140] or the sales foregone on account of the infringing act.[141]

It may be, however, that neither the depreciation of the capital value of the copyright nor the licence fee approach will prove appropriate and *Autodesk Australia Pty Ltd v Cheung*[142] is such an example. In that case, the defendant ran a computer sales business from his home and supplied a generous number of pirated computer programs to purchasers of his computers. The defendant argued that it was commercially unlikely that he would have obtained licence fees for all or even any of the programs had he been required to do so and, furthermore, that it was unlikely that purchasers would have bought all of the programs which he supplied. Wilcox J accepted this argument and in the circumstances held that it was "not logical" to apply the licence fee approach, and that the court would therefore treat the damages as being "at large". In this case the amount of damages would be determined by giving "the amount I think right as if I were a jury".[143]

Compensatory damages for infringement of copyright are not limited to pecuniary loss and, at trial in *Milpurrurru v Indofurn Pty Ltd*,[144] von Doussa J held that the personal distress, embarrassment and possible contempt caused to the indigenous artists as a result of the infringement could be considered as part of the compensatory damages. In that case, however, he declined, for other reasons, to order compensatory damages for this head of damages under s 115(2) and dealt with it as part of the additional damages.[145]

At common law the measure of conversion damages is determined as the value of the converted articles at the time of conversion. In actions under the

---

136　(1994) 130 ALR 659 at 692.

137　(1990) 94 ALR 472.

138　[1936] 1 Ch 323.

139　*Autodesk Australia Pty Ltd v Cheung* (1990) 94 ALR 472 at 475.

140　*Autodesk Australia Pty Ltd v Cheung* (1990) 94 ALR 472 at 475, referring to Blackburn CJ in *Australasian Performing Right Association Ltd v Grebo Trading Company* (1978) 23 ACTR 30 at 31.

141　*Autodesk Australia Pty Ltd v Cheung* (1990) 94 ALR 472 at 476, referring to *Birn Brothers Ltd v Keene and Co Ltd* [1918] 2 Ch 281.

142　(1990) 94 ALR 472.

143　(1990) 94 ALR 472 at 477, quoting Horridge J in *Fenning Film Service Ltd v Wolverhampton, Walsall and District Cinemas Ltd* [1914] 3 KB 1171 at 1174.

144　(1994) 130 ALR 659 at 693.

145　This decision was overturned on appeal on the basis of the directors' liability: *King v Milpurrurru* (1996) 136 ALR 327.

*Copyright Act 1968* this is generally calculated as the selling price of the goods. This is particularly important in the case of black markets where the actual price of the pirated copies may be a better estimate of their value than a fictional value calculated by reference to a putative sale of a legitimate copy by the copyright owner. Thus, in *Autodesk Inc v Yee*,[146] a case involving a student who sold compilations of pirated computer programs, the value of the pirated computer programs was assessed at $130 each, the price at which he sold them, rather than at $11,000 each which was the price at which an expert witness calculated a legitimate compilation of the programs might be sold in the unlikely event that such compilation were made. For the student this was a significant victory as he was thereby required to pay $23,530 rather than the $1,991,000 calculated by Autodesk. Conversely, the fact that the copyright owner has no market for the chattels or no desire or ability to deal with the copyright as a chose in action does not reduce the value of the chattels. In *Caxton Publishing Co Ltd v Sutherland Publishing Co Ltd*,[147] the House of Lords, on appeal, rejected the argument of the defendant that the four pages in question had only pulping value to the copyright owner, a value which was considerably less than the value of the four pages considered as a proportion of a book.

In accordance with the legal fiction that the copyright owner is the owner of the infringing copies or devices, before 1998 in actions under the *Copyright Act*, the costs of manufacturing and selling the infringing copies were not deducted from the measure of conversion damages, at least if these costs were incurred prior to the act of conversion.[148] The possible injustices caused by the fiction have been somewhat ameliorated by amendments introduced in 1998 which provide that, in assessing damages for conversion or detention, the court may take into consideration the expenses incurred by the defendant in manufacturing or acquiring the infringing copies and the time when the expenses were incurred as well as any other matters which the court considers relevant (s 116(1D)). If the infringing copy comprises only part of an article the court may take into account the importance to the market value of the article of the infringing part, the proportion the infringing part bears to the article as a whole and the extent to which it may be separated from the article (s 116(1E)).

### Additional damages

At common law, damages in addition to compensatory damages may be awarded to punish the defendant or to compensate the plaintiff when the harm caused is aggravated by the manner in which the act was done. The first is sometimes referred to as exemplary damages and the second as aggravated damages although it has been said that the distinction is hard to preserve in practice.[149] Under the *Copyright Act 1968* additional damages may be awarded in actions for infringement (s 115(4)) and in actions relating to circumvention devices, electronic rights

---

146  (1996) 139 ALR 735.

147  [1939] AC 178.

148  *Caxton Publishing Co Ltd v Sutherland Publishing Co Ltd* [1939] AC 178 at 205-206 and see Toohey J's supplementary judgment in *Fire Nymph Products Ltd v Jalco Products (WA) Pty Ltd* (1982) 47 ALR 355 at 392-393.

149  In *Uren v John Fairfax and Sons Pty Ltd* (1966) 117 CLR 118, Windeyer J at 149.

management information and broadcasting devices (s 116D(2)). In *Bailey v Namol Pty Ltd*,[150] the Full Federal Court held that these sections represented a "code" in the sense that they replace any aggravated damages that might otherwise be obtained as part of the compensatory damages.[151] Unlike the United Kingdom and New Zealand legislation, the award of additional damages is not limited to cases where compensatory damages are not "effective".

In determining whether additional damages should be awarded the court must be satisfied, on the basis of evidence,[152] that it is proper to do so having regard to the flagrancy of the breach, the need to deter similar infringements, the conduct of the defendant after the infringing act or after the defendant had been informed of an alleged infringement, whether the infringement involved any digitalisation of the copyright material, any benefit accruing to the defendant and all other matters. Flagrancy has been defined as "glaring, notorious, scandalous or blatant"[153] but mere recklessness or a willingness to take the risk that the action would not constitute an infringement is not necessarily flagrant.[154] The flagrancy relates to the flagrancy of the breach; it does not relate to the conduct of the court proceedings. Thus, in *Flags 2000 Pty Ltd v Smith*[155] which concerned an action under s 38 for the sale of an infringing Aboriginal flag, the fact that the defendant put in issue the question of the plaintiff's copyright ownership (thereby denying him the benefit of the presumption) without bringing evidence to challenge this ownership was held not to be an issue going to flagrancy although it was a matter which could be taken into account in the assessment of costs.[156] Similarly, the persistent refusal to acknowledge the subsistence or ownership of copyright of the Aboriginal artists in *Milpurrurru v Indofurn Pty Ltd*[157] was held to go to the question of costs rather than additional damages.

The list is not exhaustive and it is not necessary that each of the elements be established in order to award additional damages. Lack of flagrancy[158] or the accrual of only a small benefit to the defendant[159] have not prevented the award of additional damages. Other matters which have been taken into account in determining whether to award additional damages are the hurt caused to the plaintiff, for example, where the plaintiff's wedding photo was published in a newspaper story about the murder of her father,[160] the deliberate and secretive behaviour of a company director in setting up a new company to exploit the copyright material,[161] the fact that the infringement involved the publication of

---

150  (1994) 125 ALR 228.
151  (1994) 125 ALR 228 at 239.
152  *Prior v Lansdowne Press Pty Ltd* (1975) 12 ALR 685.
153  See, for example, Tamberlin J in *Raben Footwear Pty Ltd v Polygram Records Inc* (1997) 145 ALR 1 at 16, quoting from the *New Shorter English Dictionary*, 1993.
154  *Prior v Lansdowne Press Pty Ltd* (1975) 12 ALR 685 at 690 and *Raben Footwear Pty Ltd v Polygram Records Inc* (1997) 145 ALR 1 at 16-17.
155  (2003) 59 IPR 191.
156  (2003) 59 IPR 191, see also *Milpurrurru v Indofurn Pty Ltd* (1994) 130 ALR 659.
157  (1994) 130 ALR 659.
158  *Raben Footwear Pty Ltd v Polygram Records Inc* (1997) 145 ALR 1 at 16-17.
159  *Williams v Settle* [1960] 2 All ER 806.
160  *Williams v Settle* [1960] 2 All ER 806.
161  *Bailey v Namol Pty Ltd* (1994) 125 ALR 228.

previously unpublished material[162] and cultural harm caused by the infringement of copyright in Aboriginal art works.[163]

## Account of profits[164]

An account of profits is available as an alternative to damages under ss 115 and 116D and is available even in the case of innocent breach. Its purpose is not to punish the defendant but to prevent unjust enrichment. In the words of Windeyer J in *Colbeam Palmer Ltd v Stock Affiliates Pty Ltd*:[165]

> The distinction between an account of profits and damages is that by the former the infringer is required to give up his ill-gotten gains to the party whose rights he has infringed; by the latter he is required to compensate the party wronged for the loss he has suffered.[166]

The computations under the two remedies can therefore be very different and the plaintiff must elect between the two. The leading cases on account of profits have been concerned with the question of how the account is to be made and, in particular, which of the defendant's costs may be taken into account. In *Dart Industries Inc v Decor Corporation Pty Ltd*,[167] the High Court held that general overhead expenses in manufacturing the infringing article might be taken into account but it is a question of fact as to how the overheads may be apportioned. This question may turn on whether the defendant was utilising unused capacity in manufacturing the infringing articles but, in any event, the opportunity cost to the defendant may not be taken into account.

In that case the High Court refused special leave to cross-appeal from the Full Federal Court's decision that the profits in that case should be calculated by reference to the manufacture and sale of the whole article, in this case a plastic container with a press button seal, rather than by reference only to the infringing press button seal itself. On this question the High Court endorsed Windeyer J's decision in *Colbeam Palmer Ltd v Stock Affiliates Pty Ltd*[168] and held that it was ultimately a question of fact:

> The true rule, I consider, is that a person who wrongly uses another man's industrial property – patent, copyright, trade mark – is accountable for any profits which he makes which are attributable to his use of the property which is not his … If one man makes profit by the use or sale of some thing, and that whole thing came into existence by reason of his wrongful use of another man's property in a patent, design or copyright,

---

162  *Beloff v Pressdram Ltd* [1973] 1 All ER 241.
163  *Milpurrurru v Indofurn Pty Ltd* (1994) 130 ALR 659.
164  The leading Australian cases on account of profits in intellectual property law are in patent and trade marks (*Colbeam Palmer Ltd v Stock Affiliates Pty Ltd* (1968) 122 CLR 25 regarding trade marks, approved by the High Court in *Dart Industries Inc v Decor Corporation Pty Ltd* (1993) 179 CLR 101, a case regarding patents) but the remedy has been applied in copyright cases (see *Concrete Systems Pty Ltd v Devon Symonds Holdings Ltd* (1978) 20 ALR 677 and, for a recent example, *Quanta Software International Pty Ltd v Computer Management Services Pty Ltd* [2001] FCA 1459).
165  (1968) 122 CLR 25.
166  (1968) 122 CLR 25 at 32.
167  (1993) 179 CLR 101.
168  (1968) 122 CLR 25 at 42-43.

the difficulty disappears and the case is then, generally speaking, simple. In such a case the infringer must account for all the profits which he thus made.[169]

## Standing to sue[170]

The copyright owner has standing in actions for infringement, conversion and detention under ss 115 and 116 of the *Copyright Act 1968* where there is no exclusive licence. Where there are joint owners of copyright either owner may maintain proceedings.[171]

Special rules apply when there is an exclusive licence. Under the general law a licensee's right to sue is limited. This reflects the limited nature of a licence. The general law is changed by the *Copyright Act* which provides under Division 3 of Part V that an exclusive licensee, for the purposes of actions for infringement, conversion or detention, shall have the same rights of action and be entitled to the same remedies as if the licence had been an assignment (s 119). The rights of the copyright owner and exclusive licensee are concurrent for the purposes of infringement proceedings and, except by leave of the court, both parties must be joined. Damages, account of profits, and costs are assessed on this basis.

Under the general law, conversion and detention are wrongs against the true owner. This too is partly changed by the Act which, for the purposes of s 116, provides that the exclusive licence shall be treated as though it were an assignment. This effectively means that the copyright owner has no right of action and is not entitled to any remedies under s 116 where there is an exclusive licence.

Under ss 116A and 116B the copyright owner or exclusive licensee is expressly entitled to bring actions in relation to circumvention devices and electronic rights management information. Under s 135ANA the broadcaster is entitled to bring an action in relation to dealings with broadcast decoding devices.

A non-exclusive licensee does not have standing for infringement or other actions under the *Copyright Act* without the joinder of the copyright owner. An owner of an equitable interest has standing if the legal owner is joined.[172] In *Acorn Computers Ltd v MCS Microcomputer Systems Pty Ltd*,[173] Smithers J held that the beneficial owner could maintain their action given that the assignment had been evidenced in writing since commencement of the proceedings.

## Limitations on remedies against carriage services providers

The *US Free Trade Agreement Implementation Act 2004* introduced Division 2AA into the *Copyright Act 1968* which limits the remedies against carriage service providers for copyright infringement.

169  (1968) 122 CLR 25 at 42-43, endorsed by the High Court in *Dart Industries Inc v Decor Corporation Pty Ltd* (1993) 179 CLR 101 at 120-121.
170  For transitional provisions relating to standing of exclusive licensees, see *Copyright Act 1968* s 228.
171  *Lauri v Renard* [1892] 3 Ch 402; *Acorn Computers Ltd v MCS Microcomputer Systems Pty Ltd* (1984) 57 ALR 389.
172  *University of London Press v University Tutorial Press Ltd* [1916] 2 Ch 601.
173  (1984) 57 ALR 389.

Under s 116AG(2) there is a general limitation which provides that in certain actions for copyright infringement against a carriage service provider the court must not award damages or an account of profits, any additional damages or other monetary relief. This general limitation is subject to two important restrictions. First, the infringement must have occurred in the carrying out of a "relevant activity" and, secondly, the carriage service provider must have met certain conditions in carrying out these activities. If there is an infringement in these circumstances then the court may make alternative orders to address the infringement. Section 116AC divides the relevant activities into four categories A–D, and the conditions which must be met by the carriage service provider and the orders which may be made by the court will depend on the type of activity.

Category A activities cover the provision of facilities and services for transmitting, routing or providing connections for copyright material (including the intermediate and transient storage of copyright material during these processes) (s 116AC). In order to get the benefit of the s 116AG limitation the carriage service provider must meet certain conditions. Two of these conditions are general and apply to all categories; two are specific to the category. The general conditions are that the carriage service provider must have adopted and reasonably implemented a policy for terminating the accounts of repeat infringers; and, secondly, the carriage service provider must comply with any relevant industry code in so far as the code requires the carriage service provider to accommodate standard technical measures (such as digital water marks) used to protect and identify copyright material. The specific conditions for category A activities are that the activity must have been initiated by someone other than the carriage service provider and the carriage service provider must not have made any substantive modifications to the copyright material during transmission (s 116AH).

Category B covers the automatic caching of copyright material – it does not cover caching where the carriage service provider has manually selected the copyright material (s 116AD). In this case the carriage service provider must meet the two general conditions outlined above. In addition, the carriage service provider must ensure that any limitations on access to the material are upheld (that is, if the material is only available to subscribers to a service, for example, caching must not widen this); the carriage service provider must meet industry code standards regarding updating cached material and allowing the originating site to monitor usage of that material; the service provider must expeditiously remove or disable access to cached material if notified by the originating site that it has been removed or disabled by the originating site; and the carriage service provider must not make substantive modifications of the material as transmitted (s 116AH).

Category C covers the storing of copyright material, at the direction of the user, on a system or network controlled or operated by the service provider (s 116AE). Category D covers the referral of users to an online location using information location tools or technology (s 116AF). In these cases the carriage service provider must meet the general conditions and must not get a directly attributable financial benefit for the infringing act in relation to this storage or referral; must expeditiously remove or disable access to the stored material or the referral if the provider receives a prescribed notice that the material has been held to be infringing by a court; and the provider must comply with any prescribed procedures for removing or disabling access to stored copyright material or references (s 116AH). The interesting thing to note here is that the amendment still favours the rights of the copyright owner over the expeditious, user friendly operation of the service by manual, selective caching.

If there has been an infringement in the course of carrying out a Category A activity then the court's powers are limited to ordering the carriage service provider to terminate an account and/or take reasonable steps to disable access to an online location outside Australia (s 116AG(3)). If there has been an infringement during the course of carrying out a Category B, C or D activity the courts may order the carriage service provider to terminate a specified account; remove or disable access to infringing material or references to infringing material or "some other less burdensome but comparatively effective non-monetary order if necessary" (s 116AG(4)). In determining whether to make the order the court must have regard to the harm caused to the copyright owner or exclusive licensee; the burden on the carriage service provider; the effectiveness of the order and whether some comparable order might be less burdensome (s 116AG(5)). Section 116AI imposes a presumption that the service provider has complied with the conditions if it can point to certain prescribed evidence and there is no countervailing evidence to rebut the presumption.

## Collecting Agencies and the Copyright Tribunal

Becoming aware of the rights of the copyright owner is rather like stepping into a new dimension – suddenly the world seems quite different. Whilst many people are familiar with some aspects of copyright – that one may not copy a video, CD or book for, example – there are many other aspects of copyright which go largely unnoticed by the general public. The music played at a nightclub or in a shop or on the radio; the TV broadcast screening in a store selling electrical goods; the songs sung at school camps, in church or by a pub band; the script for the school play; the reading material produced by universities for students; the videos played in your hotel room; much of the music in films – all of these uses must be licensed or subject to an assignment in so far as they represent the exercise of one or more of the exclusive rights of the copyright holder by a third party. It would be impossible for this system to function without an effective, collective administrative framework. Neither the local priest nor the local publican, for example, has the time or resources to identify, contact and negotiate with the owner of the copyright in the words, music and sound recordings of any music which might be sung or played in the church or the pub in any week. The effective administration of copyright law on a day-to-day basis depends on the existence of collecting societies and partly on the work of the Copyright Tribunal.

Collecting societies are collective, private organisations which administer copyright, often by negotiating collective agreements with large copyright users or by registering licence schemes with the Copyright Tribunal. The collecting society may be an agent of the copyright owner, have rights assigned to it by the copyright owner or be licensed by the copyright owner in relation to certain rights. In order to accomplish its role the collecting society will often employ staff who investigate and police copyright use. It is not unusual for staff of the Australasian Performing

Right Association, for example, to pay unannounced visits to night clubs, bars and restaurants in order to detect unlicensed performances of musical work and to encourage the proprietor to take out the necessary licence for such use.

A collecting society may be declared under the Act in relation to compulsory or voluntary licence schemes. The major copyright collecting societies are:

- Australasian Mechanical Copyright Owners Society Ltd (AMCOS) which administers the right to make sound recordings of musical works.
- Australasian Performing Right Association (APRA) which administers the public performance and communication rights for musical works.
- Phonographic Performance Company of Australia is an organisation of recording companies which grants licences for public performance of sound recordings or music videos.
- Screenrights administers the compulsory licence under Part VA for copying and communicating broadcasts by educational institutions and institutions assisting people with an intellectual disability.
- Copyright Agency Limited (CAL) administers the Part VB compulsory licence for reproducing and communicating works by educational institutions and institutions assisting people with an intellectual or print disability.
- Visual Arts Copyright Collecting Agency (VI$COPY) administers the copyright of visual artists.
- Christian Copyright Licensing International Pty Ltd, Word of Life Pty Ltd and LicenSing administer copyright in church music and liturgical works.

The potential for collecting societies to abuse their monopoly power, both in relation to copyright owners and users, is recognised and the Australian Competition and Consumer Commission has considered the functioning of APRA on a number of occasions. The practice of requiring copyright owners to assign their rights to collecting societies has come under particular scrutiny. In 2000 APRA agreed, after an ACCC hearing for authorisation of APRA activities under ss 101 and 101A of the *Competition and Consumer Act 2010*, to amend its rules so as to allow copyright owners to grant non-exclusive licences to APRA rather than make an assignment of the relevant copyright.[174]

The Copyright Tribunal has limited jurisdiction under the *Copyright Act 1968* Part VI to make orders relating to compulsory licences and declared collecting agencies. In particular, in the absence of agreement between the user and the copyright owner or the copyright owner's representative, the Tribunal may determine the equitable remuneration payable under a compulsory licence. The Tribunal may also determine the terms for the use of copyright material by the Crown. The equitable remuneration for a broadcast by a commercial broadcaster or the Special Broadcasting Corporation is subject to a cap of 1 per cent of the broadcaster's gross profit. In the case of the Australian Broadcasting Corporation the cap, expressed in cents, is half of 1 per cent of the population of Australia in the case of television or radio (s 152(11)). In the absence of agreement or an order by the Tribunal the royalty on the sale or supply of a record of a musical work is

---

174 *Re Application by Australasian Performing Right Association Ltd Pursuant to ss 101 and 101A of the Trade Practices Act 1974* [2002] ACompT 2.

6.25 per cent of the retail selling price of the record (s 55(6)). In relation to Part VA and Part VB use by educational and other institutions and Crown copyright the Tribunal may, in the absence of agreement, determine the contents and terms of the sampling system, agreed system or electronic notice system to be used in calculating the remuneration.

In addition to compulsory licences, a licensor, including a collecting society, may refer a "licence scheme", which sets out a tariff of fees for particular copyright uses, to the Tribunal for approval. The advantage of a licence scheme is that it allows disputes arising under the licence to be brought to the Tribunal. In determining a dispute arising under a licence scheme the Tribunal may confirm the scheme or vary it as the Tribunal considers reasonable in the circumstances. Furthermore, in the case of a refusal to grant a licence to a person under a licence scheme or in a case where a person believes that the terms of the licence scheme are unreasonable in the circumstances, the Tribunal may, upon application by the person, make an order specifying the charges and conditions which the Tribunal believes are reasonable in the circumstances. In this case, the applicant will be treated, for the purposes of infringement proceedings, as though the person were the holder of a licence granted by the copyright holder on these terms and conditions.

Not every copyright licence may be subject to a licence scheme and s 136 sets out the licences which may be referred to the Tribunal. In relation to a literary, dramatic or musical work, these are a licence to perform the work or an adaptation of the work in public, to broadcast the work or an adaptation of the work, to make a sound recording or cinematographic film of the work or adaptation for the purposes of broadcasting and a licence to transmit electronically the work for a fee payable to the transmitter. In relation to a sound recording the licences which may constitute a licence scheme are a licence to cause the recording to be heard in public, a licence to make a copy of the recording for the purposes of broadcasting the recording and a licence to broadcast the recording in a broadcast transmitted for a fee to the person who made the broadcast. In the case where a licence scheme may be made under this section but has not been made, the Tribunal has jurisdiction to make an order specifying the charges and conditions of a licence, upon the application of a person who requires such a licence.[175]

---

175 For transitional provisions relating to licence schemes, see s 232.

# CASES

## *Acorn Computers Ltd v MCS Microcomputer Systems Pty Ltd*
### Federal Court of Australia: Smithers J
### (1984) 57 ALR 389

In an unwritten agreement between Cambridge Processor Unit Ltd (CPUL) and Acorn, CPUL purported to assign all its assets to Acorn. These assets included existing and future copyright. When Acorn took action against MCS Computers for infringement of copyright, MCS sought to have the action struck out on various grounds. One of these grounds was that Acorn was neither a legal nor equitable owner of the copyright because the formalities for assignment had not been complied with.

> **Smithers J: [392]** I did not understand Mr Archibald to contend that apart from the non-compliance with the provisions of s 196(3) of the Act there was not, on the facts alleged, possibly, or arguably, equitable ownership in Acorn of every interest which CPUL had in any relevant copyright in any literary or artistic work. It was the absence of writing which was fatal to the effectiveness of the transaction between CPUL and Acorn as an assignment of interests in the copyright. In support of this contention Mr Archibald relied, in particular, on the decision of the Court of Appeal in *Roban Jig Tool Co Ltd and Elkadort Ltd v Taylor* [1979] FSR 130 (CA). In that case the plaintiffs sued for infringement of copyright in three groups of drawings identified as S/Rob, RP, and D and N respectively. The plaintiffs' title to copyright having been put in issue, particulars were given. From these it appeared that the drawings S/Rob and D and N had been prepared for the plaintiffs by independent contractors. No other source of title was disclosed. As to the RP drawings it appeared that the same were made by one P when he was a partner of a firm the assets of which were said to have been vested in the first plaintiff upon its incorporation. The manner of vesting was not stated. It was alleged that P had made the drawings for the firm. It was held by Whitford J, the trial judge, that the claim in respect of the drawings S/Rob and D and N should be struck out as no title to the copyright therein was shown to exist. He held however, that in relation to the RP drawings, the pleading should be allowed to stand. He held that a possible inference from what was particularized was, "that the plaintiffs were and are indeed owners of some beneficial interest in the copyright in the RP drawings even though the pleadings may be defective in the sense that there is insufficient particularity and even though it may be necessary at some later stage to join the legal owner of the copyright". The plaintiffs appealed and the defendants cross-appealed. The appeal was dismissed but the cross-appeal was allowed.
>
> It was held, on appeal, that there being no facts disclosing a written assignment of copyright to the plaintiff no title was shown. So far as the plaintiffs relied on the assignment of an equitable interest it failed because of the provisions of s 53(1)(c) of the Property Law Act 1925 which is in like terms to s 53(1)(c) of the Victorian Property Law Act 1958 and requires that a disposition of an equitable interest "... must be in writing signed by the person disposing of the same, ..."
>
> It was said by Mr Archibald that the *ratio decidendi* of the Court of Appeal decision is decisive of the issue in this case so far as the applicants rely on the agreement or arrangement between Acorn and CPUL. Mr Archibald referred to the observations of Stamp LJ [1979] FSR at 140, *supra*, that there being no suggestion of any written disposition of the copyright in favour of either of the plaintiffs it followed that the statement **[393]** of claim as particularized disclosed no cause of action in respect of any of the drawings. He referred also to the observations of Ormrod LJ [1979] FSR at 143, *supra*, where his

Lordship pointed out that the pleadings plainly showed on their face that the plaintiffs were not the authors of any of the drawings and must therefore plead and prove a valid assignment or assignments in their favour. And he observed "the combined effect of s 36 of the Copyright Act 1956 and s 53(1)(c) of the Property Law Act 1925 is that in the circumstances such assignments whether they be of legal interests or equitable interests in such copyrights, must be in writing". The relevant provision in s 36 of the Copyright Act 1956 is in the same terms as s 196(3) of the Act. To my mind the question in this case is not so much whether there is in writing an assignment of copyright, but whether there was in Acorn at the commencement of the proceedings equitable ownership of the relevant copyrights.

It is to be noted, that in the *Roban Jig* case, *supra*, there was in the pleadings or particulars no suggestion that there had been a transaction for value under which it was agreed that the interest of the owner or part owner of the copyright in works was to pass to the plaintiffs and that the agreement was one of which specific performance might have been desired. It would seem that Whitford J had sensed that there was such a suggestion and it was this that persuaded him to allow the claim concerning the RP drawings to stand. But that there was such a suggestion was not accepted on appeal. In this case a transaction of the kind referred to is pleaded. The pleading does not refer to the availability of specific performance, but it does put forward a transaction susceptible of specific performance. It may be, although it is unnecessary to discuss it in this case that the element of specific enforceability is not essential to the creation of an equitable estate arising from a transaction inter partes: see *Meagher Gummow and Lehane; Equity Doctrines and Remedies* 3rd ed, p 138.

It is normally the consequence of such a transaction that, value having been given, an equitable interest in the subject thereof arises in the party giving it: see *Central Trust and Safe Deposit Co v Snider* [1916] 1 AC 266 at 272; *Fairweather v Fairweather* (1944) 69 CLR 121 at 154. In such a case the equitable interest arises not by way of transfer but by activation in Equity of the conscience of the receiver of the valuable consideration. A trust is created; there is not a transfer or assignment; there is no transmission of an equitable interest. The estate arising from a declaration of trust is appropriately spoken of as the estate created thereby; thus per Gibbs CJ in *DKLR Holding Co (No 2) Pty Ltd v Commissioner of Stamp Duties (NSW)* (1982) 40 ALR 1; 149 CLR 431. It is appropriate also to speak of the fiction that by a declaration of trust the declarant "imparts" to the beneficiary an equitable estate or interest upon which the Stamp Duties Act 1920 (NSW) operates: per Mason J in the last-mentioned case (ALR) at 21; (CLR) at 457. Where there is no transmission s 196(3) of the Act is not involved. Similarly where there is an enforceable contract to transfer property the equitable interest arising in the proposed transferee is not the product of a transfer but an exercise in creation.

In the claim made in para 27A of the amended statement of claim the applicants rely on the equitable interest which arose from the agreement to assign the copyright. It appears to me that just as prior to the 1968 Act, which provided for the legal assignment of future copyright, equity would **[394]** treat an enforceable agreement for value to assign such a right as creating an equitable interest capable of sustaining an interlocutory injunction in the absence of the legal owner, and of sustaining a perpetual injunction once the legal owner was joined as a party to the proceedings, so equity will treat as the equitable owner, and as a person entitled to commence proceedings for infringement of copyright, a person in whom there resides an enforceable right to an assignment of the relevant copyright. This appears to conform to the requirements of justice. It would not be just that a person should infringe a copyright, the right in equity to which had been acquired for value by another party from the owner merely because writing was absent and the legal owner would not become a party to the proceedings. I am therefore not persuaded that the agreement or arrangement as pleaded is not such as to confer upon Acorn equitable ownership of the relevant copyrights.

It is to be noted that in the *Roban Jig* case, *supra*, Lord Justice Stamp accepted the submission that "you may sue relying on the equitable right to property which you claim has been damaged and get in the legal title afterwards". But he pointed out that what the plaintiffs were attempting to do in that case was to commence proceedings with no title at all and to sue on a title subsequently acquired: see his Lordship's remarks [1979] FSR at 142, *supra*.

In *Performing Right Society Ltd v London Theatre of Varieties Ltd* [1924] AC 1, the matter under consideration was a claim by the equitable owner of a copyright to sue for infringement without joining the legal owner. It was conceded that the equitable owner might be granted an interlocutory injunction but that permanent relief would not be granted in the absence of the legal owner. The equitable interest had arisen by virtue of a written assignment of future copyright. Viscount Finlay pointed out that s 5 of the Copyright Act 1911 authorized an assignment in writing not only of a legal interest in copyright but of any interest whether legal or equitable. And in that case there was writing. But he said that the established rule of practice should be adhered to, namely, that the owner of the legal estate should be joined as a party. He pointed out that in the case of a refusal of the owner of the legal estate to join as a plaintiff he might be added as defendant "or if for any reason, all this were impossible, the action ought to be allowed to proceed without the presence of the legal owner".

In this case there is no joinder of the legal owner as applicant or respondent. But, soon after action brought, Acorn became the owner of the legal estate by written assignment. Assuming that the agreement or arrangement between Acorn and CPUL which is pleaded was sufficient to make Acorn the equitable owner of the relevant copyrights the question is whether the "getting in" of the legal estate by written assignment will relieve the applicants from actually joining as a party the person who was legal owner at the date of action brought but who has since ceased to be so. If the assignment to Acorn of the legal interest in the copyright to it had occurred prior to action brought the legal owner would not have been a proper party to the action. If the legal owner had been joined prior to the assignment of his interest to Acorn his presence in the action would, when the assignment was given, have become unnecessary and embarrassing. It appears to me therefore, that at this stage its presence would serve no **[395]** useful purpose and is unnecessary. Nevertheless, the assignment should be pleaded although it is something that has occurred after action brought.

### *Moorhead v Brennan*
Supreme Court of New South Wales: Bryson J
(1991) 20 IPR 161

The plaintiff novelist granted exclusive and world wide publishing rights to the defendant in respect of her novel, *Remember The Tarantella*. The defendant refused to allow the Women's Press to publish the work in England because they did not want to publish his publisher's note with it. Although the plaintiff had agreed to the inclusion of the publisher's note in the Australian publication she no longer wanted it included with her novel. Bryson J in the New South Wales Supreme Court begins by explaining why.

**Bryson J: [163]** Her insight is that references in the publisher's note to the curative tarantella danced by those bitten by the tarantula spider carry the implication that references in the novel to the dance relate to women who are sick and require some curative process. For artistic reasons she now rejects the publisher's note, and the plaintiff as author is best qualified to perceive these. ...

### [164] The implied term

The plaintiff's case rests on a term which she claims should be implied into the publishing agreement. An implied term cannot be reduced to one completely exact formulation, but the formulations put forward were that the defendant agreed that he would not impede (or that he would not obstruct) opportunities to receive royalties and fees from persons who proposed to publish the work under licence. In correspondence before action a more onerous form was put forward to the effect that the defendant would take all reasonable steps to gain royalties by licensing editions of the work to be published overseas.

A considerable body of material was put in evidence and was said to have a bearing on whether or not a term of such a kind should be implied. The defendant conducted his own case at the hearing and put in evidence many communications between the parties and other interested persons both earlier and later than the date of the agreement. Much of this is of no assistance, but it did establish the scale of the operations of the defendant, [165] and for that matter of the plaintiff, and the significance of the prospects of overseas publications in the contemplation of both parties at the time when the agreement was made.

The defendant is the only principal of Primavera Press and he and his talents and energy are its main resources. He operates as a publishing house on an extremely small scale. The 1987 publication of the novel was assisted by the Literature Board of the Australia Council. It was not in the practical world to think that the defendant as Primavera Press would also publish the novel in Britain or elsewhere overseas, and the defendant had and maintained contacts with people in the publishing world overseas and was in a good position to find any opportunities that might exist for such publications. It cannot have been in the contemplation of these parties that the defendant might pursue exploitation of the commercial opportunities relating to this novel by setting himself up as a publisher anywhere other than in Australia, or in any other way than by licensing another established overseas publisher. In another context, relating to a larger publishing house with established operations in several different countries, the basis for such an implied term may perhaps not be the same as it is in this case.

The question whether the parties contemplated that the defendant should have entire control over whether there ever would be any further publication apart from editions brought out by himself in his small publishing house in a Sydney suburb needs only to be stated for it to be seen that the parties could not have contemplated that; they could not have intended that the defendant would have the contractual right to decide, wholly on grounds suitable to himself, whether he would as it were snuff out the work apart from his own editions and see to it that it was not published overseas at all for some reason suitable to him, such as a wish to promote his own work or to promote some other author.

The licence is exclusive and worldwide so that the plaintiff could not further exploit her copyright, and there was clearly contemplation that sub-licences would be granted and half the royalties from them were to go to the plaintiff. It was not open to the defendant simply to do nothing about sub-licensing, or to take action which would prevent sub-licensing.

To my mind the alternative forms of the implied term put forward on behalf of the plaintiff both fulfil the conditions for the implication of a term referred to in the judgment of Mason J in *Codelfa Construction Pty Ltd v State Rail Authority of New South Wales* (1982) 149 CLR 337 at 347; 41 ALR 367 at 371 where his Honour set out a passage from the judgment of the Privy Council in *BP Refinery (Westernport) Pty Ltd v Hastings Shire Council* (1977) 16 ALR 363 at 376; 52 ALJR 20 at 26 in these terms: "(1) it must be reasonable and equitable; (2) it must be necessary to give business efficacy to the contract, so that no term will be implied if the contract is effective without it; (3) it must be so obvious that 'it goes without saying'; (4) it must be capable of clear expression; (5) it must not contradict any express term of the contract."

These conditions, particularly the second, third and fourth, are not easy to sever entirely from each other. To my mind it is clear from the express terms that promotion of the novel and full use of any opportunities for its publication anywhere are the heart of the parties' relationship, the genesis and aim of their dealing with each other at all, and this would be defeated if any view were taken of the contractual relation in which the defendant **[166]** could exercise an uncontrolled choice for or against taking up an opportunity for overseas licensing which was available on reasonable terms.

The observations made by Griffith CJ in *Butt v M'Donald* (1896) 7 QLJ 68 at 70–1, which have frequently been referred to, should be recalled. They were: "It is a general rule applicable to every contract that each party agrees, by implication, to do all such things as are necessary on his part to enable the other party to have the benefit of the contract."

These observations are usually cited in cases where both parties to a contract must act cooperatively to achieve a contemplated beneficial outcome, and manifestations of the parties' intentions in each particular case usually are of more significance that the influence of a general rule: see per Mason J in *Secured Income Real Estate (Australia) Ltd v St Martins Investments Pty Ltd* (1979) 144 CLR 596 at 607-8; 26 ALR 567. To my mind they are applicable in this case and the parties contemplated the receipt and sharing of overseas royalties as a benefit which the contract was to bring to each of them. The forms of implied term for which the plaintiff contends represented the workings of the reasoning in *Butt v M'Donald* on their written agreement.

The plaintiff's counsel referred me to the decision of the Court of Common Pleas in *M'Intyre v Belcher* (1863) 14 CBNS 654 at 664; 143 ER 602 at 606. Although that case is remote from the present case in time, place, subject matter and express contractual terms it is a useful illustration of the implication of a term requiring reasonable conduct to achieve a contemplated commercial outcome. In that case the principal payments to the vendor of a medical practice were to be directly related to the receipts of the purchaser from carrying on the practice, and the purchaser took some action (which the report does not state) which disabled him from carrying on the practice. The implied term was formulated as a promise to "take common and ordinary care so to carry on the business as to realise receipts".

### Lofty themes

Both parties have at times seen their dispute in wide terms, as appears from correspondence which has been put in evidence. The defendant, in his conduct of his own case, gave evidence and made submissions on subjects which ranged more widely than was necessary to address what was truly in issue. He made some contentions based on a large, indeed lofty view of the position and prerogatives of a publisher. The plaintiff at times seemed to express feelings as an author that she was morally entitled to control the manner and circumstances in which her work was republished. She took this position rather far, going so far as to threaten an overseas publisher with legal action if her work were republished with the publisher's note. However her case before me was not advocated on this wide basis; her counsel did not rely on any contention that some supposed author's moral right extends to control over everything that is published with her novel in any republication.

I do not think that it is correct to approach this case on any large views of the positions either of authors or of publishers; my decision must be based on the express and implied terms of the parties' contract. This litigation is not a vehicle for deciding broad questions about the moral rights of authors or publishers ...

## [172] Finding: the defendant broke the implied term

When assessing whether either party broke the implied term, their conduct should be weighed predominantly from the point of view of commercial considerations. Their conduct would not be weighed exclusively from that point of view if there were some commercial consideration to which it would not have been reasonable to yield. Each was the author of something, the plaintiff of the novel and the defendant of the publisher's note, and strong attachment of each can be understood.

Although the defendant in his evidence and also in submissions to me referred to other possible opportunities for British and Commonwealth publication he gave no evidence of any other concrete opportunity. There have been no real prospects of doing better than an offer for publication in London by an established publishing house prepared to pay £1200 in advances and royalty rates of 7½ per cent home and 6 per cent export. The defendant asked for 10 per cent and 8 per cent, which the The Women's Press described as hardcover royalties and were unprepared to pay. I am satisfied that the terms which The Women's Press offered were quite reasonable.

Unless there is a better offer available somewhere, a customer like The Women's Press must be right. Their requirement was just the way they do business, and was not a summons to battle on any question of censorship, sexual discrimination, oppression or gender conflict. Whatever their reasons were for imposing this condition, it is obvious from everything Ros de Lanerolle wrote at every stage that The Women's Press were completely committed to it. I find as a fact that there was not at any stage any reasonable prospect of persuading The Women's Press to publish the publisher's note or anything else written by the defendant or any other man. The Women's Press has its own publishing policy, clearly expressed, in no way a matter for apology by them and firmly adhered to.

The considerations which the defendant put forward in his correspondence with The Women's Press and maintained before me are, I am sure, quite important in some universe of discourse but it was not appropriate to argue them out with Ros de Lanerolle. In my judgment it was unreasonable to see the question whether the publisher's note appeared as important, still more unreasonable to tell a British publisher who wanted the book that the note stood the sole surviving witness to a remembered past and hoped-for future of gender detente and peaceable sexual co-existence. To insist on inclusion of the publisher's note and let a fair commercial opportunity go away on these grounds was not reasonable; it was folly. Neither the plaintiff nor the defendant had another such chance [173] of earning royalties as was broken on this point; the defendant completely disregarded the main chance, which was the opportunity for them both to get some British and Commonwealth royalties. This was a breach by the defendant of the implied term on any possible view of what the implied term required of him.

The reasonable and intelligent thing to do was accept reality and do business with The Women's Press on their terms, giving up a page and a half of publisher's note and widely publishing 350 pages of novel. The defendant's correspondence can be quoted as referring to this view as gutless opportunism but it should be described more felicitously as reasonable commercial behaviour. The loss of the opportunity to publish through The Women's Press was caused by his breach of the implied term, and the notice of termination was in my view justified and took effect on expiry according to the terms of cl 17.

# Chapter 7

# Neighbouring Rights and Indigenous Cultural Property

In this chapter we will consider three of copyright's "neighbouring rights". These are moral rights, performers' protection and resale royalty rights. Moral rights and performers' protection are granted under the *Copyright Act 1968*. Resale royalty rights arise under the *Resale Royalty Right for Visual Artists Act 2009* (Cth).

Moral rights are personal rights of the author, film maker or live performer, to be attributed in relation to a work, film or live performance and to ensure that the work, film or live performance is not subjected to derogatory treatment. The grant of moral rights to authors is required under Art 6bis of the Berne Agreement. The extension of moral rights to performers was introduced by the *US Free Trade Agreement Implementation Act 2004* (Cth), and came into effect when the *WIPO Performances and Phonograms Treaty* (Geneva, 1996) came into force in Australia on 26 July 2007.

Performers' protection gives performers in live performances an action in relation to unauthorised recording of those live performances and to any dealings with such unauthorised recordings. Performers' protection is required under the *Rome Convention for the Protection of Performers, Producers of Phonograms and Broadcasting Organisations 1961*. It is important to note that neither the moral rights of performers nor performers' protection effectively protect performers in films. Both rights are restricted to the protection of live performances, and only in relation to their sound. Performers' protection is most effective in protecting musicians against bootlegged recordings of their live performances.

Resale royalty rights came into effect in Australia in June 2010 as a result of the *Resale Royalty Right for Visual Artists Act 2009*. A resale royalty right is the inalienable right of an artist to receive a royalty on the commercial resale of an original work of visual art sold for at least $1000. The right was first introduced in France in the 1860s and came into force in the United Kingdom in 2006. It is granted in recognition of the fact that most visual artists do not have the same opportunity to exploit their work through reproduction and licensing as other creative workers. Resale royalty rights are an optional provision under Art 14ter of the Berne Agreement. The US-Australia Free Trade Agreement expressly reserved the right of the parties to introduce such measures.

In this chapter we will also take the opportunity to consider the protection of indigenous cultural property. As we have seen, the *US Free Trade Agreement Implementation Act 2004* gave joint copyright ownership to performers of expressions of folklore in any sound recordings made of that performance. The Act also gave these performers moral rights and performers' protection in relation to such performances. One of the strongest criticisms of these forms of protection is that they protect individual artists and performers but give little or no assistance to indigenous communities in relation to indigenous cultural property. We shall therefore consider attempts by indigenous communities to get around these limitations within the confines of the *Copyright Act 1968* and the possible introduction of moral rights for indigenous communities flagged by the Coalition Government in 2003.

## Moral Rights

Although Lord Mansfield based his defence of the common law origins of copyright on the moral rights of the author (see Chapter 2, "Copyright – Its Birth and Nature"), since that time courts have often disclaimed any power to protect these moral rights. In the early case of *Lee v Gibbings*,[1] for example, Kekewich J began his judgment regarding the "mutilation" of an author's work by saying:

> There are two aspects in this case, one of which had better be left alone. The other must to some extent be regarded. The one which I think had better be left alone is what I may fairly call the moral side.[2]

In that case the author's literary work was republished without its preface, table of contents, introduction, bibliographical notes or index and the publication date had been changed. Whilst ignoring the so called moral aspects of the case the judge did go on to say that the author may have a case in libel.

In *Joseph v National Magazine Co Ltd*,[3] Harman J held that an author was entitled to damages for breach of contract when a magazine publisher refused to publish his article in the form it had been submitted and in the same style. The article as rewritten by the magazine contained factual errors in the author's area of expertise (in this case jade) and, when a dispute arose between the author and the publisher, the author refused to agree that the article be published without his name attached. In this case the court was able to find that there had been a breach of an implied term in the contract that the article would be published without factual errors and in the author's style. The parties agreed that some shortening of the article might have been contemplated by them. Using similar reasoning the court in *Miller v Cecil Film Ltd*[4] found that there was an implied term in a contract between the song writer and a film production company that the song would not be attributed to someone else in the film credits.

---

1    (1892) 67 LT 263.
2    (1892) 67 LT 263 at 264.
3    [1959] Ch 14.
4    [1937] 2 All ER 464.

The disadvantages of these methods of protecting moral rights are obvious. They rely on the existence of a contract between the author and the person abusing these moral rights or they are dependent on the law of defamation – an area of law which in Australia notoriously protects the well known but offers little comfort to others. Today, however, authors of works and cinematographic film makers need not rely on these general provisions of the law but may instead rely on moral rights provided for under the *Copyright Act 1968* Part IX. Performers in live performances have also been granted moral rights under this Part as a result of the *US Free Trade Agreement Implementation Act 2004*. We shall deal with authors' moral rights and performers' moral rights separately.

## Author's Moral Rights

Before December 2000 the moral rights under the *Copyright Act 1968* were restricted to a right not to be falsely attributed as the author of a work (ss 190-192 repealed) and a limitation on the compulsory licence scheme for making records of musical works. Under s 55(2) the right to make a record of a musical work did not apply in relation to a record of an adaptation of the musical work if the adaptation "debased" the work. It was argued that these limited rights did not meet Australia's obligation under Art 6bis of the Berne Agreement which provides:

> Independently of the author's economic rights, and even after the transfer of the said rights, the author shall have the right to claim authorship of the work and to object to any distortion, mutilation or other modification of, or other derogatory action in relation to, the said work, which would be prejudicial to his honour or reputation.

In December 2000 the *Copyright Amendment (Moral Rights) Act 2000* came into effect.[5] The Act repealed the two existing moral rights and replaced them with a new extended form of moral rights in accordance with the requirements of the Berne Agreement. These rights, as set out in Part IX of the *Copyright Act 1968*, are:

- the author's right to be attributed as the author when certain "attributable acts" are done in relation to the protected subject-matter ("right of attribution", s 193);
- the author's right not to have authorship falsely attributed in the case of attributable acts (s 195AC); and
- the author's right not to have the protected subject-matter subjected to "derogatory treatment" (the "right of integrity of authorship", s 195AI).

The rights are conferred on the authors of literary, dramatic, musical and artistic works and cinematographic films.[6] The authors of a cinematographic film are the director, producer and screen writer of the film. Moral rights do not extend

---

5    For transitional provisions regarding moral rights, see *Copyright Amendment (Moral Rights) Act 2000* Sch 1 Item 3. For presumptions in relation to moral rights, see ss 195AZD, 195AZE, 195AZF and 195AZG.

6    Under s 189 a work is defined for the purposes of Part IX of the Act to include a literary, dramatic, musical or artistic work and a cinematographic film. For the sake of consistency with the rest of this text, however, we will continue to refer to works and cinematographic films separately and will use the term "subject-matter" where both types of protected material are included.

to the makers of sound recordings. Only individuals can have moral rights (s 190). Therefore, the corporate producer of a film holds no moral rights in that film which are instead vested in the screenwriter and director.

Unlike copyright, which is a property right, moral rights are personal rights which cannot be assigned (s 195AN). The author might, however, consent to someone doing an act or omission which would otherwise constitute an infringement of moral rights. The form of such consent will be considered below.

The moral rights of each author or joint author are independent of each other. The consent of one author to an act or omission affecting his or her moral rights therefore does not affect the moral rights of the other joint authors (s 195AZI re works; s 195AZJ, s 195AZK and s 195AZL re films). Section 195AN provides that joint authors may enter into a written co-authorship agreement under which each agrees not to exercise his or her right of integrity other than jointly.

The moral rights of the author continue for the duration of the copyright which is usually 70 years after the death of the author in the case of works and 70 years after publication in the case of films (s 195AN). After the death of the author the rights may be exercised and enforced by the author's legal personal representative. This is subject to the important exemption that the right of integrity in a film only lasts until the death of the director, producer or screen writer (s 195AN). In other situations, other than bankruptcy or insolvency, the author's moral rights may be exercised by the person lawfully administering the author's estate (s 195AN).

The moral rights of the author are additional to any other rights in the work, including copyright, and as a matter of practice it will be common for one person to own the copyright whilst the author retains his or her moral rights (s 192).

## Right of attribution of authorship

An author has the right to be attributed as the author of a literary, dramatic or musical work when it is reproduced, published, performed in public, communicated to the public or adapted (that is, when it is subject to an "attributable act"). In the case of artistic works, the author has a right of attribution when the work is reproduced, published, exhibited in public or communicated to the public. The authors of a film have a right of attribution if the film is copied, exhibited in public or communicated to the public. The author may nominate the manner in which he or she wishes to be identified if that is reasonable and the identification must be reasonably prominent (see ss 193-195AA). Reasonably prominent is defined in s 195AB.

The right of attribution applies to works (other than works included in films) made before or after the commencement of Part IX but only in relation to attributable acts done after this time. The right only applies to films or works included in films which were made after the commencement of Part IX. Screen writers whose names were not attributed in the past could therefore not rely on these provisions to have their name restored. It is interesting to note, however, that in the United States, quite apart from moral rights, there are moves to reinstate the names of screen writers whose names were black banned during the McCarthy era.

## Right not to have work falsely attributed

An author has the right not to be falsely attributed as the author of a work or film. Acts of false attribution are specified under ss 195AD-195AH of the *Copyright Act 1968*. It is an act of false attribution to affix a name to the subject-matter or use the subject-matter in a way that implies falsely that the author is an author of that subject-matter; affix a name which falsely implies that the subject-matter is an adaptation of the author's work or film; to deal with such subject-matter or a reproduction or copy of it, or to perform or communicate it if the attributor knows or ought reasonably to have known that there is a false attribution.

Section 195AG (as to works) and s 195AH (as to films) provide that it is also an act of false attribution to knowingly deal with a work or film which has been altered (or a reproduction or copy of such an altered film or work in it) in such a way as to imply that it is the unaltered work of the author. The right does not apply if the alteration is insubstantial or required by law to be made (s 195AG(2) as to works and s 195AH(2) as to films). This right does not give the author the right to prevent an alteration of the work and the author would have to rely on breach of contract to enforce any agreements regarding alterations.

This right applies to works and films made before or after the commencement of Part IX but only in respect to acts of false attribution done after that date. However, as one of the acts of false attribution is the dealing with films and works which have been falsely attributed, this right can indirectly reach backwards in time to overcome past acts which are now proscribed (s 195AZN).

In the first moral rights case, *Meskenas v ACP Publishing Pty Ltd*,[7] an artist's painting was attributed to another artist when it was reproduced in the *Woman's Day*. The question arose as to whether the false attribution had to be "purposely wrong" or "simply incorrect". Relying on the High Court case of *Murphy v Farmer*[8] the Federal Magistrates Court held that, as a matter of statutory construction, the moral rights remedies were restitutional rather than quasi-penal and that therefore it was sufficient that the attribution was simply incorrect.

## Right of integrity of authorship

The right of integrity is the right not to have a work or film subjected to derogatory treatment (s 195AI). Derogatory treatment is defined to encompass two distinct forms of treatment.[9] On the one hand, it covers something done to the work or film itself which materially distorts, destroys, mutilates or materially alters the work or film in a manner which is prejudicial to the author's honour or reputation. On the other hand, it covers "anything else" done "in relation to" to the work or film that is prejudicial to the author's honour or reputation. Possibly for the sake of clarity, s 195AK provides that, in relationship to an artistic work, derogatory treatment also covers exhibiting the work in public in a manner which is prejudicial to the author's honour and reputation because of the manner or place in which it is exhibited. Without such a provision it may have been difficult to

---

7    [2006] FMCA 1136.
8    (1984) 79 ALR 1.
9    See s 195AJ as to literary, musical and dramatic works; s 195AK as to artistic works; and s 195AL as to cinematographic films.

determine whether such conduct amounted to material mistreatment of the work or treatment in relation to the work. It is important to note that the prejudice is to the *author's* honour or reputation, the question is not whether the thing done is prejudicial to the work or film itself.

The difference between these two types of treatment was highlighted in *Schott Musik International GMBH and Co v Colossal Records of Australia Pty Ltd*,[10] a case which arose under the compulsory licensing provisions for making recordings of musical works previously recorded (ss 54-64). Before the introduction of the moral rights amendments this compulsory licensing scheme was subject to s 55(2) which provided that the compulsory licence did not entitle a person to make a recording of the adaptation of a musical work which "debased" the original musical work. In *Schott Musik* the defendants made a techno dance version of the "O Fortuna" chorus from "Carmina Burana" and the question arose as to whether this debased the original musical work.

The majority held that the question of whether a musical work has been debased must be determined musicologically by reference to the work. Lindgren J said that the test for debasement was whether the contentious adaptation was an "impermissible distortion, mutilation or other modification of the musical work".[11] Hill J in dissent held that debasement might also refer to how the adaptation was used. He said that "an adaptation debases a musical work where it causes a reasonable person to think less of the musical work. An example would be where an adaptation brings into the original work associations, with say a racist or terrorist group, which a reasonable person would regard as objectionable".[12]

Moral rights under the *Copyright Act 1968* take a little of both of these approaches. It covers both derogatory treatment to the work itself and derogatory treatment in the use of the work but in both cases the derogatory treatment must be "prejudicial to the author's honour".

The extent of these rights has yet to be determined. In 1982, when Malcolm Fraser was Prime Minister, the artist Clifton Pugh painted a portrait of him to be hung in Parliament House (along with portraits of previous Prime Ministers). It is said that either Malcolm Fraser or his mother disliked the portrait so much that Fraser refused to agree to its hanging. This caused a great deal of public comment but for nearly 20 years the painting was hidden away and was not seen by the public. Finally, in 2001 a now much older Fraser was shown the painting and, like so many of us, decided that he had not looked all that bad after all, all those years ago. He then agreed to the painting being exhibited and it now hangs in pride of place in the National Portrait Gallery in Canberra. This scenario illustrates some fundamental questions which will need to be determined in relation to the right of integrity. First, does a failure to do something constitute "something done in relation to a work"? Secondly, can the personal distaste of a person for the work, no matter how publicly expressed, be said to be prejudicial to the author's honour? How is this to be determined?

The right applies to films or works in films made after the commencement of Part IX. The right applies to other works made before or after the commencement

---

10  (1997) 145 ALR 483.
11  (1997) 145 ALR 483 at 498.
12  (1997) 145 ALR 483 at 493.

of the Part but only in relation to derogatory acts done after the commencement of the Part. This is subject to the proviso that it is not an infringement of the right of integrity to deal with an article which has been subjected to derogatory treatment if that derogatory treatment occurred before the commencement of Part IX (s 195AZO). Thus, this section cannot reach back to correct the wrongs of the past.

## Infringement of moral rights

The moral rights of the author may be infringed in a number of ways. It is a direct infringement of the author's moral rights to do an attributable act and either not attribute authorship or falsely attribute authorship without the consent of the author, or to authorise such acts (ss 195AO, 195AP). It is a direct infringement of moral rights to subject the subject-matter to derogatory treatment without the consent of the author or to authorise such acts (s 195AQ). It is also a direct infringement of moral rights to reproduce, publish, perform, communicate or adapt, as the case may be, a work or film which has been subjected to derogatory treatment (s 195AQ).

It is an infringement of moral rights if a person imports an article into Australia for the purpose of dealing[13] with the article if the importer knows or ought reasonably to have known that, had the article been made in Australia, it would have been an "infringing article" (s 195AU). Infringing article is defined in s 189 as an article which embodies a work or film or a reproduction, adaptation or copy of that work or film where the work or film is one in respect of which the author's rights have been infringed. It does not include works or films which have been subjected to derogatory treatment unless this derogatory treatment was a material distortion, alteration or mutilation of the work or film.

A person also infringes an author's moral rights if the person sells or otherwise deals[14] with an article which the person knows, or ought reasonably to have known, is an infringing article or, if it was imported, would have been an infringing article had it been made in Australia (s 195AV). In determining whether a person has authorised an infringement one must take into account the extent of the person's power to prevent the infringing act, the nature of the relationship between the parties and whether the person took reasonable steps to prevent or avoid the doing of the act and whether the person acted in accordance with any industry codes (s 195AVA). Section 195AVB protects internet service providers (ISPs) by providing that a person (including a carrier or carriage service provider) who provides facilities for the making of a communication is not taken to have authorised a communication for this reason only.

In each of these cases an infringement may occur in relation to the work or film considered as a whole or to a substantial part of the work or film (s 195AZH).

## Reasonableness defences

The desirability of introducing moral rights in Australia was subject to debate and its impact is difficult to assess. Whilst many people may have had sympathy

---

13    See definition of dealing in s 195AU(2).
14    See definition of dealing in s 195AV(2).

for the moral rights of painters, novelists or journalists there was concern that it may have undesirable and unpredictable effects on established industry practices. This was particularly so in view of the wide range of material covered by the provisions, from traditional literary works and public buildings to domestic architecture, computer programs, press and television advertisements and industrial drawings. Few non-industry viewers, for example, could have been happy about the idea of having to sit through screen credits for television advertisements. Few people would want to display the architect's name on their new living room extension. Even in the commercial world some people would think that a company which had purchased custom-made computer software should be able to alter the computer program without worrying about the moral rights of the computer programmer.

The result of this wide-ranging concern is a rather novel piece of legislative drafting which incorporates broad reasonableness defences based on established industry practices. Such drafting might be applauded for avoiding the traditional copyright law response of itemising numerous detailed exemptions to infringement. On the other hand, it may be considered curious that a substantially new right is subject to the practices which existed prior to this right being introduced. Practices which in the past may have been seen as "morally wrong" from the author's point of view may now be protected simply because of this prior bad practice. The courts will have an interesting time reasoning through this legislative knot.

There is, therefore, no infringement of the right to be attributed as an author or infringement of the right of integrity of authorship if the defendant establishes that it was reasonable in all the circumstances not to attribute authorship or to subject the work or film to derogatory treatment. In determining whether the treatment was reasonable, certain circumstances may be taken into account including the nature of the work or film, the purpose and manner in which it is used, the context in which it is used, the industry practice in relation to such subject-matter, any voluntary codes of practices in the industry, the difficulty or expense involved in seeking to identify the author, whether the work was made in the course of employment or a contract for services and, where there is more than one author, the views of the other authors (s 195AR as to attribution and s 195AS as to integrity of authorship).

## Defences relating to buildings and moveable art works

One of the issues which traditionally has caused great debate in the community arises in relation to the destruction of art works and the removal or destruction of site specific works, buildings and art works affixed to buildings. In the face of public criticism of a particular art work, for example, local authorities have been known to move, remove or even destroy public art works. The removal of Richard Serra's site specific sculpture, Tilted Arc, from the plaza of the Jacob K Javits Federal Building in Lower Manhattan in 1985 is one of the most famous international incidents of this type. The irony of this case is that Serra specifically designed the work to be confronting, intimidating and disruptive and this is precisely why it was moved. Not all such incidents are famous or notorious, however. On any day, building owners may wish to demolish, relocate or renovate a building in a manner which might be seen as derogatory treatment either of the building itself or of art works which are affixed to or form part of the building. For the author, any of these actions may be seen as bringing dishonour. For the community such actions may represent the loss of part of the community's cultural heritage.

The *Copyright Act 1968* seeks to address this issue in an innovative manner by providing a defence to infringement if the owner of the building or the person who wishes to destroy or move an art work first gives the author of the work an opportunity to remove and/or record the work. Different provisions apply for moveable and non-moveable works of art.

In the case of moveable art works, s 195AT(1) provides that it is not an infringement of the author's right of integrity of authorship to destroy the work if the person destroying the work gave the author a "reasonable opportunity" to remove the work from the place where it was situated. This provision is not limited to public works and so might be invoked if a person were to destroy an art work as part of a performance or demonstration, for example, even when the art work is owned by the person destroying it. It might even be invoked in the case of a private individual destroying an art work in the privacy of his or her own home if the artist can establish the necessary harm to the artist's dishonour. This may be possible in the case of a well-known artist whose works are fully catalogued but may be difficult in the case of an unknown artist whose work was bought at the local fete.

Section 195AT(4A) provides that it is not an infringement of the author's right of integrity of authorship to remove or relocate a moveable art work which is situated at a place accessible to the public and which was made for installation in that place if the person who wishes to remove or relocate the artistic work first complies with the prescribed consultation process. The process is set out in detail and requires the person to notify the author of the intention to remove or relocate the art work and to give the artist an opportunity within three weeks to seek access to the work for the purposes of recording the work and/or consulting with the person in good faith about its removal or relocation. The artist must then be given a reasonable opportunity within the next three weeks to access the work for these purposes. If the artist notifies the person that the artist wants his or her identification removed from the art work this must be complied with.

In the case of buildings or artistic works affixed to or forming part of a building a similar consultation process must be followed in the case of a change in, relocation, demolition or destruction of a building (s 195AT(2) as to artistic works affixed to or forming part of a building and s 195AT(3) as to buildings).

It has often been suggested that these consultative processes are merely gestural and will do nothing to prevent the planned treatment. If nothing else, however, the consultation provisions give the artist or architect an opportunity to mobilise public opinion in his or her favour. This is what happened in relation to the planned renovations of the front entrance to the Australian National Gallery. In early 2002 the Gallery announced that it was not proceeding with the renovations due to the fact that the architect had objected to them. The renovations have now been completed but only after many years of public discussion and negotiation between the architect and the Gallery.

## Defences relating to preservation and restoration of works and films

Disputes have also arisen regarding preservation and restoration of artistic works and cinematographic films. The continuing debate regarding the restoration of Leonardo Da Vinci's "Last Supper" and Rembrandt's "The Night Watch" are two high profile examples of such a debate. Section 195AT(5) represents an attempt to address this issue by providing that it is not an infringement of the author's right of integrity of authorship to do anything in good faith to restore or preserve a work. Whilst this section may provide a defence in cases where there is legitimate debate regarding similar actions, it may be more difficult to rely on this section to justify colourisation of films, for example.

## Consent

Copyright and moral rights are quite separate and therefore, in dealings relating to copyright, separate provision must be made with regard to moral rights by acquiring the author's written consent to do anything in relation to the work or film which might otherwise be an infringement of the author's moral rights (ss 195AW, 195AWA). Such consent may be given in relation to a work or film already in existence or not yet in existence. Section 195AWB provides that a consent obtained through duress or misleading statement has no effect. The form of consent varies according to the type of subject-matter and whether or not the author is an employee.

In the case of films, or works included in films, a consent may be given in relation to "all or any acts or omissions" occurring before or after the consent is given (s 195AW). An employee may give a consent to the benefit of the employer in relation to all works made by the employee or to be made by the employee in the future, in the course of employment.

In the case of a work which is not a film, or is not included in a film, a consent may only be given in relation to "specified acts or omissions, or specified classes or types of acts or omissions" whether occurring before or after the consent is given (s 195AWA). An employee may give a consent for the benefit of the employer but again, the acts or omissions must be specified.

The object of this difference is to offer greater protection to authors outside the film industry and, when applied to copyright subject-matter in traditional forms such as books, journal articles or paintings, the implementation of these provisions may be relatively straightforward. However, in large commercial transactions where people may be acquiring or licensing copyright, the nature of which may not yet have been contemplated, these provisions pose some difficulties. In a complex contract for the development of a new plane, for example, or in a business contract for the development of specialised, owner-specific computer hardware and software, many forms of copyright subject-matter may be generated in the course of the project, all of which may have different uses. Whether the use of this subject-matter will impinge on the author's moral rights cannot be foreseen. There are two responses to this problem, only one of which is commercially sound. The first is to draft a consent clause which specifies every possible specific act or omission which may occur. The other is to agree to negotiate at the time the relevant copyright subject-matter comes into existence.

## Actions and remedies

Under the *Copyright Act 1968* s 195AZ, the author may bring an action in respect of infringement of moral rights. Under s 195AZA the courts may award an injunction and/or damages, make a declaration that a moral right of the author has been infringed, make an order that the defendant make a public apology or that any false attribution of authorship or derogatory treatment be removed or reversed or any combination of these remedies. The provisions do not allow a person who is both the director and producer of a film, for example, to double up on damages.

In exercising its discretion, the court may take account of the knowledge of the defendant, the effect on the author's honour, the number or type of people who have seen or heard the work or film, mitigation by the defendant and the cost or difficulty associated with attributing authorship or removing a false attribution. In exercising its discretion to award an injunction the court must consider whether the parties have made an attempt to negotiate a settlement and whether the matter should be adjourned to allow negotiation (s 195AZA).

The grant of moral rights does not affect any right or remedy, civil or criminal, which the author may have had in relation to the act or omission (s 195AZB). The author may therefore resort to defamation and breach of contract actions if these are available. Any damages, however, which are recovered in one action are taken into account in assessing damages in another (s 195AZB).

## Performers' Moral Rights

Performers' moral rights, which were introduced as a result of the US- Australia Free Trade Agreement, are limited in the same way as performers' copyright and performers' protection are limited.[15] That is, the rights only attach to performers in live performances (including the conductor of a musical work (s 191B)) in so far as they relate to sound, and to recordings of these live performances (s 248A). Despite these limitations the moral rights are broad in so far as the spear carrier in the opera chorus has the same moral rights as the diva; just as the back-up singer has the same moral rights as the lead singer in a band.

Performers' moral rights closely mirror the moral rights granted to authors.[16] The performer has a right of attribution of performership (s 195ABA); a right not to have performership falsely attributed (s 195AHA) and a right of integrity of performership (s 195ALA). Performance is defined to cover circus, variety and dance acts as well as performances and improvisations of dramatic works, puppets, musical works, recitations and expressions of folklore (ss 189 and 248A) but only in so far as the performance consists of sound. Performership means participation in a performance, as the performer or one of the performers (s 189). The rights apply in relation to the whole or a substantial part of a live or recorded performance (s 195AZP). The meaning of the phrase, "expression of folklore", shall be considered below in our discussion of proposed moral rights for indigenous communities.

---

15    Performers' moral rights only subsist in relation to live performances made after the commencement of the *US Free Trade Agreement Implementation Act 2004* and of recordings made of such performances: s 195AZR.

16    For presumptions relating to subsistence of performers' copyright; performers' moral rights and performership, see ss 195AZGD-195AZGF.

Under s 195ABB the performer's right to attribution arises whenever the performance is staged or communicated to the public. In the case of a recorded performance the attributable acts are the making of a copy record of the recorded performance and communicating the recorded performance to the public. The performer's right to be attributed attaches to that performer only; it is not a right to have all performers attributed. Thus, where there is more than one performer, they each have a right to be attributed but it is not an infringement of X's right if Y is not attributed (see s 195AZQ). Sections 195ABC-195ABE provide guidance on how the performer is to be attributed.

The right not to be falsely attributed is the right not to have a person do an act of false attribution (s 195AHA). In the case of a live performance it is an act of false attribution for the person staging the performance (or a person authorised by the stager) to falsely state or imply to the audience or intended audience immediately before, during or after a performance, which is given to the public or communicated to the public, that a person is or will be performer in the performance or that the performance is or will be presented by a particular group of players (s 195AHB(1), (2), (3) and (4)). The immediacy requirement is probably meant to exclude false advertising from the prohibition but is doubtful whether it is successful.

In relation to a recorded performance, it is an act of false attribution to insert or affix (or authorise this) a person's or a group's name in or on a record in such a way as to falsely imply that the person or group is a performer in the performance. It is also an act of false attribution to deal with such a record where the attributor knows that the person or group is not a performer in the performance. Similarly, it is an act of false attribution to communicate the recorded performance to the public as being the performance of a person or group where the attributor knows that the person or group is not a performer in the performance (s 195AHB(5) and (6)).

Under s 195AHC it is an act of false attribution to deal with a recorded performance which has been altered by someone, other than the performer, as though it were an unaltered recorded performance. That is, a person cannot deal with an unauthorised abridged version, for example, or a version which has had minor expletives removed by someone other than the performer. This imposes significant limitations on the ability of the producer to unilaterally determine these matters and will need to be the subject of prerecording negotiations in the future. The right is not infringed if the alteration is insubstantial or required by law to be made or "otherwise necessary" to avoid a breach of the law.

Where there is more than one performer an act of false attribution infringes each performer's rights. Thus, if X and Y are performers and the performance is falsely attributed to X and Z this is an infringement of X and Y's moral rights (s 195AZQ(3)).

Section 195AHA(7) makes special provisions in relation to mimes and other silent performers. It provides that it is not an act of false attribution to state that a performer who participated silently in a performance performed in that performance. The Act gives an example. If X and Y present a cabaret act where X sings and Y dances silently the "performance" for the purposes of the moral rights provisions consist only of X's sounds. It is not an act of false attribution, however, to state or imply that Y is also a performer.

The right of integrity of performance is the performer's right not to have the performance subjected to derogatory treatment (s 195ALA). Derogatory treatment in relation to a live or recorded performance is defined in s 195ALB as the doing "in relation to the performance" of anything that results in the material distortion of, the mutilation of, or the material alteration to the performance that is prejudicial to the performer's reputation. This is similar to the author's right of integrity but does not include the destruction of a performance – this is arguably because the right attaches to the performance itself rather than to copies of the recorded performance. Thus, the right would not cover the mutilation of a DVD embodying the performance. You may like to consider what would constitute a mutilation of the performance. The right of integrity of performership is a right of each performer separately. Thus, if a performance starring X and Y is subjected to derogatory treatment which is prejudicial to X's reputation but not Y's reputation, only X has an action for infringement (s 195AZQ(4)).

Performers' moral rights in a live performance necessarily die with the performance itself. On the other hand, a performer's attribution rights in relation to a recorded performance continue until the copyright in the recorded performance ceases although the performer's right of integrity of performership in relation to a recorded performance only continues until the performer dies (s 195ANA). If a performer dies that performer's moral rights may be exercised by the legal personal representative but are otherwise not transmissible by assignment, will or devolution (s 195ANB).

## Infringement, defences and remedies

Performers' moral rights might be infringed directly or indirectly but this is subject to the limitation that a person, including a carriage service provider, who merely provides facilities for communicating infringing material will not be held to have authorised any relevant infringing act (s 195AXI). The infringement provisions only apply to acts or omissions occurring in Australia (s 195AXL).

A performer's right of attribution is infringed if the person does an attributable act, or authorises another person to do an attributable act, without the required identification (s 195AXA). It is a defence if the alleged infringer establishes that it was reasonable in the circumstances not to identify the performer (s 195AZD(1)). In determining whether the failure to attribute was reasonable the court must take into account the nature of the performance; the purpose, manner and context in which the performance was used; industry practice; any practice contained in a voluntary code of practice; any difficulty or expense in identifying the performer and whether the performer participated in the performance in the course of employment. It may be that the rock industry practice of personally introducing the drummer in the band might not be necessary where the drummer is playing in a brass band which is playing at the local agricultural show.

If a person does an act of false attribution in relation to a performance this is an infringement of the performer's right not to be falsely attributed (s 195AXB).

The right of integrity of performership in a live or recorded performance is infringed by a person who subjects the performance to a derogatory act or authorises such derogatory treatment (s 195AXC(2)). If a live performance is subjected to derogatory treatment and is recorded, then it is an infringement of the performer's right of integrity in the live performance to make a copy of the recorded performance, communicate the recorded performance to the public or cause the recorded performance to be heard in public (s 195AXC(3)). If a recorded performance has been subjected to derogatory treatment the performer's right of integrity of performership in respect to the recorded performance is infringed by someone who makes a copy of the recording, communicates it to the public or causes it to be heard in public (s 195AXC(4)). Section 195(3) and (4) are subject to a reasonableness defence (s 195AXE(3)).

It is a defence to an action for breach of the performer's right of integrity of performership if the treatment was reasonable in all the circumstances. The onus is on the alleged infringer. In determining whether the treatment was reasonable the court must take into account the nature of the performance; the purpose, manner and context in which the performance was used; industry practice; any practice contained in a voluntary code of practice; whether the performer participated in the performance in the course of employment; and whether the treatment was required by law or was otherwise necessary to avoid a breach of any law (s 195AXE(1) and (2)).

The Act also includes provisions relating to importation, selling and dealing with articles containing infringing material (ss 195AXF-195AXH). See s 189 for a detailed definition of infringing article.

In an action for infringement of performers' moral rights a court may grant an injunction; award damages; make a declaration; order a public apology; or order that a false attribution or derogatory treatment be removed. In exercising its discretion the court is to take into account the knowledge of the defendant; the effect on the performer's reputation; the number and categories of people who have heard the performance; anything done by the defendant to mitigate the effects of infringement; any cost or difficulty in identifying the performer or of removing a false attribution or derogatory treatment. The court must also consider whether the parties have made any attempt to negotiate a settlement (s 195AZGC).

## Dealing and consent

It is not an infringement of a performer's moral rights if the act or omission has been consented to by the performer in writing (s 195AXJ). The consent has no effect if it was given under duress or because of a false misrepresentation (s 195AXK). Except for these two requirements, the consent provisions for performers are very general (unlike those required for some authors' moral rights). Thus, the consent may be given for all or any acts or omissions occurring before or after the consent is given; it may be in relation to specified performances; to performances of a particular description; or for all performances where the performer is an employee (s 195AXJ).

Because moral rights are private, the consent of one party to an act or omission affecting his or her moral rights does not affect the rights of any other performer (s 195AZQ(5)). However, where there are two or more performers in a live or recorded performance, then they may enter into an agreement whereby each agrees not to exercise his or her right of integrity of performance except jointly with the other performer or performers (s 195ANB(4)).

## Performers' Protection

The primary function of performers' protection is to prevent the making, copying and dealing with bootleg sound and film recordings of live performances. Its reach is surprising. If you are a State of Origin fan who listened to Roy and HG's match call on Triple J radio you may have noticed that they did not play the national anthem. As soon as the chosen singer launched into song, Roy and HG put on another piece of music – usually Lionel Rose's "I Thank You". This may have been for the stirring lyrics, "when a boy becomes a man". On the other hand, you might like to consider whether this could also be explained by the fact they did not have authorisation from the performer to communicate the performance. If this is so, it is doubtful that the introduction of performers' protection was meant to restrict broadcasts of the national anthem in this way and you may like to consider whether there are any exemptions which would assist Roy and HG if they did want to broadcast the performance as part of the match call. This question is quite separate from the question of whether the communication would constitute an infringement of the national anthem itself considered as a musical or literary work.

Performers' protection was first introduced into Australia in 1989 as Part XIA of the *Copyright Act 1968* and allowed Australia in 1992 to sign the *Rome Convention for the Protection of Performers, Producers of Phonograms and Broadcasting Organisations 1961*. The provisions were strengthened as part of the *US Free Trade Agreement Implementation Act 2004*. Performers' protection only extends to live performances and therefore does not directly afford protection to actors in films or singers on sound recordings in so far as the film or sound recording was itself authorised. The performer's right, like moral rights, is a chose in action rather than a property right and cannot be assigned (s 248N).

Performance is defined in s 248A(1) as a live performance of a musical work or a dramatic work including a puppet show, a live reading, recitation or delivery of a literary work or the live performance of a dance, circus act, variety act or an expression of folklore. The Act expressly provides that the performance of the dramatic or musical work may be improvised and that performance includes the recitation and delivery of an improvised literary work. It is not necessary that there be an audience. Performances given in the classroom for the purposes of educational instructions, sporting activity, audience participation and the reading, recitation or delivery of any item of news or information are excluded from the definition of performance (ss 248A(2) and 248(1)).

The performance is protected if it is a live performance either given in Australia or given by a qualified person.[17]

The protection period for the performance commences on the day of the performance and extends for 20 years after the end of the calendar year in which the performance was made in the case of films and 50 years in the case of sound recordings of performances.[18]

In general, only performances given after the commencement of Part XIA are protected. Section 248QA creates some offences in relation to sound recordings

---

17    For the extension of performers' protection to foreign countries in accordance with Australia's international obligations, see *Copyright Act 1968* s 248A(1) and *Copyright Regulations 1969*.

18    Sections 248A, 248CA .

made before the commencement of the *Copyright (World Trade Organisation Amendments) Act 1994* (see below).

## Unauthorised use, actions and remedies

A performer may bring an action for "unauthorised use" of the performance and may be granted an injunction and/or damages, including exemplary damages, by the court (s 248J). The unauthorised use may relate to the whole performance or a substantial part of the performance (s 248A(3)). If there are two or more performers each performer must authorise the use.

There are two categories of unauthorised use under Part XIA – these are the "primary category" and the "second category" usages. Under the primary category, s 248G(1), a person makes an unauthorised use of the performance if the person:

- makes a sound recording or cinematographic film of a live performance without the authorisation of the performer; or
- communicates a live performance without the authorisation of the performer.

The recording may be "direct" or indirect. A direct recording is a sound recording or film made directly from a live performance (for example, a bootleg recording of a live concert).[19] An "indirect" recording is a sound recording or film made from a broadcast of a live performance (for example, a video taken from a television broadcast of a concert).[20] The "primary categories" of unauthorised use do not require knowledge on the part of the unauthorised user.

Under the second category of unauthorised use, s 248G(2), a person makes an unauthorised use of a performance if the person:

- copies a recording of a performance where the person knew or ought reasonably to have known that the recording was unauthorised;
- makes a copy of an "exempt recording" (see below) where the person knows or ought reasonably to have known that the copy is not an exempt recording;
- makes a copy of an unauthorised recording for use in a sound track if the person knows or ought reasonably to have known that the recording was not authorised for use in that sound track or any other sound track;
- possesses a recording of a performance for the purposes of selling, hiring, offering for trade, exposing for sale or hire or distributing for the purposes of trade in a manner which would affect the financial interests of the performer if the person knows or ought reasonably to have known that the recording was unauthorised;
- sells, hires, exhibits for trade, offers or exposes for sale or hire a recording which the person knows or ought reasonably to have known was an unauthorised recording;
- distributes a recording for the purpose of trade or for a purpose which will affect the financial interests of the performer if the person knows or ought reasonably to have known that the recording was unauthorised;
- imports a recording for sale, hire, trade etc if the person knows or ought reasonably to have known that the recording was unauthorised;

---

19   Section 248A(1).
20   Section 248A(1).

- causes a recording of the performance to be seen or heard in public if the person knows or ought reasonably to have known that the recording was unauthorised.

## Exempt recordings

There are a large number of recordings which are exempt from these provisions which closely parallel the defences to copyright infringement. The following are classified as "exempt recordings" under s 248A(1):

- a direct or indirect sound recording of a performance that is a fair dealing with the performance on the basis that it is for the purpose of criticism or review; reporting the news in a newspaper or similar journal or reporting the news by means of a communication or film;
- an indirect sound recording or film made from a broadcast, on domestic premises, solely for private and domestic use for the purpose of time shifting;
- an indirect film of a performance or a copy of that film, made solely for the purposes of the private and domestic use of the person who made it;
- an indirect film of a performance, or a copy of that film, made solely for the purposes of scientific research;
- an indirect film of a performance, or a copy of that film, where the film is made by an educational institution, an institution assisting people with a print disability or an institution assisting people with an intellectual disability, solely for educational use or for providing assistance to people with a print or intellectual disability;
- a direct or indirect film of a performance, or a copy of that film, made for the purpose of, or associated with, the reporting of news or current affairs or for the purpose of criticism or review;
- a direct or indirect sound recording or a film of a performance, or a copy of such a recording or film, made solely for the purpose of judicial proceedings or the giving of professional advice by a legal practitioner;
- a direct recording or film of a performance, or a copy of such a recording or film, made for the purpose of making a broadcast where the performer has authorised the broadcast (in which case the copy must be destroyed within 12 months);[21]
- a direct or indirect recording of a performance if the person who made the recording reasonably believes, due to a fraudulent or innocent misrepresentation made to that person, that the performer has authorised the recording. A copy of such a recording is also exempt if the person who made the copy similarly believes that the performer has authorised the making of the copy or if the copy is for one of the above-mentioned purposes.

## Offences

Many of the defences have an indictable, a summary and a strict liability version, and under s 248SA of the Act and Part 6A of the Regulations, action may be taken by way of infringement notice and penalty rather than by prosecution.

---

21    Section 248C.

The offences relating to acts done in Australia on or after the commencement of the provisions are:

- making an unauthorised direct recording during the protection period (s 248PA);
- making an unauthorised indirect recording during the protection period (s 249PB);
- making an unauthorised communication to the public during the protection period (s 248PC);
- playing unauthorised recordings publicly during the protection period (s 248PD);
- possessing equipment to make or copy an unauthorised recording (s 248PE);
- copying an unauthorised recording (s 248PF);
- making an unauthorised copy of an exempt recording (s 248PG);
- making an unauthorised copy of an authorised sound recording for the purpose of including it in a sound track (s 248PH);
- dealing with unauthorised recording (s 248PI);
- distributing unauthorised recordings (s 248PJ);
- commercial possession or importing of unauthorised recordings (s 248PK);
- exhibiting unauthorised recording in public by way of trade (s 248PL);
- importing unauthorised recording for exhibition by way of trade (s 248PM).

The Act also establishes a number to offences for acts done in Australia after the commencement of the Act but in relation to performances given before 1 July 1995. Where a single act might constitute an offence under the offences above and those following, s 248S provides that only one may be prosecuted. The offences are:

- possessing equipment for copying unauthorised sound recording (s 248QB);
- copying unauthorised sound recording (s 248QC);
- dealing with unauthorised sound recording (s 248QD);
- distributing unauthorised sound recording (s 248QE);
- commercial possession or import of unauthorised sound recording (s 248QF);
- exhibiting unauthorised sound recording in public by way of trade (s 248QG);
- importing unauthorised sound recording for exhibition by way of trade (s 248QH).

The court before which a person is charged may order the destruction or delivery up of the unauthorised recording or plates or recording equipment used or intended to be used for making an unauthorised recording (s 248T).

## Artists' Resale Rights

Artists' resale royalty rights can broadly be defined as the right of artists to receive a royalty on the second and subsequent resale of their art work. The type of work and the sales captured by the right may vary from country to country. These rights were originally known as the *droit de suite* (literally, "follow-up right") which was the name given to the first such scheme established in France in 1920.[22] Resale royalty rights are granted in recognition of the fact that visual artists do not have the same opportunities to earn money through publishing, performances and broadcast, for example, as other creators such as writers and performers.

In Australia, a resale royalty right for visual artists has been under consideration for many years and the subject of a number of reports. These include the Australian Copyright Council's *Droit de Suite: the Art Resale Royalty and its Implication for Australia 1989*; the Rupert Myer *Report of Contemporary Visual Art and Craft Inquiry 2002*; the Department of Communications, Information Technology and the Arts' *Proposed Resale Royalty Arrangement: Discussion Paper 2004*; Access Economics' *The Impact of an Australian Resale Royalty on Eligible Visual Artists 2004* (commissioned by Viscopy); and the Department of the Environment, Water, Heritage and the Arts' *Australian Resale Royalty Scheme for Visual Artists – Framework and Parameters 2004*. Resale royalties have been the subject of two Bills, the Resale Royalty Bill 2004 and the Resale Royalty Right for Visual Artists Bill 2008. Following the Second Reading Speech in 2008, the 2008 Bill was referred to the House of Representatives Standing Committee on Climate Change, Water, Environment and the Arts, which published the report on the *Inquiry into Resale Royalty Right for Visual Artists Bill 2008* in 2009. Whilst all reports broadly supported the introduction of a resale royalty for visual artists, there was considerable doubt as to whether it would benefit visual artists generally or whether it would simply be a windfall to already highly successful artists; whether limiting the right to "commercial" sales would encourage carpet bagging; and whether limiting the right to sales involving "art market professionals" would exclude significant sales by second hand dealers and some internet sales.[23] Despite these concerns, artists' resale royalty rights finally came into effect in Australia in June 2010 as a result of the *Resale Royalty Right for Visual Artists Act 2009* (Cth).

The Act defines a resale royalty right as "the right to receive a resale royalty on the commercial resale of an artwork" (s 6). A "commercial" resale is one which transfers the ownership of the work, for monetary consideration, is not the first transfer of ownership, and involves an "art market professional" (s 8). An "art market professional" is an auctioneer, the owner or operator of an art gallery, the owner or operator of a museum, an art dealer or a person otherwise involved in the business of dealing with art works (s 8). The first transfer of ownership which grounds the "resale" need not be "commercial" and would include transfers which were by way of exchange, gift or inheritance. The royalty only applies to works which are sold for at least $1000 including GST, but not including the buyers' premium (s 10). It is notable that the right arises whether or not the resale is for a profit.

Perhaps recognising the weak bargaining position of most visual artists the Act provides that the resale royalty right is "absolutely inalienable" whether by way of, or in consequence of, sale, assignment, charge, execution, bankruptcy, insolvency or otherwise (s 33). Unlike moral rights, the resale royalty right cannot

---

22   Simon Stokes, *Art and Copyright*, Hart Publishing Ltd, Oxford, 2001, p 77.

23   See House of Representatives Standing Committee on Climate Change, Water, Environment and the Arts, *Inquiry into Resale Royalty Right for Visual Artists Bill 2008*, 2009, Ch 2, <http://www.aph.gov.au/house/committee/ccwea/resaleroyalty/report.htm>.

be waived nor is an agreement to share or repay a resale royalty effective (s 34) except as between the artists themselves (s 16). However, the resale royalty right may pass by succession under s 15 and exists as a debt due to the holder of the resale royalty right by those liable to pay, that is the seller or an art market professional who is an agent in the sale (ss 19 and 20).

The resale royalty applies to "original works of visual art" created by an artist or artists, or produced under the authority of an artist or artists (s 7). The requirement of originality effectively excludes mass produced photographs, prints, films and designs for example. On the other hand, the inclusion of works produced "under the authority" of an artist recognises the studio practices of many artists, especially in the fields of sculpture and glasswork.

The range of art works is very broad and "works of visual art" is defined in s 7 to include artists' books, batiks, carvings, ceramics, collages, digital art works, drawings, engravings, fine art jewellery, glassware, installations, lithographs, multimedia art works, paintings, photographs, pictures, prints, sculptures, tapestries, video art works, weavings and "any other things prescribed by the regulations" (s 7). The definition is meant to be broad but, given the difficulty which the courts have had in defining a "work of artistic craftsmanship", for example, one can only wonder how they will cope with "fine art jewellery". The right does not extend to buildings, architectural plans and models of buildings, circuit layouts or manuscripts (s 9).

Where there is only one artist the resale royalty right is held by the "identified" artist (s 12(1)) or by the identified artist's successor in title (s 12(2)). Where there is more than one artist, the resale royalty right is held by each of the artists as tenants in common in equal shares (s 12(3)) unless they have agreed to apportion their rights differently under s 16(1). Where one or more of the artists dies, the artist's successor in title receives the share of royalties which the artist would have received had the artist been alive (ss 12(3) and 16(2)).

A person is the "identified" artist if, at the time of the resale, the person's identity as the artist is known to the seller, the buyer, any art market professional acting as an agent in the sale, the collecting society or another artist of the art work (s 13). The identified artist must meet the residency test – that is, the artist must be an Australian citizen, a permanent resident or a national, or a citizen of a reciprocating country as prescribed by regulation (s 14).[24] The successor in title must meet the residency and succession tests. Under the succession test the successor in title must be an individual, charity or a community body (or a trustee for these entities) which received its interest by testamentary disposition or under the rules of intestacy. Alternatively, the entity must be a charity, charitable institution or community body which received its interest on the winding up of a similar entity (s 15).[25]

The resale royalty right only arises in relation to art works which came into existence or which were acquired after the commencement date of the Act. Thus, no resale royalty right arises in relation to the first transfer of ownership of an art

---

24 For the residency test for corporations and unincorporated bodies see s 14. A country will be prescribed as a reciprocating country "on the basis of their implementation of Article 14ter of Berne Convention for the Protection of Literary and Artistic Works": Explanatory Memorandum to Resale Royalty Right for Visual Artists Bill 2008 clause 14.

25 For presumptions in relation to the artist see s 17.

work which was in existence at the commencement of the Act (s 11). This provision is meant to protect the property rights of art buyers who had acquired a work before they knew that they would be liable for royalties on the resale of the work.[26]

The resale royalty right continues to apply to all eligible commercial resales until the end of 70 years after the calendar year in which the artist dies. If there is more than one artist of the art work, the proportion of the resale royalty right applying to an artist continues until 70 years after the calendar year in which that artist dies (s 32).

The Copyright Agency Limited (CAL) has been appointed by the government as the collecting agency for the scheme. CAL reports that in the first 15 months of its operation, the scheme generated royalties totalling $395,302 from 1953 resales, for 330 artists (mostly indigenous artists), where the lowest royalty payment was $50 and the highest was $40,000.[27]

## Protection of Folklore and Indigenous Cultural Property

It is generally accepted that there are some significant limitations on the ability of existing copyright law, including moral rights and performers' protection, to adequately protect indigenous culture when it does not fit within the definition of a work or other subject-matter under the *Copyright Act 1968*. There is also widespread understanding that existing intellectual property law in Australia may protect individual indigenous artists, authors, performers and filmmakers, for example, but does not protect indigenous communities as the guardians of indigenous culture and knowledge. There have been a number of government reports[28] as well as numerous academic and industry writings on these issues and we will summarise the problems briefly.

First, copyright protects works only for a specified period of time and therefore does not protect ancient indigenous cultural property which may fall outside the copyright period. In the case of moral rights, the legislation provides that it applies only to subject-matter created after the introduction of moral rights legislation.

A more significant limitation is that copyright law and moral rights only apply to "works" or "subject-matter other than works" as understood in the *Copyright Act*. Copyright law does not protect culture in the abstract. Thus, cultural misappropriation in the sense of using indigenous stories, cultural motifs or styles of cultural production without actually copying a particular work (or other subject-matter) does not constitute a breach of copyright or moral rights. A non-indigenous artist who makes a dot painting similar to the Papunya style or who applies an "aboriginal style" design to a didgeridoo, for example, will not

---

26    Explanatory Memorandum to Resale Royalty Right for Visual Artists Bill 2008 clause 11.

27    Copyright Agency Ltd <http://www.resaleroyalty.org.au>. For presumptions in relation to the collecting society see s 24.

28    See Commonwealth Department of Home Affairs and Environment, *Report of Working Party on the Protection of Aboriginal Folklore*, 1981; Department of Aboriginal Affairs, *Report of the Review Committee: The Aboriginal Arts and Crafts Industry*, 1989; Commonwealth Attorney-General's Department, *Stopping the Rip-Offs: Intellectual Property Protection for Aboriginal and Torres Strait Islander Peoples*, 1994; Terri Janke, *Our Culture Our Future: Report on Australian Indigenous Cultural and Intellectual Property Rights*, 1997; Michael Davis, Social Policy Unit, Parliamentary Library, *Indigenous People and Intellectual Property Rights*, Research Paper 20, 1996-1997.

be caught by the copyright or moral rights provisions. Similarly, the copyright and moral rights provisions have traditionally not prevented non-indigenous people from publishing literary works or music or mounting performances based on indigenous stories, music or dance if these stories, music or dance have not been reduced to the form of a "work" or other subject-matter as required under the *Copyright Act* or if the appropriator has not subjectively reproduced such subject-matter if it does exist.

Finally, in so far as copyright law is based on the idea of the individual creative artist, it does not adequately recognise the claims of indigenous communities to assert control over the use of communal images or stories. As we shall see, the struggle for the recognition of communal interests lies at the heart of contemporary moves towards reform.

In this section we would like to take a brief excursion into this question of protection of cultural property to see what changes have been made to existing copyright law to recognise these problems; how indigenous communities and artists have successfully used copyright law to protect their interests, and what possibilities of reform are currently being considered to protect indigenous cultural property and communities.

## The protection of expressions of folklore

The *US Free Trade Agreement Implementation Act 2004* introduced three significant amendments which effectively extended the protection offered to performers of expressions of folklore. First, the performer became a joint owner, with the maker of a sound recording, of copyright in any sound recording made of a live performance of the expression of folklore. Secondly, the performer acquired moral rights in respect of this performance and, finally, the performer was able to exercise performers' protection in relation to the live performance.

The term "expression of folklore" is known in international law and within the discourse of intellectual property rights. In 1992 the United Nations recognised that indigenous intellectual property could, for the sake of analysis, be divided into three categories – folklore and crafts; biodiversity; and indigenous knowledge. The United Nations approach reflected a traditional distinction between the protection of knowledge under patent law and the protection of cultural artefacts under copyright law and relied partly on previous work on the definition of folklore. The WIPO *Tunis Model Law on Copyright 1976*, for example, defined folklore so as to include literary and other works passed from generation to generation and "constituting one of the basic elements of the traditional cultural knowledge". This definition attempted to avoid any time limits (which might otherwise limit copyright protection) but it still limited protection to works and other subject-matter, which were normally reduced to material form. The *Model Law for the Protection of Folklore Against Illicit Exploitation and Other Prejudicial Actions 1985* (developed by WIPO and UNESCO) went further and expressly provided that an "expression of folklore" need not be reduced to material form and included verbal expressions such as folk tales, riddles and folk poetry along with more traditional forms of expression such as musical expression, dance and artefacts. The *Copyright Act* does not define "expression of folklore" nor does it expressly provide that the expression need not be reduced to a material form. We would suggest, however, that there is no need for the expression of folklore to be reduced to a material form under the Act so long as it can be characterised as a performance, and the person who expresses the folklore can be characterised as a performer.

The exact meaning of a "performance" and a "performer" has yet to be determined. It is not clear whether the definitions of performer and performance, even though they include improvised performances, will cover fly-on-the-wall documentary situations. If a sound recording were made of children singing traditional songs or telling tales within the school playground as part of a game and without any thought of "performing" should this be considered a performance and the children characterised as performers? This problem will pose fine questions of statutory interpretation: on the one hand, there is no need for the performance to be fixed; there is no need for there to be an audience; there is no requirement for the performers to be professional; and there is no need for the performance to be other than improvised.[29] On the other hand, a performer, and the notion of performance, has traditionally imported some notion of calling and presentation for some educational or entertaining purpose, although they also have the much broader meaning of one who "does something" or the doing of something.

## Copyright protection for other indigenous cultural property

It is wrong to say that the *Copyright Act* has previously offered no protection for indigenous cultural property. Over the years individual indigenous artists, and their copyright licensees, have successfully protected their works under the *Copyright Act 1968*. In *Thomas v Brown*,[30] Harold Thomas successfully sought a declaration that he was the author and copyright owner of the artistic work which comprised the design for the Aboriginal flag. In *Flags 2000 Pty Ltd v Smith*,[31] the exclusive licensee for the distribution of the Aboriginal flag successfully sued an unauthorised distributor for infringement of the copyright in that artistic work.

On the other hand, it has been well understood, at least since *Yumbulul v Reserve Bank of Australia*,[32] that the *Copyright Act* fails to recognise the cultural claim of indigenous communities, rather than individual artists, to regulate the reproduction and use of works which have been made by an author under the authority of the community. In that case, the indigenous artist Yumbulul had come under considerable criticism from his community for allowing the Reserve Bank to reproduce his Morning Star Pole on the bicentennial $10 note. Being neither a copyright owner nor an exclusive licensee the community itself could do nothing to revoke the licence and did not have standing to take action in court. The artist did have standing but failed in his attempt to have the licence revoked on the basis of misrepresentation, deceptive conduct and mistake.

Indigenous communities were not passive in the face of these limitations and, in two important cases attempts were made to raise the issue of cultural harm

---

29    Compare the *Entertainment Industry Act 1989* (NSW) s 4(1) which defines a performer as any person such as an actor, singer, dancer, acrobat, model, musician engaged to give a performance.

30    *Thomas v Brown* (1997) 37 IPR 207.

31    *Flags 2000 Pty Ltd v Smith* (2003) 59 IPR 191.

32    *Yumbulul v Reserve Bank of Australia* (1991) 21 IPR 481.

in the context of copyright infringement.[33] In *Milpurrurru v Indofurn Pty Ltd,*[34] three bark paintings, a lino cut and three acrylic Papunya style paintings by eight leading, internationally renowned Aboriginal artists were unlawfully reproduced by the defendant who used them in carpet designs which were manufactured in Vietnam and imported into Australia. The Federal Court held that there had been direct and indirect infringement of the artists' copyright in the images and awarded damages to the artists and the legal representatives for this breach. In making his award, von Doussa J held that ordinary damages under s 115(2) of the *Copyright Act 1968* could include compensation for personal suffering, including the personal distress, embarrassment and contempt suffered by the artists within their communities as a result of the cultural harm caused by the infringement. Rather than award damages under this head, however, he assessed the serious-ness of the breach and the cultural harm caused to the applicant artists to award additional damages under s 115(4). Note that these damages did not amount to damages to the community itself for the unauthorised reproduction. Although the works could only be made by the artists under the authority of the community, the court held that this did not give the community itself any relevant property in the works in so far as the community was not a joint author of the works for the purposes of the *Copyright Act 1968.*

Four years later, von Doussa J had another chance to consider the nature of the relationship between indigenous artists, their communities and cultural prop-erty under the *Copyright Act 1968* in *Bulun Bulun v R and T Textiles Pty Ltd.*[35] Bulun Bulun and Milpurrurru were the two senior members of the Ganalbingu people in Arnhem Land. Bulun Bulun created the art work in question as part of his responsibility as an owner of the land known as Djulibinyamurr and with the authority of the people. He took action as the legal owner of the copyright in the work. Milpurrurru took action in his own right and as a representative of the Ganalbingu people, who, together with the Yolngu people, are traditional owners of the Ganalbingu country.

The applicants initially argued that the interest of the community in cultural property was an incident of native title and that this was inseparable from their interest in the land and should be recognised by the common law. In the alterna-tive, the applicants argued that the community had an equitable interest in the copyright subsisting in the artistic work which was incidental to their interest in the land and that the artist stood in a fiduciary relationship to the community in relation to the work in question.

The applicants' argument that their interest in artistic works was an incident of native title appears to be based on Brennan J's definition of native title in *Mabo v Queensland (No 2)*:

> Native title has its origin in and is given its content by traditional laws acknowledged by and the traditional customs observed by the Indigenous inhabitants of a territory. The

---

33    In her online article, "Moral Rights and Protecting the Cultural Rights of Indigenous Artists" (2000) 3 *Art & Law* <http://www.artslaw.com.au/reference/003moral_rights_indig Terri Janke succinctly explains the significance of regarding moral rights and the protection of cultural property from a community point of view.

34    *Milpurrurru v Indofurn Pty Ltd* (1994) 130 ALR 639.

35    (1998) 157 ALR 193.

nature and incidents of native title must be ascertained as a matter of fact with reference to those laws and customs.[36]

However, Brennan J's definition was subject to the ultimate limitation that "recognition by our common law of the rights and interests of the Indigenous inhabitants of a settled colony would be precluded if the recognition would fracture a skeletal principle of our legal system".[37]

In *Bulun Bulun* von Doussa J rejected the native title argument on the basis that this would amount to conflating the separate notions of ownership of land and ownership of artistic works and as such would fracture a skeletal principle of the common law.[38] In addition, the judge held that, even if the common law could recognise a communal title in copyright law, any such common law interest had been explicitly abolished by the *Copyright Act 1911*. The court, however, did find that there was a fiduciary relationship between the artist and the community in regard to the works produced under the community's authority but held that this did not give the community any right to sue for infringement of copyright in its own right. Rather, the interest simply gave the community the right to take action against the artist if the artist failed to perform his fiduciary duties. In this case there had been no such failure in so far as the artist had protected the interests of the community by taking action for infringement against the defendants.

There are currently no immediate moves afoot to grant actual copyright to indigenous communities in respect of works produced under the authority of the community. In 2003, however, the Coalition Government undertook to introduce legislation to grant moral rights to indigenous communities in respect of indigenous cultural property in which copyright subsists.[39] This would have been a significant reform in so far as it would give indigenous communities, not just the author, standing to prevent certain inappropriate, derogatory or culturally insensitive use of works and films which embody traditional knowledge and wisdom. It was expected that the rights would reflect existing moral rights for artists, that is, a right for the indigenous community to be attributed in connection with the work or film; the right of the community not to be falsely attributed and the right to prevent derogatory treatment of the work under the right of integrity provisions.

A draft of the proposed legislation was circulated for comment. Despite some serious reservations about the proposed legislation from some indigenous communities, the Coalition Government of the time advised that it would proceed with the legislation in 2006. Since then, that government has lost power and the new Labor Government has not signalled its intentions regarding moral rights for indigenous communities. This is an issue that will not disappear, however, and we can expect continued movement, especially at the international level.

---

36 (1992) 175 CLR 1 at 58.

37 (1992) 175 CLR 1 at 43.

38 For an interesting critique of this position, see Kristen Howden, "Indigenous Traditional Knowledge and Native Title" (2001) 24 *UNSWLJ* 12.

39 See the joint media release of 13 May 2003 by Senator Vanstone, then Minister for Immigration and Multicultural and Ethnic Affairs and Minister Assisting the Prime Minister for Reconciliation, and Senator Richard Alston, then Minister for Communications, Information Technology and the Arts and The Hon Daryl Williams, then Attorney-General.

# CASES

## *Bulun Bulun v R and T Textiles Pty Ltd*
Federal Court of Australia: von Doussa J
(1998) 157 ALR 193

Bulun Bulun and Milpurrurru were the two senior members of the Ganalbingu people in Arnhem Land. Bulun Bulun created an art work as part of his responsibility as an owner of the land and with the authority of the people. He took action as the legal owner of the copyright in the work. Milpurrurru took action in his own right and as a representative of the Ganalbingu people, who, together with the Yolngu people, are traditional owners of the Ganalbingu country.

### von Doussa J: [204] Why the claim is confined to one for recognition of an equitable interest

The submissions of counsel for the applicants reflected a wide ranging search for a way in which the communal interests of the traditional Aboriginal owners in cultural artworks might be recognised under Australian law. This exercise was painstakingly pursued by counsel for the applicants (and later by counsel for the Minister). That the claim was ultimately confined to one for recognition of an equitable interest in the legal copyright of Mr Bulun Bulun is an acknowledgment that no other possible avenue had emerged from the researches of counsel.

Whilst it is superficially attractive to postulate that the common law should recognise communal title, it would be contrary to established legal principle for the common law to do so. There seems no reason to doubt that customary Aboriginal laws relating to the ownership of artistic works survived the introduction of the common law of England in 1788. The Aboriginal peoples did not cease to observe their *sui generis* system of rights and obligations upon the acquisition of sovereignty of Australia by the Crown. The question however is whether those Aboriginal laws can create binding obligations on persons outside the relevant Aboriginal community, either through recognition of those laws by the common law, or by their capacity to found equitable rights *in rem*.

In *Mabo (No 2)* Deane and Gaudron JJ, after analysing the effects of the introduction of the common law of England into Australia in 1788 said, at 79 "The common law so introduced was adjusted in accordance with the principle that, in settled colonies, only so much of it was introduced as was 'reasonably applicable to the circumstances of the colony'. This left room for the continued operation of some [205] local laws or customs among the native people and even the incorporation of some of those laws and customs as part of the common law." (Some footnotes omitted.)

In 1788 there may have been scope for the continued operation of a system of indigenous collective ownership in artistic works. At that time the common law of England gave the author of an artistic work property in unpublished compositions which lasted in perpetuity: *Mansell v Valley Printing Company* [1908] 1 Ch 567 and Laddie, Prescott and Vitoria, *The Modern Law of Copyright* (1980), para 4.64. That property was lost upon publication of the artistic work. Exhibition for sale or sale constituted publication: *Britain v Hanks Bros and Co* (1902) 86 LT 765. This property interest was separate from the right recognised in equity to restrain a breach of confidence, a right which continues and was invoked in *Foster v Mountford and Rigby Ltd* (1976) 14 ALR 71. The common law of England did not protect an author of an artistic work after publication. If the common law had not been amended in the meantime by statute, an interesting question would arise as to whether Aboriginal laws and customs could be incorporated into the common law. However, the common law has since been subsumed by statute. The common law right until first publication was abolished when the law of copyright was codified by the *Copyright Act* of 1911 in the United Kingdom. That Act, subject to some modifications, became the law in Australia by s 8 of the *Copyright Act 1912* (Cth). Copyright is now entirely a creature of statute: McKeough and Stewart, *Intellectual Property in Australia* (1991) at para 504, *Copinger and Skone James on Copyright* (13th ed), paras 1-43. The exclusive domain of the *Copyright Act 1968* in Australia is expressed in s 8 (subject only to the qualification in s 8A) namely that "copyright does not subsist otherwise than by virtue of this Act".

Section 35(2) of the *Copyright Act 1968* provides that the author of an artistic work is the owner of the copyright which subsists by virtue of the Act. That provision effectively precludes any notion of group ownership in an artistic work, unless the artistic work is a "work of joint ownership" within the meaning of s 10(1) of the Act. A "work of joint authorship" means a work that has been produced by the collaboration of two or more authors and in which the contribution of each author is not separate from the contribution of the other author or the contributions of the other authors. In this case no evidence was led to suggest that anyone other than Mr Bulun Bulun was the creative author of the artistic work. A person who supplies an artistic idea to an artist who then executes the work is not, on that ground alone, a joint author with the artist: *Kenrick & Co v Lawrence & Co* (1890) 25 QBD 99. Joint authorship envisages the contribution of skill and labour to the production of the work itself: *Fylde Microsystems Ltd v Kay Radio Systems Ltd* (1998) 39 IPR 481 at 486.

In *Coe v Commonwealth* (1993) 118 ALR 193 at 200 Mason CJ rejected the proposition that Aboriginal people are entitled to rights and interests other than those created or recognised by the laws of the Commonwealth, its states and the common law. See also *Walker v New South Wales* at 45-50 and Kirby J in *Wik Peoples v Queensland* at 214. To conclude that the Ganalbingu people were communal owners of the copyright in the existing work would ignore the provisions of s 8 of the *Copyright Act*, and involve the creation of rights in indigenous peoples which are not otherwise recognised by the legal system of Australia.

### [206] Do the circumstances in which the artistic work was created give rise to equitable interests in the Ganalbingu People?

The statement of claim alleges "on the reduction to material form of a part of the ritual knowledge of the Ganalbingu people associated with Djulibinyamurr by the creation of the artistic work, the first applicant held the copyright subsisting in the artistic work as a fiduciary and/or alternatively on trust, for the second applicant and the people he represents". The foundation for this contention is expanded in written submissions made on Mr Milpurrurru's behalf. It is contended that these rights arise because Mr Milpurrurru and those he represents have the power under customary law to regulate and control the production and reproduction of the corpus of ritual knowledge. It is contended that the customs and traditions regulating this use of the corpus of ritual knowledge places Mr Bulun Bulun as the author of the artistic work in the position of a fiduciary, and, moreover, make Mr Bulun Bulun a trustee for the artwork, either pursuant to some form of express trust, or pursuant to a constructive trust in favour of the Ganalbingu people. The right to control the production and reproduction of the corpus of ritual knowledge relating to Djulibinyamurr is said to arise by virtue of the strong ties which continue to exist between the Ganalbingu people and their land.

### Was there an express trust?

The possibility that an express trust was created in respect of the artistic work or the copyright subsisting in it was not at the forefront of the applicants' submissions. In my opinion that possibility can be dismissed on the evidence in this case. ...

**[207] Did Mr Bulun Bulun hold the copyright as a fiduciary?**

In *Breen v Williams* (1996) 186 CLR 71 at 82; 138 ALR 259, Brennan CJ identified two sources of fiduciary duties, the first being the circumstances in which a relationship of agency can be said to exist, and the other is founded in a relationship of ascendancy or influence by one party over another, or dependence or trust on the part of that other. ...

**[208]** The essential characteristics of fiduciary relationships were referred to by Mason J in *Hospital Products* at 96-7:

> The critical feature of [fiduciary] relationships is that the fiduciary undertakes or agrees to act for or on behalf of or in the interests of another person in the exercise of a power or discretion which will affect the interests of that other person in a legal or practical sense.
>
> The relationship between the parties is therefore one which gives the fiduciary a special opportunity to exercise the power or discretion to the detriment of that other person who is accordingly vulnerable to abuse by the fiduciary of his position ... It is partly because the fiduciary's exercise of the power or discretion can adversely affect the interests of the person to whom the duty is owed and because the latter is at the mercy of the former that the fiduciary comes under a duty to exercise his power or discretion in the interests of the person to whom it is owed.

In *Mabo (No 2)*, Toohey J said at 200:

> Underlying such relationships is the scope for one party to exercise a discretion which is capable of affecting the legal position of the other. One party has a special opportunity to abuse the interests of the other. The discretion will be an incident of the first party's office or position.

In *Wik Peoples v Queensland* (1996) 187 CLR 1 at 95 Brennan CJ said with respect to the asserted existence of a fiduciary duty owed by the Crown to the indigenous inhabitants of the leased areas under consideration:

> It is necessary to identify some action or function the doing or performance of which attracts the supposed fiduciary duty to be observed: *Breen v Williams* (1996) 186 CLR 71 at 82. The doing of the action or the performance of the function must be capable of affecting the interests of the beneficiary and the fiduciary must have so acted that it is reasonable for the beneficiary to believe and expect that the fiduciary will **[209]** act in the interests of the beneficiary (or, in the case of a partnership or joint venture, in the common interest of the beneficiary and fiduciary) to the exclusion of the interest of any other person or the separate interest of the beneficiary. (Some footnotes omitted.)

See also the discussion of fiduciary relationships in *News Ltd v ARL* at 563-7, and Weinrib, "The Fiduciary Obligation" (1975) 25 *University of Toronto Law Journal* 1 at 4-8.

In *Hodgkinson v Simms* (1994) 117 DLR (4th) 161, La Forest J expressed the question whether a fiduciary relationship existed as being "whether, given all the surrounding circumstances, one party could reasonably have expected that the other party would act in the former's best interests with respect to the subject-matter at issue" (see also *LAC Minerals Ltd v International Corona Resources Ltd* (1989) 61 DLR (4th) 14 at 40. As the statement of Brennan CJ in *Wik* at 95 (above) reflects, the law of fiduciary relations in this country has followed that of Canada in recognising the protection of reasonable expectations as a fundamental purpose of the fiduciary concept: see also Parkinson (ed), *The Principles of Equity* (1996), PD Finn, "The Fiduciary Principle" in TG Youdan (ed), *Equity, Fiduciaries and Trusts* (1989), p. 46 and *Commonwealth Bank of Australia v Smith* (1991) 102 ALR 453 at 476.

The Court was not referred to any authority in support of the imposition of equitable principles to govern relations amongst members of a tribal group. However, the application of the principles of equity in this situation is not unknown to the common law as it has been applied outside of this country. Amongst tribal communities of African countries tribal property is regarded as being held on "trust" by the customary head of a tribal group: see SKB Asante "Fiduciary Principles in Anglo-American Law and The Customary Law of Ghana" (1965) 14 *International & Comparative Law Quarterly* 1144 at 1145. This principle received judicial recognition in *Kwan v Nyieni* (1959) 1 GLR 67 at 72-3 where the Court of Appeal of Ghana held that members of the tribal group were entitled to initiate proceedings for the purpose of preserving family property in the event of the failure of the head of the tribal group to do so. The head of the tribal group is regarded as a fiduciary: SKB Asante, at 1149.

The relationship between Mr Bulun Bulun as the author and legal title holder of the artistic work and the Ganalbingu people is unique. The "transaction" between them out of which fiduciary relationship is said to arise is the use with permission by Mr Bulun Bulun of ritual knowledge of the Ganalbingu people, and the embodiment of that knowledge within the artistic work. That use has been permitted in accordance with the law and customs of the Ganalbingu people.

The grant of permission by the djungayi and other appropriate representatives of the Ganalbingu people for the creation of the artistic work is predicated on the trust and confidence which those granting permission have in the artist. The evidence indicates that if those who must give permission do not have trust and confidence in someone seeking permission, permission will not be granted.

The law and customs of the Banalbingu people require that the use of the ritual knowledge and the artistic work be in accordance with the requirements of law and custom, and that the author of the artistic work do whatever is necessary to prevent any misuse. The artist is required to act in relation to the artwork in the interests of the Ganalbingu people to preserve the integrity of their culture, and ritual knowledge.

This is not to say that the artist must act entirely in the interests of the Ganalbingu people. The evidence shows that an artist is entitled to consider and **[210]** pursue his own interests, for example by selling the artwork, but the artist is not permitted to shed the overriding obligation to act to preserve the integrity of the Ganalbingu culture where action for that purpose is required.

In my opinion, the nature of the relationship between Mr Bulun Bulun and the Ganalbingu people was a fiduciary one which gives rise to fiduciary obligations owed by Mr Bulun Bulun.

The conclusion that in all the circumstances Mr Bulun Bulun owes fiduciary obligations to the Ganalbingu people does not treat the law and custom of the Ganalbingu people as part of the Australian legal system. Rather, it treats the law and custom of the Ganalbingu people as part of the factual matrix which characterises the relationship as one of mutual trust and confidence. It is that relationship which the Australian legal system recognises as giving rise to the fiduciary relationship, and to the obligations which arise out of it.

It is convenient at this point to dispose of an alternative submission raised as a possibility by the applicants in argument, although not seriously pressed. That is that the facts are open to the construction that there was a contract between Mr Bulun Bulun and those who gave him permission to create the artistic work (acting on behalf of the Ganalbingu people), and that the contract imposed obligations akin to fiduciary obligations, or even created an equitable interest, in the artwork. It is not inconceivable that contractual arrangements could be made between representatives of a clan and a particular artist as to the circumstances in which ritual knowledge could be incorporated into an artistic work. Arrangements between members of tribal groups have been characterised as contractual creating personal rights and obligations in Ghana – see HA Amankwar, "Recognition of Customary Law" (1994) 18 *UQLJ* 15 at 19. In accordance with ordinary principles, it would be necessary to identify the parties, the terms, the consideration for the contract and an intention to create legal relations. In the present case the evidence does not address the last three of these matters. There is no suggestion in the evidence that there was any form of express agreement of a contractual nature in which terms were agreed. It is possible, of course, for there to be a contract the terms of which arise by implication. In *BP Refinery (Western-Port) Pty Ltd v Shire of Hastings* (1977) 180 CLR 266 at 283 the Privy Council said that for a term to be applied, the following conditions (which may overlap) must be satisfied: (1) it must be reasonable and equitable; (2) it must be necessary to give business efficacy to the contract, so that no term will be applied if the contract is effective without it; (3) it must be so obvious that "it goes without saying"; (4) it must be capable of clear expression; (5) it must not contradict any express term of the contract. Whilst general evidence has been given as to the nature of Aboriginal law and customs governing the use of traditional ritual knowledge that evidence does not descend to the level of detail which would permit terms to be implied in accordance with these conditions. The evidence does not suggest that permission to create the artwork was given in circumstances which were intended to create a contractual relationship.

**The fiduciary obligation**
Central to the fiduciary concept is the protection of interests that can be regarded as worthy of judicial protection: Glover, *Commercial Equity – Fiduciary Relationships* (1995), para 3.4. The evidence is all one way. The ritual knowledge relating to Djulibinyamurr embodied within the artistic work is of great importance to members of the Ganalbingu people. I have no hesitation in **[211]** holding that the interest of Ganalbingu people in the protection of that ritual knowledge from exploitation which is contrary to their law and custom is deserving of the protection of the Australian legal system.

Under the *Copyright Act*, the owner of the copyright has the exclusive right to reproduce the work in a material form, and to publish the work. The copyright owner is entitled to enforce copyright against the world at large. In the event of infringement, the copyright owner is entitled to sue and to obtain remedies of the kind actually obtained by Mr Bulun Bulun in this case.

Having regard to the evidence of the law and customs of the Ganalbingu people under which Mr Bulun Bulun was permitted to create the artistic work, I consider that equity imposes on him obligations as a fiduciary not to exploit the artistic work in a way that is contrary to the laws and custom of the Ganalbingu people, and, in the event of infringement by a third party, to take reasonable and appropriate action to restrain and remedy infringement of the copyright in the artistic work.

Whilst the nature of the relationship between Mr Bulun Bulun and the Ganalbingu people is such that Mr Bulun Bulun falls under fiduciary obligations to protect the ritual knowledge which he has been permitted to use, the existence of those obligations does not, without more, vest an equitable interest in the ownership of the copyright in the Ganalbingu people. Their primary right, in the event of a breach of obligation by the fiduciary is a right in personam to bring action against the fiduciary to enforce the obligation.

In the present case Mr Bulun Bulun has successfully taken action against the respondent to obtain remedies in respect of the infringement. There is no suggestion by Mr Milpurrurru and those whom he seeks to represent that Mr Bulun Bulun should have done anything more. In these circumstances there is no occasion for the intervention of equity to provide any additional remedy to the beneficiaries of the fiduciary relationship.

However, had the position been otherwise equitable remedies could have been available. The extent of those remedies would depend on all the circumstances, and in an extreme case could involve the intervention of equity to impose a constructive trust on the legal owner of the copyright in the artistic work in favour of the beneficiaries. Equity will not automatically impose a constructive trust merely upon the identification of a fiduciary obligation. Equity will impose a constructive trust on property held by a fiduciary where it is necessary to do so to achieve a just remedy and to prevent the fiduciary from retaining an unconscionable benefit: *Muschinski v Dodds* (1985) 160 CLR 385 at 619-20 and *Baumgartner v Baumgartner* (1987) 164 CLR 137 at 148. By way of example, had Mr Bulun Bulun merely failed to take action to enforce his copyright, an adequate remedy might be extended in equity to the beneficiaries by allowing them to bring action in their own names against the infringer and the copyright owner, claiming against the former, in the first instance, interlocutory relief to restrain the infringement, and against the latter orders necessary to ensure that the copyright owner enforces the copyright. Probably there would be no occasion for equity in these circumstances to impose a constructive trust.

On the other hand, were Mr Bulun Bulun to deny the existence of fiduciary obligations and the interests of the parties asserting them, and refuse to protect the copyright from infringement, then the occasion might exist for equity to impose a remedial constructive trust upon the copyright owner to strengthen the standing of the beneficiaries to bring proceedings to enforce the copyright. This **[212]** may be necessary if the copyright owner cannot be identified or found and the beneficiaries are unable to join the legal owner of the copyright: *see Performing Rights Society Ltd v London Theatre of Varieties* [1924] AC 1 at 18.

It is well recognised that interlocutory injunctive relief can be claimed by a party having an equitable interest in copyright: Laddie, Prescott and Vitoria, *The Modern Law of Copyright* (1995) paras 11.79-11.81, although as a matter of practice injunctive relief will not be granted without the legal owner of copyright being joined: *Performing Rights Society Ltd v London Theatre of Varieties* at 19-20, 29, *Acorn Computers Ltd v MCS Microcomputer Systems Pty Ltd* (1984) 57 ALR 389 at 394. For an example of proceedings brought to establish the existence of an equitable interest in copyright based on a constructive trust imposed in consequence of a breach of fiduciary duty see *Missinglink Software v Magee* [1989] 1 FSR 361 at 367.

I do not consider Mr Milpurrurru and those he seeks to represent have established an equitable interest in the copyright in the artistic work. In my opinion they have established that fiduciary obligations are owed to them by Mr Bulun Bulun, but as Mr Bulun Bulun has taken appropriate action to enforce the copyright, he has fulfilled those obligations and there is no occasion to grant any additional remedy in favour of the Ganalbingu people. However, in other circumstances if the copyright owner of an artistic work which embodies ritual knowledge of an Aboriginal clan is being used inappropriately, and the copyright owner fails or refuses to take appropriate action to enforce the copyright, the Australian legal system will permit remedial action through the courts by the clan.

For these reasons, the proceedings by Mr Milpurrurru must be dismissed.

### *Meskenas v ACP Publishing Pty Ltd*
Federal Magistrates Court of Australia: Raphael FM
[2006] FMCA 1136

Mr Vladas Meskenas is a known artist. The *Woman's Day* published a photograph of Princess Mary standing in front of a portrait of Dr Victor Chang which had been painted by Mr Meskenas. Not only was the photograph printed back to front but the painting was incorrectly attributed to another artist. Evidence showed that the mistake had been caused as a result of editorial error and that *Woman's Day* had failed to print an apology despite discussions with the artist. The Federal Magistrate held that it did not matter that the false attribution had not been "purposely wrong"; it was sufficient that it was "incorrect".

**Raphael FM: The applicant's moral rights**

15. It is not in dispute that the applicant is the author of the portrait. He is therefore entitled to the three moral rights now found in Part 9 of the *Copyright Act* and derived from the *Copyright Amendment (Moral Rights) Act 2000* (Cth). The work is an artistic work in which copyright subsists. The applicant is an individual ...

16. The publication of the portrait gives rise to a requirement for an attribution of authorship under s 194(2)(d). It is clear from the photograph that the portrait itself is of significant importance and is not just incidental to the composition of the photograph. I infer from the fact that an attribution was made, albeit the wrong one, that the respondent accepted it was bound by s 194(2)(d).

17. The respondent raises two arguments to resist a finding that it has infringed the applicant's moral rights, in particular the rights not to have the authorship falsely attributed and the right of attribution. As I understand its argument in respect of the alleged infringement of the right of attribution it says that the making of a wrong attribution has the effect that the author of the work is not identified and thus it can seek to utilise the defence found at s 195AR.

18. The right of attribution expressed in s 193 is a positive right and prima facie was breached by the publication. The publication did not identify Vladas Meskenas as the author. In looking at the matters to be taken into account in deciding whether or not it was reasonable not to identify Mr Meskenas in s 195AR(2), I cannot see there is anything in the nature of the work which would prevent him from being properly identified. As I understand the evidence the portrait was signed. There was no evidence provided to me by the respondents to indicate that there was anything difficult arising out of the purpose for which the work was used in identifying him nor in respect of the manner or context in which it was used. The identification of another artist would seem to indicate that the magazine had no trouble about making an identification, albeit a wrong one. There was no evidence about any practice in the industry which was relevant, nor was there any evidence of a voluntary code or difficulty or expense as a result of identifying the author. I would not be inclined to hold that it was reasonable in all the circumstances not to identify the author.

19. The second argument put by the respondent is that there is a requirement for some form of intent in order to have infringed the author's right not to have the work falsely attributed. This raises the issue of the meaning of the word "falsely" in the context of the Act.

20. Whether "false" in the moral rights provisions of the *Copyright Act* means "purposely wrong" or simply "incorrect" is ultimately a question of statutory construction given there is no accepted definition of "false". The High Court case of *Murphy v Farmer* (1989) 79 ALR 1 (*"Murphy"*) is authority for the proposition that where a provision is properly construed as penal or quasi-penal in character, the word "false" is to be construed to mean 'purposely or deliberately or intentionally untrue'. The majority did not, however, specifically decide what the meaning of "false" is – indeed their Honours expressly stated they were not deciding the case on the basis of either attribution of meaning ...

31. I am satisfied that unless it could be suggested that there were some quasi-penal ramifications to a finding of infringement of moral rights the word "falsely" used in the context of s 194 does not require an intention and will bear the meaning of objectively incorrect.

32. The remedies for infringement of moral rights are set out in s 195AZA(1) *Copyright Act* ...

33. Quasi-penal' does not have an authoritative definition in case law. It has been used, as was seen in *Murphy*, to describe a provision where there is a pecuniary penalty for breaching a provision (ie forfeiture). Consequences of bankruptcy have been described as 'quasi-penal' ...

34. A general consideration of the provisions of s 195AZA(1) leads one to the view that the purpose of them is restitutional. This subsection can be contrasted with ss 115(4), that might well be construed as providing for a pecuniary penalty for an infringing act. I am of the view that the respondent cannot escape liability for its actions in infringing the moral right of the applicant not to falsely attribute the authorship of the painting on the ground submitted.

# Part III

# Patents

Chapter 8

# The Patent System

Patents are the oldest form of intellectual property and patent registration systems, in a form which we would recognise today, began to emerge in Europe in the late Middle Ages and in Britain in the late 15th century.

Before the establishment of the English registration system, the English Crown granted protection and safe-conduct to foreign craftsmen to enable them to practise their trade in England without interference from the local guilds. In return for this privilege the craftsmen were expected to settle in England and instruct native craftsmen in the relevant art.[1] Hulme refers to the "native cloth industry" as the first to benefit from this intervention by the Crown to promote industry. It has been said that the Crown was granting "franchises as many and such as may suffice" to foreign textile industry craftsmen. However, the grant of such a franchise was said to be for the "sake of the public good", that is, to develop English industry which had been lagging behind its Continental counterparts.[2]

The making of royal grants in medieval England took one of two forms. Either the document was folded, closed and sealed, "Literae Clausae", so that the seal needed to be broken for the document to be read, or the document was left open for anyone to be able to read it and the seal placed on the document in that state, "Literae Patens". It is suggested that the Latin word "patens", meaning "to be open", is the origin for today's "patent" which denotes a grant to an inventor.[3]

In 1474 the Venetian state passed a patent statute which contained many of the features to be found in modern patent legislation. Inventors of "new and ingenious device[s]" were granted privileges so that "devices of great utility and benefit" would be built. The object of this patent system was to stimulate indigenous invention and the inflow of technology:

> WE HAVE among us men of great genius, apt to invent and discover ingenious devices; and in view of the grandeur and virtue of our City, more such men come to us every day

---

1   E Hulme, "The History of the Patent System under the Prerogative and at Common Law" (1896) 12 *LQR* 141 at 141-143.

2   E Hulme, "The History of the Patent System under the Prerogative and at Common Law" (1896) 12 *LQR* 141 at 141-143.

3   S Ricketson, "The Law of Intellectual Property", Law Book Co, Sydney, 1984, p 860.

from diverse parts. Now, if provision were made for the works and devices discovered by such persons, so that others who may see them could not build them and take the inventor's honour away, more men would then apply their genius, would discover, and would build devices of great utility and benefit to our Commonwealth.[4]

Elizabeth I and James I made extensive use of the Crown prerogative to grant monopolies to raise revenue.[5] There appeared to be little limit to the form of these monopoly grants and they were certainly not limited to inventions. Sir Francis Drake, for example, was the recipient of a grant to import wine and the East India Company had a grant to exploit India.

The use of the Crown prerogative in this way became the subject of strong parliamentary protest and, at the end of the reign of Elizabeth I, in 1602, the Case of Monopolies, *Darcy v Allin*,[6] was decided. In that case Darcy had been granted the sole right to import playing cards and restrain their manufacture and sale by others in the realm. Thomas Allin, a haberdasher, ordered and sold playing cards for a lesser price than Darcy. Darcy sued Allin for infringing his letters patent. The Queen's Bench found for the defendant, Allin, and declared the patent void and unlawful. The court went to great pains to draw the distinction between the nature of Darcy's patent and the allowable "monopoly patents" for one's "own wit or invention". The Darcy patent, the court found, created an unreasonable restraint of trade, increased prices and tended to reduce quality.

Despite this case and the ensuing *Book of Bounty* (1610),[7] James I continued Elizabeth's practice of granting monopolies until the passing of the *Statute of Monopolies* in 1624 by the House of Commons. The *Statute of Monopolies 1623* declared all monopolies for the sole buying, selling, making or using of anything in the realm to be void. This was subject to the significant exception under s IV that monopolies might be granted in respect of appropriate subject-matter, that is, a "manner of new manufacture" made by an inventor:

> Provided also, and be it declared and enacted, that any declaration before mentioned shall not extend to any letters-patent and grants of privilege, for the term of fourteen years or under, hereafter to be made of the sole working or making of any manner of new manufacture within this realm, to the true and first inventor and inventors of such manufactures, which others, at the time of making such letters-patent or grant, shall not use, so as also they be not contrary to the law, nor mischievous to the state, by raising prices of commodities at home, or hurt of trade, or generally inconvenient; the said fourteen years to be accounted from the date of the first letters-patent or grant of such privilege, hereafter to be made, but that the same shall be of such force, as they should be, if this act had never been made and of none other.

The 14-year term of patent protection, stipulated in the *Statute of Monopolies 1623*, enabled the exclusive use of the technology for a period of two consecutive

---

4    From the Venetian statute of 1474 as quoted in G Mandich, "Venetian Patents (1450-1550)" (1948) 30 *JPOS* 166 at 176-177.

5    K Boehm, *The British Patent System, Vol 1: Administration*, Cambridge University Press, Cambridge, 1967, pp 14-15.

6    *a*.

7    James I declared the common law of patents and introduced the *Book of Bounty* (1610) as a means of gaining the support of his subjects. Common law hostility was declared toward monopolies with exceptions including patents of invention.

apprenticeships. At the end of this term of protection the patent would be available to anyone who wished to use it.

This system of patent protection as it developed through the Industrial Revolution and as it continues today is essentially two pronged. In return for the grant of a monopoly for an invention the inventor must disclose that invention to the public in "specifications" and clearly "claim" the monopoly in relation to identified aspects of that invention. The detailed description thus allows an expert to perform the invention and the limit on the claim allows others to develop the invention. The *Patents Designs and Trade Marks Act 1883* (UK) rationalised the already codified procedures for obtaining and enforcing patent rights in Britain. It was introduced in accordance with the United Kingdom's obligations under the first international patent agreement found in the *Paris Convention for the Protection of Industrial Property 1883* (the Paris Convention).

In Australia, before Federation, each Australian colony had its own Patents Act and by virtue of the United Kingdom becoming a party to the Paris Convention on 7 July 1884, Australian colonies became members of the Convention. Following Federation these Acts continued in force until the passing of the *Patents Act 1903* in exercise of the s 51(xviii) power under the Constitution. It was not until 10 October 1925 that Australia became a party to the Convention in its own right. Subsequently, the 1903 Act was repealed in favour of the *Patents Act 1952* which was based on the *Patents Act 1949* (UK). The 1952 Act established the administrative system of the Patent Office which processed applications, maintained a Register of Patents and granted a term of protection for 16 years. The Australian and British systems went their separate ways once the *Patents Act 1977* (UK) was introduced as a result of the United Kingdom joining the European Patent Convention.

These developments recognise the important influence of the various international treaties that have been established since 1883 dealing with such issues as patent administration, the scope of protection and international cooperation. We will discuss these treaties and agreements at the end of this chapter.

In 1979, following international developments, Australia introduced petty patents designed to provide protection for innovations with "a short commercially-exploitable life, such as household or office accessories, gadgets, small appliances and so on".[8] Petty patent applications were processed more quickly and cheaply than standard patents, and were granted for an initial 12-month period with a possible six-year extension. The petty patents system provided only limited avenues for opposition by third parties. In the case of standard patents a third party could oppose the grant of a patent in the first instance. In the case of petty patents, however, a third party could only oppose the extension of a patent beyond the initial 12-month period. In addition, whilst standard patents were assessed for novelty and inventiveness against international standards, petty patents were assessed only against limited domestic standards. The petty patent system has, since 2000, been replaced by the "innovation patent" system in keeping, once again, with international developments.

---

8   See Second Reading Speech of the Hon Ian McPhee, *Hansard,* House of Representatives, 21 February 1979, p 183.

In October 1990 the *Patents Act 1952* was repealed and replaced by the *Patents Act 1990* which was designed to do two things. First, the Act was said to be designed to bring "the language and the structure of the Act down to earth, so that mere mortals without law degrees have some chance of understanding what it is all about – at least in general terms".[9] Secondly, the Act was designed to implement a number of policy changes flowing from the Industrial Property Advisory Committee Report released in 1984. The Committee had recommended that the patent system be maintained but that it should be amended to enhance the fostering of indigenous innovation and development of expert markets, reduce anti-competitive conduct involving patents and to improve the efficiency of the system, for example, by streamlining procedures so as to reduce costs.[10]

This text deals with the *Patents Act 1990*, however, much of the established case law is based on the 1952 legislation. This should be kept in mind although basic principles of patent law have been maintained and the past 20 years has seen emerging trends in the case law applying the 1990 legislation, and focus on quality in the *Raising the Bar*[11] amendments to the patent law.

## Rationales for a Patent System

It might seem to be something of a paradox to grant patents for inventions when one considers that patents are monopolies and monopolies are generally seen to be contrary to the right of freedom of trade and liable to lead to high prices and low quality of goods. However, Lord Parker in the House of Lords case, *Attorney-General (Cth) v Adelaide Steamship Co*,[12] attempted to explain away this paradox simply:

> A monopoly being a derogation from the common right of freedom of trade could not be granted without consideration moving to the public ... In the case of new inventions the consideration was found either in the interest of the public to encourage inventive ingenuity or more probably in the disclosure made to the public of a new and useful article or process.[13]

The Intellectual Property and Competition Review Committee denied that there was any conflict between competition policy and intellectual property monopolies because innovation is one of the ways in which businesses compete:

> Intellectual property laws on the one hand and competition policy on the other are ... largely complementary. The intellectual property system serves to promote innovation, which is a key form of competition. Competition policy, by keeping markets open

---

9   Barry Jones, Minister for Science, Customs and Small Business, Second Reading Speech, *Hansard*, House of Representatives, 1 June 1989, p 3479.

10   See Industrial Property Advisory Committee, Part A "Reviewing the Australian Patent System", *Patents, Innovation and Competition in Australia*, 1984, p 19.

11   IP Australia embarked upon its quest to develop a stronger and more efficient system in early 2009 with a series of consultation papers commencing with the *Getting the Balance Right* (Consultation Paper, March 2009). These then resulted in the *Intellectual Property Laws Amendment (Raising the Bar) Act 2012*. The majority of amendments will come into force on 15 April 2013, one year after the date of Royal Assent; however the experimental use and regulatory use provisions came into force the day after Royal Assent.

12   [1913] AC 781.

13   [1913] AC 781 at 793.

and effective, preserves the primary source of the pressure to innovate and diffuse innovations.[14]

Machlup and Penrose[15] have identified four main rationales put forward in support of the patent system. These are the natural law thesis, the reward by monopoly thesis, the monopoly profit incentive thesis and the exchange for secrets thesis. As we saw in our discussion of copyright law, the natural law thesis, which would grant to each inventor the "fruits of his labour", was not widely adopted in common law jurisdictions although it is often said to be more acceptable in civil law jurisdictions.[16]

The three other theses presented by Machlup and Penrose are grounded in economic theory. The reward by monopoly thesis focuses on the inventor and uses another agricultural metaphor – no person should "reap without sowing". An inventor who has contributed to society by developing an invention should be able to rely on that society to reward him or her by preventing others from freely using the invention.

The monopoly profit incentive thesis focuses on the desirability of industrial development. Without making it financially worthwhile to develop new inventions, "inventions and/or their exploitation will not be obtained in sufficient measure" to encourage industrial development – hence temporary monopolies, in the form of patents, are the most effective incentive to invention.[17]

The exchange for secrets thesis marries the preceding two theses. The patent is the consideration that flows from society to the inventor for the disclosure of his or her inventions. This works on the premise that the inventor will keep the invention secret unless society somehow protects the inventor from the "free riders" we considered earlier. Society, on the other hand, considers disclosure of such secrets to encourage further industrial development. Accordingly, the granting of a patent is supposed to encourage inventive activity while the disclosure of inventions of the inventor encourages the desirable result of industrial development. Finally, it is argued, patents are a "source of technological information".[18] The patent specifications required for registration of an invention as a patent must fully describe the invention and the best possible way of performing it so that a person skilled in the relevant field would be able to replicate the invention. Patent specifications provide an invaluable source of technological information for persons undertaking research and development and attempting to build on current technologies.

---

14   Intellectual Property and Competition Review Committee, *Review of Intellectual Property Legislation under the Competition Principles Agreement. Final Report*, Executive Summary, September 2000.

15   F Machlup and E Penrose, "The Patent Controversy in the Nineteenth Century" (1950) 10 *J Econ Hist* 1. These have been refined by F Machlup in "An Economic Review of the Patent System", Study No 15 of the United States Senate Sub-Committee on Patents, Trademarks and Copyrights (1958) 85 Congress 21.

16   HI Dutton, *The Patent System and Inventive Activity During the Industrial Revolution 1750-1852*, Manchester University Press, Manchester, 1984, pp 17-29.

17   F Machlup, "An Economic Review of the Patent System", Study No 15 of the United States Senate Sub-Committee on Patents, Trademarks and Copyrights (1958) 85 Congress 21, n 16, p 21.

18   S Ricketson, *The Law of Intellectual Property*, Law Book Co, Sydney, 1984, p 860, n 4.

## Statutory Framework and System of Patent Registration

A patent is a monopoly right which grants the owner or patentee exclusive rights to exploit the patent for a fixed term of 20 years in the case of standard patents and eight years in the case of innovation patents (previously known as "petty patents"). The monopoly is granted in respect of "patentable inventions", that is an invention which is a "manner of new manufacture", that is novel and involves an inventive step and it must be in respect of an invention which is a proper subject for the grant of a patent.

In return for this grant of monopoly the inventor is required to disclose the invention to the public. Thus, an application for a patent may fail if the specifications lodged with the application do not describe the invention fully, including the best method known to the applicant for performing the invention, or if the monopoly claim is not clear.

Unlike copyright, the grant of patent rights depends on registration of the invention. This section examines the registration procedure in detail. As we shall see, designs protection, plant breeders' rights and trade marks, which are considered later in this text, are based on similar registration procedures. In the following chapters we consider the question of what is a "patentable invention" and conclude the discussion of patents with a chapter on a specific class of patents, namely, biotechnology-based patents which have been the subject of much current debate. Before that, infringement of and dealings in patents will be considered.

Like copyright law, patent law is territorial and therefore registration under the *Patents Act 1990* will provide monopoly protection for the invention in Australia only. To obtain protection in other countries owners of inventions traditionally had to make separate applications in each country. Under the *Paris Convention for the Protection of Industrial Property 1883* (Paris Convention) applicants have been assured equal treatment among member countries. Today this procedure is partly simplified by the *Patent Co-operation Treaty 1970* (PCT) establishing a system for lodging international applications, although the monopoly rights granted under the system are still territorial.

A detailed flowchart of the system of patent registration in Australia is found at s 4 of the Act. This flowchart serves as an illustration only and, where there is an inconsistency with a provision of the Act, the provision prevails. There are basically six possible stages to the patent process: application, examination, acceptance and publication, opposition, grant of letters patent, and revocation. The last of these stages highlights the fact, stated expressly in the Act, that grant or registration of a patent does not guarantee the validity of that patent.[19] Revocation may take place at any time during the patent period and often is associated with an infringement action as a form of counter-claim by an infringer of a patent. If the revocation stage is ignored for the moment perhaps the following simple flowchart (*see opposite*) serves to give an indication of the process of acquiring a patent.

The process is for the purpose of obtaining a standard patent and for the balance of the chapters devoted to patent law, the word "patent" will be synonymous with "standard patent", unless otherwise indicated. However, it should be

---

19   Section 20. Chapter 9 considers the elements of validity of a patent.

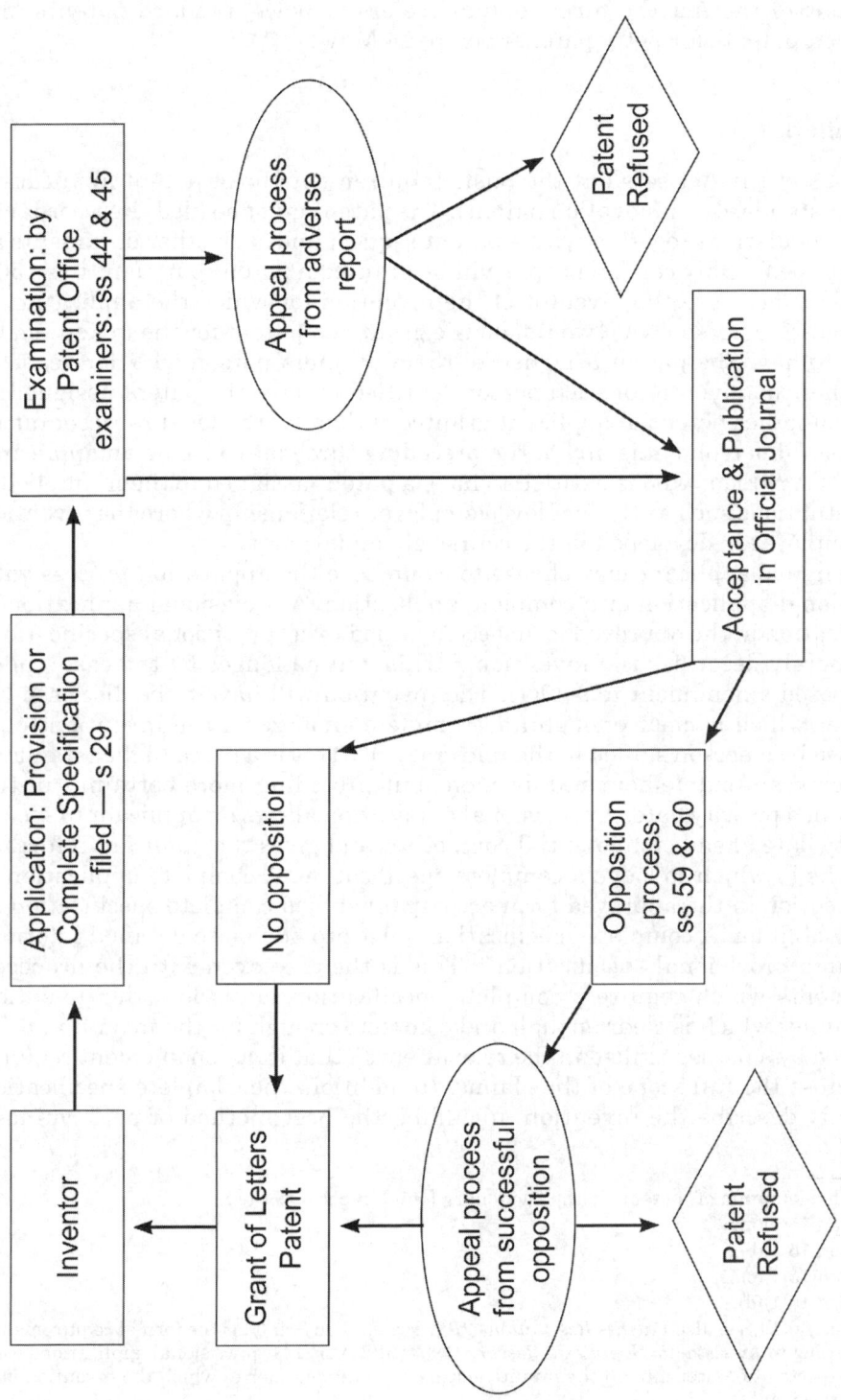

noted that in the Act the term "patent" refers to both standard patents and innovation patents (or petty patents before 24 May 2001).[20]

## Application

Section 29 of the Act sets out the basic requirements for a patent application (whether standard or innovation patent). The patent must be filed "in accordance with the regulations together with a patent request and such other documents as are prescribed". Only certain people will be granted a patent pursuant to s 15(1) of the Act. These are the inventor of the invention for which the application is being made;[21] a person who "would, on the grant of a patent for the invention, be entitled to have the patent assigned to them";[22] and a person who derives title from either the inventor or such person "entitled to have the patent assigned to them" is another potential applicant/grantee.[23] Finally, the legal representative of a deceased person being any of the preceding three may also be an applicant/grantee.[24] A person "who is entitled to have a patent assigned to them" impliedly covers situations such as the employee/employer relationship where the invention of the employee is developed in the course of employment.

An eligible applicant may choose to commence the application process with a provisional application or a complete application. A provisional application is an application in the approved form accompanied by a "provisional specification" which merely describes the invention.[25] This will no longer be the case under the proposed amendment to s 40(1). The invention will have to be disclosed "in a manner which is clear enough and complete enough for the invention to be performed by a person skilled in the relevant art". This is a much higher standard introducing an enablement requirement but providing more certainty in the securing of a priority date. A provisional application allows an applicant to secure a priority date ahead of a potential competitor and gives the applicant a further 12 months in which to lodge a complete specification. A complete application is an application in the approved form accompanied by a complete specification at the time of filing. A complete specification must provide more detailed information than a provisional specification.[26] This is the case even with the proposed amendments which require a complete specification to disclose the invention "in a manner which is clear enough and complete enough for the invention to be performed by a person skilled in the relevant art", that is, an enablement requirement across the full scope of the claims. In addition, the complete specification must fully describe the invention, including the best method of performing it

---

20   See the definition of "patent" in the Dictionary found in Sch 1 to the Act.

21   Section 15(1)(a).

22   Section 15(1)(b).

23   Section 15(1)(c).

24   Section 15(1)(d).

25   Section 40(1). See also *Patents Regulations 1991* reg 3.2 and Sch 3 for the formal requirements. According to *Anaesthetic Supplies v Rescare* (1994) 122 ALR 141, provisional applications were not expected to "enter into all the minute details as to the manner in which the invention is to be carried out".

26   Section 40(2)-(5).

known to the applicant,[27] and it must end with a claim or claims defining the invention[28] or, in the case of an innovation patent, end with at least one claim but a maximum of five claims defining the invention.[29] Section 40(3) requires that the claims be "clear and succinct and fairly based on the matter described in the specification", an issue often under consideration during patent prosecution. The fair basis requirement is proposed to change to a "supported by matter disclosed" requirement. Further, the claims must relate to one invention only.[30] In the case of micro-organisms ss 41 and 42 provide that a complete specification is satisfied if the micro-organism is deposited in accordance with s 6. The risk in making a provisional rather than a complete application has been that the description of the invention in the provisional application may not accord with what is filed in the complete specification 12 months later. If that is the case then the filing date of the provisional application will not be valid for the invention disclosed in the complete specification. This is due to the complete specification not being fairly based on matter disclosed in the provisional specification. Such a failure resulted in the eventual loss of patent protection for the sleep apnoea invention in *Rescare Ltd v Anaesthetic Supplies Pty Ltd*.[31] The proposed amendments to both s 40(1) and (3) are aimed at removing that problem.

The application, whether provisional or complete, is "taken to have been made on the filing date determined under the regulations".[32] It is this filing date that gives each claim of the specification a priority date.[33] This date is significant for a number of reasons. The term of the patent, if granted, commences from the priority date. If this is the first filing of the specification anywhere in the world then this priority date also serves as the priority date for Paris Convention applications. This gives the applicant 12 months in which to make applications for the same invention in other Convention countries and retain the priority date achieved in Australia.[34] The converse applies when an applicant has filed first in another Convention country.[35] The applicant has 12 months from that priority date to file in Australia in order to retain that priority date here.

Where an applicant wishes to take advantage of the PCT system, a single PCT application can be made designating the member countries in which protection is

---

27   Section 40(2)(a). This is in keeping with Art 29.1 of the TRIPS Agreement which requires that the disclosure be enough for a person skilled in the art to be able to carry out the invention. Further, the proposed amendments maintain this requirement.

28   Section 40(2)(b).

29   Section 40(2)(c).

30   Section 40(4).

31   (1994) 122 ALR 141.

32   Section 30.

33   However, s 43(2)(b) recognises that "the regulations [may] provide for the determination of a different date as the priority date". This is to take into account the difference between filing a provisional and a complete specification and enables the earlier date (secured by the provisional) to serve as the priority date for the invention: see *Patents Regulations 1991* regs 3.12-3.13. Under the proposed amendments, s 43(2) will be repealed and replaced such that the priority date will be determined either by the regulations where disclosure has been "clear enough and complete enough for the invention to be performed by a person skilled in the relevant art", or, the date on which a specification has been lodged.

34   However, as a general rule, the applicant must obtain a certified copy of the Australian specification and lodge that together with the complete specification in the foreign equivalent of the Patent Office when making a Convention application in the foreign jurisdiction.

35   Sections 94-96 and *Patents Regulations 1991* regs 3.12, 8.5-8.7.

sought. That application attracts an international filing date that in turn becomes the priority date of the application in Australia (and other designated countries). Although an international search of the prior art needs to be conducted followed by WIPO publishing the application, the PCT application must still comply with domestic law, especially the prescribed requirements of the Act.[36]

A strategy available to applicants faced with ever evolving research contributing to the improvement or modification of their original invention, but which may not involve an inventive step,[37] is the patent of addition. This process is limited to standard patents and enables an applicant or patentee to apply for a further patent in order to protect an improvement or modification to their main invention. It is required that the application for the main invention be examined before the application for the patent of addition and, similarly, that the patent for the main invention be sealed before the patent of addition is sealed.[38] However, while the general rule is that the patent of addition remains in force for as long as the main patent,[39] the patent of addition may be entitled to an extension[40] or even remain in force when the main patent has been revoked[41] and thereby become an independent patent. The advantage of the patent of addition is that it cannot be objected to or revoked on the basis that it does not involve an inventive step.

A further strategy, available for both standard and innovation patents, is the divisional application. This allows an applicant to file, in accordance with the regulations, a further application for another invention disclosed in the specification of the original application.[42] This is in keeping with the requirement that a patent application can only claim one invention.

## Examination

The next stage in the process of obtaining a patent is examination. An applicant must request an examination of their application in accordance with s 44(1) of the Act before this stage is instigated. Applicants have five years from lodgment of their complete specification to request examination.[43] Alternatively, the Commissioner of Patents may direct an applicant to request examination in a number of circumstances.[44]

Several tasks must first take place before formal examination can proceed. The International Patent Classification is used to classify the invention and then abstracts are prepared to assist in the searching procedure. A search report is prepared listing the prior art relevant to the issues of novelty and inventiveness of the application. The applicant then has an opportunity to review the report and

---

36    Sections 88-93 and *Patents Regulations 1991* regs 3.12, 8.1-8.14.

37    Section 25.

38    Section 81(2)-(3).

39    Section 83(1).

40    Section 83(2).

41    Section 85.

42    Section 79B in respect of standard patents and see s 79C in respect of innovation patents. The amendments to these provisions are aimed at dealing with the problem of the "continuation divisional" by limiting the time within which a divisional application can be filed, or the conversion of a standard application can be made to a divisional application.

43    *Patents Regulations 1991* reg 3.25(1).

44    Section 44(2)-(4).

the prior art listed enabling decisions about potential amendment to their application. In addition, from 1 April 2002, an applicant had a duty to disclose their own search results to the Australian Patent Office.[45] The results were to be filed by the later of when requesting examination or six months after the completion of the search (three months in the case of innovation patents).[46] However, certain prescribed searches were excluded from this requirement under s 45(3)(a) and the Patent Examiner's Manual tells us that since 22 October 2007 all searches are prescribed thereby no longer requiring their results to be provided to the Commissioner.[47] To simplify this situation, s 45(3)-(5) will be repealed under the *Raising the Bar* amendments.[48]

Meanwhile, in an attempt to bring into line all patent applications, whether PCT or not, the *Raising the Bar* amendments include the introduction of a preliminary search and opinion to be conducted by the Commissioner.[49] This is in line with a PCT conducted international search and preliminary examination and is purported to reduce the period of uncertainty for an applicant only filing in Australia while informing the public and competitors where they are free to operate.[50]

The next step is formal examination, carried out by a patent examiner in accordance with s 45 of the Act. Section 45(1) lists the relevant grounds for examination. These are:

- whether the specification complies with s 40;
- whether the invention satisfies the first three criteria for patentability specified in s 18(1), that is, that the invention is a manner of manufacture, has novelty and involves an inventive step;
- and such other matters as are prescribed.

The criteria of usefulness is not a part of the examination process although under the *Raising the Bar* amendments it will be an element of assessment during examination to reduce the risk of granting patents for inventions that do not work.[51] Similarly, s 45(1A) will be deleted so that 'prior use' is not excluded from examination and thereby reducing the risk of granting a patent for an invention that fails novelty. Similar amendments will apply to innovation patents.

---

45    Sections 101D and 45(3).

46    *Patents Regulations* regs 3.17A(2) (standard patents) and 9A.2A(2) (innovation patents).

47    See APO, *Manual of Practice and Procedure,* Vol 2 – National, July 2011, para 2.13.10: "From 22 October 2007, for all standard applications for which examination is requested after this date, and for all standard applications where the obligation to inform the Commissioner expires after this date, **all** searches are prescribed (that is, the results do not have to be provided to the Commissioner). Similarly, from 22 October 2007 for all innovation patents which the Commissioner decides to undertake examination after this date, or a third party requests examination after this date, and for all innovation patent applications where the obligation to inform the Commissioner expires after this date, all searches are prescribed (that is, the results do not have to be provided to the Commissioner)".

48    See *Intellectual Property Laws Amendment (Raising The Bar) Act 2012*, Sch 6, Part 1, Item 48.

49    Section 43A.

50    Explanatory Memorandum, Intellectual Property Laws Amendment (Raising The Bar) Bill 2011, Sch 1, Item 9.

51    Explanatory Memorandum, Intellectual Property Laws Amendment (Raising The Bar) Bill 2011, Sch 1, Item 12.

Once completed, an examination report is issued with either a favourable result or an adverse one. A favourable report indicates that there is no lawful ground of objection to the patent request and specification and leads the application to the next step in the process, that is acceptance and publication (s 49 and s 5). If, on the other hand, an adverse report ensues, the applicant may suggest amendments to the specification or claims in an attempt to remove the ground(s) of objection. Such amendments may be acceptable to the Commissioner and the acceptance procedures under s 49 are invoked.[52] Alternatively, if the applicant either does not provide an acceptable amendment or does not to the Commissioner's satisfaction deal with the ground of objection, the Commissioner can refuse the patent request and specification and must notify the applicant of the reasons.[53] An applicant then has an opportunity to appeal to the Federal Court against the decision of the Commissioner. If successful, the patent request and specification may proceed to acceptance and publication. What is important to note is that the current standard of proof under s 49 for the Commissioner to apply in determining whether the patent application meets the requirements of patentability is less than that required by the courts. This low standard relied upon the potential of low quality patents to be challenged in opposition proceedings and the assumption that the Commissioner did not have adequate information about the prior art at his or her disposal to expect a higher standard of proof. The *Raising the Bar* amendments dispel the continued validity of such arguments and have required the standard of proof be raised to an inquiry "on the balance of probabilities" in relation to both standard and innovation patents.

## Acceptance and publication

Assuming the patent request and specification are finally accepted in accordance with s 49(1) of the Act, the Commissioner must notify the applicant in writing and publish a notice of the acceptance in the *Official Journal*.[54] However, an applicant may request that the acceptance be delayed,[55] but this can only be for a limited time, that is, not beyond the time given before an application would otherwise lapse.[56]

In the case of innovation patents, if the Commissioner accepts a patent request and complete specification, then the innovation patent must be granted and sealed in the approved form.[57] The Commissioner is then required to publish a notice in the *Official Journal* confirming the grant and stating that the patent request and specification are open to public inspection.[58]

Similarly, publication of acceptance of a standard patent is accompanied by a statement that the patent request and specification are open for public inspection,

---

52   Before 1 January 2005 the Commissioner had the power to allow amendments subject to conditions. Due to the *US Free Trade Agreement Implementation Act 2004*, that power to impose conditions was repealed.
53   Section 49(7) requires that the notice be in writing and that it be published in the *Official Journal*.
54   Section 49(5) and (6).
55   Section 49(3).
56   Section 49(4).
57   Section 62(1).
58   Section 62(2).

if this has not already occurred.[59] Chapter 4 of the Act describes the processes of publication and s 55 identifies those documents to be open for public inspection whether in relation to a standard patent or an innovation patent. These are basically all documents associated with the application process.

Applicants need to be aware that they may find their specification published in the *Official Journal* "open for public inspection" before acceptance or even examination of the application as reg 4.2(3) requires such publication at the latest 18 months from the earliest priority date. The implications are significant. First, s 57(1) provides the applicant with the same right as he or she would have had if a patent for invention had been granted on the day when the specification became open for public inspection.

However, proceedings for infringement of any of the claims would not be able to be commenced until the patent was granted.[60] Second, should the application fail to be accepted, any advantage the applicant had over the invention through confidentiality would be lost, leaving the invention exposed to competition.

Where prior art is brought to the attention of the Commissioner after acceptance but before the granting of a patent, a re-examination of the application can be instituted at any time by the Commissioner prior to grant. The provisions pertaining to re-examination are to be amended to provide greater transparency. For instance, court-directed re-examination will be made in accordance with procedures to be set out in the Regulations.[61] Further, the grounds for re-examination will be expanded to the same grounds for examination.[62] In keeping with the raised standards of proof for acceptance, the Commissioner cannot refuse to grant or decide to revoke a patent unless satisfied on the balance of probabilities of the invalidity of the proposed/granted patent.[63]

## Opposition

Within three months of publication of acceptance in the *Official Journal*[64] the Minister or any other person may take action "in accordance with the regulations to oppose the grant of a standard patent".[65] Section 59 provides the only grounds upon which such an opposition action can be commenced. An opponent may argue that:

- the applicant is not entitled to a grant of patent for the invention or that another person in conjunction with the applicant is entitled to the grant;[66]
- the invention is not a patentable invention. In other words, the invention does not comply with s 18 of the Act in that the invention is not a manner of manufacture or it is not novel or does not contain an inventive step, is

---

59   Section 49(6)(b).
60   Section 57(3).
61   *Intellectual Property Laws Amendment (Raising The Bar) Act 2012*, Sch 1 Item 16 for standard patents and Item 23 for innovation patents.
62   *Intellectual Property Laws Amendment (Raising The Bar) Act 2012*, Sch 1 Item 17 for standard patents and Item 24 for innovation patents.
63   *Intellectual Property Laws Amendment (Raising The Bar) Act 2012*, Sch 1 Items 18 and 19 for standard patents and Item 26 for revocation of innovation patents.
64   *Patents Regulations 1991* reg 5.3.1.
65   Section 59.
66   Section 59(a).

not useful or was secretly used, or is for a human being or the biological processes for their generation;[67]

· the specification or claim does not comply with s 40(2) or (3)[68] (although in practice the Commissioner's delegate often allows the applicant to amend them).[69]

The final element of the second ground of opposition relates to the provisions of s 18(2) of the Act that human beings together with the biological processes for their generation cannot constitute a patentable invention. This provision was aimed at the debate over research concerning in vitro fertilisation. However, given potential developments in stem cell technology and the cloning of human beings or parts of human beings, this ground of opposition may create significant debate.

The procedures for an opposition action are prescribed in the regulations to the Act, however, s 60(2) does specify that the Commissioner must give both the applicant and the opponent a reasonable opportunity to be heard before deciding a case. In addition, the Commissioner can take into account any ground on which the opposition can be brought even if the opponent has not raised that ground in their argument.[70] Further, the standard of proof proposed under the amendments for the ground of opposition to be made out is the balance of probabilities.[71] However, before refusing the application, the Commissioner must give the applicant an opportunity to amend the application in order to remove the ground of opposition.[72] A right of appeal to the Federal Court against the Commissioner's decision is available to either party to the opposition proceedings.[73]

It should be noted that an innovation patent that has been certified can still be opposed with the purpose of revocation on the basis of one or more of the following grounds of invalidity:[74]

· the patentee is not entitled to the patent or is only entitled in conjunction with another person;
· the invention does not comply with s 18(1A)(a) or (b);
· the invention is not patentable under s 18(2) or (3); or
· the complete specification does not comply with s 40(2) or (3).

Once again the procedures are in accordance with the Regulations[75] and a right of appeal to the Federal Court is available.[76] And once again the proposed amendments will add the criterion of usefulness to the grounds of invalidity.

---

67    Section 59(b). Before 1 January 2005 this paragraph was limited to non-compliance with s 18(1) (a) or (b) only. Now, s 18(1)(c) and (d) are included in the operation of s 59(b) as is non-compliance with s 18(2); hence the repeal of the superfluous s 59(d). These changes were brought about by the *US Free Trade Agreement Implementation Act 2004*.

68    These provisions require, respectively, that the specification describe the invention fully, including the best method for performing the invention, and that the claims are clear and succinct and fairly based on the matter described in the specification.

69    Section 59(c).

70    Section 60(3).

71    *Intellectual Property Laws Amendment (Raising The Bar) Act 2012*, Sch 1 Item 15.

72    *Intellectual Property Laws Amendment (Raising The Bar) Act 2012*, Sch 1 Item 15.

73    Section 60(4).

74    Section 101M.

75    Section 101N(1).

76    Section 101N(7).

Opposition proceedings are also the subject of reform under the *Raising the Bar* amendments with provisions aimed at streamlining the system by reducing complexity and delay in the resolution of such proceedings.[77] In addition, the adverse impact of divisional applications on the opposition process is addressed in the reforms.[78] Schedule 6 to the *Raising the Bar* reforms addresses myriad issues that unnecessarily complicate the operation of the patent system, thereby bringing greater simplicity to the regime.

## Grant of letters patent

Where there is no opposition brought against the accepted patent request and specification or where an opposition action is unsuccessful, the Commissioner must grant the standard patent by sealing it in the approved form.[79] As mentioned above, an innovation patent proceeds directly to grant and sealing upon acceptance by the Commissioner. The date of the resulting patent is either the filing date of the complete specification or another date as determined by the Regulations (usually the date of filing the provisional application).[80] The term of a standard patent is 20 years from the date of the patent.[81] The term of an innovation patent is eight years from the date of the patent.[82]

The patent holder, or patentee, is given exclusive rights to exploit the invention and to authorise others to exploit the invention for the term of the patent.[83] These rights are effective in the patent area,[84] that is Australia,[85] and constitute personal property capable of assignment and devolution by law.[86]

It is important to note that the pharmaceutical industry has enjoyed special treatment in relation to the term of its patents. Only standard patents with respect to pharmaceutical substances are able to attract an extension in the term of patent protection. The process of obtaining an extension of term of patent is found in Part 3 of Chapter 6 of the Act. The rationale behind the extension of term relates to the long process of gaining regulatory approval of the pharmaceutical substance. Accordingly, the period of extension, if granted, takes into account the date of such regulatory approval, but cannot exceed five years.[87] This means that pharmaceutical substances may have patent terms of up to 25 years. However, during the extension period, the patentee cannot bring infringement proceedings against persons exploiting the pharmaceutical substance for the sole purpose

---

77    See generally, *Intellectual Property Laws Amendment (Raising The Bar) Act 2012*, Sch 3.
78    See generally, *Intellectual Property Laws Amendment (Raising The Bar) Act 2012*, Sch 3.
79    Section 61.
80    Section 65.
81    Section 67. This is in accordance with the TRIPS Agreement Art 33.
82    Section 68.
83    Section 13(1).
84    Section 13(3).
85    More specifically, the definition of patent area in Sch 1 to the Act includes Australia and its external Territories, the Australian continental shelf, the waters above that continental shelf and the airspace above Australia and its continental shelf.
86    Section 13(2).
87    Section 77.

of, for example, arranging for their own generic product to be included in the Australian Register of Therapeutic Goods.[88]

## Revocation

In line with the fact that the grant of a patent is no guarantee as to its validity, either the Commissioner or a prescribed court has the power to revoke a patent. The situations in which the Commissioner may revoke a patent are numerous,[89] but a court can only revoke a patent on the petition of the Minister or another person[90] or by way of a counter-claim for revocation by a defendant in infringement proceedings.[91]

The grounds for revocation are broader than the grounds for an opposition action and are set out in s 138(3) which provides that a patent may be revoked on one or more of the following grounds but on no other grounds:

- that the patentee is not entitled to the patent;
- that the invention is not a patentable invention;
- that the patentee has contravened a condition of the patent;
- that the patent or an amendment to a patent request or complete specification was obtained by fraud, false suggestion or misrepresentation,
- that the specification does not comply with s 40(2) or (3).

In revocation proceedings either the patent as a whole is revoked or only one or more claims in the specification may be revoked.

## International Aspects

On the international front there are two main issues regarding patent law. On the one hand, there is a difference between patent-owning countries and patent-importing countries regarding the enforcement of the patent owner's monopoly. This is particularly important in the case of pharmaceuticals and can cause great debate. India, for example, had a long-standing policy of refusing patent applications for drugs thereby allowing the production of cheap generic drugs in the interest of national health and economy.[92] Even in countries that do grant patents for drugs, international disputes may arise. In 2001, for example, in response to widespread criticism, 39 pharmaceutical companies abandoned their legal action[93] to prevent the South African government from importing cheap anti-retroviral drugs used in the treatment of HIV/AIDS. Following the collapse of the legal case one of the companies, GlaxoSmith Kline, entered into a voluntary licence with a South African drug company for that company to produce the

---

88  Section 78(1) and (2).
89  See, for example, ss 82, 134 and 137.
90  Section 138.
91  Section 121.
92  Since 2005 India's patent law permits the granting of patents for the pharmaceutical product itself not just the manufacturing process.
93  *Pharmaceutical Manufacturers' Association of South Africa v President of the Republic of South Africa*, Case No 4183/98 (filed 18 February 1998).

drugs at a cheaper price and with the payment of relatively small licence fees.[94] Today we are seeing more and more countries applying the TRIPS Protocol[95] by introducing or expanding their compulsory licence provisions to enable the production and export of generic drugs to the least-developed nations.

The second area of international activity in regard to patents relates to the facilitation of international registration and administration of patents. It is this issue which has more commonly been the subject of international agreements. The *Paris Convention for the Protection of Industrial Property 1883* (Paris Convention),[96] for example, has attempted to harmonise the operation of industrial property laws through a variety of mechanisms adopted by the Convention's member states. The term "industrial property" is used to cover patents, designs and trade marks. Australia has been a signatory to the Convention since 1925 and before that as a colony of the United Kingdom.

Article 1 of the Paris Convention stipulates that the countries to which the Convention applies "constitute a Union for the protection of industrial property". The Convention requires the guarantee of national treatment in each member country of nationals from other member countries (Art 2) and, in certain circumstances, nationals from countries not part of the Union (Art 3). The Convention does allow for independence of treatment between countries. Consequently, the grant of a patent in one member country does not oblige another member country to grant patent rights for the same invention (Art 4*bis*(1)).

The Paris Convention assists in the globalisation of patent protection by providing that the date when an application for a patent is first made in a member country shall be the priority date for subsequent applications in relation to the same invention in other member countries provided those applications are made within 12 months of the first application (Art 4).[97] The *Patents Act 1990* gives effect to this process at ss 94 to 96.

The Convention does not prescribe elements of patent validity (such as novelty, inventive step, utility, scope or rights) nor, in any detail, of substantive law. The Convention does allow the grant of limited compulsory licences (Art 5A) and provides that the inventor shall have the right to be named in the patent (Art 4*ter*). It also contains provisions dealing with the administrative framework of the Paris Convention. In the 1970s a *Declaration of Objectives* was adopted for the purpose of amending the Convention in order to promote the interests of developing countries.

---

94   In a neat circle the South African Government had previously taken action against the Indian Government in the World Trade Organization to prevent the dumping of generic drugs in South Africa WT/DS/168/1.

95   This is the term given to the introduction of Art 31*bis* after Art 31 of the TRIPS Agreement (Agreement on Trade Related Aspects of Intellectual Property) together with the Annex to the TRIPS Agreement after Art 73 of the TRIPS Agreement. This was as a result of a General Council decision in December 2005, the effect being to enable those countries capable of manufacturing generics (for example, India and Brazil) to do so under compulsory licence and export to a least-developed nation or other eligible importing member.

96   *Paris Convention for the Protection of Industrial Property 1883*, as revised at Brussels on 14 December 1900, at Washington on 2 June 1911, at The Hague on 6 November 1925, at London on 2 June 1934, at Lisbon on 31 October 1958, at Stockholm on 14 July 1967.

97   The Paris Convention Art 4 describes how the concept of priority operates in relation to trade marks and designs as well as standard and innovation patents (known as utility patents in the Convention).

Despite the assistance the Paris Convention gives to foreign applicants for patents, the process can still be an arduous one when attempting to gain patent protection worldwide. Inventors are still required to seek registration and prosecute breaches in each jurisdiction separately. The *Patent Co-operation Treaty 1970* (PCT), made under the Paris Convention, provides some reprieve from the expense and burdensome nature of this process, at least in relation to registration.

The PCT came into force in 1978 and is administered by the International Bureau of the World Intellectual Property Organization (WIPO). Australia became a member in 1980. The formal requirements and procedures to be followed are set out in the PCT and allow an applicant to file a single patent application in one member country nominating the states in which protection is sought. That application is then given an international filing date and is subject to a single search by the International Searching Authority and is assessed for novelty. Eighteen months after the priority date, the search report and the application are published. The international application is then forwarded to each state (or region)[98] designated in the application and the national processes begin, often with the payment of national fees. Although the form or content of the application may not require change from the international application before assessment under domestic law, translations may be required. The searching process at domestic level has been removed by the PCT system.

WIPO also administers the International Patent Classification system established by the *Strasbourg Agreement Concerning the International Patent Classification 1971*.[99] This uniform classification system assists in the exchange of information between patent offices and in the searching of prior art by examiners, applicants and third parties. This is achieved through varying degrees of classifications describing technology, commencing with broad sections which are divided into classes, then sub-classes and then groups. Australia acceded to this agreement in 1975.

The rapid development of biotechnology in the second half of the 20th century brought to the fore a significant difficulty in compliance with disclosure requirements for patent applications. As we have seen, a patent application must provide sufficient disclosure of the invention sought to be protected. Where the invention is or comprises a living organism, such as a genetically engineered microorganism, disclosure in the form of a documentary description is inadequate. This was recognised and resulted in yet another special agreement under the Paris Convention, namely, the *Budapest Treaty on the International Recognition of the Deposit of Micro-organisms for the Purposes of Patent Procedure 1977* to which Australia became a party in 1987. This treaty permits the deposit of a novel culture of micro-organisms with a designated "international depository authority" to facilitate the sufficient disclosure requirement for patent application purposes.

In 1989, Australia became a signatory to the *International Convention for the Protection of New Varieties of Plants 1961* (UPOV). However, before joining UPOV, the Commonwealth used the Convention as a model for its *Plant Variety Rights Act 1987*. This sui generis legislation provides protection for plant breeders

---

98    Such as Europe where the *European Patent Convention* enables the granting of patents in each of those member states designated after the successful examination of a single application by the European Patent Office in Munich.

99    It was 1975 when Australia acceded to this agreement.

in a manner separate to the patent system – an issue of great importance to Europe where the patenting of plant and animal varieties is prohibited under the *European Patent Convention*. UPOV has been revised a number of times with the most recent revision, in March of 1991, recognising new technologies and resulting in the introduction in Australia of the *Plant Breeder's Rights Act 1994* which replaced the 1987 Act. We will consider the *Plant Breeder's Rights Act* in Chapter 15.

In recent times, the TRIPS Agreement is the most significant international agreement relating to patents.[100] TRIPS recognises and reinforces the operation of the Paris Convention[101] and "[desires] to establish a mutually supportive relationship ... [with WIPO and] ... other relevant international organisations".[102] With respect to patents, Arts 27-34 deal with the scope of patentable subject-matter; the rights conferred upon a patent owner; conditions on patent applications; exceptions to rights conferred as well as other use without the authorisation of the rights holder; revocation and forfeiture; the term of protection and the burden of proof in civil proceedings concerning the infringement of process patents. It should be noted that members, when implementing TRIPS, "may, but shall not be obliged to, implement in their law more extensive protection than is required by [the TRIPS] Agreement, provided that such protection does not contravene the provisions of [that] Agreement".[103] While members are given the freedom to "determine the appropriate method of implementing the provisions of ... [TRIPS] ... within their own legal system and practice" (Art 1) they are reminded of the objectives of the Agreement at Art 7:

> The protection and enforcement of intellectual property rights should contribute to the promotion of technological innovation and to the transfer and dissemination of technology, to the mutual advantage of producers and users of technological knowledge and in a manner conducive to social and economic welfare, and to a balance of rights and obligations.

This statement of objectives goes to the core of the tension between the monopoly rights established through intellectual property regimes such as patent law and the desire to engender free trade among nations. It seems that issues relevant in Elizabethan times are still relevant today, some 400 years later.

On the issue of free trade we have seen, in recent times, a plethora of bilateral free trade agreements spring into existence. The US-Australia Free Trade

---

100 However, the *Patent Law Treaty* of 1 July 2000 (PLT), developed by WIPO as a result of negotiations in the late 1990s, is another instrument designed to contribute to establishing an international patent system. Despite Australia only having acceded to the PLT on 16 December 2008 with it coming into force on 16 March 2009, the amendments contained in the *Patents Amendment Act 2001*, were designed to bring the *Patents Act 1990* into compliance with the PLT.

101 TRIPS Agreement Part 1.

102 See the preamble or recitals to the TRIPS Agreement.

103 TRIPS Agreement. This would seem to be aimed at those jurisdictions that have not taken such a liberal view of the breadth of subject-matter capable of protection. In this regard, consider the *European Patent Convention* that prohibits the patenting of plant and animal varieties and developing nations that have refused to afford patent protection to pharmaceuticals. However, "more extensive protection" would seem to be referring to the numerous TRIPS-plus bilateral trade agreements entered into by the United States and various developing and developed countries: the US-Australia Free Trade Agreement being one.

Agreement, while accepting the relevant international treaties involving intellectual property, also required changes to the *Patents Act 1990* and resulted in changes to the *Therapeutic Goods Act 1989* to ensure that vexatious litigation would not ensue in the pharmaceutical industry.[104] In addition, the agreement reinforces a dedication of both countries to the ongoing international harmonisation efforts regarding patent laws.

---

104  See Art 17.9 on patents and Art 17.10 for specific measures regarding pharmaceutical products.

# CASES

## *Darcy v Allin*
Queen's Bench
(1602) 77 ER 1260

This is the famous Case of Monopolies which effectively limited the Crown's power to grant monopolies in the form of letters patent. In this case Queen Elizabeth I had granted a monopoly to Edward Darcy, a groom of the Privy Council, to import, make, sell and utter playing cards. In return for this grant Darcy paid the Queen 100 marks per annum. The case note explains that the monopoly was apparently granted on the basis that such a grant would prevent able bodied labourers in England from wasting their skills and talents in manufacturing playing cards when they could be "applying themselves to more lawful and necessary trades". Two questions arose. Was the grant to have the sole manufacture of the cards within the realm lawful? Was the dispensation to import the cards lawful? In each case the question which must be answered is whether the grant is within the Crown prerogative or whether it is within the power of Parliament only. (Footnotes have been deleted.)

### Report
As to the first question it was argued on the plaintiff's side, that the said grant of the sole making of playing cards within the realm, was good for three reasons. 1. Because the said playing cards were not any merchandize, or thing, concerning trade of any necessary use, but things of vanity, and the occasion of loss of time, and decrease of the substance of many, the loss of the service and work of servants, causes of want, which is the mother of woe and destruction, and therefore it belongs the benefit and liberty of the subject, and therewith agrees Forteseue in Laudibus' legum Angliae`, cap 26. ... 2. The sole trade of any mechanical artifice, or any other monopoly, is not only a damage and prejudice to those who exercise the same trade, but also to all other subjects, for the end of all these monopolies is for the private gain of the patentees; ... 3. It tends to the impoverishment of divers artificers and others, who before, by the labour of their hands in their art or trade, had maintained themselves and their families, who now will of necessity be constrained to live in idleness and beggary ... and the common law, in this point, agrees with the equity of the law of God, as appears in Deut cap xxiv ver 6 ... and it agrees also with the civil law ... **[1264]** 3. The Queen was deceived in her grant; for the Queen, as by the preamble appears, intended it to be for the weal Public, and it will be employed for the private gain of the patentee, and for the prejudice of the weal public; moreover the Queen meant that the abuse should be taken away, which shall never be by this patent, but *potius* the abuse will be increased for the private benefit of the patentee, and therefore as it is said in 21 E 3 47 in the *Earl of Kent's case*, this grant is void *jure regio*. 4. This grant is *primae impressionis,* for no such was ever seen to pass by letters patent under the Great Seal before these days, and therefore it is a dangerous innovation, as well without any precedent, or example, as without authority of law, or reason. And it was observed, that this grant to the plaintiff was for twelve years, so that his executors, administrators, wife, or children or others inexpert in the art and trade, will have this monopoly. And it cannot be intended, that Edward Darcy an Esquire, and a groom of the Queen's Privy Chamber has any skill in this mechanical trade of making cards; and then it was said, that the patent made to him was void – for to forbid others to make cards who have the art and skill, and to give him the sole making of them who has no skill to make them, will make the patent

utterly void. *Vide* 9 E 4 5 b. And although the grant extends to his deputies, and it may be said he may appoint deputies who are expert, yet if the grantee himself is not expert, and the grant is void as to him, he cannot make any deputy to supply his place … And as to what has been said, that playing at cards is a vanity, it is true, if it is abused, but the making of them is neither a vanity nor a pleasure, but labour and pains. [87 b] Arid it is true, that none can make a park, chase, or warren, without the King's licence, for that is *quodam modo* to appropriate those creatures which are *ferae naturae, et nullius in bonis* to himself, and to restrain them of their natural liberty, which he cannot do without the King's licence; but for hawking hunting, &c which are matters of pastime, pleasure, and recreation, there needs no licence, but every one may, in his own land, use them at his pleasure, without any restraint to be made, unless by Parliament, as appears by the statutes … And it is evident by the preamble of the said Act … that the importation of foreign cards was prohibited as the grievous complaint of the poor artificers cardmakers, who were not able to live of their trades, if foreign cards should be imported; as appears by the preamble, by which it appears, that the said Act provides remedy for the maintenance of the said trade of making cards, forasmuch as it maintained divers families by their labour and industry … And therefore it was resolved that the Queen could not suppress the making of cards within the realm, no more than the making of dice, bowls, balls, hawks' hoods, bells, lures, dog couples, and other the like, which are works of labour and art, although they serve for pleasure, recreation and pastime, and cannot be suppressed but by Parliament, nor a man restrained from exercising any trade, but by Parliament … And the playing at dice and cards is not prohibited by the common law … (unless a man is deceived by false dice or cards, for then he who is deceived shall have an action upon his case for the deceit) and therefore **[1265]** playing at cards, dice, &c is not *malum in se* for then the Queen could not tolerate nor license it to be done. And where King E 3 in the 39th year of his reign, by his proclamation, commanded in the exercise of archery anid artillery, arid prohibited the exercise of casting of stones and bars, and the hand and foot-balls, cock-fighting, *et alios ludos vanos* … yet no effect thereof followed, until divers of them were prohibited upon a penalty, by divers Acts of Parliament …

Also such charter of a monopoly, against the freedom of trade and traffic, is against divers Acts of Parliament … which for the advancement of the freedom of trade and traffic extends to all things vendible, notwithstanding any charter of franchise granted to the contrary or usage, or custom, or judgment given upon such charters, which charters are adjudged by the same Parliament to be of no force or effect, arid made to the derogation of the prelates, earls, barons, and grandees of the realm, and to the oppression of the commons. And by the statute of 25 E 3 cap 2 it is enacted, that the said Act of 9 E 3 shall be observed, holden, and maintained in all points. And it is further by the same Act provided, that if any statute, charter, letters patent, proclamation, command, usage, allowance, or judgment be made to the contrary, that it shall be utterly void, *vide* Magna Charter …

As to the 2nd question it was resolved, that the dispensation or licence to have the sole importation and merchandizing of cards (without any limitation or stint) not withstanding the said Act of 3 E 4 is utterly against law: for it is true, that forasmuch as an Act of Parliament which generally prohibits a thing upon a penalty, which is popular, or only given to the King, may be inconvenient to divers particular persons, in respect of person, place, time, &c for this reason the law has given power to the King, to dispense with particular persons; … But when the wisdom of the Parliament has made an Act to restrain *pro bono publico* the importation of many foreign manufactures, to the intent that the subjects of the realm might apply themselves to **[1266]** the making of the said manufactures, &c and thereby maintain themselves and their families with the labour of their hands; now for a private gain to grant the sole importation of them to one, or divers (without any limitation) notwithstanding the said Act, is a monopoly against the common law, and against the end and scope of the Act itself; for this is not to maintain and increase the labours of the poor cardmakers within the realm, at whose petition the Act was made, but utterly to take away and destroy their trade and labours, and that without any reason of necessity, or inconveniency in respect of person, place, or time, and *eo potius*, because it was granted in reversion for years, as hath been said, but only for the benefit of a private man, his executors and administrators, for his particular commodity, and in prejudice of the commonwealth. And King E 3 by his letters patent, granted to one John Peche the sole importation of sweet wine into London, and at a Parliament held 50 E 3 this grant was adjudged void ... Also admitting that such grant or dispensation was good, yet the plaintiff cannot maintain an action on the case against those who import any foreign cards, but the remedy which the Act of 3 E 4 in such case gives ought to be pursued. And judgment was given and entered, *quod querens nihil caperet per billam.*

And *nota,* reader, and well observe the glorious preamble and pretence of this odious monopoly. And it is true *quod privilegia quae re vera sunt in proejudicium republicaoe, magis tamen speciosa habent frontispicia, et boni publici proetextum, quam bonoe et legales concessiones, sed proetextu liciti non debet admitti illicilum.* And our lord the King that now is, in a book which he in zeal to the law and justice commanded to be printed anno 1610, intituled, "A Declaration of His Majesty's Pleasure, &c" p 13 has published, that monopolies are things against the laws of this realm; and therefore expressly commands, that no suitor presume to move him to grant any of them, &c.

# Chapter 9

# Elements of Patentability

At a general level it is fair to say that patents protect "inventions". However, there are great variations throughout the world as to how an invention is defined. This is an important question for, in order to be effective, patent law must be able to deal with new forms of technology and inventions. If the definition of invention is too narrow or too rigid then it is possible that whole new industries could miss out on patent protection.

The Australian approach is quite distinctive and has proved to be very flexible. Instead of asking "What is an invention?", the Australian approach is to ask, as did the judges in *Darcy v Allin*,[1] "What is a proper subject for patent protection?" Paradoxically, the Australian patents legislation does this by defining a "patentable invention" by reference to the 1623 *Statute of Monopolies*. In this chapter we see how this ancient definition has enabled Australian patent law readily to embrace new technologies, inventions and industries.

## The Legislation

The *Patents Act 1990* expressly stipulates the requirements of patentability. Section 18(1) defines the elements of a patentable invention for the purposes of a standard patent while s 18(1A) does the same for innovation patents. In both instances one must consider the definitions given to the terms "invention", which is based on the *Statute of Monopolies 1623*, and "patentable invention" in Sch 1 to the Act:

> *invention* means any manner of new manufacture the subject of letters patent and grant of privilege within section 6 of the Statute of Monopolies, and includes an alleged invention.
>
> *patentable invention* means an invention of the kind mentioned in section 18.

The *Statute of Monopolies*, it will be remembered, provided that the only proper subject for the grant of letters patent was:

> any manner of new manufacture ... [that] be not contrary to the law, nor mischievous to the state ... or generally inconvenient.

---

1    (1602) 77 ER 1260.

The *Patents Act 1990* s 18(1) requires that the invention "so far as claimed in any claim":

(a) is a manner of manufacture within the meaning of section 6 of the Statute of Monopolies; and

(b) when compared with the prior art base as it existed before the priority date of that claim:
   (i)   is novel; and
   (ii)  involves an inventive step; and

(c) is useful; and

(d) was not secretly used in the patent area before the priority date of that claim by, or on behalf of, or with the authority of, the patentee or nominated person or the patentee's or nominated person's predecessor in title to the invention.[2]

Paragraph (a) would appear to be superfluous given the definition of "invention". On the other hand, the concepts of novelty and inventive step are first required by para (b).

In order to determine whether an invention is novel and involves an inventive step there must be a comparison of the invention with the "prior art base" existing before the priority date. The "prior art base" is determined by a search done before the formal examination of the patent application.

"Prior art base" is defined in Sch 1 to the Act and varies according to whether one is determining novelty or inventiveness. In the case of inventive step (and also innovative step for innovation patents) the prior art base means:

(i)  information in a document that is publicly available, whether in or out of the patent area; and

(ii) information made publicly available through doing an act whether in or out of the patent area.[3]

For novelty, the prior art base includes the information relevant for the question of inventive step plus:

(ii) information contained in a published specification filed in respect of a complete application where:
   (A) if the information is, or were to be, the subject of a claim of the specification, the claim has, or would have, a priority date earlier than that of the claim under consideration; and
   (B) the specification was published after the priority date of the claim under consideration; and
   (C) the information was contained in the specification on its filing date and when it was published.

In s 7, the Act provides further clarification in relation to the terms novelty and inventive step. An invention will be considered novel "unless it is not novel in the light of any one of the following kinds of information, each of which must be considered separately":

(a) prior art information (other than that mentioned in paragraph (c)) made publicly available in a single document or through doing a single act;

---

2    These elements previously appeared in the *Patents Act 1952* but not as criteria for validity, rather as the grounds relevant to examination, opposition or revocation.

3    Before 1 October 2001 the act need only be done in the patent area.

    (b) prior art information (other than that mentioned in paragraph (c)) made publicly available in 2 or more related documents, or through doing 2 or more related acts, if the relationship between the documents or acts is such that a person skilled in the relevant art[4] would treat them as a single source of that information;

    (c) prior art information contained in a single specification of the kind mentioned in subparagraph (b)(ii) of the definition of "prior art base" in Schedule 1.[5]

"Prior art information" is defined as "information that is part of the prior art base" relevant to the decision of whether or not there is novelty. In effect, such information relates to either prior published patent specifications, or other publicly available information such as a single article or a connected series of articles in a scientific publication or, alternatively, a public demonstration of what effectively constitutes the invention, for example of a prototype, or another inventor's equivalent invention.

In the quest to protect traditional medicinal knowledge in recent times, the evaluation of the prior art base is crucial to the determination of the criteria of novelty in assessing the patentability of such knowledge. Can the traditional knowledge holders lay claim to a pharmaceutical patent incorporating such knowledge? Or does the traditional knowledge only form the background from which the patentable invention is derived? These are interesting but difficult questions to answer, particularly in the light of claims of biopiracy against pharmaceutical and biotechnological patent holders.

In relation to inventive step, s 7(2) provides that:

> an invention is to be taken to involve an inventive step when compared with the prior art base unless the invention would have been obvious to a person skilled in the relevant art in the light of the common general knowledge as it existed in the patent area[6] before the priority date of the relevant claim, whether that knowledge is considered separately or together with the information mentioned in sub-section (3).

Section 7(3) identifies that information as either a single piece or any combination of two or more pieces of prior art information[7] that the skilled person could have reasonably been expected to ascertain, understand, regard as relevant and combine, in the case of the two or more pieces of prior art information, before the priority date of the application in question.[8]

Once again, if we consider traditional medicinal knowledge and the criteria of inventive step, how is the prior art base defined? Is it the recorded scientific knowledge in pharmaceutical circles? Is it the knowledge held by particular

---

4    Before 1 October 2001 the choice of person skilled in the relevant art was confined to the patent area.

5    Section 7(1).

6    As mentioned in Chapter 8, the *Raising the Bar* amendments will substitute the reference to "in the patent area" with "(whether in or out of the patent area)", thereby expanding the scope of prior art available for assessment purposes.

7    Here, prior art information is once again information part of the prior art base, but this time relevant to determining whether the invention contains an inventive step. See Sch 1 to the Act.

8    The ability to consider two or more pieces of prior art in the determination of inventive step was introduced only in 2002 operating in relation to applications filed after 1 April 2002. For a discussion on the issue of prior art base and inventiveness, see *Firebelt Pty Ltd v Brambles Aust Ltd* (2002) 188 ALR 280 at 287-289. Under the *Raising the Bar* amendments, the words "to ascertain, understand, regard as relevant and" will be deleted, thereby limiting the consideration to what the skilled addressee could be reasonably expected to combine.

members of the Indigenous community from which the medicinal knowledge emanates? This raises questions of the identity of the skilled person and the nature of the common general knowledge. Their definition can be critical to the assessment of patentability as we will see. Recent initiatives from some jurisdictions rich in traditional medicinal knowledge include the creation of extensive databases of such knowledge, providing patent examiners with a searchable prior art base.[9]

Section 18(1)(c) of the Act requires that the invention be "useful" if it is to be patentable. The case law establishes that this does not mean that the invention must be useful in the sense of being worthwhile or practical but rather that it works if the specifications are followed.[10] The requirement of usefulness is therefore closely related to the requirements under s 40(2) and (3) of the Act which require that the specification fully describe the invention and that the claims are clear and succinct and fairly based on the matter described in the specification.[11] We consider the case law below.

The final element of patentability is found in s 18(1)(d) of the Act, namely, that there be no secret use of the invention in the patent area before the priority date. While there is no clarification as to what does constitute secret use, s 9 identifies uses which will not be considered as secret uses for the purposes of the Act. Accordingly, secret use does not include use that:

· is for the purpose of reasonable trial or experiment only;[12]
· occurs solely in the course of a confidential disclosure;
· is for any purpose other than the purpose of trade or commerce;[13] or
· is constituted in the disclosure of the invention to the Commonwealth, State or Territory.

Secret use would appear to be problematic for traditional medicinal knowledge. Even if the use of such knowledge can be considered to occur in the "course of a confidential disclosure" its use on injured or ill members of an Indigenous community, for example, would seem to go beyond secret use.

---

9    For example the Indian Traditional Knowledge Digital Library which has successfully prevented the patenting of many purported inventions incorporating Indian traditional knowledge without consent of the knowledge holders.

10   Article 17.9 para 13 of the United States-Australia Free Trade Agreement states: "Each Party shall provide that a claimed invention is useful if it has a specific, substantial, and credible utility". This terminology is being incorporated in the new section 7A by the *Raising the Bar* amendments – see below.

11   The United States–Australia Free Trade Agreement provides further comment in this area through paras 11 and 12 of Art 17.9:
     "11. Each party shall provide that a disclosure of a claimed invention shall be considered to be sufficiently clear and complete if it provides information that allows the invention to be made and used by a person skilled in the art, without undue experimentation, as of the filing date."
     "12. Each Party shall provide that a claimed invention is sufficiently supported by its disclosure if the disclosure reasonably conveys to a person skilled in the art that the applicant was in possession of the claimed invention, as of the filing date."

12   Consider the case *Longworth v Emerton* (1951) 83 CLR 539.

13   Consider the English Court of Appeal case, *Re Wheatley's Patent Application* (1984) 2 IPR 450, where, despite an understanding of confidentiality between the inventor and the interested party, the trading result of the arrangement negotiated before lodging a patent application cost the inventor patent protection.

As we have seen, s 18(2) expressly excludes human beings and the biological processes for their generation from the definition of patentable invention.[14] This means that, even if all the elements of patentability found in s 18(1) are satisfied, an invention pertaining to human beings, such as a clone, or the biological processes for their generation will not be granted.

Section 18(1A) deals with innovation patents and departs from the elements of patentability found in s 18(1) in relation to only two elements. Instead of requiring an inventive step, an innovation patent must contain an innovative step. This innovative step is judged in relation to the same prior art base as is an inventive step and further clarification of what constitutes an innovative step can be found in s 7(4)-(6) of the Act which has been considered for the first time in the opposition proceedings, *INC Corporations Pty Ltd v The Smith Family, MCK Pacific Pty Ltd and Foss Manufacturing Company* in 2006,[15] to be discussed later in this chapter. The exclusion in s 18(2) is applicable to innovation patents but, in addition, plants and animals, together with the biological processes for their generation, are excluded from being the subject of an innovation patent. However, s 18(4) allows a microbiological process or a product of such a process to be the subject of an innovation patent. This would seem to recognise the possibility of minor innovations in the field of microbiology and related biotechnologies.

## The Concept of "Manner of New Manufacture"

As we have seen above, an "invention" is a "manner of new manufacture" under Sch 1 and one of the elements of patentability under s 18(1) is that the invention be a "manner of manufacture within the meaning of s 6 of the *Statute of Monopolies*", that is, that it be a "manner of new manufacture". This seems to overdo the requirement that for something to qualify as an invention, it must in the first place be a proper subject for the grant of letters patent. The effect of such unfortunate drafting was the subject of two High Court cases, *NV Philips Gloeilampenfabrieken v Mirabella International Pty Ltd*[16] (the *Philips* case) and *Advanced Building Systems Pty Ltd v Ramset Fasteners (Aust) Pty Ltd*[17] (the *Ramset Fasteners* case). Stoianoff points out that the High Court in these two decisions:

> has effectively interpreted the use of the expression "manner of manufacture" in section 18(1)(a) to involve the same underlying concepts as "manner of new manufacture" in the 1952 Act. That is, the importation of the "newness" concept does not change the traditional principles, but rather this threshold requirement of "newness" is to be used in situations where the lack of subject matter [according to traditional principles] is apparent on the face of the specification.[18]

---

14  The reason for this provision was explained in the previous chapter. This exclusion would seem to be in keeping with Art 27.2 of the TRIPS Agreement although it is not clear if that is the intention of Art 27.2, particularly when the language of Art 27.3, which provides for specific acceptable exclusions, does not identify humans but confines itself to plants and animals and the biological processes for their production.

15  (2006) AIPC ¶92-183.

16  (1995) 183 CLR 655.

17  (1998) 152 ALR 604.

18  N Stoianoff, "Patenting Computer Software: An Australian Perspective" [1999] *EIPR* 500 at 505. See also APO, *Manual of Practice and Procedure – National*, July 2011, para 2.9.2.1.

Much of the case law revolves around the meaning of the concept of "manner of manufacture". The most significant Australian case on the modern meaning of this concept is the 1959 High Court case of *National Research Development Corporation v Commissioner of Patents* (the *NRDC* case).[19] This case involved a patent application for a method of killing weeds growing among leguminous fodder crops without killing those crops. This was achieved through the identification of the enzyme make-up of the weeds compared to the crops noting that when a particular hormone-based herbicide was applied, the enzymes found in the weeds would breakdown the herbicide into its active derivatives thereby bringing about the demise of the weeds. At this time the Australian Patent Office (APO) practice provided that "the word 'manufacture' … is restricted to vendible products and processes for their production, and excludes all agricultural and horticultural processes … and denies that a process for killing weeds can be within the relevant concept of invention".[20]

The High Court took a different view, stressing the importance of the "widening conception of the notion" rather than the meaning of particular words indicating that it is a "mistake" purely to look to the word "manufacture" in that way:

> It is a mistake which tends to limit one's thinking by reference to the idea of making tangible goods by hand or by machine, because 'manufacture' as a word of everyday speech generally conveys that idea.[21]

The court referred to *Morton's Rules* in the English case *GEC's Application*,[22] where Morton J formulated a test for determining whether a method or process was a manner of manufacture. These rules emphasised the need for a "vendible product":

> [M]ethod or process is a manner of manufacture if it (a) results in the production of some vendible product or (b) improves or restores to its former condition a vendible product or (c) has the effect of preserving from deterioration some vendible product to which it is applied.[23]

Dixon CJ, Kitto and Windeyer JJ, delivered a joint judgment in the *NRDC* case. They considered past interpretations of the term "vendible product" and the "emphasis upon the trading or industrial character of the processes intended to be comprehended" and pointed out:

> that a process, to fall within the limits of patentability which the context of the Statute of Monopolies has supplied, must be one that offers some advantage which is material, in the sense that the process belongs to a useful art as distinct from a fine art … that its value to the country is in the field of economic endeavour.[24]

Their Honours went on to describe how the facts in the case fit into the concept of "vendible product" noting that if a method "has as its end result an artificial effect … [or] … artificially created state of affairs … [and] … possesses

---

19   (1959) 102 CLR 252.
20   (1959) 102 CLR 252 at 268.
21   (1959) 102 CLR 252 at 269.
22   (1942) 60 RPC 1.
23   (1943) 60 RPC 1 at 4.
24   (1959) 102 CLR 252 at 275.

its own economic utility",[25] as in the *NRDC* case, then it will be held patentable.

The court also addressed the questions of whether agricultural or horticultural processes, on the one hand, or a new use of a known substance, on the other, could be a proper subject-matter for the grant of a patent. The court held that, provided the invention is a manner of manufacture and otherwise complies with the requirements of patentability under the *Patents Act 1990*, any relation to an agricultural or horticultural process should not bar the invention from patent protection.[26]

Similarly, the court held that where the patent relates to the application of newly determined properties of a known substance to a new use then this was also a "manner of new manufacture" and therefore a proper subject for the grant of a patent.[27] The court found that there was no "mere new use" in this case because the relevant property of the herbicide was not previously known and the discovery led to a new application resulting in a manner of new manufacture.[28]

This is quite a difficult point in patent law, for if it is determined that the application relates to "a claim for the use of a known material in the manufacture of known articles for the purpose of which its known properties make that material suitable"[29] or a "new use of a particular known product"[30] then this will not be a manner of new manufacture within the terms of the *Statute of Monopolies* and therefore of the *Patents Act 1990*. The High Court in the *NRDC* case was able to distinguish the case *Commissioner of Patents v Microcell Ltd*.[31] In that case a patent application for a self-propelled rocket projector comprising a tube of reinforced plastic was refused on the basis that the tube shape was known and the properties of reinforced plastic (high tensile strength and heat resistance) were known even though it had been assumed that they would probably not be suitable for use in a self-propelled rocket. Similarly, in *NV Philips Gloeilampenfabrieken v Mirabella International Pty Ltd*,[32] Philips' application for a patent for a compact fluorescent energy-saving lamp was rejected on the basis that the applicant had simply selected two known desirable characteristics of phosphors which used together would achieve the desired aims of being energy efficient and compact.[33] For a recent application of this principle, see *Belden Wire and Cable Co v Pacific Dunlop Ltd*.[34]

At common law and under statute there are also other limits to the definition of invention and the proper subject-matter for a grant of letters patent. Section

---

25    (1959) 102 CLR 252 at 277.
26    (1959) 102 CLR 252, Dixon CJ, Kitto and Windeyer JJ at 279.
27    (1959) 102 CLR 252 at 268.
28    (1959) 102 CLR 252 at 275.
29    *Commissioner of Patents v Microcell Ltd* (1959) 102 CLR 232 at 251.
30    *NV Philips Gloeilampenfabrieken v Mirabella International Pty Ltd* (1995) 183 CLR 655 at 659.
31    (1959) 102 CLR 232 at 251.
32    (1995) 183 CLR 655.
33    As a matter of procedure it should be noted that the High Court in the later *Ramset Fasteners* case pointed out that the + case was concerned with inventions "where the lack of inventive step appears on the face of the specification" and that as a general rule an inquiry as to novelty and inventive step should not be part of determining whether there is an invention to consider in the first place: *Advanced Building Systems Pty Ltd v Ramset Fasteners (Aust) Pty Ltd* (1998) 152 ALR 604.
34    (1997) 38 IPR 605.

18(2) of the Act provides that human beings and the biological processes for their generation are not patentable,[35] the *Statute of Monopolies* excludes those inventions which are contrary to law,[36] mischievous to the state or generally inconvenient[37] and the case law has traditionally excluded naturally occurring substances, mere discoveries and laws of nature[38] from the definition of invention.

In the *NRDC* case the court noted the difficulty of drawing a distinction between discovery and invention:

> The truth is that the distinction between discovery and invention is not precise enough to be other than misleading in this area of discussion. There may indeed be a discovery without invention – either because the discovery is some piece of abstract information without any suggestion of a practical application of it to a useful end, or because its application lies outside the realm of "manufacture".[39]

Accordingly, the APO *Manual of Practice and Procedure – National*, July 2011, provides the following guidance to examiners at para 2.9.2.5:

> The critical question for examiners is whether the claimed invention relates to non-patentable or patentable subject matter. This question can be answered by deciding whether the claimed invention lies in the intellectual or academic realm, or whether it lies in the technical or practical realm. Technical or practical matter is patentable.

Section 50(1)(b) allows the Commissioner to refuse a patent for:

(i) a substance which is capable of being used as food or medicine ... and is a mere mixture of known ingredients; or

(ii) a process producing such a substance by mere admixture.[40]

It has sometimes been suggested that methods of treating the human body, at least where they are therapeutic methods or surgical techniques, are not proper subjects for the grant of a patent. However, such a limitation does not seem to have been adopted by Australian courts. In *Joos v Commissioner of Patents*,[41] the High Court considered a patent application for a "process for improving strength

---

35   The direct result of this is that IVF technologies are excluded from patentability in Australia. Further, the attempt by the Australian Democrats to introduce an amendment to the *Patents Act 1990* takes this a step further (see the *Patents Amendment Bill 1996*) by seeking to exclude the patenting of genes and gene sequences.

36   As does the *Patents Act 1990* s 50(1)(a).

37   The Australian Patent Office (APO), *Manual of Practice and Procedure – National*, July 2011, provides an interesting instruction to examiners at para 2.9.3: "There is really no clear guidance as to when an invention may or may not be regarded as 'generally inconvenient'. Hence, examiners should refrain from taking this objection". After providing a list of cases that might provide guidance on the issue, the Manual goes on to advise examiners as follows: "In cases where general inconvenience might appear to be an issue, examiners should consider whether the appropriate objection is really one of anticipation [that is lack of novelty] or that the invention does not lie in the technical realm".

38   The Australian Patent Office tends to treat discoveries and laws of nature interchangeably, in accordance with *NRDC*.

39   (1959) 102 CLR 252 at 264.

40   However, as for the patentability of new drugs, if the substance is a new compound it may be patentable in its own right. If a pharmaceutical application of the new compound is later developed and there is novelty in the suggestion of the new use then the pharmaceutical use of the compound may be patentable. However, any subsequent pharmaceutical use developed generally will not attract patent protection in respect of the same compound.

41   (1972) 46 ALJR 438.

or elasticity of keratinous material" in hair and nails. The Commissioner had originally rejected the application on the basis that the invention was a process for treating parts of the body whilst attached to or growing upon the human body. The High Court to the contrary concluded that "cosmetic processes and methods are ... not of a like kind with medical prophylactic or therapeutic processes or methods". Rather, Barwick CJ pointed out that hairdressing "is an activity in the field of economic endeavour and has commercial significance as those expressions ought to be understood in relation to the grant of patents".

The Full Federal Court took this further in *Anaesthetic Supplies Pty Ltd v Rescare Ltd*,[42] where the application concerned a device and method for dealing with sleep apnoea. Although many of the claims failed because they were not fairly based on the provisional application, resulting in much of the patent being invalid, the Court did not reject the claim on the basis that it related to a method of treating the human body. The court rejected the distinction between methods of treatment of the human body for therapeutic purposes and methods of treating the human body for cosmetic purposes saying there was no justification in law or logic to distinguish a process of curative treatment from that of cosmetic treatment. So long as the process or device had a commercial application it could be a manner of manufacture regardless of its application to the human body. The decision in that case has since been upheld by the same court in *Bristol-Myers Squibb Company v FH Faulding & Co Ltd*.[43]

There are three areas of law where there has been recent debate regarding the question of whether they are manners of new manufacture and therefore proper subjects for the grant of a patent and whether they fall within the exemptions to patentability. These areas are biotechnology, computer software related inventions and business methods.

## Biotechnology

The term "biotechnology" has become synonymous with genetic engineering in recent times. However, the term predates the discovery of DNA[44] and genetic engineering, and biotechnology has traditionally been associated with fermentation processes for the production of alcoholic beverages and yeast, certain chemicals and eventually antibiotics. The common feature of these forms of production is the use of living organisms, predominantly microorganisms, in the production process. The development of recombinant DNA technology, however, has greatly extended the types of processes which might be classified as biotechnology. Recombinant DNA technology enables the production not only of new forms of living microorganisms but also of new forms of plants and animals. New biotechnology processes have enabled scientists to map the human genome and have led to the development of a new generation of pharmaceuticals and medical aids based on this knowledge. Significant innovation in this field is believed by many

---

42    (1994) 122 ALR 141.
43    (2000) 170 ALR 439. It was affirmed that the generally inconvenient argument cannot be used to invalidate patents for methods of medical treatment.
44    Deoxy-ribonucleic acid. For an excellent history of the term "biotechnology", see Max Kennedy's Letter to the Editor, "The word biotechnology is much older than most people realise" (1991) 6(3) *ABA Bulletin* 51.

people to be dependent on effective patent protection and the grant of limited monopoly rights.[45] Some have argued that patent protection is more important to biotechnology investments than other technologies.[46]

The question, however, arises as to whether biotechnology is a proper subject of patent protection and the possible basis of such protection. In particular, questions have arisen as to whether biotechnology patents are improperly protecting naturally occurring substances, mere discoveries and/or laws of nature. We might ask whether it is possible for biological material to escape the realm of nature and enter the realm of patentable subject-matter.

United States case law has distinguished between an unpatentable "product of nature" and a patentable "product derived from nature". The United States Supreme Court case, *Diamond v Chakrabarty*[47] in 1980, is the leading case for the grant of patents for living organisms and their "products" although there are earlier instances of patent offices accepting such inventions. The Australian Patent Office, for example, in *Rank Hovis McDougall Ltd's Application*[48] which was reported in 1976, accepted a claim for a process of isolating a microorganism and manipulating it into new variations but refused a claim for the naturally occurring organism itself.

Thus, the general rule still applies. Where something is naturally occurring it is not patentable unless there is some type of human intervention. Australian patent practice has been quite liberal in its attitude toward the patentability of genetic and other such inventions[49] and the level of human intervention required has not been great. Current patent law practice treats the isolation and expression of a gene outside of its natural environment as the necessary "human intervention".[50] On the other hand, applications for biological processes may fail on the basis that they fail to meet the other requirements of patentability. In Chapter 11 we take a closer look at biotechnology patents, but it is important to recognise that many natural products are currently used as pharmaceuticals. When one realises that "80 per cent of the world's population uses botanical

---

45   DS Chisum, "Patenting Living Subject Matter, DNA Sequences Encoding Proteins, Gene Therapy and Therapeutic Methods Under United States Law", *ATRIP Annual Conference Proceedings – Emergent Technologies and Intellectual Property, July 19-21, 1995*, CASRIP Publication Series No 2, 1996, p 31. See also C Arup, "Patents and Living Organisms", *Innovation, Policy and Law, Australia and the International High Technology Economy*, Cambridge University Press, Cambridge, 1993, Chapter 3, pp 66-67.

46   ES van der Graaf, *Patent Law and Modern Biotechnology*, Sanders Institute, Gouder Quint, Rotterdam, 1997, p 38.

47   447 US 303 (1980). In that case, Chakrabarty sought patent protection for a genetically engineered microorganism designed to break up crude oil spills. By majority Chakrabarty was allowed the patent protection on the basis that there was human intervention and not mere discovery.

48   (1976) 46 AOJP 3915.

49   Patent applications involving genetic manipulation cover the entire range of technologies including synthetic genes or DNA sequences; mutant forms and fragments of gene sequences; the DNA coding sequence of a gene (is this not a discovery?); protein expressed by a gene; vectors; probes for genes; host cells carrying the gene; higher plants/animals carrying the gene; organisms for expressing the gene; PCR and other such methods; regulatory DNA sequences. See *Australian Patents for Microorganisms, Cell Lines, Hybridomas, Related biological materials and their use; Genetically manipulated organisms*, IP Australia, February 1998.

50   See *Genetics Institute Inc v Kirin-Amgen Inc (No 3)* [1998] FCA 740 for a detailed judgment on point.

medicines as a first-line of treatment",[51] it is clear that traditional medicinal knowledge provides a significant contribution to society and the issue of its protection needs satisfactory resolution.

## Computer software related inventions

As a general rule, mathematical algorithms per se are not patentable subject-matter.[52] Accordingly, software alone, where "it merely implements a mathematical algorithm without having some practical application", would not constitute a manner of manufacture.[53] In the 1980s, if a claim in a patent application contained an integer or step that included software, the claim would not for that reason alone be considered unpatentable. Rather, the Australian Patent Office imported the two-part *Freeman* test, named after the US case, *Re Freeman*,[54] to assist in making a determination, namely:

(1) does the claim include subject-matter which in itself is inherently unpatentable [that is, does the claim recite a mathematical algorithm]?

(2) if so, what is the relationship between that subject-matter and the claim as a whole?[55]

In other words, if the claimed invention is not an algorithm itself but an application of the algorithm then the invention would be patentable.

The first major Australian case to confirm the patentability of software-related inventions was *IBM v Smith, Commissioner of Patents*[56] (the *IBM* case). In that case, IBM claimed "a method for producing a visual representation of a curve image from a set of control points which define the curve and which are input for each dimension and a number of intervals of the curve to be computed" comprising a series of steps. The Delegate of the Commissioner of Patents refused the application on the basis that the claim did nothing more than recite an algorithm. Burchett J, on appeal to the Federal Court, overturned the delegate's decision and referred to the alleged invention as a "commercially useful effect in computer graphics".[57] The production of the desired curve by computer was a new application to computers involving steps that were "foreign to the normal use of computers" and therefore inventive.[58] Burchett J relied on the basic principles provided by the *NRDC* case, that is, that the process must provide some material advantage, be a useful art and "that its value to the country [be] in the field of economic endeavour".[59]

---

51 John B Bremmer, "Chapter 1 Biodiversity: Reasons for the Scientific and Commercial Interest" in Natalie P Stoianoff (ed), *Accessing Biological Resources – Complying with the Convention on Biological Diversity.*, Kluwer Law International, The Hague, 2004, pp 9-10. See also Natalie P Stoianoff, "Biological Resources and Benefit Sharing: The Intersection Between Traditional Knowledge and Intellectual Property" in SK Verma and Raman Mittal (eds), *Intellectual Property Rights: A Global Vision*, Indian Law Institute, New Delhi, 2004, pp 44-45.

52 They tend to fall in the category of laws of nature, discoveries, schemes and plans, and fine arts as opposed to useful arts.

53 N Stoianoff, "Patenting Computer Software: An Australian Perspective" [1999] *EIPR* 500 at 503.

54 197 USPQ 464 (1978).

55 APO, *Guidelines for Considering the Patentability of Computer Program Related Inventions*, 1986.

56 (1990) 105 ALR 388.

57 (1990) 105 ALR 388 at 395.

58 (1990) 105 ALR 388 at 395.

59 (1990) 105 ALR 388 at 304.

This approach was affirmed by the Full Federal Court in *CCOM Pty Ltd v Jiejing Pty Ltd*,[60] and it is now accepted by the Australian Patent Office that a computer software related invention is patentable if the mathematical algorithm contained in the alleged invention allows for "a mode or manner of achieving an end result which is an artificially created state of affairs of utility in the field of economic endeavour".[61]

## Business methods

Schemes, plans and methods were not readily patentable before the *NRDC* case.[62] McKeough and Blakeney attribute this to the need for a "vendible product" as conceptualised pre-*NRDC*.[63] However, post-*NRDC*, in *Moore Paragon Australia Ltd v Multiform Printers Pty Ltd*,[64] a patent was issued for assemblies of business forms on the basis that the invention resulted in an article having a functional purpose and was associated with technological implementation, that is, a computer.

In the United States it had often been said by lower courts that business methods were excluded from patent protection. This approach was rejected in the US Court of Appeals in *State Street Bank & Trust Co v Signature Financial Group*.[65] The case involved computer software but was fought directly on the basis of the alleged exclusion of business methods. The court criticised the judicial creation of the exclusion of business methods from statutory subject-matter and held that the same legal requirements for patentability of any process or method should be applied to business methods. The patent was upheld.

In a recent Australian case, *Welcome Real-Time SA v Catuity Inc*,[66] Heerey J in the Federal Court upheld a patent for a process of operating smart cards in connection with traders' loyalty schemes. However, he treated the patent more akin to a computer software related invention, and concluded that the patent produced "an artificial state of affairs", as required by *NRDC* and confirmed by *CCOM*. He held that the patent did not involve "just an abstract idea or method of calculation" but rather produced a result "beneficial in a field of economic endeavour – namely retail trading". Heerey J stressed that the patent was not for a business method but rather for a "method and a device, involving components such as smart cards and POS terminals, in a business; and not just one business but an infinite range of retail businesses".[67] Further, he found the patent indistinguishable from the *CCOM* case and various English decisions, indicating

---

60    (1994) 28 IPR 481. This case involves a petty patent for a computer-processing apparatus for assembling text in Chinese characters. The Australian Patent Office relies on this case as the definitive Australian position on patenting of software-related inventions.

61    See APO, *Manual of Practice and Procedure – National*, July 2011, para 2.9.2.7.

62    See generally *ESP's Application* [1945] RPC 86 and *Millard v Commissioner of Patents* (1918) 24 CLR 331.

63    J McKeough and M Blakeney, *Intellectual Property Commentary and Materials*, 2nd ed, LBC, Sydney, 1992, p 340.

64    (1984) 3 IPR 270.

65    149 F 3d 1368 (1998).

66    (2001) 51 IPR 327.

67    (2001) 51 IPR 327 at 353.

that, even if a "physically observable effect" is necessary, one could be found in the "writing of new information to the Behaviour file and the printing of the coupon".[68]

As to the result in the US case, *State Street Bank & Trust Co v Signature Financial Group*, Heerey J found the decision persuasive noting that in both Australia and the US "the law has to strike a balance between ... the encouragement of true innovation by the grant of monopoly and ... freedom of competition".[69]

The Full Federal Court recently revisited the patentability of business method patents in *Grant v Commissioner of Patents*.[70] The claimed invention involved a business method for the structuring of a financial transaction in order to protect assets from legal liability.[71] It was held that the method did "not produce any artificial state of affairs, in the sense of a concrete, tangible, physical, or observable effect", rather, it was considered to be:

> [A]t best an abstract, intangible situation, namely that a hypothetical unsecured creditor who recovered judgment against a user of the method could not levy against the user's assets to the extent they were subject to the charge.[72]

This was considered to be inadequate to attract patent protection as "[a] physical effect in the sense of a concrete effect or phenomenon or manifestation or transformation is required".[73] The court held that the business method claimed was "a mere invention, an abstract idea, mere intellectual information, which has never been held to be patentable" noting the lack of a "physical consequence".[74] However, the Full Court warned against a requirement that an invention "be within the area of science and technology" relying on the High Court's decision in the *NRDC* case which emphasised "the unpredictability of the advances of human ingenuity".[75] Further, the Full Court considered whether "legal discoveries" were inventions. Interestingly, the court considered that "the interpretation and application of the law" would not have the "industrial or commercial or trading character" required by the *NRDC* case despite its economic importance:[76]

> The practice of law requires, amongst other things, ingenuity and imagination which may produce new kinds of transactions or litigation arguments which could well warrant the description of discoveries. But they are not inventions. Legal advices, schemes, arguments and the like are not a manner of manufacture.[77]

The Australian Patent Office provides the following formulation as a guide for examiners:

> It is apparent from these examples and the Grant case that it is the useful product or effect of the method considered as a whole that must result in an artificially created state of affairs, in the sense of a concrete, tangible, physical, or observable effect. The mere use of a physical form or device in the method, or a physical effect or transformation that

---

68    (2001) 51 IPR 327 at 354.
69    (2001) 51 IPR 327 at 354.
70    [2006] FCAFC 120.
71    [2006] FCAFC 120 at [1].
72    [2006] FCAFC 120 at [30]-[31].
73    [2006] FCAFC 120 at [32].
74    [2006] FCAFC 120 at [32].
75    [2006] FCAFC 120 at [38].
76    [2006] FCAFC 120 at [34].
77    [2006] FCAFC 120 at [34].

arises incidentally or indirectly in its operation will also not be sufficient to change the fundamental character of the subject matter claimed ...

Generally therefore the physical form or device in which a method is applied or operated must be directly involved or used in bringing about the "useful product". That is, the application of technology for automation of a business method (eg computerised accounting, monitoring, reporting or analysis systems) must be directly involved with the creation of the "useful product".[78]

*Grant's* case was determined solely on the issue of meeting the requirement of "manner of manufacture". The decision affirms the principles of patentability set out in the *NRDC* case with regard to determining whether or not the subject matter in question is a manner of manufacture. This is in keeping with the TRIPS requirement that patents be available without discrimination as to the field of technology.[79] In a more recent Australian decision, the idea of technology being directly involved was clarified such that:

> [T]he "concrete effect or phenomenon or manifestation or transformation" referred to must be one that is significant both in that it is concrete but also that it is central to the purpose or operation of the claimed process or otherwise arises from the combination of steps of the method in a substantial way ...[80]

The key US case that tests the boundaries of invention is *Bilski v Kappos*.[81] The patent application in that case sought protection for a claimed invention that explains how commodities buyers and sellers in the energy market can protect against the risk of price changes (hedging).[82] The US Patent and Trademark Office rejected the application on grounds the invention was an abstract idea and therefore ineligible to be patented as a business method. The matter was appealed to the Federal Court which found that the patent application failed the "machine or transformation" test. The "machine or transformation" test states a method or process is patentable if it: "is tied to a particular machine or apparatus"; "or transforms a particular article into a different state or thing".[83] The invention failed the machine or transformation test because the claims were not tied to a particular machine or apparatus. Instead, the claims related to an exchange of legal rights to purchase a commodity and so there was no transformation of something physical. This decision was further appealed to the US Supreme Court.

The US Supreme Court concluded that an invention claiming a business method is not patentable if it falls into either of the following exceptions: laws of nature; physical phenomena; or abstract ideas.[84] The court held that the invention as claimed was an abstract idea and therefore ineligible to be patented. The court concluded that the machine or transformation test is not to be used as the sole test for determining whether a business method can be patented but rather serves as a useful and important investigative tool for determining whether some claimed inventions and processes are eligible to be patented.[85]

---

78    APO, *Manual of Practice and Procedure – National*, July 2011, para 2.9.2.10.
79    TRIPS Art 27 para 1.
80    *Invention Pathways Pty Ltd* [2010] APO 10 at [38].
81    US Supreme Court, No 08-964, decided 28 June 2010.
82    US Supreme Court, No 08-964, decided 28 June 2010, per Kennedy J, at 2.
83    *In Re Bilski* 545 F 3d 943 at 954 (Court of Appeals).
84    US Supreme Court, No 08-964, decided 28 June 2010, per Kennedy J, at 5.
85    US Supreme Court, No 08-964, decided 28 June 2010, per Kennedy J, at 8.

The cases illustrate that failure at the manner of manufacture stage of inquiry is not so frequent. The following issues of novelty, innovative step and s 40 compliance are more prevalent.

## Novelty

As we have seen, under the *Patents Act 1990* s 18(1)(b)(i), novelty is a criterion for patentability. The novelty of any claim is to be assessed "when compared with the prior art base as it existed immediately before the priority date of that claim". Even if a claim in a patent application has been found to be a manner of new manufacture, it can fail for want of novelty.

When identifying the prior art base, one must consider disclosures of prior art information in documents, through conduct and through specifications publicly available anywhere in the world.[86] Information can be "publicly available" when there is disclosure to just one person where there was no understanding of confidentiality concerning the disclosure. Even publication in an obscure journal may leave a claim wanting for lack of novelty. The question to be answered is whether the invention has been "anticipated" at the time of its priority date.

The test for determining whether an invention has been anticipated is the "reverse infringement test" which was developed under the *Patents Act 1952*. Aickin J defined the reverse infringement test in the following way in *Meyers Taylor Pty Ltd v Vicarr Industries Ltd*:[87]

> The basic test for anticipation or want of novelty is the same as that for infringement and generally one can properly ask oneself whether the alleged anticipation would, if the patent were valid, constitute an infringement.[88]

The Act refers to inventions being "made publicly available" through documents or acts. While not defined in the Act, the definition of "documents" in s 25 of the *Acts Interpretation Act 1901* is useful here:

   (a) any paper or other material on which there is writing;

   (b) any paper or other material on which there are marks, figures, symbols or perforations having a meaning for persons qualified to interpret them; and

   (c) any article or material from which sounds images or writings are capable of being reproduced with or without the aid of any other article or device.

Information on computer databases is caught by this definition and the Australian Patent Office Manual also includes tape recordings, compact disks, floppy disks and photographs in its consideration of documents.

Information may be said to have been made "publicly available" even where the disclosure has been to only a small number of people. In *Sunbeam Corp v Morphy-Richards (Aust) Pty Ltd*:[89]

> A description in an obscure journal would suffice to destroy novelty provided that … the document whether or not it was read generally by the public, had been available to the public.

86   Section 7(1).

87   (1977) 137 CLR 228.

88   (1977) 137 CLR 228 at 235.

89   (1961) 180 CLR 98, Windeyer J at 111-112.

In *Dennison Manufacturing Co v Monarch Marking Systems Inc*,[90] only an expert could understand the publication but this constituted a sufficient disclosure. Even if the document is in a different language it may be enough to be a disclosure to the public.

A disclosure may be made through a number of documents but the documents must be related or connected by references. The fact that all the information needed to make the invention is available if one trawls through numerous unrelated documents and puts the information together is insufficient to constitute disclosure to the public so as to destroy novelty. In *Nicaro Holdings Pty Ltd v Martin Engineering Co*[91] (the *Nicaro Holdings* case), Lockhart J explained this principle by saying that it is not enough to make a "mosaic" of prior art:

> The invention must appear in a single disclosure, so it is not permissible to make a pattern or mosaic of or to read together various pieces of prior art in different patents. It is, however, permissible, to refer not only to the patent relied on as the source of disclosure but to another patent or other patents incorporated by reference provided that it is plain that the incorporation by reference unequivocally and plainly demonstrates that the draftsman has adopted the cross-referencing system solely as a shorthand means of incorporating a writing disclosing the invention.[92]

In addition to documentary disclosures, the invention may be made publicly available through conduct. Displaying, selling or providing the invention to a member of the public would also destroy novelty. Telling someone about the invention could render that invention publicly available unless the communication was made in confidence. A communication will not be said to have been made in confidence if it is for the purpose of attracting sales or another commercial purpose. This is because these are essentially public purposes.

The use of traditional knowledge in biologically based inventions may create a variety of outcomes as pointed out by Stoianoff in the following passage:

> If the traditional knowledge is secret and complies with the rules of confidentiality then it may not form part of the prior art base and thereby novelty is maintained. If the knowledge also forms a significant component(s) of the invention developed from the biological resource then the providers of that knowledge may have a claim as joint owners of the ensuing patent. On the other hand, if the traditional knowledge is not secret but a common practice, then it will form part of the prior art base against which [the] purported biological invention is tested. Then it becomes a question of whether such knowledge discloses the invention or whether the invention is more than the traditional knowledge.[93]

The *Patents Act 1990* provides that certain uses of an invention does not constitute prior use amounting to anticipation of the patent. Section 23 of the Act provides that use or publication on or after the priority date does not render the patent invalid. In addition, s 24(1) of the Act provides that use or publication of the invention before the priority date in "prescribed circumstances" does not affect validity of a patent if the application is made within a prescribed period. The

---

90    (1983) 66 ALR 265.
91    (1990) 91 ALR 513. This case was concerned with the infringement and cross-claim for revocation of a six-integer combination patent disclosing a method of cleaning conveyor belts.
92    (1990) 91 ALR 513 at 517.
93    Natalie P Stoianoff, "Biological Resources and Benefit Sharing: the Intersection Between Traditional Knowledge and Intellectual Property" in SK Verma and Raman Mittal (eds), *Intellectual Property Rights A Global Vision*, Indian Law Institute, New Delhi, 2004, pp 45-46.

prescribed circumstances are listed in reg 2.2 of the *Patent Regulations 1991* and include publication at a recognised exhibition, publication in relation to a learned society and any publication or use of the invention within 12 months before the filing date of the complete specification, referred to as the grace period.[94]

In *Nicaro Holdings* Lockhart J provided a modern test for lack of novelty:

> It is well established that the prior art must disclose all features of the invention embodied in the patent in suit and must do so in clear, unequivocal and unmistakable terms. The prior art must enable the notional skilled addressee at once to perceive and understand and be able practically to apply the discovery without the necessity of making further experiments. Whatever is essential to the invention must be read out of or gleaned from the prior publication.[95]

*RD Werner & Co Inc v Bailey Aluminium Products Pty Ltd*[96] clarifies this test by pointing out that "practically [applying] the discovery without the necessity of making further experiments" refers to "experiments with a view to discovering something not disclosed" and does not mean "to refer to the ordinary methods of trial and error which involve no inventive step and are generally necessary in applying any discovery to produce a practical result".[97] The prior publication must disclose the same information provided in the subsequent patent to enable a skilled person to "make the machine from what is disclosed by the prior publications".[98] Otherwise, there is no anticipation.

The *Nicaro Holdings* case also considers the issue of construction of the alleged documents of disclosure. Gummow J refers to a passage in *General Tire & Rubber Co v Firestone Tyre & Rubber Co Ltd*,[99] where the English Court of Appeal points out that both the prior publication and the claim in the patent in question "must each be construed as they would be at the respective relevant dates by a reader skilled in the art to which they relate having regard to the state of knowledge in such art at the relevant date".[100] As this is a matter of law, the courts have the function of construing these documents. Accordingly, evidence as to the technical matters, including words and expressions used in the art, must be provided in order to place the court in the position of the "person skilled in the relevant art at the relevant time". Gummow J points out that "it is not for the court by its own efforts to put itself in the position of a person skilled in the relevant art at the priority date".[101] The next issue to be determined is whether the claim is new, and that is a question of fact.

The *Nicaro Holdings* case further considers the issue of the measure of disclosure with respect to combination patents in its discussion on novelty and workshop improvements:

---

94   APO, *Manual of Practice and Procedure – National*, July 2011, para 2.4.4.6, for further details regarding the nature of recognised exhibitions and learned societies. This is also recognised in Art 17.9 para 9 of the United States–Australia Free Trade Agreement.

95   (1990) 91 ALR 513 at 517.

96   (1989) 85 ALR 679.

97   (1989) 85 ALR 679 at 706, quoting the analysis provided by Lord Reid in *C Van der Lely NV v Bamfords Ltd* [1963] RPC 61 at 71-72.

98   (1989) 85 ALR 679 at 707.

99   [1972] RPC 457.

100  [1972] RPC 457 at 485.

101  (1990) 91 ALR 513 at 524.

A prior publication doesn't amount to an anticipation of an invention claimed as a combination if it discloses some but not all of the integers of that combination.[102]

This is clearly drawn from the process of establishing infringement. For a combination patent to be infringed, the patentee must show that the defendant has taken each and every one of the essential integers of the patentee's claim. Accordingly, if the alleged infringer omits one of these essential integers, then the infringer escapes liability.[103] Conversely, where an infringing device contains the essential integers but there is a difference in respect only of an inessential integer there will be infringement because the device falls within the claim. This provides a lesson also for the determination of anticipation, namely, that it is important that the patentee, when claiming a combination, claim the essential integers only and distinguish between what is and what is not essential.

Finally, after discussing the English and Australian cases on the issue of anticipation, the court in *Nicaro Holdings* concluded that something less than a literal disclosure may suffice in determining anticipation but

> disclosure will fall short of an anticipation by description of an effective means by which the combination claimed in the patent in suit might be produced if, what is required of the skilled addressee is the exercise of any inventive ingenuity and the taking of any inventive step.[104]

Another associated issue to consider is that of prior claiming which occurs where competitors file similar applications within quick succession so that although one secures an earlier priority date, their application is not published at the time the second applicant lodges a specification. One would think that it could not be said that the second application was anticipated by prior publication. However, the 1952 Act recognised "prior claiming" as a separate ground of invalidity. Under the 1990 Act this is not the case. Instead, the "prior art base" against which novelty is to be assessed is defined to include information contained in a complete specification which was unpublished at the priority date of the patent or application under challenge (s 7(1)(c)).

The relationship between novelty and inventive step is an interesting one. In an attempt to draw a distinction, Windeyer J considered this relationship in *Sunbeam Corp v Morphy-Richards (Australia) Pty Ltd*.[105] Novelty considers the question of whether the invention has been made public somehow. Inventive step considers whether the invention is obvious to people skilled in the art to which the invention relates.[106]

However, Gummow J in *RD Werner & Co Inc v Bailey Aluminium Products Pty Ltd*[107] considers that the concepts of lack of novelty and obviousness may overlap where the activity constituting prior publication enters the fund of common general knowledge. This brings us now to the question of inventive step.

---

102  (1990) 91 ALR 513 at 527.
103  *Populin v HB Nominees Pty Ltd* (1982) 41 ALR 471.
104  (1990) 91 ALR 513 at 524 at 531.
105  (1961) 180 CLR 98.
106  (1961) 180 CLR 98 at 111-112.
107  (1989) 85 ALR 679.

## Inventive Step

In accordance with s 18(1)(b)(ii) of the *Patents Act 1990*, an invention must display an inventive step in order to be patentable. "Inventive step" is defined in s 7(2) of the Act (emphasis added):

> an invention is to be taken to involve an inventive step when compared with the prior art base *unless the invention would have been obvious to a person skilled in the relevant art in the light of the common general knowledge as it existed in the patent area before the priority date of the relevant claim*, whether that knowledge is considered separately or together with the information mentioned in sub-section (3).

The prior art base has already been considered with particular reference to the definition in Sch 1 to the Act. However, the relevant test requires a determination of the "common general knowledge", identification of the relevant "person skilled in the relevant art", and then an assessment of whether the claim is or is not obvious to such a skilled person given the common general knowledge in the patent area.

In *Lockwood Security Products Pty Ltd v Doric Products Pty Ltd (No 2)*,[108] the High Court pointed out that the "threshold of inventiveness" has actually been raised by operation of s 7(2) and (3). That is, the common general knowledge together with information described in s 7(3) need to be taken into account when assessing inventive step as against the prior art base.[109] This begs the question, what is common general knowledge? This is the second High Court Decision in relation to the "key controlled latch" invention by Lockwood. The previous decision which turned on the issue of fair basis of the claims upheld the patent. This decision considered the issue of inventive step and again the High Court upheld the patent.

It is important to understand that "common general knowledge" is not the same as the "public knowledge" concept used for the determination of novelty. Rather, Aickin J, in the High Court case of *Minnesota Mining & Manufacturing Co v Beiersdorf (Aust) Ltd*,[110] describes common general knowledge as follows:

> The notion of common general knowledge itself involves the use of that which is known or used by those in the relevant trade. It forms the background knowledge and experience which is available to all in the trade in considering the making of new products, the making of improvements in old. And it must be treated as being used by an individual as a general body of knowledge.

Aickin J states that the process in determining the common general knowledge has been described as "the making of a mosaic" of pieces of information but that such a description is misleading. The question to ask is whether the invention itself is obvious "not whether a diligent searcher might find pieces from which there might have been selected the elements which make up the patent ... [otherwise] ... there could never be a valid patent for a new combination of old integers".[111] However, it is interesting to note that the Patent Co-operation

---

108  [2007] HCA 21.
109  [2007] HCA 21 at [49].
110  (1980) 144 CLR 253 at 292.
111  (1980) 144 CLR 253 at 293. It should be noted that, at the time of Aickin J's decision, publicly available information that formed prior disclosures was not taken into consideration when determining inventive step if such information did not form part of common general knowledge: see *Lockwood*

Treaty (PCT) allows the making of a mosaic of documents for the determination of inventive step for applications filed on or after 1 April 2002.[112] Australia has followed suit by amending s 7(3) to enable consideration of "a combination of any 2 or more pieces of prior art information" that is "reasonably expected to have ascertained, understood, regarded as relevant" by a skilled person. This is also effective from 1 April 2002, and patent examiners are expected to give their reasons as to why a person skilled in the art "would be motivated to combine the disclosures of multiple documents".[113]

In a key decision of the High Court, the question of inventive step was reviewed. *Aktiebolaget Hässle v Alphapharm Pty Limited*,[114] an infringement and revocation case, considered in detail the question of what constituted common general knowledge. The formulation patent, containing the compound known as "omeprazole", was attacked on numerous grounds of invalidity with inventive step being the successful ground of attack and the subject of appeal to the Full Federal Court. The issue was:

> whether the combination of the three integers, being the core, the subcoating layer and the enteric (outer) coating, constitute an inventive step or whether such a combination of integers would have been obvious to the non-inventive skilled worker in the field of pharmaceutical formulation.[115]

The court took great pains to ensure that an expert witness, upon giving his or her opinion, gave evidence of what a hypothetical formulator would have done, not what the witness himself or herself would have done. Such evidence was considered best supported by specific facts or scientific evidence supporting the witnesses' assertions. There was little dispute in the witnesses' assertions in this case and the trial judge's assessment as to reliability was accepted.

It was affirmed that an invention is obvious "if it is shown that it would appear to anyone skilled in the art but lacking inventive capacity that to try the step or process would be worthwhile".[116] Further, the Full Federal Court held that it is "incorrect to say that an invention lacks obviousness simply because the hypothetical formulator would, or might, have been unable to say in advance which (if any) of the possibilities worth trying would have proved most satisfactory".[117] This would be so even if "the task of the hypothetical formulator would have been 'complex, detailed and laborious, involving a good deal of trial and error, dead ends and retracing of steps'."[118]

On appeal to the High Court,[119] the majority did not consider that the expression "worthwhile to try" would be synonymous with "obvious". In line with Aickin

---

*Security Products Pty Ltd v Doric Products Pty Ltd (No 2)* [2007] HCA 21 at [55]. Section 7(2) and (3) change this by lifting the restriction but still testing these prior disclosures against the objective standard of the "person skilled in the relevant art": see *Lockwood Security* at [151].

112  APO, *Manual of Practice and Procedure – National*, July 2011, para 2.5.1.1.

113  APO, *Manual of Practice and Procedure – National*, July 2011, para 2.5.2.5.6.

114  [2002] HCA 59; reversing (2000) 51 IPR 375 (FCAFC).

115  (2000) 51 IPR 375, Wilcox, Merkel and Emmett JJ at 382.

116  (2000) 51 IPR 375 at 383, quoting Buckley LJ in *Beecham Group Ltd's (Amoxycillin) Application* [1980] RPC 261 at 290-291.

117  (2000) 51 IPR 375 at 393.

118  (2000) 51 IPR 375 at 393.

119  [2002] HCA 59.

J's decision in *Minnesota Mining & Manufacturing Co v Beiersdorf*,[120] the majority noted that for inventive step to be found in a combination, the interaction between the integers is essential:

> It is the selection of the integers out of "perhaps many possibilities" which must be shown by Alphapharm to be obvious, bearing in mind that the selection of the integers in which the invention lies can be expected to be a process necessarily involving rejection of other possible integers.[121]

Therein lay the error of the Full Federal Court that focused on each integer and whether each was "at least worthwhile trying", rather than considering the interaction between the integers. The High Court, in the majority decision of Gleeson CJ, Gaudron, Gummow and Hayne JJ, rejected the Full Federal Court's line of reasoning and supported this decision with the views expressed in a series of United States cases.

With regard to what constitutes common general knowledge the Full Federal Court was careful to distinguish:

- the conducting of a literature search by a diligent searcher finding selective pieces that might make up a patent, namely by making a mosaic of documents; from
- that more appropriately understood as "common general knowledge", namely, information or knowledge which would need to be in the conscious awareness of the hypothetical non-inventive skilled worker.[122]

The issue to be determined was "whether what had to be done to achieve the step was truly a matter of inventive experiment or merely a matter of that type of trial and error which forms part of the industrial function of the addressee".[123]

The Full Federal Court determined that, while the appellants had engaged in a "successful negotiation of a 'maze of possibilities and choices'" that resulted in the "complex, detailed and laborious" development of the formulation, there was no particular inventive step.[124]

The majority in the High Court appeal agreed with the statements of Lord Buckley in *Beecham Group Ltd's (Amoxycillin) Application*,[125] namely, that when a person "versed in the art" considers the "tests" "as sufficient to warrant actual trial", that supports a finding of obviousness. In the present circumstances, the Full Federal Court was found to be in error on a number of counts:

> First, the statute does not ask whether a particular avenue of research was obvious to try so that the result claimed therefore is obvious; the adoption of a criterion of validity expressed

---

120  (1980) 144 CLR 253.

121  [2002] HCA 59 at [41].

122  (2000) 51 IPR 375.

123  English Court of Appeal in *General Tire & Rubber Company v Firestone Tyre and Rubber Company Limited* [1972] RPC 457 at 497.

124  The court was persuaded by the evidence adduced by the respondent's experts that the use of a sub coat to separate the enteric coating and core was part of the general industry knowledge and it would be a reasonable and obvious test to try a separating layer such as a sub-coating layer. The court made this determination even though it was shown that there was no Australian formulator to create omeprazole in 1986. This is because "the skilled worker is *assumed* to exist and to have the opportunity to attempt to replicate the result of the patent": (2000) 51 IPR 375 at 407.

125  [1980] RPC 261 at 290.

in terms of "worth a try" or "obvious to try" and the like begs the question presented by the statute. In a sense, any invention that would in fact have been obvious under the statute would also have been worth trying. Paragraph (e) of s 100(1) of the 1952 Act, applied to the present case, asks whether the combination claimed in claim 1 was obvious. The paragraph does not fix upon the direction to be taken in making efforts or attempts to reach that particular solution to the problem identified in the Patent. Nor does it direct an inquiry respecting each integer of the claimed combination. The paragraph asks whether "the invention ... as claimed", here the combination, was obvious, not each of its integers.[126]

Thus, in assessing "common general knowledge" the first step is to identify the field of knowledge, the second is to identify who is skilled in the relevant art, and the third is to consider what common general knowledge persons in the field would be expected to have. In *Electricity Trust (SA) v Zellweger Uster Pty Ltd*,[127] the opponent to the patent application identified a different skilled addressee from that chosen by the Supervising Examiner of Patents as the relevant skilled addressee. Consequently, no evidence was adduced by the opponent relevant to the skilled addressee identified by the examiner and the opposition failed. In reviewing the case law pertinent to the choice of skilled addressee, the examiner summarised as follows:

> [T]he hypothetical addressee is not a person of exceptional skill and knowledge, ... he is not to be expected to exercise any invention nor any prolonged research, inquiry or experiment. He must, however, be prepared to display a reasonable degree of skill and common knowledge of the art in making trials and to correct obvious errors in the specification if a means of correcting them can readily be found.[128]

This appears to be in line with the views of the Full Federal Court in *Jupiters Ltd v Neurizon Pty Ltd*[129] on whether evidence provided by two experts ought to be rejected on the basis that those two experts were considered at trial to "not [be] skilled or knowledgeable enough".[130] The court considered that such a determination "would not be a ground for rejecting the relevance of their evidence", and noted that being confronted with an "overqualified expert" is more likely the problem.[131]

The final question to ask in this process is whether, in the light of the identified common general knowledge and s 7(3) information, an inventive step is exhibited by the invention. Lockhart J in *RD Werner & Co Inc v Bailey Aluminium Products Pty Ltd*[132] put it concisely:

> [T]he court does not inquire too finely or minutely into the degree of ingenuity involved once it is satisfied that some independent invention has been applied. It is sufficient that there has been some substantial exercise of the inventive faculty.[133]

How do these principles operate, then, in the case of a pharmaceutical or biotechnological invention incorporating traditional knowledge? Is the skilled

126  [2002] HCA 59 at [72].
127  (1986) 7 IPR 491.
128  (1986) 7 IPR 491 at 498-499.
129  [2005] FCAFC 90.
130  [2005] FCAFC 90 at [154].
131  [2005] FCAFC 90 at [154].
132  (1989) 85 ALR 679.
133  (1989) 85 ALR 679 at 688.

addressee a scientifically trained biochemist or natural product chemist, an Ayuvedic practitioner, Chinese herbalist or indigenous tribal healer? Whose common general knowledge is relevant? The questions are many but need to be determined.

Restricting the common general knowledge to the "patent area" potentially excludes prior traditional or indigenous knowledge, or in fact any other scientific knowledge from countries other than Australia. It also presupposes that the skilled addressee operates with knowledge that is limited by geography, a presumption that would seem unfounded in this internet age. The *Raising the Bar* amendments recognise this situation and will remove the restriction on the scope of common general knowledge referred to in s 7(2), thereby expanding the knowledge tested to a "global" common general knowledge. The amendment is to remove the words "in the patent area" and replace with "whether in or out of the patent area". While this amendment attempts to expand the scope of the common general knowledge to be taken into account when the "person skilled in the relevant art" is asked to consider if the invention is obvious, it should be noted, however, that the same person is required also to consider the knowledge referred to in s 7(3) when making that determination. This knowledge is already expanded to "in and out of the patent area" and is in keeping with the scope of the prior art base as defined in Sch 1. The amendment to the common general knowledge is therefore in keeping with the scope of the other information able to be taken into account and the scope of the prior art base. So what are the implications of the change? Does this amendment simply remove confusion or create more? How far do we go to determine common general knowledge? Do we define it as the knowledge of Europe, Japan and the US, or Indonesia, Thailand and Peru? How do we determine a "global common general knowledge"? Is it based on the lowest common denominator or the highest? Or do we come back to what constitutes the prior art base for determining inventive or innovative step – namely, information in a publicly available document or information made public through the doing of an act somewhere in the world.

Either way the prior art base to be taken into account is global in nature. However, having a restriction on the scope of the common general knowledge implies that the person skilled in the relevant art needs to be one who is *familiar* with Australian common general knowledge. This then might dictate the choice of experts in opposition and court proceedings. The Explanatory Memorandum acknowledges this, noting that by expanding the scope of common general knowledge to global knowledge experts from around the world could be utilised in such proceedings.[134] One needs to consider who would utilise such experts from around the world. The Explanatory Memorandum makes the point that the pool of experts would become wider as a result of the amendment.[135] One question is who could better afford engaging a foreign expert – an Australian inventor or a foreign inventor? Would that expert come from a low common denominator country or a high common denominator country? What implications are there if Australia's common general knowledge was actually somewhere in the middle?

---

134  Explanatory Memorandum, Intellectual Property Laws Amendment (Raising The Bar) Bill 2011, Sch 1 Item 2.

135  Ibid

The *Raising the Bar* amendments also amend s 7(3) such that when the invention is disclosed by "a combination of two or more pieces of prior art information
that the skilled person mentioned in subsection (2) could, before the priority date
of the relevant claim, be reasonably expected to have combined". The question
is how will the courts distinguish the interpretation of "ascertained, understood
and regarded as relevant" from the "reasonably expected to have combined"?
The current test has been given recent attention in *Commissioner of Patents v
Emperor Sports Pty Ltd* where it was determined that the skilled addressee, a
football coach, would not be likely to read US patents and therefore would not be
able to ascertain that such a document would form part of the prior art base.[136]
As to whether the amendment of the current legislation to "reasonably expected
to have combined" will have much of an impact remains to be seen.

## Innovative Step

The Australian Patent Office stipulates that the inventive contribution necessary
for obtaining an innovation patent is lower than the inventive step requirement
for standard patents.[137] This is evident from the "innovative step" test provided
in s 7(4) of the *Patents Act 1990*:

> [A]n invention is to be taken to involve an innovative step when compared with the prior
> art base unless the invention would, to a person skilled in the relevant art, in the light of
> the common general knowledge as it existed in the patent area before the priority date of
> the relevant claim, only vary from the kinds of information set out in subsection (5) in
> ways that make no substantial contribution to the working of the invention.

The information set out in s 7(5) reflects the type of information relevant to
an inquiry as to novelty. However, the level of inventiveness necessary for an
invention to be considered to have an innovative step is greater than the novelty
test of being "new".[138] The Australian Patent Office explains the test of innovative
step as follows:

> An innovative step requires that the invention is not only novel, but that it also differs
> from what was already known in a way that is not merely superficial (or trivial) or
> peripheral to the invention ... The variation must be of practical significance to the way
> the invention works so as to make a "substantial contribution" to the working.[139]

This instruction is taken from the Revised Explanatory Memorandum[140] to the
implementing legislation and does not imply that an innovation patent must
not be obvious. However, the requirement of a "substantial contribution" is to be
assessed according to the merits of each invention when compared to the prior
art information.[141]

The first decision to consider the meaning of "innovative step" was an opposition to a certified innovation patent held by INC Corporation Pty Ltd relating

---

136  *Commissioner of Patents v Emperor Sports Pty Ltd* [2006] FCAFC 26.
137  APO, *Manual of Practice and Procedure – National*, July 2011, para 2.31.4.5.4.
138  Ibid.
139  Ibid.
140  Revised Explanatory Memorandum to the Patents Amendment (Innovation Patents) Bill 2000,
     item 6.
141  APO, *Manual of Practice and Procedure – National*, July 2011, para 2.31.4.5.4.1.

to materials for acoustic absorption.[142] Prior manufacturers and distributors of thermoformable sheets, namely, The Smith Family, MCK Pacific Pty Ltd and Foss Manufacturing Co Inc, opposed the innovation patent on lack of novelty and innovative step grounds. Deficiencies in evidence resulted in the opposition proceedings being dismissed. The patent holder's claims which specified weight and specific airflow resistance were considered to have made a "substantial contribution to the working of the invention" as the claims were not "merely superficial or peripheral". Perhaps this is a better formulation of the test of "substantial contribution".

The Full Federal Court more recently turned its attention to the concept of innovative step in *Dura-Post (Aust) Pty Ltd v Delnorth Pty Ltd*.[143] In that case, Delnorth Pty Ltd brought an infringement action against Dura-Post (Aust) Pty Ltd in relation to three innovation patents regarding "Roadside Posts". The appeal related to the validity of particular claims in these innovation patents. After addressing the issues of manner of manufacture and novelty the court considered the issue of innovative step and formulated the test as follows:

> In determining the issue of innovative step, the legislative provisions just mentioned oblige a Court applying them to consider and, where necessary, identify:
> (a) the invention "so far as claimed in any claim";
> (b) the "person skilled in the relevant art";
> (c) to identify the common general knowledge as it existed in Australia before the priority date; and
> (d) to ask in accordance with s 7(4), whether the invention (in (a) above) only varied from the kinds of information in s 7(5) in ways that make no substantial contribution to the working of the invention (in (a) above).[144]

The assessment of innovative step depends on the facts[145] and "substantial" contribution in the context of s 7(4) means "real" or "of substance".[146] The court recognised that "the comparison requires a functional inquiry between the invention as claimed – the claimed device or process – and the relevant prior disclosure".[147] Further, the Australian Patent Office advises its examiners that the balance of probabilities applies in relation to the examination of an innovation patent.[148] The common general knowledge relied on is that pertaining to Australia. Under the *Raising the Bar* amendments this will also change to expand the common general knowledge in the same manner as for the test of inventive step.[149]

## Utility and Section 40

Another element of patentability is that the invention must be useful (s 8(1)(c)). The requirement that the invention be "useful" or have "utility" tends to parallel

---

142  *INC Corporation Pty Ltd v The Smith Family, MCK Pacific Pty Ltd and Foss Manufacturing Company* (2006) AIPC ¶92-183.
143  [2009] FCAFC 81
144  [2009] FCAFC 81 at [54].
145  [2009] FCAFC 81 at [79].
146  [2009] FCAFC 81 at [74].
147  [2009] FCAFC 81 at [83].
148  APO, *Manual of Practice and Procedure – National*, July 2011, para 2.31.4.5.4.1.
149  *Intellectual Property Laws Amendment (Raising The Bar) Act 2012*, Sch 1 Item 4.

the concept of industrial applicability used in other jurisdictions and is also closely related to the requirements of s 40 which requires disclosure of the invention in the specifications. As we said, utility does not require that the invention be useful in the sense of being worthwhile or practical but rather that it works if the specifications are followed.

Gummow J tells us, in *Rehm Pty Ltd v Websters Security Systems (International) Pty Ltd*,[150] that the basic principle of utility was formulated in *Fawcett v Homan*[151] by Lindley LJ in the following terms:

> If an invention does what it is intended by the patentee to do, and the end attained is itself useful, the invention is a useful invention.[152]

Parker J in *In the Matter of Alsop's Patent*[153] also attributes the formulation of the test to Lindley LJ but cites his decision in *Lane Fox v Kensington and Knightsbridge Electric Lighting Co*:[154]

> [T]he well known rule is that the utility of an invention depends upon whether, by following the directions of the patentee, the result which the patentee professed to produce can in fact be produced.[155]

In the more recent case, *Martin Engineering Co v Trison Holdings Pty Ltd*,[156] Burchett J, on the issue of whether the invention as claimed in the complete specification was useful, made the following statement:

> The question, of course, is not whether the particular version or versions of the invention in fact marketed will work; the question is whether any version constructed in accordance with claim 1 will work ... there was no challenge to utility in the sense that the invention is capable of making "the wheels ... go round" ... [it] has been said that this is what is required for immunity against attack on the ground of inutility – not that an invention is commercially practical.[157]

Burchett J continued:

> It is true that, for the purposes of utility, it is necessary to consider what on their correct construction is specified in the claims; if on their correct construction they assert a monopoly, not only in respect of something useful, but also in respect of something not useful, the patent is bad.[158]

The *Raising the Bar* amendments will provide for the first time in Australia a legislative meaning for the term "useful" in a new s 7A. For an invention to meet the requirement of usefulness, the complete specification must disclose a specific, substantial and credible use.[159] The disclosure must be sufficient for a person skilled in the art to appreciate that specific, substantial and credible use

---

150  (1988) 81 ALR 79.

151  (1896) 13 RPC 398.

152  (1896) 13 RPC 398 at 405.

153  (1907) 24 RPC 733.

154  (1892) 9 RPC 413.

155  (1892) 9 RPC 413 at 417.

156  (1989) 14 IPR 330.

157  (1989) 14 IPR 330 at 336.

158  (1989) 14 IPR 330 at 337.

159  *Intellectual Property Laws Amendment (Raising The Bar) Act 2012*, Sch 1 Item 6

of the invention.[160] This amendment will implement the Australian Law Reform Commission's recommendation in its 2004 report: *Review of Gene Patenting and Human Health, Genes and Ingenuity: Gene Patenting and Human Health*. As the terminology is aligned with US law it is intended that the interpretation of "specific, substantial and credible use" be in accordance with US case law.[161] In any event, both the Australian case law and the US case law emphasise that the claims must define the area of monopoly with clarity otherwise there could be a lack of utility. This brings us to the issues raised in s 40 of the Act.[162]

First, s 40(2)(a) provides that the complete specification must "describe the invention fully, including the best method known to the applicant of performing the invention". The specification will be insufficient if it fails to achieve this requirement. Further, all specifications must have at least one claim and that claim must be clear and succinct and fairly based on the matter described in the specification.[163] Where the claim is unclear it is said to be ambiguous. However, the element of fair basis requires that the claim does not go beyond what is disclosed in the complete specification.[164]

On the distinction between insufficiency and inutility, Roskill LJ provides a concise test for each and then describes the difference in *Tetra Molectric Ltd's Application*:[165]

> "Inutility" in the statute means something which is not useful. 'Insufficiency' means something which is insufficiently described ...[166]

> [A] dividing line can fairly be drawn thus: If you cannot achieve the promised result because of deficiencies in the information given in the specification there is insufficiency. But if, following that information and having achieved mechanically that which the specification promises you will achieve by so following it, the end product will not of itself achieve that promise, then that is inutility.[167]

An alternative construction of insufficiency is that where no method whatever of carrying out the invention is disclosed by the specification, the specification is therefore insufficient to enable the invention to be properly carried into effect.[168]

As referred to in Chapter 8, the *Raising the Bar* amendments will require that the test of sufficiency of the claims provides enablement across the full width of the claims and is in keeping with the language in the European Patent Convention and the UK patent legislation. Currently, the patent applicant need only enable one of the potential embodiments of the invention while claiming

---

160  *Intellectual Property Laws Amendment (Raising The Bar) Act 2012*, Sch 1 Item 6

161  Explanatory Memorandum, Intellectual Property Laws Amendment (Raising The Bar) Bill 2011, Sch 1 Item 6, with the terms "specific" and "substantial" interpreted in accordance with *In re Fisher* 421 F 3d 1365 at 1371; 76 USPQ 2d 1225 at 1230 (Fed Cir 2005), and "credible" interpreted in accordance with *In re Marzocchi* 439 F 2d 220 at 223; 169 USPQ 367 at 369 (CCPA 1971).

162  The failure of the specification to comply with either s 40(2) or (3) is a ground for revocation (s 138(3)(f)).

163  Section 40(3).

164  On the test of fair basis and the description of a preferred embodiment, see *Lockwood Security Products Pty Ltd v Doric Products Pty Ltd* [2004] HCA 58.

165  [1976] FSR 424.

166  [1976] FSR 424 at 431.

167  [1976] FSR 424 at 432.

168  *Samuel Taylor Pty Ltd v SA Brush Co Ltd* (1950) 83 CLR 617.

others not fully disclosed. The proposed amendment to s 40(2)(a) requires that, if the bargain is to be struck between the patentee and the public, the exclusive rights granted to the patentee should only extend to that which is disclosed.[169]

Claims must be clear and succinct and not ambiguous.[170] Simultaneously, they must be fairly based on the matter contained in the complete specification and not attempt to extend the patentee's monopoly.[171] *Decor Corp Pty Ltd v Dart Industries Inc*[172] provides a discussion on both aspects. Lockhart J points out that the "lack of precise definition in claims is not fatal to their validity so long as they provide a workable standard suitable to the intended use".[173] On the point of fair basis, Lockhart J makes the following statements:

> To be fairly based the invention claimed must be the same invention which is described in the body of the specification; the claim or claims must be fairly based on what has been described and must not seek to extend the patentee's monopoly beyond this. The patentee is only permitted to claim what he has invented ... The function of the claims is to define clearly and precisely the monopoly claimed. Their primary object is to limit and not to extend the monopoly ...[174]

> In one sense it is right to say that the specification must be read as a whole, but the specification is a whole made up of several parts and those parts have different functions. It is not legitimate to reduce or enlarge the meaning of the words of a claim by glosses derived from other parts of the specification, or to confine the scope of the claims by reference to some limitation which may be found in the body of the specification but is not expressly or by inference reproduced in the claims themselves. In ascertaining the width of a particular claim it is not permissible to vary or qualify the plain and unambiguous meaning of the claim by reference to the body of the specification ... However, if an expression in the claim is not clear, it is then permissible to resort to the body of the specification in order to define or clarify the meaning of the words used in the claim.[175]

In the same case, Sheppard J provided 10 rules of construction in the interpretation of claims:

> In summary, the relevant rules of construction which may be distilled from the authorities referred to are as follows:-
> 1. The claims define the invention which is the subject of the patent. These must be construed according to their terms upon ordinary principles. Any purely verbal or grammatical question that can be answered according to ordinary rules for the construction of written documents is to be resolved accordingly.
> 2. It is not legitimate to confine the scope of the claims by reference to limitations which may be found in the body of the specification but are not expressly or by proper inference reproduced in the claims themselves. To put it another way, it is not legitimate to narrow or expand the boundaries of monopoly as fixed by

---

169  Explanatory Memorandum, Intellectual Property Laws Amendment (Raising The Bar) Bill 2011, Sch 1 Item 8
170  *Patents Act 1990* s 40(3).
171  *Ibid*. For a recent construction of "fair basis", see *Lockwood Security Products Pty Ltd v Doric Products Pty Ltd* [2004] HCA 58.
172  (1988) 13 IPR 385.
173  (1988) 13 IPR 385 at 414, citing Aickin J in *Minnesota Mining & Manufacturing Co v Beiersdorf (Aust) Ltd* (1980) 144 CLR 253.
174  (1988) 13 IPR 385 at 391.
175  (1988) 13 IPR 385 at 391.

the words of a claim by adding to those words glosses drawn from other parts of the specification.

3.  Nevertheless, in approaching the task of construction, one must read the specification as a whole.

4.  In some cases the meaning of the words used in the claims may be qualified or defined by what is said in the body of the specification.

5.  If a claim be clear, it is not to be made obscure because obscurities can be found in particular sentences in other parts of the document. But if an expression is not clear or is ambiguous, it is permissible to resort to the body of the specification to define or clarify the meaning of words used in the claim.

6.  A patent specification should be given a purposive construction rather than a purely literal one.

7.  In construing the specification, the Court is not construing a written instrument operating inter partes, but a public instrument which must define a monopoly in such a way that it is not reasonably capable of being misunderstood.

8.  The body, apart from the preamble, is there to instruct those skilled in the art concerned in the carrying out of the invention; provided it is comprehensible to, and does not mislead, a skilled reader, the language used is seldom of importance.

9.  Nevertheless, the claims, since they define the monopoly, will be scrutinized with as much care as is used in construing other documents defining a legal right.

10. If it is impossible to ascertain what the invention is from a fair reading of the specification as a whole, it will be invalid. But the specification must be construed in the light of the common knowledge in the art before the priority date.[176]

In *Lockwood Security Products Pty Ltd v Doric Products Pty Ltd*,[177] the High Court stressed that "the language [of s 40(3)] points to a comparison between the claims and what is described in the specification only, and ... does not call for any inquiry into an 'inventive step', or inventive 'merit' or a 'technical contribution to the art'."[178] This emphasises the possibility that the claims may indeed be consistent with the matter described in the specification while simultaneously failing the tests for novelty and/or inventive step or even sufficiency. The High Court pointed out that, in making an assessment under s 40(3), there is no need to take into account the common general knowledge of the skilled addressee nor the prior art as what "is essential in assessing a fair basing objection is recourse to the contents of the specification".[179] Rather there needs to be "a real and reasonably clear disclosure in the body of the specification of what is then claimed, so that the alleged invention as claimed is broadly, that is to say in a general sense, described in the body of the specification".[180] Further, the High Court emphasised that when a claim is framed in a consistory clause:

> [That] clause is not fairly based if other parts of the matter in the specification show that the invention is narrower than that consistory clause. The inquiry is into what the body

176  (1988) 13 IPR 385 at 400. Consider also the reformulation and expansion of these rules in *Flexible Steel Lacing Company v Beltreco Ltd* [2000] FCA 890.

177  [2004] HCA 58.

178  [2004] HCA 58 at [54].

179  [2004] HCA 58 at [48].

180  [2004] HCA 58 at [69], quoting Gummow J in *Rehm Pty Ltd v Websters Security Systems (International) Pty Ltd* (1988) 81 ALR 79 at 95. This point is emphasised in the recent case, *Sunnyfield Association v Cronk* [2010] FCA 143, Graham J at [64] and [65].

of the specification read as a whole discloses as the invention ... The consistory clause is to be considered by the court with the rest of the specification.[181]

The *Raising the Bar* amendments will do away with the test of "fair-basing" and introduce the test of "support" currently utilised in European and UK jurisdictions. This is an interesting development particularly when the High Court in *Lockwood* noted that "current United Kingdom law is no guide to Australian law on s 40(3)".[182] The impact foreshadowed is that there are two results which could be said to overlap with enablement under s 40(2)(a) and inventive step:

- there must be a basis in the description for each claim; and
- the scope of the claims must not be broader than is justified by the extent of the description, drawings and contribution to the art.

The Explanatory Memorandum suggests that Australian courts will have at their disposal the case law and administrative decisions of the UK and other European jurisdictions to assist in the interpretation of the proposed "support" requirement and this will enhance harmonisation.[183] While such jurisprudence may well be persuasive, Australian courts are free to interpret legislation in their own way potentially developing an alternate interpretation of the "support" requirement to that of Europe.

In practice, many objections to patents are based on s 40 and many of these objections are successful. However, as we saw in the previous chapter, this may not lead to the failure of the patent because the Commissioner will often allow rectification.[184]

## Secret Use

In contrast to s 40 objections, secret use has been described as a "free-standing ground of invalidity" requiring only one instance to be fatal to the validity of the patent in question. While there has been little case law in Australia regarding the element of "no secret use",[185] a significant review of this criteria was provided by the Federal Court in *Azuko Pty Ltd v Old Digger Pty Ltd*.[186] This case dealt with a patent infringement action and counter-claim for revocation of two patents concerning features of a hammer used in exploratory drilling in mining operations. The question that arose was whether the manufacture of a number

---

181  [2004] HCA 58 at [99].

182  [2004] HCA 58 at [67].

183  Explanatory Memorandum, Intellectual Property Laws Amendment (Raising The Bar) Bill 2011, Sch 1 Item 9.

184  Amendments are dealt with in Chapter 10 of the *Patents Act 1990* with the Commissioner's powers encompassed in ss 104, 106 and 107 of the Act. In relation to the circumstances in which the court will exercise its discretion to grant or refuse amendment of a patent under s 105, see *Novartis AG v Bausch & Lomb (Australia) Pty Ltd* [2004] FCA 835 and *Arrow Pharmaceuticals Limited v Merck & Co Inc* [2004] FCA 138 at [7]. See also *New England Biolabs, Inc v F Hoffmann-La Roche AG* [2004] FCA 1651.

185  See Heerey J in *Azuko Pty Ltd v Old Digger Pty Ltd* [2001] FCA 1079 at [105] where his Honour points out the historical rationale for this criteria being "to prevent a patentee from gaining a longer monopoly than the statutory period by enjoying a period of de facto monopoly through secret use without meeting the corresponding obligation of public disclosure".

186  [2001] FCA 1079.

of hammers before the priority date of one of the patents constituted secret use within s 18(1)(d) or fell within the exceptions found in s 9(a) and (b) of the *Patents Act 1990*.

The Federal Court decided 2:1 in favour of the patentee with Beaumont J agreeing with the judgment of Gyles J that there was no secret use. Heerey J, though, provided a broad interpretation of the term "use", thereby finding for the opponents that there was secret use of one of the patents before the priority date. His Honour drew upon English case law for assistance in this regard, particularly *Bristol-Myers Co v Beecham Group Ltd*[187] and *Fomento Industrial SA v Mentmore Manufacturing Co Limited*,[188] concluding that making the article described in the specification constituted the relevant use of the invention implying that the making was for the purposes of sale.

The majority, on the other hand, formulated a different test for "secret use", concluding that the manufacturing of the product did not amount to secret use. Gyles J drew the following arguments after analysing the relevant case law:

> [H]as what occurred amounted to a de facto extension of the patent term? The answer to this will usually depend upon whether the patentee reaped commercial benefit from what was done before the priority date. In the present case, in my opinion, there has been no de facto extension of the term of the patent by making the articles in question …
>
> To make an article for ultimate sale has, no doubt, a commercial aspect, but it does not amount to use of the product made and does not involve any de facto extension of the term of a patent claiming the product. The manufacturing of goods is not, in my opinion, commercial use of those goods.[189]

The majority's decision was coloured by the evidence adduced by the parties and the findings of fact by the primary judge. The fact that the patentee did not "sell" the hammers manufactured until after the priority date of the relevant patent strongly influenced the decision. Further, it was accepted that the order received for the hammers before the priority date was unsolicited and the patentee did not "accept" the order before the priority date. The order received was from the party testing the prototype of the invention, which would have some bearing on the exceptions provided in s 9(a) and (b), namely, reasonable trial and experiment, and confidential disclosure, respectively.

---

187  [1974] AC 646.
188  [1956] RPC 87.
189  [2001] FCA 1079 at [181] and [183].

# CASES

## National Research Development Corporation v Commissioner of Patents
### High Court of Australia: Dixon CJ, Kitto and Windeyer JJ
### (1959) 102 CLR 252

The *NRDC* case is the leading case on the modern determination of what is a proper subject for the grant of a patent as determined by the reference to "manner of new manufacture" in the *Statute of Monopolies*.

The court gave a broad interpretation of manner of manufacture, an interpretation of the requirement of newness and determined that, contrary to previous suggestions, the grant of patents in relation to food and agricultural products were proper subjects for the grant of a patent. On this basis the court allowed the appeal by NRDC against the Deputy Commissioner's direction under s 49 of the *Patents Act 1952* to delete the three claims in question from the applicant's specification.

**Dixon CJ, Kitto and Windeyer JJ: [260]** It is a requirement of the Act that an application shall be for a "patent": s 34; and "patent" is defined by s 6 to mean letters patent for an "invention." "Invention" is defined to mean "any manner of new manufacture the subject of letters patent and grant of privilege within section six of the *Statute of Monopolies*", and to include an alleged invention. Accordingly it is a subject for report under s 47 whether each claim in a complete specification defines an invention of the kind to which the expression "a manner of new manufacture" in the *Statute of Monopolies* must be understood to refer.

The complete specification in the present case contains, as has been mentioned, six claims. Those numbered 4, 5 and 6 are for **[261]** selective herbicidal compositions, and are not here in question. Claims 1, 2 and 3 are in these terms: "1. A method for eradicating weeds from crop areas containing a growing crop selected from leguminous fodder crops of the genera *Trifolium* and *Medicago*, celery and parsnip, which comprises applying to the crop areas a herbicide of the class consisting of the O-(2:4-dichlorophenoxy) –butyric and –caproic acids, their salts, esters, nitriles and amides. 2. A method for the control of weeds of the type of charlock, creeping thistle and annual nettle in a lucerne (alfalfa) crop in which a compound of the class consisting of the O-(2:4-dichlorophenoxy) –butyric and –caproic acids, their salts, esters, nitriles and amides is applied to the crop area in a concentration ranging between 1 to 2 lbs. per acre. 3. A method for the control of weeds of the type of charlock, creeping thistle and annual nettle in a clover crop in which a compound of the class consisting of the O-(2:4- dichlorophenoxy) –butyric and –caproic acids, their salts, esters, nitriles and amides is applied to the crop area in a concentration ranging between 1 to 2 lbs per acre."

The examiner, in his report under ss 47 and 48, stated objections to these three claims in the following terms: "It appears that the active substances of the invention are known. Claims 1 to 3 are not therefore directed to any manner of manufacture in that they are claims to the mere use of known substances – which use also does not result in any vendible product". ...

The power of the Commissioner under s 49(2) is discretionary, but since a requirement that claims be deleted from a specification is equivalent to a refusal of the patent for the invention claimed thereby the discretion ought not to be exercised by making such a requirement except in circumstances which would justify the refusal of a patent on a specification containing those claims and no others. The principles which govern the power to refuse a patent have been discussed recently in the case of *Commissioner of Patents v Microcell Ltd*.[190] It is shown in that case that in the portion of the definition of invention which includes in the meaning of the word an alleged invention, the word "alleged" goes only to the epithet "new" in the expression "a manner of new manufacture", and that accordingly the Commissioner may properly reject a claim for **[262]** a process which is not within the concept of a "manufacture". But the case cited shows also that even if the process is within the concept the Commissioner is not bound to accept the allegation of the applicant that it is new, if it is apparent on the face of the specification, when properly construed, that the allegation is unfounded: see also *Re Johnson's Patent*.[191] It is therefore open to the Commissioner in a proper case to direct the deletion of a claim for a process which may be seen from the specification, considered as a whole, to be "outside the whole scope of what is known as invention" because, in the words of Lord *Buckmaster*, when Solicitor-General, in *Re BA's Application*[192] it is "nothing but a claim for a new use of an old substance".[193]

But, as the *Microcell Case*[194] emphasizes, it must always be remembered how much is wrapped up in the "nothing but". Lord *Buckmaster* did not use the words without explanation:- "... when once a substance is known," he said, "its methods of production ascertained, its characteristics and its constituents well defined, you cannot patent the use of that for a purpose which was hitherto unknown".[195] And why? Because in the postulated state of knowledge the new purpose is no more than analogous to the purposes for which the utility of the substance is already known, and therefore your suggestion of the new purpose lacks the quality of inventiveness: see per *Bowen* LJ in *Elias v Grovesend Tinplate Co*.[196] Unless invention is found in some new method of using the material or some new adaptation of it so as to serve the new purpose, no valid patent can be granted: see *Moser v Marsden*;[197] *Pirrie v York Street Flax Spinning Co, Ltd*.[198] If, however, the new use that is proposed consists in taking advantage of a hitherto unknown or unsuspected property of the material, the situation is not that to which Lord *Buckmaster's* language refers. In that case there may be invention in the suggestion that the substance may be used to serve the new purpose; and then, provided that a practical method of so using it is disclosed and that the process comes within the concept of patent law ultimately traceable to the use in the *Statute of Monopolies* of the words "manner of manufacture," all the elements of a patentable invention are present: see the *Microcell Case*.[199] It is not necessary that in addition the proposed method should itself be novel or involve any inventive step: *Hickton's Patent Syndicate v Patents and Machine Improvements Co Ltd*.[200]

**[263]** This, we consider, differs not at all from the view which *Lindley* LJ expressed in the passage in his judgment in the case of *Lane Fox v Kensington and Knightsbridge Electric Lighting Co*[201] which is often cited and was referred to more than once in the argument of the present case, namely that a man who discovers that a known machine

[190] (1959) 102 CLR 232.
[191] (1937) 55 RPC 4, at p 19.
[192] (1915) 32 RPC 348.
[193] (1915) 32 RPC, at p 349.
[194] (1959) 102 CLR 232.
[195] (1915) 32 RPC, at p 349.
[196] (1890) 7 RPC 455, at p 468.
[197] (1893) 10 RPC 350, at p 358.
[198] (1894) 11 RPC 429, at p 452.
[199] (1959) 102 CLR, at pp 248, 249.
[200] (1909) 26 RPC 339.
[201] [1892] 3 Ch 424, at pp 428, 429; (1892) 9 RPC 413, at p 416.

(his Lordship might equally have said a known substance) can produce effects which no one before him knew could be produced by it has made a discovery, but has not made a patentable invention unless he so uses his knowledge and ingenuity as to produce either a new and useful thing or result, or a new and useful method of producing an old thing or result. His Lordship went on to say that the discovery how to use a known thing for a new purpose will be a patentable invention if there is novelty in the mode of using it as distinguished from novelty of purpose, or if any new modification of the thing or any new appliance is necessary for using it for its new purpose, and if such mode of user, or modification, or appliance involves any appreciable merit. But the whole passage is directed to the case of a thing which is known – not only the existence of which is known as a scientific fact, but the characteristics and properties of which are understood, so that the "appreciable merit"[202] which is requisite for a patentable invention must be found, if it is to be found at all, exclusively in something which the alleged invention has superadded to the existing knowledge concerning the thing. There is nothing in the judgment of *Lindley* LJ to justify a denial that, in respect of a process for achieving a useful result by the employment of a substance to produce effects which antecedently it was not understood to be capable of producing, the inventiveness which is essential for a valid grant of a patent may be found in the step which consists of suggesting the use of the thing for the new purpose, notwithstanding that there is no novelty or "appreciable merit" in any suggested mode of using the thing, or any modification of the thing or of an appliance necessary for using it for the new purpose. It is not decisive – it is not even helpful – to point out in such a case that beyond discovery of a scientific fact nothing has been added except the suggestion that nature, in its newly ascertained aspect, be allowed to work in its own way. Arguments of this kind may be answered as *Frankfurter* J answered them in *Funk Bros Seed Co v Kalo Inoculant Co*:[203] "It only confuses the issue," the learned Justice said, "to introduce such terms as 'the work of nature' and the 'laws of **[264]** nature'. For these are vague and malleable terms infected with too much ambiguity and equivocation. Everything that happens may be deemed 'the work of nature', and any patentable composite exemplifies in its properties 'the laws of nature'. Arguments drawn from such terms for ascertaining patentability could fairly be employed to challenge almost any patent".[204] The truth is that the distinction between discovery and invention is not precise enough to be other than misleading in this area of discussion. There may indeed be a discovery without invention – either because the discovery is of some piece of abstract information without any suggestion of a practical application of it to a useful end, or because its application lies outside the realm of "manufacture". But where a person finds out that a useful result may be produced by doing something which has not been done by that procedure before, his claim for a patent is not validly answered by telling him that although there was ingenuity in his discovery that the materials used in the process would produce the useful result no ingenuity was involved in showing how the discovery, once it had been made, might be applied. The fallacy lies in dividing up the process that he puts forward as his invention. It is the whole process that must be considered; and he need not show more than one inventive step in the advance which he has made beyond the prior limits of the relevant art. This is perhaps nowhere more clearly put than it was by *Fletcher Moulton* LJ in *Hickton's Patent Syndicate v Patents and Machine Improvements Co Ltd*[205] when he said of Watt's invention for the condensation of steam, out of which the steam engine grew: "Now can it be suggested that it required any invention whatever to carry out that idea when once you had got it? It could be done

---

[202] [1892] 3 Ch, at p 429; (1892) 9 RPC, at p 416.
[203] (1948) 333 US 127 [92 Law Ed 588].
[204] (1948) 333 US, at pp 134, 135 [92 Law Ed, at p 591].
[205] (1909) 26 RPC 339.

in a thousand ways and by any competent engineer, but the invention was in the idea, and when he had once got that idea, the carrying out of it was perfectly easy. To say that the conception may be meritorious and may involve invention and may be new and original, and simply because when you have once got the idea it is easy to carry it out, that that deprives it of the title of being a new invention according to our patent law, is, I think, an extremely dangerous principle and justified neither by reason nor authority".[206]

No-one reading the specification in the present case can fail to see that what it claims is a new process for ridding crop areas of certain kinds of weeds, not by applying chemicals the properties of which were formerly well understood so that the idea of using **[265]** them for this purpose involved no inventive step, but by applying chemicals which formerly were supposed not to be useful for this kind of purpose at all. There is a clear assertion of a discovery that a useful result can be attained by doing something which the applicant's research has shown for the first time to be capable of producing that result. This is not a claim which can be put aside as a claim for a new use of an old substance, true though it be that the chemicals themselves were known to science before the applicant's investigations began. It is a claim which denies that the chemicals are old substances in the sense in which the expression has been used in such cases as *Re AF's Application*;[207] *Re BA's Application*;[208] and *Re CGR's Application*.[209] It treats them as substances which in the relevant sense are new, that is to say as substances which formerly were known only partially and, so far as weed-killing potentialities are concerned, were unknown; and its tenor is that by an application of scientific ingenuity, combining knowledge, thought and experimentation, not only in relation to the chemicals but in relation also to the enzyme systems of certain weeds and plants, the applicant has evolved a new and useful method of destroying weeds without harming useful vegetation amongst which they are growing. It is irrelevant, even if true, that once the discovery was made that the chemicals produce a lethal reaction when applied to the weeds and produce no such reaction when applied to the crops there was no more ingenuity required in order to show how the process might be performed. The point that matters is that a weed-killing process is claimed which is distinguished from previously known processes by a feature the suggestion of which for such a process involved a step plainly inventive. ...

**[268]** The central question in the case remains. It is whether the process that is claimed falls within the category of inventions to which, by definition, the application of the Patents Act is confined. The definition, it will be remembered, is exclusive: invention means any manner of new manufacture the subject of letters patent and grant of privilege within s 6 of the *Statute of Monopolies*. The Commissioner, adopting certain judicial pronouncements to which reference will be made, emphasizes the word "manufacture" and contends for an interpretation of it which, though not narrow, is restricted to vendible products and processes for their production, and excludes all agricultural and horticultural processes. On the grounds both of the suggested restriction and of the suggested exclusion he denies that a process for killing weeds can be within the relevant concept of invention. The appellant, on the other hand, urges upon us a wider view: that there is a "manufacture" such as might properly have been the subject of letters patent and grant of privilege under s 6 of the *Statute of Monopolies* whenever a process produces, either immediately or ultimately, a useful physical result in relation to a material or tangible entity.

Section 6 of the *Statute of Monopolies* provides that the declarations of invalidity contained in the preceding provisions of the Act "shall not extend to any letters patents and graunts of privilege ... hereafter to be made of the sole working or makinge of any

---

[206] (1909) 26 RPC, at pp 347-348.
[207] (1913) 31 RPC 58.
[208] (1915) 32 RPC 348.
[209] (1924) 42 RPC 320.

manner of new manufactures within this realme, to the true and first inventor and inventors of such manufactures, which others at the tyme of makinge such letters patents and graunts shall not **[269]** use, soe as alsoe they be not contrary to the lawe or mischievous to the state by raisinge prices of comodities at home, or hurt of trade, or generallie inconvenient": *Halsbury's Statutes of England*, 2nd ed vol 17 (1950), p 619. It is of the first importance to remember always that the *Patents Act* 1952-1955 (Cth), like its predecessor the *Patents Act* 1903 (Cth) and corresponding statutes of the United Kingdom (see the *Patents, Designs and Trade Marks Act* 1883, s 46; the *Patents Act* 1907, s 93; and the *Patents Act* 1949, s 101), defines the word "invention", not by direct explication and in the language of its own day, nor yet by carrying forward the usage of the period in which the *Statute of Monopolies* was passed, but by reference to the established ambit of s 6 of that Statute. The inquiry which the definition demands is an inquiry into the scope of the permissible subject matter of letters patent and grants of privilege protected by the section. It is an inquiry not into the meaning of a word so much as into the breadth of the concept which the law has developed by its consideration of the text and purpose of the *Statute of Monopolies*. One may remark that although the Statute spoke of the inventor it nowhere spoke of the invention; all that is nowadays understood by the latter word as used in patent law it comprehended in "new manufactures". The word "manufacture" finds a place in the present Act, not as a word intended to reduce a question of patentability to a question of verbal interpretation, but simply as the general title found in the *Statute of Monopolies* for the whole category under which all grants of patents which may be made in accordance with the developed principles of patent law are to be subsumed. It is therefore a mistake, and a mistake likely to lead to an incorrect conclusion, to treat the question whether a given process or product is within the definition as if that question could be restated in the form: "Is this a manner (or kind) of manufacture?" It is a mistake which tends to limit one's thinking by reference to the idea of making tangible goods by hand or by machine, because "manufacture" as a word of everyday speech generally conveys that idea. The right question is: "Is this a proper subject of letters patent according to the principles which have been developed for the application of s 6 of the *Statute of Monopolies*?"

It is a very different question. A perusal of the definitions and quotations appearing in the Oxford English Dictionary under "manufacture" will show that the word has always admitted of applications beyond the limits which a strict observance of its etymology would suggest, and, as the present Chief Justice said **[270]** in *Maeder v Busch*,[210] a widening conception of the notion has been a characteristic of the growth of patent law. As early as 1795 it was possible for *Eyre* CJ to say that "the exposition of the statute as far as usage will expound it, has gone much beyond the letter";[211] and the width of the meaning that had already been accepted may be gauged from the statement of the same learned judge that "manufacture" extended "to any new results of principles carried into practice ... new processes in any art producing effects useful to the public": *Boulton v Bull*.[212] By 1842 it was finally settled that "manufacture" was used in the *Statute of Monopolies* in the dual sense which comprehends both a process and a product: *Crane v Price*.[213] But a question which appears still to await final decision is whether it is enough that a process produces a useful result or whether it is necessary that some physical thing is either brought into existence or so affected as the better to serve man's purposes. In some of the cases it is suggested that the process must issue in some "vendible matter"

[210] (1938) 59 CLR 684, at p 706.
[211] (1795) 1 H Bl 463, at p 492 [126 ER 651, at p 666].
[212] (1795) 1 H Bl 463, at p 492 [126 ER 651, at p 666].
[213] (1842) 1 Web PC 393; 4 Man & G 580 [134 ER 239].

or a "vendible product". The former expression was used by *Heath* J in *Boulton v Bull*[214] in the course of maintaining the opinion, which must now be considered heretical, that there could not be a patent for a method; but no such expression appears in the powerful judgment in which *Eyre* CJ maintained the opposite view and reached the conclusion in the particular case which was ultimately upheld in *Hornblower v Boulton*.[215] *Abbott* CJ in *R v Wheeler*[216] having spoken of a "thing made, which is useful for its own sake, and vendible as such",[217] went on to show that he did not find in such expressions as those any absolute test. He said (the italics are ours): "Something of a corporeal and substantial nature, something that can be made by man from the matters subjected to his art and skill, or at the least some new mode of employing practically his art and skill, is requisite to satisfy this word".[218] It is of course not possible to treat such a statement as conclusive of the question. The need for qualification must be confessed, even if only in order to put aside, as they apparently must be put aside, processes for treating diseases of the human body: see *Re C & W's Application*;[219] *Maeder v Busch*.[220] When appearing as counsel in the case last **[271]** cited, Sir George *Ligertwood* made a helpful suggestion which in effect amended the statement of *Abbott* CJ to read "... or at least some new method of employing practically the art and skill of the workman in a manual art".[221] But even so comprehensive a statement needs to be given a somewhat flexible meaning to allow for long-standing authorities such as *Forsyth v Riviere*[222] (where the patent was for a method of discharging firearms), and *Electric Telegraph Co v Brett*[223] (where the patent was for a method of giving duplicate electric signals). The truth is that any attempt to state the ambit of s 6 of the *Statute of Monopolies* by precisely defining "manufacture" is bound to fail. The purpose of s 6, it must be remembered, was to allow the use of the prerogative to encourage national development in a field which already, in 1623, was seen to be excitingly unpredictable. To attempt to place upon the idea the fetters of an exact verbal formula could never have been sound. It would be unsound to the point of folly to attempt to do so now, when science has made such advances that the concrete applications of the notion which were familiar in 1623 can be seen to provide only the more obvious, not to say the more primitive, illustrations of the broad sweep of the concept.

In a case which has been much cited in recent times, *Re GEC's Application*,[224] Morton J, as he then was, while disclaiming the intention of laying down any hard and fast rule applicable to all cases, put forward a proposition which, if literally applied, would have a narrowing effect on the law and indeed has already been found to stand as much in need as the statute itself of a generous interpretation. The proposition was that "a method or process is a manner of manufacture if it (a) results in the production of some vendible product or (b) improves or restores to its former condition a vendible product or (c) has the effect of preserving from deterioration some vendible product to which it is applied". [225] Any criticism to which this is open, as Lord *Jenkins* remarked in *Samuel Reitzman v Grahame-Chapman and Derustit Ltd*,[226] is certainly not on the score of its being too

---

[214] (1795) 1 H Bl 463, at p 482 [126 ER 651, at p 661].
[215] (1799) 8 TR 95 [101 ER 1285].
[216] (1819) 2 B & Ald 345 [106 ER 392].
[217] (1819) 2 B & Ald, at p 349 [106 ER, at p 394].
[218] (1819) 2 B Ald, at p 350 [106 ER, at p 395].
[219] (1914) 31 RPC 235.
[220] (1938) 59 CLR 684.
[221] (1938) 59 CLR, at p 696.
[222] (1819) 1 Web PC 95.
[223] (1851) 10 CB 838 [138 ER 331].
[224] (1942) 60 RPC 1.
[225] (1942) 60 RPC, at p 4.
[226] (1950) 68 RPC 25, at p 32.

wide. It is valuable for its insistence that in patent law at the present day a process may be within the concept of "manufacture" notwithstanding that it merely improves, restores, or preserves some antecedently existing thing; but in so far as it may appear to restrict the concept by its use of the expression "vendible product", it must be considered now as substantially qualified by the comments made upon it by *Evershed* J (as he then **[272]** was) in *Re Cementation Co Ltd's Application*[227] and in *Re Rantzen's Application*,[228] and by Lloyd-Jacob J in *Re Elton and Leda Chemicals Ltd's Application*.[229]

The *Cementation Case*[230] has importance here, because it decided that a process of treating a stratum of subterranean soil with chemicals may be patentable, the word "product" in *Morton* J's formulation being understood in a sense wide enough to include such a subject-matter. The process in question consisted in drilling holes from the surface to a subterranean formation which was liable to combustion, and introducing through the holes material of such a nature that it would dissociate upon the initiation of combustion, with liberation of carbon dioxide and the consequential extinguishing of the fire. For this process *Evershed* J granted a patent, observing that the emphasis in *Morton* J's "rule" was upon the three activities of production, improvement or restoration, and prevention from deterioration, and that the word "product" was used in a sense which included "that which is produced by any action, operation or work; a production; the result"; so that it denoted the subject-matter of each of the three forms of activity referred to, and was not intended to limit the conception by reference to the common acceptation of "product". ....

[The court went on to consider other cases which affected the interpretation of the Morton Rules.]

**[277]** Notwithstanding the tendency of these decisions, the view which we think is correct in the present case is that the method the subject of the relevant claims has as its end result an artificial effect falling squarely within the true concept of what must be produced by a process if it is to be held patentable. This view is, we think, required by a sound understanding of the lines along which patent law has developed and necessarily must develop in a modern society. The effect produced by the appellant's method exhibits the two essential qualities upon which "product" and "vendible" seem designed to insist. It is a "product" because it consists in an artificially created state of affairs, discernible by observing over a period the growth of weeds and crops respectively on sown land on which the method has been put into practice. And the significance of the product is economic; for it provides a remarkable advantage, indeed to the lay mind a sensational advantage, for one of the most elemental activities by which man has served his material needs, the cultivation of the soil for the production of its fruits. Recognition that the relevance of the process is to this economic activity old as it is, need not be inhibited by any fear of inconsistency with the claim to novelty which the specification plainly makes. The method cannot be classed as a variant of ancient procedures. It is additional to the cultivation. It achieves a separate result, and the result possesses its own economic utility consisting in an important improvement in the conditions in which the crop is to grow, whereby it is afforded a better opportunity to flourish and yield a good harvest.

There remains for consideration the Commissioner's contention that, even apart from the considerations which have been discussed, agricultural or horticultural processes are, by reason of their nature, outside the limits of patentable inventions. Only in comparatively recent times have statements appeared which explicitly support the

[227] (1945) 62 RPC 151.
[228] (1946) 64 RPC 63, at p 65.
[229] [1957] RPC 267.
[230] (1945) 62 RPC 151.

contention. In *Re Rau Gesellschaft's Application*,[231] an application for a patent in respect of the production by selective cultivation of lupin seeds having certain characteristics was rejected. *Luxmoore* J approved a statement by the examiner in terms which seem to run together the question whether such a process can be novel and the question whether it can be a "manufacture". It reads: "Selective breeding of animals and cultivation of plants for the obtainment of improved stocks by the rigorous selection of and breeding from the few individuals which are nearest the ideal has, as is well known, been practised from the earliest times as a part of agricultural or horticultural development, as for example in the production of **[278]** improved flowers or fruit with desired characteristics in the progeny, and the exercise of art or skill in these directions has not been regarded as coming within the term 'manufacture'". (There had been earlier cases in which applications relating to agriculture had been refused on other grounds; for instance, *Re Hamilton-Adam's Application*,[232] where the process was one for rotation of crops, and the ground taken was that although there was a discovery there was no improvement in the method of carrying out any agricultural operations). It must often happen in a sphere of human endeavour as old as that of primary production that a newly-devised procedure amounts to nothing more than an analogous application of age-old techniques; and where that is the case, want of novelty is a fatal objection to a patent. It may be conceded, moreover, that if there were nothing that could properly be called a "product" of the process, even an ingenious new departure would be outside the limits of patentability. In *Re RHF's Application*[233] *Morton* J approved a statement of the examiner which had been made to illustrate that the vendible product test enunciated in the *GEC Case*[234] was not definitive. The statement was that fruit and other growing crops, although the assistance of man may be invoked for their planting and cultivation, do not result from a process which is a "manner of manufacture". This may be agreed. However advantageously man may alter the conditions of growth, the fruit is still not produced by his action. But in the *Standard Oil Development Co's Case*,[235] where a patent was sought for a selective herbicidal process, it emerged from the examiner's report that an "established Office practice" had grown up of denying that any agricultural or horticultural process could be a "manner of manufacture". Upon this, *Lloyd-Jacob* J made no comment, and the office view has since been adhered to: *Re Dow Chemical Co's Application*;[236] *Re Canterbury Agricultural College's Application*.[237] The proposition seems an example of a generalization not supported by the reasons leading to the conclusions in the particular instances from which the generalization is drawn. If it means that there is some consideration wrapped up in the label "agricultural or horticultural" which necessarily takes a process outside the area of patentability even though it is a novel process and of sufficient inventiveness, the consideration is not easy to identify. There seems to be here a classic illustration of thinking in terms of the everyday concept of manufacture instead of following **[279]** the lines along which, over a long period, the courts have given effect to the real purpose and operation of s 6 of the *Statute of Monopolies*. The cases of *Lenard's Application*[238] (pruning to reduce mortality from disease in clove trees) and *NV Philips' Gloeilampenfabrieken Application*[239] (a method for producing a new form of poinsettia) both seem to depend on the view that

[231] (1935) 52 RPC 362.
[232] (1918) 35 RPC 90.
[233] (1944) 61 RPC 49.
[234] (1942) 60 RPC 1.
[235] (1951) 68 RPC 114.
[236] [1956] RPC 247.
[237] [1958] RPC 85.
[238] (1954) 71 RPC 190.
[239] (1954) 71 RPC 192.

the process in question was only one for altering the conditions of growth, so that the contemplated end result would not be a result of the process but would be "the inevitable result of that which is inherent in the plant" (as it was expressed in the case last cited).[240] A distinction has necessarily to be drawn between cases of this class and cases of methods employing micro-organisms; see the *Commercial Solvents Corporation v Synthetic Products Co Ltd*[241] and *Adhesives Pty Ltd v Aktieselskabet Dansk Gaerings-Industri*;[242] *Virginia-Carolina Chemical Corporation's Application*,[243] for in the latter class of cases the process is analogous to a chemical process in that, given the micro-organisms and the appropriate conditions, the desired result inevitably follows from the working of the process: see *Re Joseph Szuecs Application*.[244]

We are here concerned with a process producing its effect by means of a chemical reaction, and the ultimate weed-free, or comparatively weed-free condition of the crop-bearing land is properly described as produced by the process. The fact that the relevance of the process is to agricultural or horticultural enterprises does not in itself supply or suggest any consideration not already covered which should weigh against the conclusion that the process is a patentable invention.

## *Advanced Building Systems Pty Ltd v Ramset Fasteners (Aust) Pty Ltd*

High Court of Australia: Brennan CJ, Gaudron, McHugh,
Gummow and Kirby JJ
(1998) 152 ALR 604

The facts of the case and the rather complex case history are included within the following extract.

**Brennan CJ, Gaudron, McHugh and Gummow JJ:**

**[605] Introduction**

1. Standard Patent No 544832 ("the Patent") was issued under the Patents Act 1952 (Cth) ("the Act") to a United States corporation, The Burke Company ("the second appellant"), and was sealed on 28 October 1985. The term of the Patent was 16 years commencing on 27 August 1981. The basic application had been filed on 23 October 1980 and it is that date which provides the priority date by which questions of novelty and obviousness of the claims are to be assessed. By registered assignment dated 22 November 1990, the second appellant assigned the Patent to Advanced Building Systems Pty Limited ("the first appellant").

2. The invention claimed in the Patent relates to hoisting attachments and methods for erecting prefabricated concrete walls on building sites. There are two claims defining the invention. The second is narrower than the first. It is unnecessary for the issues which arise on this appeal to set out their text.

3. In proceedings instituted in the Federal Court of Australia, the appellants alleged that Ramset Fasteners (Aust) Pty Limited ("the respondent") had infringed the claims of the Patent by the selling or supplying by way of hire of two lift systems for tilt-up walls. The components of these systems were described as the "Ramset Frimeda Rapid Lift System" and the "Ramset Face Lift Tilt Up System" ("the Ramset systems") ...

---

[240] (1954) 71 RPC, at p 194.
[241] (1926) 43 RPC 185.
[242] (1935) 55 CLR 523.
[243] [1958] RPC 35, at p 37.
[244] (1956) 73 RPC 25.

**[606]** 7. Hill J delivered two judgments. In the first, delivered 23 April 1993,[245] his Honour held that the respondent failed on its cross-claim for revocation. In the second, delivered 13 April 1995,[246] his Honour held that the infringement case against the respondent failed but that it had contravened s 52 of the Trade Practices Act. Hill J granted the appellants injunctive relief under that statute but held that the first appellant had failed to make good its damages claim.

8. The respondent appealed to the Full Court of the Federal Court. The appellants cross-appealed, principally against the rejection by Hill J of their damages claim under the Trade Practices Act. The Full Court (Lockhart, Beazley and Sackville JJ) allowed the appeal and dismissed the cross-appeal.[247] In place of the orders made by Hill J, the Full Court ordered that the appellants' application be dismissed and the Patent be revoked. Thus there were no issues of infringement left for determination. The basis for an award of damages under the Trade Practices Act was removed and the cross-appeal was dismissed because the claim for damages depended on the validity of the Patent. The Full Court did not consider all of the grounds of alleged invalidity. That of obviousness or lack of an inventive step, based upon s 100(1)(e) of the Act, had been abandoned at the commencement of the trial before Hill J. This had great significance for the conduct of the appeal to the Full Court. It removed from consideration any objection to validity that the combination claimed in claims 1 and 2 of the Patent did not involve an inventive step and so lacked subject matter.

9. With respect to anticipation or lack of novelty, Hill J had held that none of the prior publications relied upon by the respondent was sufficient to make out the case under s 100(1)(g) of the Act that, on the priority date of the claims, 23 October 1980, the invention was not novel in Australia.[248] The Full Court did not consider the ground of appeal disputing the trial judge's dismissal of the case based on lack of novelty. Rather, it determined the appeal and ordered revocation, on the footing that the respondent had made out its case under s 100(1)(d) that the invention claimed was not an invention within the meaning of the Act 1903.[249] ...

## Combination claims

**[607]** 12. Each of the claims in the Patent is for an apparatus which comprises a combination of elements or integers. In *Welch Perrin & Co Pty Ltd v Worrel*,[250] this Court (Dixon CJ, Kitto and Windeyer JJ) considered the validity of a patent for an invention for a mechanical hay rake. Referring to the specification, their Honours said:[251]

> It was not seriously disputed that it is for a combination, in the sense that word bears in patent law. That is to say, what is described is a machine, the elements of which are all well known and simple mechanical integers, but combined so that they are not a mere collocation of separate parts, but interact to make up a new thing.

This notion of a "new thing" includes a new result, "that is, a new way of **[608]** achieving an old purpose or the fulfilment of a new purpose",[252] and "a new combination of features to obtain an improved result".[253] The significance of the exclusion of a "mere

[245] *Advanced Building Systems Pty Ltd v Ramset Fasteners (Aust) Pty Ltd* (1993) 26 IPR 171
[246] *Advanced Building Systems Pty Ltd v Ramset Fasteners (Aust) Pty Ltd* (1995) AIPC 91-129
[247] *Ramset Fasteners (Aust) Pty Ltd v Advanced Building Systems Pty Ltd* (1996) 66 FCR 151
[248] *Advanced Building Systems Pty Ltd v Ramset Fasteners (Aust) Pty Ltd* (1993) 26 IPR 171 at 184-8
[249] *Ramset Fasteners (Aust) Pty Ltd v Advanced Building Systems Pty Ltd* (1996) 66 FCR 151 at 168
[250] (1961) 106 CLR 588
[251] (1961) 106 CLR 588 at 611
[252] *Palmer v Dunlop Perdriau Rubber Co Ltd* (1937) 59 CLR 30 at 67. See also at 71-5
[253] *Meyers Taylor Pty Ltd v Vicarr Industries Ltd* (1977) 137 CLR 228 at 249; 13 ALR 605

collocation of separate parts" appears from the statement by Aickin J in *Minnesota Mining and Manufacturing Co v Beiersdorf (Australia) Ltd*[254] that it is "the interaction" between the integers which is "the essential requirement". It is this which supplies the inventive step and denies an allegation of lack of subject-matter in the case of a valid combination patent.

## The appeal

13. The issue in this Court is whether the Full Court, in purported reliance upon par (d) of s 100(1), strayed into consideration of issues that would have arisen if the ground of revocation in question had been obviousness (par (e)) which had not been before Hill J, and lack of novelty (par (g)), which it itself had put to one side. If the appellants are successful, it is accepted that the consequence would be that the matter would be returned to the Full Court for its consideration of the remaining issues on the appeal. If the result was that the validity of the Patent was upheld, it would be necessary for the Full Court to consider the merits of the cross-appeal which it had dismissed as a consequence of the decision that the Patent was invalid.

## The Statute of Monopolies

14. Section 6 of the Act contains the definition:

> "invention" means any manner of new manufacture the subject of letters patent and grant of privilege within section 6 of the Statute of Monopolies, *and includes an alleged invention.* [emphasis added]

A definition in similar terms had been contained in s 4 of the Patents Act (Cth) ("the 1903 Act") and that in turn followed the definition in s 46 of the Patents, Designs, and Trade Marks Act 1883 (UK) ("the 1883 Act"). The phrase "and includes an alleged invention" is directed to the inquiry at the stage of examination of an application before the decision as to acceptance.[255] The present case involves revocation after grant.

15. The Act defines the word "invention" by reference to "the established ambit" of s 6 of the Statute of Monopolies 1623 (Eng) (21 Jac I c 3) ("the Statute of Monopolies").[256] This statute severely restricted the prerogative power to grant monopolies but the proviso thereto contained in s 6 formed the basis of subsequent development of patent law. In Australia, the right question under the 1952 statute is:[257]

> Is this a proper subject of letters patent according to the principles which have been developed for the application of s 6 of the Statute of Monopolies?

So far as relevant, s 6 stated:

> That any Declaration before-mentioned shall not extend to any Letters Patents and Grants of Privilege for the Term of Fourteen Years or under, hereafter to be made, of the **[609]** sole Working or Making of any Manner of new Manufactures within this Realm, to the true and first Inventor and Inventors of such Manufactures, which others at the Time of Making such Letters Patents and Grants shall not use, so as also they be not contrary to the Law, nor mischievous to the State, by raising Prices of Commodities at home, or Hurt of Trade, or generally inconvenient: The said Fourteen Years to be accounted from the Date of the first Letters Patents, or Grant of such Privilege hereafter to be made, but that the same shall be of such Force as they should be, if this Act had never been made, and of none other. ...

---

[254] (1980) 144 CLR 253 at 266; 29 ALR 29

[255] *Rogers v Commissioner of Patents* (1910) 10 CLR 701 at 706, 708, 713; *Commissioner of Patents v Microcell Ltd* (1959) 102 CLR 232 at 245-6

[256] *National Research Development Corp v Commissioner of Patents* (1959) 102 CLR 252 at 269

[257] *National Research Development Corp v Commissioner of Patents* (1959) 102 CLR 252 at 269

**[610] The judgments in the Federal Court**

19. The primary judge considered three advertisements published in Australia before the priority date and concluded in respect of each of them that it did not amount to an anticipation, that is to say, it did not render either claim of the Patent not novel in Australia on the priority date. His Honour identified the alleged anticipations as the Burke advertisement, the Frimeda advertisement and the RFA Systems advertisement in the English *Concrete Year Book* of 1980. Further, in the Complete Specification for the Patent under the heading "Description of the Prior Art", upon which the patentee claimed inventive improvements, it was stated:

> The type of hoisting attachment with which the present invention is concerned is shown in US patent 3,883,170.

20. As we have indicated above, the Full Court's judgment proceeded upon the basis of the abandonment at the trial of the allegations of obviousness and put to one side the issue whether the primary judge had erred in rejecting the case for invalidity based on the alleged anticipations.[258] Upon that footing, the Full Court **[611]** nevertheless decided that the claims in the Patent did not have the "inventive merit" which, in the Full Court's view, was required for an invention within the meaning of the Act. It followed that the Patent was revoked under s 100(1)(d). In considering whether the invention claimed in the Patent was an "invention" within the meaning of s 100(1)(d), the Full Court said:[259]

> In our view, for the reasons we have given, it is necessary to take into account the publications in Australia before the priority date. These are as follows:
>
> (a)  the advertisement inserted by Burke into a United States publication;
>
> (b)  the Frimeda advertisement in a 1977 German publication; and
>
> (c)  the advertisement which appeared in The *Concrete Year Book* 1980, an English publication ...

Once these publications are taken into account, we agree with his Honour's conclusion that the invention claimed in the Australian patent involved no inventive step.

> A combination patent may be valid even if each integer, when considered separately, is well known; but in that case the combination itself must be new.

21. The use of the phrase "inventive step", which appears in par (e) of s 100(1), would suggest that the Full Court was revoking the Patent for obviousness. That was not open to the Full Court in the light of the conduct of the trial. In any event, there was no finding by the Full Court that the three publications which it said it had "taken into account" had, as to any one or more of them, entered into the body of common general knowledge in Australia, with the result that the combinations claimed in the Patent lacked any inventive step. Such a finding would have been necessary if the Full Court were to order revocation of the Patent under s 100(1)(e) of the Act.

22. The Full Court also spoke in the above passage of the need for the combination to be "new", but the issue of novelty had been put aside. The Full Court referred to authorities[260] which, in truth, deal with inventiveness and subject-matter, that is to say, with obviousness rather than novelty. The Court continued:[261]

> All the integers of the Australian invention had previously been revealed in the US patent and in publications in Australia. This leads to the conclusion that there is no

---

[258] *Ramset Fasteners (Aust) Pty Ltd v Advanced Building Systems Pty Ltd* (1996) 66 FCR 151 at 169

[259] (1996) 66 FCR 151 at 167.

[260] *Welch Perrin & Co Pty Ltd v Worrel* (1961) 106 CLR 588 at 611; *Minnesota Mining and Manufacturing Co v Beiersdorf (Australia) Pty Ltd* (1980) 144 CLR 253 at 266; 29 ALR 29; *Elconnex Pty Ltd v Gerard Industries Pty Ltd* (1991) 32 FCR 491 at 509-10; 105 ALR 247; *Fallshaw Holdings Pty Ltd v Flexello Castors and Wheels plc* (1993) 26 IPR 565 at 570

[261] (1996) 66 FCR 151 at 168.

new combination in the Australian patent. It is not a true combination patent; but a mere collocation of well-known integers.

It follows that the clutch as claimed in the Australian patent was not a manner of new manufacture at the priority date, and thus is not capable of supporting the validity of the Australian patent. There is no inventive merit beyond what was already publicly known. There is therefore no invention for the purposes of s 100(1)(d) of the Act.

23. The phrase "inventive merit" requires consideration because it appears to have been determinative of the conclusion that there was no invention.

24. It is no objection to the validity of a patent granted under the Act that it is commercially impracticable; its utility depends upon whether, by following the teaching of the complete specification, the result claimed is produced.[262] Inutility, for which s 100(1)(h) of the Act provides, was not a ground on which revocation was sought in the Full Court.

[612] 25. Further, "an invention which comes to a man by a happy flash of inspiration or without any prolonged experiment or thought may be as good a subject-matter of a patent as one which has only been arrived at after long and difficult experiments",[263] and a valid patent might be obtained under the Act "for something stumbled upon by accident [or] remembered from a dream"[264] if it otherwise satisfied the requirements of the legislation.

26. The expressions "inventive merit" and "appreciable merit" appear to have come into use during the development in the last century of modern patent law. The notion of "merit" was used by the courts[265] and by commentators, including Fletcher Moulton,[266] to express what under the Act is conveyed by the principles concerning novelty and, more frequently, inventive step. By the beginning of this century, it had no distinct and independent doctrinal meaning: it was used sometimes in reference to subject-matter, sometimes in reference to novelty. The phrase invites error through imprecision of legal analysis.

### The construction of s 100 of the Act 1952

27. The primary question on this appeal is whether the Full Court erred in construing s 100(1) of the Act by treating para (d) thereof as having, on the case as then presented to the Full Court, and independently of paras (e) and (g), an operation which imported some elements in the requirements of novelty and an inventive step ...

[614] 35. However, these matters did not touch the present litigation as it stood in the Full Court. The phrase "inventive merit" appears to have led the Full Court into an assumed construction of s 100(1)(d) which was at odds with the structure of s 100 and diverted it from consideration of the question (obviousness having been abandoned) of whether any other prior publications destroyed the novelty of either or both of the claims of the Patent.

---

[262] *Lane Fox v Kensington and Knightsbridge Electric Lighting Co* [1892] 3 Ch 424 at 430-1

[263] *Longbottom v Shaw* (1891) 8 RPC 333 at 337

[264] *Wellcome Foundation Ltd v VR Laboratories (Aust) Pty Ltd* (1981) 148 CLR 262 at 286; 34 ALR 213

[265] For example, *Harwood v Great Northern Railway Co* (1860) 2 B & S 194 at 208; 121 ER 1044 at 1050; *Penn v Bibby* (1866) 2 Ch App 127 at 136; *Hinks & Son v Safety Lighting Co* (1876) 4 Ch D 607 at 615-616; *Longbottom v Shaw* (1891) 8 RPC 333 at 338; *Lane Fox v Kensington and Knightsbridge Electric Lighting Co* [1892] 3 Ch 424 at 429. See also *National Research Development Corp v Commissioner of Patents* (1959) 102 CLR 252 at 263

[266] *The Present Law and Current Practices for Letters Patent for Inventions*, 2nd ed (1897) pp 89-95

**Philips v Mirabella**

36. Nothing decided in *NV Philips Gloeilampenfabrieken v Mirabella International Pty Ltd*[267] requires any different result on this appeal. The Full Court referred to *Philips*.[268] However, this Court should accept the submission by the appellants that Philips is not determinative of this appeal.

37. In that case, revocation was sought under s 138(3)(b) of the 1990 Act. This is significantly different in structure from s 100 of the 1952 statute.[269] The grounds **[615]** of revocation in s 138(3) of the 1990 Act do not distinguish obviousness and novelty as the 1952 Act does by creating particular grounds to which the special qualification in s 100(2) applies. Rather, s 138(3)(b) of the 1990 Act, by incorporating the definitions of invention in s 18(1)[270] and of patentable invention in Sched 1 of that Act, imports the elements which are found separately in s 100(1) of the 1952 Act. Again, the "prior art base" specified in s 18 is a concept not found in the 1952 Act and is defined in Sched 1 as including information in a publicly available document.

38. *Philips* came on appeal to this Court on a grant of special leave confined to the construction of s 18(1)(a) of the 1990 Act.[271] But it was decided upon a construction of the introductory words of s 18(1), namely "a patentable invention is an invention that".[272] Reference to the definition of "invention" in the Dictionary which constitutes Sched 1 to the 1990 Act was held to have imported into the introductory words the requirement that a manner of new manufacture for the purposes of the Statute of Monopolies should appear on the face of the specification.[273]However, the judgments gave some consideration to the old law which applied before and under the previous statute. Under that law, as the doctrine with respect to obviousness and lack of inventive step developed in the nineteenth century, it was decided that a claim for "nothing but" a new use of an old substance lacked the quality of inventiveness.[274] There also were instances in which this

---

[267] (1995) 183 CLR 655; 132 ALR 117

[268] (1996) 66 FCR 151 at 165, 166-7, 169

[269] Section 138(3) states:
"After hearing the application, the court may, by order, revoke the patient, either wholly or so far as relates to a claim, on one or more of the following grounds, but no other ground:
  (a) that the patentee is not entitled to a patent
  (b) that the invention is not a patentable invention
  (c) that the patentee has contravened a condition of the patent
  (d) that the patent was obtained by fraud, false suggestion or misrepresentation
  (e) that the amendment of the patent request or the complete specification was made or obtained by fraud or false suggestion or misrepresentation."

[270] Section 18 provides:
"(1) Subject to subsection (2), a patentable invention is an invention that, so far as claimed in any claim:
  (a) is a manner of manufacture within the meaning of section 6 of Statute Monopolies; and
  (b) when compared with the prior art base as it existed before the priority date of the claim by, or on behalf of, or with the authority of, the patentee or nominated person or the patentee's or nominated person's predecessor in title to the invention.
  (c) is useful; and
  (d) was not secretly used in the patent area before the priority date of that claim by, or on behalf o, or with the authority of, the patentee or nominated person or the patentee's pr nominated person's predecessor in title to the invention.
  (2) Human beings, and the biological processes for their generation, are not patentable inventions."

[271] (1995) 183 CLR 655 at 656; 132 ALR 117

[272] (1995) 183 CLR 655 at 663, 666; 132 ALR 117 at 121

[273] (1995) 183 CLR 665 at 663-4; 132 ALR 117

[274] *Commissioner of Patents v Microcell Ltd* (1959) 102 CLR 232 at 251; *National Research Development Corp v Commissioner of Patents* (1959) 102 CLR 252 at 262. See also *Elias v Grovesend Tinplate Co* (1890) 7 RPC 455 at 468; *Henry Berry & Co Pty Ltd v Potter* (1924) 35

lack of inventive step was admitted on the face of the specification. If so, a grant might properly be refused in the first instance on the footing that the admission of the lack of an inventive step itself disentitled the applicant to argue that even an alleged invention was disclosed.[275] If such an application had proceeded to grant, the grant would be liable to revocation under s 100(1)(e).

[616] 39. In *Philips*, the appellant failed in its attempt to establish that although a claimed use was nothing but a new use of an old substance this could still be a proper subject of letters patent under the 1990 Act where this character of the claimed use was apparent on the face of the specification.[276] Rather, Brennan, Deane and Toohey JJ decided that:[277]

> if it is apparent on the face of the specification that the quality of inventiveness necessary for there to be a proper subject of letters patent under the Statute of Monopolies is absent, one need go no further.

It was unnecessary to adduce evidence of the prior art base and to compare the invention claimed with the prior art base for the purposes of s 18(1)(b) if the absence of inventiveness appeared on the face of the specification.[278] Their Honours also said that:[279]

> it would border upon the irrational if a process which was in fact but a new use of an old substance could be a "patentable invention" under s 18 if, but only if, that fact were not disclosed by the specification.

40. The present case is not in that category of cases, considered in *Philips*, where the lack of an inventive step appears on the face of the specification. It concerns the validity of combination claims in the light of prior publications. It will be recalled that the Full Court went beyond the text of the specification and placed decisive weight upon the disclosures in the Burke advertisement, the Frimeda advertisement and the RFA Systems advertisement in the *Concrete Year Book* of 1980. In that respect, the Full Court was in error in considering under the ground of revocation in s 100(1)(d) matters that could have arisen under other grounds, namely obviousness and lack of novelty, but which either did not arise or were put to one side.

### Orders

41. The appeal to this Court should succeed and the matter should be remitted to the Full Court of the Federal Court. The Full Court should determine the remaining grounds of appeal and, depending upon that outcome, re-determine the cross-appeal. The appellants should have their costs of the appeal in this Court. The costs of the proceedings in the Full Court should await the ultimate determination of all the issues before that Court.

### Kirby J: [dissenting] ...

[618] 47. "Invention" is defined in s 6 of the 1952 Act as follows:

> "invention" means any manner of new manufacture the subject of letters patent and grant of privilege within section 6 of the Statute of Monopolies, and includes an alleged invention;

---

CLR 132 at 138-40, 141-2; Fletcher Moulton, *The Present Law and Practice Relating to Letters Patent for Inventions* (1913) pp 25-37

[275] *In the Matter of an Application for Patent by Compagnies Reunies des Glaces et Verres Speciaux du Nord de la France* (1930) 48 RPC 185 at 188; *Commissioner of Patents v Microcell Ltd* (1959) 102 CLR 232 at 250. See also *R v Patents Appeal Tribunal; Ex Parte Swift & Co* [1962] 2 QB 647 at 661

[276] (1995) 183 CLR 655 at 663; 132 ALR 117

[277] (1995) 183 CLR 655 at 664; 132 ALR 117 at 122

[278] (1995) 183 CLR 665 at 659; 132 ALR 117

[279] (1995) 183 CLR 655 at 667; 132 ALR 117 at 124

It is worth observing, in elaboration of the comment made above, that these provisions are, for relevant purposes, indistinguishable from the corresponding provisions in the 1990 Act.[280]

### The holding in *Philips*

48. The majority of this Court in Philips[281] summarised the main issue on "invention" there arising in the following terms:

> [619] In essence, Philips' argument is that the members of the Federal Court fell into error by failing to recognise that s 18(1)(b)'s requirements of novelty and inventive step (when compared with the identified applicable prior art base) are exclusive and exhaustive in so far as inventiveness (whether of step or idea) is concerned with the result that, if those requirements are satisfied, it is simply irrelevant that the subject matter of the claim as identified in the specification lacks the quality of inventiveness required by the principles which have been developed for the application of s 6 of the Statute of Monopolies. Expressed in other words, Philips' argument is that the fact that a claimed use is "nothing but ... a new use of an old substance" and therefore "outside the whole scope of what is known as an invention" under traditional principles of patent law will not of itself preclude it from being a proper subject of letters patent under the Act. In our view, Philips' argument should be rejected. Our reasons for rejecting it diverge, however, from the reasons advanced in Mirabella's primary argument which focused upon the phrase "manner of manufacture" in para (a) of s 18(1). The primary focus of inquiry should, as we have indicated, be upon the opening words ("... a patentable invention is an invention that ...") of that subsection which impose a threshold requirement which must be satisfied before one reaches that contained in the body of para (a).

49. The majority in *Philips* acknowledged the internal tension in a legislative scheme which, in effect, imposes a threshold requirement of "newness" or "inventiveness", and then proceeds to impose more specific requirements of novelty and of an inventive step.[282] However, the majority justified this scheme on two bases. First, their Honours stated that there was no construction of the provisions which was not susceptible to some legitimate criticism. Secondly, they pointed out that the interpretation favoured accorded with traditional principles of patent law.

50. In formulating the threshold test of "newness", the majority[283] referred to *Re BA's Application*,[284] in which it was held that a claim which is "nothing but a claim for a *new use of an old substance*" is a claim which lies outside the scope of an "invention". Their Honours also referred[285] to the holding in *Commissioner of Patents v Microcell Ltd*,[286] to the effect that a "claim for the use of a known material in the manufacture of known articles for the purpose of which its known properties make that material suitable ... cannot be subject matter for a patent".

---

[280] 1990 Act s 18(1) ("a patentable invention is an invention ...") and the definition of invention in Sch 1 (which is identical to that in the 1952 Act).
[281] (1995) 183 CLR 655 at 663 132 ALR 117 at 121 (footnotes omitted)
[282] (1995) 183 CLR 665 at 664; 132 ALR 117
[283] (1995) 183 CLR 655 at 661; 132 ALR 117
[284] (1915) 32 RPC 348 at 349, quoted with approval in *Commissioner of Patents v Microcell Ltd* (1959) 102 CLR 232 at 247 and *National Research Development Corp v Commissioner of Patents* (1959) 102 CLR 252 at 262 (emphasis added)
[285] (1995) 183 CLR 655 at 661; 132 ALR 117
[286] (1959) 102 CLR 232 at 251

## The present patent application

51. In my view, this Court's holding in Philips is determinative of the present appeal. In so concluding, I consider that, for the reasons which the Full Court gave, the judges there correctly decided the following points:

1. The patent was not a true combination patent – but a mere collocation of well-known integers.[287]

2. In determining whether an alleged invention was a "manner of new manufacture" within the statutory definition, a court is not confined to the face of **[620]** the specification itself. Such a test is consistent with the broad interpretation of "newness" which has been adopted by this Court in past cases.[288] As the majority in *Philips* stated:[289]

[I]t would border upon the irrational if a process which was in fact but a new use of an old substance could be a "patentable invention" … if, but only if, that fact were not disclosed by the specification.

Two arguments may be raised against such a contention. The first is that the phrase "so far as claimed in any claim of the complete specification" in s 100(1)(d) confines the decision-maker to considering only the specification. This proposition can be rejected quite readily. Sections 100(1)(e) (inventive step) and 100(1)(g) (novelty) also contain the phrase "so far as claimed in any claim of the complete specification". Yet it is plain that, in considering whether an alleged invention is obvious or novel, it is necessary to go beyond the face of the specification in determining these qualities. If the phrase does not restrict the inquiry under s 100(1)(e) and 100(1)(g), it can hardly be said to restrict the inquiry under s 100(1)(d).

The second argument against going beyond the face of the specification when considering s 100(1)(d) is that the construction of s 100(1) specifically authorises the decision-maker to go beyond the specification when considering novelty and inventive step. This Court, it is argued, should prefer a construction of the legislation which preserves a discrete role for s 100(1)(d) to one in which there is overlap between it and the tests of novelty and inventive step. Accordingly, as the legislature has clearly indicated those materials outside the specification which may be taken into account under s 100(1)(e) and 100(1)(g), the inquiry under s 100(1)(d) should be confined to the face of the specification.

The chief flaw in this argument is the presumption that it is possible to determine, without going beyond the specification, whether an alleged invention satisfies s 100(1)(d), and hence, within s 6, is a "manner of new manufacture the subject of letters patent and grant of privilege within section 6 of the Statute of Monopolies". Yet s 6 of the Statute of Monopolies (Imp) (21 Jac I c 3) states a broad test indeed. It provides that a patent shall only be granted if the alleged invention:

[B]e not contrary to the Lawe nor mischievous to the State, by raising of the prices of Comodities at home, or hurt of Trade, or generallie inconvenient.

Such an investigation could not be undertaken without regard being had to matters outside the specification. The s 100(1)(d) test is one of substantial breadth. Inevitably, it must overlap with the tests of novelty and inventive step.

For these reasons, it is my view that in deciding whether the alleged invention is a manner of new manufacture, ie has the necessary qualities of "newness" as explained, a court may look to prior publications, including the three published advertisements to which the Full Court directed its attention in this case.[290]

[287] *Ramset Fasteners v Advanced Building Systems* (1996) 66 FCR 151 at 168

[288] *Commissioner of Patents v Microcell Ltd* (1959) 102 CLR 232 at 251; *NV Philips Gloeilampenfabrieken v Mirabella International Pty Ltd* (1995) 183 CLR 655 at 661-4; 132 ALR 117

[289] (1995) 183 CLR 655; 132 ALR 117 at 124

[290] *Ramset Fasteners v Advanced Building Systems* (1996) 66 FCR 151 at 167-9

3. Adopting this approach, the alleged invention does not satisfy the test set out **[621]** in s 100(1)(d) of the 1952 Act 1949,[291] in light of the interpretation by this Court in *Philips* of the corresponding provision in the 1990 Act. In particular, it fails to do so when the three advertisements,[292] referred to by the Full Court, are taken into account. These publications could not be taken into account in considering the issue of obviousness, as they cannot be shown to have entered the body of common general knowledge in Australia. But in determining newness, in the sense of a manner of new manufacture, the decision-maker is permitted to go beyond the face of the specification.

52. In the present case, the alleged invention was "the provision of an elongated lever arm to which a remote release cable was attached, for use in face-lift tilt-up applications".[293] The elongated lever arm had the advantage of ensuring that the bolt could not release the wall section being lifted into position during the hoisting operation. Putting the three advertisements to one side, the elongated lever arm would arguably satisfy the test of newness. However, once the advertisements to which I have referred are taken into account, it is clear that the provision of an elongated lever arm was not "new" in the required sense. I therefore agree with the Full Court's finding that "the clutch as claimed in the Australian patent was not a manner of new manufacture at the priority date".[294] It thus lacked the defined quality necessary to be an "invention". That fact justified revocation of the patent.

53. The only point upon which I would, with respect, differ with the reasoning of the Full Court is in the way in which that Court expressed its finding on issue (3) above. The joint reasons describe what I would term a lack of "newness" as an absence of "inventive merit".[295] The latter term should, in my opinion, be avoided. It has the potential to be confused with a challenge to a patent on the basis that it did not involve an "inventive step". The problem is compounded by their Honours' use of the phrase "inventive step"[296] in the course of considering whether the alleged invention satisfied s 100(1)(d) of the 1952 Act.

54. The tests of newness and inventive step are distinct. In considering whether an inventive step is involved, the decision-maker's attention is directed towards the issue of whether the claimed invention would have been obvious to a non-inventive operative in the field, equipped with the common general knowledge in that field as at the priority date.[297] The test of newness is directed to whether the alleged invention is nothing more than the new use of an old substance.[298] In answering the second question, the Court is not restricted to consideration of materials forming part of the common general knowledge in a particular field. It may take into account just the kinds of publications to which the Full Court paid attention.

**Differences from the majority**
55. It is desirable that I indicate briefly why I disagree with the majority's findings in this appeal:

**[622]** 1. In my respectful view, the majority's reasoning is founded on an overly narrow reading of the holding in *Philips*. The use of the phrase "inventive merit" by the Full Court was unfortunate, as I have agreed. But what the Full Court there had in

---

[291] *Ramset Fasteners v Advanced Building Systems* (1996) 66 FCR 151 at 166-7
[292] *Ramset Fasteners v Advanced Building Systems* (1996) 66 FCR 151 at 167
[293] *Ramset Fasteners v Advanced Building Systems* (1996) 66 FCR 151 at 166
[294] *Ramset Fasteners v Advanced Building Systems* (1996) 66 FCR 151 at 168
[295] *Ramset Fasteners v Advanced Building Systems* (1996) 66 FCR 151 at 166, 167
[296] *Ramset Fasteners v Advanced Building Systems* (1996) 66 FCR 151 at 167
[297] *Wellcome Foundation Ltd v VR Laboratories (Aust) Pty Ltd* (1981) 148 CLR 262 at 270; 34 ALR 213
[298] *Commissioner of Patents v Microcell Ltd* (1959) 102 CLR 232 at 247

mind was clearly not that the patent was obvious, nor that it lacked novelty. As I have pointed out, the Full Court had already put both of these grounds to one side and so their Honours were clearly not referring to those grounds. Instead, the ground upon which they determined invalidity was that explained by this Court in *Philips* – namely that the alleged invention did not satisfy the general threshold test of "newness", ie the necessary quality of inventiveness involved in a manner of new manufacture within the Statute of Monopolies.

2. It is disingenuous, in my respectful opinion, to suggest that the Full Court's use of the word "new" should be interpreted as a reference to novelty, as the majority suggest. The test of newness was explicitly stated by this Court in *Philips*.[299] As this Court has made clear, the test of newness is distinct from the test of novelty. It is the former that the Full Court proceeded to apply. It was not only that Court's duty to do so. It was a correct application of the law.

3. As a corollary of this distinction, it follows that the same matters might fall to be considered both when deciding newness, and when addressing novelty and inventive step. The overlap of the grounds stated in the legislation has long been recognised[300] and is acknowledged by the majority themselves. A notion of newness is inherent in the concept of novelty (s 100(1)(g)) as it is in the concept and definition of "invention" itself: s 100(1)(d). The test of newness is, in this respect, a threshold one. Thus, the same matters that might be relevant to a consideration of newness might, if that test be satisfied, also be taken into consideration in determining the issues of novelty and inventive step. Likewise, simply because a matter might be relevant to the issue of novelty or inventive step, it does not follow that it cannot arise when newness is being assessed for the purpose of deciding whether an item of manufacture reaches the threshold test of being an "invention" at all ...

## *Nicaro Holdings Pty Limited v Martin Engineering Company*
### Federal Court of Australia: Lockhart, Jenkinson and Gummow JJ
### (1990) 91 ALR 513

The patent in this case related to a "Belt Cleaner Mounting Arrangement" which was to be used in the mining industry to clean conveyor belts. Conveyor belts were cleaned by scraping devices and evidence established that there were certain problems with these including residue, space around the belt and down time for maintenance. The abstract described the cleaning device in the following terms "a track mounted conveyor belt cleaner wherein individual belt scraper blades are affixed to sleeve members which slide linearly along a support member positioned generally transverse to the direction of travel of the belt to be cleaned. The sleeves are slide mounted on the support member such that they may freely slide from one end to the other but are fixed against either rotational or vertical movement and provide for repair or replacement of wiper blades without requiring conveyor belt shutdown".

In a cross-claim the appellants sought revocation of the patent on the basis of want of utility, lack of novelty and obviousness. The trial judge rejected the cross-claims on each of these grounds and the appellant appealed to the Full Federal Court solely on the ground of lack of novelty.

In his decision on appeal Gummow J considered two legal questions – first, what is the relationship between obviousness and novelty. In particular, if the

[299] (1995) 183 CLR 655 at 663-4; 132 ALR 117
[300] *Sunbeam Corp v Morphy-Richards (Aust) Pty Ltd* (1961) 180 CLR 98 at 112

invention differed from the prior art only in a way which might be called a "workshop improvement", could it still be said that the prior art anticipated the invention? Secondly, when assessing novelty how is the court to treat mosaics? In particular, could the court refer to a series of papers if they referred by cross-references to each other?

The Full Federal Court held that in this case none of the prior publications anticipated the patent in question. The court further held that listing the name of another patent at the bottom of a specification under the title "References Cited in the File of this Patent" was an insufficient cross-reference to constitute the documents as a "single source of information as the source of the art". Therefore, the patents could not be read together to determine anticipation. On these bases the appeal on want of novelty failed.

> **Gummow J: [524]** The Patent is in respect of an invention entitled "Belt Cleaner Mounting Arrangement". It claims a new combination of integers. Claim 1 is for a combination which comprises six integers. I set out the text of this claim later in these reasons. It was accepted by both sides that if the attack upon claim 1 failed then any attack upon the other claims also would fail. Hence, attention was directed solely to claim 1.
>
> Burchett J referred to the need for conveyor belts used in the mining industry and elsewhere for the transport of materials to be cleaned, generally by some form of scraping. The evidence showed that a number of devices had been adopted and that, at least in the United States, patents for such equipment had been granted over at least a forty year period before 1977. In the Complete Specification for the Patent, there is reference to the prior art and it is said that difficulties have been presented with respect to repair or replacement of blade elements used in the scraping devices. An object of the invention claimed in the Patent is said to be to obviate or minimise these disadvantages. The disadvantages are stated as follows: "The load may leave a residue which may build up on the scraper or scrapers, and on the means by which they are applied to the belt. Maintenance may be rendered more difficult by construction of space under and in the vicinity of the belt, and particularly at the point of discharge of its load. The minimisation of loss of the productive operation of the belt during any stoppage for maintenance of scraping equipment is a consideration of some importance."

[The judge set out the two legal questions to be addressed and then answered them in the following way.]

> **[527]** I turn to consider the first of the legal issues.
>
> **Novelty and workshop improvements**
> A prior publication does not amount to an anticipation of an invention claimed as a combination if it discloses some but not all of the integers of that combination: *Minnesota Mining and Manufacturing Co v Beiersdorf (Australia) Ltd* (1980) 144 CLR 253 at 298, per Aickin J. That proposition is of considerable importance on this appeal.
>
> It is important for a patentee to claim only the essential integers in a combination and to distinguish what is essential from what is inessential. This is because to establish infringement of a combination patent the patentee must show that the defendant has taken each and every one of the essential integers of the plaintiff's claim; if on its true construction the claim is for a particular combination of integers and the alleged infringer omits one of them, the infringer escapes liability: *Populin v HB Nominees Pty Ltd* (1982) 59 FLR 37 at 41. Further, where what is in question is an inessential integer, a device which contains the essential integers will fall within the **[528]** claim, whether or not an inessential integer is replaced by an obviously equivalent device or omitted altogether; hence, the expression "mechanical equivalent": *Walker v Alemite Corporation* (1933)

49 CLR 643 at 650, 657; *Sunbeam Corporation v Morphy-Richards (Australia) Pty Ltd* (1961) 35 ALJR 212 at 217; Blanco White, *Patents for Inventions*, 4th ed, para 2-208.

On the other hand, the expressions "workshop adjustment", "workshop improvement" and "workshop alteration" are usually employed in relation to obviousness: Blanco White, *Patents for Inventions*, 4th ed, para 4-212. They are used in the sense of something a skilled workman would have come to, proceeding along previous lines of inquiry and having regard to what was known or used.

In *Meyers Taylor Pty Ltd v Vicarr Industries Ltd* (1977) 137 CLR 228 at 235, Aickin J said: "The basic test for anticipation or want of novelty is the same as that for infringement and generally one can properly ask oneself whether the alleged anticipation would, if the patent were valid, constitute an infringement (see, eg *Harwood v Great Northern Railway Co* (1865) 11 HLC 654 at 681). Here no prior object and no object according to a prior document involved or incorporated all the integers of any one of the claims and could therefore possibly constitute an infringement. Accordingly I am satisfied that the objection of want of novelty has not been made out."

There was some discussion before us as to the significance of the reverse infringement test as a criterion for judging anticipation. In the *Meyers Taylor* Case, *supra*, Aickin J was dealing with alleged anticipation of a combination patent; none of the alleged anticipations incorporated all the integers of any one of the claims. Therefore, as his Honour said (137 CLR at 235) none of them "could therefore possibly constitute an infringement". In such a situation, the adequacy of the reverse infringement test will be readily apparent, given the fatal effect upon an infringement suit of omission from the alleged infringement of an essential integer. But Aickin J described this test only as "generally" applicable. Where the alleged anticipation is a paper publication, particularly a prior patent specification, there may be ground for debate in a comparison with the specification in suit as to the presence of inessential integers and mechanical equivalents. King J pointed this out in his judgment at first instance in *Werner's* case, *supra* (ALR at 702). There may also be dispute whether what has been disclosed sufficiently reveals an essential integer, in the light of the principles in *Hill v Evans* (1862) 4 De G F & J 288: see *Werner's* case (ALR at 683) per Lockhart J.

The appellants sought, somewhat tentatively, to pray in aid the principles of "purposive" construction of patent specifications, described by Lord Diplock in *Catnic Components Ltd v Hill & Smith Ltd* [1982] RPC 183 and discussed in several decisions of this Court. The particular point at issue in that case concerned whether the defendant escaped infringement because, whereas one of the integers of the claimed invention spoke of a rear support member "extending vertically", the alleged infringement included a member inclined at 6° or 8° from the vertical. A reduction of this order had a negligible effect upon function. The House of Lords found infringement. One may observe that such a result in an Australian court would have caused no great surprise to the reader of *Commonwealth Industrial Gases Ltd v MWA Holdings Pty Ltd* (1970) 44 ALJR 385 at 388. I would not treat the House of Lords as having propounded any novel principle or new **[529]** category of "non-textual infringement", and this Court has treated the decision in that light: *Populin v HB Nominees Pty Ltd* (1982) 59 FLR 37 at 42-43; *Rehm Pty Ltd v Websters Security Systems (International) Pty Ltd* (1988) 81 ALR 79 at 91-92. Certainly there is, in my view, no significant assistance to be gained in dealing with the issues that arise in this case from the *Catnic* case, concerned as those issues are with lack of novelty.

At the heart of the first of the legal issues on the present appeal is the correct description of that area of activity which is not specifically dealt with in the alleged anticipation but nevertheless sufficiently made apparent to the skilled addressee to enable one to say there has been an anticipation within the principles stemming from *Hill v Evans*, *supra*.

There has been some drift in the authorities as to the degree of rigour with which the alleged anticipation is to be tested. (As is illustrated by the discussion of the English authorities by Falconer J in *Genentech Inc's (Human Growth Hormone) Patent* [1989] RPC 613 at 629-633, selection patents may require special attention, but that is a matter for another day.) It was settled in *Savage v DB Harris & Sons* (1896) 13 RPC 364 at 368-369, per Lindley LJ, that the degree of disclosure in an alleged paper anticipation does not have to be so great as to amount to a full description of the invention allegedly anticipated, including the best method of performing it in the sense now required by s 40 of the Patents Act. Something less will do for sufficient disclosure to constitute an anticipation.

The position in England under the Patents Act 1949 (UK) appears from *General Tire & Rubber Co v Firestone Tyre & Rubber Co Ltd* (1972) RPC 457 at 485-486, a passage described as "much quoted and useful" by Lord Wilberforce in *EI Du Pont De Nemours & Co (Witsiepe's) Application* [1982] FSR 303 at 310-311. In this passage, the English Court of Appeal, in dealing with anticipation by prior publication, had said (emphasis supplied):

"If the prior inventor's publication contains a clear description of, or clear instructions to do or make, something that would infringe the patentee's claim if carried out after the grant of the patentee's patent, the patentee's claim have been shown to lack the necessary novelty, that is to say, it will have been anticipated. The prior inventor, however, and the patentee may have approached the same device from different starting points and may for this reason, or it may be for other reasons, have so described their devices that it cannot be immediately discerned from a reading of the language which they have respectively used that they have discovered in truth the same device; but if carrying out the directions contained in the prior inventor's publication will inevitably result in something being made or done which, if the patentee's patent were valid, would constitute an infringement of the patentee's claim, this circumstance demonstrates that the patentee's claim has in fact been anticipated.

"If, on the other hand, the prior publication contains a direction which is capable of being carried out in a manner which would infringe the patentee's claim, but would be at least as likely to be carried out in a way which would not do so, the patentee's claim will not have been anticipated, although it may fail on the ground of obviousness. *To anticipate the patentee's claim the prior publication must contain clear and unmistakable directions to do what the patentee claims to have invented*: *Flour Oxidizing Co Ltd v Carr & Co Ltd* (1908) 25 RPC 428 at 457, line 34, approved in *BTH Co Ltd v Metropolitan Vickers Electrical Co Ltd* (1928) 45 RPC 1 at 24, line 1. A **[530]** signpost, however clear, upon the road to the patentee's invention will not suffice. The prior inventor must be clearly shown to have planted his flag at the precise destination before the patentee."

This passage also was approved and applied by Stephen J in *Washex Machinery Corporation v Roy Burton & Co Pty Ltd* (1974) 49 ALJR 12 at 18. But it is apparent from other Australian authority that what was said by the English Court of Appeal has to be read with some qualifications.

One begins with the judgment of Latham CJ in *Acme Bedstead Co Ltd v Newlands Bros Ltd* (1937) 58 CLR 689. The Chief Justice cited what was said by the Privy Council in *Pope Appliance Corporation v Spanish River Pulp & Paper Mills Ltd* [1929] AC 269 at 276. This was a passage in which their Lordships in turn had adopted what had been said in the 1908 and 1928 decisions referred to in the above extract from the judgment of the English Court of Appeal in the *General Tire* case. Latham CJ (58 CLR at 700-701) said: "It is contended, however, that there is no justification for, to put it shortly, adding common knowledge to an alleged paper anticipation and thus depriving a patent of subject matter. It is urged that the authorities show that a paper anticipation must show, and precisely show, the whole of the claimed invention in order to be an anticipation at all, and that, if an alleged anticipation does not satisfy this requirement, it should be ignored: see *Pope Appliance Corporation v Spanish River Pulp and Paper Mills Ltd* [1929] AC 269 at 276. But a given specification is not to be read as in a vacuum. The reader must be regarded as having at least the common knowledge of the art. If a competent work-man, seeing either a given specification or an article in actual use, could, upon a defect being pointed out, devise, without the exercise of any inventive ingenuity, a means of overcoming the defect, there would not be invention in the result which he so achieved."

In the same decision, at 707, Dixon J referred to the: "... well-settled rule that a prior paper publication, giving information that does not become part of common knowledge, does not invalidate a subsequent patent unless it supplies enough information to enable a person of proper skill in the art to produce the mechanical device or appliance or carry out the process claimed in the later specification."

Twenty-five years later, in *C Van der Lely NV v Bamfords Ltd* [1963] RPC 61 at 71, Lord Reid said: "The law regarding anticipation derives from Lord Westbury's statement of it in *Hill v Evans* (1862) 4 De G F & J 288. There are two branches of this statement. The first is that 'a person of ordinary knowledge of the subject would at once perceive and understand and be able practically to apply the discovery without the necessity of making further experiments.' The appellants maintain that even if the skilled man could perceive in the *photograph* all the integers in claim 1 he would not apply the discovery without making further experiments. But Lord Westbury must have meant experiments with a view to discovering something not disclosed. He cannot have meant to refer to the ordinary methods of trial and error which involve no inventive step and are gener-ally necessary in applying any discovery to produce a practical result. ... The other requirement is that 'the information given by the prior publication must for the purposes of practical utility be equal to that given by the subsequent patent.' There may be cases where the skilled man has to have the language of the prior publication translated for him or where he must get from a scientist the meaning of technical terms or ideas with which he is **[531]** not familiar, but once he has got this he must be able to make the machine from what is disclosed by the prior publication. This part of Lord Westbury's statement appears to have been universally accepted, and I need only refer to the latest authority in this House, *Martin v Millwood* [1956] RPC 125" (emphasis added).

In the High Court of Australia, in *Olin Corporation v Super Cartridge Co Pty Ltd* (1977) 51 ALJR 525 at 536, Stephen and Mason JJ referred with apparent approval to the passage I have quoted from the speech of Lord Reid ...

It follows from the English authorities as they have been applied in Australia that, whilst *Hill v Evans* does not require a literal disclosure and something less may suffice, and whilst an alleged paper anticipation is to be treated as read by a skilled addressee, a disclosure will fall short of an anticipation by description of an effective means by which the combination claimed in the patent in suit might be produced, if what is required of the skilled addressee is the exercise of any inventive ingenuity and the taking of any inventive step.

Any references in this context to workshop improvements or variations should not be understood as importing into this field of novelty concepts of obviousness. There may be room for disagreement upon the English authorities as to what degree of activity by the skilled addressee may be called for in respect of an alleged anticipation for it still to suffice to destroy novelty. In my view, the way in which the English authorities have been treated by the High Court supports the position as stated by Lord Reid in **[532]** *Van der Lely's* case, *supra*. It is also to be borne in mind that the notional addressee of the alleged anticipation is a skilled addressee with common general knowledge of the art. But his Lordship was not saying that an alleged anticipation of a combination claim, which did not include an integer thereof, nevertheless would constitute an effective disclosure if what was required of a skilled addressee to produce that claimed combination was the taking of an obvious and non-inventive step by way of workshop improvement.

In *RD Werner & Co Inc v Bailey Aluminium Products Pty Ltd* (1989) 85 ALR 679, King J, at first instance, used the terms "workshop variation" and "mechanical equivalent" in the course of dealing with an objection to grant for want of novelty (see 85 ALR at 703). I accepted the proposition, drawn from his Honour's reasoning, that where the alleged anticipation disclosed all the essential integers of the claimed combination, the conclusion as to lack of novelty which would follow therefrom was not avoided and the invention claimed would not be saved "merely because there were differences which might be described as mere mechanical equivalents or workshop variations" (see 85 ALR 679 at 708, 716). The use of the expression "workshop variation" was not designed to introduce any concept of the presence or absence of a further step which was an inventive step or any notions drawn from the law as to obviousness. (It may be noted that in *Sunbeam Corporation v Morphy-Richards (Australia) Pty Ltd* (1961) 35 ALJR 212 at 220, Windeyer J, when dealing with want of novelty, spoke simply of the doctrine of mechanical equivalents.) In any given case, there may well be an overlap between novelty and obviousness on the evidence before the Court, and to use a mechanical equivalent may be to effect a workshop variation; but that should not encourage any blurring between the legal norms of novelty and obviousness.

Where, in a case such as the present, the question is whether one or more integers of a claimed combination is not disclosed in an alleged anticipation, and it is said that what is disclosed does sufficiently reveal that integer within the principles of *Hill v Evans*, it will not be helpful to ask whether variations between the anticipation and the claimed combination answer the description "workshop improvement". Perhaps recognising this, in reply counsel for the appellants put his case simply on the alternative basis that the differences represented no more than the substitutions of mechanical equivalents, thereby bringing his case back to the legal mainstream. But, as will later appear, to add an essential integer otherwise missing from a claimed combination would not ordinarily be to supply a "mechanical equivalent". The reasoning in the infringement cases, to which I have referred, suggests the contrary.

I return to consider whether the appellants' submissions succeed on the merits of this case, after dealing with the second legal issue.

*Mosaics and cross-references*

What is the rationale underlying the prohibition against the making of mosaics? If this is perceived, then one will be better equipped to consider whether the appellants are correct in their suggested qualification.

In *Acme Bedstead Co Ltd v Newlands Bros Ltd, supra*, at 703-704, Starke J quoted what was said by Fletcher-Moulton LJ in *British Ore Concentration Syndicate Ltd v Minerals Separation Ltd* (1909) 26 RPC 124 at 147. **[533]** His Lordship said (emphasis added): "It cannot be too carefully kept in mind in patent law that, in order to render a document a prior publication of an invention, it must be shown that it publishes to the world the whole invention – ie, all that is material to instruct the public how to put the invention in practice. It is not enough that there should be suggestions which, taken with suggestions derived from other *and independent* documents, may be shown to foreshadow the invention or important steps in it. Since the date of the vigorous protest of Lord Justice James in *Von Heyden v Neustadt* (50 LJNS Ch 128) against such a 'mosaic' of prior publications this has been a universally accepted and most salutary principle. It applies with exceptional force in cases where the alleged prior publications are the Specifications of unsuccessful inventions which have accordingly never passed into public general knowledge but have rightly been forgotten.

"All my past experience emphasizes in my mind the justice of this rule. The industrial and scientific problems, which face mankind, are being attacked all over the world by busy inventive minds from the most varied points of view. When some lucky inventor has been successful in solving the problem and – whether for the purposes of an action or otherwise – the records of past failure or incomplete success are searched, it is common to find that suggestions or adumbrations of each of the various steps, by which he has achieved his result, are to be found in some one or other of the works of those who have gone before him, though in different connection and forming part of a different and probably unsuccessful process. When such records are selected from a mass of antecedent publications and put in an isolated form before a Court, there is a danger of their giving rise to a suspicion of a general lack of novelty in the successful invention. But it must be remembered that these alleged prior publications are the product of a selection made with a knowledge of the successful invention, and that probably hundreds of proposals equally promising, but which point in wholly different directions, have been rejected in the search by reason that they do so. It is somewhat as though one were to decry the merit of a prospector who had discovered that sands were auriferous by showing that after due rejection of most of the non-metallic particles from a handful of sand the gold may be made to appear visible to the naked eye."

In his article "Having Regard to What was Known and Used" (1972) 88 *LQR* 341 at 343, Mr Gratwick QC, after referring to the case law as it had developed up to the end of the last century, said:

"It is clear that, by this time, the importance of dealing separately with the issues of lack of novelty and obviousness had become well appreciated, even though the language used in the judgments was not always chosen as carefully as it might have been.

"While the division between these two heads of objection was becoming appreciated, the law relating to lack of novelty was developing certain quite clear and strict rules. Thus, ever since *Von Heyden v Neustadt* (1880) 50 LJ Ch 126 it has been accepted without hesitation that, if a given prior document does not disclose the whole of the invention, the deficiency cannot be made good from another document unless there is a cross-reference between them. ..."

## *Minnesota Mining And Manufacturing Co v Beiersdorf (Australia) Ltd*
### High Court of Australia: Barwick CJ, Stephen, Mason, Aickin and Wilson JJ
### (1980) 144 CLR 253

The patent for "breathable" surgical tape was challenged in a cross-claim on the grounds of obviousness, that is, that the alleged invention did not involve an inventive step. In this case the High Court considered the requirements of an inventive step.

**Aickin J: [287]** The *Patents Act* 1952-1973 ("the *Patents Act* 1952") s 100(1) sets out the grounds upon which a patent may be revoked of which grounds (e) and (g) are material. They are as follows:

"(e) that the invention, so far as claimed in any claim, was obvious and did not involve an inventive step, having regard to what was known or used in Australia on or before the priority date of that claim"

"(g) that the invention, so far as claimed in any claim, was not novel in Australia on the priority date of that claim".

In *HPM Industries Pty Ltd v Gerard Industries Ltd*[301] ("the *HPM Case*") Williams J, sitting as a single justice, held that in s 100(1)(e) the words "known or used" embraced more than the common general knowledge of a skilled worker in the relevant field at the priority date. He said:[302]

---

[301] (1957) 98 CLR 424.
[302] (1957) 98 CLR, at p 437.

"Paragraph (g) appears to accept the law relating to want of novelty as it existed at the date of the *Patents Act*. But par (e) appears to have widened the law relating to want of subject matter. It requires the Court to have regard to what is known or used in Australia before the priority date of the claim, and the words 'known or used' appear to embrace more than what had become commonly known or used or in other words more than the common general knowledge of a skilled craftsman in the particular art on that date."

**[288]** Williams J referred to the decision of the Court of Appeal in *Allmanna Svenska Elektriska A/B v Burntisland Shipbuilding Co Ltd*[303] ("*Allmanna Svenska*") and to the observations of the House of Lords in *Martin and Biro Swan Ltd v H Millwood Ltd*[304] and said:[305]

"It is clear from these discussions that in deciding what was obvious, it is necessary to consider what would have been obvious to the hypothetical skilled craftsman in the state of knowledge in the particular art existing at the priority date of the patent and that this knowledge consists of everything disclosed by the literature on the subject (including prior specifications), and revealed by the articles then in use and of the common general knowledge."

The English legislation with which those cases dealt was not in the same form as the relevant sections of the *Patents Act* 1952, and in effect added to the equivalent of par (g) the concluding words of par (e). The Court of Appeal held the same words should be given the same meaning in each paragraph with the consequence referred to by Williams J.

It may be thought curious that a change in the language used in the ground of want of novelty should produce a change in the law with respect to obviousness, but this was not the subject of any comment by Williams J. However there was no such change in the Australian legislation.

As I have elsewhere observed I think it clear that the Full Court in *John McIlwraith Industries Ltd v Phillips*[306] did not indorse that view but merely proceeded upon the assumption that it was correct, since in the circumstances of that case no different result would have followed if the other view had been taken. The point has been referred to in a number of subsequent cases before single justices of the Court where they have regarded themselves as obliged to follow the view adopted by Williams J, leaving it to a Full Court to re-examine the matter if the necessity should arise. See per Windeyer J in *Sunbeam Corporation v Morphy-Richards (Aust) Pty Ltd*[307] and per Gibbs J in *Universal Oil Products Co v Monsanto Co*[308] each expressing some doubt on the matter. I referred to the point in *Meyers Taylor Pty Ltd v Vicarr Industries Ltd*[309] and in *Graham Hart (1971) Pty Ltd v SW Hart & Co Pty Ltd*.[310] The latter case was before the Full Court but it was not necessary for **[289]** the purpose of deciding it to deal with the question of whether the decision in *Allmanna Svenska* is properly applicable to the *Patents Act* 1952.

In the present case it is desirable, that that question should be put at rest. In order to examine it, a consideration of the history of the English and Australian Patents Acts is necessary.

---

[303] (1952) 69 RPC 63, at pp 68-70.
[304] [1956] RPC 125.
[305] (1957) 98 CLR 438.
[306] (1958) 98 CLR 529.
[307] (1961) 35 ALJR 212, at pp 217-219.
[308] (1972) 46 ALJR 658, at pp 659-660.
[309] (1977) 137 CLR 228, at pp 236-237.
[310] (1978) 141 CLR 305, at p 329.

Section 26 of the *Patents, Designs, and Trade Marks Act*, 1883 (Imp) provided that a patent might be revoked on a petition to the Court and in sub-s (3) the single ground was stated as follows:

"Every ground on which a patent might, at the commencement of this Act, be repealed by scire facias shall be available by way of defence to an action of infringement and shall also be a ground of revocation."

That section did no more than continue in operation the existing common law. In Australia the *Patents Act* 1903 dealt with revocation in s 86(3) in the same manner, as follows:

"Every ground on which a patent might at common law be repealed by scire facias shall be available as a ground of revocation."

The *Patents, Designs, and Trade Marks Act*, 1883 (Imp) was repealed by the *Patents and Designs Act*, 1907 (Imp) which however reproduced in s 25(2) that provision in the same form as the 1883 Act. By the *Patents and Designs Act*, 1932 (Imp) s 25(2) was substantially amended. The new sub-section set out in detail the various grounds upon which a patent might be revoked and concluded with the precautionary words "and upon any other ground upon which a patent might, immediately before the first day of January 1884, have been repealed by scire facias". Paragraphs (a) to (p) have been treated as doing no more than reproducing and restating the grounds formerly available at common law – see per Lord Macmillan in *Mullard Radio Valve Co Ltd v Philco Radio and Television Corp of Great Britain Ltd*[311] and per Lord Diplock in *Bristol-Myers Co v Beecham Group Ltd*.[312]

In Australia however s 86(3) of the *Patents Act* 1903 was not changed until 1952. During the 1930s a committee under the chairmanship of Sir George Knowles presented four reports upon the *Patents Act* and drew up a Bill to give effect to its recommendations. That Bill was introduced into the Parliament in 1939 but the outbreak of war prevented its enactment. A further committee was appointed in 1950 and is referred to below.

**[290]** In 1944 a committee (the Swan Committee) was appointed in England to consider what changes in the *Patents and Designs Act*, 1932 (UK) were desirable and it reported in 1947.

The report of the Swan Committee led to the passing of the Patents Act, 1949 (UK) which introduced among other changes the provisions relating to priority dates. The Swan Committee recommended that pars (e) and (f) of the grounds for revocation should be as follows;

"(e) That, subject as in this sub-section provided, what is claimed in any claim of the complete specification was not new.

(f) That what is claimed in any claim of the complete specification was obvious and did not involve any inventive step, having regard to what was known or used before the priority date of the said claim."

However in the Patents Act, 1949 (UK) those grounds of objection were expressed differently. Thus par (e) of s 32 was as follows:

"that the invention, so far as claimed in any claim of the complete specification, is not new having regard to what was known or used, before the priority date of the claim, in the United Kingdom;"

and par (f) was as follows:

"that the invention, so far as claimed in any claim of the complete specification, is obvious and does not involve any inventive step having regard to what was known or used, before the priority date of the claim, in the United Kingdom;"

---

[311] (1936) 53 RPC 323, at p 329.
[312] [1974] AC 646, at p 679.

Thus the words which previously formed part of the ground of obviousness were added to the previous wording of the ground of novelty. That language however was not adopted in the Australian *Patents Act* 1952.

Possible reasons for this difference in language between those grounds as set out in the 1932 United Kingdom Act and as set out in the 1949 United Kingdom Act are discussed in Mr Gratwick's interesting paper entitled "Having Regard to What Was Known and Used", *Law Quarterly Review*, vol 88 (1972), p 341. It is clear however that the report of the Swan Committee cannot be used to elucidate the reasons for the change, because it did not recommend it. Moreover, whatever those reasons may have been, it is equally clear that they have no bearing on the proper construction of the provisions of s 100 of the *Patents Act* 1952 for the provisions are not the same; the Australian Act being in substantially the same form as the recommendation of the Swan Committee, the differences not being relevant for present purposes.

[291] The Swan Committee's report and the 1949 United Kingdom Act were available to a subsequent committee established in Australia, of which Mr Justice Dean was the chairman. It was set up in 1950 and reported in 1952. The *Patents Act* 1952 reproduces the Bill recommended by the Dean Committee, virtually without alteration. The earlier committee had considered the *Patents and Designs Act*, 1932 (UK) and in par 97 it referred to the provisions in s 25(2) of that Act and prepared a Bill which attempted to define exhaustively the grounds upon which a patent might at common law be repealed by scire facias. The Bill so prepared copied the English "drag-net" provision which expressly incorporated anything else which might have been available under scire facias. The Dean Committee recommended that the present s 100 be adopted which reproduces substantially the provisions of s 25(2) of the *Patents and Designs Act*, 1932 (UK) though the language differs in a number of respects. However pars (e) and (f) of s 25(2) of the 1932 United Kingdom Act were adopted without any material change save for the addition of the references to the priority date. The Dean Committee recommended some minor changes and said in par 25:

"In 1932 the British Act set out the grounds upon which a patent might be revoked. In the previous report it was recommended that these be adopted, and that the same grounds should be available to a defendant setting up the invalidity of the patent as a defence to an action for infringement. We agree with this recommendation and at the same time we have attempted to define the various grounds with precision."

The Bill as recommended by the Dean Committee did not contain the "drag-net clause" and was enacted in the form as recommended.

Having regard to the history of the legislation it is necessary to return to the decision of Williams J in the *HPM Case*.[313] It is clear from the passages quoted above from his judgment that he regarded s 100 of the *Patents Act* 1952 as having made a substantial change in the pre-existing law for he says that prior to that Act it was not legitimate to have regard to any and all prior publications, including prior specifications, as well as upon common general knowledge and articles in common use.

He failed to advert to the fact that the words in the *Patents Act* 1952 were for all material purposes identical with those of the 1932 United Kingdom Act which Lord Macmillan had said in [292] 1932 reproduced the common law. It also appears from the reasons for judgment[314] that the case for the defendant in the *HPM Case* was based, not upon prior published specifications or any combination of them, but upon evidence of common general knowledge in the relevant art. Williams J said however that the decisions in *Allmanna Svenska*[315] and *Martin and Biro Swan Ltd v H Millwood*

---

[313] (1957) 98 CLR 424.
[314] (1957) 98 CLR, at p 439.
[315] (1952) 69 RPC 63.

*Ltd*[316] required that prior publications not forming part of common general knowledge should be taken into account. From the nature of the issue it is clear that it was not necessary so to decide in order to deal with the case itself. Indeed Williams J made an express finding[317] that the information relied upon had become part of common general knowledge of those engaged in the particular art. Accordingly his observations on this point must be regarded as obiter dicta.

For those reasons I am satisfied that we should not regard the observations of Williams J in the *HPM Case* as correctly stating the law in Australia. It is not a matter of overruling the decision because, as I have said, it was based upon a different ground. The dicta however should not be followed.

Williams J. did not deal expressly with the question whether in the case of an allegation of obviousness it is possible to "make a mosaic" out of existing publications not forming part of common general knowledge but it is nonetheless clear that he regarded such a course as open in view of the contrasting statement quoted above on novelty. The notion of common general knowledge itself involves the use of that which is known or used by those in the relevant trade. It forms the background knowledge and experience which is available to all in the trade in considering the making of new products, or the making of improvements in old, and it must be treated as being used by an individual as a general body of knowledge. I do not with respect think that it is correct to describe that process as the making of a mosaic although it has often been so described, a usage which however may be misleading. The process of applying such common general knowledge to the solution of a problem is not a process of picking out individual pieces of information and combining them, including inferences from known facts and known principles, as well as the application of such principles. The making of a mosaic prohibited in the case of an allegation of want of novelty is the picking out of individual items of information from prior publications or prior objects and assembling them together so as **[293]** to give them an appearance of unity and then alleging that such mosaic reveals the very thing claimed. That is an understandable, though not a permissible, process.

In the case of alleged lack of an inventive step the question of making a mosaic must operate (if at all) in a very different matter. An allegation of want of inventive step is not made out by saying you may take one or two, or twenty-one or twenty-two, prior publications and then select from them appropriate extracts or pieces of information, which will add up to the invention claimed and so demonstrate that it was obvious. So to proceed is to mistake the nature of an invention and the nature of the objection of obviousness. The question is, is the invention itself obvious, not whether a diligent searcher might find pieces from which there might have been selected the elements which make up the patent. If this were not so, there could never be a valid patent for a new combination of old integers. The proper question is not whether it would have been obvious to the hypothetical addressee who was presented with an ex post facto selection of prior specifications that elements from them could be combined to produce a new product or process. It is rather whether it would have been obvious to a non-inventive skilled worker in the field to select from a possibly very large range of publications the particular combination subsequently chosen by the opponent in the glare of hindsight and also whether it would have been obvious to that worker to select the particular combination of integers from those selected publications. In the case of a combination patent the invention will lie in the selection of integers, a process which will necessarily involve rejection of other possible integers. The prior existence of publications revealing those integers, as separate items, and other possible integers does not of itself make an alleged invention obvious. It is the selection of the integers out of, perhaps many possibilities, which must be shown to be obvious.

---

[316] [1956] RPC 125.
[317] (1952) 98 CLR, at p 441.

It is in relation to this process that the misuse of hindsight is most common. When once an idea or an object or a process or a combination, admittedly novel, has been published, it is very easy to say after perhaps months of search and study in the Patent Office and the public libraries that the integers into which the patent might be dissected could be found scattered amongst the prior documents by a person who already knew the solution to the problem and therefore knew what to look for and what to discard. But that process does not demonstrate lack of an inventive step. The opening of a safe is easy when the combination has been already provided.

**[294]** It is pointless to say, as some witnesses did in the present case that given the description in the claims in the patent they could with the aid of some prior specifications have produced the end product. This is an extreme example of the ex post facto dissection of an invention which has been vigorously criticized in many courts.

It is worth quoting yet again the words of Fletcher-Moulton LJ in *British Westinghouse Electric and Manufacturing Co Ltd v Braulik*[318] where he said:

"I confess that I view with suspicion arguments to the effect that a new combination, bringing with it new and important consequences in the shape of practical machines, is not an invention, because, when it has once been established, it is easy to show how it might be arrived at by starting from something known, and taking a series of apparently easy steps. This ex post facto analysis of invention is unfair to the inventors, and in my opinion it is not countenanced by English Patent Law."

Similar statements may be found in many cases; see, eg, per Latham CJ in *Palmer v Dunlop Perdriau Rubber Co Ltd*.[319]

It may be observed that in the cases where obviousness is in issue very often the larger the number of prior publications which are relied upon as together establishing absence of an inventive step, the more likely it is that the alleged invention was not obvious for the wider one has to look to find all the integers the less likely it is that it would have been obvious to put them together in the particular manner in which the inventor did.

It may be noted that even in England where the process of making a mosaic out of prior publications is regarded as permissible under the *Patents Act* 1949 it is still necessary that the mosaic must be one which "can be put together by an unimaginative man with no inventive capacity" – see per Lord Reid in *Technograph Printed Circuits Ltd v Mills and Rockley (Electronics) Ltd*.[320]

There may be some fields of endeavour in which those who work therein study and make themselves familiar with all patent specifications as they become available for inspection in one or in many countries so that what was contained therein becomes common general knowledge in that particular trade or field of manufacture in the country in question. Examples are provided by *Vidal Dyes Syndicate Ltd v Levinstein Ltd*[321] and *British Celanese Ltd v Courtaulds Ltd*.[322] Indeed in the present case **[295]** it appears that the first appellant in its establishment in the United States at one time had employees who did just this in the field of adhesives. But this is not so in all fields or in all countries. There was no evidence in the present case that those working in Australia in the field of adhesives or of surgical tapes followed such a practice or that any of the specifications relied upon was part of the common general knowledge of those working in these fields in Australia.

The respondent relied upon a number of prior specifications which had been available in Australia for public inspection before the priority date as providing a basis for the

[318] (1910) 27 RPC 209, at p 230.
[319] (1937) 59 CLR 30, at pp 60-61.
[320] (1972) RPC 346, at p 355.
[321] (1912) 29 RPC 245, at pp 279-280.
[322] (1933) 50 RPC 259, at p 280.

argument that the invention claimed was obvious. For the reasons which I have set out above I do not regard such specifications as capable of sustaining that argument without evidence that they were part of common general knowledge at that time. There was no such evidence and accordingly it is not necessary for me to examine those specifications. I turn therefore to the question of obviousness without reference to the prior publications.

The respondent provided no evidence of the state of relevant common general knowledge in Australia. Some evidence was given by the appellants' witnesses of the kind of tapes in use before the priority date and of their disadvantages which demonstrated the nature of the advance made by the invention. This evidence related to the use of surgical tapes in hospitals and in medical practice, and showed the nature of the advance which this invention made over the products then on the market and in use at the priority date. This evidence showed what kind of products would have been the common general knowledge in Australia as well as the nature of the problem awaiting solution.

Sister Stahl who was Assistant Matron in charge of operating theatres at Sydney Hospital gave evidence that she had trained at Sydney Hospital from 1956-1960 and continued there as a Theatre Sister until 1964. From 1964-1968 she was the Supervisor of the Cardiac and Neurosurgery Operating Theatres and in 1968 became the Charge Sister of Operating Theatres and in 1971, Assistant Matron in charge of theatres at Sydney Hospital. She said that when she first began nursing, zinc oxide strapping and sticking plaster were used as surgical tapes and she stated that the disadvantages of the older types of tape were that it was extremely difficult to remove and this took up nursing time and caused a strain on nurses and on patients. She said that it could often be removed only with the aid of ether or a solvent, both of which were painful to patients. She said that **[296]** irritation from the older tapes was common and generally a residue of adhesive was left on the skin and in addition many patients were allergic to the material. She said that this caused problems, particularly where wounds required frequent changing of dressing, and that the older type surgical tapes caused difficulty as well as occupying substantial amounts of nursing time. She also said with the older types of tape the skin often softened and became macerated. She said that she became aware of Micropore tape in the early 1960s and found it easy to remove and less painful from the point of view of the patient. She found it useful where dressings had to be frequently changed in that it avoided allergies and irritations to the skin and avoided maceration of the skin. She said it reduced the time and trouble needed to remove wound dressings. She also said that it was easier to handle in the operating theatre and that it had replaced the old zinc oxide tapes.

Mr Rose, a surgeon practising in Sydney also gave evidence. He had numerous qualifications in surgery, being a Fellow of the Royal College of Surgeons of England and of the Royal Australian College of Surgeons and the American College of Surgeons. He had for a substantial time been Honorary Surgeon at the Royal North Shore Hospital and other hospitals. He said that he first became aware of Micropore tape in approximately 1963-1964 and that prior to that time during his experience as a surgeon since graduating in 1933 the type of tape used was that known as "Elastoplast" or its equivalent which consisted of a woven backing applied to which was an adhesive generally containing zinc oxide. He said the disadvantages of those tapes were that they caused irritation to patients on application and removal and that in about ten per cent of cases caused allergic reactions or blistering. They did not permit the skin to breathe and irritation of the skin resulted and the risk of infection was increased. He said that because of those disadvantages it was necessary to disturb dressings sooner than was desirable and that as it was not possible to see through the tapes discharge from wounds was not visible, and the process of healing could not be estimated. He also said that they were difficult to handle with rubber gloves in an operating theatre because of the extreme stickiness and they had to be cut with scissors. He said that since about 1963-1964 he had used Micropore tape and that its usage had increased to the extent that it was used for all dressings after operations in the vast majority of cases. He said that it had a number of advantages including that under normal conditions of surgical use it did not **[297]** stretch with normal hand pulling but could be easily torn. He stated that it did not irritate the skin with normal patients in any way and that all pores in it allowed sweat and other secretions of the skin or the wound to seep through and evaporate and that the progress of healing could be observed to a "fair extent". He also said that it was easier to handle in the operating theatre with rubber gloves and that the fact that the skin could breathe through the minute pores was one of its great advantages, whilst the fact that it permits skin closures without stitches where there are small wounds was also a great advantage. Finally he stated that use of Micropore had obliterated complaints which he had heard for many years from patients and other practitioners arising out of the defects of the older type of surgical tape.

Dr Rose also produced two articles from the *Lancet*, a well known medical journal circulating in Australia, written in 1955 and 1956 indicating the need for a porous tape with a less difficult and irritating adhesive and pointing out that existing so-called porous dressings were only partially porous. The fact was however that more than four years went by before the present invention was made in the United States and the patent applied for in Australia. The evidence shows however that its merits were readily recognized in Australia and it had come into very common use at least by the middle of the 1960s. The publications produced by Mr Rose demonstrated that a breathable surgical tape with a non-irritating adhesive was known to be desirable, but the problem of producing such a tape remained unsolved until the present invention was made in 1959. Neither Sister Stahl nor Mr Rose was cross-examined. The remaining witness on the state of the art in Australia at the priority date was Mr Thomas who was formerly employed in Australia by Johnson and Johnson Pty Ltd, manufacturers of surgical dressings and sutures. He said that prior to 1960 some nonwoven surgical products were just coming into use. Examples to which he referred were drapes, used to mask off areas adjoining an operative site, hand towels and some surgical dressings. He said that prior to 1960 there were no products having both an adhesive and a nonwoven backing in use in Australia.

The evidence as to the position in Australia at the priority date thus shows that there was a known need for an improved adhesive surgical tape, the existing adhesive tapes having well known disadvantages. The advantages of a "breathable" tape had been known at least since 1955 but that need had not been satisfied by any product on the market or disclosed in the medical **[298]** field or in the field of the suppliers of surgical supplies, including tapes. That evidence further shows that when introduced on the market this tape met that need, and had substantial commercial success, notwithstanding that it may have been slow to "take off" because of price. These are well recognized indications of inventiveness though they are not in themselves decisive. In the present case however they contribute to the conclusion that there was an inventive step. There was nothing in common general knowledge which pointed to this solution to the known problem which awaited solution.

It appears that before the trial judge there was no argument presented on the objection that the patent had been anticipated by some prior publication and no such argument was presented before this Court at the hearing. However in written argument submitted by the respondent in reply a submission was made which was expressed in terms both of anticipation and obviousness. It is not altogether clear whether it was intended to raise the question of anticipation but it is desirable to deal with it as if it did raise that point. I am satisfied that the Salditt patent did not deprive the invention of novelty because, although it discloses some of the integers of the combination it does not disclose all of them. Because the information contained in the Salditt specification was not common general knowledge in Australia at the relevant time I do not need to examine it in relation to obviousness.

It was no doubt the discovery of the Ulrich adhesive which was the first step towards a suitable non-irritating adhesive but the Ulrich patent, even assuming it to be common general knowledge in Australia at the relevant time, did not reveal anything about the capacity of that adhesive to become or to be made microporous. The existence of that adhesive does not make the combination of integers in claims 7, 8 and 9 obvious. The further steps to the combination were not obvious.

132. For those reasons I am of opinion that claims 7, 8 and 9 of the patent were valid and have been infringed. I would allow the appeal and dismiss the respondent's cross-appeal.

## Lockwood Security Products Pty Ltd v Doric Products Pty Ltd
High Court of Australia: Gleeson CJ, McHugh, Gummow,
Hayne and Heydon JJ
[2004] HCA 58

This case considered the validity of a patent for a door lock. The specification included a consistory clause and described a preferred embodiment. The court considered whether the central claim was "fairly based" on the matter described in the specification or travelled beyond it. In particular the court considered whether the test of fair basing involves consideration of "merit", "inventive step", "technical contribution to the art" or general "fairness". The court also considered whether the grounds of invalidity under the *Patents Act 1990* must be kept distinct.

**Gleeson CJ, McHugh, Gummow, Hayne and Heydon JJ:** 42. It is convenient first to discuss some aspects of s 40(3), then to analyse the reasoning of the courts below, and then to examine the reasons why Doric's arguments, so far as they differ from that reasoning, must be rejected.

**The construction of s 40(3): separate consideration of each ground of invalidity**
43. The language of the legislation suggests that it is wrong to employ reasoning relevant to one ground of invalidity in considering another.

44. *Section 18 compared with s 40.* Section 18 of the Act is in Ch 2, headed "Patent rights, ownership and validity". Section 18 sets out requirements which go to the nature and subject-matter of patents. In contrast, s 40 appears in Ch 3, which is headed "From application to acceptance", and which deals with the filing, examination and acceptance of patent applications. Section 40 sets out requirements that are certainly important: in the specification, patentees give the public directions about how the advantages of the invention may be obtained after the patent expires, while in the claims, patentees warn their rivals what they must not do before the patent expires.[323] The requirements of s 40, however, unlike those of s 18, say nothing about the nature or subject-matter of patents, and go more to the form that specifications must take. Both the differences in the requirements which ss 18 and 40 and impose, and their respective locations in the Act, suggest that s 18 issues have no relevance to s 40. So far as s 18 refers to "patentable inventions" and s 40 to "inventions", that conclusion is also supported by the definition in Sched 1 of the Act of "invention" as including an "alleged invention".

45. *Separation of matters going to and grounds of invalidity.* That conclusion is also supported by the fact that the s 45(1) matters which an applicant can ask the Commissioner to conduct an examination into, the s 59 grounds on which a patent application may be

[323] *Rehm Pty Ltd v Websters Security Systems (International) Pty Ltd* (1988) 81 ALR 79 at 94-95 per Gummow J; *CCOM Pty Ltd v Jiejing Pty Ltd* [1994] FCA 1168; (1994) 51 FCR 260 at 277 per Spender, Gummow and Heerey JJ.

opposed and the s 138(3) grounds for revoking a patent are separately stated in the paragraphs of each section.

46. *The distinctness of the grounds of invalidity.* It is common in patent infringement litigation for invalidity to be alleged, and for more than one ground of invalidity to be relied on. Certain matters of fact and construction may be relevant to more than one issue. Thus common general knowledge is relevant not only to issues of construction by the skilled addressee, which underlie the infringement inquiry and interact with issues of validity,[324] but also to obviousness.[325] Other factual matters may be relevant to more than one ground of invalidity.[326] The issues may "intersect and overlap".[327] However, as Doric conceded in this Court, the grounds of invalidity themselves are, and must be kept, conceptually distinct. In particular, as Doric also conceded, a lack of fair basing is a distinct ground for revocation. Hence the "inventiveness" or "meritoriousness" of, or the technical contribution made by, the specification are issues to be examined if there is an objection under s 18(1)(b) of the Act for want of novelty or absence of an inventive step (ie obviousness). There is no reason to introduce them into the fair basing question.

47. The contrary is suggested by reading in isolation a statement of Blanco White, on which the trial judge relied.[328] It is that the fair basing objection "overlaps others to a large extent". A footnote gave as illustrations of those "others" the objections based on ss 18(1)(a), 18(1)(b)(ii) and 18(1)(c) of the Act. Blanco White did not support that statement by the citation of any authority. The passage which preceded the statement contradicted it. It said:[329]

> "It is an objection to the validity of a patent that any claim is 'not fairly based on the matter disclosed in' the complete specification. *This is a matter arising essentially on the contents of the complete specification.* Subject to that, the objection would appear to include the old objection that 'the claim claims more than what the patentee invented if he invented anything.' The modern rule thus becomes: the inventor is not entitled to claim a monopoly more extensive than is necessary to protect that which he has *himself (in his specification) said* is his invention."

48. If all that is essential in assessing a fair basing objection is recourse to the contents of the specification, there is no call, for example, for an examination (except on construction questions) of common general knowledge (which is essential when considering an objection based on want of an inventive step), or of prior art (which is essential when considering novelty (s 7(1)). And Blanco White's statement is contradicted by Australian authority. A specification can comply with s 40 even though what it claims has been invented is not a patentable invention because it is not novel or it is obvious.[330] Each of the grounds of invalidity referred to in ss 18(1)(a), 18(1)(b)(i), 18(1)(b)(ii) and 18(1)(c)

---

[324] *Welch Perrin & Co Pty Ltd v Worrel* [1961] HCA 91; (1961) 106 CLR 588 at 610 per Dixon CJ, Kitto and Windeyer JJ.

[325] Section 7(2) of the Act and *Firebelt Pty Ltd v Brambles Australia Ltd* (2002) 76 ALJR 816 at 821-823 [31]-[36] per Gleeson CJ, McHugh, Gummow, Hayne and Callinan JJ; [2002] HCA 21; 188 ALR 280 at 287-289.

[326] *Sunbeam Corporation v Morphy-Richards (Aust) Pty Ltd* [1961] HCA 39; (1961) 180 CLR 98 at 111-112 per Windeyer J.

[327] *Kimberly-Clark Australia Pty Ltd v Arico Trading International Pty Ltd* [2001] HCA 8; (2001) 207 CLR 1 at 19 [34].

[328] *Patents For Inventions*, 5th ed (1983) at §4-801: see *Doric Products Pty Ltd v Lockwood Security Products Pty Ltd* [2001] FCA 1877; (2001) 192 ALR 306 at 348 [236].

[329] Blanco White, *Patents For Inventions*, 5th ed (1983) at §4-801, footnotes omitted (emphasis added).

[330] *Rose Holdings Pty Ltd v Carlton Shuttlecocks Ltd* [1957] HCA 48; (1957) 98 CLR 444 at 449 per Williams J.

is distinct from the others.[331] Thus there is a "logically precise"[332] and "fundamental" difference[333] between the objection for want of novelty and the objection for want of an inventive step.[334] The lack of inventive step ground of invalidity is distinct from all the others, including fair basing.[335] A patent can be successfully challenged on the ground that the claims are not fairly based even though every other possible ground of challenge fails.

49. *Section 40 grounds analysed.* The distinctness of the grounds of invalidity can also be illustrated by comparing the fair basing objection with those most closely connected with it, namely the failure to describe the invention fully, and the failure to claim clearly and succinctly. Section 59(c) of the Act creates as grounds for opposition, and s 138(3)(f) creates as grounds for invalidity, non-compliance with s 40(2) or (3). They are commonly called "s 40 points", and they do form a genus in that it is not necessary to look at common general knowledge at the priority date, except in construing the patent.[336] But the genus contains several distinct grounds. Section 40(2) deals with the "complete specification", that is, with a document which concludes with the claims defining the invention (s 40(2)(b)), and in which the material preceding the claims is commonly called the "body of the specification", or the "specification" for short. In assessing whether a patent complies with the requirement of s 40(2)(a) that the complete specification must describe the invention fully, it is necessary to take into account the whole of the complete specification – both the body of the specification and the claims.[337] On the other hand, when assessing whether there is fair basing within the meaning of s 40(3), it is necessary to split the patent into the claims and the body of the specification, in order to see whether the former are fairly based on the matter described in the latter.[338] These statutorily compelled differences in the mode of analysis point against any overlap in the provisions when considered as grounds of opposition or invalidity.

### The construction of s 40(3): irrelevance of "inventive step", "merit" and "technical contribution to the art"

50. To some extent, various of the judgments below assume that the relevant test under s 40(3) requires a comparison between the claims and the "inventive step",[339] or a comparison between the claims and the "merit" of the invention,[340] or a com-

[331] *CCOM Pty Ltd v Jiejing Pty Ltd* [1994] FCA 1168; (1994) 51 FCR 260 at 291 per Spender, Gummow and Heerey JJ.

[332] *Sunbeam Corporation v Morphy-Richards (Aust) Pty Ltd* [1961] HCA 39; (1961) 180 CLR 98 at 111 per Windeyer J.

[333] *Graham Hart (1971) Pty Ltd v S W Hart & Co Pty Ltd* [1978] HCA 61; (1978) 141 CLR 305 at 330 per Aickin J.

[334] *Advanced Building Systems Pty Ltd v Ramset Fasteners (Aust) Pty Ltd* [1998] HCA 19; (1998) 194 CLR 171 at 181-182 [10]-[11] per Brennan CJ, Gaudron, McHugh and Gummow JJ. For the history see *R D Werner & Co Inc v Bailey Aluminium Products Pty Ltd* (1989) 25 FCR 565 at 594-601 per Gummow J (Jenkinson J concurring).

[335] *Advanced Building Systems Pty Ltd v Ramset Fasteners (Aust) Pty Ltd* [1998] HCA 19; (1998) 194 CLR 171 at 184 [16] per Brennan CJ, Gaudron, McHugh and Gummow JJ.

[336] *Welch Perrin & Co Pty Ltd v Worrel* [1961] HCA 91; (1961) 106 CLR 588 at 610 per Dixon CJ, Kitto and Windeyer JJ.

[337] *Kimberly-Clark Australia Pty Ltd v Arico Trading International Pty Ltd* [2001] HCA 8; (2001) 207 CLR 1 at 12-13 [14] and [16].

[338] *Kimberly-Clark Australia Pty Ltd v Arico Trading International Pty Ltd* [2001] HCA 8; (2001) 207 CLR 1 at 12 [15].

[339] *Lockwood Security Products Pty Ltd v Doric Products Pty Ltd* [2003] FCAFC 29; (2003) 56 IPR 479 at 496 [72]-[73] per Wilcox J, 503 [102] per Merkel J.

[340] *Lockwood Security Products Pty Ltd v Doric Products Pty Ltd* [2003] FCAFC 29; (2003) 56 IPR 479 at 502 [100] per Merkel J.

parison between the claims and the "technical contribution to the art" made by the patent.[341]

51. There are some key features of the legislation which suggest that these assumptions are wrong.

52. *The imprecision of "inventive merit"*. This Court has recently warned against use of the expression "inventive merit". It was employed in the 19th century to express ideas now relevant to what is novel and to what is an inventive step (ss 18(1)(b)(i) and (ii) of the Act). "The phrase invites error through imprecision of legal analysis."[342]

53. *The language of s 40(3)*. Further, conceptions like "inventive step", "merit" and "technical contribution to the art" find no support in the statutory language of s 40(3). Section 40(1) speaks of a provisional specification describing "the invention" and s 40(2)(a) speaks of a complete specification describing "the invention fully". Section 40(2)(b) speaks of the claims "defining the invention". Section 40(4) speaks of the claims relating "to one invention only". Although s 40(3) does not use the word "invention", this context suggests, and the parties agreed, that the requirement in s 40(3) that the claims be fairly based on the matter described in the specification is a requirement that they be fairly based on the matter in it that discusses the "invention" (an expression which includes the "alleged invention"). In s 40(1), "invention" means "the embodiment which is described, and around which the claims are drawn".[343] It has the same meaning in s 40(2).[344] So far as s 40(3) implicitly refers to an invention, it must bear the same meaning there. It does not mean the "inventive step taken by the inventor" or the "advance in the art made by the inventor".[345] Nor does it refer to inventive "merit" or to any "technical contribution to the art".

54. Even if s 40(3) did not impliedly refer to an invention, the language points to a comparison between the claims and what is described in the specification only, and again it does not call for any inquiry into an "inventive step", or inventive "merit" or a "technical contribution to the art".

### Section 40(3) in the light of pre-statutory authorities

55. Sometimes s 40(3) is discussed by reference to authorities decided before the first statutory ancestor of s 40(3) was introduced in the United Kingdom by s 4(4) of the *Patents Act 1949* (UK) ("the 1949 UK Act"), and in Australia by s 40(2) of the *Patents Act 1952* (Cth) ("the 1952 Act"). A leading example is *Mullard Radio Valve Co Ltd v Philco Radio and Television Corporation of Great Britain Ltd*. There are phrases in it which give some support to the glosses relating to "merit" and "technical contribution" appearing in the courts below. Thus Lord Macmillan said:[346]

> "The fact that an article of obvious construction is discovered to give a valuable and new benefit if employed in a particular way does not *entitle* the discoverer to prevent everyone else from making that article. A patentee is granted his monopoly in order to protect the invention which in his specification he has communicated to

[341] *Doric Products Pty Ltd v Lockwood Security Products Pty Ltd* [2001] FCA 1877; (2001) 192 ALR 306 at 347-348 [235]-[236] per Hely J.

[342] *Advanced Building Systems Pty Ltd v Ramset Fasteners (Aust) Pty Ltd* [1998] HCA 19; (1998) 194 CLR 171 at 188 [26] per Brennan CJ, Gaudron, McHugh and Gummow JJ.

[343] *AMP Inc v Utilux Pty Ltd* (1971) 45 ALJR 123 at 127 per McTiernan J; revd on other grounds: *Utilux Pty Ltd v AMP Inc* (1974) 48 ALJR 17; *Kimberly-Clark Australia Pty Ltd v Arico Trading International Pty Ltd* [2001] HCA 8; (2001) 207 CLR 1 at 14-15 [21] per Gleeson CJ, McHugh, Gummow, Hayne and Callinan JJ.

[344] *Kimberly-Clark Australia Pty Ltd v Arico Trading International Pty Ltd* [2001] HCA 8; (2001) 207 CLR 1 at 15 [21].

[345] *Kimberly-Clark Australia Pty Ltd v Arico Trading International Pty Ltd* [2001] HCA 8; (2001) 207 CLR 1 at 15 [21].

[346] (1936) 53 RPC 323 at 346-347.

the public. He is not *entitled* to claim a monopoly more extensive than is necessary to protect that which he has himself said is his invention. In the present case I think that in Claim 2 the Patentee has claimed more than his inventive idea *entitles* him to protect. He has not *earned the right* to say that no one else shall be permitted in manufacturing valves to connect the electrode nearest the anode with the cathode." (Emphasis added.)

Lord Macmillan went on to say:[347]

"The consideration which the patentee gives to the public disclosing his inventive idea *entitles* him in return to protection for an article which embodies his inventive idea but not for an article which, while capable of being used to carry his inventive idea into effect, is described in terms which cover things quite unrelated to his inventive idea, and which do not embody it at all. ...

It is undoubtedly the case that a claim may be too wide, in the sense that it claims protection for that for which the patentee is not *entitled* to protection, or that it gives him a wider protection than his discovery *entitles* him to receive. In the present instance the Patentee has claimed a monopoly of all valves with a certain feature of construction although the *merit* of his invention does not lie in that feature but in the utilisation in a particular and limited way of a valve containing that feature of construction. In so doing he has in my opinion over-reached himself and his claim is wider than the law will support." (Emphasis added.)

56. Lord Macmillan's speech has been relied on in cases on s 40(2) of the 1952 Act in this Court[348] but not in a manner essential to the result. The fact that that speech was dealing with objections based on novelty and obviousness,[349] and was delivered at a time when there was no statutory equivalent to s 40(3) of the Act, however, requires that it be used with great care.

57. In *CCOM Pty Ltd v Jiejing Pty Ltd*,[350] the Full Court of the Federal Court said of *Mullard*:

"[T]he House of Lords had been concerned to find a rationale for disconformity between the body and claims in a complete specification, in the absence of express statutory provision. The rationale was found in the concept of the disclosure as the consideration for the monopoly delimited by the claim. But, in applying *Mullard* to what since 1952 are express statutory provisions, some caution is needed lest the history swamp the new text."

It was for this reason that in *Olin Corporation v Super Cartridge Co Pty Ltd*[351] Barwick CJ stressed the importance of abandoning tests developed at a time when the idea underlying the present s 40(3) did not take a statutory form, and concentrating instead on the statutory language.

"The question whether the claim is fairly based is not to be resolved ... by considering whether a monopoly in the product would be an undue reward for the disclosure. Rather, the question is a narrow one, namely whether the claim to the product being new, useful, and inventive, that is to say, the claim as expressed, travels beyond the matter disclosed in the specification."

---

[347] (1936) 53 RPC 323 at 347.

[348] *Montecatini Edison SpA v Eastman Kodak Co* (1971) 45 ALJR 593 at 597 per Gibbs J; *Olin Corporation v Super Cartridge Co Pty Ltd* [1977] HCA 23; (1977) 180 CLR 236 at 263 per Stephen and Mason JJ.

[349] *Mullard Radio Valve Co Ltd v Philco Radio and Television Corporation of Great Britain Ltd* (1936) 53 RPC 323 at 339. An application to amend claim 2 of the *Mullard* patent which was made to Morton J after the House of Lords decision succeeded ((1938) 55 RPC 197) but the Court of Appeal upheld an appeal against the allowance of the amendment ((1938) 56 RPC 1).

[350] [1994] FCA 1168; (1994) 51 FCR 260 at 279 per Spender, Gummow and Heerey JJ.

[351] [1977] HCA 23; (1977) 180 CLR 236 at 240.

Barwick CJ dissented as to the construction of the patent in suit in *Olin* but the approval of his statement of principle by a unanimous court in *Kimberly-Clark Australia Pty Ltd v Arico Trading International Pty Ltd*[352] means that authorities decided before the enactment of the precursors to s 40(3), including *Mullard's Case*, should now be treated as being of very limited assistance in the construction of s 40(3).

58. The actual result in *Mullard's Case* may have been the same if s 40(3) had been in force. The conclusion was that while the invention rested on the employment of a screening grid in conjunction with a control grid, the central claim made no reference to these grids. Hence it travelled beyond the matter disclosed in the specification.[353] The idea sought to be conveyed here was sometimes expressed in the phrase "covetous claim" but, as Clauson LJ put it in a subsequent *Mullard* case,[354] the phrase was used "in no sinister sense".

59. Another authority in this category is *Palmer v Dunlop Perdriau Rubber Co Ltd*.[355] At that time, the *Patents Act 1903* (Cth) ("the 1903 Act") was in force. That authority contains statements, on which Doric placed weight, in support of allowing the appeal in that case (although the appeal was dismissed because the Court was evenly divided). Because they precede the enactment of legislation separating out fair basing as a ground of invalidity, they do not assist in construing s 40(3).[356] The statements relied upon fasten on the difficulty that can arise in some combination claims, of covering validly more than the particular aggregation of integers stated in the claims. While to some extent the language of Rich J turns on the claim being "too wide",[357] other parts of the language employed by him and by Dixon J go more to the clarity of claims ("indefinite in the extreme",[358] "a vague claim", "most indefinite"[359]). And in saying that, outside the operation together of the specific elements of the combination, "subject matter would fail", Dixon J's reasoning appears to proceed on the basis of a lack of inventiveness, ie obviousness.[360] Further, the statements of Rich J are preceded by passages indicating that the issue under debate by him was obviousness.[361] Latham CJ, who favoured dismissing the appeal, and with whom McTiernan J agreed, said obviousness was the most difficult issue.[362] Further, the case involved a patent to achieve an old result (vulcanised battery cases) by new means. It is thus distinct from the present case, which involves a patent to

[352] [2001] HCA 8; (2001) 207 CLR 1 at 12 [15] per Gleeson CJ, McHugh, Gummow, Hayne and Callinan JJ.

[353] *Mullard Radio Valve Co Ltd v Philco Radio and Television Corporation of Great Britain Ltd* (1936) 53 RPC 323 at 345 per Lord Macmillan.

[354] *Mullard Radio Valve Co Ltd v British Belmont Radio Ltd and Juviler* (1938) 56 RPC 1 at 21.

[355] [1937] HCA 43; (1937) 59 CLR 30 at 64-65 per Rich J, 76-78 per Dixon J. In the latter passage Dixon J in turn relied on *Mullard Radio Valve Co Ltd v Philco Radio and Television Corporation of Great Britain Ltd* (1936) 53 RPC 323 at 345 per Lord Macmillan and 350 per Lord Roche.

[356] Section 36 of the 1903 Act provided: "A complete specification must fully describe and ascertain the invention and the manner in which it is to be performed, and must end with a distinct statement of the invention claimed." Section 86(3) provided: "Every ground on which a patent might at common law be repealed by *scire facias* shall be available as a ground of revocation." The judgments in *Palmer* contain no reference to s 36 of the 1903 Act.

[357] *Palmer v Dunlop Perdriau Rubber Co Ltd* [1937] HCA 43; (1937) 59 CLR 30 at 65.

[358] *Palmer v Dunlop Perdriau Rubber Co Ltd* [1937] HCA 43; (1937) 59 CLR 30 at 65 per Rich J.

[359] *Palmer v Dunlop Perdriau Rubber Co Ltd* [1937] HCA 43; (1937) 59 CLR 30 at 77 per Dixon J.

[360] *Palmer v Dunlop Perdriau Rubber Co Ltd* [1937] HCA 43; (1937) 59 CLR 30 at 78.

[361] *Palmer v Dunlop Perdriau Rubber Co Ltd* [1937] HCA 43; (1937) 59 CLR 30 at 64.

[362] *Palmer v Dunlop Perdriau Rubber Co Ltd* [1937] HCA 43; (1937) 59 CLR 30 at 59 ("The most difficult question in this case is that of subject matter").

achieve a new result by existing means used in combination, and which falls within the principle stated in *Shave v H V McKay Massey Harris Pty Ltd*:[363]

"When a combination claim states an invention which gives an old result by a new means, the monopoly is limited, at any rate prima facie, to the new means. But when by a new application of principle the inventor has obtained a new result or thing, even when it be done by a combination, he may claim all the alternative means by which the thing or result may be achieved."

60. For the purposes of s 40(2)(a), it is not necessary for the inventor to disclose all the alternative means; it is enough that there is disclosure in the sense of enabling the addressee of the specification to produce something within each claim without new inventions or additions or prolonged study of matters presenting additional difficulty.[364] The trial judge held that s 40(2)(a) was satisfied in this case.

61. In the circumstances *Palmer's Case* is not a guide to the construction of s 40(3), and in any event the problem it dealt with is distinct from the present one.

62. To some extent Dixon J saw *Palmer's Case* as turning on the fact that on its true construction the specification disclosed that the invention – a mould for producing vulcanised rubber boxes – depended on the telescoping action of the core of the mould within the mould, whereas the relevant claim referred only to a "power-actuated mechanism forcing relative movement between the mould lining and the core" without any limitation to telescoping action.[365] That reasoning is consistent with s 40(3), because the unconditional claim travelled beyond the conditional matter in the specification.

**The construction of s 40(3): irrelevance of post 1977 United Kingdom cases**
63. It is necessary to bear in mind, in examining United Kingdom cases, that in 1977 the language of fair basing disappeared from the United Kingdom legislation on its being changed to give effect to the European Patent Convention. Section 14(5)(c) of the *Patents Act 1977* (UK) ("the 1977 UK Act") provided instead that the claims had to "be supported by the description" of the invention in the specification.[366]

64. The patent in suit in *Biogen Inc v Medeva plc*[367] related to a DNA sequence coding for hepatitis B virus antigen to stimulate the production of antibodies, and claimed priority from an earlier application ("Biogen 1"). If Biogen 1 did not support in the necessary sense the patent in suit then the patent was invalid because it was conceded that the invention was obvious when the application for it had been filed.[368] The House of Lords upheld the decision of the Court of Appeal which, reversing Aldous J,[369] held the patent invalid. Biogen 1 described one recombinant procedure for making the necessary antigen but this did not justify the claim made by the later patent for any recombinant method for making the antigen. The claimed invention was too broad.[370]

65. Doric cited *Biogen* in support of a submission that Lord Hoffmann was of opinion, "in a very closely related context", that the Patentee's argument in this case was "mechanistic and impoverished". Doric referred to a statement by Lord Hoffmann:[371]

---

[363] [1935] HCA 39; (1935) 52 CLR 701 at 709 per Rich, Dixon, Evatt and McTiernan JJ.
[364] *Kimberly-Clark Australia Pty Ltd v Arico Trading International Pty Ltd* [2001] HCA 8; (2001) 207 CLR 1 at 17 [25].
[365] *Palmer v Dunlop Perdriau Rubber Co Ltd* [1937] HCA 43; (1937) 59 CLR 30 at 32, 34 and 77.
[366] *CCOM Pty Ltd v Jiejing Pty Ltd* [1994] FCA 1168; (1994) 51 FCR 260 at 276.
[367] [1996] UKHL 18; [1997] RPC 1 (HL).
[368] [1996] UKHL 18; [1997] RPC 1 at 52 per Lord Hoffmann (Lords Goff of Chieveley, Browne-Wilkinson, Mustill and Slynn of Hadley concurring).
[369] [1995] RPC 25.
[370] [1996] UKHL 18; [1997] RPC 1 at 51-52.
[371] [1996] UKHL 18; [1997] RPC 1 at 52.

"[C]are is needed not to stifle further research and healthy competition by allowing the first person who has found a way of achieving an obviously desirable goal to monopolise every other way of doing so."

Doric also relied on the following passage:[372]

"[T]here is an important difference between the 1949 and 1977 [UK] Acts which make decisions on the earlier Act an unsafe guide. Section 72(1)(c) of the 1977 [UK Act] is not only intended to ensure that the public can work the invention after expiration of the monopoly. It is also intended to give the court in revocation proceedings a jurisdiction which mirrors that of the Patent Office under section 14(3) or the [European Patent Office] under article 83 of the [European Patent Convention], namely, to hold a patent invalid on the substantive ground that, as the [European Patent Office] said ... , the extent of the monopoly claimed exceeds the technical contribution to the art made by the invention as described in the specification. In the 1949 [UK] Act, this function was performed by another ground for revocation, namely that the claim was not 'fairly based on the matter disclosed in the specification' (section 32(1)(i)). The requirement of sufficiency was therefore regarded as serving a narrower purpose. But the disappearance of 'lack of fair basis' as an express ground for revocation does not in my view mean that [the] general principle which it expressed has been abandoned. The jurisprudence of the [European Patent Office] shows that it is still in full vigour and embodied in articles 83 and 84 of the [European Patent Convention], of which the equivalents in the 1977 [UK] Act are section 14(3) and (5) and section 72(1)(c)."

66. Section 72(1)(c) provides that a patent may be revoked on the ground that "the specification of the patent does not disclose the invention clearly enough and completely enough for it to be performed by a person skilled in the art". It and its corresponding provision creating a positive duty of disclosure, s 14(3), do not resemble the Australian fair basing requirement in s 40(3) of the Act, but are closer to s 40(2)(a) creating a duty to describe the invention fully. Further, Australia is not party to the European Patent Convention. The courts of Australia are not bound by what the European Patent Office says, and do not regard it as "jurisprudence". The language of the 1949 UK Act[373] continues to be reflected in Australia in s 40(3) of the Act. Lord Hoffmann's reasoning suggests that in the United Kingdom the fair basing test has gone, rather than that it has survived.

67. The inapplicability in Australia of the reasoning in *Biogen* is heightened by the fact that Lord Hoffmann applied the words "mechanistic and impoverished", not to the patentee's argument under consideration, but to a "general rule of European patent law that an invention was sufficiently disclosed if the skilled man could make a single embodiment."[374] That happens also to be the rule recognised in this Court's construction of s 40(2)(a) in *Kimberly-Clark Australia Pty Ltd v Arico Trading International Pty Ltd*.[375] This criticism of an important aspect of Australian law, as reflected in s 40(2)(a) of the Act, suggests that current United Kingdom law is no guide to Australian law on s 40(3). (The same is true of the treatment in *Biogen*[376] of obviousness.[377]) Doric was frank enough to boil the House of Lords' reasoning down to the following Voltairean

[372] *Biogen Inc v Medeva plc* [1996] UKHL 18; [1997] RPC 1 at 54.

[373] Section 4(4) provided: "The claim or claims of a complete specification must relate to a single invention, must be clear and succinct, and must be fairly based on the matter disclosed in the specification."

[374] *Biogen Inc v Medeva plc* [1996] UKHL 18; [1997] RPC 1 at 48.

[375] [2001] HCA 8; (2001) 207 CLR 1 at 16-17 [25].

[376] [1996] UKHL 18; [1997] RPC 1 at 45.

[377] *Aktiebolaget Hässle v Alphapharm Pty Ltd* [2002] HCA 59; (2002) 212 CLR 411 at 429 [40], 431-432 [48]-[49] per Gleeson CJ, Gaudron, Gummow and Hayne JJ.

aphorism: "Since the fair basis doctrine no longer exists, it is necessary to invent it." That is not an approach open to this Court.

### The approach required by s 40(3)

68. *Erroneous principles.* The comparison which s 40(3) calls for is not analogous to that between a claim and an alleged anticipation or infringement. It is wrong to employ "an over meticulous verbal analysis".[378] It is wrong to seek to isolate in the body of the specification "essential integers" or "essential features" of an alleged invention and to ask whether they correspond with the essential integers of the claim in question.[379]

69. *"Real and reasonably clear disclosure".* Section 40(3) requires, in Fullagar J's words, "a real and reasonably clear disclosure."[380] But those words, when used in connection with s 40(3), do not limit disclosures to preferred embodiments.

"The circumstance that something is a requirement for the best method of performing an invention does not make it necessarily a requirement for all claims; likewise, the circumstance that material is part of the description of the invention does not mean that it must be included as an integer of each claim. Rather, the question is whether there is a real and reasonably clear disclosure in the body of the specification of what is then claimed, so that the alleged invention as claimed is broadly, that is to say in a general sense, described in the body of the specification."[381]

Fullagar J's phrase serves the function of compelling attention to the construction of the specification as a whole, putting aside particular parts which, although in isolation they might appear to point against the "real" disclosure, are in truth only loose or stray remarks.

### The reasoning of the courts below

70. *Conflation of obviousness and s 40(2)(a) with fair basing.* The reasoning of the trial judge is of some importance to Doric, because no judge in the Full Court specifically adopted the trial judge's reasoning, and Doric, while not actually conceding that the reasoning in the Full Court was wrong, said it did not wish "to take too much time" defending it, defended it with very little relish and conceded that its primary approach was not to be found there. But some of the difficulties in the Full Court's reasoning are also present in that of the trial judge. One difficulty was an apparent conflation of the issue of fair basing with the issue of insufficiency of description or the issue of obviousness. The best Doric could do was to deny that in the courts below there was, despite appearances, any conflation of that kind, but to concede that if the conflation had taken place, the reasoning was unsustainable. The denial fails and the concession is sound. However, there are additional difficulties in the reasoning.

71. *Wilcox J.* In a section of his reasons headed "Discussion about fair basis, insufficiency and obviousness", Wilcox J expressed agreement with the trial judge's conclusions on fair basing.[382] He then discussed obviousness in a fashion critical of the trial judge, but later said that it was not necessary to express any final conclusion about obviousness, nor

---

[378] *CCOM Pty Ltd v Jiejing Pty Ltd* [1994] FCA 1168; (1994) 51 FCR 260 at 281 per Spender, Gummow and Heerey JJ.

[379] *CCOM Pty Ltd v Jiejing Pty Ltd* [1994] FCA 1168; (1994) 51 FCR 260 at 281 per Spender, Gummow and Heerey JJ.

[380] The expression was used by Fullagar J in *Société des Usines Chimiques Rhône-Poulenc v Commissioner of Patents* [1958] HCA 27; (1958) 100 CLR 5 at 11 in relation to s 45(5) of the 1952 Act, which required that a claim in a specification lodged under the 1952 Act be "fairly based on matter disclosed" in a specification lodged under the 1903 Act. The expression has been applied to s 40(3): *CCOM Pty Ltd v Jiejing Pty Ltd* [1994] FCA 1168; (1994) 51 FCR 260 at 281-282 per Spender, Gummow and Heerey JJ.

[381] *Rehm Pty Ltd v Websters Security Systems (International) Pty Ltd* (1988) 81 ALR 79 at 95 per Gummow J.

[382] *Lockwood Security Products Pty Ltd v Doric Products Pty Ltd* [2003] FCAFC 29; (2003) 56 IPR 479 at 495-497 [69]-[77].

to express a view on sufficiency of description. At the start of that section of his reasons, he said that there was a common fundamental question affecting the three issues referred to in the heading: "what, exactly, was the invention the subject of the patent?"[383] That is true, in the sense that once that question is answered, it becomes possible to consider whether the invention is fully described, whether the claims are fairly based on it, and whether it is obvious. But the question must precede, rather than accompany or follow, any resolution of those three issues. The correct way of answering the question is to examine the body of the specification in order to see what it describes as the invention. This Wilcox J did not immediately do. Instead of discussing the issue of "invention" – part of the s 40(3) question – he discussed the issue of "inventive step" which relates to the s 18(1)(b)(ii) question of what a skilled but non-inventive worker would have seen as obvious in the light of common general knowledge. His Honour said that at the trial the Patentee had adopted an inconsistent case about what the invention was. Whether or not that is so, Wilcox J then observed that, as in this Court, the Patentee "took the unequivocal position that the inventive step was the addition of the widely-expressed sixth integer." He then said:[384]

> "However, it can hardly be an inventive step simply to say that the solution to the problem of the inside lock not being responsive to an outside actuator is to make it so. That tells the addressee nothing ...
>
> If, contrary to my opinion, the addition of the widely-expressed sixth integer was thought to be an inventive step, [the Patentee] would face a serious difficulty in relation to obviousness".

72. In assessing whether the invention claimed by a patentee is fully described or fairly based, it is necessary to take into account, apart from common general knowledge so far as it casts light on questions of construction, only what is said about it in the specification, independently of whether it is a "patentable invention", and, in particular, independently of whether it is a patentable invention on the ground that it is not obvious. The first and third of the three sentences quoted in the above passage centre on "inventive step" – a s 18(1)(b)(ii) but not a s 40(3) issue. The second, as Doric conceded in argument, appears to make a different point about whether the invention is fully described for s 40(2)(a) purposes. No part of this passage explains why the claims are not fairly based on the invention claimed in the consistory clause. Any force in the points made is immaterial to the fair basing question. For the reasons given above, the various grounds of invalidity ought to have been kept distinct.[385]

73. *Branson J.* Her Honour reasoned thus:[386]

> "[T]he invention as the [Patentee] seeks to define it is merely an idea; it is not a 'patentable invention' within the meaning of s 18(1) of [the Act]. It is probably not important whether the concept of an outside key which automatically releases the lock is said not to be a manner of manufacture within the meaning of s 6 of the Statute of Monopolies, or as [Doric] contended, not to involve an inventive step, or as the primary judge found, too broad to provide a fair basis for the claims of the specification which must relate to one invention only (s 40 of the Act). The important thing is that one cannot patent an idea or a mere principle."

To the contrary, it is important whether it is s 18(1)(a), or s 18(1)(b)(ii), or s 40(3) that applies. This is partly so because the Particulars of Objection contain nothing about

---

[383] *Lockwood Security Products Pty Ltd v Doric Products Pty Ltd* [2003] FCAFC 29; (2003) 56 IPR 479 at 495 [69].

[384] *Lockwood Security Products Pty Ltd v Doric Products Pty Ltd* [2003] FCAFC 29; (2003) 56 IPR 479 at 496 [72]-[73].

[385] See [43]-[49] above.

[386] *Lockwood Security Products Pty Ltd v Doric Products Pty Ltd* [2003] FCAFC 29; (2003) 56 IPR 479 at 498 [86].

s 18(1)(a), or the patenting of an idea or mere principle, and Doric conceded that it did not put the case that way. It is also because none of these complaints is identical with or overlaps with the others: they are conceptually distinct, as Doric also conceded.

74. *Merkel J.* Merkel J's reasoning depended on a distinction between the invention claimed by the Patentee and its "merit", or what it "really disclosed". He said:[387]

"As latch assemblies commonly have features (i)-(v), ... the practical effect of claim 1 is a claim of a monopoly in respect of latch assemblies with those features and the additional feature (vi) of an outside actuator that renders the locking means inactive. The *'merit'* of the invention disclosed in the specification, and the *'real and reasonably clear'* disclosure of the invention, concerns the manner in which an outside actuator can achieve the object of providing a key controlled latch which can be released from the locked position by the outside actuator. But claim 1 does not claim protection for that invention. Rather, it claims protection for a standard latch assembly which has a *'lock release means'* constituted by *'something which causes an operation to occur'* from the outer side of the latch assembly, which renders the *'locking means inactive'*. But the invention really disclosed in the specification is the manner in which the lock release means has been achieved. ...

Claim 1 is wide enough to embrace any form of lock release means operable by an actuator on the outer side of the latch assembly, notwithstanding that that type of lock release means was not invented by the patentee and so does not use the patentee's *inventive steps* disclosed in the specification, being the lock release means described in [the passage describing a preferred embodiment after the consistory clause as quoted above[388]]." (Emphasis added.)

75. The expression "merit" is derived from Lord Macmillan's speech in *Mullard's Case*.[389] But, as discussed above,[390] "merit" plays no role in the statutory test, and Lord Macmillan's approach is no guide to the meaning of s 40(3). It follows that the test applied by Merkel J was incorrect.

76. Further, the distinction drawn between those forms of lock release that were "invented" by the Patentee and those that were not has several difficulties.

77. First, the distinction fails to apply the correct test, which calls for a comparison of the claim or claims with the matter described in the specification – not just with a preferred embodiment.

78. Secondly, the distinction reveals a confusion between the question "What is the invention here?" – the answer to which is "A new combination of integers including integer (vi)" – and the question whether each integer was an invention or an inventive step (the passage uses both expressions). Claim 1 does not claim a monopoly in any integer by itself. Paragraph (ii) of s 18(1)(b), applied to the patent in suit, requires that the combination claimed in claim 1 involve an inventive step, not that each or any integer involve an inventive step. It is only necessary that each integer form part of a full description of the invention (s 40(2)(a)), and that in their totality in any given claim they be described clearly and succinctly and be fairly based (s 40(3)). All the integers were either conceded or found to be part of a full description and to be clear and succinct. The inventiveness of particular integers is irrelevant, both to the inventiveness of a combination of them and to whether there is fair basing.

79. Thirdly, the distinction also contradicts (without any reasoning, as Doric accepted) the trial judge's conclusion that the specification taught that a "lock release means" may

---

[387] *Lockwood Security Products Pty Ltd v Doric Products Pty Ltd* [2003] FCAFC 29; (2003) 56 IPR 479 at 502-503 [100] and [102].

[388] See [11].

[389] (1936) 53 RPC 323 at 347.

[390] See [50]-[57].

take "any suitable form"[391] and that, on the evidence, and having regard to common general knowledge in the field at the priority date, the invention was not obvious and involved an inventive step.[392]

80. *The trial judge.* The reasoning of the trial judge was as follows.[393] The trial judge, having repeated the statement of principle by Barwick CJ in *Olin*,[394] recorded Doric's submission that claim 1 travelled beyond the matter disclosed in the specification, because while the Patentee had come up with a particular device – the preferred embodiment – which solved the problem identified in the Patent, the Patent went further and claimed all ways of solving that problem. He then recorded the Patentee's submission that "the words in the specification match the words of the claim, hence the claims are necessarily 'fairly based' on the specification." He said:[395]

"This is too narrow an approach to the question. The notion of 'travels beyond' requires consideration of what is truly disclosed by the specification in terms of a 'real and reasonably clear' disclosure."

The word "truly" has its source in *Atlantis Corporation Pty Ltd v Schindler*.[396] The trial judge continued:

"That this is so is recognised by the decision of the Full Court [in that case] where claim 1 was couched in the same terms as the description of the invention in the specification. But the court did not allow that coincidence of language 'to disguise the fact' that the invention disclosed in the body of the specification 'is truly' one which was subject to limitations as to use. The claims, however, were to pure apparatus claims, not subject to any limitations as to use. The claims therefore travelled beyond, and were found to be not fairly based on the matter described in the specification. Hence claim 1, and all other claims since they were dependent on it, were held to be invalid."

81. The trial judge then adopted from English cases[397] the expression "technical contribution to the art". He continued:[398]

"The structure of the specification in the present case refers to a known problem in relation to typical latch assemblies: key operation of the latch from the outside of the door does not release the inner handle, and as a result people may be locked in. The technical contribution to the art ... is the disclosure that the solution to the problem is the use of the outside lock to release the lock on the inside handle, coupled with the disclosure of one way of doing that in terms of the preferred embodiment.

Doric submits that the technical contribution made by the patentee, other than the preferred embodiment, is obvious, but I have declined to uphold that submission because of the evidentiary factors to which I have earlier referred. However, the fair basis objection overlaps with other grounds of invalidity, including obviousness:

---

[391] *Doric Products Pty Ltd v Lockwood Security Products Pty Ltd* [2001] FCA 1877; (2001) 192 ALR 306 at 316 [39].

[392] *Doric Products Pty Ltd v Lockwood Security Products Pty Ltd* [2001] FCA 1877; (2001) 192 ALR 306 at 343 [211]-[212].

[393] *Doric Products Pty Ltd v Lockwood Security Products Pty Ltd* [2001] FCA 1877; (2001) 192 ALR 306 at 346-348 [231]-[236].

[394] [1977] HCA 23; (1977) 180 CLR 236 at 240.

[395] *Doric Products Pty Ltd v Lockwood Security Products Pty Ltd* [2001] FCA 1877; (2001) 192 ALR 306 at 347 [234].

[396] (1997) 39 IPR 29.

[397] *Biogen Inc v Medeva plc* [1996] UKHL 18; [1997] RPC 1 at 54 per Lord Hoffmann (Lords Goff of Chieveley, Browne-Wilkinson, Mustill and Slynn of Hadley concurring); *Raychem Corp's Patents* [1997] EWHC 372; [1998] RPC 31 at 41-42 per Laddie J.

[398] *Doric Products Pty Ltd v Lockwood Security Products Pty Ltd* [2001] FCA 1877; (2001) 192 ALR 306 at 347-348 [235]-[236].

see Blanco White, *Patents For Inventions* [, 5th ed (1983) at §4-801]. I agree with [Doric's] submissions that the specification does not contain a real and reasonably clear disclosure of matters broader than the particular embodiment. Yet the patent claims a latch assembly which contains [lock release means] (which may take any suitable form) which is responsive to the operation of the second actuator so as to render the locking means inactive, no matter what means or mechanism is employed to achieve that result. It follows that claims 1-6 are not fairly based upon the specification."

82. In oral submissions to this Court, counsel for Doric found the first two sentences of the last paragraph something of an embarrassment and was not able to say what the point of including them was unless they related to the next two sentences. If they do, the Full Court's confusion between issues of obviousness and fair basing would appear to exist here as well. That is also suggested by the fact that in one of the English cases[399] from which the expression "technical contribution to the art" is derived, it appears under the heading "Claims to known or obvious desiderata" and precedes a discussion of invalidity on grounds of obviousness. But putting those first two sentences aside, the following difficulties remain.

83. The first is that the statutory test as expounded by Barwick CJ does not call for any evaluation of whether the breadth of the claims exceeds "the technical contribution to the art embodied in the invention", merely for an evaluation of whether the claims travel beyond the matter described in the specification.

84. The second is that in the passages quoted above, the trial judge defined the invention relatively narrowly as "the use of the outside lock to release the lock on the inside handle, coupled with the disclosure of one way of doing that". That is contradicted by other passages[400] in which the trial judge accepted that the invention was as described in the consistory clause set out in the specification – a "lock release means which is responsive to operation of the second actuator to render the locking means inactive."

85. The third is that the use of the word "real" suggests that the trial judge was applying a test which looked beyond the description of the invention as it appeared in the specification for some preferred embodiment of, or some optimal method of performing, the invention.

86. Fourthly, the trial judge relied on the proposition, seemingly asserted by Blanco White, that the fair basing objection overlaps with obviousness, which was criticised above.[401]

87. Finally, it is necessary to consider the trial judge's citation of *Atlantis Corporation Pty Ltd v Schindler*[402] for the proposition that to couch a claim "in the same terms as the description of the invention in the specification" did not of itself, by that mere "coincidence of language", establish fair basing. That proposition is correct, but it is not fatal to the Patentee's position in this case. A "coincidence of language" between a claim and part of the body of a specification does not establish fair basing if that part of the language of the specification does not reflect the description of the invention in the light of the specification as a whole. In the *Atlantis Case*, the specification, read as a whole, described an apparatus limited to a particular use as a sub-soil drainage system. The claims, however, were "pure apparatus" claims without that limitation on use. The Full Court of the Federal Court of Australia refused to construe them narrowly so as to conform with the description in the specification. A statement in the specification of a

[399] *Raychem Corp's Patents* [1997] EWHC 372; [1998] RPC 31 at 41-42 per Laddie J.

[400] *Doric Products Pty Ltd v Lockwood Security Products Pty Ltd* [2001] FCA 1877; (2001) 192 ALR 306 at 311 [13]-[14] and [17], 316-317 [39], 349 [241] and 350 [247].

[401] At [47]-[48].

[402] (1997) 39 IPR 29.

description of the invention in similar language to the first claim was not treated as the description of the invention. While the Full Court did not engage in close textual analysis, it did distinctly hold that the statement in the specification:[403]

> "should not be allowed to disguise the fact that the invention disclosed in the body of the specification is truly 'a sub-soil drainage method based on a particular apparatus' or 'a particular apparatus in its application to sub-soil drainage'. The claims, however, are 'pure apparatus claims'. They are not subject to any limitation as to use. They travel beyond, and are not fairly based on, the matter described in the specification."

In short, the case is distinguishable. Here, the Patentee does not rely on mere "coincidence of language": it contends that the language used, unlike that employed in the *Atlantis Case*, does describe the invention.

## Lockwood Security Products Pty Ltd v Doric Products Pty Ltd (No 2)

High Court of Australia: Gummow, Hayne, Callinan,
Heydon and Crennan JJ
[2007] HCA 21

This is the second case in relation to the Lockwood patent for a key operated door lock. This time the respondent challenged the validity of the Lockwood patent on the grounds of lack of inventive step. The patent included both a broad claim comprising a bare combination of integers and a narrow claim providing a "preferred embodiment" of those integers. The Court considered whether the combination of integers would be obvious to a person skilled in the relevant art and therefore lacking inventiveness.

**Gummow, Hayne, Callinan, Heydon and Crennan JJ:**

### 36. The inventive step in the Patent

37. Both Lockwood and Doric characterised the inventive step as the adding of integer (vi), "lock release means which is responsive to said operation of the second actuator so as to thereby render said locking means inactive", to a known product, the Lockwood 001, which contained integers (i)-(v).

38. It seemed to be accepted by Lockwood that the inventive step was the same for the broad claim, claim 1, as it was for the narrower claim, claim 13, the claim at the centre of this appeal, which included integers (vii) and (viii) set out in claim 12 as well as integers (ix) and (x). Lockwood did not identify a separate inventive step by reference to the combination of integers in claim 13, while it sought to reserve its rights in respect of the broader claim, claim 1.[404] At the outset of the appeal there was no suggestion in argument that claim 13 and claims dependent on it could or should be severed from the main claim, claim 1.[405] That may be explained, at least in part, by the statement in the Full Court that the two extra integers of claim 13, integers (ix) and (x), "saved it from lack of novelty, but [they] are both part of common general knowledge."[406] However, in supplementary written and oral submissions Lockwood accepted that when a court is considering whether a claim is obvious, a narrow claim in a specification may be treated differently from a broad claim. Doric did not disagree with that general proposition, as,

---

[403] *Atlantis Corporation Pty Ltd v Schindler* (1997) 39 IPR 29 at 50 per Wilcox and Lindgren JJ. Lockhart J also held that the patent did not satisfy s 40(2)(b): at 36.
[404] *Brugger v Medic-Aid Ltd* [1996] RPC 635 at 656 per Laddie J.
[405] cf *Raleigh Cycle Co Ltd v H Miller & Co Ltd* (1949) 66 RPC 253.
[406] (2005) 226 ALR 70 at 91 [111(e)].

for example, when a narrow claim defines the invention by use of more integers,[407] as can be observed in claim 7.

### The historical development of the requirement for an inventive step

39. It is important to refer to some basic principles that were engaged in this matter. These are principles that have been stated or referred to in earlier decisions, particularly decisions of this Court. We do not intend, however, and are not to be taken as suggesting, any reinterpretation of what was decided in those cases. Nonetheless, the recognition and application of these basic principles is fundamental to a proper understanding of the issues that arose in the litigation between the parties.

40. Lack of novelty as a ground for invalidating a patent had its origins in the United Kingdom through the *Statute of Monopolies*[408] enacted in 1623, which provided for the grant of Letters Patent for the "sole working or making of any manner of new manufactures" to the "true and first inventor". Within this context, novelty embraced not only the issue of anticipation, but also the issue of whether a thing produced required "some exertion of mind that could properly be called invention".[409]

41. Obviousness, or lack of an inventive step, was not clearly recognised as a separate ground of invalidity until late in the 19th century when a contemporary writer stated that the ground of invalidity emerged "as a brake upon the too rapid progress of patents for analogous uses".[410] This development continued early in the 20th century.[411] It became commonplace to note in the cases that, in addition to novelty, it is necessary to ask separately whether an invention is "ingenious",[412] or to recognise as Lockhart J said much more recently in *R D Werner & Co Inc v Bailey Aluminium Products Pty Ltd*[413] ("*R D Werner*"):

"Invention means more than novelty. Novelty alone will not sustain a patent."

42. The historical development of the distinction between novelty and obviousness, identified by Windeyer J in *Sunbeam Corporation v Morphy-Richards (Aust) Pty Ltd*,[414] is explained by Aickin J in *Minnesota Mining and Manufacturing Co v Beiersdorf (Australia) Ltd*[415] ("*Minnesota Mining*"). That explanation is amplified by Lockhart J and Gummow J in *R D Werner*[416] and reiterated in this Court in *Aktiebolaget Hässle v Alphapharm Pty Limited*[417] ("*Alphapharm*").

43. Briefly, the first Australian patent legislation, the *Patents Act 1903* (Cth), imported into Australian law the principles in place in the United Kingdom. "Invention" was defined to mean "any manner of new manufacture the subject of letters patent and

[407] See s 40(2)(b) of the Act.

[408] 21 Jac 1 c 3, s 6.

[409] *Tatham v Dania* (1869) Griffin Pat Cas 213 at 214 per Willes J. See also *Morgan & Co v Windover & Co* (1890) 7 RPC 131 at 134 per Lord Halsbury LC.

[410] Edmunds, *The Law and Practice of Letters Patent for Inventions*, 2nd ed (1897) at 84.

[411] Blanco White, *Patents for Inventions and the Protection of Industrial Designs*, 5th ed (1983) at 55.

[412] Cunynghame, *English Patent Practice*, (1894) at 77; Roberts, *The Grant and Validity of British Patents for Inventions*, (1903) at 37. See also *Britain v Hirsch* (1888) 5 RPC 226 at 232 per Cotton LJ: there must be "sufficient invention to justify a monopoly"; *Cole v Saqui* (1888) 6 RPC 41 at 44 per Lindley LJ: there must be some "ingenuity in that which is new"; and *The Edison Bell Phonograph Corporation Limited v Smith* (1894) 11 RPC 389 at 398 per Lord Esher MR: it must not be "so easy that any fool could do it".

[413] (1989) 25 FCR 565 at 574.

[414] [1961] HCA 39; (1961) 180 CLR 98 at 111-112.

[415] [1980] HCA 9; (1980) 144 CLR 253 at 289-291.

[416] (1989) 25 FCR 565 at 573-575, 594-601 respectively.

[417] [2002] HCA 59; (2002) 212 CLR 411 at 422-423 [19]-[20] per Gleeson CJ, Gaudron, Gummow and Hayne JJ.

grant of privilege within section six of the Statute of Monopolies".[418] Consonant with the cognate United Kingdom legislation, revocation by *scire facias* – essentially a writ to show cause – could be ordered upon a person's petition to the relevant court on the basis of any ground which would have been available at common law.[419]

44. The *Patents and Designs Act 1932* (UK) introduced a consolidated list of grounds for the revocation of a patent.[420] One of the grounds provided that a patent could be revoked if the invention was not new;[421] but a further ground of revocation could be invoked if the invention "is obvious and does not involve any inventive step having regard to what was known or used prior to the date of the patent".[422] That constituted a different formulation of the old ground of "want of subject matter" with the test becoming an overtly qualitatively test rather than a quantitative one.

45. Although the Knowles Committee was established in 1935 to consider changes to Australian patent law in the light of these developments in the United Kingdom, it was not until the recommendation of the Dean Committee in 1952[423] that the *Patents Act 1952* (Cth) ("the 1952 Act") was passed. That legislation implemented similar changes in Australia, including a consolidated list of grounds for revocation. This legislation contained s 100(1)(e), which provided for revocation if a claim "was obvious and did not involve an inventive step, having regard to what was *known or used* in Australia on or before the priority date of that claim" (emphasis added).

46. This was the first legislative recognition in Australia that obviousness, or lack of inventive step, constituted a ground of revocation which was independent of lack of novelty, despite the fact that such a distinction had been made in legislation in the United Kingdom nearly 20 years earlier. The Act which governs the Patent here commenced on 30 April 1991, and introduced ss 7 and 18. Now the current requirements for an inventive step differ from those to be found in s 100(1)(e) of the 1952 Act, as explicated in *Minnesota Mining*.[424] In 1991 the legislature raised the threshold of inventiveness, compared with the 1952 Act, by requiring consideration not only of what was "known or used" but also of additional information which was publicly available. These provisions will be considered in more detail later in these reasons.

47. Although *Alphapharm* was decided in relation to a patent registered under the 1952 Act, what was said in the reasons of the majority in that case about the historical development of the law in relation to obviousness and the requirement for an inventive step is relevant and applicable to the current law of obviousness in Australia.[425] Particular note may be made of the warning in *Alphapharm* against the misuse of hindsight in relation to patents which are a new and inventive combination of known integers.[426]

---

[418] *Patents Act 1903* (Cth), s 4.

[419] *Patents Act 1903* (Cth), s 86(3). See also, for example, the *Patents, Designs, and Trade Marks Act 1883* (UK) 46 & 47 Vict c 57, s 26. Following changes made in the *Patents and Designs Act 1907* (UK), the *Patents Act 1909* (Cth) was passed in Australia.

[420] Section 3 inserted a new s 25(2) into the *Patents and Designs Act 1907* (UK).

[421] Section 25(2)(e).

[422] Section 25(2)(f). This ground was later amended by the *Patents and Designs Act 1949* (UK): s 14(1) inserted a new s 25 into the *Patents and Designs Act 1907* (UK), including s 25(1)(f), such that a patent could be revoked if "the invention ... is obvious and does not involve any inventive step having regard to what was known or used, before the priority date of the claim, in the United Kingdom".

[423] The report of the Knowles Committee was contained in the report of the later Dean Committee: *Report of the Committee Appointed by the Attorney-General of the Commonwealth to Consider what Alterations are Desirable in The Patent Law of the Commonwealth*, 1952.

[424] [1980] HCA 9; (1980) 144 CLR 253 at 287ff per Aickin J.

[425] [2002] HCA 59; (2002) 212 CLR 411 at 427 [33] ff.

[426] [2002] HCA 59; (2002) 212 CLR 411 at 423-424 [21], with reference to *Technograph Printed Circuits Ltd v Mills & Rockley (Electronics) Ltd* [1972] RPC 346 at 362 per Lord Diplock, and

In *Alphapharm*, the majority of this Court drew attention to the divergence between the Australian and the United Kingdom patent systems[427] and of the "shift in grundnorm"[428] concerning inventiveness which has occurred in the United Kingdom, following the Convention on the Grant of European Patents in 1973 and the subsequent enactment of the *Patents Act 1977* (UK).[429]

48. A similar development in relation to obviousness took place in the United States. The patent regime there originated from the English system; however, since the passing of the first patent statute in 1790,[430] a number of divergences have occurred. The most recent codification is the *Patent Act 1952* (US).[431] Although primarily restating the law as it stood up to that point in time, it also introduced the concept of "non-obviousness" as a legislative requirement for patentability in § 103. This took place in circumstances where obviousness had been recognised and applied in courts as early as 1850.[432]

49. The emergence of the independent requirement for an inventive step, first in case law, then in legislative requirements for patentability as occurred in the United Kingdom, the United States and Australia, has always reflected the balance of policy considerations in patent law of encouraging and rewarding inventors without impeding advances and improvements by skilled, non-inventive persons.[433] The terms of ss 7(2), 7(3) and 18(1)(b)(ii) of the Act, and the different but cognate sections in the *Patents Act 1977* (UK), reflect the intention of both legislatures to "rebalance" those policy considerations, by raising the threshold of inventiveness.

50. Previously, only common general knowledge was taken into account when assessing an inventive step. Now, additional information which was publicly available as at the priority date must also be taken into account. Broadly speaking, s 7(3) has as its purpose the specification of the additional publicly available information ("s 7(3)

---

also *Olin Corporation v Super Cartridge Co Pty Ltd* [1977] HCA 23; (1977) 180 CLR 236 at 262 per Stephen and Mason JJ. See also *Minnesota Mining* [1980] HCA 9; (1980) 144 CLR 253 at 293 per Aickin J.

[427] [2002] HCA 59; (2002) 212 CLR 411 at 429 [42] ff.

[428] [2002] HCA 59; (2002) 212 CLR 411 at 432 [49].

[429] Pumfrey J in *Glaxo Group Ltd's Patent* [2004] RPC 43 has responded to those passages in *Alphapharm* thus (at 858 [41]): "Both the Scylla of considering nothing obvious except that to which the skilled man is driven and the Charybdis of considering every invention obvious that can be decomposed into a sequence of obvious steps must be avoided. The former is unfair to industry because it stifles natural development. The latter is unfair to inventors and not countenanced by English patent law".

[430] *Patent Act 1790* (US) 1 Stat 109.

[431] 35 USC.

[432] *Hotchkiss v Greenwood* 52 US 248 at 266 (1850), in which it was determined that while the claimed invention was "new" in that it had not been made using its particular constituent materials before, it was "destitute of ingenuity or invention". See also *Graham v John Deere Co of Kansas City* 383 US 1 at 17-18 (1966), where the Supreme Court addressed four considerations under the rubric of non-obviousness: the extent of the prior art; the degree of difference between the prior art and the claimed invention; the level of skill of the ordinary worker in the industry; and evidence of secondary considerations such as a long felt want in the industry, or commercial success. The continuing authority of *John Deere* was affirmed by the Supreme Court in *KSR International Co v Teleflex Inc* (30 April 2007); the Court also disapproved recent Federal Circuit decisions that a combination claim is obvious only if the prior art, the nature of the problem to be solved or the knowledge of the ordinary skilled worker in the art, reveals "some teaching, suggestion, or motivation" to combine known elements of the prior art. See also *Moy's Walker on Patents*, 4th ed (2006), vol 3, ch 9; Federico, "Commentary on the New Patent Act", (1993) 75 *Journal of the Patent and Trademark Office Society* 161 at 180-183; and Federico, "Origins of Section 103", (1977) 5 *American Patent Law Association Quarterly Journal* 87.

[433] *Société Technique de Pulverisation Step v Emson Europe Ltd* [1993] RPC 513 at 519 per Hoffmann LJ.

information") which must be added to common general knowledge for the purposes of deciding whether an alleged invention is obvious when compared with the prior art base.

### General principles concerning inventive step

51. Although the threshold of inventiveness has been raised as explained by the legislative changes referred to above, case law developed previously continues to be relevant, not least because the legislation employs many familiar terms, such as "common general knowledge". That makes it necessary to briefly refer to general principles of continuing relevance before turning to consider the legislative provisions in more detail.

52. In *Alphapharm*, this Court reiterated that "obvious" means "very plain",[434] as stated by the English Court of Appeal in *General Tire & Rubber Co v Firestone Tyre and Rubber Co Ltd*.[435] The majority in *Alphapharm* also confirmed that the question of whether an invention is obvious is a question of fact, that is, it is what was once a "jury question".[436] Broadly speaking, the question is not a question of what is obvious to a court.[437] As well as being a question of fact, the question of determining whether a patent involves an inventive step is also "one of degree and often it is by no means easy",[438] because ingenuity is relative, depending as it does on relevant states of common general knowledge. This difficulty is further complicated now by the need, in some circumstances, to consider s 7(3) information as well as common general knowledge.

53. Further, as recognised in *Beecham Group Ltd's (Amoxycillin) Application*,[439] as a basic premise, obviousness and inventiveness are antitheses and the question is always "is the step taken over the prior art an 'obvious step' or 'an inventive step'"? An inventive step is often an issue "borne out by the evidence of the experts".[440] There is no distinction between obviousness and a lack of inventive step.[441] A "scintilla of invention"[442] remains sufficient in Australian law to support the validity of a patent.[443] In *R D Werner* Lockhart J stated that there must be "some difficulty overcome, some barrier crossed".[444] This is consonant with older authorities in the United Kingdom which recognised that

---

[434] [2002] HCA 59; (2002) 212 CLR 411 at 427 [34] per Gleeson CJ, Gaudron, Gummow and Hayne JJ, 444 [85] per McHugh J, 463 [144] per Kirby J, 477 [190] per Callinan J.

[435] [1972] RPC 457 at 497.

[436] [2002] HCA 59; (2002) 212 CLR 411 at 443 [79].

[437] *Technograph Printed Circuits Ltd v Mills & Rockley (Electronics) Ltd* [1972] RPC 346 at 355 per Lord Reid.

[438] See *John McIlwraith Industries Ltd v Phillips* [1958] HCA 43; (1958) 98 CLR 529 at 536 per Dixon CJ; *Alphapharm* [2002] HCA 59; (2002) 212 CLR 411 at 427 [33] citing *Société Technique de Pulverisation Step v Emson Europe Ltd* [1993] RPC 513 at 519 per Hoffmann LJ.

[439] [1980] RPC 261 at 290 per Buckley LJ, as referred to in the majority reasons of this Court in *Alphapharm* [2002] HCA 59; (2002) 212 CLR 411 at 423 [20]; cf *Genentech Inc's Patent* [1989] RPC 147 at 274 per Mustill LJ.

[440] *Raleigh Cycle Co Ltd v H Miller & Co Ltd* (1946) 63 RPC 113 at 136 per Lord Greene MR.

[441] *Benmax v Austin Motor Co Ltd* (1953) 70 RPC 284 at 288 per Evershed MR.

[442] *Woolworths Ltd v W B Davis and Son Ltd Inc* (1942) 16 ALJ 57 at 59 per Williams J.

[443] *Alphapharm* [2002] HCA 59; (2002) 212 CLR 411 at 431 [48], referring to *HPM Industries Pty Ltd v Gerard Industries Ltd* [1957] HCA 47; (1957) 98 CLR 424 at 436 per Williams J. See also *Meyers Taylor Pty Ltd v Vicarr Industries Ltd* [1977] HCA 19; (1977) 137 CLR 228 at 249 per Aickin J. It was also noted in *Alphapharm* that the present position in the United Kingdom may require something more than a "scintilla of invention", which was once sufficient. See, for example, *Thomson v The American Braided Wire Company* (1889) 6 RPC 518 at 527-528 per Lord Herschell; for a more recent example, see *Cleveland Graphite Bronze Coy v Glacier Metal Coy Ld* (1950) 67 RPC 149 at 156 per Lord Normand.

[444] (1989) 25 FCR 565 at 574; see also *Allsop Inc v Bintang Ltd* (1989) 15 IPR 686 at 701 per Bowen CJ, Beaumont and Burchett JJ; *Elconnex Pty Ltd v Gerard Industries Pty Ltd* (1992) 25 IPR 173 at 182 per Lockhart J.

some inventiveness was required[445] to distinguish patentable advances over the prior art from advances which "any fool"[446] could devise. It also accords with the requirement in the United States that for an invention to be "non-obvious"[447] it must be "beyond the skill of the calling".[448]

54. The essential question to be posed when considering obviousness under the 1952 Act was outlined by Aickin J in *Wellcome Foundation Ltd v VR Laboratories (Aust) Pty Ltd*[449] ("*Wellcome Foundation*"). Section 101(1) of the 1952 Act set out the grounds upon which a patent might be revoked. Section 101(1)(e) relevantly provided:

"that the invention, so far as claimed in any claim, was obvious and did not involve an inventive step, having regard to what was *known or used* in Australia on or before the priority date of that claim." (emphasis added)

55. In considering whether experiments by an inventor were relevant to the issue of obviousness, in *Wellcome Foundation*, Aickin J[450] stated:

"It is as well to bear in mind that the question of obviousness involves asking the question whether the invention would have been obvious to a non-inventive worker in the field, equipped with the *common general knowledge* in that *particular field* as at the priority date, *without regard to documents in existence but not part of such common general knowledge*." (emphasis added)

56. "Common general knowledge" was well understood as being "part of the mental equipment of those concerned in the art under consideration",[451] and *Minnesota Mining* had confirmed that what was "known or used" in Australia was confined to common general knowledge, which was explained as:[452]

"the background knowledge and experience which is available to all in the trade in considering the making of new products, or the making of improvements in old".

The effect of *Minnesota Mining* and *Wellcome Foundation* was that for the purpose of determining inventiveness prior disclosures which were publicly available information, but which were not part of common general knowledge, were excluded from consideration. In the case of *Minnesota Mining*, a number of prior specifications available for public inspection in Australia before the priority date which were not part of common general knowledge were excluded from consideration.

57. Whether a patent is obvious under the Act is still to be determined by reference to the hypothetical non-inventive worker in the field (now a "person skilled in the relevant art" (ss 7(2) and 7(3)) equipped with common general knowledge, as stated by Aickin J in *Minnesota Mining* and followed since.[453] Therefore it is irrelevant whether the invention was arrived at as a matter of chance or luck or the result of long experiment or great

---

[445] (1989) 25 FCR 565 at 574; see also *Allsop Inc v Bintang Ltd* (1989) 15 IPR 686 at 701 per Bowen CJ, Beaumont and Burchett JJ; *Elconnex Pty Ltd v Gerard Industries Pty Ltd* (1992) 25 IPR 173 at 182 per Lockhart J.

[446] *The Edison Bell Phonograph Corporation Limited v Smith* (1894) 11 RPC 389 at 398 per Lord Esher MR.

[447] *Patents Act 1952* (US), § 103.

[448] *Graham v John Deere Co of Kansas City* 383 US 1 at 15 (1966), as referred to in *Allsop Inc v Bintang Ltd* (1989) 15 IPR 686 at 701 per Bowen CJ, Beaumont and Burchett JJ, and *Leonardis v Sartas No 1 Pty Ltd* (1996) 67 FCR 126 at 146 per Burchett, Hill and Tamberlin JJ.

[449] [1981] HCA 12; (1981) 148 CLR 262.

[450] [1981] HCA 12; (1981) 148 CLR 262 at 270, with whom Gibbs, Stephen, Mason and Wilson JJ agreed.

[451] *Lektophone Corporation v S G Brown Ltd* (1929) 46 RPC 203 at 225.

[452] [1980] HCA 9; (1980) 144 CLR 253 at 292 per Aickin J.

[453] *Alphapharm* [2002] HCA 59; (2002) 212 CLR 411; *Firebelt Pty Ltd v Brambles Australia Ltd* [2002] HCA 21; (2002) 76 ALJR 816; 188 ALR 280; see also, for example, *Elconnex Pty Ltd v Gerard Industries Pty Ltd* (1992) 25 IPR 173; *Allsop Inc v Bintang Ltd* (1989) 15 IPR 686.

intellectual effort.[454] However, reference to and use of prior disclosures, in existence but not part of the common general knowledge, has now been extended. This has the result that the limitation in Aickin J's statement of principle, emphasised above, no longer applies, a topic about which more will be said later. The objective approach to determining obviousness is equally applicable to a combination patent.[455]

58. As to the position in the United Kingdom, in *Technograph Printed Circuits Ltd v Mills & Rockley (Electronics) Ltd*,[456] Lord Reid construed the phrase "having regard to what was *known or used*, before the priority date"[457] as meaning "what was or ought to have been known to a diligent searcher".[458] Lord Diplock went further than that and accepted that the words meant everything in the public domain, which in that case included patent specifications in the United Kingdom, as well as foreign ones which were available in the Patent Office.[459]

59. Lord Reid's construction was preferred and approved in *General Tire & Rubber Co v Firestone Tyre and Rubber Co Ltd*,[460] but s 2(2) of the *Patents Act 1977* (UK) now provides that the "state of the art" for the purposes of determining obviousness includes everything in the public domain:

> "all matter (whether a product, a process, information about either, or anything else) which has at any time before the priority date of the invention been made available to the public (whether in the United Kingdom or elsewhere) by written or oral description, by use or in any other way."

### Patentability of ideas

60. For the purposes of considering this Patent and its treatment in the Courts below, it is instructive to start with an old but frequently repeated description of the processes of invention by Fletcher Moulton:[461]

> "An invention may, and usually does, involve three processes. Firstly, the definition of the problem to be solved or the difficulties to be overcome; secondly, the choice of the general principle to be applied in solving this problem or overcoming these difficulties; and thirdly, the choice of the particular means used. Merit in any one of these stages, or in the whole combined, may support the invention".[462]

Distinctions between the *idea* or concept or principle informing an invention and the *means* of carrying it out or embodying it in a manner of new manufacture have long been made despite certain expressions of caution from time to time.[463] In *Hickton's Patent*

---

[454] *Advanced Building Systems Pty Ltd v Ramset Fasteners (Aust) Pty Ltd* [1998] HCA 19; (1998) 194 CLR 171 at 187 [25] per Brennan CJ, Gaudron, McHugh and Gummow JJ; *Wellcome Foundation* [1981] HCA 12; (1981) 148 CLR 262 at 279 per Aickin J, citing *Dow Corning Corporation's Application* [1969] RPC 544 at 560 per Graham J; see also *Flexible Steel Lacing Company v Beltreco Ltd* (2000) 49 IPR 331 at 367 [166] per Hely J; and *Crane v Price* (1842) 4 Man & G 580 at 605 [134 ER 239 at 249] per Tindal CJ delivering the judgment of the Court.

[455] *Alphapharm* [2002] HCA 59; (2002) 212 CLR 411 at 429 [41]; *Minnesota Mining* [1980] HCA 9; (1980) 144 CLR 253 at 293 per Aickin J.

[456] [1972] RPC 346.

[457] Section 32(1)(f) of the *Patents Act 1949* (UK) (emphasis added), which was cognate with s 100(1)(e) of the 1952 Act.

[458] [1972] RPC 346 at 355.

[459] [1972] RPC 346 at 361

[460] [1972] RPC 457 at 497.

[461] Fletcher Moulton, *The Present Law and Practice Relating to Letters Patent for Inventions*, (1913) at 24 (footnotes omitted).

[462] See also Australian Patent Office, *Patent Office Notes on the History of the British and Commonwealth Patent Acts and the Law Relating to Letters Patent of Inventions in Australia*, 5th ed (1974) at 23-24.

[463] See, for example, Blanco White, *Patents for Inventions and the Protection of Industrial Designs*, 5th ed (1983) at 95-96.

*Syndicate v Patents and Machine Improvements Company Ltd,*[464] Fletcher Moulton LJ stated that "invention may lie in the idea, and it may lie in the way in which it is carried out, and it may lie in the combination of the two".[465]

61. In a sense, an idea *simpliciter* cannot be patented, as no patent will be granted except to a manner of manufacture within s 6 of the *Statute of Monopolies*. An idea which is part, even the main part, of an inventive step "has got to end in a new method of manufacture".[466] When an idea is incorporated into a means for carrying out an idea, the idea itself can be taken into account when considering validity, and inventiveness may repose largely in the idea. As a matter of language, it is almost inevitable that the subject matter of an invention which involves an improvement to a known combination will be spoken of as "an idea" or "a concept", as occurred here, and invention may lie in "the idea of taking the step in question".[467] To the extent that such language is used, an inventive step can be "having an insight which, although simple, genuinely requires an act of insight rather than a mere development and application of existing ideas".[468]

62. In dealing with a question of obviousness under the *Patents Act 1949* (UK) in *Windsurfing International Inc v Tabur Marine (Great Britain) Ltd*[469] Oliver LJ isolated the "inventive concept" when he set out a four-step process to be taken when approaching the question of obviousness:[470]

> "The first [step] is to identify the *inventive concept* embodied in the patent in suit. Thereafter, the court has to assume the mantle of the normally skilled but unimaginative addressee in the art at the priority date and to impute to him what was, at that date, common general knowledge in the art in question. The third step is to identify what, if any, differences exist between the matter cited as being 'known or used' and the alleged invention. Finally, the court has to ask itself whether, viewed without any knowledge of the alleged invention, those differences constitute steps which would have been obvious to the skilled man or whether they require any degree of invention." (emphasis added)

63. The "inventive concept" is important for what has come to be regarded in the United Kingdom as a "structured"[471] approach to determining obviousness under the current statutory definition.[472] In *Biogen Inc v Medeva plc*[473] Lord Hoffmann said:

> "A proper statement of the *inventive concept* needs to include some express or implied reference to the problem which it required invention to overcome." (emphasis added)

---

[464] (1909) 26 RPC 339.

[465] (1909) 26 RPC 339 at 348.

[466] *In re IG Farbenindustrie AG's Patents* (1930) 47 RPC 289 at 309 per Maugham J (in argument).

[467] *Olin Mathieson Chemical Corporation v Biorex Laboratories Ltd* [1970] RPC 157 at 192 per Graham J; see generally *Terrell on the Law of Patents*, 16th ed (2006) at 276-277.

[468] *Molnlycke AB v Procter & Gamble Ltd (No 5)* [1994] RPC 49 at 132 per Nicholls VC, delivering the judgment of the Court.

[469] [1985] RPC 59.

[470] [1985] RPC 59 at 73-74.

[471] *Molnlycke AB v Procter & Gamble Ltd (No 5)* [1994] RPC 49 at 115 per Nicholls VC, delivering the judgment of the Court.

[472] By s 1(1)(b) of the *Patent Act 1977* (UK), a patent may only be granted for an invention if it involves an "inventive step", and s 3 provides: "An invention shall be taken to involve an inventive step if it is not obvious to a person skilled in the art, having regard to any matter which forms part of the state of the art by virtue only of section 2(2) above (and disregarding section 2(3) above)". Section 130(7) provides that various provisions including ss 2 and 3 are framed so as to have the same effects as corresponding provisions of the European Patent Convention, the Community Patent Convention and the Patent Co-operation Treaty.

[473] [1997] RPC 1 at 45.

64. As noted in *Alphapharm*,[474] that statement may reflect the "problem and solution" approach apparently mandated by the European Patent Convention. That "problem and solution" approach has the inevitable effect that an idea which constitutes an addition to the existing stock of knowledge needs to be specifically characterised as an idea of doing a new thing, or an idea of the way of achieving a previously known goal, or the idea of a particular solution in relation to achieving a certain goal.[475]

65. Although the recognition of the need to identify an "inventive idea" justifying a monopoly is not new in Australia,[476] the developments in the United Kingdom, which emphasise the need to identify the "inventive concept" in terms of "problem and solution", have raised the threshold of inventiveness. This has been exemplified by a number of relevant English cases since 1977.[477]

66. Such developments were considered and distinguished in *Alphapharm*.[478] This Court rejected confining the question of obviousness to a "problem and solution" approach, particularly with a combination patent. This should not be misconstrued. The "problem and solution" approach[479] may overcome the difficulties of an *ex post facto* analysis of an invention, which may be unhelpful in resolving the question of obviousness.[480] However, it is worth repeating that the "problem and solution" approach may be particularly unfair to an inventor of a combination, or to an inventor of a simple solution,[481] especially as a small amount of ingenuity can sustain a patent in Australia. Ingenuity may lie in an idea for overcoming a practical difficulty in circumstances where a difficulty with a product consisting of a known set of integers is common general knowledge.[482] This is a narrow but critical point if, as here, the circumstances are that no skilled person in the art called to give evidence had thought of a general idea or general method of solving a known difficulty with respect to a known product, as at the priority date.

67. When considering the patentability of ideas it is necessary to remember that a "manner of manufacture" requires "something of a corporeal and substantial nature".[483] The expansion of "a manner of new manufacture" through case law which has been "characteristic of the growth of patent law"[484] came to rest with the acknowledgment in *National Research Development Corporation v Commissioner of Patents* ("the *NRDC* case")[485] that any attempt to fetter the exact meaning of "a manner of new manufacture" could never be sound.[486] ...

### Construction of ss 7(2) and 7(3)

150. The proper construction of ss 7(2) and 7(3) has been considered in *Firebelt Pty Ltd v Brambles Australia Ltd*[487] ("*Firebelt*"). In recognising that s 7(3) relaxes the previous

---

[474] [2002] HCA 59; (2002) 212 CLR 411 at 429 [40].

[475] *Biogen Inc v Medeva plc* [1997] RPC 1 at 34 per Lord Hoffmann.

[476] *Commissioner of Patents v Microcell Ltd* [1958] HCA 58; (1959) 102 CLR 232 at 249 per Dixon CJ, McTiernan, Fullagar, Taylor and Windeyer JJ.

[477] See for example, *Haberman v Jackel International Ltd* [1999] FSR 683 at 706 [45] per Laddie J; *Glaxo Group Ltd's Patent* [2004] RPC 43.

[478] [2002] HCA 59; (2002) 212 CLR 411 at 428-429 [38]-[40].

[479] *HPM Industries Pty Ltd v Gerard Industries Ltd* [1957] HCA 47; (1957) 98 CLR 424 at 437 per Williams J.

[480] *Meyers Taylor Pty Ltd v Vicarr Industries Ltd* [1977] HCA 19; (1977) 137 CLR 228.

[481] *Haberman v Jackel International Ltd* [1999] FSR 683 at 698 [29] per Laddie J.

[482] *Molnlycke AB v Procter & Gamble Ltd (No 5)* [1994] RPC 49.

[483] *R v Wheeler* (1819) 2 B & Ald 345 at 350 [106 ER 392 at 395] per Abbott CJ.

[484] *Maeder v Busch* [1938] HCA 8; (1938) 59 CLR 684 at 706 per Dixon J.

[485] [1959] HCA 67; (1959) 102 CLR 252.

[486] [1959] HCA 67; (1959) 102 CLR 252 at 271 per Dixon CJ, Kitto and Windeyer JJ.

[487] [2002] HCA 21; (2002) 76 ALJR 816 at 821-823 [31]-[36]; [2002] HCA 21; 188 ALR 280 at 287-289.

rule under the 1952 Act which forbade the use of prior disclosures not proved to be part of the common general knowledge at the priority date, this Court approved a statement by Burchett J in the Federal Court where he noted that s 7(3) in its pre-2001 version is limited:[488]

> "by the words 'being information that the skilled person ... could, before the priority date of the relevant claim, be reasonably expected to have ascertained, understood and regarded as relevant to work in the relevant art in the patent area'. And if a prior [disclosure] passes those tests, it must still be able to be said that, if that [disclosure] had been considered by the hypothetical skilled person together with the common general knowledge at the relevant time, 'the invention would have been obvious'."

151. That passage, noting the words of limitation in s 7(3), reflects the two statutory tests which have already been mentioned: the s 7(2) test of whether an invention is obvious when compared with the prior art base, and the s 7(3) test of whether information is to be included in the prior art base, each test to be determined objectively by the standard of "a person skilled in the relevant art".

152. Given the history, context, purpose and specific words of limitation in s 7(3), all of which were addressed by this Court in *Firebelt*,[489] the phrase "relevant to work in the relevant art" should not be construed as meaning relevant to any work in the relevant art, including work irrelevant to the particular problem or long-felt want or need, in respect of which the invention constitutes an advance in the art. The phrase can only be construed as being directed to prior disclosures, that is publicly available information (not part of common general knowledge) which a person skilled in the relevant art could be expected to have regarded as relevant to solving a particular problem or meeting a long-felt want or need as the patentee claims to have done. Otherwise the words of limitation in the last 40 words of s 7(3) would have no role to play. Any piece of public information in the relevant art would be included, as is the case with the much broader and quite different formulation in the cognate provisions in the United Kingdom,[490] which do not depend on the standard of a skilled person's opinion of the relevance of the information.

153. The question of what a person skilled in the relevant art would regard as relevant, when faced with the same problem as the patentee, is to be determined on the evidence. The starting point is the subject matter of the invention to be considered together with evidence in respect of prior art, common general knowledge, the way in which the invention is an advance in the art, and any related matters. It should be mentioned that the starting point is not necessarily the inventive step as claimed, or even agreed between parties, because the evidence, particularly in respect of a combination of integers, may support a different inventive step.

154. There was no real disagreement that, however one characterised the problem to be solved, it was a problem with a known product, the Lockwood 001, which was a rim mounted lock. There was no disagreement that each of integers (i)-(v) (in claim 1) and (ix) and (x) (in claim 13) was part of common general knowledge because each was a feature of the Lockwood 001. There was no challenge by Doric to the primary judge's finding that storeroom locks containing integer (vi) were not part of common general knowledge.

155. Irrespective of the breadth of claim 1, the person skilled in the relevant art would be seeking to resolve a problem known to exist with a rim mounted lock. The only locks identified as falling within claim 13 and dependent claims were rim mounted locks. Claim 13 did not cover any lock which was not a rim mounted lock with detent means which moved axially.

---

[488] *Tidy Tea Ltd v Unilever Australia Ltd* (1995) 32 IPR 405 at 414.
[489] [2002] HCA 21; (2002) 76 ALJR 816 at 823 [36]; [2002] HCA 21; 188 ALR 280 at 289.
[490] *Patents Act 1977* (UK), s 2(2) set out above at [58].

156. The Full Court recognised that Mr Freestone's evidence was directed to the internal workings of various locks which "may well be apposite to the design of a new rim mounted lock, such as an improvement of the old 001".[491] The extra integers of claim 13 (integers (ix) and (x)) deal with the internal workings of the combination claimed, insofar as claim 13 has a cam and a detent means which moves substantially radially of the cam axis.

157. There was no evidence from any witness that he would have regarded storeroom locks as relevant to the combination of integers in claim 13, and it was uncontested that the storeroom locks did not have the locking means of claim 13, such locking means being referable to rim mounted locks.

158. Relevantly, the combination of integers in claim 13 included detent means which moved radially of the axis of the cam, such detent means being absent from the storeroom locks which contained detent means which moved axially.

159. Further, there was evidence that detent means which moved radially of the axis of a cam were a feature relevant to ensuring outside security after having entered and shut a door. Any solution to the "locked in" problem with the Lockwood 001 needed to preserve that outside security without an occupant of the premises becoming locked in. The storeroom locks which employed detent means which moved axially did not give outside security unless a deliberate step was taken to lock oneself in. The storeroom locks were not perceived as being subject to any problem as they were not necessarily required to give outside security against entry.

160. Comparison of the combination of features in the storeroom locks and the combination in claim 13, tends to show that storeroom locks taught away from the invention as claimed in claim 13. That comparison does not immediately lead to any conclusion that the storeroom locks were relevant to the advance in the art represented by the invention in claim 13, or to a conclusion that the invention in claim 13 was somehow obvious on its face.

161. The comparison assists in understanding the evidence of witnesses in relation to their perception of the problem with the Lockwood 001 and possible solutions. Mr Garland, a person of inventive faculty, said that if he had been asked to solve the problem he would have considered locks which were rim mounted and those which were not. However, he did not mention storeroom locks, with which he was familiar, as relevant locks to which he would have had regard in solving the problem. He referred only to the DS60 lock (which was not rim mounted and which had a spring biased to the unlatched position and detent means which moved radially to the longitudinal axis) as relevant to solving the problem. Mr Alchin did not mention any storeroom locks, with which he was familiar, as relevant locks to which he actually had regard. He gave evidence that he was inspired by the DS60 lock. However, the primary judge found he was inspired by the new Lockwood 001. Finally, such documentary evidence as there was in relation to the inventor, Mr Blanch, did not contain any reference to storeroom locks.

162. As determined by Hely J, the relevant art was the "manufacture and design of locks".[492] This was a form of shorthand to describe the field relevant to the invention in claim 13, as Lockwood did, as that of rim mounted locks. This is explained, at least in part, by the fact that detent means which operated radially of the axis of the cam were a characteristic of rim mounted locks. The evidence from all persons skilled in the relevant art showed that the prior art base with which the invention in claim 13 needed to be compared depended on the particular combination of integers in claim 13, including integers (ix) and (x).

---

[491] (2005) 226 ALR 70 at 108 [168].
[492] (2001) 192 ALR 306 at 335 [165].

163. The Lockwood 001 was rim mounted and employed a detent means which moved radially of the axis of the cam; and whilst it ensured outside security against entry, it had the disadvantage of potentially causing a person to be "locked in". It was that combination, and not the integers considered singly, which appears to have affected the skilled persons' perceptions of what was relevant, in the prior art before the priority date, to solving the problem.

164. The skilled persons who gave evidence treated "work in the relevant art" as "work" relevant to resolving the "locked in" problem with the Lockwood 001. None of them contemporaneously regarded the information conveyed by the storeroom locks as relevant to that work and none of them possessed the solution in claim 13, despite their familiarity with one or other of the storeroom locks. Mr Garland understood the workings of the storeroom locks and was well aware of the potential seriousness of the "locked in" problem with the Lockwood 001. He was briefed, as an inventive person, to design a rim mounted dead latch to compete with the Lockwood 001. If he had thought of the solution to the "locked in" problem before the priority date he would have passed it on to Doric. He conceded that solutions he now sees in the field have been seen as he was "looking back on [the particular problem]".

165. The evidence of what actually happened before the priority date in terms of what was considered by skilled persons (one of whom was inventive) to be relevant to the problem cannot be displaced by constructing a prior art base for claim 13 by reference to the broader claim 1, or by preconceived ideas of the inventive step involved. The facts here lead to the conclusion that the information conveyed by acts of sales of the storeroom locks, assessed by reference to the statutory test in s 7(3), does not qualify as s 7(3) information for inclusion in the prior art base for claim 13.

166. It is not, strictly speaking, necessary to go further. But let it be assumed that the information qualified for inclusion in the prior art base for claim 13, pursuant to s 7(3). On that assumption, the question which s 7(2) requires to be asked is: "If that information had been considered by a person skilled in the relevant art together with common general knowledge would the invention in claim 13 have been obvious?" The evidence permits only one answer to that question: No.

167. The correct application of s 7(2) in the light of these reasons leads to the conclusion that the combination of integers contained in the invention which is the subject matter of claim 13 involves an inventive step over the prior art base.

**Conclusions**

168. The conclusions arrived at may be summarised as follows. The Full Court erred in finding that there was an "implicit 'corollary' admission" in the Patent specification which led to the result that the solution to the problem with the Lockwood 001 was part of common general knowledge. The Full Court correctly construed the references to "ascertained" and "understood" in s 7(3) of the Act. The Full Court correctly treated the art relevant to the Patent as the manufacture and design of locks. The Full Court was never invited to distinguish between what was "relevant" in respect of claim 1 and what was "relevant" in respect of claim 13 and it did not do so. The Full Court's finding that the sales of the storeroom locks could reasonably be regarded as s 7(3) information leading to the result that the alleged invention in claim 1 would have been considered obvious can hardly be criticised when it is recognised that storeroom locks fall within claim 1, and that the subject matter of claim 1 includes locks which were not rim mounted and rim mounted locks, as well as locks with detent means which moved axially, and locks with detent means which moved radially. However, the inferential conclusion of the Full Court, that claim 13 was obvious because claim 1 was obvious, was erroneous, as has been explained in these reasons.

169. Although it is not necessary to this appeal to make any determination in respect of claim 1, a comparison of information disclosed by the sale of storeroom locks with the combination of integers in claim 1 might lead a court to conclude that there was plainly no inventive step involved in that claim when compared with the prior art base enlarged by the information conveyed by sales of the storeroom locks.

# Chapter 10

# Patents – Rights, Infringement and Dealing

## The Exclusive Rights of the Patentee

The exclusive rights given by a patent to its patentee (or owner) are granted by the *Patents Act 1990* s 13. The patentee is given the exclusive rights to "exploit" the invention protected by the patent and to authorise another person to exploit the invention.[1] The patent has effect throughout the patent area,[2] that is Australia.

"Exploit" is defined in Sch 1 to the Act which provides that:

> *exploit*, in relation to an invention, includes:
>     (a) where the invention is a product – make, hire, sell or otherwise dispose of the product, offer to make, sell, hire or otherwise dispose of it, use or import it, or keep it for the purpose of doing any of those things; or
>     (b) where the invention is a method or process – use the method or process or do any act mentioned in paragraph (a) in respect of a product resulting from such use.

The words bear some resemblance to the language under the 1952 Act which conferred upon the patentee the exclusive rights to "make, use, exercise and vend"[3] and, in *Pinefair Pty Ltd v Bedford Industries Rehabilitation Association Inc,*[4] it was held that the meaning of the words "make" and "use" would follow the meaning ascribed those words in the 1952 legislation. Accordingly, case law under the 1952 Act continues to be relevant in determining the extent of the patentee's rights. Case law on the meaning of these terms is considered below in the context of infringement proceedings.

These rights are very broad and cut across the rights of a chattel owner in a manner quite different from that which we have seen in relation to copyright. Taken strictly, the exclusive rights of the patentee are so broad that the purchaser of a patented device, say a lettuce crisper or a particular type of lock, could not

---

1    Section 13(1).
2    Section 13(3). See also the definition of "patent area" in the Dictionary found in Sch 1 to the Act.
3    *Patents Act 1952* s 69.
4    (1998) 87 FCR 458.

sell that device in a garage sale or even use it without the express authority of the patentee. However, because use of the product and the right to sell a chattel are assumed to be two of the usual aspects of ownership the courts have readily implied a licence to use and sell patented products or processes lawfully sold to the purchaser (as well as products of a patented process). The implied licence may be displaced by express provisions and notice. In *National Phonograph Co of Australia Ltd v Menck*,[5] for example, a dealer whose contract was at an end was found to have infringed a patent because he had been given notice by the terms of the past contract that the goods could not be sold or dealt with in the infringing manner.

The courts have also held that there is an implied licence to repair a patented product or product of a patented process. As Lord Halsbury said in *Sirdar Rubber Co Ltd v Wallington Weston and Co*[6] a person has an implied licence to "prolong the life of a licensed article" by repairing it but the person "must not make a new one under the cover of repair". He noted that this principle was difficult to apply in practice. In *Solar Thomson Engineering Co Ltd v Barton*[7] it was accepted that this implied licence extended to a person contracted by the purchaser or licensee to repair the product and that merely keeping one part of a licensed article did not necessarily mean that the product had been repaired rather than a product made. However, in that case the judge held that the replacement of rubber rings on a pulley was a repair having regard to the commercial viability of this practice, the industry practice and the way in which the pulleys had been sold.

This generous approach by the courts to implied terms in patent licences may be compared to the much more restrictive approach adopted in relation to copyright as discussed in *Interstate Parcel Express Co Pty Ltd v Time-Life International (Nederlands) BV*.[8]

It has been assumed by some writers that the use of the term "exploitation" restricts the rights to commercial uses and dealings. This question does not seem to have been directly addressed by the courts but, as we shall see in our consideration of designs law, courts have readily assumed that non-commercial exercise of the rights of the registered owner of a design would constitute an infringement. We would suggest that the use of the term "use" within the definition of exploitation clearly indicates that a similarly wide approach should be taken in regard to patent law.

However, the implications of such an approach bring us back to the question of traditional knowledge. Consider a patented pharmaceutical product that has its origins in a plant used by healers in an Indigenous community.[9] The active chemical compound found in the plant is patented worldwide. Does the Indigenous community observed by the bioprospector have a claim over the patent that the bioprospector obtained? Is the Indigenous community infringing the patent by using the plant to heal the sick as they have done for centuries? If the Indigenous community had participated in the development of the drug and obtained some

---

5     [1911] AC 336.

6     (1907) 24 RPC 539 at 543.

7     [1977] RPC 537 at 554.

8     (1977) 138 CLR 534. See Chapter 4, "Exclusive Rights of the Copyright Owner, Actions and Offences".

9     For example, the active ingredients of tipir used by the Wapishana in the Amazon basin to stop bleeding and prevent infections.

level of ownership or rights over the patent there may not be an issue of infringement. But what if their only contribution was to point out to the bioprospector the plant used for healing and the bioprospector did the rest of the scientific analysis and development? Can the community be prevented from continuing their ancient practice? We address this issue later in this chapter.

## Infringement of Patent Rights

There are three forms of patent infringement. Although the *Patents Act 1990* provides no definition of direct infringement it can be inferred from s 13 that there will be a direct infringement of the exclusive rights of the patentee if a person exploits the patent without the authorisation of the patentee or authorises another person to do this. It is also an infringement under s 117 to supply a product to another person where use of that product would constitute an infringement of the patent. This is referred to as infringement by supply or "contributory infringement".

### Relevant test

Patent infringement is not established by comparing two products side by side but by comparing the allegedly infringing product with the invention as claimed in the specifications. Using our example above, if we consider a newly discovered active chemical compound claimed in the specifications of a patent for an ensuing pharmaceutical, that chemical compound in its natural state or extracted from natural sources is unlikely to be an infringement of the claim.[10] This is usually due to such claims being limited to the pure form of the chemical compound often defined by physical and other characteristics.[11] Accordingly, use of the natural form of the chemical compound by the traditional knowledge holders in an Indigenous community is unlikely to constitute an infringement.

Thus, in determining whether infringement has occurred the first step is to analyse the specifications and this requires a decision as to how those specifications will be interpreted. Traditionally, the courts employed a literal interpretation of the specification resulting in a rather narrow construction of the claimed invention. Applying this test of construction, small differences between the specifications and the allegedly infringing product would be adequate to stave off a finding of infringement. Even a mere mechanical equivalent of the patented product could survive the accusation of infringement. While creating a boon for increased competition the literal interpretation process confounded the whole point of the patent monopoly.

This situation was somewhat rectified by the "pith and marrow" approach provided by the House of Lords in *Clark v Adie*,[12] an infringement case concerning an "improved horse clipper". Under the pith and marrow approach the "essential integers" of the invention are identified by reference to the specifications. An

---

10    Philip W Grubb, *Patents for Chemicals, Pharmaceuticals and Biotechnology, Fundamentals of Global Law, Practice and Strategy*, Clarendon Press, Oxford 1999, p 214.

11    Ibid, p 213.

12    (1875) 10 Ch App 667.

infringement was said to have occurred if each and every one of these essential integers was adopted by the allegedly infringing product. Conversely, there would be no infringement unless all of the essential integers were taken. This meant that where an allegedly infringing article or process could be shown to have adopted each and every essential integer of the patented invention there would be an infringement even though mere mechanical equivalents were used to replace the inessential integers of the invention.

The judgment of James LJ provides the classic statement of the "pith and marrow" test in *Clark v Adie*:

> The patent is in the entire combination, but there is, or may be, an essence or substance of the invention underlying the mere accident of form; and that invention, like every other invention, may be pirated by a theft in a disguised or mutilated form, and it would be in every case a question of fact whether the alleged piracy is the same in substance and effect or is a substantially new or different combination.[13]

The House of Lords also considered the question of a combination patent where a further minor invention forms a subordinate part or integer of the whole. In those circumstances it would be necessary for the patentee to draft the claims of the specification so as to make it clear that protection is sought, not only for the invention as a whole, but for those subordinate integers as well. The court would then have to take those specifically claimed integers into account when assessing the alleged infringement.[14]

The English courts eventually built on the "pith and marrow" approach and developed what is now referred to as the purposive approach, first espoused in *Catnic Components Ltd v Hill & Smith Ltd*.[15] The invention concerned galvanised steel lintels, a support structure used in spanning the spaces above window and door openings in cavity walls usually built of bricks. The lintels involved a trapezoid box-girder structure for its strength and rigidity comprising two horizontal plates joined by a plate "extending vertically". The infringing lintel's "vertical" plate was six degrees off the perpendicular and so the question was whether such a lintel infringed the claimed invention. In other words, was a plate extending vertically only referring to the perpendicular (or 90 degrees to the horizontal) or could it extend to minor variants.

Lord Diplock pointed out that in order to come to the "pith and marrow" of an invention, one must adopt a purposive construction of the specification:

> [A] patent specification is a unilateral statement … by which (the patentee) informs (the skilled addressee) what he claims to be the essential features of the new product or process for which the letters patent grant him a monopoly. It is those novel features only that he claims to be essential that constitute the so-called "pith and marrow" of the claim. A patent specification should be given a purposive construction rather than a purely literal one derived from applying to it the kind of meticulous verbal analysis in which lawyers are too often tempted by their training to indulge.[16]

---

13  (1875) 10 Ch App 667 at 675.
14  (1875) 10 Ch App 667.
15  [1981] FSR 60.
16  [1981] FSR 60 at 67. It is interesting to note that the approach in Catnic is being utilised in patent infringement cases throughout Europe but allegedly without uniformity of result. See M Franzosi, *Three European Cases on Equivalence – Will Europe Adopt Catnic?* IIC Vol 32 2/2001, 113.

In concluding there to be an infringement, Lord Diplock pointed out that:

> [T]he expression 'extending vertically' ... is perfectly capable of meaning positioned near enough to the exact geometrical vertical to enable it in actual use to perform satisfactorily all the functions that it could perform if it were precisely vertical.[17]

His Lordship came to this conclusion using a builder familiar with ordinary building operations as the skilled addressee and noting that the variation of 6 degrees had no material effect on the way in which the invention operated.

The "pith and marrow" approach, together with the purposive construction of the specification, was acknowledged and applied in Australia by the Full Federal Court in *Populin v HB Nominees Pty Ltd*.[18] In that case, the court dealt with an appeal regarding the alleged infringement of a combination patent for a sugar cane planting machine. In relation to construction of the claims, the court said:

> It has often been said that the claims operate as a disclaimer of what is not specifically claimed ... They therefore determine the extent of the patentee's monopoly. The patentee must be vigilant to claim only the essence of the invention. This is particularly so in relation to a combination patent. It is important to claim only the essential integers in the combination or to distinguish what is essential from what is inessential. For to establish infringement of a combination patent, the patentee must show that the defendant has taken each and every one of the essential integers of the patentee's claim. Therefore if, on its true construction, the claim in a patent claims a particular combination of integers and the alleged infringer of it omits one of them he will escape liability.[19]

However, omitting an inessential part and replacing it with an equivalent does not provide an alleged infringer with an escape from liability. This acknowledges the doctrine in *Clark v Adie*. The court endorsed Gibbs J's statement in *Olin Corporation v Super Cartridge Co Pty Limited*[20] that the principle was accepted but that its limitations must be recognised:

> [T]he principle that there may be infringement by taking the "pith and marrow" or the substance of an invention does not mean that there will be an infringement where the patentee has by the form of his claim left open that which the alleged infringer has done. And it does not affect the fundamental rule that there will be no infringement unless the alleged infringer has taken all of the essential features or integers of the patentee's claim.[21]

The Full Federal Court in *Populin* applied the purposive construction espoused in *Catnic* and noted that:

> [T]he complete specification must not be read in the abstract but in the light of common knowledge in the art before the priority date bearing in mind that what is being construed is a public instrument which must, if it is to be valid, define a monopoly in such a way that it is not reasonably capable of being misunderstood ... The essential features of the product or process for which it claims a monopoly are to be determined not as a matter of abstract uninformed construction but by a common sense assessment of what the words used convey in the context of then-existing published knowledge.[22]

---

17   [1981] FSR 60 at 67.
18   (1982) 41 ALR 471.
19   (1982) 41 ALR 471 at 475.
20   (1977) 14 ALR 149.
21   (1977) 14 ALR 149 at 157.
22   (1982) 41 ALR 471 at 476.

The result was that no infringement was found because the defendant's machine omitted what the Full Court considered an essential integer in the combination. Compare this result with *Nesbit Evans Group Australia Pty Ltd v Impro Ltd*,[23] where the Full Federal Court once again applied the purposive construction in both the majority and dissenting decisions. In that case, what the dissenting judgment considered an essential integer, which would have led to the defendant's escape from liability for infringement as it was omitted, was not considered an essential integer by the majority judgment. The result, of course, was infringement and emphasises once again the importance of the construction of the claims of the patent in the process of determining infringement. A Federal Court case that neatly reviews this process of determining infringement is *Root Quality Pty Ltd v Root Control Technologies Pty Ltd*.[24] In that case Finkelstein J (sitting alone) considered the issue of construction in some detail and referred to *Improver Corporation v Remington Consumer Products Ltd*:[25]

> In this connection reference should be made to *Improver Corporation v Remington Consumer Products Ltd* [1990] FSR 181, where Hoffmann J (as his Lordship then was) said that when the issue is whether a feature embodied in an alleged infringement, which falls outside the primary or literal meaning of a claim (a feature which he called the "variant"), was nevertheless within its language as properly interpreted, the court should ask "Lord Diplock's three questions": (1) Does the variant have a material effect upon the way the invention works? If yes, the variant is outside the claim. If no: – (2) Would this (that is, that the variant had no material effect) have been obvious at the date of publication of the patent to a reader skilled in the art? If no, the variant is outside the claim. If yes: – (3) Would the reader skilled in the art nevertheless have understood from the language of the claim that the patentee intended that strict compliance with the primary meaning was an essential requirement of the invention? If yes, the variant is outside the claim.
>
> It must always be borne in mind that an element of a claim that appears not to be necessary for the invention may nevertheless be regarded by the patentee as essential for some reason that is not apparent: *Société Technique de Pulverisation Step v Emson Europe Ltd* [1993] RPC 513 at 522. Accordingly, the court should act with some care before it broadens a claim in reliance upon a purposive construction of the words used in the specification.[26]

Applying the *Improver* questions, Finkelstein J found that the patent had been infringed.

Lord Hoffman revisited the *Catnic* case and the *Improver* decision in *Kiren-Amgen Inc v Hoechst Marion Roussel Limited*.[27] That case was concerned with the production of human erythropoetin (EPO) in cell culture, one process and product of which was patented by Kiren-Amgen Inc. Infringement proceedings were brought against the defendants in relation to their EPO product, with the result being the revocation of certain claims (which will be discussed in Chapter 11) and the conclusion that there was no infringement. Lord Hoffman took the opportunity to clarify how the *Improver* questions he devised, dubbed "the Protocol

---

23    (1997) 39 IPR 56.
24    (2000) 177 ALR 231.
25    [1990] FSR 181.
26    (2000) 177 ALR 231.
27    [2004] UKHL 46.

questions" by the Court of Appeal in *Wheatly v Drillsafe Ltd*,[28] worked with the principle of purposive construction espoused in *Catnic*:

> When speaking of the 'Catnic principle' it is important to distinguish between, on the one hand, the principle of purposive construction which I have said gives effect to the requirements of the Protocol, and on the other hand, the guidelines for applying that principle to equivalents, which are encapsulated in the Protocol questions. The former is the bedrock of patent construction, universally applicable. The latter are only guidelines, more useful in some cases than in others.[29]

On the meaning of "purposive construction", Lord Hoffman pointed out that one does not extend or go "beyond the definition of the technical matter for which the patentee seeks protection in the claims", rather one needs to consider the language of the claim and how the person skilled in the art would have understood it.[30] His Lordship notes that the construction is objective and requires the interpretation of the language to be in accordance with a reasonable person's understanding of the words used.[31]

The Full Federal Court has reviewed the principles of construction in a number of recent infringement actions.[32] In *Fresenius Medical Care Australia Pty Ltd v Gambro Pty Limited*,[33] the patent allegedly infringed concerned a system for the preparation of fluid used in medical procedures such as haemodialysis. Both the patentee, Gambro, and the alleged infringer, Fresenius, are manufacturers of medical equipment and machines used for haemodialysis and the Fresenius system was held to infringe various claims of the Gambro patent. In holding so, the Full Court noted that in order to construe the claims the entire specification must be read. However, regard must be given to the words of the claims and to the choice of the patentee to exclude from the claims "matters, integers or aspects of the invention that have been referred to in the body of the specification".[34] A purposive construction requires that "the essential integers are determined by a common sense assessment of what the words of the claims convey in the context of then-existing published knowledge".[35] This is important as the Full Court noted in an extract from Gyles J in *Grove Hill*:

> A patentee cannot eat the cake and have it too by persuading a court to construe a claim more widely than the patentee was prepared to risk when framing the claims under the guise of purposive construction.[36]

The idea that a purposive construction may result in too wide a construction was reinforced by the Full Federal Court in *Jupiters Ltd v Neurizon Pty Ltd*,[37]

---

28    [2001] RPC 133 at 142.

29    *Kiren-Amgen Inc v Hoechst Marion Roussel Limited* [2004] UKHL 46 at [52]. For an example of the "Protocol questions" being adopted in Australian case law, see the judgment of Merkel J in *PhotoCure ASA v Queen's University at Kingston* [2005] FCA 344.

30    [2004] UKHL 46 at [34].

31    [2004] UKHL 46 at [32].

32    See also the trial judge decision in *Sachtler GMBH & Co KG v RE Miller Pty Ltd* [2005] FCA 788 where the principles of construction and infringement were comprehensively reviewed.

33    [2005] FCAFC 220.

34    [2005] FCAFC 220 at [94].

35    [2005] FCAFC 220 at [91].

36    [2005] FCAFC 220 at [93].

37    [2005] FCAFC 90.

where the respondent's patent for a prize awarding system used in electronic gaming machines was held to be infringed by the appellant's system. The Full Court was mindful of this danger in coming to its conclusion that infringement had occurred. After summarising the basic principles of construction, the court added:

> [T]he area of invention with which this proceeding is concerned is a particularly narrow one. It is one in which business rivals are striving to invent around the patented inventions of others and within narrow regulatory limits. In such a context it is, in our view, important to recognise that claims made for an invention may need to be formulated narrowly to avoid invalidity. While accepting the primacy of purposive construction in interpreting patents, such a construction may well provide little by way of illumination where, as here, the inventive context is a cramped one. It is not appropriate to take a claim carefully drawn to avoid invalidity and then permit a wider "purposive" construction of it for infringement purposes.[38]

This clearly indicates a preference for a narrower construction of the claims that are the subject of infringement proceedings. Interestingly, the above cases espousing such a trend were still able to find infringement. Is this development in the principles of construction and infringement an attempt by the courts to sanction greater competition or simply ensuring that the scope of patent protection does not get out of hand?

In the more recent case of *Kimberly-Clark Australia Pty Limited v Multigate Medical Products Pty Limited*,[39] the Full Court of the Federal Court reviewed the principles of construction acknowledging the summary found in the unanimous decision of the court in *Jupiters Ltd v Neurizon Pty Ltd*,[40] but equally reinforcing the principles espoused by Lord Hoffman in *Kiren-Amgen Inc v Hoechst Marion Roussel Limited*.[41] The dispute concerned three patents for a "Single Step Sterilisation Wrap System" held by Kimberly-Clark Australia Pty Limited and comprising two separate sheets. The allegation of infringement was against a similar product by Multigate Medical Products Pty Limited but which comprised only one sheet folded over to create two layers. The Full Court dismissed the infringement action and the cross-claim for invalidity of the key claims in the patents. Greenwood and Nicholas JJ explained the manner in which words in the specification need to be construed

> There are words used in patent claims that have no ordinary meaning apart from their technical or scientific meaning. There are also words used in patent claims that have a technical or scientific meaning as well as an ordinary meaning. In the latter situation the words may have been intended to be used in accordance with their technical or scientific meaning or in accordance with their ordinary meaning. Expert evidence may be received to assist in determining which of these meanings was intended.[42]

Their Honours considered it necessary to read the specification as a whole whether there is ambiguity in the claim language or not. Giving words their ordinary meaning may not be without difficulty as the context in which those words are

---

38    [2005] FCAFC 90 at [68].
39    [2011] FCAFC 86.
40    [2005] FCAFC 90.
41    [2004] UKHL 46.
42    [2011] FCAFC 86 at [39].

used may vary that meaning.[43] Their Honours went on to consider the principle of purposive construction:

> There are two aspects to the principle which requires that a patent specification be given a purposive rather than a purely literal construction. The first concerns the well recognised need to read words in their proper context. The second is directly related to the nature and function of a patent specification. It is a document that is taken as intended to be read through the eyes of the skilled addressee who is equipped with the common general knowledge in the relevant art. The question is what, in an objective sense, such a person would understand the relevant words of the claim to mean. Ultimately, however, it is the claim that must be construed, and it is not permissible to vary or qualify the plain and unambiguous meaning of the claim by reference to the body of the specification ...[44]

In a separate judgment, Emmett J considered the necessity of giving a specification a purposive construction which is objective in nature and not one which is "subjectively concerned with what the author meant to say".[45] His Honour pointed out that such a construction "is concerned with what a reasonable person to whom the patent is addressed would have understood the author to be using the words to mean".[46] Emmett J goes on to explain that the person skilled in the art relevant to the invention is the notional addressee who would use their common general knowledge in the reading of the specification and in so doing, would recognise that the purpose of the specification "is both to describe and to demarcate an invention".[47] His Honour further explained:

> The purpose of a patent specification is simply to communicate the idea of an invention. An appreciation of that purpose is part of the material that is used to ascertain the meaning. However, purpose and meaning are different. Purposive construction does not mean that one is extending or going beyond the definition of the technical matter for which the patentee seeks protection in the claims. The question is what a person skilled in the art would have understood the patentee to be using the language of the claim to mean. Accordingly, for that purpose, the language chosen is of critical importance. The specification is a document in words of the patentee's own choosing, which will usually have been chosen upon skilled advice.[48]

This indicates that a purposive construction does not mean that a carefully drawn claim would be interpreted more widely. Rather a purposive construction must heed the choice of words and the interpretation that a person skilled in the art would have given them.

## Making and using

It is important to understand that in determining whether the rights of the patentee have been "used" or "made" one does not look for similarity in appearance between the patented product and the final accused article but whether a process or product comprising the essential integers have been made, used, sold

---

43    [2011] FCAFC 86 at [39]-[40].
44    [2011] FCAFC 86 at [41].
45    [2011] FCAFC 86 at [13].
46    [2011] FCAFC 86 at [13].
47    [2011] FCAFC 86 at [14].
48    [2011] FCAFC 86 at [14].

etc. Thus, a patented product might be "made" or "used' in an infringing manner even if it is "temporarily masked" by some chemical reaction,[49] for example, or if it is used or made only temporarily in the process of making another product.

Thus, in *Pinefair Pty Ltd v Bedford Industries Rehabilitation Association Inc*,[50] a majority in the Full Federal Court held that if, in the process of manufacturing a product, a patented product is made and then altered to be non-infringing, there will still be an unauthorised "use" or "making" of the patented product, at least if the use is not an "unimportant" or "trifling" part of the process.[51] In that case, the invention in question was a roll of timber garden edging comprising sliced treated pine joined together by "elongated" wire. The appellants attempted to avoid patent infringement by manufacturing a similar product but at the last moment the appellants cut the "elongated" material holding their pine logs together so that the pieces were held together by short bits of wire. Both parties agreed that the final product was not an infringement of the patent but the respondents successfully argued that the fact that the logs were joined by the elongated material *during* the process of manufacture amounted to an infringing exploitation of the patent.

Mansfield J explained this principle by reference to the patentee's market for the patented product (or process):

> There emerges in my view an appropriate focus on the market for the product the subject of the patent as the sole preserve of the (patentee) so that the manufacture and use of the product to the commercial advantage of the (defendants) would infringe the Patent … the defendants were taking commercial advantage of the patent. They were not doing it in some peripheral or transitory way.[52]

In so far as this statement looks to the patentee's market we would suggest that it provides a useful guide to understanding why similarity between the patented and accused products is not necessary to prove infringement. On the other hand, in so far as the statement suggests that only a commercial use or making by the alleged infringer constitutes infringement we would suggest that the statement be treated with caution.

## Importing

Applying these principles to importation cases has proved to be difficult. In particular the following problems have arisen:

- Is it an infringement of a product patent to import a product lawfully made outside the jurisdiction?
- Is it an infringement to import a product which has been manufactured outside the jurisdiction using a patented product? Does it make a difference if this use is lawful or unlawful?
- Is it an infringement to import a product made by using a patented process, either lawfully or unlawfully, outside the jurisdiction?

---

49    *Smith Kline & French Laboratories Ltd v Attorney-General (New Zealand)* [1991] 2 NZLR 560.
50    (1998) 87 FCR 458.
51    (1998) 87 FCR 458, Mansfield J at 469 approving the trial judge's reasoning.
52    (1998) 87 FCR 458 at 470.

- Does it matter whether the use of the product or process was part of the final process of manufacture, an intermediary step or an initial step in the manufacture of the imported product?

The small amount of English case law on this issue is not conclusive and is largely influenced by the early history of patent law which gave a patentee an exclusive right to import products made by a patented process even if the goods themselves were not new in the patent area.[53] In *Saccharin Corp Ltd v Anglo-Continental Chemical Works Ltd*,[54] Buckley J endorsed this principle and extended it. In that case the plaintiff was the owner of a patent for an improved method of deriving ortho-toluene sulpho-chloride from coal tar. Saccharin was made by a well known method of synthesising ortho-toluene sulpho-chloride. The defendants imported into the United Kingdom some saccharin made from ortho-toluene sulpho-chloride which itself had been derived outside the United Kingdom using the plaintiff's improved process. Buckley J at trial held that this was an infringement of the patentee's right to import any product made by a patented process even if the process was used in an early stage of manufacturing rather than just in the final stages of manufacture.

In *Beecham Group Ltd v Bristol Laboratories Ltd and Bristol-Myers Company*,[55] the House of Lords had an opportunity to consider the modern application of this principle. In that case the defendants held a product patent in a penicillanic acid (6–APA) and processes for preparing it; they also held product patents in derivatives of 6-APA and process patents for deriving these products; they also held product patents in compounds of one of these derivatives. One of these compounds was a very effective form of penicillin and was marketed as ampicillin. The patents were taken out in both the United Kingdom and the United States. The defendants, who were licensed to exercise these patents in the United States, discovered that it could treat the ampicillin in such a way that a compound could be formed which had a different molecular structure to ampicillin but which, upon coming into contact with water, would revert to ampicillin. The defendants called this product hetacillin and imported it into the United Kingdom in direct competition with ampicillin. The courts treated hetacillin as ampicillin "temporarily masked".

The House of Lords held that there was an infringing importation in this case in so far as the process patents had been used in the making of hetacillin. However, Lord Diplock, in a judgment approved by other members of the bench, expressed real concern about extending the *Saccharin* principle to the use of patented products in the manufacture of imported goods. In the particular circumstances of the case this question did not need to be determined but you may like to consider whether such an extension effectively globalises the patentee's patent area.

In a recent Australian case, infringing pregnancy testing devices were imported by MDS Diagnostics Pty Ltd.[56] The action was brought against not only the importing companies but also the managing director as a joint tortfeasor.

---

53 *Elmslie v Boursier* (1859) LR 9 Eq 217 and *Von Heyden v Neustadt* (1880) 14 Ch D 230.
54 (1900) 17 RPC 307.
55 [1977] FSR 217.
56 *Inverness Medical Switzerland GmbH v MDS Diagnostics Pty Ltd* [2010] FCA 108.

In analysing the meaning of "authorise" in s 13 of the *Patents Act 1990*, Bennett J considered the meaning comparable to that found in s 101 of the *Copyright Act 1968*:

> It is an infringement of the patentee's exclusive rights not only to exploit an invention but also to authorise another person to exploit it (s 13 of the 1990 Act). The word "authorise" in s 13 has the meaning in the comparable context of the Copyright Act (*Bristol-Myers Squibb Company v F H Faulding & Co Ltd* [2000] FCA 316; (2000) 97 FCR 524 at [97] per Black CJ and Lehane J; see also *Rescare* at 155 per Gummow J). A person authorises an infringement if he or she "sanctions, approves or countenances'" the infringement (*University of New South Wales v Moorhouse* [1975] HCA 26; (1975) 133 CLR 1 at 12 per Gibbs J, at 20-21 per Jacobs J (McTiernan ACJ agreeing); Cooper at [137]-[140] per Kenny J (French J agreeing)). As Burchett J said in *Kimberly-Clark Australia Pty Ltd v Arico Trading International Pty Ltd* (1998) 42 IPR 111 at 129 (appeal allowed on validity, but not on infringement), s 13 at least embraces the case where a person 'made himself a party to the act of infringement' (*Walker v Alemite Corp* [1933] HCA 39; (1933) 49 CLR 643 at 658 per Dixon J).[57]

Her Honour found that the Managing Director, Dr Appanna, had authorised the company to sell the infringing products:

> He had the power to prevent those acts and some duty to interfere. Express or formal permission is not essential and inactivity or indifference may reach a degree from which authorisation or permission may be inferred ... Dr Appanna authorised MDS to sell the infringing products. I am satisfied that he had the power to prevent the companies from committing the acts of exploitation ... He arranged for the sourcing of the products and personally participated in the distribution of those products. Dr Appanna sanctioned, approved and countenanced the sale of products that infringed Inverness' exclusive right to exploit the invention of the first patent and the second patent.[58]

## Infringement by supply or contributory infringement

Before 1990 it was established that a person was not liable for infringement if the person merely provided parts for the assembly of a patented product although there may have been infringement if the person supplied all of the parts, at least when this was a normal way of supplying the product in question. Thus, in *Walker v Alemite Corp*,[59] the High Court held that there was no infringement of a combination patent where a part to be used in that combination patent had been supplied. Conversely, in *Windsurfing International Inc v Petitt*,[60] the supply of a complete sailboard in a kit form was held to be an infringement of the patent in the sailboard having regard to the fact that sailboards were normally sold in kit form.[61] The court in that case noted that the infringing supplier also included instructions for assembly of the sailboard and advertised an assembled sailboard. The court held that if the whole of a patented machine was being sold

---

57    [2010] FCA 108 at [194].
58    [2010] FCA 108 at [203].
59    (1933) 49 CLR 643. See also *Dunlop Pneumatic Tyre Co v David Moseley & Sons Ltd* [1904] 1 Ch 612 at 619.
60    [1984] 2 NSWLR 196.
61    This is the point that distinguished the case from *Walker v Alemite Corp* (1933) 49 CLR 643. See Waddell J in *Windsurfing International Inc v Petitt* [1984] 2 NSWLR 196 at 207.

then liability for infringement could not be avoided by selling that machine in parts that could easily be put together.[62]

The *Patents Act 1990* s 117 has attempted to extend this liability by providing that the supply of a product by one person to another is infringement of the patent by the supplier (unless the supplier is the patentee or licensee) if use of the product supplied would infringe the patent.

Section 117 provides:

117(1) If the use of a product by a person would infringe a patent, the supply of that product by one person to another is an infringement of the patent by the supplier unless the supplier is the patentee or licensee of the patent.

(2) A reference in subsection (1) to the use of a product by a person is a reference to:

  (a)  if the product is capable of only one reasonable use, having regard to its nature or design – that use; or

  (b)  if the product is not a staple commercial product – any use of the product, if the supplier had reason to believe that the person would put it to that use; or

  (c)  in any case – that the use of the product in accordance with any instructions for the use of the product, or any inducement to use the product, given to the person by the supplier or contained in an advertisement published by or with the authority of the supplier.

The effect of this provision has been said to "strike a balance between competing interests", namely, protection against infringement of a patent on the one hand and "recognising the right of a supplier to freely trade its products in the market place" on the other hand.[63]

The application of this provision to process patents has been the subject of some disagreement. In *Rescare Ltd v Anaesthetic Supplies Pty Ltd*,[64] Gummow J, then in the Federal Court, held that the supply of parts (being tubes) for the assembly of the sleep apnoea device was not an infringement of the process patent (although it would constitute an infringement of the product patent). He came to this conclusion by way of a narrow reading of s 117 and s 13. First, he noted that a process patent was infringed only by its use or by selling the "products of the process". In this case there were no products of the process and therefore there could be no product supplied which would come within s 117.

This decision was subject to some criticism and in *Leonardis v Theta Developments Pty Ltd*,[65] Williams J in the Supreme Court of South Australia expressly rejected such an application of the section. He held that there could be an infringement of a process patent by using the process and that such an infringement might be contributed to by the supply of a product (not necessarily the product *of that* process) which would allow such use:

If the manner of use of an article by the distributor himself in accordance with instructions would infringe a patent then the supply of the article in those circumstances (with instructions for use) will also infringe; that is the effect of s 117(1).[66]

62   *Dunlop Pneumatic Tyre Co v David Moseley & Sons Ltd* [1904] 1 Ch 612 at 619.
63   *Collins v Northern Territory* [2006] FCA 1698 at [1].
64   (1992) 111 ALR 205.
65   (2000) 51 IPR 546.
66   (2000) 51 IPR 546 at 567.

On appeal this particular issue was not argued.[67] In fact, it was not even determined whether the patent was a process patent or not. An authoritative determination of this difference, therefore, has yet to be made.

In *Collins v Northern Territory*,[68] the application of s 117 to process patents was revisited. Mr and Mrs Collins held an Australian patent for the method of producing blue cypress oil from bark and timber. The Australian Cypress Oil Company Pty Ltd (ACOC) infringed that patent when producing the oil from timber removed from Crown land in the Northern Territory. The patentees brought an action of contributory infringement against the Northern Territory as it licensed ACOC to enter on Crown land to harvest and remove timber in order to use the bark and wood to produce cypress oil. Mansfield J found that the licences granted by the Northern Territory to ACOC did not amount to a "supply" under s 117(1) as they were merely permissive.[69] Secondly, contributory infringement by way of the operation of s 117(2)(b) could not be made out as the timber was held to be a staple commercial product.[70] Accordingly, it didn't matter that the Northern Territory was aware of the potentially infringing use of the bark and wood from the removed trees.

Collins appealed to the Full Court of the Federal Court which reversed the decision of Mansfield J, thereby finding in favour of Collins on both issues. The Northern Territory then obtained leave to appeal to the High Court. While not successful on the issue of supply, the High Court[71] did find in favour of the Northern Territory on the issue of the timber being a staple commercial product, thereby avoiding liability under s 117(2)(b):

> The phrase "staple commercial product" means a product supplied commercially for various uses. This does not mandate an enquiry into whether there is "an established wholesale or retail market" or into whether the product is "generally available" even though evidence of such matters may well be sufficient to show that a product is a "staple commercial product". The relevant enquiry is into whether the supply of the product is commercial and whether the product has various uses. Leaving aside the supply to ACOC, the timber here was supplied on commercial terms to various licensees for a variety of non-infringing uses. Accordingly, the Northern Territory is protected by the limitation in s 117(2)(b).[72]

## Actions for infringement

Infringement of a standard patent can occur after the date of publication of the complete specification.[73] However, proceedings can only be commenced against the infringer after the standard patent has been granted[74] and, in the case of an innovation patent, after certification.[75]

---

67   *Theta Developments Pty Ltd v Leonardis* [2002] FCAFC 170.
68   [2006] FCA 1698.
69   [2006] FCA 1698 at [25]-[26].
70   [2006] FCA 1698 at [38]-[41].
71   *Northern Territory v Collins* [2008] HCA 49.
72   [2008] HCA 49 at [145] per Crennan J with Hayne and Heydon JJ agreeing.
73   Section 57(1).
74   Section 57(3).
75   Section 120(1A).

Either the patentee or an exclusive licensee can commence infringement proceedings in a prescribed court[76] or in such other court having jurisdiction to hear and determine the matter.[77] Where an exclusive licensee commences the infringement proceedings the patentee must be joined as a party to those proceedings either as co-plaintiff or as defendant.[78] The limitation period for commencing infringement proceedings is either three years from the day on which the relevant patent is granted or six years from the day on which the infringing act was done, whichever is the later (s 120(4)).

A defendant may mount a counter-claim for revocation in an infringement proceeding.[79] This is a significant factor in patent management in so far as the grant of a patent is no guarantee of validity and is vulnerable to attack at any time. The decision to commence infringement proceedings should therefore be made in the knowledge that revocation of the patent or one or more of its claims may be the result. The patentee's case should accordingly be prepared to defend the counter-claim. In particular, the prior art base should be reviewed carefully as part of the case preparation.

A successful patentee may be granted an injunction upon such terms as the court thinks fit and either damages or an account of profits, whichever the patentee chooses.[80] Before that, an interlocutory injunction may be granted to restrain threatened infringement of the patent. In order to obtain this injunction a serious question to be tried must be made out by the patentee regarding the alleged infringement.[81] Further the patentee must show that without the injunction it will suffer irreparable harm and that damages would be an inadequate form of compensation.[82] Finally, the test is on the balance of convenience that the injunction be made.[83] Once infringement is found, it is now possible for the court to award exemplary damages having regard to the flagrancy of the infringement, the need for deterrence, the conduct of the infringing party and whether any benefit has accrued to the infringer, and all other relevant matters.[84]

Damages and account will not be awarded in the case of innocent infringement. In order to establish innocent infringement the defendant must satisfy the court that "at the date of infringement, the defendant was not aware, and had no reason to believe, that a patent for the invention existed".[85] This is not easy to establish because the legislation deems the defendant to have knowledge of the patent, unless established to the contrary, where there has been substantial sales

---

76    In Sch 1 to the Act, "prescribed court" is defined as the Federal Court of Australia, the Supreme Court of a State of Australia, the Supreme Court of the Australian Capital Territory, the Supreme Court of the Northern Territory, or the Supreme Court of Norfolk Island.

77    Section 120(1).

78    Section 120(2). Further, where the patentee is joined as a defendant the patentee will not be liable for costs unless the patentee takes part in the proceedings and enters an appearance: s 120(3).

79    This tactic is specifically recognised in s 121.

80    Section 122(1).

81    See *Hexal Australia Pty Ltd v Roche Therapeutics Inc* [2005] FCA 1218, Stone J at [17]-[22]. See also *Pharmacia Italia SpA v Interpharma Pty Ltd* [2005] FCA 1675.

82    Ibid.

83    Ibid.

84    Section 122(1A) introduced in 2006.

85    Section 123(1).

or use of the patented products in the patent area and those patented products have been marked indicating the Australian patent.[86]

Pecuniary remedies may be restricted in two further circumstances. Where a complete specification has been amended after first publication (that is, after being open to public inspection) then any infringement before the date of the decision or order allowing or directing the amendment will not be subject to an award of damages or account of profits "unless the court is satisfied that the specification without amendment was framed in good faith and with reasonable skill and knowledge"[87] or the priority date of the amended claim is determined in accordance with s 114 of the Act. Secondly, where a defendant has obtained a non-infringement declaration[88] prior to the patentee bringing successful infringement proceedings against the defendant, that defendant will not be liable for an account of profits or for damages in relation to actions occurring before the date of the infringement determination.[89]

Section 128 is similar to s 202 of the *Copyright Act 1968* and provides relief against a person who has made unjustified threats of infringement proceedings by way of "circulars, advertisements or otherwise". The relief granted could amount to a declaration that the threats are unjustified, an injunction to stop the threats[90] and recovery of damages sustained as a result of those threats.[91] The relevant court is free to grant such relief to the applicant in such proceedings unless the patentee can satisfy the court that there is infringement of the patent and the applicant has not shown such patent to be invalid.[92] Accordingly, in a s 128 application, the patentee can counter-claim for infringement.[93] Mere notification of the existence of a patent or an application for a patent is not a threat under s 128.[94] A legal practitioner or registered patent attorney acting in their professional capacity on behalf of a client is not liable to proceedings under s 128.[95]

## Defences and Compulsory Licences

There are very few defences to patent infringement. We have already mentioned three of these. Thus, it is a defence to infringement that the patentee is a party to a contract containing a restrictive condition under s 144. It is also a defence to

---

86   Section 123(2).

87   Section 115(1).

88   See Part 2 Chapter 11 of the Act. A non-infringement declaration allows exploitation of an invention where there may be some question as to infringement: ss 125-127. The declaration will only be given after the applicant has notified the patentee of the proposed use and offered to pay for advice as to whether the proposed use would infringe or not.

89   Section 127.

90   In *Occupational and Medical Innovations Limited v Retractable Technologies Inc* [2007] FCA 1364, the respondent was found to have made unjustifiable threats of infringement proceedings but no injunction was granted as the threats were constrained to a particular time and a considerable period had elapsed since those threats; no further threats were made and nor was it likely that there would be such threats into the future.

91   Section 128(1). For innovation patents, see s 129A.

92   Section 129.

93   Section 130.

94   Section 131.

95   Section 132.

infringement if the alleged infringer has previously been granted a declaration of non-infringement under Chapter 2 of the Act.

Under s 118 it is a defence to infringement if the patented invention is used on board a foreign vessel exclusively for the needs of that vessel, and that vessel only temporarily or accidentally comes in the patent area; the patent rights of the patentee in the patent area are deemed not to be infringed. Similarly, where the patented invention is used in the construction or working of a foreign aircraft or land vehicle and that aircraft or vehicle comes in the patent area only temporarily or accidentally, once again, the patent rights of the patentee are deemed not to be infringed.

Prior use will also constitute an exemption from infringement pursuant to s 119 of the Act. This is an unusual provision as under normal circumstances prior use of the invention will amount to anticipation or lack of novelty and thereby prevent the issue of a patent. However, it has been suggested that where prior use is by someone other than the patentee and such use has been secret use, then the invention has not been made available to the public and s 18(1)(d) has not been contravened. However, the exemption operates in very specific circumstances. First, the person seeking the exemption must have been exploiting or taking definite steps to exploit the product, method or process claimed in Australia immediately before the priority date of the claim.[96] Ceasing or abandoning to do any of these acts, other than temporarily, would be fatal to obtaining the exemption.[97] Further, the person seeking the exemption must not have derived the subject-matter of the invention from the patentee or the patentee's predecessor in title.[98] This would seem to provide a solution for our Indigenous community, in our example at the beginning of this chapter, continuing its ancient practice of using healing plants even if such use could be considered an infringement of a product patent.

A new exemption regarding experimental use was announced in 2007 although no legislation was provided until the *Raising the Bar* amendments.[99] The amendments exempt potentially infringing acts that were carried out for "experimental purposes" with the term "experimental" being given its ordinary English meaning.[100] In addition, an inclusive list of acts that would qualify as being for experimental purposes have been provided in the new s 119C(2). Acts falling under this exemption include: determining the scope and validity of the invention, how it works and how to improve it, and determining whether one's own actions would be construed as an infringement of the patent. It is intended that for this exemption to apply the primary purpose must be an experimental purpose.[101] If, for example, the experimental purpose is secondary to another purpose, such as a commercial purpose, then the exemption will not apply.[102]

---

96    Section 119(1).

97    Section 119(2).

98    Section 119(3).

99    *Intellectual Property Laws Amendment (Raising The Bar) Act 2012*, Sch 2 Item 1, inserting new s 119C.

100   Explanatory Memorandum Intellectual Property Laws Amendment (Raising The Bar) Bill 2011, Sch 2 Item 1.

101   Explanatory Memorandum Intellectual Property Laws Amendment (Raising The Bar) Bill 2011, Sch 2 Item 1.

102   Explanatory Memorandum Intellectual Property Laws Amendment (Raising The Bar) Bill 2011, Sch 2 Item 1.

There is a special provision relating to pharmaceuticals. Section 78 provides that where the patent period is extended for pharmaceuticals there is no infringement if a person exploits the pharmaceutical substance for a non-therapeutic purpose. Before the 2006 amendments, this included doing something for the purposes of registering goods in the Australian Register of Therapeutic Goods or its overseas equivalents. This aspect is considered in Chapter 11 in the light of the United States–Australia Free Trade Agreement. In the *Raising the Bar* amendments, this special exemption for infringement is extended to non-pharmaceutical products that require regulatory approval.[103]

The Act provides for a compulsory licence for exploitation of the patent for the services of the Commonwealth or the State. This compulsory licence is narrower than the compulsory licence for Crown copyright in so far as it is restricted to exploitation which is "necessary" for the proper provision of those services "within Australia". The patentee is able to seek a declaration requiring the Commonwealth or State to cease exploiting the invention where it is no longer necessary for the proper provision of services of the Commonwealth or State.[104]

In addition, Chapter 12 of the Act provides that a person willing to work the patent may apply to a prescribed court for an order requiring the patentee to grant the applicant a licence.[105] The court can only make such an order if satisfied that the applicant tried for a reasonable period, without success, to obtain authorisation to work the patent on reasonable terms and conditions, the reasonable requirements of the public regarding the invention have not been satisfied and the patentee has not given a satisfactory reason for failing to exploit the patent.[106] The meaning of "reasonable requirements of the public" is explained in detail in s 135 of the Act. In the alternative, if the court is satisfied that "the patentee has contravened, or is contravening, Part IV of the *Competition and Consumer Act 2010* or an application law (as defined in section 150A of that Act) in connection with the patent" then a compulsory licence may be ordered.[107] Where the licence is ordered, it cannot be an exclusive licence to work the patent, nor can it be assigned except as part of the sale of the business holding the licence.[108] However, it is possible to later obtain a revocation of the patent after the grant of the compulsory licence.[109]

## Offences

The Act allows only authorised patent attorneys to write specifications, and the offences under the Act primarily relate to other people performing these functions. Thus, s 201 contains a number of offences relating to people carrying on business as patent attorneys. Section 202 provides that a legal practitioner may not prepare a specification or related document unless acting under the instructions of a patent attorney or on the direction of a court to amend it. Section 202A extends a similar prohibition to a person who is a member of a partnership but is

103  *Intellectual Property Laws Amendment (Raising The Bar) Act 2012*, Sch 2 Item 1, new s 119B.
104  Section 165.
105  Section 133(1).
106  Section 132(2).
107  Section 133(2)(b).
108  Section 133(3).
109  Section 134.

not a patent attorney. Under s 203 a patent attorney may not practise or hold him or herself out to be a patent attorney at an office where specifications are prepared unless that person is in regular attendance at that office. Each of these offences is subject to a five-year limitation period and is subject to a pecuniary penalty.

Further, there are a series of miscellaneous offences contained in Chapter 18 of the Act pertaining to the Patent Office and its staff. A person cannot make false representations about the Patent Office by implying the Office is connected with their business.[110] A penalty of $3000 is applicable but also such action may be in breach of ss 18 and 29 of the *Australian Consumer Law* (substantially reproducing ss 52 and 52 of the repealed *Trade Practices Act 1974*) and result in further consequences. Similarly, a person cannot falsely represent that they have a patent or innovation patent or that a product sold by them is patented or the subject of an application.[111] Penalties of $6000 are applicable in most instances but prosecutions in relation to standard patents require the consent of the Minister.

In proceedings before the Commissioner of Patents, a failure to comply with a summons,[112] a refusal to give evidence[113] and a failure to produce documents or articles[114] constitute offences and are met with penalties of up to $3000. However, the ground of lawful excuse is sufficient defence.[115]

Actions of the Commissioner, Deputy Commissioner and other Patent Office employees may also attract offences. Section 182 requires that officers are not to traffick in inventions (other than their own) and, if found to be in contravention of this provision, not only will there be a penalty of $6000 to consider but also the purchase, sale, acquisition, assignment or transfer in question will be deemed void. Officers also cannot assist in the preparation of a specification or associated documents unless they are the inventor[116] and they cannot search Patent Office records except in their official capacity.[117] There is also a prohibition against unauthorised disclosures of information regarding matters under the *Patents Act 1990* or *1952*,[118] but the heaviest penalty applies to unauthorised disclosure of information by persons to whom s 71 of the *Safeguards Act* applies.[119] This legislation refers to the *Nuclear Non-Proliferation (Safeguards) Act 1987* and such an unauthorised disclosure attracts a penalty of two years' imprisonment.[120]

## Dealing with Patents

### Ownership

As we have seen, s 15(1) of the Act provides that a person is entitled to the grant of a patent and therefore "ownership" of the patent, if the person is the inventor;

---

110 Section 177.
111 Section 178.
112 Section 179.
113 Section 180.
114 Section 181.
115 Sections 179(2), 180(2) and 181(2).
116 Section 185(a).
117 Section 185(b).
118 Section 183.
119 Section 184.
120 Ibid.

someone entitled to an assignment of the patent; someone who derives title from the inventor or a person entitled to an assignment of the patent or the legal representative of a deceased person being one of the previous three potential owners.[121] Typically, the "inventor" is either an individual or a group of individuals working together and who, more often than not, developed the invention in the course of their employment. We have discussed the employment relationship in the context of copyright law but some additional practical matters may now be mentioned.

Unlike the *Copyright Act 1968* which specifically provides that copyright subject-matter made in the course of employment is owned by the employer,[122] the *Patents Act 1990* is silent on the matter. Modern employment contracts, however, often contain provisions for the assignment to the employer of future intellectual property created by the employee in the course of employment. In the absence of such an express clause the courts have readily implied such a term in a contract of employment[123] or found that the employee holds the invention on trust for the employer as a result of the employee's fiduciary obligations to the employer.[124] But this depends on what falls within the scope of employment. If *Electrolux Ltd v Hudson*[125] can serve as a guide, then, when a person is employed in a position that does not require the development of products or processes, that person is under no obligation to their employer to assign their inventions even if such inventions are related to the business of the employer. Such a result would be clear if the employee was, for example, employed in administration or sales and used his or her own resources and developed the invention in his or her own time. However, if the resources, trade secrets, know how or technology of the employer were used; or if the level of trust in and responsibility of the employee were significant, the scale may be tipped toward the employer and an assignment implied.[126]

However, the decision in *University of Western Australia v Gray*[127] is authority for the view that such implied terms of assignment from employee to employer will not necessarily prevail in the university or research and development context. Dr Gray, was employed by the University of Western Australia (the University) from 1985 to teach, conduct and stimulate research. French J (as he then was) recognised that Dr Gray's research "carried with it the possibility that he would develop inventions capable of attracting patent protection". The statutes and regulations of the University as well as its Patent Regulations were incorporated into the terms of Dr Gray's appointment. At the time of his employment, Dr Gray had been engaged for some years in researching the treatment of liver cancer by using microspheres. During his continued research in this area whilst employed by the University, he devised, in conjunction with others at the University,

---

121 It should also be noted that pursuant to s 15(2), and in line with Australia's international treaty obligations, there is no requirement of Australian citizenship.

122 See the discussion of the meaning of course of employment in Chapter 6, "Dealing With Copyright".

123 See, for example, *Triplex Safety Glass Co v Scorah* (1938) 55 RPC 237.

124 See *Fine Industrial Commodities v Powling* (1954) 71 RPC 253 in relation to directors. See also RP Meagher, *Jacob's Law of Trusts in Australia*, 6th ed, Butterworths, Sydney, 1997.

125 [1977] FSR 312.

126 See *Worthington Pumping Engine Co v Moore* (1902) 20 RPC 41 and cf *Charles Selz Ltd's Application* (1954) 71 RPC 158.

127 At first instance before French J as he then was: [2008] FCA 498; appeal to the Full Federal Court: *University of Western Australia v Gray* [2009] FCAFC 116. Leave to appeal to the High Court was refused.

various microsphere technologies. Patent applications were made in respect of the inventions said to have been developed in relation to the various technologies. Dr Gray subsequently became a director of Sirtex Medical Limited (Sirtex). In 1997 Sirtex acquired the intellectual property rights arising out of the inventions from Dr Gray and the Cancer Research Institute.

French J noted that:

> [The University's] case against Dr Gray and Sirtex was critically dependent upon the proposition that it was an implied term of Dr Gray's contract of employment that intellectual property developed in the course of his employment belonged to [the University] ... [However, a]bsent express agreement to the contrary, rights in relation to inventions made by academic staff in the course of research and whether or not they are using university resources, will ordinarily belong to the academic staff as the inventors under the Patents Act 1990. The position is different if staff have a contractual duty to try to produce inventions. But a duty to research does not carry with it a duty to invent.[128]

His Honour found that Dr Gray did not have a duty to invent anything.[129]

The evidence suggested that all the inventions, except for one, were made by Dr Gray and the other academic staff outside their employment at the University. Further, the provisions of the University's regulations which purported to vest intellectual property rights in the University or interfere with the intellectual property generated by its academic staff were not valid. The University was not authorised by the *University of Western Australia Act 1911* (WA) to make regulations acquiring property from others or to interfere with their rights. The University's breach of fiduciary duty claim also failed because it did not establish that it had any rights or interests in any of the inventions. The resulting appeal to the Full Court of the Federal Court was concerned with whether Dr Gray was under a "duty to invent" and therefore the implied term of assignment to the University would apply. Lindgren, Finn and Bennett JJ upheld the decision of French J and found for Dr Gray:

> Such a deemed contingent duty to invent requires an untenable implication. It is not what Dr Gray's terms of employment required; there is no 'necessity' for it being implied by law into the employment contracts of university staff; and, importantly, it is inconsistent with the researcher's freedom to share and to publish research results.[130]

Leave to appeal to the High Court was then sought by the University but not granted. It would appear that, certainly in the case of university staff, for a university to have a valid claim over the inventions of its staff the best way is through an express term in the contract of employment. This had already been confirmed in the judgment of Nettle J in *Victoria University of Technology v Wilson*,[131] where the university had claimed a constructive trust in the patent granted to its former employees for an electronic international trading system that was partly developed during the course of employment. His Honour explained:

> [T]he mere existence of the employer/employee relationship will not give the employer ownership of inventions made by the employee during the term of the relationship. And

---

128   [2008] FCA 498 at [12].
129   [2008] FCA 498 at [1360].
130   [2009] FCAFC 116 at [197].
131   [2004] VSC 33.

that is so even if the invention is germane to and useful for the employer's business, and even though the employee may have made use of the employer's time and resources in bringing the invention to completion. Certainly, all the circumstances must be considered in each case, but unless the contract of employment expressly so provides, or an invention is the product of work which the employee was paid to perform, it is unlikely that any invention made by the employee will be held to belong to the employer.[132]

However, Nettle J did find for the university on the issue of breach of fiduciary duty noting that:

> [S]ubject to contract, it remains unquestionable that professional employees owe to their employers fiduciary obligations not to profit from their position at the expense of the employer and to avoid conflicts of interest and duty. Accordingly, even if an employee is generally speaking free to work for someone else, he or she must avoid work which could conflict with the interests of the employer that the employee is paid to serve. Correspondingly, in the absence of full and frank disclosure and consent, a professional employee remains bound to account to the employer for gains derived as a result of the employee's fiduciary position and for opportunities of which the employee may learn in the course of employment; lest the employee otherwise be swayed by considerations of personal interest.[133]

The result was that due to such breach of fiduciary duty the two former academics were held to be holding their shares in the patent holding company in constructive trust for the university.[134] The question of fiduciary duty was also raised in Gray's case. In relation to the University of Western Australia, the court did not find that Gray breached any fiduciary duty over his inventions (although Sirtex was successful in its cross-claim against Gray in relation to his fiduciary duty to Sirtex) as the University "failed to establish that it had any rights or interests in any of the inventions even if they were made by Dr Gray or others in the course of their employment as researchers with" the university.[135]

## Joint ownership

Where there are two or more owners they each own an equal and undivided share in the patent; each may exercise the exclusive rights for his or her own benefit without accounting to the others; but none can license or assign the patent without the consent of those others (s 16).[136]

If there is more than one inventor, each of the joint inventors must be a party to an application for registration. In *Stack v Davies Shephard Pty Ltd*,[137] the Federal Court interpreted this strictly and held that if only one inventor proceeds with the patent application without an assignment from the other inventors, even though consent may have been given by the other inventors, that patent application will fall foul of s 15 of the Act.[138] This was brought home in the Full

---

132 [2004] VSC 33 at [104].
133 [2004] VSC 33 at [149].
134 [2004] VSC 33 at [225].
135 [2008] FCA 498 at [1567].
136 However, the rights and obligations of a trustee or of the legal representative of a deceased person are not affected by this "fall back" position: see s 16(3).
137 (2001) 51 IPR 513.
138 (2001) 51 IPR 513 at 523.

Federal Court decision, *University of British Columbia v Conor Medsystems Inc*,[139] where the majority held that where two or more persons are specified in the patent application, they must each be entitled under s 15 and if one is held not to be so entitled then none of the persons specified is entitled.

However, who is the inventor when a concept for an invention is created by one party who confidentially discloses this to another party for the purpose of having a prototype developed? This situation was considered by the Full Court of the Federal Court in the case of *Polwood Pty Ltd v Foxworth Pty Ltd*.[140] The invention comprised both a process and apparatus for the production of plant growth media using organic waste. Consequently, the patent included claims to a process and method for producing the media, and also claims to the apparatus for implementing the process. The court considered the full specification and claims when attempting to determine what comprised the invention or inventive concept, noting that "the invention may consist of a combination of elements" or concepts and that these might be contributed by different individuals.[141] Accordingly, the court held that there was joint ownership in the patented invention.

The Commissioner may be requested by any of the joint owners to give directions with respect to co-owned patents, for example, in the case of a dispute between the owners.[142] The Commissioner must provide an opportunity for a hearing before giving a direction,[143] and such direction must not be inconsistent with the terms of an agreement between the patentees nor affect the rights or obligations of a trustee or of the legal representative of a deceased person.[144]

Chapter 19 of the Act provides for the keeping of a register and official documents by the Patent Office including dealings with and transfers of patents.[145] The register does not include dealings relating to trusts.[146] The *Patents Regulations 1991* require that sufficient evidence is provided to enable the Commissioner to be reasonably satisfied that the person seeking to register a prescribed interest in the patent is entitled to the interest claimed.[147]

## Assignment, licensing and tying arrangements

The exclusive rights of the patentee are personal property capable of assignment and devolution by law (s 13(2)).[148] Like copyright, patent rights are divisible that is, part only of the patent may be assigned for a particular geographical area or for a particular use.[149] An assignment must be in writing and signed by both the assignor and assignee.[150]

---

139  [2006] FCAFC 154.
140  [2008] FCAFC 9.
141  [2008] FCAFC 9 at [53].
142  Section 17.
143  Section 17(3).
144  Section 17(4).
145  Section 187.
146  Section 188.
147  *Patents Regulations 1991* reg 199.1(2).
148  For a discussion of the meaning of devolution by law, see Chapter 6, "Dealing With Copyright".
149  Section 14(2).
150  Section 14(1).

The patentee has many avenues for exploiting the invention protected by his or her patent. Rather than making, hiring, selling or using the invention directly, the patentee might prefer to license those rights to another party in return for a licence fee and or royalties. Such licences may be express or implied, inclusive or exclusive. That is, depending on the commercial risks involved in licensing a particular patent, a licensee may only accept exclusive rights to the patent in the patent area. This would exclude the patentee from exploiting the patent in the patent area for the duration of the exclusive licence.[151] Alternatively, if there is immense commercial potential for the patent, the patentee may wish to grant several non-exclusive licences in the patent area to ensure full market exposure, and therefore maximise returns. Accordingly, the patentee needs to consider how long the licence should endure, whether there should be an option to renew the licence for another term, the nature of the fees and royalties and whether annual minimums can be prescribed, the territorial boundaries of the licence (if not the entire patent area) and the field of use of the patent (particularly if the invention is a tool that can be used in many industrial applications).

The *Patents Act 1990* proscribes "tying arrangements" being imposed in patent dealings. Section 144(1) provides that a condition in a contract relating to the sale or lease of a patent or a licence to exploit a patent, will be void if the effect of the condition would be:

- to prohibit or restrict the buyer, lessee or licensee from using a product or process (whether patented or not) supplied or owned by a person other than the seller, lessor or licensor (or their nominees); or
- to require the buyer, lessee or licensee to acquire a product not protected by the patent from the seller, lessor or licensor (or their nominees).

Section 144(1A) provides that a condition in a such a contract is void if it prohibits or limits the buyer, lessee or licensee from applying for an examination of the patent. Section 144(4) provides that it is a defence to infringement proceedings that the patent is, or was at the start of the proceedings, the subject of a contract containing a proscribed condition. If the patentee offers a new contract to the parties (whether or not they accept them) which grants the same rights but does not contain the offending condition then s 144(4) ceases to apply and infringement might be found. In this case, however, the patentee is not entitled to damages or an account of profits (s 144(5)).

The patentee may avoid the effect of these provisions if he or she proves that the buyer, lessee or licensee had an opportunity to acquire, lease or license the patent on reasonable terms without the condition and the contract allows that person to avoid liability under the condition upon the giving of three months notice and payment of compensation.[152]

---

151  As a consequence, s 120 enables an exclusive licensee to sue for infringement. See the definition of "exclusive licensee" in Sch 1 (Dictionary).
152  For the amount of compensation, see s 144(2)(b).

# CASES

## *Peter Populin and Lewis Populin v HB Nominees Pty Ltd*
Federal Court of Australia: Bowen CJ, Deane and Ellicott JJ
(1982) 59 FLR 37

In this case the question arose as to whether the respondent's machine for plant-ing sugar cane infringed the appellant's patent despite their differences. The judgment considers the "pith and marrow" test for determining infringement.

**Bowen CJ, Deane and Ellicott JJ: [38]** The appellants are the owners of Letters Patent No 487810 which created patent rights to an invention relating to a machine and a method for planting sugar cane. The respondents, after the date of the appellants' patent, manufactured and sold a machine which the appellants considered was an infringement of their patent and in respect of which they sued for infringement in the Supreme Court of Queensland. The Supreme Court (Connolly J) held that there had been no infringement and the appellants have appealed to this Court.

Prior to the invention, it had been common practice to plant sugar cane by using a machine in which the cane was fed manually in long sticks into the machine where it was chopped into small lengths or billets and planted in a trench and covered by the machine as it moved across the previously prepared field. It had also been the practice until sugar cane harvesters were developed to cut the sugar cane manually. However, with the use of these harvesters, cane harvested by machine could be chopped into billets which were suitable for planting.

The appellants and their co-inventor, Guiseppe Scalia, (who has since assigned his rights in the patent to the appellants) decided to develop a planting machine which would enable chopped billets obtained from sugar cane harvesters to be used. This, however, confronted them with a problem. Whereas, in the existing planting machines, long sticks of cane were taken from a neat stack and fed manually into the planting machine to be chopped into billets and planted, a different means would have to be developed in order to ensure that the pre-chopped billets would be fed regularly and efficiently into the planting mechanism of the machine. As they said in their specification, the billets would be dumped into a supply bin "with random orientation". They therefore had to concentrate on the means whereby the billets so dumped could be fed into the planting mechanism.

An embodiment of the invention is described in the specification. It consists of a planting head, a rather small bin attached to the planting head and a large supply bin to the rear used for storing bulk cane. Cane from the bulk storage container is fed into the relatively small supply bin by means of a conveyor. The relatively small supply bin is defined as being such that the weight of sugar cane billets capable of being contained when supplied with random orientation in the bin and filled to a normal maximum level is "small compared with the weight of one ton".

In order to feed cane to the planting head a conveyor moves continuously through the small bin. It is claimed that by having the conveyor moving through a small bin containing relatively few billets, these billets are in a state of continual agitation. This movement together with a feature of having the floor of the bin steeply angled towards the conveyor causes the billets to align **[39]** themselves so as to be picked up by the flights of the conveyor. They are then lifted to the planting shute and guided to the planting head. If a surplus of billets is picked up by the conveyor there is an ejection means towards the top of the conveyor which removes the surplus billets and returns them to the bin. The billets are finally dropped in an end to end relationship along the planting path.

The respondents' machine (the Binder machine) also utilizes ready cut cane billets. It consists of a planting head and a large cane hopper. The cane billets are loaded with random orientation into the large hopper. They are then fed into the planting head by means of a conveyor which constitutes the front wall of the hopper. Immediately adjacent to the conveyor is a trough, the bottom floor of which is steeply angled down towards the conveyor. However, this trough continues on below the bottom of the conveyor and contains fungicide. In effect, the conveyor moves within this trough. There is a small space between the conveyor and the lower edge of the angled floor. According to the respondents, billets of cane are able to drop between the conveyor and the angled floor into the fungicide at the bottom of the trough. They are then picked up by the flights of the conveyor for carriage upwards and over to the planting head. According to the respondents it does not matter if a large volume of cane is above the bottom of the conveyor and in practice the respondents' machine is filled so that billets of cane are resting against the conveyor to a height somewhat short of the top of the conveyor and below the ejector mechanism. The cane billets taken up by the conveyor to the planting head are duly positioned and planted in an end to end relationship along the planting path.

Although after the hopper is filled the cane billets rest for some distance up the conveyor, as the machine proceeds this level falls and the main quantity of billets carried is in the back of the container. To ensure that these may be advanced selectively to the conveyor the floor of the back of the rear part of the container may be hydraulically raised pivoting at about the point where the bottom of the trough is angled down towards the conveyor. The hydraulic raising of the hopper floor is thus used to cause billets to slide forward into the trough.

Mr Binder applied for a patent (No 43809/79). In his specification, which he agreed was the same as the machine complained of, he uses the term "hopper" for that part of the container which may be raised by the hydraulic ram, and the term "tank" for what has been referred to as the "trough".

While the appellants claim that the restriction of billets going to the conveyor to those which are in the relatively small bin permits turbulence and assists in orientation, the respondents' claim they have found that this is unnecessary and that it is for this reason they are able to fill the large container to quite some distance up the conveyor. However, it is plain that when the conveyor of the Binder **[40]** machine takes up cane billets it does so from the bottom. If any billets get on to the cleats from those which are stacked high up the conveyor, these will be knocked off by the ejector means. One reason why this must be so for the Binder machine to operate in the manner intended is that only those billets at the bottom will have been dipped in the fungicide. It further seems plain that the sloping floor of the trough coupled with a degree of turbulence within the trough tends to orient the cane billets so they will be properly taken by the cleats on the conveyor. Mr PL Mizzi, an Engineer called by the respondents, agreed in evidence that one of the purposes of the small trough or tank was to get the billets moving around and to sort themselves out in line with the cleats of the conveyor although he thought the main purpose was to hold the fungicide. He said that in the tank the billets were turbulent and that in moving around some rotate and align themselves with the cleats. On the other hand, in the hopper section the cane was static. Mr BD Schmidt, another Engineer called by the respondents, agreed in evidence that the idea of the Binder machine was to take the material from the hopper into the tank where it was dipped in fungicide and went up the cleats. He agreed that the billets in the tank would be in a state of turbulence which would decrease as one moved away from the conveyor and there would be a fairly clear division between those billets which were in a state of turbulence and those which were not. He expressed the opinion that the greater load of cane on top in the case of the Binder machine would tend to suppress that turbulence.

Although there was claimed to be a difference of philosophy in the construction of the two machines, and undoubtedly the Binder machine adds the function of dipping the billets in fungicide and operates on the basis that the load of cane may be such as will tend to suppress turbulence, nevertheless there is a good deal that is common in the philosophy. What happens in the operation of both machines regarding orientation of the cane billets is very similar.

The question before us is largely one of fact. The learned trial Judge does not appear to us to have misconceived the principles to be applied and the question before this Court is whether he has applied those principles correctly to the facts of the case. The credibility of the witnesses is not in issue, and this Court, sitting on appeal, is therefore in as good a position as the trial Judge to decide on the proper inferences to be drawn from the facts. In the course of so deciding, it should, however, give due respect and weight to the conclusion of the trial Judge (see *Warren v Coombs* (1979) 142 CLR 53).

Section 40 of the *Patents Act 1952*, provides that a complete specification shall fully describe the invention including the best method of performing it known to the applicant and shall end with a **[41]** claim or claims defining the invention which shall be clear, succinct and fairly based on the matter described in the specification.

Many patents are combination patents. That is to say, they consist of the combination of a number of known integers which work in relation to one another so as to produce a new or improved result. This is the case with the invention claimed in the appellants' patent. None of the elements claimed is new in itself. What is new is the working relationship of the various elements to produce a new and improved machine for planting cane. Because of the requirements of provisions such as s 40, it has become the practice to set out in the claim, sometimes at great length, the elements or integers of the invention. As in this case it is also common for the first claim to be added to or varied in the subsequent claims. This progressively adds elements to the combination, which tend to make an attack upon the grounds of want of subject matter or want of novelty more difficult. The effect is progressively to narrow the area of monopoly claimed.

It has often been said that the claims operate as a disclaimer of what is not specifically claimed (eg *Walker v Alemite Corporation* (1933) 49 CLR 643 per Dixon J at p 656). They therefore determine the extent of the patentee's monopoly. The patentee must be vigilant to claim only the essence of the invention. This is particularly so in relation to a combination patent. It is important to claim only the essential integers in the combination or to distinguish what is essential from what is inessential. For to establish infringement of a combination patent, the patentee must show that the defendant has taken each and every one of the essential integers of the patentee's claim. Therefore if, on its true construction, the claim in a patent claims a particular combination of integers and the alleged infringer of it omits one of them he will escape liability.

At the same time, however, the courts have avoided too technical or narrow a construction of claims. In *Radiation Limited v Galliers and Klaen Pty Limited* (1938) 60 CLR 36 Dixon J at p 51 said: "But, on a question of infringement, the issue is not whether the words of the claim can be applied with verbal accuracy or felicity to the article or device alleged to infringe, it is whether the substantial idea disclosed by the specification and made the subject of a definite claim has been taken and embodied in the infringing thing."

It is in reliance on this approach that the courts have held that a defendant will not escape infringement by adopting what are immaterial variations, for example, by omitting an inessential part or step and substituting another part or step as its equivalent (see *Marconi v British Radio Telegraph and Telephone Co Limited* (1911) 28 RPC 181 per Parker J at p 217). It was considerations such as this that led early in the history of patent law to the development of what has been termed **[42]** the "pith and marrow" or "pith and substance" test. The classic statement of it is found in the judgment of James LJ in

*Clark v Adie* (1875) 10 Ch App 667 at p 675 where he said: "The patent is in the entire combination, but there is, or may be, an essence or substance of the invention underlying the mere accident of form; and that invention, like every other invention, may be pirated by a theft in a disguised or mutilated form, and it would be in every case a question of fact whether the alleged piracy is the same in substance and effect or is a substantially new or different combination".

The existence of this doctrine is still recognized by the High Court. But its limitations must be borne in mind. Thus in *Olin Corporation v Super Cartridge Co Pty Limited* (1977) 14 ALR 149 at p 157, Gibbs J (as he then was) after referring to the above passages said: "The statements in these passages are still good law; see *C Van der Lely NV v Bamfords Limited* [1963] RPC 61 at p 75. However, as was pointed out in *C Van der Lely* at 78 and 80, the principle that there may be infringement by taking the 'pith and marrow' or the substance of an invention does not mean that there will be an infringement where the patentee has by the form of his claim left open that which the alleged infringer has done. And it does not affect the fundamental rule that there will be no infringement unless the alleged infringer has taken all of the essential features or integers of the patentee's claim; See *Rodi & Weinenbirger AG v Henry Showell Limited* [1969] RPC 367 especially at 383-4."

In *Minnesota Mining & Manufacturing Co v Beiersdorf (Aust) Limited* (1980) 29 ALR 29 at pp 52-53, Aickin J, with whose judgment Barwick CJ, Stephen, Mason and Wilson JJ all expressed agreement, wrote:

"Notwithstanding the undoubted fact that the doctrine of *Clark v Adie* (1875) LR 10 Ch App 667 concerning the taking of the pith and substance of an invention, but nonetheless staying outside the express words of the claim, is less often applicable at the present time than it was at the time of that decision, it remains the law that a defendant may not take the substance of an invention unless the wording of the claims make it clear that the relevant area has been deliberately left outside the claim.

"The authorities which demonstrate this to be so are collected in the judgment of Gibbs J, in *Olin Corporation v Super Cartridge Co Pty Ltd* (1977) 51 ALJR 525 at 530; 14 ALR 149 at 157, and need not be repeated here". (See also *Beecham Control Group Limited v Bristol Laboratories Ltd* [1978] RPC 153 at p 200.)

The complete specification must not be read in the abstract but in the light of common knowledge in the art before the priority date **[43]** bearing in mind that what is being construed is a public instrument which must, if it is to be valid, define a monopoly in such a way that it is not reasonably capable of being misunderstood (see generally *Welch Perrin & Co Pty Limited v Worrel* (1961) 106 CLR 588 at p 610). The essential features of the product or process for which it claims a monopoly are to be determined not as a matter of abstract uninformed construction but by a common sense assessment of what the words used convey in the context of then-existing published knowledge. As Lord Diplock (with whom the other members of the House of Lords agreed) commented in *Catnic Components Limited v Hill & Smith Limited* (1981) 7 FSR 60 at pp 65-66: "… a patent specification is a unilateral statement by the patentee, in words of his own choosing, addressed to those likely to have a practical interest in the subject matter of his invention (ie "skilled in the art"), by which he informs them what he claims to be the essential features of the new product or process for which the letters patent grant him a monopoly. It is those novel features only that he claims to be essential that constitute the so-called "pith and marrow" of the claim. A patent specification should be given a purposive construction rather than a purely literal one derived from applying to it the kind of meticulous verbal analysis in which lawyers are too often tempted by their training to indulge …".

In the light of these principles it is necessary to construe the claims and to see whether the respondents' machine has taken the essential integers of what the patentees saw fit to claim. For the purpose of this Appeal it is, we think, sufficient to consider in detail only claim 1. All the other claims which are alleged to be infringed incorporate claim 1 and a decision on claim 1 will dispose of the matters which have been argued before us.

In one of the exhibits claim 1 is conveniently set out in lettered paragraphs as follows: "*Claim 1 of Patent No* 487,810 1. Apparatus for planting sugar cane comprising – (a) a planting unit having a relatively small bin (as hereinbefore defined) for receiving a supply of randomly orientated sugar cane billets; (b) a conveyor having a plurality of conveyor elements mounted at spaced locations on an endless support means which is arranged to be driven at a rate proportional to the progress of the apparatus along a planting path; (c) the conveyor having a forward run extending upwardly from the bin to an elevated station such that in operation the billets in the bin are taken up by the conveyor elements as they move through the bin; (d) means for guiding the billets from the elevated station so as to be deposited on the ground with the axis of each billet extending generally in the direction of said planting path; (e) said bin having a floor at an angle to the horizontal and extending downwardly towards the portion of said forward run of the conveyor which extends through the bin **[44]** whereby billets fall towards said forward run; (f) the dimensions and shape of said conveyor elements and said bin being such that in general at least one and sometimes a plurality of billets tend to be taken up by each conveyor element; (g) means for ejecting surplus billets from the conveyor elements located at an elevated position and causing ejected billets to be returned to the bin; (h) a relatively large supply container having walls and a floor; (i) wheel means on which the container can be moved when towed by an associated vehicle; and (j) conveyor means operable selectively to advance a stream of sugar cane billets from a bulk supply of billets randomly orientated in said container to said bin, there being provided; (k) means for mounting said supply container for co-operation with the planting unit whereby in use billets reaching the top of the conveyor means are dropped into the relatively small bin; and (1) the size and shape of the bin being such that when filled normally the billets can move relative to one another in the bin as billets are taken up by the conveyor elements, a supply of billets sufficiently orientated relative to the longitudinal direction of the conveyor elements being available to be taken up by the conveyor elements."

The first element in the claim (para (a)) is "a planting unit having a relatively small bin … for receiving a supply of randomly orientated sugar cane billets". The phrase "relatively small bin" is defined in the specification as follows: "The term 'relatively small supply bin' is hereby defined as meaning that the weight of sugar cane billets capable of being contained when supplied with random orientation in the bin and filled to a normal maximum level is small compared with the weight of one ton". In relation to this bin the specification states that it is thought that by limiting the weight of billets within it, effective orientation of the billets is possible in part due to the tumbling action induced in the mass of billets on operation of the conveyor.

The claim then proceeds to describe in detail the conveyor which extends through the bin, its relation to the bin and the floor of the bin which slopes towards the conveyor. We think it is important to note that in this portion of the claim (paras (b) to (g) inclusive) the patentee is at pains to describe in detail the nature of the conveyor whereas when "conveyor means" are mentioned subsequently, no such detail is provided. It is also important to note that the conveyor as described extends upwardly from the bin so that in operation the billets in the bin are taken up by the conveyor elements as they move through the bin (see para (c)).

The element which the claim then describes is a "relatively large supply container". This expression is obviously used in contra distinction to the "relatively small bin". This container has "walls and a floor". It does not in terms state that the walls extend on all sides of the container. The verb "to contain" in the *Shorter Oxford Dictionary* is defined as including "to hold together, to keep under **[44]** control, restrain, – restrict, confine". "Container" is not separately defined but obviously includes a thing which has that effect.

We do not think the word "container" necessarily requires something which has all its sides enclosed. It is, however, plain that the small bin and the supply container are two quite separate elements in the claim.

According to the claim the apparatus also has "wheel means on which the (supply) container can be moved when towed by an associated vehicle". We find it difficult to regard the existence of wheel means of this character as essential to the claim. This part of the claim could, in our view, properly be regarded as satisfied by provision of means whereby the relatively large supply container can move in co-operation with the planting unit by, for example, being attached to it. The concept of the supply container being "towed" on "wheel means" tends, however, to emphasise that the small bin and the supply container are separate elements in the claim.

Much of the argument surrounded the meaning of the next element in the claim, that is to say, "conveyor means operable selectively to advance a stream of billets from a bulk supply" in the relatively large container to the relatively small bin. We have already noted that the claim does not describe at length the conveyor means as it does the conveyor which operates within the relatively small bin. It does, however, describe the conveyor means by reference to function, that is to say, "to advance a stream of sugar cane billets" from a bulk supply in the container to the bin. Obviously this can be achieved by a conveyor of the type previously described in the claim. Needless to say, if a strict meaning is to be given to the word "conveyor", it would be construed as requiring an apparatus on which the billets are carried from the container to the bin. We are, however, of the view that the phrase "conveyor means" would cover any mechanism which is operable selectively and has the effect of advancing billets from the container to the bin. A mechanism such as a hydraulic arm tilting a container could conceivably answer this description. Again, however, the concept of the connection between the small bin and the supply container being by way of "conveyor means" serves to underline the separate nature of the two.

The final part of the claim which calls for comment is that there be means for mounting the container for co-operation with the planting unit whereby in use billets reaching the top of the conveyor means are dropped into the relatively small bin. Here the debate surrounded the word "top", it being argued that this indicated that what was in mind was a conveyor similar to that depicted in the drawings which are part of the specification, the top being the uppermost point over which the billets are carried from the container and dropped into the bin. However, we are of opinion that the word "top" when used in relation to a conveyor could describe that part of such a mechanism from which the billets drop into a bin [46] even if it be for some reason horizontal or downwardly inclined towards the smaller receptacle. It is, in any event, doubtful whether this represents an essential element of the patentees' claim in which case a mechanical equivalent adopted by another party may not save that party from being held to have infringed.

In the Supreme Court, Connolly J held there had been no infringement because the Binder machine does not have two quite separate containers. In addition to the terms of actual claim (see above) he placed some reliance upon the following passage in the patent specification: "The present invention is based on the concept of delivering a large supply of sugar cane billets, for example, of the order of one ton or more, into a supply container which has conveyor means operable selectively during a planting operation to advance the billets to fall into a small supply bin which co-operates with a conveyor of a planting unit". His Honour's view as to the importance of the quite separate nature of the small bin and the supply container appears from the following passage from his judgment: "One must read the claim as a whole and so read, together with the body of the specification, it defines, on its proper construction, an invention in which the containers are deliberately separated for the purpose of ensuring that an unacceptable weight of billets is not held in the small bin from which the billets are taken up by the discharge conveyor".

There can be no doubt that reading claim 1 as a whole it describes an invention in which there are two containers quite distinct and separate. The relatively small bin is part of the planting unit. The relatively large supply container is described as having walls and a floor and is represented as being capable of being moved on wheel means when towed by an associated vehicle being connected with a small bin by conveyor means operable selectively and being mounted for co-operation with the planting unit which as has been said includes the small bin.

On the present state of authority, it appears to us that the outcome of the appeal ultimately depends upon whether the quite separate nature of the small bin as part of the planting unit and the large container as an associated receptacle should properly be seen as an essential feature of the invention described in the claim which the patentees formulated. If it is not essential, the use of an equivalent mechanism to produce similar results to those claimed for the patented invention will not prevent the respondents from being held to have infringed. On the other hand, if it be an essential feature and is not present in the machine adopted by the respondents, there will be no infringement. Their machine will be outside the area of the monopoly which the patentees saw fit to claim notwithstanding that it adopts and uses concepts and ideas which are incorporated in the patented invention.

[47] The respondents' machine uses a good deal more of the concept of the appellants' invention than was conceded by the respondents' Counsel. It, nevertheless, appears to us that the separate nature of the small bin and the supply container is an essential feature of the patented invention. As has been seen, the separate and distinct nature of the two appears plainly from the words of the patentees' claim and is emphasised and underlined by the nature and description of some of its elements. We agree with Connolly J's conclusion that the separation is a deliberate and essential feature of the actual concept of the patented invention. We are satisfied that the respondents have not adopted that particular feature. It is true that the trough at the front of the defendant's hopper, on the one hand, and the rear part of it with an upwardly moveable floor and rear side, on the other, might if they existed quite separately be properly described as two separate containers. However, when combined as they are in the defendant's machine, they lack this quality. They are, instead, elements of one large container.

It follows that the respondents have not infringed the patent and that the appeal should be dismissed with costs.

## *National Phonograph Co of Australia Ltd v Menck*
Privy Council: Lord McNaughten, Lord Atkinson, Lord Shaw of Dumferline,
Lord Mersey and Lord Robson
[1911] AC 336

A patent grants the patentee a monopoly to exploit the patent. Applied strictly this means that a person who buys a patented product cannot sell or even use that product. In this case Menck had a contract to sell and deal with the goods as a dealer/supplier. The contract came to an end and Menck relied on his rights as the owner of the product to continue dealing with the goods. The Privy Council, in an appeal from the High Court of Australia, considered how the rights of a chattel owner might be reconciled with the rights of the patentee. The judgment of their Lordships was delivered by Lord Shaw of Dumferline.

**Lord Shaw of Dumferline: [347]** To begin with, the general principle, that is to say, the principle applicable to ordinary goods bought and sold, is not here in question. The owner may use and dispose of these as he thinks fit. He may have made a certain contract with the person from whom he bought, and to such a contract he must answer. Simply, however, in his capacity as owner, he is not bound by any restrictions in regard to the use or sale of the goods, and it is out of the question to suggest that restrictive conditions run with the goods. The judgment of Swinfen Eady J in *Taddy v Sterious*[153] is plainly sound. It would be contrary to the public interest and to the security of trade, as well as to the familiar rights attaching to ordinary ownership, if any other principle applied.

The real point of difficulty is the enforcement of that principle without impinging upon something else, namely, the right of property granted by the State and by way of monopoly to a patentee, and his agents and licensees, "to make, use, exercise, and vend the invention, ... in such manner as to him seems meet." This is, of course, with reference to the grant of the right as a sole right, that is to say, put negatively, with a power to exclude all others from the right of production, &c, of the patented article, and also with reference to the imposition of conditions in the transactions of making, using, and vending, which are necessarily an exception by statute to the rules ordinarily prevailing.

In the opinion of their Lordships it is perfectly possible to adjust the incidence of ownership of ordinary goods with the incidence of ownership of patented goods in such a manner as to avoid any collision of principle. In their Lordships' **[348]** view this has been done for a long period of years in England by decisions which are consistent and sound.

[The court canvassed the reasons of the Chief Justice in the Australian High Court.]

There is no doubt that, if the doctrine contended for by the appellants and affirmed by the dissentient judges in the Court below were to be given effect to, namely, that the conditions imposed by the patentee run with the goods, a radical change in the law of personal property would have been made. But if that latter view be an extreme view, and if the restriction upon alienation, use, or otherwise of the chattel purchased be a restriction arising from the fact that the person who has become **[349]** owner has done so with the knowledge brought home to him of the limitation of his rights of alienation or otherwise, then there seems to be no radical change whatever. All that is affirmed is that the general doctrine of absolute freedom of disposal of chattels of an ordinary kind is, in the case of patented chattels, subject to the restriction that the person purchasing them, and in the knowledge of the conditions attached by the patentee, which knowledge is clearly brought home to himself at the time of sale, shall be bound by that knowledge and accept the situation of ownership subject to the limitations. These limitations are merely the respect paid and the effect given to those conditions of transfer of the patented article which the law, laid down by statute, gave the original patentee a power to impose. Whether the law on this head should be changed and the power of sale sub modo should be withdrawn or limited is not a question for a Court. It may be added that where a patented article has been acquired by sale, much, if not all, may be implied as to the consent of the licensee to an undisturbed and unrestricted use thereof. In short, such a sale negatives in the ordinary case the imposition of conditions and the bringing home to the knowledge of the owner of the patented goods that restrictions are laid upon him.

These principles harmonize the rights of the patentee with the rights of the owner. They are not, in their Lordships' opinion, novel, nor did they start, as might appear to be the view of the case law adopted by some of the judges in the Court below, with the judgment of Wills J in the case of *Incandescent Gas Light Co v Cantelo*.[154]

[The court considered some cases preceding *Incandescent Gas Light Co v Cantelo*.]

---

[153] [1904] 1 Ch 358.
[154] 12 Rep Pat Cas 262.

**[350]** Then in 1895 there occurred the case of *Incandescent Gas Light Co v Cantelo*.[155] As the judgment has been much canvassed, and as, in their Lordships' opinion, it forms undoubtedly a leading authority in the law of England, these passages from the opinion of Wills J may be cited: "The sale of a patented article carries with it the right to use it in any way that the purchaser chooses to use it, unless he knows of restrictions. Of course, if he knows of restrictions, and they are brought to his mind at the time of the sale, he is **[351]** bound by them. He is bound by them on this principle: the patentee has the sole right of using and selling the articles, and he may prevent anybody from dealing with them at all. Inasmuch as he has the right to prevent people from using them or dealing in them at all, he has the right to do the lesser thing, that is to say, to impose his own conditions. It does not matter how unreasonable or how absurd the conditions are. It does not matter what they are, if he says at the time when the purchaser proposes to buy or the person to take a licence: 'Mind, I only give you this licence on this condition,' and the purchaser is free to take it or leave it as he likes. If he takes it, he must be bound by the condition. It seems to be common sense, and not to depend upon any patent law or any other particular law." As to the attempt, however, to bind a purchaser to a condition not brought to his notice at the time of the sale, such an attempt cannot succeed. The purchaser "had bought it subject to no condition, and the bringing of a condition to his mind after the sale was completed will not do, and it ought not to do. It would be a most oppressive thing that any person who bought a box of this kind, and who happened to find out before he used the thing that it was covered with a label of this kind – it would be a most oppressive thing if he were bound to observe the conditions which are upon it." So far as this judgment is concerned, it will be seen that it only put with force and clearness what had been the result of authority in England for about at least a quarter of a century on the two main points, namely, first, the effect of sale without conditions, and, secondly, the limitation of the rights of an owner who buys a patented article with knowledge of the conditions. It may be said to have introduced a third element which was really a clearing up of the other two, namely, that the imposition or knowledge of restrictive conditions must occur at the time of sale, and that a purchaser who has made his bargain is not bound to conform to conditions which are attempted to be subsequently imposed upon him.

[The court then considered cases following *Incandescent Light Co v Cantelo*.]

**[353]** In their Lordships' opinion, it is thus demonstrated by a clear course of authority, first, that it is open to a licensee, by virtue of his statutory monopoly, to make a sale sub modo, or accompanied by restrictive conditions which would not apply in the case of ordinary chattels; secondly, that the imposition of these conditions in the case of a sale is not presumed, but, on the contrary, a sale having occurred, the presumption is that the full right of ownership was meant to be vested in the purchaser; while thirdly, the owner's rights in a patented chattel will be limited if there is brought home to him the knowledge of conditions imposed, by the patentee or those representing the patentee, upon him at the time of sale. It will be observed that these propositions do not support the principles relied upon in their absolute sense by any of the judges of the Court below. On the one hand, the patented goods are not, simply because of their nature as chattels, sold free from restriction. Whether that restriction affects the purchaser is in most cases assumed in the negative from the fact of sale, but depends upon whether it entered the conditions upon which the owner acquired the goods. On the other hand, restrictive conditions do not, in the extreme sense put, run with the goods, because the goods are patented.

Applying these principles to the present case, the result is this: the respondent, Mr Menck, has been acquitted of every charge of violation of contract which was laid against him by the appellants. He has also succeeded in shewing that the claim made by the

[155] 12 Rep Pat Cas 262.

appellants as patentees was in its nature extreme and unsound in law. But he made this mistake: he assumed that, being guiltless of violation of contract, he was as free as an ordinary member of the public who had acquired possession of articles embodying the appellants' patent. His misfortune, however, consists in this, that by the very fact that **[354]** he entered into contractual relations with the appellants he has become seized with the knowledge of the conditions on which they dispose of their goods, and he is not free to propone the plea that such conditions have not been brought home to him. When he therefore announced his intention to deal in these articles as ordinary articles of commerce, he must be held to have pursued a mistaken course, the course of treating himself as an unrestricted instead of a restricted trader. In this particular case the result may involve some hardship to him, but their Lordships cannot see their way to a departure from the principle that a restriction rests upon a purchaser of goods which are covered by a grant of patent, and which have come into the possession of a purchaser in the full knowledge of the restrictions imposed by the patentee upon their disposal. Notwithstanding the most able presentment of his case by his counsel, Mr Levinson, their Lordships are of opinion that in the one particular referred to it cannot be given effect to.

## *Root Quality Pty Ltd v Root Control Technologies Pty Ltd*
Federal Court of Australia: Finkelstein J
(2000) 177 ALR 231

The invention in question was Root Control Technologies' pot plant container for plants which were to be transplanted, usually in a commercial setting. The question was whether there had been an infringement despite the differences between Root Control technologies and Root Quality's pots. Finkelstein J, sitting alone in the Federal Court, applied a purposive test to determine this question.

**Finkelstein J:**

[The judge summarised the law on construction of specifications and concluded that in *Catnic Components Ltd v Hill and Smith Ltd*[156] Lord Diplock "was not only dealing with principles of construction but also setting out the proper approach to questions of infringement". The judge continued:]

> **[242]** 42. In this connection reference should be made to *Improver Corporation v Remington Consumer Products Ltd* [1990] FSR 181, where Hoffmann J (as his Lordship then was) said that when the issue is whether a feature embodied in an alleged infringement, which falls outside the primary or literal meaning of a claim (a feature which he called the 'variant'), was nevertheless within its language as properly interpreted, the court should ask "Lord Diplock's three questions": (1) Does the variant have a material effect upon the way the invention works? If yes, the variant is outside the claim. If no: – (2) Would this (that is, that the variant had no material effect) have been obvious at the date of publication of the patent to a reader skilled in the art? If no, the variant is outside the claim. If yes: – (3) Would the reader skilled in the art nevertheless have understood from the language of the claim that the patentee intended that strict compliance with the primary meaning was an essential requirement of the invention? If yes, the variant is outside the claim.
>
> 43. It must always be borne in mind that an element of a claim that appears not to be necessary for the invention may nevertheless be regarded by the patentee as essential for some reason that is not apparent: *Société Technique de Pulverisation Step v Emson*

---

156 [1982] RPC 183.

*Europe Ltd* [1993] RPC 513 at 522. Accordingly, the court should act with some care before it broadens a claim in reliance upon a purposive construction of the words used in the specification.

44. It seems that the following is the position that now pertains. Before *Catnic*, the subject matter of a patent was defined in accordance with the literal meaning of the claim. Nevertheless, if the substance (pith and marrow) or mechanical equivalent of the claim was taken, there would be an infringement. The rules were made necessary to render patents useful. The change brought about by *Catnic* was that a patent specification is to be given a purposive and not a literal construction. The question to be determined under this approach is whether the patentee intended strict compliance with an element of the invention to be an essential requirement of the invention. On this basis the former approach, that is, whether the "pith and marrow" or substance of a claim has been taken, is no longer necessary.

45. In Australia the so-called 'purposive approach' to construction has been adopted (see *Populin v HB Nominees Pty Ltd and Binder* (1982) 41 ALR 471; *Nesbit Evans Group Australia Pty Ltd v Impro Ltd* (1997) 39 IPR 56) although some cases imply that the former approach can still have application: see *Populin* at 475-477; see also JW Dwyer and A Dufty (eds) *Lahore on Patents Trademarks and Related Rights* (1996) pars 18,135 and 18,140. On the other hand when the *Improver* questions are posed and answered, it is difficult to see what can be achieved by recourse to the "pith and marrow" approach.

46. With the above considerations in mind I turn back to the question whether each root guiding recess must converge in a hole. To place myself in the position of being able to answer this question from the point of view of someone with a practical interest in the subject matter, I have evidence from a number of witnesses to which reference will be made.

47. If the language of the claim is clear, then the meaning of that language cannot change by reference to what appears in the specification. But the words of the claim must read in light of the specification as a whole and given a meaning in that context. Once construed it is not permissible to extend or narrow **[243]** the ambit of the claim by reference to the specification: see generally *Conoco Specialty Products (Inc) v Merpro Montassa Ltd* [1994] FSR 99 at 106 and the cases there cited. Thus if, expressly or by necessary implication, something is indicated in the descriptive part of the specification to be an essential feature of the invention, the patentee is bound by that assertion: *JK Smit & Sons Inc v McClintock* [1940] SCR 279 at 295. Likewise, if a feature of the invention is said to be inessential, the court should not go behind that statement.

48. The approach that I will adopt is to consider the claim in its unamended form to discern what was intended and then to consider whether the meaning has changed following the amendments. Usually, the task of construction is best undertaken by taking the claim as it currently stands and ascertaining its meaning, having regard to the nature of any amendments made. In this case, for reasons which will become apparent, a different approach is called for. It is not an approach which, I believe, will lead to error.

49. The proper construction of the specification is a matter of law: see generally *Dècor Corporation Pty Ltd v Dart Industries Inc* (1988) 13 IPR 385 at 400. It is, however, a task that must be undertaken through the eyes of the person to whom the specification is directed, that is the person skilled in the art or science to which the specification relates: *Vidal Dyes Syndicate Ltd v Levinstein Ltd and Read Holliday & Sons Ltd* (1912) 29 RPC 245 at 272; *Osram Lamps v Pope Electric Lamp Co* (1917) 34 RPC 369 at 391. It is this person who may give expert evidence to inform the court what is the generally accepted meaning of technical terms and also to explain how things actually work: *American Cyanamid Company v Ethicon Ltd* [1979] RPC 215 at 254.

50. There will be cases, however, where expert evidence is not admissible on the question of construction. Sometimes the text of the specification will be couched in

language with which all lawyers are familiar, containing no technical or trade terms calling for explanation. In that event the court of construction can determine for itself, unassisted by experts, the relevant meaning, as it does with any other instrument. In its unamended form the specification of the patent in suit falls into this category at least so far as concerns the issue presently under consideration.

51. Whether each recess must end in a hole is the subject of express comment in the specification. An embodiment of the invention is described by reference to a number of drawings. According to those drawings, especially figures 1, 2 and 3, each root guiding recess leads to a hole. However, the specification states: "It is not essential that each recess leads towards a respective hole, but this is the preferred arrangement". Further, according to the specification when the strip is overlapped, in order to hold the ends in their overlapped condition a fastener is required. Examples of various fasteners are given. One is a tie which passes through a number of aligned holes. These holes are no longer capable of air pruning the roots of a plant.

52. There can be no doubt that, in their unamended form, it was not an essential aspect of the claims that each protuberance end in a hole. First, the wording of the principal claims (claims 1, 4 and 8) expressly provided that only some, and not all, recesses should converge to a hole. Second, there is the express statement to that effect in the descriptive part of the specification. Finally, as the descriptive part shows, some of the holes may be blocked by a releasable fastening device.

[244] 53. Have the amendments brought about a change in construction? The first point to note about these amendments, taking claim 1 as the example, is that a literal reading of the claim, in isolation from the remainder of the specification, now requires each recess to converge to a hole. In my opinion, however, it does not necessarily follow that an element that had not been an essential requirement of the invention has become essential. In the first place, the fact that when read literally the claim requires each recess to end in a hole, is not enough for the skilled addressee to conclude that this feature is essential. To determine whether that is truly so, other matters must be taken into account. In the second place, although the claims were amended, there was no amendment to the statement in the specification that this was not essential to the invention. While that statement remains in the specification it cannot be ignored unless it is possible to conclude that the amendments are so inconsistent with the statement such that the statement must yield to the new language. An analogy might be drawn with an implied amendment of a statute. In reality, however, there is no inconsistency. The amended claims can be read, as claims sometimes are, as containing the features of the preferred embodiment of the invention.

54. The cross-respondents say that one object of the amendments to claim 1 was to restrict the scope of the claim to a strip of material which had, as an essential feature, each truncated conical form ending in a hole. They refer to what was said by counsel for the patentee on the amendment application to reinforce this point. I do not accept that the specification can be construed by reference to direct statements of intention. A specification is addressed not to the public but to persons skilled in the particular art of the patent under review. In construing the patent, the addressee is not entitled to interrogate the inventor nor to take into account what the inventor may have said about his invention. *A fortiori* in the case of an assignee who amends the specification.

55. Nevertheless, I accept that as a result of the amendment, the issue is not as clear as it was beforehand. Therefore I intend to consider also whether strict compliance with the feature is required by reference to the questions suggested in *Improver*. To undertake that task it will be necessary to consider the matter by reference to the alleged infringing products. It is only by having regard to those products that the particular "variant" can be identified. It will also be appropriate to consider the evidence on the effect of the variant.

56. In early 1997 the original proprietor of the patent in suit, Ronneby Tree Farm Pty Ltd, was placed under administration pursuant to Part 5.3A of the *Corporations Law.* On 20 January 1997 Mr Lawton, who until then was a director of the company, was dismissed from office. Shortly thereafter he took charge of Root Quality. By this I mean that Mr Lawton became responsible for the affairs of Root Quality although he did not become one of its directors. As he said: "I do all of the physical activities of Root Quality personally. I conduct all of the manufacturing, the design, the sales and the accounting". Being an undischarged bankrupt, Mr Lawton could not accept office as a director of Root Quality: see s 229(1) of the *Corporations Law*, being the provision in force in 1997; see now s 206B(3).

57. Since September or October 1997 (Mr Lawton said that it was "in the spring of '97") Root Quality has been in the business of selling plant growing containers or panels that can be assembled to form a plant growing container. The features of these containers, or the panels from which they are constructed, have changed over the years. It is important to consider these changes. For **[245]** convenience I will refer to the different versions of the container, or the panels for that container, by the description employed by the parties, although at times there was some confusion concerning which particular container had a particular designation. Root Quality refers to each of its containers as the Rocketpot. Four different versions of the Rocketpot have been developed. Each is given a different designation, from Mark 1 through to Mark 4. Only three of the containers are the subject of the infringement claim.

58. The first container manufactured and sold by Root Quality is referred to as the Mark 1 Rocketpot. The evidence shows that this container has all of the features of claim 1 of the patent in suit, including the fact that it was made from a single panel. For a number of reasons Root Quality discontinued production of the Mark 1 container in about January 1998. Mr Lawton said that one reason was his concern that the container might infringe the patent in suit. Be that as it may, Root Control brings no claim for infringement in respect of the Mark 1.

59. The Mark 2 Rocketpot container is different from the Mark 1 in that it is assembled from more than one panel. Mr Lawton sometimes referred to it as a "two panel product", although the container is usually made from three or four panels. However, nothing turns on that point. Each panel contains all of the features of the strip referred to in claim 1 except the following. The overlapping ends of each panel are held in their overlapping position by two screw threaded fasteners. The fasteners are inserted through the aligned holes on each of the nested cusps of the overlapping edge portions.

60. The Mark 3 Rocketpot container came onto the market in August 1998. It has the features of the Mark 2 with one exception. It has two rows of root guiding recesses that do not end in a hole. Those rows are the upper two rows of the container in its assembled condition.

61. Mr Lawton explained the importance of leaving the upper two rows of recesses without holes. He said that a plant must be flooded with water at the time of planting. The removal of the holes enables full water saturation to take place by allowing water to be retained within the container. This was said to be of great value to the life of a plant. Mr Lawton said "top up nursery watering and after-market watering are made much quicker and more effective by omission of the holes. In hostile after-market storage areas it can make a major contribution to tree survival."

62. There is both truth and exaggeration in what Mr Lawton said. The evidence shows that when a plant is placed into a container, potting mixture is put around the plant and sometimes mulch is placed on the surface of the mixture. The container is filled to the brim with potting mixture because the mixture consolidates and after a short time settles to a level of approximately one inch below the top of the container . Upon being placed into the container the plant must be watered. However working practices differ. Some

nurseries flood the newly transplanted plant by using a hand-held hose. Most nurseries now use an automated or computer controlled dripper or spray watering system that does not flood the container.

63. I accept that the absence of holes is a useful feature. But the degree of usefulness has been significantly overstated by Mr Lawton. Mr Davidson, a tree surgeon, was called by the cross-respondents to give evidence. He explained that the initial flood watering takes place immediately after the plant has been placed in the container. At this time the surface level of the potting mixture is at the top of the container. Accordingly, the absence of holes will have little effect on the capacity of the container to retain water. However, as the surface level drops the **[246]** capacity to retain water will increase. Mr Davidson said that some retail nurseries still hand water their plants rather than use an automated sprinkler system. For those nurseries watering will be a little easier when the two top rows of the container do not have cusps that end in a hole.

64. Important as regards the Mark 3 Rocketpot container is the fact that the absence of holes in the top rows of the container will not affect the air root pruning that is achieved by the use of the container. The reason is obvious. Once the surface level of the potting mixture settles below the top of the container roots will not extend to the vicinity of the top two rows. The evidence also shows that if one or two of the overlapping holes are taken up with a fastening device this will have no effect on the growth of the root system.

65. There is one aspect of the Mark 3 Rocketpot container that requires separate comment. Mr Lawton gave evidence that Root Quality did not sell single panels from which a Mark 3 container could be made. He said that the panels were sold in sets of either three or four, dependent upon the size of the container that was required by the purchaser. There was no evidence of Root Quality having sold a single panel so that a purchaser could make one small container. But there was evidence of a threat to do so. After the commencement of this proceeding, the former solicitors for Root Quality wrote a letter dated 9 November 1998 to Root Quality's patent attorneys as follows:

> We are instructed by Mr Peter Lawton that he has recently developed a new version of the Rocketpot root container which will be displayed by representatives of Root Quality Pty Ltd at an industrial exhibition which commences this Thursday.
>
> Our client's patent attorneys have advised that the new product does not infringe the SpringRing patent owned by your client. However we would be pleased to receive your opinion regarding the same prior to the unveiling of the product in public. A sample of the smaller size of the new product will be available for inspection at our office.

66. Mr Schlicht, an attorney with Phillips Ormonde & Fitzpatrick, took up the invitation to inspect the sample. He described the container that he was shown as a Rocketpot container with the two top rows of root guiding recesses unpunched. He said that it was made from a single panel. He took possession of the sample but unfortunately did not retain it.

67. Mr Lawton was asked how this particular version of the Mark 3 Rocketpot container had come into existence. He said that his solicitor had requested him to produce it for the purpose of discussions with Mr Schlicht. I do not accept this explanation. Mr Lawton also said that the sample was never displayed at an industry exhibition. That may be true. It seems to me that Mr Lawton originally intended to sell a single panel version of the Mark 3 Rocketpot but decided not to do so for fear that it might infringe the patent in suit.

68. The Mark 4 Rocketpot container seems to have been first manufactured some time during 1999, but the evidence is unclear on this point. In all relevant respects it has the same features as the Mark 3, although its precise status is unclear. In an affidavit Mr Lawton deposed that "the Mark 4 is being implemented progressively". Yet during his cross-examination he said that production was limited to an "experimental batch" and

that it was not intended for it to be manufactured for sale. There is not sufficient evidence for me to resolve this inconsistency, but at least I am entitled to infer that there is a threat to sell the Mark 4 Rocketpot.

[247] 69. With this background in mind I now come back to the *Improver* questions. For the purposes of those questions there are two variants. The first is that some aligned holes are taken up by the screw fastening means. The second variant is that two rows of recesses do not end in a hole. The first question is whether these variants have a material effect on the way in which the invention works. The specification says that "the main aims of the invention are to provide containers which guide primary roots radially outwardly towards holes in the container walls. As the roots approach the holes they are air pruned resulting in secondary roots branching from the length of the primary roots and thereby forming a well matted and cohesive root ball which is ideal for transplantation." From what I have already said it is clear that the variants will not affect the way in which the invention will facilitate the growth of the root ball in the desired fashion. In the case of the Mark 2 Rocketpot there is a loss of only six or eight air pruning holes and that is not sufficient to affect the capacity of the container to function as a root pruning container in the desired manner. With the plants grown in either the Mark 3 or Mark 4 Rocketpot, the roots will not extend to the areas of the upper two rows above the surface of the potting mixture.

70. The second question is whether the fact that the variants do not have a material effect on the invention would be known to the skilled addressee. Here I must say some more about this person. The identity of the skilled addressee occupied a little time during the hearing. Both parties proceeded on the basis that the skilled addressee was not to be found in one discipline, but in two. The skilled addressee, or the judge adopting the mantle of the skilled addressee, is relevant for a variety of purposes in patent law. He is the person to whom the patent is addressed and who must construe it. He is the person whose knowledge will determine whether a patent is novel. He is the person who will judge whether a patent is obvious. The skilled addressee has been given various descriptions. Sometimes he is the "notional skilled addressee" (*Electricity Trust of South Australia v Zellweger Uster Pty Ltd* (1986) 7 IPR 491 at 500), sometimes the "uninventive skilled worker in the particular field" (*Leonardis v Sartas No 1 Pty Ltd* (1996) 67 FCR 126 at 146), sometimes the "non-inventive worker in the field" (*Wellcome Foundation Ltd v VR Laboratories (Aust) Pty Ltd* (1981) 148 CLR 262 at 270; *Minnesota Mining and Manufacturing Company v Beiersdorf (Australia) Ltd* (1980) 144 CLR 253 at 293), sometimes the "person skilled in the art" (*Genentech Inc v Wellcome Foundation Ltd* (1989) 15 IPR 423 at 545; *Tetra Molectric Ltd v Japan Imports Ltd* [1976] RPC 547 at 583) and sometimes the "non-inventive hypothetical skilled addressee" (*Innovative Agricultural Products Pty Ltd v Crawshaw* (unreported, Federal Court of Australia, Lee J, 19 August 1996 at par 90)).

71. Generally speaking the skilled addressee is the person who works in the art or science with which the invention is connected. In *Plimpton v Malcolmson* (1876) 3 Ch D 531 Jessel MR said (at 556):

> What is meant is that if [the invention] is a manufacture connected with a particular trade, the people in the trade shall know something about it; if it is a thing connected with a chemical invention, people conversant with chemistry shall know something about it.

In *Catnic* Lord Diplock said (at 242) that skilled addressees are "those likely to have a practical interest in the subject matter of [the] invention". A variety of people may have that interest. There are those who might wish to make or construct the invention, those who may wish to compound the invention and [248] those who may wish to use the invention. The skilled addressee seems to me to be a relative expression which does not identify any specific person. Because the patent is directed to a person interested in making, constructing, compounding or using the invention (see eg s 27(3)(b) of the *Patent Act 1993* (Canada); *International Standard Electric Corporation v Ooms* 157 F 2d 73 (1946)), this hypothetical person, the patent lawyer's "reasonable man", may be required to be skilled in more than one art. Such a person might be thought of as the composite being, mentioned by Buckley LJ in *Tetra Molectric*, above, at 583. It may be preferable not to search for a composite addressee but a team whose combined skills are to be employed. In *General Tire & Rubber Company v Firestone Tyre & Rubber Company Ltd* [1972] RPC 457 at 485, Sachs LJ said:

> The construction of these documents is a function of the court, being a matter of law, but, since documents of this nature are almost certain to contain technical material, the court must, by evidence, be in the position of a person of the kind to whom the document is addressed, that is to say, a person skilled in the relevant art at the relevant date. If the art is one having a highly developed technology, the notional skilled reader to whom the document is addressed may not be a single person but a team, whose combined skills would normally be employed in that art in interpreting and carrying into effect instructions such as those which are contained in the document to be construed.

72. Although for some purposes the skilled addressee must be a team, in considering whether it would have been obvious that the variants do not have a material effect on the way in which the invention works, the relevant member of the team, if there need be a team, is the person who intends to use the invention. This would be a horticulturalist or nurseryman. A number of witnesses had the relevant expertise, including Drs May and Yau. Dr May said that the alleged infringing containers "would function, in the sense of root control, in exactly the same manner as the … SpringRing container". Dr Yau gave evidence to the same effect. Their evidence on this aspect was not challenged. So, we have an affirmative answer to the second question.

73. The final *Improver* question is whether the patent specification makes it obvious to the skilled addressee that the variants could not have been intended to be excluded from what is specified in the claim. The skilled addressee in this case would find the clear statement in the specification that it is inessential that each recess end in a hole. He would discover that the specification contemplates that some holes would be taken up with a fastening device. He would be aware of the amendments and the potential for repugnancy. But he would note that when the claims were amended the remainder of the specification remained intact. The skilled addressee would conclude, as I do on his behalf, that the variants were not intended to be excluded from the claim.

74. So far what I have said leads to the conclusion that unless the patent in suit is invalid, selling or offering to sell panels for the Mark 2 and Mark 3 Rocketpot is an infringement of the patent, and threatening to sell panels for the Mark 4 Rocketpot is a threat to infringe the patent. The conduct would infringe the first claim according to the principle that selling the component parts of an article which is protected by a patent amounts, in substance, to selling the article: *Rotocrop International Ltd v Genbourne Ltd* [1982] FSR 241 at 259. This is not a case, such as *Walker v Alemite Corporation* (1933) 49 CLR 643, where only some components of an article are sold. In *Walker* Dixon J said (at 658) that the exclusive property in a combination invention is not infringed by the sale of the components. That particular rule does not apply when all of the components of **[249]** a combination invention are sold by a person who knows and intends that the ultimate purchaser would assemble the invention. The conduct would infringe the twelfth claim because the panels can be formed into a container. This is true both in cases of a single panel, although the formation would not be easy, and multiple panels.

## *Pinefair Pty Ltd v Bedford Industries Rehabilitation Association Inc*
### Federal Court of Australia: Foster, Mansfield and Goldberg JJ
### (1998) 87 FCR 458

The invention in question was a roll of timber garden edging comprising sliced treated pine joined together by "elongated" wire. The appellants, attempting to avoid patent infringement, manufactured a similar product but in the final stages of manufacture cut the "elongated" material holding their pine logs together. Both parties agreed that the final product was not an infringement of the patent but the respondents successfully argued that the fact that the logs were joined by the elongated material during the process of manufacture amounted to an infringing exploitation of the patent.

**Mansfield J: [465]** The product the subject of the Patent in its primary claim was identified by the learned trial judge as consisting of seven integers as follows:
"1.  Edging material suitable for retaining earth comprising an assembly of a plurality of post elements …
2.  each of generally half-round cross-section …
3.  with side edges defined by the intersection of a substantially flat rear face and a curved front face …
4.  the elements being disposed in side-by-side relationship with the side edges of adjacent elements either abutting or being slightly spaced …
5.  elongated band means connected by connecting means to each element …
6.  whereby the assembly is able to be deformed about axes parallel to the said elements but not significantly about transverse axes …
7.  said band means either extending along the rear face of the elements in which case the connecting means comprises staples interconnecting the band means with the said rear face of each element or passing through holes extending laterally through each element substantially parallel to the rear face thereof, which holes constitute the said connecting means."

As the matter was argued, it is not necessary to address separately the other claims in the Patent.

It was common ground on the appeal that the final form of the Pinefair product did not infringe the Patent because there was no longer an elongated plastic band joining each post element. The process of slicing that band on the flat surface or rear of the post elements after the stapling step, and after the **[466]** cutting of the 600mm length post elements into four by 150mm (or other length as required) post elements, was introduced after the Deed, and after the events leading up to the Deed. It was introduced precisely to achieve that end. It serves no useful functional purpose.

Thus it was necessary for the respondent to establish that the Patent was infringed by the appellants in the course of their manufacturing process. That gave rise to the need to address firstly whether a product patent could be infringed during the process of manufacture of a product which did not itself infringe the product patent, and if so secondly, whether in the particular circumstances of this matter such infringement had occurred. It is plain that the Patent is a product patent, rather than a process patent …

The respondent acknowledged that, for present purposes, the relevant elements of that definition were the terms "make" or "use". Its case on appeal was based upon the proposition that the appellants, in the course of manufacturing the Pinefair product, did make or use the product the subject of the Patent, and so had infringed the respondent's exclusive right to exploit its invention.

In my view, in an appropriate case the process of manufacture of a particular product may infringe a product patent, by making or using the product the subject of the product patent during that process. It is really no more than a question of fact whether there has been a relevant "making" or "use" of the patented product in the process of manufacture of the ultimate non-infringing product. For example, if the manufacturing process of the respondent involved manually slicing the elongated band joining the post elements only immediately before packing and distribution for sale, there would clearly be a time at which there would be in existence the product the subject of the patent itself then suitable for use as garden edging, as it would satisfy each of the seven integers of the Patent.

The 'infringing importation' cases are generally concerned with the question of whether that which is done or proposed to be done within the jurisdiction in respect of an imported product constitutes an infringing "use" of the imported product within the jurisdiction: *Smith Kline & French Laboratories Ltd v Attorney-General (New Zealand* [1991] 2 NZLR 560; *Saccharin Corporation v Anglo-Continental Chemical Works Ltd* (1900) 17 RPC 307; *Dunlop Pneumatic Tyre Co Ltd v British & Colonial Motor Car Co* (1901) 18 RPC 313; *Pfizer v Ministry of Health* [1965] AC 512. In those cases, the **[467]** manufacture of the imported product, if effected within the jurisdiction, would itself infringe the patent in suit.

In *Saccharin*, the Court also addressed whether the manufacture of the product itself, if done within the jurisdiction, would constitute infringement of the patent in suit. Buckley J said (at 319):

"If the patented process were the last stage in the production of the article sold, the importation and sale of the product would, in my opinion, plainly be an infringement. Does it make it any the less an infringement that the article produced and sold is manufactured by the use of the patented process which is subjected to certain other processes? In my opinion it does not. By the sale of saccharin, in the course of the production of which the patented process is used, the Patentee is deprived of some part of the whole profit and advantage of the invention, and the importer is indirectly making use of the invention."

In *Beecham Group Ltd v Bristol Laboratories Ltd* [1978] RPC 153, similar issues were addressed. In that case, one particular issue was whether the use within the jurisdiction of the imported article infringed a particular product patent because, in the course of manufacture of the imported article, the article which was the subject of the product patent was made as an intermediate product in that manufacture. Russell LJ delivering the judgment of the Court of Appeal (Russell and Stamp LJJ and Brightman J) concluded that the defendants' production of a certain chemical made use of two patented products of the plaintiff and one patented process of the plaintiff, and so infringed the relevant product patents and process patent. Their Lordships did not regard legislative changes to have altered that conclusion, and said (at 185-186):

"The truth of the matter, as we see it, is that the law, in applying the language of the grant by letters patent of the monopoly to protect the invention of a new process for producing an article or substance, has found it, and established it as, a common-sense necessity to embrace in that language the product without which the process is a meaningless exercise. In our judgment, the cases relied upon by the plaintiff remain good law, and a claim to the product of a claimed process is not necessary. (We do not, of course, refer to a case in which the product per se is novel but might be produced by a different process: there a product claim would be valuable)."

That case went on appeal to the House of Lords. The appeal was dismissed. The speech of Lord Diplock, with which Viscount Dilhorne, and Lords Simon of Glaisdale, Salmon and Fraser of Tullybelton agreed, recognised the particular issues in the following terms (at 200):

"In the instant case Beechams have invited your Lordships to extend it from claims for processes for manufacturing products to claims for new products in themselves; so that if a patented product is used as a starting point in the manufacture of the imported article or formed as an intermediary at any stage in the course of its manufacture, this constitutes an infringement of the claim to the patented product, even though no part of the process of manufacture of the imported article infringed any claim to a new process by the patentee, and even though the imported article is wholly different in composition, characteristics and usefulness from the patented product."

His Lordship then affirmed the conclusion of the Court of Appeal (at 203), but with the reservation that the lawful use overseas of a product in the **[468]** manufacture of a different product, then imported and sold, should not, within the jurisdiction, constitute infringement of a product patent for the first product. Lord Simon addressed that issue in his short additional speech in the following terms (at 204):

"I would have thought that some formula might be devised whereby the Saccharin doctrine could be extended so as to cover, say, 6-APA playing a significant part in the manufacture of a semi-synthetic penicillin, but not of a wholly different product like, say, glue."

In the present circumstance, where it is contended that the product the subject of the Patent was manufactured by the appellants, and that some unnecessary embellishment or alteration to it was then made by a further manufacturing step designed to avoid the consequence that the product as ultimately manufactured infringed the Patent, such considerations as concerned their Lordships in *Beecham* do not arise. If the infringement claim is made out as a matter of fact, it will be because, whatever the manufacturing process, there was manufactured in that process the product the subject of the Patent as an integral step. There is no scope in the present circumstances for the stage at which the product the subject of the Patent comes into existence during that manufacturing process, if it does, to be described as unimportant or trifling (cf *Wilderman v FW Berk & Co Ltd* [1925] Ch 116) or as constituting an insignificant part of or step in the Pinefair product as ultimately manufactured.

The question, in my judgment simply becomes one of whether as a matter of fact the product the subject of the Patent was made or used by the appellants in the course of manufacturing the Pinefair product. As Rich J said in *Walker v Alemite Corporation* (1933) 49 CLR 643 at 650, the question "entirely depends upon the claiming clauses in the [patent] specification".

It seems to me that there are three possible stages at which the product the subject of the Patent may have been made in the course of that manufacturing process. The first such stage is the stage between the stapling tower from which emerges 600mm post elements connected by the elongated plastic band and the point where the post elements are cut into shorter lengths. Between those points, if the manufacturing program was to produce 150mm post elements, the elongated plastic banding would comprise four separate ribbons of banding which would flow back to the roller of elongated plastic bands. The second such stage is the stage between the cutting function, where the 600mm post elements are cut into 150mm post elements or other lengths as required, and the slicing function where the elongated band is sliced at the flat surface of each post element so as to remove the "elongated band" feature of the integers of the primary claim under the Patent. The third such stage is that between the stapling tower and the point where the slicing function occurs, that is the combination of stages one and two described above.

I do not think that the third stage as described above could constitute the making or use of the product the subject of the Patent. As counsel for the appellants submitted, the assembly of post elements at that point would not be suitable for retaining earth because (assuming the other integers of the claim were met) there would be a product comprising a plurality of post elements connected by elongated banding, but comprising a mix of

600mm post elements and with four tails of 150mm post elements (or a lesser number if the manufacture was for some different length of post element) flapping loosely. In my judgment that compendious "product" is clearly not suitable for retaining [469] earth, and so does not satisfy the first of the integers identified by the trial judge.

The question is not so readily answered in respect of the first and second stages which I have described above.

I note that the learned trial judge said as to the word "make":

"The word "make" is an ordinary English word with wide meaning. *Terrell on The Law of Patents* 14th Ed 1994, p 176 observes that for this reason, no difficulty should arise with the word. Where the invention is a product, what must be made is the whole product, not constituent parts, and the "making" is not complete until the final step is carried out which results in the complete infringing article: see Lahore at para 18,205. In the present case, the final step to complete the infringing article has occurred before the cutter severs the plastic strip at each post element."

After considering authorities as to the meaning of the word "use", his Honour said:

"In the present case the creation of edging material that has all the integers of claim 1 of the Patent as a step in the manufacture of the Pinefair product constitutes a "use" of the invention as the respondents are taking commercial advantage of the invention to advance them in the market place, even though at the point of sale the Pinefair product has been altered so that it no longer possesses all the integers of the claim."

I respectfully agree in each instance with his Honour's observations.

His Honour concluded that the making of edging material having all the integers of the primary claim under the Patent and its subsequent use in the manufacture of the Pinefair product was neither an unimportant nor a trifling part of that manufacturing process and so infringed the Patent.

In respect of the first stage described above, each of the seven integers comprising the primary claim under the Patent exists as a matter of fact. In reaching that conclusion, I have had careful regard to the submissions of counsel for the appellants on that question. There is no specification in the patent that the post elements be of a particular height. Nothing was identified in the material before the Court to suggest that post elements of 600mm in length were not within the description "edging material suitable for retaining earth". As Goldberg J's description of the appellants' manufacturing process indicates, between the stapling tower and the point where the post elements were cut into shorter lengths, there was a plurality of post elements. The other integers of that claim are also met. It was put, however, that the product the subject of the Patent was not "made" nor "used" at that point in the manufacturing process of the respondents because there was never a product capable of use, without more, during the process. That is because the "product" was, at one end, still attached to the roll of plastic banding which passed under the stapling tower for stapling to the post elements and, at the other end, was attached to four 150mm strips of post elements after the cutting process which themselves then (after the elongated band was sliced) extended until cut into marketable lengths. The exploitation of a patent may occur notwithstanding that the product the subject of a patent is not reproduced in its ultimate commercial form or forms: *Pfitzner* at 571-573; *Smith Kline & French Laboratories Ltd v Attorney-General (New Zealand)*. In the latter case, there was an importation of certain drug samples to apply for and obtain consent from the Minister of Health to their distribution. The imported drug samples embodied the invention in the appellant's patent, but the distribution was not to occur until after that patent had expired. It was held, [470] nevertheless, that the patent was infringed as the conduct complained of constituted a "use" of the patented invention. Cooke P said (at 562):

"In my opinion, as a matter of the ordinary use of language, whether now or (one would suppose) in earlier centuries, to send an embodiment of the invention to a government authority for approval is plainly a use of it. Without doubt, too, Douglas acted for the commercial advantage or springboard of being more ready to launch into the market when the patent expired. This seems to me an infringement of both the letter and the spirit of the grant."

Hardie Boys J said (at 566):

"These cases serve to delineate not only the limits of the experiment principle, but also the bounds of permissible activity, between what is and what is not use for commercial advantage. Doubtless experimentation will usually have an ultimate commercial objective; where it ends and infringement begins must often be a matter of degree. If the person concerned keeps his activities to himself, and does no more than further his own knowledge or skill, even though commercial advantage may be his final goal, he does not infringe. But if he goes beyond that, and uses the invention or makes it available to others, in a way that serves to advance him in the actual market place, then he infringes, for the market place is the sole preserve of the patentee."

From each of those judgments there emerges in my view an appropriate focus upon the market for the product the subject of the Patent as the sole preserve of the respondent, so that the manufacture and use of that product to the commercial advantage of the appellants would infringe the Patent. It is apparent that the appellants were taking commercial advantage of the Patent. They were doing so not in some peripheral or transitory way. Their manufacturing process ultimately included a step by reason of which the Pinefair product did not infringe the Patent. It was a cosmetic rather than a functional step. Until then, looking at the "spirit" of the Patent in suit, the product the subject of the Patent had been brought into existence and had been used towards the Pinefair product as ultimately marketed. The fact that, at this stage of the manufacturing process, an object existed which required the simple process of cutting the elongated band to be commercially marketable does not, in my judgment, lead to a conclusion that the product the subject of the Patent in the circumstances was not made, or was not used.

The same process of reasoning, with one qualification, leads me to the view that the second stage of the manufacture of the Pinefair product described above, namely its state between the point where the post elements are cut into shorter lengths and the point where the elongated band connecting those post elements is sliced at the post elements, also involves an infringement of the Patent by the making and use of the product the subject of the Patent at that stage.

The one qualification is that it is not totally clear to me whether the proximity of the points at which the post elements are cut into shorter lengths and at which the elongated connecting band at the rear of the post elements is cut is such that there is no "plurality of post elements" between those points. The learned trial judge did not need to make a specific finding on that topic, but it appears probable from the evidence that there are either two or three post elements between those points at the time when the next adjoining post elements to them are being respectively cut into shorter lengths at one end **[471]** and having the elongated connected band sliced to remove its 'elongated' characteristic at the other. If that were so, in my judgment, the second stage of the appellants' manufacturing process which I have described above would also constitute an infringement of the Patent. In the light of my reasons and conclusion above, it is not necessary finally to decide that issue ...

## *Leonardis v Theta Developments Pty Ltd*
### Supreme Court of South Australia: Williams J
### (2001) 51 IPR 546

The defendants supplied building spacers with instructions for use. Williams J held that this amounted to an infringement under s 117 of the combination patent for both the product and the process. He explicitly rejected Gummow J's interpretation of ss 117 and 13 in *Rescare Ltd v Anaesthetic Supplies Pty Ltd*.[157]

**Williams J: 11. Liability for contributory (or indirect) infringement**
**[566]** 86. In the previous section I have concluded that the corporate defendants RBS and Podfix Pty Ltd have offered Podfix 2 for sale in terms of a brochure which is in evidence. (The brochure includes an illustration of Podfix 1 and the bottom cover spacer). This raises the question as to the distributors' liability for aiding abetting or procuring the infringement of a process claim where the only link between the defendant and the infringing use of the process is the fact of sale together with instructions for use; bearing in mind the limited practical application of Podfix 2, the further question also arises as to the consequences of selling an article so as to procure (rather than merely facilitate) a patent infringement by the customer.

87. The point is covered by s 117 of the Patents Act 1990 when read in conjunction with s 13(1) and the definition of "exploit" in the dictionary to the Act (Sch 1 and s 3). The provisions read as follows:

117(1) If the use of a product by a person would infringe a patent, the supply of that product by one person to another is an infringement of the patent by the supplier unless the supplier is the patentee or licensee of the patent.

(2) A reference in subsection (1) to the use of a product by a person is a reference to:

(a)  if the product is capable of only one reasonable use, having regard to its nature or design-that use; or

(b)  if the product is not a staple commercial product-any use of the product, if the supplier had reason to believe that the person would put it to that use; or

(c)  in any case-the use of the product in accordance with any instructions for the use of the product, or any inducement to use the product, given to the person by the supplier or contained in an advertisement published by or with the authority of the supplier."

Section 13(1) provides:

Subject to this Act, a patent gives the patentee the exclusive rights, during the term of the patent, to exploit the invention and to authorise another person to exploit the invention.

"Exploit" is defined in Sch 1 as follows:

"exploit", in relation to an invention, includes:

(a)  where the invention is a product-make, hire, sell or otherwise dispose of the product, offer to make, sell, hire or otherwise dispose of it, use or import it, or keep it for the purpose of doing any of those things; or **[567]**

(b)  where the invention is a method or process-use the method or process or do any act mentioned in paragraph (a) in respect of a product resulting from such use;

88. Section 117 has been drafted to cover a number of situations. I need only address that which arises where the relevant conduct is the sale (or offer for sale) of a product

---

157  (1992) 111 ALR 205.

together with some instructions in circumstances where it may be anticipated that the instruction (if obeyed) will involve the use of a patented method or process and therefore an anticipated exploitation.

89. In case of an invention in respect of a method or process claim, the patentee has the exclusive right (inter alia) to use the method or process. The application of the patented process to any article would amount to an infringement and it is irrelevant for this argument whether the article itself is the subject of patent rights.

90. Section 117 contains a definition clause which deals with the manner of use of an article in particular circumstances for the purpose of considering infringement. If the manner of use of an article by the distributor himself in accordance with instructions would infringe a patent then the supply of the article in those circumstances (with instructions for use) will also infringe; that is the effect of s 117(1).

91. A contrary view was expressed by Gummow J in *Sartas No 1 v Koukourou* and in *Rescare Ltd v Anaesthetic Supplies* and upon appeal Lockhart J affirmed that approach. Heerey J in *Bristol-Myers Squibb v Faulding* also took the same approach as did Gummow J. However, on appeal in *Bristol-Myers Squibb Co v FH Faulding & Co Ltd* (2000) 46 IPR 553 the Full Court of the Federal Court rejected the views expressed by Gummow J in *Rescare* and reiterated in *Sartas*.

92. In *Bristol-Myers Squibb* the appellant relied upon a method claim for the administration of the drug Taxol for the treatment of cancer. The properties of Taxol had been known for many years but its administration presented problems in terms of side effects. The invention lay in a method of infusing a limited and specific dosage over a comparatively short and specific time so as to enable it to be suitable for outpatients use. It was argued that use of Taxol in accordance with the respondent's product information guide would involve infringement of the appellant's invention.

93. In upholding the appellant's argument under s 117(2)(c) that there was infringement by the supply of the drug with instructions, the Full Court, Black CJ and Lehane J, said at IPR 582-3 [87]–[88]:

> Paragraph (c) raises a more complex question. The appellant's argument commenced with the uncontroversial proposition that use of taxol in accordance with the product information guide or the protocols would infringe the petty patents; the next step was that the guide and the protocols were instructions (in the sense of directions or recommendations) given by the respondent for the use of the taxol which it supplied, and we accept that proposition. Then, it was said, s 117(1) applied, having regard to the dictionary in subs (2), as follows:
>
> > "If the use of [taxol] by a [medical practitioner], in accordance with any instructions for the use of taxol … given to the [medical practitioner] by the [respondent] …, would infringe [either of the petty patents], the supply of that [taxol] by [the respondent] to [the medical practitioner] is an infringement of the [petty patent] by the [the respondent] unless [as was not the case] the [respondent] is the patentee or a licensee of the [petty patent]."
>
> It may be said immediately that there is considerable force in that way of looking at it. It involves, after all, a literal application of the words of s 117. The respondent, **[568]** however, contended for a different approach, the one adopted by Heerey J. According to that approach, the starting point is not s 117 but the definition of "exploit". Where an invention is a method or process, use of a product exploits the invention only if the product is one which results from use of the method or process. Section 117, the argument proceeds, is concerned only with a case where the use of a product by a person would infringe a patent (because the person, not the patentee or a licensee, exploited it); and, where the patent is for a method or process, that will not be so unless the product is one which results from the use of that method or process.

94. The Full Court cited with approval an article by Ms Ann Monotti in (1995) 6 AIPJ 217 where she deals with the fallacy which she perceived in the approach of Gummow J in *Rescare Ltd* and *Sartas No 1*. In the latter case Gummow J said at 495:

"Further, where ... what relevantly is claimed is a method or process, exploitation occurs, *other than by use of the method or process*, only by the doing of an act mentioned in par (a) of the definition of 'exploit'. There must be an act done 'in respect of a product resulting from such use'. Here, unlike the situation with the chemical process example, there is no such product derived from the activity of the customer, still less any such product supplied by Sartas so as to attract the operation of s 117. In my view, s 117 has no application to the claims in question."

95. However, as Ms Monotti points out, the definition of exploit in the case of a method claim includes "the use of the method or process" which means that applying a patented method to an article (whatever its origin) must result in an infringement (if not authorised by the patent holder). Therefore if the manufacturer were to use a spacer itself in accordance with the instructions there will be an infringement; likewise (by applying the definition in s 117(2)(c)), supplying a product in such circumstances to another with instructions constitutes infringement.

In *Bristol-Myers* at IPR 585, [95] the joint judgment continues:

... it is perhaps a pity that the drafter chose to use the phrase "use of a product", which contains such a clear reference to the terminology of par (a) of the definition of "exploit". But s 117 provides its own dictionary, in subs (2). And our paraphrase of s 117(1), incorporating subs (2)(c), shows, in our view, that the construction urged by the appellant is not only a possible construction but a literal one. That literal construction being consistent with the apparent purpose of the provision, it is, in our view, plainly to be preferred.

96. I note that on this issue Finkelstein J was in agreement with the other members of the Court: see IPR 600, [162].

97. I will treat *Bristol-Myers* as having now determined the issue and binding upon me. The Full Court judgment only became available after I had reserved my judgment but counsel has drawn it to my attention.

98. In these circumstances, the corporate defendants in the present case will be liable if they distributed Podfix 2 with instructions for use which infringed the method or process Claim 1 of the Leonardis patent.

### *University of Western Australia v Gray*
Full Court of the Federal Court of Australia: Lindgren, Finn and Bennett JJ
[2009] FCAFC 116

Dr Gray was employed by the University of Western Australia (the University) from 1985 to teach, conduct and stimulate research. At the time of his employment, Dr Gray had been engaged for some years in researching the treatment of liver cancer by using microspheres. During his continued research in this area whilst employed by the University, he devised, in conjunction with others at the University, various microsphere technologies. Patent applications were made in respect of the inventions said to have been developed in relation to the various technologies. Dr Gray subsequently became a director of Sirtex Medical Limited (Sirtex). In 1997 Sirtex acquired the intellectual property rights arising out of the inventions from Dr Gray and the Cancer Research Institute. The University brought an action against Dr Gray and Sirtex on several grounds and on the whole French J (as he then was) found against the University. The following extract is from the appeal to the Full Court of the Federal Court of Australia which was concerned with whether Dr Gray was under a "duty to invent" and therefore an implied term of assignment to the University would apply.

### Lindgren, Finn and Bennett JJ: Applicable legal principles

135. We will refer, first, to the general principles governing the implication of a term by law into a contract and, then, to the specific considerations applying to the implication of a term into an employment contract such as would entitle the employer to an invention made by the employee.

#### (a) Implication of a term in law

Terms implied in fact are individualised gap fillers, depending on the terms and circumstances of a particular contract. Terms implied in law are in reality incidents attached to standardised contractual relationships, or perhaps more illuminatingly, such terms can in modern US terminology be described as standardised default rules": *Society of Lloyds v Clementson* [1995] CLC 117 at 131.

See also *Byrne* at 447 ff; and generally, Furmston (ed), *The Law of Contract* (3rd ed, 2007), 3.21-3.25; *Cheshire and Fifoot's Law of Contract* (9th Aust ed), 10.50-10.54; Carter, Peden and Tolhurst, *Contract Law in Australia* (5th ed, 2007), [11-12]-[11-16]; Peden, "Policy Concerns Behind Implication of Terms in Law" (2001) 117 LQR 459 where this subject is helpfully analysed.

136. We begin with what is well accepted. (i) Terms implied in law are "legal incidents of the particular class of contract" to which they respectively relate: *Codelfa Construction Pty Ltd v State Rail Authority of NSW* [1982] HCA 24; (1982) 149 CLR 337 at 345. They are to be found in many commonly occurring types of contract – sales, employment, landlord and tenant, doctor-patient, etc. (ii) They are not based upon the intention of the parties, actual or presumed, in a given instance, although the provenance of a particular term may well have been the commonplace use of such a term in earlier times in contracts of that type, so establishing what later would become the default rule: see *Byrne* at 449. (iii) Neither are they founded on the need to give efficacy to a contract: *Codelfa Construction* at 345; although, as has often been recognised, there can be a deal of overlap between terms implied in law and terms implied in fact in particular contractual settings: see eg *Hughes Aircraft Systems International v Airservices Australia* (1997) 76 FCR 151 (*Hughes Aircraft Systems International*) at 193. While implication in law is also said to be based on "necessity", that necessity, as will be seen, is informed by "more general considerations than mere business efficacy": *Lister v Romford Ice and Cold Storage Co Pty Ltd* [1956] UKHL 6; [1957] AC 555 (*Lister*) at 576. (iv) Implication of a term in law yields to the contrary intention of the parties as expressed in their contract or because of inconsistency with the terms that have been agreed: *Castlemaine Tooheys Ltd v Carlton & United Breweries Ltd* (1987) 10 NSWLR 468 (*Castlemaine Tooheys*) at 492B-C; *Shell UK Ltd v Lostock Garage Ltd* [1977] 1 All ER 481 (*Shell UK*) at 487.

137. The matters that need to be considered for present purposes are, first, the requirement that there be a recognised or commonly occurring class, type, or kind of contract: *Breen v Williams* [1996] HCA 57; (1996) 186 CLR 71 (*Breen*) at 103; *Shell UK*, at 487; and, secondly, the test to be satisfied if the implication is to be made.

138. The class requirement has been recognised in many cases. All that needs to be emphasised about it here is that it can be formulated and satisfied at differing levels of generality depending upon the nature of the implication sought to be made. So while one type of term may quite appropriately be implied in a class of contract cast in very general terms, eg in a contract of employment the employee's duty to obey lawful and reasonable directions given by the employer that fall within the scope of the employment (eg *McManus v Scott-Charlton* (1996) 70 FCR 16 at 21; *Macken's Law of Employment*, [5.360] (6th ed, 2009)), another term may be of such a character as to be implied only

into a recognisable sub-category of that larger class. In *Scally v Southern Health and Social Services Board* [1992] 1 AC 294 (*Scally*), for example, a term was implied into an employment contract obliging the employer to give notice to its employees of changes to their contributory pension scheme, but this implication was limited to a sub-category or type of contract having quite particular characteristics ...

139. There has been a degree of uncertainty, and increasing controversy, as to the burden of the test to be applied – if there be a single test – in making an implication in law. What is presently clear is that the implication requires a justification greater than merely that of "reasonableness": see *Scally* at 215; *Castlemaine Tooheys* at 488-489; but see also *Crossley v Faithful & Gould Holdings Ltd* [2004] EWCA Civ 293; [2004] 4 All ER 447 (*Crossley*) at [33]-[36]; for the different position in US jurisprudence see *Restatement of Contracts, Second,* SS204. Something more is needed. The test most commonly stated or asserted is that of "necessity" ...

### (b) Implied terms and employee inventions

148. Neither party contends that French J erred in his extended comparative analysis of, or in his conclusions upon, the common law relating to employee inventions: [112]-[157]. In these circumstances it is unnecessary that we essay a like survey of the law, although it will be necessary, given the nature of the errors now ascribed to his Honour, to emphasise certain aspects of the common law in relation both to employee inventions and employee secrecy.

149. We would add by way of preface that we are aware of both the shifts in emphasis and the tensions that have attended the evolution of the principles we are about to discuss. We note in particular that there has over time been a tendency at common law to increase the presumption of ownership in favour of the employer: see Cornish and Llewellyn, *Intellectual Property: Patents, Copyright, Trade Marks and Allied Rights,* 7-03 (6th ed, 2007). For a more traditional view more favourable to employees, see *Re Marshall and Naylor's Patent* (1900) 17 RPC 553. There continue to be tensions between a variety of employment-related implied terms and general equitable principles, particularly fiduciary ones: see eg *Vokes Ltd v Heather* (1945) 62 RPC 135 (*Vokes*) at 141-142; *British Celanese Ltd v Moncrieff* [1948] Ch 564 at 167. Given UWA's grounds of appeal, it is unnecessary to explore these matters. We should emphasise, though, for the sake of completeness, that we have not considered at all any bearing that an employee's duty of fidelity allegedly may have on an employer's entitlement to claim an employee's invention: cf Monotti & Ricketson, *Universities and Intellectual Property,* 5.58-5.59 (2003); Dean, *The Law of Trade Secrets and Personal Secrets,* Ch 5 (2nd ed, 2002); Poole, "Employee's Rights in Respect of Patent, Designs and Copyright Material", (1979) 3 Auckland UL Rev 355. As already noted, UWA's late attempt to plead such a duty was refused.

150. As both parties have sought to rely upon the observations of Nettle J in *Victoria University of Technology* on implied terms and the ownership of inventions, we take them as our starting point. As his Honour acknowledged, his observations crystallise the leading English authorities on this subject which have been accepted in this country (at [104]):

> The law is well settled upon the position of an officer or employee who makes an invention affecting the business of his or her employer. It is an implied term of employment that any invention or discovery made in the course of the employment of the employee in doing that which he is engaged and instructed to do during the time of his employment, and during working hours, and using the materials of his employers, is the property of the employer and not of the employee. Having made a discovery or invention in course of such work, the employee becomes a trustee for the employer of that invention or discovery, and he is therefore as a trustee bound to give the benefit of any such discovery or invention to his employer. But the mere existence of the employer/employee relationship will not give the employer ownership of inventions

made by the employee during the term of the relationship. And that is so even if the invention is germane to and useful for the employer's business, and even though the employee may have made use of the employer's time and resources in bringing the invention to completion. Certainly, all the circumstances must be considered in each case, but unless the contract of employment expressly so provides, or an invention is the product of work which the employee was paid to perform, it is unlikely that any invention made by the employee will be held to belong to the employer.

151. The fundamental idea said to inform when and why an employee's trusteeship of an invention arises is not hard to find and is deeply rooted in the general character of what in times past was described as the master-servant relationship. Viscount Simonds and Lord Reid both made this plain in *Sterling Engineering Co Ltd v Patchett* [1955] AC 534 (*Sterling Engineering*). Viscount Simonds stated (at 543):

It is elementary that, where the employee in the course of his employment (ie, in his employer's time and with his materials) makes *an invention which it falls within his duty to make* (as was the case here) he holds his interest in the invention and in any resulting patent as trustee for the employer. [Emphasis added]

The implied term procuring this result his Lordship considered (at 544) was:

… only an implied term in the same sense that it is an implied term, though not written at large, in the contract of service of any workman that what he produces by the strength of his arm or the skill of his hand or the exercise of his inventive faculty shall become the property of the employer.

Likewise Lord Reid stated (at 547):

No doubt the respondent was the inventor and in the ordinary case the benefit of an invention belongs to the inventor. But at the time when he made these inventions he was employed by the appellants as their chief designer and *it is, in my judgment, inherent in the legal relationship of master and servant that any product of the work which the servant is paid to do belongs to the master*: I can find neither principle nor authority for holding that this rule ceased to apply if a product of that work happens to be a patentable invention. [Emphasis added]

For a like view where the work product was a copyright article, see *Report of the Committee to Consider the Law on Copyright and Design* (1977), Cmnd 6732, (UK) para 571. Unless varied or excluded by the parties, the implied term was "the ordinary rule inherent in the parties' relationship of master and servant" (per Lord Reid at 548).

152. Unsurprisingly, express contractual stipulation apart, with the employer's entitlement turning on that which it was the employee's "duty" to do – and for which the employee was paid – the recurrent preoccupation in the case law has been in each instance with the actual subject matter and purpose of the employee's engagement itself and with the question: "[w]hat is it that he is employed to do?"; cf *LIFFE Administration & Management v Pinkava* [2007] EWCA Civ 217; [2007] 4 All ER 981 (*LIFFE*) at [97]. The end of this inquiry is to ascertain whether, if at all, it was part of an employee's engagement with his or her employer to utilise his or her "inventive faculty" (cf *Sterling Engineering* at 544; *Vokes* at 136) in an agreed way or for an agreed purpose for the benefit of, or to further the purposes of, the employer. To use the shorthand of *Electrolux Ltd v Hudson* [1977] FSR 312 at 326, was the employee "employed to make or discover inventions at all?", or, as French J put it, did the employee have "a duty to invent?"

153. If the employee's invention is the, or a, product of what he or she was employed to do, and did do, it will belong to the employer unless otherwise agreed: see eg *British Reinforced Concrete Engineering Co Ltd v Lind* (1917) 34 RPC 101 (*British Reinforced Concrete*); *Adamson v Kenworthy* (1932) 49 RPC 57; *Triplex Safety Glass Co v Scorah* [1938] 1 Ch 211 (*Triplex Safety Glass*); and see also *Electrolux Ltd*, at [97]. In such a case, it would be "inconsistent with [the employee's] duty to appropriate to himself an invention of this kind": *Edisonia Ltd v Forse* (1908) 25 RPC 546 at 552.

154. By way of contrast, if (a) the employee was not engaged to use his or her inventive capacity at all (cf *Re Charles Selz Ltd's Patent Application* (1954) 71 RPC 158); or (b) was so engaged only by way of additional duties to use his or her inventive capacity as and when asked (*Spencer Industries Pty Ltd v Collins* [2003] FCA 542; (2003) 58 IPR 425) or only for an agreed purpose, the employer would have in case (a) no claim on the employee's invention at all and in case (b) such a claim only if the invention resulted from a task the employee was asked to perform by way of additional duty or if the invention was related to the effectuation of the agreed purpose.

155. We note in passing that it can, on occasion, be factually difficult to define the subject matter over which a particular employee's inventive responsibility to the employer extends. This may be, for example, because (a) the employee's engagement gives him or her considerable discretion in determining the area of inventive inquiry he or she will pursue for the employer's benefit; or (b) the employee's managerial and inventive responsibilities combined are such that he or she, as a fiduciary, is obliged to give the employer the benefit of any invention developed in the course of his or her employment that is germane to the employer's business (see eg *Fine Industrial Commodities Ltd v Powling* (1954) 71 RPC 253; see also *British Syphon Co Ltd v Homewood (No 2)* [1956] All ER 897 which is probably better explained as a breach of fiduciary duty case); or (c) the employee's inventive responsibilities evolve over the course of the employment as a result, for example, of the employment tasks changing: see eg *British Reinforced Concrete*, at 109.

156. To illustrate the care that needs to be taken in determining what a person is employed to do, Jacob LJ in the *LIFFE* case helpfully indicated (at [97]) that this may not be revealed by looking at an employee's day-to-day work:

> Take for instance a research chemist working on a cancer cure for the last ten years. Suppose he came up with a cure for arthritis. He could not seriously contend that he owned the invention because he was day-to-day working on a cancer cure. His duty as a research chemist is clearly wider than his day-to-day work.

157. What needs to be said about the definitional problem which can exist in defining the subject matter encompassed by the implied term is that it differs little, if at all, from the parallel problem in fiduciary law of defining "the subject matter over which the fiduciary obligations extend" (*Birtchnell v Equity Trustees, Executors & Agency Co Ltd* [1929] HCA 24; (1929) 42 CLR 384 at 408) for the purposes of the conflict of duty and interest rule.

158. Finally, because the implied term turns critically on what the employee has been engaged to do, it does not seem to us to be decisive that the employer is publicly or privately owned.

### (c) The employee's duty of confidentiality

159. We refer to this matter, not because the secrecy obligation of any UWA employee is in issue in this proceeding, but because it is a factor that informs our conclusions on the implied term aspect of the appeal. As with employee inventions, so also with confidentiality, the law is an unhappy mixture of equitable obligation (the duty of confidence and fiduciary obligation) and implied terms (particularly, but not only, the duty of good faith and fidelity): see Dean, [4.35] ff; Stafford and Ritchie, [4.3] ff, [5.207] ff.

160. All that is necessary for present purposes is that we refer briefly and in general terms to the protection afforded an employer against unauthorised disclosure during, or after, the currency of the employment relationship of confidential information communicated to, or acquired by, an employee in the course of his or her employment. The case law is voluminous: see generally, Dean; Stafford and Ritchie; and Toulson and Phipps, *Confidentiality*, (2nd ed, 2006).

161. Express contractual stipulation apart, an employee's duty of confidence to his or her employer can arise by way of implied contract or as a matter of equitable obligation.

The scope of the duty will be the same in both cases despite their "different conceptual origins": *Concut Pty Ltd v Worrell* [2000] HCA 64; (2000) 176 ALR 693 at [26]. In employer-employee cases, however, the historical tendency has been to treat the matter as one of implied contract: see eg *Ansell Rubber Co Pty Ltd v Allied Rubber Industries Pty Ltd* [1967] VR 37 at 41; Dean, [2.85], [2.95]; but see Meagher, Gummow & Lehane's *Equity Doctrines and Remedies*, (4th ed, 2002) [41-020].

162. As was indicated in *Ansell Rubber*, at 40, an obligation of confidence (whether contractual or equitable) may come into existence –

... by reason of the nature of the relationship between persons, or by reason of the subject-matter and the circumstances in which the subject-matter has come into the hands of the person charged with the breach.

It is clear that, in the employment setting, provided the information communicated to, or acquired by, an employee in the course of his or her employment has the necessary quality of confidentiality, ie it is relatively secret (*Franchi v Franchi* [1967] RPC 149 (*Franchi*), at 153); is not trivial (*Coco v AN Clark (Engineers) Ltd* [1969] RPC 41 (*Coco*) at 48); and is not public property or public knowledge (*Saltman Engineering Co Ltd v Campbell Engineering Co Ltd* (1948) 65 RPC 203 (*Saltman Engineering Co*) at 215), the courts will readily find that the employee is subject to a duty of confidence and that the unauthorised use or disclosure of the information by the employee will be an actionable wrong (see Gurry, *Breach of Confidence* (1984), Ch 8).

163. Importantly for present purposes, among the now well accepted factors pointing towards the confidentiality of a particular piece of information are the following: (i) When information has been produced or obtained only after the expenditure of time, or money, either by way of research or in the application of skill and ingenuity, its confidentiality is indicated (*Saltman Engineering Co*; *Interfirm Comparison (Australia) Pty Ltd v Law Society of New South Wales* [1975] 2 NSWLR 104 at 117; *H & R Block v Sanott* [1976] 1 NZLR 213) as it is when another person could acquire or duplicate the same information only by going through the same process (*Cranleigh Precision Engineering Ltd v Bryant* [1966] RPC 81 at 88-89); and see generally Gurry, 70-71. (ii) The novelty or originality of the process, technique or product which the information encapsulates is an important indicator that the information itself is not already in the public domain, although novelty is not a pre-requisite: *Saltman Engineering Co*, at 216; Gurry, at 83. What is required in the cases of technical, scientific and business information is "some product of the human brain which is relatively secret": *Coco* at 47.

164. An important aspect of the duty of confidence in employment settings is that the duty subsists after the termination of the employment so as to preclude disclosure or use of subsisting confidential information held by the ex-employee which was derived from his or her previous employment: see eg *Triplex Safety Glass*; *United Sterling Corporation Ltd v Falton* [1974] RPC 162; Ricketson & Cresswell, *The Law of Intellectual Property: Copyright, Designs & Confidential Information* (2nd ed 1999) [25.170]; and see generally, Dean [4.145]-[4.250]. While an ex-employee is entitled to make full use of the general knowledge, skill and experience – the "know-how" – which as a result of the previous employment has become his or her own (*E Worsley & Co Ltd v Cooper* [1939] 1 All ER 290 at 309-310), what the employee cannot do is to use or disclose confidential information that

can fairly be regarded as a *separate part of the employee's stock of knowledge* which a man of ordinary honesty and intelligence would recognise to be the property of his old employer, and not his own to do as he likes with:

*Printers & Finishers Ltd v Holloway (No 2)* [1965] RPC 239 at 255. A considerable body of case law has now evolved to aid in the process of differentiating the protectable from the non-protectable: see eg *Faccenda Chicken Ltd v Fowler* [1987] Ch 117; Dean [4.145] ff; Toulson and Phipps, 14-006 – 14-024. What is important to note for present purposes is that the duty of confidence can pose a significant obstacle to the mobility of employees engaged in research-related employment having applications in science or technology.

165. We emphasise the above for the following reason. Where an employee is engaged in an inventive capacity for the benefit of his or her employer, that employment will commonly result both in the disclosure to the employee of confidential information and the generation of such information by the employee. In respect of such information, the employee would ordinarily be precluded from disclosing it either to other employees or to third parties without the employer's consent, express or implied. In saying this we acknowledge that internal disclosures may, and often will, be a necessary part of the employment, as where the employee's research is being undertaken as part of a team effort and disclosure to other members of the team is impliedly authorised.

166. The importance of the duty of confidence for present purposes is that it buttresses and supplements the patent system by providing "trade secret" protection (i) before a patent has been applied for, and (ii) in relation to ideas and concepts which for some reason cannot be patented: Cornish, "Rights in University Innovations", (1992) 14(1), *EIPR*, 13.

167. Finally, an employer that is owed a duty of confidence by its employees may by its own act strip information otherwise subject to that duty of its quality of confidentiality by making it public as, for example, by publishing a patent specification revealing it: *O. Mustad & Son v Dosen* [1963] RPC 41; *Franchi* …

### Grounds of appeal 1-5 and 8 …

181. Although UWA changed its stance on the implied term during the hearing before us, it finally accepted (Transcript 159) that it was required to establish that Dr Gray's employment contract was one of the class or type in which the employee invention term would be implied. To that end, and to put the matter shortly, UWA contended, first, that there was no relevant distinction between a university as an employer and any other employer; and, secondly, that Dr Gray's contractual duty to undertake research was, in the circumstances, sufficient to bring it within the class of contract attracting the implied term.

182. We disagree with both contentions. The first disregards the distinctiveness of universities (such as UWA); the second disregards both the distinctiveness of academic "employment" in universities (such as UWA) and the terms and research circumstances of Dr Gray's own employment. As French J properly recognised, both of these matters had to be considered in determining whether Dr Gray's contract of employment stood within or apart from the class or type of contract that attracted the implied term at law. There was in this sense a "threshold question": [1365].

183. First, there is the distinctiveness of UWA as a university. As we earlier indicated, UWA is a special purpose statutory corporation. It was created to serve the public purposes served by a "university" (as the language of its Act makes plain: see the preamble to the Act and s 2). As such, UWA is, at least, an institution of higher education offering courses and providing research facilities in various disciplines and having amongst its acknowledged powers and privileges that of conferring degrees: cf *Shorter Oxford English Dictionary*, vol 2 "university" (5th ed, 2002); UWA Act, s 29.

184. We accept that UWA has not been immune from the forces, financial and otherwise, that are forcing changes in the character of the university sector in Australia. As French J noted, UWA has engaged in commercial activities, as have done "most, if not all, universities". The evidence put on by UWA as to the range, character and significance of such activities of UWA was slight, though it hoped on the appeal that we would take judicial notice of these matters: cf *Evidence Act*, s 144(1) (Cth). What is notable for present purposes is that there is nothing in the evidence to suggest that those commercial activities have displaced, either totally or if in part to what extent, UWA's traditional public function as an institution of higher education in favour of the pursuit of commercial purposes (if it lawfully could do so under its Act). Its function, in other words,

was not limited to that of engaging academic staff for its own commercial purposes. Accordingly, we agree with French J that on the evidence Dr Gray was not required to advance a commercial purpose of UWA when selecting the research he would undertake.

185. A further distinctive feature of many, but not all, universities (including UWA) is that their academic staff are part of the membership that constitutes the corporation and as such are bound by the statutes, regulations, etc of the university. Their membership is integral to their status and place in the university. To define the relationship of an academic staff member with a university simply in terms of a contract of employment is to ignore a distinctive dimension of that relationship.

186. Secondly, there is the distinctiveness of academic employment in a university. The two faceted character of an academic staff member's relationship with a university – ie as member and as employee – is "not without significance" as French J observed ([1361]). It probably is the case – though it is not a matter we need explore – that some of the practices revealed in the evidence in this matter (not repudiated by UWA), and the underlying values which seem to inform them, are more likely to be referable to understandings that have been traditionally associated with membership. The seeming freedom to choose the subject or line of research and the manner of its pursuit and the freedom to decide when and how to publish the products of one's research to the extent that these subsist, sit uneasily with employment notions such as the implied duty of an employee to obey all lawful and reasonable instructions of the employer within the scope of the employee's employment, or to maintain the secrecy of confidential information generated in the course of employment. Yet they are apparent manifestations of the contested value of "academic freedom": Cornish, "Rights in University Innovations", at 2-3. …

193. This leads us to consider the circumstances of Dr Gray's employment and of the research environment in which he worked, upon which French J relied to negative the implication that UWA sought.

194. First, his Honour found that under his contract of employment Dr Gray had no duty to invent anything, though he had a duty to research and to stimulate research: "He was working for a university" (at [1360]). To put the matter as we earlier put it, he had not been engaged to use his inventive faculty in an agreed way or for an agreed purpose, for UWA's benefit. While his duty to research was in an applied science, it cannot for that reason be transformed into a duty to invent, notwithstanding that his actual research, in fact, carried the possibility of developing inventions capable of attracting patent protection.

195. We reject UWA's contention to the contrary and we agree with the primary Judge's reasons and conclusions. The insuperable difficulty in UWA's submissions is that Dr Gray's employment duties did not even require him to perform tasks from which inventions might result. The subject matter and the manner of discharge of his duty to research were in his discretion. He was not employed to invent. UWA put on extensive written submissions criticising French J's use of the formula "duty to invent". The shorthand expression is widely used in scholarly writing: see Dean, 238 ff; Monotti and Ricketson, 6.56-6.67. As so used, and as used by French J, its meaning is self-evident and unobjectionable.

196. UWA has sought to circumvent his Honour's conclusion in the following way. Though Dr Gray was entitled to determine the subject and manner of his research, if what he chose to do required him to bring his inventive faculty to bear, then the doing of that research should, it is said, be regarded as that which he was engaged to do and for which he was paid. Any invention resulting from his so doing should, in consequence, attract the implied term.

197. Such a deemed, contingent duty to invent requires an untenable implication. It is not what Dr Gray's terms of employment required; there is no "necessity" for it being implied by law into the employment contracts of university academic staff; and,

importantly, it is inconsistent with the researcher's freedom to share and to publish research results.

198. Secondly, French J regarded the freedom to publish the results of research, including invention, notwithstanding that the publication might destroy patentability, as another circumstance telling against the implication. From what we have already said about the constraining character of the duty of confidence and of its underpinning of the implied term relating to employee inventions, the importance of this particular "freedom" is self-evident. We earlier referred both to Dr Burton's evidence, accepted by his Honour, on the Gray group's "strong commitment to the publication and dissemination of research results", and of Professor Barber's evidence of the "kudos and reputation" that UWA desired "from academic publication in the peer-reviewed literature". While we do not suggest that Dr Gray and his researchers may not have controlled the time and manner of their publications, the evidence clearly suggests that Dr Gray enjoyed the freedom to publish that French J found. He was not constrained by a secrecy obligation.

199. As noted earlier in its submissions, UWA appears to have accepted that this was the case. In its oral submissions, it contended, seemingly for the first time, that a prohibition on publication arose only if and when "an invention" had been developed and then only by virtue of reg 7 of the Patents Regulations. We have already indicated that those regulations were devoid of significance for the purposes of UWA's contract claim. In any event, reg 7 was not itself a free standing prohibition. It was a proscription that arose once a particular point in a regulatory régime was reached. In the circumstances of this matter that point was not, and could not have been, reached, because UWA had abandoned the Patents Regulations régime in favour of an "alternative pathway": see "The Patents Regulations" above.

200. Thirdly, French J considered that the extent to which Dr Gray and those working with him were expected to and did solicit funds for their research was another circumstance militating against the implication. We accept as a starting point that the solicitation of funds from public or private sources for the purposes of conducting research is not a phenomenon unique to universities. It is commonplace in the private sector: cf *Industry Research and Development Act 1986* (Cth). What was "a striking feature of this case" ([161]) was the amount of time and effort devoted by Dr Gray and his researchers in applying for research grants, and the extent of their dependence on their success. UWA may have wished to foster, but seemingly could not fund, Dr Gray's research. To the extent that the *Sterling Engineering* principle has nascent in it the idea that the employer pays the researcher and, in significant degree, for the research itself, it can be said, without criticism of UWA that, if sustained, the suggested implied term would allow UWA to reap where various entities had sown. Importantly, it is implicit in what French J said that Dr Gray was raising the funds for his research, the metes and bounds of which he determined, though UWA received and managed the funds. Further, it also can probably be inferred that the grants were made to Dr Gray as an established researcher and not to UWA as such, although its involvement as institutional manager of the grant would also be taken into account by the funding body. So considered, the "grant factor" can properly be said to be a consideration that further weakens UWA's claim to the benefits of any inventions so generated.

201. UWA seeks to counter this argument by saying that Dr Gray's post-contractual conduct cannot be used to negate an implication into a contract.

202. After referring to this factor and to the necessity, consistent with the kind of work Dr Gray was doing, to enter into collaborative arrangements, French J went on to use Dr Gray's experience to characterise "the role of the researcher at UWA" in the area in which Dr Gray was working. His Honour described that as being "required ... to act as entrepreneurs in securing the resources which would enable them to carry out their work": [1366]. It was immediately following this that his Honour made the following important observation:

The circumstances of his employment were a long way removed from the situations which gave rise to the common law implications discussed in the English cases.
In these circumstances we consider that the proper complexion to place upon what his Honour said is that he was describing the known context and shared expectations of the parties in relation to raising funds for research at the time of contracting, using what happened post-contract as the manifestation of what was anticipated. We would add that we were not taken to any evidence which suggested what contractual arrangements, if any, there were as to the raising of funds for research by UWA or by Dr Gray. If there was no such arrangement, we see nothing impermissible in French J having regard to Dr Gray's subsequent behaviour in fund raising to negative the suggested implication.

203. The fourth and final negativing circumstance adverted to by the primary Judge was the necessity, consistent with research of the kind he was doing, for Dr Gray to enter into collaborative arrangements with external organisations. The evidence was replete with instances of such collaborations and of information exchanges between Dr Gray and his researchers on the one hand and between them and researchers in other institutions on the other. Informative examples of both processes at work can be seen in the evolution of the research on the binding of Yttrium90 to microspheres (see [277]-[300]) and the use made in it of notes of Dr Self of St Vincent's Hospital written in 1984: see also [1469].

204. Implicit in his Honour's reliance upon the collaborations is the appreciation that the need for inter-institutional cooperation in the research being conducted tells against the exclusive appropriation of its product to one institution (ie UWA) via an implied term in the event that an invention is made. Further, and we consider importantly, the evidence on collaboration and information exchanges in Dr Gray's field of research suggests that some level of sharing of research results and know-how was a necessary and accepted practice in the particular research community so as to increase "the stock of available knowledge": cf *Taylor v Taylor* [1910] HCA 4; (1910) 10 CLR 218 (*Taylor*) at 224.

205. As we earlier noted, the principles governing terms implied by law themselves raise a threshold question which French J correctly identified. The onus is on the proponent of the term to show that the contract is of a class, type or kind to which the legal implication applies: [1365]. Save in cases of first impression, the discharge of that onus will pose few problems. Thereafter the question becomes one as to whether the terms agreed by the parties to the contract are inconsistent with, or negate, the implied term. The opponent of the implication bears this onus. The present case is of the former variety. …

210. Like the primary Judge, in reaching this conclusion we have found it unnecessary to consider the judgment of Nettle J in the *Victoria University of Technology* case. That was a clear case of misappropriation of a corporate opportunity in breach of fiduciary duty. While Nettle J considered, as we have noted, the applicability of the implied term relating to employee inventions and rejected it in respect of academic staff members, he was not called upon to consider, and did not consider, the question whether universities were different as a category of employer. For that reason we have derived little assistance from that case.

211. We would also add that, while our conclusion recognises a distinction between the ownership of employee inventions in universities and in private sector business entities, we should not be taken as suggesting that the solution reached by use of the implied term in law is necessarily a desirable one in either case. What we do emphasise is that there are clear reasons for not implying such a term as to inventions in a case such as this. If a less crude and more fair and reasonable result is to be achieved which balances the respective interests of a university and its academic staff members, this will need to be done by or under legislation or, if it could be devised, by an express contractual régime appropriate to the circumstances of the individual case.

# Chapter 11

# Biotechnology Patents

## Introduction

Jeremy Rivkin's assertion that we are living in the Biotech Century[1] would appear to be well supported given the significant attention bestowed upon biologically derived inventions and the patents protecting them. The boundaries of biotechnology have been alluded to in Chapter 9, such as the fermentation-based industries, genetic engineering and agricultural industries. A broader view might use the expression "life science industries"[2] enabling the inclusion of pharmaceuticals, particularly those derived from natural products, medical devices and therapeutic treatments incorporating biotechnological products and the list goes on. In his *Guide for Scientists* wishing to protect biotechnological inventions back in 1988, Roman Saliwanchik described just how broad biotechnology could be:

> The scope and application of biotechnology research is extremely broad. The techniques used in this research are derived largely from the classical fields of physics, chemistry, biology, and molecular biology. The fruits of this research promise to have a profound effect on numerous disciplines including pharmaceutical, agricultural, medicinal, and environmental sciences.[3]

However biotechnology is defined, the common denominator is often the same. There is invariably some use of biological material anywhere from a complete living organism down to its genetic make-up. This is acknowledged in the Australian Biotechnology Report 2001:

> Biotechnology is a broad term for a group of technologies based on the application of biological processes. It has diverse applications in medicine, agriculture, food processing, manufacturing and environmental management. The term "modern biotechnology" is used to distinguish recent, research based activities from traditional fermentation technologies such as bread, cheese or beer making, and animal and plant breeding, which were the

---

1   See generally, J Rifkin, *The Biotech Century: harnessing the gene and remaking the world*, Tarcher Putnam, New York, 1998.

2   See G Dutfield, *Intellectual Property Rights and the Life Science Industries, A Twentieth Century History*, Ashgate, Hampshire, 2003.

3   R Saliwanchik, *Protecting Biotechnology Inventions, A Guide For Scientists*, Science Tech Publishers, Madison, 1988.

first examples of biotechnology. Modern biotechnology includes a range of techniques from recombinant DNA technology, molecular and cellular biology, biochemistry and immunology through to information technology. Gene technology is a specific subset of biotechnology, based on the manipulation and modification ("recombination") of the genetic material of living organisms to develop new characteristics, processes and products.[4]

We will see that much of the controversy that surrounds biotechnological development and proprietary rights in such development revolves around the common component of all lifeforms – the chemical deoxyribonucleic acid or DNA. DNA is the building block of the genes that define a living organism. The past 30 years have seen an explosion in the science of genetics, that is, the science of genes and heredity. Genes are the units that control the function, reproduction and development of a living organism.[5] The differences in genes provide the differences between and among species.[6] Genes are responsible for the production of an organism's proteins, controlling the amount, timing and location of the production of the organism's proteins.[7]

The procedures that have become commonplace in the genetic engineering field of biotechnology are such things as gene sequencing, gene modification, cloning and the "creation" of new life forms. The result has been a great deal of discussion in the political, ethical and religious arenas. The law, on the other hand, has not always been able to accommodate such rapid change and consequently we have seen the stretching of traditional viewpoints in the patent laws in this area together with additional issues such as the following: Who owns a person's genetic material? Who owns the genetic material of a plant or animal native to a geographical location? Should new species of living organisms be patentable in the first place? Should stem cells derived from a human foetus be patentable?

The issue of the patentability of living organisms, other biological materials such as genes and related biotechnological products has been the subject of significant review and controversy in recent times in Australia.[8] By this we refer to the question whether such subject-matter is "appropriate" for the grant of

4    Biotechnology Australia, Freehills and Ernst & Young, *Australian Biotechnology Report*, (2001, cited in *Genes and Ingenuity Report Gene Patenting and Human Health*, ALRC, Report 99, June 2004, p 401.

5    N Stoianoff, *Genetics*, Chapter 3, 20.12 "Medical Technology", *The Laws of Australia*, Vol 20 Health & Guardianship, [68]; see also, House of Lords Select Committee on Science and Technology, *Regulation of the United Kingdom Biotechnology Industry and Global Competitiveness*, HMSO, London, 1993, pp 12-14.

6    N Stoianoff, *Genetics*, Chapter 3, 20.12 "Medical Technology", *The Laws of Australia*, Vol 20 Health & Guardianship, [68], where it is stated: "Minor differences in the function of a large number of genes are responsible for individuality within a species whereas a major change in the function of a single gene pair may result in genetic diseases"; see also Report of the Australian Health and Ethics Committee, *Human Gene Therapy and Related Procedures*, NHMRC, Canberra, November 1993, p 2.

7    N Stoianoff, *Genetics*, Chapter 3, 20.12 "Medical Technology", *The Laws of Australia*, Vol 20 Health & Guardianship, [72].

8    Beginning with *Genes and Ingenuity Report Gene Patenting and Human Health*, ALRC, Report 99, June 2004; and then more recently the Myriad controversy led to: the Senate Community Affairs Reference Committee Inquiry into Gene Patents resulting in a Report in November 2010; the private member's Bill, *Patent Amendment (Human Genes and Biological Materials) Bill 2010*; which in turn led to another Senate Inquiry, this time by the Legal and Constitutional Affairs Legislation Committee resulting in a report in September 2011 recommending that the Senate

letters patent. The *Patents Act 1990* does not specifically include nor exclude such subject-matter, other than in the exclusion of "human beings, and the biological processes for their generation".[9] Rather, s 18(1) of the Act sets out the elements of patentability as discussed in Chapter 9. Accordingly, if an invention satisfies these elements it will be patentable, be it biological in nature or not. This is, of course, in line with Art 27.1 of TRIPS which requires that there be no discrimination as to the field of technology capable of protection.

In Australia there has been very little in the way of judicial consideration of the patentability of such subject-matter. However, the Australian Patent Office (APO), under the jurisdiction of IP Australia, sets out a series of principles or statements as to the patentability of microorganisms, cell lines, hybridomas, related biological materials and their use, and genetically manipulated organisms. While these principles serve as some guidance to those seeking patent protection for their inventions, they are no substitute for judicial consideration. Even so, they have shaped the way in which the APO treats patent applications for living organisms and biotechnological products. This may change depending on the outcome of the current test case challenging the patenting of human genes – namely, *Cancer Voices Australia v Myriad Genetics Inc*, which puts into question the validity of the patent for the BRCA 1 genetic mutation.

## The Rationale for Biotechnology Patents

In Chapter 8 we considered the historical development of patent law and the rationale behind the patent system. According to Lord Parker in *Attorney General (Cth) v Adelaide Steamship Co*,[10] the patent system encourages "inventive ingenuity" with the result being "a new and useful article or process" for the ultimate benefit of society. It is often claimed that without the provision of a temporary monopoly to thwart "free-riders", there would not be the necessary investment in research and development to bring about innovation and thereby the technological advancement of a society.[11]

As for the biotechnology industry, significant innovation is considered dependent on patent protection as the necessary financial base needed for research and development would not make itself available otherwise.[12] However, Arup states that "[p]atent rights provide no guarantee to the state that inventions will be

---

not pass the Bill; meanwhile the Australian court action, *Cancer Voices Australia v Myriad Genetics Inc*, was heard by the Federal Court in February 2012.

9     See *Patents Act 1990* s 18(2).

10    [1913] AC 781, House of Lords.

11    See Industrial Property Advisory Committee, *Part A Reviewing the Australian Patent System, Patents, Innovation and Competition in Australia*, 1984. See also Intellectual Property and Competition Review Committee, *Review of Intellectual Property Legislation under the Competition Principles Agreement. Final Report*, September 2000.

12    See DC Chisum, *Patenting Living Subject Matter, DNA Sequences Encoding Proteins, Gene Therapy and Therapeutic Methods Under United States Law*, ATRIP Annual Conference Proceedings – Emergent Technologies and Intellectual Property, July 19-21, 1995, CASRIP Publication Series No 2 1996, p 31. See also C Arup, *Innovation, Policy and Law, Australia and the International High Technology Economy*, Cambridge University Press, Melbourne, 1993, Chapter 3, pp 66-67.

stimulated or to the holder that inventions will be successful",[13] but goes on to recognise that patents form part of the overall strategy of the biotechnology industry, and indeed other technology industries, to "capture the benefits of innovation".[14]

Perhaps the most important purpose of the patent system from the point of view of the financial investor in biotechnology is the security of legal recourse should the research and ensuing invention be infringed by "free-riders". That is, the ability to exclude others from exploiting one's invention for a significant period of time provides a greater opportunity to recoup investment costs and ultimately make a profit, not to mention creating a well defined asset which is able to be traded for access to other biotechnology.[15]

However, while investors are not assured of a return in relation to research and development in biotechnology, without the expectation of the basic security of patent protection finance for the industry would more than likely be stifled. This is particularly poignant when we recognise that most biotechnology firms do not exploit their inventions directly but rather sell the rights to such exploitation.[16] It is common for a biotechnology company in Australia to develop its invention to the pre-clinical stage and seek an offshore multinational (often pharmaceutical) company to take a licence of the technology.[17] This is usually due to the cost of clinical trials necessary for registration under the *Therapeutic Goods Act 1989* before the resultant pharmaceutical can be marketed. The length of the process for gaining market-ing approval is recognised as an impediment to the full exploitation of a patent protecting the product. That is why an extension of up to five years is available to pharmaceutical substances.[18] However, the extension does not prevent producers of generic products from "springboarding", namely, gearing up to hit the market upon expiry of the patent. That is why the patentee's competitors are not considered to be infringing the patent during the extension term if the form of the invention being exploited is not the pharmaceutical substance[19] or the purpose of exploiting the pharmaceutical substance is other than for a therapeutic use.[20] Exploiting a pharmaceutical patent to obtain regulatory approval from the Therapeutic Goods Administration or its equivalent overseas is an exemption to infringement even

---

13    C Arup, *Innovation, Policy and Law, Australia and the International High Technology Economy*, Cambridge University Press, Melbourne, 1993, Chapter 3, p 66.

14    C Arup, *Innovation, Policy and Law, Australia and the International High Technology Economy*, Cambridge University Press, Melbourne, 1993, Chapter 3, p 66.

15    ES van der Graaf, in *Patent Law and Modern Biotechnology*, Sanders Institute, Gouder Quint, Rotterdam, 1997, p 38.

16    OECD, *An Overview of Biotechnology Statistics in Selected Countries*, 2003, p 13.

17    *Genes and Ingenuity Report Gene Patenting and Human Health*, ALRC, Report 99, June 2004, p 404.

18    *Patents Act 1990* s 77. A pharmaceutical substance is defined as "a substance (including a mixture or compound of substances) for therapeutic use whose application (or one of whose applications) involves: (a) a chemical interaction, or physico-chemical interaction, with a human physiological system; or (b) action on an infectious agent, or on a toxin or other poison, in a human body; but does not include a substance that is solely for use in in vitro diagnosis or in vitro testing: *Patents Act 1990* Sch 1.

19    *Patents Act 1990* s 78(b).

20    *Patents Act 1990* s 78(a).

where no extension of patent term has been granted.[21] If, however, the products are required to be exported from Australia to a foreign jurisdiction for approval purpose then the exemption from infringement will only apply if the patent term has been extended.[22] This exemption from infringement is to be extended to all technologies that require regulatory approval but only for the purpose of obtaining such approval and thereby preventing the simultaneous stockpiling of the generic version of the patented product.[23]

This patent extension process was the subject of debate in relation to the implementation of the US-Australia Free Trade Agreement and resulted in significant amendments to the *Therapeutic Goods Act 1989*. Schedule 7 to the *US Free Trade Agreement Implementation Act 2004*, which commenced on 1 January 2005, requires persons applying for registration or listing of therapeutic goods (other than therapeutic devices) to provide one of two certificates. The applicant will either have to certify that they do not propose to market those therapeutic goods in a way or in circumstances that would infringe a patent,[24] or they would have to certify that they propose to market the therapeutic goods before the expiry of a relevant patent and that they have notified the patent owner of their application to include goods in the Australian Register of Therapeutic Goods.[25] If the certificate is false or misleading in a material particular, it will be an offence and attract a penalty.[26]

Schedule 7 introduces another certification regime for parties who undertake patent infringement proceedings against a person who has lodged a certificate under the above new requirements of the *Therapeutic Goods Act 1989*. This regime is design to discourage vexatious actions brought by patent owners to prevent the introduction of cheaper generic drugs on the market. A pecuniary penalty of up to $10 million dollars may apply if the certificate provided by the patentee is false or misleading or an undertaking in the certificate is breached.[27] The patentee must certify that the infringement proceedings are commenced in good faith, will be conducted without unreasonable delay, and there are reasonable prospects of success.[28]

Where the patentee has sought an interlocutory injunction against a party who has applied for registration of a pharmaceutical under the *Therapeutic Goods Act 1989*, the patentee may be liable for damages if the principal infringement proceedings are discontinued without consent or are dismissed and the court declares that the patentee was acting vexatiously or there were no reasonable grounds for taking the action in the first place.[29] For this provision to apply, the

---

21  *Patents Act 1990* s 119A(1), effective 25 October 2006.
22  *Patents Act 1990* s 119A(2), effective 25 October 2006.
23  *Intellectual Property Laws Amendment (Raising The Bar) Act 2012*, Sch 2 Item 1, new s 119B. The Explanatory Memorandum explains that there are a variety of other technologies that require regulatory approvals, such as medical devices and agricultural chemicals, and that there is no reason why they should be treated differently from pharmaceutical products.
24  *Therapeutic Goods Act 1989* s 26B(1)(a).
25  *Therapeutic Goods Act 1989* s 26B(1)(b).
26  *Therapeutic Goods Act 1989* s 26B(2).
27  *Therapeutic Goods Act 1989* s 26C(5).
28  *Therapeutic Goods Act 1989* s 26C(3).
29  *Therapeutic Goods Act 1989* s 26D(5).

applicant seeking registration with the Therapeutic Goods Administration must have provided notice to the patentee in the circumstances that they intend to market their goods before the expiry of the patent.[30]

The question arises as to what these provisions are trying to achieve. The penalties are heavily skewed against the patentee but perhaps such a regime is necessary to ensure that the patent system is not abused. After all, pharmaceuticals have the advantage over all other inventions by having the opportunity for a longer monopoly term.

## Ethical Considerations

There have been some efforts to try to limit patent protection pertaining to the latest developments in the biotechnology industry. These mostly relate to lifeforms and genetic "discoveries", with the limits based on both ethical grounds and equity based grounds. For instance, the use of intellectual property systems such as patents to obtain exclusive ownership over biological resources, products and processes derived from plants and animals has been considered "biopiracy", an attempt by the industrialised "North" to enclose the "biological commons" of the developing "South".[31] Further, the patenting of genes have been considered contrary to moral values and nature,[32] but the greatest ethical and religious concerns relate to the patenting of human genes.[33] If we accept the complete complement of human genes (the human genome) to be "the common heritage of humanity", espoused by both UNESCO[34] and HUGO's Ethics Committee,[35] then it is difficult to comprehend how a single corporation could obtain an exclusive right over such common heritage. Concerns over an individual's right to self-determination is said to confuse physical property rights with the intangible property rights conferred by a patent.[36]

But how does one close the floodgates after they have been opened?[37] This is certainly evident when we consider that a United States patent for yeast was

---

30   *Therapeutic Goods Act 1989* s 26D(1)(a).

31   V Shiva, *Protect or Plunder, Understanding Intellectual Property Rights*, Zed Books Ltd, London, 2001, p 49; for a discussion, see NP Stoianoff, "Biological Resources and Benefit Sharing: the Intersection between Traditional Knowledge and Intellectual Property" in SK Veerma and R Mittal (eds), *Intellectual Property Rights A Global Vision*, Indian Law Institute, New Delhi, 2004, p 46.

32   In Europe, the objection of being contrary to *ordre public* has been raised by various groups opposing patents for genes and genetic technologies. The concept of *ordre public* is similar in nature to the concept of "generally inconvenient" in Australian patent law.

33   *Genes and Ingenuity Report Gene Patenting and Human Health*, ALRC, Report 99, June 2004, p 72.

34   United Nations Educational, Scientific and Cultural Organization, see specifically Art 12(a) of the *Universal Declaration on the Human Genome and Human Rights*, 11 November 1997, UNESCO.

35   Human Genome Organisation's Ethics Committee, *Statement on the Principled Conduct of Genetics Research*, 1996.

36   *Genes and Ingenuity Report Gene Patenting and Human Health*, ALRC, Report 99, June 2004, p 72.

37   See, for example, the proposed *Treaty for a Lifeforms Patent-free Pacific and Related Protocols*, August 1995, and the *Patents Amendment Bill 1996* (Commonwealth of Australia) which, had it passed, would have effectively excluded the patenting of genes and gene sequences.

obtained by Louis Pasteur in 1873.[38] Interestingly, this predates the *Chakrabarty* patent[39] by more than a century and yet the subject-matter in each instance concerned single celled lifeforms. More importantly, the question is whether, in fact, ethical considerations come into the question of patentability given the rationale behind the system. One might ask, then, what is the purpose of the "generally inconvenient" exception to patentability?

Certainly, the APO does not consider it their role to determine whether a particular subject-matter is patentable or not based "solely on matters of ethics or social policy".[40] Nor has it been perceived in Australia as the role of the courts to do so. Rather, such matters are considered appropriate for Parliament to decide. Lockhart J, in *Anaesthetic Supplies Pty Ltd v Rescare Limited* (the *Rescare* case),[41] stressed this point in relation to the question of the patentability of medical treatment inventions, noting:

> There is no statutory provision in Australia prohibiting the grant of a patent for a process of medical treatment of a human ailment or disease in a human being. It is noteworthy that Parliament had the opportunity to exclude methods of treating the human body when it enacted the 1990 Act, but the limit of the exclusion was s 18(2), namely: 'human beings, and the biological processes for their generation, are not patentable inventions' ...[42]

The same argument applies in relation to living organisms generally, their genes and other biotechnological inventions. The reason why humans and the biological processes for their generation were specifically excluded from patentability relates to the ethical concerns associated with the direction of research pertaining to *in vitro* fertilisation developing in Melbourne at the time. This reinforces the view that such ethical considerations in relation to what is to be excluded from patentability is a question for Parliament and the opportunity has presented itself since the enactment of the 1990 Act.[43] Clearly, a specific exclusion was perceived necessary to ensure that *human beings and the biological processes for their generation* would not be patented. Does this mean, therefore, that, but for the express exclusion, *human beings and the biological processes for their generation* would be appropriate subject-matter for letters patent? This is an interesting question given the current debates about stem cell technology and cloning of human beings – particularly since studies show that one-third of the over 2000 patent applications for human and animal stem cells lodged worldwide by May 2002 have been granted.[44]

Further, Lockhart J's point is particularly poignant when one considers that in the 1980s patent offices around the world were dealing with numerous

38    USP 141,072, cited in PW Grubb, *Patents for Chemicals, Pharmaceuticals and Biotechnology*, Clarendon Press, Oxford, 1999, p 225.

39    *Diamond v Chakrabarty* 447 US 303 (1980).

40    See APO, *Manual of Practice and Procedure – National*, July 2007, ¶2.9.1.2.

41    (1994) 28 IPR 383.

42    (1994) 28 IPR 383 at 400.

43    This opportunity was in the form of an attempt by a sitting member of the Australian Democrats to introduce an amendment to the *Patents Act 1990* (see the *Patents Amendment Bill 1996*) which would, if enacted, effectively exclude the patenting of genes and gene sequences. This has not succeeded.

44    *Genes and Ingenuity Report Gene Patenting and Human Health*, ALRC, Report 99, June 2004, p 379.

applications pertaining to the development of the biotechnology industry including the Harvard or Oncomouse affair and other transgenics,[45] not to mention the fact that in 1990 the Human Genome Project had just commenced.[46] One could conclude that, by not excluding such inventions, the Australian Parliament was acting in full knowledge of the commercial potential surrounding the biotechnology industry. Alternatively, one could also conclude that interest groups expressing ethical concerns about the development of that industry did not make a mark in Australian social policy until the late 1990s.[47] Whatever view is taken the issue is the same, as Wilcox J confirms, also in the *Rescare* case,[48] the courts should not be resorting to ethics and social policy "in order to engraft onto a recently enacted statute an exception that parliament has chosen not to adopt" as that would be to "usurp [parliament's] role" when "the courts have no special expertise" in these matters.[49]

## The Elements of Patentability

When considering the elements of patentability under Australian law one must keep in mind Australia's obligations under the TRIPS Agreement.[50] TRIPS confirms the basic concepts of what constitutes patentable subject-matter and these concepts are therefore common to most jurisdictions; namely, whether the subject-matter of the invention is a product or process, whether the invention is novel and inventive, and whether the invention is useful or capable of industrial application.[51] However, perhaps the most relevant obligation contained in Art 27.1, for the purposes of this chapter, is the requirement that "patents shall be available for any inventions, whether products or processes, in all fields of technology".

In Australia, the *Patents Act 1990* expressly stipulates the requirements of patentability. Section 18(1) defines the elements of a patentable invention

---

45 The "Harvard mouse" or "Oncomouse" affair refers to the patent for a transgenic mouse developed, as a medical research tool, to be susceptible to breast cancer. The mouse was transgenic in that human genes were inserted into the genetic structure of the mouse through recombinant DNA methods producing a new "animal variety". The patent was granted in the United States of America in 1988 but received much opposition from green and other lobby groups in Europe and Canada, given that this was the first time that a patent was being sought over a higher life form. For a brief history of genetic technology patents, see *Genes and Ingenuity Report Gene Patenting and Human Health*, ALRC, Report 99, June 2004, p 66.

46 M Kirby, "Intellectual Property and the Human Genome" (2001) 12 *AIPJ* 61.

47 For example, the *Consensus Conference* in 1999 regarding the labelling of GMOs in food.

48 *Anaesthetic Supplies Pty Ltd v Rescare Ltd* (1994) 28 IPR 383.

49 (1994) 28 IPR 383 at 425.

50 The Agreement on Trade-Related Aspects of Intellectual Property Rights.

51 In particular, Art 27 at para 1 states that:
    Subject to the provisions of paragraphs 2 and 3, patents shall be available for any inventions, whether products or processes, in all fields of technology, provided that they are new, involve an inventive step and are capable of industrial application. See footnote 5. Subject to paragraph 4 of Article 65, paragraph 8 of Article 70 and paragraph 3 of this Article, patents shall be available and patent rights enjoyable without discrimination as to the place of invention, the field of technology and whether products are imported or locally produced.
    Footnote 5 acknowledges the interchangeability of the terminology "inventive step" and "non-obviousness", and, "industrial applicability" and "useful". Paragraphs 2 and 3 of Art 27 indicate what may be excluded from patentability.

for the purposes of a standard patent while s 18(1A) does the same for innovation patents. These have been considered in Chapter 9, namely, manner of manufacture, novelty, inventive step (or innovative step for innovation patents), usefulness or utility, and no secret use.

## Human beings

Further, s 18(2) provides the express exclusion to patentable inventions referred to above, namely, human beings and the biological processes for their generation. This exclusion would seem to be in keeping with the general exclusion provided in Art 27.2 of TRIPS which enables members

> to exclude from patentability inventions, the prevention within their territory of the commercial exploitation of which is necessary to protect ordre public or morality, including to protect human, animal or plant life or health or to avoid serious prejudice to the environment, provided that such exclusion is not made merely because the exploitation is prohibited by their law.

However, when we consider the specific exclusions permitted in Art 27.3, human beings are not mentioned while plants and animals and the biological processes for their production are capable of specific exclusion.[52] This is an interesting situation bringing us back to the question of whether, without a specific exclusion, human beings and the biological processes for their generation can be appropriate subject-matter for letters patent.

As for the scope of s 18(2) of the *Patents Act 1990*, the APO provides guidance at ¶2.9.5 of the APO, *Manual of Practice and Procedure – National*, July 2011. Keeping in mind that there is a lack of judicial consideration, the APO refers to the decision of the Deputy Commissioner in *Fertilitescentrum AB and Luminis Pty Ltd's Application* [2004] APO 19:

> The correct interpretation of s 18(2) is ascertained by recognizing a human being as being in the process of generation from the time of the processes that create a fertilized ovum (or other processes that give rise to an equivalent entity) up to the time of birth.[53]

Further, the Deputy Commissioner recognises that a "fertilized ovum and all its subsequent manifestations" will constitute a human being for the purposes of the prohibition.[54] This in turn is further clarified in the APO Manual at ¶2.9.5 as "fertilized ova and equivalents, zygotes, blastocysts, embryos, fetuses, and totipotent human cells including those cells that are the products of nuclear transfer procedures".

---

52   Article 27 at para 3 states that:
     "Members may also exclude from patentability:
     (a)  diagnostic, therapeutic and surgical methods for the treatment of humans or animals;
     (b)  plants and animals other than micro-organisms, and essentially biological processes for the production of plants or animals other than non-biological and microbiological processes. However, Members shall provide for the protection of plant varieties either by patents or by an effective sui generis system or by any combination thereof. The provisions of this subparagraph shall be reviewed four years after the date of entry into force of the WTO Agreement."
53   APO, *Manual of Practice and Procedure – National*, July 2011, ¶2.9.5.
54   APO, *Manual of Practice and Procedure – National*, July 2011, ¶2.9.5.

The Deputy Commissioner goes on to determine that "all biological processes applied from fertilisation to birth – so long as the process directly relates to the generation of a human being"[55] are prohibited under s 18(2). The APO Manual provides an extensive list of such excluded biological processes at ¶2.9.5 but perhaps the list of inventions the APO considers not to contravene s 18(2) is more telling, namely:

> [P]rocesses for cryopreservation of gametes, methods for preimplantation genetic analysis of gametes, and processes of methods for determining the developmental progress or viability of a fertilised ovum, blastocyst or embryo, by analysis of culture or incubation media.[56]

Stem cells, on the other hand, could be clear of the operation of s 18(2) or could quite squarely fit into the operation of s 18(2). These cells can divide indefinitely as well as differentiate into any type of cell. The three types of stem cells have varying qualities which will result in a different application of s 18(2). Human embryonic stem cells are pluripotent, meaning they can differentiate into a variety of cell types, but are not considered totipotent as they cannot develop into an entire human being. This means that human embryonic stem cells and their cell lines are likely to be considered patentable. However, human embryos

> are considered to be human beings within the meaning of the s 18(2), and consequently human embryos and processes for generating or culturing human embryos for any purpose, including the harvest of stem cells, are not patentable and contravene s 18(2).[57]

On the other hand human adult stem cells are not derived from embryos and are more likely multipotent in nature having only limited capacity to differentiate.[58] Consequently, both the cells and the process of harvesting or isolating such adult stem cells fall outside the operation of s 18(2).[59] Conversely, human totipotent stem cells do have the capacity to develop into an entire human being and accordingly such cells, together with the process of obtaining such cells, are not patentable pursuant to s 18(2).[60]

The "contrary to law" objection found in s 50(1)(a) of the *Patents Act 1990* may operate in conjunction with s 18(2). For instance, an invention that contravenes s 18(2) such as certain types of cloning would also fall foul of the *Prohibition of Human Cloning Act 2002* or even the *Research Involving Human Embryos Act 2002*. The APO Manual requires examiners to include the s 50(1)(a) objection in their report in addition to the s 18(2) objection.[61]

It is interesting to note that inventions, comprising human genes, tissues and cell lines *per se* have not been identified by the APO as contravening s 18(2). This would imply that they are patentable if all the other statutory requirements

55   APO, *Manual of Practice and Procedure – National*, July 2011, ¶2.9.5.

56   APO, *Manual of Practice and Procedure – National*, July 2011, ¶2.9.5.

57   APO, *Manual of Practice and Procedure – National*, July 2011, ¶2.9.5.1.

58   APO, *Manual of Practice and Procedure – National*, July 2011, ¶2.9.5.1.

59   APO, *Manual of Practice and Procedure – National*, July 2011, ¶2.9.5.1.

60   APO, *Manual of Practice and Procedure – National*, July 2011, ¶2.9.5.1. Consider also the situation of human/non-human totipotent hybrids where human nuclear material is present in the resultant cell. In *Woo-Suk Hwangs Application* (2004) APO 24 IP, the APO considered that the human characteristics present would fall foul of s 18(2).

61   APO, *Manual of Practice and Procedure – National*, July 2011 ¶2.9.5.1.

are met. However, if we follow the line of reasoning of Lockhart and Wilcox JJ in the *Rescare* case,[62] much more is implied. One could argue that the specific exclusion implies that all *non-human* beings and the biological processes for their generation are patentable (as standard patents). In other words, microorganisms, plants and animals and the biological processes for their generation ought to be patentable subject-matter, provided there is compliance with the statutory requirements.

The situation is somewhat different for innovation patents. As mentioned in Chapter 9, innovation patents are also subject to the exclusion in s 18(2). In addition, s 18(3) excludes plants and animals together with the biological processes for their generation from being the subject of an innovation patent.[63] However, innovation patents can be obtained for a microbiological process or a product of such a process to be the subject of an innovation patent pursuant to s 18(4).

Clearly, the primary element to be addressed is the question of manner of new manufacture. Without satisfying this element there is no point in testing whether the purported invention satisfies the remaining elements of patentability.[64] The only exception to this is the application of the exclusion in s 18(2) of the Act. If one is attempting to patent a human being or biological process for generating a human being, then the purported invention fails before the test of manner of new manufacture can be applied. At the end of 2010 an attempt had been made to introduce another exception to patentability by introducing para (b) to s 18(2), thereby excluding from patentability:

> biological materials including their components and derivatives, whether isolated or purified or not and however made, which are identical or substantially identical to such materials as they exist in nature.[65]

This led to numerous submissions and a recommendation by the Legal and Constitutional Affairs Legislation Committee of the Senate not to pass the Bill.[66] This would seem in line with the outcome of two earlier reports. The Senate Community Affairs Reference Committee Inquiry into Gene Patents also did not recommend an express prohibition on the patenting of human genes and genetic products.[67] The outcome of the Advisory Council of Intellectual Property – Review of Patentable Subject Matter (ACIP Report) was not in favour of another specific

---

62   *Anaesthetic Supplies Pty Ltd v Rescare Ltd* (1994) 28 IPR 383.

63   The fact that this exclusion is specifically made in respect of innovation patents confirms that s 18(2) of the *Patents Act 1990* does not encompass any lifeform other than humans. However, consider *Woo-Suk Hwang's Application* [2004] APO 24 relating to an interspecies hybrid embryo.

64   Although the contrary view has been taken by House of Lords in *Biogen Inc v Medeva plc* (1997) 36 IPR 438 (HL). See specifically Lord Hoffman at 449, but note that the *Patents Act 1977* (UK) does not have a definition for "invention" while the *Patents Act 1990* (Cth) does have a definition in the form of the statutory element, "manner of [new] manufacture".

65   *Patent Amendment (Human Genes and Biological Materials) Bill 2010.*

66   Senate Legal and Constitutional Affairs Legislation Committee, Patent Amendment (Human Genes and Biological Materials) Bill 2010, September 2011, p 65. Specifically, on p 64, the Committee concluded:
     [T]he committee does not agree that the Bill represents an effective solution to the problems which may be caused by patents over human genes and biological materials. In particular, the committee is concerned that proposed amendments in the Bill, which are focused on addressing a specific issue, could have a large number of unintended consequences across the entire patent system with indeterminate impacts on a range of industries and sectors.

67   Senate Community Affairs References Committee, Gene Patents, November 2010, pp 99-100.

exclusion, preferring the introduction of a general exclusion on ethical grounds and a redefining of patentable subject-matter "using clear and contemporary language".[68] The Legal and Constitutional Affairs Legislation Committee of the Senate was in favour of this course of action.

Meanwhile, there are other elements to patentability. The requirements of novelty and inventiveness concentrate on the comparison of the prior art base with the purported invention, not whether the purported invention is appropriate subject-matter for patent protection. The issue of usefulness or utility goes to the question of construction of the patent specification and its claims which impact upon the question of invention. And it would seem that what judicial opinion there exists in this field of technology has been in relation to compliance with s 40. The issue of secret use goes to whether the purported invention has been used in such a fashion as to constitute a fatal disclosure of the invention. These elements of novelty, inventiveness, utility and no secret use are therefore reliant upon the facts of the individual application and perhaps comprise the more technical side of the inquiry.

## Manner of New Manufacture

As we have seen in Chapter 9, an "invention" is a "manner of new manufacture". A discussion of the general principles and relevant cases can be found in that chapter. However, as noted above, much of the case law revolves around the meaning of the concept of "manner of manufacture" with *National Research Development Corporation v Commissioner of Patents* (*NRDC* case),[69] determined by the High Court some 53 years ago, being the most significant case on point today. The case is significant also from the point of view that it deals with a biologically based process, namely, the eradication of weeds growing among leguminous fodder crops. Further, one could describe the invention as the practical application of the discovery of a naturally occurring property in a living organism. The application of the herbicide based on this property was not previously known and the discovery led to a new application resulting in a manner of new manufacture.[70]

But a mere *discovery*[71] or *law of nature*[72] would not be patentable. The *NRDC* case points out the difficulty of drawing a distinction between discovery and invention but notes that, for there to be invention, there must be a practical application of the discovery to a useful end.[73] The APO provides that a claimed invention must lie in the technical or practical realm for it to be patentable.[74] But the High Court in the *NRDC* case actually provided further clarification. If there is "an artificial effect" or "artificially created state of affairs" and the invention

---

68  ACIP, Patentable Subject Matter, Final Report, December 2010, pp 2-20.

69  (1959) 102 CLR 252.

70  (1959) 102 CLR. 252.

71  See, for example, Lindley LJ in *Lane-Fox v Kensington & Knightsbridge Electric Lighting Co (Ltd)* (1892) 9 RPC 413 at 416.

72  The APO tends to treat discoveries and laws of nature interchangeably, in accordance with the *NRDC* case.

73  (1959) 102 CLR 252 at 264.

74  APO, *Manual of Practice and Procedure – National*, July 2011, ¶2.9.2.5.

"possesses its own economic utility" then it is patentable.[75] And this applies even where the invention relates to an agricultural or horticultural process.[76]

A similar development has occurred with the human treatment exception. It is now generally accepted that, provided they have commercial application, both a therapeutic or curative treatment and a cosmetic treatment may constitute a manner of manufacture.[77] The only argument standing in the way of such a conclusion would be on the ground of general inconvenience. However, the concept of general inconvenience has not been the subject of much judicial guidance. But in the instance of medical treatment, it was affirmed, by the Full Court of the Federal Court of Australia, that the generally inconvenient argument cannot be used to invalidate patents for such methods.[78] In fact, the APO specifically instructs its examiners to avoid it as a ground of objection, preferring the argument that the invention does not lie in the technical realm or fails for lack of novelty.[79]

What the above developments illustrate is that the courts, in addition to the APO, are increasingly reluctant to exclude a particular field of technology from patentability on the basis of "inappropriate" subject-matter. Rather, in keeping with the requirements of TRIPS Art 27.1, there is an increasing trend to acknowledge that any technology is appropriate subject-matter for the grant of letters patent provided that the claimed invention consists of an "artificially created state of affairs" or is a "useful art as distinct from a fine art" and has "economic utility" or "its value to the country is in the field of economic endeavour".[80] This confirms, though, that mere discoveries or laws of nature still fall outside of the concept of a manner of new manufacture.

The question then arises as to on what basis a living organism or other biological material or biotechnological products attain patent protection in Australia. The primary issue has been whether living organisms and biological material can escape the realm of nature and enter the realm of patentable subject-matter. The difficulties that have arisen are concerned with the above-mentioned concepts of naturally occurring substance, mere discovery or law of nature. The case law in the USA has distinguished between a "product of nature" and a "product derived from nature" with the first being unpatentable while the second providing possibilities of patentability. It was the US Supreme Court case of *Diamond v Chakrabarty*[81] that has been attributed with the fame of paving the way for the grant of patents for manipulated living organisms and their "products". In that case, Chakrabarty

75   (1959) 102 CLR 252 at 277.

76   (1959) 102 CLR 252 at 279 per Dixon CJ, Kitto and Windeyer JJ.

77   *Anaesthetic Supplies Pty Ltd v Rescare Ltd* (1994) 28 IPR 383. Also confirmed in *Bristol-Myers Squibb Company v FH Faulding & Co Ltd* (2000) 46 IPR 553.

78   *Bristol-Myers Squibb Company v FH Faulding & Co Ltd* (2000) 46 IPR 553. In this case petty patents for the administration of taxol were in question. Taxol is a naturally occurring cancer treatment drug that, of itself, is not patentable; the claims here related to the method of administration of the drug.

79   APO, *Manual of Practice and Procedure – National*, July 2011, ¶2.9.3.

80   See *CCOM Pty Ltd v Jiejing Pty Ltd* (1994) 28 IPR 481; (1994) AIPC ¶91-079 and, more specifically, see APO, *Manual of Practice and Procedure – National*, July 2011, ¶2.9.2.7, wherein it was confirmed that the alleged software-based invention must be "an artificially created state of affairs of utility in the field of economic endeavour".

81   447 US 303 (1980).

sought patent protection for a genetically engineered microorganism designed to break up crude oil spills. In a majority decision, Chakrabarty was allowed the patent protection on the basis that there was human intervention and not mere discovery. The Supreme Court recognised that the new bacterium was "not nature's handiwork" but that of the inventor, and that the characteristics of the new bacterium were markedly different from those found in nature.[82]

But there are earlier instances of patent offices accepting such inventions, such as the Pasteur patent referred to above. In Australia, the APO considered the *Rank Hovis McDougall Ltd's Application*.[83] In that case the process of isolating a microorganism from soil and manipulating it into new variations as well as the variants themselves were considered patentable while the naturally occurring organism itself, isolated using standard techniques, could not be patented.[84] In essence, some form of "technical intervention" was required. There was no objection on the ground that the invention was living, but, for a naturally occurring microorganism to not represent a discovery, "a claim to a pure culture in the presence of some specified ingredients would satisfy the requirement of technical intervention".[85]

Further, the APO historically dealt with biotechnological applications through the chemical inventions division until such time as expertise was developed in biotechnology. Accordingly, it is no coincidence that, when dealing with the issue of discoveries, chemical substances and microorganisms have been treated similarly. This is illustrated in the guidance provided in the APO, *Manual of Practice and Procedure – National*, July 2011, at ¶2.9.2.5:

> A chemical substance or microorganism which is discovered in nature without any practical application is a "mere chemical curiosity" and not patentable subject matter.
>
> More commonly in examination, the specification provides some practical application for the isolated substance or microbe. Although such subject matter is potentially patentable, examiners should consider whether the claims distinguish the microbe or substance from those forms which already exist in nature.
>
> Thus, the discovery of a microorganism, protein, enatiomer or antibiotic in nature can be claimed in its isolated form or as substantially free of (perhaps, specified) impurities. Also a gene can be claimed as the gene per se (as long as the claim does not include within its scope the native chromosome of which the gene forms part) or as the recombinant or isolated or purified gene.

Accordingly, the general rule still applies – where something is naturally occurring it is not patentable. However, where there is some type of human intervention involved, such as genetically altering a living organism, this would indicate that the invention is some form of manner of new manufacture. And this construction accords with the principles obtained from the *NRDC* case.

In the Australian Law Reform Commission's Genes and Ingenuity Report, June 2004, reference was made to the 1988 joint statement made by the Japanese

---

82    447 US 303 at 309-310 (1980).

83    (1976) 46 AOJP 3915.

84    The commissioner pointed out that, in addition to the issue of "discovery", the claim for the naturally occurring organism would fail for lack of novelty as at the priority date because the naturally occurring organism was in existence in Australia at that time.

85    APO, *Manual of Practice and Procedure – National*, July 2007, ¶2.9.2.14.

Patent Office, the United States Patent and Trade Mark Office and the European Patent Office:

> Purified natural products are not regarded as products of nature or discoveries because they do not in fact exist in nature in an isolated form. Rather, they are regarded for patent purposes as biologically active substances or chemical compounds and eligible for patenting on the same basis as other chemical compounds.[86]

This quite clearly accords with Australian Patent Office practice. But the European Union went one step further and implemented, after many years of negotiation, the Biotechnology Directive from 6 July 1998.[87] Article 5(2) of the Directive clarifies the treatment of genes derived from the human body:

> An element isolated from the human body or otherwise produced by means of a technical process, including the sequence or partial sequence of a gene, may constitute a patentable invention, even if the structure of that element is identical to that of the natural element.

At face value, such a treatment blurs the line between discovery and invention. One can only hope that novelty and inventive step are met to distinguish the invention from the discovery. Clearly, emphasis needs to be given to "technical process" in determining patentability.

Australian patent practice has been quite liberal in its attitude toward the patentability of genetic and other such inventions.[88] The degree of human intervention necessary in order to consider a gene sufficiently altered from its natural state has not been great. And this holds true when considering the outcome of the erythropoietin case, *Genetics Institute Inc v Kirin-Amgen Inc (No 3)*.[89] In that case the invention concerned the use of recombinant DNA techniques to produce commercial quantities of erythropoietin (EPO), a protein produced in the human body responsible for maintaining sufficient red blood cells, and disclosed the protein coding sequence necessary to produce EPO. The only issues of concern turned out to be related to s 40, namely fair basis and clarity.

It is clear that current patent law practice treats the isolation and expression of a gene outside of its natural environment as the necessary "human intervention".[90] This is interesting when contrasted with the decision in *Rank Hovis McDougall Ltd's Application*.[91] Lawson points out that "a cloned gene or gene sequence is arguably similar to an isolated soil bacteria – it is the same as the gene or gene sequence found in nature and has been 'discovered' using

---

86   *Genes and Ingenuity Report Gene Patenting and Human Health*, ALRC, Report 99, June 2004, p 124.

87   *Directive 98/44/EC of the European Parliament and of the Council on the Legal Protection of Biotechnology Inventions*.

88   Patent applications involving genetic manipulation cover the entire range of technologies including: synthetic genes or DNA sequences; mutant forms and fragments of gene sequences; the DNA coding sequence of a gene (is this not a discovery?); protein expressed by a gene; vectors; probes for genes; host cells carrying the gene; higher plants/animals carrying the gene; organisms for expressing the gene; PCR and other such methods; regulatory DNA sequences. See *Australian Patents for: Microorganisms, Cell Lines, Hybridomas, Related biological materials and their use; Genetically manipulated organisms*, IP Australia, February 1998.

89   [1998] FCA 740.

90   See *Genetics Institute Inc v Kirin-Amgen Inc (No 3)* [1998] 740 FCA for a detailed judgment on point. See also *Synaptic Pharmaceutical Corporation v Astra Aktiebolag* [1998] APO 49.

91   (1976) 46 AOJP 3915.

standard techniques".[92] But this ignores the fact that isolating bacteria from soil could be seen as simply removing an entire living organism from a dense, opaque and complex nutrient environment, the soil, and placing it into a translucent and comparatively homogeneous nutrient environment, such as an agar plate, making it easy to separate out and observe. The bacteria, in each case, maintain their separateness from the medium and are alive, growing and multiplying in the presence of the medium. Contrast this with a gene sequence that was, before its isolation, an integral part of a strand of genes in a DNA molecule located in the nucleus of a living cell. The gene in its natural state forms part of that living cell and contributes to the functioning of that cell. Isolated and expressed, albeit using standard techniques, that gene is not the same as it was in the living cell.

Further, Jacobs and Van Overwalle note that there is one school of thought that "sees DNA as simply a chemical molecule" capable of patent protection like any other chemical compound.[93] This is quite evident in the decision of the Court of Appeal of the Federal Circuit in *Association for Molecular Pathology v Myriad Genetics Inc*[94] where Lourie J (representing the majority), after analysing the US Supreme Court decision in *Diamond v Chakrabarty*, pointed out:

> The distinction, therefore, between a product of nature and a human-made invention for purposes of § 101 turns on a change in the claimed composition's identity compared with what exists in nature. Specifically, the Supreme Court has drawn a line between compositions that, even if combined or altered in a manner not found in nature, have similar characteristics as in nature, and compositions that human intervention has given "markedly different," or "distinctive," characteristics … Applying this test to the isolated DNAs in this case [namely BRCA 1 an BRCA 2], we conclude that the challenged claims are drawn to patentable subject matter because the claims cover molecules that are markedly different—have a distinctive chemical identity and nature—from molecules that exist in nature.[95]

Interestingly, in the process of Lourie J addressing the arguments of the plaintiffs and the amicus brief from the US government, the distinctions raised above between isolated bacteria and isolated DNA are pertinent:

> It is suggested that holding isolated DNAs patent eligible opens the door to claims covering isolated chemical elements, like lithium; minerals found in the earth, like diamonds; atomic particles, like electrons; and even organs, like a kidney, and a leaf from a tree. None of these examples, however, as far as we can discern, presents the case of a claim to a composition having a distinctive chemical identity from that of the native element, molecule, or structure. Elemental lithium is the same element whether it is in the earth or isolated; the diamond is the same lattice of carbon molecules, just with the earth removed; the kidney is the same kidney, the leaf the same leaf. Some may have a changed form, quality, or use when prepared in isolated or purified form, but we cannot tell on this record whether the changes are sufficiently distinctive to make the composition markedly different from the one that exists in nature. In contrast, a portion of a native DNA

---

92  C Lawson, "Patenting Genetic Materials: Old Rules May be Restricting the Exploitation of a New Technology" (1999) 6 *Journal of Law and Medicine* 373 at 380.

93  P Jacobs and G Van Overwalle, "Gene Patents: A Different Approach" [2001] EIPR 505.

94  Case No 2010-1406, decided 29 July 2011, <http://www.cafc.uscourts.gov/images/stories/opinions-orders/10-1406.pdf>.

95  Case No 2010-1406, p 41.

molecule—an isolated DNA—has a markedly different chemical nature from the native DNA. It is, therefore, patentable subject matter.[96]

Lourie J went on to deal with the arguments of the dissent and then on to the 30 years of practice of the USPTO in granting patents for DNA molecules indicating that this practice is not inconsistent with s 101 of the US legislation, concluding that if there is to be a change it must come from Congress.[97] The method claims comparing or analysing two gene sequences, on the other hand, were held not to be patentable as they covered only abstract mental processes.[98] Meanwhile, the method claim "to screening potential cancer therapeutics via changes in cell growth rates" was held to be patentable subject-matter.[99] It should be noted that Moore J, while concurring on most issues, drew a distinction between longer chain and shorter chain isolated DNA but refrained from finding against the patentability of the BRCA 1 and BRCA 2 genes.[100] Meanwhile, Bryson J concurred on the method claims and on the patentability of cDNA claims but dissented on the BRCA gene claims and gene fragment claims.[101] The difficulty with this appeal is that it does not provide a clear majority decision with Lourie J and Moore J reaching the same conclusion utilising different paths.

However, where the real issues may lie in this inquiry is in the examination of the other elements of patentability and certainly there have been examples where the element of inventive step has been at issue.[102] Before we discuss the other elements of patentability, the views of IP Australia provide some insight into why cases like *Genetics Institute Inc v Kirin-Amgen Inc (No 3)*[103] have treated genes and their corresponding proteins as patentable subject-matter.

## IP Australia Guidelines

Over a decade ago, IP Australia made a point of listing the "range of patentable inventions for standard patent applications which involve microorganisms, cell lines, hybridomas and other related biological materials".[104] This publication then went on to state that standard patent protection could be obtained for inventions *involving*:

- "genotypically or phenotypically modified living organisms [such as] genetically modified bacteria, plants and non-human organisms ...";
- "DNA and genes (including human DNA and genes) which have for the first time been identified and copied from their natural source and then

---

96    Case No 2010-1406, p 46.
97    Case No 2010-1406, p 48.
98    Case No 2010-1406, p 49.
99    Case No 2010-1406, p 54.
100   Case No 2010-1406, p 18 (Moore J).
101   Case No 2010-1406, p 2 (Bryson J).
102   See, for example, the British case, *Genentech Inc v Wellcome Foundation Ltd* [1989] RPC 147, on the patenting of tissue plasminogen activator, and compare the result in the Hepatitis C case, *Chiron Corp v Organon Teknika Ltd (No 3)* [1994] FSR 202.
103   [1998] FCA 740.
104   In the publication: *Australian Patents for: Microorganisms, Cell Lines, Hybridomas, Related biological materials and their use; Genetically manipulated organisms*, IP Australia, February 1998.

> manufactured synthetically as unique materials with a definite industrial use …";
- "products of such living matter".[105]

The first question that arises in considering this statement is what is meant by "inventions *involving*" such phenomena? The term "involving" could imply that something more might be required than the list provides for there to be a patentable invention. There is no clarification of this point but if a standard thesaurus is consulted, words like "include", "entail", "contain", "comprise" etc , appear as synonyms for "involve". Each gives an impression of open-endedness. That is, the use of the term "involving" implies that the invention is not solely defined by the phenomena described in the list. But this vagueness may or may not be intended.

As for genotypically or phenotypically modified organisms these are clearly outside the realm of "naturally occurring" and display the necessary human intervention for classification as a manner of new manufacture. But DNA and genes first identified would seem to still be in the realm of naturally occurring.[106] Accordingly, the additional requirements that such DNA or genes be "copied from their natural source and then manufactured synthetically as unique materials with a definite industrial use" would seem to provide the necessary human intervention for classification as a manner of manufacture.[107] Thirdly, given that the "products of such living matter" are therefore derived from non-naturally occurring modified organisms, genes or DNA, then such products by implication would also not be naturally occurring and would fall in the realm of manner of new manufacture.

The next statement in the IP Australia publication provides an inclusive list of "[t]he range of patentable inventions *involving* genetic manipulation found in Australian standard patent applications".[108] These are:

- "synthetic genes or DNA sequences" – clearly involving human intervention;
- "mutant forms and fragments of gene sequences" – again, one would expect involving human intervention;

---

105 IP Australia, *Australian Patents for: Microorganisms, Cell Lines, Hybridomas, Related biological materials and their use; Genetically manipulated organisms*, February 1998, p 1. This has since been updated into an online document, current as at 9 September 2011, with the list somewhat simplified:
  - genotypically or phenotypically modified living organisms, for example, genetically modified bacteria, plants and non-human organisms (patenting of plant varieties is described in Plant Breeder's Rights)
  - DNA, RNA, chromosomes and genes (including human DNA and genes)
  - products of such DNA, RNA and genes including polypeptides and proteins.
  at <http://www.ipaustralia.gov.au/get-the-right-ip/patents/about-patents/what-can-be-patented/patents-for-biological-inventions/> 6 February 2012.
106 Compare this to the developments concerning chemical or pharmaceutical patent.
107 The updated guidance provided on the IP Australia website provides more clarity on this point:
  For example, DNA or genes in the human body are not patentable. A DNA or gene sequence that has been isolated may be patentable.
  Patent specifications must also describe a specific use for a biological material. For example, if the invention relates to a gene, the specification must disclose a specific use for the gene, such as its use in the diagnosis or treatment of a specific disease, or its use in a specific enzymatic reaction or industrial process.
  at <http://www.ipaustralia.gov.au/get-the-right-ip/patents/about-patents/what-can-be-patented/patents-for-biological-inventions/> 6 February 2012.
108 *Australian Patents for: Microorganisms, Cell Lines, Hybridomas, Related biological materials and their use; Genetically manipulated organisms*, IP Australia, February 1998, p 2.

- the isolated or recombinant state of a DNA coding sequence for a gene – this recognises that to claim the sequence otherwise than isolated or recombinant would be attempting to protect the naturally occurring DNA sequence;
- "the protein expressed by the gene" – could provide confusion if the protein produced naturally is the same in every way, but then resort to the way chemical patents are treated may be necessary here;
- vectors containing the gene are common tools created by biotechnologists;
- "probes for the gene" are clearly an artificially created state of affairs with potential economic utility;
- "methods of transformation using the gene", while a manner of manufacture may have initial issues of "newness" and of novelty, such methods would certainly require an investigation of inventive step;
- anti-sense DNA (which is the sequence used to regulate the gene), while requiring human intervention, might again raise the issue of inventive step;
- host cells and higher plants or animals manipulated to carry the gene fall into the realm of transgenics which are clearly not naturally occurring;
- "organisms for expression of the gene" and "general recombinant DNA methods" are reminiscent of the traditional fermentation biotechnologies using modified bacteria and yeasts and can be clearly manners of new manufacture; and, finally,
- "DNA sequences ... including regulatory sequences such as promoters".

The above list seems to recognise that a mere discovery of biological material cannot be patented, an "artificially created state of affairs" must be the result.[109] IP Australia continues and explicitly states the tests that must be met before a patent can be granted in this field of technology. These tests are basically a restatement of the elements appearing in s 18(1) of the Act. The first test requires the subject-matter to involve "the technical intervention of a technologist applying their inventive ingenuity to produce something distinguishable from the natural source material".[110] This test seems to combine the manner of new manufacture concept with the inventive step concept which would appear to be in keeping with the case law pertaining to the threshold "newness" test.[111]

The second test requires the subject-matter to be "new in the sense of not previously being publicly available [that is, novel]".[112] Once again IP Australia

---

109  Compare the list of patentable subject-matter for plants found in *Australian Patents for Plants*, IP Australia, p 1, namely, new plant varieties; plant components such as genes and chromosomes; reproductive material such as seeds, whole plants, cuttings, cells or protoplasts; products from plants such as fruits, flowers, oils, starches, chemicals and pharmaceuticals; and plant material used in industrial processes, for example cell lines, plant tissue culture etc.

110  See also *Australian Patents for Plants*, IP Australia, p 1, wherein the same test applies for plant patents.

111  Namely, *NV Philips Gloeilampenfabrieken v Mirabella International Pty Ltd* (1995) 183 CLR 655 and *Advanced Building Systems Pty Ltd v Ramset Fasteners (Aust) Pty Ltd* (1998) 152 ALR 604 (see Chapter 9). In the updated online version IP Australia separates these out into a distinct manner of manufacture element and a test for inventiveness as compared to the prior art: at <http://www.ipaustralia.gov.au/get-the-right-ip/patents/about-patents/what-can-be-patented/patents-for-biological-inventions/> 6 February 2012.

112  *Australian Patents for: Microorganisms, Cell Lines, Hybridomas, Related biological materials and their use; Genetically manipulated organisms*, IP Australia, February 1998, p 2.

points out that "a patent cannot be granted for materials in their naturally occurring state" nor that patent protection can be afforded to "materials which have previously been made publicly available".[113] The third test goes to the issue of disclosure and drafting of the specification in the vein of the requirement of usefulness or utility and the requirements of s 40 of the Act. In other words, the third test requires that the subject-matter is "fully described in the sense that sufficient information is provided to allow the technologist to make the product or perform the process without having to resort to invention".[114]

The final test requires demonstrated industrial use, which brings us full circle back to the manner of new manufacture if we follow the *NRDC* case. This demonstrated use must be fully described and not merely a speculation as to future uses of the subject-matter.[115] Accordingly, as with all patent applications, the other elements of patentability require consideration before a final determination can be made as to the patentability of biologically based inventions.

## Novelty and Inventive Step

The elements of novelty and inventive step are discussed in general in Chapter 9 and it is clear that the identification of the prior art base is crucial to determining both novelty and inventive step. In fact, naturally occurring products would seem to comprise such a prior art base. Further, the use of such naturally occurring products through traditional medicinal practices would also form part of that prior art base[116] against which an invention would be judged. The question is how different must the invention be to avoid being accused of lack of novelty or inventive step?

In the words of the Royal College of Pathologists of Australasia (RCPA):

> Natural materials are only novel in the sense that they have not previously been discovered by humans. Natural DNA sequences are the result of over a billion years of evolution and exist independent of the inventors.[117]

That statement implies that the process of isolating and purifying genetic material is not enough to distinguish that material from its natural state. On the other hand, it has also been pointed out that "genetic materials do not exist in nature in an isolated or purified form".[118] There needs to be some level of human

---

113 *Australian Patents for: Microorganisms, Cell Lines, Hybridomas, Related biological materials and their use; Genetically manipulated organisms*, IP Australia, February 1998, p 2. Once again the same test applies for plant patents: see *Australian Patents for Plants*, IP Australia, p 1.

114 *Australian Patents for: Microorganisms, Cell Lines, Hybridomas, Related biological materials and their use; Genetically manipulated organisms*, IP Australia, February 1998, p 2. Again the same test applies for plant patents: see *Australian Patents for Plants*, IP Australia, p 2, with the added comment that the best method of performing the invention known to the inventor must be described.

115 *Australian Patents for: Microorganisms, Cell Lines, Hybridomas, Related biological materials and their use; Genetically manipulated organisms*, IP Australia, February 1998, p 2.

116 Consider the attempt to patent medicinal uses of tumeric in the United States and the successful opposition brought by the Indian government on the basis of anticipation.

117 As cited in *Genes and Ingenuity Report Gene Patenting and Human Health*, ALRC, Report 99, June 2004, p 133.

118 *Genes and Ingenuity Report Gene Patenting and Human Health*, ALRC, Report 99, June 2004, p 134.

intervention to bring about the isolation and purification. On the question of novelty, IP Australia submitted to the ALRC:

> In order to be acceptable, patent claims must not include within their scope anything which occurs already, either artificially or naturally. As a consequence, patents are not granted for genetic materials which already exist in the body of any living thing. The same principle applies to all chemical compounds which have been newly isolated from nature.[119]

But perhaps a more technical argument from a representative of the very organisations that would be seeking such patents, GlaxoSmithKline, can shed some more light on why patents for genetic material would satisfy novelty.[120] In their submission to the ALRC, GlaxoSmithKline pointed out that patent claims are frequently framed in the form of cDNA or complementary DNA which generally does not occur in nature.[121] Instead, cDNA "is a copy of the naturally occurring genomic DNA but lacking the interspersed intron sequences".[122] The ALRC accepted that genetic materials in nature are not sufficient to preclude a finding of novelty for an isolated and purified version of that material.[123] However, gene sequence databases in existence at the time of invention would constitute prior art information that could result in a lack of novelty as would other usual forms of disclosure.[124]

This brings us to the unanimous decision of the House of Lords in *Kirin-Amgen Inc v Hoechst Marion Roussel Limited*.[125] This was an appeal regarding infringement and revocation proceedings brought in relation to Kirin-Amgen Inc's patent for the production of the protein, erythropoietin (EPO), by recombinant DNA technology. Lord Hoffman found that claim 26 which claimed the protein as "the product of the expression in a host cell of an exogenous DNA sequence according to claim 1"[126] failed on the ground of anticipation. This was due to the existence of prior art regarding urinary EPO or uEPO, collected and purified from the urine of aplastic anaemia patients. Accordingly, since the natural product had been extracted and isolated before the patent in question and there was no significant difference between the natural product and the synthesised product, as they were both produced in eucaryotic hosts (namely human beings) novelty would not be satisfied.

Where the real difficulty lies for the patenting of genetic materials is in the question of inventive step. Clearly, this can only be determined on a case-by-case

---

119  As cited in *Genes and Ingenuity Report Gene Patenting and Human Health*, ALRC, Report 99, June 2004, p 134.

120  *Genes and Ingenuity Report Gene Patenting and Human Health*, ALRC, Report 99, June 2004, p 134.

121  *Genes and Ingenuity Report Gene Patenting and Human Health*, ALRC, Report 99, June 2004, p 134.

122  As cited in *Genes and Ingenuity Report Gene Patenting and Human Health*, ALRC, Report 99, June 2004, p 134.

123  *Genes and Ingenuity Report Gene Patenting and Human Health*, ALRC, Report 99, June 2004, p 135.

124  *Genes and Ingenuity Report Gene Patenting and Human Health*, ALRC, Report 99, June 2004, p 135.

125  [2004] UKHL 46.

126  [2004] UKHL 46 at [12].

basis as for novelty. But the processes for gene sequencing and isolating genes have become routine and heavily automated over time, thereby raising the level of common general knowledge. Consequently, a person skilled in the art may not need to engage their inventive ingenuity to come to the solution. In other words, the process of achieving the invention claimed may be an obvious step to take for a skilled person.

IP Australia, in its submission to the ALRC, stated that only a small number of patents are granted for genetic material "on the basis that the means of identifying and isolating [the] genetic material was inventive".[127] Rather it is the purpose to which the genetic material can be put, usually through the inventive identification of a useful property, that will define the patentable invention, even where standard processes for isolating the genetic material are employed.[128] The identification of the usefulness of the invention is necessary to comply with the utility requirement of patentability.[129]

## Disclosing Biotechnology Inventions

Internationally, the late 1960s and 1970s saw the development of the biotechnology industry with its use of recombinant DNA technology and manipulation of microorganisms for industrial purposes. During this period it was also recognised that, in order to obtain patent protection for this burgeoning field, there had to be a way of describing the biological material forming part of the invention. Disclosure is the question at hand and hence the need to comply with the rules found in s 40 of the *Patents Act 1990*.

This brings us to the *Budapest Treaty on the International Recognition of the Deposit of Microorganisms for the Purposes of Patent Procedure 1977* of which Australia is a signatory. Although the purpose of this Treaty was to find an acceptable method of providing sufficient disclosure of an invention incorporating a microorganism, by establishing International Depository Authorities, its mere existence confirms the international recognition that microorganisms can be appropriate subject-matter for patenting. However, the Budapest Treaty does not define "microorganism". The result has been that a greater range of biological materials have been accepted as depositable subject-matter than one would expect.[130] The range of materials capable of deposit under the Budapest Treaty include:

- Cells – from bacteria to eukaryotic (higher living organism) cell lines;
- Organisms used for gene expression, such as bacteria and yeasts;

---

127  As cited in *Genes and Ingenuity Report Gene Patenting and Human Health*, ALRC, Report 99, June 2004, p 141.

128  As cited in *Genes and Ingenuity Report Gene Patenting and Human Health*, ALRC, Report 99, June 2004, p 141.

129  For a detailed discussion on the requirement of usefulness, see *Genes and Ingenuity Report Gene Patenting and Human Health*, ALRC, Report 99, June 2004, pp 142-159.

130  See IP Australia, *The Budapest Treaty and Australian Patents*, 1998. See now Depositing Micro-organisms, updated 29 September 2011 at <http://www.ipaustralia.gov.au/get-the-right-ip/patents/about-patents/what-can-be-patented/depositing-micro-organisms/> 6 February 2012.

- Genetic vectors including plasmids, bacteriophages or viruses;
- Yeast, algae, protozoa, eucaryotic cells, cell lines, hybridomas, viruses, plant tissue cells, spores and other hosts containing vectors, DNA, RNA, genes and chromosomes;
- Purified nucleic acids (the building bricks of proteins); and
- Other materials such as "naked" DNA, RNA, plasmids.

However, the International Depository Authority in Australia, the Australian Government Analytical Laboratories (AGAL), imposes some limits. While bacteria, yeasts, fungi and other known human and animal pathogens are accepted, they are only accepted up to hazard categorisation WHO Classification Risk Group 2. Further, only those materials that can be preserved without significant change to their properties with the preservation techniques in use are accepted. In addition, AGAL accepts nucleic acid preparations and phages but not microorganisms requiring special attention in relation to storage, animal, plant, algal, and protozoan cultures, nor viral, rickettsial and chlamydial agents. Despite these restrictions, IP Australia accepts deposits made in International Depository Authorities overseas and so the scope of acceptable deposits in AGAL are not reflective of the scope of subject-matter accepted by IP Australia, or the APO.

In the case of gene technology inventions the application of s 40 has been considered by the Federal Court in *Genetics Institute Inc v Kirin-Amgen Inc (No 3)*.[131] Heerey J concluded that the patent "discloses a 'principle capable of general application' and discloses a beneficial property which is common to the class". This went contrary to the House of Lords case, *Biogen Inc v Medeva plc*,[132] but his Honour was able to distinguish that case on the basis that the Biogen 1 patent did not disclose the relevant coding sequence as was achieved by Kirin-Amgen. However, it has been suggested that Kirin-Amgen's broad claims are unlikely to be accepted today given the developments in the technology.[133]

Further, in *Kirin-Amgen Inc v Hoechst Marion Roussel Limited*,[134] the question of sufficiency arose in relation to claim 19, which again claimed the protein EPO as "the product of the expression of an exogenous DNA sequence".[135] His Lordship pointed out that the claim over the product, EPO, failed "because the last-minute amendment to distinguish the product from the natural EPO turned out to [be] based upon the false premise that all uEPO had the same molecular weight".[136] The difficulty arose in the comparison between the specifications and the claims. The specifications provided a number of purification methods different from each other but not indicating which one would produce the result in claim 19, that is, one which distinguishes the recombinant EPO from the urinary EPO. Accordingly, Lord Hoffman agreed with the trial judge in determining that claim 19 was not sufficiently enabled and therefore it was held to be invalid. His Lordship pointed out that "having invented a perfectly good and ground-breaking

131 [1998] FCA 740.

132 (1996) 36 IPR 438.

133 *Genes and Ingenuity Report Gene Patenting and Human Health*, ALRC, Report 99, June 2004, p 160.

134 [2004] UKHL 46.

135 [2004] UKHL 46 at [12].

136 [2004] UKHL 46 at [132].

process for making EPO and its analogues, they [Amgen] were determined to try to patent the protein itself, notwithstanding that, even when isolated, it was not new".[137] It was the question of prior art and sufficiency of expression regarding the product derived from the sequence that resulted in the narrowing of protection afforded to the patentee. While potentially a blow to the protection of natural product chemistry, the decision does give some hope that the elements of patentability operate to reward true invention.

---

137  [2004] UKHL 46 at [13].

# CASE

## Genetics Institute, Inc v Kirin-Amgen, Inc (No 3)
### Federal Court of Australia: Heerey J [1998] FCA 740

**HEEREY J: Introduction**

Genetics Institute, Inc (Genetics) appeals from a decision of the Commissioner of Patents given by his delegate Deputy Commissioner Mr D Herald on 19 October 1995. Genetics was one of two opponents to Australian Patent Application No 600650 (the Amgen patent) brought by the respondent Kirin-Amgen, Inc (Amgen). The Deputy Commissioner found that the claims of the patent were novel and involved an inventive step. He found that three claims did not comply with s 40 of the *Patents Act 1952* (Cth) because they involved "some minor lack of clarity" and that five claims were not fairly based. He considered that the defects could be readily overcome and allowed Amgen to propose appropriate amendments. He otherwise held that the opposition failed.

The present appeal is confined to the requirements of s 40. Genetics' case is that the invention claimed:

   (i)  is not fairly based on the matter disclosed in the specification (s 40(2));

  (ii)  does not fully describe the invention (s 40(2)(a)); and

 (iii)  contains claims which are not clear and succinct and do not clearly define the invention (s 40(2)).

By a cross-appeal Amgen appeals from that part of the Deputy Commissioner's decision which found some claims lacked clarity or were not fairly based.

*The Field of the Invention*

The claimed invention relates generally to recombinant procedures which make it possible to produce polypeptide proteins. More particularly the invention concerns the use of recombinant DNA techniques to produce commercial quantities of erythropoietin.

*Erythropoietin*

Erythropoietin (EPO) is a protein, normally produced in the liver of the foetus and in the kidney of adults, which plays a major role in regulating the rate of red blood cell formation. EPO is responsible for maintaining a sufficient number of red blood cells to oxygenate body tissues adequately. Red blood cells under the control of EPO are formed predominantly in the bone marrow.

EPO is rare. It is only produced in a few cells. Moreover it is a highly regulated gene; it is only "switched on", even in those few cell types in which it is found, during particular limited windows of time.

The existence of EPO was postulated in 1906 and confirmed in 1953. By 1975 it was known that small amounts of EPO were excreted by the kidneys and that urine provided a source for urinary EPO (uEPO) but only in limited quantities. Publications in 1977 showed that foetal liver was a source of EPO (Zanjani et al) and that the urine of aplastic anaemia patients over-produced EPO (Goldwasser et al). But neither blood nor urine is a practical source of EPO for therapeutic use. Thus until recombinant EPO (rEPO) became available there existed a need for a product which could fulfil the protein's therapeutic role.

In 1983 the only publicly available information concerning the structure of EPO (that is its amino acid sequence) was a putative amino acid sequence for the first 26 amino acids of the protein.

*Genetic information and DNA*

The genetic material of any organism is the substance that carries the information determining the properties of that organism. It is the information contained in the genetic material that determines, for example, the colour of flowers and that fish have gills. The genetic material is also responsible for transferring the genetic information from parent to progeny. All the genetic information of an organism is collectively referred to as its genome. The genetic material in all organisms, apart from viruses, is a form of nucleic acid called DNA (short for deoxyribonucleic acid). Thus the complete genetic material of an organism is called its genomic DNA (gDNA).

DNA is a large molecule of repeating subunits called nucleotides. Four different types of nucleotides are found in DNA: adenine (A), guanine (G), thymine (T), and cytosine (C). Nucleotides are commonly referred to as bases.

The nucleotides (A, G, T and C) are joined together end to end in a linear fashion forming a long string of bases. The linear order of bases along a DNA strand is called the DNA sequence. Every DNA strand has a proper direction in which it should be read, ie the 5' (five prime) to 3' (three prime) direction. This direction is related to the orientation of the sugar-phosphates that are part of the nucleotides. A DNA molecule consists of two of these long strands of nucleotides. The two strands of a DNA molecule are held together by chemical (hydrogen) bonds between bases on opposite strands; A always pairs with T, and C always pairs with G. As a result of this base pairing between DNA strands, DNA resembles a ladder; the paired bases are analogous to the rungs while the sugar phosphate groups of the nucleotides are the side rails. These carefully matched strands twist into a compact spiral commonly referred to as the double helix, discovered by Crick and Watson in 1953.

The consistent pairing of A to T and G to C is referred to as complementarity, thus one strand of DNA in the double helix is complementary to the other. The complementary nature of DNA allows for its faithful reproduction and also enables the ready identification of specific DNA sequences by gene probes.

There is another type of nucleic acid called ribonucleic acid, referred to by its abbreviation RNA. RNA, like DNA, is made of a linear chain of nucleotides. (The sugar of RNA (ribose) is slightly different to the one found in DNA (deoxyribose).) Unlike the large double-stranded DNA, RNA molecules have only one strand and are shorter than the DNA molecules, being derived from the transcription (see infra) of particular regions of the DNA.

The genetic information carried in the DNA governs the day-to-day function of a cell through its expression in the form of proteins. All biological reactions are accomplished by proteins which are in effect little engines which have specific functions within the organism. As has been mentioned, EPO is a protein. A length of DNA sequence that codes for production of an entire protein is called a gene. All proteins are assembled from building blocks called amino acids by a complex apparatus that works under the direction of genetic information provided by a nucleic acid sequence. Each gene includes a sequence of nucleotides that directly determines the sequence of amino acids in a corresponding protein. The amino acid sequence in turn determines the function of the protein. All proteins of the cell are therefore determined by the sequence of the genetic material.

Amino acids are represented in DNA by different triplet combinations (triplet codons) of the bases A, C, G and T. A triplet codon is identified simply by the letters representing the bases of each of its nucleotides, eg, GGA and TAG. For example, having G in the first position, G in the second position, and A in the third position of the triplet codon, would encode the amino acid glycine and a table in common use lists the triplet-amino acid relationships. As there are 64 possible combinations of 3 bases to encode 20 amino acids, there is a degree of what is called degeneracy in the coding such that a single amino acid can be encoded by several different base triplets.

In the making of a protein, the genetic information contained in the DNA instructs the cellular machinery through a two-stage process of expression (manufacture) that involves an intermediate molecule. The first stage of expression is transcription, the process by which parts of the genetic message encoded in the DNA are rewritten in the form of a temporary molecule called messenger RNA (mRNA). This also allows the level of gene expression to be varied and controlled, by regulating the amount of mRNA that is made. The DNA molecule serves as a template, but in this case, the complementary strand is the temporary, intermediate molecule, mRNA. The second stage of expression is translation, in which the genetic message now coded for in mRNA is translated by complex structures called ribosomes into a sequence of amino acids to form the encoded protein …

*Proteins*

As mentioned, proteins are molecules of complex structure which are composed of sub-units of amino acids, of which there are 20 different types. Amino acids are linked together in a linear fashion to form a chain which is referred to as a polypeptide chain.

Protein structure can be viewed from four aspects which are termed the primary, secondary, tertiary and quaternary structure. The primary structure of the protein refers to the amino acid sequence of the polypeptide chain. The secondary and tertiary structure of a protein refers to the particular manner in which the polypeptide chain is folded into a unique three-dimensional structure. The quarternary structure is present when individual proteins combine to make a multi-protein structure.

*Glycosylation of Proteins*

Many proteins (including EPO) are modified by the addition of one or more carbohydrate chains to some of the amino acids. The carbohydrate chains consist of a string of individual units or residues called monosaccharides (also commonly called sugars). The attachment of carbohydrate chains to a protein is called glycosylation, and the completed protein is called a glycoprotein.

The total amount of sugar added to a protein can be quite substantial. For example about 40 per cent of the weight of the EPO glycoprotein is made up of added sugar, the rest being the polypeptide chain.

Monosaccharides exist in a particular ring form, either a six-membered pyranose ring or the less common five-membered furanose ring. Sugars that exist as six-membered rings are called hexoses. The numbers and types of sugars attached at glycosylation sites depend upon the cell making the glycoprotein. Therefore when a DNA sequence is introduced into a host cell, such as a CHO (Chinese hamster ovary) cell the protein that is expressed may have different sugars attached compared to the same protein made in a different host cell such as a COS-1 (monkey kidney) cell.

*Introns and mRNA Splicing*

Originally it was assumed that a mRNA transcript would have the same sequence as the DNA from which it was transcribed. While this remains essentially true for bacteria, comparison of DNA in plant and animal cells with mRNA revealed that in many instances the DNA contained sequences which were absent from its mRNA transcript.

By comparing DNA sequences with mRNA molecules from the cytoplasm of a cell, scientists found that most plant and animal DNA contains "intervening sequences" which are normally removed in their totality from the mRNA transcript before the mRNA transcript is shuttled to the cytoplasm for translation. These intervening DNA sequences are referred to as "introns", while the portions of the DNA that code for a portion of the protein sequence are called "exons" (see Figure 1). The presence of introns in genes is unique to plants and animals and, indeed, bacteria are unable to distinguish between exons and introns. The size and position of introns within genes appears to be random: some introns are short in length while others consist of hundreds or even thousands of bases.

Most plant and animal genes consist of an alternating series of exons and introns. The exons are the sequences which code for the protein and are transcribed into mRNA, which information is then translated into an amino acid sequence to form a protein. The introns carry no information relevant to the formation of a protein, and their primary function, if any, is unknown. Thus during transcription the mRNA copy of gDNA must go through a process in which the introns are removed (mRNA splicing) before the protein can be made (see Figure 1).

By comparing the nucleotide sequence of mature mRNA with that of the gDNA sequence from which it was transcribed, the junctions between exons and introns in the DNA sequence can be assigned.

*Genetic engineering*
The amount of DNA present in each set of chromosomes in each cell of a human (or most of the higher animals) is approximately 3 billion base pairs. An average gene contains about 1,000 – 2,000 bases of protein-coding information, although the entire gene itself, including control sequences and introns, may be much larger. Thus, to isolate and clone a single human gene from the entire human genome is to embark on a search among an amount of DNA which could contain up to three million genes. This problem has been likened to looking for an ant on Mount Everest.

At first sight, these numbers suggest that gene hunting would be impossible. However, by 1983 powerful tools had been developed to make it possible to isolate a gene of interest, reconstruct it by joining it with DNA sequences from quite different sources, place it into a simpler foreign system, and replicate the gene many times to give a large amount of that single gene. The product is often described as recombinant DNA and the technique as genetic engineering. With these techniques, genes that would not have otherwise been accessible could be isolated, cloned, and characterised. As part of this process, restriction enzymes (sometimes referred to as "molecular scissors") cut DNA at predefined sequences which are characteristic for a particular enzyme.

Another important cloning tool of genetic engineering is the vector. The vector is a special piece of DNA which is able to carry foreign DNA into a living host cell and to replicate autonomously in that host cell. Vectors are usually derivatives of naturally-occurring small DNA molecules. A critical feature of any vector is that it should possess a site at which foreign ("exogenous") DNA can be inserted without disrupting any essential function of the vector.

A vector has the ability to replicate autonomously in a host cell of DNA. Using the host cell's replication machinery the vector DNA, including the foreign gene, is replicated and can be perpetuated indefinitely as a population of clones.

A clone can be defined as a large number of molecules or cells, all identical to one another, and to an original ancestral molecule or cell from which they are derived by replication. A sequence of DNA can be cloned by inserting exogenous DNA into a vector, introducing the vector into a host cell, and then growing the host cell. Cloning of DNA is made possible by the ability of host cells to continue their usual life-style after additional sequences of DNA (vector and exogenous DNA) have been incorporated into their genome.

Many vectors are used to express an exogenous DNA insert, by introducing a vector carrying a gene into a host cell. In this process the introduced gene is transcribed and translated to make a protein product. The gene can be altered so that the host cell is instructed to make large amounts of the new protein. In this way what is normally a rare and difficult to produce protein such as EPO can be made in abundance and purified for use as a drug.

The host cells can be bacteria or various cell lines derived from different mammals. Two commonly used host cells are CHO cells, which derive from Chinese hamster ovary, and COS-1 cells, which derive from monkey kidney. These cell lines can be propagated in laboratories. They readily take up foreign DNA.

Using specialised enzymes, vectors and host cells, it has been possible to prepare what are called gene libraries. There are two main types of libraries: genomic and cDNA.

The former is a collection of small pieces of DNA, contained within the self-replicating vectors, that represents the entire genome of the individual from which the DNA was made. A cDNA library is also a collection of small pieces of DNA but it represents only that part of the gDNA which has been transcribed in mRNA by the cell(s) from which the cDNA was made. Thus the content of a cDNA library is limited to the DNA which is actually transcribed in the cells used to construct the library. cDNA libraries have the advantage that they contain the exon sequences reassembled into a contiguous protein coding sequence after the removal of the introns.

To make a genomic library of an organism, the DNA from any somatic cell of that organism is cut into fragments usually ranging in size from 5 to 30 kilobases (a kilobase (kb) is one thousand nucleotide bases). These fragments are a random assortment of stretches of DNA that may or may not include an entire gene. The fragments are inserted into an appropriate vector. Typically, bacterial host cells are transformed with the vector for cloning.

To make a cDNA library, complementary DNA (cDNA) must first be generated. mRNA can be used as a template to make cDNA molecules. This process is called reverse transcription since it is the opposite of the normal transcription process (ie mRNA obtained from DNA).

Genomic and cDNA libraries may contain hundreds of thousands of different recombinants, each representing a different segment of DNA attached to a plasmid or bacteriophage DNA. In order to select a particular colony or plaque containing a desired gene from a bacterial plate, a technique called colony or plaque hybridisation was in use in 1983.

As explained above, bases of each strand of double stranded DNA are bound to each other through chemical bonds. The chemical bonds occur between A (adenine) and T (thymine), and G (guanine) and C (cytosine). These bases are therefore referred to as being complementary to each other. By the end of 1983, it was possible to synthesise by chemical methods a short stretch of DNA, an oligonucleotide probe, with a defined sequence of bases. Such a molecule can then be used to identify a complementary strand in a mixture of DNA molecules, eg, a genomic or cDNA library, simply by adding it to the library under appropriate conditions. In a process, called hybridisation, the probe will find its complementary partner (target) and form a double-helical structure with it as long as such a partner exists in the mixture. The hybridisation reaction can readily be carried out under conditions which will distinguish between a perfect match of a probe and its target, and the situation in which the probe has bound to a DNA sequence in a library but one or more base pairs are mismatched.

In order to fish out a particular gene from a library capable of containing up to three million genes, it is necessary to construct a probe with a complementary sequence that will anneal to the gene of interest, but not to the rest of the DNA. If the DNA sequence of the gene of interest was known in 1983, probe design was a relatively straightforward task. Amino acid sequence information could also be used in designing probes, but if little or nothing was known about the DNA sequence of interest, isolating the clone from a library would have been a daunting task.

*Confirmation*

A significant aspect of all gene cloning efforts in 1983 and today is confirmation that the DNA isolated by hybridisation screening actually encodes the protein of interest. Because the genetic code is universal, a given coding sequence should have the same meaning in all situations. Once the "target gene" (synthetic DNA, cDNA or gDNA) of the desired polypeptide is obtained, it can be introduced into a host cell, either bacterial, animal or plant, by a vector. The host cell treats this new DNA as its own and can be made to transcribe it and translate the resulting mRNA causing synthesis of the encoded protein.

The polypeptide is said to have been expressed. That is, the polypeptide can be obtained by the steps of (i) inserting the DNA into a plasmid (vector), (ii) incorporating the plasmid into a host cell, and (iii) culturing the host cell. One caveat is that the commonly used bacterial hosts will not undertake post-translational modifications such as the addition of sugars; nor will they be capable of properly translating a gene that contains intron sequences.

*The Amgen Patent*
The invention is entitled "Production of Erythropoietin". The inventor states by way of background:

> "The present invention relates generally to the manipulation of genetic materials and, more particularly, to recombinant procedures making possible the production of polypeptides possessing part or all of the primary structural conformation and/or one or more of the biological properties of naturally-occurring erythropoietin."

The inventor identifies three known alternative methods which can be employed to develop DNA sequences which will encode the protein of interest:

 (i) the isolation of a double stranded DNA sequence from gDNA;
 (ii) the chemical manufacture of a DNA sequence which provides a code for a polypeptide of interest; and
 (iii) the in vitro synthesis of a double stranded DNA sequence by enzymatic reverse transcription of a small mRNA which has been isolated from donor cells (cDNA).

(Chemical manufacture – method (ii) – has not become an issue in the present proceeding.)

The inventor states that when the entire sequence of amino acid residues of the desired polypeptide is not known the cDNA method is preferable, although it is first necessary to have available a source of donor cells having an abundance of mRNA which encodes the polypeptide of interest. The inventor states that the use of gDNA is the least common of the three methods. The inventor continues to identify the problem to be overcome (p 9 lines 21-27):

> "There thus continues to exist a need in the art for improved methods for effecting the rapid and efficient isolation of cDNA clones in instances where little is known of the amino acid sequence of the polypeptide coded for and where 'enriched' tissue sources of mRNA are not readily available for use in constructing cDNA libraries."

The inventor notes that attempts to obtain EPO in good yield from plasma or urine have been relatively unsuccessful. After discussing probing strategies the specification then proceeds to the "detailed description" which reveals the steps the inventor took. I gratefully adopt the summary contained in the Deputy Commissioner's decision as follows (CB121):

> "The major part of the 'detailed description' of the invention involves ten examples which:
>
> > '... are specifically directed to procedures carried out prior to identification of EPO encoding monkey cDNA clones and human genomic claims, to procedures resulting in such identification, and to the sequencing, development of expression systems and immunological verification of EPO expression in such systems.'
>
> In essence, the specification details:-
>
> > – the identification of monkey EPO using a cDNA library;
> > – the identification of human EPO using a human Genomic library;
> > – the construction of vectors containing erythropoietin-encoding DNA;
> > – the development of mammalian host expression systems;
> > – manufactured genes encoding human erythropoietin and analogues thereof having preference codons for expression in certain hosts; and
> > – antibodies for identifying erythropoietin."

The specification ends with 56 claims. Those claims, as the Deputy Commissioner noted, fall into four categories:

* claims limited by the DNA sequence encoding human or monkey EPO (claims 14, 17, 18, 39, 45, 46 and 55);
* claims limited to variations of those sequences (claims 33 and 34);
* claims that are not limited to human or monkey EPO (claims 1, 33 and 48); and
* claims to an antibody recognising small parts of those sequences (claim 48).

Claim 1 is in these terms:

"A purified and isolated polypeptide having the primary structural conformation and one or more of the biological properties of naturally-occurring erythropoietin and characterized by being the product of procaryotic or eucaryotic expression of an exogenous DNA sequence."

*The Deputy Commissioner's decision*
The essence of the Deputy Commissioner's decision on the fair basing issue is contained in the following paragraphs (CB133):

"The attack on fair basis is essentially that the claims should be limited to the specific sequences of tables 5 and 6, to methods for producing those sequences, and to variants of those sequences specifically referred to.

Tables 5 and 6 disclose the specific DNA sequences for human and monkey erythropoietins. The specification also teaches that as a result of the invention DNA hybridization processes can be used to locate the erythropoietin gene position "in the human, monkey and other mammalian species['] chromosomal map". This statement is made presumably in reliance upon the well-known substantial homology of gene sequences across species. Further, it is well known that there is a redundancy in the DNA coding for any particular amino acid; and that one can make conservative substitutions for amino acids without making significant changes in the properties of the protein. It seems to me that, properly considered, the discovery of a natural DNA sequence is tantamount to the discovery of a class of compounds – which class would be readily understood by a person skilled in the art. Accordingly I am satisfied that there is sufficient teaching to provide a fair basis to claims to erythropoietin unlimited either by species or specific structure. (And I would also observe that if it was subsequently found that a particular variation of the sequence gave rise to new and surprising results, the law of selections would apply.)"

This is a convenient point to note the way I have approached the Deputy Commissioner's decision. The appeal is of course a complete rehearing and included a great body of evidence which was not before the Deputy Commissioner. However I have found the Deputy Commissioner's reasons helpful as providing a conceptual framework for the complex and technical issues in this case.

*Onus and Standard of Proof*
It was not disputed that Genetics, as opponent, bore the onus of proof. In reality this is an original proceeding: *Kaiser Aluminium & Chemical Corporation v Reynolds Metal Co* (1969) 120 CLR 136 at 142. The principles governing refusal of a patent application are stated in *Commissioner of Patents v Microcell Ltd* (1959) 102 CLR 232 at 244-5:

"… it is well settled that the Commissioner ought not to refuse acceptance of an application and specification unless it appears practically certain that letters patent granted on the Specification would be held invalid. As Menzies J has pointed out, he will not normally have before him the material necessary for the formation of a concluded opinion. Moreover, whereas refusal of acceptance is final, acceptance is not: the application may be opposed after acceptance on any of the grounds mentioned in s 56, and, if a patent is granted, its validity is open to attack in proceedings for infringement or for revocation. So, in *McDonald v Commissioner of Patents* [(1913)

15 CLR 713] (a case in which the validity of a patent granted on the specification may be thought to have been very doubtful) this Court allowed an appeal from the Commissioner, Griffith CJ saying: 'I think that it is only in a clear case, where it is obvious that a patent cannot be granted, that the Commissioner should reject an application altogether' [at 717].

On the other hand, it is not to be overlooked that the Commissioner has a duty to the public as well as to the applicant for a patent, and, if it appears manifest that a valid patent could not be granted, the Commissioner not merely has power, but is under a duty, to reject the application under s 46."

Similarly in *Farbwerke Hoechst Aktiengesellschaft Vormals Meister Lucius & Bruning v Commissioner of Patents* (1971) 45 ALJR 235 at 239 Gibbs J said:

"In the case of an appeal against a refusal by the Commissioner to accept a specification, the Appeal Tribunal will allow the appeal unless it clearly appears that a patent granted on the specification will be invalid, because a refusal is final whereas an acceptance is not".

In *Martin v Scribal Pty Ltd* (1954) 92 CLR 17 at 97, Taylor J said:

"… it is right to construe a claim with an eye benevolent to the inventor and with a view to making the invention work – this is an application of the old doctrine ut res magis valeat quam pereat."

There was some argument about a passage in the joint judgment of Stephen and Mason JJ in *Olin Corporation v Super Cartridge Co Pty Ltd* (1977) 14 ALR 149 at 172 where their Honours, speaking of the patent then in suit, said:

"This is not a case in which the inventor has conceived of and brought into existence an entirely new or revolutionary product which stands so far in advance of, and apart from, previous developments that it works a radical transformation in the field in which it is introduced, as, for example, the invention of the electric light globe. In such a case the inventive step or the merits of the invention may be so great that it may be proper to reward the patentee with a monopoly in the product or article, unlimited by reference to the actual process according to which it is produced. Then it may be said the monopoly conferred is proportionate to the great benefit which has been given to the public by the patentee's disclosure. Such a case, so it seems to us, is far removed from the present where the invention, though possessing the requisite element of inventive ingenuity to support the process claim, is not of a kind to justify a claim to the product whether made pursuant to the process or not."

Although Barwick CJ agreed generally with Stephen and Mason JJ (at 151) it may be doubted whether he agreed with the passage just stated. His Honour said (at 152):

"The question whether the claim is fairly based is not to be resolved, in my opinion, by considering whether a monopoly in the product would be an undue reward for the disclosure. Rather, the question is a narrow one, namely whether the claim to the product being new, useful, and inventive, that is to say, the claim as expressed, travels beyond the matter disclosed in the specification."

The remaining member of the Court, Gibbs J, did not discuss the point.

Counsel for Genetics did not shrink from submitting that the passage in the judgment of Stephen and Mason JJ was wrong. He contended, correctly I think, that it was not part of the ratio in Olin. Also, in my view, it would add a complicating new issue to cases of this nature if the Commissioner, or the Court on appeal or in a revocation suit, had to make a finding as to whether an invention worked a "radical transformation". For example, it might well be said that the Amgen patent, although undoubtedly of great therapeutic benefit and commercial importance, does not rank with the electric light globe, or the steam engine, or the printing press. It is not a case where the inventor is the first to set foot on a new continent. Rather, the evidence discloses that recombinant technology in general was well known at the priority date but there was a race to obtain a recombinant version of this particular protein.

In any event, I do not approach the case on the basis that the Amgen patent discloses any kind of super invention in the sense discussed. The question is whether the specification provided a "real and reasonably clear" disclosure of the invention: see generally *CCOM Pty Ltd v Jiejing Pty Ltd* (1994) 122 ALR 417 at 432-437.

As to clarity, the claim must

"define clearly and with precision the monopoly claimed so that others may know the exact boundaries of the area within which they will be trespassers. Their primary object is to limit and not to extend the monopoly.

… The claims must undoubtedly be read as part of the entire document, and not as a separate document; but the forbidden field must be found in the language of the claims and not elsewhere."

*Electric & Musical Industries Ltd v Lissen Ltd* (1938) 56 RPC 23 at 39. See also *Martin v Scribal Pty Ltd* (1954) 92 CLR 17 at 59.

*Applicable Statute*

The parties were not in agreement as to whether s 40 of the 1952 *Patents Act 1977* or s 40 of the 1990 *Patents Act* was applicable. Despite some drafting differences, it was accepted that both had the same effect. I agree with counsel for Genetics that the 1952 Act is applicable. The validity of a patent application which was commenced prior to the commencement date of the 1990 Act (30 April 1991) and not finally dealt with or determined by that date is by virtue of the provisions of Ch 23 of the 1990 Act to be determined under the 1952 Act: see especially s 234(2) and (3).

Section 40 of the 1952 Act is as follows:

"40(1) A complete specification –

(a) shall fully describe the invention, including the best method of performing the invention which is known to the applicant; and

(b) shall end with a claim or claims defining the invention.

(2) The claim or claims shall be clear and succinct and shall be fairly based on the matter described in the specification."

*Priority date*

Of a number of possible priority dates, the earliest is 13 December 1983, that being the earliest of a number of claimed priorities based on United States patent applications. In the circumstances of the present case it is in the interests of Amgen to have as late a priority date as possible (the later the date, the more knowledge available to the skilled addressee and the less difficulty in working the invention). Since 13 December 1983 was accepted, tacitly at least, by both sides, I shall treat that as the priority date.

*Skilled Addressee*

The relevant skilled addressee is a molecular biologist skilled in the production of recombinant proteins.

*Witnesses*

All witnesses were thoroughly and skillfully cross-examined. I was particularly impressed with the evidence of Professors Mattick, Gray and Schofield who were called on behalf of Amgen. I feel confident in relying on their testimony.

*Genetics' Primary Case – Fair Basing*

Genetics argued that the claims are "avariciously" broad because they purport to include human EPO cDNA which is not disclosed by the specification. It was said that the invention only disclosed

(i) the isolation from a genomic library of the gene that encodes human EPO; and

(ii) the isolation from a cDNA library of the gene that encodes monkey EPO.

and the subsequent expression of these proteins in host cells.

There was said to be no relevant disclosure of the isolation of the gene that encodes human EPO by the use of a cDNA library.

*Conclusion on Genetics' Primary Case*

I accept Amgen's argument that the object of the invention was to produce biologically active EPO in sufficient quantities for therapeutic use. The problem was that no one knew the sequence of the DNA encoding for EPO. Once the sequence was disclosed in the specification, the skilled addressee could use that sequence to produce EPO with existing technology.

That sequence is disclosed in Table VI. The intron/exon boundaries in the gDNA are disclosed and identified. They are identified by the use of monkey cDNA and two boundaries are confirmed by comparison with the tryptic fragments of urinary EPO set out in Table I.

One of the splice sites was further verified by sequencing of the human cDNA clone (see p 49 of the specification). Further, the splice site at exon 3/4 was at a region of perfect homology between the monkey and the human sequences (Schofield CB3199). Table I also provided sequence confirmation for about 75 per cent of the protein. In addition, N-terminal sequencing of the CHO produced EPO was identical to that of the naturally occurring urinary EPO. The coding sequence is correct from its 5' end to its 3' end and produced rEPO (recombinant EPO) with the full range of biological activity tested. Finally, in addition to the coding region, Table VI discloses substantial 5' and 3' untranslated regions that provide a description of a wide population of cDNAs that could be isolated from transfected host cells (see Symons T161-162). As Professor Symons acknowledged, one could easily tailor the 5' and 3' ends of the genomic DNA (as was done in Example 7B), insert that modified gDNA into a COS or CHO cell and isolate back out a cDNA that contained the coding region and the tailored 5' and 3' ends.

The evidence clearly demonstrates that a skilled addressee would have relied on the information in Table VI as disclosing the human cDNA sequence. In particular, I accept the evidence of Professor Mattick:

"The patent specification, however, unequivocally states that the inventor made cDNA encoding human EPO, sequenced it, and used that sequence to confirm an amino acid difference between human and monkey EPO, both of which are disclosed in the patent specification." (CB 2977)

"The real value of a cDNA sequence is the information which it reveals. This information is provided in Table VI in the patent specification and can be used to obtain a physical copy of the cDNA if required, using standard techniques known to persons ordinarily skilled in the field." (CB 3025)

"The essential value of a 'cDNA' sequence is not as a physical entity but in the information it contains about the DNA protein-coding sequence. This information can be obtained by generating a cDNA and sequencing it, as did the inventor of the [Amgen] patent application. Because this information originates from the genomic DNA, this same information is provided by a genomic sequence when the intron and exon boundaries are provided, as they are in the patent specification." (CB 2977)

See also Professor Schofield (CB3191, T636 and T640) and Professor Klinken (CB2834).

*The information the patent gives – an analogy*

In the course of argument there was some discussion of analogies.

Counsel for Genetics likened the Amgen case to that of a treasure hunter who discovers a map giving directions to buried treasure on a desert island. Counsel said that Amgen were trying to prevent anyone else from obtaining the treasure, even by a route different from the one shown on the map.

However a more apt analogy in my view is that of treasure in a castle. The castle has many gates, each with a combination lock (this being a modern castle). The combination for each lock is the same. Anyone who knows the combination can enter the castle. Finding the treasure may require some further time and trouble but this will merely be a matter of carefully searching through every room and cupboard in the castle. The critical knowledge is the combination of the locks. Without that, it is impossible to enter the castle. Once you have that, entry can be obtained through any gate. With reasonable time and effort the treasure will be discovered.

I think the protein coding sequence, the essential information contained in Table VI, is analogous to the combination of the castle locks.

To extend the analogy, it may be that the first time Amgen entered the castle the gate was reached by a particularly difficult route. It was necessary to swim across a crocodile-infested moat. But once the combination is known anyone can simply walk across the drawbridge and open the main gate.

Thus once the protein coding sequence is known, the same route (gDNA) does not have to be followed. Nor need the tissue source be the same.

*Biogen Inc v Medeva Plc*
Important guidance is provided by the recent decision of the House of Lords in *Biogen Inc v Medeva plc* [1997] RPC 1. As far as I am aware, this is the first reported decision on patent litigation in the area of genetic engineering at ultimate appeal level in the United Kingdom or Australia.

The patent in suit was for an artificially constructed molecule of DNA carrying a genetic code which, when introduced into a suitable host cell, would cause that cell to make antigens of the virus hepatitis B (HBV).

One of the issues in the case was whether, for the purposes of fixing the priority date, the invention was supported by matter disclosed in an earlier patent application called Biogen 1: *Patents Act* (UK) s 5(2)(a). According to *Asahi Kasei Kogyo KK's Application* [1991] RPC 485, this meant that for matter to be capable of supporting an invention it had to disclose the invention in a way which would enable it to be performed by a person skilled in the art, in other words there had to be "enabling disclosure".

Lord Hoffmann, with whom all other members of the House agreed, commenced his discussion of this issue by noting a decision of the Technical Board of Appeal of the EPO in *Genentech I/Polypeptide expression* (T292/85) [1989] OJ EPO 275 (EPO here stands not for erythropoeitin but for European Patent Office). Lord Hoffmann said of that case (at 48-49):

"... the applicants had invented a general principle for enabling plasmids to control the expression of polypeptides in bacteria and there was no reason to believe that it would not work equally well with any plasmid, bacterium or polypeptide. The patent was therefore granted in general terms. ...

In fact the Board in Genentech I/Polypeptide expression was doing no more than apply a principle of patent law which has long been established in the United Kingdom, namely, that the specification must enable the invention to be performed to the full extent of the monopoly claimed. If the invention discloses a principle capable of general application, the claims may be in correspondingly general terms. The patentee need not show that he has proved its application in every individual instance. On the other hand, if the claims include a number of discrete methods or products, the patentee must enable the invention to be performed in respect of each of them.

Thus if the patentee has hit upon a new product which has a beneficial effect but cannot demonstrate that there is a common principle by which that effect will be shared by other products of the same class, he will be entitled to a patent for that product but not for the class, even though some may subsequently turn out to have the same beneficial effect: see *May & Baker Ltd v Boots Pure Drug Co Ltd* (1950) 67 RPC 23, 50. On the other hand, if he has disclosed a beneficial property which is common to the class, he will be entitled to a patent for all products of that class (assuming them to be new) even though he has not himself made more than one or two of them.

Since *Genentech I/Polypeptide expression* the EPO has several times reasserted the well established principles for what amounts to sufficiency of disclosure. In particular, in *Exxon/Fuel Oils* (T 409/91) [1994] OJ EPO 653, paragraph 3.3, the Technical Board of Appeal said of the provision in the European Patent Convention equivalent to section 14(5)(c) of the Act:

'Furthermore, Article 84 EPC also requires that the claims must be supported by the description, in other words, it is the definition of the invention in the claims that needs support. In the Board's judgment, this requirement reflects the general legal principle that the extent of the patent monopoly, as defined by the claims, should correspond to the technical contribution to the art in order for it to be supported, or justified.'" (Bold emphasis added)

Before the trial judge (Aldous J) and in the Court of Appeal the issue was regarded as being whether Biogen I disclosed a method of making the antigen HBsAG as well as the antigen HBcAG. Lord Hoffmann's view was that the Court of Appeal should not have disturbed the affirmative answer of Aldous J to that question. However his Lordship continued (at 50):

"But the fact that the skilled man following the teaching of Biogen 1 would have been able to make HBcAg and Bag in bacterial cells, or indeed in any cells, does not conclude the matter. I think that in concentrating upon the question of whether Professor Murray's invention could, so to speak, deliver the goods across the full width of the patent or priority document, the courts and the EPO allowed their attention to be diverted from what seems to me in this particular case the critical issue. It is not whether the claimed invention could deliver the goods, but whether the claims cover other ways in which they might be delivered: ways which owe nothing to the teaching of the patent or any principle which it disclosed.

It will be remembered that in Genentech I/Polypeptide expression the Technical Board spoke of the need for the patent to give protection against other ways of achieving the same effect 'in a manner which could not have been envisaged without the invention'. This shows that there is more than one way in which the breadth of a claim may exceed the technical contribution to the art embodied in the invention. The patent may claim results which it does not enable, such as making a wide class of products when it enables only one of those products and discloses no principle which would enable others to be made. Or it may claim every way of achieving a result when it enables only one way and it is possible to envisage other ways of achieving that result which make no use of the invention.

One example of an excessive claim of the latter kind is the famous case of *O'Reilly v Morse* (1854) 56 US (15 How) 62 in the Supreme Court of the United States. Samuel Morse was the first person to discover a practical method of electric telegraphy and took out a patent in which he claimed any use of electricity for 'making or printing intelligible characters, signs, or letter, at any distances'. The Supreme Court rejected the claim as too broad. Professor Chi sum, in his book on Patents (vol 1, SS 1.03[2]) summarises the decision as follows:

'Before Morse's invention, the scientific community saw the possibility of achieving communication by the "galvanic" current but did not know any means of achieving that result. Morse discovered one means and attempted to claims all others.'" (Bold emphasis added)

Lord Hoffmann then applied those principles to the Biogen 1 patent as follows (at 51-52):

"I return therefore to consider the technical contribution to the art which Professor Murray made in 1978 and disclosed in Biogen 1. As it seems to me, it consisted in showing that despite the uncertainties which then existed over the DNA of the Dane particle – in particular, whether it included the antigen genes and whether it has introns – known recombinant techniques could nevertheless be used to make the antigens in a prokaryotic host cell. As I have said, I accept the judge's findings that the method was shown to be capable of making both antigens and I am willing to accept that it would work in any otherwise suitable host cell. Does this contribution justify a claim to a monopoly of any recombinant method of making the antigens? In my view it does not. The claimed invention is too broad. Its excessive breadth is due, not to the inability of the teaching to produce all the promised results, but to the fact that the same results could be produced by different means. Professor Murray had won a brilliant Napoleonic victory in cutting through the uncertainties which existed in his day to achieve the desired result. But his success did not in my view establish any new principle which his successors had to follow if they were to achieve the same results. The inventive step, as I have said, was the idea of trying to express subsequence eukaryotic DNA in a prokaryotic host. Biogen 1 discloses that the way to do it is to choose the restriction enzymes likely to cleave the Dane particle DNA into the largest fragments. This, if anything, was the original element in what Professor Murray did. But once the DNA had been sequenced, no one would choose restriction enzymes on this basis. They would choose those which digested the sites closest to the relevant gene or the part of the gene which expressed an antigenic fragment of the polypeptide. The metaphor used by one of the witnesses was that before the genome had been sequenced everyone was working in the dark. Professor Murray invented a way of working with the genome in the dark. But he did not switch on the light and once the light was on his method was no longer needed. Nor, once they could use vectors for mammalian cells, would they be concerned with the same problem of introns which had so exercised those skilled in the art in 1978. Of course there might be other problems, but Biogen 1 did not teach how to solve them. The respondents Medeva, who use restriction enzymes based on knowledge of the HBV genome and mammalian host cells, owe nothing to Professor Murray's invention." (Non-italicised emphasis in original; bold emphasis added).

A critical feature of the case for present purposes is that the Biogen 1 patent did not disclose the coding sequence. In narrating the state of the art at the relevant time, Lord Hoffmann said (at 38):

"In 1978, however, the HBV genome had not yet been sequenced. A reliable technique for sequencing had been invented by Professor Gilbert, but it was laborious and slow. It was not until six months after the filing of Biogen 1 that the whole genome was sequenced by Valenzuela and others in the University of California at San Francisco (Nature, Vol 280, 815-819). The genes which coded for the antigens were found to have no introns. It is because of this discovery and other advances in the state of the art that Biogen conceded that, by the date of its European filing [21 December 1979], the method by which HBV antigens could be made was obvious. But the information was not available in 1978."

The inventor had purified some DNA from a Dane particle and cut it into fragments with restriction enzymes chosen to digest the DNA at as few sites as possible. (The Dane particle had been discovered by D S Dane et al in 1970. It is a circular molecule of DNA in a protein core surrounded by a protein surface and is the infective agent of HBV.) The inventor then employed established techniques of recombinant DNA technology to legate the fragments to a ready-made and commercially available vector pBR322 and introduce that to E.coli.

The principal claim in the patent was, as Lord Hoffmann pointed out (at 40), for any recombinant DNA molecule which expressed the genes of any HBV antigen in any host cell. Moreover the invention had claimed a generalisation of the method actually used. As Lord Hoffmann said (at 40) the inventor

> "… had made his DNA molecule from a standard pBR322 plasmid and large fragments from Dane particle DNA, chosen simply on the basis that they should be large. This was a technique imposed upon him by lack of information about the coding sequences. Thereafter, he employed conventional means to express the DNA in a conventional bacterial host. The claim was for any method of making a DNA molecule which would achieve the necessary expression."

The fundamental difference which distinguishes the present case from Biogen is that in the Amgen patent the coding sequence is disclosed. The patent thus discloses a "principle capable of general application" and discloses a beneficial property which is common to the class. It cannot be said of it that it "discloses no principle which would enable other products [of the class] to be made".

### Source of Tissue

Genetics argued that it was critical for the production of EPO via the human cDNA route to have an "enriched" human tissue source, that is to say a cell or cell type which was, at the time, producing EPO mRNA in quantities which could be reliably detected. It was contended that at the priority date such a tissue was not identified and therefore a cDNA library which could contain EPO cDNA was not available.

However the evidence shows that at the priority date foetal liver was recognised as a source of human EPO: see the paper by Professor Congote of McGill University, Montreal published in 1977 (CB 2880) and also Zanjani et al 1977 (CB 2887), and 1981 (CB 1183) and Sherwood (CB1621) which although published in 1984 reviews scientific knowledge which had been in existence for some time and would have been available to the skilled addressee in 1983.

But, in any case, with the sequence information disclosed in the Amgen patent a reliable probe could be created to screen tissues in which EPO was being made at quite low levels, such as adult human kidney. Further, non-human cells (eg COS-1 or CHO cells) transfected with human EPO gDNA all became suitable sources from which EPO mRNA might be extracted: Professor Klinken (CB2836), Professor Mattick (CB2996, 3003), Professor Schofield (T652-4).

### Difficulty of Production

Genetics argued that, assuming a suitable source tissue was available, obtaining human EPO cDNA would not have been straightforward or reliable. For example, the mRNA might not be correctly spliced, or might be otherwise aberrant. Considerable evidence was presented concerning two attempts to isolate a human EPO cDNA from cells transfected with gDNA. One was within the laboratories of Amgen by Dr Lin (p 55 and Figure 3 of specification and confidential Exhibit PLM 21). The other was that of Wojchowski et al (CB 2124). In both cases the resultant cDNA was unusual in some respect. Significantly however, this could be quickly recognized by reference to the sequence presented in the patent and steps taken using routine methods available in 1983 to obtain a complete and uninterrupted protein coding sequence. In the case of Wojchowski et al this was the construction of a hybrid sequence composed partly of cDNA and partly of gDNA. A substantial body of evidence was presented therefore that human cDNA or DNA sequences containing an uninterrupted coding region could be obtained: Professor Mattick (CB 2989), Professor Klinken (CB 2841-2), Professor Gray (CB 2679, 2681), Professor Schofield (CB 3185-6). I find this evidence persuasive. Genetics has not discharged the onus on this issue.

And in any case, once the sequence is disclosed the skilled addressee need not follow any particular route to the invention, but may take the most convenient one: Professor Mattick (CB 2978-8, 2995), Professor Schofield (CB 3193), Professor Symons (T285, 295). Once you have the combination, it is not necessary to brave the crocodiles in the moat again.

There was also significance in the fact that Genetics produced no evidence of a failed attempt to make the invention work in accordance with the specification. The nearest approach was the evidence of Dr Olsen, an employee of an American firm called Human Genomic Sciences (HGS). In 1993 HGS had constructed over 250 cDNA libraries representing normal and malignant tissue, foetal and adult. At the request of a German licensee of Genetics they searched in those libraries but were unable to identify EPO.

However, HGS did not use a radio labelled probe specific for EPO to isolate an EPO cDNA as is taught by the patent (T354). Furthermore the majority of the libraries were constructed from tissue sources that were not known to express EPO. In fact no effort was made to confirm that the tissues had first made EPO mRNA (T354-6). Moreover the primer design was very poor (T423).

In any case it is not disputed that human EPO mRNA is rare. The point is that the invention enables you to find it in a library using routine screening methods even though the mRNA may be very rare indeed: Mattick (T440-1).

*The meaning of "cDNA"*

There was considerable evidence and argument as to the meaning which the expression "cDNA" would convey to a skilled addressee at the priority date. The Genetics case was that the expression meant, and meant only, a physical entity, that is to say a DNA molecule that is the product of a laboratory process in which mRNA is copied into DNA using the enzyme reverse transcriptase. The resultant DNA molecule contains the entire protein coding region and very substantial parts of the 5' and 3' untranslated sequences.

Amgen did not dispute that "cDNA" could bear the meaning contended by Genetics. However Amgen argued that the expression could, according to context, also bear several secondary meanings including not only DNA molecules but also information – in this case the protein coding sequence of EPO.

In construing language, whether technical or trade terms or ordinary English words, context is everything. A party who asserts that a word can bear a particular meaning (which his opponent accepts) will often find it difficult to establish that the word can never, in any context, bear some other meaning for which his opponent contends. As Dixon J said in *Herbert Adams Pty Ltd v Federal Commissioner of Taxation* (1932) 47 CLR 222 at 228-229:

> "… it is always less difficult to show that a word has a wider meaning than it is to establish a specialized use. For an extension of meaning involves no abandonment of the use in respect of things to which it would in any case apply; but a uniformly restricted application among any class of persons is necessary in order to establish that it has among them a narrower meaning and that meaning only."

On the evidence, I do not think Genetics has made out its case on this issue.

More fundamentally however, the question of meaning was approached by both sides as though a finding as to which meaning "cDNA" bore would resolve a legal issue. In a forensic context, a dispute as to the meaning of words frequently has such a consequence. For example, in Herbert Adams the issue was whether "sponge" fell within the meaning of the term "cakes" in sales tax legislation. The High Court held that it did. As a result, the goods were not exempt from sales tax.

I am not persuaded that the present case is of that character. While the term "cDNA" appears on a few occasions in the Amgen patent, including in the claims, it does not do so in any context where it could be said the skilled addressee would or would not be able to work the invention, depending on the meaning "cDNA" conveyed. In other words, this is not a case where the specification says "take cDNA and do such and such with it" and the Court is asked to find that "cDNA" would convey to a skilled addressee meaning X and that, given that meaning, the addressee could not produce something answering the description of the claims. Rather I think the question is whether, given the information in the specification, and regardless of what label is put on that information, the skilled addressee could produce the invention claimed.

*Clarity*

Genetics argued that a number of the claims lacked clarity.

It was said that the use of the term "primary structural conformation" was not clear. I accept the contention of counsel for Amgen that the term "primary structural conformation" is clear and means "amino acid sequence". The amino acid sequence of naturally-occurring human and monkey EPO is disclosed in the specification in Tables V, VI and VII. The skilled addressee would understand the term "primary structural conformation" to mean the amino acid sequences of human EPO and monkey EPO disclosed in those Tables: Professor Klinken (T609-612).

The skilled addressee would further have understood claim 1 (and the other polypeptide claims, namely, 2-13, 16, 38, 45-54 and 56) to include amino acid sequences of EPO of additional species which could be obtained by using a probe based on the nucleotide sequences disclosed in the Tables, using standard techniques available in the art in December 1983: Genetics concession (T250), Professor Mattick (CB3017), Professor Schofield (CB3199).

In addition to having an amino acid sequence of naturally occurring EPO, a polypeptide of claim 1 must also have one or more of the biological properties of EPO. The hearing officer considered that the term "biological property" was unclear. Accordingly Amgen seek an amendment which would insert at p 18 line 14 of the specification the following:

"The term 'biological property of naturally-occurring erythropoietin' is herein defined to include the in vivo or in vitro activity of immunological function or characteristic of naturally-occurring erythropoietin which (1) causes bone marrow cells to increase production of reticulocytes or red-blood cells, or (2) causes bone marrow cells in culture to increase iron uptake or hemoglobin synthesis, or (3) enables an erythropoietin-specific immunological response or production of erythropoietin-specific antibodies."

In my opinion this amendment is necessary and appropriate and the patent should be amended accordingly.

A skilled addressee would have been able to determine whether a polypeptide had such a property using standard tests for EPO activity, namely, radioimmunassay, in vitro assay and in vivo assay (as disclosed in the Specification), as at December 1983: Professor Mattick (CB3003-5).

The additional and last integer of the claim, that is, "characterised by being the product of procaryotic or eucaryotic expression of an exogenous DNA sequence" is a description of the physical characteristics of the polypeptides of the claim. This may be referred to as a "limitation by result": see *No-Fume Ltd v Frank Pitchford & Co Ltd* (1935) 52 RPC 231, 238. Thus the claim is not a process claim.

Genetics also complained of lack of clarity in claims 33 and 34 which were as follows:

"33. A DNA sequence coding for a polypeptide analog of naturally-occurring erythropoietin.

34. A DNA sequence coding for [phe15] hEPO, [Phe49] hEPO, [Phe145] hEPO, [His7] hEPO, [Asn2des-Pro2 through Ile6] hEPO, [des-Thr163 through Arg166] hEPO or [27-55] hEPO."

However the evidence establishes that a skilled addressee could routinely have made substitutions to the amino acid sequences and thereby obtained EPO analogues or variants: Professor Mattick (CB2989-90, 3024, 3022-5) Professor Firkin (CB2328-9).

*Glycoproteins – Claim 39*
On pp 64-65 of the specification it is stated:

"A preliminary attempt was made to characterize recombinant glycoprotein products from conditioned medium of COS-1 and CHO cell expression of the human EPO gene in comparison to human urinary EPO isolates using both Western blot analysis and SDS-PAGE. These studies indicated that the CHO-produced EPO material had a somewhat higher molecular weight than the COS-1 expression product which, in turn, was slightly larger than the pooled source human urinary extract. All products were somewhat heterogeneous. Neuraminidase enzyme treatment to remove sialic acid resulted in COS-1 and CHO recombinant products of approximately equal molecular weight which were both nonetheless larger than the resulting asialo human urinary extract. Endoglycosidase F enzyme (EC 3.2.1) treatment of the recombinant CHO product and the urinary extract product (to totally remove carbohydrate from both) resulted in substantially homogeneous products having essentially identical molecular weight characteristics.

Purified human urinary EPO and a recombinant, CHO cell-produced, EPO according to the invention were subjected to carbohydrate analysis according to the procedure of Ledeen, et al. Methods in Enzymology, 83 (Part D), 139-191 (1982) as modified through use of the hydrolysis procedures of Nesser, et al, Anal.Biochem., 142, 58-67 (1984). Experimentally determined carbohydrate constitution values (expressed as molar ratios of carbohydrate in the product) for the urinary isolate were as follows: Hexoses, 1.73; N-acetylglucosamine, 1; N-acetylneuraminic acid, 0.93; Fucose, 0; and N-acetylgalactosamine, 0. Corresponding values for the recombinant product (derived from CHO pDSVL-gHueEPO 3-day culture media at 100 nM MTX) were as follows: Hexoses, 15.09; N-acetylglucosamine, 1; N-acetylneuraminic acid, 0.998; Fucose, 0; and N-acetylgalactosamine, 0. These findings are consistent with the Western blot and SDS-PAGE analysis described above.

Glycoprotein products provided by the present invention are thus comprehensive of products having a primary structural conformation sufficiently duplicative of that of a naturally-occurring erythropoietin to allow possession of one or more of the biological properties thereof and having an average carbohydrate composition which differs from that of naturally-occurring erythropoietin."

Claim 39 is for:

"39. A non-naturally occurring glycoprotein product of the expression in a non-human eucaryotic host cell of an exogenous DNA sequence consisting essentially of a DNA sequence encoding human erythropoietin said product possessing the in vivo biological property of causing human bone marrow cells to increase production of reticulocytes and red blood cells and having an average carbohydrate composition which differs from that of naturally occurring human erythropoietin."

It is now common ground that the figures for Hexoses (1.73 and 15.09) are an error. It is not common ground that they would have been so recognised at the priority date. Amgen had the tests done by an expert glycobiologist, Dr Yu, who apparently did not pick up the error.

Genetics argued that the passage quoted on pp 64-65 meant that all the glycoprotein products of the invention (ie recombinant proteins expressed in COS-1 or CHO cells although not in bacteria) must have as one of their three characteristics "an average carbohydrate composition which differs from that of naturally-occurring erythropoietin". Therefore, it was said, there was no support for any claim to a polypeptide product which does not exhibit the feature of an average carbohydrate composition which differs from that of naturally occurring EPO. No claims other than claim 39 deal with this feature. Hence, it was said, they are not fairly based. Claim 39 does deal with it, but in an unclear way because it does not give any guide as to the extent of the difference.

I do not agree with the Genetics construction argument. The expression "comprehensive of" can ordinarily indicate inclusion of something within a greater whole. In the specification I think it is used in that sense. The specification is not saying that this particular feature is an essential element of all products of the invention.

However there remains the problem of the incorrect hexose data and the suggested lack of clarity in claim 39.

Amgen sought an amendment. In its final form this amendment had the effect of omitting the paragraph on p 65 commencing "Purified human urinary EPO ..." and concluding with "... analysis described above". In other words the specification as amended would only refer to the Western blot and SDS-PAGE analysis as a standard of comparison.

But this would posit a vague and uncertain criterion expressed in terms of "somewhat higher molecular weight" and "slightly larger" size. There is no practical utility since such a test would rely on an analytical procedure which is known to have a degree of imprecision and require direct comparison to human urinary erythropoietin, a substance that is particularly difficult to obtain. (As to this see Professor Symons T283, Dr Browne T516.) Since there is no other test disclosed relative to claim 39 I think it should be removed from the patent, along with the passage commencing with "A preliminary attempt ..." on p 64 and ending with "... naturally-occurring erythropoietin" on p 65.

*Cross-Appeal*
Amgen formally cross-appealed against the Deputy Commissioner's rejection of some claims, but was content to accept the amendments proposed.

I shall therefore order that, in addition to the insertion of the definition of "biological properties" and the deletion of claim 39 and the associated passage at pp 64-65 already referred to, amendments be made in terms of Amgen's notice of proposed amendments dated 21 May 1998.

**Part IV**

**Passing Off, Trade Marks and Related Actions**

---

Chapter 12

# Passing Off and Related Actions

For some traders, their most valuable form of intellectual property is their name, reputation or goodwill. The value of a university's reputation, or the name of NIKE, COCA COLA, MAMBO, SESAME STREET or ROLLS ROYCE, is something that is built up over time and, in order to maintain its value, it needs to be protected and managed wisely. Overuse of the name, either lawfully or unlawfully, may dilute the value of the name. On the other hand, the value of a small trader's name may be "swamped" by a large international trader who enters a market using that name.

The law has developed three main ways to protect such property. One may register a trade mark under the *Trade Marks Act 1995*. Such registration will give the registered owner a limited monopoly right to use that mark as a trade mark in relation to the goods and services in respect of which it is registered. Secondly, one might protect a mark, name, reputation or goodwill by way of a common law action for passing off. This action preceded the development of the statutory regime for the registration and protection of trade marks but continues to be a powerful weapon in the hands of traders in respect of their mark, names, goodwill or reputation, whether or not they have a registered trade mark. Finally, a trader may rely on the consumer protection provisions of the *Competition and Consumer Act 2010* (Cth), in particular ss 18 and 29 of Sch 2 to the Act, known as the *Australian Consumer Law* (ACL). These provisions substantially reproduce ss 52 and 53 of the repealed *Trade Practices Act 1974* and proscribe misleading or deceptive conduct in the course of trade or commerce, including conduct which misrepresents a trade or other connection between traders

In the case of a registered trade mark it is common to take action on all three grounds against a person who makes an unauthorised use of the trader's mark and it is possible that the defendant may be found liable in each case. However, it is important to remember that the three actions are quite distinct. In particular, whilst trade mark legislation protects against the mere misuse of a registered trade mark in certain circumstances, passing off and the ACL provisions protect against misrepresentation.

In this part of the text we examine these three different avenues for protecting the name, mark, reputation and goodwill of a trader. In this chapter we examine passing off and ss 18 and 29 of the ACL, relying on the well-developed jurisprudence of ss 52 and 53 of the repealed *Trade Practices Act 1974*. In the following two chapters we will turn to the statutory regime for the registration and protection of trade marks. As you read these chapters you might also like to consider how far you can use copyright law to protect a trade name or mark.

## Passing Off

Passing off is a tort of misrepresentation not misappropriation. The classic case of passing off is said to have occurred when a person uses the plaintiff's common law trade mark, name or other device in such a way as to misrepresent that the goods or services with which the person is dealing have originated with the plaintiff. In the early passing-off case of *Perry v Truefit*,[1] for example, Lord Langdale MR explained the action in the following terms:

> A man is not to sell his own goods under the pretence that they are the goods of another man.[2]

The action is not restricted to this misrepresentation and the tort quickly developed to cover a broader range of misrepresentations which suggest a connection between the goods and services of the plaintiff and defendant. As we shall see, a relevant misrepresentation has been made out where the defendant has misrepresented that the defendant's products are the products of the plaintiff; that the defendant's products have a characteristic which is generally associated with the plaintiff or the plaintiff's products; that the plaintiff has endorsed or sponsored the defendant's product; that there is some commercial association between the plaintiff and the defendant's goods and services; or that the plaintiff uses the defendant's product.

Over the years some commentators have suggested that there is no longer any requirement to prove a relevant misrepresentation in order to establish passing off and that the mere unauthorised use of another's name or image would be sufficient to prove the case.[3] Under this analysis, the tort has become, or should become, an action of misappropriation similar to the celebrity rights which are granted in some jurisdictions. The Civil Code of the State of California, for example, provides actions for persons against the unauthorised use of the person's name, voice, signature, photograph or likeness for advertising and other commercial purposes. The action is based on the concept of misappropriation, rather than misrepresentation, and applies to both living and deceased persons (ss 3341 and 3344.1).

Two successful passing-off cases run by Paul Hogan in the late 1980s to prevent people using names, words and images associated with the film, *Crocodile Dundee*, and the fictional character, Mick Dundee, marked the highpoint of this purported development of celebrity rights in Australia (see *Hogan v Koala Dundee*

---

1    (1842) 6 Beav 66.

2    (1842) 6 Beav 66 at 73.

3    For a discussion of these academic arguments, see J McMullan, "Personality rights in Australia" (1997) 8(2) *AIPJ* 86; B Katekar, "Coping with character merchandising: passing off unsurpassed" (1996) 7(4) *AIPJ* 178.

*Pty Ltd*[4] and *Pacific Dunlop Ltd v Hogan*).[5] However, despite the many words spilled on this matter by commentators, the courts have not accepted such a position. As Pincus J said in *10th Cantanae Pty Ltd v Shoshana Pty Ltd and Sue Smith*,[6] "[p]utting this more shortly, passing-off is not necessarily constituted by the mere ... use of someone's name or picture or the name or picture of a well-known fictitious character".[7]

It is interesting to note, however, that the contrary might be true: passing off may occur even where there has been no misappropriation. This was demonstrated in the High Court case of *Campomar Sociedad Limitada v Nike International Ltd*.[8] In that case the appellant Spanish company had a long-standing trade mark, NIKE, which was registered in Australia in relation to toiletries and cosmetics, including perfumes. The company started marketing NIKE SPORTS PERFUME. Nike International, the well known sports wear manufacturer, sought to prevent this use by challenging the validity of the appellant's trade mark (on the basis that it was likely to deceive or cause confusion) and by alleging passing off and breach of what was then s 52 of the *Trade Practices Act*. Nike International had not registered the trade mark NIKE in Australia in respect of toiletries or perfumes and therefore could not sue for breach of trade mark. The High Court, in a unanimous decision, upheld the validity of Campomar's trade mark registration (on the basis that it was not a source of confusion or deception *at the time* it was registered even though it could be a source of confusion and deception today). The court, however, also held that the Spanish company was liable for passing off and misrepresentation under the old *Trade Practices Act 1974* even though there was no question of misappropriation because the company was using its own registered trade mark.

## The Elements of Passing Off

In order to establish passing off it is necessary not only to prove a relevant misrepresentation but also that the plaintiff has a reputation, and that the plaintiff has suffered actual or potential damage as a result of the misrepresentation. These three elements are sometimes referred to as the "classical trinity" of passing off.[9] The classical trinity identifies the elements of the action but cannot be said to wholly define the action for it does not tell us what type of misrepresentation is required, what type of reputation might be protected, or the type of damage which will ground the action.

In *Erven Warnink BV v J Townend and Sons (Hull) Ltd*,[10] Lord Diplock gave the following, more detailed, formulation of the action:

> [T]he ... cases make it possible to identify five characteristics which must be present in order to create a valid cause of action for passing off: (1) a misrepresentation (2) made by

---

4    (1988) 83 ALR 187.

5    (1989) 87 ALR 14.

6    (1987) 79 ALR 299.

7    (1987) 79 ALR 299 at 306.

8    (2000) 202 CLR 45.

9    Nourse LJ in *Consorzio del Proscuitto di Parma v Marks and Spencer plc* [1991] RPC 351 at 368-369.

10   [1979] 2 All ER 927.

a trader in the course of trade, (3) to prospective customers of his or ultimate consumers of goods or services supplied by him, (4) which is calculated to injure the business or goodwill of another trader (in the sense that this is a reasonably foreseeable consequence) and (5) which causes actual damage to a business or goodwill of the trader by whom the action is brought or (in a quia timet action) will probably do so.[11]

Even this statement cannot be treated as a complete or sufficient definition of the action. As Lord Diplock himself said, and as Deane J emphasised in *Moorgate Tobacco Co Ltd v Philip Morris Ltd (No 2)*:[12]

> In seeking to formulate general propositions of English law, however, one must be particularly careful to be aware of the logical fallacy of the undistributed middle.[13] It does not follow that because all passing off actions can be shown to present the characteristics, all factual situations which present these characteristics give rise to a cause of action for passing off.[14]

In *ConAgra Inc v McCain Foods (Aust) Pty Ltd*,[15] Gummow J noted the limitations of treating either of these statements as a definition of the action and warned that "the law of passing off contains sufficient nooks and crannies to make it difficult to formulate any satisfactory definition of [it] in short form". The judge concluded that, nevertheless, the "classical trinity" of reputation, misrepresentation and damage, does serve to emphasis "three core concepts" in this area of law.[16] On this basis, but keeping in mind the limitations of the formulation, we consider the elements of passing off by reference to these three core concepts.

## Reputation

Passing off developed as an action for the grant of an equitable remedy of injunction or account of profit in an ancillary action to a common law action in deceit.[17] As a matter of legal principle, the equitable remedies were only available for the protection of a proprietary interest and the question arose as to what proprietary interest was protected by the action of passing off.

In *AG Spalding and Bros v AW Gamage Ltd*,[18] Parker LJ held that the proprietary interest protected by the law of passing off was not simply a proprietary interest in the name, mark, slogan or other indicia of the plaintiff but in the "business or goodwill likely to be injured".[19] In the words of Wilberforce J in

---

11    [1979] 2 All ER 927 at 932-933.

12    (1984) 156 CLR 414.

13    A classic example of the fallacy of the undistributed middle is the syllogism: "All dogs have four legs; cats have four legs therefore all cats are dogs". Similarly, it is incorrect to say: "All actions for passing off have these characteristics; this action has these characteristics therefore this action is an action for passing off".

14    (1984) 156 CLR 414 at 443-444 paraphrasing Lord Diplock's own warning in *Erven Warnink BV v J Townend and Sons (Hull) Ltd* [1979] 2 All ER 927.

15    (1991) 106 ALR 465.

16    (1991) 106 ALR 465 at 518.

17    See Way CJ's discussion in *Weingarten Bros v G and R Wills and Co* [1906] SALR 34 and Gummow J's history of the action in *ConAgra Inc v McCain Foods (Aust) Pty Ltd* (1991) 106 ALR 465.

18    (1915) 32 RPC 273.

19    (1915) 32 RPC 273 at 284.

*Norman Kark Publications Ltd v Odhams Press Ltd*,[20] in a passage approved by Gummow J in *ConAgra Inc v McCain Foods (Aust) Pty Ltd*:[21]

> The basis of the action, as shown in *Spalding v Gamage* (1915) 32 RPC 273, is a proprietary right, not so much in the name itself, but in the goodwill established through use of the name in connection with the plaintiff's goods.[22]

In *Inland Revenue Commissioners v Muller and Co's Margarine Ltd*,[23] Lord McNaughten defined this proprietary interest, or goodwill, as the "benefit and advantage of the good name, reputation and connection of a business … the attractive force which brings in custom".[24] This was a taxation case which determined that, at least for the purposes of taxation, "goodwill" is a property right which is attached to a business and is limited to the territory in which the business is conducted. It followed from this determination that goodwill could not be sold apart from the business to which it was attached and, if the business and the goodwill were sold, then the dealing was said to have taken place where the business itself was located even though the business may have been known elsewhere. Thus, if a business and its goodwill were sold in Germany, this was not a dealing for taxation purposes in England even if, on account of this goodwill, the business had a reputation in England.

On the basis of this understanding of goodwill a body of case law developed in which it was assumed that, in an action for passing off, the plaintiff had to carry on a business in the jurisdiction before he or she could ground an action for passing off because it was only in this situation that the plaintiff might be said to have a proprietary interest which might be protected by the action. The fact that the plaintiff was known in the jurisdiction would, on this analysis, be insufficient to ground the action.[25]

The question came before the Full Federal Court in Australia in *ConAgra Inc v McCain Foods (Aust) Pty Ltd*.[26] In that case the plaintiff ConAgra carried on a business in the United States which included the sale of frozen food products called "Healthy Choice" which were sold in a distinctive get-up. The defendant noted the success of the product in the United States and introduced a frozen food range in Australia which it called "Healthy Choice" and which was in a similar distinctive get-up. The trial judge found as a matter of fact that the plaintiff did not have a reputation in Australia, did not carry on business in Australia and therefore held that the action did not succeed. On appeal the plaintiff argued that there was no need to have a business in Australia, that mere reputation was enough and even mere reputation was not required if the defendant had acted fraudulently. The Full Federal Court accepted that the plaintiff need not have an actual business in the jurisdiction but held that the plaintiff did need a reputation in the jurisdiction. On the question of reputation Lockhart J said:

---

20    [1962] RPC 163.

21    (1991) 106 ALR 465 at 528.

22    [1962] RPC 163 at 167.

23    [1901] AC 217.

24    [1901] AC 217 at 223-224.

25    For a discussion of the prior case law, see Gummow J in *ConAgra Inc v McCain Foods (Aust) Pty Ltd* (1991) 106 ALR 465.

26    (1991) 106 ALR 465.

It is quite right to say that the reputation of a business cannot be severed from the business itself or a person who owns it, each is inevitably entwined with the other. Reputation is a result of the carrying on of business. But it is, in my view, wrong to assert in 1992 that the law of passing off cannot protect a plaintiff or his goods (or services) in a country where he does not carry on business or has ceased to carry on business or has no place of business … it is not a necessary element of the tort.[27]

On the question of fraud Lockhart J said that the basis of the action was a misrepresentation which made a reference to the business reputation of the plaintiff. Therefore, it was logically impossible for there to be a passing off without misrepresentation or reputation, even where there was fraud.[28] (The converse question, of whether fraud is a necessary element of the action, is discussed below.)

Reputation does not rely on the consumer knowing the name of the producer or manufacturer. Thus, in *Birmingham Vinegar Brewery Co v Powell*,[29] the respondents had for many years manufactured a sauce called Yorkshire Relish. The appellants started to manufacture a sauce which was sold as "Yorkshire Sauce". The respondents were successful in an application for an injunction even though there was evidence that the customer "does not know or care who the manufacturer is" because it was established that "it is a particular manufacture he desires. He wants Yorkshire Relish to which he has been accustomed, and which … has been made exclusively by the plaintiff for a great number of years".[30] In the words of Lord Herschell:

> I think that the fallacy of the appellant's argument rests on this: that it is assumed that one trader cannot be passing off his goods as the manufacture of another unless it is shewn that the persons purchasing the goods know the manufacturer by name, and have in their mind when they purchase the goods that they are made by a particular individual. It seems to me that one man may quite well pass his goods as the goods of another if he passes them off to people who will accept them as the manufacture of another, though they do not know that other name at all.[31]

A business reputation may belong to a class of persons rather than an individual or single business. Thus, in *J Bollinger v Costa Brava Wine Co Ltd* (the "Champagne case"),[32] Bollinger and 11 other wine makers from the Champagne district of France sought an injunction to prevent Costa Brava from describing its Spanish grown and produced wine as "champagne" or "Spanish Champagne". They argued that it was only the producers of the Champagne region of France who were entitled to refer to their wines as having been made by the method associated with this region and that their reputation as a class had been harmed by the misrepresentation. They were successful, even though the court noted that at the time of the action there were 150 manufacturers

---

27   (1991) 106 ALR 465 at 503.
28   (1991) 106 ALR 465 at 507.
29   [1897] AC 710.
30   [1897] AC 710 at 713 per Lord Halsbury.
31   [1897] AC 710 at 715.
32   [1960] Ch 262. This was just one in a line of alcoholic beverages cases in passing-off law including the sherry case, *Vine Products Ltd v MacKenzie and Co Ltd* [1969] RPC 1 and the Scotch Whisky case, *John Walker and Sons Ltd v Henry Ost and Co Ltd* [1970] 2 All ER 106 and the Advocaat case, *Erven Warnick BV v J Townend and Sons (Hull) Ltd* [1979] 2 All ER 927.

entitled to use the term in the region and that this number was likely to expand in the future.[33]

In *Erven Warnink BV v J Townend and Sons (Hull) Ltd*,[34] the House of Lords noted that the same principle applied whether there was a small or large number of claimants although, as Lord Diplock remarked:

> The larger it is the broader must be the range and quality of products to which the descriptive term used by the members of the class has been applied, and the more difficult it must be to show that the term has acquired a public reputation and goodwill denoting a product endowed with recognisable qualities which distinguish it from others of inferior reputation that compete in the same market.[35]

The Champagne case came to be accepted as authority for the proposition that the reputation of a number of plaintiffs might be associated with a quality of the goods and services rather than simply the origin of the goods and services. However, in *Erven Warnink BV v J Townend and Sons (Hull) Ltd*, the defendants sought to have the Champagne case restricted to reputations associated with the geographical locality of the manufacture of, or other trade dealings with, the product in question. In that case the plaintiffs were the Dutch manufacturers and distributors of Advocaat, an alcoholic drink made from eggs and spirits which was made mainly in Holland, but also in other countries, and sold throughout the world including England. Seeking to benefit from the popularity of Advocaat, the defendant English company began marketing a different type of alcoholic drink, made out of dried eggs and sherry, as "Old English Advocaat" (rather than "egg-flip" which was how such a drink had previously been marketed). The House of Lords found that the word Advocaat had become distinctive of the plaintiff's egg and spirit drink and was a valuable part of their goodwill.[36] The House of Lords also held that there was no reason in logic or policy to restrict the qualities which might support such a valuable goodwill to words or phrases referring to geographical locality.[37]

The fact that reputation need not be exclusive has been important in ensuring that any member in a chain of commercial dealings may take an action in passing off to protect its reputation in relation to that chain. The courts have not always clearly identified the basis of the rights of the various parties which are being protected in such cases. In some cases it may be that there are separate reputations being protected, in other cases it may be that the parties share a reputation similar to that shared by the manufacturers of the Champagne region of France. In *Childrens Television Workshop Inc v Woolworths (NSW) Ltd*,[38] there were

---

33   Note, in the related Australian cases of *Comite Interprofessionel du Vin de Champagne v NL Burton Pty Ltd* (1981) 38 ALR 664, the Federal Court declined to grant an interlocutory injunction banning the use of the term "champagne" and "imported champagne" on sparkling wines imported from Spain. The court found, for the purposes of the proceeding, that in Australia people used the term champagne to refer to a sparkling white wine and/or wine fermented in the bottle (the "methode champenoise"). The term was not solely related to wine produced in the Champagne region of France.

34   [1979] 2 All ER 927.

35   [1979] 2 All ER 927 at 934.

36   [1979] 2 All ER 927, Lord Diplock at 943.

37   [1979] 2 All ER 927, Lord Diplock at 935.

38   [1981] 1 NSWLR 273.

three plaintiffs. These were Jim Henson, the creator of the Muppets, the Childrens Television Workshop which had an exclusive licence to use the Muppets in "Sesame Street" and an Australian business which was in early negotiations for a licence to distribute the Muppets to retail outlets. Helsham CJ in Eq held that the third plaintiff did not have a reputation in the required sense, that the Childrens Television Workshop did and that he did not need to make up his mind about Henson himself.

These cases assume that it is only a business reputation, rather than a personal reputation, which is protected by the action, although the business connection required to establish this reputation has been liberally interpreted. In the 1960 case of *Henderson v Radio Corporation Pty Ltd*,[39] for example, two professional ballroom dancers, the Hendersons, sought an injunction to have their unnamed photograph removed from a record of ballroom dancing music. The court found that the Hendersons had a reputation in the field of ballroom dancing and that, for the identified audience, the use of the photograph amounted to a misrepresentation that the Hendersons had recommended the record. The couple were held to be "engaged in business, using that expression in its widest sense to include professions and callings"[40] and passing off was held to have occurred.

In the 1988 case of *Hogan v Koala Dundee Pty Ltd*,[41] the plaintiffs argued the case on the basis that "it is possible to bring a passing off suit in respect of an image, including a name, unconnected with any business at all".[42] In that case the well-known personality and actor, Paul Hogan, and a firm which owned the merchandising rights for the film *Crocodile Dundee*, were granted an injunction to prevent a small retail company from exploiting an image of a koala bear wearing a sleeveless vest, holding a big knife and sporting a bush hat with teeth in its band. The outfit was similar to the outfit worn by the fictional character played by Hogan in the film. The company also used the term DUNDEE COUNTRY as a label, name and feature in its shops. Pincus J claimed to have accepted the plaintiff's submission unreservedly but it is interesting to note that he did identify a business connection of some sort:

> The assumption appears to me to be correct. I think the law is, at least in Australia, that the inventor of a sufficiently famous fictional character having certain visual or other traits may prevent others using his character to sell their goods and may assign the right to use the character. Furthermore, the inventor may do these things even where he has never carried on any business at all, other than the writing or making of the work in which the character appears.[43]

At the time the case was decided it was heralded by some in the academic literature as the arrival of a new tort of misappropriation of personality which

39    (1960) 1A IPR 620.

40    (1960) 1A IPR 620 at 636.

41    (1988) 83 ALR 187.

42    (1988) 83 ALR 187 at 196.

43    (1988) 83 ALR 187 at 188 at 196. Pincus J based his decision on the remark in *Henderson v Radio Corporation Pty Ltd* (1960) 1A IPR 620 that injury to a reputation would, without more, be accepted as proof of damage. However, in that case it must be remembered, the court was only referring to business reputation as it had always been understood in passing-off law. Also see Manning J's remarks on this issue in *Henderson v Radio Corporation Pty Ltd* at 640; and *Illustrated Newspapers Ltd v Publicity Services (London)* [1938] 1 Ch 414 at 422.

would protect everyone's reputation, both personal and private. By virtue of this new tort, it was suggested, any person might prevent his or her image being used in an advertising campaign, for example, without consent.[44] However, this was an overstatement of the case and, even in *Hogan v Koala Dundee Pty Ltd*,[45] the plaintiffs were held to have been involved in business at least in so far as they wrote the script and made the film in which the fictional character appeared. Furthermore, since this case courts have continued to insist on the necessity of establishing a reputation which is a "saleable commodity"[46] in order to ground an action in passing off.

## Proving reputation

A person has a reputation for the purposes of passing off if it can be established that, at the time the alleged passing off occurred,[47] "a substantial number of persons" would be "potential customers of the plaintiff within the jurisdiction if the plaintiff's goods and services were marketed at that time".[48] This is a question of fact which is established by showing that the name, mark or other indicia has acquired a secondary meaning so that it is distinctive of the plaintiff's goods or services. As Lord Wilberforce said in *Norman Kark Publications Ltd v Odhams Press Ltd*,[49] "[t]he plaintiff must show that the name has become distinctive of his goods, and that a reputation has attached to them under the name in question".[50]

The name, mark or other indicia which may be a vehicle for such a reputation is not closed. Lord Scarman, in *Cadbury Schweppes Pty Ltd v Pub Squash Co Pty Ltd*,[51] a Privy Council case on appeal from Australia, said:

> The tort is no longer anchored, as it was in the 19th century formulation, to the name or trade mark of a product or business. It is wide enough to encompass other descriptive material, such as slogans or visual images, which radio, television or newspaper advertising campaigns can lead the market to associate with a plaintiff's product, provided always that such descriptive material has become part of the goodwill of the product. And the test is whether the product has derived from the advertising a distinctive character which the market recognises.[52]

---

44    See J McMullan, "Personality rights in Australia" (1997) 8(2) *AIPJ* 86; B Katekar and "Coping with character merchandising: passing off unsurpassed" (1996) 7(4) *AIPJ* 178.

45    (1988) 83 ALR 187.

46    See Manning J in *Henderson v Radio Corporation Pty Ltd* (1960) 1A IPR 620 at 645.

47    *Cadbury Schweppes Pty Ltd v Pub Squash Co Pty Ltd* (1980) 32 ALR 387.

48    Gummow J in *ConAgra Inc v McCain Foods (Aust) Pty Ltd* (1991) 106 ALR 465 at 538. For an interesting application of this test in the South African context in relation to trade marks, see *McDonald's Corp v Joburgers Drive-Inn Restaurant Pty Ltd* (1996) 36 IPR 11 where it was established that many black South Africans would not recognise McDonalds but white South Africans and middle class black South Africans who were the intended market for McDonalds would recognise the name.

49    [1962] RPC 163.

50    [1962] RPC 163 at 167.

51    (1980) 32 ALR 387.

52    (1980) 32 ALR 387 at 393.

Thus, advertising slogans (as in *AG Spalding and Bros v AW Gamage Ltd*),[53] product names (*Erven Warnink BV v J Townend and Sons (Hull) Ltd*),[54] photographs (*Henderson v Radio Corporation Pty Ltd*),[55] images of fictional characters (*Hogan v Koala Dundee Pty Ltd*),[56] and packaging, get-up and even the shape of the product have all been found to be distinctive in the sense that they distinguished the plaintiff's goods or services from those of another or that they had acquired a secondary meaning which was distinctive of the plaintiff's goods and services. In *Williams Edge and Sons Ltd v William Nicholls and Sons Ltd*,[57] for example, the particular get-up of a laundry "blue bag"[58] which comprised an unmarked bag attached to a stick and made no reference to the plaintiff by name, was held to have become sufficiently distinctive to be the vehicle of the plaintiff's reputation.

It may be difficult to prove that a descriptive or functional term, or common get-up has acquired a secondary meaning so as to be distinctive of the plaintiff's goods and services. For example, if a manufacturer decided to call its soap "SOAP", it might be quite difficult, but not impossible, to prove that consumers treated this term as a term which referred particularly to the manufacturer's soap rather than as a term which described the product. Thus, in *McCain International Ltd v Country Fair Foods Ltd*,[59] McCain International was unsuccessful in its attempt to prevent Country Fair launching a new product, "Birds Eye Oven Chips" to compete with its "McCain's Oven Fried Chips". The English Court of Appeal held that the term "oven chips" was descriptive and, as a matter of fact, in the 18 months in which it had been used, had not acquired a secondary meaning which was distinctive of the plaintiff's product and a vehicle for the plaintiff's reputation. Similarly, if a feature is mundane or in common use it may be difficult to prove that it carries a reputation. Thus in *Nutrientwater Pty Ltd v Baco Pty Ltd*[60] the familiar trade get-up of bottled enhanced water – that is clear packaging, wide mouth, rainbow coloured labels across the product range – was held not to be associated with the plaintiff but rather with the product range as a whole. There have, however, been cases where the plaintiff has been able to protect such features.

In the early case of *Reddaway v Banham*,[61] for example, the plaintiff had for many years made and sold belts which it called "Camel Hair Belts". The defendant started selling belts under this name and sought to justify the use on the basis that the term was purely descriptive (the belts were made of camel hair).[62] The House of Lords rejected the argument on the basis that, even though the phrase was descriptive, the phrase "Camel Hair Belt" had in fact acquired a secondary meaning so that use of the term was thought by consumers to refer to the plaintiff's product. Similarly, the fact that the term "Equity Access" was partly

---

53  [1915] 32 RPC 273.
54  [1979] 2 All ER 927.
55  (1960) 1A IPR 620.
56  (1988) 83 ALR 187.
57  [1911] AC 693.
58  Ask your grandparents or another older person why people may have used a blue bag.
59  [1981] RPC 69.
60  [2010] FCA 2.
61  [1896] AC 199.
62  This fact, it seems came as a surprise to both parties in the case.

descriptive of the financial service offered did not prevent it being protected in *Equity Access Pty Ltd v Westpac Banking Corporation*.[63] In the words of Hill J in that case, there is no black and white distinction between descriptive terms and "fancy" terms either in law or in practice:

> The reality is that there is a continuum … The closer along the continuum one moves towards a merely descriptive name the more a plaintiff will need to show that the name has obtained a secondary meaning, equating it with the products of the plaintiff … and the easier it will be to see a small difference in names as adequate to avoid confusion.[64]

A similar approach has been adopted in relation to functional features. For example, the fact that the stick on the blue bag in *Williams Edge and Sons Ltd v William Nicholls and Sons Ltd*[65] had a utilitarian purpose did not prevent it, as a matter of principle, from protection and, as a question of fact, it was found that customers associated the get-up with the plaintiffs. Finally, even where the defendant otherwise legitimately uses a name this may still amount to passing off in so far as the use of that name amounts to a misrepresentation because the name is the vehicle of the plaintiff's reputation. This was a bit of a shock to the unsuccessful defendant in *Southorn v Reynolds*[66] one might imagine. In that case, the defendants had gone so far as to employ an unskilled person named Southorn in an attempt to justify the use of the plaintiff's name, Southorn, on the clay tobacco pipes which the defendants were selling. Similarly, in the NIKE case discussed at the beginning of this chapter, the legitimate use of the word NIKE amounted to a misrepresentation in so far as the word was a vehicle for Nike International's reputation. In both cases the use of the name was held to amount to passing off. As Stephen J noted in the s 52 case of *Hornsby Building Information Centre Pty Ltd v Sydney Building Information Centre Ltd*,[67] it is possible that a statement may carry with it the relevant false representation even if it is literally true.

Over the years defendants have sought to argue that, as a matter of legal principle, descriptive terms, functional items, get-up in common use, or the use of a person's real name cannot amount to passing off. As the cases above illustrate, however, there is no such principle and in each case the question of whether the particular mark, name or other indicia is distinctive of the plaintiff's goods and services remains one of fact.

## Misrepresentation

The distinctive feature of passing off is that it involves a misrepresentation, by way of statement or conduct, which "passes off" some connection between the defendant, or the defendant's goods and services, and a plaintiff with the requisite reputation. That is, not every misrepresentation in the course of trade amounts to passing off. The case law has identified a relevant misrepresentation where the defendant has misrepresented that the defendant's products are the

---

63   (1989) 16 IPR 431.
64   (1989) 16 IPR 431 at 448.
65   [1911] AC 693. Contrast *Collins Debden Pty Ltd v Cumberland Stationery Co Pty Ltd (No 2)* [2005] FCA 1398 regarding a desk calendar design.
66   (1865) 12 LT 75.
67   (1977) 140 CLR 216 at 228.

products of the plaintiff or that the defendant's products have a characteristic which is generally associated with the plaintiff or the plaintiff's products. The relevant misrepresentation has also been established where the defendant has misrepresented that the plaintiff has endorsed or sponsored the defendant's product, that there is some commercial association between the plaintiff and the defendant's goods and services, or that the plaintiff uses the defendant's product. This last example is known as "reverse passing off". We consider these in turn.

In *AG Spalding and Bros v AW Gamage Ltd*,[68] Gamage, a sports retailer, acquired a stock of old Spalding Bros "Orbs" (as Spalding footballs were known) which Spalding had sold to a waste merchant because they were made from out-dated moulded technology and had been subject to consumer complaints. Gamage advertised the Orbs for sale at half the Spalding price using terms which Spalding itself had used in advertising its latest model sewn football. Gamage was found liable for passing off on the basis that they had misrepresented that their goods had a quality associated with the new Spalding orbs. Similarly, in *Erven Warnink BV v J Townend and Sons (Hull) Ltd*[69] (the Advocaat case), the defendant's use of the term Advocaat was held to amount to a misrepresentation that their egg flip, made from dried eggs and sherry, had a quality associated with the plaintiff's drink, which was made of eggs and spirits.

In *Henderson v Radio Corporation Pty Ltd*,[70] the defendant was held to have misrepresented that the plaintiffs had endorsed the ballroom dancing record on which their unnamed photograph had appeared. This decision was generally embraced as a conventional application of the principles of passing off. However, the application of these principles was subject to some criticism following the two Hogan cases.

We have set out the facts of *Hogan v Koala Dundee Pty Ltd*[71] above. *Pacific Dunlop Ltd v Hogan*[72] involved another use of images from the movie *Crocodile Dundee*. In that case the defendant had produced a television commercial for Grosby shoes which was based on a take-off of the famous knife scene in *Crocodile Dundee*. The actors in the commercial were clearly not the actors, Linda Kozlowski or Paul Hogan, although the male character was dressed in an exaggerated Mick Dundee outfit. Having been set upon by a mugger wearing leather shoes the Mick Dundee character vanquishes the attacker with the words, "You call those shoes ... these are shoes".

In the first Hogan case Pincus J declined to base his decision on the "legal fiction" that the audience would think that Hogan or his company had endorsed the products or even that the audience would have thought of this. Instead, he held that the misrepresentation was that there was some commercial association between the defendant and Paul Hogan and the merchandising company.[73] In the second Hogan case the misrepresentation was held to have been that "the advertisement could not have been shown without Mr Hogan's consent or approval".[74]

---

68 [1915] 32 RPC 273.
69 [1979] 2 All ER 927.
70 (1960) 1A IPR 620.
71 (1988) 83 ALR 187.
72 (1989) 14 IPR 398.
73 *Hogan v Koala Dundee Pty Ltd* (1988) 83 ALR 187.
74 *Pacific Dunlop Ltd v Hogan* (1989) 14 IPR 398 at 403.

Pincus J's judgment has sometimes been taken as a criticism of the need to prove any misrepresentation in a passing-off action and as the leading case for the development of celebrity rights in Australia. Whether you agree with this reading of his decision or not it is notable that, since the Hogan cases, Australian courts have expressly required something more than the mere use of the name or image in order to establish a relevant misrepresentation. Thus, in *Gary Honey v Australian Airlines Ltd and House of Tabor*,[75] the athlete Gary Honey was unsuccessful in his passing-off action against both Australian Airlines, which had used his photograph on a poster, and against a charismatic Christian organisation, which had used the photograph from the poster on the cover of a book. In the first case, although Honey's name was used and the poster was likely to be distributed amongst sporting establishments who would recognise him, Northrop J held that there was no representation of a connection between the airline company and Honey in so far as the company's name was relatively insignificant in the poster design and the poster was one of a series of sports posters produced by the airline company, many of which showed amateur and unknown sportspeople. In the case of the book, Honey's name was not used and the fact that the book would be distributed to a small group of charismatic Christians who might not recognise him, together with the fact that the photo was typical of covers used on such publications, led the judge to conclude that there had been no relevant misrepresentation.

The typical example of reverse passing off is to say that Celebrity X uses the defendant's shampoo. However, the reverse representation may be more subtle. In *Taco Company of Australia Inc v Taco Bell Pty Ltd*,[76] a large United States restaurant chain opened two Taco Bell restaurants in Sydney suburbs even though they knew that there was an existing Australian Taco Bell in Bondi. It was held that this conduct amounted to a misrepresentation by the United States company that the Bondi restaurant was part of the United States company's chain. (See also *Cambridge University Press v University Tutorial Press*.)[77]

These cases illustrate an interesting problem. If non-legally trained members of the public incorrectly assume that no one can use a celebrity's name or image (or the name or image of a famous fictional character) without consent, does this mean that the celebrity can prove misrepresentation simply on the basis of the use of these words or images and the erroneous assumption of the public?

The question was considered directly in the s 52 case of *McWilliam's Wines Pty Ltd v McDonald's System of Australia Pty Ltd*[78] where the appellants used the term "BIG MAC" in an advertising campaign in relation to their wines. On appeal the Federal Court held that there is no misleading or deceptive conduct under s 52 if any misconception is based on the "erroneous assumption" of the customer. In that case it was said that the only reason a customer would have the misconception that there was a connection between the two companies was because the customer had an "erroneous assumption" that only a person authorised by McDonald's could use the name BIG MAC. This seemed to be a neat

---

75    (1990) 18 IPR 185.
76    (1982) 42 ALR 177 at 204-206.
77    (1928) 45 RPC 335.
78    (1980) 33 ALR 394.

way around the problem but, in *Taco Company of Australia Inc v Taco Bell Pty Ltd*,[79] in relation to another s 52 application, Deane and Fitzgerald JJ denied the existence of such a general principle and pointed out that no conduct can mislead or deceive unless it is based on some erroneous assumption, for example, the erroneous assumption that the person making the representation is speaking the truth.[80] The judges held that the question of what assumptions the audience might hold and the fancifulness of such assumptions were just two of the factors to be taken into account in determining whether, as a question of fact, there had indeed been misleading or deceptive conduct for the purposes of s 52 of the *Trade Practices Act 1974*. There was some legitimate debate as to whether this was the appropriate approach to take in relation to passing-off actions as well as s 52 actions but, in *Campomar Sociedad Limitada v Nike International Ltd*,[81] the High Court took this approach in relation to both and denied the existence of a general principle of erroneous assumption in Australia in either a passing-off action or in an action under the Act.[82]

If a person uses the plaintiff's mark, name or other indicia but disclaims any relevant connection between the parties then there will be no relevant misrepresentation for the purposes of grounding passing off. In *Sony Music Australia v Tansing*,[83] for example, the defendants released a bootleg recording of Michael Jackson. The cover of the recording carried the words "Michael Jackson King of Pop" but there was held to be no passing off because the cover also had disclaimers such as the word "Unauthorised" written in bold red across the front of the cover and the phrases "the unauthorised recordings", "this live recording and its release has not been authorised by Michael Jackson or his record company" and "this sound recording may not be of the same quality as an authorised release". On the other hand, the fact that the defendants had stamped "Unauthorised" on the front of their cans of DUFF BEER, a beer which up until then had been the fictional preferred drop of Homer Simpson, did not allow the defendant to escape liability for passing off because the court found that "given the irreverent nature of (The Simpsons series) it is by no means beyond reasonable argument that the disclaimers would reinforce, rather than negate or diminish, any association with the series".[84]

Even if it is determined that the relevant misrepresentation has been made there will be no passing off if it is determined that the misconception arose out of the plaintiff's conduct. For example, in *Taco Company of Australia Inc v Taco Bell Pty Ltd*,[85] although it was determined that the public might think that there was a connection between the American company's chain and the Australian restaurant this was held not to constitute passing off by the Australian company. This was

---

79 (1982) 42 ALR 177.
80 (1982) 42 ALR 177 at 200-201.
81 (2000) 202 CLR 45.
82 (2000) 202 CLR 45 at 83-88 as to s 52 of the *Trade Practices Act 1974* and at 89 as to passing off, citing *10th Cantanae Pty Ltd v Shoshana Pty Ltd* (1987) 79 ALR 299 at 324-325 and *Hogan v Pacific Dunlop Ltd* (1988) 83 ALR 403 at 426.
83 (1993) 27 IPR 649.
84 Tamberlin J in *Twentieth Century Fox Film Corp v South Australian Brewing Co Ltd* (1996) 34 IPR 247 at 254.
85 (1982) 42 ALR 177.

because the misconception was caused by the fact that the American company had entered the market after the Australian company. On the other hand, this misconception did lead to a finding of passing off by the American company.

On the other hand, it is possible for there to be an honest concurrent use of a name so that neither party can maintain a passing-off action. As Finkelstein J put it in *Colorado Group Ltd v Strandbags Group Pty Ltd*:[86]

> In a passing off action, where two traders have a reputation in the same or similar names that are concurrently being used 'neither of them can be said to be guilty of any misrepresentation. Each represents nothing but the truth, that a particular name or mark, is associated with his goods or business'[87] … If in such circumstances there might be confusion that is just 'one of the misfortunes which occur in life', but it is not actionable as a passing off.[88]

The question of misrepresentation in passing-off actions is inseparable from the question of reputation in so far as no person will be misled by the use of the plaintiff's name, mark or other indicia unless that name, mark or indicia has acquired a secondary meaning whereby it has in fact become distinctive of the plaintiff's goods and services. Therefore, just as it could be difficult to establish that a descriptive term is a vehicle for the plaintiff's reputation so it may be difficult, if the defendant uses this descriptive term, to establish that the defendant is making a relevant misrepresentation. If a defendant uses the plaintiff's name "SOAP", for example, it may be difficult, but not impossible, to prove that the defendant is making a representation about the product's connection with the plaintiff rather than merely using the name in a descriptive sense. However, in the two cases discussed above, *Reddaway v Banham*[89] and *Williams Edge and Sons Ltd v William Nicholls and Sons Ltd*,[90] the plaintiffs were successful in establishing the relevant misrepresentation. In cases where descriptive names have been used the courts have found that even small differences in a competitor's name will prevent the use of the name from constituting passing off.[91]

It is not necessary for the defendant to have an intention to deceive in order to establish passing off, although, in the absence of such intention, the plaintiff's remedies may be limited to an injunction. As Lord Morris said in a phrase adopted by the High Court in *Hornsby Building Information Centre v Sydney Building Information Centre*,[92] "trading must not only be honest but must not even unintentionally be unfair".[93]

On the other hand, deception, fraud and sharp practices alone are insufficient to establish passing off. In *Cadbury Schweppes Pty Ltd v Pub Squash Co*

---

86   [2006] FCA 160 at [53].
87   Citing *Habib Bank Ltd v Habib Bank AG Zurich* [1981] 1 WLR 1265 at 1275 per Oliver LJ.
88   Citing *Marengo v Daily Sketch and Daily Graphic Ltd* [1992] FSR 1 at 2.
89   [1896] AC 199.
90   [1911] AC 693.
91   *Office Cleaning Services Ltd v Westminster Window and General Cleaners Ltd* (1946) 63 RPC 39, cited by Stephen J in *Hornsby Building Information Centre v Sydney Building Information Centre* (1977) 140 CLR 216 at 229. Stephen J said that the approach applied a fortiori to s 52 actions where the action was to protect the interests of third parties (at 230).
92   (1977) 140 CLR 216 at 228.
93   Lord Morris in *Parker-Knoll Ltd v Knoll International Ltd* [1962] RPC 265 at 278, quoted by Stephen J in *Hornsby Building Information Centre v Sydney Building Information Centre* (1977) 140 CLR 216 at 228.

*Pty Ltd,*[94] for example, the trial judge had determined that there had been no relevant misrepresentation even though the defendant had acted "in a deliberate and calculated fashion to take advantage of the plaintiff's past efforts in developing SOLO"[95] and had consciously adopted the get-up and style of the plaintiff's advertisement to profit from the plaintiff's success with its drink SOLO. The appellants (the SOLO makers) argued that the trial judge had misdirected himself by failing to take the plaintiff's intention to deceive into account when considering the misrepresentation. The Privy Council rejected the argument and endorsed the trial judge's statement that one must guard against finding fraud "merely because there had been an imitation of another's goods, get-up, method of trading or trading style". The Privy Council repeated that even fraud was insufficient to establish the necessary misrepresentation but noted that where an intention to deceive is found "it is not difficult for the court to infer that the intention has been, or in all probability will be, effective".[96] As Gummow J explains in *10th Cantanae Pty Ltd v Shoshana Pty Ltd and Sue Smith,*[97] the rules relating to fraud or intention to deceive arise out of general legal principles in so far as the common law action for damages for passing off arose out of the action for deceit whilst the equitable remedy of account was only available in the case of persistence after notice.[98] An injunction, on the other hand, is available without proof of fraud.

Finally, the representation must be made in Australia. In *Ward Group Pty Ltd v Brodie and Stone plc,*[99] a case relating to representations made on a United Kingdom website, Merkel J was inclined to find that there had been no misrepresentation in Australia because the representation had not been targeted at Australian consumers but was made to the world at large. Although the judge claimed that this was in accordance with authorities[100] and distinguished *Dow Jones and Co Inc v Gutnick,*[101] he did not decide the passing-off matter on this basis but rather on the basis that there had been no damage proven.

## Misrepresentation and domain names

A domain name is the textual name for an internet address. Domain name registration is regulated by private, not-for-profit registration bodies and partly co-ordinated by ICANN (Internet Corporation for Assigned Names and Numbers, another private, not-for-profit organisation) which administers the Domain Name System (DNS) in respect of technical matters. Registration of domain names is on a first-come first-served basis and is subject to few substantive limitations

---

94   (1980) 32 ALR 387.
95   Quoted by the Privy Council on appeal in *Cadbury Schweppes Pty Ltd v Pub Squash Co Pty Ltd* (1980) 32 ALR 387 at 396.
96   (1980) 32 ALR 387 at 395, citing Lindley J in *Slazenger and Sons v Feltham and Co* (1889) 6 RPC 531 at 538.
97   (1987) 79 ALR 299.
98   (1987) 79 ALR 299 at 319-321.
99   (2005) 215 ALR 716.
100 See the judge's own decision in *Bray v F Hoffman-La Roche* (2002) 118 FCR 1 and *Norbert-Steinhardt and Son Ltd v Meth* (1961) 105 CLR 440.
101 (2002) 210 CLR 575.

regarding what type of name might be registered. Neither the registrars nor ICANN considers substantive issues such as whether the applicant has any connection with the name sought to be registered or whether the name is a trade mark, business name or in any other way connected with a third party.

Any disagreements regarding use of a domain name may be settled by way of mediation procedures established by the Uniform Domain Name Dispute Resolution Policy which is administered by ICANN. Some countries, such as the United States, also have specialist legislation relating to domain names and cybersquatting.[102] Cybersquatting refers to the practice of registering a well-known name as a domain name and then seeking to sell that domain name to a business or other entity which has an interest in protecting that name or using it as its own domain name. Alternatively, disputes may be resolved by reference to general legal principles such as the law of passing off, trade mark infringement or misleading or deceptive conduct.

In the English case of *British Telecommunications plc v One in a Million Ltd*,[103] the respondent was a dealer in domain names and had registered names such as virgin.org, marksandspencer.co.uk, ladbrokes.com, britishtelecom.co.uk, bt.org, britishtelecom.com and burgerking.co.uk which it sought to sell. The prices varied considerably. They had offered to sell burgerking.com.uk to Burger King for £25,000 plus VAT, for example, and bt.org to British Telecommunications for £4500 plus VAT. A number of organisations, including British Telecommunications, took action against One in a Million for passing off and trade mark infringement.

The respondent submitted that the mere registration of such domain names did not amount to a passing off and that no damage or likelihood of damage could be proven. Lord Aldous rejected these arguments. He held that the fact that a search of a domain name register would reveal One in a Million's name as the company registered to use that domain name would amount to a misrepresentation that the registrant was "connected or associated with the name registered and thus the owner of the goodwill in the name". He further concluded that registration of the domain name "is an erosion of the exclusive goodwill in the name which damages or is likely to damage" the plaintiff.[104]

We would suggest that this case is at the far reach of passing off and not wholly consistent with Australian law as it has developed since the Hogan litigation. Although certain uses of domain names would amount to passing off, it is suggested that mere registration does not make a relevant misrepresentation under Australian law. Furthermore, it is possible that not every use of a name as a domain name or part of a domain name would constitute a passing off. The use of the domain name kyliefanclub.com.au, for example, might not amount to a misrepresentation that Kylie has endorsed or sponsored the site and the reference to "fan club" might be seen as a disclaimer of such a connection.

---

102 *Domain Name Piracy Prevention Act 1999* (US), the *Anticybersquatting Consumer Protection Act 1999* (US), the *Trademark Cyberpiracy Protection Act 1999* (US) and the *Satellite Viewers Act 1999* (US).

103 [1998] 4 All ER 476.

104 [1998] 4 All ER 476 at 497.

## Proving misrepresentation

In order to prove the necessary misrepresentation in a passing-off action it is not enough to show that people may be "confused" or "caused to wonder" whether there was a relevant connection between the plaintiff and the defendant. Rather, the plaintiff must establish that a "significant segment" of those seeing the representation would be likely to associate the defendant's goods and services with the plaintiff.[105]

The relevant part of the public which must be considered are the same people to whom the question of reputation is addressed – that is, a substantial number of people who are potential customers of those goods and services[106] or a "significant section of the people who are likely to be exposed to the conduct of which complaint is made".[107] This would not include an extraordinarily stupid person, as Franki J confirms:

> Broadly speaking it is fair to say that the question is to be tested by the effect on a person, not particularly intelligent or well informed, but perhaps of somewhat less than average intelligence and background knowledge, although the test is not the effect on a person who is, for example, quite unusually stupid.[108]

Where the representation is not made to identified individuals the court must, in order to determine whether there has been a misrepresentation, identify a class of persons to whom the representation is made and make an objective attribution of characteristics to the ordinary or reasonable person of that class and the likely reactions of members of the class to the alleged misrepresentation.[109] Whilst this class is often the potential customers of the goods and services this is not always the case and there may be more than one class. In *Knight v Beyond Properties Pty Ltd*,[110] a case involving the use of the name "Mythbusters" on a television show, the judge identified two different classes – the first was "members of the television viewing public", the second was "TV broadcasters and television production executives".

An interesting issue arose in *Anakin Pty Ltd v Chatswood BBQ King Pty Ltd*,[111] relating to the use of Chinese characters in a business name. Having found that the famous BBQ King Restaurant in Sydney's city had a significant reputation the question was whether the lesser known BBQ King in the suburb of Chatswood had misrepresented a relationship between the two restaurants for the purposes of passing off and related actions. The court acknowledged that the Chinese characters used by each restaurant differed and found that Chinese speaking customers were therefore significantly less likely to be misled into thinking there was a relevant relationship between the two restaurants. However,

---

105  Wilcox J in *10th Cantanae Pty Ltd v Shoshana Pty Ltd and Sue Smith* (1987) 79 ALR 299 at 301.

106  Gummow J in *ConAgra Inc v McCain Foods (Aust) Pty Ltd* (1991) 106 ALR 465 at 538.

107  Franki J in *Taco Company of Australia Inc v Taco Bell Pty Ltd* (1982) 42 ALR 177 at 181, citing *Snoid v Handley* (1981) 38 ALR 383 at 388.

108  Franki J in *Taco Company of Australia Inc v Taco Bell Pty Ltd* (1982) 42 ALR 177 at 181, quoting himself in *Annand and Thompson Pty Ltd v Trade Practices Commission* (1979) 25 ALR 91 at 102.

109  *Campomar Sociedad, Limitada v Nike International Ltd* (2000) 202 CLR 45 at [103].

110  [2007] FCA 70 at [30].

111  [2008] FCA 1467.

the relevant section of the public was not only Chinese speaking customers in Chatswood and Sydney but included significant numbers of English speaking customers who formed "an appreciable part of the clientele of the respondent's restaurant" even though Chinese speaking customers were still in the majority.[112]

In determining whether there has been a misrepresentation the court will look at the overall purchasing experience and not simply the design of the product. Thus in *Playcorp Group of Companies Pty Ltd v Peter Bodum A/S*[113] the production, importation and sale of a cheaper knock-off version of a Bodum coffee plunger was not itself enough to establish passing off having regard to the packaging, naming and price of the articles.

In that case Bodum could be understood to be a "victim of its own success" because its reputation as the producer of sophisticated products meant that it had "a separate and distinct identity from look-alike products" which made it difficult for Bodum to successfully sue for passing off.[114] Bodum's situation was similar to that of the makers of Maltesers in *Mars Australia Pty Ltd v Sweet Rewards Pty Ltd*.[115] In that case Mars Australia was unsuccessful in its passing-off action because "the principle component in the Maltesers get-up is the word 'Maltesers', (and) it is very unlikely that any ordinary consumer of chocolate confectionery could mistake something which is not called a Malteser for a Malteser".[116]

It has been suggested that the misrepresentation in a passing-off case must continue "up to the point of sale". Thus, in *Cadbury Schweppes Pty Ltd v Pub Squash Co Pty Ltd*,[117] the defendants had designed and launched a lemon soft drink which was sold in a can which was similar in colour to the plaintiff's SOLO can; it had a similar medallion device on the can and was supported by an advertising campaign which took up the macho images associated with the plaintiff's drink. The Privy Council held that there was no confusion except in the initial casual picking up of the can and that neither can was picked and bought under a mistaken belief that it was the drink of the other party.

The *Pub Squash* case was relied on by the defendants in their s 52 application in *Taco Company of Australia Inc v Taco Bell Pty Ltd*[118] to suggest that the necessary misrepresentation was not established because the misrepresentation did not continue up to the point of sale. The defendants conceded that a customer of the Bondi Taco Bell might assume that the Granville Taco Bell restaurant was connected with the Bondi restaurant if they just looked it up in the telephone book. If, however, the customer went to the restaurant in Granville he or she would quickly realise that they were not connected because the two restaurants were quite different. The Granville restaurant was more like a fast food outlet whilst the Bondi restaurant was a more traditional sit down affair. The Full Federal Court held that there was no such general principle in relation to a s 52 action and suggested (obiter) that no such general principle applied in the case of

---

112  [2008] FCA 1467 at [103].
113  [2010] FCA 23.
114  [2010] FCA 23 at [121].
115  [2009] FCA 606.
116  [2009] FCA 606 at [32].
117  (1980) 32 ALR 387.
118  (1982) 42 ALR 177.

passing off either.[119] However, we would suggest that it is possible to distinguish the two actions. In the absence of a continuing misrepresentation in a passing-off action, it may be difficult to establish the necessary element of damage. As damage is not a requirement under s 52 of the *Trade Practices Act 1974* or s 18 of the ACL, such a continuing misrepresentation would not be necessary.

The relevant date for determining whether there has been a misrepresentation is the date of the commencement of the conduct complained of. Therefore, if the plaintiff only gains a reputation after the action complained of there will be no misrepresentation. If, for example, an Australian business used a name or device of an American company there would be no misrepresentation if the American company did not have a reputation in Australia at the time the Australian business first adopted the name or device. The fact that the American company subsequently became famous and well known in Australia would not change this.

## Damage

Proving damage is an essential element in an action for passing off although, where it is proven that a defendant has the object of causing some people to deal with the defendant on the basis of a misrepresentation, the court may infer that the defendant has in fact achieved his or her purpose.[120] This inference will not always be drawn and, in *Central Equity Ltd v Central Corporation Pty Ltd*,[121] Drummond J declined to make the inference where the applicant had failed to give any evidence of customers being misled (and thereby causing damage to the plaintiff) even though the respondent had carried on the opposed activity for some time. On this basis he held the respondent not liable for passing off, although he did hold the respondent liable for misleading or deceptive conduct under s 52 of the *Trade Practices Act 1974*.

Damage in a passing-off action may take different forms. In the classic form of passing off, where the defendant passes his or her goods off as the goods of the plaintiff, the damage proven might be the loss of sales on account of the diversion of trade to the defendant (*Reddaway v Banham*).[122] Where the misrepresentation relates to a quality of the plaintiff's goods or services, as in the Champagne, Advocaat and Spalding cases, the plaintiff's reputation may be diluted in such a way as to amount to damage to that reputation.

In the endorsement and sponsorship cases the damage to reputation has been held to be the loss of the opportunity of the plaintiff to negotiate a fee for the use of his or her name or image in the field of endeavour in which that reputation is established. Thus, in *Henderson v Radio Corporation Pty Ltd*,[123] the damage proven was the loss of the opportunity for the Hendersons to place their approval on other ballroom dancing records. Where the misrepresentation relates to a "connection" between the plaintiff and the defendant, the damage to the reputation might similarly be found to be the loss of the opportunity to exploit

---

119  (1982) 42 ALR 177 at 199.
120  *Woollen Mills Ltd v FS Walton and Co Ltd* (1937) 58 CLR 641 at 657.
121  (1995) 32 IPR 481.
122  [1896] AC 199.
123  (1960) 1A IPR 620.

the reputation. In the Hogan cases, however, the plaintiffs sought an injunction only and the question of the actual damage or the exact amount of damage caused was not addressed in detail.

The damage may also lie in the loss of potential to expand and develop the plaintiff's goodwill. This has been particularly significant in the case of companies which may have a reputation but no business, as yet, in Australia (see *McIlhenny Co v Blue Yonder Holdings Pty Ltd*,[124] for example, regarding the use of the name "Tabasco").

*Ward Group Pty Ltd v Brodie and Stone plc*[125] is an example of a passing-off case where no damage was proven. In that case the only evidence of sales were those generated as a result of trap purchases made by the applicant's solicitors. In addition, because the product, RESTORIA anti-greying hair cream, had a common origin and was of similar quality and standard to the Australian product, the representations on the United Kingdom website could not have harmed the Australian goodwill.

## Remedies

The remedies available for the action are damages or an account of profits and/or an injunction. In accordance with the action's common law origins in deceit, damages will not be awarded for passing off without proof of fraud and, in accordance with equitable principles, an account of profits will not be awarded for innocent misrepresentation, although an account may be ordered in the case of persistence after notice. An injunction may be granted without proof of fraud[126] and a quia timet injunction may be granted without proof of damage having occurred.

The *Trade Marks Act 1995* s 230 provides that in certain limited circumstances damages will not be awarded in a passing-off case arising out of the use of a registered trade mark. This is when the defendant in the passing-off case is the registered owner or an authorised user of the trade mark and that trade mark is substantially identical with or deceptively similar to the plaintiff's trade mark. The limitation only applies if the defendant can satisfy the court that, at the time the defendant began to use the trade mark the defendant was unaware, and had no reasonable means of finding out, that the trade mark of the plaintiff was in use and that, when the defendant did become aware, he or she immediately ceased to use the trade mark in relation to the goods and services for which the plaintiff's trade mark was registered. The narrowness of this limitation means that it is rarely relied upon.

## Actions under the Competition and Consumer Act

Today, in addition to a passing-off action, a person who wishes to protect his or her business reputation against a misrepresentation by another may take

---

124  (1997) 149 ALR 496.

125  (2005) 215 ALR 716. For a discussion of trap purchases, see *CC Wakefield and Co Ltd v Purser* (1934) 51 RPC 167.

126  See *10th Cantanae Pty Ltd v Shoshana Pty Ltd and Sue Smith* (1987) 79 ALR 299, Gummow J at 319-321.

proceedings under the *Competition and Consumer Act 2010* s 18 or s 29 which are found in Sch 2 which is headed "The Australian Consumer Law". Sections 18 and 29 of the *Australian Consumer Law* (ACL) replace ss 52 and 53 of the *Trade Practices Act 1974* "without substantive change".[127] Under the *Competition and Consumer Act 2010* a court has power to grant an injunction (s 232 of the ACL) or damages (s 236 of the ACL) in relation to conduct in contravention of these provisions. Breach of s 29 of the ACL is also an offence under the Act (s 151 of the ACL). Section 18 of the ACL, which replaces s 52 of the *Trade Practices Act 1974*, provides:

> A person must not, in trade or commerce, engage in conduct that is misleading or deceptive or is likely to mislead or deceive.[128]

Section 29 of the ACL replaces s 53 of the *Trade Practices Act 1974* and proscribes certain specified false representations. These include false representations as to standard, quality, value, grade, composition, style or model or as to the particular history or previous use of the goods and services; sponsorship, approval or affiliation agreements; the place of origin of the goods or that a particular person has agreed to acquire the goods or services. The specific nature of these misrepresentations means that s 18 provides a broader and more flexible remedy for trade competitors seeking to protect their interests and we shall therefore concentrate on s 18 in this section.

In *Hornsby Building Information Centre Pty Ltd v Sydney Building Information Centre Ltd*,[129] the High Court directly considered the question of whether an action under the old *Trade Practices Act 1974* for an infringement of s 52 could be taken by a trade competitor or whether the fact that the relevant Part of the Act was headed "Consumer Protection" meant that only consumers, or those with an interest in consumer protection, could take action under the Act. Applying general principles of statutory interpretation, the High Court held that the application of the section should not be artificially restricted in this way and that the unambiguous meaning of the words of the section should be applied so that a trade competitor could take action under these provisions. Such an approach would also apply under the new Act.

There are three factors necessary to establish a breach of s 18 of the ACL. These are, that there be a "person", that the person engage in conduct which is "misleading or deceptive" or "likely" to mislead or deceive; and that this conduct occur "in trade or commerce".

The reference to a "person" rather than a "corporation" is the only significant change between s 18 of the ACL and s 52 of the old *Trade Practices Act 1974*. Together with ss 5 and 6 of the *Competition and Consumer Act 2010* it extends the ACL to cover natural persons in situations where the Commonwealth has power to do so, for example, in trade and commerce among the States, within Territories, between Australia and outside Australia, and in relation to contracts dealing with

---

127  See Explanatory Memorandum to Trade Practices Amendment (Australian Consumer Law) Bill (No 2) (Cth) 2010 at [3.2].

128  Compare s 52 of the *Trade Practices Act 1974* which provided that "A *corporation shall* not, in trade or commerce, engage in conduct that is misleading or deceptive or likely to mislead or deceive" (emphasis added).

129  (1977) 140 CLR 216.

the use of postal, telegraphic and telephonic services. Where these provisions do not succeed in covering a natural person, proceedings might be commenced under State and Territory fair trading Acts.

The phrase, "trade or commerce" is defined in the Act as trade and commerce within Australia or between Australia and places outside Australia (s 4). Trade and commerce has been broadly defined in the case law to include conduct which "is not at arm's length", for example, conduct by co-operatives.[130] However, it is only in so far as the conduct occurs "in" trade or commerce that it will be caught by s 18. Conduct which is incidental to trade and commerce will not be caught. Thus, in *Concrete Constructions (NSW) Pty Ltd v Nelson*,[131] the High Court held that a representation made by one employee to another was not a representation "in" the course of trade or commerce.    Conduct has been held to be misleading or deceptive if it leads into error or is likely to do so. Merely causing confusion or uncertainty is not enough.[132] There is no need to prove intent or fraud although s 4 of the ACL provides that where a corporation makes a representation as to any future matter without reasonable grounds the misrepresentation shall be taken to be misleading. In the absence of evidence to the contrary the corporation will, in these circumstances, be deemed not to have had reasonable grounds (s 4(2) of the ACL).

## The difference between passing off and s 18 of the ACL

In the wake of *Hornsby Building Information Centre Pty Ltd v Sydney Building Information Centre Ltd*,[133] it became common for plaintiffs to plead actions under passing off and the *Trade Practices Act 1974* together. However, in that case the High Court held that s 52 was a separate action and not a mere statutory re-enactment of the law of passing off and warned against confusing the two. The High Court also noted that the courts' long experience with passing off should not be ignored in s 52 cases but that this experience would not always be a "safe guide".[134] Developing these themes in *Parkdale Custom Built Furniture Pty Ltd v Puxu Pty Ltd*,[135] the High Court held that the operation of s 52 was not to be read down either by reference to the action of passing off nor by reference to the "detailed treatment of limited monopolies of intellectual and industrial property in specific statutes".[136]

There are two major differences between s 18 of the ACL and passing off. First, s 18 covers misleading and deceptive conduct where no question of passing off arises. A person might be found liable under s 18 when that person misrepresents that a product has been subjected to independent testing, for example, even though this misrepresentation makes no reference to any other person and causes

---

130  See *Re Ku-ring-gai Co-operative Building Society Ltd* (1978) 22 ALR 621 at 649.
131  (1990) 169 CLR 594.
132  *Parkdale Custom Built Furniture Pty Ltd v Puxu Pty Ltd* (1982) 149 CLR 191 and *Hornsby Building Information Centre Pty Ltd v Sydney Building Information Centre Ltd* (1977) 140 CLR 216.
133  (1977) 140 CLR 216.
134  (1977) 140 CLR 216 at 227.
135  (1982) 149 CLR 191.
136  (1982) 149 CLR 191, Mason J at 205.

no damage to another's reputation. Despite this very broad application of the section it has been said that most of the proceedings brought under the old *Trade Practices Act* s 52 were by competitors seeking to restrain conduct which could be characterised as passing off.[137] This, too, is likely to be the case in relation to s 18 of the ACL.

Secondly, it is not necessary to prove damage to a person's reputation in order to establish an infringement of s 18 of the ACL. Thus, in *Central Equity Ltd v Central Corporation Pty Ltd*,[138] although the applicant proved a relevant misrepresentation for the purposes of passing off it failed to prove any damage to its reputation and the court declined to infer such damage. On this basis the action for passing off failed whilst the infringement of the legislative provisions was established.

Arising from these two major differences certain principles follow. First, it is not necessary to prove that the plaintiff and the defendant are in a common field of activity or that the plaintiff has any connection with the defendant's trade. However, if the alleged misrepresentation is in fact one which relates to the plaintiff's reputation then it will be necessary to prove, as a question of fact, that the plaintiff does indeed have a reputation in relation to which the misrepresentation might be made. Thus, in *Hornsby Building Information Centre Pty Ltd v Sydney Building Information Centre Ltd*,[139] the plaintiff failed in its s 52 action against Hornsby Building Information Centre because the plaintiff was unable to prove that the name, Sydney Building Information Centre, was distinctive of its reputation and was subsequently unable to establish that any use of that name by the Hornsby business would amount to a misrepresentation of an affiliation between the two centres.

In proving misleading or deceptive conduct under s 18 of the ACL the audience is not restricted to that audience which is common to the plaintiff and the defendant. Thus, in *Central Equity Ltd v Central Corporation Pty Ltd*,[140] the audience was not only the potential purchasers of real estate, the industry in which the defendant operated, but included members of the public who might have dealings with the plaintiff as investors or lessors or lessees of commercial property.

It is not necessary to prove that the misleading or deceptive conduct under s 18 of the ACL has continued up to the point of sale although it may be that such conduct is necessary in order to establish passing off (see the discussion of *Cadbury Schweppes Pty Ltd v Pub Squash Co Pty Ltd*[141] and *Taco Company of Australia Inc v Taco Bell Pty Ltd*[142] above). As we noted above, this possible difference may be explained by the fact that damage need not be proved under s 18 of the ACL but, in *Taco Company of Australia Inc v Taco Bell Pty Ltd*, Deane and Fitzgerald JJ also explained the difference by reference to the broader purposes

---

137   RV Miller, *Miller's Annotated Trade Practices Act*, 18th ed, Law Book Co, Sydney, 1997, p 280. Miller also provides a helpful list of cases and case summaries for passing-off type cases under s 52 of the *Trade Practices Act 1974* at pp 280-285.

138   (1995) 32 IPR 481.

139   (1977) 140 CLR 216.

140   (1995) 32 IPR 481.

141   (1980) 32 ALR 387.

142   (1982) 42 ALR 177.

of s 52 and the *Trade Practices Act*. This means that a late disclaimer, which may be effective in passing-off cases to avoid liability, may only go to the type of relief in ACL cases. As Flick J said in *AMI Australia Holdings Pty Ltd v Bade Medical Institute (Aust) Pty Ltd*:

> Conduct may remain misleading or deceptive even though there may only be transient confusion. A subsequent correction may seek to address any confusion which may have been initially experienced — but, by then, a consumer may have been entangled in the "*marketing web*" of those who engage in such conduct. A correction may, however, be relevant to the relief to be granted.[143]

## Proving misleading or deceptive conduct

In determining whether the relevant conduct is misleading or deceptive under s 18 of the ACL there must be a misrepresentation: a mere tendency to cause confusion or uncertainty is insufficient in itself (see *Taco Company of Australia Inc v Taco Bell Pty Ltd*).[144] The plaintiff may rely on any meaning which is reasonably open to a significant number of the relevant audience. Thus, in *Talmax Pty Ltd v Telstra Corporation Ltd*,[145] the relevant audience were readers viewing a Telstra newspaper supplement regarding the "preselection" which was to be conducted whereby telephone users could choose between Optus and Telstra as their carrier for long distance and international calls. The supplement featured an article on Kieran Perkins including a photo of him finishing a swimming race, wearing a cap with the Telstra logo on it. The pool also featured a Telstra logo. The trial judge held that this did not amount to a misrepresentation that Perkins endorsed Telstra's competition for telephone subscribers; that Perkins was sponsored by Telstra; or that Perkins consented to the use of his name and image in the advertisement. This finding was overturned on appeal.

On appeal, the Supreme Court of Queensland criticised the trial judge who had considered "the meaning which the material complained of would convey to a 'careful reader' who undertook an 'analysis of the supplement' and 'would have observed a contrast with other articles which were clearly endorsements'".[146] The Supreme Court, relying on *Taco Co of Australia v Taco Bell Pty Ltd*,[147] rejected this test where the material complained of was an advertisement directed to the general public through a popular newspaper:

> [T]he "target" readership accordingly included "the astute and the gullible, the intelligent and the not so intelligent, the well educated as well as the poorly educated, men and women of various ages pursuing a variety of vocations" and the appellants could rely on any meaning which was reasonably open to a significant number of the newspaper readership.[148]

---

143 [2009] FCA 1437 at [192].
144 (1982) 42 ALR 177, approved by the High Court in *Campomar Sociedad Limitada v Nike International Ltd* (2000) 202 CLR 45.
145 [1997] 2 Qd R 444.
146 [1997] 2 Qd R 444 at 446.
147 (1982) 42 ALR 177 at 202.
148 [1997] 2 Qd R 444 at 446.

The question of whether the conduct is misleading or deceptive or is likely to mislead or deceive is a question of fact,[149] to be determined by the court applying an objective test.[150] The question should not be determined by reference to empirical evidence as to the actual reaction of potential or actual customers and the court "must not surrender in favour of any witness its own independent judgement".[151] In *McWilliam's Wines Pty Ltd v McDonald's System of Australia Pty Ltd*,[152] Smithers J went so far as to suggest that there was only "sparse" authority for the view that evidence of public reaction had any relevance whatsoever.[153]

The fact that there may be proof of actual misconception in the mind of a customer may be persuasive but is not conclusive in determining whether there has been misleading or deceptive conduct. In particular, if a misconception is not referable to the conduct of the defendant there will be no infringement of s 18 of the ACL. Thus, in *Parkdale Custom Built Furniture Pty Ltd v Puxu Pty Ltd*,[154] there was evidence that customers had in fact been misled as to the manufacturer of lounge suites due to the fact that an independent retailer had hidden the labels identifying the appellant as the actual manufacturer. The High Court held that the question for the court was not whether people had been misled but whether the appellant's conduct amounted to misleading or deceptive conduct. On this basis the appellant was held not to have infringed s 52 of the *Trade Practices Act 1974*. Although the matter has not been determined, in practice this approach has also been adopted in passing-off actions.

In that case the High Court also held that in determining whether the conduct of the defendant is misleading or deceptive it is assumed that customers will take reasonable care to protect their interests. The amount of care will depend on the type of product dealt with and the circumstances in which it is sold. Thus, in *Parkdale Custom Built Furniture Pty Ltd v Puxu Pty Ltd*,[155] it was considered reasonable that a person buying a $1500 lounge suite would look at the labels and compare the prices of different look-alike lounge suites. In that case the appellant had manufactured a cheaper version (the RAWHIDE range) of the respondent's expensive leather lounge suite (the CONTOUR range) and had labelled it in the usual way. That is, the appellant had attached a label to the bottom of the cushions with its name and the name of its lounge suite on it. The High Court found that there was no conduct by the appellant which amounted to misleading or deceptive conduct when all these circumstances were taken into account even though the two lounges were practically identical.

---

149 Deane and Fitzgerald JJ in *Taco Company of Australia Inc v Taco Bell Pty Ltd* (1982) 42 ALR 177 at 199-200 point out that even though it is a question of fact the decision of the court will, by its very nature, commonly be read as though it were a statement of legal principles but that the reader should guard against such a misconstruction.

150 *Snoid v Handley* (1981) 38 ALR 383 at 391.

151 Lord Morris in *Parker-Knoll Ltd v Knoll International Ltd* [1962] RPC 265 at 279, approved in *McWilliam's Wines Pty Ltd v McDonald's System of Australia Pty Ltd* (1980) 33 ALR 394 at 399.

152 (1980) 33 ALR 394.

153 (1980) 33 ALR 394 at 399. For a survey of the use of empirical evidence in passing-off cases see Vicki Huang, Kimberlee Weatherall and Elizabeth Webster, *The Use of Survey Evidence in Australian Trade Mark and Passing Off Cases*, Intellectual Property Research Institute of Australia Working Paper No 5/11, IPRIA, Melbourne, August 2011.

154 (1982) 149 CLR 191.

155 (1982) 149 CLR 191.

# CASES

## *Erven Warnink BV v J Townend and Sons (Hull) Ltd*
House of Lords: Lord Diplock, Viscount Dilhorne, Lord Salmon, Lord Fraser of
Tullybelton and Lord Scarman
[1979] 2 All ER 927

The classic form of passing off prevented traders passing off their goods as the
goods of another. In this case the House of Lords explained how the action had
grown so as to prevent traders passing off their goods as having a quality associated with another. In this case, the English traders, cashing in on the popularity
of Dutch Advocaat, renamed their eggflip "Old English Advocaat". A group of
Dutch manufacturers brought an action for passing off.

> **Lord Diplock: [929]** My Lords, this is an action for 'passing off', not in its classic form
> of a trader representing his own goods as the goods of somebody else, but in an extended
> form first recognised and applied by Danckwerts J in the Champagne case (*Bollinger v
> Costa Brava Wine Co Ltd*. The ratio decidendi of that case was subsequently adopted as
> correct by Cross J in the Sherry case (*Vine Products Ltd v Mackenzie & Co Ltd*[156]) and by
> Foster J in the Scotch Whisky case (*John Walker & Sons Ltd v Henry Ost & Co Ltd*[157]).

[The judge set out the facts of the case.]

> **[930]** True it is that it could not be shown that any purchaser of Keeling's Old English
> Advocaat supposed or would be likely to suppose it to be goods supplied by Warnink or
> to be Dutch advocaat of any make. So Warnink had no cause of action for passing off
> in its classic form. Nevertheless, the judge was satisfied: (1) that the name 'advocaat'
> was understood by the public in England to denote a distinct and recognisable species of
> beverage; (2) that Warnink's product is genuinely indicated by that name and has gained
> reputation and goodwill under it; (3) that Keeling's product has no natural association
> with the word 'advocaat'; it is an egg and wine drink properly described as an 'egg-flip',
> whereas advocaat is an egg and spirit drink; these are different beverages and known as
> different to the public; (4) that members of the public believe and have been deliberately
> induced by Keeling to believe that in buying their Old English Advocaat they are in
> fact buying advocaat; (5) that Keeling's deception of the public has caused and, unless
> prevented, will continue to cause, damage to Warnink in the trade and the goodwill of
> their business both directly in the loss of sales and indirectly in the debasement of the
> **[931]** reputation attaching to the name 'advocaat' if it is permitted to be used of alcoholic
> egg drinks generally and not confined to those that are spirit based.
>
>     These findings, he considered, brought the case within the principle of law laid down
> in the Champagne case by Danckwerts J and applied in the Sherry and Scotch Whisky
> cases. He granted Warnink an injunction restraining Keeling from selling or distributing
> under the name or description 'advocaat' any product which does not basically consist
> of eggs and spirit without any admixture of wine.

[These facts were accepted by the Court of Appeal and were not challenged in
the House of Lords.]

> **[932]** My Lords, *AG Spalding & Bros v AW Gamage Ltd*[158] and the later cases make it
> possible to identify five characteristics which must be present in order to create a valid

---

[156] [1969] RPC 1.
[157] [1970] 3 All ER 106, [1970] 1 WLR 917.
[158] (1915) 32 RPC 273.

cause of action for passing off: (1) a misrepresentation (2) made by a trader in the course of trade, (3) to prospective customers of his or ultimate consumers of goods or services supplied by **[933]** him, (4) which is calculated to injure the business or goodwill of another trader (in the sense that this is a reasonably foreseeable consequence) and (5) which causes actual damage to a business or goodwill of the trader by whom the action is brought or (in a quia timet action) will probably do so.

In seeking to formulate general propositions of English law, however, one must be particularly careful to beware of the logical fallacy of the undistributed middle. It does not follow that because all passing-off actions can be shown to present these characteristics, all factual situations which present these characteristics give rise to a cause of action for passing off. True it is that their presence indicates what a moral code would censure as dishonest trading, based as it is on deception of customers and consumers of a trader's wares, but in an economic system which has relied on competition to keep down prices and to improve products there may be practical reasons why it should have been the policy of the common law not to run the risk of hampering competition by providing civil remedies to everyone competing in the market who has suffered damage of his business or goodwill in consequence of inaccurate statements of whatever kind that may be made by rival traders about their own wares. The market in which the action for passing off originated was no place for the mealy mouthed: advertisements are not on affidavit; exaggerated claims by a trader about the quality of his wares, assertions that they are better than those of his rivals, even though he knows this to be untrue, have been permitted by the common law as venial 'puffing' which gives no cause of action to a competitor even though he can show that he has suffered actual damage in his business as a result.

Parliament, however, beginning in the 19th century has progressively intervened in the interests of consumers to impose on traders a higher standard of commercial candour than the legal maxim caveat emptor calls for, by prohibiting under penal sanctions misleading descriptions of the character or qualify of goods; but since the class of persons for whose protection the Merchandise Marks Acts 1887 to 1953 and even more rigorous later statutes are designed are not competing traders but those consumers who are likely to be deceived, the Acts do not themselves give rise to any civil action for breach of statutory duty on the part of a competing trader even though he sustains actual damage as a result: *Cutler v Wandsworth Stadium Ltd*;[159] and see *London Armoury Co Ltd v Ever Ready Co (Great Britain) Ltd*.[160] Nevertheless the increasing recognition by Parliament of the need for more rigorous standards of commercial honesty is a factor which should not be overlooked by a judge confronted by the choice whether or not to extend by analogy to circumstances in which it has not previously been applied a principle which has been applied in previous cases where the circumstances although different had some features in common with those of the case which he has to decide. Where over a period of years there can be discerned a steady trend in legislation which reflects the view of successive Parliaments as to what the public interest demands in a particular field of law, development of the common law in that part of the same field which has been left to it ought to proceed on a parallel rather than a diverging course.

The Champagne case came before Danckwerts J in two stages: the first[161] on a preliminary point of law, the second[162] on the trial of the action. The assumptions of fact on which the legal argument at the first stage was based were stated by the judge to be:[163]

---

[159] [1949] AC 398.
[160] [1941] 1 All ER 364, [1941] 1 KB 742.
[161] [1960] Ch 262.
[162] [1961] 1 WLR 277.
[163] [1960] Ch 262 at 273.

'(1) The plaintiffs carry on business in a geographical area in France known as Champagne; (2) the plaintiffs' wine is produced in Champagne and from grapes grown in Champagne; (3) the plaintiffs' wine has been known in the trade for a long **[934]** time as "Champagne" with a high reputation; (4) members of the public or in the trade ordering or seeing wine advertised as "Champagne" would expect to get wine produced in Champagne from grapes grown there and (5) the defendants are producing a wine not produced in that geographical area and are selling it under the name of "Spanish Champagne".'

These findings disclose a factual situation (assuming that damage was thereby caused to the plaintiff's business) which contains each of the five characteristics which I have suggested must be present in order to create a valid cause of action for passing off. The features that distinguished it from all previous cases were (a) that the element in the goodwill of each of the individual plaintiffs that was represented by his ability to use without deception (in addition to his individual house mark) the word 'champagne' to distinguish his wines from sparkling wines not made by the champenois process from grapes produced in the Champagne district of France was not exclusive to himself but was shared with every other shipper of sparkling wine to England whose wines could satisfy the same condition and (b) that the class of traders entitled to a proprietary right in 'the attractive force that brings in custom' represented by the ability without deception to call one's wines 'champagne' was capable of continuing expansion, since it might be joined by any future shipper of wine who was able to satisfy that condition

My Lords, in the Champagne case the class of traders between whom the goodwill attaching to the ability to use the word 'champagne' as descriptive of their wines was a large one, 150 at least and probably considerably more, whereas in the previous English cases of shared goodwill the number of traders between whom the goodwill protected by a passing-off action was shared had been two, although in the United States in 1898 there had been a case, *Pillsbury-Washburn Flour Mills Co Ltd v Eagle*,[164] in which the successful complainants to the number of seven established their several proprietary rights in the goodwill attaching to the use of a particular geographical description to distinguish their wares from those of other manufacturers.

It seems to me, however, as it seemed to Danckwerts J, that the principle must be the same whether the class of which each member is severally entitled to the goodwill which attaches to a particular term as descriptive of his goods is large or small. The larger it is the broader must be the range and quality of products to which the descriptive term used by the members of the class has been applied, and the more difficult it must be to show that the term has acquired a public reputation and goodwill as denoting a product endowed with recognisable qualities which distinguish it from others of inferior reputation that compete with it in the same market. The larger the class the more difficult it must also be for an individual member of it to show that the goodwill of his own business has sustained more than minimal damage as a result of deceptive use by another trader of the widely-shared descriptive term. As respects subsequent additions to the class, mere entry into the market would not give any right of action for passing off; the new entrant must have himself used the descriptive term long enough on the market in connection with his own goods and have traded successfully enough to have built up a goodwill for his business.

For these reasons the familiar argument that to extend the ambit of an actionable wrong beyond that to which effect has demonstrably been given in the previous cases would open the floodgates or, more ominously, a Pandora's box of litigation leaves me unmoved when it is sought to be applied to the actionable wrong of passing off.

---

[164] (1898) 86 F 608.

## *Henderson v Radio Corporation Pty Ltd*
Supreme Court of New South Wales: Evatt CJ, Myers and Manning JJ
(1960) 1A IPR 620

The plaintiffs were professional ballroom dancers whose unidentified photographs were the main image used on the cover of a ballroom dancing record. This case is important for its consideration of the type of misrepresentation which will ground an action for passing off.

**Evatt CJ and Myers J: [634]** The respondents have contended that the acts of the appellant were likely to lead to the belief that the business of the appellant was connected with the business of the respondents because, it was said, the picture of the respondents on the record cover would lead buyers of the record to believe that the respondents recommended the record as providing good music for ballroom dancing.

Four witnesses were called on this issue on behalf of the respondents. They were the president of an association of dancing teachers, the secretary of another such association, a theatrical agent and the assistant secretary of the trade union to which the professional dancers belong. Each said in substance that when he saw the record he recognised either Henderson or Henderson and his wife and gathered from the fact that their pictures were on the cover, that they had sponsored – that is, recommended or approved – the record, or were associated in some way with it. The appellant called no evidence on this aspect. His Honour did not express any adverse view of these witnesses but he did not accept the view that buyers of the record would come to the same conclusion as the witnesses.

However, the facts relevant to this issue, including the evidence to which we have referred, are not in dispute. The only question is the proper inference to be drawn from them, and in those circumstances we are entitled to form our own opinion: *Benmax v Austin Motor Co Ltd* [1955] AC 370.

Unaided by evidence, one might consider that the dancing figures merely indicate the type of music on the record and that it is not possible to come to the conclusion for which the respondents contend. But one is not unaided by evidence and, having regard to the fact that the record was primarily intended for professional dancing teachers, and to the uncontradicted evidence of four experts in that field, we are of opinion that the proper finding is that the class of persons for whom the record was primarily intended would probably believe that the picture of the respondents on the cover indicated their recommendation or approval of the record. The only rational purpose of the wrongful use of the respondents' photograph on the disc container was to assist the sale of the disc it contained.

This false representation was not only made by the appellant, but would almost inevitably lead to a similar false representation on the part of every shopkeeper who might buy the records from the appellant and sell them or display them for sale.

**[635]** It still remains to be considered whether that finding establishes the necessary element of deception, namely, that the business of the appellant was connected with the business of the respondents. In our opinion it does.

The representation that the respondents recommended the record is an inducement to buy it. The recommendation can only be attributed to the respondents in their capacity of professional dancers, that is, a recommendation made in the course of their professional activities, and means that as professional dancers they have associated themselves with the appellant in promoting sales of the record, and that amounts to a connection, in respect of the marketing of the record, between the business of the respondents and the business of the appellant.

The point is not without authority. In *British Medical Association v Marsh* (1931) 48 RPC 565 at 574, Maugham J referring to the professional cases on passing off, said that they did not establish the proposition that if a tradesman puts forward a remedy as having been prescribed by, or sold for the benefit, or with the approval of a medical man, the latter would have no remedy.

> What it is necessary in such a case to prove is, either positive injury, or in a quia timet action, a reasonable probability of injury; and if that is done, I, for my part, see no reason why such an action should not succeed.

In our opinion the evidence established a passing off by the appellant and, subject to proof of injury, as to which we will have something to say later, the respondents, were entitled to relief by way of injunction.

## *Hogan v Koala Dundee Pty Ltd*
### Federal Court of Australia: Pincus J
### (1988) 83 ALR 187

Paul Hogan and a firm which owned the merchandising rights for the film *Crocodile Dundee* brought an action in passing off against a small retail company which used an image of a koala bear wearing a sleeveless vest, holding a big knife and sporting a bush hat with teeth in its band (similar to the outfit worn by Hogan in *Crocodile Dundee*). The company also used the term DUNDEE COUNTRY as a label, name and feature in its shops. This case is probably at the extreme limit of the movement towards "extended passing off" which occurred in the 1980s. It is also an extreme example of treating passing off as misappropriation.

**Pincus J: [196]** *Extended passing off suit*
The case was argued before me on behalf of the applicants on the assumption that it is possible to bring a passing off suit in respect of an image, including a name, unconnected with any business at all. That assumption appears to me correct. I think the law now is, at least in Australia, that the inventor of a sufficiently famous fictional character having certain visual or other traits may prevent others using his character to sell their goods and may assign the right so to use the character. Furthermore, the inventor may do these things even where he has never carried on any business at all, other than the writing or making of the work in which the character appears.

The characteristics of such a suit are not necessarily precisely the same as those of the older type. In particular, an assignment of a right in a character need not assign any business. Further, merely accidental uses of images invented by another will not necessarily give any cause of action to the inventor.

It is necessary to examine some of the more recent authorities. I do not propose, however, to say much about the English cases. Except in certain specific areas, English law has not progressed (if the changes are in truth progress) much beyond the traditional notion of passing off, namely suggesting that what are in fact goods or services of the defendant are produced by the plaintiff, and misrepresentations closely similar to that central type. This may be illustrated by reference to two authorities. In the *Pub Squash* case, heard in 1980, the Privy Council substantially approved of the trial judge's having treated an "image-filching" piece of litigation on the basis of an inquiry "... whether the consuming public was confused or misled by the get-up, the formula or the advertising of the respondent's product into thinking that it was the appellants' product": *Cadbury Schweppes Pty Ltd v Pub Squash Co Pty Ltd* (1980) 32 ALR 387 at 393.

Then in the *Kojak* case (*Tavener Rutledge Ltd v Trexapalm Ltd* [1977] RPC 275), the contest was between two parties seeking to use the connection of the then well-known television series with lollipops. On the assumption that the defendant had a licence to use the image, the plaintiff having none, the plaintiff succeeded, because it was first into the field. It is true that in the *Kojak* case, and in some other English decisions, one finds statements to the effect that misleading the public as to a product's "associations" or the like can be passing off, but the actual results of the decisions in the United Kingdom show clearly enough that protection of images *simpliciter* is but embryonic there.

The first important Australian case is *Henderson v Radio Corp Pty Ltd* [1960] SR (NSW) 576. The plaintiffs were professional ballroom dancers and not record producers. Their fame was such that they were held entitled **[197]** to stop makers of gramophone records of dancing music from using photographs of the plaintiffs on the record covers. The plaintiffs could perhaps have succeeded on the basis that the public might have assumed that they had something to do with the making of the records, although they were not identified by name. However, the New South Wales Supreme Court took broader ground. It was held the plaintiffs were entitled to succeed on the bases that

(1)  the plaintiffs were being represented to have recommended or approved the records (at 592, 593);

(2)  the plaintiffs' reputation had been wrongfully appropriated (at 595).

It is true that the second ground was advanced as an answer to the contention that no injunction could go because damage was not proved, but the court described the misappropriation of reputation as "an injury in itself, no less, in our opinion, than the appropriation of ... goods or money" (per Evatt CJ and Myers J at 595).

In *Childrens Television Workshop Inc v Woolworths (NSW) Ltd* [1981] 1 NSWLR 273, Helsham CJ in Eq restrained the defendants from selling toys resembling characters in the television series "Sesame Street". The judge held that the first plaintiff had: "... a business reputation, in the sense that it is its imprimatur, by licence, that permits the character merchandising or image related merchandising in dolls to take place; it is behind the commercial exploitation of its characters as dolls as licensor" (at 280).

His Honour went on to say that it was part of the business of each of the first two plaintiffs to get their character reproductions onto the market in various forms through licensing arrangements (at 280) and that: "By exposing for sale deceptively similar goods, the public are likely to be misled into believing that the defendants' goods are in the same sense the plaintiffs' goods, linked to the plaintiffs through the same sort of arrangement" (at 281).

This is a narrower ground of liability than that used in *Henderson's* case. It ties character merchandising more closely to the traditional form of passing off and is authority that there is no need for the plaintiff to be in the business of making goods to justify a passing off suit; the business of licensing them is enough. There appear to me, with respect, to be difficulties in using the test adopted in the *Childrens Television* case (Were the goods represented to be licensed?), as a basis for development of rights of this sort, and these are referred to below.

In *Moorgate Tobacco Co Ltd v Philip Morris Ltd* (1984) 156 CLR 414; 56 ALR 193; 3 IPR 545, the reasons of Deane J, which were agreed in by the other members of the High Court, were, so far as relevant to the present problem, concerned mainly to deny the existence of a tort of unfair competition; the subject of image merchandising was not a central theme. But his Honour said that the rejection of a general action for unfair competition or unfair trading had not "... for example, prevented the adaptation of the traditional doctrine of passing off to meet new circumstances involving the deceptive or confusing use of names, descriptive terms or other indicia to persuade purchasers or customers to believe that goods or services have an association, quality or endorsement which belongs or would belong to goods or services of, or associated with, another or others: see, eg, *Warnink v Townend & Sons (Hull) Ltd* [1979] **[198]** AC at 739ff; *Henderson v Radio Corp Pty Ltd* [1960] SR(NSW) 576" (CLR at 445; ALR at 214).

This dictum gives added authority to the reasoning in *Henderson's* case, as well as to the result in that case. I stress particularly the use of the word "association", as meaning a connection other than one relating to "quality or endorsement".

An example of persuading people that goods or services have an association which properly belongs to other goods is the Formula I car driver who races with advertising signs on his helmet, clothing and car, visible on television to hundreds of millions of people. Although the driver may be loosely spoken of as "endorsing" the products advertised, that is so only in the sense that their names appear in connection with him; nobody really thinks that he is expressing a view about the particular brands of products thus publicised. (See per Lord Bridge of Harwich in *"Holly Hobbie" Trade Mark* (1984) 10 FSR 199 at 202.4.) Nor, in my opinion, are those who see the race on the track or on television necessarily going to know whether the driver is in the business of collecting fees to publicise products. For all the public knows, any licence is given by the racing company for which the driver works, or by some other entity.

Suppose such a driver has his car associated with an unlicensed product, as in *Motschenbacher v RJ Reynolds Tobacco Co* (1974) 498 F 2d 821. There the tobacco company used a picture of a car looking like Motschenbacher's and put the name of its cigarettes on it. That conduct was held to be unlawful, at the suit of Motschenbacher, on the basis that people thought he had been sponsored by the cigarette company. But how was Motschenbacher or the public hurt by that? Motschenbacher's harm was that he was denied a fee which he would have charged; but he could only exact a fee if the law recognised his right to stop people using images associated with him — so the argument becomes circular. The real point is whether the right of property in his name and reputation as a driver is entitled to protection.

The essence of the wrong done in the *Motschenbacher* and *Childrens Television* cases and those like them is not in truth a misrepresentation that there is a licensing or sponsoring agreement between the applicant and the respondent. It is in the second ground taken in the *Henderson* case, namely wrongful appropriation of a reputation or, more widely, wrongful association of goods with an image properly belonging to the applicant.

I would make three comments, then, on the use of reasoning of the type just discussed. First, it appears to me that there is a degree of artificiality in deciding image-filching cases like the *Childrens Television* case on the basis that the vice attacked is misleading the public about licensing arrangements. Secondly, the point is of special importance in the present case, where it cannot be held, either for the purposes of the law of passing off or under the Trade Practices Act, that the public have been led to think that there is a precisely known kind of commercial connection with Paul Hogan or the film. Thirdly, the process of considering the views of people in the respondent's shop as to whether they think there is a licence from the applicants, or that of simply attempting to form an unaided opinion on the subject, involves ascertaining the public's views on the state of the law about character advertising, rather than their views on any factual matter. Those of the public who say they think a licence must be behind the use of **[199]** "Dundee" and the koala image are guessing as to the law's requirements – and guessing on a point which is a little unsettled.

A recent appellate decision dealing with this sort of case is that of the Full Court of the Federal Court in *10th Cantanae Pty Ltd v Shoshana Pty Ltd* (1987) 79 ALR 299; 10 IPR 289. The court consisted of Wilcox J, Gummow J and me. The case concerned an alleged misuse of the name and identity of a television personality. The complaints of passing off and breach of the Act failed on the facts. Wilcox J and I agreed that no wrong had been done because the personality was insufficiently identified. But his Honour's view as to the legal principles involved was, I think, closer to that of Gummow J, who dissented on the fact, than to mine.

Wilcox J said that in the United States the claim would "fall within that aspect of the law of privacy which is called 'appropriation'" and that *Henderson's* case "goes some distance towards covering the appropriation cases". His Honour went on:

"I see no reason to exclude the application of the law of passing off from a case such as the present, provided that the court were satisfied that the advertisement published by the appellants would be read as containing a representation that Ms Smith endorsed, or was otherwise associated with, the Blaupunkt video recorder. It is true that, even under the *Henderson* approach, the protection offered by the law of passing off is limited to persons 'engaged in business, using that expression in its widest sense to include professions and callings': see per Evatt CJ and Myers J at 593. However, Mr Smith was so engaged at the time of the relevant publications. If the advertisement could be read as representing that the second respondent was the 'Sue Smith' of the advertisement, it could accurately be said that there was a representation that the advertised product was one with which she was associated. And it would not be inappropriate to grant relief. However debased the currency or endorsement may have become, in my opinion it cannot yet be said that readers of advertisements remain unaffected by the introduction into an advertisement of a respected name" (ALR at 300; IPR at 290).

I read this dictum of Wilcox J as affording general support to character merchandising suits, on the basis of the first ground in *Henderson's* case, and, perhaps, the second also. His Honour's opinion would suggest that an implied representation that the person in question was "associated" with a product, and proof that his or her introduction into an advertisement would affect readers, might be enough to ground liability.

Gummow J's reasons included the following remarks: "The injury of which the plaintiff complains in many passing off suits will be loss of sales by diversion or apprehended diversion of business. But, as Dixon J pointed out in *Turner v General Motors (Australia) Pty Ltd* (1929) 42 CLR 352 at 368, the court intervenes to protect the business reputation of the plaintiff from misappropriation and that protection is not confined to cases where loss simply consists in diversion of trade. ... This certainly means that there may be such misappropriation where the defendant's goods or services are shabby or second-rate, albeit not in direct competition with those of the plaintiff: ... But the principle also applies where, regardless of any question of inferior quality, the defendant wrongfully deprives the plaintiff of a right to bestow for value his recommendation of the goods or **[200]** services of a third party. This is established for Australia by *Henderson v Radio Corp Pty Ltd* [1960] SR(NSW) 576 at 592-5 ..." (ALR at 318; IPR at 308-9).

It should be noted, in particular, that this passage tends towards treating misappropriation of a reputation as enough, at least where the complaint is by one who might otherwise have been able to get money for licensing the use of his name. In my reasons in the *10th Cantanae* case I took a narrower view of the legal rights of such an applicant than did my brethren. I also remarked of the *Moorgate* case that: "... the question whether the law of passing off gives protection to the alleged proprietary right, 'in gross', in the use of a well-known name, is left open" (ALR at 305; IPR at 295).

That question does not arise directly here, but a cognate one does: whether there is such protection for a well-known image, including a name. The other two members of the Full Court, in the *10th Cantanae* case, used language inclining to support the view that there is such protection.

Here, Mr Chesterman QC argued that the koala image was akin to a parody of the image of Paul Hogan in the film and he relied upon certain United States parody cases: *Warner Bros Inc v American Broadcasting Companies Inc* (1983) 720 F 2d 231; *Universal City Studios Inc v Casey & Casey Inc* (1985) 622 F Supp 201 and *Universal City Studios Inc v T-Shirt Gallery Ltd* (1986) 634 F Supp 1468. He contended that people would be likely to think that, if the respondents were using "Crocodile Dundee" images in the shop by licence, Paul Hogan's face would not have been replaced by that of a koala, nor would all mention of Paul Hogan's name have been omitted. I agree. In my opinion, however, there is nevertheless a clear representation of association with the film's images. Mr Chesterman pointed out that each of the elements complained of is by itself common enough. For example, koalas are, as are bush hats and, perhaps less so, hats with teeth in the band and so forth, but the combination of images is something else again.

### Cadbury Schweppes Pty Ltd v Pub Squash Co Pty Ltd
Privy Council: Lord Wilberforce, Lord Edmund-Davies, Lord Fraser
of Tullybelton, Lord Scarman and Lord Roskill
(1980) 32 ALR 387

Pub Squash cashed in on the success of the Solo lemon campaign which had been run on television and radio and is remembered primarily for the way the male character dribbled the Solo down his chin. Over the life of the campaign the dribble became a virtual cascade.

**Lord Scarman: [394]** The critical question in this case proved to be: were customers, or potential customers, led by the similarities in the get-up and advertising of the two products into believing that Pub Squash was the Cadbury Schweppes product? Or, if no deception be proved, was there a real probability of deception? The trial judge addressed himself to this question of fact first when considering the claim in "passing off", and secondly when stating his conclusions on the alternative claim of unfair trading. In respect of passing off, he asked himself whether the respondent did sufficiently distinguish its product from Solo. He answered the question as follows: "… it can readily be seen that they are different. This, however, is not necessarily enough, for one must take into account the nature of the market-place and the habits of ordinary purchasers (see, for example, *Saville Perfumery Ltd v June Perfect Ltd* (1941) 58 RPC 147, 174-5 *Tavener Rutledge Ltd v Specters Ltd* [1959] RPC 83, 88-9). As I have pointed out earlier, it is not uncommon, albeit that it is not the universal practice, both in supermarkets, and in mixed businesses and milk-bars which have self-selection display refrigerators for products such as Solo and Pub Squash to be displayed alongside each other; and in those cases in which they are not, they are, none the less displayed in close proximity to each other. Further, as I have pointed out, the purchase of **[395]** a soft drink is often a casual transaction. These two features of the market seem to explain most, if not all, of the cases of incorrect selection of which evidence has been given…. But even accepting, as I do, that by reason of the nature of the market-place and of the habits of purchasers, mistakes are likely to, and do, in fact, occur, the evidence would seem to demonstrate that in most, although not all, cases in which there has initially been a wrong selection by a customer, or the wrong product has been offered by the shopkeeper, the error has been recognized before the purchase has been completed. … This being so, it seems to me that the defendant has sufficiently differentiated its product from that of the plaintiff's."

This answer, it is true, related to the effect of get-up as a cause of confusion and was not addressed to the problems of the advertising campaign. Nor, when he gave it, was the judge directing his attention, let alone making any findings, upon the conduct of Mr Brooks or any of the other officers of the respondent company in the marketing of their product.

When, however, he came to consider the claim of unfair trading, he examined in detail, and made a number of adverse findings upon, their conduct in the development and marketing of Pub Squash. He stated his findings and conclusion on this aspect of the case in a remarkable passage which, because it is the key to a full understanding of his judgment, their Lordships quote in full:—

**(vii)** *Conclusion*

"From what I have written above it will appear that it is my view that, as from a time being no later than the later part of August 1974, the defendant, having by means of one or more of its officers become aware of the successful launch of Solo in Victoria and of the sale of Solo in Southern New South Wales, and, thus, appreciating that in all probability the Victorian 'launch' would be followed by a large-scale 'launch' of Solo upon the New South Wales market, set out in a deliberate and calculated fashion to take advantage of the plaintiffs' past efforts in developing Solo and of the plaintiffs' past and anticipated future efforts in developing a market for a product such as Solo, and that, in particular the defendant, by its officers, sought to copy or to approximate the formula for Solo, and chose a product name and package for the defendant's proposed product derived from, and intended to gain, the benefit of the plaintiffs' past and anticipated advertising campaign, and the plaintiffs' package for their product.

"Notwithstanding these findings, it is my view, as I have earlier indicated, that, as the facts, as I have earlier found them, do not reveal any relevant misrepresentation on the part of the defendant as to its goods, the plaintiffs have not made out a case for relief based upon the expanded concept of 'passing off' or upon 'unfair trading'."

Put very shortly, the learned trial judge concluded that there was no "relevant misrepresentation", no deception or probability of deception. The competition developed by the respondent and its officers took advantage of the appellants' promotion of their own product, but never **[396]** went so far as to suggest that Pub Squash was the product of the appellants, or merely another name for Solo. It might have been expected that he would have inferred from these findings the existence of confusion and the fact of deception: but after a long trial and a detailed examination of the evidence he refused to take the step of drawing the inference. His decision, taken very deliberately and with full awareness of what the respondent and its officers did in promoting their product, is, whether right or wrong, entitled to the greatest respect.

Counsel for the appellants accepted that the issue of deception was crucial. In submitting that the judge fell into error, he sought to rely on three points. He submitted first that the judge misled himself by the way in which he "compartmentalized" his judgment; secondly, that he misled himself by an error of law as to the relevant date for establishing the necessary goodwill or reputation of the plaintiff's product; and thirdly, that his conclusion was contrary to his primary findings of fact.

First, the "compartmentalization" point. The appellants' submission may be summarized as follows: Counsel attributed the error, into which, on his submission, the judge fell, to the structure of the judgment. The judge, as their Lordships have already noted, dealt with the cause of action in passing off first. At that stage he made no findings as to the conduct of the respondent's officers, Mr Brooks and his colleagues. He found that there was no "relevant misrepresentation on the part of the defendant as to its goods" without considering the defendant's intentions. But intention is relevant. Having found no misrepresentation, he then considered the case of unfair trading. He now found as a fact that the respondent set out deliberately to take advantage of the appellants' efforts to develop the market for Solo; but this was of no consequence, since he had already found no deception or misrepresentation. Had the learned judge appreciated that the case must be considered as a whole, and not in separate compartments, he would have had regard to the respondent's intention in determining whether there was deception or the probability of deception; and, had he done so, only one conclusion was possible: namely, that the respondent was passing off its goods as the goods of the appellants.

This is a formidable submission.

Where an intention to deceive is found, it is not difficult for the court to infer that the intention has been, or in all probability will be, effective: *Slazenger & Sons v Feltham & Co* (1889) 6 RPC 531, per Lindley LJ at 538. But in dealing with the issue of deception the learned judge directed himself correctly and made the comment, which is also good law, that "… the court must be on its guard against finding fraud *merely* because there has been an imitation of another's goods, get-up, method of trading or trading style (see, for example, *Goya Ltd v Gala of London Ltd* (1952) 69 RPC 188)."

After a very careful consideration of the judgment as a whole, their Lordships do not think that in the arrangement of the subject-matter of his judgment the judge allowed himself to overlook the importance, **[397]** subject to safeguards, of a defendant's intention when deciding the issue of deception.

Once it is accepted that the judge was not unmindful of the respondent's deliberate purpose (as he found) to take advantage of the appellants' efforts to develop Solo, the finding of "no deception" can be seen to be very weighty: for he has reached it, notwithstanding his view of the respondent's purpose. But it is also necessary to bear in mind the nature of the purpose found by the judge. He found that the respondent did sufficiently distinguish its goods from those of the appellants. The intention was not to pass off the respondent's goods as those of the appellants but to take advantage of the market developed by the advertising campaign for Solo. Unless it can be shown that in so doing the respondent infringed "the plaintiffs' intangible property rights" in the goodwill attaching to their product, there is no tort: for such infringement is the foundation of the tort: see Stephen J in *Hornsby Building Information Centre Pty Ltd v Sydney Building Information Centre Pty Ltd, supra.*

In their Lordships' view, therefore, the first submission fails. And, once the conclusion is reached that the judge did not allow the structure of his judgment to mislead him, the submission recoils upon itself. The finding of the judge becomes, by its rejection, immensely strengthened.

The second submission is less formidable. The judge, it is conceded, misdirected himself in holding that the relevant date for determining whether a plaintiff has established the necessary goodwill or reputation of his product is the date of the commencement of the proceedings (ie 1 June 1977). The relevant date is, in law, the date of the commencement of the conduct complained of, ie 8 April 1975, when the respondent began to market Pub Squash: *Norman Kark Publications Ltd v Odhams Press Ltd* [1962] RPC 163. Despite his error, the learned judge did direct his mind to the facts as they were in "the early months of 1975". He found that by then Solo had attained a significant level of recognition and acceptance in the market and went on to consider, and make findings upon, "the nature and extent of the goodwill and reputation which Solo had, *by early 1975* (emphasis supplied), attained, and which it thereafter maintained". This submission, therefore fails.

Their Lordships now turn to the main attack upon the judge's conclusion. His primary findings, which the appellants accept, should, it is submitted, have led him to conclude that there was confusion amongst buyers and deception by the respondent.

The judge's analysis of the nature of the goodwill or distinctive reputation which Solo had acquired by April 1975 cannot, in their Lordships' view, be challenged. The reputation he found to be that of "a lemon squash type of soft drink, marketed under the name of Solo, packaged, principally in yellow cans bearing a rondel-like or medallion-like device …, and widely advertised on television by advertisements featuring a rugged masculine figure". He was not, however, persuaded that *any of the variants* upon the phrase "those great old squashes like the pubs used to make" and "a man's drink" were generally associated **[398]** with Solo (emphasis supplied). He based his negative conclusion upon his understanding of the evidence of "the confusion witnesses", especially those members of the consuming public, who were called, and upon his view of the nature and effect of the advertisements for Solo, of which he said that "he had regard to two particular types …, namely: the fact that television is principally a visual medium so that the 'audio' tends to have less impact than the visual image, and, secondly, the fact that, no matter what variation be worked upon it, the phrase 'those great old squashes the pubs used to make' is essentially descriptive of the *type* of product advertised — it does not, of itself, *identify*, or denote the origin of, the product being advertised (cf and cp the slogan in issue in *Chemical Corporation of America v Anheuser-Bush Inc* (1962) 306 F 2d 433)". The appellants' challenge is to the negative conclusion. In their Lordships' opinion, it fails to displace either the judge's inference, based on his analysis of the nature of the market in which the two products were sold, or his finding that the advertising of Pub Squash, intended though it was to win a share of the market from its competitor Solo, led to no significant confusion or deception. He accepted that on occasions there was confusion at the point of sale: but he found, and there was plenty of evidence on which he could find, that the confusion was almost always corrected before the moment of sale. Such confusion as there was arose, in his view, from the casual attitude of many purchasers in the market to the product offered and not from any failure of the respondent sufficiently to distinguish its product from Solo.

He found that "the principal, if not the only, part of the market in which the wrong product has been selected or given, is in relation to cans". He saw the two cans: he refused to hold that, because Solo became known as being sold in yellow cans, it "thereby became entitled to a monopoly" of sale or that the mere fact the defendant adopted a yellow can for its product dictated a finding of "passing off". He was unable, on the evidence, to find that the consuming public associated yellow cans only with Solo.

Nevertheless, the judge recognized that the similarity in size and shape of can (which was a stock size and shape in the trade), and in colour made it "incumbent" upon the respondent to distinguish its package from that of Solo. He looked at the cans and commended that "it can readily be seen that they are different" and then proceeded to analyse the market and the effect of such confusion as there was in the way already described.

When the judge turned to consider the effect of the radio and television advertising, he rejected the submission that either of the two themes used in these media had become the property of the appellants in the sense in which the word "property" is used in this class of case. They were descriptive of the product (perhaps even eloquently descriptive), but never became a distinguishing feature. There was ample evidence to support his rejection of this submission, and their Lordships are in no position to substitute for his assessment of the effect of the Solo advertising campaign a different assessment or to challenge his analysis of the market, ie the character of the buying public.

[399] In reaching his conclusion of fact that the respondent had "sufficiently" distinguished its product from Solo, the judge had not only to conduct an elaborate and detailed analysis of the evidence, which he certainly did, but to bear in mind the necessity in this branch of the law of the balance to be maintained between the protection of a plaintiff's investment in his product and the protection of free competition. It is only if a plaintiff can establish that a defendant has invaded his "intangible property right" in his product by misappropriating descriptions which have become recognized by the market as distinctive of the product that the law will permit competition to be restricted. Any other approach would encourage monopoly. The new, small man would increasingly find his entry into an existing market obstructed by the large traders already well known as operating in it

For these reasons their Lordships are of the opinion that the appeal fails ...

# Chapter 13

# Trade Marks

Trade marks[1] generate passion. Not only are they powerful, privately owned symbols of wealth, globalisation and consumerism but they also form part of the landscape of our lives. One can say that trade marks are cultural artefacts which are bearers of immense aesthetic and emotional effects.

This aspect of trade marks is well recognised, even by the High Court. In *Campomar Sociedad Limitada v Nike International Ltd*,[2] the High Court noted that trade marks "may play a significant role in ordinary public and commercial discourse, supplying vivid metaphors and compelling imagery disconnected from the traditional function of trade marks to indicate the source of origin".[3] The High Court quoted Judge Kozinski writing extra judicially who said:

> Trademarks are often selected for their effervescent qualities, and then injected into the stream of communication with the pressure of a fire hose by means of mass media campaigns. Where trademarks carry so much communicative freight, allowing the trademark holder to restrict their use implicates our collective interest in open and free communication.[4]

There is another face to trade marks, however, which is not so well recognised. That is, trade marks are voracious devourers of culture. No identifiable, cultural product is safe from appropriation by trade mark owners in search of a good mark. Thus, the iconic name of WALTZING MATILDA has been registered as a trade mark in respect of all types of products and services from tents to business management. The goddess NIKE has given her name not only to gym clothes and shoes but to motor engines and tools. UGG boots, once an affectionate name for a particular style of sheepskin boot, is now registered in relation to a wide range of shoes, clothing and headware. ROOIBOS, an African word for tea, is registered in Australia for teas generally. HIGH FIVE, FIVE STAR, GIVE ME FIVE and

---

1    For transitional arrangements, see *Trade Marks Act 1995* Part 22.
2    (2000) 202 CLR 45.
3    (2000) 202 CLR 45 at 67.
4    (2000) 202 CLR 45 at 67, quoting from "Trademarks Unplugged" (1993) 68 *NYUL Rev* 960 at 973. In support of this view the High Court also cited Kozinski J in *New Kids on the Block v News America Publishing Inc* 971 F 2d 302 (1992) in the Court of Appeals Ninth Circuit, and Kitto J in *Clark Equipment Co v Registrar of Trade Marks* (1964) 111 CLR 511 at 513-515.

FIVE AND DIME are all registered trade marks as are the SOUTHERN CROSS, the HAPPY BUDDHA, CAPTAIN COOK and NED KELLY.

This tendency of trade marks to appropriate and devour culture is one which members of the public often decry by way of the appeal that we should not "fence off the commons" and that we should "protect the public domain". However, it seems that trade mark law has little concern with "protecting the commons". Rather trade mark law is primarily concerned with providing trade mark owners with a simple method of protecting their marks against non-genuine users: most infringement cases in Australia are against trade mark pirates who fake SEIKO watches and POLO shirts, for example, rather than against genuine competitors with similar marks.

At the same time, by providing broad grounds for challenging registration, the Act does seek to protect competition and trade by ensuring that genuine competitors are not disadvantaged by the registration of a mark which they might need to use honestly in the course of trade.

In addition, it is important to remember that the trade mark owners' rights are quite limited. The trade mark owner only has the right to use the mark "as a trade mark" in relation to nominated goods and services (s 20); and this right is only infringed by a person who uses the trade mark "as a trade mark" (s 120). This means that a person who includes a COCA COLA sign in a painting is not guilty of trade mark infringement (although, it must be admitted, they might be liable for infringement under the *Copyright Act 1968*). A person who sings Waltzing Matilda in the shower does not infringe the trade mark in relation to tents.

In this chapter we will consider the limits of trade marks – what can be registered as a trade mark and how the trade mark registration can be challenged or restricted. We will also consider the special protection offered to well-known marks, such as NIKE, the WIGGLES and BIG MAC. We will conclude the chapter with a consideration of the other two types of marks protected under the Act; these are the collective mark and the certification mark. In the next chapter we will examine the rights of the trade mark owner and infringement of those rights; offences relating to trade marks and the law relating to dealing with trade marks.

## Legislative Framework

The first Australian trade marks Act after Federation was passed in 1905 as an exercise of the Commonwealth Parliament's legislative powers to make laws with respect to "trade marks" under s 51(xviii) of the Constitution. The *Trade Marks Act 1905* allowed for the registration of "trade marks" but also allowed the registration of "workers' marks" (which indicated that the goods had been made by an Australian worker or association of workers) and the "Commonwealth mark" (which indicated that, in the opinion of both Houses of Parliament, the conditions of the workers involved in the manufacture of the goods were fair and reasonable). The constitutional validity of the legislation in relation to workers' marks was successfully challenged in *Attorney-General (NSW) v Brewery Employees Union NSW*,[5] when the High Court held that the term trade mark,

---

5    (1908) 6 CLR 469.

within the terms of the Constitution, did not cover every type of mark used in connection with trade but:

> meant a mark which was a visible symbol of a particular type of incorporeal or industrial property consisting in the right of the person engaged in trade to distinguish by a special mark goods in which he deals, or with which he has dealt, from the goods of other persons.[6]

In particular, Griffith CJ noted, a trade mark is a form of property which distinguishes the goods as having been dealt with by a particular person (even if the name and identity of that person is not known).[7] The Commonwealth mark was not challenged in the High Court but was repealed in 1912.

The *Trade Marks Act 1905* was replaced by the *Trade Marks Act 1955* which in turn was repealed and replaced by the current *Trade Marks Act 1995*. In accordance with Australia's international treaty obligations, the types of marks protected under the legislation have been gradually extended beyond the narrow limits envisioned by the High Court in *Attorney-General (NSW) v Brewery Employees Union NSW*. Today a trade mark may be registered not only in relation to goods but also services. In addition, the *Trade Marks Act 1995* protects collective trade marks (Part 15), certification trade marks (Part 16) and defensive trade marks (Part 17). A collective trade mark is similar to the old workers' mark and identifies the goods or services as having been dealt with by members of an association (s 162). A certification trade mark is a mark by which a person certifies that the goods or services have a particular quality, origin, are made of a certain material or have some other characteristic such as accuracy (s 169). Under the defensive trade mark provisions the owner of a well-known trade mark is able to register that trade mark in relation to goods and services even though the trade mark owner has no intention of trading in those goods and services (s 185). The defensive trade mark therefore cannot be attacked for non-use. In this chapter, and in accordance with the legislative usage, we use the term trade mark to refer to trade marks which are not collective, certification or defensive trade marks.

Australia's trade mark legislation operates within an international framework of treaty protection. In addition to the *Paris Convention for the Protection of Industrial Property 1883*, Australia has signed the *Nice Agreement Concerning the International Classification of Goods and Services for the Purpose of Registration of Marks 1957* (entered into force by Australia on 8 April 1961), the TRIPS Agreement (administered by the World Trade Organization of which Australia has been a member since its inception on 1 January 1995), the *Trademark Law Treaty 1994* (entered into force by Australia on 21 January 1998), the *Singapore Treaty on the Law of Trademarks 2006* (entered into force by Australia on 16 March 2009), and the *Agreement and the Protocol Relating to the Madrid Agreement Concerning the International Registration of Trademarks 1989* (entered into force by Australia on 11 July 2001). Under the Madrid Protocol and Agreement an international system of registration for trade marks is established whereby registration in a member country allows registration in another member country without loss of priority date. These arrangements are covered by regulations made under s 189A of the *Trade Marks Act 1995*.

---

6     (1908) 6 CLR 469 at 512-513.
7     (1908) 6 CLR 469 at 513.

# Definition of a Trade Mark

As we have seen, the High Court in *Attorney-General (NSW) v Brewery Employees Union NSW*[8] held that it is not every mark used by a trader in the course of trade which is a trade mark but only those marks which, "distinguish ... goods in which he deals, or with which he has dealt, from the goods of other persons".[9]

This definition of a trade mark has been adopted in successive trade marks legislation. The *Trade Marks Act 1995* s 17 defines a trade mark as:

> a sign used, or intended to be used, to distinguish goods or services dealt with or provided in the course of trade by a person from goods or services so dealt with or provided by any other person.

The *Trade Marks Act 1955* s 6, by comparison, provided that a trade mark must "show a connection" in the course of trade between the goods and services on the one hand and the person entitled to use the mark on the other, "whether with or without the identity of the person". This may seem to be narrower than the current definition but the case law on the 1955 definition gave a very broad definition of "a connection in the course of trade" and there has been no indication from the courts that they read the 1995 definition any more widely than this. The case law applying to the 1955 definition may therefore still prove useful for determining the meaning of a trade mark under the 1995 Act.

In the 1956 case of *Mark Foy's Ltd v Davies Coop and Co Ltd*,[10] the High Court approved the statement in the *Yeast-Vite Case*[11] that a trade mark showed a connection between the respondent and the goods and services if it "indicate[s] the origin of the goods in the respondent by virtue of manufacture, selection, certification, dealing with or offering for sale".[12] This statement has been accepted as a positive requirement that a trade mark must function as a "badge of origin" although this must be understood in a very broad sense. As Gummow J said in *Johnson and Johnson Australia Pty Ltd v Sterling Pharmaceuticals Pty Ltd*,[13] a case relating to the 1955 definition:

> The registered trade mark serves to indicate, if not the actual origin of the goods and services, nor their quality as such, the origin of that quality in a particular business, whether known or unknown by name.[14]

Conversely, a mark was not a trade mark under the 1955 Act if it was used merely as a descriptive term[15] or a name or as a ghost mark[16] rather than to show a connection between the trader and the goods or services in question. Thus, in *Imperial Group Pty Ltd v Philip Morris and Co Ltd*,[17] a case which is discussed in more detail below, registration was successfully challenged on the basis that

---

8    (1908) 6 CLR 469.
9    (1908) 6 CLR 469 at 512-513.
10   (1956) 95 CLR 190.
11   (1934) 51 RPC 110.
12   (1934) 51 RPC 110 at 115, approved by the High Court in *Mark Foy's Ltd v Davies Coop and Co Ltd* (1956) 95 CLR 190 at 203.
13   (1991) 21 IPR 1.
14   (1991) 21 IPR 1 at 25.
15   *Mark Foy's Ltd v Davies Coop and Co Ltd* (1956) 95 CLR 190.
16   [1982] FSR 72.
17   [1982] FSR 72.

the mark was being used as a "ghost mark" rather than as a trade mark – that is, the applicant was seeking to register it simply to prevent competitors registering similar marks rather than to show a connection in the course of trade between the goods in question and the applicant. These principles continue to apply under the 1995 Act and will be considered in more detail below.

## What is a sign?

Today, a wide range of signs might function as a trade mark. A sign is defined in s 6 to include:

> the following or any combination of the following, namely, any letter, word, name, signature, numeral, device, brand, heading, label, ticket, aspect of packaging, shape, colour or scent.

This 1995 definition extends the old definition of a sign (previously known as a "mark") in so far as it includes shape, colour, scent and aspects of packaging.

Before 1995 it was often argued that a trade mark must be applied to a product and therefore the product itself could not be a trade mark. It was on this basis, for example, that the shape of the Coca Cola bottle was denied registration as a trade mark in the United Kingdom in 1986.[18] As a result of the amendments introduced by the *Trade Marks Act 1995* it is now accepted that the shape of a product or its packaging may be a trade mark so long as it meets the other criteria for registrability; thus, a shape would probably not be registrable if it were determined by the function of the product, for example. The shape of the Coca-Cola bottle has been registered in Australia as a trade mark since 1998 and, in 2002, following a long dispute, Kenman Kandy's rather cuddly spider shaped lollies were held by the Full Federal Court to be registrable as a trade mark in respect of those lollies.[19]

Colour was always permitted as one aspect of the trade mark.[20] Thus, Gillette has registered the copper and black surface of its batteries; Smith Kline Beecham has registered maroon and gold as applied to the surface of a capsule; and in 1985 a single colour was registered for the colour pink as applied to Pink Batts. The express reference to colour in the 1995 Act will therefore probably have little effect on the practice of the Trade Marks Registrar in relation to registration of colour and the registrability of a colour remains subject to the general principles.[21] Thus, the colour green would be unlikely to be registered in relation to vegetables as colours which are commonly used with the particular trade are not likely to be capable of distinguishing one trader's goods from another.[22] In comparison, there was no evidence that the colour pink was related in such a way to fibreglass insulation batts, and in *Philmac Pty Ltd v Registrar of Trade Marks* Mansfield J suggested that an "out of left field" colour choice might be registrable.[23]

---

18    *Coca-Cola Trade Marks* [1986] RPC 421.

19    *Kenman Kandy Australia Pty Ltd v Registrar of Trade Marks* (2002) 56 IPR 30.

20    Under s 70 a trade mark may be registered with limitations as to colour and, if there are no limitations, then it is taken to be registered in all colours.

21    For further discussion on the registrability of colour as trade marks, see *Trade Marks Office Manual of Practice and Procedure*, Part 21 para 4.5.

22    See *Luk Lamellen and Kupplungsbau Beteiligungs KG* [2003] ATMO 12 where yellow was rejected in respect of oil and grease used for technical purposes.

23    (2002) 56 IPR 452 at 474.

The first scent trade mark was apparently granted in the United States in 1990 for a "high impact, fresh floral fragrance reminiscent of plumeria blossoms" in relation to embroidery yarn.[24] Like other forms of trade marks these applications are subject to the general principles of registrability and it is therefore unlikely that a pine smell would be registered in relation to a cleaning product or that a perfume would be registered in its own right if it is found that another trader might want to use this scent in the ordinary course of trade.

## Registration, Rejection, Opposition, Cancellation and Rectification

The 1995 Act introduced a presumption of registrability[25] which brought the registration procedure for trade marks even closer to the patents procedure. The trade mark procedure requires an application, examination, acceptance, notification of acceptance in the *Official Journal*, possible opposition, registration and finally notification of registration in the *Official Journal*. Registration is initially for 10 years but may be renewed indefinitely. The mark is registered in relation to specified classes of goods and services. The classes are set out in Sch 1 to the *Trade Marks Regulations 1995* and are also readily accessed on IP Australia's website. The owner (s 27) or joint owners (s 28) of the trade mark may apply for registration of the mark.

The Registrar may reject an application for registration on grounds set out in Part 4, Division 2 of the Act (ss 39-44). A person may oppose the registration on grounds set out in Part 5, Division 2 (ss 57-62A) and the registration might be cancelled or amended under Part 8, Division 2 (ss 85-88). Part 9 (ss 92-105) provides for cancellation of the trade mark on the basis of non-use. In addition the Registrar may impose limits on the applicant's rights under ss 23, 24 and 25 of Part 3.

There are six grounds under Part 4, Division 2 for rejection of the application for registration of the trade mark. These are:

- the trade mark is prescribed by the regulations (s 39);
- the trade mark cannot be represented graphically (s 40);
- the trade mark is incapable of distinguishing the applicant's goods or services (s 41);
- the trade mark is scandalous or contrary to law (s 42);
- the trade mark is likely to deceive or cause confusion (s 43); or
- the trade mark is substantially identical with or deceptively similar to another trade mark registered in relation to the same or related goods and services (s 44).

In accordance with the presumption of registrability the Registrar must accept the application unless satisfied that the application has not been made in accordance with the Act or there are grounds to reject it (s 33). This provision changes the onus from the 1955 Act under which it was the applicant's affirmative duty to prove registrability. It is interesting to note that these grounds do not give

---

24 *Re Clarke* 17 USPQ 2d 1238 (1990). For further discussion of scent trade marks, see *Trade Marks Office Manual of Practice and Procedure*, Part 21 para 7.

25 For a discussion of the presumption of registrability, see *Pfizer Products Inc v Karam* [2006] FCA 1663.

the Registrar the right to reject the application on the basis that the applicant is not the owner or does not intend to use the mark as a trade mark (s 27).

The grounds for opposition are set out in ss 57 to 62A. Section 57 provides that registration of a trade mark may be opposed on the same grounds as provided for rejection except that an opposer cannot oppose on the basis that the sign cannot be graphically represented. In addition, an opposer may raise the following objections:

- that the applicant is not the owner of the trade mark (s 58);
- that the opponent used a similar trade mark earlier (s 58A);
- that the applicant is not intending to use the trade mark as a trade mark (s 59);
- that the trade mark is similar to a trade mark which has acquired a reputation in Australia (s 60);
- that the trade mark contains a false geographical indication (s 61);
- that the application was amended contrary to the Act or that the Registrar accepted the application on the basis of false representations in material particulars (s 62); or
- that the application was made in bad faith (s 62A).

A "person aggrieved" may apply to a prescribed court for an order to the Registrar to rectify the register by cancelling or amending an entry or by attaching a condition or limitation to the registration of the trade mark. A person is aggrieved if "there is a reasonable possibility of the applicant being appreciably disadvantaged in a legal or practical sense by the register remaining unrectified": *Ritz Hotel Ltd v Charles of the Ritz Ltd.*[26]

This general rule was approved by the Full Federal Court in *Health World Ltd v Shin-Sun Australia Pty Ltd.*[27] The Federal Court held that if the marks of the mover and the challenged trade mark are not deceptively similar it would be difficult to prove that the mover was an aggrieved person.[28] Furthermore, the mere fact that the marks of the moving party and the challenged mark are deceptively similar or the mark is misleading is not sufficient to establish that the mover is an aggrieved person – there must be a "reputational impact".[29] The Full Court held that the possibility of disadvantage in a legal or practical sense does not arise from the possibility of deceptive similarity alone. The owner of a mark is an aggrieved person for the purposes of s 88(1) of the Act where, by reason of the reputation of their mark, another mark would be likely to deceive or cause confusion. However, the High Court in *Health World Ltd v Shin-Sun Australia Pty Ltd*[30] interpreted the "aggrieved person" standard more broadly, and overturned the approach taken by the Full Federal Court. In their joint judgment, French CJ, Gummow, Heydon and Bell JJ held that the "aggrieved person" standard should be interpreted liberally because of the public interest in maintaining the integrity and purity of the register.[31] The security of the register:

---

26    (1988) 15 NSWLR 158 at 193.
27    (2009) 174 FCR 218 at 225.
28    (2009) 174 FCR 218 at 226.
29    (2009) 174 FCR 218.
30    (2010) 240 CLR 590.
31    (2010) 240 CLR 590 at 597. For recent application of this principle by the Federal Court, see *Austin, Nichols and Co Inc v Lodestar Anstalt* (2011) 90 IPR 310 at 320.

should be prevented from being eroded by applications for rectification or removal by busybodies or "common informers or strangers proceeding wantonly" or persons without any interest in the Register or the functions it serves beyond gratifying an intellectual concern or reflecting "merely sentimental motives". Applications of that kind, by clogging up and causing delay in the courts, would cause an unnecessary cloud to hang over registrations. The purpose of avoiding this outcome is reflected in the standing requirements in ss 88 and 92. Applications by persons who are not aggrieved are positively inimical to the fulfilment of the statutory purposes through the Register.[32]

An application to rectify the register may be made on the following grounds:

- any ground of opposition referred to above (s 88(2)(a));
- the registered mark contains a sign which, since registration, has become generally accepted within the trade as the sign that describes or is the name of an article, substance or service (ss 87 and 24); or
- the registered mark contains a sign which is the name of, or describes, an article, substance or process that was formerly patented and the patent has been expired for at least two years and the sign is the commonly known way to describe or identify the article, substance or process (ss 87 and 25);
- to correct an error (s 85);
- that an amendment was obtained by fraud, false suggestion or misrepresentation (s 88(2)(b));
- that, at the time of applying for rectification, the use of the trade mark is likely to cause confusion or deception for some reason other than those provided for under s 43, s 44 or s 60 (s 88(2)(c));
- an entry on the register was made or amended as a result of fraud, false suggestion or misrepresentation (s 88(2)(e));
- that a condition or limitation has been contravened (s 86); or
- non-use (ss 92-105).

Under s 89 the court has a discretion not to order cancellation or rectification under s 85, s 87 and s 88 (except for the grounds involving fraud, false suggestion or misrepresentation) if the ground complained of did not arise due to any act or fault of the registered owner.

We now consider the most significant of these grounds for rejection, opposition and rectification.

## Grounds for Challenging Trade Marks

### Ownership and intention to use and non-use (ss 58, 59, 92-105)

*Ownership*

The "owner" of a trade mark may apply for registration of the mark if the person:

- is using or intends to use the mark in relation to the goods and services;[33]
- the person has authorised or intends to authorise another person to use the mark in relation to goods and services;

---

32  (2010) 240 CLR 590 at 598 (footnotes omitted).

33  Section 7(4) and (5) provides that "use of a trade mark in relation to goods" and "use of a trade mark in relation to services" means use of the trade mark upon, or in physical or other relation to, the goods (including second-hand goods) and in physical or other relationship to the services.

- the person intends to assign the mark to a body corporate that is about to be constituted with a view to using the mark in relation to goods and services (s 27).

The owner of the trade mark is not necessarily the creator or originator of the mark in the copyright sense (although this may be taken into account) but is the person who first uses the mark as a trade mark within the jurisdiction. In *Shell Co of Australia Ltd v Rohm and Haas Co*,[34] Dixon J in the High Court said in relation to the requirement of proprietorship under the *Trade Marks Act 1905*:

> The basis of a claim of proprietorship in a trade mark so far unused has been found in the combined effect of authorship of the mark, the intention to use it upon or in connection with the goods and services and the applying for registration.[35]

In *Aston v Harlee Manufacturing Co*,[36] Harlee Manufacturing was the registered owner in the United States of the mark, TASTEE FREEZ, in connection with iced confectionery. The mark was widely used in the United States through franchising arrangements. Aston, having heard of the mark in the United States, applied to have it registered in Australia. There was some, though very little, evidence of use of the mark in Australia by Aston. Applying the principles from *Shell Co of Australia Ltd v Rohm and Haas Co*,[37] Fullagar J in the High Court found that Aston was entitled to registration of the mark as the first proprietor of the mark in Australia.

Because the lodging of an application is prima facie proof of ownership of the mark,[38] the Registrar has no practical avenue for rejecting an application on the basis that the applicant is not the owner or does not intend to use the mark as a trade mark although non-ownership is a ground for opposition and rectification.[39]

### Use of the trade mark

The requirement that the owner have used or intends to use the mark in relation to goods and services has been interpreted to mean that the owner has used or intends to use the mark "as a trade mark" in relation to goods and services.

The concepts of "use" and "use as a trade mark" are central to the operation of the trade marks regime. They arise in relation to proprietorship and registration; a trade mark may be expunged from the register on the basis of non-use and, finally, a trade mark is infringed if a person, without authorisation, uses the trade mark "as a trade mark" but not otherwise.

The meaning of "use" and "use as a trade mark" are dealt with in ss 6, 7, 8, 9 and 228 of the Act. "Use of a trade mark in relation to goods" means use of

---

34  (1948) 78 CLR 601.
35  (1948) 78 CLR 601 at 627.
36  (1960) 103 CLR 391.
37  (1948) 78 CLR 601.
38  *Shell Co of Australia Ltd v Rohm and Haas Co* (1948) 78 CLR 601 and *Aston v Harlee Manufacturing Co* (1960) 103 CLR 391.
39  In *Food Channel Network Pty Ltd v Television Food Network GP* (2010) 185 FCR 9 at 18 and 20 (Keane CJ, Stone and Jagot JJ), the Full Federal Court recently confirmed that the general rule as to onus of proof that a party who asserts must prove applies to opposition proceedings under ss 58 and 59 of the Act. Further, the court held that the onus lies on the opponent.

the trade mark upon, or in relation to, the goods (including second-hand goods (s 7(4)). "Use of a trade mark in relation to services" means use of the trade mark in physical or other relation to the services (s 7(5)). A trade mark is said to be "applied to" material things if it is woven in, impressed on, worked into or affixed or annexed to the material thing (s 9(1)). A trade mark is "applied in relation to" goods or services if it is applied to any covering, document, label, reel or thing which the goods might come in or be provided with in the course of trade (this includes packaging and instruction booklets) or if it is used in a manner which is likely to lead persons to believe that it refers to, describes or designates the goods or services (s 9(1)(b)). Advertising pamphlets for a cruise, for example, might come within this definition, as would a person dressed up as the mark (Crazy Ron and Ronald McDonald, for example). The Act specifically states that a trade mark is taken to have been "applied in relation to" goods and services if it is used on a signboard; or in an advertisement (including a television advertisement); or in an invoice, wine list, catalogue, business letter, business paper, price list or other commercial document (s 9(1)(c)). The fact that the trade mark has been altered does not prevent the Registrar or court finding that it has been used (s 7(1)).

The Act states that "to avoid any doubt" an aural representation of a word, letter, name or numeral mark is use as a mark (s 7(2)). One would have to assume that the aural use of an aural mark is also use as a mark. Thus the use of the name McDONALDS in a radio advertisement would be use of a trade mark, the playing of a registered jingle would be use of the mark, but the description of the green and yellow of a BP station would not be.

The use may be by an owner or an authorised user (s 7(3)) and an "authorised user" is defined as a person who uses the trade mark under the control of the trade mark owner (s 8(1)). Under the control includes having quality control or financial control (s 8(3) and (4)). These provisions are very important in managing franchise operations, for example.

A mark is positively used as a trade mark if it functions as a badge of origin in the broad sense although this need not be its only use.[40] Negatively, there are many ways a sign or mark may be used other than as a trade mark. In *Beecham Group plc v Colgate-Palmolive Co*,[41] for example, Colgate Palmolive sought to register 11 variations on a blob of triple striped toothpaste. The Registrar rejected 10 of these applications on the basis that Colgate-Palmolive could not demonstrate that it intended to use the signs as trade marks and did not counter the opposition allegation that it had simply sought to register the full range of marks so as to gain a monopoly in the field of toothpaste gimmicks. The one version which the Registrar did accept was the most stylised depiction of the toothpaste blob. Similarly, in *ACI Operations Ltd v Amcor Limited*,[42] an application for the registration of a recycling sign on plastic bottles was rejected on the basis that the sign was used as a recycling symbol rather than as a trade mark, although the delegate of the Registrar acknowledged that a mark could in theory perform the two roles.

To constitute a use as a trade mark the use must be in the course of trade in the goods and services themselves although this trade need not amount to actual

40   *Shell Company of Australia Ltd v Esso Standard Oil (Australia) Ltd* (1963) 109 CLR 407.
41   (2001) 58 IPR 161.
42   [2001] ATMO 34 and see *Amcor Ltd v ACI Operations Pty Ltd* (2000) 53 IPR 608.

sales and dealings with the goods. Trade in the trade mark itself is insufficient to establish use of the mark as a trade mark. Thus, in *Woolly Bull Enterprises Pty Ltd v Reynolds*,[43] the rather fruitless attempts of the plaintiff to interest traders in using the Red Bull mark did not amount to a use and, in *Moorgate Tobacco Co Ltd v Philip Morris Ltd*,[44] "merely preliminary discussions and negotiations about whether the mark would be used" was not a relevant use.

This principle effectively operates to limit speculative registration of trade marks. The idea of registering GRASS or ECSTASY, for example, in the faint hope of cashing in on a change of government policy regarding illicit drugs is unrealistic unless the applicant is prepared to become a trader in the meantime. At the time of writing, THE GAP had a lapsed trade mark comprising an image and the word GRASS in relation to class 3 goods which includes perfumes and essential oils. The Sunraysia company has maintained an ECSTASY trade mark at least since 1924 in relation to foods and beverages. The more recent versions of this mark provide that the registration does not extend to food or beverages in the nature of pharmaceuticals or drugs.

In *Moorgate Tobacco Co Ltd v Philip Morris Ltd (No 2)*, the High Court explained use of a trade mark for the purposes of establishing proprietorship in the following way:

> The cases establish that it is not necessary that there be an actual dealing in the goods bearing the trade mark before there can be a local use of the mark as a trade mark. It may suffice that imported goods which have not actually reached Australia have been offered for sale in Australia under the mark: *Re Registered Trade Mark "Yanx"; ex parte Amalgamated Tobacco Corporation Ltd* (1951) 82 CLR 199 or that the mark has been used in an advertisement of the goods in the course of trade: *Shell Co of Australia v Esso Standard Oil (Australia) Ltd* (1963) 109 CLR 407. In such cases, however, it is possible to identify an actual trade or offer to trade in the goods bearing the mark or an existing intention to offer or supply goods bearing the trade mark.[45]

In that case the provision of cigarettes showing the mark KENT GOLDEN LIGHTS was held not to be a relevant use because the cigarettes were not intended for sale and the sample was more properly characterised as a sample of the trade mark although this is not always an easy distinction to draw.[46]

On the other hand, not every sale of goods bearing the mark constitutes a relevant use. In *Imperial Group Pty Ltd v Philip Morris and Co Ltd*,[47] the plaintiff had manufactured a cigarette called MERIT. They believed that this name would not be registrable (because it lacked distinctiveness) and therefore it sought to register the mark NERIT as a "ghost mark" in relation to cigarettes. At the time of registration the plaintiffs were not using the NERIT mark, they had no intention to exploit the mark commercially but knew that they might have to use it within the next five years to avoid cancellation of the mark on the grounds of non-use. The plaintiffs discovered that the defendants intended to launch a brand of cigarettes under the name MERIT. In order to ensure that

---

43   (2001) 51 IPR 149.
44   (1984) 156 CLR 414.
45   (1984) 156 CLR 414 at 433-434.
46   Compare *Settef Spa v Riv-o-land Marble Co (Vic) Pty Ltd* (1987) 10 IPR 402 where the trade marks attached to samples of marble wall finish.
47   [1982] FSR 72.

they would be able to sue for the breach of the ghost mark the plaintiffs made a small commercially non-viable release of a cigarette called NERIT. The English Court of Appeal applied a negative test to determine whether this was use as a trade mark and held that this was not use of a mark as a trade mark, it "was not a use at all. It had the unreal qualities of a ghost mark which the plaintiffs always intended it to be".[48]

As the High Court emphasised in the *Moorgate* quote above, the use must be in Australia. Thus, an overseas manufacturer uses the mark in Australia when the goods are imported and displayed or offered for sale in Australia,[49] even if the goods have not yet arrived in Australia.[50] The use of the mark on an overseas manufacturer's correspondence received in Australia was an appropriate use in *Thunderbird Products Corp Pty Ltd v Thunderbird Marine Products Pty Ltd*.[51] The fact the Australian importer removed the trade mark before selling the goods might not be sufficient to deny the usage by the overseas manufacturer.[52] In the case of export goods, s 228 provides that the application of a mark or any other relevant action in Australia to goods or services for export is a use in Australia.

The Federal Court in *Ward Group Pty Ltd v Brodie and Stone plc*[53] has taken a narrow approach in determining what internet use constitutes use of a trade mark in Australia for the purposes of infringement. In that case Ward Group, the owner of an Australian registered trade mark (RESTORIA) for anti-greying hair cream, took action against a United Kingdom company, Brodie, which manufactured and distributed a similar product under the same name for which it was the registered owner in the United Kingdom. The hair cream was advertised and sold on the internet by United Kingdom website owners who had purchased the products from Brodie. Although the website gave prices in Australian dollars as well as other currencies, and provided shipping prices for Australia, there was no evidence of any sales in Australia through the websites other than a number of trap purchasers made by Ward's solicitors.[54] This is not surprising as the rate of exchange meant that the United Kingdom products would be more expensive for Australian purchasers. In relation to the trap purchases the website owner sent a confirmation of payment together with a receipt number to the trap purchasers (either by email or by directing the purchaser to a page) but the word RESTORIA did not appear on the confirmation. In addition, the goods were delivered to the trap purchasers. The question arose as to whether either the advertising or the sale was a use in Australia.

---

48    [1982] FSR 72 at 78.

49    *Estex Clothing Manufacturers Pty Ltd v Ellis and Goldstein Ltd* (1967) 116 CLR 254.

50    *Re Registered Trade Marks 'Yanx'; Ex parte Amalgamated Tobacco Corporation Ltd* (1951) 82 CLR 199.

51    (1974) 131 CLR 592.

52    *Blackadder v Good Roads Machinery Co Inc* (1926) 38 CLR 332. This case displays a brevity and sense of "fair play" which we no longer see in Australian intellectual property cases.

53    (2005) 215 ALR 716. For recent consideration of this decision by the Federal Court, see *International Hair Cosmetics Group Pty Ltd v International Hair Cosmetics Ltd* [2011] FCA 339, Logan J at [45]-[47], [56] and [59].

54    For a discussion of the courts' attitude to trap purchases and the expected safeguards, see *CC Wakefield and Co Ltd v Purser* (1934) 51 RPC 167 which was cited favourably in *Ward Group Pty Ltd v Brodie and Stone plc* (2005) 215 ALR 716.

A statement made elsewhere is usually said to have been made in the place that it is received – see, for example, *Norbert Steinhardt and Sons Ltd v Meth*[55] regarding an unjustified threat written in the United States and received by mail in Australia and compare the High Court defamation case of *Dow Jones and Company Inc v Gutnick*.[56] In *Dow Jones* the High Court commented that, in determining where an action takes place, one might distinguish between those cases "like trespass or negligence, where some quality of the defendant's conduct is critical" in which case "it will usually be very important to look to where the defendant acted". In cases such as defamation, on the other hand, one might need to look at "where the consequences of the conduct were felt".[57] This would suggest that in the case of passing off, for example, it might be where the statement was received that was significant, whilst in the case of trade mark use it is where the defendant acted that is significant.

In *Ward's* case, as we saw in the previous chapter, Merkel J drew a different distinction which he said distinguished the facts of this case from those in *Dow Jones*. He drew a distinction between a statement "made to the world at large" and one "directed or targeted at people in a particular jurisdiction".

> When such publications or statements are made to the world at large, and not to persons or subscribers in a particular jurisdiction, there is some difficulty in regarding them as having been made by a website in a particular jurisdiction. However, where the publication or statement is directed or targeted at persons or subscribers in a particular jurisdiction there is no difficulty in treating them as having been made and received in that jurisdiction ...[58]

Applying this test, Merkel J held that the advertising in *Ward* did not amount to a use in Australia but that, subject to any defences, the confirmation of the trap purchase did amount to a use in Australia.[59]

In reading Merkel J's decision at the end of the chapter you may like to consider whether the distinction he draws is useful in the context of internet communications or even whether such a distinction is necessary given that a mark may be registered as a trade mark in the name of multiple people in multiple jurisdictions throughout the world, all of whom want to advertise on the web.

It is sometimes suggested that *Imperial Group Pty Ltd v Philip Morris and Co Ltd* is authority for the proposition that the use must be bona fide. This is not strictly correct. The Act in question (the *Trade Marks Act 1938* (UK)) provided that a trade mark registration could be amended on the basis that at the time of registration the applicant had no intention to use the mark as a trade mark. This provision made no reference to the requirement of good faith. The Act also provided that a trade mark could be cancelled on the basis of non-use, which included non bona fide use. The Court of Appeal found against the plaintiff on both grounds.

---

55   (1961) 105 CLR 440.
56   (2002) 210 CLR 575.
57   *Dow Jones and Company Inc v Gutnick* (2002) 210 CLR 575 at [43].
58   *Ward Group Pty Ltd v Brodie and Stone plc* (2005) 215 ALR 716 at [40].
59   The consent defence was established in this case because Merkel J held that Ward had consented to the use by authorising the trap purchases and he distinguished this case from other trap purchases cases on the basis that, apart from the trap purchase, there was no other use in Australia at all.

This distinction is maintained under the current Australian Act and the requirements of bona fides or good faith arises today only in relation to expungement for non-use. The difference between a bona fide use and a non bona fide use can be demonstrated by comparing the "NERIT" case[60] and *Electrolux Ltd v Electrix Ltd*.[61] In *Electrolux Ltd v Electrix Ltd*, the plaintiffs had registered the names ELECTROLUX and ELECTRUX but had continued to market their vacuum cleaners under the name of ELECTROLUX. During this same period the defendants had marketed a vacuum cleaner under the name of ELECTRIX. Following the end of the Second World War the defendants developed a renewed marketing plan which was successful in increasing their market share. Electrolux, as part of their strategy to compete against Electrix, decided to challenge their use of the word ELECTRIX as an infringement of Electrolux's registered trade mark ELECTRUX. In order to ensure that their action for infringement would not be defeated by an application for removal on the basis of non-use they, under advice from their lawyers one assumes, renamed their cheaper vacuum cleaner ELECTRUX and marketed it as such. The Court of Appeal held that this was a bona fide use of the trade mark because it was "an ordinary and genuine use", it was "substantial" and it was "not spasmodic or merely temporary". The fact that the plaintiffs used it in this way to gain a forensic advantage did not amount to mala fides because "a man whose title gives him certain rights ought not ... be held to be acting otherwise than *bona fide* if he takes steps to perfect his title".[62]

On the other hand, when the plaintiffs wanted to protect the ghost mark NERIT in *Imperial Group Pty Ltd v Philip Morris and Co Ltd*,[63] they only produced a small number of NERIT cigarettes, they were distributed to a limited number of retail outlets owned by them, many of the cigarettes were returned and they only had two production runs spaced over a period of years. The court applied the *Electrolux* test to determine that this was not a relevant use. The court found that it was not an ordinary and genuine use, it was spasmodic and temporary and it was not substantial.

A person aggrieved may succeed in an application for the cancellation of a trade mark registration for non-use in two different circumstances. A trade mark may be removed from the register upon such an application if, at the time the trade mark owner applied for registration, the trade mark owner had no intention in good faith to use the trade mark in Australia (or authorise such use or assign the right to exercise such use) and in fact has not used the trade mark in Australia at all or has not used the trade mark in good faith in Australia at any time up to one month before the application for removal (s 92(4)(a)).[64] A trade mark may also be removed if it has been on the register for a continuous period of three years (up to one month before the removal application) and at no time during that period has the registered owner used the trade mark or used the trade mark in good faith in Australia (s 92(4)(b)). In *E and J Gallo Winery v Lion Nathan Australia*

60    *Imperial Group Ltd v Philip Morris and Co Ltd* [1982] FSR 72.
61    (1953) 71 RPC 23.
62    (1953) 71 RPC 23 at 36.
63    [1982] FSR 72.
64    For a broad interpretation of the concept of "authorised use" within the context of s 92(4)(a) or (4)(b), see *Pioneer Computers Australia Pty Ltd v Pioneer KK* (2009) 176 FCR 300 at 331-332.

*Pty Ltd* the High Court interpreted "in good faith" to mean that the "use must be ordinary and genuine".[65] The High Court also reiterated that for s 92(4)(b) the use must be in the course of trade.[66]

In *Estex Clothing Manufacturers Pty Ltd v Ellis and Goldstein Ltd*[67] the High Court held that the registered owner did not have to personally use the goods in Australia but was required to "project" the goods into the course of trade in Australia:

> [W]hen an overseas manufacturer projects into the course of trade in this country, by means of sales to Australian retail houses, goods bearing his mark and the goods, bearing his mark, are displayed or offered for sale or sold in this country, the use of the mark is that of the manufacturer.[68]

In *E and J Gallo Winery v Lion Nathan Australia Pty Ltd*[69] the Full Federal Court held that simply because a mark was used in the course of trade in Australia this did not amount to a use by the *registered owner*. In this case, the BAREFOOT trade mark had been applied by the registered owner to wines in the United States. Some of these wines had been exported to Germany to a German wholesaler. A company had subsequently bought wines from the German wholesaler and then exported them to Australia where they had been sold and otherwise used in the course of trade. However, this course of trade was not by the registered owner. The registered owner had engaged in a course of trade with the German wholesale company but "objectively considered" there was no course of trade between Gallo and the company selling wines in Australia or any other party in Australia.[70] It is interesting that the court did not rely on the subjective intent of the registered owner but on the course of trade "objectively considered". In this case both the primary judge and the Full Federal Court found that there had been no use of the BAREFOOT trade mark in Australia as there had been no intentional projection of the marked goods into the Australian market.[71] However, the High Court reversed this finding, holding that there is no separate requirement of knowingly projecting goods into the Australian market. The High Court held that there will be use of the trade mark by the owner if the goods arrive in Australia with the trade mark affixed, and remain in the course of trade.[72] With respect to the standard of use that was sufficient to maintain registration, the High Court held:

---

65    (2010) 241 CLR 144 at 168. For further discussion of the good faith requirement, see *Liquideng Farm Supplies Pty Ltd v Liquid Engineering 2003 Pty Ltd* (2009) 175 FCR 26 at 35-37; *Pawlyshyn v Novatech SA* [2010] ATMO 17; *KD Rausch Pty Ltd v Oettinger Brauerie* [2003] ATMO 69.

66    *E and J Gallo Winery v Lion Nathan Australia Pty Ltd* (2010) 241 CLR 144 at 163 (French CJ, Gummow, Crennan and Bell JJ). See also *Rothman's Ltd v WD and HO Wills (Australia) Ltd* (1955) 92 CLR 131 at 138-139.

67    (1967) 116 CLR 254.

68    (1967) 116 CLR 254 at 271.

69    (2009) 175 FCR 386.

70    (2009) 175 FCR 386 at 403.

71    *E and J Gallo Winery v Lion Nathan Australia Pty Ltd* (2008) 77 IPR 69 at 97-100; affirmed on appeal (2009) 175 FCR 386 at 398-403.

72    See *E and J Gallo Winery v Lion Nathan Australia Pty Ltd* (2010) 241 CLR 144 at 165-166 (French CJ, Gummow, Crennan and Bell JJ).

Whilst a single act of sale may not be sufficient to prevent removal, in the case of genuine use, a relatively small amount of use may be sufficient to constitute "ordinary and genuine" use judged by commercial standards.[73]

The use must be use as a trade mark and the onus is on the registered trade mark owner to show such use (s 100(1)(c)). Under s 100(3)(c) the registered owner is taken to have rebutted the allegation if the non-use was due to circumstances which were an obstacle to the use of the mark during that period. The circumstances may have affected traders generally or only the registered owner. In *Pierre Fabre SA v Marion Laboratories Inc*,[74] Marion Industries successfully opposed an application to have its mark cancelled for non-use when it was able to show that, despite its "constant and energetic endeavours"[75] it had so far failed to obtain marketing approval for its drug in Australia. The delay was due to the detailed examination requirements rather than any shortcoming by the company.

### Incapable of distinguishing the applicant's goods or services (s 41)

Under s 41 an application for registration of a trade mark must be rejected if the mark is not capable of distinguishing the applicant's goods and services from the goods and services of another person. This is also a ground for opposition and cancellation. The ground is not concerned with general principles of protecting the commons but, rather, is concerned with regulating relationships between competitors. It raises many of the issues previously considered in passing-off actions.

The Act provides a three-step process for determining whether or not the mark is capable of distinguishing in this manner.

First, the Registrar must take into account whether the mark is "inherently adapted" to distinguish (s 41(3)).

Secondly, if the Registrar is unable to decide the question on this basis then the Registrar must consider not only the extent to which the mark is inherently adapted to distinguish but also the use or intended use of the mark by the applicant and any other circumstances (s 41(5)).

Finally, if the Registrar finds that the mark is not inherently adapted to distinguish goods but that it does in fact distinguish goods and services because the applicant has used the trade mark before the filing date then the mark is treated as capable of distinguishing the goods and services (s 41(6)).

Thus, under the 1995 Act a mark must have some inherent capacity to distinguish unless it has prior acquired distinctiveness. An applicant cannot rely on the fact that the mark may acquire distinctiveness in the future. This scheme is different from the 1955 Act under which every mark had to have some degree of inherent adaptability. Thus, in *Clark Equipment Co v Registrar of Trade Marks*,[76] the fact that the mark MICHIGAN was 100 per cent distinctive on the basis of its acquired adaptability did not make it registrable because it lacked any "inherent

---

73   *E and J Gallo Winery v Lion Nathan Australia Pty Ltd* (2010) 241 CLR 144 at 168-169 (French CJ, Gummow, Crennan and Bell JJ).

74   (1986) 7 IPR 387. See also *Paragon Shoes Pty Ltd v Paragini Distributors (NSW) Pty Ltd* (1988) 13 IPR 323 for the discretionary factors courts may take into account in refusing an application to cancel even where there has been non-use.

75   (1986) 7 IPR 387 at 390.

76   (1964) 111 CLR 511.

adaptability". Today this same mark would be registrable under s 41(6) on the basis of its acquired distinctiveness before registration.

In *Clark Equipment Co v Registrar of Trade Marks*, Kitto J held that a mark was inherently adapted to distinguish if it is not a mark which another person will want or need to use in the course of trade in the goods or services:

> [T]he question of whether a mark is adapted to distinguish [may] be tested by reference to the likelihood that other persons, trading in goods of the relevant kind and being actuated only by proper motives – in the exercise, that is to say, of the common right of the public to make honest use of words forming part of the common heritage, for the sake of the signification which they ordinarily possess – will think of the word and want to use it in connexion with similar goods or in any manner which would infringe a registered trade mark granted in respect of it.[77]

This test emphasises that the test is concerned with trade usage rather than free speech and *Clark Equipment Co v Registrar of Trade Marks* is a good example of the application of the principle. The court held that the mark MICHIGAN used in relation to earth-moving equipment was not inherently capable of distinguishing the goods because Michigan was a well-known manufacturing centre in the United States.[78] It was likely that other dealers would want to use this term in relation to their earth-moving equipment because it was the place of origin of the goods.

In *Burger King Corporation v Registrar of Trade Marks*, Gibbs J held that a mark is "inherently" adapted to distinguish if its ability to distinguish is "something that depends on the nature of the mark itself – it is not something which can be acquired".[79] In *Clark Equipment Co v Registrar of Trade Marks*, Kitto J also stated that it is something which must be considered "quite apart from the effects of registration".[80] Kitto J's test above, which outlines the principles for determining whether a mark is inherently adapted to distinguish, and Gibbs J's comments on the nature of inherent adaptation, have been referred to by several Federal Court and Trade Mark Office decisions under the current Act.[81]

In *Oxford University Press v Registrar of Trade Marks*,[82] a case decided under the 1955 Act, the university argued that because Oxford University Press was so well known no person could really be said to be acting with proper motives if that person applied the name "Oxford" to tapes, films and discs containing information. The court's implied rejection of this argument might be explained

---

77    (1964) 111 CLR 511 at 513-514.
78    Similarly, in *Colorado Group Ltd v Strandbags Group Pty Ltd* (2007) 164 FCR 506, the Full Federal Court held that the word "Colorado" was not inherently adapted to distinguish various items, including bags and backpacks, as it was a State in the United States. For recent consideration of this case in the Federal Court, see *Yarra Valley Dairy Pty Ltd v Lemnos Foods Pty Ltd* (2010) 191 FCR 297 at 308-312.
79    (1973) 128 CLR 417 at 424.
80    (1964) 111 CLR 511 at 513.
81    For example, see the following Full Federal Court decisions: *TGI Friday's Australia Pty Ltd v TGI Friday's Inc* (2000) 100 FCR 358, Wilcox, Kiefel and Emmett JJ at 366; *Kenman Kandy Australia Pty Ltd v Registrar of Trade Marks* (2002) 56 IPR 30, French J at 44-45, Lindgren J at 52-53, Stone J at 66-67; *Colorado Group Ltd v Strandbags Group Pty Ltd* (2007) 164 FCR 506, Kenny J at 515-516, Allsop J at 539.
82    (1990) 17 IPR 509, Jenkinson J at 516-517.

on the basis that a mark's inherent adaptability cannot be tested by reference to its acquired distinctiveness.

It is therefore important to distinguish between inherent adaptability and acquired distinctiveness. As Bennett J explained in *Unilever Australia Ltd v Societe des Produits Nestle SA*:[83]

> The power of advertising may mean that any product other than a pure description may acquire the capacity to distinguish a trader's goods regardless of whether or not it does so at any particular time … Acquired distinctiveness is achieved only because the relevant community has, since the priority date, been educated to see the mark as an indicator of the origin of particular goods. An inherent capacity is an "essential permanent characteristic" and "intrinsic" to the trade mark.

Evidence of use is therefore limited in determining inherent capacity. It is useful in determining that the mark has acquired distinctiveness before the application so as to fall within the s 41(6) provisions for registrability. It may also be used to argue that because it now distinguishes it must have had *some* inherent capacity to distinguish at the time it was registered.

Inherent adaptability to distinguish is not an absolute value and there are varying degrees to which a mark might be said to be inherently adapted to distinguish the applicant's goods and services from the goods and services of another. The level of inherent adaptability may be said to be measured against the likelihood of alternative legitimate trade usage as defined by Kitto J above. A photograph of an applicant who trades in the goods in question or the actual signature of the applicant trader are examples of marks which are very highly inherently adapted to distinguish the goods and services. There would be very little likelihood of another person using those marks in connection with trade in those goods. A photograph of the product, on the other hand, would have little or no inherent adaptability because any trader in those goods would be likely to use such a photograph in the course of trade in relation to those goods. A stylised drawing of an inner spring, for example, was held not to be a "distinctive" device under the 1955 Act.[84] Between these extremes there are many levels of inherent adaptability measured against this likelihood test.

A note to s 41 provides:

> Trade marks that are not inherently adapted to distinguish goods and services are mostly trade marks that consist wholly of a sign that is ordinarily used to indicate:
> (a) the kind, quality, quantity, intended purpose, value, geographical origin, or some other characteristic, of goods or services: or
> (b) the time of production of goods or the rendering of services.

On the other hand, the 1955 Act contained a list of categories that may have been taken to be inherently capable of distinguishing. These were the name of someone represented in a special manner; a signature of a person; an invented word and a word not having direct reference to the character or quality of the goods in respect of which the registration is sought; and not being, in ordinary signification, a geographical or surname.[85]

---

83 (2006) 154 FCR 165 at [29].
84 *Eclipse Sleep Products Inc v Registrar of Trade Marks* (1957) 99 CLR 300.
85 *Trade Marks Act 1955* s 24.

Neither the s 41 note nor the 1955 Act have legislative effect today and reference to these provisions for the purpose of determining inherent adaptability is
by way of guidance only. In addition, the *Trade Marks Office Manual of Practice
and Procedure* Part 22 provides a detailed consideration of the possible inherent adaptability of various types of marks. The Registrar considers two and
three letter marks including initials; monograms; abbreviations and acronyms;
phonetic equivalents of words; punctuated words; composite marks with letters;
words relating to kind, quality, quantity, intended purpose, value and time of
production; foreign words; slogans, phrases and multiple words (TOYS R US is
registrable, "Best for Baby Best for You" is not); marks containing Mister (MISTER
SPEEDY is more inherently adapted than MR DONUT); Doctor (DOCTOR LAWN
is inherently adapted, LAWN DOCTOR is not); Ultra (ULTRA SUEDE and
ULTRBRA have little or no inherent adaptability); and World (SPORTS WORLD
has less inherent adaptability than FUN-WORLD). The Registrar also considers "e" marks, domain names, "Smart" marks, geographical names, surnames,
famous names, signatures, corporate names, numerals, pharmaceutical names
and images. Despite the wide range of marks which may have to be considered
the test for determining inherent adaptability is today standard – that is – what
is the likelihood of alternate legitimate trade usage by the public? We consider
some of these categories in turn.

Names, whether a full name or a surname, are unlikely to be inherently
adapted to distinguish if the name is common. As a matter of practice the
Registrar consults the *Search For Australian Surnames* and, if there are more
than 750 people in Australia with that name, then it is prima facie not considered
inherently adapted to distinguish. If the name is presented in a fancy way it may
decrease the likelihood of another person using the mark in relation to the goods
but the courts traditionally applied this rule strictly under the 1955 Act.[86]

Geographical names are normally not inherently adapted to distinguish if the
name refers to the origin of the goods or has come to be associated with a quality.
Sheffield in relation to steel goods, Michigan in relation to farming machinery,
Champagne in relation to wines or New York in relation to just about anything
are likely to be used by another person in relation to those goods. On the other
hand, a place which is little known in Australia or which is not thought of in relation to those goods might have inherent adaptability and might be registrable.[87]

Emotive phrases such as "Have a break ...";[88] and "Go on ..."[89] have been
refused registration because they lack inherent capacity to distinguish on the
basis that they are mere exhortations to buy and used "purely in an advertising
sense and not in a trade mark sense at all".[90] It has also been suggested that
"Thank God it's Friday" as opposed to "TGI Friday's" would be refused registration on the same grounds.[91]

---

86    See two cases under the *Trade Marks Act 1905* (UK), *Fanfolds Ltd's Application* (1928) 45 RPC
      325 and *Standard Camera Ltd's Application* (1952) 69 RPC 125.
87    See *"Farah" Trade Mark* [1978] FSR 234 and *"Magnolia" Trade Mark* [1897] 2 Ch 371.
88    *Nestle SA's Trade Mark Application (Have a Break)* [2004] FSR 2.
89    *Unilever Australia Ltd v Societe des Produits Nestle SA* (2006) 154 FCR 165.
90    *Unilever Australia Ltd v Societe des Produits Nestle SA* (2006) 154 FCR 165 at [41].
91    *TGI Friday's Australia Pty Ltd v TGI Friday's Inc* (2000) 100 FCR 358.

Invented words or marks are perhaps the simplest way to forge an inherently adapted mark. However, mere spelling variations or phonetic equivalence does not automatically entitle a mark to registration but is assessed in accordance with the general test. Thus, "Rohoe" would today probably not be registrable on the basis of inherent adaptability because of the likelihood of other rotary hoe traders using the word in a legitimate manner in the course of trade.[92]

Descriptive terms are likely to lack the required inherent adaptability. In *Burger King Corporation v Registrar of Trade Marks*,[93] the use of the term WHOPPER in relation to burgers was held to lack the requisite inherent adaptability under the 1955 Act because it was likely that a trader in burgers would use this term in relation to burgers. However, under the 1995 Act both the word WHOPPER and a flame device surrounding the word have been registered as trade marks by application of s 41(6).

A mark is unable to distinguish the applicant's product if, before registration, it has become the common name for a product or services: see *Shredded Wheat Co Ltd v Kellogg Co (GB)*[94] regarding the SHREDDED WHEAT mark. The usage must be tested at the time of registration although an acquired common name may be grounds for cancelling or amending the register under ss 87, 24 and 25 below.

In *Mark Foy's Ltd v Davies Coop and Co Ltd*,[95] Mark Foy's had registered TUB HAPPY as a trade mark in relation to clothing. In infringement proceedings the defendant counter-claimed that the mark was not registrable under the 1955 Act because it made a "direct reference to the character or quality of the goods". Today such a challenge would be mounted under s 41 on the basis that the mark was not capable of distinguishing the goods and in particular that it had no inherent adaptability. The High Court split in its decision. Dixon CJ, in the majority, held that the mark did not make a direct reference to the quality of the goods but merely suggested a "gladsome carelessness *à propos* of the tub".[96] Kitto J, in the minority, held that the mark did make a direct reference to the character of the goods because "'Tub' obviously refers to the wash tub ... 'Happy' as applied to garments and in relation to the wash tub, would readily convey ... that they came out of the wash in a condition of enhanced well-being, as if they actually took delight in the tub".[97] The difference of the two approaches lies in the different ways the two judges treated the requirement of "directness" in that case. Today, however, there is no reference to "directness" and inherent adaptability under s 41 is determined according to the general test.

The question of whether a mark has acquired adaptability to distinguish under s 41(6) is "entirely one of fact".[98] The evidence which may establish such actual distinctiveness was considered by Branson J in *Blount Inc v Registrar of Trade Marks*.[99] The mark in question, OREGON plus an oval device, was held

---

92   Compare the 1905 approach to this question in *Howard Auto-Cultivators Ltd v Webb Industries Pty Ltd* (1946) 72 CLR 175.

93   (1973) 128 CLR 417.

94   *Shredded Wheat Co Ltd v Kellogg Co (GB)* (1940) RPC 137.

95   (1956) 95 CLR 190.

96   (1956) 95 CLR 190 at 195.

97   (1956) 95 CLR 190 at 206.

98   *Blount Inc v Registrar of Trade Marks* (1998) 40 IPR 498, Branson J at 508.

99   (1998) 40 IPR 498 at 509.

to be not inherently capable of distinguishing the manufacturer's wide range of products. However, the judge accepted evidence of use, promotion and affidavit evidence from consumers, wholesalers and retailers to establish that the mark was in fact distinctive. The judge acknowledged that proof of use or promotion does not, without more, demonstrate distinctiveness.[100] "Nevertheless", Branson J continued, "commonsense suggests that significant promotion and use ... will have a tendency to enhance, rather than diminish, the trade mark's capacity to distinguish". Conversely, absence of promotion and use may be significant in establishing lack of distinctiveness. In relation to affidavit evidence the judge noted that the evidence came from a pool of people having trade contacts with the applicant. However, the affidavits did refer to broader consumer responses to the mark and "it is not ... necessary as a matter of law for a statistically sound market survey to be undertaken".[101]

## Applying these tests to shape and colour signs

Since the extension of trade marks to include colour, shape and scent the courts have emphasised that the traditional test for inherent adaptability taken from *Clark Equipment Co v Registrar of Trade Marks* (1964)[102] should be applied: see *Kenman Kandy Australia Pty Ltd v Registrar of Trade Marks*[103] regarding shapes and *Philmac Pty Ltd v Registrar of Trade Marks*[104] regarding colour. Thus, in *Kenman Kandy* the court acknowledged that a shape may lack inherent adaptability if a trade competitor would be likely to want to use the mark because it was part of the function or nature of the product itself. The court gave *Koninklijke Philips Electronics NV v Remington Products Australia Pty Ltd*[105] as an example of such a case, where the triple round head of an electric shaver was held to be part of its function and therefore incapable of distinguishing the applicant's product. Similarly in *Mayne Industries Pty Ltd v Advanced Engineering Group Pty Ltd*,[106] a case involving an "S" shaped "fence dropper", Greenwood J in the Federal Court held that there had been no use of the shape as a trade mark because of the substantial functional elements of the goods in question.[107] However, in *Global Brand Marketing Inc v YD Pty Ltd*,[108] a case involving trade mark use of a mark consisting of the shape of a shoe with a distinctive pattern on the sole, Sundberg J held that there was trade mark infringement by the defendant's use of a similar pattern on the sole of its shoe as the soles acted as a badge of origin indicating a

---

100  (1998) 40 IPR 498 at 509, endorsing *British Sugar plc v James Robertson and Sons Ltd* [1966] RPC 281 at 286 and 302.

101  (1998) 40 IPR 498 at 509.

102  (1964) 111 CLR 511.

103  (2002) 56 IPR 30.

104  (2002) 56 IPR 452.

105  (2002) 177 ALR 167.

106  (2008) 166 FCR 312.

107  The following cases also suggest a cautionary approach when deciding the issue of whether a shape mark has been used as a trade mark in the context of applications for interlocutory injunctions: *Sebel Furniture Ltd v Acoustic and Felts Pty Ltd* (2009) 80 IPR 244; *Outdoor Power Products Pty Ltd v Silvan Australia Pty Ltd* [2005] FCA 1696.

108  (2008) 76 IPR 161.

connection in the course of trade between the goods.[109] In *Coca-Cola Co v All-Fect Distributors Ltd*,[110] the Full Federal Court held that the defendant's marketing and sale of a cola-flavoured confectionery, which was shaped like the contour glass bottle in which Coca-Cola was traditionally sold and which had the word "Cola" inscribed on it, infringed Coca-Cola's registered trade mark (a contour drawing of the glass bottle in which Coca-Cola was sold). The Full Court held that there had been use as a trade mark as the defendant had used the features of the confectionery so as to indicate the origin of the confectionery, and further that the confectionery was likely to cause consumers to wonder whether it might be the case that the confectionery came from the same source as Coca-Cola.[111]

In *Re Application by Chocolaterie Guylian NV*[112] the delegate of the Registrar of Trade Marks rejected the application for registration of a shell shape in relation to chocolates on the basis that the shape was not inherently adapted to distinguish chocolates because it was a well-known ordinary shape in the chocolate trade which other chocolate makers would like to use to increase their market appeal. In addition, there was no evidence of prior use of the shape so the delegate also rejected the application for registration under s 41(6) on the basis of acquired distinctiveness through prior use. Indeed, in several cases the Trade Marks Office has rejected evidence that the use of a shape or colour of goods or their packaging was use as a trade mark, particularly where the sign served a functional purpose.[113]

In *Chocolaterie Guylian NV v Registrar of Trade Marks*,[114] a later case involving *Guylian* seahorse shaped chocolates, Sundberg J in the Federal Court found that one of the factors which resulted in the mark not acquiring distinctiveness was that the evidence illustrated that the shape had been simply used to attract consumers and provide an example of the type of goods sold:

> The evidence is that other traders were selling sea shell chocolates for some time before the priority date. In that context, it does not seem to me likely that consumers would conceive of the seahorse shape on Guylian's boxes as a trade mark, so much as simply an example of the novelty shapes that Guylian manufactures. I also note that there is a lack of precision in the evidence as to the timing, duration and location of much of the packaging, advertising and point of sale material. Most of the evidence (in particular, the

---

109 For further explanation of Sundberg J's reasoning, see (2008) 76 IPR 161 at 176.

110 (1999) 96 FCR 107.

111 113(1999) 96 FCR 107 at 121-123.

112 (1999) 46 IPR 201.

113 For example, see: *Application by Multix Pty Ltd* (2004) 64 IPR 128; *Effem Foods v Nestle SA* [2008] ATMO 55 (but reversed on appeal, see *Mars Australia Pty Ltd (formerly called Effem Foods Pty Ltd) (ACN 008 454 313) v Société des Produits Nestlé SA* (2010) 86 IPR 581); *Re Application by August Storck KG* (2003) 57 IPR 242; *Re Application by Cadbury Ltd* (2002) 55 IPR 561; *Re Application by Conewich Enterprises Ltd Partnership* (2002) 59 IPR 558; *Re Application By Dualit Ltd (Toaster Shapes)* (2001) 52 IPR 593; *Re Application by Effem Foods Pty Ltd* (2000) 49 IPR 139; *Re Application by Luk Lamellen Und Kupplungsbau Beteiligungs KG* (2003) 57 IPR 248; *Re Chocolaterie Guylian NV* [2007] ATMO 30; *Saramar LLC* [2000] ATMO 117. In *Societe Des Produits Nestle SA v Aldi Stores (a Limited Partnership)* [2010] FCA 218, a case where the opposition was withdrawn and which involved chocolate-coated confectionery bars, Nicholas J in the Federal Court set aside a Trade Marks Office decision which found that consumers had only become educated to the function of the shape of the chocolate-coated bars as opposed to its use as a trade mark.

114 (2009) 180 FCR 60.

sales sheets, magazine catalogues and website extract) appeared to be quite recent, in the two to three years leading up to the priority date and beyond. Absent, for example, was any evidence about how the seahorse shape had been used between the time it entered the market in 1980 and the end of the 1990s. It is not at all clear what use, in a trade mark sense, was made of the seahorse shape by Guylian over that period.[115]

In *Philmac Pty Ltd v Registrar of Trade Marks*,[116] Mansfield J identified four situations where a colour might be held to lack inherent adaptability within the *Clarke Equipment* test – these are when the colour serves a utilitarian function, for example, as a light reflector or heat absorber; where the colour has a recognised meaning such as red for danger or green for environmentalism; and where the colour has an economic purpose, for example, where it is the naturally occurring colour of the product. Finally, a colour may lack inherent adaptability where there is a proven competitive need for use of colour and an honest trader would naturally think of that colour in relation to those goods and services – terracotta in relation to piping, beech in relation to wood, for example. In this last case the court might have regard to the risk of "colour depletion".[117] Furthermore, in determining whether the mark had in fact acquired distinctiveness in order to be registrable under s 41(6) Mansfield J said that two issues needed to be addressed. First, had the colour been used "as a trade mark" before application? Second, if it had, had it acquired distinctiveness having regard to the evidence of its use as a trade mark?

In *Philmac*,[118] the court held that not only had the colour terracotta been used as a trade mark before registration but that the evidence showed that it had acquired the necessary distinctiveness before that date as a result of this use. Similarly, in *Mars Australia Pty Ltd (formerly called Effem Foods Pty Ltd) (ACN 008 454 313) v Société des Produits Nestlé SA*,[119] a case involving the registration of the colour purple for pet food, Bennett J reversed the earlier decision of the Trade Marks Office and accepted that there was sufficient evidence to show that the mark had acquired distinctiveness.[120] In the lengthy litigation between Cadbury and Darrell Lea, in which Cadbury claimed an exclusive right to use the colour purple in relation to the sale and marketing of chocolate, the Trade Marks Office finally accepted in part that the colour purple had acquired distinctiveness in relation to block chocolate and boxed chocolate.[121] By contrast, in *Woolworths Ltd v BP plc (No 2)*[122] the fact that survey evidence indicated that consumers

---

115 (2009) 180 FCR 60 at 92-93.
116 (2002) 56 IPR 452.
117 (2002) 56 IPR 452 at 472.
118 *Philmac Pty Ltd v Registrar of Trade Marks* (2002) 56 IPR 452.
119 (2010) 86 IPR 581.
120 (2010) 86 IPR 581 at 587-588. The decision of the delegate of the Registrar of Trade Marks found that although there was evidence of consumer education, it was not sufficient to overcome the s 41(6) objection: see *Effem Foods v Nestle SA* [2008] ATMO 55. For other Trade Marks Office decisions in which single colour trade marks have been held to fall under s 41(6), see: *Re Application by Veuve Clicquot Ponsardin, Maison Fondée En 1772* (1999) 45 IPR 525 (orange for wine and champagne); *Flower Carpet Pty Ltd* [2001] ATMO 35 (pink for flower pots); *Re Application by Cadbury Ltd* (2002) 55 IPR 561 (purple for chocolate).
121 See *Darrell Lea Chocolate Shops Pty Ltd v Cadbury Ltd* (2006) 69 IPR 386. For the final case in this protracted litigation, see *Cadbury Schweppes Pty Ltd v Darrell Lea Chocolate Shops Pty Ltd (No 8)* (2008) 75 IPR 557, which involved consideration by Heerey J in the Federal Court of passing-off and consumer protection legislation.
122 (2006) 154 FCR 97.

"associated" the colour green with BP stations was not sufficient to allow registration under s 41(6). In that case the Full Federal Court held that the colour green had not been used as a trade mark before registration, rather it was the colours green and yellow together that had been used in this way.

## Substantially identical or deceptively similar to another trade mark (ss 44 and 60)

Subject to the discretions mentioned below, s 44 requires the Registrar to reject an application for a trade mark that is substantially identical with or deceptively similar to another registered trade mark registered in relation to "similar" or "closely related" goods and services. If the applicant's mark is being registered in relation to goods then the mark will be compared to marks with an earlier priority date which are registered for "similar" goods or "closely related" services (s 44(1)). If the applicant's mark is being registered in relation to services it will be compared to marks with an earlier priority date which are registered in relation to "similar" services and "closely related" goods (s 44(2)). Substantial identity or deceptive similarity is also a ground for opposition and rectification.

The Registrar has a discretion not to reject an application on this ground if satisfied that there has been an "honest concurrent user" of the marks or other circumstance. In this case the Registrar may impose conditions on the applicant's trade mark (s 44(3)). The Registrar may not reject an application on this ground if satisfied that the applicant had used the mark continuously up to the priority date of the other registered mark (s 44(4)).

### Similar goods and services and closely related goods and services

Goods and services are "similar" if they are the "same as the other" goods or services or "if they are of the same description" as the other goods and services (s 14). In *Southern Cross Refrigerating Co v Toowoomba Foundry Pty Ltd*,[123] the High Court held that the question was not determined by reference to the classifications under the legislation but was essentially a question of fact to be determined by reference to the nature of the goods, the use of the goods and the trade channels through which they were bought and sold.[124] In that case, the court held that refrigerators were not the same as or of the same description as windmills and pumps. On the other hand, in *McCormick and Co Inc v McCormick*,[125] Kenny J held that instant batter on the one hand and spices, condiments, seasonings and essences for flavouring food on the other hand were similar goods. In coming to this decision the judge relied on expert evidence of chefs that the purpose of battering was to enhance the flavour of food.

The question of whether goods are "closely related" to a particular service is usually decided by reference to their functional relationship. French J in *Registrar of Trade Marks v Woolworths Ltd*[126] said:

---

123 (1954) 91 CLR 592.
124 (1954) 91 CLR 592 at 606, citing *Jellinek's Application* (1946) 63 RPC 59.
125 (2000) 51 IPR 102.
126 (1999) 45 IPR 411.

The relationship may, and perhaps in most cases will, be defined by the function of the service with respect to the goods. Services which provide for the installation, operation, maintenance or repair of goods are likely to be treated as closely related to them.[127]

French J referred to television sets and television repair services, tailoring and curtain sales and perhaps fish and a fish restaurant as examples of closely related goods and services. A supermarket and the goods sold in it were held not to be closely related in *Registrar of Trade Marks v Woolworths Ltd*,[128] although this decision was criticised by the minority for failing to give due weight to the phenomena of generic name-brand goods.

Section 60 provides that registration may also be opposed on the ground that the mark is substantially identical with or deceptively similar to a trade mark which before the priority date had acquired a reputation in Australia and, because of that reputation, the use of the mark would be likely to deceive or confuse.[129] The reputation must be in respect to the goods and services for which the applicant was seeking registration. This section significantly enlarges the scope of the proceedings in so far as the mark does not need to be registered in relation to these goods and services.

### Substantial identity and deceptive similarity

In *Shell Co of Australia Ltd v Esso Standard Oil (Australia) Ltd*,[130] Windeyer J, in the High Court, drew a distinction between "substantial identity" and "deceptive similarity" in the context of infringement proceedings:

> In considering whether marks are substantially identical they should, I think, be compared side by side, their similarities and differences noted and the importance of these assessed having regard to the essential features of the registered trade mark and the total impression of resemblance or dissimilarity that emerges from the comparison ... On the question of deceptive similarity, a different comparison must be made ... The marks are not now to be looked at side by side. The issue is not abstract similarity but deceptive similarity.[131]

In *Australian Woollen Mills Ltd v FS Walton & Co Ltd*,[132] the High Court held that the question of deceptive similarity is determined by reference to the impression or recollection of the mark which a viewer would carry away and retain and the marks "should not be compared side by side".[133] In the words of French J in *Registrar of Trade Marks v Woolworths Ltd*:[134]

---

127    (1999) 45 IPR 411 at 424.

128    (1999) 45 IPR 411.

129    The general standard for deception and confusion is the same for the purposes of ss 44 and 60. For example, see *Toddler Kindy Gymbaroo Pty Ltd v Gymboree Pty Ltd* (2000) 100 FCR 166 at 191-193; *Pfizer Products Inc v Karam* [2006] FCA 1663 at [47]; *Kimberly-Clark Worldwide Inc v Goulimis* (2008) 253 ALR 76 at 86-87.

130    (1963) 109 CLR 407.

131    (1963) 109 CLR 407 at 414. This issue was not considered on appeal and the distinction is generally applied in registration proceedings.

132    (1937) 58 CLR 641 at 658. Further, "Evidence of actual cases of deception, if forthcoming, is of great weight" (at 658). On the relevance of evidence, see also *Bing!Software Pty Ltd v Bing Technologies Pty Ltd (No 1)* (2008) 79 IPR 454; *Wingate Marketing Pty Ltd v Levi Strauss and Co* (1994) 28 IPR 193 at 226, 231.

133    (1937) 58 CLR 641 at 658.

134    (1999) 45 IPR 411.

It requires assessment of the effect of the challenged mark upon the minds of potential customers. Impression or recollection taken away from the point at which the challenged mark is observed will be the basis of any belief about a connection between the new and the old marks. The effect of spoken description must be considered. What confusion or deception may be expected is to be based upon the behaviour of ordinary people. As potential buyers of goods they are not to be credited with high perception or habitual caution. Exceptional carelessness or stupidity may be disregarded. The question ultimately is not susceptible of much discussion.[135]

A trade mark is taken to be "deceptively similar" to another trade mark if "it is likely to deceive or cause confusion" (s 10). The question of whether the relevant person is likely to be deceived or confused is determined according to Kitto J's "wonderment" test and the principles set out in *Southern Cross Refrigerating Co v Toowoomba Foundry Pty Ltd*:[136]

> While a mere possibility of confusion is not enough – for there must be a real, tangible danger of its occurring – it is sufficient if the result of the user of the mark will be that a number of persons will be caused to wonder whether it might not be the case that the two products come from the same source. It is enough if a reasonable person entertains a reasonable doubt.[137]

In that case Toowoomba Foundry Pty Ltd, which had a trade mark registered in relation to well-drilling and boring machinery, milking machines, engines and windmills, opposed the registration of Southern Cross's trade mark in relation to gas and electrical refrigerators. They opposed the application on the basis that the mark was deceptively similar or substantially identical to their marks in respect of similar or related goods. They also opposed on the basis that the mark was likely to deceive or cause confusion. They failed on the first ground because the goods were not of the same description but they succeeded on the second ground. The wonderment test, however, applies in relation to both grounds.

The likely deception or confusion must be determined by reference to the prospective or potential customers for the goods and services; the deception or confusion need not extend up to the point of sale; it must be considered taking all the surrounding circumstances into account and is determined at the date of the application for registration.[138] There is no need to establish actual confusion on the part of potential customers. Kitto J's test for likely deception or confusion was approved on appeal to the Full Bench of the High Court.

The principles have been accepted in relation to s 44 and s 60 actions under the 1995 Act and, in *Registrar of Trade Marks v Woolworths Ltd*,[139] French J noted that the use of the word "likely" does not import a requirement that it be more probable than not that the mark has that effect.

Deception or confusion may arise because of phonetic similarity between the signs (Bali Bras and Berlei Bras),[140] because of visual similarity between the signs

---

135 (1999) 45 IPR 411 at 427.
136 (1954) 91 CLR 592.
137 (1954) 91 CLR 592 at 595.
138 *Southern Cross Refrigerating Co v Toowoomba Foundry Pty Ltd* (1954) 91 CLR 592 at 595.
139 (1999) 45 IPR 411.
140 *Berlei Hestia Industries Ltd v Bali Co Inc* (1973) 129 CLR 353. But compare *Deeko Australia Pty Ltd v Decor Corporation Pty Ltd* (1988) 11 IPR 531.

or because of similarity in the idea between the signs (for example, if both marks showed two men striving in athletic events).[141]

All the circumstances of the possible sale and dealing with the goods or services may be taken into account in determining whether there is deceptive similarity (*Southern Cross Refrigerating Co v Toowoomba Foundry Pty Ltd*[142]). This includes the types of shops in which the goods or services are provided and how they will be displayed; whether customers have an opportunity to examine the goods; whether orders are likely to be made over the phone where aural similarity would be more important or in writing when visual similarity would be more important. In *Registrar of Trade Marks v Woolworths*,[143] in a split decision, the Full Federal Court held that the notoriety of the applicant could be taken into account when assessing deceptive similarity. In that case the applicant's mark, "Woolworths Metro", was held not to be deceptively similar to the registered mark "Metro" on the ground that Woolworths was so well known that this visual and aural aspect of the sign would be its most significant aspect. Similarly, in *Mars Australia Pty Ltd v Sweet Rewards Pty Ltd*,[144] Perram J held that the defendant's "Malt Balls" were used descriptively, and were not deceptively similar to the registered "MALTESERS" trade mark as: "consumers are so familiar with Maltesers that they could not possibly be confused by the Malt Balls packaging – more formally, there is no likelihood of imperfect recollection by them of the Maltesers mark leading to confusion".[145]

The question of deception or confusion is determined not by reference to the actual use of the mark but by reference to the possible use of the mark. Thus, in *Berlei Hestia Industries Ltd v Bali Co Inc*,[146] the fact that Berlei bras were inexpensive and mass produced and sold in different types of shops and that Bali Bras were "speciality items" did not prevent the likely deceptive similarity because Bali Bras could extend their trade to the mass-produced market if they so desired.

In *Campomar Socieda, Limitada v Nike International Ltd*,[147] the High Court held that even in rectification proceedings the date for assessing the likely deception and confusion was the date of the original application for registration of the mark, not the date of the application for rectification. That case was decided in 1994. Campomar Socieda Limitada started to market a "sports perfume" in Australia in 1993. The perfume was called NIKE. Campomar Socieda had applied for registration of the mark in 1986 and it was registered without opposition in 1989. Campomar had held trade marks for perfume in other jurisdictions since 1940. Nike International Ltd, the owner of the trade mark NIKE which was registered in Australia in relation to athletic shoes and sports wear, applied to have Campomar Socieda Limitada's trade mark NIKE expunged from the

---

141  *Jafferjee v Scarlett* (1937) 57 CLR 115. See also *Dial and Sangel Pty Ltd v Sagitur Services Systems Pty Ltd* (1990) 96 ALR 181.

142  (1954) 91 CLR 592.

143  (1999) 45 IPR 411.

144  (2009) 81 IPR 354 at 376.

145  The trial decision of Perram J was unanimously affirmed on appeal by the Full Federal Court, see *Mars Australia Pty Ltd v Sweet Rewards Pty Ltd* (2009) 84 IPR 12.

146  (1973) 129 CLR 353.

147  (2000) 202 CLR 45.

register on the basis that it was deceptive and confusing. To the surprise of many, Nike International failed in its application under the *Trade Marks Act 1955* even though the High Court accepted that the Spanish company might have been "cashing in" on the fame of the NIKE mark and that there may have been some likelihood of consumer confusion today.[148]

In rejecting Nike's argument that a registration should be cancelled at any time during its life if it became deceptive or confusing the High Court said that Nike's argument was based on a misunderstanding. Nike International's argument, it said, was founded on the "proposition that the supreme, or at least, predominant interest manifested in the 1955 Act is the maintenance of the integrity of the Register against any apparent condonation of misleading or deceptive practices". The court noted that trade mark law is "more complex than this proposition would suggest" and the Act "struck a balance between competing interests".[149] The court identified some of these interests. The consumer has an interest in relying on the trade mark as a badge of origin but the registered owner has an interest in treating the trade mark as a form of valuable property which might be assigned or licensed. There may be some conflict if owners of similar registered trade marks both wish to extend their trade into other areas. The owner of a large well-known trade mark may fear the "dilution" of the value of that mark if another person, no matter how small or non-competitive, were to use it. At the same time, a small trader may fear that a large trader, through the power of advertising, could "swamp" a small trader's mark, even if that small trader had been using it for years. There may be a conflict between the long-term user of an unregistered mark and the registered owner of a trade mark. There may be competing public interests between the desire to prevent restrictive trade practices and the desire to maintain the value of a trade mark.

The NIKE decision was made under the *Trade Marks Act 1955*. As you read recent cases you may like to consider the weight given by different courts to these interests and whether the balance is struck differently in the current Act.

## Likely to deceive or cause confusion (s 43)

Section 43 provides that an application for registration of a trade mark with respect to particular goods and services must be rejected:

> if, because of some connotation that the trade mark or a sign contained in the trade mark has, the use of the trade mark in relation to those goods or services would be likely to deceive or cause confusion.

The test for determining whether the mark is likely to deceive or confuse is Kitto J's "wonderment test" and principles from *Southern Cross Refrigerating Co v Toowoomba Foundry Pty Ltd*.[150]

The *Macquarie Dictionary* defines "connotation" as "that which is connoted; secondary implied or associated meanings (as distinguished from *denotation*): *the word 'bum' has connotations of vulgarity*". A generic computer thesaurus gives

---

148  Nike International did, however, succeed in its two actions of passing off and misleading and deceptive conduct, under the former s 52 of the *Trade Practices Act 1974*.

149  (2000) 202 CLR 45 at 65.

150  (1954) 91 CLR 592 at 595.

the following synonyms: nuance, suggestion, implication, association, subtext, undertone or overtone. "Denotation" is defined by the *Macquarie Dictionary* as, inter alia, "the meaning of a term when it identifies something by naming it (distinguished from *connotation*)".

The use of the term "connotation", which is new to the 1995 Act, effectively separates s 43 (confusing or deceptive) from s 44 (substantial identity and deceptive similarity) as grounds to reject, oppose or cancel the registration of the mark. Section 44 excludes marks not because of something inherent in or suggested by the mark but because of some actual or external similarity between the mark and another mark. Section 43, on the other hand, excludes only those marks which, because of something inherent in the mark or which is suggested by the mark itself, is likely to cause confusion or deception. Section 43 is therefore not a ground to exclude a mark on the basis of its similarity with another mark. Note that the 1955 Act did not distinguish between these two grounds in the same way and in cases where there was similarity between two signs it was usual to take action under both s 28(2) (likely to deceive or cause confusion) and s 33 (substantial identity and deceptive similarity) of the 1955 Act.

The use of the term "connotation" may also partially distinguish s 43 from s 41 (those marks not capable of distinguishing goods and services) on the basis that s 43 excludes marks because of the connotation of the sign whilst s 41 excludes marks because of their denotative qualities (that is, they describe something or name something other than the goods or services in question). However, as *Executors of the Estate of Diana, Princess of Wales v Masterson*[151] (extracted below) illustrates, this distinction is not clear cut.

The Trade Marks Office Manual notes specific instances of signs that are likely to be refused registration under s 43.[152] These are signs that are likely to cause deception or confusion in regard to:

- geographical indications for wine;
- plant variety names;
- International Non-Proprietary Names (generic names for pharmaceutical substances) and INN stems; and
- marks suggesting endorsement, license or approval.

Examples of trade marks which have been held to be deceptive or confusing are the ORLWOOLA mark in relation to clothes,[153] YANX in relation to cigarettes[154] and MICKEY MOUSE in relation to radios.[155]

In establishing a s 43 case it is necessary for the opponent to identify the likely confusion or deception. Thus, in the ORLWOOLA[156] case, the matter of confusion was the quality of the clothes, in the YANX[157] case the deception arose from the false geographical reference and in the MICKEY MOUSE[158] case the

---

151  (2001) 52 IPR 264.
152  *Trade Marks Office Manual of Practice and Procedure*, Part 29 para 4.
153  *Re Trade Mark "Orlwoola"* (1990) 26 RPC 850.
154  *Ex parte Amalgamated Tobacco Corp Ltd* (1951) 82 CLR 199.
155  *Radio Corporation Pty Ltd v Disney* (1937) 57 CLR 448.
156  *Re Trade Mark "Orlwoola"* (1990) 26 RPC 850.
157  *Ex parte Amalgamated Tobacco Corp Ltd* (1951) 82 CLR 199.
158  *Radio Corporation Pty Ltd v Disney* (1937) 57 CLR.

confusion or deception arose from the false representation of a connection between the applicant and the Disney company and Walt Disney himself.[159]

In *Executors of the Estate of Diana, Princess of Wales v Masterson*,[160] the mark in question was an ornate device in the shape of a wreath with the words DIANA'S LEGACY IN ROSES in cursive script around the bottom of the device and an ornate "D" in the centre of the device. The applicant sought to register the mark in relation to live roses. The Hearing Officer found that there was no evidence that the public, at least in Australia, believed that the estate of the Princess entered into commercial merchandising agreements in relation to words and images associated with the late princess and therefore the use of the mark in Australia was not likely to deceive or confuse the Australian public. He held that the case could be distinguished both from the passing-off cases such as the Hogan cases[161] and from the MICKEY MOUSE case.[162] On the first point he said that a member of the public would expect an actor, personality or sports star to commercialise his or her image but one would not expect such a thing from a princess. In relation to the MICKEY MOUSE case he said that, while MICKEY was invented and created by Disney and formed part of Disney's intellectual property, there was no evidence that the Princess was in this relationship with the estate. This is a circular argument, however, and does not appear to take the distinction any further.[163]

## Common description for product or service (ss 24, 25 and 87)

The Act provides a special mechanism for cancelling or amending a registration in two situations where a trade mark has become, post registration, the common name for a product or service.

Section 24 applies where a trade mark contains a sign that, after the date of registration, becomes generally accepted within the relevant trade as the sign that describes or names an article, substance or service. Section 25 applies where a registered trade mark contains a sign that describes or is the name of an article, substance or service which has been exploited or used under a patent; the patent has expired or ceased for at least two years and the sign is the only commonly known way to describe or identify the article, substance or service.

Under s 87 a prescribed court, on the application by an aggrieved person, may order the cancellation or amendment of the register in any cases where ss 24 or 25 apply. The court has a discretion to allow the trade mark to remain on the register subject to any limitations or conditions. These provisions are not absolutely necessary because, as we shall see in the next chapter, ss 24 and 25 also operate to restrict the exclusive rights of the trade mark owner.

---

159  Latham CJ, Rich and McTiernan JJ in the majority in *Radio Corporation Pty Ltd v Disney* (1937) 57 CLR 448.
160  (2001) 52 IPR 264.
161  *Hogan v Koala Dundee Pty Ltd* (1988) 83 ALR 187; *Pacific Dunlop Ltd v Hogan* (1989) 14 IPR 398.
162  *Radio Corporation Pty Ltd v Disney* (1937) 57 CLR 448.
163  (2001) 52 IPR 264 at 273. Under the *Trade Marks Act 1955* s 30 an applicant for a mark consisting of the name or image of a famous person, alive or dead, could be required to provide a consent from the person or the person's estate to use that name or image. There is no similar requirement under the 1995 Act but, as a matter of practice, the Registrar will still request such a consent.

Section 24 may not apply when the general use of the name has arisen because the trade mark owner has widely licensed the use of the trade mark. In *Australian Co-operative Foods v Norco*,[164] Bryson J thought that, to the contrary, the wide use of licensing agreements for use of the mark LITE WHITE in relation to milk products was evidence that the name was not considered a generally accepted description or name for the product but was instead regarded as a form of personal protected property. Conversely, the section will apply where the trade mark owner has failed to protect the mark. In the case of patented articles, substances or services s 25 will apply at least where the name refers to a new substance which is known by no other name: see *James A Jobling and Co Ltd v James McEwan and Co Pty Ltd*[165] regarding the use of the name PYREX and *Linoleum Manufacturing Co v Nairn*[166] regarding LINOLEUM.

The common name grounds are very narrow and, in particular, s 24 only applies if the trade mark became the common description after registration and s 25 only applies once a patent has expired or ceased. These limitations are perhaps surprising for lay people. In the public debate over the registration of the UGG mark in respect of sheep skin boots many lay commentators stressed that UGG boots may have been a common name for pilots' boots in the Second World War, before any mark was registered. This precludes the s 24 grounds being made out but, if it can be established that UGG was the commonly accepted name for the boots before registration, then the mark could be challenged on the basis that it is incapable of distinguishing the applicant's product under s 41.

### Scandalous or contrary to law (s 42)

There have been few cases relating to the rejection of a trade mark on the basis that it is scandalous or contrary to law. The Trade Marks Office Manual has adopted the *Macquarie Dictionary* definition of "scandalous" as meaning "disgraceful to reputation; shameful or shocking", or "defamatory or libellous, as a speech or writing".[167] In this context trade marks incorporating the words "Jesus" for jeans[168] and "Mecca"[169] and "Hallelujah"[170] in relation to women's clothing have been rejected on the ground that they are scandalous. On the other hand, the use of the word "Quaker" in relation to alcohol has been said obiter not to be scandalous.[171] This was because there was no law against drinking and that not even the Quakers were total teetotallers. The question of whether the material is scandalous must be determined at the time of application.[172]

---

164 [1999] NSWSC 274. For other cases where evidence that the sign had become generally accepted was held to be insufficient, see *Alcon Inc v Bausch and Lomb (Australia) Pty Ltd* (2009) 83 IPR 210 at 234; *Mantra Group Pty Ltd v Tailly Pty Ltd (No 2)* (2010) 183 FCR 450 at 477-479.
165 [1933] VLR 168.
166 (1878) 7 Ch 834.
167 *Trade Marks Office Manual of Practice and Procedure*, Part 30 para 2.
168 *Maglificio Calzifico Torinese SPA's Application* (1982) 37 AOJP 1764.
169 *Mecca* (1955) 25 AOJP 938.
170 *Hallelujah Trade Mark* [1976] RPC 605.
171 *Re Ellis and Co's Trade Mark* (1904) 21 RPC 617.
172 *Hallelujah Trade Mark* [1976] RPC 605 at 607.

A trade mark is contrary to law if the use of the mark is proscribed by another statute or its use would constitute a breach of another person's rights. There are a number of statutes which proscribe the use of certain marks as trade marks including the *Advance Australia Logo Protection Act 1984*[173] and the *Defence Act 1903*.[174]

In *Advantage Rent-A-Car v Advantage Car Rental Pty Ltd*,[175] the Full Federal Court rejected an argument by the Registrar that only the courts and not the Registrar could determine this question in relation to "more complex" situations such as breach of copyright. In that case the court held that the trade mark application constituted an infringement of the copyright in another trader's trade mark as an artistic work and therefore should have been rejected on the basis that it was contrary to law.

## False geographical indication (s 61)

A false geographical indication is likely to deceive or confuse under s 43 however, the fact that a mark contains a false geographical indication is also a separate ground for opposition under s 61. The *Australian Wine and Brandy Corporation Act 1980* (which was passed in accordance with Australia's international TRIPS obligations) governs the labelling, sale, import and export of grape products with a false description or presentation. Any false geographical indication in relation to grape products might therefore also render the mark unregistrable under s 42.

The application of s 61 relating to geographical indications was considered in detail by Bennett J in *Bavaria NV v Bayerischer Brauerbund eV*.[176] The case involved a trade mark comprising a medallion/crest with the words "Bavaria" across the middle and "Holland" and "Beer" beneath. The application was opposed by the Bavarian Brewery Association (Bayerischer Brauerbund eV, "BBA") which represented Bavarian beer makers. The term Bavarian beer had traditionally been associated with a method of beer making which had spread throughout Europe in the 19th century. The *Trade Mark Act s* 6 defines a geographical indication in relation to goods to mean:

> a sign that identifies the goods as originating in a country, or in a region or locality in that country, where a given quality, reputation or other characteristic of the goods is essentially attributable to their geographical origin.

Bennett J held that a geographical indication must be formally recognised and that prior long term use short of such formal recognition is insufficient.[177] The recognition must also extend to the characteristics, as required under s 6.

In this case Bennett J found that that LADY BAVAIA and BAYERISCHES BIER were recognised geographical indications. The evidence in support of this was the registration by the BBA of a trademark LADY BAVARIA with the words GENUINE BAVARIAN BEER which indicated a connection between the mark

---

173  See *Re Kelly* (1987) 8 IPR 667.
174  For a list of such Acts, see the *Trade Marks Office Manual of Practice and Procedure*, Part 30 Annex A1.
175  (2001) 52 IPR 24.
176  (2009) 177 FCR 300.
177  (2009) 177 FCR 300 at 327.

and the characteristics and origin of the goods; the registration of BAYERISCHES BIER ("Bavarian Beer") by the German Government under Council Regulation (EC) 1347/2001 as a protected geographical indication (PIG); and the existence of bi-lateral treaties between Germany and other states (not including Australia) regarding the use of BAYERISCHES BIER. However, Bennett J held that the trade mark in question did not actually contain or consist of either of these signs as required by s 61. We have included an extract of Bennett J's reasoning as this is one of the few cases dealing directly with this issue.

## Proscribed signs (s 39)

Section 18 provides that regulations may proscribe certain signs. The trade marks proscribed by the regulations are a rather eclectic group. They are words such as "Patent", "By Royal Letters Patent", "Copyright" and their related symbols; the words "To counterfeit this is a forgery"; a representation of the Arms, flag or seal of the Commonwealth, a State or Territory or Australian town; marks notified by the International Union for the Protection of Industrial Property; the words "Austrade", "C.E.S", "Olympic Champion", "Repatriation", "Returned Airman, Soldier or Sailor".[178] The regulations also set down the grounds for rejection of an international application under the Madrid Protocol.[179]

## Graphic representation (s 40)

A trade mark must be able to be represented graphically. Although most of the registrable signs are by nature visual, and therefore capable of being represented graphically, problems can arise in relation to sound and scent trade marks. The *Trade Marks Office Manual* assumes that a sensory trade mark is represented graphically by words (and gives as an example "CLIP, CLOP, MOO").[180] The Manual requires that this graphic representation should be lodged with a precise and accurate description of the trade mark (for example, "The trade mark consists of the sound of two steps taken by a cow on pavement, followed by the sound of a cow mooing").[181] If the trade mark consists of a tune the tune should be represented graphically by the score of the tune and a description should also be lodged (for example, "The trade mark is a sound mark. It comprises the sound of dogs barking to the traditional tune 'Greensleeves' as rendered in the audio tape accompanying the application").[182] Similarly, the Manual assumes that a scent is represented graphically if it is written in words ("the scent of apple blossoms") together with a description ("The application is a scent mark, consisting of the smell of apple blossoms applied to car tyres").[183] The Manual states that the graphical representation must be in a form that conveys information to the ordinary person, and expressly excludes the use of highly technical data

---

178  *Trade Marks Regulations 1995* reg 4.15 and Sch 2.
179  *Trade Marks Regulations 1995* reg 4.15A.
180  *Trade Marks Office Manual of Practice and Procedure*, Part 21 para 6.1.
181  *Trade Marks Office Manual of Practice and Procedure*, Part 21 para 6.1.
182  *Trade Marks Office Manual of Practice and Procedure*, Part 21 para 6.1.
183  *Trade Marks Office Manual of Practice and Procedure*, Part 21 para 7.1.

such as "infrared spectroscopy; vacuum, fractional and molecular distillation; nuclear magnetic resonance; vacuum fractionation; 'electronic nose' analysis and chromatographic techniques".[184]

## Special Rules for Well-known Marks

Under s 185 a special mark, known as a defensive mark, may be registered for well-known marks.[185] The advantage of registering a well-known mark as a defensive mark is that certain provisions do not apply to defensive marks. In particular, a defensive trade mark can be registered in respect of goods and services even if the trade mark owner does not, or does not intend to, use the mark in relation to these goods and services and a defensive trade mark cannot be challenged on the basis of non-use.

There are currently 310 defensive marks registered, or pending registration, lodged by about 100 companies. These include everything from the shape of the COKE bottle and the NIKE symbol to DOROTHY THE DINOSAUR and The WIGGLES. BIG MAC is now registered as a defensive mark in relation to educational and similar material (not being computers). A defensive trade mark is ancillary to a registered trade mark – that is the mark must already be registered in relation to particular goods and services and can only be registered by the owner of that trade mark. Under s 185(1), a defensive mark will be registered only in relation to particular goods and services if "because of the extent to which (the) registered trade mark has been used" in relation to its current goods and services then "it is likely" that its use in relation to other goods and services will be taken to indicate that there is a connection between those goods and services and the owner of the trade mark (s 185). The defensive mark cannot, therefore, be used to make a universal claim which would give the owner an absolute monopoly on the use of the mark.

## Collective Marks

A collective mark is a sign used or intended to be used by a member of an association in relation to goods and services dealt with or provided in the course of trade by members of the association to distinguish them from goods and services dealt with or traded by non-members (s 162). In accordance with general usage an unincorporated association is a group of people with a common purpose and formal structure who do not have a separate legal identity. They include societies, clubs and perhaps trade unions. Any member of the association may exercise the rights of the registered owner in accordance with the rules of the association and may not prevent another member from so exercising these rights (s 165). A collective mark may not be assigned or transmitted (s 166).

---

184 *Trade Marks Office Manual of Practice and Procedure*, Part 21 para 7.1.

185 For a history of defensive marks, see the decision of the delegate of the Registrar of Trade Marks in *AT and T Corporation* [2001] ATMO 96 which suggests that the defensive mark was recognised in cases such as *Eastman Photographic Material Co Ltd v Griffiths Cycles Corp Ltd* (1898) 15 RPC 105 and *Southern Cross Refrigerating Co v Toowoomba Foundry Pty Ltd* (1954) 91 CLR 592 before it was codified.

## Certification Marks

The distinctive feature of a certification mark is that its use certifies that the goods or services have a particular quality, accuracy or other characteristic such as origin, material or mode of manufacture (s 169). When applying for registration of a certification mark the applicant must lodge a set of rules which will govern the use of the mark (s 173(1)). The rules must specify various requirements such as who may be approved to use the mark; the process for determining whether goods and/or services meet the certification requirements; when an approved user may use the mark; the procedure for resolving disputes about whether goods and/or services meet the certification requirements and any other issues (s 173(2)). The Registrar must forward the application to the Australian Competition and Consumer Commission (ACCC) who must approve it before acceptance (ss 174, 175 and 176). A certification mark may be assigned only with the consent of the ACCC (ss 180 and 180A).

# CASES

## *Aston v Harlee Manufacturing Co*
High Court of Australia: Fullagar J
(1960) 103 CLR 391

Harlee Manufacturing was the registered owner of the trade mark "Tastee Freez" in the United States. Although Harlee Manufacturing had an extensive franchised business in the United States they had not used the trade mark in Australia, nor done anything to suggest they would use the trade mark in Australia. Aston, having heard the name and having failed to reach agreement with Harlee Manufacturing for an Australian franchise, registered the mark in Australia. Harlee Manufacturing objected and also sought to register a mark. The Registrar, under the *Trade Marks Act 1905* s 27, sought an order from the court to determine who was the proprietor under that Act and who had the right to register the mark in Australia.

**Fullagar J: [396]** Aston in 1950 and up to the end of 1952 was resident in Honolulu. He was a member of the Dairy Queen National Trade Association, which was apparently an organization of persons engaged in the **[397]** same class of business as Harlee and using the name "Dairy Queen" as a trade mark or trade name. Towards the end of 1950 he decided to endeavour to enter into "the soft-serve business" in Australia, and he sent a man named La Delle to Australia to survey the position for him. He says that it was La Delle who suggested to him at this time that "Tastee Freez" would make a good name for an ice cream product. I do not believe this. I can find no reason to believe that Aston had ever heard of the mark "Tastee Freez" until he heard of it as Harlee's mark, but he was engaged in a similar class of business, and it is very likely that he had heard of it before he visited Australia, and before he had any contact with Harlee. In June 1951 he visited Australia himself, and, while he was in this country, he instructed patent attorneys in Sydney to lodge applications for the registration of several trade marks, but he either elected not to apply (as he says in one place) or through some oversight omitted to apply (as he says in another place) for the registration of "Tastee Freez". In December 1951 he went to the United States to attend a conference of the Dairy Queen Association, and, while in that country, visited the office of Harlee in Chicago, where he had conversation with Maranz with reference to the granting by Harlee to him of Tastee Freez franchises overseas. Maranz says that in the course of these conversations he informed Aston fully of Harlee's activities and plans in the United States and elsewhere, and Aston was given a copy of Harlee's agreement with franchise-holders and a list of the Harlee machines. Maranz does not say that there was any specific mention of Australia in his conversations with Aston.

Aston returned to Honolulu early in 1952. After his return a somewhat desultory correspondence, extending over a period of about eighteen months, took place between him and Harlee. I shall have to refer to this correspondence later. Mr *King* described it as constituting negotiations between Aston and Harlee as to the terms of a franchise to be granted by Harlee to Aston for Australia and certain other countries. Mr *Bannon* said that it showed that Aston was interested only in the Harlee machines. Up to a point, I cannot find anything in any of Aston's letters which suggests to me, or would be likely to suggest to Harlee, that Aston was interested in anything but the Harlee machines. The parties may have been to some extent at cross purposes. The correspondence begins with a letter of 29th February 1952 from Aston to Harlee, and the reply of Harlee of 10th

March 1952 made it plain that Harlee was not interested in the sale of any machine or machines, and was interested only in a franchise agreement. Aston's letters, **[398]** apart from making it clear that he is anxious to get some Harlee machines, are very vague. On 23rd April 1953, for no clear reason that I can find, Harlee wrote that it was "puzzled and worried" as to why Aston intended to operate "on an individual basis rather than operate as a Tastee Freez". In reply to this Aston wrote a letter, in the course of which he said: "My intentions were never to use your equipment, only as a Tastee Freez operation." This is perhaps ambiguous, but a little later in the letter he said: "My sincere intentions have never been only to operate under the name of Tastee Freez. You have a wonderful organization and am naturally interested in all your know-hows, international advertising and all your promotion ideas, and I would be proud to be a Tastee Freez franchise-holder and a member of your organization. Please send along an agreement as you have proposed for my signature on the basis of the arrangements you have made with Attilio Castigliano and Mario Rigat of Italy." There is no ambiguity about this, but nothing came of it.

The correspondence began, as I have said, on 29th February 1952. It ended with a letter from Harlee of 8th July 1953. In December 1952 Aston left Honolulu and came to reside permanently in Sydney. It is to be noted that it was at an early stage in this correspondence that Aston (14th May 1952) caused the application for the registration of "Tastee Freez" as his trade mark to be lodged in Australia. At no time did he inform Harlee that he intended to make this application or that he had made it.

I have said that Harlee has never used the mark in question in Australia in any way. Nor has Aston ever used the mark substantially in Australia. He said that about the end of 1956 there was some use of it in one or two towns in the Riverina, but no particulars of this alleged use were given.

The case seems to me to be one of considerable difficulty. What s 27 doubtless primarily contemplates is the case where two or more rival claimants for the same mark, or nearly identical marks, assert a title acquired by user. In the present case there has been, even up to the present time, no relevant user of the mark in question by either party in Australia, but it does not follow that neither party is entitled to register the mark. Section 32 of the Act provides that any person claiming to be the proprietor of a trade mark may apply to the Registrar for the registration of his trade mark. The right to registration depends, therefore, on proprietorship of a mark. The conception of proprietorship, other than proprietorship acquired by a user which has made the mark distinctive of the applicant's goods, is a difficult conception, but it has been **[399]** explained by *Dixon* J in *Shell Co of Australia Ltd v Rohm and Haas Co*,[186] where his Honour refers to the history of the English legislation. His Honour quotes *Cotton* LJ as saying in *In re Hudson's Trade Marks*:[187] "The difficulty is this: Is a man to be considered as entitled to the use of any trade mark when he has never used it at all? That is a difficulty, but I think the meaning is this. If a man has designed and first printed or formed any of those particular and distinctive devices which are referred to in the first part of s 10, he is then looked upon as the proprietor of that which is under that Act a trade mark, which will give him the right so soon as he registers it."[188] *Dixon* J then sums up the position by saying: "It is clear enough from the course of legislation and of decision that an application to register a trade mark so far unused must, equally with a trade mark the title to which depends on prior user, be founded on proprietorship. The basis of a claim to proprietorship in a trade mark so far unused has been found in the combined effect of authorship of the mark, the intention to use it upon or in connection with the goods and the applying for

---

[186] (1949) 78 CLR 601, at pp 625 et seq.
[187] (1886) 32 Ch D, at p 319, 320.
[188] (1949) 78 CLR, at p 626.

registration".[189] "Authorship", says his Honour a little later, "involves the origination or first adoption of the word or design as and for a trade mark".[190]

The passage quoted above requires careful consideration in relation to the present case. In the first place, I do not think that the requirement of "authorship" means that the applicant must be the true and first inventor: he has not to establish anything analogous to what an applicant for letters patent for an invention must establish. I do not think that an opponent of an application for registration of a trade mark could succeed by saying *merely* "I thought of it first", or even "I thought of it first, and communicated it to the applicant." It is otherwise if the opponent has used the mark in relation to goods. In *Re Hick's Trade Mark*,[191] *Holroyd* J, speaking for a Full Court, said: "In order to substantiate his application to be placed on the register for this word he must have claimed to be the proprietor, and the word 'proprietor' must be taken to mean the person entitled to the exclusive use of that name. If there is anyone else who would be interfered with by the registration of the word 'Empress' in the exercise of a right which such person has already acquired to use the same word in application to the same kind of thing, then Hicks **[400]** ought not to have been put on the register for that trade mark ...".[192] The reference in this passage to a "right acquired" does not, of course, mean that an opponent, or a person aggrieved on a motion to expunge, must show that he has acquired such a right to the mark at common law as would enable him to maintain an action for passing off.

In the second place, it would appear that an applicant may be the "author" of a trade mark, although he has deliberately copied or adopted a mark registered in a foreign country in respect of the same description of goods. In *Re Registered Trade Mark "Yanx";  Ex parte Amalgamated Tobacco Corporation Ltd*,[193] *Williams* J said: "To try and register in Australia a word which the applicant to the knowledge of the respondent is using elsewhere on its cigarettes is sharp business practice. But it is not in itself fraudulent or a breach of the law".[194] (I would think myself that it may or may not, according to circumstances, constitute "sharp business practice".) Again, it is otherwise if the opponent or person aggrieved has used the mark, for prior user by the foreign proprietor negatives the claim of the Australian applicant to "authorship". But the user must be user in Australia: the most extensive user by another person in foreign countries will not avail by itself to defeat an applicant for registration in this country. It has been said, however, that the Courts frown on these borrowings from abroad, and very slight evidence of user in Australia has been held sufficient to protect the proprietor of a foreign trade mark: *Seven Up Co v OT Ltd*.[195] A good example is *Blackadder v Good Roads Machinery Co Inc*.[196] That was clearly, I think, not a case of fraud. The vital fact was that, as the Court held, the goods were to be regarded as having "come into the Australian market" bearing the trade mark "Winner". Another good example – perhaps an extreme example – is the *Yanx Case*.[197] But, where there has clearly been no user at all in Australia, an applicant for a trade mark identical with a mark registered in a foreign country is entitled to be regarded, so far as Australia is concerned, as the "author" of the mark. I can see no reason why this should not be so. In *Seven Up Co v OT Ltd*,[198] *Williams* J, after citing certain English

[189] (1949) 78 CLR, at p 627.
[190] (1949) 78 CLR, at p 628.
[191] (1897) 22 VLR 636.
[192] (1897) 22 VLR, at p 640.
[193] (1951) 82 CLR 199.
[194] (1951) 82 CLR, at p 202.
[195] (1947) 75 CLR 203, at p 211.
[196] (1926) 38 CLR 332.
[197] (1951) 82 CLR 199.
[198] (1947) 75 CLR 203.

authorities, said: "In my opinion the effect of these cases is that in the absence of fraud it is not unlawful for a trader to become the registered proprietor under the *Trade Marks Act* of a mark which has been used, however extensively, by another trader as a mark for similar goods in a foreign **[401]** country, provided the foreign mark has not been used at all in Australia at the date of the application for registration."[199] *Latham* CJ quoted this passage with approval[200]on an appeal from *Williams* J, which was dismissed.

There is another element mentioned by *Dixon* J in the *Shell Co's Case*,[201] which is stated as essential to the proprietorship of an unused trade mark. That element is the intention of the applicant for registration to use it upon or in connexion with goods. As to this I need only say that I do not regard his Honour as meaning that an applicant is required, in order to obtain registration, to establish affirmatively that he intends to use it. There is nothing in the Act or the Regulations which requires him to state such an intention at the time of application, and the making of the application itself is, I think, to be regarded as prima facie evidence of intention to use. I cannot think that the Registrar is called upon to institute an inquiry as to the intention of any applicant, and I think that, on an opposition or on a motion to expunge, the burden must rest on the opponent, or the person aggrieved, of proving the absence of intention. Again, I do not think that "intention" in this connexion ought to be regarded as meaning an intention to use immediately or within any limited time. A manufacturer of (say) confectionery would, I should suppose, be entitled to register three trade marks in relation to confectionery, though he intended only to use two of them and had not made up his mind as to which two he would use. If he in fact does not use any of them for the period specified in s 72, the unused mark or marks may be expunged under that section. On the other hand, a manufacturer of confectionery, who had no intention of ever manufacturing motor cars, might be held disentitled to register a mark in relation to motor cars: the effect of *In re Registered Trade-Marks of John Batt & Co*,[202] is, I think, correctly stated in the first paragraph of the headnote to the report of the case before *Romer* J and the Court of Appeal.

A claim to proprietorship of a trade mark will be defeated if it is proved that to give effect to it would be to involve a fraud upon another person. A recent example is the case of *Farley (Aust) Pty Ltd v JR Alexander & Sons (Q) Pty Ltd*,[203] where *Williams* J held that a registration had been fraudulently obtained, on the ground that a promise not to use the mark after existing stocks **[402]** had been disposed of had "lulled the applicant" (*sc* for expungement) "into a state of false security".[204] It would appear that something short of fraud may suffice to defeat an application for registration, or support an application for expungement. Thus *Latham* CJ in the *Seven Up Case*[205] said: "User in Australia would be relevant. So also would facts establishing a breach of confidential relations or any fraud".[206]

I have now stated the facts which I regard as relevant and the principles which I think I have to apply, and I now come to the first question which I have to determine. That is the question whether Aston is entitled, for the purposes of his application of 14th May 1952, to be regarded as the proprietor of the trade mark "Tastee Freez".

Prima facie he is, in my opinion, so entitled.

---

[199] (1947) 75 CLR, at p 211.
[200] (1947) 75 CLR, at p 216.
[201] (1949) 78 CLR, at p 627.
[202] [1898] 2 Ch 432; [1899] AC 428.
[203] (1946) 75 CLR 487.
[240] (1946) 75 CLR, at p 492.
[205] (1947) 75 CLR 203.
[206] (1947) 75 CLR, at p 215.

# Ward Group Pty Ltd v Brodie and Stone plc
Federal Court of Australia: Merkel J
(2005) 215 ALR 716

A United Kingdom based website owner advertised and sold a product over the internet using a name which was registered in Australia and the United Kingdom as a trade mark. The question arose as to whether this was a use in Australia. In relation to advertising Merkel J draws a distinction between statements "made to the world at large" and statements "directed or targeted at people in a particular jurisdiction".

### Merkel J: Trade mark infringement

37. Determining when the website proprietors first used the Restoria mark in Australia is not without difficulty. That issue turns on when the proprietors first advertised for sale or sold UK Restoria products *in* Australia in a manner that used the Restoria mark. The website proprietors' advertising on the Internet of products for sale was a marketing of those products to the world at large and I am not satisfied that it was a marketing that was specifically targeted or directed at, or was specifically intended to be acted upon by, consumers in Australia. It is correct that Australia was listed in a "drop down" country box, together with numerous other countries, as a destination to which products may be shipped. Also, on the Westons website, an Australian dollar price was quoted together with other currencies as an indicative conversion price of a number of products. However, I am not satisfied that those circumstances indicated a specific intention that the particular goods in question were being marketed to consumers in Australia in a manner that would differ from the way in which those, and other, goods were being offered to consumers around the world. Rather, the circumstances indicate no more than that the website proprietors expected that there may be potential consumers in Australia, in the same way as they expected that there may be potential customers elsewhere in the world, that might be interested in purchasing *any* of the products advertised on their websites.

38. In *Hoffman-La Roche* at 45 [145]-[146] I considered the question of when a statement originating outside of Australia is made and received in Australia:

"In a different context, Mason CJ, Deane, Dawson and Gaudron JJ in *Voth v Manildra Flour Mills Pty Ltd* (1990) 171 CLR 538 observed at 567-568:

'In some cases an act passes across space or time before it is completed. Communicating by letter, telephone, telex and the like provide examples.'

However, after also observing that generally the tort of negligent misstatement is committed where the statement is received and acted upon their Honours pointed out that the statement may be received in one place and acted upon in another. They stated:

'If a statement is directed from one place to another place where it is known or even anticipated that it will be received by the plaintiff, there is no difficulty in saying that the statement was, in substance, made at the place to which it was directed, whether or not it is there acted upon.'…"

39. In *Norbert Steinhardt & Son Limited v Meth* (1961) 105 CLR 440 at 442 Fullagar J stated that a groundless threat of patent infringement "is to be regarded as made at the time when, and at the place where, it is received by the person to whom it is addressed". In that case, a letter containing the relevant threats was written in the USA and received in England, and his Honour found that the threats were made in England.

40. A similar approach has been taken in relation to publications or statements made on the Internet. When such publications or statements are made to the world at large, and not to persons or subscribers in a particular jurisdiction, there is some difficulty in regarding them as having been made by a website in a particular jurisdiction. However,

where the publication or statement is directed or targeted at persons or subscribers in a particular jurisdiction there is no difficulty in treating them as having been made and received in that jurisdiction…

41. On the facts of the present case the first occasion on which the website proprietors would be considered to have intended to use and used the Restoria mark *in* Australia was when they accepted the orders placed by the trap purchasers in respect of the UK Restoria products in terms that used the Restoria mark. The reason I have arrived at that conclusion is that prior to that time the trap purchasers were downloading a representation made on the Internet to the world at large, and not a representation intended to be made to, or directed or targeted at, them in Australia. Thus, I do not accept the contention made by the Ward Group that the use of the Restoria mark by the website proprietors on the Internet, without more, was a use of the mark by them in Australia.

42. Although *Dow Jones v Gutnick* was relied upon by the Ward Group, that case was concerned with whether an alleged defamation published on the Internet, which was downloaded by subscribers to that publication in Victoria, occurred in Victoria. Unlike the present case, where the focus is on when the website proprietors' infringing use of the Restoria mark occurred in Australia, the focus of the alleged defamation was on where the damage to reputation occurred: see *Dow Jones v Gutnick* at 606-608. As the allegedly defamatory publication was made available to subscribers in Victoria on the Internet, no issue arose about the publication of that material in Victoria. Therefore that case is of no assistance to the Ward Group.

43. In summary, the use of a trade mark on the Internet, uploaded on a website outside of Australia, without more, is not a use by the website proprietor of the mark in each jurisdiction where the mark is downloaded. However, as explained above, if there is evidence that the use was specifically intended to be made in, or directed or targeted at, a particular jurisdiction then there is likely to be a use in that jurisdiction when the mark is downloaded. Of course, once the website intends to make and makes a specific use of the mark in relation to a particular person or persons in a jurisdiction there will be little difficulty in concluding that the website proprietor used the mark in that jurisdiction when the mark is downloaded.

44. The first occasion on which there would have been a specific use of the Restoria mark *by* the website proprietors *in* Australia was when the trap purchasers were informed in Australia that their order had been accepted, in terms that used the Restoria name when referring to the UK Restoria product. In this case the confirmation web pages and emails that were downloaded by the trap purchasers did not refer to the Restoria mark. However, I am prepared to assume that the downloading of the acceptance of the order involved an implicit use of the Restoria mark by the website proprietor. There was also a further use of the mark in Australia by the website proprietors when the UK Restoria products were delivered by them to the trap purchasers in Australia. Both uses were uses of the mark in Australia that fall within the terms of s 120(1).

[The judge then went on to find that the consent defence applied to these uses.]

### *Philmac Pty Ltd v Registrar of Trade Marks*
Federal Court of Australia
(2002) 56 IPR 452

Philmac applied to register the colour terracotta in relation to its polypipe agricultural fittings. The Registrar initially rejected the application on the basis that it did not have any inherent capacity to distinguish the goods and did not in fact distinguish them. On appeal the court considered the application of the

*Clark Equipment* test to colour marks. The court agreed that there was no inherent capacity to distinguish but found that the colour did in fact distinguish the applicant's goods on the basis of prior use of a trade mark.

**Mansfield J: [472]** 60. In the present application, the consequence of a grant of registration would be to prevent any other trader in goods of the same description from using not only that shade of terracotta specifically described and visually represented in the application in respect of the goods to which the application relates, but all other shades of colour that might be described as deceptively similar to that colour. That conclusion, in my judgment, is relevant to the legitimate or honest use test set out in *Clark Equipment*. That is, (to superimpose the words of the test to the context of colour marks) the limited palate of colours available to a trader at the very least renders it more likely that other persons trading in goods of the relevant kind and being actuated only by proper motives – in the exercise, that is to say, of the common right of the public to make honest use of the colours forming part of the common heritage, for the sake of the signification which they ordinarily possess – will think of a colour and want to use it in connection with similar goods in a manner which would infringe a registered trade mark granted in respect of it. Stating the proposition in that way equates it with what has become known in international jurisprudence as the "colour depletion" argument.

61. The USA Federal Court in *Re Owens-Corning Fiberglas Corporation* 774 F 2d 1116 (1985) (*Pink Batts*) rejected a "colour depletion theory" asserted in an earlier case. In *Campbell Soup Co v Amrour & Co* 138 F 2d 4 (7th Cir 1950) the applicant was denied registration of labels that were half red and half white. The court held that if the applicant were to "monopolize red in all its shades the next manufacturer [could] monopolize orange in all its shades and the next yellow in the same way. Obviously, the list of colours would soon run out. The court in *Pink Batts* considered that approach inconsistent with the legislative framework that provided that colour was capable of registration as a trade mark. It stated at 1122 that "where there is no competitive need for colors to remain available, the color depletion argument is an unreasonable restriction on the acquisition of trademark rights".

62. I consider the qualification in that statement to be of critical importance in this matter. In my view, it is not inconsistent with the conclusion in *Pink Batts* that in circumstances where there is a proven competitive need for colours to remain available, it is not an unreasonable restriction on the acquisition of trade mark rights to have regard to that competitive imperative and preclude the granting of a monopoly in a colour applied to goods.

63. In the present application I have concluded on the evidence that colour has been and continues to be applied to irrigation fittings and related products by manufacturers as a means of coding their products for measurement compatibility and other purposes. That evidence includes the evidence of Philmac that its products manufactured for export to overseas markets are coloured so as to identify them as products manufactured for that purpose, and evidence of the Registrar that Philmac's most significant market competitor Plasson has applied the colours red, burgundy and "red-pink" to its rural compression fittings since 1998. I note also the use by the manufacturer Iplex of the colour blue on the nuts of its metric compression fitting so as to identify it as a metric product. The use of colour as a means of distinguishing between products with different measurement and performance specifications is also evident in the broader irrigation market. ...

**[473]** 64. Having regard to that evidence, I have reached the conclusion that in the narrow class of goods in respect of which the Philmac application relates, and less relevantly in the wider irrigation market, there is indeed a competitive need for colours to remain available. That conclusion is relevant, in my view, to the test in *Clark Equipment*. The proven existence of a competitive need for colours to remain available in my view places the present application in the same class as an application for registration of a purely descriptive word. That is because the existence of that competition renders it more likely in fact that "other traders are likely, in the ordinary course of their business and without any improper motive to desire to use [it] in connection with their goods": see the discussion of *Faulding* at [47] above.

65. By approaching the matter in that way, despite what the USA Federal Court in *Pink Batts* defined as a "colour depletion argument", I do not mean to suggest that a single colour applied to goods may never be inherently adapted to distinguish an applicant's goods from those of other traders. Such a conclusion would be inconsistent with the provisions of the Act that contemplate that a colour may serve as a trade mark. The definition of a sign in the Act provides that a colour may be a sign in its own right, and not merely as an element of another species of sign such as a logo or aspect of packaging. It would therefore not be in accordance with the Act to reject a trade mark purely on the basis that rejection would secure a monopoly over part of what is in reality a limited resource. However, having regard to the above principles and the test in *Clark Equipment*, I consider that the circumstances in which a colour applied to goods will be inherently adapted to distinguish are limited to the following:

- the colour does not serve a utilitarian function: that is, it does not physically or chemically produce an effect such as light reflection, heat absorption or the like;
- the colour does not serve an ornamental function: that is, it does not convey a recognised meaning such as the denotation of heat or danger or environmentalism;
- the colour does not serve an economic function: that is, it is not the naturally occurring colour of a product and registration of that colour in respect of that product would not thereby submit competing traders to extra expense or extraordinary manufacturing processes in order to avoid infringement;
- the colour mark is not sought to be registered in respect of goods in a market in which there is a proven competitive need for the use of colour, and in which, having regard to the colour chosen and the goods on which it is sought to be applied, other properly motivated traders might naturally think of the colour use it in a similar manner in respect of their goods.

66. I have concluded that the mark applied for does not serve the functions set out in the first three of those points. The fourth point raises two considerations. First, whether there is a competitive need for the use of colour. I have concluded that on the present application there is such a need. Second, the likelihood of properly motivated traders naturally thinking of the relevant colour and wishing to apply it to their goods should be considered in the context of both the colour **[474]** the subject of the application and the goods in respect of which registration of the trade mark is sought. It is to that second consideration that I now turn.

67. … I conclude from that evidence that Philmac struck on the colour terracotta not because it was an unnatural and unusual choice for application to compression fittings for irrigation piping, but because it was an obvious and apt choice for application to that type of goods. It follows that at the time of the Philmac application, another honest trader might also legitimately desire to apply the colour to the same class of goods. Were the colour chosen a lilac purple (a colour chosen by way of example only) the application might give rise to different considerations. While I am not prepared to hypothesise on such an application, in my view counsel for the Registrar correctly identified that in some circumstances the choice of a colour with respect to particular goods might on rare occasions amount to an "out of left field choice" and therefore assist the registrability of a colour mark, notwithstanding the competitive need for the use of colour in the relevant market. It was submitted, and I am inclined to agree, that the application of the colour pink to insulation batts is such a case: see *Pink Batts*. In my view such an application might lead the court to consider that the mark applied for was, *to some extent*, inherently

adapted to distinguish and therefore cause the application to fall for consideration under the less stringent test set out in s 41(5) of the Act. Those considerations do not arise on this application. The colour terracotta, or any shade of colour deceptively similar to it, applied either to rural compression fittings or more generally to farming irrigation products is, in my view, a combination that an honest trader in those products might legitimately desire to use.

68. Applying the test in *Clark Equipment*, the Philmac mark is, therefore, not inherently adapted to distinguish Philmac's goods from those of other traders.

[The judge did, however, find the mark registrable on the basis that because of its usage it did in fact distinguish the goods under s 44(6).]

## *Woolworths Pty Ltd v BP plc (No 2)*
### Federal Court of Australia: Heerey, Allsop and Young JJ
### (2006) 154 FCR 97

As part of its worldwide "Project Horizon" BP changed the colour scheme and get-up of its stations and sought to register its new green as a trade mark on the basis of acquired distinctiveness through prior use as a trade mark. The court held that, although customers "associated" the colour with BP stations, the colour had not been used as a trade mark before registration and had not acquired distinctiveness in this trade mark sense.

**The Court: The requirements of s 41(6) and use as a trade mark**

72. Section 41(6)(a) of the Act requires the applicant to establish at least two things: first, that there has been use of the trade mark that is the subject of the application before the filing date, being, of course, use as a trade mark; and, second, that because of the extent of that use before the filing date the trade mark does distinguish the designated goods or services as those of the applicant ...

77. Whether or not there has been use as a trade mark involves an understanding from an objective viewpoint of the purpose and nature of the use, considered in its context in the relevant trade. How the mark has been used may not involve a single or clear idea or message. The mark may be used for a number of purposes, or to a number of ends, but there will be use as a trade mark if one aspect of the use is to distinguish the goods or services provided by a person in the course of trade from the goods or services provided by any other persons, that is to say it must distinguish them in the sense of indicating origin...

80. Woolworths submitted that, during the relevant period, the letters "BP" and the logo with the letters "BP" surrounded by the yellow outline of a shield, had each been used as a trade mark, but not the colour green. It also submitted that, even if some of BP's advertisements were to be regarded as using the colour green as a trade mark, BP had not established the distinctiveness called for by s 41(6) as at the relevant filing dates.

81. ... In *Philmac Pty Ltd v Registrar of Trade Marks* (2002) 126 FCR 525; 56 IPR 452; [2002] FCA 1551 at [71], Mansfield J said that for the purposes of applying s 41(6) to a colour mark two issues needed to be addressed. The first is whether the use of the colour in the manner described in the application has, prior to the date of the application, constituted use of the colour as a trade mark. The second issue is whether the trade mark applied for does in fact distinguish the applicant's products, having regard to evidence concerning the actual use of the colour as a trade mark. We agree with that approach. Thus, s 41(6) requires specific consideration of the extent to which BP has used each of the marks applied for as a trade mark before the date of filing and whether that use was sufficient to distinguish the designated goods and services as being those of BP: *Blount*

*Inc v Registrar of Trade Marks* (1998) 83 FCR 50 at 60; 40 IPR 498 at 507; [1998] FCA 440.

82. In our view, there are obvious dangers in approaching these issues by reference to the get-up of the service stations. The foremost danger, perhaps, is that the inquiry will be diverted into an examination of the distinctiveness of the colour green alone, and away from the questions posed by s 41(6). That danger must be heightened where the evidence clearly showed that BP had used the colour green in ways, and as part of other trade marks, that did not correspond with the trade marks that were the subject of the applications in suit. For the purpose of s 41(6), the focus of the inquiry should be the use of the marks applied for, rather than use of colour as part of the get-up or packaging of goods generally: compare *British Sugar plc v James Robertson & Sons Ltd* [1996] RPC 281 at 302. Woolworths submitted that the primary judge was diverted in this way, and as a result incorrectly concluded that the trade marks the subject of the applications had been used by BP, either at all or to such an extent that they did distinguish BP's goods and services. We agree with this submission ...

87. This context makes clear that BP had used green and yellow (or gold) as a combination of colours (often against a white background) for many years as its corporate colours to identify BP and to distinguish its services and products from those of other oil companies. In that context, and as part of that combined usage of colours, green was an important part of its get-up and in that way part of the method of identifying and distinguishing BP products and services. We do not see the colour green, however, as having been used, separately, as a trade mark. Nevertheless, as a prominent element of the colour scheme of BP, the colour green would no doubt be capable of founding a mental association with BP if used alone, depending on the context.

88. One then comes to the changes brought about by the implementation of "Project Horizon". Photographs of BP service stations introduced as part of "Project Horizon" were placed into evidence. These reveal a significantly more extensive use of green in the livery of the service stations. In these photographs the yellow strip on the fascias of the canopy and buildings was largely eliminated, as were the white borders, and the white background on the main signage was eliminated. Yellow was, however, still used. The prominent "BP" mark was in yellow. The often-used word "welcome" placed prominently on the fascia of the canopy was in yellow. The prices on the price board were in yellow numbers. The word "workshop" to identify same on the building fascia was in yellow. On the main identification sign, the words, letters and numbers "car wash", "workshop", "24 hrs", "autogas" and "shop" were in yellow. Yellow colouring was used for the conveying of information, through numbers and letters that clearly contrast with the surrounding green. In the context of the history of BP's use of colour these uses of yellow would have been understood as the subsidiary company colour alongside the predominating green. In other words, the colours green and yellow were still being used to identify or brand the stations. The use of green was extensive, and certainly more extensive than previously. It can be said to predominate in the colour scheme of the service stations, though it was visibly and noticeably accompanied by yellow in that two-colour scheme ...

99. Taking all the evidence together the following can be said. First, in the context of the oil industry in which a small number of companies had, for many years, used colours to distinguish their goods and services from the goods and services of competitors. Before 1989, BP used green and yellow to distinguish its service stations, goods and services from those of its competitors.

100. Second, by 1989, BP made a deliberate decision to change what might be called the colour branding of BP. Green was to be, and was, used more extensively than yellow in the livery of service stations and in advertising. It continued, however, to be used with yellow.

101. Third, on the fascias of buildings, petrol pumps, signage boards, (including poster boards, pole signs and price boards), and spreaders in service stations (the parts of service stations referred to in the endorsements), green was used as the predominant colour, but only with yellow. This use of green as the predominant colour, with the use of yellow, can be understood as trade mark use, replacing the use of green and yellow given approximately equal weight and prominence as the company's brand colours before 1989.

102. Fourth, the question arises whether, after 1989, the advertising reveals not only the use of predominantly green with yellow as the company's colours and as a trade mark, but also the use, as a trade mark, of green alone. This question cannot be answered simply by attempting to find an advertisement without yellow present, although there is no such advertisement in evidence. For the conclusion to be drawn that green alone was being used by BP as a trade mark prior to 1991 or 1995, one must understand the material as stating to the ordinary person that, green alone was being used as a badge of origin to distinguish BP's goods and services from those of its competitors.

103. Some of the print media referring to "green stations" and the "green light" clearly sought to use green in this way. Overall, however, it is difficult to conclude that the colour green was used by BP before 1991 and 1995 as a trade mark other than by its use of green as the predominant colour in conjunction with yellow. Certainly, on the evidence, in relation to the parts of the service station referred to in the endorsements, green has always been used in conjunction with yellow.

104. The fact that from a distance the predominant green of the colour of the service station (in particular the fascias of the canopy and buildings and any pole sign) would be noticed, and would assist the motorist in identifying the existence of a BP service station, is not sufficient to transform the use of green predominantly with yellow into the use of green as a trade mark. The fact is that the fascias had yellow logos and marks prominently placed on them, the main identification signs had the green and yellow logo and mark, as well as yellow script, the price boards had a green background and yellow writing, the pumps and spreaders had yellow logos and marks.

105. After the change brought about by "Project Horizon", green predominated in the colour scheme of the service station, but at all times it was used with yellow as the subsidiary, but ever present companion. Looking at all the advertisings, print, television and point of sale material, we conclude that the colours used to distinguish BP's goods and services from those of its competitors in the parts of the service stations referred to in the endorsements were its existing brand colours, green and yellow, with a marked and clear predominance of green. Green, alone, was not used as a trade mark in the parts of the service stations referred to in the endorsements. BP stressed, however, the educative role of that part of the advertising which stressed green – that told the reader of the "Green BP stations" and to "stop at the green light". But even if it be assumed that there was some trade mark use of green alone in the particular print advertisements to which we have referred, the evidence is inadequate to elevate that to the point where it establishes the matters referred to in s 41(6).

106. Taking all of the evidence into account, including the absence of evidence as to the frequency of specific print or television advertising, we are unable to conclude that any trade mark use of colour by BP at the relevant times has been other than green as the dominant colour in conjunction with yellow as the subsidiary colour.

## *Southern Cross Refrigerating Co v Toowoomba Foundry Pty Ltd*
High Court of Australia: Kitto J (on trial); Dixon CJ, McTiernan, Webb,
Fullagar and Taylor JJ (on appeal)
(1954) 91 CLR 592

Toowoomba Foundry Pty Ltd had a trade mark registered in relation to well-drilling and boring machinery, milking machines, engines and windmills. It opposed the registration of Southern Cross's trade mark SOUTHERN CROSS in relation to gas and electric refrigerators on the basis of substantial identity and deceptive similarity between the marks and on the basis of deception and confusion. They failed on the first ground because the goods were not of the same description. They succeeded on the second and at trial Kitto J set out his wonderment test and principles for establishing deception and confusion. Note that this action was under the 1905 Act so the onus was on the applicant to prove that there would be no deception and confusion. Today, however, there is a presumption of registrability.

### ON TRIAL
**Kitto J: [594]** In relation both to the English and to the Australian section there are certain propositions which I think may be accepted as established by the cases. I take them, substantially, from the judgment of *Romer* J, (as he then was), in *In re Jellinek's Application*[207] (i) [*this principle related to onus which has now been reversed (ed)*] **[595]** (ii) It is not necessary, in order to find that a trade mark offends against the section, to prove that there is an actual probability of deception leading to a passing-off. While a mere possibility of confusion is not enough – for there must be a real, tangible danger of its occurring (*Reckitt & Colman (Australia) Ltd v Boden*;[208] *Sym Choon & Co Ltd v Gordon Choons Nuts Ltd*[209]) – it is sufficient if the result of the user of the mark will be that a number of persons will be caused to wonder whether it might not be the case that the two products come from the same source. It is enough if the ordinary person entertains a reasonable doubt. (iii) In considering the probability of deception, all the surrounding circumstances have to be taken into consideration (this includes the circumstances in which the marks will be used, the circumstances in which the goods will be bought and sold, and the character of the probable purchasers of the goods: *Jafferjee v Scarlett*[210]). (iv) In applications for registration, the rights of the parties are to be determined as at the date of the application.

### ON APPEAL
**Dixon CJ, McTiernan, Webb, Fullagar and Taylor JJ: [607]** We have thought it necessary to make some reference to the matters proper for consideration in relation to this issue under s 25 for the argument of the appellant seizes upon them and asserts that once these matters have been considered and the relevant issue answered in favour of an applicant it is impossible to say that the use by him, with respect to his goods, of the trade mark in question would be "likely to deceive" within the meaning of s 114. Whilst conceding that the likelihood of deception is not as great where, in no sense, can it be said that an applicant's goods are the same or of the same description as those of an opponent, it is quite clear that the latter finding by no means disposes of the relevant inquiry under s 114. To suggest that it does really confuses the nature of the inquiry which arises under s 25 for

---

[207] (1946) 63 RPC 59 at 78.
[208] (1945) 70 CLR 84, at pp 94, 95.
[209] (1949) 80 CLR 65, at p 79.
[210] (1937) 57 CLR 115, at p 120.

it is not sufficient in order to reach the conclusion that an applicant's goods are of the same description as those of an opponent, merely, to find that in the course of marketing there is a likelihood of deception taking place; the inquiry is much more limited and must be answered in favour of the applicant unless upon an examination of the material matters the conclusion is justified that the applicant's goods ought to be regarded as being of the same description as those of the opponent. This is far from saying that if the evidence shows a probability or likelihood of deception such a conclusion would be justified. Indeed, if it were not a distinct and separate inquiry it would be impossible to reconcile the multitude of cases – of which *In re Jellinek's Application*[211] and *Reckitt & Colman (Australia) Ltd v Boden*[212] are themselves examples – in which it has been thought necessary to consider the likelihood of deception notwithstanding a finding that the respective goods of the applicant and the opponent were not the same or of the same description.

The question whether it is likely that deception will result from the use of a mark which is the same as, or which closely resembles, **[608]** a trade mark already in use may, and frequently will, require the consideration of matters additional to and distinct from those which are relevant to an inquiry under s 25. It may be of importance to see whether the registered mark is general or special in character and to ascertain the extent of its reputation. Again, it may be important to see whether the goods in respect of which it is registered constitute a narrow class or a wide variety of goods as also will be the question whether the goods of both the applicant and the opponent will be likely to find markets substantially in common areas and among the same classes of people. It is, of course, for the person applying for registration to establish that there is no likelihood of confusion and we agree with *Kitto* J that registration should be refused if it appears that there is a real risk that "the result of the user of the mark will be that a number of persons will be caused to wonder whether it might not be the case that the two products came from the same source"; it is, of course, not necessary that it should appear that the user of the mark will lead to passing-off: see per *Morton* J (as he then was) in *In re Hack's Application*.[213] Further, it is not enough for the applicant "to negative the likelihood of confusion in relation to the actual trade carried on by the opponent at the time of registration and to the manner in which the latter then uses his mark. The applicant must also take into account all legitimate uses which the opponent may reasonably make of his mark within the ambit of his registration": *Reckitt & Colman (Australia) Ltd v Boden* per *Dixon* J (as he then was).[214]

The second branch of the appellant's argument asserted that the question of fact under s 114, which was decided adversely to him, should, upon the evidence, have been decided otherwise. In our opinion, there was, however, abundant evidence to justify his Honour's conclusion; there was evidence which his Honour found "entirely convincing" and we find it of equal cogency. Not only was there evidence which established the probability of confusion but, also, quite substantial evidence of actual confusion. But the appellant claims that any actual or probable confusion had proceeded or would proceed from a belief that the respondent had a monopoly of the "Southern Cross" mark. This mistaken belief, it was said, alone had led to the actual confusion deposed to and this circumstance operated to strip the evidence of real weight. We do not agree. In part the confusion resulted from the use by the appellant of a mark which had long and widely been used by the respondent, in part from the fact that it was a mark which had been used by the **[609]** latter with respect to such diverse objects as both manual and power well-drilling and boring machinery, milking machines and engines and windmills, in part from the fact

---

[211] (1946) 63 RPC 59.
[212] (1945) 70 CLR 84.
[213] (1940) 58 RPC 91, at p 103.
[214] (1945) 70 CLR, at pp 94, 95.

that in the course of business those articles frequently are and have, for a long time, been sold in country stores where, side by side with them, domestic refrigerators are stocked and sold, and last, but not least, from the circumstance that the name "Southern Cross" is a mark of a general character and – as appears from what we have already said – of a wide and varied significance. A careful scrutiny of the evidence convinces us that the respondent made out a clear case, not only that a user of the mark by the appellant for the purposes proposed by it would be likely to deceive, but that it has already done so in a not inconsiderable number of cases. In those circumstances we do not propose, nor do we think it necessary to traverse the whole of the facts again.

For the reasons given we are of opinion that the appeal should be dismissed.

## Executors of the Estate of Diana, Princess of Wales v Masterson
### Australian Trade Marks Office: T Williams (Hearing Officer)
### (2001) 52 IPR 264

The executors of the estate of the Princess of Wales opposed the registration of a trade mark comprising an ornate device in the shape of a wreath with the words DIANA'S LEGACY IN ROSES in cursive script around the bottom of the device and an ornate "D" in the centre. In this extract the Hearing Officer addressed the opposition on the s 43 ground of deception and confusion. You may also like to read the reasons regarding s 60.

### T Williams (Hearing Officer):

[271] *Ground (ii) Deceptive or Confusing Connotation (s 43)*
Section 43 reads:
*Trade mark likely to deceive or cause confusion*
An application for the registration of a trade mark in respect of particular goods or services must be rejected if, because of some connotation that the trade mark or a sign contained in the trade mark has, the use of the trade mark in relation to those goods or services would be likely to deceive or cause confusion
Section 43, when used in opposition to registration, requires an opponent to show that:
   (a) there is a connotation in the proposed mark or in one of its parts; and
   (b) because of this, the trade mark is likely, when in use, to deceive or cause confusion.
*TGI Friday's Australia Pty Ltd v TGI Friday's Inc* (2000) 173 ALR 127, 48 IPR 513 is the most recent authoritative decision on the meaning of "connotation". The case confirms that the connotation must be in the mark itself and cannot be determined as the result of external considerations, such as reputation.

[272] *(a) Connotation of the mark*
The opponents submit that there are five connotations contained within the mark (four singular and one composite) which are likely to deceive or cause confusion. The alleged connotations and the opponents' submissions in relation to them are as follows:
   (a) "Diana's" – that the late Princess was commonly, if not universally, referred to as "Diana" prior to her death. The opponents rely upon the matters set out in the statutory declarations of Lady McCorquodale and Mr Hughes to support this.
   (b) "Legacy" – that the *Oxford English Dictionary* defines "legacy" as a "gift left in a will or something handed down by a predecessor". When combined with the word "Diana", this indicates a clear connection with the late Princess.

(c) "Rose" and "Roses" – that a "Princess of Wales" rose was available for fundraising purposes both before and after the Princess's death, marketed, apparently, by the British Lung Foundation. Further, the rose is a symbol of England, and the Princess was, prior to her divorce, the presumptive Queen Consort of England.

(d) The stylised "D" – that the stylised "D" and the encircled rose in the centre of the proposed trade mark contain a connotation of the Princess, although Professor Ricketson admitted, at hearing, that this was "Perhaps not a direct connotation".

(e) That the words "Diana's Legacy in Roses" and the stylised "D" together convey a clear indication of the late Princess.

There is no evidence to suggest that a person in Australia would necessarily associate roses, or the "Princess of Wales" rose in particular, with the Princess. Even so, I am reasonably satisfied that the overall impression of the mark, limited to live roses, is one that evokes a memory of Princess Diana. In fact, Mr Heerey on behalf of the applicant, stated during his submissions that the applicant did not deny that the trade mark was a reference to the late Princess. Accordingly, I find that the trade mark does carry a connotation of the late Princess. However, without more, merely invoking a reference to a deceased celebrity cannot deceive or confuse.

*(b) Whether the connotation is likely to deceive or cause confusion*
The appropriate standard when testing for deception or confusion was recently set down by French J in *Registrar of Trade Marks v Woolworths Ltd* (1999) 45 IPR 411; at 426; AIPC 91-499; at 39,695 [43]. In considering the phrase "likely to deceive or cause confusion", his Honour said:

> The use of the word "likely" in this context does not import a requirement that it be more probable than not that the mark has that effect. The probability of deception or confusion must be finite and non-trivial. There must be a "real tangible danger of it occurring".

The Trade Marks Office *Draft Manual of Practice and Procedure* Part 29 para 4 states as follows, in regard to s 43 prior to acceptance:

> If the inclusion of the name or representation is likely to lead the ordinary buying public to the conclusion that the person whose name or representation appears in the trademark, has endorsed the product or services in some way, then a ground for rejection exists unless the applicant has permission to use the name or representation in the trade mark upon the product or in relation to the services specified in the application.

[272] I believe that a similar approach is necessary in relation to that section when it is used as a basis for a ground of opposition. The question becomes: has a ground of opposition been established?

Professor Ricketson referred me to the cases of *Radio Corporation Pty Ltd v Disney* (1937) 57 CLR 448, and *Sabrina Trade Mark* (1959) 29 AOJP 1988. Shortly stated, the decision in *Disney* recognised that the relevant characters' names were so closely associated in the public mind with the name of their owner that their use by another party was likely to cause deception when applied to radios. However, I believe that the *Disney* case can be distinguished from the present one. The characters in the *Disney* case were the invention and intellectual property of their owner. As characters, the trade marks did not exist before their creation by Disney.

In the present case, the Princess was a well-known public figure well before this application was filed. There is a complete lack of evidence of commercialisation of her name during her lifetime. This tends to confirm what I think is general knowledge, that members of the Royal family do not allow their names to be commercialised. There is nothing in the evidence that satisfies me that the Estate or Memorial Fund changed this position, at least as it existed in Australia, before the priority date.

As to the *Sabrina* case, I believe that the Deputy Registrar was probably swayed by the fact that, under the old legislation, the onus was quite notoriously on the applicant to negative the likelihood of deception or confusion. He said, emphasis and parenthesised material added:

> I consider that the average purchaser would, when seeing the name Sabrina (a well-known English television personality) ... wonder whether the goods had any association with the stage personality. I think that many purchasers *might* consider that the person well-known by the name Sabrina had some direct association with the goods ...

The matter was not ultimately decided by reference to the likelihood of deception or confusion. Probably because of this, it is not entirely clear to what extent the Deputy Registrar was convinced that a real tangible risk was present. Nor is it clear that he saw the doubt in question as what has been called, in many cases over time, a reasonable doubt, present in the mind of a person who has been given cause to wonder, rather than one who is indulging in mere idle speculation

The opponents submitted that, in the present case, it is clear that the Estate of the Princess, as the exclusive owner of all intellectual property related to the Princess, had carried out large-scale licensing of intellectual property rights relating to Princess Diana through the Memorial Fund. However, neither the opponents nor the declarants have provided any basis for this assertion and I am not satisfied that their asserted exclusive right exists. Even if it does, the Estate would still need to establish that the mark itself incorporates a connotation that the product to which it is applied has some sponsorship or approval by the Estate or the Memorial Fund. Again, there is no evidence before me that indicates that any person in Australia would assume that the trade mark connoted such sponsorship or approval. The newspaper articles exhibited as part of Mr Hughes' declaration merely show that an Australian reader might be aware that a Memorial Fund had been established, and that endorsed products might be available. However, this is not sufficient for me to find that the mark in question will give rise to a connotation of connection, sponsorship, approval or endorsement by the Estate or Memorial Fund. In fact, and as Mr Heerey **[274]** submitted, the same articles may have the effect of negativing any connotation which could have been raised by the mark, by pointing to the amount of unauthorised merchandising which was taking place.

Nor do I believe that the internet search results or the books about the Princess, referred to in the first Hughes declaration, assist in this regard. With regard to the internet searches, there is no indication that any of the searches identify sites which mention the Estate or the Memorial Fund. Where sites do contain such references, such as those contained in Ex SH6 to the second Hughes declaration, no details are provided of actual visits by Australians. It is not open to me to assume that a reasonable number of visitors to the site were Australians: *Advantage Rent-A-Car v Advantage Car Rental Pty Ltd* (2000) 49 IPR 129; AIPC 91-582. In relation to the books, there is no mention at all of any apparent connection to the Estate or Memorial Fund.

The fact that there have been sales of authorised products in Australia is of no real assistance in the present case. The evidence indicates neither how nor whether these products were identified as "official", nor what constitutes the "well known trade marks of the Princess". Further, it is not apparent on the face of the evidence that any of the products were available in Australia, with or without an official endorsement, before the priority date.

Those things being so, it is now necessary for me to make my own assessment of what will be a typical person's knowledge of the late Princess, her Estate and/or the Memorial Fund and what, consequently, they will be likely to make of the connotation that is present in the mark. I think it was common knowledge that there were fundraising activities conducted in memory of or in relation to the late Princess. I believe that consumers, when they see a product which relates in some way to a deceased celebrity such as the Princess, will do either or both of two things. First, they may buy the product because it has a particular attribute. That attribute is likely to be the inclusion of the name or likeness of the celebrity. In such a case, the buyer's decision to purchase is not actually made on the basis that the product or service has a particular endorsement, approval or source

If the buyer does purchase the product because of a supposed association or endorsement with a deceased celebrity, today's consumers are, I believe, likely enough to look for some evidence of such an association or endorsement. This is particularly so where the name is that of a deceased person who, during her life, appears to have carefully avoided the commercialisation of her name. She was, in this respect, apparently unlike those people who might be expected, in principle, to be likely to trade on a reputation. This is not a case where, in life, the person created a connotation linked directly to the goods. The Princess of Wales never was to roses what Stradivarius was to violins, for instance. Neither was she to roses what an actor and businessman such as Paul Hogan is to shoes[215] or souvenir shops,[216] nor what a prominent sportsperson may be to sporting equipment. In my opinion, there is nothing in the mark itself to give the imprimatur of endorsement. No independent evidence, in either anecdotal or survey form, has been placed before me to contradict this finding

I therefore find that no ground has been established under s 43.

[The hearing officer then considered the claim based on s 60 but found that there was no relevant trade mark with a reputation in Australia.]

## Bavaria NV v Bayerischer Brauerbund eV
Federal Court of Australia: Bennett J
[2009] FCA 428

The case involved a trade mark comprising a medallion/crest with the words "Bavaria" across the middle and "Holland" and "Beer" beneath. The application was opposed under *Trade Marks Act 1995* s 61 by an association of Bavarian beer makers on the basis that the mark contained a false geographical indication. The court held that it was only the use of formally recognised geographical indications which were caught by s 61.

**Bennett J:** *Does the trade mark contain or consist of a sign that is a geographical indication for goods originating in Bavaria?*
158. The answer to this question does not depend on impression or the likely impression made on a consumer. It requires the trade mark to be looked at in its totality to decide if it contains or consists of a sign recognised in Germany as indicating that the beer comes from Bavaria and that is has a quality, reputation or other characteristic attributable to its origin.
159. The signs recognised in Germany do not equate to the trade mark.
160. Essentially, BBA contends that GENUINE BAVARIAN BEER (from the Lady Bavaria trade mark) and BAYERISCHES BIER are geographical indications, that this establishes that 'Bavaria' and 'Bavarian' are also geographical indications for beer and that the trade mark contains or consists of a sign that is a geographical indication by virtue of the words BAVARIA or BAVARIA BEER (disregarding the interspersed HOLLAND).

---

[215] *Hogan v Pacific Dunlop Ltd* (1988) 20 FCR 314; 83 ALR 403; 12 IPR 225.
[216] *Hogan v Koala Dundee Pty Ltd* (1988) 83 ALR 187; 12 IPR 508.

161. I do not accept that contention. The Act requires that the trade mark application contain a sign that is itself recognised in Germany. The recognised signs are the Lady Bavaria trade mark which includes the phrase GENUINE BAVARIAN BEER and BAYERISCHES BIER, which translates as BAVARIAN BEER. 'Bavarian Beer' is not the same as 'Bavaria' or 'Bavarian Holland Beer'. As was said by the Delegate, Bavaria is the name of a German State, while BAYERISCHES BIER refers to beer that comes from Bavaria. They are not the same. Section 61(1) requires that the geographical indication itself be contained in the trade mark. The section does not refer to a sign that is substantially the same as or deceptively similar to the geographical indication, or refer to an evocation or imitation of the geographical indication. The trade mark does not contain 'Bavarian', 'Bavarian Beer' or even 'Bavaria Beer'. One cannot just ignore the word HOLLAND that appears between BAVARIA and BEER, nor the difference between Bavaria, the name of the State in Germany, and the description of the kind of beer that has the quality that BBA contends is associated with Bavarian beer.

162. BBA has adduced evidence of German text books published in 2002 on geographical indications which recognise the designation 'Bavaria' for use with particular beers. I do not accept that evidence as sufficient for the purposes of the Act to establish that 'Bavaria' when used for beer is a recognised sign for the purposes of the definition of a 'geographical indication' under the Act. Indeed, BBA's submissions concentrate on various ways in which 'Genuine Bavarian Beer' or 'Bayerisches Bier' were recognised as signs. None of them are either 'Bavaria' or 'Bavaria Holland Beer', which are the signs which could be said to be contained within the trade mark. It is not a question of translation. I accept that a translation should be made for the purposes of comparison. It is not to the point that, in Germany, a Bavaria NV trade mark was found to infringe BAYERISCHES BIER as a PGI. The ground of opposition in these proceedings is based on s 61 and s 6 of the Act. As noted by the Delegate, s 6 contains no mention of a geographical indication encompassing signs which are substantially identical with or deceptively similar to a geographical indication or those that evoke or 'allude to' a protected designation as, apparently from the German decision, does the law in that country regarding infringement of a PGI.

163. The opposition based on s 61(1) of the Act does not succeed. I will, however, proceed to consider the defence provided for in s 61(2)(c) of the Act.

# Chapter 14

# Trade Marks – Rights, Infringement and Dealings

## Rights

Under the *Trade Marks Act 1995* s 20(1) the registered owner of a trade mark has the exclusive right to use the trade mark or authorise another person to use the trade mark "as a trade mark" in relation to the goods and services in which it is registered. The owner also has the right to obtain relief if the trade mark is infringed (s 20(2)).

The extent of the trade mark owner's rights are subject to four significant limitations which, we would suggest, reflect the Act's interest in ensuring that trade competitors are able to conduct their business. Two of these limitations have been discussed previously in so far as they also provide grounds for cancelling or rectifying a trade mark registration.

As we have seen, s 24 applies where a registered mark contains a sign which, following registration, has generally come to be accepted within the trade as the name of an article, substance or service. Under s 24(2) the registered owner of such a mark does not have an exclusive right to use, or authorise the use of, the sign or the trade mark in relation to those articles, substances or other goods, or services of the same description. The exclusive rights will be taken to have ceased from the day on which the sign first became generally accepted as determined by the court. Thus, South Australian Brewing Co's trademark, SHOWDOWN, has arguably become the generally accepted term for the two AFL football clashes between the Adelaide Football Club and the Port Adelaide Football Club.[1]

Section 25 applies where a registered trade mark contains a sign that describes or names a formerly patented article, substance or service which has become the commonly known way to describe or identify the article, substance or service provided that the patent has ceased or expired for at least two years. Under s 25(2) if this happens the registered owner does not have any exclusive rights to use, or authorise the use, of the trade mark or sign in relation to those

---

1    See *South Australian Brewing Co Pty Ltd v Carlton and United Breweries Ltd* [2001] FCA 902 where this point was argued but not decided.

articles, substances or other goods or services of the same description. The rights cease to subsist two years after the patent ceased or expired.

Section 23 applies where two or more substantially identical or deceptively similar trade marks have been registered, whether in relation to the same or to different goods and services. In this case, a trade mark owner of any one of these marks does not have the right to prevent the registered owner of any of the other trade marks from using his or her trade mark "except to the extent that the first-mentioned owner is authorised to do so under the registration of his or her trade mark". Despite the circularity of this provision, its effect is to limit the rights of the trade mark owner so that the trade mark owner can only prevent someone else using the same trade mark in relation to actual goods and services for which it is registered; the trade mark owner effectively loses the right to sue for infringement by the use of substantially identical or deceptively similar trade marks or by the use of the registered trade mark in relation to related goods and services.

Under s 20(4) the rights of the trade mark owner are subject to any limitations or conditions imposed. These limitations may include limitations relating to the mode of use, the territory of use or use in relation to exported goods or services (s 6).

Finally, s 20(5) provides that if the trade mark is registered in the name of two or more persons as joint owners of the mark, the rights granted to those persons are to be exercised as if they were the rights of a single person.

## Infringement

Under s 120 of the Act a trade mark is infringed in three different ways. Under these s 120 provisions, infringement becomes harder to prove as the use moves further away from the goods and services for which the trade mark is registered. Thus, the trade mark owner's rights are infringed if a person, without consent, uses a "substantially identical" or "deceptively similar" sign "as a trade mark":

- in relation to the goods and services in respect of which the mark is registered (s 120(1));
- in relation to goods or services which are of the "same description" or "closely related to"[2] the goods or services for which the mark is registered. However, in this case there is no infringement if the alleged infringer establishes that the use of the mark is not likely to deceive or cause confusion (s 120(2));
- in relation to "unrelated" goods or services, if the registered mark is well known in Australia. This section only applies if, because of the fact that the mark is well known, its use in relation to the unrelated products is thought to indicate a connection between those products and the trade mark owner. It must also be established that, on account of such use, the interests of the owner are likely to be adversely affected (s 120(3)). "Unrelated" goods and services are products which are not in the same class as the registered

---

2    For the meaning of these terms, see Chapter 13, "Substantially identical or deceptively similar to another trade mark (ss 44 and 60)".

trade mark, are not of the "same description", and are not "closely related to" the products for which the mark is registered.

Under s 121 a trade mark owner may prohibit certain acts in relation to the use of the trade mark and the doing of any of these acts in the course of trade also constitutes an infringement of the trade mark. Thus, the registered owner may, by notice, prohibit a person from:

- applying or using the trade mark in physical relation to products where the state, condition, get-up, or packaging has been altered (s 121(2)(a));
- altering, partially removing or obliterating a trade mark applied to registered goods or used in physical relation to them (s 121(2)(b));
- removing or obliterating a trade mark used in relation to registered goods or in physical relation to them without also removing or obliterating associated material (s 121(2)(c));
- applying another trade mark to registered goods or using another trade mark in physical relation to them (s 121(2)(d));
- using the trade mark on registered goods or in physical relation to them in a manner which would injure the reputation of the trade mark (s 121(2)(e)).

These provisions give Coca-Cola, for example, great control over the refrigerators and other signage which they might supply to retailers. You might like to consider whether problems of authorisation would arise if, say, a school child put graffiti on the Coke sign in a shop. A person does not infringe s 121 if the person acquired the goods in good faith without being aware of the notice of prohibition, or acquired a title through such a person.

The relief available for infringement is an injunction, and damages or an account of profits (s 126). If the defendant has applied for the removal of the mark from the register for non-use then the plaintiff is not entitled to damages or an account of profits for infringing use during the period of non-use (s 127). The *Trade Marks Act* also provides an action against a person who makes groundless threats of legal proceedings (s 129).

## Substantially identical or deceptively similar

It has been held that the test for substantial identity and deceptive similarity for the purposes of infringement is different from the test for substantial identity and deceptive similarity for the purposes of registrability. In particular, it has been determined in *Polaroid Corporation v Sole N Pty Ltd*[3] that the principles of Kitto J's "wonderment test" from *Southern Cross Refrigerating Co v Toowoomba Foundry Pty Ltd*[4] should not be applied in so far as that test takes "passing off" type considerations into account.

In that case, the plaintiffs owned a trade mark POLAROID in respect of anti-glare devices and light polarising material which they manufactured and distributed. The defendants owned the trade mark SOLAROID for a similar material which, in practice, they used for tinting windows and cars. The defendant used the name on its brochures referring to their tinting service and to the

---

3    [1981] NSWLR 491.
4    (1954) 91 CLR 592.

material used and they also used the word as part of their business name. The plaintiffs did not provide a tinting service. This fact would be significant if the principles from *Southern Cross Refrigerating Co v Toowoomba Foundry Pty Ltd*[5] were applied.

However, the plaintiffs argued that, in determining whether marks were substantially identical or deceptively similar for the purposes of infringement, the surrounding circumstances should not be considered and only the marks themselves should be compared. They based their argument on the principle that infringement was of the mark itself, not of the use of the mark.

The defendants argued that all the circumstances, including the price differences, the different markets and use of the material, should be taken into account in accordance with the *Southern Cross Refrigerating Co v Toowoomba Foundry Pty Ltd* principles.

Kearney J held that the statutory definition of substantial identity and deceptive similarity as causing deception and confusion only applied in the case of registration proceedings. He accepted the argument of the plaintiff on the basis that the role of the court in infringement proceedings was to uphold and support the monopoly granted by the Act.[6]

## Use as a trade mark

An infringement occurs if a person "uses" the trade mark "as a trade mark". For an infringement to occur the mark must therefore be "used" in the appropriate way and that use must be "as a trade mark" in Australia.

The question of whether the mark is used "as a trade mark" raises similar issues to those considered in the previous chapter on the definition of a trade mark and intention to use the mark. Before 1955 the requirement was implied in relation to both registration and infringement but under the 1995 Act it is expressly referred to in relation to infringement.[7] The pre-1955 cases may therefore be referred to in order to determine the parameters of such a use.

In *Shell Co of Australia Ltd v Esso Standard Oil (Australia) Ltd*,[8] the High Court held that the question of whether a mark is used as a trade mark is determined by referring to the purpose and nature of the use, common trade usage and how the mark is displayed.[9] The case law indicates that a mark is not used as a trade mark if it simply refers to the reputation or renown of the trade mark owner; if it is used to refer to the trade mark owner's product; if it is used as a name or as a description; or if it is not used as a badge of origin.

Some cases are relatively straightforward. For example, in *Irvings Yeast-Vite Ltd v Horsenail*,[10] there was held to be no infringement of the plaintiff's

---

5    (1954) 91 CLR 592.

6    [1981] NSWLR 491 at 497.

7    In *Mark Foy's Ltd v Davies Coop and Co Ltd* (1956) 95 CLR 190 at 204, the High Court applied *Irvings Yeast-Vite Ltd v Horsenail* (1934) 51 RPC 110 and held that the words "as a trade mark" were implied in the infringement provisions proscribing use of the trade mark.

8    (1963) 109 CLR 407.

9    (1963) 109 CLR 407 at 426, cited with approval more recently by Gummow J in *Johnson and Johnson Australia Pty Ltd v Sterling Pharmaceuticals Pty Ltd* (1991) 101 ALR 700.

10   (1934) 51 RPC 110.

YEAST-VITE mark when the defendant sold tablets with a label saying "Yeast Tablets a substitute for Yeast-Vite", because this did not indicate any connection in the course of trade between the product and the trade mark owner. In *Unilever Australia Ltd v Karounos*, there was held to be no infringement of Karounos' trade mark REAL, when Unilever included the words "Real Soup" above its Rosella mark on a tomato soup. The fact that the words were in smaller type than the word "Rosella" was indicative that the word was being used in a descriptive sense rather than as a trade mark.[11] In *Pepsico Australia Pty Ltd v The Kettle Chip Company Pty Ltd*,[12] the Full Federal Court held that the defendant's use of the phrase "Kettle cooked potato chips" was not use as a trade mark of the registered mark "KETTLE", but instead was a description of the cooking process. In *Nature's Blend Pty Ltd v Nestle Australia Ltd*,[13] both at first instance and on appeal, the court found that the defendant's use of the words "luscious Lips" did not infringe the registered trade mark "LUSCIOUS LIPS", but instead was a description of the defendant's confectionery contained in its Retro Party Mix product.

On the other hand, Mark Foy's trade mark "TUB HAPPY" was held to have been infringed by the defendant's label "EXACTO COTTON GARMENTS TUB HAPPY COTTON FRESH BUDGET WISE", on the basis that the use of the term was held not to be purely descriptive but distinguished the defendant's goods from those of other traders. The fact that the defendant's use suggested that the requisite connection was with EXACTO rather than Mark Foy's did not change the nature of the use.[14]

The importance of context is central in deciding whether there has been use as a trade mark. For example, in *Aldi Stores Ltd Partnership v Frito-Lay Trading Co GmbH*,[15] the prominent position of the words "Cheezy Twists" on the front of the defendant's snack packets was important in satisfying the court that there was use as a trade mark. In *Top Heavy Pty Ltd v Killin*,[16] the court found that the defendant's use of the registered trade mark "CHILL OUT" (for clothing) on the front of T-shirts did not constitute trade mark use as it was purely decorative. The importance of context led Lindgren J to state in *Perfection Fresh Aust Pty Ltd v Top Class Fruit Supply Pty Ltd* that "There is not a clear demarcation between trade mark usage and descriptive usage".[17] In *Anheuser-Busch Inc v Budejovický Budvar, Národní Podnik* with respect to trade mark use Allsop J said: "The task is to examine the way the words are used in their context, including the totality of the packaging, to assess their nature and purpose in order to see whether they are used to distinguish the goods from goods of others".[18]

Difficult problems arise when the mark is used in such a way that the user gets the benefit of the trade mark owner's reputation or the goodwill built up in the mark but does not actually use the mark to refer to the relevant connection.

11   (2001) 52 IPR 361.
12   (1996) 33 IPR 161.
13   (2010) 86 IPR 1; (2010) 87 IPR 464 (Full Federal Court).
14   *Mark Foy's Ltd v Davies Coop and Co Ltd* (1956) 95 CLR 190.
15   (2001) 190 ALR 185 (Full Federal Court).
16   (1996) 34 IPR 282.
17   [2002] FCA 1636 at [25].
18   (2002) 56 IPR 182 at 227.

In *Johnson and Johnson Australia Pty Ltd v Sterling Pharmaceuticals Pty Ltd*,[19] the defendants purposely set out to devalue the plaintiff's trade mark CAPLETS by using it as a generic term on their packaging to refer to their own capsule shaped tablet. The word was used in smaller lettering than the defendant's own trade mark. This was held not to be an infringing use because, in the words of Gummow J:

> [T]he appellant has not used "Caplets" on its packaging so as to invite persons to purchase the product in the packaging which is to be distinguished from the products of other traders, partly because "Caplets" is used in relation to them.[20]

In *Shell Company of Australia Ltd v Esso Standard Oil (Australia) Ltd*,[21] the defendants, Shell, made a television commercial featuring a cartoon humanised oil drop which somewhat resembled Esso's trade mark blob. In the advertisement the little oil drop slides through mesh, shows off its patent and gets an injection (a petrol additive, Windeyer J assumes in the first instance).[22] The High Court held that in this advertisement "the purpose and only purpose that can be seen in the appearance of the little man on the screen is that it unites the quickly moving series of pictures as a whole, namely the purpose of conveying by a combination of pictures and words a particular message about the qualities of Shell petrol".[23] The purpose was not to show a connection in trade between a person (here Shell) and the mark. This case, decided in 1963, is an extreme example of the application of the badge of origin principle to the definition of a trade mark and its use. You might like to consider whether such a strict application of the principle would be made today.

Referring to a trade mark as a badge of origin does not mean that passing off principles are imported into trade mark law. A trade mark, unlike the indicia in passing-off law, is protected in its own right, not simply in so far as it refers to the reputation of its owner. In *Saville Perfumery Ltd v June Perfect Ltd*,[24] for example, the House of Lords, referring to the *Trade Marks Act 1938* (UK), relied on the function of the trade mark as a badge of origin to hold that there could be an infringement of a trade mark even where the trade mark was used with printed matter which indicated that the product did not originate with the trade mark owner. Viscount Maugham quoted the Master of the Rolls:

> But this circumstance, relevant though it may be upon the question of passing off is immaterial upon the question of infringement. In an infringement action, once it is found that the defendant's mark is used as a trade mark, the fact that he makes it clear that the commercial origin of the goods indicated by the trade mark is some business other than that of the plaintiff, avails him nothing, since infringement consists in using the mark as a trade mark, that is, as indicating any origin.[25]

This reasoning may still apply in the case of s 120(1) infringements in relation to the goods and services for which the mark is registered but there is a real

---

19    (1991) 101 ALR 700.
20    (1991) 101 ALR 700 at 726-727.
21    (1963) 109 CLR 407.
22    (1963) 109 CLR 407 at 413.
23    (1963) 109 CLR 407 at 425.
24    (1941) 1B IPR 440.
25    (1941) 1B IPR 440 at 464.

question as to how far this principle should apply in the case of s 120(2) and (3) infringements where there is a requirement of deception or confusion (s 120(2)) or a positive requirement to show a connection in the course of trade (s 120(3)).[26]

Courts have had to go through quite complex contortions trying to apply these principles to find that using a genuine mark in relation to second-hand goods is not a use of the mark as a trade mark even when the defendant is dealing in those goods. However, it appears to be settled that if a genuine mark is used in relation to products which have originated from the trade mark owner this is not a use of the mark as a trade mark by a second-hand dealer in those products. (See *Fender Australia Pty Ltd v Bevk*[27] as to second-hand guitars and *Wingate Marketing Pty Ltd v Levi Strauss and Co*[28] as to second-hand Levi jeans.) Although it has been held that in these cases the dealer was not using the mark to show a connection between the dealer and the goods the cases are better understood today as an application of the doctrine of exhaustion (see discussion of s 123 below).

# Defences

## Name and other trade usages (s 122)

Under s 122 a trade mark is not infringed if:

- the person uses, in good faith, his or her name, the name of his or her place of business or his or her predecessor's name or name of place of business (s 122(1)(a));
- the person uses a sign, in good faith, to indicate the kind, quality, quantity, intended purpose, value, geographical origin, or some other characteristic of the goods or services or the time of production of the goods or services (s 122(1)(b));
- the person uses, in good faith, the trade mark to indicate the intended purposes of the goods (in particular as accessories or spare parts) or services (s 122(1)(c));
- the person uses the trade mark for comparative advertising (s 122(1)(d));
- the person exercises a right to use a trade mark given to the person under the Act (s 122(1)(e)). This applies where the defendant is using his or her own valid, registered mark or is authorised to use the mark by an authorised owner;[29]
- the court is of the opinion that the person could obtain registration of the mark in his or her own name if the person were to apply for it (s 122(1)(f)). This section might apply where there has been a purported assignment of the mark, where there has been a concurrent use or where there has been a prior use;
- the person uses a trade mark that is substantially identical with or deceptively similar to the first-mentioned trade mark, and the court is of

26   See *Marc A Hammond Pty Ltd v Papa Carmine Pty Ltd* (1976) 15 ALR 179 for an example of the deception or confusion defence.
27   (1989) 89 ALR 89.
28   (1994) 28 IPR 193.
29   *Spillers Ltd's Application* (1954) 71 RPC 234.

the opinion that the person would obtain registration of the substantially identical or deceptively similar trade mark in his or her name if the person were to apply for it (s 122(1)(fa));
- the usage is within a condition or limitation, or disclaimer (s 122(1)(g) and (2)).

In *Hy-Line Chicks Pty Ltd v Swifte*,[30] Windeyer J appears to have suggested, obiter, that the name of the person's business, Hy-Line Poultry Farm, was the name of the defendant's place of business for the purposes of s 64(1)(a) of the *Trade Marks Act 1955*, which is the equivalent of s 122(1)(a) of the 1995 Act. It was not clear whether this was because it was the name of the business or because the business was carried on at Hy-Line Farm but, in *Angove's Pty Ltd v Johnson*,[31] the second option was adopted by the Full Federal Court. The court in that case held that any reference to the city, town, suburb, street or street number (or farm name?) of the business might allow the use under this defence. In this case the business name, "St Agnes Liquor Store", was held to be covered by the exemption in so far as the business was situated in the suburb of St Agnes.

The use of the name is in good faith if it is "an honest use ... with no intention to deceive anybody or without any intention to make use of the goodwill which has been acquired by another trader".[32] The use may be in good faith even if it causes some confusion[33] and this applies even if the person continues to use the name having been made aware of possible confusion.[34]

The defences relating to the quality, purpose and comparative advertising repeat many of the themes already examined in relation to use as a trade mark. The cases referred to above are therefore applicable to the determination of this defence.

## Consent, parallel importation and second-hand goods (s 123)

Section 123 provides that there is no infringement if the trade mark has been applied by or with the consent of the "registered owner" of the trade mark. This section, introduced in the 1995 Act, incorporates the doctrine of exhaustion which had developed under previous case law. Thus, there is no infringement of a trade mark if the person sells second-hand goods bearing the trade mark if the marks were applied to those goods with the consent of the owner.[35]

How this section will be applied in relation to parallel importation is so far unclear. Under the 1955 Act the original manufacturer and registered trade mark owners were unsuccessful in their attempt to halt the parallel importation of Bailey's Irish Cream in *R and A Bailey and Co Ltd v Boccaccio Pty Ltd*.[36] In that case the question of consent was not argued and the case was decided on the basis that a trade mark was a badge of origin not a badge of control.

---

30  (1966) 115 CLR 159 at 161.
31  (1982) 43 ALR 349.
32  *Baume and Co Ltd v AH Moore Ltd* [1958] 1 Ch 907 at 921.
33  *Parker-Knoll Ltd v Knoll International Ltd* [1962] RPC 265 at 275.
34  *Angove's Pty Ltd v Johnson* (1982) 43 ALR 349.
35  *Fender Australia Pty Ltd v Bevk* (1989) 89 ALR 89; *Wingate Marketing Pty Ltd v Levi Strauss and Co* (1994) 28 IPR 193.
36  (1986) 6 IPR 279.

In *Revlon Inc v Cripps and Lee Ltd*,[37] the English trade mark owner, who was a subsidiary of an American company, was held to have impliedly consented to the importation of cosmetics which carried a trade mark applied with the consent of the American company. The consent was partly implied from the relationship between the companies and partly from the fact that the product carried an endorsement which read "Revlon, New York, Paris and London".

In *Fender Australia Pty Ltd v Bevk*,[38] on the other hand, Burchett J in the Federal Court held that Fender Australia, the registered trade mark owner in Australia and sole distributor of Fender guitars in Australia, had not consented to the application or use of the trade mark in Australia on Fender guitars bought in the United States and imported and sold in Australia. Rather, the parallel importation of the genuine articles was an infringement of the Australian company's trade mark. Similarly, in *Sporte Leisure Pty Ltd v Paul's International Pty Ltd (No 3)*,[39] Nicholas J in the Federal Court found that the trade marks had not been applied with the consent of the registered owner. In this case, the respondent had imported garments which bore the applicant's registered trade marks. The respondent relied upon the s 123 defence, and argued that the trade marks had been applied in Pakistan pursuant to a licence agreement with the applicant. Nicholas J upheld the applicant's claim for trade mark infringement, and found that pursuant to the licence agreement the consent of the owner only extended to garments produced for sale to regular customers in India.

An entirely different approach was taken in *Transport Tyre Sales Pty Ltd v Montana Tyre Rims and Tubes Pty Ltd*,[40] decided under the 1995 Act. In this case the Japanese manufacturer of the tyres in question had made a revocable assignment of the trade mark to the sole Australian distributor of the tyres, Transport Tyres. Before this registration Montana had imported the same tyres which it had purchased in Singapore. The tyres were marked with the manufacturer's trade mark. Montana relied on the s 123 defence and argued that the mark had been applied in Singapore with the consent of the Japanese owner and therefore there was no infringement of the mark in Australia.

The plaintiffs, on the other hand, argued that a trade mark was territorial in function and therefore the trade mark which was applied in Singapore was a different legal entity to the trade mark registered in Australia (even though they were otherwise identical). In this case the consent had not been given in relation to the Australian mark but for the application of the Singapore mark. The Full Federal Court rejected this argument. It held that, whilst the rights of the trade mark owner were territorial, the trade mark itself, as a sign, was not. The court held that the rights of the owner were exhausted upon application of the mark and that the application of any principle of territoriality to the sign itself was incompatible with international marketing and manufacturing practices.

Note that this case was only argued in relation to tyres purchased before Transport Tyres became the registered owners in Australia and therefore serious questions remain as to which registered owner must give the relevant consent.

---

37    [1980] FSR 85.

38    (1989) 89 ALR 89.

39    (2010) 275 ALR 258.

40    (1999) 162 ALR 175.

Unlike the *Copyright Act 1968*, which contains detailed provisions relating to who is the registered owner for the purpose of parallel importing, there are no similar provisions under the *Trade Marks Act 1995* and we might expect future cases to address this issue.

### Prior continuous use (s 124)

Section 124 of the *Trade Marks Act 1995* contemplates that there may be an honest concurrent user of a registered and unregistered mark and impliedly condones some confusion in relation to the trade marks register and the use of marks. Under s 124(1) a person is not liable for infringement if he or she uses a substantially identical or deceptively similar trade mark in relation to similar or closely related goods and services if the person or the person's predecessor in title has continuously used the unregistered mark in relation to those goods and services from a date before the priority date or the date that the registered owner or his or her predecessor in title first used the trade mark (whichever is earlier). Section 124(2) provides that if the unregistered trade mark has continuously been used only in a particular area of Australia, s 124(1) only applies to the use of the trade mark by the person in that area.

This exemption has been very narrowly interpreted and, in *Hy-Line Chicks Pty Ltd v Swifte*,[41] Windeyer J declined to find the necessary continuous user in relation to "chickens and other bred poultry". In this case the defendant had a poultry farm, produced eggs, bred chickens for their egg production and even sold some live chickens. They had recently started selling day-old chicks. Windeyer J held that this was insufficient and that they had only a short and non-continuous user as the producers of day-old chickens.

### Dealing

Because a trade mark has traditionally been regarded as a badge of origin it was sometimes argued, on the basis of *Bowden Wine Ltd v Bowden Brake Co Ltd*,[42] that no trade mark can be sold, licensed or otherwise dealt with unless the business to which it is attached is sold or licensed with it. This is an overstatement and such a broad interpretation was rejected by the High Court in *Pioneer Kabusiki v Registrar of Trade Marks*.[43] The court held that the general rule is that a trade mark may be assigned, licensed or otherwise dealt with so long as it does not sever the connection between the registered owner and the products or cause the trade mark to become deceptive. This connection, the court insisted, need only be "slight such as selection, or quality control or control of the user in the sense in which a parent company controls a subsidiary".[44]

This statement is arguably still correct as a statement of general principle and successive trade marks statutes have simply liberalised the procedures and altered the burden of proof relating to trade mark dealings. Under the *Trade*

---

41    (1966) 115 CLR 159.
42    (1941) 31 RPC 385.
43    (1977) 137 CLR 670.
44    (1977) 137 CLR 670 at 683.

*Marks Act 1905* s 58, for example, an assignment of a trade mark without the goodwill of the business was said to be invalid unless it could be established that the mark had in fact become distinctive of the assignee's goods. Under the *Trade Marks Act 1955* s 82, on the other hand, a trade mark could be assigned with or without the goodwill of the business but an assignment without the goodwill would be invalid if it could be confused with the assignor's use. The Act expressly provided that the assignment was not invalid if, as a matter of fact, the mark was distinctive of the assignee's goods.

There were no express provisions in these Acts relating to licensing although from 1948 on the Acts allowed the registration of "permitted users" of the mark.[45] The registered user provisions were not compulsory and it was accepted by the High Court in *Pioneer Kabusiki v Registrar of Trade Marks*[46] that licensing was permitted with or without registration of the user.

The *Trade Marks Act 1995* does not make any dramatic changes to this position although, for the first time, the Act expressly provides that a trade mark is a form of personal property (s 21). The Act provides that a trade mark may be assigned or transmitted wholly or partially in relation to the goods and services for which it is registered (s 106(1), and (2)). Unlike copyright and patents, however, a trade mark may not be partially assigned or transmitted in relation to use of the trade mark in a particular geographical area (s 106(2)). The Act provides further that the assignment or transmission may be with or without the goodwill of the business concerned in the relevant goods and/or services (s 106(3). The 1995 Act has no provision for the registration of permitted users although it does recognise "authorised users" for the purposes of establishing standing to object to the importation of infringing articles.[47] The Act provides that an assignment must be registered (ss 107-111). Like its predecessors, the 1995 Act maintains some limitations in so far that, if the dealing severs the requisite connection, then the mark may be susceptible to challenge for non-user.

## Domain Names

Well-known trade marks have been a popular target for cybersquatters who appropriate the mark as a domain address. The general principles of registration and infringement of trade marks apply in this case. Domain names may be registered as a trade mark if they are distinctive, not deceptive or confusing and not substantially identical with or deceptively similar to a trade mark registered in the jurisdiction. If the mark is simply being used as an address its registration might be challenged on the basis of non-use as a trade mark or lack of intention to use it as a trade mark. In the case of infringement the registered owner must establish that it is being used as a trade mark. This is not always so if the name is simply being used as an address.

Attempts are being made to set up a regulatory structure which will meet the interests of both trade mark owners and domain name users although there are some considerable difficulties in joining these different types of usages. The current

---

45  *Bowden Wine Ltd v Bowden Brake Co Ltd* (1941) 31 RPC 385.
46  (1977) 137 CLR 670.
47  See definition of "authorised user" in s 8.

system of trade marks, for example, allows similar marks to co-exist in different geographical areas and in relation to different goods and services. Internet domain names, on the other hand, do not function like this. They are international and omnipresent and are not readily regulated in regard to the type of product or service (if any) in relation to which they are used. Trade marks in Australia are registered by IP Australia whilst domain names are registered internationally under a not-for-profit system of registration co-ordinated by ICANN (Internet Corporation for Assigned Names and Number). Different domains (.com; .org; .net, for example) may also be registered by different bodies. However, progress is being made internationally to provide a satisfactory response to these issues. In jurisdictions such as the United States, anti-cybersquatting legislation has been passed.[48] In June 1998, the World Intellectual Property Organization (WIPO) undertook an international consultation to develop recommendations concerning legal issues associated with domain names, including domain name dispute resolution. WIPO's findings were finalised on 30 April 1999 with the publication of a Final Report.[49] The recommendations contained in the Final Report were adopted by ICANN, and the Uniform Domain Name Dispute Resolution Policy (UDRP) was established as a dispute resolution procedure for resolving domain name disputes.[50] The UDRP has been a very popular method for resolving disputes, and since its inception in December 1999 the WIPO Arbitration and Mediation Center has administered over 21,430 proceedings under the UDRP (or UDRP-related policies).[51] Complainants must submit to the UDRP in the event of a dispute, and adjudicating panellists are required to adhere to the UDRP when deciding a dispute.[52] While there is no formal doctrine of precedent implemented in UDRP proceedings, all written decisions of panellists are publicly available and frequently referred to, particularly where consensus has emerged about a particular issue.[53] A number of 'providers' or organisations, such as WIPO, and the Asian Domain Name Dispute Resolution Centre, have also been approved by ICANN to provide a dispute resolution service under the UDRP.[54]

To date, there has been very little Australian case law on trade marks and online infringement, and the vast majority of decisions in this area have

---

48   See the *Domain Name Piracy Prevention Act 1999* (US), the *Anticybersquatting Consumer Protection Act 1999* (US), the *Trademark Cyberpiracy Protection Act 1999* (US) and the *Satellite Viewers Act 1999* (US).

49   *The Management of Internet Names and Addresses: Intellectual Property Issues*, Final Report of the WIPO Internet Domain Name Process *http://wipo2.wipo.int*, <http://www.wipo.int/amc/en/processes/process1/report/index.html>.

50   The UDRP is available on ICANN's website: <http://www.icann.org/en/udrp/udrp.htm>. The Australian Uniform Dispute Resolution Policy (auDRP) for .au domain names is similar to and based on the UDRP. The policy was prepared by auDA. The auDRP is available at <http://www.auda.org.au/audrp/audrp-overview/>.

51   See generally WIPO, *WIPO Domain Name Dispute Resolution Statistics* <http://www.wipo.int/amc/en/domains/statistics/>.

52   The rules for the resolution of disputes under the UDRP are available online. See *Rules for Uniform Domain Name Dispute Resolution Policy* (the "Rules"), ICANN <http://www.icann.org/en/dndr/udrp/uniform-rules.htm>.

53   See D Lindsay, "International Domain Name Law: ICANN and the UDRP", Hart Publishing, Portland, 2007, pp 130-133.

54   See ICANN, *List of Approved Dispute Resolution Service Providers* <http://www.icann.org/en/dndr/udrp/approved-providers.htm>.

originated from the United States, European Union and the United Kingdom.[55] It is for this reason that *Mantra Group Pty Ltd v Tailly Pty Ltd (No 2) (Mantra)*[56] attracted considerable attention when it was handed down by Reeves J in the Federal Court in March 2010.[57] This case is an important decision as it signals the direction Australian courts may take when dealing with trade mark law in the new sphere of online infringement. The *Mantra* case involved the Circle on Cavill apartment complex in Surfers Paradise, Queensland. The complex included 644 residential apartments. Mantra was the exclusive onsite rental agent for the apartments, however it did not have a monopoly over the offsite rental services for the complex. The respondent Tailly had approximately 39 apartments in the complex to sub-let. Mantra was the registered owner of various trade marks incorporating the words CIRCLE ON CAVILL and MANTRA. Mantra claimed that Tailly had infringed its registered trade marks by the way it used the internet and its domain names for its online advertising and marketing, and by "typosquatting" or "domain mimicry" (ie where a domain name is registered by a deliberate misspelling of another domain name).[58] Mantra also claimed that Tailly had breached relevant sections of the former *Trade Practices Act 1974* by using those words and logos in a false, misleading and/or deceptive way. Tailly argued that it had used those words in a descriptive sense, as opposed to using the words as a trade mark. Further, Tailly claimed that it used the words CIRCLE ON CAVILL in good faith to indicate the geographical origin of the accommodation services it was offering. Finally, Tailly filed a cross-claim under s 87 of the *Trade Marks Act 1995* arguing that Mantra's trade marks using the words "Circle on Cavill" should be cancelled as they had "become generally accepted in the trade of subletting apartments in Surfers Paradise as the sign that describes the name of the Circle on Cavill apartment complex".[59] Reeves J rejected Tailly's arguments outright and found that there had been use of the relevant words as a trade mark. In considering the issues in the case, Reeves J spent considerable time examining the nature of the internet, and how both parties used the internet for their online advertising and marketing.[60]

Interestingly, in deciding the major question in this case: that is, whether the words were used as a trade mark, Reeves J demonstrated no hesitation at all in drawing from established case law to apply core trade mark infringement

---

55  See generally M Davison, T Berger and A Freeman, *Shanahan's Australian Law of Trade Marks and Passing Off,* 4th ed, Lawbook Co, Sydney, 2008, pp 861-917.

56  (2010) 183 FCR 450.

57  Interestingly, the Federal Court has recently considered other cases involving trade marks and domain names: *Solahart Industries Pty Ltd v Solar Shop Pty Ltd* [2011] FCA 700, Perram J at [50] (for a useful summary of whether use of a domain name constitutes use as a trade mark); *Sports Warehouse Inc v Fry Consulting Pty Ltd* (2010) 186 FCR 519 (whether use of a domain name constitutes use as a trade mark under s 41(5) of the Act).

58  Mantra gave evidence that out of the 16 domain names held by Tailly, 13 were found to begin with the word "Circle", or letter "e" followed by the word "Circle", and one domain name began with the word "Cavill". Further, nine of these 14 domain names used the word (or a misspelling of the word) "Cavill". Mantra also gave evidence that Tailly manipulated Google search results by using the words "Circle on Cavill" frequently in the source codes for its websites, and by paying for advertising on Google as a sponsored link using similar terms to "Circle on Cavill". See *Mantra* (2010) 183 FCR 450 at 458-460.

59  (2010) 183 FCR 450 at 453.

60  (2010) 183 FCR 450 at 455-461.

principles to a newly emerging area of law (see the extract from the case at the end of this chapter).

## Offences

It is an offence to falsify or unlawfully remove a trade mark which has been applied to goods and services in the course of trade (s 145); to falsely apply a trade mark to goods or services being used in the course of trade (s 146) or to manufacture or possess dies and other equipment knowing that it is likely to be used in contravention of these provisions (s 147).

It is an offence to intentionally sell or deal with goods knowing or reckless to the knowledge that they have had a falsified trade mark applied to them or that a registered trade mark has been unlawfully removed from them or a registered trade mark has been falsely applied to them (s 148).

Section 151 provides that no person shall make a representation that a mark is a registered trade mark unless the person knows or has reasonable grounds to believe that the mark is registered in Australia. A person is also prohibited from making similar representations regarding part of a mark, the exclusive rights of the person or conditions or limitations attaching to the mark.

In addition to these substantive offences the Act also proscribes certain conduct in relation to the registration of the mark.[61]

## Current Developments: The Intellectual Property Laws Amendment (Raising the Bar) Act 2012 (Cth)

After two years of public consultation, and more than half a year in Parliament, the *Intellectual Property Laws Amendment (Raising the Bar) Act 2012* (Cth) (the Act) received Royal Assent on 15 April 2012. The majority of amendments will come into force in another 12 months, allowing for Regulations to be drafted. The Act amends the *Trade Marks Act 1995* (Cth), as well as the *Patents Act 1990* (Cth), the *Copyright Act 1968* (Cth), the *Designs Act 2003* (Cth) and the *Plant Breeder's Rights Act 1994* (Cth). The amendments have been divided into six Schedules. Schedules 1 and 2 specifically relate to patent reforms, while Schs 3-6 deal with reform in all other areas, including patents.[62] Schedule 3 is titled "Reducing delays in resolving patent and trade mark applications", and amends the *Trade Marks Act 1995* (Cth) by introducing changes into trade mark opposition procedure with the aim that disputes will settle more quickly and inexpensively. Schedule 4 is titled "Assisting the operations of the IP profession", and amends both the *Patents Act 1990* (Cth) and the *Trade Marks Act 1995* (Cth) to allow patent and trade mark attorneys to incorporate. The Act also extends client-attorney professional privilege to the same level of privilege that currently exists between client-lawyer. Currently, although communications with Australian

---

61   Sections 152, 153, 154, 156, 157.

62   For a summary of the specific items introduced by the Act in relation to trade marks legislation, see B Elkington and A Roy, "The *Intellectual Property Laws Amendment (Raising the Bar) Bill 2011* (Cth) and its impact on the *Trade Marks Act 1995* (Cth)" (2011) 85 *IP Forum* 25.

attorneys attract professional privilege, communications with foreign attorneys are not afforded the same degree of privilege (unlike client-lawyer privilege which extends to communications with foreign legal professionals). The underlying aim of Sch 4 is to rectify the current anomalies which exist between the ways in which patent and trade mark attorneys can operate as a business and the ways in which other professionals, such as legal professionals, can operate. Schedule 5 is titled "Improving mechanisms for trade mark and copyright enforcement", and addresses concerns relating to penalties for trade mark counterfeiting – which are lower than those for copyright infringement.[63] Schedule 5 introduces improved mechanisms for trade mark (and copyright) enforcement by increasing penalties for trade mark infringement, and by revising the "notice of objection" scheme for Customs to seize counterfeit trade mark (or copyright) goods. Finally, Sch 6 is titled "Simplifying the IP system", and amends the trade marks legislation (and also the *Patents Act 1990* (Cth), *Designs Act 2003* (Cth) and *Plant Breeder's Rights Act 1994* (Cth)) to implement a number of changes to remove procedural hurdles and streamline processes for an increasingly global and electronic environment. The *Intellectual Property Laws Amendment (Raising the Bar) Act 2012* is one of the most comprehensive revisions to Australia's intellectual property regime and introduces significant changes to trade marks practice and procedure.

---

63    For example, see Advisory Council on Intellectual Property, *Review of Trade Mark Enforcement*, 2004, pp 22-24 <http://www.acip.gov.au/library/reviewtmenforce.pdf>; IP Australia, *Review of Penalties and Additional Damages Trade Marks Act 1995 Options Paper*, 2008, p 3 <http://www.ipaustralia.gov.au/pdfs/news/2008-11-26%20Review%20of%20penalties%20and%20additional%20damages%20in%20the%20Trade%20Marks%20Act%201995.pdf>.

# CASES

## *Polaroid Corporation v Sole N Pty Ltd*
Supreme Court of New South Wales: Kearney J
[1981] 1 NSWLR 491

The parties accepted Windeyer J's judgment in *Shell Co of Australia Ltd v Esso Standard Oil (Australia) Ltd*[64] that when considering whether the marks are substantially identical they should be compared side by side but when considering whether the marks were deceptively similar one should have regard to the total impression. The parties disagreed on how this should be applied and, in particular, disagreed as to whether all the surrounding circumstances should be taken into account in accordance with Kitto J's principles in *Southern Cross Refrigerating Co v Toowoomba Foundry Pty Ltd*.[65]

**Kearney J: [496]** Reverting to the principal point, the plaintiff's mode of applying the criteria as analysed by Windeyer J (1963) 109 CLR 407, at pp 414, 415) requires the exclusion of elements which might be described as passing-off considerations and confines the inquiry accordingly.

On the other hand the defendants contend that while passing-off considerations are not relevant under s 62(1) in a direct sense, nevertheless, in a case under s 62(1), it is permissible to look to the use of the mark. They further submit that, notwithstanding the distinction between sub-s (1) and sub-s (2) of s 62, which is so strongly emphasized by the plaintiffs, the use to which such mark is put is not irrelevant under sub-s (1). The defendants rely upon the long-established terminology adopted in trade mark law, both on the early authorities and in the statutory provisions, and submit that the wording of s 62(1) should not be given a radically different effect without a clear indication to that effect in the Act.

Thus, the defendants submit that the test of "deceptively similar" takes one back to the definition section, s 6(3), which provides:

"For the purposes of this Act, a trade mark shall be deemed to be deceptively similar to another trade mark if it so nearly resembles that other trade mark as to be likely to deceive or cause confusion."

The defendants then say that therefore the inquiry concerning deceptive similarity under s 62(1) necessarily encompasses factors and considerations outside the marks themselves.

Further support for this approach on the part of the defendants is sought to be derived from such decisions as that of *Southern Cross Refrigerating Co v Toowoomba Foundry Pty Ltd* (1954) 91 CLR 592. The defendants point to the passage in the judgment of Kitto J (at pp 594, 595) setting out the matters to be taken into account in considering the question of the likelihood to deceive, or associated questions of confusion. In effect, the defendants submit that the tests which were so formulated in relation to an application for registration under s 114 of the former Commonwealth Act apply also in relation to the question of deceptive **[497]** similarity arising to be determined under s 62. The defendants also refer on this point to the decisions of the House of Lords in *Berlei (UK) Ltd v Bali Brassiere Co Inc* [1969] 1 WLR 1306; [1969] 2 All ER 812 and of the Privy Council in *Hannaford and Burton Ltd v Polaroid Corporation* [1976] 2 NZLR 14. These cases were not, of course, cases of infringement, but applied criteria appropriate to applications for

---

64    (1963) 109 CLR 407 at 414-415.
65    (1954) 91 CLR 592.

expungement or registration where the wide-ranging inquiry embraces inter alia, the risk of confusion in the minds of a substantial number of persons and other factors mentioned in the *Southern Cross Refrigerating Case* (1954) 91 CLR 592, at p 608.

It seems to me that this proposition of the defendants is not a valid approach to the question raised for determination under s 62. The definition in s 6(3) is not directed to a case such as the present of a contest between a registered mark and another mark. It is concerned only with a competition between two trade marks, and is limited to that situation. It is directed rather to situations necessitating comparison of trade marks under such sections as s 33, s 34, s 58(3) and s 82(2) of the Act: see also *Smith Kline and French Laboratories Ltd's Trade Mark Applications* [1976] RPC 511, at p 532, per Lord Diplock. So far as the authorities are concerned to which the defendants refer, I do not consider that they have significant bearing on the matters raised for consideration and determination in dealing with the question of infringement under s 62. They were concerned, as previously mentioned, with different situations involving wider considerations than are admissible under s 62(1). As counsel for the plaintiff phrased it, these cases involve a different universe of discourse from that involved when the court is measuring the monopoly of a party already on the register and thus entitled to the protection and assistance provided by the Act in aid of the right so held.

Therefore, I uphold the plaintiff's first proposition coupled with its contention as to exclusion of passing-off elements in limiting the inquiry called for under s 62(1).

The defendants further submitted that it was proper to look at the market, and in this regard suggested that the products of the plaintiffs are in a more expensive range, and also that they are provided to a different class of customer from that applicable in the case of the defendants' goods. For the same reasons as outlined above, I do not consider that matter of this kind is appropriate to be considered under the tests stated in s 62.

The same comment is to be made as to the defendants' submission that the absence of evidence of actual confusion is to be taken into account. Here again, this question is completely outside the range of the inquiry required under s 62.

In further answer to these further submissions of the defendants, it might be added that it is not a question of the manner in which the plaintiffs use their marks, but rather a question of which market, and the extent of the market which the plaintiffs are to be treated as free to use. The only question posed under s 62 is whether the defendants have trespassed into any part of that area reserved to the plaintiffs by virtue of their proprietorship of the registered marks. This question is to be determined by reference to potential use in such area by the defendants of the first defendant's mark: see *Marc A Hammond Pty Ltd v Papa Carmine Pty Ltd* [1976] 2 NSWLR 124, at p 128; *Berlei Hestia Industries Ltd v Bali Co Inc* (1973) 129 CLR 353, at p 362, per Mason J.

**[498]** Applying the tests referred to by Windeyer J ((1963) 109 CLR 409, at pp 414, 415, 416) to the two subject marks, the plaintiffs point to the fact that, viewed as a whole, the only difference upon which the defendants can rely is in the first letter of the subject words, and that, so far as substantial identity is concerned, both in respect of essential features and total impression, the similarity is such as to constitute substantial identity. On this point the defendants contend that the words have different connotations, the word "solar" involving a concept of sun; whereas "Polaroid" or "Polar" evoke an entirely different concept; so that ordinary people would not think of any connection between the two words. The plaintiffs assert that there is a common concept evoked by both words, namely that of light; whereas the defendants suggest that this would not occur to the ordinary person, considering the two words side by side, as creating substantial identity. The defendants further rely strongly upon the fact that the differences in the one letter between the two words are highly significant, because it is the first letter of each word, and it is located in the accented syllable in each of the words.

It seems to me that, considering the two marks side by side, they are not substantially identical in regard to the essential features of the marks. Nor do I have a total impression of resemblance between them to the extent of substantial identity. The first letter in each word conveys to my mind a difference between the words which constitutes an essential feature of each of them, so as to preclude a finding that the registered marks and the defendants' mark are substantially identical.

As to deceptive similarity, the impression here to be considered is of course different from that of the impression to be considered in viewing the two marks side by side. As emphasized by Windeyer J ((1963) 109 CLR 407, at p 415) it is an impression based on recollection which may be an imperfect recollection of the plaintiffs' marks that persons of ordinary intelligence and memory would have, and on the other hand, the impression that such persons would get from the defendants' mark. It seems to me that, in applying this test, the similarity between the two marks is such as to qualify as deceptive similarity. The deceptiveness, I consider, flows not only from the degree of similarity itself, but also from its effect considered in relation to the circumstances of the goods, the prospective purchasers and the market covered by the plaintiffs' monopoly. The two words are in the general impression created, so alike that I consider that there is a strong likelihood of confusion arising from the deception created by such similarity.

Accordingly, I would uphold the plaintiffs' claim that an infringement has occurred in the use of the defendants' mark.

### *Mark Foy's Ltd v Davies Coop and Co Ltd*
High Court of Australia: Dixon CJ, Williams and Kitto JJ
(1956) 95 CLR 190

Mark Foy's took an action for infringement against Davies Coop for the use of its trade mark TUB HAPPY. Davies Coop counter-claimed that the mark was not registrable. This case considers both the registrability of a descriptive sign and the concept of "use as a trade mark" for the purposes of infringement.

**Williams J: [199]** The first question is whether the words "tub happy" are registrable as a trade mark under s 16(1)(d) of the *Trade Marks Act*. To qualify they must be words having no direct reference to the character or quality of articles of clothing. In his speech in *Eastman Photographic Materials Co Ltd v Comptroller-General of Patents, Designs and Trade Marks* ("Solio" Case)[66] Lord *Herschell* explained the meaning of this qualification. He said: "any word in the English language may serve as a trade-mark the commonest word in the language might be employed. In these circumstances it would obviously have been out of the question to permit a person by registering a trade-mark in respect of a particular class of goods to obtain a monopoly of the use of a word having reference to the character or quality of those goods. The vocabulary of the English language is common property: it belongs alike to all; and no one ought to be permitted to prevent the other members of the community from using for purposes of description a word which has reference to the character or quality of goods".[67] The introduction of the word "direct" into the paragraph is explained by the following passage in *Kerly on Trade Marks*, 7th ed (1951), p 127: At first the qualification was "A word or words having no reference to the character or quality of the goods, and not being a geographical name ... The decisions on the clause, however, and especially those prior to the *Solio Case*,[68] tended to prevent the registration of words having a merely indirect reference to the character or quality of

---

[66] [1898] AC 571.
[67] [1898] AC, at p 580.
[68] [1898] AC 571.

the goods; the framers of the Act of 1905 therefore introduced the word 'direct' to qualify 'reference' with the object of extending the class of registrable words, or at all events of making the object of the Legislature more clear." One example of words that have been held to have a direct reference to the character or quality of the goods will be found in *Pilippart v William Whiteley Ltd* (*"Diabolo" Case*)[69] where *Parker* J (as he then was) held that this word denoted the top used in the well-known game of diabolo just as cricket applied to a set of stumps would directly suggest the use to which the stumps were to be put. Another example will be found in *In re Colgate & Co's Application*[70] to register the word "ribbon" in respect of a dentrifice. The same learned judge refused the application on the ground that the word referred to a character or quality of the goods because it described the manner in which the dental cream would **[200]** come out of the tube and lie on the brush in the shape of a ribbon. Reference may also be made to two cases in each of which ordinary English words were held to have a reference to the character or quality of the goods. In *In re Keystone Knitting Mills Ltd's Application*[71] the noun "charm" in respect of hosiery being wearing apparel was held to have the same significance as the adjective "charming" and to describe in a laudatory sense the character or quality of the goods. As Lord *Hanworth* said: "I think one has to look at the word which is registered, not in its strict grammatical significance, but as it would represent itself to the public at large who are to look at it and to form an opinion as to what it connotes".[72] In *In re Joseph Crosfield & Sons Ltd's Application*[73] the noun "perfection" when applied to household soap was held to have the same meaning as the adjective "perfect" and as such to be a mere laudatory epithet which could be used to describe the character or quality of any goods and as such open to all the world and incapable of being registered. On the other hand in *In re Compagnie Industrielle Des Petroles' Application*[74] *Warrington* J (as he then was) allowed "Motorine" to be registered in respect of lubricating oils, any exclusive use of the word "motor" being disclaimed. His Lordship said: "I cannot see how the word 'Motorine' has any direct reference to the character or quality of those goods. No doubt it suggests that in some way they are oils which are to be used in connection with a motor, but beyond that it has no reference either to their character or their quality, and such reference as the use of the two syllables of the word 'motor' in the word 'Motorine' as to the character or quality seems to me not to be that direct reference which the present Act contemplates".[75] So too in *In re la Marquise Footwear's Application*[76] *Evershed* J (as he then was) held that the word "Oomphies" in relation to shoes was registrable. Although the word "oomph" had a meaning of sex appeal derived from a popular cinema actress it had no direct reference to any character or quality of ladies' footwear. His Lordship said: "where you take an ordinary word in common use properly applicable in its ordinary meaning to the class of goods to which it is sought to be applied by the applicant, the Court must be slow to give to the applicant in effect a monopoly of that epithet. Where you take a word which is exceedingly uncommon by comparison, I think that somewhat different considerations apply and, if you say that it has a direct reference, you are going to assume **[201]** that this word, which I assume not to be an invented word, has a much more precise significance and a much greater circulation than, I think, on the evidence

---

[69] (1908) 25 RPC 565.
[70] (1913) 30 RPC 262; (1913) 29 TLR 326.
[71] (1928) 45 RPC 421.
[72] (1928) 45 RPC, at p 426.
[73] (1909) 26 RPC 837; [1910] 1 Ch 130.
[74] (1907) 24 RPC 585.
[75] (1907) 24 RPC, at p 592.
[76] (1946) 64 RPC 27; [1946] 2 All ER 497.

plainly it has".[77] Any reference that the words "Tub Happy" have to the character or quality of articles of clothing is very remote. They are in the nature of a coined phrase. Inanimate objects including articles of clothing cannot have the character or quality of happiness whether they are in a tub or not. But the defendants' case is that the common metaphorical use of the adjective would convey to prospective buyers of the fabrics that the cotton emerged from the wash tub more attractive than ever in appearance with fibres and colours as good if not better than ever. Therefore, so it is said, the words are a description of the character or quality of the goods and moreover are not entitled to registration. This claim gives far too specific a meaning to the vague figurative use of the word "happy" in connection with "tub". Like so many expressions used in advertisements no definite or actual meaning seems to belong to the combination "Tub Happy". There is a cloudy suggestion only about it that all will be well in a wash tub but that is all. The attitude of mind of those who glance at such advertisements may be affected favourably by some sort of vague association of ideas but it falls a long way short of conveying any meaning to them. To say that articles of clothing are tub happy is in the ordinary use of English meaningless. The words contain at most a "covert and skilful allusion" to the quality of washability which is characteristic of articles of clothing made of some kinds of material including cotton. At most they create an impression that this is what they are intended to convey. They do not trespass upon the rights of other traders to use any ordinary English words or phrases referring to the washable qualities of their goods. They do not attempt to "enclose and appropriate as private property certain little strips of the great open common of the English language". No doubt the words are intended to "contain a meaning a meaning is wrapped up in them if you can only find it out.": see the speech of Lord *Macnaghten* in the *Solio Case*.[78] And it may not be hard to find out that meaning but the words do not refer in any ordinary sense, laudatory or otherwise, to any character or quality of articles of clothing, still less do they do so directly.

The conclusion that the words "Tub Happy" are registrable under s 16(1)(d) of the *Trade Marks Act* because they have no direct reference to the character or quality of articles of clothing **[202]** goes a long way towards deciding the ground on which his Honour ruled against the defendants. There is nothing in the registration of these words to prevent the defendants describing their cotton goods as having the qualities of washability, freshness and cheapness, and in particular the first of these qualities. The whole English language is open to them, even the most up to date English, if the defendants wish to refer to these qualities "in a modern descriptive sense". In *JB Stone & Co Ltd v Steelace Manufacturing Co Ltd*[79] Lawrence LJ said: "In my opinion the object of s 44" (of the English *Trade Marks Act 1905* which corresponds to s 53A of the Commonwealth Act) "was to safeguard traders in cases where the registered trade mark consisted of more or less descriptive words forming part of the ordinary English language, without the use of which other traders would find some difficulty in describing certain qualities of their goods; but was never intended and does not operate to enable a trader to make use of a rival trader's registered trade mark consisting of a fancy word having no reference to the character and quality of the goods in order more readily to sell his own goods".[80] In *de Cordova v Vick Chemical Co*[81] Lord *Radcliffe*, delivering the judgment of the Privy Council, said: "However that may be, it seems plain on the facts of this case that 'Vapour Rub' cannot be regarded in Jamaica as a 'bona fide description' of the character or quality of the appellants' goods … . If the makers of the goods which the appellants are selling

---

[77] (1946) 64 RPC, at p 32; [1946] 2 All ER, at pp 499, 500.
[78] [1898] AC, at p 583.
[79] (1929) 46 RPC 406.
[80] (1929) 46 RPC, at p 417.
[81] (1951) 68 RPC 103.

desire to inform their customers that the properties of their ointment are such that, if it is rubbed on the chest or throat, it will give off a healing vapour which can be inhaled through the mouth or nose, there is nothing to prevent them from doing so. But that would be something different from what they have done hitherto".[82] Section 53A of the *Trade Marks Act* protects the use by any person of any bona fide description of the character or quality of his goods. But that means a description and not a mere suggestion in fanciful language. It does not protect an attempt by the defendants to usurp a metaphorical phrase like "Tub Happy" however magnetic the force of its public appeal may be.

The remaining question is whether the rights conferred on the plaintiff by s 50 have been infringed. The defendants have used the exact words of the plaintiff's trade mark so that the plaintiff need not rely on s 53. It is contended that the plaintiff's rights have not been infringed because the defendants have not used the words as a trade mark at all, but only descriptively as a laudatory **[203]** or puffing expression to extol the goods. They rely on the speech of Lord *Tomlin*, concurred in by Lord *Atkin* and Lord *Russell of Killowen*, in the *Yeast-Vite Case* in the House of Lords.[83] The Act there in question was the English *Trade Marks Act 1905-1919* and the particular section under review was s 39 which corresponds to s 50 of the Commonwealth Act. The definition of "trade mark" in the English Act was the same as the definition in the Commonwealth Act of 1912. There was no section in the English Act corresponding to s 53 of the Commonwealth Act. The plaintiffs were the proprietors of the registered trade mark "Yeast Vite" and it was held that this mark was not infringed by the defendant selling in his shop a preparation labelled "Yeast Tablets a substitute for Yeast-Vite" which was not the plaintiff's preparation. Lord Tomlin said: "Now the act which the appellants contend amounts in law to an infringement of their exclusive right as registered proprietors of the trade mark is the use by the respondent upon the bottles in which he sells his preparation of the phrase 'Yeast Tablets, a substitute for Yeast-Vite.' This is clearly a use of the word 'Yeast-Vite' on the respondent's preparation to indicate the appellant's preparation and to distinguish the respondent's preparation from it. It is not a use of the word as a trade mark, that is, to indicate the origin of the goods in the respondent by virtue of manufacture, selection, certification, dealing with or offering for sale".[84] His Lordship continued: "The question therefore here … is, what is the property right of the appellants and has it been infringed? It is true that the language of the definition of a trade mark contained in s 3 of the Act of 1905 cannot without some change of form be read directly into s 39, but it is equally true that the language of s 39 must carry with it some implied limitation, unless it is to be given a meaning extending its operation altogether outside the scope of the *Trade Marks Acts*. The phrase 'the exclusive right to the use of such trade mark' carries in my opinion the implication of use of the mark for the purpose of indicating in relation to the goods upon or in connection with which the use takes place, the origin of such goods in the user of the mark by virtue of the matters indicated in the definition of 'trade mark' contained in s 3".[85] Mr May contended that the speech by Lord Tomlin is not applicable to the Commonwealth Act, first because of the difference between the two Acts in the definition of trade mark since the definition in the 1912 Act was omitted and the existing definition substituted for it, and secondly, because of the **[204]** presence in the Commonwealth Act of s 53 which has no counterpart in the English Act. But the reasoning of his Lordship appears to be equally applicable to the Commonwealth Act despite these differences. If the defendants in the present case had advertised that their Exacto cotton frocks washed as well as the plaintiff's Tub Happy frocks it could not be said that the words "Tub Happy"

---

[82] (1951) 68 RPC, at pp 107, 108.
[83] (1934) 51 RPC 110.
[84] (1934) 51 RPC, at p 115.
[85] (1934) 51 RPC, at p 116.

were used by the defendants in relation to goods to indicate a connection in the course of trade between the goods and themselves. They would only be used in support of a claim that their cotton goods washed as well as the plaintiff's Tub Happy goods. In such a case the words "Tub Happy" would not be used as a trade mark within the meaning of the present definition. Section 50 states that the proprietor of a registered trade mark has the exclusive right to the use of the trade mark upon or in connection with the goods in respect of which it is registered. This appears on its face to mean that no one but the proprietor can use the trade mark upon or in connection with the goods in respect of which it is registered for any purpose. One purpose within the section would appear to be the use of the trade mark by an opponent for the purpose of claiming that his goods were a substitute for those of the proprietor. It does not matter that the identity of the proprietor of the trade mark is unknown to the public. It is the trade mark which identifies the goods and the sale of goods that have acquired a reputation could be seriously prejudiced by an opponent offering his goods as substitutes for them. But in the *Yeast-Vite Case*[86] the House of Lords narrowed the meaning of s 50 by implying after the words "the exclusive right to the use of the trade mark" the words "as a trade mark". Their Lordships held that the exclusive rights of the registered proprietor are only infringed if the trade mark is used as a trade mark for the purpose mentioned in the definition. This construction must be applied to s 50 of the Commonwealth Act and the presence of s 53 in that Act can make no difference. Section 53 is really an appendage to s 50 and its function is to widen the definition of infringement so as to include cases where the defendant does not use the identical trade mark but uses a mark substantially identical with it or so nearly resembling it as to be likely to deceive. But the alleged infringement must still be the use of the plaintiff's trade mark or some mark substantially identical with it as a trade mark.

But the *Yeast-Vite Case*[87] does not assist the defendants. They are not using the words "Tub Happy" in the same way as the defendant was using the words "Yeast-Vite" in that case. They **[205]** are advertising the words "Tub Happy" and emphasizing them in relation to their own cotton garments for the purpose of indicating a connection in the course of trade between the goods and themselves. The public are not being invited to compare the "Exacto" goods of the defendants with the "Tub Happy" goods of the plaintiff. They are being invited to purchase goods of the defendants which are to be distinguished from the goods of other traders partly because they are described as "Tub Happy" goods. In *Aristoc Ltd v Rysta Ltd*[88] Viscount *Maugham* cites the following appropriate passage from the judgment of Lord *Greene* MR in *Saville Perfumery Ltd v June Perfect Ltd*:[89] "In an infringement action, once it is found that the defendant's mark is used as a trade mark, the fact that he makes it clear that the commercial origin of the goods indicated by the trade mark is some business other than that of the plaintiff avails him nothing, since infringement consists in using the mark as a trade mark, that is, as indicating origin".[90] Needless to say, if the defendant uses the words of the plaintiff's trade mark as indicating origin it is still an infringement notwithstanding that the defendant always adds his own name: *Kerly on Trade Marks*, 7th ed (1951), p 445.

---

[86] (1934) 51 RPC 110.
[87] (1934) 51 RPC 110.
[88] [1945] AC 68.
[89] (1941) 58 RPC 147, at p 161.
[90] [1945] AC, at p 94.

## *Shell Company of Australia Ltd v Esso Standard Oil (Australia) Ltd*

High Court of Australia: Dixon CJ, McTiernan, Kitto, Taylor and Owen JJ

(1963) 109 CLR 407

Shell used a humanised oil drop similar to Esso's trade mark oil drop in a short advertising film. This case indicates the narrow view previously taken of the phrase "use as a trade mark". Would the courts come to a different view today on the basis of the wider definition of trade mark under the *Trade Marks Act 1995*?

**Kitto J: [421]** The conduct of the appellant which the learned primary Judge held to have constituted infringement consisted in causing two advertising films, of the animated cartoon variety, to be exhibited to the public in the course of television programmes. The films were projected on to a screen during the hearing, on the agreed footing that what was there seen should be treated as evidence in the case. We have accordingly witnessed a screening of the films ourselves. In each film a "humanized" oil drop is made to personify the appellant's Shell petrol, and to perform a series of exuberant antics designed, in conjunction with some letterpress and the spoken word, to create in the minds of viewers a feeling of pleasure at recognizing desirable attributes in Shell petrol. In the course of his merry pranks, the Shell Eulenspiegel constantly changes in shape and expression. He always has a head the shape of an oil drop drawn to a peak at the top, and generally the head is supported, without a neck, by a body bifurcated to indicate short legs with feet turned outwards. Arms and hands take up varying positions, and what passes for a face expresses varying emotions. On some occasions the figure, in the course of its mutations, approaches fairly closely in appearance to the respondent's trade marks; but the name "Esso" is never **[422]** seen, and the changes of appearance follow one another so swiftly that the viewer can hardly gain more than a general impression of a Protean creature who could be, having regard to some of his manifestations at least, the man whom the respondent has registered as its trade mark, but could equally be another member of the same tribe. It may be assumed for present purposes, however, that in the course of each film the figure takes on, at least for a moment or two now and then, an appearance substantially identical with that of the trade marks.

The question, then, is whether such a user of the oil drop figure as takes place by the exhibition of the films on television involves infringement of the trade marks. It is a question not to be answered in favour of the appellant merely by pointing to the brevity of the occasions when substantial identity is achieved. The assumption I have made means, of course, that if the oil drop figure as appearing in some of the individual frames of the films were transferred as separate pictures to another context the use of the pictures in that context could be an infringement. But the context is all-important, because not every use of a mark which is identical with or deceptively similar to a registered trade mark infringes the right of property which the proprietor of the mark possesses in virtue of the registration. Section 58(1) of the *Trade Marks Act 1955-1958* (Cth) defines that right as the right to the exclusive use of the trade mark in relation to the goods in respect of which the trade mark is registered; and s 62(1) adds that a registered trade mark is infringed by a person who, not being the registered proprietor, or a registered user using by way of permitted use, uses a mark which is substantially identical with or deceptively similar to the trade mark, in the course of trade, in relation to goods in respect of which the trade mark is registered. ...

**[424]** The crucial question in the present case seems to me to arise at this point. Was the appellant's use, that is to say its television presentation, of those particular pictures of the oil drop figure which were substantially identical with or deceptively similar to the respondent's trade marks a use of them "as a trade mark"? **[425]** With the aid of the definition of "trade mark" in s 6 of the Act, the adverbial expression may be expanded so that the question becomes whether, in the setting in which the particular pictures referred to were presented, they would have appeared to the television viewer as possessing the character of devices, or brands, which the appellant was using or proposing to use in relation to petrol for the purpose of indicating, or so as to indicate, a connexion in the course of trade between the petrol and the appellant. Did they appear to be thrown on to the screen as being marks for distinguishing Shell petrol from other petrol in the course of trade?

Clearly they were used so that the figure in all its varying forms would be understood as representing Shell petrol for the purposes of the disjointed tale that is told. But the connexion in the films between the oil drop man and the petrol he symbolizes is a connexion limited by the purpose of the occasion. At every point of the exhibition, whether the resemblance to the respondent's trade marks be at the moment close or remote, the purpose and the only purpose that can be seen in the appearance of the little man on the screen is that which unites the quickly moving series of pictures as a whole, namely the purpose of conveying by a combination of pictures and words a particular message about the qualities of Shell petrol. This fact makes it, I think, quite certain that no viewer would ever pick out any of the individual scenes in which the man resembles the respondent's trade marks, whether those scenes be few or many, and say to himself: "There I see something that the Shell people are showing me as being a mark by which I may know that any petrol in relation to which I see it used is theirs." And one may fairly affirm with even greater confidence that the viewer would never infer from the films that every one of the forms which the oil drop figure takes appears there as being a mark which has been chosen to serve the specific purpose of branding petrol in reference to its origin. No doubt if, later, the viewer were to come across the respondent's trade mark used in relation to petrol his recollection of the films might lead him to think that the appellant, taking advantage of a reputation created for the oil drop figure by means of the films, had adopted the figure, in one of its forms, as a mark for its petrol. But that would be quite a different matter from inferring, while sitting in front of his television set, that the figure in one or more, some or all, of its exhibited forms was being placed before him there as a trade mark for Shell petrol.

## *Transport Tyre Sales Pty Ltd v Montana Tyre Rims and Tubes Pty Ltd*
Federal Court of Australia: Beaumont, Heerey and Emmett JJ
(1999) 162 ALR 175

In this case the Japanese manufacturer of the tyres in question had made a revocable assignment of the trade mark to the sole Australian distributor of the tyres, Transport Tyres. Before this registration Montana had imported the same tyres which it had purchased in Singapore. The tyres were marked with the manufacturer's trade mark, which was formed by the moulding on the tyres. Montana relied on the s 123 defence and argued that the mark had been applied in Singapore with the consent of the Japanese owner and therefore there was no infringement of the mark in Australia. You might wish to read this case in its entirety for its treatment of the registration and ownership of trade marks.

### Beaumont, Heerey and Emmett JJ: [187] INFRINGEMENT
65. That moulding, it is common ground, is substantially identical with the Trade Marks. Transport Tyre contended that the sale of such tyres would involve the use of that mould-

ing as a trade mark in relation to the tyres and that such sale involves using a sign as a trade mark in relation to goods within the meaning of s 120.

66. Having regard to the terms of s 9, it is clear that the moulding has been applied to or in relation to the tyres by Ohtsu. At the time when the moulding was placed on the tyres in question, Ohtsu was the registered owner of the Trade Marks. Montana contended, therefore, that it was entitled to the benefit of s 123 because it is a person who used registered trade marks in relation to tyres, being goods that are similar to goods in respect of which those trade marks are registered and the trade marks had been applied to, or in relation to, the tyres by Ohtsu.

67. Transport Tyre, on the other hand, contended that the moulding on the tyres was not a trade mark within the meaning of s 123 because it was not a sign used or intended to be used in Australia. Transport Tyre contended that the term "trade mark" when it is used in s 123 means a sign used or intended to be used in Australia and that there was no evidence that, at the time when the moulding was placed on them, the tyres in question were intended to be projected into the course of trade in Australia. On the contrary, an inference should be drawn, so it was said, that the tyres in question were intended to be projected into trade in Singapore. Thus, since the tyres in question were not intended to be projected into the course of trade in Australia, the moulding on them was not a trade mark within the meaning of s 123. Therefore, even though it might have been applied to or in relation to the tyres by Ohtsu at a time when Ohtsu was the registered owner of the Trade Marks, s 123 has no application.

68. The basis for Transport Tyre's contention is the decision of the High Court **[188]** in *Estex Clothing Manufacturers Pty Ltd v Ellis & Goldstein Ltd* (1967) 116 CLR 254. In that case, the respondent was a manufacturer in England of women's dresses, jersey suits and coats which it sold by wholesale and was registered under the provisions of the Trade Marks Act as the proprietor of two trade marks "EASTEX". The appellant was a New South Wales company which also manufactured articles of women's clothing. The appellant applied for an order that the trade marks in question be removed on the ground that during the relevant period of three years there was no use in good faith of the trade marks by the respondent.

69. During the relevant three year period, the respondent had manufactured and sold to Australian retail traders for resale in Australia substantial quantities of garments with "Eastex" tags and labels sewn on or otherwise attached to the garments. The sales made by the respondent to the Australian retail traders were made in England and the garments, in each instance, were the subject of an FOB contract and property in them passed upon shipment in London. However, during the three year period such garments were displayed for sale and sold in Australia by those retail traders.

70. The question was whether, in those circumstances, there had been a use in Australia of the trade marks by the respondent during the relevant three year period. The appellant contended that there had been no act of the respondent in Australia which could be said to constitute a use by it in Australia of the marks. The High Court said the following (at 271):

> ... when an overseas manufacturer projects into the course of trade in this country, by means of sales to Australian retail houses, goods bearing his mark and the goods, bearing his mark, are displayed or offered for sale or sold in this country, the use of the mark is that of the manufacturer.

71. The High Court considered that in the circumstances of that case, the respondent was the only person who had the right to use the marks and the retailer to whom the garments had been sold for resale did not, in any relevant sense, "use" it.

72. Transport Tyre contended that it follows from that conclusion that the expression "trade mark" when used in the Act must be taken to refer to a mark in relation to goods which are intended to be projected into the course of trade in the Australian market. It was

said, therefore, that the term "trade mark" must, whenever used in the Act, be construed as a reference to the rights which were under the Trade Marks Act 1995 and not to rights which are conferred or which might exist in some other jurisdiction. In particular, the term must be so construed when it appears in s 123. Such an approach, however, in our view confuses the rights which arise from the registration of a trade mark under the Act on the one hand and the physical representation or manifestation of the sign which is registered on the other hand.

73. Section 20(1) of the Trade Marks Act relevantly provides as follows:

If a trade mark is registered, the registered owner of the trade mark has ... the exclusive rights:

(a) to use the trade mark; and

(b) to authorise other person to use the trade mark;

in relation to the goods and/or services in respect of which the trade mark is registered.

74. In addition, under s 20(2) the registered owner of a trade mark also has the right to obtain relief under the Act if a trade mark has been infringed.

**[189]** 75. A trade mark is defined in s 17 as:

... a sign used, or intended to be used, to distinguish goods or services dealt with or provided in the course of trade by a person from goods or services so dealt with or provided by any other person.

76. The term "sign" is defined in s 6 as including the following or any combination of the following:

... any letter, word, name, signature, numeral, device, brand, heading, label, ticket, aspect of packaging, shape, colour, sound or scent.

77. Thus, the term "trade mark" is a physical manifestation. A physical manifestation, or sign, may be registered. When the Act speaks of a "trade mark" it is concerned only with something which is capable of being a sign, albeit a sign which is used or intended to be used to distinguish goods or services from other goods or services in the course of trade.

78. The rights conferred by s 20 must, of course, be taken to have some territorial limitation. It would not be competent for the Parliament of Australia to provide for exclusive rights to use a trade mark in relation to goods throughout the world. However, that limitation has nothing to do with the physical representation or manifestation of the sign which comprises a trade mark.

79. In other words, while the rights conferred by the Trade Marks Act may be territorially limited in the manner indicated above, the term "trade mark" imports no territorial limitation at all. Thus, a sign may be applied, within the meaning of s 9, to goods or in relation to goods or services in any part of the world. It is nevertheless capable of being a trade mark within the meaning of the Act, notwithstanding that it is applied to the goods or in relation to goods or services outside of Australia. It is also capable of being a trade mark within the meaning of the Act, whatever may have been the intention, if any, of the person who *applied* the mark. ...

83. Senior Counsel for Transport Tyre sought to obtain support for the alternative conclusion by reference to a decision of the English Court of Appeal and by reference to extrinsic materials relating to the enactment of the Trade Marks Act. A distinction was drawn between the so called competing theories relevant to the question of "parallel imports". The two theories are described as **[190]** the doctrine of "exhaustion of rights" and the doctrine of "territoriality". The former is said to involve the exhaustion of a trade mark proprietor's rights to control the disposition of goods bearing its mark once the goods are put on the market. The latter provides that a proprietor's rights in one country should be completely independent of the rights in another country. ...

87. ... s 123 was said to bear a closer resemblance to s 4(3)(a) of the Trade Marks Act of the United Kingdom. That section relevantly provides as follows:

(3) The right to the use of a trade mark given by registration as aforesaid shall not be deemed to be infringed by the use of any such trade mark as aforesaid by any person

    (a)  in relation to goods connected in the course of trade with the proprietor or a registered user of the trade mark if, as to those goods, or a bulk of which they form part, the proprietor or the registered user conforming to permitted use has applied the trade mark and has not subsequently removed or obliterated it, or has at any time expressly or impliedly consented to the use of the trade mark …

88. The effect of s 4(3)(a) was considered by the Court of Appeal in *Colgate Palmolive Ltd v Markwell Finance Ltd* [1989] RPC 497. In that case, the Court proceeded on the assumption that registered trade marks had been applied to goods in Brazil by the registered proprietor of the trade marks. Nevertheless, the Court held that s 4(3)(a) was not attracted in the circumstances of that case. Lloyd LJ said (at 533) the following:

What then does section 4(3)(a) mean when it refers to the proprietor applying the trade mark? It must mean the United Kingdom trade mark in respect of which he has been granted his exclusive right under section 4(1). It cannot mean or, which is more important for **[191]** present purposes, even include the Brazilian trade mark. The fact that the marks are identical is … wholly irrelevant. Just as the United Kingdom parliament can not create trade mark protection in Brazil, so any application of the Brazilian trade mark cannot affect the proprietor's exclusive right in respect of the United Kingdom trade mark. If the marks had been different, this would have been so obvious as to amount to a truism.

But the fact that the marks are identical does create a theoretical difficulty. [Counsel] accepted [and rightly accepted] that if the marks had been different, there would have been nothing to stop the proprietor applying the United Kingdom mark in Brazil, or the Brazilian mark in the United Kingdom. Thus, [the proprietor] could have manufactured, or procured the manufacture of, goods for the United Kingdom marketed in Brazil, applied the United Kingdom mark in Brazil, and then exported them to the United Kingdom. [The registered proprietor] would then have been entitled to the benefit of the United Kingdom registration in respect of such goods, and been subject to the exception created by section 4(3)(a). In other words the place where the mark is applied is immaterial, what matters is which mark has been applied.

How does this work when the mark is the same? How is one to determine which mark has been applied? I can see no alternative but to look to the intention of the proprietor at the time he applies the mark. Then comes the inevitable supplementary question: How is the proprietor's intention to be determined? Is the test subjective or objective? … On the facts of the present case it does not matter. Whether one adopts a subjective or objective approach, it is clear beyond doubt that [the registered proprietor] applied the Brazilian mark.

89. With great respect to his Lordship, such an argument confuses the physical sign with the rights conferred by trade mark legislation. There is no reason to conclude that s 4(3)(a), when it says "if … the proprietor … has applied the trade mark" is referring to anything other than the physical manifestation of the trade mark. A registered trade mark is a sign recorded in the Register. The only question is whether that sign has been applied.

90. A different conclusion would require a quite impractical enquiry in order to determine whether s 123 had any application. His Lordship's argument would require that enquiry be made as to the intention, whether determined subjectively or objectively, of the proprietor of a registered trade mark, when it physically applies the sign which comprises the trade mark to goods. For example, it would be necessary in a case such as the present one, to enquire whether it was the sign which is registered in Japan as distinct from the sign which is registered in Australia which the proprietor intended to apply. When the

signs are identical, in the sense that the signs recorded in each register are identical to each other, such an enquiry would be no more than an exercise in metaphysics.

91. For example, it is easy to imagine a manufacturer who markets his goods world-wide with a trade mark which is registered in identical terms in numerous countries. Such goods might be produced on a continuous production line. Such a manufacturer may not, at the time of the actual application of the trade mark, give any consideration to the country in which each individual item of production would ultimately be marketed. It would follow from the argument of Lloyd LJ that in those circumstances s 123 would have no application to any of the goods. Assuming that there are equivalent provisions to s 123 in other jurisdictions, those equivalent provisions would also have no application to any of the goods. No sale of the goods in any such jurisdiction would have the benefit of s 123.

## *Mantra Group Pty Ltd v Tailly Pty Ltd (No 2)*
### Federal Court of Australia: Reeves J
### [2010] FCA 291

This case involved the infringement of Mantra's registered trade marks on the internet, and provides an interesting illustration of how existing legal principles can be used to address the rapidly evolving area of trade mark law and online infringement. In this case, the court discussed how the internet operates within the context of trade mark infringement, whether there was use of words either substantially identical with or deceptively similar to registered trade marks in domain names and on websites, metatags, search engine keywords, inter alia.

**Reeves J:** 50. From these submissions and the various authorities I was referred to by counsel, I take the relevant legal principles on this infringement issue to be as follows:

(a) Use as a trade mark is use of the mark as a "badge of origin" in the sense that it indicates a connection in the course of trade between goods or services and the person who applies the mark to those goods or services. It has been described as "planting a flag to identify the fact you are in a particular trader's territory": see *Johnson & Johnson Australia Pty Ltd v Sterling Pharmaceuticals Pty Ltd* (1991) 30 FCR 326 ("*Johnson & Johnson*") at 342 per Burchett J and 347 per Gummow J; *Coca-Cola* 96 FCR 107 at [19]; and *Global Brand Marketing Inc v YD Pty Ltd* (2008) 76 IPR 161 ("*Global Brand*") at [45] per Sundberg J;

(b) In determining whether a sign is used as a trade mark, one does *not* ask whether the sign indicates a connection between the alleged infringer's services and those of the registered owner. Instead, one asks whether the alleged infringer has used the sign so as to indicate that the origin of the services was in itself: see *Coca-Cola* 96 FCR 107 at [20], [28] and *Global Brand* 76 IPR 161 at [47];

(c) The latter question is the question that has to be determined at this threshold stage: see *Coca-Cola* 96 FCR 107 at [30]. The determination of this threshold question only involves an examination of the impugned mark, not the registered trade mark: *Global Brand* 76 IPR 161 at [49];

(d) In assessing whether the alleged use is use as a trade mark, the Court is required to examine the purpose and nature of the use in its context. This includes factors such as the positioning of the sign, the type of font used, the size of the words or letters, and the colours which are used, as well as how the sign is applied to the advertising material in question: see *Shell Company of Australia Ltd v Esso Standard Oil (Australia) Ltd* (1963) 109 CLR 407 ("*Shell Company*") at 422 per Kitto J; *Johnson & Johnson* 30 FCR at 347 per Gummow J; *Sports Break Travel Pty Ltd v P & O Holidays Ltd* (2000) 50 IPR 51 ("*Sports Break*") at [14] per Burchett J; *Christodoulou v Disney Enterprises Inc* (2005) 156 FCR 344 at [35] per Crennan J; and *Anakin Pty Ltd v Chatswood BBQ King Pty Ltd* (2008) 250 ALR 620 at [60]-[61] per Branson J;

(e)  This assessment of the purpose and nature of the use of the sign is objective, ie by reference to what a member of the public could be expected to understand by its use: see *Shell Company* 109 CLR at 425 per Kitto J; *Sports Break* 50 IPR 1 at [14] per Burchett J and *Aldi Stores Ltd Partnership v Frito-Lay Trading Company GmbH* (2001) 190 ALR 185 ("*Aldi*") at [76] per Lindgren J;

(f)  The words (of a mark) may be used to describe the goods or services concerned, but still serve as a badge of trade origin: see *Johnson & Johnson* 30 FCR at 343, 347; and *Coca-Cola* 96 FCR 107 at [26]. The question is whether consumers are being invited to purchase the services on the basis that they are to be distinguished from that of other providers of those services *partly because* they are described by the words used: see *Johnson & Johnson* 30 FCR at 347-348 per Gummow J; *Coca-Cola* 96 FCR 107 at [26]; and cf *Aldi* 190 ALR 185 at [23] per Hill J and [60] per Lindgren J;

(g)  It has been doubted whether the mere registration of a domain name containing the words of a trade mark constitutes the use of those words as a trade mark for the purposes of s 120 of the *Trade Marks Act*: see *CSR Ltd v Resource Capital Australia Pty Ltd* (2003) 128 FCR 408 ("*CSR Ltd*") at [42] per Hill J and the cases referred to. However, if the registered domain name is linked to a website that contains advertising material that promotes goods or services in relation to which the trade mark is registered, this combination of use could constitute use as a trade mark under s 120 of the *Trade Marks Act*. This is all the more so if the advertising material on the website also uses the words of the trade mark to promote the goods or services concerned. In considering whether these situations constitute trade mark use, it will be necessary to apply the general principles set out above to the particular circumstances: see the discussion in *Shanahan* at [115.1050].

# Part V

# Designs, Plant Breeder's Rights, Circuit Layouts and Confidential Information

---

## Chapter 15

# Designs

It is often surprising for lay people to discover that designs law protects the way an object looks, not the way it works. In this sense it is closer to copyright law than to patent law. However, in so far as designs law has traditionally protected industrial products, is based on a system of registration and grants an exclusive right to the registered owner to use the product, as well as to import, sell, hire or otherwise dispose of or authorise any of these actions, designs law also displays certain characteristics of patent law.

The *Designs Act 2003* (Cth) came into effect on 17 June 2003 and replaced the *Designs Act 1906* (Cth) which had itself been the subject of significant amendments. The introduction of the 2003 Act was the result of more than a decade of review, commentary and discussion and to a great extent follows the recommendations of the Australian Law Reform Commission Report No 74, *Designs*, released in 1995.[1] The Explanatory Memorandum to the Designs Bill 2002 outlined the Bill in the following manner:

> The proposed changes to the design system include a more streamlined registration system, better enforcement and dispute resolution procedures, stricter eligibility and infringement tests and clearer definitions.[2]

We would also suggest that the 2003 Act significantly extends the exclusive rights of the registered owner. Despite these changes, it is still fair to say that the statutory structure for the protection of intellectual property in designs has not changed greatly during the history of designs protection although the range of designs protected has expanded and the requirement for registration has varied.

The first designs statutes provided protection for the lucrative textile industry in 18th century England. *An Act for the Encouragement of the Arts of Designing and Printing Linens, Cottons, Calicoes, and Muslins, by vesting the Properties*

---

1    See Designs Law Review Committee, *Report on the Law Relating to Designs*, AGPS, Canberra, 1973; Lahore J et al, *Inquiry into Intellectual Property Protection for Industrial Designs* AGPS, Canberra, 1991; Australian Law Reform Commission Report No 74, *Designs* 1995; and the Bureau of Industry Economics, Occasional Paper 27, *The Economics of Intellectual Property Rights for Design*, AGPS, Canberra, 1995.

2    Explanatory Memorandum to Designs Bill 2002, Outline.

*thereof in the Designers, Printers, and Proprietors for a Limited Term* commenced in 1787 (27 Geo III c 38). In 1839 the protection was extended to other types of fabrics (2 and 3 Vict c 13) and then to articles of manufacture (2 and 3 Vict c 17). Like copyright law, these disparate statutes were consolidated in 1842, a consolidation which resulted in the *Designs Act 1842* (UK) (5 and 6 Vict c 100). The significant feature of the 1842 Act was the introduction of a registration system for the protection of designs.

In the Australian colonies before Federation, designs protection applied both as imperial legislation and separate colonial legislation. Following Federation the *Designs Act 1906* was passed on the basis of Federal Parliament's power under s 51(xviii) of the Constitution. Like its United Kingdom forebears, Australian designs protection was called a "copyright" in designs even though it afforded monopoly rights to the designer independent of subjective copying. It was not until 1981 that this nomenclature was dropped from the Australian legislation. The 1906 Act was subject to four major reviews, the most important of which was the Australian Law Reform Commission's Report in 1995.

Designs are covered by the *Paris Convention for the Protection of Industrial Property 1883* (the Paris Convention) which was signed by the United Kingdom on Australia's behalf in 1884 and which Australia signed on its own behalf in 1925. The Paris Convention establishes the principle of national treatment of designs (Art 2) and provides that a design application in a Convention country shall enjoy, for the purposes of filing in another country, a right of priority if an application is filed in that second country within six months of the original application (see Art 4).

The *Hague Agreement Concerning the International Deposit of Industrial Designs* was completed in 1925 and establishes an international deposit system for the registration of designs. Although Australia has not yet signed the Agreement, under the *Designs Regulations 2004* an application at the International Bureau will be treated as though it were an application in a Convention country for the purposes of establishing priority. Convention countries are set out in Sch 1 to the *Designs Regulations 2004*. Similarly, although Australia has not signed the *Locarno Agreement Establishing an International Classification of Industrial Design 1968*, the *Designs Act 2003* relies on these classifications for the purposes of registering designs under the Act. Designs are also covered by the TRIPS Agreement (Arts 25 and 26) and the US-Australia Free Trade Agreement (Art 17.8).

## What is a Registrable Design?

In everyday language, when people speak of the design of a product they usually mean the way a product functions, its ease of operation, its ergonomic qualities, its environmental characteristics, its durability, safety features, value for money or the way it looks and feels.[3] As we have already said, however, the *Designs Act 2003* does not seek to protect design in this broad sense – it protects design only in so far as it relates to the visual appearance of a product.

---

3    See Australian Law Reform Commission Report No 74, *Designs*, 1995 paras 2.3-2.19 for a discussion of the nature of design.

On the other hand, people sometimes speak of a design with little regard to any product at all. If one were to speak of the design of a painting, a computer icon or screen saver, for example, it is possible that design is here being used in a more abstract sense without reference to the product to which it is applied. This is an important distinction because under the *Designs Act 2003* it is only in so far that a design is a design in relation to a product that it is protected.

This double limitation on the scope of a registrable design, that is, that it only protects visual appearance and only in so far as it applies to a product, derives from the definition of design under the Act. Under s 5 of the *Designs Act 2003* design is defined in the following terms:

> *Design*, in relation to a product, means the overall appearance of the product resulting from one or more visual features of the product.

This is reinforced under s 8 which provides:

> In this Act, a reference to a design is a reference to a design in relation to a product.

A product is defined under s 6 as "a thing that is manufactured or handmade" and includes part of a product, an assembled kit and a thing which is of indefinite dimensions (such as a cornice or piping). Visual feature is defined inclusively under s 7 as "in relation to a product, includes the shape, configuration, pattern and ornamentation of the product". Section 7 provides that it does not include the feel of a product or the materials used in a product. In the case of a product of indefinite dimensions, a visual feature does not include the indefinite dimension or more than one repetition of a repeating pattern. Section 7 also provides that a visual feature may (but need not) serve a functional purpose.

Considered together these provisions provide a broad definition of design which excludes both an article apart from its visual appearance and visual features apart from their application to a product. In addition they largely reflect the case law on the definition of a design under the *Designs Act 1906*. We shall consider these terms in more detail.

## A product

The *Designs Act 2003* s 6 defines a product as a "thing" which is manufactured or handmade. By comparison, the 1906 Act required that a design be "applicable to" an "article". The Australian Law Reform Commission suggested that "product" was a more contemporary term than "article"[4] and thought that there would be no substantive difference introduced by virtue of this change in terminology. However, you might like to consider whether today we are more likely to include intangible, commercial goods and services within the definition of a product when we would not have included them within the definition of an article. A software application or service, for example, would be thought by many to be a product but not an article. However, the requirement that a product be a "thing" would seem to restrict the reference to tangible objects and would not include the shape of the water coming from a fountain or a 3D laser image projected into space. At the same time, the fact that a product must be manufactured or handmade

---

4     Australian Law Reform Commission Report No 74, *Designs*, 1995, para 4.9.

would exclude the human body. A hairstyle applied to a live head would therefore not be registrable under the Act but a hairstyle applied to a wig or a mannequin might be.

Under the 1906 Act, which required that a design be "applicable to" an "article", courts developed a rather complex and idiosyncratic definition of "article" (so as to limit the extent of designs protection to the visual features of a particular article rather than the protection of visual features per se). For example, it was held that a thing whose only function was to carry a design was not an article for the purposes of the Act. This effectively excluded traditional artistic works such as paintings, drawings, maps and plans[5] from the *Designs Act 1906*. Thus, in *Re Littlewood's Pools Ltd*,[6] the lines drawn on a piece of paper to make a football pools betting coupon were held not to be a design applied to "an article". If the thing to which the alleged design was applied had another function apart from carrying the design then it was not excluded under this provision. Therefore, packaging could have been an article for the purposes of the *Designs Act 1906* and, in *Hutchence v South Seas Bubble*,[7] a T-shirt on which an INXS poster was printed was held to be an article under that Act. This reasoning did not translate to the digital environment very well because it was difficult to say that a computer screen, for example, was not an "article" within the terms of the Act. However, in *Re Application by Altoweb Inc*,[8] it was held that an icon appearing on a computer screen did not constitute a design under the 1906 Act because it was not "applied to" the screen.[9] Under the 1906 Act buildings and other structures which are constructed in situ were also generally excluded from registration on the ground that either the design could not be said to have been applied to an article which was built in situ (*Re RH Collier*)[10] or because buildings were not articles: see *Re Concrete Ltd*,[11] where it was held that an article under the *Patents and Designs Act 1907* (UK) was something which could be transported either in one piece or in parts and therefore did not include an air raid shelter which was to be constructed on site. In *Tefex v Bowler*,[12] Rath J rejected an argument that a swimming pool, which was constructed off site and afterwards transported to the site, lost its character as an article because it was then installed permanently in the ground as a fixture.[13]

The 1906 *Designs Act* also provided that articles which were "primarily literary or artistic in character" could be excluded from registration under that Act. In accordance with this provision the Regulations provided that articles on which there is printing being bookjackets, calendars, certificates, forms or other documents, dressmaking patterns, greeting cards, labels, leaflets, maps, plans, postcards, stamps or transfers were not registrable under the 1906 Act.[14] Medals

---

5    *Re Application by Hansley* (1987) 10 IPR 365.
6    (1949) 66 RPC 309.
7    (1986) 64 ALR 330.
8    (2002) 55 IPR 656.
9    (1990) 23 IPR 145 at 147.
10   (1937) 54 RPC 255.
11   (1939) 57 RPC 121.
12   (1981) 40 ALR 326.
13   (1981) 40 ALR 326 at 330.
14   The Australian Law Reform Commission appeared to view these exclusions as an historical anomaly in so far as, since 1989, two-dimensional works applied to the surface of an article were

were also excluded from registration under this provision. No similar exclusion exists under the new Act and Regulations (although certain designs are still proscribed including medals; designs relating to the use of the word ANZAC; currency; scandalous designs; and the Arms, flag or seal of the Commonwealth, State, Territory, city, public authority or other country: s 43 and reg 4.06).

The question rises as to whether the limitations built on the requirement that the design be "applicable to an article" continue to apply under the 2003 Act now that it provides that the design must "result" from the visual features of the "product". Given the rather unsatisfactory and tenuous nature of the reasoning in the application of these principles under the old Act there is little to recommend their importation into the 2003 Act. Furthermore, the Designs Office of IP Australia is proceeding on the basis that these limitations no longer apply. However, neither of these reasons is decisive and we must turn to the statute. As a matter of statutory interpretation it seems that there is no reason why an oil painting, for example, cannot be accepted as a product and the design be understood as the overall appearance of that oil painting resulting from its visual features. In the case of buildings the situation remains unclear. The 2003 Act might cover buildings built in situ on the basis that they are handmade things and there is no requirement that a thing be transportable.

The s 6 definition of a product includes "a component part of a complex product ... if it is made separately from the product" and complex product is defined in s 5 as a product comprising at least two replaceable component parts permitting assembly and reassembly of the product. It is interesting to compare this to the 1906 Act which defined an article to include "parts of an article". In *Richsell Pty Ltd v Khoury*,[15] it was said that this reference was "intended to deal with items such as buttons and handles which are made separately but are intended to be incorporated into other articles".[16] In that case the court held that the back cushion of a lounge suite did not constitute an article separately made because the cushion was "simply an integral part of the chair and the lounge".[17] Under the 2003 Act, buttons and handles would presumably be characterised as products in their own right and the cushions would normally not be said to be a replaceable part of a complex product. On the other hand, component parts of a complex product might include a set of products. Under the 1906 Act the applicants in *Re Aspro-Nicholas Ltd*[18] sought to register a design for "encapsulated tablets", that is five tablets in a transparent capsule, the whole to be taken together as one dose. Graham J held that a combination of articles, including a container and its contents, might be an article for the purposes of the *Registered Designs Act 1949* (UK) where the articles are "not at random but in a particular way or in a particular relationship to each other". In this case the encapsulated tablets might be an article but a "pair of lamb chops wrapped by the butcher in a polythene bag" would not be.[19] Similar reasoning may apply to a complex product.

---

not caught within the definition of corresponding design under the ss 74-77 (copyright/designs overlap provisions) of the *Copyright Act 1968*.

15   (1995) 32 IPR 289.
16   (1995) 32 IPR 289 at 296.
17   (1995) 32 IPR 289 at 296.
18   (1969) 21 RPC 645.
19   (1969) 21 RPC 645 at 650.

Products with indefinite proportions, such as guttering and hoses, have traditionally caused problems for designs legislation. This was partly because they might not be considered an article but more importantly, it was considered logically difficult to determine precisely what the protected design was. An article of indefinite proportions was theoretically capable of an infinite number of variations. This problem was simply exacerbated if the pattern or design on the guttering or hose, for example, did not repeat. This in turn made it difficult to prove infringement of an article with indefinite proportions.

Under the 2003 Act an article with one or more indefinite proportions might still be registered as a product but only if a cross-section taken across the indefinite proportion is itself fixed or at least repeats in a regular pattern; and/or all the dimensions remain in proportion; and/or the cross-sectional shape remains the same throughout even though the size of that cross-section varies in a regular way; and/or it has a pattern or shape which repeats itself.

Thus, one could not register a yarn which is infinitely changing (in colour, size and shape), for example, but one could register a yarn which repeats its colour or shape. One could also register a garden hose with a regular pattern; a tube which increases from narrow to large in a definite ratio throughout its length; or guttering which remains the same throughout its length.

## Visual feature and overall appearance

Visual feature, in relation to a product, includes the shape, configuration, pattern or ornamentation of the product (s 7). Under the *Designs Act 1906* the terms pattern, ornament, shape and configuration were interpreted broadly and, in *Smith, Kline and French Laboratories Ltd's Design Application*,[20] Graham J referred to dictionary definitions of pattern being "a decorative or artistic design" and ornament being "anything used or serving to adorn".[21] Broadly speaking, it can be said that shape and configuration refer to three-dimensional aspects of design and pattern refers to two-dimensional aspects of design applied to the surface of a product although, of course, this is very loose.

When applying to register a design it is not necessary to identify what aspects of shape, configuration, pattern or ornamentation are sought to be protected although under the 1906 Act it was usual to put in an optional statement of monopoly in the form of "an application for aspects of shape applied to a jug" (for example). Courts recognised that the four aspects are overlapping and were reluctant to find an application invalid on the basis that the statement of monopoly may have identified the "wrong" aspects of a design. An embossed edging on a plate, for example, might be considered an aspect of shape, configuration, pattern or ornamentation. The court's approach is expressed in *Samuel Heath and Sons Ltd v Rollason*,[22] where Lord Herschell said that the object of the equivalent definition clause under the *Patents, Designs, and Trademarks Act 1883* (UK) was to make the word design "as extensive as possible" and there was no intention to draw "sharp, hard and fast distinctions" between aspects of shape, configuration,

---

20   [1974] RPC 253.
21   [1974] RPC 253 at 260.
22   [1898] AC 499.

pattern or ornamentation.[23] In that case the statement of monopoly accompanying the design limited the monopoly to "aspects of pattern applicable to a coffin-plate". The appellants sought to have the design removed from the register on the basis that the depression in the centre of the coffin plate was not part of the "pattern" but part of the shape or configuration. The House of Lords rejected the argument on the basis that the terms were not mutually exclusive.[24] Under the 2003 Act the applicant need not put in a statement of monopoly but the old law is useful for understanding the scope of the meaning of visual features.

It is interesting to note that colour is neither referred to in the inclusive definition of visual feature nor excluded from that definition under the 2003 Act. Under the 1906 Act, the general practice was that a colour was registrable if it was used in such a way as to constitute a pattern, for example, but it was generally thought that a colour was not a form of ornamentation in itself. Thus, under the 1906 Act the coloured pellets in a capsule might constitute a registrable design in so far as they formed a pattern[25] but a piece of plain yellow cotton was not registrable because it did not exhibit any aspect of pattern and, it seems, that courts did not accept that mere colour was a form of ornamentation. It was said that "colour or colouring *per se* does not constitute design".[26]

The treatment of colour was considered in *Review 2 Pty Ltd v Redberry Enterprise Pty Ltd*,[27] a case relating to a wrap-around dress whose design registration included a colour representation. In that case, Kenny J held that the use of a colour representation was "relevant to determining the extent of the monopoly sought and given".[28] The weight to be given to colour, however, depended on the "nature of the product and the relative importance of the different features in the registered design".[29] In this case, an informed user would regard the colour as an element of the pattern that forms part of the overall look of that registered design.[30] Kenny J quoted Graham J in *Smith, Kline and French Laboratories Ltd's Design Application*:[31]

> [C]olour cannot be ignored, though normally differences in colour are unlikely to be important. Colour may or may not make a material difference, depending on the circumstances and nature of the design in question.[32]

When looking at a design it is important to remember that the design is the "overall appearance" of the product resulting from the visual features of the product. By comparison, as we shall see, when determining the distinctiveness of a design one looks to the "overall impression" of the design. This raises the interesting question of whether the internal appearance of a product is registrable.

The inside of the lid of a jewellery box, for example, would certainly be registrable as a design. The inside of a Kinder Surprise chocolate would probably be

---

23   [1898] AC 499 at 501.
24   [1898] AC 499 at 501.
25   *Smith, Kline and French Laboratories Ltd's Design Application* [1974] RPC 253 at 260.
26   Assistant Comptroller in *Re Associated Colour Printers Ltd* (1937) 54 RPC 203 at 206.
27   (2008) 173 FCR 450.
28   (2008) 173 FCR 450 at [52].
29   (2008) 173 FCR 450 at [52]
30   (2008) 173 FCR 450 at [53].
31   [1974] RPC 253.
32   *Smith, Kline and French Laboratories Ltd's Design Application* [1974] RPC 253 at 261.

registrable.[33] The inside of a golf ball on the other hand, might be considered a design in so far as it relates to the "overall appearance" of the product but the Designs Office has suggested that such a design would fail to be registered on the basis that it lacks distinctiveness on the basis of its "overall impression".[34]

This raises the further question as to when the overall appearance of the product should be assessed. It may be that the product is to be assessed when in use, or at rest or plugged in or not plugged in. The Designs Manual, in fact, claims that the features of a thing must be assessed when the product is "at rest". In the case of electrical products the Designs Office has said that the product should be assessed when it is not plugged in.[35] This is a difficult position to support and seems to contradict the decision in *Koyo Seiko Kabushiki Kaisha's Application*[36] where the transient graphic icons applied to a display screen in a digital watch were held to be registrable even though they were not visible at all times and presumably, were not visible at all when there were no batteries.

## Functionality[37]

A visual feature may, but need not, serve a functional purpose (s 7). This provision, which was first introduced in 1981, overturns the case law on functionality which had held that where a shape was solely dictated by function then it was not registrable as a design. Courts were divided as to when a shape was "solely dictated by function".

Even though a design which is attributable to function may now be protected under the *Designs Act* it is only the specific appearance of the article which is protected and not the function itself. In *Firmagroup Australia Pty Ltd v Byrne and Davidson Doors (Vic) Pty Ltd*,[38] the High Court said:

> Specificity of shape and configuration must be conveyed by a registrable design; features of a design which do no more than convey the idea of a general shape appropriate to the function which the article is intended to perform and which are consistent with a variety of particular shapes in articles copying those features are not amenable to protection by the Act.[39]

In accordance with general principles there will be no infringement of the design if only the function of the article is copied. Thus, in *Firmagroup*, although the alleged infringer had adopted the appellant's idea of a combined door handle and recessed lock which functioned as a lock and handle on a roller door, there was no infringement of the appellant's registered design because the alleged infringer had not applied the appellant's squat design but had instead applied a streamlined design which was held to be sufficiently visually different so as not to constitute an infringement under the 1906 Act. In *Dart Industries Inc v*

---

33    Compare *Ferrero's Design* [1978] RPC 473.
34    *Designs Examiner's Manual* D05.4.4 as at 31 July 2007.
35    *Designs Examiner's Manual* D05.3.2 as at 31 July 2007.
36    [1958] RPC 112.
37    For an interesting review of the statutory protection of functional aspects of an article under designs law, see Gummow J in *Hosokawa Micron International Inc v Fortune* (1990) 97 ALR 615.
38    (1987) 180 CLR 483.
39    (1987) 180 CLR 483 at 487.

*Decor Corporation Pty Ltd*,[40] the respondent's lettuce crisper was found not to have infringed the applicant's registered design for a lettuce crisper because, although they had produced a functionally similar article, the two articles were not sufficiently visually similar to constitute an infringement.[41]

Under the 1906 Act, "principles and methods of construction of a product" were also expressly excluded from protection. Despite this, courts consistently held that a design was not excluded from registration because it was *also* a method or principle of construction. This is well illustrated in *Kestos Ltd v Kempat and Vivian Fitch Kemp*,[42] a case regarding an application for registration of a design for a bra. A bra that is described simply as two basically triangular and conical shaped pieces of fabric supported at the top and around the back by elastic straps would fail as a design because it would fail to identify the "individual and specific appearance" (old Act) or visual feature (new Act) of the bra for which registration was sought. In *Kestos*, however, the combination of a drawing of the bra and a detailed description of the bra which defined it visually as well as in terms of construction was accepted as a design.

## A Design Must be New and Distinctive

Under the 1906 Act a design was registrable if it was new or original. The courts never effectively defined originality and the test for novelty was thought by many to be too low, allowing registration of a design which demonstrated only minor differences from existing designs. The 2003 Act attempted to raise the registration bar by requiring that a design be new *and* distinctive (where each of these terms is defined differently) and by broadening the prior art base. In addition, the *Designs Act 2003* has harmonised the tests for registrability with the infringement tests so as to effectively introduce a reverse infringement test for registration similar to that applicable under the *Patents Act 1990*.

The *Designs Act 2003* s 15 provides that a design is a registrable design if the design is new and distinctive when compared to the prior art base for the design as it existed before the priority date of the design. Under s 16 a design is new unless it is identical to a design that forms part of the prior art base; and a design is distinctive unless it is substantially similar in overall impression to a design that forms part of the prior art base. In *World Technologies (Aust) Pty Ltd v Tempo (Aust) Pty Ltd*,[43] a case relating to the appellant's design for a bagless vacuum cleaner, the Federal Court provided an extraordinarily narrow interpretation of newness. In that case the prior art included a photograph of the vacuum cleaner in question. However, because it only showed one aspect of the vacuum cleaner the judge was not prepared to say that it was identical to the design before him. Given this narrow definition of new, distinctiveness will therefore in practice be the primary consideration for registration.

---

40    (1989) 15 IPR 40.

41    As we shall see, this test for infringement was very strict under the 1906 Act and required that the "individual and specific appearance" of the design be imitated.

42    (1935) 53 RPC 139.

43    [2007] FCA 114.

The definition of distinctiveness refers to overall impression in relation to a design rather than to the overall appearance of the product. We would suggest that this requires one to consider not just the visual features of the product in an abstract way but the overall impression caused by the application of those visual features to a particular product. In addition, it may also be that the impression must be considered in the overall context of the design including the type of product and the ability of the designer to be innovative. This broad reading of the test partly reflects the earlier case law on the meaning of distinctive and is partly reflected in s 19 of the new Act which sets out the factors to be considered in assessing substantial similarity in overall impression.

Section 19 provides that the person or court making the assessment is to give more weight to similarities than to differences (s 19(1)). This provision is intended to overcome the perception that under the 1906 Act both courts and the Registrar concentrated on differences to such an extent that even very small variations from an existing design would entitle an applicant's design to registration.

In addition, the person is to have regard to the prior art base (s 19(2)(a)) and, if there is a statement of newness and distinctiveness, they are to have particular regard to those features and, if those features relate only to part of the design, have particular regard to that part of the design but within the context of the design as a whole (s 19(2)(b)). Where only part of the design is substantially similar then the person is to have regard to the importance, amount and quality of the part in the context of the design as a whole (s 19(2)(c)). Finally, the person is to have regard to the freedom of the creator of the design to innovate (s 19(2)(d)).

This last provision reflects the problem of finding that a product such as a chair is new and distinctive when by nature products such as chairs seem to allow little room for innovation. As Jacobs J said in *D Sebel and Co Ltd v National Art Metal Co Pty Ltd*[44] (a case under the 1906 Act):

> I think that it is most important to bear in mind in relation to such an article as a chair, that one cannot or should not expect to find some startling novelty or originality. The element of novelty or originality will of necessity be likely to be within a small compass. I do not mean thereby that any difference of shape, outline, proportion or placement of components will thereby constitute novelty of design, but provided I see a substantial difference from the fundamental form and from the development in the trade up to the time of the application for registration, then I do not think that it is sufficient to point to a number of elements of similarity to past design in order to show that the design is not new or original.[45]

In considering these factors the person must apply the standard of an informed user, that is, of a person who is familiar with the product to which the design relates or with products which are similar to the product to which the design relates (s 19(4)).

The standard of the informed user replaces the older requirement that the design "be judged by the eye". The new test is objective[46] and focuses on the "user" or consumer rather than the designs expert. The "informed user" is one who has more "familiarity" than one might expect of the "average consumer".[47] The

---

44    (1965) 10 FLR 224.
45    (1965) 10 FLR 224 at 226.
46    (2008) 173 FCR 450 at [20].
47    (2008) 173 FCR 450 at [19].

standard of the informed user was reviewed extensively by Kenny J in *Review 2 Pty Ltd v Redberry Enterprise Pty Ltd*.[48]

Who is the informed user? Plainly, the informed user must be a person who is familiar with the product to which the design in question relates. Moreover, the informed user must be a *user* of the class of product in question, in this case, ladies' garments, or perhaps, more narrowly, ladies' dresses. A designer or manufacturer of such garments is not an informed user merely because he or she designs or manufactures them. Further, this user is not simply an ordinary consumer: the user must be an *informed* user.[49]

In the case of the dress in question, Kenny J distinguished between "women who subscribe to fashion magazines (such as *Vogue* or *Collezioni* that illustrated the prior art in this case) and have particular knowledge of, and familiarity with, fashion trends" and those other women "who lack such knowledge and familiarity".[50]

The requirement for distinctiveness owes something to the case law under the 1906 Act. As we have seen, under that Act, a design was not registrable unless it was "new or original". The courts never effectively distinguished between the two concepts and, in determining registrability, the courts resorted to the concept of distinctiveness where distinctiveness referred to a characteristic of the design considered in its overall context. Lockhart J formulated a test for distinctiveness in *Dart Industries Inc v Decor Corporation Pty Ltd*[51] which was approved by Davies and Spender JJ in *Richsell Pty Ltd v Khoury* on appeal:[52]

> For a design to be protected there must be a special or distinctive appearance, something in the design which captures and appeals to the eye. To have that effect, the design must be noticeable and have some perceptible appearance of an individual character: *AMP Inc v Utilux Pty Ltd* [1972] RPC 103.[53]

Despite the similarities of this formulation with the current statutory definition it is worth noting that the old formulation arguably emphasises the inherent distinctiveness of the design over its comparative distinctiveness although, in practice, the courts often did compare designs to the prior art base.

## Examples of designs which may lack distinctiveness

Because the determination of distinctiveness requires a comparison of the overall impression of the design, and design is defined as the overall appearance of the product resulting from one or more visual features of the product, then the question of distinctiveness requires one to consider both the appearance of the product and the product itself. Problems of distinctiveness may therefore arise when similar visual features are applied to different products. For example, is the particular orange stripiness of a ceramic Garfield cat comparable to the same particular orange stripiness applied to a ceramic Garfield cat shaped mug or a

---

48    (2008) 173 FCR 450.
49    (2008) 173 FCR 450 at [19].
50    (2008) 173 FCR 450 at [27].
51    (1989) 15 IPR 403 at 408-409.
52    (1995) 32 IPR 289.
53    *Dart Industries Inc v Decor Corporation Pty Ltd* (1989) 15 IPR 403 at 408-409.

plain ceramic glass? Problems may also arise where the visual appearance of the product is quite different but the product itself is simply a minor design variation in the context of the trade. For example, is a cushion with a button in the middle distinctive when compared to an otherwise identical cushion which has a sewn middle?

The case law reveals five main situations where the question of innovation and registrability have traditionally posed particular problems. These are when the design applies known features to different products; when the design comprises a mere conjunction of old features; when the design differs from existing designs only in "immaterial details"; when the design is a mere "trade variation" of an existing design and when the design is an "obvious adaptation" of an existing design. These situations are likely to arise in practice under the 2003 Act but may need to be addressed differently. We shall therefore consider them by reference to both the old case law and the current test.

In *Re Clarke's Design*,[54] the question arose as to whether a lampshade which had initially been designed for an oil lamp could be said to be new or original when it was adapted for use on a then new electric lamp. The court held that it was not new or original even though a chimney had been omitted from the electric version of the lampshade:

> The design must be new or original with reference to the kind of article for which it is registered, meaning by kind of article, not the class of article mentioned in the schedule to the rules,[55] but the kind of article having regard to its general character and use. A design might be new for a coal-shuttle but not for a bonnet. On the other hand, a design for a shape for a lamp shade can hardly be new if it is old for an oil lamp.[56]

Although this would no longer qualify as a new design under the *Designs Act 2003* (because it is not identical to a design in the prior art base) we would suggest that *Clarke's* test is still useful in determining distinctiveness under the *Designs Act 2003*. In so far as the test requires one to consider the product to which the design is applied it reflects the current law: the test for distinctiveness refers to a design and, as we have seen, s 8 provides that a design is a reference to a design in relation to a product. The question of the product to which the design is applied is therefore indirectly imported into the question of distinctiveness.

A more difficult question relates to the range of products which might be compared for the purposes of proving distinctiveness. *Re Clarke's Design* held that the products need not be identical, that one would consider a "kind of article having regard to its general character and use" and that the products need not be in the same designs class under the Act. Thus, a design for an iron furnace

---

54  [1896] 2 Ch 38.

55  Before 1981 the *Designs Regulations* contained 14 categories of articles for which a design could be registered. As a matter of practice it may have been thought that if a person registered a design for one or more categories of articles the person effectively left the field open for another person to apply the design to articles in other categories. However, this was not the legal position. In *Re Read and Greswell's Design* (1889) 42 Ch D 260 at 262, Chitty J held that that a design must be " 'new or original' in fact and not ... 'new or original' as to some particular class of goods. It cannot be said to be new or original if it is already being applied to articles of an analogous character". In 1981 the regulatory categories were dropped and today a design is registered in respect of a named article and whether its application to another article is substantially new or original is a question or fact in each case.

56  [1896] 2 Ch 38 at 45.

has been held not to be of the same character and use as a wooden door for a sideboard[57] whilst, in *MacPhee v Peters Foods Australia Pty Ltd*,[58] Hill J in the Federal Court was "tempted" to say that a cheesecake flavoured DRUMSTICK ice cream was of the same general character as a cheesecake in a cone but did not have to come to a conclusion on the matter.

We would suggest that the difference between newness and distinctiveness ensures that products other than those for which the design is to be registered must be considered in determining whether designs are distinctive, that is, whether they are similar in overall impression. We would also suggest that there is nothing in the *Designs Act 2003* which restricts the comparison to products within the same Locarno classification. We therefore suggest that other products may be considered and that, as a matter of fact, the closer the products are in general character the more likely they are to be similar in overall impression when a similar design is applied to them.

Under the 1906 Act a combination of features which were not themselves new or original could still constitute a new or original design when used in combination but this was a question to be determined as a question of fact in each case. This principle was endorsed by Jacobs J in *D Sebel and Co Ltd v National Art Metal Co Pty Ltd*[59] in considering the design for a chair:

> It is also true no doubt that a mere conjunction of old features does not necessarily result in a new design. However, it may do so and it seems to me that when one is dealing with furniture design, and with the obvious limitations that exist in the addition of new features, one should not be astute to deny novelty upon the ground that there is not some wholly new feature of design incorporated. Design in such a field is a subtle thing and, provided it is distinctive to the trained eye, I think that registration should not be denied in view of the element of subtlety which is involved in the combination of old features in a particular way and the manner in which they are applied.[60]

Under the 2003 Act a similar result may emerge in so far as the question is not whether old or known components, such as a chair leg or bottom, are used but whether there is a substantial similarity in overall impression taking into account s 19(2)(d) which requires the informed user to have regard to the fact that the creator of a chair does not have much freedom to innovate.

Under the 1906 Act it was difficult to establish the requisite innovation if the design only differed in "immaterial details" from a previous design and these variations were either "trivial and unimportant" (*Samuel Heath and Sons v Rollason*)[61] or were mere "trade variants" in common use.[62] Registrability could be refused to a trade variant even where the difference between the new and old design were not trivial and unimportant. Thus, in *J Rapee and Co Pty Ltd v Kas*

---

57    *Hecla Foundry Co v Walker, Hunter and Co* (1889) 14 App Cas 550.

58    (2003) 60 IPR 51.

59    (1965) 10 FLR 224.

60    (1965) 10 FLR 224 at 227, approved by Kelly ACJ in *Australian Building v Woodman McDonald (Glass) Pty Ltd* (1986) 7 IPR 91 at 97.

61    [1898] AC 499 at 503.

62    Again, the emphasis is on the nature of the product within its trade context rather than on the visual appearance of the product. For a discussion of common use, see *Ullrick Aluminium Pty Ltd v Dias Aluminium Products Pty Ltd* [2006] FCAFC 119.

*Cushions Pty Ltd*,[63] Gummow J held that even though the form of tufting used on a cushion was not an immaterial difference it still failed to be new or original because it was a mere trade variation. He gave as an illustration the example of a rocking horse. If a galloping horse were put on a base which was usually used for a bucking horse this would not be an immaterial difference but it may be a mere trade variant which would disentitle the design from registration.[64]

We would suggest that a similar result may not be possible under the new Act and the fact that a design is a trade variant is not of itself a reason for exclusion under the new Act. Certainly one can imagine many galloping rocking horses which could hardly be said to be similar in overall impression to a bucking rocking horse, even though, as a matter of trade practice, one might be said to be a trade variant of the other in so far as it is a result which "a competent craftsman could achieve if he or she wanted to": see Davies and Spender JJ's definition of trade variant in *Richsell Pty Ltd v Khoury*.[65]

Under the 1906 Act a design might be found to lack originality or novelty if it was an "obvious adaptation" of a prior design applied to an analogous article. In *Dover Ltd v Nurnburger Celluloidwaren Fabrik Gebruder Wolff*,[66] for example, the application of a machined tooled pattern to a bicycle handle was held to be an obvious adaptation of the application of the pattern to an unidentified "analogous article". The concept of obvious adaptation should have no place to play under the 2003 Act and the focus should be on whether the new product is distinctive by reference to both the similarity of the product and the visual appearance overall – that is by reference to the overall impression.

## Prior art base

In determining whether a design is new and distinctive the court must judge the design against the "prior art base", that is, against designs which have been published within or outside Australia; used publicly in Australia or registered in Australia before the "priority date" (s 15). The priority date of a design disclosed in a design application that meets the minimum filing requirements is defined

63    (1989) 90 ALR 288.

64    (1989) 90 ALR 288 at 301-302.

65    The meaning of trade variant was considered in *Richsell Pty Ltd v Khoury* (1995) 32 IPR 289 where the design in question comprised a variation made to the back of an arm chair which simply added a known pleating effect to a previously unpleated back. On appeal the Full Federal Court held that this was not a new or original design but a mere "trade variant", a term which was defined as follows:

>    The change did not alter the basic features which made the "Apollo" distinctive. Looking at the photographs, it seems to us that the designs of the "Sherwood" and "Apollo" chairs and lounges are the same, save that the "Sherwood" has adopted a trade variant for the upper back cushion. We use the term "trade variant" as referring to a variation which a competent craftsman could achieve if he or she wished to do so. The upper back cushions are certainly different but the "Sherwood" cushion does not strike us as being a particularly distinctive feature. It may be that the design of the "Sherwood" cushion is novel, in the sense that the precise combination has not previously been achieved. But the elements, nevertheless, are not surprising, unusual or unfamiliar. The impression we have is that the fundamental design of the "Apollo" is unchanged, merely that there has been a change in appearance to one part of the articles. Even the feature of ruffling of the fabric was maintained, even enhanced in the "Sherwood" design. (Davies and Spender JJ at 294-295)

66    [1910] 2 Ch 25 at 28-29.

in s 27 as the filing date of the design application (see below for the meaning of minimum filing requirements). The Regulations contain special rules in relation to designs previously filed in a Convention country. Once a design application has been lodged a later publication, use or registration will not render the design invalid even though it has not otherwise been disclosed.

The prior art base is defined in s 15 as consisting of:

· designs publicly used in Australia;
· documents published within or outside Australia; and
· designs where the design is disclosed in a design application, that design has an earlier priority date and the first time that the design is made available for public inspection (as required under s 60) is on or after the priority date of the new design. That is, even if the design has not been disclosed but has been registered, it forms part of the prior art base. This provision maintains the importance of the priority date and registration under the designs regime.

Before 1981, prior use was included within the concept of prior publication and therefore a prior use would not destroy originality or novelty unless it disclosed the design to the public. In 1955 in *Re Wolanski's Registered Design*,[67] for example, a neck-tie support was found not to have been published or disclosed to the public when it was worn in such a way that an onlooker could not determine its shape. Furthermore, the court held that the fact that the wearer had himself seen the design did not constitute a disclosure to the public.

After 1981 prior use under the 1906 Act became a separate ground for limiting registration of a design. However, unlike the current provisions, this use was not expressly restricted to public use. If one followed the reasoning in the English patents case, *Re Wheatley's Patent Application*,[68] it could have been argued that, under the post-1981 provisions of the 1906 Act, there was no requirement that the prior use disclose the design to the public.[69] This strict interpretation of prior use, however, would have had the unfortunate result that under the *Designs Act 1906* designs which had been used only by the designer could be excluded from registration even where the use was for the purposes of experimentation and testing. This is because, unlike the *Patents Act 1990*, there was no protection for experimentation and testing. The 2003 Act clarifies the position by requiring that the use be public and in Australia. In *World Technologies (Aust) Pty Ltd v Tempo (Aust) Pty Ltd*,[70] the Federal Court was "not disposed to hold" that sending samples to an Australian retailer for examination and testing for the purposes of determining the commercial suitability of the product was a public use in Australia and declined to make a finding. The court did hold, however, that the provision of a single sample to a government department for the purpose of receiving a certificate of approval for an electrical item was not a public use.[71]

---

67    (1953) 88 CLR 278.
68    (1984) 2 IPR 450.
69    See also *Safe Sport Australia Pty Ltd v Puma Australia Pty Ltd* (1985) 4 IPR 120 at 125 and *Richsell Pty Ltd v Khoury* (1994) 30 IPR 129.
70    [2007] FCA 114.
71    [2007] FCA 114 at 68.

Publication is the disclosure of the design in a document to the public. The 2003 Act extends the prior art base to include publications outside Australia. It is therefore unnecessary for decision makers to determine where a website, for example, has been published. Publication is generally found to have occurred when visual representations of the design have been circulated. Visual representations in trade catalogues,[72] a publication of a colour photograph on a website and a jpeg file sent to an advertising company,[73] patent applications and design applications have been held to be prior publications for the purposes of the 1906 Act. In order to constitute a publication the design must be disclosed with "reasonable clarity". Thus, in *J Rapee and Co Pty Ltd v Kas Cushions Pty Ltd*,[74] the applicant had registered a design for a chair pad with five circular stitched "tufting" points which gave the cushion a dimpled effect. The respondent challenged the validity of the registration on the basis of prior publication. Gummow J found that, although photographs of similarly shaped tufted cushions had appeared in the Sears Roebuck and the Ikea catalogues, the photographs did not disclose what form of tufting had been used and therefore there was no publication of the design. In Gummow J's words:

> [I]f such material is to constitute prior publication, then the reader must from a fair perusal of the material be able at least to see the design in his mind's eye and the design or something substantially the same as the design should be disclosed with reasonable clarity.[75]

Because the Act protects the overall impression of a product resulting from one or more visual features of the product, it would be rare that a purely written description will be found to have disclosed a design with the requisite clarity. However, such a finding may not be impossible. As Kitto J said in *Re Wolanski's Registered Design*,[76] regarding an application to cancel registration under the 1906 Act, the question "is not whether there is identity between the representations themselves but whether there is identity between the ideas of shape which they respectively convey".[77]

A publication has been held to have been made to the public if it is "publicly available" even if it has not actually been disclosed to an individual member of the public.[78] In *A Pressler and Co Ltd v Gartside and Co (of Manchester) Ltd*,[79] a textile design was held to have been made publicly available because it was held in the library of the Calico Printers Association where, according to Luxmore J, "[i]t has always been kept open for inspection ... at any rate since 1911 by members of (the Association), by their customers, and indeed, by such members of the public as (the Association) were ready to allow to inspect it without any condition of any kind".[80]

---

72   *Stratford Auto Components Ltd v Britax (London) Ltd* [1961] RPC 197.
73   *World Technologies (Aust) Pty Ltd v Tempo (Aust) Pty Ltd* [2007] FCA 114.
74   (1989) 90 ALR 288.
75   (1989) 90 ALR 288 at 297.
76   (1953) 88 CLR 278 at 280.
77   (1953) 88 CLR 278 at 280.
78   *J Rapee and Co Pty Ltd v Kas Cushions Pty Ltd* (1989) 90 ALR 288, Gummow J at 297.
79   (1933) 50 RPC 240.
80   (1933) 50 RPC 240 at 246, repeated by Gummow J in *J Rapee and Co Pty Ltd v Kas Cushions Pty Ltd* (1989) 90 ALR 288 at 297.

## Specific exclusions

In determining whether a design is new and distinctive the Act sets out a number of factors which must be disregarded. The person making the decision must disregard certain authorised exhibitions; certain unauthorised uses occurring just before registration; certain official disclosures; and certain non-industrial uses of artistic works. In more detail these exclusions are:

- any publication or use of the design with the consent of the owner or predecessor in title in situations provided under the Regulations (s 17). These are exhibitions at an official international exhibition within the meaning of Art 11 of the *Paris Convention for the Protection of Industrial Property* or Art 1 of the *Convention Relating to International Exhibitions* or an exhibition recognised by the Registrar (reg 2). The Regulations set out the formalities required in order to qualify under this exemption;
- any publication or use of the design made by a person who derived or obtained use of the design from the registered owner (or the registered owner's predecessor in title) where the publication or use was without the consent of the registered owner but only if a design application in relation to that design is made within six months of that publication or use (s 17 and reg 2);
- any information given by the registered owner or with the registered owner's consent or by a predecessor in title of the registered owner to the Commonwealth, State or Territory, or a person authorised by the Commonwealth, State or Territory to investigate the design or anything done for the purposes of such an investigation (s 17);
- Under s 18 the prior use of an artistic work does not constitute a prior publication of a "corresponding design", nor does it deprive the design of newness or distinctiveness, unless the previous use consisted of selling, hiring, offering or exposing for sale a product to which the corresponding design was applied industrially and this use was with the consent of the registered owner. This exemption does not apply in regard to articles which would otherwise not be registrable under s 43(1) because they are prescribed by the Regulations, they are protected under the *Olympic Insignia Protection Act 1987*, or the design is a design in relation to an integrated circuit. This exemption is discussed immediately below.

## Prior use of artistic work under s 18

As we have seen, ss 74 to 77A of the *Copyright Act 1968* provide that once a "corresponding design" of an artistic work has been industrially applied and products embodying that corresponding design have been dealt with, then there is no infringement of the copyright in the artistic work if one reproduces the work by embodying a corresponding design in a product. A corresponding design in relation to an artistic work is defined under the *Copyright Act* s 74 as "visual features of shape or configuration which, when embodied in a product, result in a reproduction of that work, whether or not the visual features constitute a design that is capable of being registered under the *Designs Act 2003*". That is, the provisions do not apply to two-dimensional aspects of pattern or ornamentation for example. "Embodied in", in relation to a product, includes woven into, impressed on or worked into the product.

As previously discussed in Chapter 5, "Balancing the Interests", the exemption has two main effects. First, it operates to prevent an industrial designer from indirectly getting protection for a design for the period of the copyright rather than for the shorter period of the designs monopoly.[81] Secondly, it functions in such a way that the designer risks losing significant protection for an industrial design unless it is registered under the *Designs Act*.

Section 18 of the *Designs Act*, despite its superficial similarity to the copyright provisions, has quite a different operation. It enhances the designer's protection by providing that, even though a design may have been disclosed to the public by the prior use of an artistic work, this does not take away the design's novelty or distinctiveness so long as the use of the artistic work was not an industrial application and the design is a "corresponding design" in relation to the artistic work. The section only applies where the person seeking to register the corresponding design is also the owner of the copyright in the artistic work or seeks registration with the consent of the copyright owner. "Corresponding design" has the same meaning as it does under the *Copyright Act* and therefore the section only applies in relation to shape and configuration.

It is sometimes thought that the purpose of s 18 is to provide a practical solution to the problem caused by the fact that a design often starts life as an artistic work, such as a plan or diagram, and that the existence of such a plan or a diagram should not take away the novelty or distinctiveness of the design. However, as a matter of principle such a "practical solution" would not be necessary because the existence of the plan or diagram has not traditionally taken away the novelty or distinctiveness of the design unless the plan or diagram has been publicly disclosed. We would therefore suggest that a more important function of the section is to encourage value adding by allowing the copyright owner to exploit an artistic work by developing it as a design to be applied to a product in some way other than by the simple application of the artistic work as a pattern or ornament on the surface of a product. It is this second purpose, rather than the first, which is reflected in the case law.

In *Water Recreations Pty Ltd v Fairmile Pty Ltd*,[82] for example, it was held that a corresponding design is different from an artistic work as a matter of statutory construction. In that case plans for waterslide components were drawn up by an architect for the defendant who subsequently engaged the plaintiff to make a waterslide. With the consent of the architect the plaintiff registered designs for waterslide components made in accordance with the architect's plans. After delivery of the waterslide to the defendants the defendants made flop moulds of the waterslide and used the moulds to reproduce the waterslide. In an action for infringement the defendants challenged the validity of the registration for lack of novelty or originality and the plaintiffs relied on the *Copyright Act 1968* s 17A. In the Federal Court, Olney J rejected the plaintiffs' argument on the basis that, as a matter of statutory interpretation there must be some difference between the

---

81   *Copyright Act 1968* ss 74-77A.
82   (1982) 42 ALR 273.

"artistic work" and the "corresponding design". In this case, he said, the design applications "were not applications for registration of a corresponding design of an artistic work, but were applications for registration of the artistic work itself".[83] He continued that had the artistic work been a model of the components and drawings or plans had been drawn from this model then those drawings would have been "corresponding designs".[84]

There is much to commend Olney J's approach in so far as it allows the development of designs from pre-existing artistic works but subjects plans and diagrams for the design to the ordinary rules of disclosure. However, it must be admitted that this narrow interpretation of corresponding design has not been applied in the application of ss 74-77A of the *Copyright Act 1968*. On the other hand, even if one rejects Olney J's approach as based on an incorrect definition of corresponding design then the ordinary rules of disclosure are still partially imported into s 18. Section 18 provides that the exemption does not apply if the prior use of the artistic work "consisted of or included the sale, letting for hire or offering or exposing for sale or hire of articles to which the design has been applied industrially". Under s 18(3) "applied industrially" has the same meaning as s 77 of the *Copyright Act 1968* and reg 17 of the *Copyright Regulations 1969*. As we have seen, this may include a single application for an industrial purpose.

## Registration Procedure

Most countries, including Australia, continue to have a registered designs system. A registered system has the advantage of openness – designers are able to see what their competitors are doing; they are able to identify the owner of a design for the purposes of licensing agreements and the register provides the designer with an easy way to notify competitors of the claim to exclusive rights in the design. Like the patents register, the designs registration system does not guarantee the validity of the design although the register is prima facie evidence of any particulars entered in it (s 118).

The registration procedure under the *Designs Act 2003* is quite straightforward and involves three distinct steps – application; registration or publication of the design within six months of application and an optional examination of the registered design at any time. Only a design which has been registered and examined may be the subject of infringement proceedings.

This new procedure makes two important changes to the designs system. First, it abolishes the requirement for a substantive examination to be conducted before registration. Under the *Designs Act 2003* the Registrar is only required to determine whether an application meets the formal requirements before registration. Any substantive examination, where the question of whether the design is new and distinctive is considered, takes place following registration. Although this examination is largely optional, no infringement proceedings may be conducted in relation to a design which has not been examined (s 73). Secondly,

---

83  (1982) 42 ALR 273 at 281.
84  (1982) 42 ALR 273 at 281. Olney J's decision was followed by the Delegate of the Registrar of Designs in *Warner v Commercial Systems Australia Pty Ltd* (1995) 33 IPR 534.

the new system gives the applicant an option to publish the design rather than to register it. Publication without registration does not give the applicant any exclusive rights in the design but it does prevent any other person registering the design because the design will lack novelty and distinctiveness on account of the publication. The publication will also destroy novelty and distinctiveness for the applicant and therefore any decision to publish will preclude the applicant from registering the design in the future.

## Application

Under s 21 any one or more persons may file an application in respect of a design. Although the application may be filed by any person the application must specify the "entitled person or persons" in relation to the design. An entitled person is defined under s 13 as the person who created the design (the designer); the designer's employer or contractor if the design was created under contract or in the course of employment; a person deriving title from one of these people; a person entitled to have the exclusive rights in the design assigned to him or her once the design is registered; or the legal representative of any of these people. It does not include someone who has assigned their rights or from whom the rights have wholly devolved.

The courts pay particular attention to the question of whether a design was created "in the course of employment". "If the employee was employed to make or discover inventions of the type ultimately produced, then that is work for which the employer has paid and the employer is entitled to benefit from the invention. If the employee does not have any general duty to invent or duty of creativity, then the only basis upon which an invention can be said to have been created "in the course of employment" is if it has been created pursuant to a specific direction by the employer to undertake work which results in the creation of the invention".[85]

The application may be in respect of one design in relation to one product; it may be a common design in relation to more than one product; it may be more than one design in relation to one product or it may be more than one design in relation to more than one product so long as each product belongs to the same class under the *Locarno Agreement Establishing an International Classification of Industrial Design 1968* (s 22). A common design is not defined under the Act.

If the application meets the minimum filing requirements – that is, the application indicates that what is filed is meant to be a designs application, it identifies the applicant and the applicant's contact details and it includes a representation of each design (s 21 and reg 3.01) – the Registrar will notify the applicant of the application's filing date (that is, the day on which the application meets the minimum filing requirements reg 3.05); advise the applicant that he or she has six months in which to either publish or register the design (s 24); and the Registrar publishes details of the application (s 25).

---

85  *Courier Pete Pty Ltd v Metroll Queensland Pty Ltd* [2010] FCA 735 at [19]. See also Chapter 6, "Dealing with Copyright".

## Registration or publication election

Within six months of the filing date the applicant must elect to either publish the design or register the design (s 35). If the application is in relation to more than one design then the applicant may seek publication of part of the application and registration of other parts of the application if the applicant so desires (s 36). If the applicant makes no request in relation to some of these designs then the Registrar may allow the applicant to request publication in the future but will not allow registration of those designs. If the applicant does not request either publication or registration within the prescribed period the application lapses (s 33).

If the applicant requests registration of the design the Registrar must register the design if it meets the formalities requirements; that it is in fact a common design where necessary; that the products are in the same Locarno Agreement class where necessary; and the Registrar is not required to refuse registration under s 43 (see below). If the Registrar is required to register the design the Registrar must enter details in the register; issue a certificate of registration and publish a notice that the design has been registered (s 45). Note that the Registrar is not required to conduct a substantive examination of the design before registration.

The Registrar must refuse registration under s 43 if the design is prescribed by the Regulations (see reg 4.06 and the definition of design above); if the design is a protected design under s 18 of the *Olympic Insignia Protection Act 1987* (Cth); if the design is an integrated circuit, part of or a mask for an integrated circuit; if the Registrar has given the applicant an opportunity to amend the application and the applicant has not done so; or if the design is subject to a prohibition order under s 108. Under s 108 the Registrar may prohibit or restrict publication of information about the subject-matter of a design application if the Registrar thinks it is necessary or expedient to do so in the interests of the defence of the Commonwealth.

If the applicant requests publication of the design rather than registration, the Registrar must publish the design if the documents satisfy the formal requirements under the Regulations (s 57). The Act allows the Registrar to request amendments to the application in order to meet the publication requirements (ss 57-59).

## Revocation relating to entitled persons

A person may at this time, without an examination of the design, apply for revocation of a design registration on the basis that a person who was an entitled person at the time of registration was not included in the registration or because a person who was an original registered owner was not an entitled person at that time. The Registrar is required to revoke the registration if the allegations are established after the original applicants have been given a chance to be heard. This is a strict ground which appears to put a heavy burden on the applicant to ensure that all original registered owners are in fact entitled persons and that all entitled persons are in fact registered as original owners (ss 51-56).

## Examination

Following registration any person, a court or the Registrar on his or her own motion, may require the Registrar to conduct an examination of the design.[86] An examination is conducted to determine whether registration should be revoked on the ground that it is not a registrable design under s 15, that is, that the design is not new and distinctive, or because it is a prescribed design under s 43 (ss 63-65 and reg 5.02. For the s 43 grounds, see above). If the grounds are made out then the Registrar must revoke the registration and publish a notice to this effect (s 68). The Act provides some limited scope for the Registrar to amend the register to avoid revocation (s 66). If the Registrar determines upon examination that there is no ground for revocation, or that there is no ground to amend the register, then the Registrar must issue a certificate of examination and publish a notice advising that an examination has been conducted and that infringement proceedings may now commence (s 67).

## Term of registration

The term of registration is five years from the filing date and may be renewed for a further five years (ss 46 and 47). The registration ceases if the registration is revoked; the applicant has not paid the prescribed fees; the registered owner surrenders the registration; or if the copyright expires in an artistic work which was a corresponding design which did not destroy the novelty of the design by virtue of s 18 of the *Designs Act 2003* (ss 48-49). See prior use of artistic work under s 18 above.

# Rights and Infringement

The rights of the registered designs owner have been substantially increased under the *Designs Act 2003* to include the use of a product embodying a registered design for the purposes of trade or business. This brings the 2003 Act closer to the model of patent law and further away from the copyright law model.

Under s 10 the owner of a registered design has the exclusive right:

- to make or offer to make a product which embodies the design (s 75(5));
- to import such a product into Australia for sale, or for use for the purposes of trade or business;
- to sell, hire or otherwise dispose of, or offer to sell, hire or otherwise dispose of such a product or to keep the product for such purposes;
- to use such a product in any way for the purpose of trade or business or to keep the product for such purposes;
- to authorise any of these acts.

Breach of the first of the exclusive rights is called a primary infringement. Breach of the remaining rights is called a secondary infringement (s 75(5)). The

---

86  The Registrar must discontinue an examination if a court action commences in relation to the design and must not commence an examination where such proceedings are pending. The court may, however, order the Registrar to commence or continue an examination (s 63).

classification of an infringement as a primary or secondary infringement may have implications as to whether or not damages may be awarded: see s 75 and Remedies, below.

A person infringes a registered design under s 71 if the person, without consent:

- makes or offers to make a product, in relation to which a design is registered, which embodies a design that is identical to, or substantially similar in overall impression to, the registered design;
- imports such a product into Australia for sale, or for use for the purposes of trade or business;
- sells, hires or otherwise disposes of, or offers to sell, hire or otherwise dispose of such a product;
- uses such a product in any way for the purpose of trade or business; or
- keeps such a product for any of these purposes.
- In determining whether an allegedly infringing design is substantially similar in overall impression to the registered design, the court is to consider those factors which are to be taken into account in determining newness and distinctiveness under s 19, that is, the court is to give more weight to similarities than to differences; the development of the prior art base; any statement of newness; the amount, quality and importance of that part if only part of the design is substantially similar and the freedom of the creator of the design to innovate; and if there is no statement of newness the court must have regard to the design as a whole. In applying these tests the court is to apply the standard of the informed user. These factors have been discussed in detail above.

There are two significant changes between the 1906 Act and the 2003 Act in relation to infringement. First, under the 1906 Act a design monopoly was infringed if a person applied an obvious or fraudulent imitation of the design. The use of the term "imitation" suggested that there was a requirement of actual copying (similar to a breach of copyright) rather than an application of a design in innocence and without knowledge of the registered design (similar to patents infringement). The 2003 Act does not require any subjective copying and is more aligned to the patents model of monopoly protection.

Secondly, the test for infringement under the 2003 Act is much wider than that which developed under the old case law. Under the 2003 Act a design is infringed if a person makes or deals with a product which embodies a design which is identical to, or substantially similar in overall impression to, a registered design. By comparison, under the 1906 Act it was held that there was no infringement unless the "individual and specific appearance" of the design had been taken.[87] This strict test was applied in *Firmagroup Australia Pty Ltd v Byrne and Davidson Doors (Vic) Pty Ltd*[88] where a handle for opening a roller door was held to be non-infringing even though it incorporated the same distinctive

---

87    The phrase is taken from *Russell-Clarke on Copyright in Industrial Designs*, 5th ed, Sweet & Maxwell, London, 1974, p 27, and approved in *Re Wolanski's Registered Design* (1953) 88 CLR 278 at 279-280; *Kestos Ltd v Kempat and Vivian Fitch Kemp* (1935) 53 RPC 139 at 151 and *Firmagroup Australia Pty Ltd v Byrne and Davidson Doors (Vic) Pty Ltd* (1987) 180 CLR 483 at 487-489.

88    (1987) 180 CLR 483.

arrangement of inset grip, flat key and lock but where one of the handles was squat and the other was slimmer and more streamlined.

This case is also important for illustrating the application of the function/design dichotomy in designs law. Thus, the court explained its decision by reference to the rule that there will be no infringement of the design if only the function of the design, rather than the visual appearance of the design, is taken.

Despite the requirement that the infringement be of a "registered" design, in *Turbo Tek Enterprises Inc v Sperling Enterprises Pty Ltd*[89] (a case concerning importation of articles to which a fraudulent imitation had been applied under the old Act), it was held that there might be a fraudulent imitation under the 1906 *Designs Act* even though the design had not in fact been registered at the time the fraudulent imitation was applied to the article. In that case an application had been lodged and the court held that it was in accordance with the statutory framework, and the principle of priority, the protection should apply from the time of the application rather than from the time of registration. The manufacturers in that case (rather than the importers) had reason to believe that the design would be subject to some type of protection, be it patent, copyright or designs protection.[90] This reasoning would probably not apply under the *Designs Act 2003* because under the new Act an infringement takes place "during the term of registration" of the design (s 71) which is calculated from the filing date. The filing date is the date when the applicant meets the minimum requirements and, in practice, this will often be the date on which the application was lodged.

## Offences

In addition to the action for infringement there are a number of offences created under the *Designs Act 2003* ss 131-135. It is an offence to make false entries in the register and to make a representation that a design is registered.[91] It is an offence to make any representation which might suggest that one's business office is, or is officially connected with, the Designs Office. It is an offence to fail to appear before the Registrar, fail to answer a question put by the Registrar, fail to produce a document or article to the Registrar or swear or make an affirmation before the Registrar when required, without lawful excuse (unless the requirement would tend to incriminate the person). It is an offence for the Registrar, Deputy Registrar or an employee of the Designs Office or the Public Service to traffic in registered designs unless that person is the registered owner or has acquired the registered design by devolution of will or by operation of law.

## Defences and Compulsory Licence

There are only two defences and one compulsory licence under the *Designs Act 2003*. These are the repair defence and the defence of consent (which may allow parallel importation). A compulsory licence is available for Crown use and supply of designs.

---

89   (1989) 88 ALR 524.
90   See also *Elconnex v Gerard Industries* (1995) 105 ALR 247.
91   Section 45.

## Repair defence (s 72)

The *Designs Act 2003* introduced a new repair defence under s 72. In lay terms when we speak of a repair we might mean a repair to restore a product's function or a repair to restore a product's appearance. For example, in the vehicle industry a repair might restore the function of the car by replacing a bolt and nut within the engine mount or the repair might restore the appearance of the car by replacing its front panel or bumper bar. Often, a repair will do both – however, the *Designs Act 2003* only covers those repairs that restore the appearance of a product.

The *Designs Act* provides that there is no infringement of a registered design if a person uses, or authorises another person to use, a product embodying the design where the product is a component part of a complex product and the use is for the purpose of repairing the complex product "so as to restore its overall appearance in whole or part".

Repair is defined to include restoring or replacing a decayed or damaged part to good and sound condition and replacing any incidental items when restoring or replacing these items. That is, generally speaking, the part must be damaged or decayed in order for the repair defence to be effective. Section 73(d), however, extends the defence to cover maintenance of a complex product. Thus, if as part of the maintenance of a car or other complex product, parts are normally replaced or restored before they are decayed or damaged then the repair defence is effective.

Use is defined as making; offering to make; importing for sale or for trade or business; selling, hiring or disposing of the product; using the product in any other way for business or trade and keeping the product for the purpose of doing any of these things (s 73(5)). Thus, the repair defence is available not just to consumers but to spare parts dealers, importers and manufacturers.

Under s 72(3)(a) a repair is only taken to have restored the overall appearance of a complex product in whole if the overall appearance of the complex product immediately after the repair is not materially different from its overall original appearance. Thus, the repair defence does not extend to anything which improves the appearance or visual features of the complex product and so one could not rely on the repair defence to replace a rear spoiler on a car by a fancier, more streamlined one, for example. Under s 73(3)(b) a repair is taken to restore the overall appearance of a complex product in part if any material difference between the original overall appearance of the complex product and the overall appearance of the complex product immediately after repair is solely attributable to the fact that only part of the complex product has been repaired. Thus, if three panels of a car are damaged and the person can only afford to repair two of the panels then the repair defence will be effective. In determining these matters the court must apply the standard of the informed user (s 73(4)).

The repair defence is substantially narrower than other options canvassed by the government before the *Designs Act 2003* was introduced. The government rejected a suggestion that spare parts be wholly excluded from registration as designs; it also rejected the possibility of only excluding spare parts which "must fit" (so as to ensure functionality) or "must match" (so as to ensure that appearance might be protected) a complex product. Finally, the government rejected a proposal that the registrability of a spare part be determined by an appropriate competition authority.

## Consent and parallel imports (s 71(2))

Section 71(2) provides that a person does not infringe a registered design if the person imports a product which embodies a design which is identical to or substantially similar in overall impression if the product embodies that design with the licence or authority of the registered owner of the design. If the "registered owner" includes a registered owner of the design in an overseas jurisdiction then this section would allow parallel importation of designs. If the "registered owner" only covers a registered owner of a design registered in Australia then this provision is very narrow and, arguably, otiose. The 2003 Act is not clear as to the meaning of registered owner and, thus, the problems identified in the discussion of parallel imports and trade marks also arise in relation to designs under this Act. The Act needs to be amended to clarify this problem.

## Crown use and supply (ss 95-105)

The *Designs Act 2003 ss* 95-105 grants a compulsory licence to the Crown whereby the Commonwealth or State, or a person authorised by the Commonwealth or State, may use the design for the service of the Crown or State. Subject to s 105, the use is restricted to use necessary for the services of the State or Commonwealth within Australia. Under s 105, the Commonwealth, or a person authorised by the Commonwealth, may supply goods embodying the design, to a foreign country for the defence of that country. The Commonwealth may sell the product to the foreign country and may also sell excess products to any other person.

# Dealing and Actions

Section 10 provides that the exclusive rights of the registered owner are personal property capable of assignment or devolution by will or operation of law. The registered owner or owners may assign, in writing, all or part of the registered owner's interest in the design and the assignment must be signed by the assignor and assignee. An assignment may be for a particular geographical location (s 11).

Under s 12 a registered owner may deal with his or her interest as an absolute owner and give good discharges for any consideration for such dealing. These rights are subject to any rights appearing on the register to be vested in other people under s 114. In addition, the right does not protect a person who deals with the owner otherwise than as a bona fide purchaser for value without notice of any fraud on the part of the registered owner. Equities in relation to a registered design may also be enforced against the registered owner, except to the prejudice of a purchaser in good faith for value.

Under s 114 the assignee or assignor of a registered design may ask the Registrar to record the assignment on the register, as may a person who has become the owner through devolution, by will or by operation of law.

The registered owner of a registered design is the person or persons whose names are entered on the register (s 14). If there are two or more registered owners they are entitled to equal undivided shares in the exclusive rights and may each exercise these rights without the consent of the other owners except that no owner may assign or license an exclusive right without consent. These dealing rights are subject to any contrary agreement entered into between the owners (s 14).

Unlike other intellectual property regimes, an exclusive licensee does not have a right to take an action for infringement under the new Act; this right is reserved to the registered owner of a registered design (s 73). There is no provision for actions in conversion and detinue under the *Designs Act 2003* although there is provision for an action for unjustified threats (ss 77-81).

The remedies available for infringement under the *Designs Act* are similar to the other intellectual property statutory regimes. The design's owner may seek an injunction and, at the option of the plaintiff, either damages or an account of profits (s 75). The court has the power to refuse damages or to award an account of profits if the defendant satisfies the court that, in the case of direct infringement, the defendant was not aware that the design was registered and that the defendant had taken all reasonable steps to ascertain whether a monopoly in the design existed. In the case of secondary infringement, the defendant must establish that, at the time of infringement, the defendant was not aware, and could not reasonably be expected to be aware, that the design was registered. It is prima facie evidence that the defendant was aware that the design was registered if the product was marked so as to indicate that it was registered. A defendant to an action for infringement may apply, by way of counter-claim, to have the register rectified by expunging the registration of the design in question.

# CASES

## *World of Technologies (Aust) Pty Ltd v Tempo (Aust) Pty Ltd*
### Federal Court of Australia: Jessup J
### [2007] FCA 114

This is one of the first cases under the *Designs Act 2003* to apply the test of newness and distinctiveness. The case relates to a bagless vacuum cleaner made in China and the judge is certainly very cautious in his test of newness.

### Jessup J: Cross-claim for Revocation

58. Under s 15(1) of the Designs Act, a design is a "registrable design" if it is "new and distinctive" when compared with the "prior art base for the design" as it existed before the priority date. By subs (2) the "prior art base" consists of three items, including "designs publicly used in Australia" and "designs published in a document within or outside Australia". By s 16(1) a design is new "unless it is identical to a design that forms part of the prior art base". A design is distinctive "unless it is substantially similar in overall impression to a design that forms part of the prior art base". In considering the matter of substantial similarity, I am required, by s 19(1) of the Act, to give more weight to similarities between the subject design and the prior art base than to differences between them. In the present case, the application for design registration did not include a statement of newness and distinctiveness, in which circumstances I am required, by s 19(3) of the Designs Act, to have regard to the appearance of the design as a whole. If I am satisfied that the subject design was not a registrable design within the meaning of s 15(1) of the Designs Act at the priority date, I am empowered to revoke the registration of the design pursuant to s 93(3)(a) of the Act.

59. In the circumstances of the present case, the priority date is the date of application for registration, 16 June 2005.

60. The respondent relies first upon the publication, at the Canton Fair in April 2005, of a brochure depicting the appearance of the MC-801 vacuum cleaner, for the purposes of s 15(2)(b) of the Designs Act. The original of that brochure is before the court. I have compared the brochure with the design as registered. It is common ground that the vacuum cleaner shown in each document is one and the same product. The copy of the registered design which is before the court is a photocopy. The representations of the vacuum cleaner in it are less distinct than the corresponding printed colour photographs appearing on the Suzhou Fak brochure of April 2005. Further, in the design as registered the product is shown in side view (both sides), in bottom view, in top view, in back view, in front view, in back perspective view and in front perspective view. As represented on the brochure, the product is shown only in front perspective view. For that reason, I am unable to conclude that the design is identical to that shown in the brochure. Accordingly, I do not hold that the design is not new for the purposes of s 16(1) of the Designs Act.

61. However, I consider that the design as applied for and subsequently registered is substantially similar in overall impression to the design disclosed in the Suzhou Fak brochure of April 2005. Although shown on the brochure in front perspective view only, the impression obtained from that angle permits the viewer to make a reasonable assessment not only of the side, but also of the front, of the vacuum cleaner. Assuming, as I do, that the product is symmetrical, I take it that the other front perspective view would convey the same impression. Further, the item is displayed on the brochure in such a way as to permit the viewer to gain a reasonably good impression of the appearance of the

product from the top. The only faces of the product which it is impossible to perceive from the brochure are those of the rear and of the underside. Notwithstanding these omissions, I consider that the vacuum cleaner is sufficiently represented on the Suzhou Fak brochure to give a good impression of the appearance of the design of the product as a whole, as required by s 19(3) of the Designs Act. Taking that approach, I find that the design for which the applicant applied for, and subsequently secured, registration is substantially similar in overall impression to that which appeared on the printed brochure for the MC-801 vacuum cleaner distributed at the Canton Fair in April 2005. The latter was a design published in a document outside Australia and was, accordingly, part of the prior art base for the purposes of registrability.

## *Macrae Knitting Mills Pty Ltd v Lowes Ltd*
High Court of Australia: Starke, Dixon, Evatt and McTiernan JJ
(1936) 55 CLR 725

A swimming suit is held to lack the necessary novelty for registration under the 1906 Act. Would it be registrable as distinctive under the *Designs Act 2003*?

**Dixon J: [730]** In the present case the object of the design, considered independently of the Act, is plainly to produce a bathing garment which not only will have a particular appearance but in fit and fastening will have also a particular practical effect. The latter element is, of course, to be disregarded in considering the questions of novelty and infringement which we are to decide. The *Designs Act* is concerned with shape and configuration, not function. The whole bathing garment is registered as a design and, therefore, the whole **[731]** bathing garment must be considered. The part for which novelty is now claimed is the strapping at the back. Of the modes of strapping which were in practice many have been placed before the court by means of pictures put in evidence. As might be imagined, they exhibit a great variation in detail. Doubtless, form, configuration and appearance did not constitute the sole motive which led people to adopt one or the other of the various arrangements of straps. More substantial considerations played their part. But configuration and shape would not be disregarded.

In the present design the configuration is not an exact reproduction of any shown in the pictures. But the configuration does not, in my opinion, show any distinctiveness in its departure from prior models. The general appearance presented by many of the entire garments formerly in use is the same. Innumerable variations in the relative sizes and positions of back and shoulder straps are possible. However varied, in function they are a mere equivalent. In appearance also they are substantially equivalent. Originality or novelty are not qualities to be ascribed to the configuration produced by the variation. In my opinion the bathing garment is not a new or original design.

If a contrary opinion had been formed by the court, the question of infringement might have presented some difficulty. The view which *Nicholas* J took of infringement was necessarily hypothetical. His hypothesis was that novelty or originality was discovered in slight variations. If, so, there could not be an infringement without a very exact resemblance between the two things. But it is unnecessary to say more on the subject of infringement.

In my opinion the suit failed because the registration of the alleged design was invalid.

## *Re Clarke's Design*
English Court of Appeal: Lindley, Lopes and Kay LJJ
[1896] 2 Ch 38

In this case the accused design was a lamp shade for an electric light. The shape of the lamp shade had previously been applied to a gas lamp but not to an electric light, electric lights having previously been unknown. The court held that the lamp shade was neither new nor original but do you think it would also fail the distinctiveness test under the *Designs Act 2003*?

**Lindley LJ: [44]** I pass now to the shape for which the design is applicable, and to the inquiry whether at the date of its registration such shape was new or original and not previously published in the United Kingdom. It is not easy to determine what distinction, if any, is intended to be drawn between novelty and originality; but if there is any difference the design need not be both new and original. The Act applies to designs which are new or original provided they have not been previously published in the United Kingdom. In considering the novelty or originality of a design it must always be borne in mind that the applicability of the design to manufactured articles is the matter which has to be determined. This was pointed out in *Saunders v Weil*,[92] the Abbey spoon-handle case. From the wording of ss 47, 58, and 60, it might be thought that if a design had never been applied to articles comprised in one of the classes of goods into which manufactured articles are divided for the purposes of the Act, such design might be protected for that class even if it had been previously applied to goods of a different class. But it has been decided that if a design is really old in its application to some manufactured article its application to a new substance will not necessarily entitle it to protection, although such substance may not fall within the class to which the first article belongs. In *In re Bach's Design*,[93] a lamp-shade in the shape of a rose, but made in linen, was registered for goods in class 12. It was held that a lamp-shade of the same shape, but made in china, and which had been registered for goods in class 14, was not entitled to protection, and it was removed from the register accordingly. Although the substances were dissimilar the shape was the same, and the articles having that shape were both lamp-shades – that is, they were both of the same kind and used for the same purpose. Again, in *In re Read and Greswell's Design*,[94] a lamp-shade made of **[45]** paper, shaped like a chrysanthemum, was registered in class 5, and a similar design for a lamp-shade of the same shape was expunged from the register, although it was registered for goods in class 12 and was made of linen and paper. In this last case Chitty J[95] said that, "to be capable of being registered a design must be 'new or original' in fact, and not, as is suggested, 'new or original' as to some particular class of goods. It cannot be said to be new and original if it is already being applied to articles of an analogous character." The learned judge was obviously referring to the classes of goods mentioned in the schedule to the Designs Rules, and the words referring to articles of an analogous nature shew that the learned judge did not intend by the words "new or original in fact" to decide that a design must be new or original in the sense of never having been seen before as applied to any article whatever. In *Walker, Hunter & Co v Falkirk Iron Co*,[96] and *Hecla Foundry Co v Walker, Hunter & Co*,[97] a design for the shape of an iron furnace-door was protected, although wooden

---

[92] [1893] 1 QB 470.
[93] 42 Ch D 661.
[94] 42 Ch D 260.
[95] 42 Ch D 262.
[96] 4 Rep Pat Cas 390.
[97] 14 App Cas 550.

doors of the same shape for sideboards and other articles of furniture were old. The things shaped were for such different purposes and their uses were so dissimilar that the design for one of such things was held to be new or original, although it was old for the other. What then is the test to be applied to a case such as that before us? The design must be new or original with reference to the kind of article for which it is registered, meaning by kind of article, not the class of article mentioned in the schedule to the rules, but the kind of article having regard to its general character and use. A design may be new for a coal-scuttle, but not for a bonnet. On the other hand, a design for a shade of a gas-lamp can hardly be new if it was old for an oil-lamp. In the present case the design registered is for the shape of an electric lamp, or, rather, of the shade for an electric light. It follows from what has been stated above that the shape may be new or original in its application to electric lamps, which are modern inventions, and yet be neither new nor original in its application to gas or oil lamps. **[46]** If when registered the design was not new or original for all lamps, if the shape was common for such lamps as were used before electric lighting was invented, the design is one to which the Act does not apply, and the design ought to be expunged. Electric lighting being new, every lamp or lamp-shade adapted to it for the first time may be said to be new or original if attention is paid only to its application to the new method of lighting. But it is absurd to suppose that the application of an old shaped lamp or shade to an electric light could be protected under this Act. There must be some novelty or originality in the shape as applied to sources of light in order that a design for the shape of a lamp can be protected. How, then, does this case stand? On the one side it is contended that there is nothing new or original in this design for the shape of lamps; on the other it is contended that this particular shape of lamp has never been seen before. The truth must be ascertained by looking at the shape of this particular design and by comparing it with the shapes of lamps or shades previously known. This method of determining such a question is not only dictated by good sense, but is warranted by decided cases: see *Hecla Foundry Co v Walker, Hunter & Co.*[98]

Applying this method to the present case, using my own eyes and attending to the evidence adduced on both sides, the conclusion at which I have arrived is that the design registered is nothing more nor less than an old and well known lamp or lamp-shade, with the omission of a part which was wanted for gas or oil burners, but which is useless for an electric light.

## *J Rapee and Co Pty Ltd v Kas Cushions Pty Ltd*
Federal Court of Australia: Gummow J
(1989) 90 ALR 288

The applicants sought to register a design for a cushion with a particular form of tufting. Photos of similar cushions had been published before the priority date and the question arose as to what level of disclosure is needed to destroy novelty under the 1906 Act.

**Gummow J: [301]** ... s 17(1)(a) of the Australian legislation is directed to a design which:
> "(a) differs only in immaterial details or in features commonly used in the relevant trade from a design that, before the priority date in respect of the application for registration, was registered, published or used in Australia in respect of the same article ..."

In *Sebel & Co Ltd's Application (No 1)* [1959] RPC 12, an application for registration for a design of a rocking horse was unsuccessful. In upholding the decision of the hearing

---

[98] 14 App Cas 550.

officer, Lloyd-Jacob J said (at 18): "Registration is to be denied to a design which is the same as a published design or differs from it only in immaterial details or in features which are variants commonly used in the trade. The March 1956 issue of *Playthings* at pp 201 and 202 and the August 1956 issue of the same journal overleaf to p 64 carry illustrations of toy bouncing horses in which the shape of the stands is substantially identical with that in the design in suit. The detailed design of horse mounted on such stands presents differences which are evident on inspection, for the magazine illustrations relate to horses in a 'bucking' or 'leaping' attitude, whilst the design in suit presents the animal with all four legs outstretched such as used to be thought appropriate to a 'galloping' position. Such differences cannot be said to be immaterial, for they could reasonably be thought to be of significance. But a modification of the 'bucking' or 'leaping' toy horse illustrated in these periodicals which are of American origin so as to substitute upon the same shape of stand a 'galloping' horse in the traditional pose common to rocking horses in English homes for generations past would be to utilise a feature which is an obvious variant, and one which is and has for years been in use."

Both this case and Lloyd-Jacob J's decision in *Sebel & Co Ltd's Application (No 2)* [1959] RPC 19 at 24, indicate that a feature of a design which is not an immaterial detail may still be a variant commonly used in the trade. In what follows, as to validity, I direct attention to common trade variants.

[302] I bear in mind both that each of the designs must be looked at as a whole and that a design is not invalid merely because it contains a number of elements of similarity to earlier designs, if there are other elements that are different: *D Sebel & Co Ltd v National Art Metal Co Pty Ltd* (1965) 10 FLR 224 at 227, per Jacobs J.

I have described the features of the designs and the evidence of the trade witnesses and of various documentary publications (particularly Exs 4D 10B, 10C, 11A and 12C) which were published (in the relevant sense) before the priority date. As I have said, all of the features of the first and second designs are shown before the priority date to have been well known and commonly used in the relevant trade of cushion and chair pad manufacture and reupholstery; further, (tufting methods aside) designs have been published for chair pads which to the eye are shaped in the same way as the first design. This is not a case such as *Britvic Ltd's Application* [1960] RPC 201, where a disclosure in one trade catalogue was insufficient to establish a common trade variant. What has happened here may properly be described as the adoption of features commonly used in the trade and the registration of designs for combinations thereof. It is true, as the witnesses agreed, that no particular one of the publications relied on sufficiently discloses chair pads of the squarish shape of the designs with tufting points effected by circular stitching. But this method of tufting was well known and used with other cushions and chair pads, for example, the Eos product (Ex 8). The use of this method of tufting rather than buttoning and straight stitching, in my view, would not present an effect which went beyond the impression of a substitution of a known alternative: cf *Sebel & Co Ltd's Application (No 2), supra*, at 24. As I have said, something may be a not immaterial detail but may still be a variant commonly used in the trade.

My conclusion is that the first design is invalid because it differs only in features commonly used at the priority date of 23 August 1984 in the relevant trade from designs published or used in Australia in respect of chair pads. What I have said concerning the first design applies to the second design, with the additional observation that the evidence would indicate that the use of five rather than four tufting points was a well known trade variant. Thus, the second design also would be invalid. But that is not all.

The second design was registered pursuant to s 25D of the Act, on the footing that the use of the fifth tufting point meant that it differed from the first design only in immaterial details or in features commonly used in the relevant trade. The cancellation of the first design means that the registration of the second design no longer is deemed to have come into force when the application for the first design was made (ie 23 August 1984); its priority date will be the date of the application (ie 19 July 1988). This follows from the inter-action between s 21 and s 25D of the Act. The consequence is that the second design is invalid, not only for the reason given above, but also because the second design differed only from the first in a feature commonly used in the trade, and the first design had a prior registration in respect of the same article as the second design, within the meaning of s 17(1)(a). This paragraph is directed not only at designs previously published or used, but at prior registrations. The first design is such a registration

## *Firmagroup Australia Pty Ltd v Byrne and Davidson Doors (Vic) Pty Ltd*

High Court of Australia: Wilson, Brennan, Deane, Dawson and Gaudron JJ
(1987) 180 CLR 483

Firmagroup registered a design for a combined door handle and lock for a garage door. The respondents produced another combined door handle and lock which was more squat in appearance than the registered design. Under the *Designs Act 1906* this was held not to be an infringement of the design. The case is generally considered the most restrictive interpretation of infringement under the 1906 Act. Do you think the infringement test has been broadened under the 2003 Act? Note also the application of the function/design dichotomy in designs law.

> **Wilson, Brennan, Deane, Dawson, Gaudron JJ: [485]** The question is whether the **[486]** respondents' article is a "fraudulent or obvious imitation" of the registered design. A representation of the respondents' article appears in appendix "B" (at 490). A visual comparison of the registered design with the respondents' article reveals some points of similarity and some of distinction.
>
> Looking from the front, both the registered design and the respondents' article consist of a flat rectangular plate in which a keyhole is set and, beside the plate, a recessed rectangular handgrip. Before the appellant created the design which was granted registration, the locking units attached to metal roller doors consisted of rectangular plates in which a keyhole was set standing out from the surface of the screen so that a hand could grip the lower or upper surface in order to lift or lower the door. King J found that the registered design incorporated a "new concept of design in products of its kind", and he identified the "new main features" as "a more elongated rectangular shape than was previously known and a recessed handle". These new features are common to the registered design and to the respondents' article. In both the design and the article, the plate section (containing the keyhole) and the handgrip section are placed side by side horizontally; in both, the upper, lower and front surfaces of the plate and handgrip sections are continuous, extending without a break from one section to the other. King J found that the respondents consciously adopted "salient features of [the appellant's] design, namely, the recessed handle and a face plate lengthened laterally to accommodate the recess and the lock side by side". Although his Honour found that "salient features of construction" had been taken from the registered design, he held that the respondents had produced a different design distinct from the registered design.
>
> The registered design and the respondents' article are dissimilar in proportion (the design being rather squat, the article much slimmer); in the comparative size of the plate and handgrip sections (the handgrip section being larger than the plate section in the design, the two sections being of the same size in the respondents' article); in the vertical line which, on the respondents' article but not in the design, visually divides the plate section from the handgrip section; in the width of the front surface surrounding the recess

of the handgrip (the design showing a rather thick edging, the respondents' article being slender of line around the recess); in the angularity of the recess (in the design the recess is sloped, in the article the recess is virtually right-angled) and in the shape of the ends (the design showing a deep and irregular base designed to fit the corrugation of the panels in the metal screen of the door, the **[487]** ends of the article being thin and abutting flat onto the metal screen).

When a design satisfies the statutory definition of "design" by reason of its applicability "to the purpose of ... shape, or configuration, of an article", the monopoly conferred by registration does not extend to the features of the design which do not determine the article's unique shape or configuration, and this is so although the design may be applied to make a new and useful article. The Act is concerned with shape and configuration, not function.[99] Specificity of shape and configuration must be conveyed by a registrable design; features of a design which do no more than convey the idea of a general shape appropriate to the function which the article is intended to perform and which are consistent with a variety of particular shapes in articles copying those features are not amenable to protection by the Act. In *Pugh v Riley Cycle Co Ltd*,[100] Parker J said:

"The difficulty arises where the conception, thus arrived at, is not a definite conception as to shape or configuration, but only a conception as to some general characteristic of shape or configuration, necessitated by the mode or principle of construction, the definite shape or configuration, being, consistently with such mode or principle of construction, capable of variation within wide limits. To allow the registration of a conception of such general characteristics of shape or configuration might well be equivalent to allowing the registration of a conception relating to the mode or principle of construction."

The principle is stated in *Russell-Clarke on Copyright in Industrial Designs*,[101] in a passage which has been judicially approved:

"What he gets a monopoly for is one particular individual and specific appearance. If it is possible to get several different appearances, which all embody the general features which he claims, then those features are too general, and amount to a method or principle of construction."[102]

The definition of "design" was amended by the *Designs Amendment Act 1981* (Cth) and now expressly excludes "a method or principle of construction". But that exclusion, which was contained in s 93 of the Patents and Designs Act 1907 (UK) (see now s 1(3) of the Registered Designs Act 1949 (UK)), gives **[488]** statutory expression to what was previously implied in the true conception of a design in the earlier statute law.[103] The notion that a feature which does no more than identify a general characteristic of shape is a method or principle of construction and is therefore outside the protection of the Act appears in what this Court said in *Malleys Ltd v JW Tomlin Pty Ltd*:[104]

"It is not the function of design to indicate a process of manufacture; indeed, anything amounting to a method of construction that would permit differences of shape spells invalidity."

The only design features that are susceptible of protection are those features which convey the idea of "one particular individual and specific appearance", to repeat the phrase from *Russell-Clarke*. No design should be so construed as to give to its proprietor

---

[99] *Macrae Knitting Mills Ltd v Lowes Ltd* (1936), 55 CLR 725, at p 730, per Dixon J.

[100] [1912] 1 Ch 613, at pp 619-620.

[101] 5th ed (1974), p 27.

[102] See *In re Wolanski's Registered Design* (1953), 88 CLR 278, at pp 279-280; *Kestos Ltd v Kempat Ltd* (1935), 53 RPC 139, at p 151.

[103] *Stenor Ltd v Whitesides (Clitheroe) Ltd*, [1948] AC 107, at p 121.

[104] ante, p 124.

a monopoly in a method or principle of construction. The registration of the appellant's design thus gives no monopoly for the making of an article combining a plate in which a keyhole is set and a recessed handgrip; nor in our opinion does it give a monopoly for the making of an article combining a rectangular plate in which a keyhole is set and a recessed rectangular handgrip placed alongside horizontally. The idea of shape or configuration conveyed by those features is altogether too general to attract statutory protection If the appellant's design was no more precisely specified than that, registration ought to have been refused.

But the appellant's registered design does convey a particular idea of the shape of a particular combination unit, though the features which convey that idea are not the features on which the appellant relies to establish that the respondents' article is an infringing imitation of the registered design. The particular idea of shape conveyed by the registered design is of a rather squat combination unit with the surface of the plate section extending into a broad surround of the recessed handgrip, a sloping recess in the handgrip, an absence of symmetry between the plate and handgrip sections of the unit and ends which are thick and irregularly shaped. These features, however, serve to distinguish the registered design from the respondents' article. What the respondents took from the registered design were not design features susceptible of protection; they were features which, although intended to make an article to which they were applied more useful than similar articles then in use, were insufficiently precise to convey an idea of unique shape or **[489]** configuration. Such general functional features are not protected by the Act, however novel, useful and commercially significant they may be. Section 30(1)(a) of the Act does not expand the protection conferred by registration so that an article which copies such general functional features is held to infringe the monopoly granted by registration. As the points of similarity between the registered design and the respondents' article are general functional features, the article is not an "imitation" of the registered design within the meaning of that term in s 30(1)(a).

Special leave was granted in this case chiefly to consider the distinction between "obvious" and "fraudulent" imitations. On analysis, that question does not arise. However, nothing that was submitted in argument before this Court casts doubt upon the brief but accurate description of obvious and fraudulent imitations in Malleys Case.

In our opinion King J correctly summed up the position in these findings:

"My conclusion is that although there are common features of construction in the compared designs, it must appear, to find fraudulent imitation, that the overall distinctive appearance of the registered design has been taken. In this case salient features of construction are taken, but the whole unit has been so redesigned to incorporate them that a different design has been produced. Thus the change in balance of the features and the lengthening of the article are not mere disguise but are themselves salient features of the defendants' design which are novel and unique in that design."

We would dismiss the appeal.

### *Dart Industries Inc v Decor Corporation Pty Ltd*
Federal Court of Australia: Lockhart, Jenkinson and Gummow JJ
(1989) 15 IPR 403

This case illustrates the application of the infringement test under the 1906 Act as the court compares lettuce crispers. Although the 2003 Act is meant to make it easier to prove infringement do you think a different decision would arise under that Act?

**Lockhart J: [410]** The consequence of s 30(1) of the Act is that there is infringement of a registered design in any one of three cases: namely, where the design which has been applied by the defendant is:

(a)  the registered design itself;

(b)  an obvious imitation of the registered design; or

(c)  a fraudulent imitation of the registered design.

An obvious imitation is one which is not the same as the registered design but is a "copy apparent to the eye notwithstanding slight differences": *Malleys Ltd v JW Tomlin Pty Ltd* (1961) 35 ALJR 352 at 354. The question must be looked at as one of substance and by examining the essential features of the design: *Oliver & Co v Thornley & Co* (1896) 13 RPC 490; *Hanfstaengl v WH Smith & Sons* (1905) 21 TLR 291; *Wallpaper Manufacturers Ltd v Derby Paper Staining Co* (1925) 42 RPC 443; *Dunlop Rubber Co Ltd v Golf Ball Developments Ltd* (1931) 48 RPC 268 per Farwell J at 281; *Benchairs Ltd v Chair Centre Ltd* [1974] RPC 429 per Graham J at 437; *Firmagroup Australia Pty Ltd v Byrne and Davidson Doors* **[411]** *(Vic) Pty Ltd, supra*, at 41. A closer correspondence between the registered design and the accused design is necessary to satisfy the test of obvious imitation rather than fraudulent imitation.

In distinguishing the concepts of "obvious imitation" and "fraudulent imitation", the oft-cited passage from the judgment of Farwell J in *Dunlop Rubber Co Ltd v Golf Ball Developments Ltd, supra*, at 279–80 is useful and apposite:

"Now with regard to the two words 'fraudulent' or 'obvious', in my judgment 'obvious' means something which, as soon as you look at it, strikes one at once as being so like the original design, the registered design, as to be almost unmistakable. I think an obvious imitation is something which is very close to the original design, the resemblance to the original design being immediately apparent to the eye looking at the two. With regard to the word 'fraudulent', fraudulent I think does presuppose a knowledge of the registered design. I think it would be difficult for a court to come to the conclusion that an imitation was fraudulent unless the court was satisfied that the registered design had been known to the author of the alleged infringing design, and further, it seems to me that 'fraudulent' imports something in the nature of making use of the registered design. It does not necessarily import deliberate intention to steal the property of the owner of the registered design. It does not import any intention to be fraudulent, because a person may be the author of a fraudulent imitation believing perfectly honestly that he has so altered the registered design as to make them two different designs, and so far as his own mind and his own intention are concerned, he may be honest in that sense. But fraudulent imitation seems to me to be an imitation which is based upon, and deliberately based upon, the registered design, and is an imitation which may be less apparent than an obvious imitation; that is to say, you may have a more subtle distinction between the registered design and a fraudulent imitation, and yet the fraudulent imitation, although it is different in some respects from the original, and in respects which render it not obviously an imitation may yet be an imitation perceptible when the two designs are closely scanned and accordingly an infringement."

In *Malleys'* case, supra, at 354 the High Court described a fraudulent imitation as being: "… a copy with differences which are both apparent and not so slight as to be insubstantial but which have been made merely to disguise the copying."

A design may be an obvious imitation within the meaning of s 30(1)(a) of the Act notwithstanding that the person who puts the obvious imitation on the market may not know of the registered design. By contrast, a fraudulent imitation presupposes a knowledge of the registered design and making use of it by the author of the alleged infringing design: *Dunlop Rubber Co Ltd v Golf Ball Developments Ltd, supra*, per Farwell J at 279; *Lewis Falk Ltd v Jacobwitz* (1944) 61 RPC 116 per Morton J at 122; *Firmagroup, supra,* at 41. It follows that, whereas visual comparison will establish whether the article alleged to infringe the registered design applies the registered design or an obvious imitation of it, something more is required to establish whether there has been a fraudulent imitation.

As I observed in *Firmagroup* at 41 the use of the word "fraudulent" in the Act is perhaps somewhat unfortunate since fraudulent in this context does not necessarily connote dishonesty. The essence of fraudulent **[412]** imitation is that the respondent's design has knowingly, consciously or deliberately been based on or derived from the registered design and neither dishonest intent nor deliberate or conscious intention to copy is a necessary element: *Grafton v Watson* (1884) 51 LT (NS) 141 especially per Cotton LJ at 144; *Pugh v Riley Cycle Co, supra*, per Parker J at 202; *Lewis Falk Ltd v Jacobwitz, supra*.

It is the necessary corollary of a finding that a design is entitled to statutory protection so as to confer the monopoly on the person in whose name it is registered, that the design is one which involves some unique feature of pattern, shape, configuration or ornament applicable to an article, and not being a method or principle of construction. If registration of a design is to confer anything useful upon the registered owner then questions of infringement must not be determined by a narrow or overly technical approach when comparing the registered design and the design of the offending article.

First impressions are important in determining whether there is infringement of a registered design. An essential purpose of the statutory scheme of design registration is to confer a monopoly upon the owner of the design for a limited period so that he may be rewarded for his inventiveness by exploiting the design commercially. Section 30 of the Act, specifying the circumstances in which a registered design may be infringed, should be interpreted having regard to the objects of the legislative scheme. In particular, it should be recognised that s 30 is intended to ensure that persons other than those entitled to the benefit of a registered design cannot produce or market articles which are derived by imitation, whether obvious or disguised, of the registered design and which are likely to be regarded by others who may acquire them as those of the registered design owner. There are, of course, two associated purposes here. One, that of encouraging and rewarding invention by the proprietor of the registered design, exhibits an analogy with the law of patents. The other, preventing confusion between articles bearing the registered design and infringing articles, has common elements with common law principles as to passing off.

The visual comparison test is obviously an important and sensible test to employ, having regard to the second purpose identified above, because purchasers of articles will in practice use their eyes in deciding whether to acquire, by purchase or otherwise, a particular article. It is for this reason that the principle is now well established by the courts that precise mathematical comparisons or matters of measurement or ratios, which form no part of the mental picture which the eye conveys to the brain of the shape or configuration suggested by the design, are not to be applied as the test of infringement. Appearance to the eye is the critical issue, and the decision of the trial judge is to be given particular weight unless some error in his judgment has been demonstrated: *Dalgety Australia Operations Ltd v FF Seeley Nominees Pty Ltd* (1986) 6 IPR 361 per Fisher J at 367 and Beaumont J at 373-4.

I compare now the appearance of the respondent's article which is alleged to infringe the registered design with the registered design itself. On first impression there are obviously similarities between the respondent's article and the figures appearing in the registered design, in particular Fig 5. It must be remembered, however, that Fig 5 represents a cross-section of the depicted bowl and lid; hence the cross hatching shows the cross-section by **[413]** some form of external or outer cutting. The other figures are probably a more reliable measure of comparison, although I certainly take Fig 5 into account. Each lid has a dome-like appearance and a rim at the circumference. Walls on both the respondent's container or bowl and the registered design curve inwardly and culminate in a base with a fairly squat appearance.

However, there are distinct and perceptible differences between the two. The critical and most obvious difference lies in the dome of the lid itself. Although the trial judge found that the visual concept of a bowl with a domed lid intended for the keeping of lettuce was familiar to persons aware of what was on the market on 16 August 1979, the domed lid used in the prior art was distinctly different from the domed lid represented by the registered design. The appellant's earlier product, being the only prior art in the area of lettuce crispers which the trial judge found to be relevant, had a small and only slightly raised dome which occupied only a portion, perhaps one-half, of the total area of the lid; whereas the dome of the lid in the registered design extends close to the outer rim of the lid and is the dominant feature of the lid and of the combination lid and bowl. The domes of the registered design and of the respondent's article are similar, but there are obvious differences. The essential difference between the two lids is that the dome on the respondent's article is distinctly higher than the dome on the registered design, although there are other differences including small differences between the rims on the lids themselves.

A second difference is in the bowl. The side wall of the respondent's bowl begins from the top downwards with approximately the same vertical fall as that contained in the registered design, but curves inwardly at a distinctly higher point than does the wall of the registered design. The lower part of the respondent's bowl conveys the appearance of a more continuous and gradual curve than the more rigid and pronounced curve of the lower part of the registered design.

The third difference, but a less distinct one, lies in the comparison of the bases of the respondent's article with the registered design. The base of the bowl in the registered design is smaller in height than that of the respondent's article and contains at its top a small curved area, whereas the base of the respondent's article is higher and more perpendicular than that of the registered design.

Doubtless there are other differences between the registered design and the respondent's article which can be measured by appropriate instruments, but this is not the test to be applied for determining questions of infringement under the Act.

Based on first impression and on later impressions formed by several examinations and comparisons between the registered design and the respondent's product, in my opinion the respondent's article plainly involves no application of the design itself. Nor is there any obvious imitation of the registered design.

As to the question of fraudulent imitation some examination of the trial judge's findings is required. The managing director of the respondent, Mr Davis, gave evidence at the trial. He said in essence that the respondent wished to produce a lettuce keeper as a companion to a product which it had already marketed, being a lettuce shaker of spherical form. It was not suggested to Mr Davis in cross-examination that his company had **[414]** deliberately based its design upon the product of the appellants or that it had deliberately copied it. Nor was it suggested that any differences were adopted for the purpose of disguising any fact of copying.

The designer of the respondent's product is a Mr Carlson who also gave evidence. He said that he had the idea in mind of a "ball" concept for the lettuce crisper before he saw products of the appellants. He said that the conception which he had initially formed as to the ball design did not alter after he had examined the samples produced to him of the Tupperware products, being the products of the appellant, prior to his producing concept drawings for the Decor product. He gave evidence as to the reasons for his adoption of the various features of the Decor design, none of which involved copying or disguising and copying of the appellants' product or design. This evidence was not challenged. He said that he was not asked to copy the registered design and that he did not copy it. His

Honour appears to have accepted the evidence of Mr Carlson. Although his Honour did not expressly state that he accepted such evidence, its acceptance appears to me to be implicit in his Honour's findings of fact. An element of doubt arises from the statement by his Honour that the respondent "was helped" by the sample of the appellant's product which was placed before Mr Carlson and the design development inherent in the product over and above the prior art consisting of the article produced by the appellant earlier. Although his Honour did not define the respects in which this help was afforded, in my view it cannot be inferred that his Honour rejected any material part of Mr Carlson's evidence.

The evidence does not therefore support a finding that the respondent knowingly, consciously or deliberately based its design upon the registered design or that the respondent's design was derived from that of the appellant so as to constitute a fraudulent imitation of the appellant's design.

It was submitted on behalf of the appellants that the trial judge erred in that he approached the comparison through the eye of an expert in design looking at the matter in considerable detail instead of in terms of visual impact. The trial judge stated the test which he applied, namely, that the requisite comparison is between the offending article and the registered design, that the required comparison is visual and must be made by the court.

His Honour did say that the court should take into account common trade knowledge and usage in the class of articles to which the registered design relates and cited *Phillips v Harbro Rubber Co* (1920) 37 RPC 233 per Lord Moulton at 239-40 as authority for that proposition. His Honour stated the result of his comparison of the registered design with the respondent's article, noting similarities and the major points of difference. It is true that in his examination his Honour stated in some detail the particular differences which he observed; but this does not in my view detract from his Honour's findings as to the differences. His Honour plainly approached the comparison as a matter of visual impact correctly, and not as an expert in design, and he did not look in undue detail at the matter.

It was also submitted that his Honour erred in that he did not consider the design and the article said to infringe the design separately and together, comparing the mental picture which the court retains of the registered **[415]** design with the infringing article, and that he failed to note that the respondent's article was more like the registered design than the registered design was similar to the prior art.

His Honour did not state whether he considered the designs of the registered design and of the respondent's product separately and together and whether he compared the mental picture he had of the registered design with the accused article. Nor, in my view, was it necessary that he make any such express statement. It is obvious from his Honour's reasons for judgment that he compared the registered design and the respondent's product carefully and in accordance with accepted principles. No error in this respect has been established.

# Chapter 16

# Plant Breeder's Rights

Although there is nothing in theory to prevent a plant variety from being patented under the *Patents Act 1990* there is a practical difficulty in the case of conventionally bred plants. That is, in the case of conventionally bred plants the patent will always be susceptible to a challenge on the basis of obviousness.

Partly in order to meet this limitation and partly in order to meet its international obligations, Australia has developed specialised legislation to allow the protection of new plant varieties regardless of their method of breeding. Today in Australia, plants may be registered under the *Patents Act* (in the case of non-conventionally bred plants) and/or under the specialised plant variety legislation, the *Plant Breeder's Rights Act 1994*. The *Plant Breeder's Rights Act 1994* was passed in order to allow Australia to meet its obligations under the *International Convention for the Protection of New Varieties of Plants 1961* (UPOV) as revised in 1972, 1978 and 1991.[1] The Act repealed and replaced the *Plant Variety Rights Act 1987*.[2]

The Act grants monopoly rights to breeders (the grantee) to produce, reproduce, condition, sell, import, stock or offer to sell (hereafter "deal" with) propagating material for distinctive, uniform and stable (DUS) plant varieties which have not previously been exploited.[3] It does not grant a monopoly in the plants themselves (except to the extent that the plant may be propagating material in its own right) nor in the process of reproducing the plant.[4] These rights are known as plant

---

1  In the Second Reading Speech it was said that the Act was also in harmony with the United Nations *Agenda 21*, the *International Convention for the Conservation of Biological Diversity* (both arising out of the 1992 Earth Summit), the Food and Agriculture Organisation's *Undertaking on Plant Genetic Resources* 1981 and the *General Agreement on Tariffs and Trade* (GATT). Since then GATT has become the TRIPS Agreement (with requirements regarding plant breeder's rights set out in Art 27) and the Undertaking has become the *International Treaty on Plant Genetic Resources for Food and Agriculture 2001*.

2  For transitional provisions, see ss 81-86. For an application of the transitional provisions see *Elders Rural Services Australia Ltd v Registrar of Plant Breeder's Rights* [2011] FCA 384.

3  Section 43.

4  Section 10 provides that the Act does not permit the granting of PBR in a plant variety unless (1) Australia is a signatory to the *International Convention for the Protection of New Varieties of Plants* as set out in the Schedule to the Act and the grant is appropriate to give effect to Australia's obligations under that Convention or (2) the breeding of the plant constitutes an invention for

breeder's rights or PBR. An important feature to note is that these rights, other than the rights to reproduce or export to certain countries, are exhausted after the first sale (s 23).

The Act contains limited exemptions to infringement including an exemption for acts done for private, experimental and breeding purposes (s 16). The most important of the exemptions is the farmer's right to reserve and reproduce seed and other propagating material (s 17). In addition, there is a limited compulsory licence scheme which ensures public access to new plant varieties (s 19) and to meet obligations under State, Territory and other Commonwealth legislation (s 18).

The *Plant Breeder's Rights Act 1994* is structured in a similar way to the *Patents Act 1990* in so far as there is a requirement of registration and the rights of the grantee are in the nature of a grant of monopoly.

## Registrable Plant Varieties

Under s 44 of the Act the Secretary of the Department is required to grant registration to an applicant if the Secretary is satisfied that:

- there is such a variety;
- the variety is registrable under s 43;
- the applicant is entitled to make the application;
- the grant of the right is not prohibited by the Act;[5]
- the right has not been granted to another person;
- the name of the variety complies with s 27;[6]
- propagating material of the variety has been deposited with a approved genetic resource centre; and
- relevant fees have been paid.

A plant is defined to include fungi and algae and hybrids but does not include bacteria, bacteroids, mycoplasms, viruses, viroids and bacteriophages.[7] A plant variety is defined in accordance with the International Code of Botanical

---

the purposes of s 51(xviii) of the Australian Constitution. Regarding the constitutionality of the *Plant Breeder's Rights Act 1994*, see *Grain Pool of Western Australia v Commonwealth* (2000) 202 CLR 479.

5     Under s 42, regulations may be made excluding certain plant varieties from registration although no regulations are currently in force under this section. A hybrid of prohibited varieties could also be prohibited.

6     Under s 27 a name may be a word with or without other letters or numbers; it must not cause confusion, be contrary to law, scandalous or offensive, be prohibited by regulation, include a trade mark registered in respect of live plants, plant cells or plant tissue; and must comply with the *International Code of Botanical Nomenclature* and subsidiary codes. It may be a person's name so long as the person has consented (if the person is alive) or the legal representative of the person has consented (if the person has been dead for less than 10 years). The name may include the name of a corporation or other organisation if that body agrees. If a plant variety has been previously registered in another country which is a contracting party to the UPOV then the plant must be registered in Australia with that name if it is complying, although it may also be registered with a synonym by which the plant will be known and sold in Australia.

7     Section 3. This definition does not strictly reflect any one accepted scientific definition of a plant but rather reflects the history of legislative protection in so far as algae had previously been excluded from protection under the *Plant Varieties Act 1987*.

Nomenclature and the International Code of Nomenclature for Cultivated Plants. Thus, a plant variety is a plant group which is contained within the lowest taxonomic rank of a particular species;[8] it must be able to be defined by the expression of characteristics resulting from the genotype of each individual within the group (that is, a genetic trait such as colour or number of leaves); it can be distinguished from any other group by the expression of at least one of these characteristics (that is, the genetic trait must distinguish the plant from other plants in the same taxon) and is "functional" in so far as it is capable of being propagated unchanged.[9] A plant variety may include a plant whose genome has been altered by genetic material that is not from plants.[10]

Section 43 provides that a plant variety is registrable if:

- the variety has a breeder;
- the variety is distinct;
- the variety is uniform;
- the variety is stable; and
- the variety has not been exploited or has only recently been exploited.

It is a normal part of the biological process for plants to spontaneously mutate. It is much more difficult to reproduce this mutation or maintain the mutation in any stable form. The requirements of registrability as set out in s 43 ensure that mere one-offs do not receive protection. In addition, contrary to popular wisdom, the Act does not necessarily grant monopoly rights either in discovered plant varieties (because there would be no breeder) nor in plant varieties which may have been traditionally used in other cultures (because they would often have been exploited). If the discovered or traditional varieties have been subsequently subjected to selective propagation in order to develop a distinctive, uniform and stable plant variety then this new variety may be registered. In such a case both the discoverer and the selective propagator are defined as breeders for the purposes of acquiring rights.[11]

Under the Act a plant is distinct if it is "clearly distinguishable from any other variety whose existence is a matter of common knowledge".[12] The Plant Breeder's Rights Office requires that distinctiveness be determined by way of an objective comparison with the most similar varieties of common knowledge and that both qualitative and quantitative characteristics must be recorded. The Office recommends that morphological features are preferred (especially those not affected by environmental factors such as height) but that DNA, protein profiles and performance attributes might also be used. It is necessary to demonstrate "clear repeatable varietal differences".[13]

---

8    The taxonomic hierarchy under the *International Code of Botanical Nomenclature* is Family – Genus – Species – Subspecies or Varieties. Under the *International Code of Nomenclature for Cultivated Plants* the taxonomy is Family – Genus – Cultivar. In the case of cultivated plants, therefore, the lowest ranking taxon is usually a cultivar. In the case of other plants the lowest ranking taxon is usually a subspecies or variety.

9    Section 3.

10   Section 6.

11   See definition of "breeding" in s 5.

12   Section 43(2).

13   IP Australia, *Criteria for Protection* <http://www.ipaustralia.gov.au/get-the-right-ip/plant-breeders-rights/pbr-application-process/criteria-for-protection/ index.html>.

The Act is especially concerned to ensure that varieties grown, developed and tested overseas will maintain their characteristics in Australia and s 38 lists the circumstances when an overseas test growing will be sufficient to demonstrate that a plant variety has a particular characteristic for the purposes of the Act.

A plant variety is uniform if it is "uniform in its relevant characteristics" on propagation, subject to any expected variation arising from its particular features of propagation.[14] The Plant Breeder's Rights Office provides a table of the accepted number of "off-types", that is plants which do not conform to all distinctive characteristics of the variety. The number depends on whether the plant is fully self-pollinated, partially self-pollinated or cross-pollinated and there are special UPOV technical guidelines for specified species.[15]

A plant variety is stable if its "relevant characteristics" remain unchanged after repeated propagation.[16] The Plant Breeder's Rights Office requires that breeders of plants that are propagated from seed must demonstrate this stability over two generations. In the case of plant varieties which are to be vegetatively propagated, the demonstration of uniformity will usually satisfy the requirement of stability.[17]

A variety will be taken not to have been exploited or recently exploited if, at the date of lodging the application, plant material of the variety or material harvested from the variety:

- has not been sold by or with the consent of the breeder;
- has not been sold in Australia more than one year before that date;
- has not been sold in a contracting party state more than six years before that date in the case of tree or vine varieties;
- has not been sold in a contracting party state more than four years before that date in the case of other varieties (s 43).

It is not necessary that the "sale" be a sale in the strictly technical, common law sense of the term. Under s 3 "sell" is defined to include "letting on hire and exchanging by way of barter". A "sale" with restrictive conditions attached, which formed part of a larger transaction where there was at least nominal consideration has been held to be a sale for the purposes of the equivalent section under the *Plant Varieties Act 1987*.[18]

"Plant material" is defined to include propagating material, harvested material and products obtained from harvested material (s 43(10)).

## Plant Breeder's Rights

Section 11 of the *Plant Breeder's Rights Act 1994* provides that PBR in a plant variety is the exclusive right to do certain acts in relation to propagating material of the variety or to authorise another person to do these acts. Propagating

---

14   Section 43(3).

15   IP Australia, *Criteria for Protection* <http://www.ipaustralia.gov.au/get-the-right-ip/plant-breeders-rights/pbr-application-process/criteria-for-protection/ index.html>.

16   Section 43(4).

17   IP Australia, *Criteria for Protection* <http://www.ipaustralia.gov.au/get-the-right-ip/plant-breeders-rights/pbr-application-process/criteria-for-protection/ index.html>.

18   *Sun World International Inc v Registrar, Plant Breeder's Rights (Formerly Plant Variety Rights)* (1998) 158 ALR 98.

material is defined as any part or product from which another plant of the same variety can be produced.[19] The product or part may be used either separately or with other parts or products of the plant. Thus, propagating material may include seeds, seedlings, cuttings and even cut flowers unless those parts have been treated so as to prevent them being used for reproduction. The grantee of PBR has the exclusive right to do the following acts:

- produce or reproduce the propagating material. Reproduction means any process whereby the number of units of propagating material that can be grown is increased.[20] However, the processes covered by the right do not include growing a plant larger or the development of a cell or tissue or plant part into a single plant of that variety;[21]
- condition the propagating material for the purposes of propagation. Conditioning is defined very broadly as cleaning, coating, sorting, packaging, or grading propagating material and any other similar treatment undertaken for the purposes of preparing the material for propagation or sale;[22]
- offer the propagating material for sale;
- sell the propagating material;
- import the propagating material; and
- stock the propagating material for any of the above purposes.

It has been argued that these rights should extend to all varieties derived from the registered variety. However, the legislature has rejected this approach on the basis that this would act as a disincentive to innovation. On the other hand, if only the smallest of changes would lead to the grant of new rights to a different breeder then the value of the first rights would be reduced and similarly act as a disincentive. The Act attempts to strike a balance by providing that PBR (in this debate known as the first breeder's rights) extend not only to propagating material for the production or reproduction of the initially registered plant variety but also to propagating material for "dependent plant varieties" (s 13) and "essentially derived varieties" (s 12). A grantee may seek a declaration from the Secretary that a second variety is an essentially derived variety under s 40 whether or not that second variety is registered (s 40). If the Secretary finds that there is a prima facie case that the second variety is an essentially derived variety, the Secretary may require test growings to be conducted to rebut this (s 41).

A "dependent plant variety" is one which is not clearly distinguishable from the initial variety, is clearly distinguishable from varieties in common knowledge at the time of the grant of PBR to the initial variety and any other plant which cannot be produced except by repeated use of such varieties.[23] An "essentially derived plant variety" is one that is predominantly derived from the initial plant variety; retains the essential characteristics resulting from the genotype or genetic structure of that variety; and does not exhibit any "important (as distinct from cosmetic)" features that differentiate it from that other variety (s 4).

---

19　See definition in s 3.
20　See definition of "reproduction" in s 3.
21　See definition of "process" in s 3.
22　Section 3.
23　Section 13.

There has been little disagreement regarding dependent plant varieties but there has been much discussion regarding the proper limits of essentially derived varieties. This discussion became especially strident in the 1980s and 1990s with the development of new gene technologies which were commonly believed to allow the insertion of a new gene at a late stage of plant breeding with little effort, research or risk on the part of the gene technology party. Contemplation of such practices gave rise to the "First Breeder's Nightmare"[24] which played on the fear that a plant breeder who spent years developing a better variety of wheat (for example) would lose the value of this investment if a chemical company could, at the last moment, make a small and simple change to the genetic structure of the improved variety so as to make it pest resistant, for example. It was believed that it was wrong to allow the chemical company to claim breeder's rights for this new variety because the chemical company was "not really interested in" plant breeding and shouldn't "really" benefit from the monopoly at the expense of "legitimate" plant breeders.

However, in February 2002 the Expert Panel on Breeding reported to the Department of Agriculture, Fisheries and Forestry that the nightmare was simply that, a nightmare. The Panel rebutted the notion that gene technology was easy and risk free. The Panel also noted with approval that the fears expressed by the "First Breeder's Nightmare" appear to have abated and that, in practice, the chemical and plant breeding industries have learned to work together by cross-licensing agreements and other similar commercial arrangements to their joint commercial advantage. The Panel therefore rejected a proposal to extend the definition of essentially derived varieties to include these genetically modified plants.[25]

Partly because of the ephemeral nature of plant stock, and partly as a response to breeder demands, the *Plant Breeder's Rights Act 1994* deems both the harvest (s 14) and the products of the harvest (s 15) of a PBR-protected variety to be propagating material to which s 11 applies in certain circumstances. In *Cultivaust Pty Ltd v Grain Pool Pty Ltd* the Full Federal Court commented obiter that this deeming provision only applies where the harvest or the product of the harvest is not itself propagating material.[26] The circumstances in which the deeming provisions apply are that the original propagating material was produced or reproduced without the authorisation of the grantee and that the grantee "does not have a reasonable opportunity to exercise the grantee's right in relation to" this original propagating material. The Full Federal Court in that case further commented that the opportunity to exercise one's rights should not be confused with the opportunity to take an action for infringement but did not otherwise explain the meaning of the phrase.[27] We would suggest, however, that if the grantee has had an opportunity to negotiate a royalty

---

24    *Clarification of Plant Breeding Issues under the* Plant Breeder's Rights Act *1994. Draft Report of the Expert Panel on Breeding*, February 2002.

25    *Clarification of Plant Breeding Issues under the* Plant Breeder's Rights Act *1994. Draft Report of the Expert Panel on Breeding*, February 2002.

26    See *Cultivaust Pty Ltd v Grain Pool Pty Ltd* [2004] FCA 683; *Cultivaust Pty Ltd v Grain Pool Pty Ltd* [2005] FCAFC 223. Special leave to appeal this decision to the High Court was refused: *Cultivaust Pty Ltd v Grain Pool Pty Ltd* [2006] HCATrans 333.

27    *Cultivaust Pty Ltd v Grain Pool Pty Ltd* [2005] FCAFC 223 at [57].

payment but failed to reach agreement (as happened in the *Cultivaust* matter itself) this would constitute a reasonable opportunity to exercise the grantee's rights. Finally, the deeming provision does not apply to the harvest of farm saved seed kept for the farmer's use but does apply to excess seed saved by the farmer (s 14(2)).

The doctrine of exhaustion is fundamental to the nature of PBR. Under this doctrine, the plant breeder's rights, other than the right to produce or reproduce the propagating material, are exhausted once the propagating material has been sold by the grantee or with the consent of the grantee (s 23). Thus, if seeds or rose cuttings are sold by the grantee then the purchaser may sell, condition, import or stock them but may not reproduce them for the purpose of selling more cuttings or seeds. The purchaser may also export the material provided the export is to a country which provides PBR and the purpose is for final consumption. If a grantee wants to get round the doctrine of exhaustion (for example, if the grantee wants to prevent on-selling of the vine cuttings for a grape variety) then the grantee should license the use of the propagating material rather than assign it. However, the doctrine of exhaustion was interpreted narrowly at first instance in *Cultivaust Pty Ltd v Grain Pool Pty Ltd*.[28]

In that case, the Western Australian Grain Board exported barley for malting. Like other grains, barley is propagating material in its own right, as well as being the harvest of propagating material. Some of the exported barley came from seed bought directly from or under the licence of the grantee; some of the barley was harvested from first generation farm-saved seed; and some of the barley was harvested from second and subsequent generations of farm-saved seed. Without discussing the doctrine of exhaustion in any great detail, Mansfield J assumed that propagating material which was harvested from second or subsequent generations of farm-saved seed could not be said to have been sold and was therefore not yet caught by the doctrine of exhaustion. This is an unfortunate decision, in so far as the original seed had been sold to the farmer who had kept the harvest from which the second and third generation crops where grown only in accordance with his or her statutory rights to do so under s 17.[29]

The general rule of duration is that PBR begins on the day that the grant is made and extends for 25 years in the case of trees and vines and 20 years in the case of other varieties (s 22(2)). This is subject to the provisions that, in the case of dependent varieties, PBR commences on the day the grant is made in relation to the initial variety or the day the dependent variety comes into existence, whichever is the later, and lasts for the duration of PBR in the initial variety (s 22(4)). In the case of essentially derived varieties the PBR extends from the day of the declaration that the variety is essentially derived and continues until the end of the initial variety's term (s 22(5)). Regulations may be made to provide for a longer period for varieties in a specified taxon (s 22(3)).

---

28    [2004] FCA 683.
29    The question was not considered on appeal although the Full Court did comment obiter that the trial judge's dealing with exhaustion "appears to be unexceptional": *Cultivaust Pty Ltd v Grain Pool Pty Ltd* [2005] FCAFC 223 at [55].

## Exemptions and Compulsory Licences

There are two exemptions to infringement of PBR which are designed to protect traditional farm, breeding and private usage. Under s 16 there is no infringement of PBR if the act in s 11 is done privately and for a non-commercial purpose. Nor is an act an infringing act if it is done for experimental purposes or for breeding another plant variety. Home gardeners, for example, may take plant cuttings from their geraniums so as to produce propagating material for another geranium. A commercial nursery owner might clean and coat registered propagating material with rooting hormone (that is, condition it)[30] to use it in experiments regarding preferred growing mediums or for breeding a new variety using that propagating material.

Under s 17, a farmer who legitimately obtains propagating material (either by purchase or by previously exercising his or her farmer's rights) may condition or reproduce harvested propagating material. The farmer may condition only so much of the harvested propagating material as is required for the farmer's use for reproductive purposes but there is no limit on the farmer's right to reproduce. The limitation will not limit the amount that may be conditioned or reproduced but will allow infringement proceedings to be taken where conditioned material is found in such quantities as to suggest that it is not for the farmer's use in reproduction.

Mansfield J gave a narrow definition of farmers' rights at first instance in *Cultivaust Pty Ltd v Grain Pool Pty Ltd*,[31] where he held that, although there was an implied right to grow, sell and export the harvest from first generation farm-saved seed, there was no such implied right to similarly deal with the harvest from second and subsequent generations of farm-saved seed. In the light of this decision farmers are advised to ensure that there is an express right for them to retain, grow and otherwise deal with the harvest from each generation of farm-saved seed. This matter was not considered on appeal.[32]

Before the *Plant Breeder's Rights Amendment Act 2002*, s 18 of the Act also provided an exemption for any s 11 act done in relation to propagating material that enabled the propagating material to be used as a food, a food ingredient or as fuel, or for any other purpose which did not involve the production or reproduction of the propagating material. This exemption was relied on successfully by the Western Australian Grain Pool in the *Cultivaust* case to allow the sale of barley for malt.

The food exemption was in accordance with UPOV 1961 and 1978 which effectively limited plant breeder's rights to productive and reproductive uses. However, UPOV 1991 dramatically extended the scope of PBR by providing that, subject to the doctrine of exhaustion, plant breeder's rights extended to dealing with propagating material generally and were not restricted to dealing for the purposes of production and reproduction. The rights under UPOV 1991 were not

---

30   See definition of "condition" in s 3.

31   [2004] FCA 638.

32   *Cultivaust Pty Ltd v Grain Pool Pty Ltd* [2005] FCAFC 223. This interpretation has been accepted in principle by the government in the *Australian Government Response to the Advisory Council on Intellectual Property Report* "A Review of Enforcement of Plant Breeder's Rights", 2010, p 7 <http://www.acip.gov.au/library/pbr_enforcement_response.pdf>.

limited by a food exemption. In Australia the rights of the plant breeder have always been wider than the mere right to produce or reproduce the variety in question although, historically, these rights were subject to significant exemptions including the food exemption. The abolition of the food exemption effectively brings the Australian Act back into line with the UPOV standards although one might question the global advisability of this and it is notable that few countries have actually taken PBR this far. The use of propagating material for private, non-commercial food or fuel use is still protected by s 16.

There are two compulsory licence schemes under the Act (ss 18 and 19). Section 19 imposes a duty on the grantee to take all reasonable steps to ensure reasonable public access to the plant variety. Reasonable access means making propagating material of reasonable quality available to the public in sufficient quantities to satisfy demand.

If a person believes that the grantee has failed to do this then that person, any time after two years of the grant being made, may apply to the Secretary to license, on behalf of the grantee, a person to sell propagating material for the variety or to produce propagating material for sale. The person who makes the application must be a person affected by the grantee's failure to ensure reasonable access.[33] Under s 19(11) the Secretary may certify at the time of granting PBR that the particular plant variety in question has no "direct use as a consumer product" and thus is not subject to this compulsory licence. The meaning of this phrase has not been determined within the context of the Act. However, under the *Competition and Consumer Act 2010*, a consumer use does not include an acquisition for the purposes of re-supply or for use in trade or commerce.[34] It has been suggested that this type of exclusion might effectively be used to prevent public access under s 19 to inbred lines which are said to have a high commercial but low consumer value:

> In combination, as male and female parents, inbred lines give rise to hybrids that are vigorous, high yielding, and, as a consequence, in demand by consumers. Inbred lines individually would ordinarily have no direct consumer use since they lack vigour, yield poorly and lack quality. However, inbred lines are costly to develop, contain important genetic components and are commercially valuable to the breeder for their ability as parents of vigorous hybrid offspring which are of direct consumer use. Commercial plant breeders maintain inbred lines under tight security and they are unwilling to transfer them to areas and countries where they perceive there may be a risk of unauthorised dissemination.[35]

The second compulsory licensing scheme was introduced under the *Plant Breeder's Rights Amendment Act 2002*. Under the new s 18, any person is allowed to perform a s 11 act in relation to propagating material where that act is necessary to meet the person's obligations under another State, Territory or Commonwealth Act. This section facilitates the operation of compulsory statutory marketing schemes.

---

33    There are detailed procedural provisions for the Secretary to follow in establishing this licensing scheme including a requirement that the Secretary invite interested parties to apply for the grant of such a licence. See s 19(3)-(10).

34    *Competition and Consumer Act 2010* s 3(2).

35    *Halsbury's Laws of Australia*, Intellectual Property, para 240-7015 footnote 3 (referring to the *Trade Practices Act 1974*).

## Infringement, Actions and Offences

Under s 53 and subject to the exemptions, compulsory licences and the doctrine of exhaustion (ss 16, 17, 18, 19 and 23), PBR is infringed:

- by a person doing any of the s 11 acts, without consent, in relation to the variety or a dependent variety;
- a person claiming, without consent, the right to do any of these acts;
- a person using the name of the registered variety in relation to any other plant variety in the same denominational class or a plant of any other variety of the same denominational class.[36]

In addition to infringement there are two categories of offence created by the *Plant Breeder's Rights Act 1994*. A person commits an "infringement offence":

- if the person intentionally or recklessly does a s 11 act which would be an infringement under s 53 (s 74; 500 penalty points). A prosecution may be made even if infringement proceedings have been commenced against the person (s 74(2)).

A person[37] commits a "non-infringing offence":

- if the person intentionally or recklessly makes a false statement in an application or other document given to the Secretary or Registrar (s 75(1), six months' imprisonment);
- if a person intentionally or recklessly represents that he or she is the grantee of PBR when he or she is not (s 75(2); 60 penalty points);
- if a person intentionally or recklessly represents that his or her PBR in one variety extends to another on the basis that it is a derived or essentially derived variety when it is not (s 75(3), 60 penalty points);
- if a person intentionally or recklessly represents that a plant is a variety in which PBR has been granted when it is not (s 75(4), 60 penalty points).

In an action for infringement the court may award an injunction and either damages or an account of profits (s 56). This is subject to the proviso that damages may not be awarded for innocent infringement. A person will be taken to have innocently infringed if the person satisfies the court that at the time of infringement the person was not aware of, and had no reasonable grounds for suspecting, the existence of the right.[38] In an action for infringement the defendant may counter-claim for a revocation of the grant of PBR (s 54).

In order to avoid possible infringement proceedings a person who intends to perform an act which is described in s 11 may apply to the court for a declaration that performance of the act would not constitute an infringement. Although there need not have been an assertion of PBR by the grantee the court will not make the declaration unless the applicant has, before that application, written to the

---

36    The reference to a "class" is an indirect reference to the taxonomic hierarchies under the *International Code of Botanical Nomenclature* and the *International Code of Nomenclature of Cultivated Plants*. See definition of "plant class" in s 3.

37    For the liability of directors, servants and agents of a corporation for ss 74 and 75 offences, see s 76.

38    For a more detailed consideration of these remedies, see Chapter 6, "Dealing With Copyright".

grantee regarding the performance of the act. In such a proceeding the validity of the grant of PBR may not be challenged (s 55).

In 2005, in response to the high level of industry dissatisfaction with the effectiveness of the Act's enforcement provisions, the Advisory Council on Intellectual Property (ACIP) was asked to inquire, report and make recommendations to the Australian Government on the enforcement of PBR in Australia. The ACIP Report was released in 2010 and the government has since responded. The government accepted a number of recommendations, the most significant of which are the introduction of an Information Notice System which would enable PBR owners to obtain information from suspected infringers; moving some PBR matters to the Federal Magistrates Court; and the introduction of exemplary damages.[39] At the time of going to press none of these suggested changes has been implemented.

## Registration Process

The registration process is similar to that established for the registration of standard patents. Following the lodging of an application in the prescribed form (s 26) the Secretary assigns a priority date which is usually the date of application (s 28) unless the applicant has previously made a "foreign application" in a contracting state within the past 12 months (s 29). Under s 30 the Secretary is required to accept or reject the application "as soon as practicable" after the application is lodged.

The Secretary must accept the application if there is no applicant with an earlier priority date in relation to the same material; the application conforms with s 26; and the application establishes a prima facie case for treating the plant variety as distinct from other varieties. The Secretary must reject the application if not satisfied with these requirements. The Secretary must notify the applicant and the public in both cases. The application is quite detailed and includes a brief description of the plant including photographs, the name of the variety and particulars of the breeding program and breeding location.

Upon acceptance the Secretary will require a specimen of any indigenous plant to be deposited with the herbarium (s 44(2)) and the applicant will have the status of a provisional grantee until the application is "disposed of" (s 39). The application is disposed of if the Secretary notifies the applicant that the Secretary is satisfied that a grant will not be made or is unlikely to be made; if the application has been withdrawn; or if the Secretary has decided not to proceed with the application. The provisional status will also lapse if the Secretary is satisfied that the applicant has given an undertaking to another person that the applicant will not commence proceedings for infringement (s 39). The policy purpose for this provision is unclear but it may be that such behaviour is taken to corrupt the registration process by limiting possible objections to the registration. It is therefore comparable to s 144 of the *Patents Act 1990*.

Within 12 months of the application being accepted (or such longer period as allowed by the Secretary) the applicant must provide a detailed description of the

---

39    *Australian Government Response to the Advisory Council on Intellectual Property Report* "A Review of Enforcement of Plant Breeder's Rights", 2010, pp 4-11 <http://www.acip.gov.au/library/pbr_enforcement_response.pdf>.

plant variety (s 34). Failure to do so is taken to be a withdrawal of the application (s 34(2)). The description must contain particulars of the characteristics which distinguish the plant variety and details of growing tests conducted to prove that the variety is distinct, uniform and stable (s 34(3) and (4)). The Secretary is required to publish this description (s 34(5)).

Following acceptance, and up to six months after the publication of the description, an objection may be lodged under s 35 by any person who considers that his or her "commercial interests would be affected by the grant of the PBR" and who considers that the Secretary could not have been satisfied that the application conformed to the prescribed form under s 26(2) or that the application otherwise conformed with matters referred to in s 44(1)(b)(i) to (viii) that is, that there is such a plant variety; that the plant is registrable with s 43; that the applicant is entitled to make the application; that the grant is not prohibited by the Act; that the right has not been granted to another person; that the name complies with s 27; that propagating material has been deposited at an approved genetic resource centre; and that a specimen has not been supplied to the herbarium as required by the Secretary.

These s 44 provisions are also the same grounds on which the Secretary must grant the rights following acceptance, examination of the application (including the detailed description) and the determination of objections. In addition, the Secretary must be satisfied that all fees have been paid (s 44(1)(b)(i)-(ix)). If the Secretary is not satisfied of all of these grounds then the Secretary must refuse to grant the right (s 44(3)). Section 49 provides a procedure whereby the Minister may have conditions imposed on the grant of PBR in the public interest.

The *Plant Breeder's Rights Act 1994* provides for revocation of PBR upon application by a person whose interests are affected by the grant of PBR (s 50(8)) or by the declaration (s 50(9)). The Secretary must revoke if he or she becomes aware that facts existed which, if known before the grant or the declaration, would have led to a refusal to grant the PBR or declaration. The Secretary is also obliged to revoke if required fees have not been paid (s 50(1)). The Secretary has a discretion to revoke if the grantee fails to notify the Secretary of an assignment of the PBR as required under s 21; or if the grantee has not complied with a condition attached to the licence in accordance with s 49 (s 50(2)); or if the person has not conducted the required growing tests under s 37 (s 50(9)). In addition, revocation may be counter-claimed in infringement proceedings on the ground that the plant is not a variety or that facts exist that would have led the Secretary to refuse the grant had the Secretary known of them (s 54).

At any time following acceptance the Secretary may require the applicant to conduct a test growing of the plant variety to which the application, an objection or a request for revocation relates. The Secretary may require the applicant to supply plants, propagating material and information so that the Secretary may conduct the tests or, alternatively, require the person to make suitable arrangements for an approved person to conduct the tests (s 37). The cost of the test growing must be paid by the applicant if it relates to acceptance of the application; by the objector if it relates to an objection; or the person making a request for revocation unless the objection or revocation is successful in which case the applicant must bear the cost (s 37(5)).

# CASE

## *Cultivaust Pty Ltd v Grain Pool Pty Ltd*
Federal Court of Australia: Finn, Emmett and Bennett JJ
[2005] FCAFC 223

The Western Australian Grain Pool sold and exported barley for malting purposes. It declined to pay royalties to the plant breeder or its exclusive licensee for this use in respect of barley harvested from farm-saved seed. The Grain Pool relied on its statutory right to reproduce farm-saved seed and its defence under the now repealed s 18. Section 18 provided that there was no infringement of PBR if the act were done so that the propagating material could be used as food, a food ingredient or fuel. The Full Federal Court found in favour of the Grain Pool on the basis of the s 18 defence but this judgment is still very interesting for the court's approach to the relationship between farm-saved seed, the doctrine of exhaustion and the ss 14 and 15 deeming provisions which extend PBR to the harvest and product of PBR protected varieties where the harvest or product is not itself propagating material.

### Finn, Emmett and Bennett JJ: SCHEME OF PLANT BREEDER'S ACT
2. Under s 11 of the Plant Breeder's Act, subject to ss 16, 17, 18, 19 and 23, a plant breeder's right ('PBR') in a plant variety is the exclusive right to do, or to licence another person to do, the following acts in relation to propagating material of the plant variety:
  (a)  produce or reproduce the material;
  (b)  condition the material for the purpose of propagation;
  (c)  offer the material for sale;
  (d)  sell the material;
  (e)  import the material;
  (f)  export the material;
  (g)  stock the material for the above purposes.
3. Section 3(1) of the Plant Breeder's Act contains definitions. Thus, propagating material in relation to a plant of a particular plant variety relevantly means any part or product from which another plant with the same essential characteristics as that variety can be produced. Reproduction in relation to propagating material of a plant of a particular variety means any process whereby the number of units of that propagating material that have the capacity to grow into independent plants is multiplied. Propagation in relation to a living organism means the growth, culture or multiplication of that organism.
4. Curiously, the term conditioning in relation to propagating material is defined as meaning:
  'cleaning, coating, sorting, packaging or grading of the material, or any other similar treatment, undertaken *for the purpose of preparing the material for propagation or sale.*' [Emphasis added by Court]
That is to say, the term is defined as undertaking certain treatment for the purpose of the propagation **or** sale of relevant material.
5. On the other hand, s 11(b) refers to conditioning for the purpose of propagation, thus apparently excluding conditioning for the purpose of sale. In so far as s 11(b) refers to the act of conditioning propagating material for the purpose of propagation, the definition of '*conditioning*' seems inapt. To apply the definition strictly in s 11(b) is to say that to condition material for the purpose of propagation means to undertake certain treatment of relevant material, for the purpose of preparing the material for propagation or sale,

for the purpose of propagation. To make sense of s 11(b), it should probably be taken to mean undertaking relevant treatment for the purpose only of propagation. Accordingly, undertaking any such treatment for the purpose of preparing the material for sale is not one of the acts comprised in the exclusive right that constitutes PBR.

6. Such convoluted language indicates the difficulties that arise when '*plain English*' is employed in legislation. In his speech on the second reading of the bill for the Plant Breeder's Act, the relevant minister, somewhat fatuously, said that '*the plain English used ... should promote a better understanding of ... the legislation on which the Plant Breeder's Rights Scheme will be based*'.

7. Sections 14(1) and 15 respectively extend PBR to harvested material in certain circumstances and to products obtained from harvested material in certain circumstances. Under s 14(1), s 11 operates as if certain harvested material were propagating material and under s 15, s 11 operates as if certain products made from harvested material were propagating material. Thus, ss 14(1) and 15 make sense in a context where harvested material, or products obtained from harvested material, would not, but for their operation, be propagating material. Accordingly, the grantee of the PBR has the exclusive right to do, or to licence another person to do, in relation to that non-propagating material, the acts referred to s 11.

8. Section 14(1) is predicated upon three prerequisites and s 15 is predicated upon four prerequisites. The first two prerequisites in each section are the same. They are:
- propagating material of a plant variety covered by PBR is produced or reproduced without the authorisation of the grantee; and
- the grantee does not have a reasonable opportunity to exercise the grantee's right in relation to the propagating material.

The reference to an opportunity to exercise the grantee's right is a reference to a reasonable opportunity to exercise the exclusive right to do, or to licence another person to do, the acts referred to in s 11. The reasonable opportunity refers to the exercise of those rights in relation to the propagating material that is produced or reproduced without the authorisation of the grantee.

9. However, s 14(2) limits the operation of s 14(1), by reference to s 17. Section 17(1) relevantly provides that, if a person engaged in farming activities legitimately obtains propagating material, either by purchase or by previous operation of s 17, for use in that person's farming activities and that person subsequently harvests further propagating material from plants grown from the first mentioned propagating material, there is no infringement of the PPR by:
- the conditioning of so much of that further propagating material as is required for the person's use for reproductive purposes; or
- the reproduction of that further propagating material.

Section 14 applies to so much of the material harvested by a farmer from propagating material conditioned and reproduced in the circumstances set out in s 17(1) as is not itself required by the farmer, for the farmer's own use for reproductive purposes.

10. Thus, the effect of ss 14 and 17 is that a person engaged in farming activities (a 'farmer'), who legitimately obtains propagating material by purchase, may harvest further propagating material from plants grown from the propagating material so purchased and may condition that further propagating material for the farmer's use for reproductive purposes and may reproduce that further propagating material. The farmer may do those same acts in relation to a third generation of propagating material harvested from that second generation of propagating material. The farmer will not infringe PPR by doing so. Section 14(1) will not apply to the harvested material that consisted of propagating material used for those purposes. However, s 14(1) will apply to all other material harvested from any of that propagating material.

11. [The Court referred to s 18.]

12. Section 23 is a further qualification of s 11, in so far as it provides that PBR does not extend to any act referred to in s 11 in certain circumstances. Thus, it will not infringe PBR to do any act referred to in s 11 in relation to propagating material *after the propagating material has been sold* by the grantee or with the grantee's consent. However, there is a qualification on that qualification: PBR will nonetheless be infringed by an act referred to in s 11 if the act involves:

- *further* production or reproduction of the material; or
- the export of the material, for a purpose other than final consumption, to a country that does not provide PBR.

For reasons given later, it is unnecessary to express any view on the specific operation of s 23(1) in the scheme of the Act.

## ALLEGED INFRINGEMENT OF PBR BY THE GRAIN POOL

13. By s 6 of the *Grain Marketing Act 1975* (WA) ('the Grain Marketing Act'), the Grain Pool of WA ('the Grain Pool') was established as a body corporate. Under s 18A of the Grain Marketing Act, the objects of the Grain Pool were to maximise the net returns to persons ('producers') who deliver grain to a grain pool, by securing, developing and maintaining markets for grain and grain products and by minimising costs as far as practicable. Under s 18B, the functions of the Grain Pool were to control the marketing of *prescribed grain* that was to be exported or sold for export from the Commonwealth and to promote and market, in markets within and outside the Commonwealth, grain delivered to the Grain Pool by producers. Under s 20, barley was a prescribed grain.

14. By s 22 of the Grain Marketing Act, the Grain Pool was to be the sole marketing authority of prescribed grain that was to be exported, or sold for export, from the Commonwealth. Under s 22(2), no person, other than the Grain Pool or a person authorised by the Grain Pool, was to export a prescribed grain or sell a prescribed grain for export from the Commonwealth. Under s 22(2)(a), no person was permitted to purchase, take delivery of or receive from any person, other than the Grain Pool, a prescribed grain that was to be exported or sold for export from the Commonwealth.

15. Section 24 of the Grain Marketing Act provided that the Grain Pool was, on such terms and conditions as it thought fit, to establish and maintain a pool or separate pools for the marketing of a particular prescribed grain produced in a season. Under s 25, the Grain Pool was to receive, for the prescribed grain pool, any prescribed grain that was produced in the season to which the prescribed grain pool related. Under s 29, where the Grain Pool received grain for a pool, the grain was vested in the Grain Pool, freed and discharged from all trusts and encumbrances and, under s 31(1), the Grain Pool was authorised to sell grain so vested in it to such persons, at such prices, and on such terms, as the board of directors of the Grain Pool thought fit.

16. The Grain Marketing Act was repealed by the *Grain Marketing Act 2002* (WA). By the operation of s 46 of, and item 4 of Schedule 1 to that Act, the liabilities of the Grain Pool immediately before the commencement of that Act became liabilities of the first respondent, Grain Pool Pty Limited. More particularly, item 4(2) of Schedule 1 to that Act provided that any proceeding or remedy that, immediately before that commencement, might have been brought, continued or available against the Grain Pool may, on or after that day, be brought or continued and was available against Grain Pool Pty Limited.

17. On 19 January 1990, the fourth respondent, the State of Tasmania ('Tasmania'), in the guise of its Department of Primary Industry ('the Tasmanian Department'), was granted plant variety rights under the *Plant Variety Rights Act 1987* (Cth) ('the Plant Variety Act') in relation to the '*Franklin*' variety of the *Vulgare* species of the *Hordeum* genus. *Hordeum Vulgare* is commonly known as barley. Those rights were to expire on 6 April 2009. The Plant Variety Act was repealed by s 78 of the Plant Breeder's Act but, by s 82 of the Plant Breeder's Act, the PBR granted to Tasmania under the Plant Variety

Act continue to have effect as if those rights had been granted under the Plant Breeder's Act. By an agreement made on 31 January 1992 between Tasmania and the appellant, Cultivaust Pty Limited ('Cultivaust'), Tasmania granted to Cultivaust the exclusive right to sell and produce Franklin barley throughout the world and to grant to others rights to sell and produce Franklin barley.

18. In March 1991, the crop improvement branch of the Western Australian Department of Agriculture notified the Tasmanian Department that it wished to proceed with commercial evaluation of Franklin barley for malting in Western Australia. It was agreed that two tonnes of Franklin barley seed would be supplied for such evaluation at the standard price. The Tasmanian Department stipulated that the two tonnes of Franklin barley were to be supplied on the understanding that all grain produced in Western Australia would be used for malting and none would be retained for further seed multiplication. The Western Australian Department of Agriculture agreed to abide by those terms. However, despite that arrangement, one of the producers who participated in growing trials in the 1991/1992 season retained about 10 tonnes of the 50 to 55 tonnes of Franklin barley grain harvested. The balance, as with the other Franklin barley grown in the trials, was delivered to the Grain Pool pursuant to the Grain Marketing Act.

19. In the first half of 1992, Kirin Australia Pty Ltd ('Kirin') approached the Tasmanian Department for supplies of Franklin barley for malting in Western Australia. During 1992 and in the next succeeding few years, Kirin acquired quantities of Franklin barley direct from Tasmania, totalling in excess of 16,000 tonnes over three or so years.

20. During 1992, the Grain Pool decided that it would become involved in a large scale trial of Franklin barley. Quantities of Franklin barley were supplied for the 1992 crop, largely through dealings between Cultivaust and Joe White Maltings Limited ('Joe White'). It was agreed that Joe White would procure about 200 tonnes of Franklin barley for growing trials in 1992 and the Grain Pool would be responsible for the allocation and distribution of that Franklin barley. There were also direct dealings between Cultivaust and the Grain Pool for the supply of Franklin barley for the 1992 crop.

21. Thus, from May 1992, Franklin barley was grown and harvested by producers in Western Australia and was then delivered to the Grain Pool pursuant to the provisions of the Grain Marketing Act. Over the seasons 1991/1992 to 1999/2000, the Grain Pool received and handled some 326,000 tonnes of Franklin barley, of which about 131,000 tonnes were sold to maltsters for malting for beer or whiskey. Those sales were either to Western Australian based maltsters or for export to maltsters in China, Chile, Japan and South Africa. The balance of the Franklin barley, about 195,000 tonnes of lesser quality, was sold for animal feed. The Grain Pool did not stock, offer for sale, export or sell any of the Franklin barley for the purpose of its being used to propagate further Franklin barley.

22. Neither Tasmania, nor Cultivaust on behalf of Tasmania, authorised the Grain Pool to deal with the Franklin barley grown in Western Australia in the manner described above.

**THE PROCEEDING ...**

29. The appeal was concerned solely with the questions of whether, by offering for sale, selling, or exporting Franklin barley, or stocking Franklin barley for those purposes, the Grain Pool infringed Tasmania's PBR and whether the primary judge erred in the exercise of his discretion in ordering Cultivaust and Tasmania to pay Western Australia's costs of the consolidated proceeding. As to the first question, the appeal turns on the meaning and effect of s 18 of the Plant Breeder's Act in the circumstances outlined above.

[The court held that the s 18 defence at the time, that is that the act was done for the purpose of producing food, a food ingredient or fuel, applied. This defence has since been repealed.]

55. It follows that s 18 had the effect that the acts of the Grain Pool about which Cultivaust complains did not infringe Tasmania's PBR in Franklin Barley. In view of that conclusion concerning the operation of s 18, it is not necessary to express any opinion on the operation of s 23(1). While that provision might have been of significance in relation to a claim against a producer of Franklin barley, it would have no application to the Grain Pool, in circumstances where the acts referred to in s 11 engaged in by the Grain Pool did not involve '*further production or reproduction*' of Franklin barley. The primary judge dealt with s 23 in a manner in that appears to be unexceptionable.

56. In dealing with s 14 of the Plant Breeder's Act the primary judge considered the meaning of s 14(1)(b), which is in the same terms as s 15(b). The primary judge, in dealing with whether Tasmania had a '*reasonable opportunity to exercise the grantee's right in relation to Franklin barley produced or reproduced without its authorisation*', the primary judge characterised Tasmania's '*rights*' [sic] as '*exclusive, but negative*' and said that the exercise of '*those rights*' [sic] involved, if necessary, action under s 54 of the Plant Breeder's Act. However, s 54 simply provides that that an action for an infringement of PBR in a plant variety may be begun in the Federal Court.

57. His Honour's characterisation may involve a confusion of the concept of *exercising* the right that constitutes PBR with the concept of *enforcing* rights that arise under the Plant Breeder's Act by reason of infringement of the right, conferred by the Plant Breeder's Act, that constitutes PBR. That is to say, if s 14(1) be relevant, the primary judge may have misconstrued s 14(1)(b) in failing to distinguish between the grantee's right under s 11 and the secondary rights that arise by reason of infringement of that right, as provided for in s 53(1). In the light of the conclusion reached above, it is unnecessary to resolve that question but it should not be thought that his Honour's view of ss 14(1)(b) and 15(b) would necessarily be endorsed if the question arises in the future.

# Chapter 17

# Circuit Layouts

## The Nature of the Rights

The *Circuit Layouts Act 1989*[1] creates a "copyright like" intellectual property right. The Act grants exclusive rights to the maker of an eligible circuit layout (eligible layout) and indirectly protects integrated circuits made in accordance with an eligible layout. The Act, which was passed in anticipation of the World Trade Organization's *Treaty on Intellectual Property in Respect to Integrated Circuits 1989*, was assented to on 22 May 1989 and commenced on 1 October 1990.[2] Before its introduction circuit layouts may have been protected either as a registered design under the *Designs Act 1906* or as an artistic work under a broad definition of sculpture under the *Copyright Act 1968*.

A circuit layout is a diagram for the construction of an integrated circuit. An integrated circuit is a microelectronic semiconductor comprising interconnected transistors and other components. An integrated circuit might be analogue, digital or both. A digital integrated circuit is commonly called a computer chip. The Act defines these terms in more detail. A circuit layout is defined as "a representation, fixed in any material form, of the three-dimensional location of the active and passive elements and interconnections making up an integrated circuit". The Act is only concerned with integrated circuits which are intended to perform an electronic function (that is, computer chips). The Act defines an integrated circuit as "a circuit, whether in final form or an intermediate form, the purpose, or one of the purposes, of which is to perform an electronic function, being a circuit in which the active and passive elements, and any of the interconnections, are integrally formed in or on a piece of material".[3]

An eligible layout is defined as an "original" circuit layout produced by an eligible person[4] or first commercially exploited in Australia or an eligible foreign

---

1   Regarding the constitutionality of the *Circuits Layout Act 1989*, see *Nintendo Co Ltd v Centronics Systems Pty Ltd* (1994) 181 CLR 134.

2   For transitional provisions, see *Circuit Layouts Act 1989* s 7 and the High Court case of *Nintendo Co Ltd v Centronics Systems Pty Ltd* (1994) 181 CLR 134 at 144-148.

3   Section 5.

4   An eligible person is defined as an Australian citizen or resident; a citizen, national or resident of an eligible foreign country; or a body corporate incorporated under the law of a State or Territory or eligible foreign country: s 5.

country.[5] There has been no case law on the meaning of original under the *Circuit Layouts Act 1989* but s 11 provides that, without limiting the meaning of "original", a circuit layout will not be original if its making involved no creative contribution by the maker or it was commonplace at the time it was made. The term therefore appears to be closer to the requirements under the *Designs Act 1906* than the concept of originality under the *Copyright Act 1968*.

Under s 16 the Act grants exclusive rights to the owner of an "eligible layout". These are known as EL rights.[6] The EL rights are granted for a term of 10 years after the integrated eligible layout is made or, if the layout is commercially exploited within 10 years of being made, then 10 years after the date that the eligible layout was first commercially exploited.[7] The EL rights are the right to:

- directly or indirectly copy the layout in material form (s 16(1)) or to authorise such copying (s 9);
- make or authorise the making of an integrated circuit in accordance with the layout or a copy of the layout (s 16(2) and s 9); and
- exploit or authorise the exploitation of the layout commercially in Australia (s 16(3) and s 9).

There is no registration procedure required under the Act. However, s 39 provides that, if a prescribed label is included on the layout, integrated circuit, package or article incorporating an integrated circuit made in accordance with an eligible layout, this label will be prima facie evidence in infringement proceedings that any person dealing with the layout or integrated circuit had been notified of the existence of the EL rights in the layout. This will be particularly important in proving commercial dealing with knowledge under s 19(3) or refuting the innocent dealings defence under s 20(3).

## Infringement

Under s 19 of the *Circuit Layouts Act 1989* the EL rights are infringed if a person without the consent of the owner of the eligible layout:

- copies or authorises the copying of the layout (s 19(1));
- makes or authorises the making of an integrated circuit in accordance with the layout (s 19(2)); or
- commercially exploits or authorises the commercial exploitation in Australia of the eligible layout if the person knows or ought reasonably to have known that he or she is not authorised by the owner to do so (s 19(3)).

The EL rights are infringed if these acts are done in relation to a substantial part of the layout, copy or integrated circuit.[8]

---

5    Section 5. Eligible foreign countries are set out in Sch 3 to the *Circuit Layouts Regulations 1999*. Section 42 of the Act provides that no country may be declared to be an eligible foreign country unless it is a party to a Convention to which Australia is also a party or which Australia has taken steps to become a party or unless the Governor-General is satisfied that adequate provision is or will be offered for circuit layouts made by an eligible person or first commercially exploited in Australia.
6    Section 5.
7    Section 5.
8    Section 13.

Commercial exploitation is defined in s 8(1). Commercial exploitation of an eligible layout is taken to have occurred if the layout, a copy of the eligible layout or if an integrated circuit made in accordance with the eligible layout is:

- sold, let for hire or otherwise distributed by way of trade;
- offered or exposed for sale, hire or other distribution by way of trade; or
- imported for the above purposes.

This includes dealings where the circuit layout is incorporated into another thing such as a video game, washing machine or other digital device.

A copy of a circuit layout or an integrated circuit made in accordance with a circuit layout shall be taken to have been commercially exploited if it is:

- sold, let for hire or otherwise distributed by way of trade;
- offered or exposed by way of trade; or
- imported for the purpose of sale, letting for hire or other distribution by way of trade.

In *Nintendo Co Ltd v Centronics Systems Pty Ltd*,[9] the parties agreed that the onus lay on the plaintiff, Nintendo, to prove that the defendant had the requisite knowledge but there was disagreement as to what that requisite knowledge must be. The High Court held that it was not sufficient to establish that the defendant commercially exploited the eligible layout in question knowing or constructively knowing that it did not have the authorisation of Nintendo as the actual owner of the eligible layout. Rather, the plaintiff had to establish that the defendant had actual or constructive knowledge of the existence of the eligible layout and that he or she did not have a licence from the owner, whoever that owner might be. On the facts the plaintiff had discharged this onus. The High Court's broad interpretation effectively protects the innocent dealer who may not know nor have the facilities to establish whether there is an eligible layout in the goods in question and who the owner of the EL rights is.

# Defences

Defences to infringement are set out in ss 22-25 of the *Circuit Layouts Act 1989*.

## Innocent commercial dealings

There is no infringement of EL rights if a person deals with an "unauthorised" integrated circuit if at the time the person acquired the circuit the person did not know and could not be expected to know that the circuit was unauthorised. An unauthorised circuit is one made in accordance with an eligible layout without the licence of the owner. This defence lasts only so long as the person remains innocent (s 20(1)).[10]

---

9    (1994) 181 CLR 134.

10    For a consideration of s 20, see *Nintendo Co Ltd v Centronics Systems Pty Ltd* (1994) 181 CLR 134 at 153-159.

## Private use

There is no infringement if a copy of the layout is made, or an integrated circuit is made, in accordance with the layout for the private use of the person who makes the copy or integrated circuit (s 21(1)). If the copy or integrated circuit is commercially exploited or distributed in such a way as to prejudice the interests of the owner this is not a private use (s 21(2)).

## Research and teaching

There is no infringement if a copy or copies of the layout are made or an integrated circuit is made in accordance with the layout for research or teaching purposes (s 22).

## Evaluation and analysis

There is no infringement of EL rights if a copy or copies of the layout are made for the purposes of evaluation and analysis or an original circuit layout is made based on this analysis (s 23(1)) or an integrated circuit is made for the purposes of evaluation or analysis or an original circuit layout is made which is based on such an integrated circuit (s 23(2)). Original circuit layouts made under these provisions may be copied or commercially exploited (s 23(1)(d) and (2)(d)). Copies or integrated circuits made for these purposes may also be copied or commercially exploited (s 23(1)(c) and (2)(c)).

## Layouts and circuits previously dealt with commercially

If a person acquires a copy of an eligible layout or of an integrated circuit made in accordance with an eligible layout as a result of the commercial exploitation of the eligible layout in Australia then that person may in turn commercially exploit the eligible layout or integrated circuit in Australia (s 24).

Section 24(2) provides that where such an integrated circuit (made in accordance with an eligible layout) contains a copy or an adaptation of a work protected under the *Copyright Act 1968* then the commercial exploitation is not an infringement of the copyright in the work (say under ss 37 and 38 of the *Copyright Act*) unless the copy or adaptation of the work was itself an infringement of copyright.

In *Avel Pty Ltd v Wells*,[11] the Full Federal Court explained the purpose of s 24 in these terms:

> Section 24(1) has the effect, inter alia, of ensuring that there is no prohibition on parallel importing of integrated circuits made in accordance with an eligible layout. If an eligible layout is exploited by the making of an integrated circuit, such as a ROM, s 24(1) ensures that if the ROM chip is purchased overseas and imported into Australia for the purposes of sale, that act of importation would not be an infringement of the EL rights, nor would the sale in Australia of that chip infringe those rights.

---

11    (1992) 108 ALR 97.

Subsection (2) is concerned with the situation where an integrated circuit may contain a copy or adaptation of a work entitled to protection under the provisions of the Copyright Act. But for the provisions of subs (2), the importation of such an integrated circuit, for example for the purposes of sale and the subsequent sale, while not infringing the EL rights (s 24(1)) would breach the provisions of either or both of ss 37 and 38 of the Copyright Act. This impediment upon the importation of integrated circuits into Australia for the purposes of sale or other exploitation and any subsequent exploitation is removed by providing that in such a case there will be no infringement of the copyright rights, unless the making of the copy or adaptation, which is contained in the integrated circuit, was itself an infringement of copyright. It is the proper interpretation of this subsection which has given rise to the controversy between the parties.[12]

In that case Avel had an exclusive licence to import and sell certain video games in Australia. This included an exclusive copyright licence in the computer programs stored on the integrated circuits in the video games. The defendant Wells knowingly imported and dealt with these video games in such a way as to constitute an infringement of ss 37 and 38 of the *Copyright Act 1968*. The question arose as to whether s 24(2) of the *Circuit Layouts Act 1989* applied so as to give them a defence against infringement.

The parties agreed that the ROM (Read Only Memory) in the video game was an integrated circuit "made in accordance with an eligible layout". Avel argued, however, that the other memory devices which comprised a blank integrated circuit (bought from a circuit manufacturer) into which a computer program had been added for the purpose of running the video game was not an "integrated circuit made in accordance with an eligible layout" and could not be said to "contain" a copyright work. The Full Court on appeal rejected this argument and the respondents were able to rely on the s 24(2) defence.

## Compulsory licence for defence or security use

The Act provides that the Commonwealth, or a person authorised in writing by the Commonwealth, may do any act comprised in the EL rights if the act is for Australian defence and security and the Commonwealth or an authorised person has unsuccessfully taken all reasonable steps to obtain a licence from the owner of the EL rights on reasonable terms (s 25). Section 25 contains provisions relating to notice, subsequent dealings and terms for such use.

## Actions and Dealings[13]

The person who makes an eligible layout is the first owner of the EL rights[14] unless the layout is made under a contract of employment, contract for services or an apprenticeship.[15] Agreements may be entered into modifying the effects of the employment, services and apprenticeship provisions.[16] EL rights are a form

---

12    (1992) 108 ALR 97 at 103.
13    For presumptions as to ownership and subsistence, see *Circuit Layouts Act 1989* ss 37 and 38.
14    For transitional provisions regarding ownership, see s 16(4).
15    Section 16.
16    Section 16(3).

of personal property and may be assigned (in writing), licensed or devolve by operation of law[17] and, under s 44, future EL rights may be assigned.[18]

Both the owner and an exclusive licensee (but not a non-exclusive licensee) may take an action for infringement of EL rights except that an exclusive licensee may not take an action against the owner of the EL rights. The rights and remedies of the exclusive licensee are concurrent with those of the owner[19] and the same defences may be raised against the exclusive licensee as against the owner.[20] Except in an action for an interlocutory injunction, neither the owner nor the exclusive licensee may proceed without joining the other except by leave of the court. There is a limitation period of six years established by the Act.[21]

In an action for infringement the court may grant an injunction and either an account of profit or damages. This is subject to the proviso that no damages may be awarded for innocent infringement, although an account of profits may be. Additional damages may be awarded in appropriate circumstances including in cases of flagrant breach.[22] Provision is made for the apportionment of damages, account and costs between the owner and the exclusive licensee.[23]

Like the other intellectual property regimes, a person may take action against someone who has made groundless threats of legal proceedings.[24]

---

17 Section 45.
18 Section 44.
19 Section 30.
20 Section 32.
21 Section 28.
22 Section 27.
23 Sections 33-36.
24 Section 46.

# Chapter 18

# Confidential Information

Some say we are living in an information age[1] where power and the control of information have become synonymous. Whether we agree with this statement or not we can at least say that information may be a valuable commodity that takes many forms – from simple client lists[2] to traditional knowledge of indigenous peoples[3] to highly technical trade secrets developed as precursors to patent applications. For this reason it is important to consider confidential information within the context of intellectual property law. This is especially so when we recognise that the same tensions exist for the protection of such information as do for copyright and patent protection. On the one hand, protection against those who would "reap without sowing" is important as a form of encouragement or reward for the development of new knowledge. On the other hand, society's interests lie in the free flow of information into the public domain enabling maximum exploitation. Consequently, if what you are trying to protect does not fit within any of the other categories of intellectual property you might consider whether it is possible to protect it as confidential information.

Article 1 of the TRIPS Agreement specifically includes "undisclosed information" within its definition of intellectual property and Art 39 of the Agreement imposes obligations on members to provide protection for this information. The rationale behind such protection of undisclosed information is to "ensure effective protection against unfair competition".[4]

In Australia, this obligation is said to be more than satisfied by the general law of breach of confidence. The action for breach of confidence is not restricted to the protection of information having a commercial value but might be used to protect spousal communications[5] and pillow talk, for example, as well as professional communications and government secrets.

---

1   Intellectual Property and Competition Review Committee, *Review of Intellectual Property Legislation Under the Competition Principles Agreement*, Final Report, 2000, p 90.
2   For example, *Faccenda Chicken Ltd v Fowler* [1985] FSR 114. See also *Orica Investments Pty Ltd v McCartney* [2007] NSWSC 645 for a recent discussion on what constitutes confidential client information.
3   For example, *Foster v Mountford and Rigby Ltd* (1976) 14 ALR 71.
4   TRIPS Art 39.1.
5   For example, *Duchess of Argyll v Duke of Argyll* [1967] Ch 302.

# Invasion of Privacy

There have been two developments over the past decade which have had an indirect relationship with this action. In Australia privacy laws have been enacted which regulate the way in which private information is handled.[6] In addition, the High Court in *Australian Broadcasting Corporation v Lenah Game Meats Pty Ltd*[7] (*Lenah Games Meats*) had cause to consider the question of whether a tort of invasion of privacy might be developed in Australia. In that case Gummow and Hayne JJ suggested that the decision in *Victoria Park Racing and Recreation Grounds Co Ltd v Taylor*[8] would not prevent the development of such a tort[9] but concluded that, if a tort dealing with "unjustified invasion of privacy" were to develop, it could only "benefit natural, not artificial, persons" and therefore would offer no relief to the corporation in that case.[10] The tort has attracted much attention since this case including being the subject of consideration in a number of cases and law reform inquiries.

In the 2003 case, *Grosse v Purvis*,[11] the plaintiff's claim against the defendant was essentially in relation to the act of stalking. The District Court of Queensland found that the offence of unlawful stalking[12] involved an invasion of the privacy of the plaintiff.[13] The elements of an action for the invasion of privacy, which the court found were made out, were said to comprise the following:

    (a) a willed act by the defendant,

    (b) which intrudes upon the privacy or seclusion of the plaintiff,

    (c) in a manner which would be considered highly offensive to a reasonable person of ordinary sensibilities,

    (d) and which causes the plaintiff detriment in the form of mental psychological or emotional harm or distress or which prevents or hinders the plaintiff from doing an act which she is lawfully entitled to do.[14]

Meanwhile, in the 2004 Federal Court trial, *Kalaba v Commonwealth*,[15] Heerey J did not consider that the law had developed sufficiently to support an independent tort for invasion of privacy and the Full Court did not grant leave to appeal Heerey J's decision.[16] That case concerned the Commonwealth's inquiry into records regarding Mr Kalaba's internment in a concentration camp during World War II. In another 2004 case, *Giller v Procopets*,[17] this time before the Victorian Supreme Court, several causes of action were brought in relation

---

6    See the *Privacy Act 1988* which was recently amended to extend its power of regulation to the private sector in response to developments internationally such as the EU Directive on data protection.

7    (2001) 185 ALR 1.

8    (1937) 58 CLR 479.

9    (2001) 185 ALR 1 at 31.

10    *Australian Broadcasting Corp v Lenah Game Meats Pty Ltd* (2001) 185 ALR 1 at 50. See also *Grosse v Purvis* [2003] QDC 151 where Skoien SJDC of the District Court of Queensland considered the scope of such an action to protect against intrusions "upon the privacy or seclusion of the plaintiff" and set out essential elements for such an action to succeed.

11    [2003] QDC 151.

12    *Criminal Code* (Qld) s 359E.

13    [2003] QDC 151 at [420].

14    [2003] QDC 151 per Senior Judge Skoien at [444].

15    [2004] FCA 763.

16    *Kalaba v Commonwealth* [2004] FCAFC 326.

17    [2004] VSC 113.

to the distribution and publication of videotapes showing the sexual encounters between the plaintiff and the defendant. Breach of confidence, intentional infliction of mental harm and breach of privacy were all argued and all dismissed with the court concluding that Australian law had not developed sufficiently to recognise an action for breach of privacy.[18] On appeal, the majority of the Victorian Court of Appeal held that there was a breach of confidence and that, in line with the outcome of various English decisions, the plaintiff was entitled to compensation for the mental distress and embarrassment caused by the publication of the videotapes.[19]

Returning to the lower courts, in 2007 Judge Hampel of the Victorian County Court considered that the tort of invasion of privacy had achieved growing recognition as the string of cases since *Lenah Game Meats* had demonstrated. The case was *Doe v Australian Broadcasting Corporation*,[20] where a rape victim had her identity and other personal information revealed in the news bulletins of a radio station. Judge Hampel found the ABC liable for both breach of confidence and breach of the tort of invasion of privacy, and that the publication of the personal information was unjustified, noting the need for balance between freedom of speech and protection of privacy.[21] What this judgment does point out is the connection between the action for breach of confidence and the tort of invasion of privacy:

> As the analysis of the decisions referred to under breach of confidence demonstrates, development of a tort of invasion of privacy is intertwined with the development of the cause of action for breach of confidence. What is seen to underpin both causes of action is the acceptance or recognition of the value of privacy as a right in itself deserving of protection. That in turn, springs from a recognition of the value of, and importance of the law recognising and protecting human dignity.[22]

It seems, however, that the higher courts in Australia simply cannot entertain utilising a tort of invasion of privacy and this holds true in the United Kingdom as well. It should be noted that in the House of Lords decision, *Campbell v MGN Limited*,[23] Lord Nicholls of Birkenhead made the following comments on the issue of an action for "invasion of privacy" in the United Kingdom:

> In this country [the United Kingdom], unlike the United States of America, there is no over-arching, all-embracing cause of action for 'invasion of privacy': see *Wainwright v Home Office* [2003] 3 WLR 1137. But protection of various aspects of privacy is a fast developing area of the law, here and in some other common law jurisdictions. The recent Court of Appeal of New Zealand in *Hosking v Runting* (25 March 2004) is an example of this. In this country development of the law has been spurred by enactment of the Human Rights Act 1998.[24]

His Lordship went on to explain that "wrongful disclosure of private information" was one aspect of invasion of privacy and that the action for breach of confidence provided the equitable protection for such wrongful disclosure.[25] His Lordship also pointed out the need to weigh up the competing human rights of freedom

---

18   [2004] VSC 113 at [188].
19   *Giller v Procopets* [2008] VSCA 236.
20   [2007] VCC 281.
21   [2007] VCC 281 at [163]-[164].
22   [2007] VCC 281 at [148].
23   [2004] UKHL 22.
24   [2004] UKHL 22 at [11].
25   [2004] UKHL 22 at [12]-[13].

of expression and respect for private and family life in making a determination under an action for breach of confidence.[26] In the recent United Kingdom case *Mosley v News Group Newspapers Limited*,[27] a claim was brought against the *News of the World* for having published articles, images and video footage of the former FIA President, Max Mosley, involved in an orgy. The High Court case relied on the action for breach of confidence and the unauthorised disclosure of personal information in breach of the right of privacy under Art 8 of the *European Convention on Human Rights and Fundamental Freedoms* (the Convention). In awarding the plaintiff £60,000 in damages, the court found that there was no public interest or other justification for the intrusion on the personal privacy of the plaintiff. Once again no separate tort of invasion of privacy was relied on – rather, legislative enactment of the principles of the Convention through the *Human Rights Act 1998* (UK) complemented the action for breach of confidence.

In Australia there have been two specific inquiries as to whether legislation should be enacted to provide a mechanism that acknowledges the principles of a tort of invasion of privacy.[28] Both the Australian Law Reform Commission (ALRC) and the New South Wales Law Reform Commission (NSWLRC) released consultation papers and reports dealing with privacy. The NSWLRC recommended a statutory action to deal with invasion of privacy in a manner similar to that in the United Kingdom, enabling a balanced approach between protection of privacy and maintaining the public interest such as free speech and flexibility in determining the most appropriate remedy given the circumstances.[29] The ALRC undertook a far broader review of privacy but also dealt with the issue of invasion of privacy recommending that a statutory action only be created for cases of serious invasions of privacy[30] and only where there is a reasonable expectation of privacy and the claimant has met the "highly offensive to a reasonable person" test.[31] On 23 September 2011, the Commonwealth Government released an issues paper, *A Commonwealth Statutory Cause of Action for Serious Invasion of Privacy*. Submissions were due by 18 November 2011 but there is yet to be a report from the Attorney-General's Department and there is no further advancement of the notion of a general tort of invasion of privacy. Accordingly, this chapter is confined to a discussion of the action for breach of confidence and does not deal with either the potential for a tort of invasion of privacy or the existing or potential privacy legislation.

## History and Nature of the Action for Breach of Confidence

The action for breach of confidence originated with the famous case of *Prince Albert v Strange*.[32] This case also indirectly raised interesting questions about the

---

26   In Australia, such an assessment is considered under the defence of justification dealt with later in this chapter.

27   [2008] EWHC 1777 (QB).

28   The Victorian Law Reform Commission addressed the issue as part of the *Surveillance in Public Places Final Report* 18 (2010).

29   See NSWLRC, *Consultation Paper 1 Invasion of Privacy*, May 2007, and *Invasion of Privacy Report 120*, April 2009.

30   ALRC, *Report 108, Australian Privacy Law and Practice*, May 2008, Recommendation 74-1.

31   ALRC, *Report 108, Australian Privacy Law and Practice*, May 2008, Recommendation 74-2.

32   (1849) 47 ER 1302. Although some refer to the equitable doctrine regarding trustee responsibility in *Keech v Sandford* (1726) 2 Eq Ca Ab 741; 22 ER 629, as the "starting point": see,

relationship between copyright law and breach of confidence. In that case, Queen Victoria and Prince Albert made some etchings of their dog and other personal domestic subjects and delivered these etchings to a private printer for printing. The defendant somehow obtained the etchings and produced a catalogue that did not reproduce the etchings but gave detailed written descriptions of them with commentary and criticism. The defendant readily admitted that the Queen and Prince Albert had "property" (perhaps in the nature of copyright?) in the etchings and that he could not reproduce or exhibit the etchings themselves. However, he argued that the Queen and Prince Albert had no property in the information which he imparted about the content of the etchings and that he was free to make use of this in any way he saw fit. Perhaps surprisingly, the Lord Chancellor found that the plaintiffs did have "property" in the information and also found against the defendant on the grounds of breach of trust, breach of confidence and contract. There are two things to note about this case. First, it is unlikely that such a case could be argued on the basis of copyright today. Secondly, it is difficult when reading the case to determine whether the confidential information is protected as a form of property in its own right, as a breach of an equitable duty or as a breach of contract.

The modern basis of breach of confidence was explored in *Saltman Engineering Co Ltd v Campbell Engineering Co Ltd.*[33] In that case a manufacturer was engaged by a client to produce tools based on drawings supplied by the client. The manufacturer exceeded its rights by producing and selling the same tools on its own account. The Master of the Rolls, Lord Greene, held that the equitable obligation of confidence arose apart from any contractual obligation between the parties.[34] A plaintiff could ground an action for breach if the plaintiff could establish that confidential information obtained directly or indirectly from the plaintiff was used by the defendant without the consent of the plaintiff.[35] This implies that it is the "confider" who "owns" the information for the purposes of breach, not the "creator" of that information.[36] Thus, in *Schering Chemicals Ltd v Falkman*,[37] the court found an implied duty not to use information to the detriment of the confider. Even if there is an express clause, the equitable obligation of confidentiality may take over where that express clause is considered an unreasonable restraint of trade[38] or where the express clause is unduly limited.[39]

In Australia, an attempt was made by Fullagar J to determine the jurisdictional basis of the action for breach of confidence in *Deta Nominees Pty Ltd v Viscount Plastic Products Pty Ltd.*[40] In that case, which concerned a trade secret in the manufacture of plastic drawers, his Honour identified two classes of actions

---

for example, Gowans J in *Ansell Rubber Co Pty Ltd v Allied Rubber Industries Pty Ltd* [1967] VR 37.

33    (1948) 65 RPC 203.
34    (1948) 65 RPC 203 at 216.
35    (1948) 65 RPC 203 at 213.
36    *Fraser v Evans* [1969] 1 QB 349. Although, it depends on the arrangement. Note, also, that this principle does not apply in all circumstances. See *Privacy Act 1988*.
37    [1981] 2 All ER 321.
38    *TV Shopping Network v Scutt* (1998) 43 IPR 451 at 459; see also *Deta Nominees Pty Ltd v Viscount Plastic Products Pty Ltd* [1979] VR 167 at 190, and *Titan Group Pty Ltd v Steriline Manufacturing Pty Ltd* (1990) 19 IPR 353 at 388.
39    *FSS Travel and Leisure Systems Ltd v Johnson* [1999] FSR 505.
40    [1979] VR 167.

– those based on contract and those based on equity.[41] In the High Court case of *Moorgate Tobacco Co Ltd v Philip Morris Ltd (No 2)*,[42] Deane J explained the equitable jurisdiction of the action in the following terms:

> It is unnecessary ... to attempt to define the precise scope of the equitable jurisdiction to grant relief against an actual or threatened abuse of confidential information not involving any tort or any breach of some express or implied contractual provision, some wider fiduciary duty or some copyright or trade mark right. A general equitable jurisdiction to grant such relief has long been asserted and should, in my view, now be accepted ...[43]

His Honour put to rest the suggestion that the protection of confidential information was based on property. He held that the "rational basis [for such an exclusive equitable jurisdiction] does not lie in proprietary right",[44] but rather, the action for breach of confidence "lies in the notion of an obligation of conscience arising from the circumstances in or through which the information was communicated or obtained".[45] This is reminiscent of Lord Denning MR in *Fraser v Evans*,[46] who held that the jurisdictional basis for the action was the "duty to be of good faith". In the United States a similar view has been taken:

> Therefore the starting point for the present matter is not property or due process of law, but that the defendant stood in confidential relations with the plaintiffs, or one of them. These have given place to hostility, and the first thing to be made sure of is that the defendant shall not fraudulently abuse the trust reposed in him. It is the usual incident of confidential relations.[47]

However, both the Canadian and New Zealand courts seem reluctant to make such a stand. Sopinka J of the Supreme Court of Canada, for example, preferred to treat the action as *sui generis* although he recognised that it may have its foundations in contract, equity and property.[48] The Court of Appeal of New Zealand has preferred not to dwell on the grounding of the duty of confidence, claiming that common law and equity "are mingled or merged" and that therefore a "full range of remedies should be available" for such a breach.[49]

In the tax law cases on "know how" the Australian courts have also chosen not to characterise that information as a form of property.[50] As Latham CJ says in

---

41    The equitable class is further divided by Fullagar J into that which protects the "property" of a person and that where use or publication of the information would be unconscionable.

42    (1984) 156 CLR 414

43    (1984) 156 CLR 414 at 437.

44    (1984) 156 CLR 414 at 437-438. Consider also Gummow J in *Smith Kline & French Laboratories (Australia) Ltd v Secretary, Department of Community Services and Health* (1990) 17 IPR 545 at 592. For a more detailed discussion on the issue of information as property, see RP Meagher, WMC Gummow and JRF Lehane, *Equity: Doctrines and Remedies*, 3rd ed, Butterworths, 1992, pp 877-880, paras [4116]ff.

45    *Moorgate Tobacco Co Ltd v Philip Morris Ltd (No 2)* (1984) 156 CLR 414 at 437-8.

46    [1969] 1 QB 349.

47    *EI Dupont de Nemours Powder Co v Masland* 244 US 102 (1917) as quoted in the judgment of Sheppard, Wilcox and Pincus JJ in *Smith Kline & French Laboratories (Australia) Ltd v Secretary, Department of Community Services and Health* (1991) 20 IPR 643 at 656.

48    *Lac Minerals Ltd v International Corona Resources Ltd* (1989) 61 DLR (4th) 14; 16 IPR 27.

49    *Aquaculture Corp v New Zealand Green Mussel Co Ltd* (1990) 19 IPR 527, Cooke P at 529.

50    Note that the use of the term "know how" in such tax cases is more likely a reference to trade secrets rather than the concept "know how", explored later in this chapter.

*FCT v United Aircraft Corp*,[51] although "[k]nowledge is valuable ... [it] is neither real nor personal property" even where that knowledge is secret or confidential.[52] In order for there to be a duty of confidence, there must be an obligation that the recipient of the confidential information will not deal with that information other than as the confider has permitted. In the words of Lord Denning MR in *Seager v Copydex (No 1)*,[53] "the broad principle of equity [is] that he who has received information in confidence shall not take unfair advantage of it". And this duty of confidence, even as an implied obligation, has been held to be assignable in equity to a new owner of an existing business.[54]

This has been accepted despite not being able to classify confidential information as property. In *TS & B Retail Systems Pty Ltd v 3Fold Resources Pty Ltd (No 3)*,[55] Finkelstein J confirmed that since confidential information is not property it therefore cannot be assigned.[56] His Honour went on to explain that the impact of *O Mustad & Son v Dosen*[57] was that the purchase of a "company's business included the benefit of trade secrets" such that an employee's contractual obligation of confidence would be able to be relied on by the purchaser to restrain a disclosure by such an employee in breach of their obligation.[58] It should be noted, therefore, that this chapter is concerned with the equitable action for breach of confidence. As explained by Campbell J in *AG Australia Holdings Limited v Burton*:[59]

> The law recognises three different ways in which an obligation of confidentiality might arise. The first is by an express provision in a contract, the second is by an implied term in a contract. The third is an obligation recognised in the exclusive jurisdiction of equity.[60]

As a general rule, the express commitment in a contract would take priority in defining the extent of the obligation of confidence.[61] However, there may be circumstances where the express contractual provision is found to be unenforceable and, in those situations, the courts have been prepared to accept an implied term of confidentiality or even an equitable obligation of confidence.[62] It has also been accepted that an equitable duty may stand side by side with an existing contractual duty of confidence or may even be used in preference.[63] The following

---

51   *FCT v United Aircraft Corp* (1943) 8 CLR 525 at 534.

52   However, income tax cases alternate between treating the profits derived from trade secrets as income on the one hand and capital on the other depending on whether the trade secrets are "licensed" to many parties or sold outright to only one party: consider *Rolls Royce Ltd v Jeffrey* [1962] 1 All ER 801 as to licensing and *Moriarty v Evans Medical Supplies Ltd* [1957] 3 All ER 718 as to the outright sale. Such a treatment is consistent with treating the trade secrets as proprietary in nature.

53   [1967] 2 All ER 415 at 417.

54   See *Mid-City Skin Cancer & Laser Centre v Zahedi-Anarak* [2006] NSWSC 844, where a doctor employed by a medical practice is held to continue his obligation of confidence to the practice's new owner even though the doctor did not remain an employee of the practice.

55   [2007] FCA 151.

56   [2007] FCA 151 at [75].

57   [1964] 1 WLR 109.

58   [2007] FCA 151 at [75].

59   [2002] NSWSC 170.

60   [2002] NSWSC 170 at [73].

61   [2002] NSWSC 170 at [75].

62   [2002] NSWSC 170 at [75].

63   *Optus Networks Pty Ltd v Telstra Corporation Ltd* [2010] FCAFC 21 per Finn, Sundberg and Jacobson JJ at [38].

provides an analysis of the equitable action for breach of confidence but it should be noted that the case law will often involve a combination of the three ways in which the obligation of confidence might arise.

## Action for Breach of Confidence

Megarry J set out the elements of the action for breach of confidence in *Coco v AN Clark (Engineers) Ltd*.[64] First, the information sought to be protected "must 'have the necessary quality of confidence about it'".[65] This concept has its origins in the judgment of Lord Greene MR in *Saltman Engineering Co Ltd v Campbell Engineering Co Ltd*.[66] Secondly, the information must have been imparted in such a way as to "import ... an obligation of confidence".[67] Finally, the plaintiff must show that there is an "unauthorised use of that information to the detriment of the party communicating it", that is, the plaintiff.[68]

In Australia, the formulation of the action for breach of confidence was expanded to four elements by Gummow J in *Smith Kline & French Laboratories (Australia) Ltd v Secretary, Department of Community Services and Health*:[69]

- the information claimed to be subject to the obligation of confidentiality must be identified "with specificity, and not merely in global terms";
- this information must not be common or public knowledge but have "the necessary quality of confidence";
- the circumstances in which the information was received must "import an obligation of confidence"; and
- misuse of that information must be actual or threatened and clearly without the confider's consent.

Gummow J did not include, in the last element, the stricter requirement of detriment to the confider as stipulated in *Coco v AN Clark (Engineers) Ltd*. In line with Megarry J's intention in that case to aim toward a broader formulation which did not require detriment, Gummow J grounded the action in the obligation of conscience:

> The obligation of conscience is to respect the confidence, not merely to refrain from causing detriment to the plaintiff. The plaintiff comes to equity to vindicate his right to observance of the obligation, not necessarily to recover loss or to restrain infliction of apprehended loss.[70]

This sits well with the basic right of other intellectual property "owners" to exclude others from using or exploiting that intellectual property simply because they have that monopoly right and not because any harm has occurred. But this seems to bring us back to the issue of proprietary rights and the nature of confidential information. Meagher, Gummow and Lehane do not deny the role

---

64  [1969] RPC 41.
65  [1969] RPC 41 at 47.
66  (1948) 65 RPC 203 at 215.
67  *Coco v AN Clark (Engineers) Ltd* [1969] RPC 41 at 47.
68  *Coco v AN Clark (Engineers) Ltd* [1969] RPC 41 at 47.
69  (1990) 17 IPR 545.
70  (1990) 17 IPR 545 at 584.

played by the notion of property in the development of the action and explain this situation as follows:

> The point is that the effect of the protection given endows confidential information with some proprietary characteristics, although they are not the reason for equitable intervention.[71]

Overall, there is no clear case law on whether detriment to the owner or confider of the information is a factor in determining liability for breach of confidence. However, Deane J in *Moorgate Tobacco Co Ltd v Philip Morris Ltd (No 2)*[72] does point to the need for the plaintiff to have a "substantial concern" to preserve confidentiality for relief to be available in an action for breach of confidence. In cases concerning government information, such as *Commonwealth v John Fairfax & Sons Ltd*,[73] detriment to the public interest needs to outweigh the interest in freedom of speech for there to be a breach of confidence. Mason J puts this down to the different interests of executive government compared to the personal, private and proprietary interests of the citizen for which this equitable action has been developed.[74] To this end, "when equity protects government information it will look at the matter through different spectacles".[75]

## Information claimed to be confidential

If we are to commence our exploration of the four elements we need to start with a discussion on the information that has attracted protection under the action for breach of confidence. Certainly, a consequence of Gummow J's formulation has been to encourage the careful drafting of confidentiality contracts or deeds so as not to fall foul of the requirements in equity. That is, defining what information is claimed as confidential has required "owners" to identify and describe their confidential information with precision and avoid ambit claims.[76] But such contracts or deeds tend to be associated more with commercially valuable information.

There appear to be three broad categories of information in respect of which the action for breach of confidence will apply: commercially valuable information, personal information and government information. In addition, there is growing support for recognising the importance of traditional knowledge of indigenous peoples and the action for breach of confidence may, in certain circumstances, serve as an appropriate form of protection for such knowledge.[77]

---

71    RP Meagher, WMC Gummow and JRF Lehane, *Equity: Doctrines and Remedies*, 3rd ed, Butterworths, Sydney, 1992, p 878, para [4117].

72    (1984) 156 CLR 414 at 438.

73    (1980) 147 CLR 39. See in particular, Mason J at 51-52.

74    (1980) 147 CLR 39 at 51-52.

75    (1980) 147 CLR 39 at 51-52.

76    This is supported by the judgment of Mason J in *O'Brien v Komesaroff* (1982) 150 CLR 310 at 326-328 where a failure to define precisely the purported confidential information (in this case schemes or arrangements for the minimisation of taxation) would undermine an action for breach of confidence. See also Mummery LJ in *FSS Travel and Leisure Systems Ltd v Johnson* [1999] FSR 505 at 512 on the issue of precision in pleadings.

77    See, for example, the current work of the World Intellectual Property Organisation in this field and consider also the report, *Intellectual Property Needs and Expectations of Traditional Knowledge Holders*, WIPO, Geneva, 2001.

Commercially valuable information encompasses trade secrets or business information. This can range from highly technical processes, formulae and machines to customer lists, price lists or financial information. This type of information has been the subject of numerous cases concerning the employer/ employee relationship.[78] The common example is where an ex-employee makes use of confidential information of their previous employer and either commences business in competition with that employer[79] or provides that information to a competitor of the employer, often the new employer.[80]

Within the context of an employment relationship it is often necessary to distinguish between "know how" and confidential information. "Know how" falls short of confidential information in so far as it represents the confidant's (employee's) accumulated experience and knowledge in a particular line of work or field. Often, such experience or knowledge is not peculiar to the particular employer but only peculiar to the relevant industry. Hence, "know how" is a more general form of knowledge whilst confidential information in the nature of "trade secrets" has a greater association with the particular employer.[81] Information that represents a "natural increase in skill and aptitude gained in the course of service"[82] can therefore be used elsewhere by the employee without recourse from the employer. However, "information which can fairly be regarded as an identifiably separate part of the employee's stock of knowledge such as chemical formulae or a list of customers committed to memory",[83] that is, specifically acquired information, will be capable of protection as confidential information. As Young J said in *Forkserve Pty Ltd v Pacchiarotta*:[84]

> There is a distinction between confidential information and know-how. An employee is entitled to take with him or her, when quitting employment, general knowledge and skills acquired whilst an employee. Those general skills or know-how become part of the employee's personal property, even though he or she would not have acquired them had it not been for the employer. Of course I am speaking of cases where there is no contractual restraint.

It is in the public interest that this distinction be maintained in so far as it prevents the imposition of an unreasonable restraint on an employee. Whilst there is a public interest in protecting confidential information it is also desirable that employees be able to use experience, skill and knowledge, or know how,

---

78  A McRobert, "Breach of Confidence: Revisiting the Protection of Surreptitiously Obtained Information" (2002) 13 *AIPJ* 69 at 70.

79  See, for example, *Speed Seal Products Ltd v Paddington* [1986] 1 All ER 91; *Ormonoid Roofing & Asphalts Ltd v Bitumenoids Ltd* (1930) 31 SR (NSW) 347; and *Forkserve Pty Ltd v Pacchiarotta* (2000) 50 IPR 74.

80  See, for example, *Coral Index Ltd v Regent Index Ltd* [1970] RPC 147.

81  See, for example, Harper J's discussion on what is a "trade secret" in *GlaxoSmithKline Australia Ltd v Ritchie* [2008] VSC 164 at [49]-[50]; and Hodgson JA's decision in *Del Casale v Artedomus (Aust) Pty Ltd* [2007] NSWCA 172 at [37]-[43].

82  RP Meagher, WMC Gummow and JRF Lehane, *Equity: Doctrines and Remedies*, 3rd ed, Butterworths, Sydney, 1992, p 865, para [4103].

83  RP Meagher, WMC Gummow and JRF Lehane, *Equity: Doctrines and Remedies*, 3rd ed, Butterworths, Sydney, 1992, p 865, para [4103]. See also *Robb v Green* [1895] 2 QB 1 at 13 on the issue of deliberately memorising information.

84  (2000) 50 IPR 74 at 78.

gained from prior employers and be in a position to continue to make a living from their chosen field of work.[85]

Information gained during employment that is either publicly available or trivial in nature falls short of protectable confidential information. On the other hand, specifically identified "trade secrets" developed by the employer, such as a method of production, are likely to fall into the category of protectable confidential information.[86] However, there is a grey area identified in *Faccenda Chicken Ltd v Fowler*[87] by Goulding J at first instance, that is, information that is treated as confidential during the term of employment, but which is absorbed and becomes part of the skill and knowledge of the employee.[88] In Australia, such information may still be protected provided that there is an express covenant or agreement to that effect, and that stipulation is not an unreasonable restraint of trade.[89] But how far does that go with, say, customer lists? Do we draw a distinction between an employee remembering customers on the one hand and obtaining a customer list or memorising a customer list on the other, as Bryson J does in *Weldon & Co v Harbinson*?[90] In *Forkserve v Pacchiarotta*,[91] Young J relies on the proposition provided in Heydon:[92]

> "The employee cannot remove, whether by using paper or using memory, a material part of the former employer's business records; but the employee can approach a particular customer or client whom that employee can recall without a list or deliberate memorisation". That proposition is, I believe, supported by the decision of *Peninsular Real Estate Ltd v Harris* [1992] 2 NZLR 216 at 221.[93]

White J in the New South Wales Supreme Court has taken a similar view in the recent case, *Orica Investments Pty Ltd v McCartney*,[94] where contractual restraints of trade and confidentiality obligations were upheld against a past owner/employee of a business. The court made the following points in regard to an employee's obligation of confidence:

> The identity of suppliers to Bronson & Jacobs was not itself confidential information. However ... the contact details for individual suppliers, such as the names, email addresses and telephone numbers of the individuals employed by the suppliers responsible for deciding with whom to place orders or enter into distribution arrangements, was confidential information ... There is no difference in principle between an employee making a list of the email addresses of customers or suppliers for the purpose of making use of such a list in a competitive business which the employee proposes to establish,

---

85    *Stevenson Jordan & Harrison Ltd v MacDonald & Evans* (1951) 69 RPC 1 and see also *TV Shopping Network Ltd v Scutt* (1998) 43 IPR 451.

86    *Ansell Rubber Co Pty Ltd v Allied Rubber Industries Pty Ltd* [1967] VR 37; see also *Ormonoid Roofing & Asphalts Ltd v Bitumenoids Ltd* (1930) 31 SR (NSW) 347 at 355.

87    [1984] ICR 589.

88    [1984] ICR 589 at 589-590; also repeated by the English Court of Appeal [1987] Ch 117 at 133-134.

89    *Wright v Gasweld Pty Ltd* (1991) 22 NSWLR 317 at 339-341. Contrast this with the judgment of the English Court of Appeal in *Faccenda Chicken Ltd v Fowler* [1987] Ch 117 at 133-134.

90    *Weldon & Co v Harbinson* [2000] NSWSC 272 at [72].

91    *Forkserve Pty Ltd v Pacchiarotta* (2000) 50 IPR 74.

92    Heydon, *The Restraint of Trade Doctrine*, 2nd ed, Butterworths, Sydney, 1999, p 80.

93    *Forkserve Pty Ltd v Pacchiarotta* (2000) 50 IPR 74 at 78.

94    [2007] NSWSC 645.

and the employee forwarding the emails to his or her computer so as to have access to those addresses.[95]

There is a wide range of commercially valuable information which might be protected as confidential information such as ideas for television shows and other forms of entertainment.[96] If a person approaches a broadcaster or producer with a concept for, say, a television series then that information might be protected under copyright law in certain limited circumstances. However, if the idea has not been reduced to material form or does not have the requisite coherency to constitute a "work" for the purpose of copyright law, then the only way to protect this information might be by way of an action for breach of confidence.

Personal information may also be treated as confidential information depending on the nature of the relationship between confider and confidant and the nature of the information revealed. The classic example of spousal communication is found in *Duchess of Argyll v Duke of Argyll*,[97] where the Duchess sought an interlocutory injunction to prevent the communication and publication of marital communications with her husband pertaining to her private life and personal affairs. Ungoed-Thomas J considered marital communications to be confidential noting that, even where one party subsequently becomes guilty of adultery, the other party is not released from the obligation to preserve the earlier "close confidence and mutual trust between husband and wife".[98] The extent of the protected relationship is not clear, however. Information relating to the confider's sexual behaviour in a lesbian relationship was considered confidential in nature in *Stephens v Avery*[99] even though the communication was only between friends and not under the umbrella of a marital relationship. This implies that certain types of personal information will be inherently confidential, or have a "necessary quality of confidence" – the second element in the action for breach of confidence.

Such a conclusion is in line with recent developments in Australia and the United Kingdom discussed earlier in relation to the protection of personal information through a potential tort of invasion of privacy. This is illustrated in the Naomi Campbell case[100] decided by the House of Lords in May 2004 with a majority of three to two in favour of Ms Campbell. In that case the *Mirror* newspaper published an article about Naomi Campbell's drug addiction complete with photographs of her leaving a Narcotics Anonymous (NA) meeting. The details of her addiction and therapy were said to have come from a fellow attendee at NA and passed on to the newspaper. In his dissent, Lord Hoffman analysed two developments in the law of confidence noting, first, that there is no need under English law for the existence of a prior confidential relationship to imply a duty

---

95   [2007] NSWSC 645 at [254]. The New South Wales Supreme Court has produced a number of recent decisions on the issues of restraint of trade and the obligation of confidence: see, for example, *Portal Software v Bodsworth* [2005] NSWSC 1179; *Cactus Imaging Pty Ltd v Peters* [2006] NSWSC 717; *Australian Regional Wholesalers v Stafford* [2007] NSWSC 572; and *Bromhead v Graham* [2007] NSWSC 609.

96   *Talbot v General Television* [1980] VR 224; *Fraser v Thames Television* [1984] QB 44.

97   [1967] 1 Ch 302.

98   [1967] 1 Ch 302 at 332.

99   [1988] 2 All ER 477.

100  *Campbell v MGN Limited* [2004] UKHL 22.

of confidence,[101] and, secondly, that due to the developments in human rights law at the European Union level and domestically in the UK, private information has been identified as "something worth protecting as an aspect of human autonomy and dignity".[102]

Other examples of personal information include the identity of a person where, for example, that person is participating in an investigation or is a police informant,[103] and even information "which, if made public, could threaten the social structure of a minority".[104] In the first instance, where a person has provided information on the basis that his or her identity be kept confidential, Yeldham J saw "no reason why his identity should not be treated as confidential information".[105] In the second instance, secret tribal folklore of a group of Aborigines was considered confidential information in *Foster v Mountford and Rigby Ltd*.[106] This would suggest that secret tribal medicines might also attract such protection providing an avenue for protecting, what has been commonly termed "traditional knowledge" of indigenous peoples. Considering recent developments in biotechnology based on accessing unique non-human biological resources indigenous to particular countries or regions, such recognition would go some way towards satisfying the benefit sharing provisions of the *Convention on Biological Diversity 1992*.

The final category of confidential information is government information. The ability to protect purported confidential government information depends on the weighing of public interests. Where the information is concerned with past government activities, *Commonwealth v John Fairfax & Sons Ltd*[107] has considered such information as not warranting protection because discussion of public affairs and keeping the public informed were considered in the public interest.[108] In that case, Mason J indicated that if disclosure was to injure public interest then such information would be protected as confidential.[109] Thus, if there were current issues of national security, sensitive government policy or relations with foreign governments at stake, that might be sufficient to tip the balance in favour of treating such information as confidential. The issue of public interest is nicely encapsulated in the following passage by McHugh JA in the "Spycatcher case", *Attorney-General (UK) v Heinemann Publishers Australia Pty Ltd*:[110]

> But governments act, or at all events are constitutionally required to act, in the public interest. Information is held, received and imparted by governments, their departments and agencies to further the public interest. Public and not private interest, therefore, must

101 [2004] UKHL 22 at [47]-[48].

102 [2004] UKHL 22 at [49]-[50].

103 See, for example, *G v Day* [1982] 1 NSWLR 24; and *Falconer v Australian Broadcasting Corporation* [1992] 1 VR 662.

104 See GE Dal Pont and DRC Chalmers, *Equity and Trusts in Australia and New Zealand*, 2nd ed, LBC Information Services, 2000, p 149, in reference to *Foster v Mountford and Rigby Ltd* (1976) 14 ALR 71.

105 *G v Day* [1982] 1 NSWLR 24 at 35.

106 (1976) 14 ALR 71.

107 (1980) 147 CLR 39.

108 (1980) 147 CLR 39 at 52.

109 (1980) 147 CLR 39 at 52.

110 (1987) 10 NSWLR 86

be the criterion by which equity determines whether it will protect information which a government or governmental body claims is confidential.[111]

## Quality of confidence

Information has the "necessary quality of confidence" if it is not in the "public domain", that is, it is neither public property nor public knowledge.[112] The public domain is not limited to national boundaries. For example, if a previously secret process or product is the subject of a patent application in one country and a specification is published and made available to the public in that country then the information will lose its necessary quality of confidence even in other countries because patent attorneys from other countries will have access to that information.[113] The information will also lose its quality of novelty for the purposes of another patent application.[114] In addition, certain information has been held to lack the necessary quality of confidence altogether. Information pertaining to "crimes, wrongs and misdeeds" are examples.[115]

The TRIPS Agreement attempts to define when undisclosed information is protectable. Under Art 39 para 2, there is express recognition that natural and legal persons can prevent non-consensual disclosure, acquisition and use of information in their control provided that the following three requirements are met; namely, that the information:

- is secret;
- has commercial value because it is secret; and
- has been subject to reasonable steps to maintain its secrecy.[116]

This element of secrecy is crucial to a finding of the necessary quality of confidence in Australian law. How is this determined? Fullagar J in *Deta Nominees Pty Ltd v Viscount Plastic Products Pty Ltd*[117] proposes a "reasonable man" test:

> [W]ould a person of ordinary intelligence in all the circumstances of the case, including, inter alia, the relationship of the parties and the nature of the information and the circumstances of its communication, recognise this information to be the property of the other person and not his own to do as he likes with? ... recognising that the nature of the information itself is relevant to that inquiry.[118]

This test is consistent with the criteria proposed in the earlier decision of Gowans J in *Ansell Rubber Co Pty Ltd v Allied Rubber Industries Pty Ltd*[119] (the

---

111  (1987) 10 NSWLR 86 at 191.

112  *Saltman Engineering Co Ltd v Campbell Engineering Co Ltd* (1948) 65 RPC 203 at 215.

113  *Franchi v Franchi* [1967] RPC 149

114  *Franchi v Franchi* [1967] RPC 149. This is why the priority date of a patent application is so significant – the 12-month period following first application provides protection against loss of novelty (or secrecy) of the invention.

115  *Corrs Pavey Whiting & Byrne v Collector of Customs (Vic)* (1987) 74 ALR 428, Gummow J at 450.

116  Further, a special provision has been included regarding undisclosed tests and data prepared for the purposes of approving the marketing of pharmaceutical or agricultural chemical products: TRIPS Art 39.3.

117  [1979] VR 167.

118  [1979] VR 167 at 193.

119  [1967] VR 37.

*Ansell Rubber* case) who held that the conduct of the confider in relation to the alleged confidential information assists in the determination of the "necessary quality of confidence". In the *Ansell Rubber* case Gowans J refers to six criteria, found in American law, for the determination of whether business information or trade secrets could be said to have the necessary quality of confidence. One must have regard to:

- the extent that the information is known outside the business of the employer;
- the extent that employees and others involved in the business know the information;
- the extent of measures taken to guard the secrecy of the information;
- the value of the information to the employer and its competitors;
- the amount of effort or money expended to develop the information;
- the ease or difficulty of properly acquiring or duplicating the information.[120]

In the *Ansell Rubber* case, the plaintiff sought to protect the confidentiality of the improvements and method of operation of its patented machine for the production of rubber gloves. However, two employees, with full knowledge of the trade secrets of the plaintiff and the secrecy obligations in place, acted together with others in the establishment of a glove manufacturing business in competition with the plaintiff. The plaintiff sought injunctions to restrain those former employees from using the trade secrets to manufacture rubber gloves. In applying the above six criteria, Gowans J found that there were trade secrets, that those trade secrets constituted confidential information and that the employees knew that the trade secrets were confidential and that by using those trade secrets for their own benefit they were in breach of their obligations. This result was achieved without the benefit of an express contract of secrecy. Rather, Gowans J found that when one of the defendants commenced employment with the plaintiff, he was told of the importance of the machinery and processes to the success of the business, that the unique methods were developed by the plaintiff and that the secrecy of those methods were jealously guarded, that it was the plaintiff's policy to keep such information private and that the employee knew that the design, construction and operation of the machinery was not to be disclosed. Accordingly, the conduct of the confider was instrumental in reaching such a determination. We would suggest that the same holds true where the information sought to be protected is not a trade secret but is personal information or government information.

The loss of secrecy can lead to the end of the obligation of confidence. For example, where publication of the information occurs by or with the consent of the owner of the information, or without prior breach by the receiver of the information, then the obligation of confidence is likely to lapse. However, where there is publication due to the activities of the receiver of the information, then the owner of the information may still have remedies against the receiver in the form of injunctive relief and damages or an account of profits.

The circumstances necessary for secrecy to be maintained are not clear. On the one hand, the disclosure of the identity of a police informant on television was

---

120  [1967] VR 37 at 49-50.

held not to have destroyed the secrecy of that person's identity in *G v Day*.[121] On the other hand, in *Commonwealth v Walsh*, the sale of a limited number of publications containing government secrets was held to have destroyed the necessary quality of confidence needed to restrain further publication.[122] The cases relating to personal information and government information on the whole support the view that the nature of disclosure of the allegedly confidential information will determine whether secrecy has been lost to the public domain. In determining the nature of disclosure a number of factors need to be weighed against each other such as: the nature of the medium of disclosure, for example television or court proceedings; the duration of such disclosure, such as short and impermanent television or radio reports compared to various forms of print media; the circulation of that disclosure, such as the national public compared to the participants in a court hearing (although broadcasts themselves are not permanent they may have been captured on the internet such as on YouTube and have a wide and long period of circulation); and public policy considerations pertaining to the nature of the information, such as the new identity of a police informer.

The circumstances can be further complicated by the operation of a confidentiality agreement. In *Maggbury Pty Ltd v Hafele Australia Pty Ltd*,[123] the confider sought to enforce a perpetual confidentiality obligation on the part of the confidant. In that case Maggbury Pty Ltd (Maggbury) developed a new foldaway ironing board assembly and filed patent applications for the alleged invention. Soon after the applications were made interest was shown in the new foldaway ironing board by the Australian arm of a German manufacturer. After much negotiation the parties entered into confidentiality agreements protecting the invention in order to allow Hafele Australia Pty Ltd (Hafele) an opportunity to inspect the prototype and associated information with a view to entering into licence arrangements. The agreements restrained Hafele from using the information for any purpose other than for assessment and set up a perpetual obligation not to use the information for any purpose whatsoever without the informed consent of Maggbury. However, through the operation of the patenting process, and in particular the PCT application process discussed briefly in Chapter 8, the details of the invention were published approximately 19 months after the earlier priority date.

This brought much of the information protected by the confidentiality agreements into the public domain and, as in *Franchi v Franchi*,[124] this meant that the information lost its quality of confidence. Hafele took advantage of this situation and its parent company commenced manufacturing a variation of Maggbury's foldaway ironing board and distributed these in Australia through Hafele. Maggbury sought to enforce the confidentiality obligations on Hafele and obtain an injunction restraining further use of that information. As the patent application had not yet been granted at this stage the only avenue open was breach of the confidentiality contracts. The majority decision of the High Court, comprising Gleeson CJ, Gummow and Hayne JJ, held that contractual restraints

---

121  [1982] 1 NSWLR 24.
122  (1980) 147 CLR 61.
123  (2001) 185 ALR 152.
124  [1967] RPC 149.

would not operate at the time of a breach if the subject-matter had lost its quality of confidence because it had entered the public domain as a result of the actions of the confider. Interestingly, Kirby J, in dissent, did not consider the restraint of trade doctrine applicable in the circumstances finding that the confidentiality agreements were breached. His Honour determined that injunctive relief was proper in the circumstances:

> In the present matter, Hafele not only agreed, in terms, that it would not use "the Information" irrespective of whether it was, or became, publicly available. Hafele also expressly agreed, in cl 13.3, that Maggbury "shall be entitled to" an injunction in the event of a breach. Why should Hafele now be heard to resist the remedy to which it expressly agreed in respect of the precise circumstances that have occurred? ...[125]

And on the issue of injunctions in relation to information, his Honour said:

> Before granting an injunction in relation to information, a court will consider the extent of the dissemination of the information. If the information has become publicly available, a court may nevertheless order an injunction to prevent the defendant using the information. The court might elect to order a temporary "springboard" injunction to prevent the defendant gaining an unfair advantage[126] if a permanent injunction would be pointless.[127] Yet here, the primary judge found that dissemination of Hafele's wall-mounted foldaway ironing board was "small" and a comparable product had not previously been seen on the market. The primary judge also found that Hafele's conduct in breach of the agreements diminished Maggbury's capacity to exploit its designs.[128]
>
> In circumstances where the copying was found to be "substantial"[129] and where the injunction granted was confined to preventing the use of "the Information" embodied in the materials provided by Maggbury on the strength of the agreements, the justification for injunctive relief is overwhelming.
>
> I reach this conclusion without deciding whether an additional justification lies in the fact that the breaches of the confidentiality agreements proved against Hafele were deliberate and flagrant.[130]

Callinan J, also dissenting, applied the restraint of trade doctrine to the confidentiality agreements and determined that the restrictive covenants were reasonable in the circumstances:

> The parties were engaged in commercial dealings and the respondents were on an equal footing with the appellants, if not on a superior commercial footing to them.[131] They took their own legal advice. The covenant with the appellants that the respondents entered into simply forbade them from making use of information that was provided to them by

---

125   (2001) 185 ALR 152 at 173.

   [126] *British Franco Electric Pty Ltd v Dowling Plastics Pty Ltd* [1981] 1 NSWLR 448 at 451.

   [127] Dean, *The Law of Trade Secrets*, (1990) at 305-307.

   [128] Byrne J found that distribution of the respondents' board would have a "special [adverse] impact" on the appellants: *Maggbury Pty Ltd v Hafele Australia Pty Ltd* (unreported, SC (Qld), 22 January 1999), p 29.

   [129] *Maggbury Pty Ltd v Hafele Australia Pty Ltd* (unreported, SC (Qld), 22 January 1999) at p 21 per Byrne J.

130   (2001) 185 ALR 152 at 173-174.

   [131] *North Western Salt Co Ltd v Electrolytic Alkali Co Ltd* [1914] AC 461 at 471 per Viscount Haldane LC; *English Hop Growers v Dering* [1928] 2 KB 174 at 181 per Scrutton LJ; *Esso Petroleum Co Ltd v Harper's Garage (Stourport) Ltd* [1968] AC 269 at 300 per Lord Reid, 320 per Lord Hodson, 324 per Lord Pearce; *Amoco Australia Pty Ltd v Rocca Bros Motor Engineering Co Pty Ltd* (1973) 133 CLR 288 at 316 per Gibbs J.

the appellants: the restraint was designed to prevent the respondents from obtaining the benefit of the appellants' wall-mounted invention in ways that would harm the business of the appellants. The covenant left the respondents with their pre-existing freedom to trade, and did not otherwise interfere with their business.[132] It could not be said to injure the public by stifling competition. Indeed, as one court has suggested, striking down such restraints might have adverse consequences on trade:[133]

> The owners of new and unpatented products would hesitate before transmitting the information and making the disclosures essential to bring about meaningful negotiations.

All these considerations, in my view, lead to the conclusion that the restraint went no further than was necessary in the interests of both parties and offended no public interest. Even on the current law of restraint of trade, the covenant can and should be given effect.[134]

It is interesting to note in this case that, had the patent been granted, Maggbury would have been able to bring infringement proceedings against Hafele for those infringements committed after the first publication of the applications, that is, when applications are open for public inspection as notified in the *Australian Official Journal of Patents*. This would indicate that Hafele's actions, while considered by the majority of the High Court not to be a breach of confidence, were at risk of constituting an infringement of potential patent rights. Hafele's strategy not to wait until a determination was made as to the granting of patents to Maggbury indicated Hafele's belief that ultimately no patents would be granted and this was based on independent patent advice sought from their own attorneys.[135] It is interesting also to note that the High Court was not asked to consider the issue of when it would be reasonable for a confidant to start using confidential information once it became public knowledge. Such an issue is assisted by the operation of the "springboard doctrine".

A person who receives confidential information is not necessarily precluded forever from using that information if it becomes public knowledge. The rights of the receiver to use that information are governed by the "springboard doctrine". The doctrine was explained by Roxbough J in *Terrapin Ltd v Builders' Supply Co (Hayes) Ltd*:[136]

> [A] person who has obtained information in confidence is not allowed to use it as a spring-board for activities detrimental to the person who made the confidential communication, and spring-board it remains even when all the features have been published or can be ascertained by actual inspection by any member of the public.[137]

In other words, the receiver of the information cannot unfairly benefit from the receipt of the information but similarly should not be any worse off than a member of the general public. How this is gauged depends on the nature of the

---

[132] *Esso Petroleum Co Ltd v Harper's Garage (Stourport) Ltd* [1968] AC 269 at 298 per Lord Reid, 309 per Lord Morris of Borth-y-Gest, 316-17 per Lord Hodson. While these comments are directed to the scope of the restraint of trade doctrine, I can see no reason why keeping intact a pre-existing freedom should not factor in the reasonableness of the restraint.

[133] *Biodynamic Technologies Inc v Chattanooga Corporation* 644 F Supp 607 (1986) at 611.

134 (2001) 185 ALR 152 at 179.

135 A search of the Australian Patent Register reveals that all applications by Maggbury Pty Ltd have lapsed.

136 [1967] RPC 375.

137 [1967] RPC 375 at 391-392.

disclosure of the information.[138] For example, if the information is associated with a product, then once that product has entered the public domain the period of time necessary for a competitor to reverse engineer that product would represent the period of time a confidant ought to wait before being able to make use of the information pertaining to the product.[139] Where the disclosure of information is basic in nature and does not reveal all details necessary to make use of the confider's information, then the springboard would operate so as to restrain the confidant from using the confidential information provided to them until such time as it would take for the undisclosed information to be ascertained.

Employees have a special duty of fidelity to their employers which is more stringent than the general equitable duty of confidence. However, once the employment contract comes to an end the duty of fidelity also comes to an end and an employer cannot rely on this duty to prevent an ex-employee from disclosing non-confidential information properly acquired. On the other hand, if the information acquired had been dealt with by the employer in such a way as to maintain its quality of confidence, as seen in the *Ansell Rubber* case discussed above, then the ex-employee may be liable for breach of confidentiality if he or she uses that information.[140]

## Receipt of information in confidence

The third element in Gummow J's formulation of the action for breach of confidence is whether the circumstances import an obligation of confidence. The inquiry into this element is very closely tied to the inquiry as to whether the information has the necessary quality of confidence. Under *Coco v AN Clark (Engineers) Ltd*,[141] the question of whether the information has been passed on so as to impose a duty of confidence is determined by the reasonable man test. Megarry J provided the following test:

> It seems to me that if the circumstances are such that any reasonable man standing in the shoes of the recipient of the information would have realised that upon reasonable grounds the information was being given to him in confidence, then this should suffice to impose upon him the equitable obligation of confidence.[142]

In *Smith Kline & French Laboratories (Australia) Ltd v Secretary, Department of Community Services and Health*,[143] it was held that there must have been an understanding at the time of receiving the information that it is confidential.

---

138  Where the confidant or recipient of the information is the party who brought that information into the public domain, for example by publication of a brochure or as part of a patent specification as in *Speed Seal Products Ltd v Paddington* [1986] 1 All ER 91, it has been held that in order to prevent such a confidant from abusing their position of confidence they should be restrained from using such information. Compare this view with that of Lord Goff in the Spycatcher case, *Her Majesty's Attorney-General v The Times Newspapers Ltd* (1988) 13 IPR 75.

139  See, for example: *Saltman Engineering Co Ltd v Campbell Engineering Co Ltd* (1948) 65 RPC 203 at 215; and, more recently, *Re Titan Group Pty Ltd v Steriline Manufacturing Pty Ltd* [1990] FCA 402.

140  *Faccenda Chicken Ltd v Fowler* [1986] 1 All ER 617; *Orica Investments Pty Ltd v McCartney* [2007] NSWSC 645; and *Mid-City Skin Cancer & Laser Centre v Zahedi-Anarak* [2006] NSWSC 844.

141  [1969] RPC 41.

142  [1969] RPC 41 at 48.

143  (1990) 17 IPR 545.

The nature of any pre-existing relationship of the parties may, however, be taken into account as evidence of this understanding. In the decision of the Full Federal Court in *Smith Kline & French Laboratories (Australia) Ltd v Secretary, Department of Community Services and Health*,[144] a number of circumstances were identified as relevant to a determination of the existence of confidentiality:

> To determine the existence of confidentiality and its scope, it may be relevant to consider whether the information was supplied gratuitously or for a consideration; whether there is any past practice of such a kind as to give rise to an understanding; how sensitive the information is; whether the confider has any interest in the purpose for which the information is to be used; whether the confider expressly warned the confidee against a particular disclosure or use of the information – and, no doubt many other matters.[145]

A confidence cannot be forced upon an unwilling recipient and, in the absence of a pre-existing relationship, the party communicating the information must give the recipient an opportunity to reject the communication of information.[146] Where, however, the information was solicited by the recipient or deliberate steps were taken to acquire the information, then confidentiality over that information can be implied.[147] This is also the case where the information was obtained "improperly or surreptitiously" as in the case *Franklin v Giddens*.[148] In that case the stealing of cuttings from the plaintiff's orchard provided the defendants with the "genetic information" necessary to grow nectarines which were identical to the plaintiff's and which therefore allowed them unfairly to compete directly with the plaintiff. This was held to be an infringement of the plaintiff's confidentiality rights. In direct contrast, the lawful tapping of phones in a police investigation has been considered not to impart a duty of confidence upon the person listening to the telephone conversations.[149] However, the issue of improperly or surreptitiously obtaining information is not necessarily the focal point in a determination of whether it can be implied that the information was received in confidence. Rather, what may be the determining issue is whether, in such cases, the information would be recognised as confidential in nature. Gleeson CJ made the following observation in *Australian Broadcasting Corporation v Lenah Game Meats Pty Ltd*:[150]

> [E]quity may impose obligations of confidentiality even though there is no imparting of information in circumstances of trust and confidence. And the principle of good faith upon which equity acts to protect information imparted in confidence may also be invoked to "restrain the publication of confidential information improperly or surreptitiously obtained" (*Commonwealth v John Fairfax & Sons Ltd* (1980) 147 CLR 39 at 50 per Mason J citing *Lord Ashburton v Pape* [1913] 2 Ch 469 at 475 per Swinfen Eady LJ). The nature of the information must be such that it is capable of being regarded as confidential.

---

144  (1991) 20 IPR 643.

145  (1991) 20 IPR 643 at 655.

146  For an example of the result when the opportunity to reject the communication is not given, see *Fractionated Cane Technology Ltd v Ruiz-Avila* (1987) 8 IPR 502.

147  *Johns v Australian Securities Commission* (1993) 178 CLR 408.

148  [1978] Qd R 72.

149  See *Malone v Commissioner of Police of the Metropolis (No 2)* [1979] 2 All ER 620. Compare this result with the opposite finding in *Francome v Mirror Group Newspapers Ltd* [1984] 2 All ER 408 where the telephone tap was unlawful.

150  (2001) 185 ALR 1 at 11.

In *Australian Broadcasting Corporation v Lenah Game Meats Pty Ltd*,[151] the respondent brought an action to restrain the appellant from broadcasting a videotape made surreptitiously and unlawfully by a group opposed to the way in which the respondents slaughtered brush tail possums for meat processing. In order to ground such a restraint in an action for breach of confidence the slaughtering process filmed, according to Gleeson CJ, would have to be confidential in nature.[152] But Gleeson CJ did not find that the slaughtering methods filmed were confidential in nature. There was no "private act" as Laws J considered necessary in *Hellewell v Chief Constable of Derbyshire*.[153] Gleeson CJ pointed out:

> If the activities filmed were private, then the law of breach of confidence is adequate to cover the case. I would regard images and sounds of private activities, recorded by the methods employed in the present case as confidential. There would be an obligation of confidence upon the persons who obtained them, and upon those into whose possession they came, if they knew, or ought to have known, the manner in which they were obtained.[154]

The activities filmed were not shown to be private in any other sense than the fact that they were carried out on private property. Gleeson CJ noted that there is "no bright line" between what is or is not private and indicated that "there is a large area in between what is necessarily public and what is necessarily private":

> An activity is not private simply because it is not done in public. It does not suffice to make an act private that, because it occurs on private property, it has such measure of protection from the public gaze as the characteristics of the property, the nature of the activity, the locality, and the disposition of the property owner combine to afford. Certain kinds of information about a person, such as information about a person, such as information relating to health, personal relationships, or finances may be easy to identify as private; as may certain kinds of activity, which a reasonable person, applying contemporary standards of morals and behaviour, would understand to be meant to be unobserved. The requirement that disclosure or observation of information or conduct would be highly offensive to a reasonable person of ordinary sensibilities is in many circumstances a useful practical test of what is private.[155]

This comparison with personal information is an interesting one given that the facts of the case are concerned with what one might consider a method of manufacture, although, the circumstances are quite consistent with the media cases and hence the concern over privacy would seem paramount. We suggest, however, that if the slaughtering process had been a trade secret of the respondents then perhaps the reasoning in *Franklin v Giddens*[156] would operate to ground an injunction on the basis that the information was confidential in nature.

The above statement by Gleeson CJ has been the subject of much comment and featured in both the majority and dissenting judgments in the *Naomi Campbell* case.[157] In dissent Lord Nicholls of Birkenhead cautions in relation to the use of the "highly sensitive" formulation found in the passage above:

---

151  (2001) 185 ALR 1 at 11.
152  (2001) 185 ALR 1 at 11.
153  [1995] 4 All ER 473 at 476.
154  (2001) 185 ALR 1 at 12.
155  (2001) 185 ALR 1 at 13.
156  [1978] Qd R 72.
157  *Campbell v MGN Limited* [2004] UKHL 22.

[T]he 'highly offensive' phrase is suggestive of a stricter test of private information than a reasonable expectation of privacy. Second, the 'highly offensive' formulation can all too easily bring into account, when deciding whether the disclosed information was private, considerations which go more properly to issues of proportionality; for instance, the degree of intrusion into public life, and the extent to which publication was a matter of proper public concern. This could be a recipe for confusion.[158]

The majority judgments far more readily embraced Gleeson CJ's formulation. Lord Hope of Craighead, in noting the trial judge's application of the formulation, confirmed its usefulness "in cases where there is room for doubt".[159] However, his Lordship went on to note:

The test is not needed where the information can easily be identified as private. It is also important to bear in mind its source, and the guidance which the source offers as to whether the information is public or private.[160]

The trial judge was right to consider the information regarding the therapy Naomi Campbell undertook for her drug addiction, such as her regular attendance at Narcotics Anonymous meetings, to be "easily identifiable as private" and "worthy of protection".[161] Even so, in his conclusion, the trial judge echoed the words of Gleeson CJ's formulation finding the disclosure as to the nature of Ms Campbell's therapy for drug addiction, comprising the attendance at Narcotics Anonymous meetings, to be "highly offensive to a reasonable person of ordinary sensibilities".[162] Lord Hope agreed with the trial judge's conclusion and identified who the reasonable person might be:

The mind that has to be examined is that, not of the reader in general, but of the person who is affected by the publicity. The question is what a reasonable person of ordinary sensibilities would feel if she was placed in the same position as the claimant and faced with the same publicity.[163]

The majority judgment of Baroness Hale of Richmond agrees with Lord Hope and points out Gleeson CJ's formulation is not intended to be the only test "particularly in respect of information which is obviously private, including information about health, personal relationships or finance".[164] Rather, she considers the "reasonable expectation of privacy" to be a threshold test to be followed by a balancing exercise between the interest in keeping the claimant's information private and the interest in the recipient publishing that information.[165] This aspect is considered later in the chapter.

## Unauthorised use of the information

Where the recipient of confidential information either discloses or uses that information beyond the purpose for which it was given then such disclosure or use will

---

158 [2004] UKHL 22 at [22].
159 [2004] UKHL 22 at [94].
160 [2004] UKHL 22 at [94].
161 [2004] UKHL 22 at [95].
162 [2004] UKHL 22 at [96].
163 [2004] UKHL 22 at [99].
164 [2004] UKHL 22 at [136].
165 [2004] UKHL 22 at [137].

be unauthorised and therefore in breach of confidence.[166] This is so whether the misuse is intentional, unintentional, subconscious or negligent.[167]

In order to determine whether there is unauthorised use and in order to obtain a remedy to restrain such unauthorised use it is necessary to identify exactly what information is alleged to be confidential and for what purposes it may be used or disclosed.[168] The identification of the confidential information needs to be accurate and not merely global, at least for the purposes of enforce-ability of an injunction. The High Court of Australia could not grant protection in equity for the alleged confidential information in *O'Brien v Komesaroff*[169] as there was a failure to identify what part of the information in question was not common knowledge. This is a clear example of not being able to identify the scope of protection.

Further, difficulties may arise where the recipient is working in the same field as the confider and may have prior knowledge of the subject-matter sought to be protected by the confider. The question in these circumstances turns on the evidence of such prior knowledge. In *Seager v Copydex Ltd*,[170] the plaintiff, during negotiations in relation to its carpet grip invention, disclosed information to the defendant in relation to a carpet grip not covered by its patent. The defendant rejected both products but produced its own carpet grip for distribution. While not infringing the plaintiff's patent, the defendant's carpet grip was held to have been possible only with the knowledge of the plaintiff's alternative design which was not in the public domain. Accordingly, Lord Denning MR found for the plaintiff. The opposite result would have been possible if the defendant could show that it had designed its carpet grip before receiving the information from the plaintiff as in *Johnson v Heat & Air Systems Ltd*.[171] In that case the defendants were able to substantiate their prior knowledge with evidence of their work.

As for the purpose for which the information is disclosed, there are two Australian cases that explore this issue with different results. In each case, the information sought to be protected was disclosed to a government instrumental-ity. In *Castrol Australia Pty Ltd v EmTech Associates Pty Ltd*,[172] the plaintiff submitted confidential marketing documents to the Trade Practices Commission (now the Australian Consumer and Competition Commission) for the purpose of assessment as to whether those materials complied with consumer protection requirements of the *Trade Practices Act 1974*. As a result of the information disclosed, the Commission considered the plaintiff to be in breach of other provisions under that Act and sought to prosecute. The plaintiff claimed that the use by the Commission of the confidential information for this purpose was beyond that for which the information was disclosed. In finding for the plaintiff, Rath J weighed the public interest in the disclosure of the offending information

---

166 Cf *Smith Kline & French Laboratories (Australia) Ltd v Secretary, Department of Community Services and Health* (1990) 17 IPR 545 (FCA, Gummow J); (1991) 20 IPR 643 (FCA, FC).
167 *Seager v Copydex Ltd* [1967] 2 All ER 415.
168 See, for example, *O'Brien v Komesaroff* (1982) 150 CLR 310; *Corrs Pavey Whiting & Byrne v Collector of Customs (Vic)* (1987) 74 ALR 428.
169 (1982) 150 CLR 310.
170 [1967] 2 All ER 415.
171 (1941) 58 RPC 229.
172 (1980) 33 ALR 31.

against the confidentiality of the information determining that the "purpose did not extend to any investigation of the plaintiff's advertising with a view to a prosecution of the plaintiff".

In *Smith Kline & French Laboratories (Australia) Ltd v Secretary, Department of Community Services and Health*,[173] the appellant supplied information to the respondent pertaining to its patented chemical, cimetidine, with a view to having it approved by the respondent for importation and marketing as a treatment for stomach ulcers. The issue arose as to how far such a purpose extends where the respondent uses such information in the assessment of a generic drug by another pharmaceutical company, Alphapharm. The appellant claimed that such a use is beyond the purpose for which the information was supplied and sought to restrain the respondent's use of the information for the evaluation of Alphapharm's generic version of cimetidine. The Full Court's determination turned on whether the respondent's use of the information would amount to the taking of an unfair advantage of the information:

> To avoid taking unfair advantage of information does not necessarily mean that the confidee must not use it except for the confider's limited purpose. Whether one adopts the "reasonable man" test suggested by Megarry J or some other, there can be no breach of the equitable obligation unless the court concludes that a confidence reposed has been abused, that unconscientious use has been made of the information.[174]

The public interest was a major factor in the court's determination:

> There is the distinction between use of confidential information in a way of which many people might disapprove, on the one hand, and illegal use on the other. Not only the administration of business and government, but ordinary communication between people, might be unduly obstructed by use of too narrow a test, such as that which the appellants put forward here. This is amply illustrated by the facts of the present case in which the evidence clearly showed the substantial interference with vital functions of government, in protecting the health and safety of the community, which could ensue if the appellant's primary submission were accepted. It is our view that the "blanket" protection of the SK&F B1 data which the appellants sought, as well as the rather more limited protection suggested during the hearing in this court, would go well beyond any obligation which ought to be imposed on the Secretary.[175]

But this is a curious result implying that all applicants seeking approval of their generic drugs can rely on the technical information tests and data previously prepared and supplied by the patentee of the original drug. Surely it would be in the better interests of the community if each applicant was put to the test by providing independent information concerning their own generic drug rather than relying on information that is not specific to that particular drug. Further, this case would appear to be in breach of Australia's subsequent obligations under TRIPS which provides that undisclosed tests and data prepared for the purposes of approving the marketing of pharmaceutical or agricultural chemical products should be protected against disclosure, unless necessary to protect the public, and should be protected against unfair commercial use.[176]

---

173  (1991) 20 IPR 643.
174  (1991) 20 IPR 643 at 656.
175  (1991) 20 IPR 643 at 657.
176  TRIPS Art 39.3.

Third parties receiving or using information supplied by someone acting in breach of their duty of confidence may also be subject to an injunction regarding the continued use of that information. Such a liability would arise upon actual or constructive notice of the breach, if the third party was not aware of the breach from the outset.[177] Accordingly, the innocence of the third party is a relevant consideration in determining liability to pay compensation or an account of profits.[178] The extent to which the third party has detrimentally changed their position may also be taken into account. Finally, if the plaintiff is able to show that the third party encouraged or participated in the recipient's breach of confidentiality then other remedies by way of "contractual interference" or "interference with rights" may be sought.[179]

## Defences

A defendant in an action for breach of confidentiality may have two defences – that the disclosure was justified or that the disclosure was made under legal compulsion. In the first case, the defendant must prove that there was a just cause or excuse for disclosing the information because an iniquity would result without such disclosure. The iniquity rule, established by *Gartside v Outram*,[180] provides that there will be no breach of confidence where misconduct is disclosed to proper authorities in the public interest. However, it does not follow that general publication will not leave the defendant open to pecuniary relief.

In Australia, the High Court in *Attorney-General (UK) v Heinemann Publishers Australia Pty Ltd*[181] supported the need for the public interest in disclosure to outweigh the public interest in confidences for a breach of confidence to be excused. This public interest approach appears to be confined to cases involving government information.[182] As for confidences between private parties, the iniquity rule would appear to apply with the public interest exception only operating where the information discloses a crime, misdeed or civil wrong.[183]

In the *Naomi Campbell* case, public interest disclosure is given a broader meaning to that provided in Australia. In that case five elements of personal confidential information were identified through publication in the *Mirror*.[184] However, two of those elements were considered justified in that Ms Campbell had previously lied to the media, publicly denying that she was a drug addict,[185] and, secondly, that "the fact that she was receiving treatment for the condition was not in itself intrusive".[186] Clearly there is no government information here

---

177  *Fraser v Evans* [1969] 1 QB 349; *Ansell Rubber Co Pty Ltd v Allied Rubber Industries Pty Ltd* [1967] VR 37 at 49-50; *Johns v Australian Securities Commission* (1993) 178 CLR 408.
178  *Wheatley v Bell* [1982] 2 NSWLR 544.
179  Such tortious actions have been suggested by McKeough and Stewart in *Intellectual Property in Australia*, 2nd ed, Butterworths, 1997, pp 90-91.
180  (1856) 26 LJ Ch 113
181  (1988) 165 CLR 30.
182  Consider the discussion on the availability of such a defence in Campbell J's decision in *AG Australia Holdings Limited v Burton* referred to above.
183  *Corrs Pavey Whiting & Byrne v Collector of Customs (Vic)* (1987) 74 ALR 428, Gummow J at 450.
184  *Campbell v MGN Limited* [2004] UKHL 22 at [88].
185  [2004] UKHL 22 at [89].
186  [2004] UKHL 22 at [89].

nor is there a crime, misdeed or civil wrong that required reporting, unless the public false statement made by Ms Campbell regarding drug addiction could be considered a "misdeed". Rather, the balancing exercise that must be conducted in the United Kingdom revolves around the adoption of the right to respect for private life and the right to freedom of expression adopted from the European Convention on Human Rights.[187] Lord Hope explains:

> The effect of these provisions is that the right to privacy which lies at the heart of an action for breach of confidence has to be balanced against the right of the media to impart information to the public. And the right of the media to impart information to the public has to be balanced in its turn against the respect that must be given to private life.[188]

The publication of the remaining elements of confidential information was held to have been in breach of confidence, predominantly due to those elements being concerned with the nature of her therapeutic treatment.

Disclosure under legal compulsion may be required by statute either to a government body or some other person or it may be ordered by a court for the purposes of litigation. In this case, however, the recipient or the person or body receiving the information under legal compulsion may also be subject to the obligation of confidentiality.[189]

---

187 See also *Mosley v News Group Newspapers Limited* [2008] EWHC 1777 (QB).
188 [2004] UKHL 22 at [105].
189 *Smith Kline & French Laboratories (Australia) Ltd v Secretary, Department of Community Services and Health* (1991) 20 IPR 643 (FCA FC); *Johns v Australian Securities Commission* (1993) 178 CLR 408.

# CASES

## *Prince Albert v Strange*
High Court of Chancery: The Lord Chancellor
(1849) 47 ER 1302

Prince Albert sought an injunction to prevent the defendant from publishing a catalogue which described (but did not reproduce) etchings made by Queen Victoria and Prince Albert. The defendant had acquired the etchings via a third party who had a contract with the Queen and Prince Albert to print the etchings. The case is interesting in so far as it shows how even the Lord Chancellor at this time had difficulty conceptualising the nature of the duty of confidence.

**Lord Cottenham:**

[The Lord Chancellor held that the Prince had property in the unpublished etchings in the nature of copyright and on this basis could prevent the publication of the catalogue. Today, copyright legislation could not be relied on to offer such a wide-ranging protection to the ideas conveyed by the etchings.]

[1311] But this case by no means depends solely on the question of property; for a breach of trust, confidence or contract itself would entitle the Plaintiff to the injunction. The Plaintiff's affidavit states the private character of the work or composition, and negatives any licence or authority for publication (the gift of some of the etchings to private friends not implying any such licence or authority); and states distinctly the belief of the Plaintiff that the catalogue, and the descriptive and other remarks therein contained, could not have been compiled, except by means of the possession of the several impressions of the etchings, surreptitiously and improperly obtained. To this case no answer is made, the Defendant saying only, that he did not at the time believe the etchings to have been improperly obtained, but not suggesting any mode by which they could have been properly obtained, so as to entitle the possessor to use them for publication.

If, then, these compositions were kept private, except as to some given to private friends, and some sent to Mr Brown, for the purpose of having certain impressions taken, the possession of the Defendant, or of his partner Judge, must have originated in a breach of trust, confidence or contract in Brown, or some person in his employ, taking more impressions than were ordered, and retaining the extra number; or in some person to whom copies were given, which is not to be supposed, but which, if it were the origin of the possession of the Defendant, would be equally a breach of trust, confidence or contract, as was considered in the case of *The Duke of Queensberry v Shebbeare* (2 Eden, 329). And upon the evidence on behalf of the Plaintiff, and the absence of any explanation on the part of the Defendant, I am bound to assume that the possession of the etchings or engravings, on the part of the Defendant or Judge, has its foundation in a breach of trust, confidence or contract, as Lord Eldon did in the case of Mr Abernethy's Lectures, as reported in 3 Law Journal, 209; and upon this ground, also, I think the Plaintiff's title to the injunction sought to be discharged fully established.

The observations of Vice-Chancellor Wigram, in *Tipping v Clarke* (2 Hare, 393), are applicable to this part of the case. He says "Every clerk employed in a merchant's counting-house is under an implied contract that he will not make public that which he learns in the execution of his duty as clerk. If the Defendant has obtained copies of books, it would very probably be by means of some clerk or agent of the Plaintiff; and if he availed himself surreptitiously of the information, which he could not have had except from a person guilty of a breach of contract in communicating it, I think he could not be permitted to avail himself *of* that breach of contract."

In this opinion I fully concur and I think that this – the case supposed by Sir J Wigram – has actually arisen, or must from the evidence be assumed to have arisen, in the present, and the consequence must be what Sir J Wigram thought would follow. Could it be contended that the clerk, although not justified in communicating copies of the accounts, would yet be permitted to publish the substance and effect of them?

In that, as in this case, the matter or thing of which the party had obtained knowledge being the exclusive property of the owner, he has a right to the interposition of this Court to prevent any use being made of it; that is to say, he is entitled to be protected in the exclusive use and enjoyment of that which is exclusively his own.

This was the opinion of Lord Eldon, expressed in the case of *Wyat v Wilson*, in the year 1820, respecting an engraving of George III, during his illness; in which, according to a note with which I have been furnished by Mr Cooper, he said, "If one of the late king's physicians had kept a diary of what he had heard and seen, this Court would not, in the king's lifetime, have permitted him to print or publish it."

### *Forkserve Pty Ltd v Pacchiarotta*
Supreme Court of New South Wales: Young J
(2000) 50 IPR 74

The defendants were ex-employees of the plaintiff. The plaintiff sought to prevent them using information, in the nature of a client list.

**Young J: [75]** 5. The plaintiff's suspicions grew until it was convinced that the defendants had taken some notebooks containing the names and addresses of the plaintiff's customers and that the defendants were openly canvassing those customers. The plaintiff accordingly commenced these proceedings by summons on 13 May 1999, seeking orders restraining the defendants from soliciting or approaching for the purpose of provision of servicing of forklifts any persons or companies whose names had been obtained by the defendants from the plaintiff's records with consequential orders. On 3 September 1999, a statement of claim was filed seeking such injunctions, an order for delivery up of records, damages under section 1317HD of the Corporations Law and ancillary orders.

6. The principal claim in the pleadings and in the affidavit evidence was that the business of the plaintiff was conducted as follows. Each serviceman, including the two defendants, was issued with a small, spiral bound notebook which could be put in the serviceman's pocket. The procedure that was laid down **[76]** was that when a serviceman finished a job he would ring in to the base and the person in control of the base would give the serviceman the name of the next customer to be serviced and that the employee would write down the name and address of the customer in the spiral bound notebook and then proceed to that address. Mrs Jack gave evidence that this procedure was devised because it would be very easy for a serviceman to take with him a notebook in his pocket, jot down the information and proceed to the address. The plaintiff claims that when the defendants left its employ, there were no notebooks which the defendants had used left on the premises and, accordingly, it must follow that the notebooks were in the possession of the defendants. This, it claimed, is reinforced by the fact that the defendants had in fact called on some of the then customers of the plaintiff and, indeed, some former customers of the plaintiff are now customers of the first defendant.

7. The defendants' reply was simply that they did not have any notebooks. They admit that they generally surveyed the potential market and that this would have included customers of the plaintiff. They deny that the first defendant specifically targeted any such

customers or that the second defendant assisted him. The first defendant believes that of his 45 current customers, only 6 were former customers of the plaintiff. The evidence was that the plaintiff had about 450 customers.

8. Having set the scene, it is convenient to consider the issues that arise in this case under the following heads:

(A) Credibility of witnesses.

(B) Did the defendants remove any notebooks?

(C) Did the defendants by using notebooks or any other material use confidential information of the plaintiff?

(D) The issues arising under s 232 of the Corporations Law.

(E) Whether any remedy should be given.

(F) The result of the case including the question of costs. ...

[77] 17. The plaintiff bears the onus and virtually relies on evidence of general practice. As I accept the defendants' denials, it must follow that I must find that the plaintiff has not established that the defendants took the notebooks or utilised them.

18. (C) The question is whether, in using the notebooks or other material, the defendants used confidential information of the plaintiff. Various general propositions should be noted before I deal with the facts of this particular case.

[78] (1) There is a distinction between confidential information and know-how. An employee is entitled to take with him or her, when quitting employment, general knowledge and skills acquired while an employee. Those general skills or know-how become part of the employee's personal property, even though he or she would not have acquired them had it not been for the employer. Of course I am speaking of cases where there is no contractual restraint.

(2) At the very least, without a contractual restraint a former employer is not entitled to restrain a former employee from competing with the employer after termination of the employment.

(3) An employee is not entitled to appropriate to himself or herself the employer's confidential information which he or she came to know in the course of the employment: *Ormonoid Roofing & Asphalts Ltd v Bitumenoids Ltd* (1930) 31 SR (NSW) 347 at 355. Generally what is confidential information is a question of fact: *Wright v Gasweld Pty Ltd* (1991) 22 NSWLR 317 at 334-5. Generally speaking, a useful way of testing whether information is confidential information is the tripartite classification made by Goulding J in *Faccenda Chicken v Fowler* [1984] ICR 589 at 589-590, conveniently repeated in the judgment of the English Court of Appeal which affirmed that decision which is reported in [1987] Ch 117 at 133-134. Goulding J said that the three classes were essentially, in my paraphrase:

(1) Information of a trivial nature or which is easily accessible;

(2) Know-how which may have originally been confidential, but which has become part of the employee's skill and knowledge;

(3) Specific trade secrets so confidential that even though they may necessarily have been learned by heart, and even though the servant may have left the service, they can not be used for anyone's benefit but the master's.

19. I would note that normally, lists of customers and their requirements may constitute confidential information: see *Robb v Green* [1895] 2 QB 315. However, as Bryson J shows in *Weldon & Co v Harbinson* [2000] NSWSC 272 at [67]-[72], such information is not necessarily confidential, or may be at a low order of confidentiality, depending on the particular circumstances; see also *Wright v Gasweld Pty Ltd* (1991) 22 NSWLR 317 and my decision in *Kone Elevators Pty Ltd v McNay* (1997) 19 ATPR ¶41-563. Even though the actual result in that case was reversed by the Court of Appeal at (1997) 19 ATPR ¶41-564, those matters were not gainsaid.

20. Bryson J, in the *Weldon case* at [72], dealt with a distinction between a written list of customers and an employee remembering who the customers were. There is some doubt in the authorities as to how far an employee can make use of his or her memory of customers as distinct from a list. I consider that the proposition in Heydon, *The Restraint of Trade Doctrine*, 2nd ed, Butterworths, Sydney, 1999, p 80, correctly states the law, namely, "The employee cannot remove, whether by using paper or using memory, a material part of the former employer's business records; but the employee can approach a particular customer or client whom that employee can recall without a list or deliberate memorisation". That proposition is, I believe, supported by the decision of *Peninsular Real Estate Ltd v Harris* [1992] 2 NZLR 216 at 221.

21. I should note that there is an additional complication in that the so-called lists in the notebooks were not made by the plaintiff, but (assuming they existed) were actually made by the servicemen themselves. However, as it would seem the plaintiff company always owned the notebooks, the probability is that even **[79]** though the entries were made by the servicemen, the notebooks, including the entries, were the property of the plaintiff; see *Health Services for Men Pty Ltd v D'Souza* (2000) 48 NSWLR 448.

22. With these considerations in mind, I turn to the facts of the case.

23. In the absence of it being established that the defendants removed any notebooks or other documents, the mere fact that the defendants called on some people who were customers of the plaintiff would not of itself be sufficient to constitute a breach of confidential information.

24. There is no evidence to enable me to come to the conclusion that there was a deliberate memorisation of any records of the plaintiff.

25. Mr Johnson relies on pieces of evidence such as the fact that the business card of Mr Clark of Plumbers Supplies at Penrith was on the desk of Mr Walls, the business development manager of the plaintiff during December 1998, and that the evidence clearly shows that the defendants made special efforts to canvass Mr Clark early in January 1999. Although this and a couple of other incidents raise suspicion, I do not consider that even with this material it is more likely than not that the defendants used confidential information to their own advantage.

26. (D) Section 232(5) and (6) of the Corporations Law as in effect in December 1998 is as follows:

"232(5) An officer or employee of a corporation, or a former officer or employee of a corporation, must not, in relevant circumstances, make improper use of information acquired by virtue of his or her position as such an officer or employee to gain, directly or indirectly, for an advantage for himself or herself or for any other person or to cause detriment to the corporation.

(6) An officer or an employee of a corporation must not, in relevant circumstances, make improper use of his or her position as such an officer or employee to gain, directly or indirectly, an advantage for himself or herself or for any other person or to cause detriment to the corporation".

27. It is the Corporations Law in force as at December 1998 and January 1999 to which I must look. However, as is common, the sections have been rearranged and the corresponding provisions are now in ss 182-184 of the Corporations Law in its present form.

28. As I said in *Rosetex Company Pty Ltd v Licata* (1994) 12 ACSR 779, the general coverage of the obligations under s 232 are not to any major extent wider than the duties under the general rules of equity. There are some extensions made by the statute in that there is taken away some problems of privity, there is conferred a statutory right to receive damages or compensation where under the general law there would only be an account of profits and other ancillary advantages. However, generally speaking, if there has been no improper use of information under the general equitable principles, there is no improper

use of information under the statute. This is logically so when one remembers that sections like s 232 were originally taken by the drafters of the 1958 Victorian Companies Act and the Companies Act 1961 (NSW) from the equitable duties set out by Romer J in *Re City Equitable Fire Insurance Company Ltd* [1925] Ch 407.

29. Thus it follows that as there is no breach under the general rules of equity, there is no breach under s 232.

30. Mr Beale, who appeared for the defendants, suggested in his submissions that an employee under s 232(5) and (6) should be read down to an employee in the nature of an officer of the corporation, that is, some sort of executive **[80]** employee. The argument is one that can briefly be expressed by saying noscitur a sociis. I do not consider this argument is correct, and favour the submission of Mr Johnson that "employee" must be read widely. However, that has still not enabled the plaintiff to succeed under this head.

31. It follows that as the plaintiff fails on the merits, no remedy should be given.

## *Maggbury Pty Ltd v Hafele Australia Pty Ltd*
High Court of Australia: Gleeson CJ, Gummow, Kirby, Hayne and Callinan JJ
(2001) 185 ALR 152

In this case, Maggbury Pty Ltd (Maggbury) sought to enforce a perpetual confidentiality obligation on the part of Hafele Australia Pty Ltd (Hafele), the Australian arm of a German manufacturer. Maggbury had developed a new foldaway ironing board assembly and filed patent applications for the alleged invention. Soon after the applications were made, interest was shown in the new foldaway ironing board by Hafele and after much negotiation the parties entered into confidentiality agreements protecting the invention. Hafele was then allowed to inspect the prototype and associated information with a view to entering into licence arrangements. The agreements restrained Hafele from using the information for any purpose other than for assessment and set up a perpetual obligation not to use the information for any purpose whatsoever without the informed consent of Maggbury. However, through the operation of the patenting process, the details of the invention were published approximately 19 months after the earliest priority date.

This brought much of the information protected by the confidentiality agreements into the public domain and meant that the information lost its quality of confidence. Hafele took advantage of this situation and its parent company commenced manufacturing a variation of Maggbury's foldaway ironing board and distributed these in Australia through Hafele. Maggbury sought to enforce the confidentiality obligations on Hafele and obtain an injunction restraining further use of that information. As the patent application had not yet been granted at this stage the only avenue open was breach of the confidentiality contracts. The majority decision of the High Court, comprising Gleeson CJ, Gummow and Hayne JJ, follows.

**Gleeson CJ, Gummow and Hayne JJ:** [162] 38. In this Court, Maggbury and Gisma seek orders which would have the effect of restoring the position established by the orders of Byrne J, in particular the injunctive relief against Hafele Australia and Hafele. Of that injunctive relief, it should be observed that the restraints imposed upon Hafele Australia and Hafele are not conditioned by any limitation reflecting the need for existing and continued confidentiality of the information conveyed by the documents and prototype referred to in the injunction. Indeed, Maggbury and Gisma submit as a principal plank of their appeal that the injunctions enforce negative stipulations contained in the first and second agreements which, on their proper construction, continue "forever" and do not depend upon the continuation of secrecy or lack of public disclosure.

39. Given the conclusions reached in the Court of Appeal as to the quantum and significance of the public disclosure, which should be accepted, it is essential for the appellants in this Court to put their case in that way. Nevertheless, their submission should be rejected and the attempt to reinstate the injunctive relief given by the primary judge should fail.

40. It is necessary first to construe the provisions of the two agreements upon which the primary judge founded the injunctive relief. The evident and primary purpose of the agreements was to facilitate discussions to consider the commercial exploitation of the invention claimed in PN4147, PN4592 and later in the PCT application. The Recitals indicate this. The fact that the discussions were taking place was to be kept secret: cl 4.

[163] 41. There was no express obligation imposed upon Maggbury to make any disclosures for the purposes of the discussions with the Hafele companies. Rather, the two agreements assume that this will occur and that Maggbury will show or provide items within the definition of the information. The agreements do impose specific obligations upon the Hafele companies respecting the use of the information. At one level these are concerned with the treatment of the very items themselves. The requirement for their return to Maggbury if the discussions collapse is an example. At another level, the restraints fix not upon objects or chattels, but operate more broadly upon the information embodied therein (for example, in the prototypes) or stated or otherwise communicated (as in the drawings).

42. It is apparent from the references in the agreements to patent applications that the agreements contemplated the placing in the public domain of significant features of the information in this second and broader sense. The agreements impose no express obligation upon Maggbury to pursue PN4147 to grant or to make and pursue any other applications. But they assume Maggbury's intention to do so and thereby provide in patent monopoly rights a legal foundation for the commercial exploitation of the product. However, the discussions between the parties might never come to fruition. The agreements also contemplated that eventuality with the Hafele companies being obliged to return materials to Maggbury when the purpose was spent. That is what in fact came to pass after, in the meantime, what the Court of Appeal found was, for practical purposes, full public disclosure of the substance of the claimed invention.

43. Upon the proper construction of the agreements, did the restraints upon use continue to operate after the public disclosure and the collapse of negotiations? It was said by Lord Diplock that:[190]

> ... if detailed semantic and syntactical analysis of words in a commercial contract is going to lead to a conclusion that flouts business commonsense, it must be made to yield to business commonsense.

Of course, what in respect of a particular contract comprises "business commonsense", as an apparently objectively ascertained matter, may itself be a topic upon which minds may differ and in respect of which an imputed consensus is impossible. Here the difficulty arises not from the need for detailed semantic and syntactical analysis of the language used in the agreements, but from the use therein of simple terms such as "at any time hereafter" and "forever". Is this a case where "something must have gone wrong with the language"?[191]

---

[190] *Antaios Compania Naviera SA v Salen Rederierna AB* [1985] AC 191 at 201.
[191] *Investors Compensation Scheme Ltd v West Bromwich Building Society* [1998] 1 WLR 896 at 913; [1998] 1 All ER 98 at 115 per Lord Hoffmann.

44. In *Staffordshire Area Health Authority v South Staffordshire Waterworks Co*,[192] the English Court of Appeal construed the phrase "at all times hereafter" in the price-fixing provision of a water supply contract made in 1929 between a hospital and a water authority as importing an obligation to supply only until the agreement had been terminated on reasonable notice; there was no express power of termination.[193] In *Harbinger UK Ltd v GE Information Services Ltd*,[194] the same court construed an obligation in a software supply contract to provide after sales **[164]** service "in perpetuity" and in return for an annual payment as continuing until the customer and the end users no longer were willing to pay for these services; that willingness might be expected to diminish as the software became obsolescent.

45. Ordinarily, the obligations relating to the use and disclosure of the information would be construed as limited to subject-matter which retained the quality of confidentiality at the time of breach or threatened breach of those obligations. An expression of a contrary intent should, as Judge Learned Hand put it in *Picard v United Aircraft Corporation*,[195] be explicit. This is because:[196]

> ... the applicant is proposing to broadcast the invention to the world at large, reserving as his protection only the claims which he may secure; and there is ordinarily no reason to suppose that he means to exact any greater protection against the promisor than he will have against others. At any rate, if he does, he should say so.

The same judge later expressed the point slightly differently in *Conmar Products Corporation v Universal Slide Fastener Co*.[197] Speaking of the relationship between employer and employee, his Honour said:[198]

> Conceivably an employer might exact from his employees a contract not to disclose the information even after the patent issued. Of what possible value such a contract could be, we find it hard to conceive; but, if an employer did exact it, others would perhaps be obliged to turn to the specifications, if they would use the information. Be that as it may, we should not so construe any secrecy contract unless the intent were put in the most inescapable terms; and the plaintiff's contract had none such.

46. Similar reasoning may be discerned in the litigation which in 1928 reached the House of Lords as *O Mustad & Son v Dosen* but which was not reported until 1963.[199] The House of Lords dismissed the appeal from the English Court of Appeal. The judgments in the Court of Appeal are not reported but extracts, particularly from the judgment of Atkin LJ, are set out in the judgment of Roskill J in *Cranleigh Precision Engineering Ltd v Bryant*.[200] Dosen, as Roskill J put it:[201]

> ... had entered into a written agreement under which he expressly agreed that he would not disclose information of which he might get an insight in consequence of his work.

After the commencement of the action in England seeking injunctive relief against Dosen, the appellants, upon legal advice and thinking that the step would protect their

---

[192] [1978] 1 WLR 1387; [1978] 3 All ER 769.
[193] Earlier authorities are noted by Menzies J and Windeyer J in *Amalgamated Television Services Pty Ltd v Television Corporation Ltd* (1969) 123 CLR 648 at 654, 655 and discussed in Carnegie, "Terminability of Contracts of Unspecified Duration", (1969) 85 *Law Quarterly Review* 392.
[194] [2000] 1 All ER (Comm) 166.
[195] 128 F 2d 632 (1942).
[196] 128 F 2d 632 at 637 (1942).
[197] 172 F 2d 150 (1949).
[198] 172 F 2d 150 at 156 (1949)9
[198] [1964] 1 WLR 109 (n); [1963] 3 All ER 416; [1963] RPC 41.
[200] [1965] 1 WLR 1293 at 1314-15; [1964] 3 All ER 289 at 298-9.
[201] [1965] 1 WLR 1293 at 1314; [1964] 3 All ER 289 at 298.

position, made a patent application, the specification in respect of which was published in the United Kingdom. Dosen successfully contended that the secret the subject of the patent application thus had been published to the world and that he was free from any obligation of secrecy under the contract or **[165]** otherwise. In the Court of Appeal, Atkin LJ construed the contractual obligation as one "not to acquaint strangers with [the employer's] trade secrets".[202] His Lordship concluded:[203]

> It seems to me, therefore, that there was a complete publication to the public of the construction and operation of the machine, the construction and operation of which was alleged in the proceedings to be a trade secret, and from that moment it appears to me quite plain that that which before might have been a trade secret, was a trade secret no longer. Now, what is the result of that? It appears to me that the result is that there is no longer any subject matter upon which the agreement could operate.

That statement is to be read with the later remark by Lord Buckmaster in the House of Lords:[204]

> The important point about the patent is not whether it was valid or invalid, but what it was that it disclosed, because after the disclosure had been made by the appellants to the world, it was impossible for them to get an injunction restraining the respondents from disclosing what was common knowledge. The secret, as a secret, had ceased to exist.

In the Court of Appeal, Lawrence LJ had put the matter slightly differently by emphasising that it was the plaintiffs who, by their own act, had made public the essential part of the trade secret which they then sought to restrain Dosen from communicating. His Lordship said:[205]

> [B]y applying for a patent, it seems to me that they have destroyed the foundation of their action.

47. *Cranleigh* is authority that different considerations apply where (i) the publication was in a patent granted to an unrelated third party and (ii) the relationship between the litigants is that of employer and employee and therefore involves fiduciary or other equitable obligations as well as those founded simply in contract.[206]

48. However, in *Attorney-General v Guardian Newspapers Ltd (No 2)*, Lord Goff of Chieveley said that *Cranleigh* did not:[207]

> ... support any general principle that, if it is a third party who puts the confidential information into the public domain, as opposed to the confider, the confidant will not be released from his duty of confidence.

His Lordship added that he recognised:[208]

> ... that a case where the confider himself publishes the information might be distinguished from other cases on the basis that the confider, by publishing the information, may have implicitly released the confidant from his obligation.

Those remarks respecting release are readily applicable where the relationship is equitable rather than contractual, as is the present case.

49. The present appeal does not involve the putting of the information into the public domain by a third party or a relationship between the plaintiff and the **[166]** defendant which is governed purely by equitable principles. Here, the first question is one of construction of the two agreements. It may be that the legal rights to which the agreements,

[202] [1965] 1 WLR 1293 at 1315; [1964] 3 All ER 289 at 299.
[203] [1965] 1 WLR 1293 at 1315; [1964] 3 All ER 289 at 299.
[204] [1964] 1 WLR 109 at 111; [1963] 3 All ER 416 at 418; [1963] RPC 41 at 43.
[205] [1965] 1 WLR 1293 at 1316; [1964] 3 All ER 289 at 299.
[206] *Concut Pty Ltd v Worrell* (2000) 75 ALJR 312 at 317-18 [26]; 176 ALR 693 at 700-701.
[207] [1990] 1 AC 109 at 285.
[208] [1990] 1 AC 109 at 285.

so construed, give rise may, in particular circumstances, for example concerning the conduct of the plaintiff, not attract equitable relief. But that would be another matter.

50. A construction of the restraints in the two agreements which gave them a limited temporal operation after public disclosure and after failure of the negotiations might be supported as the contractual imposition upon the Hafele companies of a "head start" handicap. This would reflect the advantage to those companies, over the position of competitors who had not dealt with Maggbury, in having had access to the information over a period preceding its public disclosure.[209] Public disclosure occurred at the latest in February 1997. It may be accepted for present purposes that a contractual restraint of this nature upon the Hafele companies would not exceed the reasonable protection of the interests of Maggbury. It is unnecessary to determine the point. This is because what the appellants seek from this Court is the restoration of an absolute perpetual and unconditional injunction, granted as if the confidential quality of the information in question still persists.

51. What then is the effect, upon their proper construction, of the contractual restraints in question here? Three provisions are particularly in point. Clause 5.1 obliged the Hafele companies to "treat" the information as "confidential". The agreements contained no warranty by Maggbury that the information had this character at the date of the agreements or that it would have that character when disclosed or supplied by Maggbury during the negotiations with respect to the purpose. Clause 5.1 obliged the Hafele companies to deal with the information when supplied or disclosed during the negotiations on the agreed footing that it had this confidential character. However, were it not for the provisions of cl 11.1, cl 5.1 might properly be construed as not obliging the disclosees to continue to accept that the information had the confidential character after it had been disclosed publicly by Maggbury itself. The obligation to "treat" the information as "confidential" answers the description in the first sentence of cl 11.1 as one of the "obligations of confidence set out in this Agreement". Clause 11.1 states it as a condition of the agreement that the Hafele companies "forever" observe those obligations.

52. Further, cl 5.6 forbids the use without consent of the information "for any purpose" "at any time" thereafter. Both cl 5.1 and cl 5.6 use "Information" in the broader of the senses referred to earlier in these reasons. Thus they do not proceed on the footing that, for example, after the prototypes had been returned no further obligations subsist with respect to the information derived from inspection of the prototypes.

53. The terms of cll 5.1 and 5.6 as so construed would, on the findings of Byrne J, found the injunctive relief, unlimited in time, respecting the wall-mounted Hafele model. It is not fairly open to avoid that result by construing these provisions as having as their subject-matter only information which at the time of the alleged breach of covenant retains a confidential character which it had when first disclosed by Maggbury. The emphatic temporal extensions applied to cl 5.1 by cl 11.1 and the terms of cl 5.6 are expressions of [167] "explicit" intent[210] and are put in "inescapable terms".[211] Any implied term to other effect would contradict the express terms.

54. The question then arises as to whether these contractual terms are subjected to and survive the application of the restraint of trade doctrine. Undoubtedly the provisions impose restraints upon the activities of the Hafele companies, as is apparent from the terms of the injunction. They restrict the liberty of the Hafele companies in the future to conduct their operations and dealings with third parties in such manner as they think fit. The Hafele parties undoubtedly are in "trade" and the activities restrained are part of that

---

[209] cf *United States Surgical Corporation v Hospital Products International Pty Ltd* [1983] 2 NSWLR 157 at 228-33 (reversed on other grounds (1984) 156 CLR 41).

[210] *Picard v United Aircraft Corporation* 128 F 2d 632 (1942) at 637.

[211] *Conmar Products Corporation v Universal Slide Fastener Co* 172 F 2d 150 (1949) at 156.

trade. Contrary to the submissions pressed for the appellants, the restraints which they seek to have enforced in this litigation are not of the same character as terms of licences to use intellectual property. In the judgments in *Breen v Williams*[212] there is discussion of the distinction between property in particular records or other chattels and the protection of the information conveyed thereby or embodied therein.[213] Whatever else may be said of the notion that confidential information is to be regarded as proprietary in nature, that analysis cannot be sustained where the information has become available from public sources as a result of disclosures by the party asserting that quality of confidence. Other intangible proprietary rights such as those conferred by the law of copyright are not involved. Allegations of the subsistence and the infringement of copyright were removed from the further amended statement of claim. The source of the rights which the appellants seek to enforce is found in contract. In particular in the contractual obligation imposed upon the Hafele companies to treat or deal with the information as having the quality of confidence.

55. Why then does the common law doctrine respecting restraint of trade not apply? The appellants submit that the doctrine does not apply because the Hafele companies could carry on their trade without relying upon the particular disclosures by Maggbury by, for example, having recourse to the public domain and their own previously acquired skills and experience. But that circumstance does not demonstrate that the doctrine has no application. In *Peters (WA) Ltd v Petersville Ltd*,[214] the Court has recently considered the cases in which it has been said that some restraints are not of a nature to which the doctrine applies. In particular, the Court rejected the criterion of "fettering existing freedom" associated with statements in the speeches of Lord Reid, Lord Morris of Borth-y-Gest and Lord Hodson in *Esso Petroleum Co Ltd v Harper's Garage (Stourport) Ltd*.[215] The Court also rejected the principle of exclusion by reference to "sterilisation" associated with the speech of Lord Pearce in *Esso*.[216] The Court left open for further consideration in an appropriate case the identification by Lord Wilberforce in *Esso*[217] of species of restraint which have become generally accepted as part of the structure of a trading society. The present appeal is not the occasion for dealing with that subject. This is because, as is apparent from the **[168]** tenor of submissions throughout this litigation, the notion of a contractual restraint in respect of publicly available information is far from attaining general acceptance of the kind of which Lord Wilberforce spoke.

56. The fact that the restraint can be said to have freely been bargained for by the parties to the contract provides no sufficient reason for concluding that the doctrine should not apply. All contractual restraints can be said to be of that character.

57. The result is that the doctrine applied to the restraints we have identified and rendered them invalid, subject to their justification as reasonable in the interests of the public and the parties. The respondents correctly emphasise that such an enterprise was not undertaken at the trial. Further, it may be added that there would be substantial difficulty in doing so.

58. Reference has been made earlier in these reasons to the provision respecting severance in cl 16.10. It is unnecessary to determine whether the restraints in question here could be severed or read down. If read down, this would be on the footing that the restraints did not operate where, at the time of the breach or threatened breach in question,

---

[212] (1996) 186 CLR 71.
[213] See the judgments of Brennan CJ (1996) 186 CLR 71 at 80-2, Dawson and Toohey JJ at 88-90, Gaudron and McHugh JJ at 101-2, Gummow J at 126-9.
[214] (2001) 75 ALJR 1385; 181 ALR 337.
[215] [1968] AC 269 at 298, 306-9, 316-17.
[216] [1968] AC 269 at 328-9.
[217] [1968] AC 269 at 335.

the subject-matter had lost its confidential quality and had entered the public domain as the result of steps taken by or to be attributed to Maggbury.

59. The appeal against the orders made by the Court of Appeal should be dismissed with costs. There has been no cross-appeal by the respondents against the award of $5,000 damages made by the Court of Appeal.

# Index